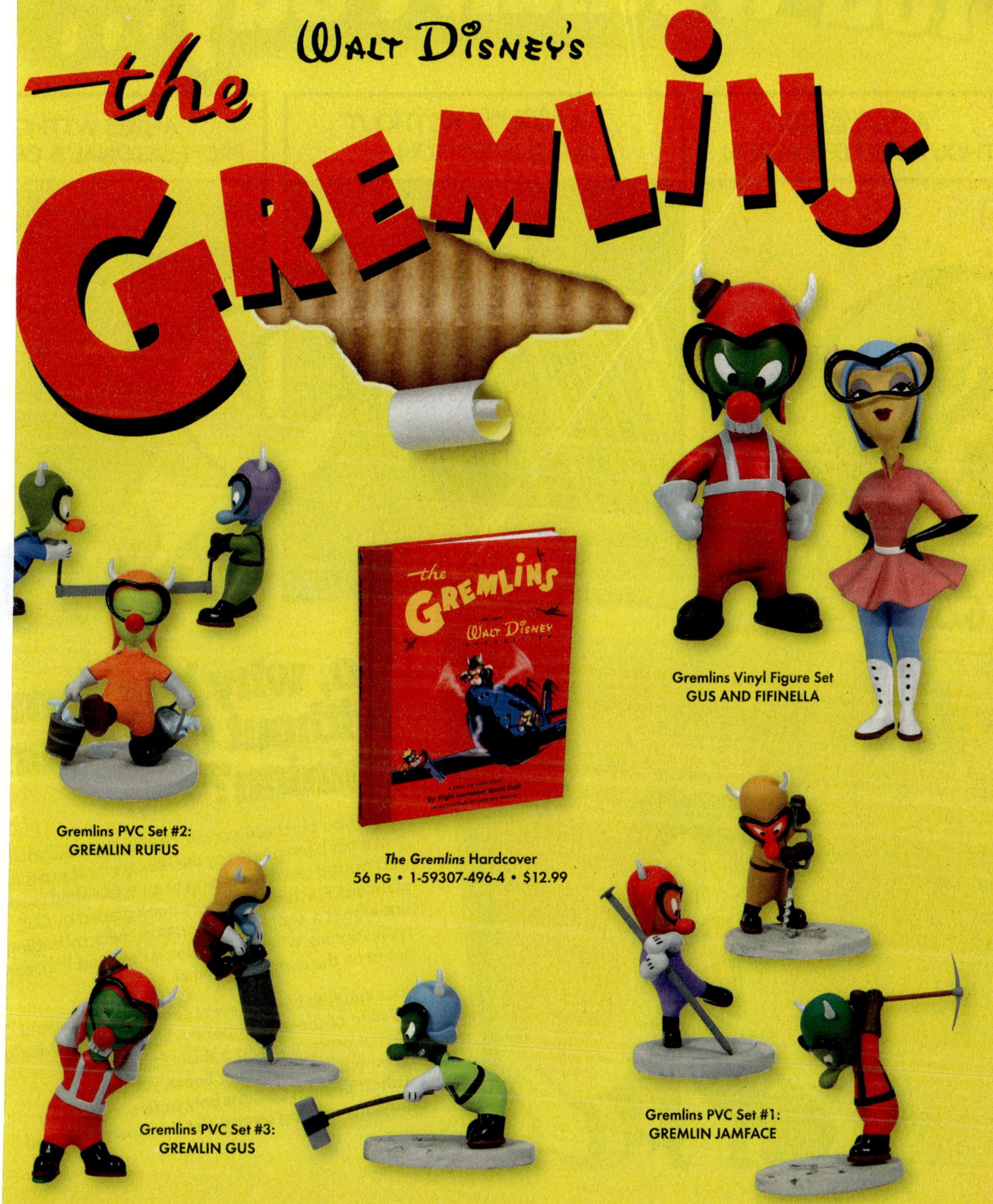
Walt Disney's
the Gremlins
the Gremlins
Walt Disney
Gremlins Vinyl Figure Set
GUS AND FIFINELLA
Gremlins PVC Set #2:
GREMLIN RUFUS
The Gremlins Hardcover
56 PG • 1-59307-496-4 • $12.99
Gremlins PVC Set #3:
GREMLIN GUS
Gremlins PVC Set #1:
GREMLIN JAMFACE

You wouldn't buy...

...A **DIAMOND** WITHOUT CERTIFICATION

...A **HOUSE** WITHOUT AN INSPECTION

...A **CAR** WITHOUT A PROFESSIONAL'S OPINION

So, why buy comics without the expert's opinion?

When you purchase a comic certified by CGC, you know that it has been graded by the hobby's most experienced and trusted team, according to an established grading standard. Furthermore, every book graded by CGC undergoes a thorough restoration check by leading professionals. When restoration is detected, it's clearly noted on the certification label.

Once certified by CGC, every comic is encapsulated in a state-of-the-art, tamper-evident holder, providing superior protection and stability for long-term enjoyment. **For your comic books, you deserve certification from CGC, the only expert, impartial, third-party grading service. Get the expert's opinion!**

When a Comic Book becomes a Treasure

P.O. Box 4738 | Sarasota, Florida 34230 | 1-877-NM-COMIC (662-6642) | www.CGCcomics.com

An Independent Member of the Certified Collectibles Group

Do your mousework

Trust the leading FREE **auction archive database** to give you the edge you need

Whether you collect or buy and sell, you need the most accurate information out there. Lucky for you there's LiveAuctioneers.com. It's the world's leading auction archive database. Search millions of lots to find even the most obscure Disney-related items, see color pictures and get real-world results. Value your collection. Find items up for sale. And do it all absolutely free of charge.

Visit LiveAuctioneers.com today.

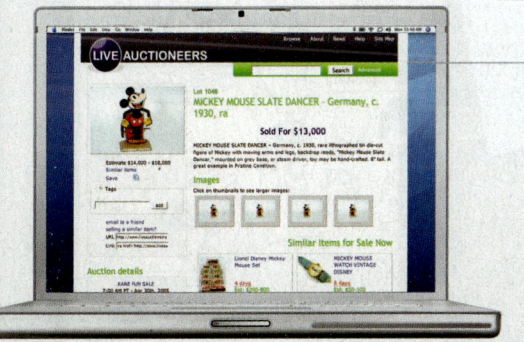

Search by any term; get results plus items coming up for bid; full-color images; view similar items; set alerts; save searches — conduct your research with us, free

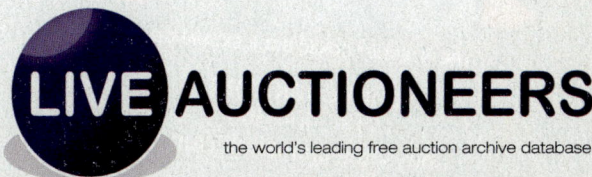

the world's leading free auction archive database

COMICLINK AUCTIONS

The Auction Choice of Smart Sellers

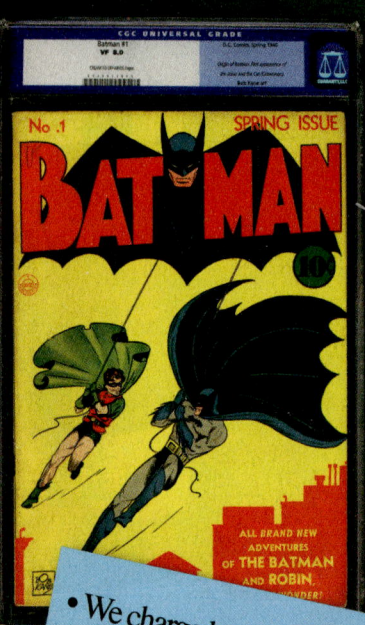
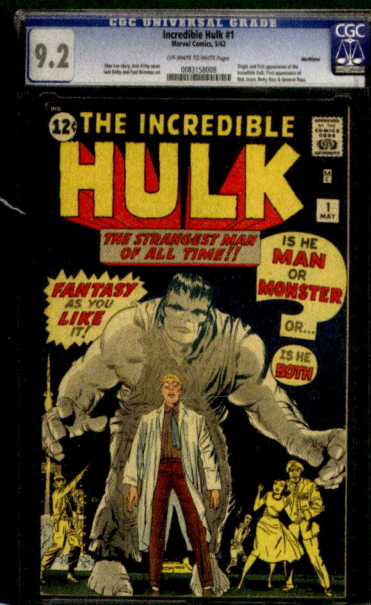

ALL THESE SOLD AT RECORD PRICES

- We charge half the commission of other auction houses
- We get the highest realized prices
- We offer generous interest-free advances
- We don't charge fees for unmet reserves (you can only win)
- We have been in the comic business longest and have the most relevant bidders

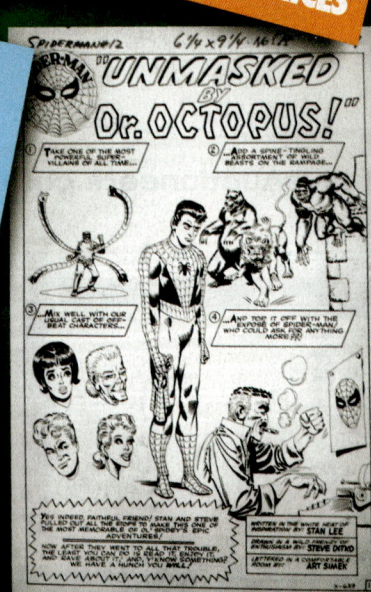

THE INTERNET COMIC BOOK EXCHANGE

comiclink.com
718-246-0300
buysell@comiclink.com

THE OFFICIAL PRICE GUIDE TO DISNEY COLLECTIBLES

2nd Edition

by TED HAKE

FOR GEMSTONE PUBLISHING

J.C. Vaughn, **Executive Editor & Associate Publisher**
Brenda Busick, **Creative Director** • Brandon G. DeStefano, **Editor**
Mark Huesman, **Production Coordinator** • Tom Gordon III, **Managing Editor**
Jamie David, **Director of Marketing**
Heather Winter, **Office Manager**
Stacia Brown, **Editorial Coordinator**

RANDOM HOUSE
INFORMATION GROUP
NEW YORK

HOUSE OF COLLECTIBLES

GEMSTONE PUBLISHING, INC.

NOTICE: Values for items pictured in this book are based on the author's experience, consultations with a network of advisors including collectors specializing in various categories, and actual prices realized for specific items sold through private sales and auctions, including the catalogs of Hake's Americana & Collectibles internet, mail and telephone bid auctions. The values offered in this book are approximations influenced by many factors including condition, rarity and demand, and they should serve only as guidelines, presenting an average range of what one might expect to pay for the items. In the marketplace, knowledge and opinions held by both sellers and buyers determine prices asked and prices paid. This is not a price list of items for sale or items wanted by the author or publisher. The author and the publisher shall not be held responsible for losses that may occur in the purchase, sale or other transaction of property because of information contained herein. Efforts have been made to present accurate information, but the possibility of error exists. Readers who believe they have discovered an error are invited to mail corrective information to the author, Ted Hake, c/o Gemstone Publishing, 1966 Greenspring Drive, Timonium, MD 21093. Verified corrections will be incorporated into future editions of this book.

Copyright ©2007 by Gemstone Publishing, Inc.

All rights reserved in accordance with U.S. and International copyright law. No part of this work may be reproduced or transmitted in any form or by any means, electronic or mechanical, without written permission from the publisher.

Front Cover: Front Cover: Pluto, Snow White, Mickey Mouse, Minnie Mouse, Donald Duck, and Tinker Bell ©2007 The Walt Disney Company. All rights reserved. **Spine:** The Wicked Queen from Snow White ©2007 The Walt Disney Company. All rights reserved.

All characters depicted in this book are ©2007 their respective copyright holders. All rights reserved.

THE OFFICIAL® PRICE GUIDE TO DISNEY COLLECTIBLES (2nd Edition) is an original publication of Gemstone Publishing, Inc. and House of Collectibles. Distributed by The Random House Information Group, a division of Random House, Inc., New York and simultaneously in Canada by Random House of Canada Limited, Toronto. This edition has never before appeared in book form.

House of Collectibles
Random House Information Group
1745 Broadway
New York, New York 10019

www.houseofcollectibles.com

House of Collectibles is a registered trademark and the H colophon is a trademark of Random House, Inc.

Random House is a registered trademark of Random House, Inc.

Published by arrangement with Gemstone Publishing.

ISBN: 978-0-375-72262-2

Printed in China

10 9 8 7 6 5 4 3 2 1

Second Edition: September 2007

Ted Hake is recognized as the founding father of America's collectibles industry. He began Hake's Americana & Collectibles in 1967, the first auction house to specialize in 20th century American popular culture. Disney collectibles have been his primary specialty for forty years. His early initiatives in hundreds of collecting areas contributed significantly to establishing collectibles as a major interest for millions of Americans. Over the years, Hake has shared his expertise by writing sixteen reference/price guides covering such subjects as presidential campaign artifacts, pin-back buttons and vintage collectibles in the areas of advertising, comic characters, cowboy characters and television. He is a frequent guest on radio, was an appraiser on the first two seasons of the PBS series *The Antiques Roadshow* and is a featured expert on the History Channel's 2003 program *History of Toys*. In 2004, Hake sold the business to Diamond International Galleries but he continues as Hake's Chief Operating Officer. Hake's four annual catalogue and internet (www.hakes.com) auctions, sales lists and books are produced at the company's home office in Timonium, Maryland.

OTHER BOOKS BY TED HAKE:

The Button Book
(out of print)

Buttons In Sets
With Marshall N. Levin

Collectible Pin-Back Buttons 1896-1986:
An Illustrated Price Guide
With Russ King

The Encyclopedia of Political Buttons 1896-1972
Political Buttons Book II 1920-1976
Political Buttons Book III 1789-1916

The Encyclopedia of Political Buttons: 2004 Revised Prices for Books I, II, III

Hake's Guide to Advertising Collectibles
100 Years of Advertising from 100 Famous Companies
(out of print)

Hake's Guide to Comic Character Collectibles
An illustrated Price Guide to 100 Years of Comic Strip Characters
(out of print)

Hake's Guide to Cowboy Character Collectibles
An Illustrated Price Guide Covering 50 Years of Movie & TV Cowboy Heroes
(out of print)

Hake's Guide to Presidential Campaign Collectibles
An Illustrated Price Guide to Artifacts from 1789-1988

Hake's Guide to TV Collectibles:
An illustrated Price Guide
(out of print)

Hake's Price Guide to Character Toys, 6th Edition

Non-Paper Sports Collectibles:
An Illustrated Price Guide
(with Roger Steckler)

Sixgun Heroes: A Price Guide to Movie Cowboy Collectibles
With Robert Cauler

A Treasury of Advertising Collectibles
(out of print)

For ordering information write the author at:
Hake's Americana & Collectibles
1966 Greenspring Drive, Suite 400
Timonium, MD 21093
Or visit: www.hakes.com

TABLE OF CONTENTS

About the Author/Other Books 7
Acknowledgements 11
Introduction 14
Price Guide Overview 15
  Types of Items 16
  Dates of Issue, Abbreviations 17
  Sizes 17
  Guide Values 18
  Definitions: Good, Fine,
    Near Mint 18
  Paper/Cardboard, Metal,
    Celluloid 18
  Other Materials.....................20
  Collect For Personal
    Enjoyment 21
  The Search 22
  Shows, Magazines &
    Price Guides 23
  Clubs and Collectibles Industry
    News/Events 24
  The Purchase 24
  Reproductions & Fantasies....25
  Preserving It 27
  Time To Sell? 28
Market Report
  by John K. Snyder Jr
  & J.C. Vaughn. 29
Traded for a Toon
  by Brandon G. DeStefano 40
Lost & Found
  by J.C. Vaughn..........................43
Snow White's Homecoming
  by J.C. Vaughn & Brandon G.

DeStefano 52
Educating Mickey
  by John K. Snyder Jr.
  & J.C. Vaughn 60
Disney Timeline 66
President's Letter 86
Pricing Section 87

COLLECTIBLE CATEGORIES:
A Bug's Life 88
Absent-Minded Professor 89
Adventures of Ichabod
  & Mr. Toad............................89
Aladdin 90
Alice Comedies........................92
Alice in Wonderland 92
Annette Funicello 98
Aristocats, The 102
Babes in Toyland...................104
Baby Weems 106
Bambi 107
Beauty and the Beast 118
Bedknobs and Broomsticks ..120
Ben and Me............................121
Black Cauldron, The 121
Black Hole, The 122
Bongo 124
Carl Barks Writer and Artist ..126
Cars...131
Chip 'n' Dale 132
Chip 'n' Dale Comics 134
Chronicles of Narnia 137
Cinderella 139

Clarabelle Cow 146
Darby O'Gill
  and the Little People 147
Davy Crockett........................147
Dell Giant Comics 161
Disneyana Convention 168
Disneyland 172
Disneyland Paris 186
Disneyland TV Show.............186
Donald Duck, Daisy
  & Nephews.........................187
Donald Duck Comics 279
DuckTales 287
Dumbo 288
Elmer Elephant 296
EPCOT 298
Fantasia 299
Ferdinand the Bull 312
Finding Nemo 315
Flip the Frog 317
Four Color Comics 321
Fox and the Hound, The 351
Fun and Fancy Free 351
Gnome-Mobile 353
Goofy 353
Gremlins 361
Hardy Boys, The 364
Herbie the Love Bug.............364
Hercules 365
Horace Horsecollar...............367
Hunchback
  of Notre Dame, The 369
In Beaver Valley 369

TABLE OF CONTENTS

Title	Page
Incredibles, The	370
James and the Giant Peach	371
Johnny Appleseed	372
Johnny Tremain	372
Jungle Book, The	373
Lady and the Tramp	378
Lambert, The Sheepish Lion	382
Legend of Sleepy Hollow, The	383
Lilo and Stitch	383
Lion King, The	384
Little Hiawatha	386
Little Mermaid, The	387
Little Toot	388
Littlest Outlaw, The	388
Living Desert, The	389
Ludwig Von Drake	389
Make Mine Music	391
Mary Poppins	392
Melody Time	395
Mickey Mouse, Minnie & Nephews	397
Mickey Mouse Comics	615
Mickey Mouse Club (TV)	619
Mickey Mouse Clubs	634
Modern Pinbacks	637
Mulan	689
Multi-Character	689
Nightmare Before Christmas, The	703
Nikki, Wild Dog of the North	706
Old Yeller	706
One Hundred and One Dalmatians	706
Oswald, the Lucky Rabbit	709
Pecos Bill	711
Pegleg Pete	712
Perri	712
Pete's Dragon	713
Peter Pan	714
Pinocchio	723
Pirates of the Caribbean	758
Pluto	759
Pocahontas	771
Pollyanna	772
Pop-Up Books	773
Posters	777
Promotional Comics	786
Reluctant Dragon, The	801
Rescuers, The	802
Robin Hood	803
Robin Hood, The Story Of	804
Rocketeer, The	804
Saludos Amigos	805
Shaggy Dog, The	806
Silly Symphonies	808
Sleeping Beauty	818
Snow White and the Seven Dwarfs	823
So Dear To My Heart	873
Song of the South	873
Spin and Marty	876
Susie, The Little Blue Coupe	877
Swamp Fox	877
Swiss Family Robinson	877
Sword in the Stone, The	878
That Darn Cat	879
Three Caballeros, The	880
Three Little Pigs, The	884
Three Lives of Thomasina, The	902
Toby Tyler	902
Tokyo Disneyland	903
Tonka	904
Toy Story	905
Treasure Island	909
Tron	910
Twenty Thousand Leagues Under the Sea	910
Uncle Scrooge	911
Uncle Scrooge Comics	919
Walt Disney	927
Walt Disney's Comics and Stories	931
Walt Disney Studio	965
Walt Disney World Resort	978
Walt Disney's Wonderful World	983
Who Framed Roger Rabbit	984
Willie the Operatic Whale	986
Winnie the Pooh	987
World War Two Disneyana	997
Zorro	1002
Bibliography	1015
Appendix: Disney Books	1016

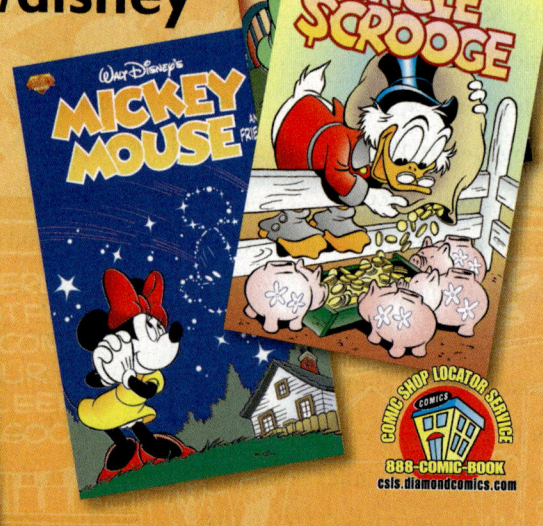

Disney
COMICS & COLLECTIBLES

© 2007 Disney Enterprises, Inc.

GEMSTONE PUBLISHING

Gemstone's current and back issue comics available at bookstores, comic specialty stores, and online at:

www.gemstonepub.com/disney

Gladstone back issues and collectibles available at:

www.carlbarks.org

For a comprehensive overview of Disney and other giants in the entertainment industries, be sure to visit Geppi's Entertainment Museum located at Camden Yards in Baltimore, Maryland. For more information, go to:

www.geppismuseum.com

ACKNOWLEDGEMENTS

Many contributors joined forces to make our original and this second edition guide possible. I'm indebted to Maurice Sendak who gave me access to his collection of vintage Mickey items. Doug and Pat Wengel, noted Disneyana collectors and dealers kindly provided photos of many rare 1930s Disney tin wind-up toys and consulted with me on the values. Thanks also to David Smith, Walt Disney Archives Director, for information on Disney copyright markings used on merchandise since 1930.

There are numerous items pictured in this guide provided by their actual creators. From the 1930s into the 1970s, Gordon Gold and his father Sam Gold, known as the "premium king," created thousands of toys used as sales incentive premiums. Over the past decade, Hake's Americana & Collectibles offered at auction many of these toys from the Golds' archive where usually one example of each was preserved. Items in the guide of this origin are noted "Gordon Gold Archives." Our guide also includes the original art for numerous toy concept designs by Disney character merchandising executive Al Konetzni. As the "idea man" in Disney's New York office from 1953 to 1981, Konetzni proposed toy concepts to Disney's many licensees. His most famous creation is the Disney school bus design lunch box which became the best selling lunch box ever. In 1999, Disney honored Konetzni with the title "Disney Legend."

Three collectors made major contributions to this comprehensive guide. John K. Snyder, Jr., President of Diamond International Galleries, of which Hake's Americana is a division, made many pieces from his personal collection available and used his specialized knowledge of the nationwide toy market to prepare our Disneyana recent sales Market Report. Melissa Bowersox created our extensive section on modern Disney pins and revised the values for our second edition. Steve Geppi, the CEO of Diamond International Galleries and Diamond Comic Distributors, made the creation and continuation of this guide possible, as well as offering access to his personal Disneyana collection.

Our in-depth and uniquely informative section on Disney posters combines photos from Russ Cochran and Bruce Hershenson with pricing assistance from Bruce Hershenson and Peter Merolo.

For additional photos and information, my thanks to Dan Morphy, Tom Sage Jr., and Shanelle Weaver of Morphy Auctions, Gary Selmonsky for items from his collection, Harrison Judd for photos of the Sendak collection, Carl Lobel, Phil Hecht, Jamie Hillstead, and Paul Merolle.

Many hours of research were needed to create our Disney category histories and featured articles. Thanks are gratefully extended to Tema Zerbe, David Gerstein, Charlie Roberts, and Mark Squirek.

The scope and detail of this guide requires contributions from many people on the production staffs of three Diamond companies. At Hake's Americana, a special thanks to my assistant Joan Carbaugh, General Manager Alex Winter and Mike Bollinger, Jack Dixey, Mark Herr, Kelly McClain, Kevin McCray, Linda Snyder, Sara Snyder, Mark Squirek, and Sally Weaver.

At Diamond International Galleries, headed by John K. Snyder, Jr., for production and marketing assistance, my thanks to Melissa Bowersox, Jamie David, Joe McGuckin, Mike Wilbur, and Heather Winter. All our efforts came together under the auspices of Gemstone Publishing. A special thanks to Robert M. Overstreet for use of information from his authoritative reference *The Official Overstreet Comic Book Price Guide*. Shouldering much of the responsibility for this guide's integration and look are Brandon DeStefano, Editor; Mark Huesman, Production Coordinator; and Brenda Busick, Creative Director. My thanks to each and a special acknowledgement to Tom Gordon III for his recommendations and coordination of the hundreds of item additions to the second edition. Also at Gemstone, thanks to Executive Editor and Associate Publisher J.C. Vaughn.

Rounding out our numerous contributors on various fronts, my appreciation is extended to Ken Chapman, John Hone, Steve Ison, Ken Sequin, Jim Halperin, Ed Jaster, Bill Hughes, Harry Matetsky, Dave Anderson, David Callahan, Bruce Hamilton, Joe and Nadia Mannarino, Robert Rogovin, Jay Parrino and Tom Tumbusch. Special credit goes to my wife, Jonell, both for her support and insightful ideas.

From myself and everyone in the Diamond family of companies, we thank our advertisers for their support of our second edition. We also appreciate the support of our audience and urge our readers to mention this guide when responding to advertisements.

INVEST IN THE BEST.

The long-standing leader in high-quality archival supplies, E. Gerber Supply Products understands why every one of its valued customers is serious about this deceptively simple sentiment. Why else would they choose its archival products – the finest preservation and storage supply products on the market – to keep their collectibles pristine and resistant to the ravages of age?

The answer is simple: E. Gerber Supply Products offers serious protection for the serious collector. And its customers only demand the best. **Shouldn't you?**

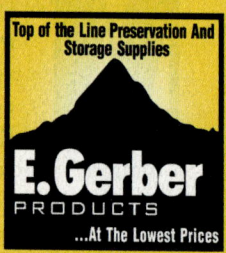

Top of the Line Preservation And Storage Supplies

E. Gerber PRODUCTS ...At The Lowest Prices

Formerly "Snugs"™

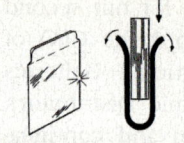

Made from 4 mil thick Mylar®.
Dimensions are width x height plus two - 7/8" non-foldable flaps.

Item#	Size	Description	50	200	1000
700R	7 x 10 1/2	Current Comics- 1990's	$19.25	$63.00	$276.00
725R	7 1/4x 10 1/2	Standard Comics - 1970's-90's	$19.50	$64.00	$282.00
775R	7 3/4 x 10 1/2	Silver/Golden Comics - 1950's-70's	$20.00	$66.00	$288.00
800R	8 X 10 1/2	Golden Age Comics - 1940's-50's	$21.25	$70.00	$306.00
825R	8 1/4 x 10 1/2	Super Golden Age Comics	$22.25	$73.00	$318.00
550R	5 x 5 1/2	Compact Disc	$12.50	$42.00	$180.00
625R	6 1/4 x 8 5/8	Reader's Digest & Paperbacks	$19.00	$62.00	$270.00
875R	8 3/4 x 11 1/2	Large Comics, Mag. & Letter	$24.25	$78.00	$348.00
900R	9 x 11 1/2	Standard Magazines	$29.50	$97.00	$420.00
914R	9 x 14 1/2	Legal Size	$35.50	$116.00	$504.00
950R	9 1/2 x 12 1/4	Sheet Music, Large Magazines	$31.25	$106.00	$468.00
1013R	10 x 13	Playboy Magazine (no flaps)	$34.75	$115.00	$504.00
	Add Shipping & Handling		$2.00	$7.00	$22.00

Item#	No Flaps Size	Description	10	50	200
1114R	11 1/2 x 14 1/2	Lobby Cards & Photos	$13.50	$55.25	$190.00
1117R	11 1/2 x 17 1/2	Portfolio, Art	$16.00	$66.00	$228.00
1218R	12 1/2 x 18 1/2	Tabloid, Art	$18.00	$75.50	$258.00
1313R	13 x 13	Record	$19.25	$80.50	$288.00
1418R	14 3/4 x 18 1/2	Original Art, Posters	$21.50	$86.50	$300.00
1422R	14 3/4 x 22 3/4	Window Card Poster	$28.75	$115.25	$408.00
1518R	15 1/2 x 18 1/2	Art, Photo, Poster	$22.00	$90.00	$312.00
1524R	15 1/2 x 24 1/2	Newspaper, Poster	$30.00	$122.50	$426.00
1620R	16 1/2 x 20 1/2	Photo, Original Art	$27.50	$114.00	$396.00
1721R	17 1/2 x 21 1/2	Art, Newspaper	$28.50	$116.50	$408.00
1824R	18 1/2 x 24 1/2	Art, Photo, Maps	$36.50	$150.00	$522.00
2136R	21 1/2 x 36 1/2	Maps, Art, Posters	$48.00	$198.00	$696.00
2436R	24 1/2 x 36 1/2	Newspapers, Posters	$52.00	$212.50	$744.00
3626R	36 1/2 x 26 1/2	Maps	$60.50	$249.50	$864.00
2819R	28 3/4 x 19 1/2	Maps, Atlas Pages	$47.00	$193.25	$672.00
2822R	28 3/4 x 22 3/4	Half-Sheet, Poster	$49.25	$201.50	$714.00
4331R	43 x 31	Posters, Maps	$84.00	$345.50	$1,200.00
4836R	48 1/2 x 36 1/2	Newspapers, Maps	$106.00	$434.50	$1,512.00
	Add Shipping & Handling		$5.00	$10.00	$35.00

CGC Storage Box

The official storage box of the CGC!

Official CGC Storage Box

Holds up to 30 CGC-"slabbed" comics
Durable construction withstands
200 pounds of pressure

Item#	Size	Description	Price per:	1-10	11-50	51+
514	15x8 1/2x13	CGC Storage Box		$4.50	$3.30	$2.75
545	15 1/4x9 7/8x14 1/4	CGC Magazine Storage Box		$4.50	$3.30	$2.75
		Add Shipping & Handling*		$8.00	$20.00	$40.00

Corrugated Comic Carton

ACID FREE BOXES

Grey corrugated. Acid-free, 3% buffered, 200 lb strength. Min. ph of 8.5 throughout. Life time acid-free storage. Box plus separate lid.

The boxes have had a **3% calcium carbonate buffer** added, which maintains an acid-free alkaline ph content of 8.0-8.5 throughout, not just on the surface.

All boxes fold flat for shipping. Easy snap up assembly. Does not require glue nor tape.

Sold in Packs of 5 Boxes

Item#	Size	Description	Price per:	5	20	50
13	15 x 8 x 11 1/2	Silver/Golden Comics		$45.00	$175.00	$400.00
15	15 x 9 1/4 x 12 1/2	Super Golden/Magazines		$47.50	$185.00	$450.00
		Add Shipping & Handling*		$8.00	$24.00	$49.00

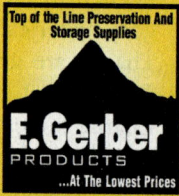

Top of the Line Preservation And Storage Supplies

E. Gerber PRODUCTS ...At The Lowest Prices

The Best Protection at the Best Price!

For a complete list of our affordable archival products, please call us toll-free at

1-800-79-MYLAR

from 8:00 a.m. to 5:00 p.m. EST, or mail your request to:

E. Gerber Products • 1720 Belmont Avenue
Suite C • Baltimore, MD 21244
Fax: 1-410-944-9363
e-mail: archival@egerber.com

www.egerber.com

DON'T FORGET OUR TOP-QUALITY BACKING BOARDS!

We can provide any custom size to fit your needs! Boards are genuine acid-free, virgin wood, cellular fiber that meets strict U.S. Government standards for archival storage. Both styles are white on both sides, and contain 3% calcium carbonate buffer throughout, maintains ph of 8.0

FULL-BACK
- 42 mil, Acid-free,
- 3% Buffered Backing Board

HALF-BACK
- 24 mil, Acid-free
- 3% Buffered Backing Board

* Minimum Shipping Charge $7.00   Mylar® by Dupont Co. or approved equivalent.

PLEASE NOTE: All returns are subject to a 10% restock fee. Returned items must be undamaged and unopened unless otherwise approved.

COLLECTORS:
Make Your Next Big Find a Great Comics Shop!

COMIC SHOP LOCATOR SERVICE
888-COMIC-BOOK
comicshoplocator.com

By phone and online, millions of people around the world have used the Comic Shop Locator Service to find comic book specialty stores in their areas!

Sponsored By

FREE COMIC BOOK DAY
1st Saturday In May
www.freecomicbookday.com

INTRODUCTION

Welcome to the second edition of the most comprehensive price guide devoted to the entire spectrum of Disney collectibles. The acceptance and success of our first edition published in 2005 is gratifying and we thank our readers for the opportunity to expand those efforts.

This edition features new articles, updated historical information for each section, hundreds of added items and a total review and fine tuning of the guide values. Still, our original goal is unchanged. This guide's purpose is to document, date and evaluate, at current market prices, potentially all forms of collectibles that comprise the term Disneyana. While we include many items related to Disney's recent movies and authorized collectible releases, naturally our slant is towards the older material which matches the focus of most collectors.

In the first edition, I stated "The universe of collectors who share our interests is immense." That remains true, although we are also in a fascinating period of first generation collections in transition. As I prepared the introduction for this book's first edition, my search of the Disney Collectibles category on eBay resulted in 52,061 listings. Now close to two years later, the same search has decreased to 47,911 listings.

Both numbers are somewhat amazing, since they represent thousands of people paying fees for listing and commissions to sell their items. Even more amazing is the larger body of collectors purchasing these items. And, finally, squaring my amazement factor, on eBay this day a mere 2,462 items are in the pre-1968 Vintage Disneyana category. This number of vintage Disney collectibles, the focus of most collectors, has been decreasing over the last few years and reflects the fact that a finite number of objects were preserved prior to the mid-1960s when the concept of a collectible, and its potential value, was realized.

Since 1967 I have been searching out Disney collectibles treasured by their original owners and thus saved from oblivion. When Hake's Americana & Collectibles began, from the very first, Disneyana was among the auction's most popular categories. Now, forty years later, many collections that Hake's auctions helped to build are coming to the marketplace. This is a natural occurrence for all collectibles hobbies that attracted a large number of collectors from the mid-1960s and later. In most cases, if the collector bought prudently and with an eye to quality, over the ensuing years the marketplace has rewarded the investment. Today's collector benefits from this turn-over as rare items long absent from the marketplace make brief return appearances before once again being absorbed into a collection for private enjoyment.

While the price changes from our 1967 inaugural year until 2007 have been remarkable, three things remain constant: the appeal of Disney collectibles spans all generations, wonderful items are available to Disney collectors from all time periods and in all price ranges and there always seems to be new exciting discoveries, regardless of the Disney collecting category.

The Disneyana market since our first edition of this guide has been solid and broad. Rarely offered items, many coming from the collections assembled decades ago, consistently achieve record prices. I hope this guide contributes to making the pursuit of Disney collectibles both more enjoyable and more profitable for both the casual collector and the many for whom Disney collecting is a paramount pastime.

Ted Hake
March, 2007

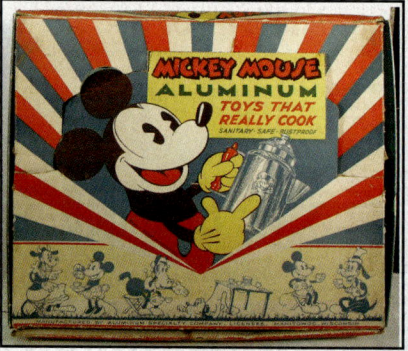 

Mickey Mouse Aluminum Cookware Set 16x13" box containing 13 aluminum pieces and paper napkins 1930s.

PRICE GUIDE OVERVIEW

Our guide contains 137 sections detailing Disneyana collecting areas such as specific characters, movie or television program titles, in-house Disney studio material and more. Every type of Disney-associated collectible is included regardless of age, construction material and purpose. The vast majority of listed items are broadly defined as toys, but also listed are animation cels, original art, studio Christmas cards, World War II insignia designs and more. There are also sections on Oswald the Rabbit with items from the era when Disney was producing Oswald cartoons, a section on Flip the Frog, a character created by early Disney associate Ub Iwerks, and a section on the "duck artist" Carl Barks.

The section arrangement is in alphabetical order. Each section is introduced with a history of the subject. The individual items are photo-illustrated and designated with a letter abbreviation of the section title plus a sequential item number. The photo caption code matches the code accompanying that item's description. Quotation marks in the item's title denote words actually appearing on the item. Where possible, the exact name used by the item's maker or sponsor is used in the title, although these words are not in quotations unless they actually appear on the item.

Following the item title is the year of issue if known exactly or stated as c. for circa if the date is approximate. Following the date, most items are detailed by the item's maker, publisher or sponsor name along with relevant details of size, number of pages, identifying marks, number in a set, and so on.

The description ends with three current market values for the item in Good, Fine and Near Mint condition. It is most important to read the introductory section defining these condition terms to properly understand and use the values specified for each item.

If only a single value is given, typically for items issued within the past decade, that value is for an item in Near Mint condition. For the Disney poster section two values are given for examples either Very Good or Very Fine.

Disney-related comics could be a book unto themselves. We know that many Disney collectors would like to collect some books, but find the varied listings difficult to understand. We have simplified our listings with this in mind. The term "Disney comics" refers to all comic books that featured a Disney character, movie or theme. Specific books are referred to by their own individual title.

Print runs on Disney comics were among the largest ever. This means that many early comics can be purchased for very affordable prices. Since the number of Disney comics easily reaches into the thousands, we have decided to use 1962 as a rough cut-off date when listing Disney comics. This decision was not arbitrary. It roughly coincides with the year that Dell stopped publishing the Disney books and the line was picked up by a new company, Gold Key. However, that time line is still a bit blurry as several fine books deserved to be listed.

"Mickey Mouse Magazine" Vol. 1 No. 6 from 1934. Collectors can get into the swing of things with early vintage Disney memorabilia. This magazine was a premium issued by various dairy companies.

Listing every Disney item in one guide is impossible, but like Mickey "A to Z" from Whitman, 1936, we cover the bases from A Bug's Life to Zorro.

PRICE GUIDE OVERVIEW

Walt Disney's Comics And Stories Vol. 1 No. 1 from 1940. Disney is a timeless tradition as seen in Disney Comics which continue on today allowing many generations to enjoy the classic characters and stories.

Disney comics appeared under many different titles. While several characters had their own regular books, there are three anthology-type books that need to be set apart. They are *Four Color*, *Dell Giant* and *Walt Disney's Comics and Stories*.

Where a full series of comics was published under one title, such as *Walt Disney's Comics and Stories*, we have listed all the issues under that title instead of listing them by the character or characters featured in each book.

For *Four Color*, an anthology title that included characters from many different Disney projects as well as other companies, we have listed only the Disney-themed issues chronologically, omitting the non-Disney issues. Correspondingly, the numbering sequence will show gaps between these issues in which Disney appeared.

When a character or movie appears in the *Four Color* series, we have listed a reminder with that character's historical introduction. For instance, the film *Babes in Toyland* has its own section of collectibles, but the comic adaptation is pictured under *Four Color* #1282.

Dell Giant was also an anthology title that was home to many different characters. Since Dell did not start numbering *Dell Giant* consecutively until ten years after they started publishing the series, these issues are listed alphabetically by character or title, with the publication date listed after the title.

Since many Disneyana enthusiasts specialize their areas of collecting, there will be some instances of items listed in two categories. This is particularly true of comic books featuring the work of Carl Barks.

For titles featuring individual characters, such as Mickey Mouse, Donald Duck and Uncle Scrooge, we have listed the earliest issues, and you will find them listed by character name. In most cases, the early issues and selected later issue are listed.

As the years passed, the license for Disney books was acquired by new publishers. We have listed that transition in text at the appropriate place during the run of that title. Where possible, we have included examples of the new publisher's work.

The prices listed with each book have been derived from the 2007 edition of *The Official Overstreet Comic Book Price Guide*. The most important factors in determining the price are the grade and scarcity of the issue. We have listed the prices for comics graded 2.0 (Good), 6.0 (Fine) and 9.2 (Near Mint -).

TYPES OF ITEMS

Disney collectibles come in all shapes and sizes, made from a diversity of materials. This guide includes examples of everything from the earliest Disney years to the most recent. Sizes range from 13/16" pin-back buttons to a 9-foot long outdoor banner promoting the French publication "Le Journal de Mickey."

While the majority of items are of United States origin, Disney, for decades, has been a worldwide marketer. Accordingly, our listings include numerous items intended for distribution in Australia, Canada, France, Italy, Germany, Great Britain, Japan, Netherlands, Norway, South America and other areas.

Aside from product advertising collectibles, original art and other Disney Studio-related collectibles, most items we list are "toys." Webster's New World Dictionary defines a toy as "any article to play with, especially playthings for children." This definition includes both store-bought toys as well as those distributed as a premium by a sponsor. Premium toys may be free or sometimes require a small payment and/or proof of purchase of the sponsor's product.

While guide listings are comprehensive, they are selective and

PRICE GUIDE OVERVIEW

by no means all inclusive. Items included are not necessarily more common or rarer than items not included.

DATES OF ISSUE

Within each category, items are listed chronologically by decade starting with the earliest specific year, followed by the earliest approximate year followed by those items of an unknown year but approximated to the earliest decade. The sequence then repeats for each successive decade. When a specific year or decade is open to question, the date is listed with the abbreviation c. for circa.

To determine issue dates, most often the copyright date is used when this is obviously consistent with the date of issue. Other primary sources for dating include Disney merchandise catalogues, wholesale or retail toy catalogues, and newspaper or other advertisements. When an item was available over several years, the earliest known date is specified. Most original art used to create cartoons or animated features is undated and obviously pre-dates the movie's release date, but the release date is typically used since the creation date is unknown.

Other dating clues may come from the character's design. For example, most five-fingered Mickeys are circa 1930 and of European origin. Similarly, most Mickeys prior to 1938 are referred to as having "pie-eyes" due to the white notch accents on the eyes. Mickeys with solid black pupils generally began in 1938. Of course, there are exceptions. Most notably, all the Mickeys from his revival era of the mid-1960s until today which are created with pie-eyes to capture his vintage appearance.

If an item depicts multiple characters, who is shown and when that character was introduced may help establish a date. The name of a manufacturer in business during particular years or the use of synthetic materials introduced in a certain era may also help establish a date.

While there are Disney movie promotional items, largely posters, prior to 1930, the vast percentage of Disney collectibles were issued between 1930 and now. One of the following copyright notices usually appears on an item issued during these specific years. However, there are exceptions and overlaps as licensees sometimes used an older copyright notice if an item was in production when the rule changed and Disney adopted a new copyright specification. Along with the copyright notices are a few dates that relate to information sometimes found on the items, tags or packaging. Disney's first character merchandise contract dates to February 3, 1930 with the New York City novelty firm Geo. Borgfeldt & Co.

1930-32: © Walter Disney, © W.E. Disney, © Walter E. Disney
1932-9/30/38: © Walt Disney Enterprises, © W.D.E., © Walt Disney Ent.
9/30/38 – 2/6/86: © Walt Disney Productions, ©WDP
2/6/86 – current: © The Walt Disney Company, © Walt Disney Co., © Disney
May 1, 1943 – June 30, 1963: Postal zone numbers in use by large and some medium-sized cities.
July 1, 1963 – current: ZIP codes in use.
1975: Universal Product Codes (UPC) begin on packaging.
1970s: Two letter state name abbreviations become standard.

ABBREVIATIONS

Three abbreviations are used very frequently for recurring descriptive purposes.

c. = circa. An approximate date.
cello. = celluloid. Usually referring to a pin-back button or other small collectible having a protective covering of this substance. The term and abbreviation are also used for convenience to indicate similar latter day substances, such as acetate or thin plastic, which gradually replaced the use of flammable celluloid coverings after World War II.
litho. = lithographed process. Usually referring to a pin-back button or other small collectible with the design printed directly on metal, usually tin, rather than "cello" version wherein the design is printed on paper with a celluloid protective covering.

ADDITIONAL ABBREVIATIONS:
BLB = Big Little Book series by Whitman Publishing Co.
BTLB = Better Little Book series by Whitman Publishing Co.
KFS = King Features Syndicate
K.K. Publications = Kay Kamen Publications
WDE = Walt Disney Enterprises
WDP = Walt Disney Productions

SIZES

Most items in the guide are detailed by exact measurements of size. The format for three-dimensional objects is two measurements followed by a third specifying depth, length or height. For items of standardized sizes such as Big Little Books or comic books, sizes are not specified.

Uncle Scrooge keeps a strong hand on his finances. Knowing the value of your collectibles will not only help you make prudent acquisitions, but also shrewd sales. Uncle Scrooge figurine 1950s by Hagen-Renaker.

GUIDE VALUES

Values in this guide are estimations of retail prices for each item in Good, Fine and Near Mint condition. The prices stated are based on the author's 40 years of experience in auctioning and selling all types of popular culture collectibles, with a concentration on Disneyana since 1967. Most prices are based on actual sales at auction during the past decade, adjusted for any lapse of time and with the extreme results of an occasional "bidder war" eliminated.

Also considered were sales lists, show prices, transactions between individuals and advice from collectors and dealers with expertise in certain specialties.

Few vintage items are still truly Mint, so the highest grade listed for each item is Near Mint. However, there are those rare exceptions. Strictly Mint items with no traces of wear might command 25% or even more than the listed Near Mint value. Those items falling between the specified grades are termed Very Good or Very Fine. A reasonable approximation of value for these items would be the midpoint value between Good and Fine or Fine and Near Mint.

Original packaging, particularly if illustrated and appealing in design, is highly valued by many collectors. This applies usually to toys of a three-dimensional nature and includes mail order premiums. While premium mailer envelopes and boxes are not usually illustrated, the package often included an instruction sheet, order form or premium catalogue; collectors do consider these important. Thus, a wind-up toy illustrated original box or a "complete" premium package may add 50%-100% to the value of the basic toy. In many cases, the price guide evaluations take these options into account and specify separate values for toy and box or premiums complete as issued in mailer and Near Mint.

DEFINITIONS: GOOD, FINE, NEAR MINT

Value has three primary determining factors: rarity, demand, and condition. Of these, condition is paramount. If a very rare, very desirable item has a significant condition problem, a large part of the potential buyer universe ceases to exist.

Accurately assessing an item's condition is a crucial step in using the Good, Fine and Near Mint prices specified in this guide. For any given item, issued before the advent of collector targeted items intended to be preserved, the percentage of items still surviving in Near Mint condition is likely to be very small. This low supply, coupled with collector demand for outstanding condition, accounts for the disproportionately high values assigned to Near Mint examples versus those in Fine or Good. Furthermore, the survivability of an item depends on its material construction. The chances of a bisque figure remaining Near Mint over seventy years far exceeds those for a comic book. Thus, the value increase between Fine and Near Mint for a bisque is typically proportional whereas for a comic book the increase is a geometric progression. To correctly compare prices encountered in the marketplace with the values specified in this guide, the following condition definitions must be understood and applied. Condition factors vary according to an item's basic materials and those materials generally fall into the following four categories.

PRICE GUIDE OVERVIEW

This Pinocchio Good Housekeeping card stock sign from 1940 is just one example of the numerous materials used in producing Disney memorabilia over the years. Many store signs and promotional displays are scarce due to the materials used and their size.

PAPER/CARDBOARD

Near Mint: Fresh, bright original crisply-inked appearance with only the slightest perceptible evidence of wear, soil, fade or creases. The item should lay flat, corners must be close to perfectly square and any staples must be rust-free.

Fine: An above average example with attractive appearance but moderately noticeable aging or wear including: small creases and a few small edge tears; lightly worn corners; minimal browning, yellowing, dust or soiling; light staple rust but no stain on surrounding areas; no more than a few tiny paper flakes missing. Small tears repaired on blank reverse side are generally acceptable if the front image is not badly affected.

Good: A complete item with no more than a few small pieces missing. Although showing obvious aging, accumulated flaws such as creases, tears, dust and other soiling, repairs, insect damage, mildew and brittleness must not combine to render the item unsound and too unattractive for display.

METAL

Near Mint: Painted or lithographed tin objects, such as toys, must retain at least 97% original color with only a few non-obtrusive random small scratches or rub marks. An object with un-painted metallic finish, such as a ring, must retain 90% or more of its original bright finish metallic luster as well as any accent coloring on the lettering or design. Badges must have the original pin intact and rings must have near perfect circular bands. Any small areas missing original luster must be free of rust, corrosion, dark tarnish or any other defect that stands out enough to render the naked eye appearance of the piece less than almost perfect.

Fine: An above average item with moderate wear. Painted items must retain 80% of original color. Metallic luster items should retain at least 50%. There may be small, isolated areas with pinpoint corrosion spotting, tarnish or similar evidences of aging. Badges must have the original pin, although perhaps slightly bent, and rings must have bands with no worse than minor bends. Although general wear does show, the item retains an overall attractive appearance with strong, bright color or luster.

Good: An average well-used or aged item missing about 35% paint or nearly all metallic luster. Badges may have a replaced pin and ring bands may be distorted or obviously reshaped. There may be moderate but not totally defacing evidence of bends, dents, scratches, corrosion, etc. Aside from a replaced pin, completeness is still essential.

This c. 1931 Mickey Mouse Sparkler with original box is a classic toy which features a sparking action.

Mickey Mouse Converse Sneakers button from c.1935. Celluloid buttons have a circular metal rim on the reverse, called a collet, to hold the image paper and celluloid covering in place. Lithographed tin buttons are paint on metal so no collet is needed.

CELLULOID OR LITHOGRAPHED TIN PIN-BACK BUTTONS

Near Mint: Both celluloid and lithographed tin pin-backs retain the original, bright appearance without visual defects. For celluloid, this means the total absence of staining (known as foxing to button collectors). There can be no apparent surface scratches when the button is viewed directly; although when viewed at an angle in reflected light, there may be a few very shallow and small hairline marks on the celluloid surface. The celluloid covering must be totally intact with no splits, even on the reverse where the celluloid covering is folded under the collet, a metal ring that holds the parts together. Lithographed tin buttons may have no more than two or three missing pinpoint-size dots of color and no visible scratches. Even in Near Mint condition, a button image noticeably off-center, as made, reduces desirability and therefore value to some price below Near Mint depending on the severity of the off-centering.

Fine: Both styles of buttons may have a few apparent scattered small scratches. Some minor flattening or a tiny dent noticeable to the touch, but not visually, is also acceptable. Celluloids may have a very minimal amount of age spotting or moisture stain, largely confined to the rim area, not distracting from the graphics and not dark in color. There may be a small celluloid split on the reverse by the collet, but the celluloid covering must still lay flat enough not to cause a noticeable bump on the side edge. Lithographed tin buttons may have only the slightest traces of paint roughness, or actual rust, visible on the front. A variation of the celluloid pin-back is the celluloid covered pocket mirror which holds a glass mirror on the reverse rather than a fastener pin. Condition definitions for pocket mirrors match those for celluloid buttons except a fine condition item may have clouded or smoked mirror and some streaks of missing silvering. A cracked mirror typically reduces desirability to the level of Good condition.

Good: Celluloid pin-backs may have moderate dark spotting or moisture stain not exceeding 25% of the surface area. There can be some slight evidence of color fade, a small nick on the front celluloid, or a small celluloid split by the reverse collet causing a small edge bump. Dark extensive stain, deep or numerous scratches and extensive crazing of the celluloid covering each render the button to a condition status of less than Good and essentially unsalable. Lithographed tin buttons must retain strong color and be at least 75% free of noticeable surface wear or they too fall into the likely unsalable range.

OTHER MATERIALS

(Ceramic, Glass, Wood, Fabric, Composition, Rubber, Plastic, Vinyl, etc.)

Near Mint: Regardless of the substance, the item retains its fresh, original appearance and condition without defect. Only the slightest traces of visually non-distracting wear are acceptable.

Fine: Each material has its own inherent weaknesses in withstanding time, typical use or actual abuse as follows:

Ceramic, porcelain, china, bisque and other similar clay-based objects are susceptible to edge chips. These are acceptable if minimal. Glazed items very typically develop hairline crazing not considered a flaw unless hairlines have also darkened.

Glass is fragile and obviously susceptible to missing chips, flakes or hairline fractures but acceptable in modest quantity.

Wood items, as well as the faithful likeness composition wood, generally withstand aging and use well. Small stress fractures or a few small missing flakes are acceptable if the overall integrity of the item is not affected.

Fabric easily suffers from weave splits or snags plus stain spots are frequently indelible. Weaving breaks are generally

PRICE GUIDE OVERVIEW

Donald Duck large celluloid roly-poly from the 1930s. Celluloid toys are difficult to locate in high grade as they have a tendency to break easily.

acceptable in limited numbers but fabric holes are not. Stains may not exceed a small area and only a blush of color change.

Composition items, typically dolls or figurines, tend to acquire hairline cracks of the thin surface coating. This is commonly expected and normally acceptable to the point of obvious severity. Color loss should not exceed 20% and not involve critical facial details.

Rubber items, either of solid or hollow variety, tend to lose original pliability and evolve into a rigid hardness that frequently results in a warped or deformed appearance. Some degree of original flexibility is preferred or at least minimal distortion.

Plastic and vinyl items have a tendency to split at areas of high stress or frequent use. This is frequently expected and excused by collectors up to the point of distracting from overall appearance or function.

Good: Items of any material are expected to be complete and/or functional. Obvious wear is noticeable, but the item retains its structural soundness. Wear or damage must not exceed the lower limits of being reasonably attractive for display purposes.

COLLECT FOR PERSONAL ENJOYMENT

If you care about the psychology of collecting, much research and speculation is available for study. Most collectors view the collecting "bug" as a blessing, others without the "bug" may see collecting as a curse.

Some people believe collectors are born, it's in the blood from the get-go. Other people might be able to identify some event early in life that instilled the desire to collect. Still others come to collecting as adults upon exposure to objects that resonate personally and launch a search for similar treasures.

Collectors are always searching. Collecting is mostly about what objects are already owned and what is desired to make the collection better. Usually, collectors aren't motivated by a need to show off their collection, but interest by others is welcomed. Building the collection is a process of self-expression and the satisfaction that it creates is rationale enough.

Here are a few thoughts on a related but different subject – why collecting in general and collecting Disneyana in particular make sense.

As we proceed through our lives, we all acquire a multitude of objects. Indeed, the acquisition of objects is one of the most basic human traits. Our cave men ancestors who put forth the effort to acquire that extra measure of food, fur, firewood, weapons and tools were the ones likely to survive the longest.

In today's society, most of us rather quickly and easily acquire the necessities for day-to-day living. Many of us have the time, energy, money and intellectual curiosity to acquire objects beyond the necessities. We are able to acquire objects that bring us a sense of satisfaction and enjoyment. Our lifetime accumulations make us all collectors in a general sense, but when we seek out, acquire and appreciate a particular type of object we have a focus, the hallmark of a true collector.

So why does collecting make sense? Many other recreational pursuits share with collecting a wide range of psychological and emotional benefits. These may include simply providing a means of relaxation to offering opportunities for communication and interaction with people who share a common interest. The pursuits which bring these benefits often require financial expenditures and often the money spent is irretrievably gone. The bonus that accrues to astute collectors is that rather than dissipating financial resources, they are actually increasing their wealth over time as they acquire objects with the potential to gain in value.

Since the mid-1960s, the buy-

PRICE GUIDE OVERVIEW

Donald's Better Self booklet by Whitman from 1939 features Donald as an angel and also a devil. While searching for items for your collection make sure you balance prudence with temptation.

ing and selling of collectibles has grown to a multi-billion dollar industry. This is rather amazing considering that Webster's New World Dictionary defines "collectible" as "any of a class of old things, but not antiques, that people collect as a hobby, specifically a thing of no great intrinsic value."

Collectors spending billions on things "of no great intrinsic value" must have clear goals in mind and be rewarded with benefits or this economic activity would never have grown to its present level. If one's goals are solely financial, that person is more properly termed an investor than a collector. For collectors, financial benefits are often an important consideration and a positive bonus, but there are more important considerations. Collectors feel passionate about the objects they seek and search for them with enthusiasm. The collector identifies with those objects emotionally. There is recognition intellectually of an item's historical importance or appreciation of its physical qualities. Sometimes, as with Disneyana collecting, the emotional connection with objects is intensely personal.

Amazingly, there are few Americans alive today who were not the childhood owner of some type of Disney character toy. Disney characters are imbedded in our deepest psyche and, indeed, the phenomenon is worldwide. Our memories of childhood, both the trials and triumphs, stay with us until our demise. Some say, in a negative way, the collectors of Disneyana or toys in general are out to recapture their youth. The reality is that collectors of these objects never lost their youth. They are collected as a way to keep us in touch with our youth. Disneyana collections bring our past experiences to life in a physical form to be sensed visually and tactically and thus enhancing precious memories. Developing all the nuances of astute collecting and the evolution of a collector's focus takes time. The journey is rewarding in many ways. In contrast to our daily obligations and concerns, collecting is an adventure to be savored, a way to express and enjoy our passions. Collecting Disneyana is about having fun. It's a positive experience and it makes sense.

THE SEARCH

Even if a collector is precisely focused on a specific area of Disneyana collecting, he needs a framework of knowledge against which potential acquisitions may be evaluated. Honing these skills is an evolving process which should be an enjoyable journey of appreciation. The goal is to absorb the knowledge and develop the techniques that enable the collector to evaluate objects and recognize quality when it presents itself.

The resources to acquire this framework of knowledge are both plentiful, and with the Internet, more accessible than ever. There are websites devoted to specific Disney characters, filmographies, etc. For toy collectors there are museums, reference books and clubs. We list some useful resources at the end of this section.

Disney clubs or clubs devoted to a particular type of collectible (banks, salt & pepper sets, etc.) publish member rosters and hold conventions. It's useful to find and meet collectors in the local area who share similar interests and travel to conventions, shows and in-person auctions. Observing and participating are the building blocks of an educated collector. An excellent source to learn about happenings in the world of Disney and character toys, both old and new, is Scoop! a free e-newsletter sponsored by the publisher of this book, Gemstone Publishing and Diamond International Galleries (visit www.hakes.com and click on the *Scoop* logo).

When it comes to finding items, newer collectors who don't thoroughly know the nuances of their items of interest are advised to know their dealer. Unlike Internet auction sites where both the authenticity and condition of the items may be misrepresented, innocently or with malice, there

PRICE GUIDE OVERVIEW

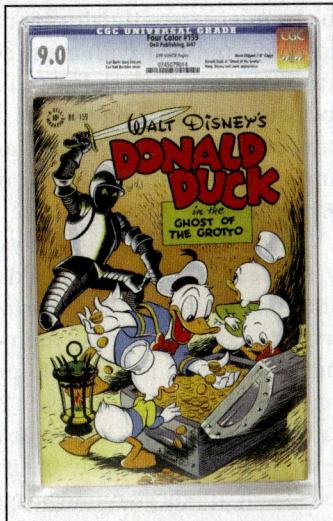

Four Color #159 CGC certified 9.0 from the Davis Crippen pedigree collection. Hunting for that next item for your collection is sometimes like searching for buried treasure.

are many nationally known sources for guaranteed authentic material such as Hake's Americana & Collectibles and the dealers advertising in this guide.

As a collector's knowledge and confidence in his focus area grows, he may safely expand his searches for items with less concern about overpaying or purchasing reproductions. Although the odds of a significant find vary greatly, potential sources include garage sales, flea markets, newspaper want ads, local auctions, antique shops or multi-dealer co-ops, general or specialized show venues, Internet auction sites, and in-person or catalogue/ phone/ Internet bidding specialized auctions with a field of nationwide or even worldwide bidders.

If the venue is an auction, some beforehand preparation is recommended. Is authenticity guaranteed or are items sold "buyer beware?" Know the terms of sale including bidding increments, applicable buyer's premium and return policy. If at all possible, personally inspect items of interest. If that isn't possible, ask condition questions in advance or deal with auctioneers whose condition statements are known to be accurate and trustworthy. Decide in advance what each item of interest is worth to you. One approach is to pick an amount you would be happy to pay and a second amount as the maximum you are willing to pay. Remember to calculate and add in any buyer's premium the auction may require. Do not exceed your maximum without careful consideration. There are, however, those special items. Will the extra bid paid now to acquire a special piece have much future significance or will the loss of the item be overshadowed by regret for a missed opportunity? The answer is part of the process of knowing ourselves and becoming astute collectors.

Here are resources useful to Disney collectors. Some specifically focus on Disneyana (*), others on popular culture collectibles in general:

SHOWS

All American Collectors Show - Glendale Civic Auditorium, Glendale, CA. (www.allamerican-cal.com or 310-455-2894)

Antique and Collectible Toy & Doll World Show - Kane County Fairgrounds, St. Charles, IL. (708-457-3888)

Atlantique City World's Largest Antique Show - Atlantic City, NJ Convention Center, F&W Publications (800-526-2724)

Dan Morphy's Antique Toy, Doll, Holiday & Advertising Show - York Fairgrounds Expo Center, York, PA (717-335-3435)

MAGAZINES & PRICE GUIDES

Antique Toy World (magazine), P.O. Box 34509, Chicago, IL, 60634 (773-725-0633)

The "E" Ticket (Disneyland Park specialty magazine), P.O. Box 8597 Mission Hills, CA 91346-8597 (www.the-e-ticket.com)

Hake's Price Guide to Character Toys, (6th edition, nearly 15,000 items pictured and priced), Random House and Gemstone Publishing. (www.hakes.com or toll-free 866-404-9800)

Overstreet Comic Book Price Guide, (37th edition) Random House and Gemstone Publishing (www.gemstonepub.com or toll-free 888-375-9800)

Tomart's Disneyana Update (magazine), Tomart Publications, 3300 Encrete Lane, Dayton, OH 45439-1944 (937-294-2250)

Toy Shop (magazine), F&W Publications, 700 E. State St, Iola, WI 54990 (800-258-0929)

CLUBS AND COLLECTIBLES INDUSTRY NEWS/EVENTS

NFFC – The Club for Disney Enthusiasts. An international, non-profit organization "committed to preserving and sharing the rich legacy of Walt Disney." Sponsors

PRICE GUIDE OVERVIEW

local chapters, publishes a newsletter and holds conventions. P.O. Box 19212, Irvine, CA (www.nffc.org or 714-731-4705).

Scoop – http://scoop.diamondgalleries.com, a free e-newsletter devoted to weekly coverage of collectibles industry news and events with many special features on character collectibles, celebrities, auction price highlights, new discoveries and more. Sponsored by Gemstone Publishing and Diamond International Galleries. To sign up visit www.hakes.com and click on the Scoop logo.

THE PURCHASE

The diversity of Disneyana available to the collector is both staggering and, at the same time, marvelous. There are myriad areas of specialization available for not only types of items but also time periods and price ranges. Each offers the collector rich opportunities for fun, immersion in our shared popular culture history, the creation of a wonderful assemblage of objects and, with wise selections, the potential for financial appreciation.

The golden rule of collecting is simple – collect what you enjoy. Along the way, educate yourself by enjoying shows, auctions, publications, conventions and fellow collectors.

When a purchase is made, the collector is putting his knowledge and instincts to the test. He is operating in a marketplace created by people with a shared interest in owning a particular object. Because Disneyana has a forty-year track record of being collected by 'modern day' collectors, many items have established values as

Don't let you're emotions cloud your judgment when making a purchase like the Donald Duck figurine c.1940 depicted here in an angry rage.

our guide demonstrates. Still, for each collector, the value of an item may be quite subjective and based on personal experience, preferences and emotions.

For vintage collectibles, as opposed to new creations designed for collector appeal, the rules of supply and demand are important, but actually secondary to the critical third factor of condition.

Supply, or rarity, is an assessment of availability. One important fact is that rarity does not automatically equate to value. Rare items without the support of much collector interest will stay at low to moderate prices. Other much more available items, immensely popular with many collectors, achieve high dollar values, especially in top condition. An example is the 1934 Mickey and Minnie Hand Car toy by Lionel Corporation.

Vintage collectibles, for a variety of reasons, were produced in finite quantities and have various survival rates. Factors include length of time an item was in production and its intended use. For example, a Vernon Kilns figurine meant to sit on a display shelf is more likely to survive undamaged than a wooden pull toy with paper labels designed for the active four year old. Some items, such as gum wrappers or toy boxes, were frequently discarded immediately after purchase.

Often, rarity is further increased as surviving examples enter collections to be held long-term. For example, many collections assembled in the 1960s and 1970s era of greater availability were brought to market in the 1990s and purchased by new owners who may hold them for a quarter century or longer.

Demand is an assessment of popular appeal. Levels of interest may vary over time and in some narrow specialties even be influenced by the actions of just a few individual collectors. The important issue for a person selecting a collecting focus is to find a subject with a demand level that results in a value structure comfortably in tune with available finances. Collecting goals must realistically match collecting resources.

Condition, in establishing values, is the third and frequently most influential critical consideration. Rarity and demand being equal, an item with a significant condition problem results in the elimination of a large percentage of the potential buyers. An item in exceptionally choice Near Mint or Mint condition will add to the universe of potential buyers. It seems everybody wants "mint" or close to it. Because the supply of vintage items in this best condition range is limited, costs are disproportionately high. However, the higher costs of collecting at this condition level will likely be justified and pay dividends down the road when it is time to sell.

There are numerous additional factors that influence an item's perceived value. Among these are considerations of historical importance, provenance, physical size, aesthetic qualities and subject qualities that may attract interest from several distinct groups of collectors. For example, the Lionel Mickey and Minnie Hand Car appeals to three groups: train collectors, wind-up collectors and Disneyana collectors.

On top of this, in auctions the unknown emotional motivations of competing bidders provide the wild card factor. In auction bidding, it's wise to plan ahead and set a maximum amount for each desired item. In the heat of bidding, one can always rationalize that the first personal maximum was too conservative or optimistic and exceed it once. If that proves unsuccessful, it's time to do a reality check on desires and finances before proceeding with higher bids.

When the buying decision is imminent, reflect on whether the item conforms to your collecting focus. Does it grab your attention, pique your interest, spark your enthusiasm? Apply brutal, rigorous standards. You are taking one of many steps that together are going to play a big role in determining the future potential value of your collection. Try to buy the best example that fits your budget or that will likely ever present itself for purchase. Step up for important pieces. A few dollars "too much" now may quickly become irrelevant in terms of satisfaction and potential growth in value.

Restored items require the collector to balance many factors. How desirable do you find this item? Will an un-restored example likely be encountered soon? Is the restoration done professionally and not obvious? Is the piece sufficiently discounted in relation to an undamaged example? If the answers fit your goals and standards, make the purchase.

Restoration takes many forms depending on the material substance of the collectible. From mending a box corner split, to filling in a china mug rim flake, to the near total restoration of a lithographed tin image – nearly all things are possible for the professional restorer. The processes require skill, practice and the correct materials. Many items are made worse, rather than better, by over-confident amateurs. Responsible sellers must volunteer the degree of restoration to potential buyers.

REPRODUCTIONS & FANTASIES

Not all reproductions are created equally. Licensed or properly authorized reproductions, indelibly marked as such, allow people to own wonderful objects at reasonable prices. Unfortunately, other reproductions are created by people who deceive for profit. The collector's best defense is acquiring knowledge about a chosen specialty and patronizing dealers and auction houses who unconditionally guarantee their merchandise as authentic. Surprisingly, many big names in the auction world do not guarantee authenticity. Read the fine print prior to participating as a bidder.

Deceptive items may be broadly classified as fantasies or reproductions. In the mid-1970s, Hake's began using the term fantasy item to signify deceptive objects never licensed by the copyright owner, or an item that did not even exist during the time period that produced original and authorized collectibles.

Fantasy collectibles are produced after the fact, typically when a person, character, movie, etc. becomes the subject of collector interest. The people making fantasy items intend them to appeal to, or intentionally defraud, collectors unaware of the item's unauthorized status and relative newness. Frequently such items bear illegitimate copyright notices and spurious dates. For most collecting specialties, there are relatively few fantasy items and they are easily avoided by patronizing reputable dealers, particularly

PRICE GUIDE OVERVIEW

while gaining personal experience in a given area.

A few Disney fantasy items that come to mind are pocketwatches with both Mickey and Minnie on the dial and a Mickey pocket knife with text that falsely states its origin as the Chicago 1933 World's Fair. Particularly annoying is the "Official Store" button we illustrate. The design is authentic and was used on c. 1932 black and orange 11" square store window cards. However, the design was never used on a pin-back button. This fantasy button first appeared in the mid-1990s. To aid the deception, the curl text reads "Walt Disney 1937" (a form of copyright notice never used by Disney) and with a glued-in backpaper reading "Kay Kamen Ltd./New York/London" (another version of a spurious copyright notice never used by Disney's licensing agent).

Reproductions, undated and unmarked as such, will undoubtedly be encountered by active collectors. Happily, because Disney is so vigilant about copyright infringements, there are relatively few unlicensed and unmarked reproductions in the Disneyana collecting field. Unlike a fantasy item, the reproduction has its original, authentic counterpart. In some circumstances, a questionable item may be compared directly to a known original to determine any difference. Producing reproductions doesn't require ethics but it does require some care and skill to produce a copy with most if not all of the distinguishing features of the original. Careful observation of originals, some appreciation of the materials and manufacturing techniques in use when the original was produced and a healthy degree of skepticism are potent weapons against reproductions. Copied items very seldom match all the characteristics of the original. If any doubts surface, postpone the purchase and get a second opinion, or at least obtain a written receipt with the seller's money-back guarantee of authenticity.

Here are a few basic warnings and tips to keep in mind regarding reproductions:

Framed items – covering an item with glass, or even shrink wrap, may hide a multitude of problems. A generous layer of grime or highly reflective glare may obscure the image enough to hide what proves to be a photocopy, color laser copy or printed reproduction. Some Disney cartoon posters from the 1930s have been reproduced. We've seen these presented at local auctions in battered vintage frames under dusty and dirty glass. What might seem to be a bidding bargain price is really a scam for the unwary.

Printed items – Small single sheet paper items and cards are easy to reproduce. Color laser copies are particularly deceptive, but detectable on close inspection.

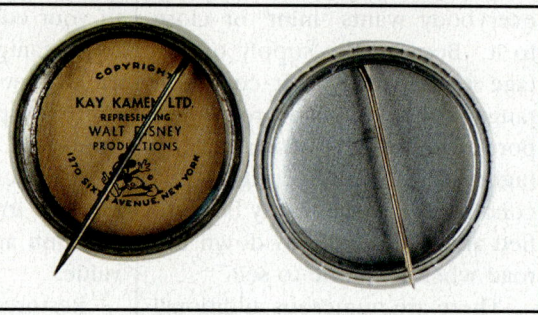

The "real" 1942 Dumbo button with four accent stars and correct back paper. The "fake" 1980s Dumbo missing the star designs and without back paper.

Sometimes the surface of a color copy is un-naturally glossy or a solid color area that should not show a printing screen pattern will reveal one with use of a magnifying glass. It's difficult to explain what to look for, but take an original, make a color copy and view both under magnification. The differences are obvious once seen. Modern technology is frequently put to use to reproduce Disney wrist or pocket watch dials as well as other deceptions. However, color and black/white reproductions of paper items will often reproduce small tears, creases or other flaws on the paper of the original item being copied. These defects may show on the photocopy while the paper used to produce the copy is actually not torn, not creased or otherwise flawed.

PRICE GUIDE OVERVIEW

The fantasy 1990s creation for "Mickey Mouse Official Store" with mis-leading 1990s created back-paper.

Pin-back Buttons - Very few buttons were made in both celluloid and lithographed tin varieties. However, a small number of lithographed tin buttons have been reproduced as celluloids. Nearly all buttons described in this guide as lithographed tin (litho.) should be regarded with much suspicion if encountered as a celluloid version. Most button reproductions are celluloid copies made by photographing celluloid originals. This sometimes results in a slightly blurred appearance, sometimes the dot screen fills in on the reproduction and sometimes the covering of thin acetate is noticeably different than the celluloid of the 1950s and earlier. A shiny metal back does not prove much. The metal used now may quickly oxidize while the metal used in the 1960s and earlier may retain its shine. The presence or absence of a "union bug" does not determine authenticity. A union bug is a small logo stamped in the metal or printed on the button paper to signify the button was produced by unionized workers.

Fortunately, only a handful of Disney button designs are reproduced. The ones we've encountered and how to distinguish them are:

Donald Duck 1984 Happy Birthday - original is 2.5" litho; repro is known in two celluloid-versions - 2 1/8" and 1.25".

Dumbo D-X (gasoline 1.25", 1942 premium) - original with four star designs and backpaper; repro without stars and no back paper.

Mickey Mouse Hose (7/8", 1930s) - original highly domed with large image and "© WALT DISNEY ENTERPRISES" on curl; repro has flat surface, smaller image, and upper/lower case curl text "© Walt Disney Enterprises."

Mickey "Buy Cote's Master Loaf" (1.25", 1937) - original has white background and Mickey image on backpaper; repro has dark cream background and no back paper.

"Mickey Mouse Globe Trotters" with no sponsor name (1.25", 1937) - original is black, white and red with "W.D." below copyright symbol; repro is black and white (no red) with "WB" below a letter "0."

"Mickey Mouse Globe Trotters" with "Pevely" sponsor name. (1.25", 1937) original is black, white and deep red with same copyright as previous item, repro red color is very pale and copyright is same as previous repro.

Mickey 1978 Happy Birthday (1.25", 1978) - original has open back with standard removable spring pin; repro has back covered by sheet metal with fixed horizontal bar pin.

"Snow White Jingle Club Member" (1.25", 1938) - original has tiny text "© 1938 WD ENT"; repro has tiny text "© 1938 W. DISNEY."

Reproductions and fantasies are a regrettable aspect of nearly all hobbies, but not cause for despair. In the normal course of enjoying and learning about a particular specialization, the ability to discern the small number of deceptive items is acquired almost automatically. Just proceed with a bit of caution at the outset and rely on fellow collectors for advice concerning reputable dealers.

PRESERVING IT

When a collectible toy is acquired, the collector becomes its custodian, responsible for its well being. This is not much of a burden and in fact should be enjoyed, but there are some basic maintenance principles to apply.

First, remove any adhesive price tags as quickly as possible. The longer these are in place the more firmly they adhere. Also, an inked price may bleed through the tag and stain the item. In most cases, a few drops of adhesive solvent will do the item no harm. Let the solvent do its work for a few seconds and usually the tag will then easily lift off without taking along surface paper or paint.

If the seller marked the item with a price in pencil, it may be left alone or erased. Above all, don't write the purchase price on

PRICE GUIDE OVERVIEW

the item. Record keeping should be done in a notebook or computer not on the item itself.

Mylar bags are recommended for acidic paper items such as comic books or magazines. Pinbacks may go into glass-covered "butterfly" mounts. However, these mounts in a stack create pressure and the glass may adhere to the paint on lithographed tin buttons. If this type of case is used, lithographed pin-backs should be stored separately in individual holders. Similarly, cels should not be stacked in a way that creates pressure or the result may be images with paint cracks. Three dimensional objects are best stored on shelves in closed cases to protect them from accumulating dust and particularly tobacco smoke residue.

Collectibles in the home face their greatest threats when stored in attics and basements or any location that receives direct sunlight. Also dangerous to many printed items are fluorescent lights, which may fade colors very quickly. Any extreme – heat, cold, light, moisture, smoke – presents dangers to be avoided. Glue, tape, pen and pencil should never be applied directly on the item. Do nothing to degrade it. It's future value depends in part on the custodial care it receives.

TIME TO SELL?

Once acquired, some collectors abhor the thought of parting with a single object. The collection becomes a fortress with a one-way door. This approach is one extreme, but if it brings satisfaction, it's the correct approach for that collector.

Another approach is to test and fine-tune judgments by periodically entering the marketplace. This concept is particularly worthwhile for the more seasoned collector whose tastes and sense of appreciation has evolved over time. Being open to "trading up" and culling earlier mistakes will likely be a valuable learning experience and a financial benefit, at least in the long term.

A collector may stay in touch with the retail marketplace without becoming a seller. This takes time and study, but is easily accomplished by attending shows or reviewing auction results. Entering the marketplace will likely provide different useful insights. Selling venues might include a hobby publication advertisement, taking a table at a show, consigning to an auction, listing items on public Internet auctions, and selling directly to a dealer or another collector.

Educate yourself regarding reproductions and fantasy items so that you don't become dejected like Pinocchio depicted here in this c. 1939 figurine.

This 1950s animation cel shows a very time conscious White Rabbit. Collectors should invest time in refining collecting skills and goals.

The potential benefits of the selling experience may include: raising the collection's quality; establishing valuable relationships with dealers, auction houses and other collectors; receiving feedback on just how astute were the original purchases of the items now for sale; and a host of other insights to help continually refine collecting goals and skills.

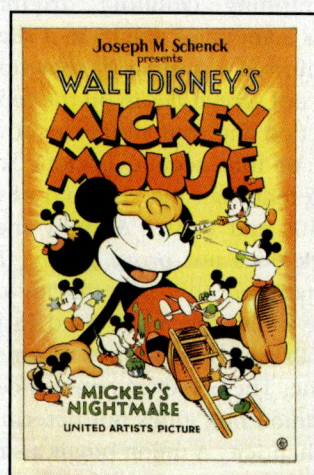

Collecting can be a nightmare if you try and amass a collection without the proper education. The information in this book can aid in making educated decisions that promote a good night's sleep.

MARKET REPORT

by John K. Snyder, Jr. & J.C. Vaughn

The market for Disneyana is strong, something we've seen confirmed time and again since the release of the first edition of *The Official Price Guide To Disney Collectibles*. Through high profile auctions, eBay transactions, catalog offerings and private sales, we've seen market support for Disney items continuing at a remarkably solid, sustained level. Enthusiasts have found confirmation of this across a wide spectrum of collectibles and in many of the specialized niches within Disneyana.

The trend has also crossed many age boundaries, both in terms of the items themselves and the people collecting them. Whether it's a one-of-a-kind, top-of-the-line original Mickey Mouse piece or something from the latest Disney-Pixar collaboration, chances are that you'll find not only a collector who is interested in purchasing it, but someone who might really surprise you with his or her collecting outlook.

This isn't unique to the world of Disneyana, but it's really found nowhere else in such a pure form.

Mickey Mouse lithographed tin bank c. 1930.

With any group of experienced collectors, sooner or later the subject of record prices is bound to come up. Considering the amount of time, effort, and capital it takes to collect at the high end, this is only natural. But don't let that distract you from the real motivation pulsing through a true collector.

COLLECTING & VALUE

What made us take our first steps in this hobby? What made us do the research, purchase (or work on) books such as this one, and reach out to our fellow enthusiasts? In the end, just as in the beginning, it's all about loving the characters and the desire to preserve them and pass them onto subsequent generations. Love them as we may, we're don't get to take them with us.

That said, although we collect for love and not for the promise of return on investment, being good stewards of our treasures does indeed include the responsibility of understanding their values. Since prices are generally the product of scarcity (or supply and demand), the rarity of the item and its value most often go hand-in-hand. When we find an item for which this seems not to apply, more often than not it is simply that the word on that particular piece has not been fully disseminated. Get the information about an artifact or group of artifacts in front of the right audience, and watch what happens.

Just as the market for the items is healthy, the marketplace of ideas has never been more active. Through print media, eBay, television, radio and the internet, there have never been more channels for prospective buyers and sellers to research and evaluate their specific items and the marketplace in general.

There are more top level auction houses than ever open to character collectibles. Can you even imagine a serious auction entity passing on the chance to offer high end Disney collectibles? Whether we speak of coloring books, pull toys, or comic books, it would be

A 1950s die-cut sign promotes Donald Duck Cola.

MARKET REPORT 2007

The earliest Mickey Mouse Club started in January of 1930 and included pinback buttons for the various ranking officers in the club.

like passing on a near-certainty. The same is true for fine art ranging from Carl Barks paintings to production pieces from classic Disney films. This also goes for magazines, cups, records, pinbacks, figurines, calendars, plates, lunch boxes, patches, club kits, cereal boxes, pop-up books, Big Little Books, movie posters, and just about every other type of Disneyana. And, of course, Disney fans have it easier than many other collectors. What other niche or area in collecting can compete with the allure and impact of the Walt Disney name?

AWARENESS

The strength of the market is reflected in the media coverage for record sales. As we intimated in the last edition, this is increasingly done in a serious fashion rather than with the incredulity that used to accompany such events. News from the world of popular culture is no longer greeted with the perennially raised eyebrow or knowing smirk.

It is difficult to understate the role of specialty publications and particularly the influence of "new media" in this. Just as in col-lectibles, the market provided a solution for the lack of awareness the old media elite used to display toward us. News sites, blogs and email newsletters have all captured readers, and their inherent ability to specialize in areas of interest and get the news out quickly has greatly motivated the mainstream press to reassess what they were doing wrong. As a result, we continue to see publications like *Forbes, Fortune, USA Today* and *The Wall Street Journal* give serious attention to collectibles.

A Flip The Frog doll by Dean's Rag Book Co. c. 1930 depicts the creation of Disney early associate Ub Iwerks.

An important factor in this – both highlighting the power of the market and reinforcing it – is the decreasing gap between the value of collectibles and liquidity. It continues to narrow rapidly. As we and others have pointed out, the ability of collectors to sell their collections or pieces of their collections

Some days the world can seem a little bit Goofy. Fortunately collectors and Disney fans alike can pass time with a smiling c. 1975 Goofy wrist watch by Bradley.

is increasing, and that in turn is increasing the viability of collectibles as an option for serious investment in the minds of the general public.

Likewise, both collectively and as individuals, we must continue to develop the professional face of the hobby. We should support the clubs, organizations, books, periodicals, conventions, dealers and spokesmen who are doing what they can and getting it right. When it comes to new products, we should encourage the firms who look to our past and see that there are plenty of lessons there that can be applied profitably to today's market. This is no time to stand around with our hands in our pockets, looking down at our feet, hoping against hope that someone will notice what we do is worthwhile and fun. In recent years the public has seen us as they have never seen us before, and we must capitalize on that. Now is the time we must seize the day, and the only way we're going to do that is to accurately gauge where we are and what we're up against.

The person who said that time is a constant probably didn't have email.

The world is speeding up. Time during a given day is a blur, as if sleep didn't exist. Email, voice mail,

MARKET REPORT 2007

A 1941 National Life and Accident Insurance Company calendar featuring Mickey, Minnie, Pluto and Donald.

internet news sites and text messages fight with more traditional forms of communication for the priorities of our attention.

When was the last time one of your friends lamented having too much time on his or her hands? With increasing frequency, we're seeing even our children's schedules regimented by school, organized functions, homework and play dates. Add to that the chaos, confusion, distresses and demands of the adult world. It's worse than an epidemic. It's a pandemic of tension, frustration and stress manifested in a struggle which results in the complete inability to make the activities of your life slow down.

Doesn't even the thought of making things slow down seem more appealing to you than ever before? Well, how about trying a new approach in which we seek to learn about the past from the things we collect? Collecting offers us one means to not only slow things down for a moment or two, but to give us a perspective when we're back in the quagmire of deadlines and difficulties. It holds out to us the chance to step out of the negative pace and into the spirit of having fun, which represents what's good for all of us.

THE BIGGER PICTURE

We still have a lot to learn about our field and how popular culture fits into history in general. For our part, we already know the overwhelming portion of what we collect was created for children. We can seek an understanding of the social and educational advances of the past through collectibles. We can dig into the background of the particular field or fields we specialize in, and learn more about each generation and increase our understanding of how the people of that period reacted to new ideas and inventions. In most cases, what those creators and manufacturers wanted was similar to what we might wish for our own children.

We know all about famous wars, popular and unpopular leaders, great moments in science and significant achievements in sports by adults. But do we know enough about their childhoods and the toys that were made for them? What do we know about the mindsets of the people who created or manufactured them or what they had to do to get them approved by adults? What do we know about how they were received by the media, school systems or what they meant to their culture?

Weren't adults in many cases trying to teach valuable lessons to their children with these toys? If you accept the point that they were and then wonder about what we're teaching kids with toys today, it's easy to reach the point where you see the wisdom of embracing such investigation. While society sometimes seems stagnant or redundant in its course, there no doubt have been a few too many good ideas and successful concepts for teaching children left behind. Maybe together we can discover some of the areas

Walt Disney's Comics and Stories #25 CGC certified 5.5.

Mary Poppins medicine spoons musical figurine by Enesco from 1964.

The Shaggy Dog doll by Gund c. 1959.

31

MARKET REPORT 2007

1934 Mickey Mouse painted variety radio by Emerson.

Elmer Elephant and Tillie Tiger figurine by Goebel from the 1950s.

Donald Duck ceramic cookie jar by Shaw from the 1950s.

that have been forgotten as we organize and document the toys produced in the past.

Since time has become so precious (it always was, of course; it's just that some of us are finally noticing it), it's more important than ever to include our families in our collecting efforts. It can be something as simple as taking them and our friends to conventions or watching the increasing number of TV programs on the subject.

As we witnessed in many collecting areas, there was already a strong back-to-family-values undercurrent moving through entertainment and collecting prior to the events of September 11, 2001. After those tumultuous events, that movement manifested itself in many different ways. For many Disneyana enthusiasts nothing changed, but they, too, have witnessed the changes in others. How we continue to respond to these changes will greatly affect how we interact with our families.

Family members should be given the chance to discuss and plan activities, and to be a part of your goals. We all get caught up in the thrill of the hunt, and it's easy to get snarled up in the blind spirit of acquisition rather than the fun-loving life-force that brought us into the game to start with. It remains a source of pride that many of the top collectors of new Disney products are women. This is fantastic and shows how our fellow enthusiasts are paving the way for collectors in other areas.

For perspective, it helps to acknowledge that we are at best custodians of these artifacts. There is a higher order to things, and even those of us who live long lives don't have this life for much more than the blink of an eye. What do we want to be remembered for? How we dispense the knowledge we acquire and share our friendship will say more about us in the end than the quantity or monetary value of our holdings.

Collecting has the ability to enrich or engulf its practitioner. Our respective focuses are the key ingredients in the mix, and they go a long way toward determining the outcome.

Steve Geppi, Ted Hake, Tom Gordon III, Brandon DeStefano, the Gemstone Publishing and Hake's Americana & Collectibles staffs, and many other contributors have put in a tremendous amount of work on this edition of *The Official Price Guide to Disney Collectibles* for the simple reason that we're eager to share our understanding of the marketplace with you. The same reasons compel us to publish the Disney comics and books like *Mickey and the Gang: Classic Stories in Verse*, as well as *The Official Overstreet Comic Book Price Guide* and other our books.

We hope you'll join us for the next edition of this guide, too, and that you'll enjoy the following representative sampling of top Disney sellers over the past two years.

John K. Snyder, Jr. is the President of Geppi's Entertainment Museum. J.C. Vaughn is the Executive Editor & Associate Publisher of Gemstone Publishing.

The Three Little Pigs ceramic figurine by Zaccagnini c. 1947.

MARKET REPORT 2007

A

Alice Gets In Dutch 1924
   One Sheet Poster $6,900

Alice In Wonderland
   Ceramic Teapot $402.50

Alice In Wonderland
   Goebel Figurine $616

Alice In Wonderland Rare
   Regal China Cookie Jar $1,176

Alice In Wonderland Queen Of Hearts
   Figural Nodder By Goebel $690

Alice In Wonderland Wrist Watch By
   US Time With Box 1950 ....$885.50

Art Of Animation, The Multi-Signed
   Book Including Walt Disney
   ....$3,360

B

Bambi Thumper Catalin Plastic
   Figural Sharpener $283.73

Black Cat Large Ceramic Figurine
   By Zaccagnini $3,163

C

Carl Barks 95th Birthday
   Commemorative Signed Limited
   Edition Prints 1996 ....$834.91

Cinderella 1958 Timex
   Wrist Watch In Packaging $560

D

Davy Crockett 1954 US Time
   Boxed Watch Set $492.80

Davy Crockett Official
   Frontier Knife Store Display $500

Disney Musician Wind-Ups By
   Marx/Linemar $1,019.20

Disney Studio Christmas
   Card For 1935 ....$287.50

Disney Studio Christmas Card
   For 1938 ....$313.09

Disney Studio Christmas Card
   For 1939 ....$411.13

Disney Studio Christmas Card
   For 1942 ....$442.75

Disney Studio-Designed Insignia
   Original Art $1,035.49

Disneykings Marx Store Display
   ....$448

Disneyland Friction Van Trailers
   Casey, Jr. Boxed Truck
   By Line Mar. $1,495

Disneyland 1956
   Postcard Folders $253

Donald Duck Band Leader Doll
   By Knickerbocker $4,312

Donald Duck Very Rare Ceramic
   Cookie Jar By Shaw $1,960

Donald Duck 1936 Hardcover
   Book With Dust Jacket....$2,142.91

Donald Duck Icy-Frost Twins Club
   Of Canada Member Button $575

Donald Duck In His Convertible
   Boxed Line Mar Car $1,581.25

Donald Duck 1936 Ingersoll
   Rare Wrist Watch..................$2,240

Donald Duck Jackets Button
   ....$410.63

Donald Duck Original Cel Set-Up
   From Der Fuehrer's Face Framed,
   Matted And Signed By Walt Disney
   ....$3,738

Donald Duck Lamp..................$1,200

Donald Duck Large Ceramic Figurine
   By Zaccagnini $2,302.30

Donald Duck Large Golfer Ceramic
   Figurine By Zaccagnini $3,738

Donald Duck Large Golfer Ceramic
   Figurine By Zaccagnini $3,738

Donald Duck 1930s
   Largest Size Bisque $863.13

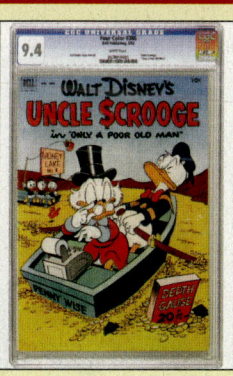

Mickey Mouse doll by Knickerbocker in Near Mint Condition
$19,096

Four Color #386 CGC Certified 9.4
$26,290

Oswald The Rabbit 1927 one sheet poster in Very Fine+ Condition
$6,900

MARKET REPORT 2007

Donald Duck Peanut Butter Club 1940s Litho. Button............$492.80

Donald Duck Pencil Drawing From Magician Mickey $585.20

Donald Duck Pencil Drawing From Mickey's Fire Brigade $277.20

Donald Duck Pencil Drawing From Moose Hunters $686.22

Donald Duck Self Control Bronze Sculpture By Carl Barks ..$1,381.15

Donald Duck Rare Toy Telephone 1938 ......$1,464.24

Donald Duck Wanna Fight Button $542.08

Donald Duck 1930s With Mandolin Bisque $747.42

Dumbo 1941 One Sheet Poster $6,900

E

Elmer Elephant Rare Celluloid Figure $398.94

Elmer Elephant Figural Celluloid Tape Measure $574.44

F

Fantasia Centaurette Figurine By Vernon Kilns $805

Fantasia Exceptional Concept Art $8,200

Fantasia Exceptional Concept Art $3,210.74

Fantasia Cut-Out Book $1,064

Fantasia Euro Disney Restaurant Exceptional China Dinnerware Set $517.50

Fantasia Nutcracker Tea Cups And Saucers By Vernon Kilns $805

Fantasia Ostrich Figurine By Vernon Kilns $805

Fantasia Nubian Centaurette Figurine By Vernon Kilns........$748

Fantasia Unicorn Figurine By Vernon Kilns $504

Fantasia Winged Nymph Vase By Vernon Kilns $460

Ferdinand The Bull Five Men In Funny Hats Rare Set Of Large Brayton Laguna Figurines $7,082.75

Ferdinand's Mama Large Impressive Ceramic Figurine By Brayton Laguna $504

Ferdinand The Bull Picador/Toreador On Horseback Rare Large Brayton Laguna Figurines $3,829.14

Flip The Frog Rare Composition Figure $1,368.89

Flip The Frog Doll By Dean's Rag Book Co. $336

Flip The Frog Rare English Doll 1930 ....$392

Four Color (Series 1) #16 CGC 7.5 ....$7,762.50

Four Color (Series 1) #16 CGC 4.5 ....$1,840

Four Color (Series 1) #16 CGC 3.5 ....$1,015.75

Four Color #9 CGC 8.0 Rockford Pedigree $5,377.50

Four Color #108 CGC 8.5........$1,380

Four Color #147 CGC 9.4......$10,755

Four Color #147 CGC 9.2........$2,390

Four Color #288 CGC 9.2 ..$5,377.50

Four Color #300 CGC 9.4 ..$7,767.50

Four Color #300 CGC 8.5......$418.25

Four Color #318 CGC 9.4 File Copy..............................$7,170

Four Color #328 CGC 9.4........$7,170

Four Color #386 CGC 9.4......$26,290

Four Color #386 CGC 9.2 File Copy............................$11,950

Large Donald Duck quacking celluloid wind-up in Near Mint Condition $8,860

Pinocchio 1942 Theater silk banner display in Good Condition $1,553.50

Peter Pan production cel and background in Very Good Condition $4,182.50

MARKET REPORT 2007

Four Color #386 CGC 9.2 .... $3,450

Four Color #386 CGC 9.0 .. $2,688.75

40 Big Pages Of
Mickey Mouse $1,840

G

Gremlins, The Hardcover
With Dust Jacket 1943 .... $1,008.47

H

Horace And Clarabelle
Large Dolls $784

Horace And Clarabelle
Bisques $1,669.61

Horace Horsecollar
Fun-E-Flex Figure $2,000

L

Lonesome Ghosts 1937
One Sheet Poster $25,300

Louie In His Dream Car Line Mar
Boxed Friction Car $1,404.15

M

Mad Doctor, The 1933
One Sheet Poster $138,000

Mary Poppins Medicine Spoons
Musical Figurine By Enesco $523

Mary Poppins Musical Teapot $805

Merry Christmas From Mickey Mouse
Rare Premium Book $925.23

Paragon China Rare Mickey And
Minnie Mouse Sandwich Plate
.... $1,940.40

Mickey And Minnie Mouse
Child's Clothing Rack $862.50

Mickey And Pluto Boxed
Celluloid Wind-Up Toy $6,325

Mickey, Donald And Goofy
Pencil Drawing From Mickey's
Fire Brigade $560

Mickey Mouse 6 Wee Little Books
Boxed Set $409.95

Mickey Mouse A Handful Of Fun
Premium Booklet $772.80

Mickey Mouse 1929 Advertising
Drawing By Les Clark $12,000

Mickey Mouse And Donald Duck
General Foods Breakfast Cereal
Display Sign $1,610

Mickey Mouse And Donald Duck
Pencil Drawing From
The Dognapper $736.65

Mickey Mouse And Pluto Pencil
Drawing From Mad Doctor
.... $431.20

Mickey Mouse And Pluto Paragon
China Mug $2,063.60

Mickey Mouse Aviation Department
Badge With Card $2,051.20

Mickey Mouse Band Leader
Musical Doll By Knickerbocker
.... $10,841.60

Mickey Mouse Big Big Color Set
Whitman Boxed Set $708.40

Mickey Mouse Big Little Set $1,495

Mickey Mouse Boxed Tea Set
By Ohio Art $1,035

Mickey Mouse Campaign Folio For ..
Movie Theater Club $1,970.46

Mickey Mouse Celluloid Squeaker
Figure 1930s $968.97

Mickey Mouse Celluloid
Wind-Up Nodder $518

Mickey Mouse Circus Train Complete
Boxed Set By Lionel $7,475

Mickey Mouse
Circus Train Boxed English Set
By Wells O' London $4,888

Mickey Mouse Club Authentic
Cast Member Outfit $2,500

Mickey Mouse Club
Sweater Emblem $460

Snow White and the Seven Dwarfs rare two-color series glass set in Excellent Condition
$6,050

Uncle Scrooge #39 original cover art by Carl Barks in Excellent Condition
$21,510

MARKET REPORT 2007

Mickey Mouse Comic Cookies Hat And Box $602.31

Mickey Mouse Comic Daily Strip 2-3-33 By Floyd Gottfredson $11,352.50

Mickey Mouse Comic Daily Strip 11-25-36 By Floyd Gottfredson $9,560

Mickey Mouse Crossing Bridge Boxed Celluloid Novelty $595.70

Mickey Mouse/Donald Duck Ring Display By Ingersoll $1,680

German Version Mickey Mouse Drummer Tin Toy $2,000

Mickey Mouse In Easter Parade Outfit Doll By Knickerbocker $11,180.40

Mickey Mouse Emerson Radio Cream Color Variety $2,164.62

Mickey Mouse English Door Knocker $308

Mickey Mouse English Electric Space Heater $1,265

Mickey Mouse Figural Lamp $863

Mickey Mouse Figural Composition Pencil Box By Dixon With Original Box $1,232

Mickey Mouse Fire Dept. Brass Shield Badge $924.00

Mickey Mouse First Rosenthal Porcelain Figurine $1,495

Mickey Mouse Fun-E-Flex Boat $1,200

Mickey Mouse German Band Figurine Set $2,300

Mickey Mouse German China Bridge Set $1,610

Mickey Mouse German Metal Figure $1,016.40

Mickey Mouse Happy Birthday Specialty Packaged Watch Set By Ingersoll $1,107.21

Mickey Mouse In Bathing Suit Celluloid Figure/Rattle With Life Preserver $3,348.80

Mickey Mouse 1933 Ingersoll Pocket Watch Boxed Example With Fob $1,680

Mickey Mouse Ingersoll First English Pocket Watch $1,663.20

Mickey Mouse Ingersoll 1935 Wrist Watch Boxed $1,232

Mickey Mouse Ingersoll 1935 Wrist Watch Boxed $1,113.20

Mickey Mouse Jack-In-The-Box $1,848

Mickey Mouse Large 17" Doll By Knickerbocker ..$2,710.40

Mickey Mouse 16" Doll By Knickerbocker $19,096.00

Mickey Mouse 1937 Ingersoll Wrist Watch Boxed $862.40

Mickey Mouse Dean's 1930s Jazzer Boxed Doll $2,710.40

Mickey Mouse Magazine 1935 #1 Fn+ $2,794.13

Mickey Mouse Magazine 1935 #1 Vg $2,031.50

Mickey Mouse Magazine 1936 Vol. 1 #5 Fn- $1,314.50

Mickey Mouse Magazine 1937 Vol. 3 #3 Vf $1,015.75

Mickey Mouse Magazine 1940 Vol .5 #2 CGC 9.2 File Copy $1,955

Mickey Mouse Milk For Better Health 3.5" Button $2,183.23

Mickey Mouse, Minnie, And Tanglefoot 1930s Button From Washington Herald Newspaper $1,150

Mickey Mouse On Trapeze Boxed Celluloid Wind-Up $1,495

Mickey Mouse Paragon China Baby's Plate $2,226.40

Mickey Mouse Picture Puzzles With Trays Rare Boxed Set $1,555.51

Mickey Mouse Racing Car Boxed Wind-Up $1,948.10

The Ugly Duckling concept art by Gustaf Tenggren in Very Good Condition $2,940

Ingersoll Donald Duck rare wrist watch in Very Fine Condition $4,312

MARKET REPORT 2007

Mickey Mouse Radio By Emerson Cream Color Variety $1,610

Mickey Mouse Recipe Scrapbook Display Sign $1,683.72

Mickey Mouse RKO Kiddie Kartoon Klub Button $672

Mickey Mouse Seed Shop Complete Boxed Store Display With Sign And Button $690

Mickey Mouse Small German Figurine Band Set......$560

Mickey Mouse Sneakers Pinback Button $1,610

Mickey Mouse Southern Dairies Ice Cream Button $794.64

Mickey Mouse The Steamroller Preliminary Poster Illustration Art 1934 ....$13,800

Mickey Mouse 1930s 9.25" Steiff Doll $1,120

Mickey Mouse 1930s 7" Steiff Doll $1,064

Mickey Mouse Washer With Box...............................$1,500

Mickey Mouse Whirligig Rare Boxed Celluloid Wind-Up Toy $2,070

Mickey Mouse Wood Jointed Figure W/Lollipop Hands 1931 ....$874.72

Mickey Mouse Zippo Lighter 1970s $264.88

Minnie Mouse At Piano China Figural Cigarette Holder $615.25

Minnie Mouse Carousel Boxed Wind-Up...........................$1,897.50

Minnie Mouse In Easter Parade Outfit Doll By Knickerbocker $1,344

Minnie Mouse Glass From Rare Musical Note Series $1,391.50

Minnie Mouse 1930s 6.5" Steiff Doll........................$1,114.96

Minnie Mouse Riding Horse Bobbing Toy 1930s $822.25

O

Oswald The Lucky Rabbit 1927 7/8" Pinback Button $873.40

Oswald The Lucky Rabbit Club 1927 7/8" Pinback Button $230

P

Pinocchio As Donkey Boy Ceramic Figurine By Zaccagnini $1,840

Pinocchio Ceramic Figurine By Brayton Laguna $618.59

Pinocchio Circus Linen Sign....$2,000

Pinocchio's Cleo Figural Pencil Sharpener................$492.80

Pinocchio Coachman Cookie/Candy Jar By Brayton Laguna $4,099.48

Pinocchio Cut-Out Book........$532.22

Pinocchio Geppetto Figurine By Brayton Laguna $920

Pinocchio Good Housekeeping Appearance Promo Sign ..$921.65

Pinocchio Honest John Ceramic Figurine By Brayton Laguna $2,080.93

Pinocchio Jiminy Cricket Figurine By Brayton Laguna $2,423.34

Pinocchio Jiminy Cricket Composition Doll By Knickerbocker $368.59

Pinocchio Jiminy Cricket Boxed Ingersoll Birthday Series Watch With Pen $1,800.64

Pinocchio Stromboli Pencil Drawing From Pinocchio ..$402.50

Pinocchio Theatre Silken Banner $1,553.50

Pinocchio RCA Victory Records 1940 Button $895.62

Pluto Large Ceramic Figurine By Zaccagnini $4,313

Pluto Marionette.......................$2,464

S

Sleeping Beauty And Prince Marx

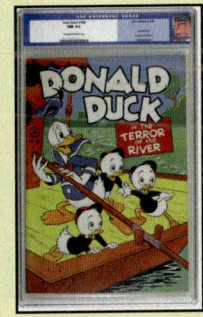

Ingersoll Three Little Pigs alarm clock with box in Excellent Condition $3,080

Fantasia exceptional concept art in Exc. Condition $8,200

Four Color #108 CGC certified 9.4 $16,730

MARKET REPORT 2007

Boxed Figure Set $1,124.13

Snow White 3.5" Button $1,101.44

Snow White Boxed Watch
 With Figurine $492.80

Snow White And The Seven Dwarfs
 Rare Figurine Set By Wade, England
 ....$1,453.46

Snow White And The Seven Dwarfs
 Boxed Set Of Glasses $1,008

Snow White And The Seven Dwarfs
 Musical Variety Pitcher By
 Wadeheath, England $2,588

Snow White The House Of The
 Seven Dwarfs From Walt Disney's
 Snow White Dean's Cut-Out Book
 ....$1,047.20

Snow White Early Storyboard
 Featuring Sleepy $800.80

Snow White Pencil Drawing
 Featuring The Witch........$1,505.63

T

Three Little Pigs Ingersoll
 Alarm Clock With Box $3,080

Three Little Pigs Fiddler Pig Boxed
 Wind-Up By Line Mar $506.35

Three Little Pigs Ceramic Figurine
 By Zaccagnini $4,600

Three Little Pigs
 China Mug $575

Three Little Pigs And
 Big Bad Wolf Wind-Up Set
 By Line Mar..........................$1,035

Three Little Pigs Ingersoll
 Pocket Watch With Fob ..$1,113.20

Three Little Pigs Wood Radio ..$1,000

Tinkerbell Bronze Sculpture
 By Marc Davis $1,150

20,000 Leagues Under The Sea
 Nautilus Submarine Boxed
 Wind-Up..................................$518

U

Uncle Scrooge #39 1962 Original
 Cover Art By Carl Barks $21,510

Uncle Scrooge Paint Book
 Original Cover Art 1960
 By Al Anderson $836.50

Ugly Duckling Concept
 Original Illustration Art 1939
 By Gustaf Tenggren..............$2,940

W

Walt's Field Day 1938
 Complete Program For Studio
 Employees Picnic $406.56

Walt Disney's Comics
 And Stories #96 1948
 Unpublished Hand-Colored
 Original Cover Art By
 Carl Barks $29,875

Walt Disney's Hiawatha
 Hardcover With Dust Jacket
 File Copy............................$227.05

Z

Zorro 1957 US Time
 Wrist Watch Boxed Set $308

Zorro 1958 School Bag..........$287.50

Zorro 1958 Outfit On Card
 ....$607.02

Zorro 1958 Marx Playset #3753
 With Original Box $715

Zorro 1958 Marx Playset #3754
 With Original Box................$8,800

Zorro 1960s Figural Ceramic
 Trinket Dish $548.17

Mickey Mouse in Easter Parade Outfit
Doll by Knickerbocker in
Very Fine Condition
$11,110

The Mad Doctor 1933 One Sheet Poster
in Very Fine/Near Mint Condition
$138,000

Mickey Mouse in Bathing Suit
Celluloid Figure/ Rattle with
Life Preserver in Fine Condition
$3,348.80

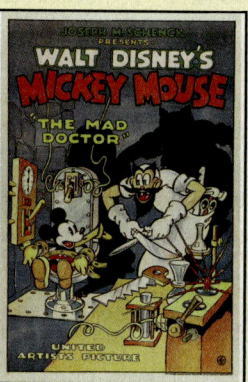

Traded for

Veteran sportscaster Al Michaels, for years the voice of ABC's Monday Night Football, earned a place in broadcasting history for his famous "Do you believe in miracles?" call of the U.S. hockey team's improbable medal-round defeat of the Soviets in the 1980 Winter Olympics. He also earned at least one bizarre footnote when he was traded by the network's parent company to rival NBC in exchange for Oswald the Lucky Rabbit.

It was history in the making. In an unprecedented trade agreement, The Walt Disney Company, parent company of both ESPN and ABC, acquired the rights to Oswald the Lucky Rabbit, Walt Disney's first creation and star of original cartoon shorts released by Universal. In trade for a mostly forgotten character from the Golden Age of animation, ESPN released the services of Emmy-award winning sportscaster Al Michaels to NBC - Universal. The deal was stuck in February of 2006 and turned over possession of the character, a key piece of Disney history which had been out of Disney's hands for nearly 70 years to The Walt Disney Company.

Between May, 1927 and August, 1928, Disney produced 26 animated shorts that featured the mischievous rabbit, backed financially by film producer Charles Mintz. With the technology of early animation growing in leaps and bounds, the quality of each Oswald short produced also took giant steps ahead. Correspondingly, so did the budgets.

After approaching Mintz concerning a higher production budget for future shorts, Disney was informed that not only was the production budget going to be slashed by twenty percent, but that Universal retained full ownership of the character. In anticipation of Disney's displeasure with the budget cuts, Mintz also approached several Disney staffers and contracted with them behind Disney's back to continue to produce Oswald shorts for Universal.

After Disney and Mintz parted ways, the responsibility of future Oswald shorts fell to Walter Lantz, a former animator for Bray Studios and, most notably, the creator of Woody Woodpecker. Lantz redesigned the character to make him cuter and to simplify his mischievous personality. Although more than 100 Oswald shorts were produced under Lantz, by the late 1930s, the characters had lost most of its previous appeal and ceased to function as a complex cartoon.

On a train ride home from the fateful split, Walt Disney created the character who would become Mickey Mouse, putting his and his company's future on one course and Oswald's on another.

Oswald continued to appear throughout the '40s, '50s and 60s in Lantz's comic book, *New Funnies* from Dell Publishing, but never again reached the audience or appeal it had under Disney's per-

Al Michaels, broadcaster and future trivia answer.

a 'TOON

by Brandon G. DeStefano

sonal supervision. Although the character has developed something of an overseas following, U.S. audiences never embraced the character as they did later Disney creations.

For years, though, The Walt Disney Company had been trying to reacquire the rights to Mickey's older, less-known sibling. Their efforts met with no success until Robert Iger was named Chief Executive Officer of the company. To the Disney family, he re-stated the company's priority to bring Oswald home.

Over the years since Walt Disney first created Oswald, his company had grown, of course. Through the addition of feature films, theme parks, cable television outlets and other businesses, the company eventually came to include the ABC television network.

Al Michaels had been with ABC for 30 years and had been the play-by-play voice of Monday Night Football since 1986. Over the course of his illustrious 30-year career at ABC, Michaels became associated with some of the greatest moments in sports history. He is one of only two sportscasters to act as play-by-play voice/host to six major American sporting events, including the Super Bowl, the World Series, the NBA Championship, the Stanley Cup Finals, the Triple Crown and the Indianapolis 500. From covering the "Miracle on Ice" to the exciting match-up of boxers, "Marvelous" Marvin Hagler and Thomas "The Hitman" Hearns, Michaels has been as much a part of American popular culture as Oswald has, which made him an enormous bargaining chip for Disney.

Monday Night Football was scheduled to end its ABC run and move to ESPN after the end of the 2005-2006 season. John Madden, Michaels' *MNF* broadcast partner, was hired for NBC's coverage of *Sunday Night Football* and the network hoped to re-team the duo by acquiring Michaels' services as well.

Since Universal Studios owned Oswald and since they are in turn owned by General Electric, which also owns NBC, it provided a great negotiating point. Both their group and The Walt Disney Company – ABC – ESPN team had something or someone the other side wanted.

The deal was struck. Oswald went to Disney, Michaels to NBC, and history was made. Michaels signed a six-year deal with NBC Universal to again be Madden's partner, and this made him the first-ever real-life person to be traded for a cartoon character.

"As the forerunner to Mickey Mouse and an important part of Walt Disney's creative legacy, the fun and mischievous Oswald is back where he belongs, at the home of his creator and among the stable of beloved characters created by Walt himself," Iger said in an ESPN.com article.

"When Bob [Iger] was named CEO, he told me he wanted to bring Oswald back to Disney, and I appreciate that he is a man of his word," said Walt Disney's daughter Diane Disney Miller in a statement. "Having Oswald around again is going to be a lot of fun."

"Oswald is definitely worth more than a fourth-round draft choice," Michaels said in the ESPN article on his unusual trade agreement. "I'm going to be a trivia answer someday!"

Brandon G. DeStefano is the Editor of Gemstone Publishing.

STEP BACK IN TIME
TO AN ERA OF SUPERB ARTISTRY AND IMAGINATION

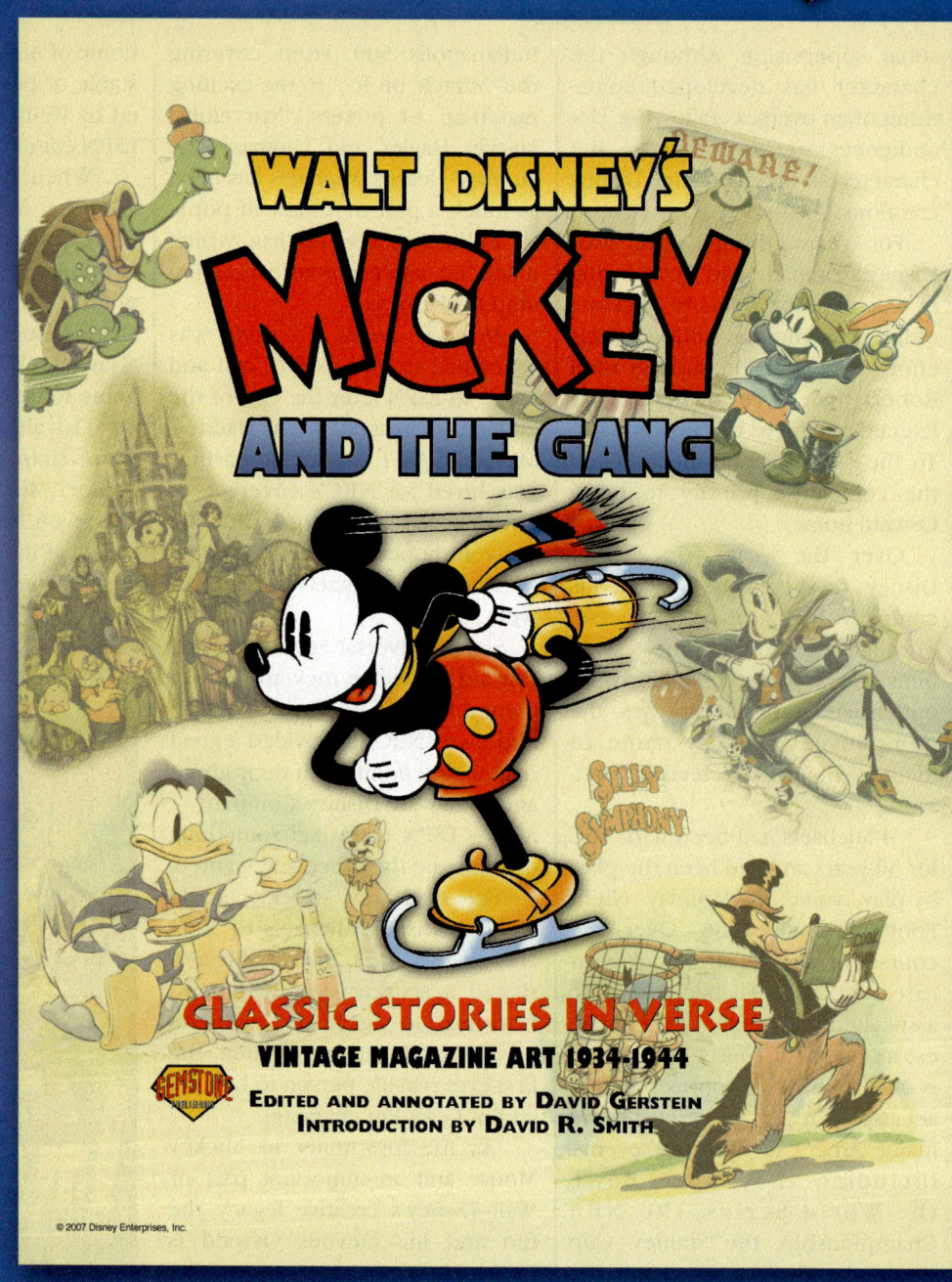

Poetic Disney stories hit the newsstands in 1934, when the famed animation studio joined in a mutual promotional plan with *Good Housekeeping* magazine. *Good Housekeeping* felt that a Disney page in each issue of their magazine would be a sales plus; Disney liked the idea of a "permanent advance publicity 'break'" for its latest cartoon shorts. Soon a monthly feature was born. From April 1934 to September 1944, new *Mickey Mouse* and *Silly Symphony* films were transformed into rollicking comic poems with masterful painted art. Now, for the first time, these funny, fascinating features are together in one book—and grounded in history via a wealth of Disney animation art and ephemera!

Walt Disney's Mickey and the Gang is available at your local book retailer. You can also order online directly from Gemstone or call 1-800-322-7978.
10⅝" x 12½"
Softcover $29.99
Hardcover $149.99

www.gemstonepub.com/disney

THE GREMLINS

by J.C. Vaughn

Mike Richardson, the founder of Dark Horse Comics, knew that he had stumbled onto something amazing, something that both as a creator and a Disneyana enthusiast whet his whistle and set off alarm bells in his head. He just had to convince Disney that they actually owned the property he wanted to license from them.

It couldn't possibly be true. A collaboration between the great Walt Disney and writer Roald Dahl, creator of *James and the Giant Peach* and *Charlie and the Chocolate Factory* was just sitting on the shelf collecting dust and cobwebs?

If one abandoned the enormous creative possibilities and thought only of the bottom line, the merchandising possibilities alone would seem limitless. But the story itself and the concept of those two creative goliaths working together appeals well beyond the notion of money. It reaches into the realm of perfection and dares to think of what should have been. It couldn't be true, could it?

Yes, it was true, and noted film

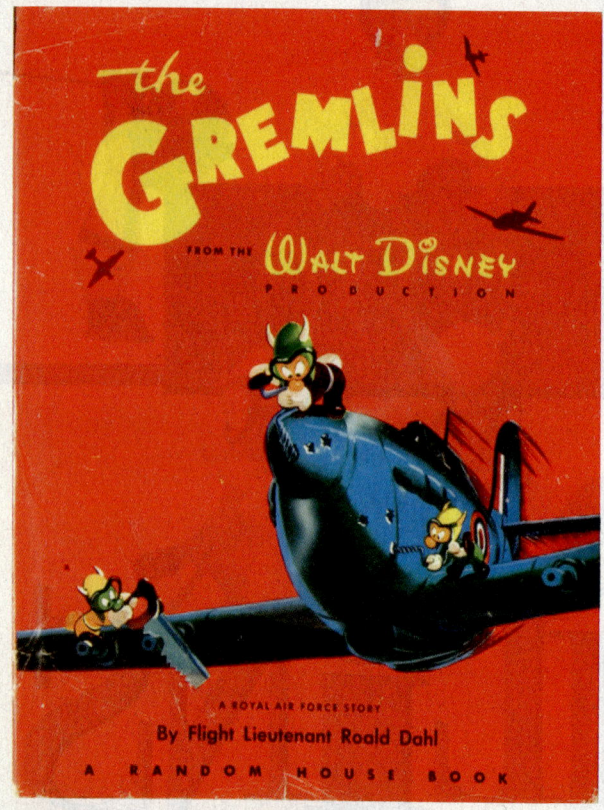
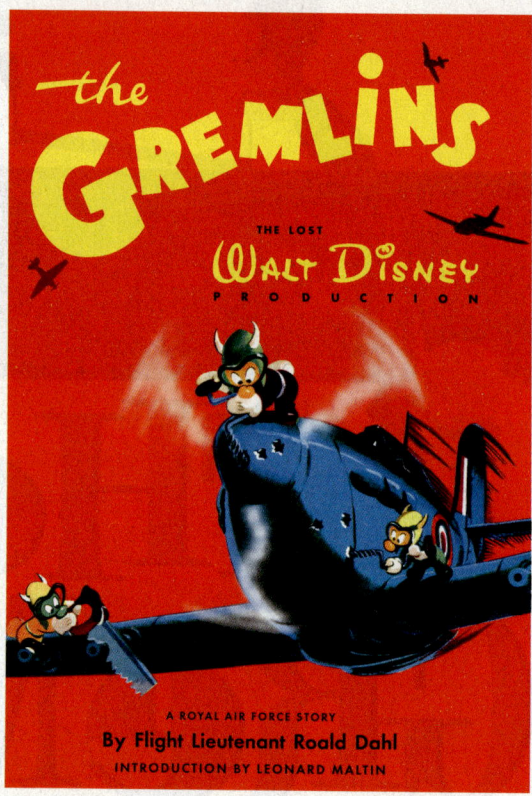

Above, left: the original Random House edition of The Gremlins (1943), and at right, the modern Dark Horse edition of Roald Dahl's no-longer-forgotten tale.

Left: Dark Horse Comics founder Mike Richardson, champion of the Gremlins.

Preceding page: a selection of Gremlins PVC figures from Dark Horse.

historian and critic Leonard Maltin was telling anyone who would listen about it via his well-versed commentary on the DVD *Walt Disney Treasures - On the Front Lines*. Any one of the thousands who saw the disc could have put the pieces together, but Richardson was electrified. A passionate and resourceful collector in addition to being a publisher of comic books and a producer of films, he knew that there had to be some magic left in the story Dahl and Disney had worked on, even if he wasn't familiar with it.

And he decided to get familiar with it in a hurry. He purchased a copy of the original 1943 storybook featuring Dahl's text and Disney animator Bill Justice's art on eBay. To his creator-historian-producer's mind it screamed potential. He asked Anita Nelson, Dark Horse's Vice-President of Licensing, to contact The Walt Disney Company about licensing the characters.

"We don't own them," was the gist of the reply.

"I've had a copy of the original *Gremlins* book for years," Maltin said. "I think I picked it up at a used-bookstore, though at the time I didn't know any of the back-story." Like Maltin, many other seasoned Disney fans might not have had all the facts, but they knew there had been Gremlins at Disney. That put them a step ahead of the lawyers.

There wasn't a lot to go on in terms of physical evidence. In addi-

Above: Disney animator Bill Justice was brought in to illustrate Roald Dahl's short story. These interior pages from The Gremlins are the result.

Right: This original 1943 glow-in-the-dark Gremlins illustration of Fifinella with three baby gremlins (known as Widgets) is one of the very rare collectibles from the film that never happened.

tion to the story book and an issue of *Cosmopolitan*, the characters had been featured in *Walt Disney's Comics & Stories* (with story and art by Pogo creator Walt Kelly). They also had been featured on a puzzle, a hand puppet, and as figures. That, though, was about the limit of what had been produced.

Armed with a copy of the book and enough enthusiasm for an army, Richardson was persistent. He asked them to check again. To their surprise – but not his – they did own the characters. A licensing deal was struck.

"The idea that we could reintroduce a book that had essentially been 'lost,' and was created through the collaboration of Walt Disney and Roald Dahl was thrilling," Richardson said. "I had no idea why this book had been left to languish, but the fact that it had was certainly a piece of luck for Dark Horse."

WHERE THEY CAME FROM

By time the United States was pulled into World War II, "gremlins" had already become the catch-all excuse of choice for RAF pilots. Whatever the problem or mistake, it was caused by the mythical little troublemakers who were said to go as far as moving runways or unscrewing bolts from airplanes mid-flight.

Author Roald Dahl enlisted in the early days of the European war, but a crash in the Sahara desert bumped him permanently from flying status in 1940. He was assigned to be a military attaché in the British Embassy in Washington, D.C.

Talking with other pilots, Dahl clearly grasped the storytelling potential of the mythical creatures and created specific characters and a story to go around them. As a member of the British military, it

Left: Fifinella, who was famously seen on squadron patches during World War II is a vinyl figure from Dark Horse.

Center: Dark Horse is also releasing a new comic book mini-series, Return of the Gremlins, a sequel to the original, written by Mike Richardson and illustrated by Dean Yeagle.

Right: The company is also working with Gentle Giant to produce the Gremlin with Pipe Statue.

was customary for him to submit the piece for approval before it could be published. Sidney Bernstein, the official to whom he sent it, immediately brought it to the attention of Walt Disney.

Disney immediately saw potential in *The Gremlins* as well, and the development of the project was undertaken. Dahl was granted leave to fly out to Hollywood, where he spent three weeks with Disney and his staff kicking around ideas and trying to come up with a workable concept.

Bill Justice was brought in to illustrate Dahl's story, which was published by Random House in 1943. As Maltin pointed out in his forward to Dark Horse's late 2006 reprint of that volume, it even bore the tag "From the Walt Disney Production." The book sold out, a small line of toys was issued, and the comic book stories were published. The possibilities for the film at one point had been so great that Walt sent his brother Roy to talk the other Hollywood studios out of doing Gremlin-inspired projects (by 1943 the use of gremlins as excuses had long since crossed the Atlantic and expanded well beyond the field of aviation).

Roy Disney was largely successful. The lone hold-out was Warner Brothers, who had two now-famous Bugs Bunny cartoons already in the works.

"I suppose there was still such a thing as honor among gentlemen in those days," Maltin said. "Leon Schlesinger begged off because

Top and middle right: two of the PVC figure sets from Dark Horse.

Bottom, right: One of Dean Yeagle's interior pages from Return of the Gremlins.

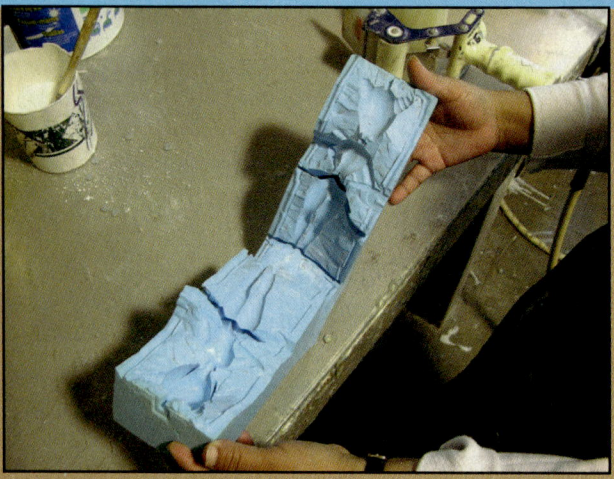

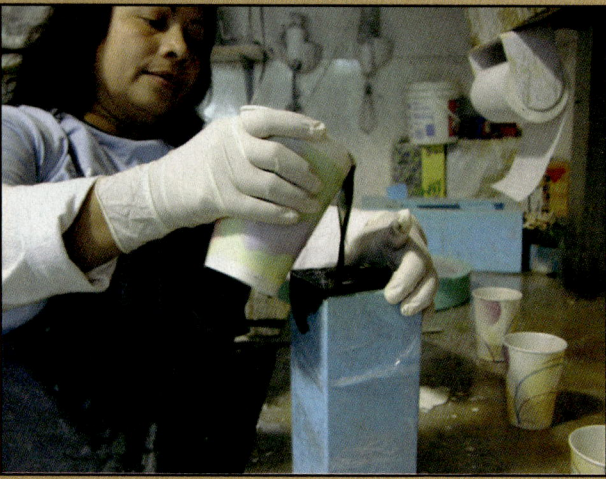

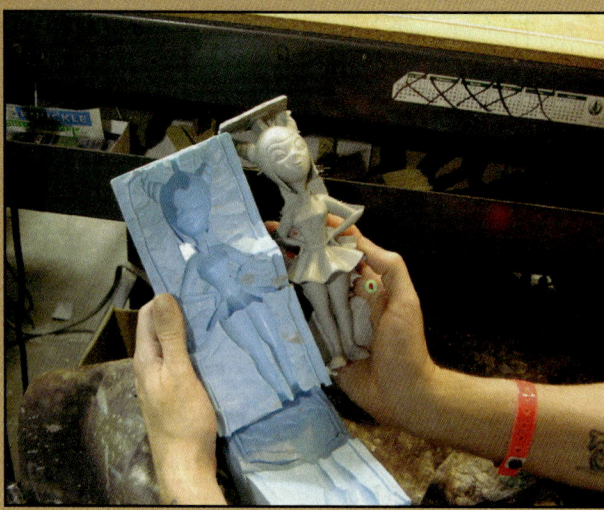

Above, from top: Step by step, the mold is created, the liquid PVC is poured in the mold, and the figure is ready to be trimmed and painted.

he'd already sunk so much money into producing his two Warner Bros. cartoons, but he agreed to take the name "Gremlins" out of the titles in deference to Roy."

Then suddenly – or at least it seems so in hindsight – the Walt Disney - Roald Dahl collaboration was over.

WHAT HAPPENED

As much as Richardson speculated that there almost certainly had to be some magic from the product of two great minds, something had happened to derail *The Gremlins*. While the movie was in development, discussion had ranged from a blend of live action and animation (such as *Song of the South* or, more recently, *Who Framed Roger Rabbit?*) or a straight animated feature.

Dahl was reportedly content to let the Disney storytellers have their way with the story after he went back to his post. It's probably important to note that this was, after all, a time of serious conflict, one for which the outcome was far from certain.

"Walt was tickled by the idea of the Gremlins at first, but then his story men realized that these 'cute' creatures were actually quite destructive--of aircraft during wartime! They could never lick that problem," Maltin said. "And remember, Roald Dahl wasn't Roald Dahl then; he'd never had anything published before."

Disney had sunk more than $50,000 into developing *The Gremlins* before the film was canceled. That was a fair amount of money at the time, even for the movie business, but the gamble on *Snow White* and subsequent successes had made the studio a serious player also spurred Walt himself to be even more of a perfectionist than he had been previously.

"Disney was famous for shutting down projects when they weren't bearing fruit. Even on *Pinocchio*, he scrapped six months' of work because he felt they were headed in the wrong direction," Maltin said. The project was destined for the shelves in the Disney Archives. Copies of the book became scarcer as did the handful of toys. The Bugs Bunny cartoons and eventually the 1984 feature film (of no relation) supplanted the original project in the minds of most filmgoers and fans. If not for the historians and collectors, the Dahl-Disney Gremlins would have probably disappeared permanently.

THE GREMLINS RETURN

But Richardson was indeed energized by what he saw on Maltin's DVD. After obtaining a copy of the original book, he set out to bring back this relatively unknown offspring of the fathers of Mickey Mouse and Charlie and the Chocolate Factory.

Dark Horse re-published the original storybook, *The Gremlins*, now with the tagline "The Lost Walt Disney Production" and a foreword by Maltin, in September 2006. The company is also producing statues, vinyl figures, PVC figures and other products. Richardson himself personally scripted the comic book revival, *The Return of the Gremlins*, illustrated by Dean Yeagle.

In the new story, Gus, a young man from America, arrives in England to claim his grandfather's house as part of his inheritance. He intends to sell it as soon as he can, particularly when he finds out the

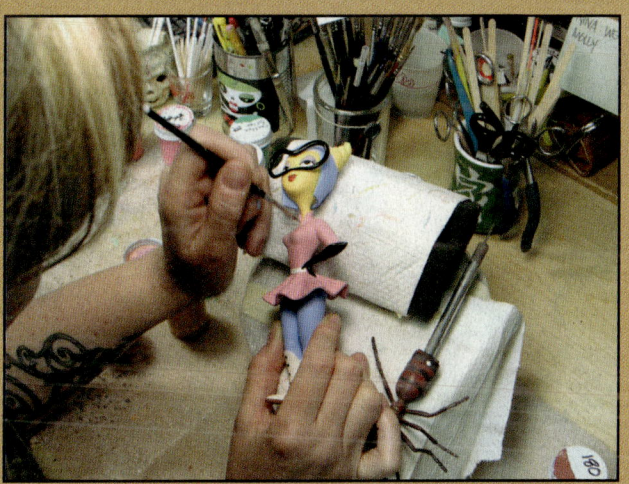

Dark Horse worked with Gentle Giant Studios and Disney (particularly George McClements) to create the physical representations of the characters. They based as much of their work as possible on 1940s concept art and other period examples.

locals think the house is haunted. Exploring further, he finds that it's not haunted; it's inhabited by Gremlins descended from those in the original story.

Richardson said he hopes that through the original book, the toys, and the new story that fans who have never heard the Roald Dahl – Walt Disney collaboration will discover it and that those who are already familiar with it will find new enjoyment.

"The history and origin of the Gremlins is pretty well unknown. I had always thought that they were characters of mythology, much like trolls and elves. The fact that these characters integrated into our culture so quickly attests to the strength of their appeal," Richardson said. "I'm extremely happy to reintroduce them to modern readers and at the same time restore credit for their creation to two creative geniuses, Walt Disney and Roald Dahl."

Gus vinyl figure

Fifinella vinyl figure

ARE YOU A DONALDIST?

don • ald • ism \ dän'-ld-iz'-em \ *n* : the research of Disney comics, and/or the fan culture that is found among Disney comics aficionados (Jon Gisle, 1973)

Go on, admit it. You like reading about comics history… but you love reading historically important comics themselves. You want a real Disney comics archival book—a thick trade paperback full of those extra-esoteric Duck and Mouse tales that just wouldn't fit in anywhere else.

You're a Donaldist! And we know where you're coming from.

Dive into the 160-page **DISNEY COMICS: 75 YEARS OF INNOVATION** for:

- Great Donald sagas by Carl Barks (a newly-restored "Race to the South Seas"), Don Rosa ("Fortune on the Rocks"), and Al Taliaferro (the seminal "Donald's Nephews")
- Never-before-reprinted Mickey tales by Floyd Gottfredson ("Mickey Mouse Music") and Romano Scarpa ("AKA Cormorant Number Twelve")
- Ducks by Daan Jippes, Dick Kinney, William Van Horn, and Daniel Branca
- Mice by Byron Erickson, César Ferioli and Paul Murry
- Renato Canini's José Carioca, Gil Turner's Big Bad Wolf—and Brer Rabbit too!

GEMSTONE PUBLISHING
presents
WALT DISNEY TREASURES VOLUME ONE
Now On Sale

(Any similarity between this book and the Disney DVDs you love to collect is purely intentional!)

www.gemstonepub.com/disney

Snow White's

After an encounter with the daughter of a pre-war Disney "Ink and Paint Girl" at his first major auction, Steve Ison turned his nascent interest in animation art into a full-fledged passion for collecting Snow White. In the years that followed, he established himself as the top Snow White collector and as an authority on the subject. He did it not only by seeking out the best pieces for his collection, but by exploring the human elements of information. In many cases he found the former Disney animators and other employees had stories to tell, and he listened. Through these methods over the course of more than two decades, Ison's Snow White collection grew in size and scope to become the stuff dreams are made of.

He staged exhibits, put together an impressive book on the subject, and continued to acquire key pieces, all with his personal focus not on the monetary value of the collection but on its historical and social significance. He believed, in his words, that "This stuff is important."

That these items were ever available in the first place illustrates how times have changed since the film was made in 1937. What would now most likely be seen as a distinct company asset was not closely guarded; over the years many of the pieces just "walked out" the door, and a number of pieces were sold to cover expenses associated with making the film in the first place. In recent years, though, under Chief Executive Officer Robert Iger, Disney has conspicuously moved closer to its roots.

This direction marked a change from the tenure of Iger's predecessor, Michael Eisner. While Eisner gave the authorization to build and maintain the Animation Research Library and storage facility, he did not appear to place any sentimen-

Wicked Queen Grimhilde in her finery—and her element—as depicted in the early scenes of Snow White and the Seven Dwarfs (1937). This image and other Snow White cel and story sketch art reprinted here: collection of Steve Ison.

Homecoming

tal value or historical importance on the vintage artwork.

With so much of the company's history in one place, perhaps the collecting world shouldn't have been surprised, but they were definitely startled this past summer when it was announced that Ison had sold his prestigious collection to Disney.

As a child, Steve Ison collected baseball cards, coins, and the like. Nothing more than a fascination with the scene in which the skeleton reaches for a drink would tip his interest in Snow White, but even then, in each area he was active in, he narrowed his focus to collect a specific niche. It was a habit that would serve him well later in life.

"I couldn't learn it all, or afford to buy it all, so I decided to narrow my collecting strategy," Ison said.

In college, he was in a singing group that had sung at Walt Disney World. There he saw an original vintage Disney cel that was being sold for $50. Being the typical college student, he couldn't afford it at the time, but started to investigate the idea of collecting animation art. He began talking with the few expert dealers and collectors he could find and started networking. He attended an auction at which he met the daughter of a Disney animation department employee. The

An interior shot from the gallery Steve Ison built in his home to showcase his collection.

Snow White sings the opening strains of "I'm Wishing," the first of the feature film's numerous hit songs. Voiced by Adriana Caselotti, Disney's first princess warbled to the words and music of Frank Churchill and Leigh Harline.

Prince Charming sits on the garden wall. A relative cipher on screen, Snow White's handsome prince had a more involved role in the film's 1937 comics adaptation, in which Queen Grimhilde forced him to fight for his freedom.

"Famed is thy beauty, Majesty; but hold, a lovely maid I see. Rags cannot hide her gentle grace; alas, she is more fair than thee." Voiced by Moroni Olsen in Snow White, the Slave in the Mirror later got a new voice—Hans Conried—and a new job as host for many later Disney TV shows.

woman's mother had been an "Ink and Paint Girl" (or "inker" for short), which was a job assigned to women because the studio found women's steady hands could ink the cels in a more fluid and competent manner. She offered him what turned out to be his first real indoctrination in this area of vintage animation art collecting. On a trip to her Michigan home, he purchased an array of pieces from a number of different Disney films.

"After buying the pieces, I instantly had this huge collection; pieces from all of the classic Disney animated features. I have never collected with profit in mind. That idea has never appealed to me. So, what I did when deciding to focus on Snow White was to sell and/or trade the pieces that were non-*Snow White*-related, the *Peter Pan*, *Mickey* and other pieces. I would pool my money into collecting only *Snow White*. My initial goal was to get a cel of every character from *Snow White*. That developed into concept and storyboard art and that eventually evolved into the collecting of the original background paintings," he said. "The only downside to the way I went about narrowing my collection was that I sacrificed some really amazing pieces of early Disney animation to focus on *Snow White*. Throughout the entire time, I've never regretted it! There are some pieces that I wish I still had, but you just can't have it all."

His collection continued to grow and as it did, Ison looked for ways to improve the public's perception of the art form.

"I've always tried to get people to understand that this is more than some 'Disney collectible;' I consider it fine art. It has never been about me. It's always been about the art and the incredible artists who created it," he said.

"In 1989, I approached the Indianapolis Museum of Art, and asked one of the directors of the museum about having an exhibit of animation art. After five years of convincing, they agreed to display my collection. By that time, the collection had evolved. It would now be possible, through the viewing of storyboards, backgrounds, drawings, and concept pieces, for even the youngest student to learn the story and production process of *Snow White*," he said.

Early storyboards and organizational story documents allowed Ison to see where there might be gaps in the story of Snow White, particularly if it was to be told in the visual form of actual art. He began filling in all of the holes in his background collection based on the original version of the storyboards, including scenes that were cut from the final version of the film. This allowed him to focus on the missing pieces while keeping his collection intact. Of the approximate 200 backgrounds that were created for *Snow White*, for instance, he ended up with over 60 of them when all was said and done.

The details of this process and the museum's interest in producing a catalog of the exhibit eventually developed into Ison's book, *Walt Disney's Snow White and the Seven Dwarfs: An Art in Its Making*, which was released in 1994 and eventually published in several languages (a miniature version of it accompanied the special edition DVD release of the film).

"It gave me the direction I needed to not only put together an exhibit, but the book, too," he said.

Snow White and her critter friends investigate the house of the absent Seven Dwarfs.

Later, hey clean it out in the "Whistle While You Work" musical number, again written and composed by Frank Churchill and Leigh Harline. Hard as it is to believe today, Snow White's animal pals got merchandise of their own in the 1930s—including a cover feature in Mickey Mouse Magazine #32 (1938).

The Seven Dwarfs "work work work work work work work, in [their] mine the whole day through!" Animator Bill Tytla's delineation of Grumpy—whose attitude changed over the course of the film from chauvinist pig to sensitive soul—marked an early character animation milestone.

Queen Grimhilde gets the bad news that not only hasn't Snow White been executed—"t'is the heart of a pig" the Queen instead holds in her hands.

"They originally planned to do a pretty straightforward, meat-and-potatoes-type of book, but I said to them, 'Let's make this really more interesting, because animation art, especially at the Disney company, is all about the story, all about personality.' I also wanted to include information on the animators who had put their personalities and talents into making *Snow White*, so I decided to fly myself and my two co-authors out to California, where I had set-up between 15 and 20 interviews that would be included in the book."

Ison's ability to arrange interviews for the book was significantly enhanced by the connections he had made through collecting.

"Over the years, I had become friends with former animators like Mark Davis, Ollie Johnson, Frank Thomas, Jim Grant, Maurice Noble and others, and every time I was in California my old friend Bill Justice would meet me at the Hilton in Burbank with a box of animation art treasures that he would sell for other people that he had worked with. I was always fair in my dealings, out of respect for them and what they had created. Over the years, there were many horror stories where some collector or dealer had cheated many of these people. I would keep the *Snow White* pieces I needed and sell or trade the rest to continue finding pieces for the book and the exhibit," he said. "So I started spending money like it was water to try and fill in the holes in the book. We then contacted The Walt Disney Company to get permission to reproduce the artwork in the book."

The company initially became aware of his collection when he contacted them about the book.

"Our first letter outlined the

exhibit itself, which was comprised of my collection. Initially, the request to do the book was rejected, but while we were out in California conducting the interviews for the book, the Disney board made the announcement that the company would be releasing *Snow White* on VHS. At that point, Disney was also just starting Hyperion Publishing, and with the release of *Snow White*, we decided to approach Hyperion with the idea of publishing the book," Ison said.

"They immediately seemed interested in the concept and asked for a prospectus, but at that point we were three-quarters of the way done with the book and had completed most of the photography. So rather than just a simple prospectus, we sent them three or four sample chapters and that was it; they immediately went for it. That's how Disney ended up publishing the book, and ultimately finding out about my collection. This ended up being a perfect situation because no one expected *Snow White* to be released on video and all of the sudden a nearly finished book on the film just fell into their laps," he said.

By 1996, Ison's collection had grown to the point where he thought that it was a truly important collection.

"I've always been surprised that The Walt Disney Company had let me, 'Joe Average' from Indiana, compile this massive collection from their first animated feature. This was their history…their legacy! If *Snow White* hadn't succeeded, we would be asking 'Walt who?' right now. I never believed in collecting for the monetary value of the pieces, but as I told my wife, in the early years of collecting, I believed

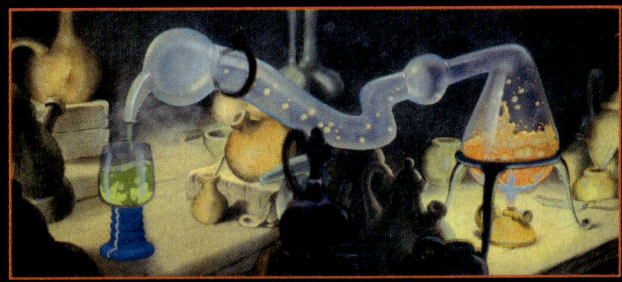

Flagons of pulsing chemicals transform Queen Grimhilde into the infamous Wicked Witch. Norm Ferguson, lead animator on the Witch, turned a fundamentally comic character design into a figure at once horrifying and cunning.

Dopey—typically animated by Fred Moore—handles the percussion section in "The Silly Song" production number.

that the art was important, and would someday be recognized as such," he said. At that point his goal was to add two or three key pieces every year, specifically backgrounds and concept art, which is what really caught his eye.

But by the mid- to late-1990s, the animation art market had taken a hit. While key pieces of classic animation art retained large percentages of their value at the time, many of the dealers and collectors of newer material had stopped collecting due to the influx of manufactured collectibles. As many unsuspecting collectors and even dealers discovered, the idea of "limited editions" meant that they were really limited in performance.

At first, such limited editions had attracted a fair amount of attention, but after they succeeded there were soon too many being produced for the market to handle. As a matter of supply and demand, this impacted the situation negatively to the point where many of the editions sold for below their issue price. Disenchanted collectors, some who never knew the difference between the limited editions and true vintage pieces, sold their collections. There was some reciprocal fallout in the vintage market as well.

Undeterred, Ison said this left him in good position to further his collection.

"I continued buying both backgrounds and concept art. I was able to add many great art pieces to my collection, during those years. It didn't really matter to me what the monetary value was," he said.

There have been some very special moments in collecting for Ison. One night while the exhibit was on display (from 1993-1994), Ison got a phone call from Diane Disney Miller, Walt's daughter, who had said that she read the forward in the book and that it had touched her. She then asked if she could come out and see the exhibit.

"Of course I told her that was definitely okay," Ison laughed. "So she flew out from San Francisco, and I picked her up at the airport. I kept her visit under wraps from both the local media and the museum staff because I felt that she was there because she had a genuine love and appreciation for the art that was a part of her father's first animated feature. After her visit to the museum, we became friends and have stayed so over the years."

While the company and now the Disney family were aware of his collection, things still had not fully clicked into place for what would eventually happen. In the forward to his book, though, he had alluded to the notion that he hoped that one day there would be a place where all of the wonderful pieces could be housed and displayed for everyone to see.

"I've always felt guilty about having all of this great art and never really being able to share it with the world. I've built several home galleries over the years, but never really made them open to the public. I even designed and built one that was a reproduction of the interior of the Dwarfs' cottage, complete with working fireplace; and all to museum specifications. Some of the art is very fragile, and it's your job, as it's steward, to preserve it."

"I've always talked about a public museum, but when Diane con-

The Seven Dwarfs pay their respects at the grave of not-yet-dead Snow White. Animator Frank Thomas captured the Dwarfs' grief in a genuinely touching sequence. Interestingly, the scene as screened marked a slight softening from its first conception: in a short moment that was animated, but didn't make the final cut, a pained, grief-stricken Dopey points directly at Snow White's presumed corpse before (as generally seen) breaking down and sobbing on Doc's shoulder. Luckily for the Dwarfs, of course—not to mention Snow White—we're only minutes away from a happily-ever-after conclusion.

tacted me about three years ago about the construction of a Walt Disney Family Museum at the Presidio in San Francisco, we talked about housing my collection there. It was planned to be the upper level of the museum, but in the end the expenses that were involved just became too much. It just broke my heart. At that point, we were building a home in the mountains of North Carolina, and I didn't want to deal with the construction of another home gallery, so I decided I would probably put the artwork into storage to protect it and hoped that maybe something would happen someday. Also, during that time, I had lent artwork to an important exhibit of vintage animation art that the Walt Disney Company was involved with in Paris, France. While there to view the exhibit, I was fortunate enough to meet Bob Iger through Lella Smith, the Executive Director of the Walt Disney Animation Research Library. Iger told me that he had read my book and had heard about my collection for years. It was very kind."

"The next night, at dinner with Lella Smith, we began discussing the possibilities of a Snow White "homecoming", about selling the collection to the company".

"Over the years I've had several people approach me about selling my collection, but I've always turned them down for fear the collection would be broken up," he said, but that wouldn't be the case with Disney purchasing it. "Over the course of the next three or four months, they came to view my collection and they couldn't believe the amount and quality of the material. It's one thing to see photos, but quite another to see these amazing pieces in person."

After the inspection, a deal was hammered out and they took possession of the collection in April of this year.

"This really came about because the upper management of Disney was, as I understand it, genuinely excited to have these pieces at the studio once again. They were very, very happy to regain this important part of the history of their company. It seems to be a whole new era at Disney these days. This decision came from the very top," he said.

Though many collectors have tried, it's difficult to go from "full speed ahead" to "stop" simply through the process of selling a collection after decades of work. Ison has already acknowledged this and has no intentions of stopping yet.

"In between the initial discussion and the final sale of my *Snow White* collection, I've begun focusing on collecting vintage *Fantasia* concept art. I chose this because, to me, this was really Walt's attempt at an art film in a medium in which he truly set the standard. I've already found some pieces that would bring a tear to the eye of the harshest art critics. I think I'll always collect in some form or another. Maybe it's a way to hold on to the past; but if it weren't for the collectors of the world, many important works of art and artifacts would be lost forever. I just happen to collect art that has it all…amazing design, beauty, and the wonderful memories it evokes every time I look at it. I miss the collection, but it comforting to know it has a good home."

Ison recreated the interior of the Dwarves' cottage to house elements of his collection. From the working fireplace to the intricately crafted walls and furniture, it was a tribute to the impact of Snow White.

EdUCATiNG

Rare 1930 Campaign Folio for Mickey Mouse Movie Theater Club.

The kind-hearted, nurturing image associated with Disneyana was neither developed by chance nor exclusively in a "good marketing" vacuum. Instead it was a reflection of Walt Disney's drive in this area. A notoriously demanding boss – particularly on the creators working closest to him – he nonetheless believed in educating his employees, and used new training to elevate the company as well as the artforms of filmmaking and animation.

"In addition to producing educational films, Walt Disney manifested his interest in education in another very important way: the education of his staff," wrote film historian J.B. Kaufman. "The legendary creative explosion at the Disney studio during the 1930s, which transformed and redefined the art of animation, didn't happen by accident. It was the result of endless study, practice, and training on the part of all the Disney artists, and it grew out of an unprecedented training program established and developed by Walt himself."

For a young man with a less-than-inspiring track record with formal education, Walt Disney was also always concerned with what society was teaching its younger members.

"In fact," reads an article on the Disney corporate website, "much of Walt's life story is focused on a commitment to education, in a variety of ways; films that helped inform people of all ages around the world; for his employees; for young people yearning to learn about music, dance, film, and more."

Under the direction of Disney and marketing director Kay Kamen, the company and its licensees undertook to develop not only highly commercial items that would be popular with children and their parents, but by and large items they would be comfortable having around their own kids.

The Brownies had humidors and the Yellow Kid advertised everything from cigarettes to liquor, but Mickey Mouse and friends stuck with toys that could teach children about the adult world. Tea sets, watches, books, craft sets, and hygiene items were matched with dolls, records, stationery, writing implements, and jewelry, among other items, to create an imitation of their counterparts in the adult world.

This, of course, is not that odd. The role most toys have played throughout history has been to educate children and to keep their minds occupied. Whether it's helping them understand transportation, comprehend science or learn how a kitchen works, toys have been there.

This education wasn't the formal sit-down-and-study type of learning. From playing at potential occupations to developing skills for social interaction, children don't pretend to be other children; they pretend to be adults.

Take the example of transportation toys, such as cars: first a youngster is content to drive the vehicle around, making squealing tire noises, making sounds for a revving engine or a police siren. Soon though, interacting with his or her peers, the behavior becomes self-correcting or group-correcting. Kids teach each other how to play correctly based on how they view adults.

by John K. Snyder & J.C. Vaughn

Mickey

Another way to see it is to reflect back on the movie *Giant*. In this Academy Award-winning 1956 film starring Elizabeth Taylor, Rock Hudson, and James Dean, the father wants the young boy to grow up to follow in his footsteps, but we see the boy instead playing with a toy doctor's kit. Through this storytelling device, which is deeply rooted in the concepts of play and education, we know that the young character isn't going to go the way his father hopes.

"Role playing toys" was a category in which Disney particularly excelled. Items such as puppets, marionettes, action figures, dolls and various costumes helped children develop their socialization skills and their understanding of the adult world.

This is not to suggest that there weren't a few products approved that in hindsight were less than useful even with the best of intentions. For instance, the social standing of smoking has changed dramatically since the 1930s, and it seems reasonable to assert that no one would expect a Mickey Mouse or Donald Duck ashtray to be made in the present era. That said, it seems unlikely that any long-lived line of merchandise wouldn't contain some questionable items.

But remember, even positive attributes weren't always recognized as such. How many teachers in days gone by confiscated comics that would "rot your brain" instead of realizing they encouraged reading? Now many leading educators clearly see their helpfulness. In fact, The Walt Disney Company is involved in a major initiative now in the pilot program stage with educators in the state of Maryland to utilize comic characters in reading development. In addition to a greater interest in reading, a likely consequence of this direction is a superior understanding of characters and eventually of collecting among the general populace.

And let's face it, characters will indeed make exercising the brain through reading and using the imagination more enticing to many students. It follows then that if characters are a part of education in childhood, there will be a predisposition to understanding the same characters later in life. While that doesn't equate to a wholesale knowledge of collecting, it does suggest that there will be more people than ever to whom the legacy may pass.

Listed below are the categories and sub-categories of toys, broken down by their educational objectives:

Role Playing
Action figures
Badges
Costumes
Dolls
Eyeglasses
Figurines
Marionettes
Masks
Paper dolls
Puppets
Pull toys
Sunglasses

Hygiene
Bubble bath containers
Combs
Hair accessories
Hairbrush
Soap
Toothbrushes
Toothbrush holders

Disneyland the Chicken of the Sea Pirate Ship Restaurant Poster from 1955.

61

Business/Business Awareness
Awards
Cash registers
Merchandise catalogues
Paperweights
Printing sets
Product containers
Stamps
Store punch-outs
Tote bags
Typewriters

Clothing
Bandannas
Beanies
Belts
Chaps
Coats
Footwear
Galoshes
Gloves
Handbags
Handkerchiefs
Hats
Helmets
Jackets
Necktie slides
Neckties
Pajamas
Patches
Pants
Rainwear
Robes
Scarves
Shirts
Shoes
Slippers
Socks
Suspenders
Sweaters
Sweatshirts
Swimsuits
T-Shirts
Tie bars
Underwear
Vests

Communication
Club newsletters
Club newspapers
Decoders
Radios
Radio guides
Radio premiums
Telephones
TV guides
TV premiums
Walkie talkies

Crafts
Clay
Doll patterns
Folders
Glue
Labels
Plaster molds
Rulers
Scissors
Stamping/printing sets
Stencils

Creativity
Animation art
Colorform sets
Coloring books
Coloring sets
Crayon sets
Drawings
Etch-a-Sketch
Fine art
Illustration art
Markers
Mobiles
Ornaments
Paint sets
Prints
Tracing books

Early Childhood Development
Baby bottles
Bathtub toys
Beanbags
Noisemakers
Pull toys
Rattles
Squeeze toys
Stroller (for dolls)
Stuffed animals

Entertainment
Beanie Babies
Bobbing head dolls
Bottle caps
Clickers
Flickers
Lithographs
Lobby cards
Magic answer boxes
Magic sets
Movie posters
Movie premiums
Movie programs
Tattoos
Trading cards
TV guides
Whistles
Wind-up toys
Wrappers
Yo-yos

Food Products, Packaging & Offers
Bread premiums
Bread wrappers
Candy

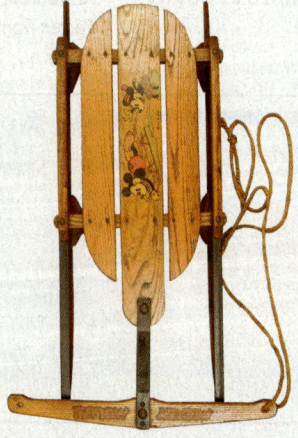

1930s Mickey Mouse Sled by S.L. Allen & Co.

Candy containers
Candy machines
Cereal
Cereal boxes
Cereal box premiums
Cracker Jack toys
Gumball machines
Ice cream lids
Juice
Juice packaging
Juice premiums
Lunch bottles
Lunch boxes
Milk
Milk premiums
Pez

Gambling
Arcade machines
Pinball machines
Punch boards
Shooting galleries
Skee ball
Slot machines

General Education
Press books
Puzzles
School bags
Show tickets
Signs
Standees
Videos
Viewers

Health & Medical
Band-aids
Doctor's kits
Emergency kits
Nurse's kits
Vitamin packaging

Homemaking/Tools
Bedspreads
Blankets
Boxes
Candles
Catalogues

Chairs
Coasters
Fans
Flashlights
Highchairs
Lamps
Needle books
Nightlights
Package seeds
Party supplies
Photo frames
Pillows
Planters
Plaques
Pottery
Rugs
Sandbox toys
Scales
Sewing kits
Sheets
Tables
Tool kits
Towels
Toy chests
Wallpaper

Jewelry & Make-Up
Barrettes
Bracelets
Chains
Charms
Cuff links
Key chains
Lapel pins
Lapel studs
Make-up kits
Necklaces
Pins
Ribbons
Rings
Stick pins

Kitchen
Baking sets
Bottles
Bowls
Cereal boxes

Cookie cutters
Cookie jars
Cooking sets
Cups
Dishes
Forks
Glasses
Knives
Mugs
Napkins
Pitchers
Placemats
Plates
Salt and pepper shakers
Soap
Spoons
Stools
Straws
Tea sets
Thermometers
Tin containers
Toy chests
Trays
Wastebaskets

Mickey Mouse doll in Easter Parade outfit by Knickerbocker c. 1930s.

Money
Banks
Billfolds
Coins
Coupons
Mechanical banks
Money clips
Paper money

Music
Instruments
Music boxes
Phonographs
Records
Sheet music
Songbooks

Organization
Albums
Scrapbooks
Stickers
Tags

Promotion & Politics
Buttons
Decals
Leaflets
Pinbacks

Pinocchio Large Composition Doll Produced in 1940 by Ideal.

Reading
Big Little Books
Bookmarks
Books
Comic books
Comic book stands
Cutout books
Flip books
Little/Big Golden books
Magazines
Paperbacks
Pop-up books
Post cards
Pulps
Punch-out sets
Scripts

Science/Academics
Animal figures
Balloons
Binoculars
Cameras
Casting sets
Chemistry sets
Codebooks
Compasses
Decoders
Detective kits
Geology kits
Globes
Gyroscopes
Ingots
Kaleidoscopes
Magnets
Magnifiers
Maps
Marbles
Mechanical toys
Microscopes
Model kits
Periscopes
Robots
Science kits
Star finders
Telescopes

Smoking
Ashtrays
Bubblegum cigars
Bubble pipes
Candy cigarettes
Lighters
Matches
Pipes

Socialization
Barbie dolls
Cards
Certificates
Christmas cards
Christmas lights
Club kits
Concert programs
Doll houses
Games
Greeting cards
Gum cards
Gum wrappers
Handbills
Handbooks
Instructions
Locks
Manuals
Medals
Membership cards
Mirrors
Musical instruments
Newsletters
Newspaper premiums
Newspapers
Notepaper
Pennants
Photos
Playsets
Radios
Transfers
Valentines
Wrapping paper
Yearbooks

Sports/Athletics/Outdoor Activities
Balloons

Baseball equipment
Basketball equipment
Boomerangs
Boxing gloves
Fishing kits
Football
Hockey
Ice skates
Kites
Lariats
Pedometers
Pinwheels
Ping-pong ball
Ping-pong paddle
Pool toys
Punching bags
Rollerskates
Sleeping bags
Sparklers
Spinners
Sporting goods
Tennis rackets
Tennis balls
Tents
Water sprinklers

Telling Time
Alarm clocks
Calendars
Clocks
Digital watches
Pocket watches
Stopwatches
Toy watches
Wristwatches

Transportation
Airplanes (toy)
Ambulances (toy)
Bicycles
Big Wheels
Boats (toy)
Buses (toy)
Car emblems
Cars (toy)
Construction equipment (toy)
Fire engines (toy)
Gasoline premiums

Gas stations (toy)
Gliders (toy)
Handcarts
Helicopters (toy)
Hot-air balloons (toy)
License plates
Motorcycles (toy)
Pogo sticks
Rockets (toy)
Scooters
Skateboards
Sirens
Sleds
Spaceships
Space toys
Trains (toy)
Tricycles
Trucks (toy)
Wagons

Visual Education
Films
Projection equipment
Movie viewers
TV sets (toy)

Weapons
Air rifles
BB guns
Cap bombs
Disc guns
Gun holsters (toy)
Guns (toy)
Knives

Slingshots
Swords
Targets
Waterguns

Weather
Snow globes
Sundials
Thermometers
Umbrellas
Weather predictors
Weather rings
Weathervanes

Writing
Blotters
Envelopes
Letter openers
Letters
Magic slates
Mailers
Penholders
Pencil boxes
Pencil erasers
Pencil holders
Pencil sharpeners
Pencils
Pens
Postcards
Stationery
Writing paper

Sport of Tycoons Bronze Limited Edition Sculpture by Paul Vought and Signed by Carl Barks. (1994)

Disney

Oswald The Lucky Rabbit Pinback Button from 1927. The earliest known Disney Related Button.

May 1920
Milton Feld contracts with Walt Disney to produce twelve short "Laugh-O-Grams" cartoons for the Newman theatre chain. These first "Lafflets" are essentially animated editorial cartoons, comically commenting on such issues as the condition of the Kansas City police force.

May 23, 1922
Walt Disney incorporates Laugh-O-Gram Films, Inc., opening a studio in Kansas City, MO. The studio will produce a series of fairy tale parodies along with the live-action/animation combination *Alice's Wonderland*. Disney himself and longtime associate Ub Iwerks act as lead animators. Young Virginia Davis performs in the live-action role of Alice.

May 14, 1923
Walt Disney opens negotiations with New York film distributor Margaret Winkler in regards to *Alice's Wonderland* and a subsequent Alice Comedies series.

October 16, 1923
Operating under the Disney Bros. name, Walt and Roy Disney sign a final contract with Margaret Winkler. The Alice series begins production at the Disneys' new Hollywood studio.

April 1, 1924
Alice's Spooky Adventure premieres. It introduces Julius the Cat, Disney's first recurring cartoon star.

June 1924
Ub Iwerks joins the staff in Hollywood, leading to an upgrade in both the studio's animation quality and the popularity of the Alice series.

March 24, 1925
Alice Solves the Puzzle premieres. It introduces Pegleg Pete (originally Bootleg Pete), the oldest Disney character still active today. Originally featured as a bear, the villainous Pete would become a cat in 1928.

January 1927
Under producer Charles Mintz, the Disney studio develops the new character of Oswald the Lucky Rabbit for Universal Pictures.

July 4, 1927
Premiere of *Trolley Troubles*, the second produced and first released Oswald cartoon.

February 1928
Charles Mintz gives Disney the choice of producing the Oswald cartoons at a lowered budget or

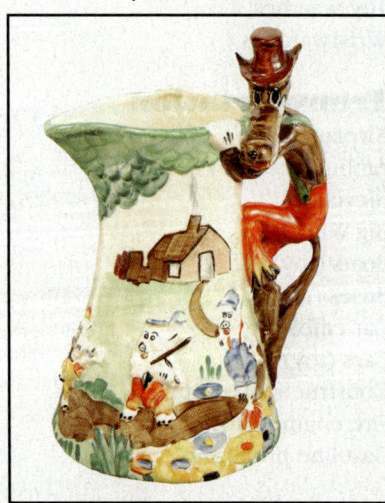

Wadeheath Three Little Pigs ceramic pitcher, 1930s.

TIMELINE

ending his association with the character. Disney chooses the latter, after which Disney and Iwerks create Mickey Mouse.

May 15, 1928
Plane Crazy, the first produced Mickey Mouse cartoon, is given a sneak preview at a Sunset Boulevard theatre. Minnie Mouse and Clarabelle Cow also debut in the cartoon.

November 18, 1928
Steamboat Willie, the third produced Mickey Mouse cartoon and the first with sound, premieres at the Colony Theatre. Pat Powers' Celebrity Pictures handles distribution and provides sound with its Cinephone system.

June 1929
Sneak preview of the first *Silly Symphony* cartoon, *The Skeleton Dance*, at Los Angeles' Cathay Circle Theatre.

June 28, 1929
Release of *The Plowboy*, introducing Horace Horsecollar, Mickey's egotistical barnyard pal.

January 13, 1930
The *New York Mirror* publishes the first Mickey Mouse daily newspaper comic strip. It is written by Walt Disney, penciled by Ub Iwerks, and inked by Win Smith.

January 21, 1930
Ub Iwerks leaves the Disney studio. Walt Disney buys out Iwerks' 20% share in the company.

February 1930
Columbia Pictures takes over distribution of Disney cartoons.

May 5, 1930
Floyd Gottfredson takes over art chores and, shortly after, plotting of the Mickey Mouse daily comic strip. He will continue work on the

German tin mechanical tin toy by Eisenmann & Co., 1930.

The Wise Little Hen Hardcover Edition by Whitman Publishing Co., 1935.

strip in various capacities until 1975.

September 5, 1930
Premiere of *The Chain Gang*, a Mickey Mouse short featuring two identical prison bloodhounds in a supporting role. The hounds mark the first use of what would become the Pluto character design.

November 1930
The first Disney publications appear: the paperback *Mickey Mouse Book* from Bibo and Lang and the hardback *Mickey Mouse Annual* #1 from English publisher Dean and Son. (The *Annual* is often misdated at 1931, but was actually published in time for the 1930 holiday season.)

DISNEY TIMELINE

Walt Disney's Sketch Book of Snow White and The Seven Dwarfs by English Publisher Wm. Collins Sons & Co. Ltd., 1938.

January 10, 1932
Mickey Mouse appears in his first Sunday newspaper comics color half-page. It is accompanied by the *Silly Symphony* Sunday half-page, which will feature such characters as Bucky Bug and José Carioca over the years.

May 12, 1932
Mickey's Revue is released. It introduces Dippy Dawg, the hayseed character soon to be renamed Goofy.

Summer 1932
United Artists takes over distribution of Disney cartoons.

July 1, 1932
Walt and Roy Disney contract with advertising agent Herman Kay Kamen, making him the company's chief licensing representative.

July 30, 1932
Flowers and Trees is released. This Silly Symphony is Disney's first color cartoon, and the first color cartoon ever to use the three-strip Technicolor process.

November 18, 1932
Disney wins his first two Oscars. The Academy Award for Short Subjects, Cartoons, is won by *Flowers and Trees*. A special additional Academy Award is given to Disney for the creation of Mickey Mouse. *Parade of the Award Nominees*, a promotional short, premieres at the Academy Award ceremony. It features the first color animation of Mickey Mouse.

December 26, 1932
Topolino, the first Disney periodical, appears on Italian newsstands courtesy of Italian publisher Nerbini. *Topolino* initially contains stories and illustrations created entirely in Italy. Several months later it begins to reprint American Disney newspaper comics as well.

January 1933
Kay Kamen and Hal Horne introduce *Mickey Mouse Magazine*, the first American Disney periodical. Its first incarnations are movie theatre and dairy giveaways. In summer 1935 it will become a standard newsstand publication.

May 27, 1933
The Silly Symphony *Three Little Pigs* is released, featuring the first appearances of the title characters and of Zeke, the Big Bad Wolf. *Three Little Pigs* will go on to win an Academy Award.

June 9, 1934
The Silly Symphony *The Wise Little Hen* premieres, introducing Donald Duck.

February 8, 1936
Mickey Mouse Weekly is issued in England by Willbank Publications. Similar to *Topolino* in format, it features a mix of locally produced comics (not all Disney-related) and American reprints.

January 9, 1937
Release of *Don Donald*, introducing Donna Duck and Donald's famous car. Donald's girlfriend would be renamed Daisy in 1940; the car, soon to receive its famous 313 license plate, remains a comics' icon today, with model kits sold by various European licensees.

May 15, 1937
Donald and Donna, the first long Donald Duck comic book story, begins serialization in *Mickey Mouse Weekly*. It is an entirely British production, drawn by William Ward.

December 21, 1937
Snow White and the Seven Dwarfs premieres. It is the first American animated feature film.

Joe Carioca Ceramic Figurine By Zaccagnini, 1947.

DISNEY TIMELINE

December 30, 1937
Paperino Giornale, the first comic book named for Donald Duck, begins weekly publication in Italy. The first issue begins serialization of Federico Pedrocchi's Paolino Paperino e il Mistero del Marte (*Donald Duck and the Secret of Mars*), the first extended length Disney comic book story to be created in Italy.

May 20, 1939
The Mickey Mouse daily strip begins serializing *Mickey Mouse Outwits the Phantom Blot*, plotted and penciled by Floyd Gottfredson, scripted by Merrill de Maris, and inked by Ted Thwaites and Bill Wright. The story introduces the Phantom Blot, Gottfredson's most important creation and the second most important Mickey villain after Pegleg Pete.

February 7, 1940
Pinocchio premieres.

April 2, 1940
Walt Disney Productions' initial public offering.

October 1940
Mickey Mouse Magazine becomes Western Publishing's *Walt Disney's Comics and Stories*, the first modern format Disney comic book. The earliest issues are mostly devoted to newspaper strip reprints.

November 12, 1940
Fantasia premieres.

February 27, 1941
Disney wins Academy Awards for Music, Best Song (for *When You Wish Upon a Star*) and Music, Best Score (for *Pinocchio*).

Summer 1941
Western Publishing's *Four Color Comics (Series I)* 13 features "The Reluctant Dragon," an animated featurette adapted to comics by Irving Tripp. This is the first American comic story to be produced exclusively for a comic book.

July 1942
Western Publishing's *Four Color Comics (Series II)* #9 features "Donald Duck Finds Pirate Gold," written by newspaper strip scripter Bob Karp and drawn by Donald cartoon storymen Carl Barks and Jack Hannah. "Pirate Gold" marked the start of Barks' lifetime association with Duck comic books.

January 1, 1943
Release of *Der Fuehrer's Face*. This wartime cartoon, in which Donald Duck dreams of leading a miserable life in Nazi Germany, will go on to win Donald his first and only Academy Award.

April 2, 1943
Release of *Private Pluto*, introducing Chip 'n' Dale.

July 18, 1944
El Pato Donald y Otras Historietas, the first Brazilian Disney comic book, begins publication from Editorial Abril. In time, Abril will become one of the foremost producers of Disney comics material, much of it centered around locally popular Disney star José Carioca.

January 1945
Roy Disney becomes President of Walt Disney Productions.

Schuco Disneyland Alweg-Monorail Boxed Set.(1962)

December 1947
Western Publishing's *Four Color Comics (Series II)* #178 features *Donald Duck's Christmas on Bear Mountain*, written and drawn by Carl Barks. The story introduces Uncle Scrooge McDuck, Barks' most important creation and the second most important Duck character after Donald himself.

January 1948
Walt Disneys Comics and Stories #88 introduces Donald's lucky cousin Gladstone Gander, another legendary Carl Barks creation.

March 20, 1948
Zip-A-Dee-Doo-Dah, a hit tune from *Song of the South*, wins the 1947 Academy Award for Best Song.

August 31, 1948
Mickey Mouse Park, named in an internal memo, circulates as the initial concept for what will become Disneyland Park.

September 1948
Kalle Anka & C:o, a Swedish version of *Walt Disney's Comics and Stories*, is issued by what will become the Egmont Publishing Group. In time, from its headquarters in Copenhagen, Denmark,

DISNEY TIMELINE

Winnie The Pooh Boxed Watch with Figurine was a 1965 Sears Exclusive By Bradley.

Egmont will become another of the foremost producers of Disney comics material.

April 1949
Italy's *Topolino* comics magazine changes formats to become a thick digest-sized comic. In its first year, *Topolino* digest features the Italian-made Dante parody *L'Inferno di Topolino* (*Mickey's Inferno*). In the 1950s and 1960s, a golden age of original Italian comics production will begin, under creators such as Romano Scarpa, Guido Martina and Giorgio Cavazzano.

October 1949
The Walt Disney Music Company is formed.

July 19, 1950
Release of *Treasure Island*, Disney's first purely live action feature film. The movie stars Bobby Driscoll as Jim Hawkins and Robert Newton in a famous performance as Long John Silver.

December 25, 1950
One Hour in Wonderland, the first Disney TV special, airs on NBC.

November 1951
Walt Disney's Comics and Stories #134 introduces the Beagle Boys, creations of Carl Barks and the Disney duck characters' most famous recurring foes.

May 1952
Walt Disney's Comics and Stories #140 introduces Gyro Gearloose, Donald Duck's inventor friend and another of Carl Barks' creations.

October 1952
Donald Duck, a Dutch version of *Walt Disney's Comics and Stories*, is issued by what will become the De Geillustreerde Pers. In time, GP (today Sanoma) will become another of the foremost producers of Disney comics material.

December 16, 1952
Walt Disney Inc. is formed to develop Disneyland.

1953
Buena Vista Distribution Company is established as the Disney studio's self-managed distribution firm.

April 1954
Walt announces that Disneylandia (as it was called early on) would open in July, 1955. ABC television executives suggest the name change to Disneyland.

July 21, 1954
Ground broken for Disneyland.

October 27, 1954
Disneyland TV show, Disney's classic one-hour variety series, debuts on ABC.

March 30, 1955
20,000 Leagues Under the Sea wins Academy Awards for Art Direction and Visual Effects.

July 18, 1955
Disneyland opens to the public.

October 3, 1955
The *Mickey Mouse Club* begins on ABC, introducing the Mouseketeers.

1958
Disneyland TV show becomes *Walt Disney Presents*.

June 14, 1959
Disneyland monorail begins operation.

September 24, 1961
Walt Disney Presents becomes *Walt Disney's Wonderful World of Color* on NBC.

December 1961
Western Publishing's *Uncle Scrooge* #36 introduces Magica De Spell, the "saucy sorceress" and second most famous nemesis of the Disney ducks.

1962
Disney initiates the Overseas

DISNEY TIMELINE

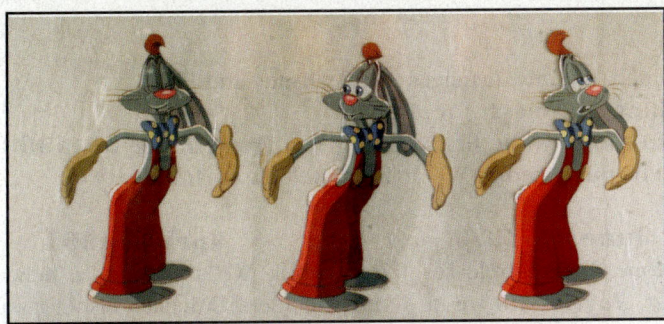
Roger Rabbit Production Test Cels.

Comics Program: in-house Burbank production of extra comic book stories in English, exclusively for publication abroad. The Overseas Program's most popular creation is Donald's cousin Fethry Duck.

1963
Central Florida is chosen as the location for what will become Walt Disney World.

August 27, 1964
Mary Poppins premieres.

1964
Walt Disney begins developing concepts for what will become EPCOT Center at Walt Disney World.

April 5, 1965
Mary Poppins wins Academy Awards for Best Actress (Julie Andrews), Best Song ("Chim Chim Cher-ee"), Musical Score, Film Editing, and Special Visual Effects.

November 15, 1965
First public announcement of plans to build a new theme park in Florida.

February 4, 1966
Winnie the Pooh and the Honey Tree is released, introducing Disney's versions of Pooh, Rabbit, Owl, Eeyore, Kanga and Roo. Tigger and Piglet, though not in the film, are still part of the ancillary marketing campaign, although the designs used for the two are markedly different from those later used in animation.

December 15, 1966
Walt Disney dies at age 65 from symptoms related to lung cancer. The recognition of his legacy consists of 48 Academy Awards and 7 Emmys. In lieu of Walt, Roy Disney is named company chairman, with Don Tatum as president and Card Walker as executive vice-president of operations.

October 18, 1967
Release of *The Jungle Book*, the last animated feature personally supervissed by Walt Disney.

December 20, 1968
Winnie the Pooh and the Blustery Day is released, introducing Disney's definitive versions of Tigger and Piglet.

June 8, 1969
Topolino #706 features "Paperinik il Diabolico Vendicatore" ("The Diabolical Duck Avenger"), written by Elisa Penna and drawn by Giovan Battista Carpi. The comic story introduces Paperinik (Duck Avenger), Donald Duck's secret superhero identity.

October 25, 1971
The Magic Kingdom opens at Walt Disney World in Orlando, Florida.

December 20, 1971
Roy Disney dies of a cerebral hemorrhage. Don Tatum becomes company chairman and Card Walker president.

July 9, 1982
Release of *Tron*, the cult classic live action film that introduces many to the concepts of computer animation.

October 1, 1982
EPCOT (Experimental Prototype Community of Tomorrow) Center opens at Walt Disney World.

April 15, 1983
Tokyo Disneyland opens. The park is operated under license from Disney by the Oriental Land Company.

April 18, 1983
The Disney Channel begins broadcasting. Initially a pay-TV network, it later becomes part of most cable companies' basic package.

March 9, 1984
Release of *Splash*, the first release by Disney subsidiary Touchstone Pictures.

September 24, 1984
Months of internal unrest at Disney end as the company formally announces Michael Eisner's elec-

DISNEY TIMELINE

tion as chairman and CEO, with Frank Wells as company president.

October 1984
Jeffrey Katzenberg takes over the position of Walt Disney studio chairman.

Summer 1985
Uncle Scrooge Goes to Disneyland and *Disneyland Birthday Party* are the first American Disney comics published under the Gladstone imprint. Gladstone, managed by Bruce Hamilton and Russ Cochran, published from 1985-1990 and again from 1993-1998. In addition reprinting Barks, Gottfredson, and foreign comics material, Gladstone produced its own stories, introducing the work of Don Rosa and William Van Horn. Byron Erickson and John Clark are the editorial team behind the new developments.

April 7, 1987
Gladstone's *Uncle Scrooge* #219 (cover date July 1987) ships to retailers. The 32-page comic book features the first authorized Disney work of writer/artist Don Rosa, today renowned as one of the foremost Scrooge delineators.

September 18, 1987
The animated TV series *DuckTales* is launched with the full-length prime time TV movie *Treasure of the Golden Suns*. Starring Scrooge McDuck, the series also introduces Launchpad McQuack.

June 13, 1988
Creation of the Magazines Division of the Walt Disney Company Italia SpA, which directly manages the publishing business for Italy. *Topolino* #1702 is the first comic book to be published by WD Italia.

June 24, 1988
Touchstone Pictures releases *Who Framed Roger Rabbit*, a live-action/animated feature largely credited with a general revival of interest in golden age cartoons. Roger Rabbit will also be treated as a major Disney star for several years, although disagreements with co-owner Amblin Entertainment will later cause the character to drop from sight.

May 1, 1989
Disney-MGM Studios opens at Walt Disney World.

November 15, 1989
Release of *The Little Mermaid*. Introducing Ariel and Sebastian, the film marks the start of what some have called Disney's "renaissance" with a new guard of animators creating a series of highly popular feature films.

June 1990
Expanding the Overseas Program into a domestic publishing arrangement, the Walt Disney Company begins publishing American comic books in-house. The effort will ultimately be unsuccessful.

November 22, 1991
Release of *Beauty and the Beast*.

April 12, 1992
Official opening date of Euro Disney Resort in Paris, France. The park will later be renamed Disneyland Paris.

November 25, 1992
Release of *Aladdin*.

April 3, 1994
Frank Wells dies in a helicopter accident. Michael Eisner assumes Wells' duties along with his own.

May 20, 1994
The Return of Jafar, an *Aladdin* sequel, is released direct-to-video. While not the first sequel to a Disney feature, Jafar is the first in what will become a long series of such films released as direct-to-video projects, eventually including *Cinderella II* (2002) and *III* (2007).

June 24, 1994
Release of *The Lion King*.

August 1994
Jeffrey Katzenberg resigns from the company. He will go on to co-found Dreamworks SKG, one of Disney's modern-day animation rivals.

August 18, 1994
Egmont Serieforlaget's *Anders And & Co.* 34/1994 features *Fantasy Island*, written and drawn by Byron Erickson and César Ferioli. The comic story begins a new tradition of modern Mickey comics in the spirit of the 1930s classics.

July 31, 1995
Disney purchases Capital Cities/ABC.

November 24, 1995
Disney/Pixar's *Toy Story*, the first computer-animated feature film, is released. It introduces Woody the cowboy doll and Buzz Lightyear.

DISNEY TIMELINE

June 1997
Disney Cruise Lines opens for business as the Disney *Magic* touring ship is launched.

April 22, 1998
Animal Kingdom opens at Walt Disney World.

December 17, 1999
Fantasia/2000 premieres at Carnegie Hall.

May 19, 2000
Release of *Dinosaur*, Disney's first self-produced computer-animated feature. While heavily merchandised, the film is not particularly successful.

April 2001
The comic book *W.I.T.C.H.* begins publication through the Walt Disney Company Italia SpA. Created by Elisabetta Gnone, Alessandro Barbucci and Barbara Canepa, the *W.I.T.C.H.* character franchise will go on to become one of Disney's most profitable in Europe.

September 4, 2001
Opening of Tokyo DisneySea. The park is operated under license from Disney by the Oriental Land Company.

March 28, 2002
Release of *Kingdom Hearts* video game. Developed by Square Co. Ltd., the game combines Disney characters with Square's *Final Fantasy* characters in a sword-and-sorcery adventure. The game's success has led to sequels and merchandising spinoffs. In the world of *Kingdom Hearts*, different Disney worlds exist in a dimension ruled by King Mickey; human boy Sora teams up with Court Wizard Donald and Captain Goofy for various quests.

June 7, 2002
Premiere of long-running *Kim Possible* TV cartoon series. The title character, a long-suffering high-school-age crime fighter, is paired with her pal (and later boyfriend) Ron Stoppable. Other characters include Ron's pet rat Rufus; boy genius Wade; and villains such as Dr. Drakken, Shego and the Mexican tycoon Señor Señor, Senior.

June 21, 2002
Release of *Lilo and Stitch*. The mischievous Stitch, "Experiment 626" of mad alien scientist Jumba Jookiba, becomes a breakout character, with numerous TV and video follow-ups over the years.

May 5, 2003
Donald Duck Adventures/Free Comic Book Day is the first American Disney comic book published under the Gemstone imprint.

May 30, 2003
Release of Pixar's *Finding Nemo*.

July 9, 2003
Release of *Pirates of the Caribbean: Curse of the Black Pearl*. Based on the famous Disney theme park rides, the Oscar-nominated live-action film starring Johnny Depp is a runaway success, leading to sequels and a merchandising juggernaut.

November 5, 2004
Release of Pixar's *The Incredibles*.

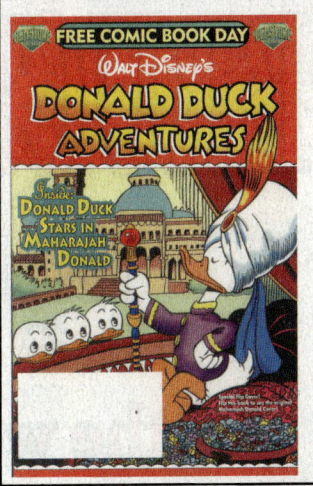

Donald Duck Adventures/Free Comic Book Day by Gemstone Publishing, Inc. (2003)

September 12, 2005
Hong Kong Disneyland opens.

September 30, 2005
Michael Eisner steps down as CEO of the Walt Disney Company. He is replaced by Robert Iger, former corporate president and COO.

October 30, 2005
Release of *Chicken Little*, Disney's second self-produced computer-animated feature. The heavily merchandised film also introduces the characters Runt of the Litter (pig), Abby Mallard (duck) and Fish Out of Water.

February 9, 2006
Disney announces agreement with NBC/Universal in which Disney acquires character rights to its version of Oswald Rabbit, together with film rights to Walt Disney's 26 Oswald cartoons. Not included in the deal are rights to any non-Disney-produced Oswald cartoons or products.

Subscribe to Antique Toy World Magazine and Enjoy 12 Issues for Only $39.95

Antique Toy World is quickly approaching its 32nd Anniversary. It is now the oldest, most specialized publication in its class. We cover everything from 19th century to post World War II playthings. We're growing too! We currently reach more than 20,000 toy collectors 12 times a year with more than 160, jam-packed pages.

Each issue includes:
- Firsthand previews and reports of major toy auctions and shows from coast to coast, plus Europe and Canada.
- Incisive insight into collecting, written by *ATW* columnists, each experts in their area of specialization.
- A Show & Auction Calendar that will prepare you for events you won't want to miss.
- Almost every page is chock full of color and black & white photography of exceptional toys we'd all like to own.
- Read about what's hot, and what's not, the market, "how to" articles, and updates on the repro scene.
- Display and classified advertising that showcases a vast array of toys, offered by leading collectors, as well as experts in repair, restoration and parts services.

Don't miss this unique opportunity to catch up on What's Happening! Subscribe to Antique Toy World Today!

The perfect gift anytime!

"One great idea or piece of vital information you've been seeking, in itself can be worth more than the cost of a subscription to Antique Toy World." —*Dale Kelley, Publisher*

ANTIQUE TOY WORLD
P.O. Box 34509, Chicago, IL 60634 • Call 773-725-0633 to subscribe

---

Save Over 50% Off the Cover Price!!!
Yes! Please send me one year (12 issues)
of Antique Toy World Magazine for only $39.95

Name _____

Address _____

Town/State/Zip _____

I would like to send
a one-year
gift subscription to:

Name _____

Address _____

Town/State/Zip _____

Make checks payable to: Antique Toy World Magazine, P.O. Box 34509, Chicago, IL 60634

The leader in character collectibles for more than 40 years!

CONSIGNMENTS WANTED • ALWAYS BUYING

ONE ITEM OR ENTIRE COLLECTIONS

AUCTIONS • SALES • EBAY

NO BUYER'S PREMIUM

HAKE'S AMERICANA & COLLECTIBLES • 1966 GREENSPRING DRIVE, SUITE 400 ✧ TIMONIU

A division of Diamond International Galleries

MD 21093 ✧ TOLL FREE (866) 404-9800 ✧ PHONE (410) 427-9440 ✧ WWW.HAKES.COM

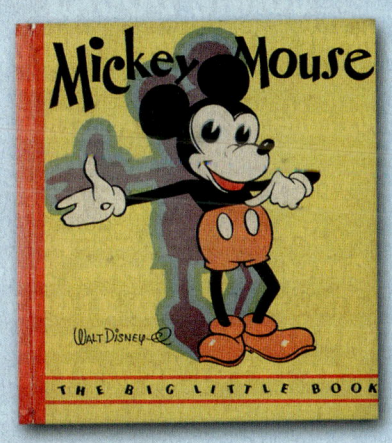

BUYING & SELLING

KOKONINO KOLLECTIBLES

160 DESERT HOLLY DRIVE ✴ SEDONA, AZ 86336
TEL: (928) 204-0086 ✴ FAX: (928) 204-1858
CELL PHONE: (928) 963-0600 ✴ E-MAIL: KOKOKOLLECTIBLES@AOL.COM

All characters ©2007 respective copyright holders. All rights reserved.

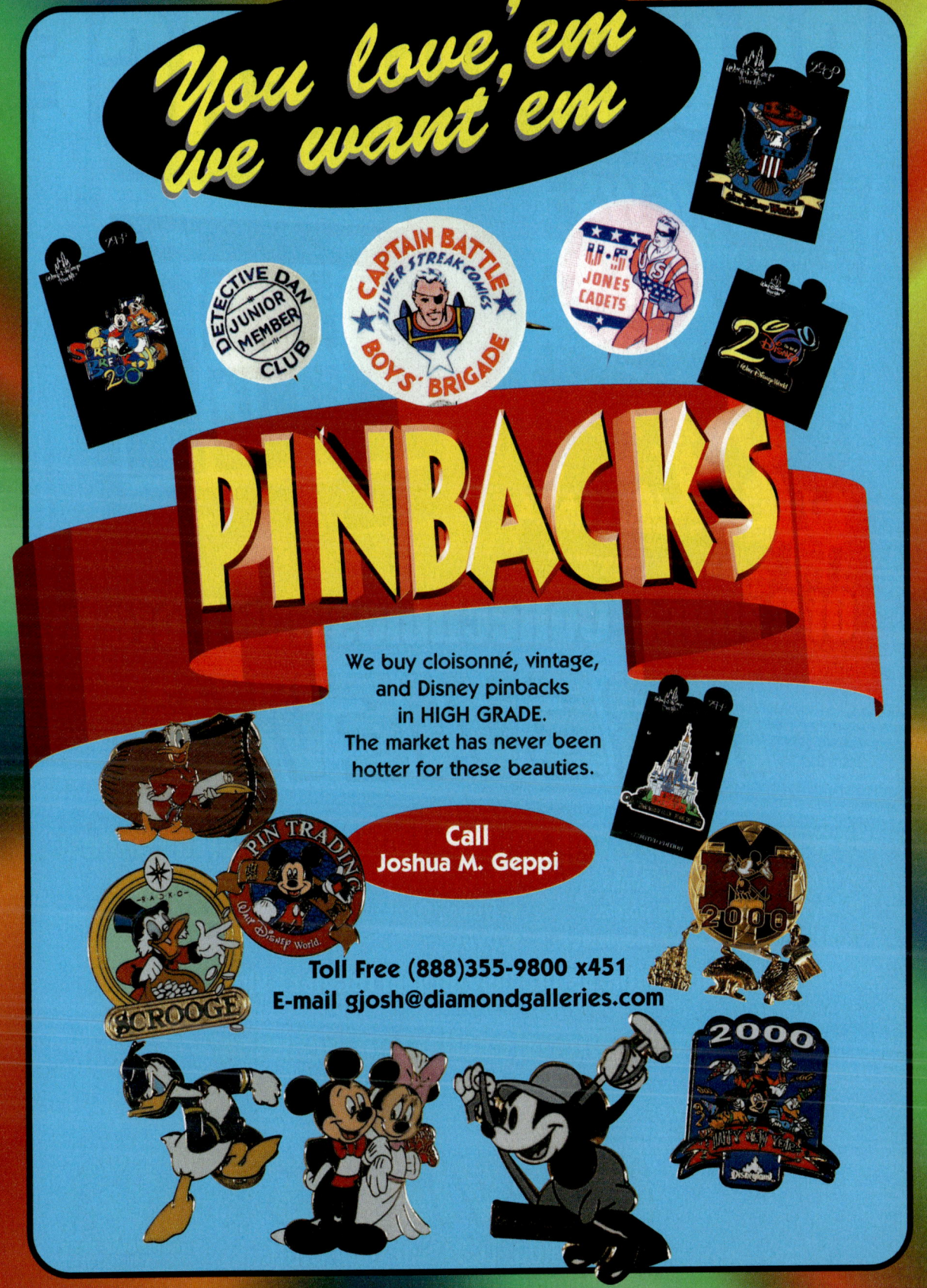

PRESENTING
Russ Cochran's Comic Art Auction

Frank McSavage color cover art for Walter Lantz's Woody Woodpecker coloring book, 1950s, sold for $570.

John Totleben cover painting for Edgar Rice Burroughs' The Return of Tarzan #2, 1997, sold for $1870.
Pat Boyette cover painting for Space 1999 #7, 1976, sold for $790.

FOR MORE THAN 33 YEARS, RUSS COCHRAN'S COMIC ART AUCTION HAS BEEN THE PIONEER AND LEADER IN THE SALE OF ORIGINAL COMIC STRIP AND COMIC BOOK ART. OUR HISTORY-MAKING SALES HAVE INCLUDED WORKS BY ALEX RAYMOND, FRANK FRAZETTA, MILTON CANIFF, AND MANY OTHERS! WHETHER YOU'RE A CONSIGNER LOOKING TO SELL OR A COLLECTOR LOOKING TO BUY, CHECK OUT RUSS COCHRAN'S COMIC ART AUCTION!

CALL FOR MORE INFORMATION!

(417) 256-2224 OR TOLL FREE (800) EC CRYPT

COMICART@RUSSCOCHRAN.COM

DAN MORPHY

"The most BANKABLE NAME in the BUSINESS"

TOP DOLLAR PAID
•CASH•

WANTED
- - - - - - - Mechanical Banks
- - - - - - - Bank Boxes
- - - - - - - Trade Cards
- - - - - - - Other Vintage Toys

DAN MORPHY
danmorphy@dejazzd.com
717.335.4569

PRESIDENT'S LETTER

When I wrote in the last edition of this guide, "It started with a rabbit," no one knew that Oswald The Lucky Rabbit would for the first time ever fall under the control of the home team, The Walt Disney Company. I also think it's safe to say that none of us expected him to be traded for Al Michaels either, for that matter.

Likewise, who knew that one of the most inspirational comebacks of 2006 and 2007 would be The Gremlins? Last seen in 1943, they were the subject of an ill-fated project that teamed *Charlie and the Chocolate Factory* creator Roald Dahl and the great Walt Disney. The creations sat somewhere in the Disney archives until my good friend Mike Richardson heard about them. Mike is the founder of Dark Horse Comics and creator of the film that brought Jim Carrey to fame, *The Mask*. He brought new life to a property that only barely had it to begin with.

And who could have expected that a great collector like Steve Ison would sell his staggering *Snow White* collection to Disney? After spending literally decades assembling its prestigious and diverse components, Steve packed up his collection and sent it home to Disney this past summer.

If you've read the articles in this edition, you've seen how all of the stories above played out. On the surface, they don't seem to have an awful lot in common other than they involve Disney and Disneyana collecting. They do, however, offer one more thing: they weren't what we expected.

Sometimes in collecting, particularly in a well-established niche such as Disneyana, we are tempted to think we've seen it all. Then something like one or all of these tales comes up and reminds us that there is still the unexpected lurking out there. As someone who's turned up a hidden collection or two in his day, this gets my blood going. What else is out there left to discover? What secrets are hidden in some collector's basement or in some forgotten filing cabinet? Wouldn't it be great to find out? That's the kind of excitement I've always found in collecting, and I bet you're the same way!

A similar kind of surprise came to us when we released the first edition of *The Official Price Guide To Disney Collectibles*. We knew it was a terrific book, to be sure, but we didn't know for certain how it would be received. It went over big. On behalf of author Ted Hake and everyone at Gemstone Publishing, I want to personally thank you for your support. Aside from our own passion for the material, you are the reason that we are able to produce this new edition.

With that in mind, if you have a moment to drop us a line, we'd really like to know what you think. Just email feedback@gemstonepub.com and tell us about it!

In the meantime, as a fellow collector, I'd like to personally invite you and all of your friends in the hobby to visit Geppi's Entertainment Museum. GEM opened in Baltimore, Maryland in September 2006 and has quickly become a well-documented phenomenon with critics and reviewers. It covers the history of popular culture in this country from 1776 to the present, and that definitely includes copious quantities of Disneyana. You can find out more about it by visiting www.geppismuseum.com.

Sincerely,

Stephen A. Geppi

Stephen A. Geppi
President and Chief Executive Officer

DDK-86
(page 198)

A BUG'S LIFE

Unless otherwise noted, prices listed for all items represent GOOD, FINE, and NEAR MINT conditions.

A Bug's Life

Pixar's second computer-animated, full-length feature from 1998 had the incredible task of following its first. *Toy Story* was so beloved by both critics and the public that anything following it was almost doomed to be less successful. Upon its release *A Bug's Life* had its detractors, but it succeeded on so many levels that it virtually eliminated comparisons. With a storyline loosely inspired by Aesop's fable of *The Ant and the Grasshopper*, the feature is centered in the world of insects. The film takes the idea of community into a world that most of us never think of. By giving that world so many distinct personalities and such a lush existence, it becomes a brand new place that no one has ever seen before. It is the idea that the story could be taking place in our very own backyard, coupled with the personalities of the insects, which drives the movie.

Flik is a well-meaning ant who, though ridiculed in his colony for his wacky inventions, nevertheless decides to defend his fellow ants against a group of free-loading grasshoppers. He ventures out and hires what he thinks are "Warrior Bugs" to defend the colony. They turn out to be performers in a flea circus.

Pixar went to great lengths to keep a sense of reality for each insect. A fly who is heckling the circus act is heard saying that "I've been in outhouses that didn't stink this bad." There is a snail who specifically orders a drink without salt. Little touches like this contributed to the film's universal appeal. The actors voicing the characters matched the high standard of the writing. Dave Foley, Julia Louis-Dreyfus, Kevin Spacey and Phyllis Diller all bring their personalities to the screen. Denis Leary is a standout as a ladybug with identity issues. The feature was directed by Andrew Stanton and John Lassiter. The soundtrack was written by Randy Newman.

Merchandise included books, toys, games and cross promotion in fast food outlets.

ABU-1

❏ **ABU-1. Giant Light-Up Ant Hill Playset,** 1998. Mattel. Coaster Catapult, Acorn Cannons, and Grasshopper Trap. Lights up. - **$55**

ABU-2   ABU-3

❏ **ABU-2. Warrior Flik Action Figure,** 1998. Mattel. Complete with Battle Nut weapons. - **$15**

❏ **ABU-3. Francis and Slim Action Figure,** 1998. Mattel. Two figures in one package, with twin blasting launchers. - **$18**

ABU-4   ABU-5

❏ **ABU-4. Enemy Hopper Action Figure,** 1998. Mattel. Kick striking action, enemy Hopper. - **$22**

❏ **ABU-5. Enemy Molt Action Figure,** 1998. Mattel. Head butting action. - **$18**

ABU-6   ABU-7

❏ **ABU-6. Hang Glider Flik Action Figure,** 1998. Mattel. Complete with leaf hang glider and Berry Blaster. - **$15**

❏ **ABU-7. Flik Action Figure,** 1998. From the Bug's Life Play Set. - **$7**

ABU-8

❏ **ABU-8. Flik Figure,** 1998. . - **$28**

(2 VIEWS)

ABU-9

❏ **ABU-9. Water Globe,** 1998. Has real magnifying glass. - **$80**

ADVENTURES OF ICHABOD & MR. TOAD

ABU-10

❏ **ABU-10. Valentine Pack,** 1998. . - **$6**

Absent-Minded Professor

This full-length black and white feature was released in March 1961. Its star, Fred MacMurray, had been known for years as a dependable screen actor, but the year before this film's release he had started a twelve year run as the kindly father in *My Three Sons* on CBS. That gave him a more solid image in the eyes of the public. His skill gives the film a grounded center that allows the most outlandish slapstick gags to take place around him and yet, still remain believable.

He played Professor Brainard, a man so absent-minded that he forgot his own wedding. Somehow, Brainard managed to create the anti-gravity material flubber, allowing people and objects to fly. The movie is packed with great special effects that are still thrilling in today's world of computer-assisted effects. The flying car is a hoot and the basketball game where the school's students use flubber to gain the upper hand is a funny sequence.

Directed by Robert Stevenson (who also directed *Mary Poppins* and is the grandson of Robert Louis Stevenson), the movie stars Nancy Olson, Ed Wynn, Keenan Wynn and Tommy Kirk. The film marks the first time that the brothers Richard M. and Robert B. Sherman wrote a song for a Disney film. They would achieve great success with *Mary Poppins*. The special effects were nominated for an Academy Award.

A sequel, *Son of Flubber* was released in January 1963 and it featured many of the same cast members. In 1997 Robin Williams starred in a remake titled *Flubber*.

The Absent-Minded Professor appears in *Four Color Comics* #1199.

Merchandise includes books and soft, rubbery imitation flubber.

AMP-1

AMP-2

❏ **AMP-1. Disney Studio Christmas Card,** 1960. 7x8" slightly textured paper. Card opens to reveal calendar for 1961. Illustration on back is for upcoming film The Absent-Minded Professor and depicts Fred MacMurray, Santa and dalmatians in his flying car. - **$10 $20 $35**

❏ **AMP-2. Movie Herald,** c. 1961. From Maryland theater. - **$4 $8 $15**

AMP-3

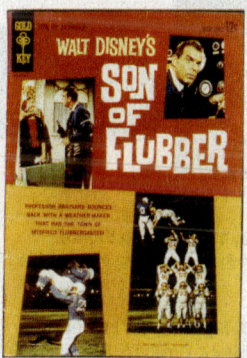

AMP-4

❏ **AMP-3. "Son of Flubber" Press Book,** 1962. 12x18" 24-page glossy paper press book. Includes many bw photo scenes from the film plus much text on the film's story and stars. There are also many different newspaper ads, several pages of merchandise including "Flubber" by Hasbro, page of promotional souvenirs including inflatable footballs and "Son of Flubber Squawky Toy," coloring contest page. - **$10 $18 $30**

❏ **AMP-4. "Son of Flubber" Comic Book,** 1963. First and only issue of this title based on the Disney film by K.K. Publications Inc. - **$5 $15 $45**

Adventures of Ichabod & Mr. Toad

Released by Disney in 1949, the year before *Cinderella*, this fine film tends to get forgotten when people talk about the greatness of Disney animation. Marketed as a single feature, this wonderful film is actually comprised of two separate tales. The first, narrated by Basil Rathbone is taken from Kenneth Graham's *The Wind in the Willows*. Wealthy and fun-loving J. Thaddeus Toad's wasteful ways may have been ruining his business at Toad Hall, but that didn't make him a thief. That is until he unwittingly trades his entire estate for a stolen car. Framed for having stolen it himself, he is imprisoned. With the help of his horse, Cyril, he gets free and ends up proving his innocence. The film is peppered with interesting characters like Ratty, Moley and Angus MacBadger.

Second up is the Washington Irving tale, *The Legend of Sleepy Hollow*. This segment is narrated by Bing Crosby. The film needed his calm tones. The pace and tenor of the film is so perfect that the horrific ending is still capable of instilling nightmares in the minds of even the bravest. The tale centers on the timid and easily frightened new schoolmaster of the town Sleepy Hollow, Ichabod Crane. Crane tries to win the heart of wealthy Katrina Van Tassel, but must contend with a rival for her affections, Brom Bones.

Sleepy Hollow deserves its name, except for one slight problem; it is haunted by the Headless Horseman. Almost fifty years later, the final sequence with the Headless Horseman riding full force is still frighteningly effective.

Clyde Geronimi and Jack Kinney directed the film. The animators included several of Disney's famed "Nine Old Men," Frank Thomas, Ollie Johnston, Ward Kimball and Milt Kahl.

Merchandise includes books and a Disneyana Convention version of the famed amusement park ride *Mr. Toad's Wild Ride* boxed car.

ADVENTURES OF ICHABOD & MR. TOAD

ADV-1

❑ **ADV-1. Mr. Toad Original Large Cel,**
1949. Movie cel. NM - **$1600**

ADV-2

❑ **ADV-2. Mr. Toad In Jail,**
1949. Classic art from the Golden Book by the late John Hench. NM - **$7800**

ADV-3

❑ **ADV-3. Three Key Cel Set-up,**
1949. Ratty, Moley and Angus MacBadger appear. NM - **$2200**

ADV-4

❑ **ADV-4. Lobby Card Group,**
1949. RKO Radio Pictures Inc. Title card and two scene cards. Title - **$20 $40 $85**
Each Scene - **$10 $20 $35**

ADV-5

❑ **ADV-5. Promotional Badge,**
1996. NM - **$22**

ADV-6   ADV-7

❑ **ADV-6. Mr. Toad Big Figure,**
1990s. Disney. Resin Big Figure of Mr. Toad. - **$225**

❑ **ADV-7. Figurine Set LE 1000,**
1990s. Disney. Limited Edition of 1000, in pewter with characters from Ichabod and Mr. Toad. - **$60**

ADV-8

❑ **ADV-8. "Mr. Toad's Wild Ride" Figure in Car,**
2002. Limited to 500. Boxed. - **$700**

Aladdin

Fueled by the energy and wit of Robin Williams, this 1992 film was a tremendous box office hit for Disney. It spawned a TV show, two sequels, and the music from the film is still delighting kids today. Aladdin is a street thief who falls in love with the sultan's daughter, Jasmine. Unfortunately, she doesn't feel the same way towards him. Aladdin is unwittingly hired by the evil vizier Jafar who uses him to find a fabled magic lamp that houses an all-powerful genie. Aladdin and his friendly monkey, Abu, find the lamp but keep it for themselves. In order to impress the Princess Jasmine, Aladdin has himself magically changed into a prince. The disguise is revealed and Aladdin must resort to his wits in order to defeat the evil Jafar. He finally wins the love of the Princess.

The film was directed by Ron Clements and John Musker. The vocal talent featured Robin Williams, Scott Weinger, Jonathan Freeman and Gilbert Gottfried. The music and lyrics were written by Alan Menken, Howard Ashman and Tim Rice. The film won Academy Awards for Best Original Score and Best Song.

The film was followed by two direct-to-video sequels, *The Return of Jafar* (1994) and *Aladdin and the King of Thieves* (1996), as well as by a long-running half-hour TV cartoon series.

Merchandise includes books, action figures, dolls, CDs and cross promotions with fast food chains.

ALADDIN

ALA-1

ALA-4

ALA-7

ALA-2

ALA-8

❑ **ALA-1. "Aladdin Fossil" Limited Editon Watch Set,**
c. 1992 Box is 5" diameter by 2" deep and contains watch set limited to 15,000. Set comes in decorative tin containing insert featuring mounds of treasure and holds the watch. Dial features Genie portrait with numerals in gold. Reverse of case has limited edition markings. Attached to box insert is goldtone metal magic lamp pin with needlepost and clutch fastener. Mint As Issued - **$70**

❑ **ALA-2. "Aladdin Fossil" Watch,**
c. 1992. Tin container 2.5x5.5x.75" deep holds watch with 1-7/8" diameter goldtone case and genuine leather straps. Dial design features Genie with expressive facial details and gives the appearance as if he is being scrunched to fit within the confines of the watch case. Mint As Issued - **$30**

ALA-3

❑ **ALA-3. "Aladdin" Limited Edition Watch,**
1993. Blue velvet pouch is 2.5x9.5" and contains nicely made watch with 1.5" diameter metal case. Dial illustration is of Genie surrounded by cloud of smoke and the word "Poof!" Reverse of case has copyright "Disney Limited Edition." There were only a total of 1500 made and used to promote the release of the video cassette and while not marked, they were tied in with a Nestle Co. promotion. Mint As Issued - **$75**

❑ **ALA-4. Aladdin TV Show Cel,**
1996. Image is 7.75x8.25" of the Sultan and Iago the parrot. Comes with color laser background. Has "Walt Disney Television Original Animation Art" seal. Near Mint As Issued - **$165**

ALA-5

ALA-6

❑ **ALA-5. Aladdin TV Show Cel,**
1996. Image is 6x6" of Aladdin, Abu and Iago. Comes with laser background. Has "Walt Disney Television Original Animation Art" seal. Mint As Issued - **$375**

❑ **ALA-6. Genie From Aladdin Cel With Matching Pencil Drawing,**
1990s. Image is 8x9.75" of Genie wearing headphones. Comes with matching lead pencil drawing on sheet of animation paper. From a numbered sequence. Cel also comes with 11x14.5" laser background depicting overhead view of Arabian city. Mint As Issued - **$135**

❑ **ALA-7. Genie Cel From Aladdin TV Show,**
1990s. Image is 10x12". From a numbered sequence. Comes with matching lead pencil drawing on sheet of animation paper. Mint As Issued - **$135**

❑ **ALA-8. "Aladdin Jafar" Disney Employee Only Watch,**
1990s. Watch comes in 2.5x10" long felt pouch with gold text and metal corner tips. Watch has intricately detailed 1.75" diameter metal case with tooled black leather straps. Color dial illustration is of Jafar while on the second hand disk is image of Iago. From a limited edition of 1075. Mint As Issued - **$70**

ALA-9

❑ **ALA-9. "Aladdin & Jasmine Original Production Art" Portfolio,**
c. 1990s. Envelope is 12x15" with die-cut windows on front and back. Cel images are of Aladdin and Jasmine. Includes photographic reproduction background and also comes with matching pencil drawing as well as certificate of authenticity. Mint As Issued - **$225**

Alice Comedies

While not exactly Walt Disney's first animation attempt, the Alice Comedies were his first solid success. Prior to the Alice Comedies, Disney had created the Laugh-O-Grams. These were a series of fairy tale parodies, but that cartoon series lost its financing when its distributor went bankrupt. In order to recover the money, he made a dental hygiene film for a Kansas City dentist titled *Tommy Tucker's Tooth* (1923). Walt then took the $500 he made from that film and used the money to finance the first film in the Alice series. That silent, black and white film, titled *Alice's Wonderland* (1923), combined live action with animation. Six year old Virginia Davis starred as Alice.

The film was never released theatrically, but it was shown to distributors. One of them, Margaret J. Winkler, liked what she saw. At the time, she was distributing the Felix cartoons. Working along with his brother Roy, Walt Disney set up shop and produced the first official short in the series, *Alice's Day at Sea* (1924). Virginia Davis reprised her role as Alice and eventually ended up doing 14 of the Alice shorts. Others who played Alice include Margie Gay, Dawn O'Day and Lois Hardwick. At one point, the cartoons were distributed by Joseph P. Kennedy and his Film Booking Offices Agency. Kennedy would eventually become the patriarch of the Kennedy political dynasty.

The series introduced two animated characters, Julius the Cat and the villainous Pete who was also known as Bootleg Pete, Pegleg Pete and Black Pete, among other aliases. After 80 years, Pete is Disney's longest running character. He recently appeared in the 2004 animated release, *The Three Musketeers*. At the start, Pete was featured as a bear, but he became a cat to face off with Mickey Mouse. It is safe to say that he has never been one of the good guys.

The continuing success of the Alice shorts enabled Disney to move to a bigger studio (the originals were created in a garage), and also hire some extra help with the animation. Those animators included Ub Iwerks, Hugh Harman, Rudolph Ising and Friz Freleng.

Merchandise that accompanied Alice comedies seems to be non-existent. There are movie posters and promotional paper for the theatre owners, but we have never seen an item licensed for retail sale.

ALC-1

☐ **ALC-1. Disney's Alice 1926 Ad Page In Exhibitor Magazine,**
1926. 9.25x12.25" Vol. 25 #8 from May 8 "Exhibitors Herald/The Independent Film Trade Paper." At the center on heavy stock are 44 pages devoted to Film Book Offices (FBO) releases from 1926-1927 season. Included among others are Fred Thomson double page ad, single page ads for Bob Custer and Tom Tyler and the wonderful facing page ads for "26 Krazy Kat Comics" and "26 Alice Comedies By Walt Disney." - **$55 $135 $225**

 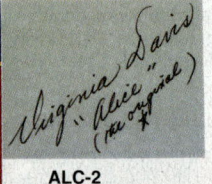

ALC-2

ALC-3

☐ **ALC-2. "Walt In Wonderland/The Silent Films Of Walt Disney" Signed Hardcover,**
1992. 9.5x11" book has 168 pages. Revised English language edition distributed by the Johns Hopkins University Press. "Virginia Davis 'Alice' (The Original (Star)." Autographed - **$10 $30 $60** Unsigned - **$5 $15 $25**

☐ **ALC-3. Virginia Davis "Alice" Autographed Disney Souvenir,**
2000. 3x6.5" blister package with 2.5x3.5" trading card and 1.5" diameter coin sold at The Disney Store. Issued as part of "The Disney Decades Coins" collector's series. Front of card features scene from 1924 silent cartoon "Alice And The Three Bears." Actress Virginia Davis is pictured on the card as well as black and white photo insert at center of coin.
Near Mint Autographed - **$30**
Near Mint Unsigned - **$15**

Alice in Wonderland

Adapting Lewis Carroll's timeless books *Alice's Adventures in Wonderland* (1865) and *Through the Looking Glass* (1871) into an animated feature would be a daunting task for anyone, even the expert hands of the Walt Disney Studios. The books contained over eighty characters that needed to come to life. Even more troublesome for the animator was that, thanks to the incredible illustrations of John Tenniel, everyone who has ever read the book had a definite and preconceived notion of what the characters should look like.

Walt Disney had been interested in the story for years. His first real success had been with the Alice Comedies. This was a series of early featurettes that mixed live action with animation. They had been initially inspired by Carroll's first book. Returning to the ideas of Lewis Carroll in 1936, Disney placed Mickey Mouse in a wonderful cartoon short titled *Thru the Mirror*. This cartoon placed Mickey in a dream world that clearly referenced Carroll's source material. With the 1951 full length animated feature film Disney was finally able to bring a direct adaptation of Carroll's stories to the screen.

Packed with incredibly imaginative sequences, the film is a non-stop ride through the surrealism of Carroll's imagination. The action starts with Alice following the White Rabbit down into a rabbit hole. In episode after episode, she encounters a fantasy world of unusual characters such as the March Hare, the Mad Hatter, the Queen and King of Hearts, Tweedledum and Tweedledee and the Cheshire Cat.

The directors on the film were Wilfred Jackson, Clyde Geronimi and Ham Luske. Animators included Milt Kahl, Ward Kimball, Marc Davis, Fred Moore, Frank Thomas, Ollie Johnston and Wolfgang Reitherman. Vocal talent included some of Disney's favorites such as Ed Wynn and Sterling Holloway. Alice was voiced by Kathryn Beaumont. The musical score was nominated for an Academy Award and included *I'm Late* by Robert Hilliard and Sammy Fain.

Merchandise for the film was fairly limited, but did include figurines, books, comics and sheet music.

ALICE IN WONDERLAND

ALW-1

❏ **ALW-1. Alice Wristwatch With Presentation Box,**
1950. U.S. Time. 5" diameter by 3" deep box. Outer box has wraparound tea party scene. Platform base holds plastic tea cup which contains watch. Near Mint Boxed - **$750** Watch Only - **$25 $50 $100**

ALW-2

❏ **ALW-2. Alice Wristwatch With Ceramic Figure,**
1951. US Time. Near Mint Boxed - **$275**

ALW-3

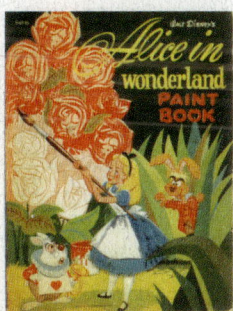

ALW-4

❏ **ALW-3. Alice In Wonderland Sticker Fun Stencil And Coloring Book,**
1951. Whitman. 10.25x12" with 18 pages. - **$30 $65 $125**

❏ **ALW-4. "Alice In Wonderland Paint Book,"**
1951. Whitman. 8.5x11" with 128 pages. - **$15 $25 $50**

ALW-5

❏ **ALW-5. "Alice In Wonderland" Publicity Stills,**
1951. Each is 8x10" glossy. - **$5 $10 $20**

ALW-6

ALW-7

❏ **ALW-6. Alice In Wonderland Concept Art,**
1951. Image is 10x4.75" featuring Alice at the tea party celebrating a very "unbirthday" by Disney artist Mary Blair. - **$3000 $6000 $12000**

❏ **ALW-7. Alice In Wonderland Animation Cel Set-Up Art,**
1951. Image is 3.5x4.25" with 11.5x13.5" background. Features the White Rabbit running down a hallway as he is "late for a very important date." - **$2000 $4000 $8000**

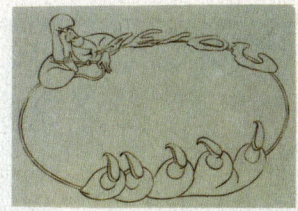

ALW-8

❏ **ALW-8. Caterpillar Animation Pencil Drawing,**
1951. Image is 5x7.5". - **$50 $100 $225**

ALW-9

ALW-10

❏ **ALW-9. "Alice In Wonderland" Campaign Book,**
1951. RKO Radio Pictures Inc. 12x18" with 28 pages. - **$50 $125 $225**

❏ **ALW-10. "Alice In Wonderland Golden Record,"**
1951. Simon & Schuster. 6.75x7.5" sleeve contains vinyl 78rpm. - **$6 $12 $25**

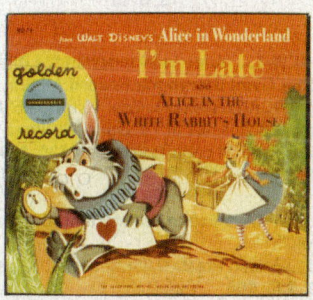

ALW-11

ALICE IN WONDERLAND

ALW-12

❏ **ALW-11. "Alice In Wonderland Golden Record,"**
1951. Simon & Schuster. 6.75x7.5" sleeve contains vinyl record. - **$8 $15 $30**

❏ **ALW-12. "Alice In Wonderland Golden Record,"**
1951. Simon & Schuster. 6.75x7.5" paper sleeve contains vinyl 78rpm. - **$6 $12 $25**

ALW-13

❏ **ALW-13. "Alice In Wonderland" Little Nipper Giant Storybook Record Album,**
1951. RCA/Western Printing. 10.5x13.25" hardcover contains pair of 10" diameter 78rpm records and 24 page storybook. - **$30 $60 $125**

❏ **ALW-14 "Alice In Wonderland Big Golden Book,"**
1951. Golden Press. 9.25x12.5" with 32 pages. - **$15 $30 $60**

ALW-14

ALW-15

ALW-16

❏ **ALW-15. "Alice In Wonderland" Movie Poster,**
1951. Half-sheet is 22x28" stiff paper. - **$125 $250 $500**

❏ **ALW-16. "Alice In Wonderland" 15 Stand-Up Figures Boxed Set,**
1951. Whitman. 7.5x12.5x1" deep box containing set of die-cut cardboard figures. Figures range in size from 2" to 6.5" tall. - **$50 $100 $150**

ALW-17

❏ **ALW-17. "Pageant" Magazine With Alice Cards,**
1951. Vol. 7, No. 2 is 5.5x7.5" featuring one-page specialty story for Alice in Wonderland that includes instructions for the set of 52 standard playing cards that are contained on the following six pages. - **$20 $40 $80**

❏ **ALW-18. Alice Figurine,**
c. 1951. Shaw. Painted and glazed ceramic 4x4x5.5" tall. - **$100 $175 $200**

ALW-19

❏ **ALW-19. "Mad Hatter" Ceramic Figurine,**
c. 1951. Shaw. Figure is 3.75" tall. - **$65 $125 $200**

ALW-20

❏ **ALW-20. "Tweedle Dee/Tweedle Dum" Ceramic Figurines,**
c. 1951. Shaw. Collars marked "Dee" and "Dum." Each is 3.75" tall. Each - **$50 $125 $200**

ALW-18

ALW-21

94

ALICE IN WONDERLAND

❑ **ALW-21. White Rabbit Figurine,**
c. 1951. Shaw. Figure is 2.5x2.75x3.5" tall. - **$50 $100 $150**

ALW-22

ALW-25

ALW-29

❑ **ALW-22. "March Hare" Figurine,**
c. 1951. Shaw. 4.5" tall. - **$75 $150 $250**

ALW-23

❑ **ALW-23. "Dormouse" Ceramic Figurine,**
c. 1951. Shaw. 2.25" tall. - **$75 $150 $250**

ALW-24

❑ **ALW-24. "Alice In Wonderland" China Cookie Jar,"**
c. 1951. Regal. 8x9x13.5" tall figural china cookie jar from a set that included salt & pepper, creamer, sugar and teapot. - **$400 $800 $1200**

ALW-26

❑ **ALW-25. "King of Hearts" China Pitcher,**
c. 1951. Regal. 7.5" tall - **$65 $125 $225**

❑ **ALW-26. "Queen of Hearts" Nodder Figurine,**
c. 1951. Goebel. 5.5" tall with Goebel markings under base including incised "Dis 69". - **$250 $500 $750**

ALW-27

ALW-28

❑ **ALW-27 "Mad Hatter" China Teapot,**
c. 1951. Regal. 7.5" tall. - **$400 $800 $1600**

❑ **ALW-28. Tweedle Dee And Tweedle Dum China Salt And Pepper Set,**
c. 1951. Regal. Each is 4.5" tall. Each - **$50 $125 $200**

❑ **ALW-29. The Walrus From Alice In Wonderland Rare Figural Decanter,**
c. 1951. Goebel. 3.5x3.5x7" tall painted and glazed ceramic. Underside has Goebel markings including full bee and incised "110." - **$125 $250 $425**

ALW-30

ALW-31

ALICE IN WONDERLAND

❑ **ALW-30. "Alice In Wonderland" Ceramic Planter,**
c. 1951. Leeds. 6.25" tall. - **$40 $75 $135**

❑ **ALW-31. "Alice In Wonderland" Glass,**
c. 1951. Glass is 4.5/8" tall and #1 from a scarcer numbered series. - **$15 $30 $60**

ALW-32

❑ **ALW-32. "Alice" In Wonderland Watch,**
c. 1953. Unmarked but by New Haven. - **$20 $40 $75**

ALW-33

❑ **ALW-33. "Alice" Ceramic Figurine,**
1950s. Hagen-Renaker. 1-7/8" tall. - **$75 $150 $250**

ALW-34

❑ **ALW-34. Mad Hatter Figurine,**
1950s. Hagen-Renaker. 2.25" tall glazed ceramic. - **$75 $150 $250**

ALW-35

❑ **ALW-35. March Hare Figurine,**
1950s. Hagen-Renaker. 2" long glazed ceramic. - **$75 $150 $250**

ALW-36

ALW-37

❑ **ALW-36. "Art Corner At Disneyland" Cel,**
1950s. White Rabbit cel. Image is 4.5x5.25". Reverse has gold foil label and stamped "This Souvenir Is From The Art Corner At Disneyland." - **$125 $275 $525**

❑ **ALW-37 "Art Corner At Disneyland" Cel,**
1950s. The King Of Hearts. Image is 4.5x4.75". Has gold foil label and ink stamp "This Souvenir Is From The Art Corner At Disneyland." - **$125 $275 $525**

ALW-38

ALW-39

❑ **ALW-38 Alice In Wonderland Bread Labels,**
1950s. Each is 2.75x2.75". Each - **$2 $5 $10**

❑ **ALW-39. "Alice In Wonderland" Fabric,**
1950s. Piece is 38x44". Maker unknown. Similar Size - **$15 $30 $60**

ALW-40

❑ **ALW-40. "Peter Puppet Playthings" Catalogue Folder,**
1950s. Cover features all three marionettes from the Alice in Wonderland series. - **$15 $25 $40**

ALICE IN WONDERLAND

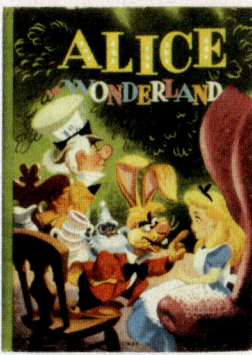

ALW-41

ALW-44

ALW-48

❑ **ALW-41. "Alice In Wonderland" Hardcover With Dust Jacket,**
1950s. Whitman. Copyright 1945, but a 1950s edition with revised jacket design. Book is 6x8.25" with 240 pages. Jacket - **$10 $20 $35** Book - **$15 $25 $40**

❑ **ALW-44. Alice In Wonderland Ceramic Teapot,**
c. 1965. Shorter & Son, England. 4.5x7.5x7" tall. No Disney copyright. - **$100 $200 $400**

❑ **ALW-48. "Alice In Wonderland" Press Book,**
1974. Measures 11x15" with 16 pages for film's re-release. - **$10 $20 $40**

ALW-42

ALW-45

ALW-46

ALW-49

❑ **ALW-45. Alice Ceramic Watch Figurine,**
1960s. Timex. Also issued in plastic variety. Ceramic - **$8 $12 $20** Plastic - **$5 $10 $15**

❑ **ALW-46. Alice Ceramic Figurine,**
1960s. Figure is 6" tall. - **$10 $20 $35**

ALW-50

❑ **ALW-49. "Alice In Wonderland" Thermos,**
1974. Aladdin. 6.5" tall plastic for the vinyl lunch box. - **$10 $20 $40**

❑ **ALW-50. "Alice In Wonderland" Vinyl Lunch Box,**
1974. Aladdin. 7x9x4" deep. - **$50 $100 $160**

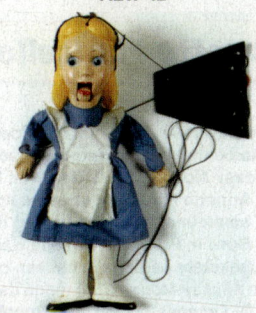

ALW-43

ALW-47

❑ **ALW-42. "March Hare Marionette,"**
1950s. Peter Puppet Playthings. 6x14x3.5" deep box contains 12.5" tall marionette with attached cardboard hand control unit. Box - **$25 $50 $100** Toy - **$35 $75 $175**

❑ **ALW-43. Alice Marionette,**
1950s. Peter Puppet Playthings. 14" tall with painted composition head, hands and legs plus fabric outfit and attached cardboard hand control unit. - **$50 $100 $200**

❑ **ALW-47. Mad Hatter And White Rabbit Ramp Walker,**
1960s. Marx. 3.5" tall plastic. - **$30 $65 $110**

ALW-51

ALICE IN WONDERLAND

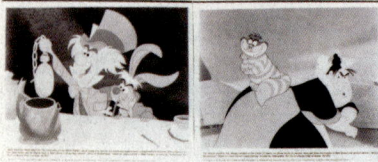

ALW-52

❑ **ALW-51. The White Rabbit Cel,**
1970s. Eastern Airlines commercial. 10.5x12.5" acetate sheet with 4.25x5" image. - **$30 $65 $140**

❑ **ALW-52. "Alice In Wonderland" Publicity Stills,**
1970s. Buena-Vista re-release. Each is 8x10". Each - **$1 $3 $6**

ALW-53

❑ **ALW-53. Alice In Wonderland Ceramic Figurines,**
1970s. White Rabbit is 2.75" tall and March Hare is 4.25" tall. Each - **$5 $15 $30**

ALW-54

ALW-55

❑ **ALW-54. Alice Figurine,**
1970s. Figure is 6" tall. - **$5 $15 $30**

❑ **ALW-55. Mad Hatter Ceramic Figurine,**
1970s. Figure is 4.5" tall. - **$5 $15 $30**

ALW-56

ALW-57

❑ **ALW-56. "Alice In Wonderland" Boxed Doll,**
1970s. Horsman. 7.75x10.75x3" deep box contains 8" tall doll from the "Walt Disney's Classics" series. Near Mint Boxed - **$65**

❑ **ALW-57. Cheshire Cat Figurine,**
1980s. Figure is 1-3/8" tall. - **$5 $10 $15**

ALW-58

❑ **ALW-58. "Alice at the Mad Hatter's Tea Party",**
Late 1980s. Crafted by master sculptor Enzo Arzenton. Edition 322. - **$4250**

ALW-59

ALW-60

❑ **ALW-59. Cheshire Cat Keychain,**
2000s. - **$10**

❑ **ALW-60. White Rabbit Keychain,**
2000s. - **$10**

Annette Funicello

Even today, many fans still consider Annette to be the most talented Mouseketeer in the *Mickey Mouse Club*. When Walt Disney first saw Annette Funicello, she was appearing in an amateur show being held at the Starlight Bowl in Burbank, CA. She was the only Mouseketeer personally chosen by Walt! The *Mickey Mouse Club* made its debut on ABC-TV October 3, 1955, and Annette became an instant celebrity. For the next ten years she starred in many properties for Disney Studios. These included the Mickey Mouse Club serials *Adventures in Dairyland*, and *Spin and Marty*. Her feature films for the Disney Studio include *The Shaggy Dog* (1959), *Babes in Toyland* (1961), and her last film for the Studio, *The Monkey's Uncle* (1965). In addition, she also released vocal recordings under the Disneyland record label.

ANNETTE FUNICELLO

From her first appearance on the *Mickey Mouse Club* she immediately became America's sweetheart. For many American young men she was the ideal girl-next-door. When she left the Disney "family," her career continued with roles in several beach movies for American International Pictures. Those movies moved her to another, almost iconic, level of fame. Her amazing career continues to this day with appearances on TV and at charity events.

She appears in Four Color Comics *#905* (with *Spin and Marty*) and #1100 (her life story). She can also be seen with Zorro on the cover of #1037.

Merchandise created during her Disney days includes books of all types, records and sheet music.

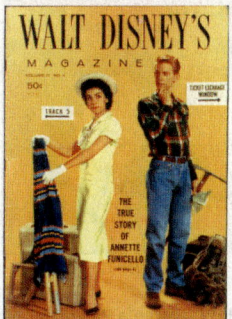
ANN-3

ANN-4

ANN-1

ANN-2

ANN-5

ANN-6

❏ **ANN-6. "Walt Disney's Magazine,"** 1959. Volume 4, #5 8x10.25". "Double Date" featuring Annette, Tommy Kirk, Roberta Shore and Tim Considine. - **$15 $30 $80**

ANN-7

ANN-8

❏ **ANN-3. "Walt Disney's Magazine,"** 1958. Magazine is 8.25x11.25" Vol. 3 #1. Cover photo is Annette and David Stollery. - **$10 $20 $50**

❏ **ANN-4. "Annette" Funicello Record,** 1959. Buena Vista Records. 7x7" paper sleeve contains 45 rpm with songs "Lonely Guitar/Wild Willie." - **$5 $15 $30**

❏ **ANN-1. "Walt Disney's Mouseketeer Annette Cut-Out Dolls,"** 1957. Whitman, 10.5x12". Contains two Annette cut-out dolls with colorful outfits and accessories. Uncut - **$25 $50 $110**

❏ **ANN-2. "Walt Disney's Magazine,"** 1958. Magazine is 8x10.25" Vol. 4 #1. Cover photo of Annette, David, Darlene, Bobby. - **$15 $30 $80**

❏ **ANN-5. Annette Funicello Record,** 1959. Buena Vista Records. 7x7" paper sleeve holding 45 rpm. - **$20 $45 $85**

❏ **ANN-7. "Walt Disney's Magazine,"** 1959. Volume 4, #4, 8x10.25". 48 pages. - **$22 $55 $110**

❏ **ANN-8. Annette Funicello Autographed "Mouseketeers Club" Wallet,** 1950s. Vinyl wallet is 3.25x4" and signed along left edge by Annette in black felt tip pen. Autographed Near Mint - **$200** Wallet Unsigned - **$25 $50 $100**

ANNETTE FUNICELLO

ANN-9

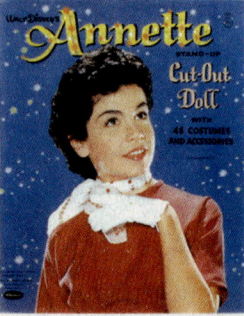

ANN-10

ANN-11

ANN-12

❑ **ANN-11. "Children's Playmate" Magazine And "Annette" Coloring Book,**
c. 1960. Magazine is 6x9" Vol. 29 #6, Nov. 1957 issue featuring two-page "Star Mousekeepers" article including group photo with Annette. Coloring book is by Whitman copyright 1961 with 128 pages. Magazine - **$10 $15 $30**
Coloring Book - **$10 $20 $40**

❑ **ANN-12. "Annette" Funicello Record,**
1961. Buena Vista Records. 7x7" paper sleeve contains 45 rpm with songs "Dream Boy/Please Please Signore." - **$12 $25 $40**

ANN-13

ANN-14

❑ **ANN-13. "This Is Annette/Her Story In 31 Photos" Book,**
1961. Preview Photos, Hollywood, Calif. Eight pages on glossy paper. - **$15 $35 $80**

❑ **ANN-14. "Annette In Hawaii" Paperdoll Book,**
1961. Whitman, 10.25x12". One Annette doll with many outfits and accessories. Uncut - **$20 $40 $85**

ANN-15

ANN-16

❑ **ANN-9. "Walt Disney Annette's Life Story" Comic Book,**
1960. Dell. Four Color Series #1100. - **$25 $75 $375**

❑ **ANN-10. "Annette Cut-Out Doll,"**
1960. Whitman. 10.25x12" cardboard folder. Set consists of 9" tall die-cut cardboard doll and comes with 48 costumes and accessories. Uncut - **$15 $40 $85**

❑ **ANN-15. "Beach Party" With Annette Movie Promo,**
1963. American International. 13.75x22" cardboard window card. The first film in the long series of beach party movies. - **$25 $50 $85**

❑ **ANN-16. "Escapade In Florence" Comic Book,**
1963. K.K. Publications. Based on two-part television show starring Annette and Tommy Carpenter. - **$10 $30 $115**

ANN-17

ANN-18

100

ANNETTE FUNICELLO

◻ **ANN-17. Lobby Cards Including Autograph,**
1964. American International Pictures. Two 11x14" cards # 1 for films "Pajama Party" and "Muscle Beach Party," both starring Annette. Latter is signed "Love-Annette Funicello." First - **$8 $15 $30** Second Signed - **$20 $40 $80**

◻ **ANN-18. "Bikini Beach" With Annette Movie Promo,**
1964. American International. 13.75x22" cardboard window card. - **$20 $40 $75**

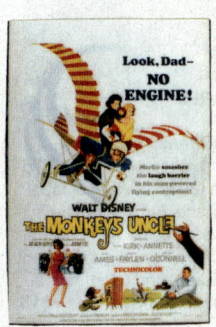
ANN-19

ANN-20

◻ **ANN-19. "The Monkey's Uncle" Window Card,**
1964. Card is 14x22" stiff paper for initial release in 1965 of film starring Annette. - **$10 $20 $40**

◻ **ANN-20. "The Monkey's Uncle" Pressbook And Supplement,**
1964. Both are 12x18". Film starred Tommy Kirk and Annette Funicello. 28-page pressbook has color with black and white contents. Merchandise items shown include Annette records, Monkey's Uncle flicker/flasher badge, sweatshirt, comic book and theater imprint balloon. The separate "Pressbook Supplement" is 6 pages in black and white featuring "The Big Promotion Yamaha Sports Cycles Ties In With The Monkey's Uncle." Pressbook - **$10 $20 $35**
Supplement - **$5 $10 $20**

ANN-21

ANN-22

◻ **ANN-21. "Annette 'Something Borrowed, Something Blue'" Record Album,**
1964. Buena Vista Records. 12.25x12.25" gatefold cardboard album cover contains 33-1/3 rpm mono record. - **$20 $40 $65**

◻ **ANN-22. "Thunder Alley" Movie Poster,**
1967. Window Card, 13.75x22" cardboard for American International film starring Annette and Fabian. - **$10 $20 $40**

ANN-23

ANN-24

◻ **ANN-23. "Annette Funicello" Fan Photo,**
1960s. Glossy 8x10" photo with facsimile signature. - **$10 $20 $35**

◻ **ANN-24. Autographed Photo,**
1960s. Photo is 8x10" glossy signed in pen "Annette Funicello." - **$50 $100 $150**

ANN-25

ANN-26

◻ **ANN-25. Annette-Related Books,**
1960s. Whitman. Two 5.75x7.75" hardcovers comprised of movie story title "The Misadventures Of Merlin Jones" from 1964 and novel "Annette And The Mystery At Smugglers' Cove." Each - **$5 $10 $15**

◻ **ANN-26. Magazines With Annette,**
1960s. Six 8.5x11" movie and/or TV fan magazines comprised of TV Star Parade 1959, Motion Picture 1959, TV Picture Life 1960, Teen Screen 1963, Screenland 1966, Sh-Boom premiere issue Vol. 1 #1, 1989. All have Annette cover article. Each - **$5 $12 $20**

ANN-27

◻ **ANN-27. Personal Christmas Card,**
1970s. Card is 3.5x7" one-sided photo and text greeting on glossy stiff paper. - **$8 $15 $30**

THE ARISTOCATS

The Aristocats

First released during the Christmas season of 1970, this Disney animated feature proved so popular that it saw theatrical re-release in 1980 and 1987. Today, it is a tremendous success on both video and DVD. *The Aristocats* has the sad distinction of being the first animated feature released by Disney Studios without the complete supervision of Walt himself.

The film is based on a story by Tom McGowan and Tom Rowe. It is centered on the lives of a mother cat and her three kittens that are living in a luxurious, well kept home. When their owner deeds her magnificent estate to the cats, they are suddenly kidnapped by a greedy and jealous butler. Left to fend for themselves in the unknown, the mother and her cats are exposed to the outside world for the first time. Eventually, they are befriended by an alley cat named Thomas O'Malley. After many adventures, they return to Paris where O'Malley, his friends, and a mouse named Roquefort deal with the butler.

As with any Disney film, the animation is superb and the music is top-notch. The main theme song was sung by Maurice Chevalier and the film included songs by Richard B. and Robert M. Sherman. Among the vocal talents were Phil Harris, Eva Gabor, Sterling Holloway, Scatman Crothers and famed ventriloquist, Paul Winchell. Directed by Wolfgang Reitherman, the film featured the animation work of Ollie Johnston, Frank Thomas, Milt Kahl and Eric Larson.

Merchandise included figurines, books and records.

ARI-1

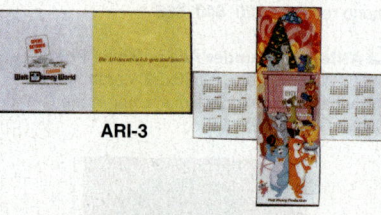
ARI-2

❏ **ARI-1. "The Aristocats" Figurine,** 1968. 3.25x3.25x7.5" tall glazed ceramic figure of Duchess with tag. - **$20 $50 $85**

❏ **ARI-2. O'Malley The Cat Cel,** 1970. Acetate sheet is 12.5x16" with 4x4.25" image. - **$50 $100 $160**

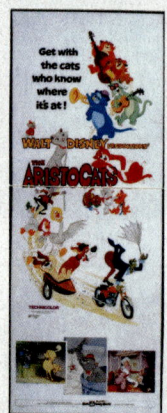
ARI-3

ARI-4

❏ **ARI-3. Disney Studio Christmas Card,** 1970. Stiff textured paper card is 5x5" closed. Four-panel folder, shown back/front and fully opened. Three panels include text titled "The Aristocats Wish You And Yours A Very Merry Christmas And A Purrrrrrfect New Year!" Fourth panel illustration is Christmas ball carried by silhouettes of Mickey, Donald and Pluto. Left and right panels are monthly calendar for 1971. Back cover is for opening of Disney World. - **$15 $30 $45**

❏ **ARI-4. "The Aristocats" Insert Poster,** 1970. Glossy stiff paper is 14x36" illustrating many of the film's characters and three film scenes. Text at bottom margin includes announcement of Oct. 1971 opening of Walt Disney World. - **$15 $30 $50**

ARI-5

❏ **ARI-5. Aristocats Kittens,** c. 1970. Enesco set of three painted plaster figurines, each 4" tall with underside maker label. Pictured examples of Marie and Toulouse each have their whiskers and felt collar with bow but are missing small tuft of life-like hair from top of head; Berloioz has whiskers and tuft of hair but felt collar is missing bow. Each Complete - **$15 $25 $50**

ARI-6

❏ **ARI-6. The Aristocats Music Box,** c. 1970. Schmid Pottery. Painted and glazed ceramic 6.5" tall on 4" diameter base. Depicts Thomas O'Malley. One of five music boxes from Schmid series. Underside has maker sticker including song title "When Irish Eyes Are Smilin'." - **$25 $50 $85**

THE ARISTOCATS

ARI-7

❏ **ARI-7. The Aristocats Music Box,**
c. 1970. Schmid Pottery. Painted and glazed ceramic 6.5" tall on 4" diameter base. Depicts the guitar player from Skat Cats Band. One of five music boxes from Schmid series. Underside has maker sticker including song title "I Want To Hold Your Hand." - **$25 $50 $85**

ARI-8

❏ **ARI-8. The Aristocats Music Box,**
c. 1970. Schmid Pottery. Painted and glazed ceramic 6.5" tall on 4" diameter base. Depicts trumpet player from the Skat Cats Band. One of five music boxes from Schmid series. Underside has maker sticker including song title "When The Saints Go Marching In." - **$25 $50 $85**

ARI-9

❏ **ARI-9. Figural Music Box,**
c. 1970. Schmid. 6.5x4" diameter painted and glazed ceramic depicting Duchess and Marie. Key-winding produces tune "La Vie En Rose." Complete with string tag and box. Box - **$1 $3 $5**
Music Box - **$25 $50 $85**

❏ **ARI-10. Figural Music Box,**
c. 1970. Schmid. 6.5x4" diameter painted and glazed ceramic depicting member of Skat Cats Band. Key-winding produces tune "Oh Sole Mio." Complete with string tag. - **$25 $50 $85**

ARI-11

❏ **ARI-11. Little Roquefort From The Aristocats Cel,**
c. 1970. 12x14" cardboard mat with 4x5" cel image and printed background. Sold at The Art Corner, Disneyland with original label on back. - **$50 $100 $175**

ARI-12

❏ **ARI-12. "The Aristocats" Re-Release Lobby Card,**
1980. Stiff glossy paper card 11x14" depicting Madam Bonfamille holding Duchess as Georges Hautecourt kisses Duchess' tail. - **$4 $8 $12**

ARI-13

ARI-14

❏ **ARI-13. "The Aristocats" Re-Release Fan Card,**
1980. Glossy stiff paper fan card 5x7" picturing The Skat Cats and the kittens. - **$5 $10 $15**

❏ **ARI-14. "The Aristocats" Re-Release Press Book,**
1980. Publicity manual 9x12" with 12 pages including film scenes, detailed text, page featuring record albums, coloring contest page, order form for giveaway balloon. - **$10 $15 $30**

THE ARISTOCATS

ARI-15

❏ **ARI-15. Aristocats Surprise Egg Figures,**
1989. Ferrero Kinder, Germany. Hand-painted hard plastic figures, 1" to 1.5" tall of O'Malley, Duchess, Berlioz, Marie, all five members of the Skat Cats band. Near Mint Set - **$75**

ARI-16

❏ **ARI-16. "Aristocats" Plush Piano,**
Sept. 7-11, 1999. Special event product offered only at the 1999 Convention. The piano is the holder for the "Aristocat" bean figures. - **$35**
7" tall "Chinese Cat" Bean Figure - **$22**
8 1/2" tall "Scat Cat" Bean Figure - **$22**
8" tall "English Cat" Bean Figure - **$22**
8" tall "Italian Cat" Bean Figure - **$22**
8" tall "Russian Cat" Bean Figure - **$22**

Babes in Toyland

In 1961, Annette Funicello and Tommy Sands were just about the biggest stars in the Disney universe, human stars that is. So it made sense for them to be teamed up in this musical. While some felt that the picture didn't live up to the standards of other Disney features, it found a second life on the Disney television show. Through annual rebroadcasts, it became a holiday favorite for many. It is especially popular with young children.

The story is based on the Victor Herbert and Glenn McDonough operetta and features the residents of Mother Goose Village. Tom the Piper's Son and Contrary Mary are to be married, but the villain Barnaby wants Mary so he can get her inheritance. Barnaby kidnaps Tom, and his helpers kidnap Mary's sheep. Tom escapes and eventually, with the help of a lot of toy soldiers and a size reduction gun, Mary and Tom are reunited.

The movie's songs are cheerful and the colors are incredibly bright. The special effects, especially the toy soldiers, are delightful. Directed by Jack Donohue, the cast includes Annette Funicello, Tommy Sands, Ray Bolger, Ed Wynn and, in a very early appearance, Ann Jillian. Disney animator and famed toy collector Ward Kimball was in charge of the unit that created the mechanical toys. It is an ingenious piece of filmmaking that serves as a reminder of Kimball's distinctive talents.

Babes in Toyland appears in *Four Color Comics* #1282.

Merchandise included books, records and Louis Marx toys.

BTL-1

BTL-2

❏ **BTL-1. "Babes In Toyland Annette Dress Designer Kit" Box Label,**
1961. Colorforms. Uncut, unused 16x19.75" glossy paper sheet only to be applied to a box lid. One of only three known examples from Colorforms archives. Near Mint - **$135**

❏ **BTL-2. Publicity Photos,**
1961. Three 8x10" glossy stills of three-dimensional toy soldier wood models. Each - **$3 $6 $12**

BTL-3

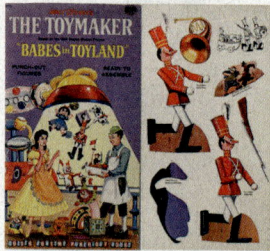

BTL-4

❏ **BTL-3. "Babes In Toyland/A Great Big Punch-Out" Book,**
1961. Whitman. Large 11x22.25" format. Front cover, back cover and 4 stiff pages contain punch-outs. Un-punched - **$20 $40 $80**

❏ **BTL-4. "Babes In Toyland/The Toymaker" Punch-Out Book,**
1961. Golden Press. 7.25x13" cover and four inside pages are thin cardboard punch-outs of Tom, Mary, Gumio, The Toymaker, Barnaby, soldiers, wooden horse, toymaking machine, toy battleship. Un-punched - **$12 $25 $50**

BABES IN TOYLAND

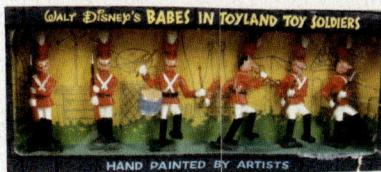

BTL-5

BTL-6

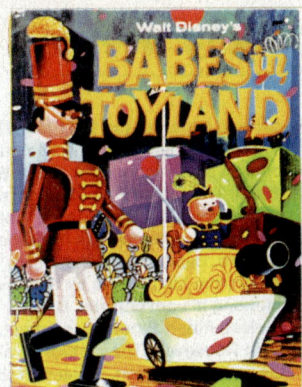

BTL-8

❑ **BTL-7. "Babes In Toyland Table Decorations" Premium,**
1961. Alcoa Wrap 10x14" one-sided stiff paper cut-out sheet of six decoration figures of "toy" soldier, clown, Indian, balloon, horse and train. Assembly instructions are on left margin. Original folded size 2.5x10". - **$5 $15 $30**

❑ **BTL-8. "Babes In Toyland Big Golden Book,"**
1961. Golden Press. 8.5x11" hardcover, 28 pages. Each page includes story art. Cover has clear lamination as published. - **$10 $25 $40**

BTL-9

❑ **BTL-9. "Babes In Toyland Golden Picture Storybook,"**
1961. Western Printing Co. 10.25x14" large format comic book, 48 pages. Cover photo is repeated front and back of Annette and Tommy Sands with toy soldiers. - **$25 $75 $350**

BTL-10

❑ **BTL-10. "Cadet From Babes In Toyland" Doll,**
1961. Gund Toys. Large 26" tall plus doll with vinyl head, stitched maker's tag. Detailed by six brass buttons on jacket front. - **$30 $65 $135**

BTL-7

❑ **BTL-5. "Babes In Toyland Toy Soldiers" Boxed Set,**
1961. Marx. 4x10x1.25" deep display window box containing six 3" tall hand-painted hard plastic Disneykins. Figures are in four poses and depicted holding rifle, drum and/or trumpet. Soldier names are "Archbald, Trustworthy, Gallant, Chivalrous, Valiant, Hooligan." - **$35 $75 $135**

❑ **BTL-6. Soldier Figure Boxed,**
1961. Marx. 2.5x7.5x1.5" deep display box holding 6.5" tall "Twistable Toy" with poseable vinyl-covered arms and legs. Boxed - **$20 $40 $80**

BTL-11

BABES IN TOYLAND

❏ **BTL-11. "Marching Soldier From Babes In Toyland" Boxed Line Mar Wind-up,**
1961. Toy is 2.25x3.25x5.75" tall tin lithographed with built-in key and comes in nicely illustrated box. Toy depicts soldier with drum attached at waist and is complete with pipe cleaner plume and rubber nose. Toy walks forward as he plays the drum. Box - $25 $60 $115 Toy - $55 $110 $175

BTL-12

❏ **BTL-12. "Babes In Toyland Game,"**
1961. Whitman. Boxed board game also including insert with illustrated spinner, large cards of "Barnaby And Reducing Gun" and die-cut cardboard soldier puzzle pieces. - $15 $30 $60

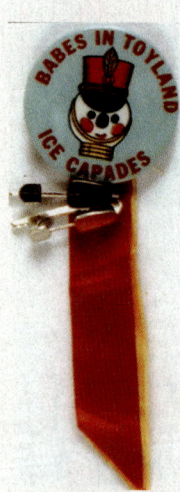

BTL-13

❏ **BTL-13. "Babes In Toyland Ice Capades" Button,**
1960s. Cello button is 2" in diameter attached by ribbon and pair of miniature metal skates. - $8 $15 $30

Baby Weems

This cartoon is part of the 1941 film *The Reluctant Dragon*, which combined animated sequences with a live-action tour of the Walt Disney Studio. The plot of *Baby Weems* was an unusual one for a Disney cartoon. Weems is an infant prodigy who can talk from the moment of birth. Because of his abilities, he is taken away from his parents by the government. Among his adventures, Baby Weems advises Albert Einstein and meets with Franklin Roosevelt. The cartoon is also remarkable for its execution. Instead of the usual lush Disney animation, the story is advanced by actual storyboards with just minimal motion added. The cartoon includes brief appearances by George Bernard Shaw, Salvador Dali and Walter Winchell. The concept came from a storyboard created by Joe Grant.

Merchandise that directly involves this cartoon is sparse, but Vernon Kilns made a beautiful ceramic figure of the character.

BWE-1

❏ **BWE-1. Baby Weems Glazed Ceramic By Vernon Kilns,**
1941. 3x4.5x5.75" tall. The only figural piece we know of. - $60 $125 $200

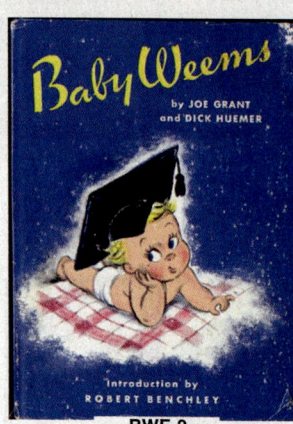

BWE-2

❏ **BWE-2. "Baby Weems" Hardcover With Dust Jacket,**
1941. 7x9.5" by Doubleday, Doran & Co. Inc. Has 64 pages with story art on every page. Near Mint With Jacket - $225 Book Only - $30 $70 $135

BWE-3

❏ **BWE-3. "Baby Weems Child's Set" Of Utensils,**
c. 1941. 4.5x8" display card marked "A Bestmaid Product" contains set of three blue hard plastic utensils, each about 5.5" long. Each utensil has same small raised full figure image of Baby Weems on tops of handles. Set Carded - $15 $30 $65
Each Loose Utensil - $3 $5 $10

Bambi

The scene of Bambi learning to walk on ice may be the most famous sequence that Disney ever produced for a feature cartoon (1942). The touching story of a year in the life of a young deer was based on Felix Salten's original 1923 story (the novel was published in 1926). Through Disney's skillful use of humor, drama and pathos, combined with superb art, Bambi learns to talk, loses his mother to a hunter, falls in love, faces a forest fire and finally, becomes a prince.

Due to the animators' lengthy studies of real animals in motion, the film has a more realistic feel than other Disney features. Audiences of all ages relate to it on different levels. The film is helped greatly by the depth of characterization that the supporting characters are given. The skill of the writers makes Thumper, Flower the Skunk, Friend Owl, The Old Stag, and Bambi's mate Faline, all fully developed individuals. The supervising director was David Hand and the animators included Frank Thomas, Ollie Johnston, Milt Kahl, Marc Davis, Ken Hultgren and Jack Bradbury. The background artists included Tyrus Wong, Art Riley and Merle Cox.

Bambi, as well as other characters from the *Bambi* film, also appear in the following issues of *Four Color Comics*: #12, 19, 30, 186 and 243. #243 was reprinted as part of the Movie Classics series by Dell Publishing.

Merchandise includes ceramic figures, books, playsets and watches. Bambi was one of the first characters to be featured on a forest fire prevention poster.

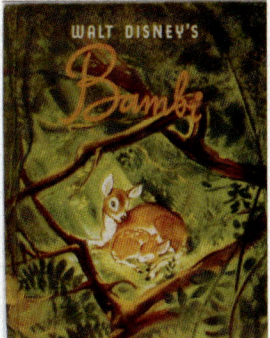

BMB-2

❏ **BMB-2. "Bambi" Book With Dust Jacket,**
1941. Simon & Schuster. 9x11.25" hardcover version with 60 illustrated story pages and "A Bambi Gallery" before the title page comprised of four full color full page pictures meant to be cut along perforated lines and then framed. Both cover and dust jacket feature same wrap-around design. Jacket - **$6 $12 $25**
Book - **$20 $35 $75**

BMB-3

BMB-4

❏ **BMB-3. "Walt Disney's Bambi" Figural Catalin Plastic Pencil Sharpener,**
c. 1941. 1.75". - **$35 $65 $110**

❏ **BMB-4. Bambi Catalin Plastic Pencil Sharpener,**
c. 1941. 1.75" long. - **$40 $75 $125**

BMB-5

❏ **BMB-5. Thumper Catalin Plastic Pencil Sharpener,**
c. 1941. 1.75" tall. - **$50 $100 $200**

BMB-6

❏ **BMB-6. Thumper Catalin Plastic Pencil Sharpener,**
c. 1941. Round style 1" in diameter.
- **$50 $100 $200**

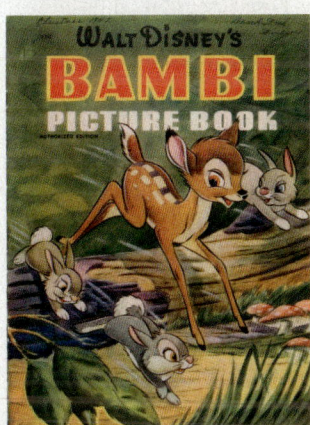

BMB-7

❏ **BMB-7. "Bambi" Linen-Like "Picture Book,"**
1942. Whitman, 9.5x13". 16 pages.
- **$20 $40 $100**

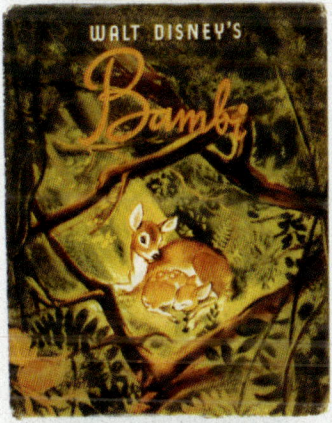

BMB-1

❏ **BMB-1. "Bambi" Book With Dust Jacket,**
1941. Simon & Schuster. 9x11.25" hardcover, 52 illustrated story pages. Jacket - **$6 $12 $25**
Book - **$12 $25 $50**

BAMBI

BMB-8

❑ **BMB-8. Bambi Cut-Out Book,**
1942. Whitman. Uncut - **$100 $200 $400**

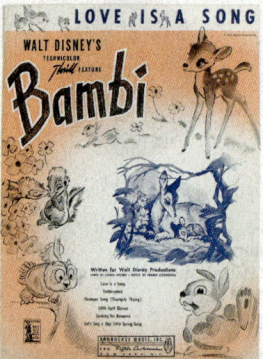
BMB-9

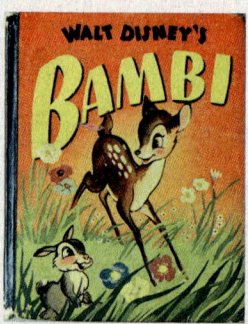
BMB-10

❑ **BMB-9. "Bambi" Sheet Music,**
1942. Folder is 9x12" for movie tune "Love Is A Song." - **$15 $30 $60**

❑ **BMB-10. "Bambi" Better Little Book,**
1942. Whitman. Book #1469. Upper corners of story art pages have additional flip-book sequence art. - **$25 $75 $160**

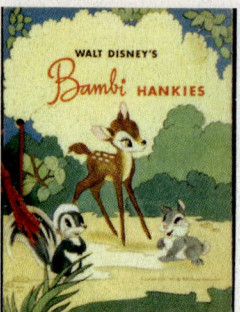
BMB-11

BMB-12

❑ **BMB-11. "Bambi Hankies" Book,**
1942. Stiff cardboard 7x9.25" storybook with eight pages of art and text. Four pages have die-cut slots for holding hankies. Book is bound by yarn string through die-cut holes as published. Complete - **$30 $60 $125**
Book Only - **$10 $20 $45**

❑ **BMB-12. "Thumper" Book,**
1942. Grosset & Dunlap. 7x8.25" hardcover, 32 pages. - **$15 $30 $60**

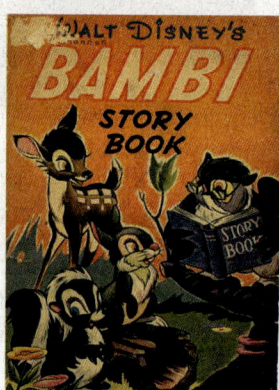
BMB-13

BMB-14

❑ **BMB-13. "Bambi Storybook,"**
1942. Whitman. 8.5x11.25" softcover #725 with 96-page illustrated story. - **$20 $40 $80**

❑ **BMB-14. Bambi Studio Fan Card,**
c. 1942. Stiff paper card 7-1/8x9.25" includes facsimile Walt Disney signature. - **$15 $30 $60**

BMB-15

BMB-16

BAMBI

◻ **BMB-15. Thumper Artwork,**
c. 1942. Art board is 7x9" centered by 5.5x7" water colored image. No markings but believed from time of Bambi film release in 1942. In a period wood frame. - **$15 $30 $50**

◻ **BMB-16. Bambi "Prevent Forest Fires" Poster,**
1943. U.S. Department of Agricultural Forest Service. Poster is 14.25x20"and reads "Please, Mister, Don't Be Careless. Prevent Forest Fires/Greater Danger Than Ever!" - **$60 $115 $165**

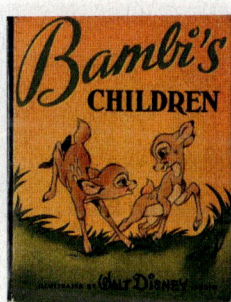
BMB-17

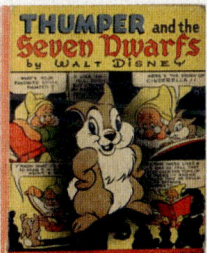
BMB-18

◻ **BMB-17. "Bambi's Children" Better Little Book,**
1943. Whitman. Book #1497. Story involves Bambi's children Geno and Gurri, written by Felix Salten and illustrated by Walt Disney Studio. - **$25 $75 $160**

◻ **BMB-18. "Thumper And The Seven Dwarfs" Better Big Little Book,**
1944. Whitman. Better Little Book #1489 "All Pictures Comics." - **$20 $60 $140**

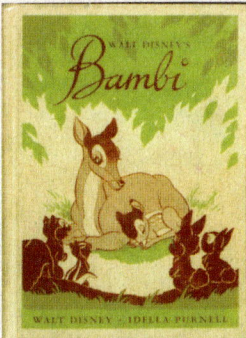
BMB-19

BMB-20

◻ **BMB-19. "Bambi" Book,**
1944. D.C. Heath & Co. Hardcover is 6.25x8.5" from educational "Walt Disney Storybooks" series, 102 pages. - **$12 $25 $50**

◻ **BMB-20. Figurine,**
1946. Figurine is 4x6x7.5" tall painted and glazed ceramic made by both American Pottery and Shaw. - **$20 $40 $75**

BMB-21

◻ **BMB-21. Thumper And His Girlfriend Figurines,**
1946. Set of 3.75" tall Thumper and 4.25" tall girlfriend painted and glazed replicas made by both Shaw and American Pottery. Each - **$15 $30 $50**

BMB-22

◻ **BMB-22. Small Figurine,**
1946. Figurine is 1.5x3x4.75" tall painted and glazed likeness. By Shaw and American Pottery. - **$15 $30 $50**

BMB-23

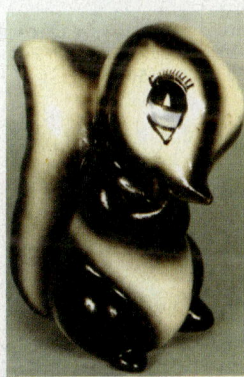
BMB-24

◻ **BMB-23. Figurine With Butterfly,**
1946. American Pottery Co. and Shaw. 3x7x7.75" tall painted and glazed ceramic. - **$25 $50 $85**

◻ **BMB-24. Flower Figurine,**
1946. Figurine 2.5x4.5x4.5" tall painted and glazed ceramic produced by both Shaw and American Pottery. - **$10 $20 $40**

BAMBI

BMB-25

BMB-26

BMB-27

❏ **BMB-25. Thumper Figurine,**
c. 1946. Shaw. 1.75" tall painted and glazed ceramic. - **$30 $65 $100**

❏ **BMB-26. Flower Toothbrush Holder Or Bud Vase,**
c. 1946. Holder is 2.5x3.5x4.25" tall painted and glazed ceramic by either American Pottery or Shaw. - **$50 $100 $150**

❏ **BMB-27. Bambi And Friends Framed Print,**
1947. New York Graphic Society. 9.5x11.5" lithographed print. - **$15 $25 $50**

BMB-28

❏ **BMB-28. Faline Figurine,**
1947. American Pottery. Large 8" tall painted and glazed version of Bambi's girlfriend in matching size to companion figure of Bambi. Figurine has foil sticker label by maker. - **$25 $50 $85**

BMB-29

BMB-30

❏ **BMB-29. Thumper Salt & Pepper Set,**
c. 1947. Leeds China Co. 3.75" tall glazed ceramic figures with over-the-glaze paint. - **$10 $20 $40**

❏ **BMB-30. "Bambi/Ingersoll" Watch Box,**
1948. Ingersoll/US Time 3.5x4.5x1" deep box only originally containing Bambi watch from a Mickey Mouse 20th birthday series of 10 different watches. Each watch came in the same style box lid design of replica film frame picturing 10 characters at birthday party. Box Only - **$75 $150 $300**

BMB-31

BMB-32

❏ **BMB-31. Bambi Watch,**
1948. U.S. Time. Issue from series featuring different Disney characters in celebration of Mickey Mouse's 20th birthday. Chromed metal case circles dial face illustration accompanied by revolving ears to serve as time pointers. Original straps are vinyl over leather. - **$75 $150 $300**

❏ **BMB-32. Bambi Luminous Dial Wrist Watch,**
1948. Ingersoll (U.S. Time). 3.25x4.25x1" deep box with 3.75" long ballpoint pen which has Mickey Mouse decal on cap. One of ten in Mickey's 20th "Birthday Series." Birthday theme lid not shown. Box With Pen - **$200 $600 $1000**
Watch Only - **$65 $250 $500**

BMB-33

BAMBI

BMB-34

❏ **BMB-33. Bambi's Friend Owl Figurine,**
1949. American Pottery Co. 3.25" tall painted and glazed ceramic, one of the few figural pieces for this character. - **$85 $175 $275**

❏ **BMB-34. "Faline" Figure,**
1949. American Pottery. Painted and glazed ceramic figue 3x8x7" tall with foil label. - **$25 $50 $85**

BMB-35

BMB-36

❏ **BMB-35. "Bambi" And "Dumbo" Record Sets By Shirley Temple,**
1949. RCA Victor. Two 7.25x7.25" sleeves, each holding two vinyl records of character story narrated by Shirley Temple. Each - **$12 $25 $40**

❏ **BMB-36. "Bambi As Told By Shirley Temple" Record Set,**
1949. RCA Victor. 10x10.75" stiff cardboard gatefold cover containing set "Y-395" of three 78 rpm records. - **$15 $30 $50**

BMB-37

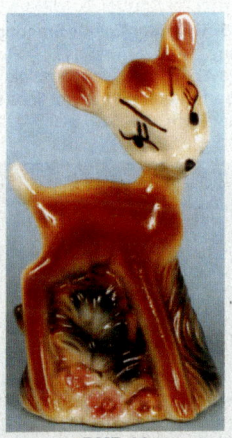

BMB-38

❏ **BMB-37. "Thumper" Wall Planter,**
c. 1949. Leeds China Co. 2.5x7.5x6.75" tall figural with flat plane back incised by name and holed for wall hanging. - **$12 $25 $50**

❏ **BMB-38. Bambi Figure Bank,**
c. 1949. Leeds China Co. 7.25" tall painted and glazed ceramic with coin slot spine. - **$20 $40 $70**

BMB-39

❏ **BMB-39. "Bambi And Thumper" Multi-Plane Painting,**
1940s. Courvoisier Galleries. Three dimensional scene in original 8x8.5x1.25" deep painted wood frame. Dimensional effect is created by painted cardboard background overlaid by two individual layers of glass. Back has label explaining how Disney uses the multi-plane technique in his studio. These were produced by Courvoisier for sale as representations of the Disney art form. Several examples were done and this is #5 in the series. - **$100 $200 $325**

 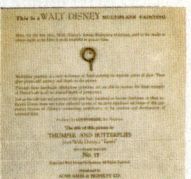

BMB-40

❏ **BMB-40. "Thumper And Butterflies" Multiplane Plaque,**
1940s. Frame is 8x8.75x1.75" deep original composition surrounding a painted cardboard overlaid by background upon two individual layers of glass images to produce a three-dimensional scene. Back has label explaining how Disney uses the multiplane technique in his studio. These were produced by Courvoisier Galleries for sale as representations of the Disney art form. Several different designs were done and this is #12 in the series. - **$85 $175 $300**

BMB-41

❏ **BMB-41. Thumper Skating Multi-Plane Painting,**
1940s. Courvoisier Galleries. 8x8.5x1.5" deep wood frame surrounding painted cardboard background upon which are mounted two individual layers of glass that bear the images and produce a 3-D scene. Depicts Thumper skating as two chipmunks watch him. Reverse of frame covered by paper label explaining how Disney uses the multi-plane technique in his studio. Produced for sale as representations of the Disney art form. #4 in the series. - **$100 $200 $325**

BAMBI

BMB-42

BMB-43

BMB-45

❏ **BMB-44. The Great Prince Glazed Ceramic Figure,**
1940s. Shaw Pottery. Walt Disney Productions sticker. 6x9.25" tall. - **$200 $400 $875**

❏ **BMB-45. Thumper Easter Standup Decorations,**
1940s. Two 4.5x6" cardboard possible candy product inserts, each with pair of flaps on back for standing. Each - **$6 $12 $18**

BMB-46

BMB-48

BMB-49

❏ **BMB-42. Flower Figurine,**
1940s. American Pottery. 3.25" tall painted and glazed figure. - **$20 $40 $75**

❏ **BMB-43. Flower's Girlfriend Figurine,**
1940s. Unmarked 2x3x3" tall painted and glazed ceramic seated pose of Miss Skunk. - **$25 $50 $75**

BMB-44

BMB-47

❏ **BMB-46. "Thumper" Planter,**
1940s. Leeds China Co. 4x4x4.5" tall figural with name and copyright incised on reverse. - **$20 $40 $75**

❏ **BMB-47. "Flower" Planter,**
1940s. Leeds China Co. 3x6.5x4.25" tall painted and glazed ceramic. Tail has incised name and Disney copyright. - **$30 $65 $100**

❏ **BMB-48. "Prevent Forest Fires" Bambi Bookmark,**
1940s. Two-sided stiff paper marker 2.5x6.25" issued by U.S. Dept. of Agriculture-Forest Service/State Forest Service. Front text is "Please, Mister, Don't Be Careless/Prevent Forest Fires." Reverse has 6" ruler edge and forest safety tips. - **$8 $15 $25**

❏ **BMB-49. "Bambi" English Hardcover,**
1940s. Collins. 8.75x11.25" with 60 pages. Bound into the front of the book are four "Extra Full Color Pictures." - **$25 $50 $100**

BMB-50

☐ **BMB-50. Flower Australian Figuine,**
c. 1950. Modern Ceramic Products. 2.75" painted and glazed likeness very similar to figurine produced by Shaw Pottery. Complete with foil sticker. - **$25 $50 $85**

BMB-51

BMB-52

☐ **BMB-51. "Songs From Bambi" Music Folio,**
1951. Walt Disney Music Co. 9x12" song book of lyrics and music, 16 pages. Content is six songs from the film including numerous small character illustrations on borders of song pages. - **$20 $40 $80**

☐ **BMB-52. "Thumper Annual" English Book With Dust Jacket,**
1952. Oldhams Press Ltd. 7.25x10"hardcover, 96 pages. Content includes about 400 illustrations for text stories, comic strip stories, puzzles, games. 32 pages are full color while the rest are single color of either orange or green plus black. Bambi and Thumper features are in addition to those for Ugly Duckling, Alice in Wonderland, Snow White, Li'l Bad Wolf, others. Jacket - **$10 $25 $50** Book - **$50 $100 $200**

BMB-53

☐ **BMB-53. "Bambi" Stereo Views Reel Set,**
1956. View-Master 4.5x4.5" envelope holding complete three reels in individual sleeves plus related story booklet. Reels are color photos of studio models. - **$5 $15 $30**

BMB-54

☐ **BMB-54. Bambi Figurine,**
1950s. Hagen-Renaker. 1.5" tall painted and glazed ceramic miniature with foil sticker. - **$40 $85 $150**

BMB-55

☐ **BMB-55. Thumper Figurine,**
1950s. Hagen-Renaker. 1.25" tall painted and glazed. - **$25 $50 $100**

BMB-56

☐ **BMB-56. Flower Figurine,**
1950s. Hagen-Renaker. 1" tall. - **$40 $75 $130**

BMB-57

☐ **BMB-57. Thumper And Miss Bunny Figurine,**
1950s. Goebel. 3.25x5.25x5.25" tall dual figurine of Miss Bunny reaching out to touch Thumper. Underside has Goebel markings and incised number "DIS 120." - **$125 $250 $400**

BMB-58

☐ **BMB-58. Bambi And Thumper Figurine,**
1950s. Goebel. 2x5.5x3.5" tall on base with full bee marking and incised "DIS 113." - **$60 $125 $250**

BAMBI

BMB-59

☐ **BMB-59. Figurine,**
1950s. Goebel. 2.5x7x7" tall painted figurine of Bambi looking down at a frog. Underside has incised "DIS 111" with Goebel markings. - **$75 $150 $250**

BMB-60

☐ **BMB-60. Friendly Owl Figurine,**
1950s. Goebel. 4.25" tall. Underside has manufacturer markings. - **$50 $100 $150**

BMB-61

☐ **BMB-61. "Thumper/Owl" Bookends,**
1950s. Goebel. 3.75x6.5x5.25" tall. Underside has Goebel markings. Pair - **$100 $200 $300**

BMB-62

☐ **BMB-62. Figurine,**
1950s. Goebel. 1x2.5x3.25" tall painted likeness with foil sticker on front and "Made In Germany" sticker on back. - **$25 $50 $85**

BMB-63

☐ **BMB-63. "Thumper" Double Figurine,**
1950s. Goebel. 4x4x3.5" tall painted figurine depicting playful pose of two rabbits, apparently meant to depict Thumper and Miss Bunny. Markings include full bee and incised "128" plus foil name sticker "Thumper." - **$75 $150 $250**

BMB-64

☐ **BMB-64. Thumper Figurine,**
1950s. Goebel. 2.5" tall painted and glazed yawning image. - **$15 $30 $60**

BMB-65

☐ **BMB-65. Bambi Vase,**
1950s. Goebel. 2.75x3x5.5" tall. Marked "DIS 42" along with full bee marking. - **$60 $125 $250**

BMB-66

☐ **BMB-66. Bambi Bud Vase,**
1950s. Goebel Pottery. 5.5" tall painted ceramic with figure at hollowed tree stump. Underside has incised "DIS 42B" and full bee marking. - **$60 $125 $250**

BAMBI

BMB-67

❑ **BMB-67. "Flower" Salt And Pepper,**
1950s. Goebel. Pair of 2.5" tall with full bee marking. - **$35 $70 $125**

BMB-68

❑ **BMB-68. "Thumper" Salt & Pepper Set,**
1950s. Goebel. Pair is 2.25" to 2.5" tall, both complete with foil stickers on chest, various Goebel markings including full bee, cork stoppers. - **$40 $80 $140**

BMB-69

❑ **BMB-69. "Thumper" Figural Ashtray,**
1950s. Goebel 4" tall ceramic figurine ashtray with hollowed body, cigarette rest above tail, opened mouth for venting smoke. Complete with foil sticker on body plus underside has Goebel markings including a full bee and incised "DIS 8." - **$40 $75 $150**

BMB-70

❑ **BMB-70. "Thumper" Figurine By Beswick,**
1950s. England. 2.25x2.25x3.75" tall painted china figurine depicting Thumper atop tree stump surrounded by flowers. Text in gold on underside of base including copyright, character name and "Beswick, England." - **$100 $200 $300**

BMB-71

❑ **BMB-71. Bambi Charm Bracelet,**
1950s. Unidentified maker but Disney copyright 6" long silvered metal link bracelet with five matching .5" tall three-dimensional charms, each finished by tiny paint accents. Two charms of Bambi are identical except facing opposite direction. Remaining charms are Thumper, Flower and Friend Owl. - **$10 $20 $40**

BMB-72

❑ **BMB-72. Bambi Planter,**
1950s. "Napco." Goebel-like design 3x4x3.5" tall painted and glazed china from a series of planters. - **$15 $30 $60**

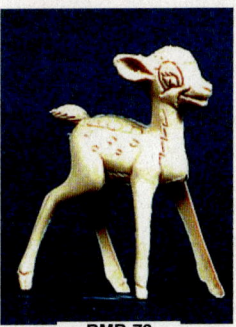

BMB-73

❑ **BMB-73. Mini-Figure,**
1950s. Marx. 2" tall soft plastic version from second series of late 1950s. - **$6 $12 $20**

BMB-74

❑ **BMB-74. Thumper German Ceramic Clock,**
1950s. J.A. Sural Hanau/Main. 7x9" high relief design. Incised with mark "10271". - **$50 $100 $200**

BMB-75

❑ **BMB-75. "Thumper Woolikin" Doll Bagged,**
1950s. F.W. Woolnough Corp. 15" tall plush doll comes in original Easter-theme drawstring vinyl bag. Doll has wire inserts in ears, vinyl face, fabric bow around neck and felt hands. Bag - **$5 $10 $15** Doll - **$20 $40 $75**

BAMBI

BMB-76

BMB-77

BMB-79

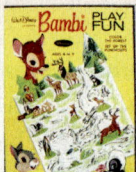  

BMB-82

❑ **BMB-76. "Steiff Bambi" Small Size,**
1950s. Germany. This smaller size Steiff is 2.5x4x6" tall. With Button And Tag - **$75 $150 $225** With Button Or Tag - **$65 $110 $165** No Button Or Tag - **$35 $65 $100**

❑ **BMB-77. "Bambi" Steiff Large Size,**
1950s. Germany. This larger size Steiff is 3x6.75x9" tall. With Button And Tag - **$100 $175 $285** With Button Or Tag - **$70 $125 $200** No Button Or Tag- **$40 $75 $115**

BMB-78

❑ **BMB-78. Bambi Figural Lamp Base,**
1950s. Unidentified maker but similar design and quality of painted and glazed ceramic figures by Leeds China Co. Actual figure height to bulb socket is 7" on 4" diameter base. - **$25 $50 $85**

BMB-80

❑ **BMB-79. "Bambi Nite Lite,"**
1950s. Hankscraft Co. 3.5x5x8" tall hard plastic. Underside has two company labels including one listing six different Disney character lights in this series. - **$25 $50 $85**

❑ **BMB-80. Unusual Bambi Inspired Salt And Pepper Set,**
c. 1950s. Glazed ceramic and brass wire figure. 2.5x3.5x4.5" tall. Top of body has a pair of hooks to attach shakers. Feet are rubber. No Disney copyright. - **$20 $40 $75**

BMB-81

❑ **BMB-81. "Bambi Flocked Press-Out Book,"**
1966. Whitman. 8.5x11" activity book #1920 with flocking accents throughout the six pages of punch-outs to form diorama scene of Bambi and forest friends. Un-Punched - **$15 $30 $65**

❑ **BMB-82. "Bambi Play Fun" Punch-Out Set,**
1966. Whitman. 8.75x11.75x1.5" deep box containing complete 10 thin cardboard sheets totaling 25 different punch-outs of Bambi, Flower, Thumper, other forest animals, trees, etc. Set includes a forest scene play sheet opening to 30x30" designed for coloring and accompanied by box of generic crayons. Un-punched - **$15 $30 $60**

BMB-83

BMB-84

❑ **BMB-83. Bambi Planter,**
1960s. Enesco. 3.5x6x5" tall painted and glazed ceramic floral holder with underside foil sticker by maker. - **$15 $30 $60**

❑ **BMB-84 . Figurine,**
1960s. Likely Enesco "Japan" 2.5x5x5.5" tall painted and glazed ceramic. - **$10 $20 $40**

BAMBI

BMB-85

❏ **BMB-85. "Bambi" And "Thumper" Soap Bottles,**
1960s. Soaky. Pair of 10" tall containers with soft plastic bodies and hard plastic removable heads. Each - **$12 $25 $40**

❏ **BMB-86. Night Light/Incense Burner Figure,**
1960s. Goebel. 2.5x4x6.25" tall china dual purpose figurine "DIS 150" with other maker markings, original electric cord and inner bulb mount with light bulb. A drop of oil is heated to produce scent and top of Bambi's head has three holes as made for this purpose. - **$35 $75 $135**

❏ **BMB-87. Bambi And Thumper Salt & Pepper Set,**
1960s. Enesco. Painted and glazed ceramic shakers comprised of 4" tall Bambi and 3.25" tall Thumper. From a series of salt & pepper sets accompanied by generic simulated wood grain plastic tray (not shown). - **$45 $80 $140**

BMB-90

❏ **BMB-89. "Bambi" Figural Ashtray,**
1960s. Goebel 3.5x4x3" tall ceramic design including 2" long figurine molded on rear upper base. Cigarette rest is on right edge. Figurine has maker's foil sticker on reverse, underside of tray has stylized bee marking plus incised "DIS 146." - **$50 $100 $200**

❏ **BMB-90. "Bambi Bayard" Alarm Clock,**
1972. France. 2x4.5x4.75" tall. Metal case back is blue, front rim "feet" are hard plastic. Has a separate butterfly piece attached above Bambi's tail and this moves as seconds tick. - **$35 $65 $100**

BMB-86

BMB-88

❏ **BMB-88. "Bambi Mini-Puppet,"**
1960s. Kohner Bros. 2.75" tall push puppet plastic toy with maker's foil sticker on base. - **$10 $20 $40**

BMB-91

BMB-87

BMB-89

BMB-92

BAMBI

❑ **BMB-91. "Bambi" Figure With Bag,**
c. 1975. Dakin Co. 8" tall poseable vinyl figure complete with die-cut gold cardboard tag plus plastic original carrying bag with grip handle. By Dakin but unmarked as this is from the era when Disney did its own distribution marked "Walt Disney Distributing Co." Near Mint Bagged - $45 Loose - $5 $15 $30

❑ **BMB-92. Figurine,**
1970s. Wade. 1.5" tall porcelain miniature. - $12 $25 $40

❑ **BMB-95. Serigraph Signed By Marc Davis,**
1980s. Acetate sheet is 11x14" with 5.5x6" animation cel image of Bambi and Thumper. Walt Disney Co. seal plus signature by Disney legend animator/designer Davis. From limited edition. Signed And Mint - $250

BMB-93

BMB-94

BMB-96

❑ **BMB-96. Limited Edition Watch,**
1993. With die-cut image and box. - $150

❑ **BMB-93. Thumper Figurine,**
1970s. Goebel. 2.25" tall painted and glazed ceramic in unusual purple and yellow coloration. Underside has incised marking "DIS 36" and foil sticker. - $12 $25 $40

❑ **BMB-94. Bambi And Flower The Skunk Vase,**
1970s. "Japan" but otherwise unmarked 6.25" tall china bud vase. - $5 $12 $25

BMB-95

BMB-97

❑ **BMB-97. Musical Water Globe,**
1999. Includes all the major characters. Bambi moves up and down as music plays. - $75

Beauty and the Beast

Upon its 1991 release, this film was hailed as the best animated film that Disney had done in years. Through a combination of peerless animation technique, (which set a technical precedent for years to come) and an imaginative, original musical score, this film captured hearts and minds like few films ever do. It was the first animated film ever nominated for an Academy Award as the Best Picture of the Year.

Still, with all the peerless animation going on, the movie would have been so much less without a well-written story. The young and beautiful Belle is caring for her father Maurice when he gets lost in the woods, stumbles into the Beast's castle, and ends up thrown into a dungeon. Belle finds her father and agrees to trade places with him. The Beast falls in love with her. He is actually an enchanted prince, who can regain his human form if she will love him back. But, she wants to be with her father, so she is allowed to return home. Gaston, Belle's jealous self-proclaimed suitor back in the village, hears of the Beast's love for Belle and decides to attack the Beast's castle. Belle returns to the castle to help and realizes her love for the Beast. With her love, the Beast ends up becoming human again.

Directed by Kirk Wise and Gary Trousdale, the film features voice actors Paige O'Hara, Robbie Benson, Richard White, Jerry Orbach and Angela Lansbury. The score was by Alan Menken and Howard Ashman. Their title song won an Academy Award. The film inspired a successful Broadway musical.

Merchandise includes books, watches, figurines, tie-ins with fast food chains. There were also spin-offs from the Broadway musical adaptation of the film.

BEA-1

❑ **BEA-1. "Beauty And The Beast Ballroom Dancing" Limited Edition Framed Cel,**
1990s. 20x28" lacquered wood frame with 9x11" cel. Limited to 500 pieces and issued with certificate. Sold out and is among the most prized Disney hand-painted editions.
Mint as issued - $1000

BEAUTY AND THE BEAST

BEA-2   BEA-3   BEA-8   BEA-12   BEA-13

❏ **BEA-2. Belle Figurine,** Classic Collection. "Dreaming of a great wide somewhere, Belle in a blue dress." - **$175**

❏ **BEA-3. Wardrobe Figurine,** Classic Collection. "You'll look ravishing in this one!" - **$150**

❏ **BEA-8. Beauty and the Beast Snow Globe,** Disney. Belle shown sitting on throne with Beast looking over and surrounded by other characters. - **$25**

❏ **BEA-12. Beast Action Figure,** 1993. From the Beauty and the Beast playset. - **$8**

❏ **BEA-13. Mrs. Potts Miniature Figure,** 1993. From the Beauty and the Beast playset. - **$8**

BEA-4   BEA-5   BEA-9   BEA-14

❏ **BEA-4. Maurice Figurine,** Classic Collection. "Is someone there?" - **$175**

❏ **BEA-5. Belle and Beast Figurine,** Classic Collection. "Tale as old, as time." - **$295**

❏ **BEA-9. Beast's Library Snow Globe,** Disney. Depicting Beast giving Belle his entire library. - **$65**

❏ **BEA-14. Plastic Cup featuring Chip,** 1993. From Beauty and the Beast. - **$10**

BEA-15   BEA-16

❏ **BEA-15. Broadway Edition Belle Fashion Doll,** 1994. 11 1/2 " tall. - **$20**

❏ **BEA-16. Broadway Edition Plush Beast Doll,** 1994. 13 " tall. - **$20**

BEA-6   BEA-7   BEA-10

❏ **BEA-6. Lenox Cogsworth,** Lenox. Ivory China with 24 karat gold. - **$50**

❏ **BEA-7. Belle and Beast Teapot,** Disney. Dancing Belle and Beast. - **$25**

BEA-11

❏ **BEA-10. Beauty and the Beast Winter Snow Globe,** Disney. Winter time and Beast's castle. - **$110**

❏ **BEA-11. Beauty and the Beast Mug,** Disney. Belle shown eating with the characters. - **$10**

BEA-17

BEAUTY AND THE BEAST

BEA-18

□ **BEA-17. Plush Baby Belle,**
2003. From Beauty and the Beast. - **$6**

□ **BEA-18. Brass Key Keepsake Collection Belle Doll,**
2004. Porcelain collectible doll, 7 1/2 " inches high. - **$10**

BEA-19

□ **BEA-19. Sparkle Princess Collection Belle Doll,**
2005. Fashion doll 11 1/2 " tall, with collectible ring. - **$12**

Bedknobs and Broomsticks

A combination of live-action and animation, this 1971 release featured many people from the same creative team that worked magic on *Mary Poppins*. It was directed by Robert Stevenson, with music by the brothers Robert B. and Richard M. Sherman. The producer-writer was Bill Walsh who based the film on the book by Mary Norton.

Set in the London of 1940, the story features a spinster studying to become an apprentice witch in the hope of helping England find a way to fight Nazi Germany. The film was not a huge hit and Disney re-edited it for a 1979 theatrical re-release. Most of the cuts were made to the musical numbers. It was nominated for several Oscars, eventually winning an Oscar for Best Special Effects. Among those who contributed to the special effects was Ward Kimball. He was responsible for the animation sequences on the Island of Naboombu. Voice actors included Angela Lansbury, Roddy McDowell, David Tomlinson and Cindy O'Callaghan.

Merchandise included records and books.

BED-1

BED-2

□ **BED-1. "Bedknobs and Broomsticks Play This Soccer Game" Punch-out Book,**
1971. Whitman 8.75x11.75". Stiff paper cover plus six pages feature "A Press-Out Set-Up Board and Playing Pieces." Un-punched - **$10 $18 $35**

□ **BED-2. "Nestle's Quik" Container With Premium Offer,**
1971. 3.25x4.25x6" tall tin and cardoard container with wrap-around label. Front and back sides advertise set of six 11x14" "Art Reproductions" color pictures featuring scenes from the film. All six are shown on the back and were available for $1 plus package code. Container - **$12 $25 $50** Set - **$15 $40 $75**

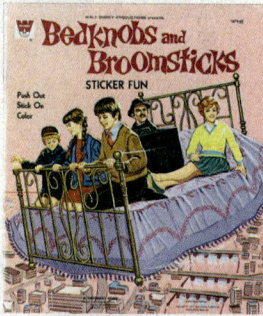

BED-3

BED-4

□ **BED-3. "Sticker Fun" Book,**
1971. Whitman. 10.5x12" stiff paper cover and twelve placement pages for bound-in six pages of cut-out stickers with glue backing. Unused - **$8 $15 $30**

□ **BED-4. "Bedknobs And Broomsticks" Books,**
1971. Whitman. 5.5x6.25" "Tell-A-Tale" titled "A Visit To Naboombu," 28 pages, and 6.75x8" Little Golden Book, 24 pages. Each - **$5 $10 $15**

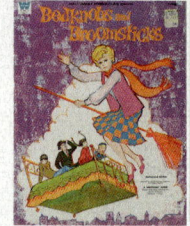

BED-5

BED-6

□ **BED-5. Paperdoll Book,**
1971. Whitman. 10x13" with stiff paper covers "London Village Pop-Out" scene; two card stock pages of punch-out dolls for Mr. Browne, Miss Price, Carrie, Charlie and Paul; six glossy paper pages of outfits and accessories. Uncut - **$10 $25 $45**

□ **BED-6. Frame Tray Puzzle Set With Slipcover,**
c. 1971. Jaymar. Set of three 9.75x12.75" in paper slipcover with diecut window. - **$10 $20 $35**

BED-7

THE BLACK CAULDRON

BED-8

❑ BED-7. "Bedknobs and Broomsticks" Lunch Box,
1972. 7x8x4" deep embossed metal by Aladdin Industries Inc. - **$20 $40 $90**

❑ BED-8. "Bedknobs and Broomsticks" Lobby Card Set w/Envelope,
1979. Set of nine re-release 11x14" glossy stiff paper lobby cards. Set **$15 $25 $50**

Ben and Me

This 21-minute cartoon featurette from 1953 tells the tale of how a church-mouse named Amos was actually the main inspiration for the inventions of Ben Franklin. The film was directed by Ham Luske and the vocal cast included Disney regulars Hans Conried and Sterling Holloway. It was based on the book of the same name by Richard Lawson. *Ben and Me* was made during a period when Disney was still producing and releasing one and two reel subjects. Today, educators use this cartoon as a way of introducing young students to an important era of American history as well as one of America's most important historical figures, Ben Franklin.

Merchandise for this short consists mainly of book and comic book spin-offs (*Four Color Comics* #539), but there are some cel reproductions being sold.

BEN-1

❑ BEN-1. Amos Mouse Pencil Drawing,
1953. 10x12" sheet of animation paper with 2.75x3.5" image in lead pencil. #58 from a numbered sequence. - **$30 $60 $125**

BEN-2

❑ BEN-2. "Ben & Me,"
1954. 7.25x8.25" hardcover from the "Cozy Corner" series by Whitman, 24 pages. - **$20 $40 $85**

The Black Cauldron

Based on Lloyd Alexander's five-book series, *The Chronicles of Prydain*, this full-length animated feature was released in July 1985. The project actually started in 1971 when Disney purchased the screen rights to all five *Prydain* volumes. The project saw many writers come and go, but the real preparation began a decade later when Joe Hale was named producer. The first thing he had to do was condense the massive storyline of the original source material. It featured over thirty characters. To make the material accessible for the screen, he took a single villain from the series, the Horned King, and gave him the attributes of several of the other villains.

Another contributing factor to the film's production was the technological updates that became available to Disney. Video cameras and computers were now able to advance the animation process to new levels.

The story focused on Taran, a young assistant pig keeper, who is trying to rescue his psychic pet pig Hen-Wen from the Horned King's castle. The King wants to use the psychic pig to find the infamous Black Cauldron. Once found, the Cauldron can be used to create an army of evil deathless warriors.

Directed by Richard Rich and Ted Berman, the film featured the work of animators such as Phil Nibblelink, Andreas Deja, Jay Jackson and Walt Stanchfield. Vocal talent included John Hurt, John Byner and Susan Sheridan.

Merchandise was relatively limited but it included books and a cereal premium.

BKC-1

❑ BKC-1. "The Black Cauldron" Movie Poster,
1985. 27x41" pre-release poster to promote the film's summer release. - **$5 $10 $25**

BKC-2

❑ BKC-2. "The Black Cauldron" Fritos Premium Wrist Watch,
1985. 1.25" diameter metal case. - **$25 $50 $75**

BKC-3

❑ BKC-3. Black Cauldron Animation Cel,
1985. 20x14" cel with certified signed sticker on front and Walt Disney Productions label on back. - **$100 $200 $300**

THE BLACK HOLE

The Black Hole

This 1979 live-action science fiction film was the first Disney production to receive a PG rating. With Disney being mostly known for high-quality animation and films based on classics, the genre of science fiction was an unusual one for the studio.

The U. S. S. Palomino spacecraft is returning to Earth when its crew sees another spacecraft, one that has been reported as missing, hanging near a black hole. That ship, the U. S. S. Cygnus, is piloted by Dr. Hans Reinhart and his robot companion Maximillian. With their robot crew, they plan to fly straight into the black hole.

The film cost $20 million to make and wasn't exactly a big success, but those that did see it were absolutely stunned by the special effects. The film was directed by Gary Nelson and starred Maximillian Schell, Ernest Borgnine, Anthony Perkins and Yvette Mimieux. The film was nominated for Academy Awards in cinematography and visual effects.

Merchandise included books, model kits and a clock.

BKH-1

BKH-2

❑ **BKH-1. "The Black Hole Colorforms Set,"** 1979. 12.5x16x1" deep. Colorful background board depicting interior of spaceship and two large sheets of die-cut vinyl pieces representing crew and robot characters. - **$8 $15 $30**

❑ **BKH-2. "The Black Hole" Lobby Card Set With Envelope,** 1979. W.D.P. Complete set of nine stiff glossy paper lobby cards, each 11x14" in original envelope. Near Mint Set - **$60**

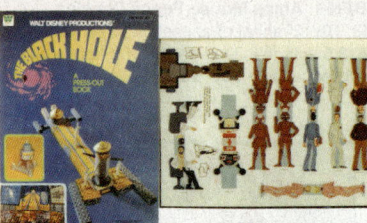

BKH-3

BKH-4

❑ **BKH-3. "The Black Hole" Punch-Out Book,** 1979. Whitman. 10x14" with stiff paper cover plus six inside pages with punch-outs. Unpunched - **$5 $10 $20**

❑ **BKH-4. "The Black Hole Puzzle,"** 1979. Whitman. 8.5x11x2" deep box contains puzzle with 15.5x18" assembled size titled "The Cygnus." - **$3 $8 $12**

BKH-5

BKH-6

❑ **BKH-5. "The Black Hole" Gum Card Set,** 1979. Topps. Set of 88 cards, each 2.5x3.5". Fronts feature photos from the film with both puzzle and text backs. Near Mint Set - **$10**

❑ **BKH-6. "The Black Hole" Canadian Lunch Box,** 1979. Aladdin. 7.5x8x4" deep plastic with high gloss sticker on front. - **$10 $20 $45**

BKH-7

BKH-8

❑ **BKH-7. "The Black Hole" Lunch Box With Thermos,** 1979. Aladdin. 7x8x4" deep embossed metal box and 6.5" tall plastic thermos. Box - **$10 $30 $65** Bottle - **$10 $20 $30**

❑ **BKH-8. Sticker Activity Book,** 1979. Whitman. 8.25x10.25" card stock cover and center two pages plus sixteen black and white activity pages, two sheets of full color punch-out stickers to form outer space diorama. - **$6 $12 $25**

BKH-9

THE BLACK HOLE

BKH-10

☐ **BKH-9. "The Black Hole" Portfolio Folders,**
1979. Mead Corp. Lot of five, each 9.5x12.5". Each - **$1 $3 $5**

☐ **BKH-10. "MPC/The Black Hole" Store Sign,**
1979. Stiff cardboard sign 17x22" advertising series of Black Hole character model kits. Signs were packaged one per case. - **$20 $50 $75**

BKH-11

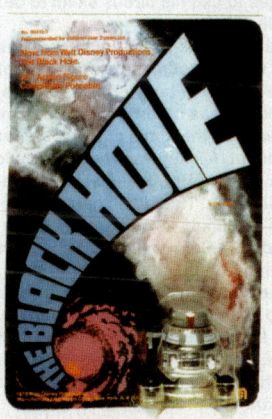
BKH-12

☐ **BKH-11. "The Black Hole" Publications,**
1979. Assortment of comic books #1-3, coloring book, activity book, all by Whitman; three novels published by Ballantine Books, Golden Press, Random House; Disneyland book/record set. Each Near Mint - **$6**

☐ **BKH-12. "The Black Hole/V.I.N.Cent" Action Figure,**
1979. Mego. 6x9" colorful blister card contains 2" tall figure. Carded - **$10 $20 $40**

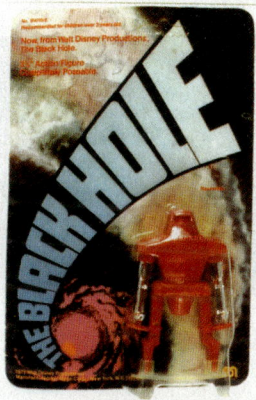
BKH-13

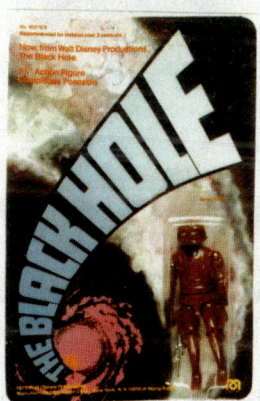
BKH-14

☐ **BKH-13. "The Black Hole/Maximillian" Action Figure,**
1979. Mego. 3.75" tall figure comes with display stand. Carded - **$5 $10 $20**

☐ **BKH-14. "The Black Hole/Sentry Robot" Action Figure,**
1979. Mego. 3.75" tall hard plastic poseable figure comes with gun. Carded - **$10 $20 $35**

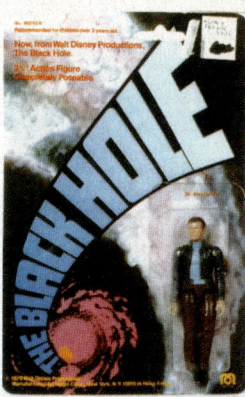
BKH-15

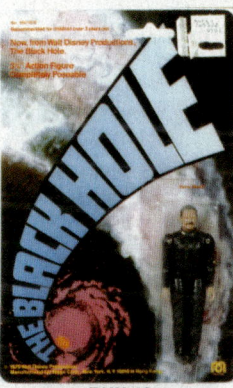
BKH-16

☐ **BKH-15. "Dr. Alex Durant" Action Figure,**
1979. Mego. 6x9" blister card holding 3.75" tall poseable hard plastic figure. Carded - **$5 $10 $20**

☐ **BKH-16. "Harry Booth" Action Figure,**
1979. Mego. 6x9" blister card holding 3.75" tall poseable hard plastic figure. Carded - **$5 $10 $20**

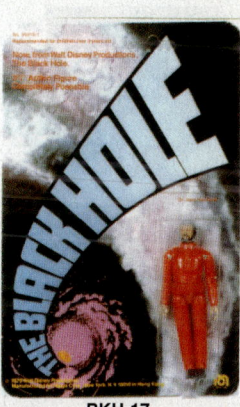
BKH-17

THE BLACK HOLE

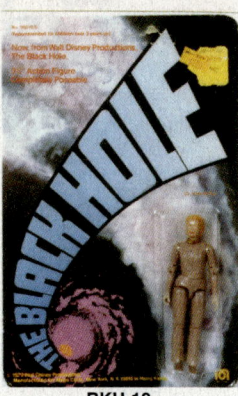

BKH-18

❑ BKH-19. "The Black Hole Maximillian" Model,
1979. W.D.P. issued by MPC. 7x14x3" deep box contains model. Un-built - **$10 $20 $40**

❑ BKH-20. "The Black Hole V.I.N.Cent" Model Kit,
1979. W.D.P. issued by MPC. 7x14x3" deep sealed color box contains MPC model copyright 1979. Model is 8.5" tall when assembled. Box includes color photos from the movie. Un-built - **$10 $20 $40**

BKH-21

BKH-23

❑ BKH-17. "Dr. Hans Reinhardt" Action Figure,
1979. Mego. 6x9" blister card holding 3.75" tall poseable hard plastic figure. Carded - **$5 $10 $20**

❑ BKH-18. "Dr. Kate McRae" Action Figure,
1979. Mego. 6x9" blister card holding 3.75" tall poseable hard plastic figure. Carded - **$5 $10 $20**

BKH-19

BKH-20

BKH-22

❑ BKH-21. "The Black Hole" Wall Clock,
1979. Wooden framed 15x19x2" deep battery-operated unit fronted by illustrated spaceships Cygnus scene print applied on fiberboard. Bottom margin has attached plastic strip with Disney name and "The Black Hole" title. - **$20 $40 $80**

❑ BKH-22. "The Black Hole" Watch,
1979. Bradley. 2.5x9.5x1" deep hard plastic box with hinged lid holding 1-3/8" diameter quartz wristwatch with dial face illustration of U.S.S. Cygnus approaching a black hole. Box - **$5 $10 $15** Watch - **$20 $40 $65**

❑ BKH-23. Black Hole Canadian Cereal Premiums,
c. 1979. Five soft plastic figural pieces issued as cereal box insert premiums. There are four identical 2.5" tall "Bob" pencil holders and a 2" tall "Dexter" figure with movable arms and legs. Each side of Dexter's body has color human face sticker depicting white child on front and black child with glasses on back. Each - **$3 $6 $10**

Bongo

Bongo is a trained bear who performs in the circus. His incredible act has made him a hit everywhere he goes. However, Bongo does not enjoy captivity or the stardom; he wants to be free to run in the woods. He escapes the circus and meets a female bear, Lulubelle. Unfortunately, she has another suitor, a gigantic grizzly named Lumpjaw, who is willing to fight to keep her. Bongo manages to use his circus skills to defeat the bully bear.

This featurette was originally released as part of the live action/animation combination feature *Fun and Fancy Free* (1947). As a feature, *Bongo* has unfortunately been overshadowed by the film's other, more famous component, *Mickey and the Beanstalk*.

The story of Bongo is based on a book by Sinclair Lewis. The film is narrated on-screen by Jiminy Cricket as voiced by Cliff Edwards. One of the highlights is a brief walk-on by Chip and Dale before they became chipmunk stars as antagonists of Donald Duck. *Fun and Fancy Free*'s live action segments were directed by Jack Kinney, Hamilton Luske, and Bill Roberts. Animation directors included Ward Kimball, Les Clark and Fred Moore.

Merchandise included records, paint books and several appearances by Bongo in Dell and Gold Key Comics.

BONGO

BON-1

BON-2

BON-3

BON-4

❑ BON-3. "Bongo Big Golden Book,"
1947. Simon and Schuster. 8.25x13.25" laminated hardcover, 28 pages and story art on every page "Based On The Disney Motion Picture Fun And Fancy Free." - **$15 $30 $75**

❑ BON-4. "Bongo" Book,
1948. Whitman. 4.5x6.25" softcover from "Story Hour Series," 32 pages of art and story. - **$10 $20 $40**

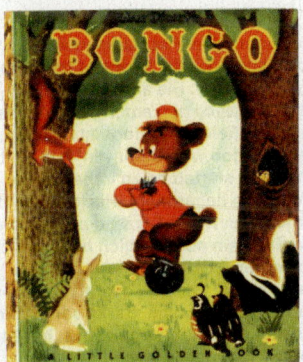
BON-5

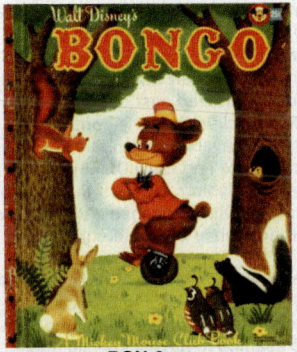
BON-6

❑ BON-1. "Bongo/Lulubelle" Hanky,
1947. Hanky is 8.5x8.5" fabric picturing him riding unicycle and waving hanky at her. - **$10 $20 $35**

❑ BON-2. "Fun And Fancy Free" Lobby Card,
1947. RKO Radio Pictures. 11x14" original issue example card #7 from set of eight. Features Bongo and includes corner inset from Mickey and the Beanstalk section. - **$20 $45 $85**

❑ BON-5. "Bongo Little Golden Book,"
1948. Book shows original copyright but was issues in mid-1950s. Simon & Schuster. 6.75x8" wtih 44 pages. - **$8 $15 $35**

❑ BON-6. "Bongo" Variety Book,
1948. This is an abbreviated version of the 44 page Little Golden Book and from the "Mickey Mouse Club Book" series by Simon & Schuster. This book has 24 pages. Book shows original copyright but was issued in mid-1950s - **$5 $12 $25**

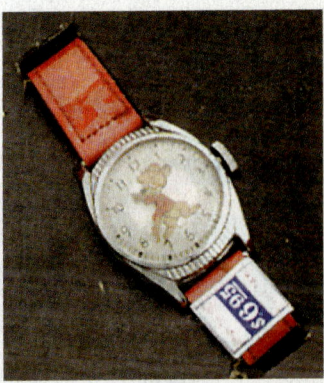
BON-7

BON-8

❑ BON-7. Bongo Watch,
1948. U.S. Time. From series of different character watches to celebrate 20th birthday of Mickey Mouse. Original vinyl over leather straps. Near Mint Boxed -**$300**
Watch Only - **$50 $100 $200**

❑ BON-8. "Walt Disney's Hanky Clock" With Bongo & Others,
c. 1950. English 7.5x7.5" die-cut stiff paper clock-shaped circus theme folder designed to hold 8x8" hanky on right half by an attached sheet of paper. Inside folder also pictures various Disney characters. - **$20 $40 $90**

BONGO

BON-9

BON-12

☐ **BON-9. "Disneyland" TV Show Dairy Promotion Large Poster,**
1955. ADA-sponsored large 19.5x58" paper poster promoting "June Is Dairy Month/Festival Of Better Living/See 'Disneyland' American Dairy Association Television Show." Circus theme art pictures Bongo and more than nine other Disney characters. - **$50 $100 $175**

BON-10

BON-11

☐ **BON-10. "From Disneyland Jiminy Cricket Presents Bongo" Record,**
1955. 10x10" cardboard sleeve contains 78rpm record "Complete Story And Songs." - **$8 $15 $25**

☐ **BON-11. "Disneyland Gloves" Store Display Box,**
1950s. Wells Lamont Corp. 8.5x11.5x3.75" deep box only originally containing assortment of Disney character fabric gloves. Exterior lid pictures Bongo, Mickey Mouse, Snow White, Dopey, Bambi, Brer Rabbit, Alice, Jiminy Cricket, Peter Pan, others. Inside lid has paper label of Mickey wearing a pair of Bambi gloves. Box bottom has three cardboard dividers. - **$15 $35 $60**

☐ **BON-12. Disney Character Bread Wrapper End Labels,**
c. 1950s. Bond Bread five 2.75x2.75" waxed paper examples utilizing day-glo color accents and a single alphabet letter to jointly form sponsor's name when entire series is collected. Pictured example labels are Bambi ("N"), Bongo ("O"), Jiminy Cricket, Thumper, both ("D"). Fifth label featuring Figaro is without a letter at margin. Each - **$6 $12 $25**

Carl Barks Writer and Artist

The connection that Barks made with the fans of Disney comics is one of the deepest in comic's history. His artistic and storytelling skills place him among the all-time greats in his field. A cartoonist by trade, he applied for a job with Disney in 1935 at the age of 34. He started as an in-betweener in the animation department. His job was to draw the "in-between" drawings that connected the main poses which had been created by other artists.

Barks quickly moved over to storyboarding cartoons. Over time, Barks contributed to upwards of thirty-five cartoons. In 1942, he worked with Jack Hannah on a comic book story that eventually appeared in Dell's Four Color #9. It was called *Donald Duck Finds Pirate Gold*. The art from that comic was later used in a Better Little Book titled *Ghost Morgan's Treasure* which was released in 1946.

In 1942, Barks left Disney and with his second wife, moved east of Los Angeles to operate a chicken farm. He continued to sell drawings to several magazines. In 1943, he started to write and draw Disney stories for Western Publishing. Western Publishing had acquired the Disney license and was now publishing Disney characters in several titles.

Barks' work began to appear regularly in *Walt Disney's Comics and Stories*. Fans of the title started to realize that some of the stories seemed to have a special quality about them. Those fans actively sought each issue and an underground fan base for those unique stories began to grow. At the time, no one knew who was drawing or writing these fantastic stories.

In 1947, Barks created Uncle Scrooge and placed him in the immortal tale, *Christmas on Bear Mountain*. He was the main artist for long Donald Duck stories until 1952 when he began the Uncle Scrooge comic book series. As time went on, fans started to speak in reverential tones about the "Good Duck Artist." Issues containing his stories became valuable on both a collecting and emotional level. People found the ducks to be as real as anything else on the market at the time.

Barks expanded the duck universe and gave it a dimensionality that was seldom found in comics. Among the characters he created for the books are Gladstone Gander in 1948, the Beagle Boys in 1951, Gyro Gearloose in 1952, and Magica de Spell in 1961.

As his work evolved, so did the world of the ducks. Readers waited anxiously for each issue and Barks never let them down. Every story was inventive, fun and often, adventurous. Finally, in 1966, at age 65, Barks voluntarily left the books. He began to work on his oil paintings and in 1968 started to take commissions for full color oil paintings. Many of those paintings featured the ducks. The paintings originally sold for $175-$200. Today, they are selling for five and six figures.

What is amazing is that Barks had never signed his comic book work! His fans had gone to great lengths to find out who was behind the amazing stories they were enjoying. In 2000, at the age of 99, Barks passed away. Today his legacy is carried on by current duck artists like Daan Jippes, Fred Milton, Victor Arriagada Rios (Vicar), Daniel Branca, Don Rosa, William Van Horn, Mau Heymans and Patrick Block.

The work that Barks did is still selling comics today. Gemstone Publishing is reprinting some of his stories every month in one of their Disney titles. They can be found in comic stores.

Merchandise that features characters that Barks created, as well as the other characters that Barks has worked on, is actively sought out by collectors.

CARL BARKS WRITER AND ARTIST

CAR-1

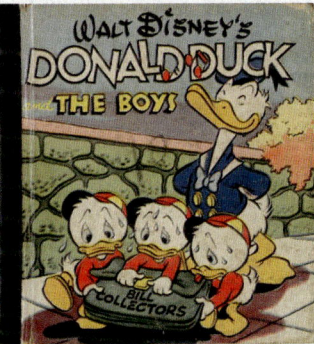

CAR-2

CAR-4

CAR-5

CAR-6

❏ **CAR-1. "Calgary Eyeopener" Magazine With Early Barks Art,**
1928. Vol. 25 #31 is 6x7", September issue of risque magazine with contents of jokes, humorous stories and cartoons. Issue has three Barks cartoons and his art appeared in this magazine until about 1934. He went to work at Disney Studio in 1935. - **$25 $50 $80**

❏ **CAR-2. "Donald Duck And The Boys" Book,**
1948. Whitman. 5.25x5.5" hardcover from "845" series, 96 pages with art on every other page by Barks. - **$50 $100 $300**

❏ **CAR-3. Handwritten And Signed Two-Page Letter,**
1974. Pair of 8.5x11" lined paper sheets, each in a different vibrant color, both inked by message dated February 26 to "Mr. Conklin." Very detailed and interesting contents, largely relating to the collectibility and availability of Barks' original art. He notes of Donald Duck "I liked Donald because I could use him in all sorts of roles. Villain, hero, cad, bully. He was a good actor."
Unique, Fine - **$400**

❏ **CAR-4. Comic Book Preliminary Page Original Art,**
c. 1974. Paper sheet is 8.5x11" illustrated in lead pencil for a Junior Woodchuck story written and drawn by Barks. This is page 11 of the 15-page story titled "Captain Outrageous." This was Barks' last Junior Woodchuck story in 1974.
Unique, Near Mint - **$425**

❏ **CAR-5. Carl Barks Autograph Matted With Photo,**
c. 1974. Art board is 8x10" with mounted high quality photograph 5x6.75". This is a re-creation of the cover for Walt Disney Comics & Stories #108. Signed in blue ink directly below the photo by Barks, signature runs 2" long. Near Mint - **$175**

❏ **CAR-6. "Newcon" Comic Convention Program Signed,**
1976. Softcover annual convention program is 8.5x11", 40 pages. Front cover photo of Barks laughing at a Howard the Duck comic book is autographed in pen "To Charlie/Carl Barks."
Unique, Fine - **$125**

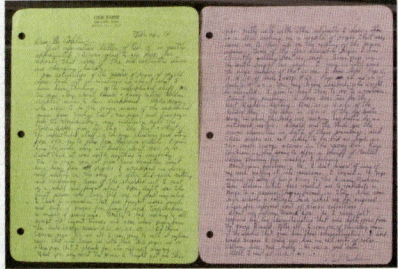

CAR-3

CAR-7

❏ **CAR-7. Carl Barks Original Pen & Ink Drawing,**
1976. Original pen and ink drawing by Carl Barks showing Uncle Scrooge and the Barks' inspired villains. - **$10,500**

CARL BARKS WRITER AND ARTIST

CAR-8

CAR-8. "Caliph Of Baghdad" Print Of Signed Barks Art,
1978. Carl Barks Studio print of exotic painting by him. Reverse description notes "Famous Figures Of History As They Might Have Looked If Their Genes Had Gotten Mixed With Those Of Waterfowl." Mint As Issued - **$300**

CAR-9 (Blue cover)

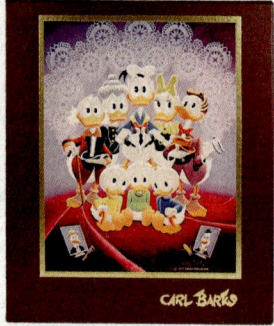

CAR-9 (Maroon cover)

❏ **CAR-9. "The Fine Art of Walt Disney's Donald Duck" Painting Book,**
1981. Features Carl Barks' oil paintings. These McDuck Editions came with burgundy or blue covers and slipcovers. This was a limited edition of 1875 books total for the two covers. Each was signed and numbered. Each Near Mint - **$1800**

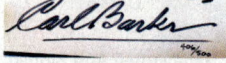

CAR-10

❏ **CAR-10. Poster-Size Print Signed,**
1987. Glossy paper enlarged reprint is 24x36" of Barks' comic book cover titled "Donald Duck In Sheriff Of Bullet Valley." Bottom margin has Barks' inked signature, one of 500 signed from a publication run of 3,000 by "Another Rainbow Publishing Co." other identifications include "Disney's Comic Classics" and "Comic Book Library No. 4." Near Mint - **$135**

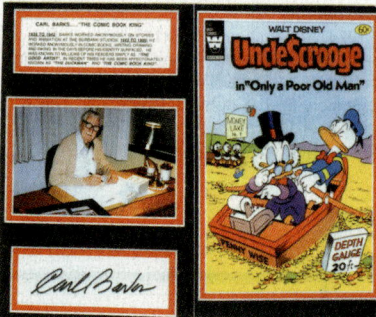

CAR-11

CAR-12

❏ **CAR-11. Carl Barks Limited Edition Autograph Display,**
1993. Overall size is 14x18". Includes comic book cover for issue #195, short biography, photo and signed card and certificate of authenticity. Only 245 issued. Mint As Issued - **$500**

❏ **CAR-12. "The Nude With The Hat" Signed Print,**
1994. German-issued 14x19" stiff glossy paper print of artwork originally done by Barks in 1939. Print is also an artist's proof with inked edition number at bottom left corner. Bottom right corner is signed by Barks in felt tip pen. Mint As Issued - **$225**

CAR-13

❏ **CAR-13. Mickey Mouse Print Of Signed Barks Art,**
1994. Walt Disney Co. produced by Brockmann Und Reichelt, Mannheim, Germany. Enlargement print of original signed sketch, resulting in 9x11" enlarged image of Mickey. Mint As Issued - **$300**

CAR-14

CARL BARKS WRITER AND ARTIST

☐ **CAR-14. Donald Duck Print Of Signed Barks Art,**
1994. Walt Disney Co. produced by Brockmann Und Reichelt, Mannheim, Germany. Print centered by large 10.5x12" portrait above Barks' completion signature. Mint As Issued - **$250**

CAR-15

☐ **CAR-15. Carl Barks Pocket Watch,**
1994. Gifted Images product. Watch features a Barks self portrait. Limited edition of 65. - **$200**

CAR-16

☐ **CAR-16. Italian Tribute Book,**
1994. Book is 8.75x9.5", 48 pages. Entirely in Italian text printed by "Comic Art" copyright by Walt Disney Co. Specialty art by Italian artists in honor of Barks in some way feature or tie-in him, Uncle Scrooge and/or Donald Duck. - **$10 $20 $40**

CAR-17

☐ **CAR-17. Carl Barks "The Barkster" Commemorative Figure,**
1995. Painted resin figure by Randy Bowen. Only 10 produced. - **$2000**

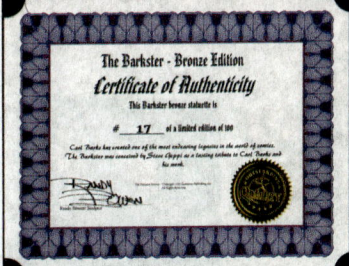

CAR-18

☐ **CAR-18. Carl Barks "The Barkster" Commemorative Figure,**
1995. Painted bronze figure by Randy Bowen. Approved by Carl Barks. Came with Certificate and videotape on which Barks discusses "The Barkster." Only 100 produced. - **$1600**

CAR-19

☐ **CAR-19. "Carl Barks 95th Birthday Commemorative" Signed Limited Edition Prints,**
1996. 11x14" pair of prints on stiff artboard from "International Museum Of Cartoon Art." Issued March 27, 1996. Each print features different western theme art of Mickey, Minnie, Horace and Clarabelle and are reproductions of the drawings Barks submitted to Disney's hiring officer in 1935 which in turn landed him a job. Only 120 number prints produced, each boldly signed by Barks in felt tip pen. Each sealed in an envelope with gold foil seal and decorative string. Mint as issued - **$800**

CARL BARKS WRITER AND ARTIST

CAR-20

❑ **CAR-20. Disneyana Convention Card Signed,**
1996. Oversized card 6.5x10.5" issued for 1996 Disneyana Convention at Walt Disney World Resort. Promotes "Self Control" limited edition bronze Donald Duck figurine on marble base, available for $1800; only 150 were produced. Card insert photo of Barks holding an Uncle Scrooge doll is signed in ink. Mint As Issued - **$55**

CAR-21

❑ **CAR-21. Carl Barks One Hundred Quackers Treasury Bill,**
1997. City of Ducksburg paper $100 dollar bill featuring Carl Barks and his signature. - **$40**

CAR-22

❑ **CAR-22. "Fifty Stingy Years" Uncle Scrooge Signed Art Tile,**
1997. Tile size is 10x13". Produced by Carl Barks Studio to commemorate the 50th anniversary of Uncle Scrooge. Signed and numbered #44 with signed certificate of authenticity. 100 produced. Mint as issued - **$1050**

(BOX FRONT)

(CLOSE-UP OF LABEL ON BACK OF BOX)

CAR-23

❑ **CAR-23. Uncle Scrooge Boxed Puzzle,**
1990s. Limited edition boxed 1000 piece puzzle. Shows Carl Barks painting "Rich Finds at Inventory Time." Made in Japan. Near Mint sealed - **$115**

(CLOSE-UP OF LABEL ON BACK OF BOX)

CAR-24

❑ **CAR-24. Uncle Scrooge Boxed Puzzle,**
1990s. Limited edition boxed 1000 piece puzzle. from the Barks' Commemorative Birthday painting "Surprise Party." Made in Japan. Near Mint sealed - **$115**

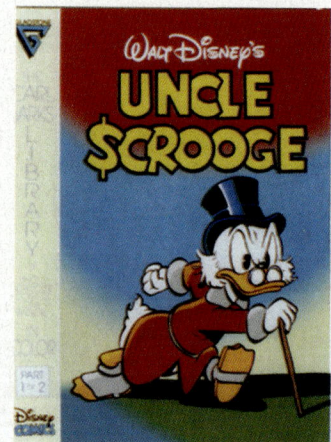

CAR-25

❑ **CAR-25. "The Carl Barks Library" Comic Book Reprints,**
1990s. Gladstone Publishing. Series of eleven full color reprint comic book stories, all by Barks. Included are issues #1 and #2 from the "Uncle Scrooge" series and the first nine issues of the "Walt Disney Comics And Stories" series. Issues have sealed trading cards. Mint As Issued - **$75**

Cars

This full-length animated film chronicles the adventures of an arrogant rookie racecar named Lightning McQueen. Finding himself lost on Interstate 40, the young racer has a series of adventures that teach him the true meaning of life. The film was an international hit upon its release on June 9, 2006. It went on to become the second most successful motion picture of 2006, albeit not quite the blockbuster for which Disney had hoped.

Cars' history can be traced back to 1998, when the preliminary script – outlining an electric car's adventures in a gas-powered world – was known as Yellow Car. After numerous script revisions and halts in production, serious work began again in or around 2001 (*A Bug's Life* and *Toy Story 2* were released in the interim). For awhile, the film was to be called Route 66, but some felt that the audience might assume it was a reference to the popular 1960s TV show of the same name. Eventually, the title *Cars* was chosen instead.

Most animated films based on humanized automobiles choose to place the characters' eyes on their headlights. Some feel that a contributing factor to *Cars*' success was the deliberate decision to place the cars' eyes on their windshields. Pixar found inspiration for this decision in Disney's 1952 animated short *Susie the Little Blue Coupe* as well as Tex Avery's *One Cab's Family* (also 1952). As with so many of Pixar's animated features, *Cars* contains many such subtle (and not-so-subtle) cultural references.

The voice-over talent in the film brought out the best in both Hollywood and NASCAR. Paul Newman, Richard Petty, Michael Keaton, Bonnie Hunt, and Pixar regular John Ratzenberger all play important roles in the feature. The lead role of Lightning McQueen was voiced by Owen Wilson. Many singled out Larry the Cable Guy's performance as Mater, a mid-1950s one-ton wrecker truck who befriends Lightning, as a highlight of the film.

Merchandising associated with *Cars* was a monstrous success. Some estimate that by the end of 2006, merchandising sales totaled over $1 billion. Among the most popular items were a series of diecast cars produced by Mattel.

Other products included shirts, books, coloring books, tattoos, and limited edition prints. (Factual note: these prints weren't cels, as the movie was not produced with cels.)

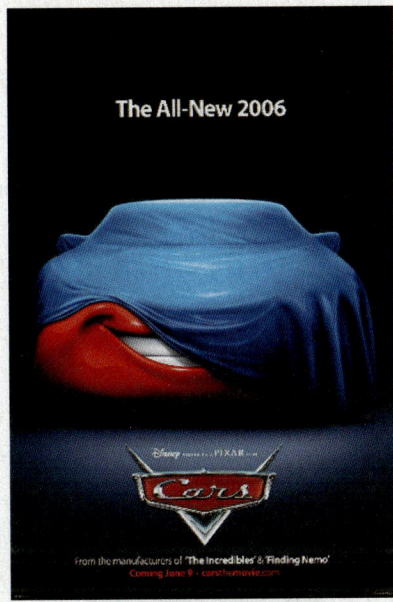

CRS-1

❏ **CRS-1. "Cars" Teaser Release Poster,** 2006. 27"x41". One Sheet. - **$40**

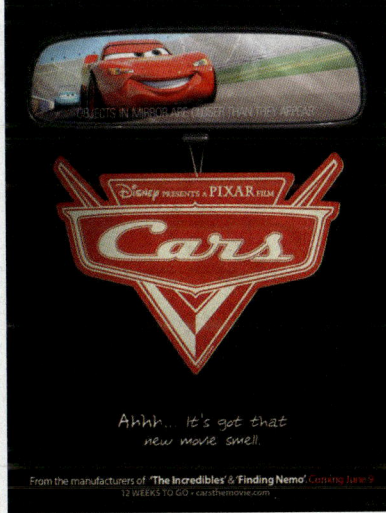

CRS-2

❏ **CRS-2. "Cars" International Teaser Poster,** 2006. 27"x41". One Sheet. - **$40**

CRS-3

❏ **CRS-3. Cars "Frosted Mini-Wheats" Cereal Box,** 2006. Kellogg's. Box is 2.5x8x11" tall with mail-in offer for a custom name license plate.
Box - **$1 $2 $3**
License Plate - **$1 $2 $3**

CRS-4

❏ **CRS-4. Lightning McQueen Pez Dispenser,** 2006. - **$1**

CARS

CRS-5

❑ **CRS-5. Doc Hudson Pez Dispenser,**
2006. - **$1**

CRS-6

❑ **CRS-6. Mater the Tow Truck Pez Dispenser,**
2006. - **$1**

CRS-7

❑ **CRS-7. Sally Pez Dispenser,**
2006. - **$1**

CRS-8

❑ **CRS-8. Cars "Lightning McQueen" Wristwatch,**
2006. Fossil. Limited edition of 2,000. - **$85**

Chip 'n' Dale

Originally, these two best friends were nothing more than one-off co-stars in a Pluto short (*Private Pluto*, 1943). They were developed by Gerry Geronomi and there was no intention of using them again. However, fate stepped in. Disney had been seeking new and different foils for Donald Duck. Jack Hannah took the two little troublemakers and fleshed out their personalities with additional future development by Bill Justice. In doing so, he made Donald's life a nightmare.

Chip 'n' Dale usually had one thing on their mind; they wanted to store mass quantities of food. They were never deliberately mean about it, but one thing was for sure, nothing was going to get in their way. Occasionally they would have to deal with someone trying to take their home, but it was the desire for food that usually drove them.

As close as they were in appearance, the chipmunks each had a distinct personality. The one thing they definitely shared was their ability to scheme. Chip, with the black nose, was a bit more on top of things and he had more business sense. Dale, with the red nose, was a lot more fun loving and a bit goofier. They worked well together and over the course of 23 different shorts, they did what they could to torment Donald.

Some feel that Chip 'n' Dale's sped-up voices may have been the inspiration for Theodore, Alvin and Simon, the three Chipmunks who had some record hits in the fifties and sixties.

Chip 'n' Dale merchandise included books, figurines and plush dolls.

C&D-1

❑ **C&D-1. Dale Story Board Art,**
1950. Sheet of paper is 6x8.25" filled by pastel art for Donald Duck cartoon 'Out On A Limb' starring Donald as tree surgeon determined to prune the tree home of Chip and Dale. Unique, Near Mint - **$225**

CHIP 'N' DALE

C&D-2

❑ **C&D-2. Chip Pencil Drawing From "Out Of Scale,"**
1951. 10x12" sheet of animation paper with 3x5x3.75" image from Donald Duck short. #30 from a numbered sequence. - **$35 $65 $135**

C&D-3

C&D-4

❑ **C&D-3. Bill Justice Personal Christmas Card With Chip & Dale,**
1958. 5.25x7" slightly textured stiff white paper card. Justice was a Disney animator from the later 1930s on and became the primary animator for Chip & Dale. Opens to reveal scene of Chip, Dale and the Justice's dog Kayak watching a home movie with image of Bill and his wife Marie projected on the screen. Back of card features the Justices with Chip & Dale using hula hoops. - **$10 $25 $55**

❑ **C&D-4. Chip Figurine By Hagen-Renaker,**
1950s. 1.25" glazed ceramic figurine with small foil company sticker. - **$50 $100 $150**

C&D-5

C&D-6

❑ **C&D-5. Dale Figurine By Hagen-Renaker,**
1950s. 1.25" glazed ceramic figurine wtih small foil company sticker. - **$50 $100 $150**

❑ **C&D-6. German Figures,**
1950s. Companion pair of 3.25" tall hollow hard plastic figures. Chip is depicted with hands in front of him. Dale has arms stretched out. Both have small loop between ears, possibly to be used as ornaments. Each has name sticker including "Walt Disney" authorization. Pair - **$125 $250 $400**

C&D-7

❑ **C&D-7. Bill Justice Personal Christmas Card,**
1960s. Stiff textured paper is 5x7.5" limited issue folder card for friends and family with specialty art by Justice, Disney animator with such films as Fantasia and Bambi to his credit as well as developing the characters Chip and Dale. - **$10 $20 $40**

C&D-8

❑ **C&D-8. Disneyland Promotion Christmas Card,**
1972. 4x10" on slightly textured stiff paper. Text mentions card originally came with admission tickets and ride books for "A Christmas Visit To Disneyland." Also notes that this was the first full year "Without The Presence Of Our Founders Walt And Roy Disney." - **$5 $15 $30**

C&D-9

C&D-10

❑ **C&D-9. Plush Dolls,**
1980s. Companion pair of 9" tall stuffed dolls, each with individual detailing plus stitched tag "Disneyland/Walt Disney World." Pair - **$8 $15 $30**

❑ **C&D-10. "Dragon Around" Signed Limited Edition Bronze Statue,**
2000. White Horse Studios. Edition of 100, signed in gold ink on front plate by animator Bill Justice. 7x10x11.25" tall. Mint As Issued - **$2100**

CHIP 'N' DALE COMICS

Chip 'n' Dale Comics

Dell Publishing counted Chip 'n' Dale's appearances in Four Color Comics before they began numbering the individual title. The dynamic chipmunks had previously appeared in Four Color Comics #517, 581, and 636.

❏ Chip 'n' Dale #6,
June 1956. - $6 $18 $75

❏ Chip 'n' Dale #9,
March 1957. - $6 $18 $75

❏ Chip 'n' Dale #4,
December 1955. - $6 $18 $75

❏ Chip 'n' Dale #7,
September 1956. - $6 $18 $75

❏ Chip 'n' Dale #10,
June 1957. - $6 $18 $75

❏ Chip 'n' Dale #5,
March 1956. - $6 $18 $75

❏ Chip 'n' Dale #8,
December 1956. - $6 $18 $75

❏ Chip 'n' Dale #11,
September 1957. - $5 $15 $60

CHIP 'N' DALE COMICS

❏ Chip 'n' Dale #12,
December 1957. - **$5 $15 $60**

❏ Chip 'n' Dale #15,
September 1958. - **$5 $15 $60**

❏ Chip 'n' Dale #18,
June 1959. - **$5 $15 $60**

❏ Chip 'n' Dale #13,
March 1958. - **$5 $15 $60**

❏ Chip 'n' Dale #16,
December 1958. - **$5 $15 $60**

❏ Chip 'n' Dale #19,
September 1959. - **$5 $15 $60**

❏ Chip 'n' Dale #14,
June 1958. - **$5 $15 $60**

❏ Chip 'n' Dale #17,
March 1959.   Info. - **$5 $15 $60**

❏ Chip 'n' Dale #20,
December 1959. - **$5 $15 $60**

CHIP 'N' DALE COMICS

❑ **Chip 'n' Dale #21,**
March 1960. - **$5 $15 $60**

❑ **Chip 'n' Dale #24,**
December 1960. - **$5 $15 $60**

❑ **Chip 'n' Dale #27,**
November 1960. - **$5 $15 $60**

❑ **Chip 'n' Dale #22,**
June 1960. - **$5 $15 $60**

❑ **Chip 'n' Dale #25,**
May 1960. - **$5 $15 $60**

❑ **Chip 'n' Dale #28,**
December 1960. - **$5 $15 $60**

❑ **Chip 'n' Dale #23,**
September 1960. - **$5 $15 $60**

❑ **Chip 'n' Dale #26,**
August 1960. - **$5 $15 $60**

❑ **Chip 'n' Dale #29,**
March 1961. - **$5 $15 $60**

CHRONICLES OF NARNIA

The Chronicles of Narnia

Produced by Walden Media and distributed by Walt Disney Pictures, this 2005 feature film is based on the first novel in C.S. Lewis' Chronicles of Narnia series. The books follow the adventures of different children who find themselves magically transported to the realm of Narnia. While there they find that in this world, magic is an everyday occurrence; animals speak; and as in many fantasy worlds, the forces of good battle the forces of evil.

At the start of the film, four children – Peter, Susan, Edmund and Lucy Pevensie – find themselves evacuated during the World War II London blitz. While staying at the country home of Professor Kirke they engage in a game of hide and seek. It is sister Lucy who first stumbles across the entranceway to the world of Narnia. During her initial stay there she meets the first of many mythological creatures, a faun named Mr. Tumnus. Tumnus tells Lucy that Narnia is currently experiencing a century-long winter in which Christmas is not celebrated. As the story unfolds, Lucy and her siblings find other entryways into the world of Narnia, and learn of the battle between the Lion Aslan and the White Witch. Each child ends up playing an important role in the history of Narnia.

While the film does have slight deviations from the novel's narrative, *The Lion, the Witch and the Wardrobe* is considered to be faithful to the intent and structure of Lewis' book. Produced at a budget of $180 million, the film has grossed over $750 million worldwide. The United States' total gross is close to $300 million.

The Lion, the Witch and the Wardrobe is the first in a planned film adaptation of the complete Chronicles of Narnia. All seven of the novels were written by Lewis between 1949 and 1955. There are over 100 million copies of the books available in over 40 languages. Scheduled for release in May 2008 is the second film in Disney's series, *The Chronicles of Narnia: Prince Caspian*.

Collectibles for the film include a successful soundtrack CD, action figures, posters, postcards, video games, and pins.

CHR-2

❏ **CHR-1. Chronicles of Narnia Pocketwatch,** 2006. Features a stainless steel case with a gold finish and ornate finish, Aslan logo on its face, and a reddish dial. Packaged in a wooden box with a classic Narnia scene on top, includes Certificate of Authenticity and serial number. Limited to 2,000 pieces - **$130**

❏ **CHR-2. Narnia Lion & Witch Bookends,** 2006. By Weta. Each side: L 8.5" x W 6" x H 13.5", fully painted, limited edition. - **$300**

CHR-4

CHR-3

❏ **CHR-3. Narnia Tumnus Maquette,** 2006. By Weta. L 7" x W 8" x H 17.5", fully painted, limited edition. - **$150**

❏ **CHR-4. Narnia Satyr Design Maquette,** By Weta. L 7" x W 8" x H 9", fully painted, limited edition. - **$150**

CHR-1

CHRONICLES OF NARNIA

CHR-5

CHR-7

❏ **CHR-7. Narnia Minoboars Maquette,**
2006. By Weta. L 7" x W 8.5" x H 12", fully painted, limited edition. **- $150**

CHR-8

CHR-6

❏ **CHR-5. Narnia Centaur Action Figure,**
2005. 5" scale. **- $8**

❏ **CHR-6. Narnia Girls on Aslan Statue,**
2006. By Weta. L 17" x W 6" x H 13.5", fully painted, limited edition.. **- $300**

CHR-9

❏ **CHR-8. Narnia Peter Action Figure,**
2005. 5" scale. **- $8**

❏ **CHR-9. Narnia Aslan Action Figure,**
2005. 5" scale. **- $8**

Cinderella

This classic animated feature made its debut in February 1950. Like many other Disney full-length features, it found its basis in a familiar fairy tale. The story of Cinderella was known by almost everyone. A poor teenage girl, horribly abused by her wicked stepmother and her two cruel stepsisters, can't go to the royal ball. With the help of her Fairy Godmother's magic, she manages to attend the ball after all. Once there, she meets Prince Charming. Unfortunately, she has to be home by midnight, since that is when the magic wears off. As midnight comes, she flees the ball. In her haste, she has left behind a single slipper. During the brief time they spent together, the Prince has fallen in love with her.

Unaware of her actual identity, the Prince searches high and low for Cinderella. Using the shoe she left behind as a test, he visits every eligible woman in the kingdom. Finally, he matches the slipper to Cinderella. Reunited at the end, she and the Prince live happily ever after.

The years prior to this film's release had not been easy ones for Walt Disney. His last few features had not done as well as hoped and he was looking for a property that would help break the doldrums that the company was going through. He saw similarities between his first real success, Snow White, and the fairy tale of Cinderella. With those similarities as a basis for potential success, he attacked the new film with everything he could. One of the major decisions he made was to shoot actors in live action so that the animators would have something very real to work from. Walt participated in every meeting, often contributing suggestions to characterization and art. His effort paid off. The film was a great success and in addition, earned a couple of Oscar nominations.

The songs were by Mack David, Jerry Livingston and Al Hoffman. Animators who worked on the film include Ward Kimball (who focused on the mice Gus and Jaq as well as the cat Lucifer), Marc Davis, Frank Thomas, Ollie Johnston, Eric Larson and Milt Kahl. Vocal talent included Ilene Woods, Mike Douglas and Verna Felton. The film was directed by Hamilton Luske and Wilfred Jackson.

Cinderella, as well as other characters from the film, appears in *Four Color Comics* #272, and 786.

Merchandise included a watch inside a clear plastic slipper; books, records and figurines.

CIN-1

❑ **CIN-1. "Cinderella Puppet Show Golden Toy Book,"**
1949. Simon & Schuster. 8.25x11.25" with die-cut pages slotted for use with puppet punch-outs. Un-punched - **$30 $85 $150**
Punched - **$20 $50 $80**

CIN-2

❑ **CIN-2. "Cinderella" Concept Art,**
1950. 5.75x8.75" by noted artist Mary Blair featuring Cinderella in her ball gown on the castle staircase. Unique, same or similar- **$2000 $4000 $7000**

CIN-3

❑ **CIN-3. Cinderella Concept Art,**
1950. Image is 7.75x5.75" featuring Cinderella and her Fairy Godmother by Disney artist Mary Blair. Unique, same or similar - **$2500 $5000**

CIN-4

❑ **CIN-4. "Cinderella Little Nipper Storybook Album,"**
1950. RCA. 10.5x12" stiff cardboard cover contains set of two 78rpm records plus bound-in, 24-page book. - **$15 $35 $75**

CIN-5

❑ **CIN-5. "Cinderella Golden Record,"**
1950. Simon & Schuster. 6.75x7.5" paper sleeve contains 78rpm on vinyl. - **$5 $10 $20**

❑ **CIN-6. "Cinderella" Hardcover,**
1950. Whitman. Cozy Corner series. 7.5x8.25" with 24 pages. - **$10 $20 $50**

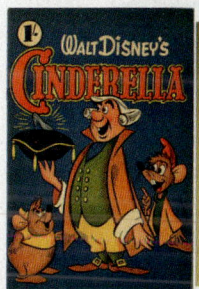

CIN-7

❑ **CIN-7. "Cinderella" Australian Book,**
1950. W.G. Publications, Sydney. Contents are 48-page black and white comic book story believed to be a reprint of the Dell Four-Color Comic #272 which was released in April 1950. - **$30 $65 $135**

CINDERELLA

CIN-8

☐ **CIN-8. "Cinderella Big Golden Book,"**
1950. Golden Press. 9.5x12.75" with 28 pages. - **$15 $30 $60**

CIN-9

☐ **CIN-9. "Quick" With Cinderella Article,**
1950. Volume 2, #17. 4x6". - **$5 $12 $25**

CIN-10

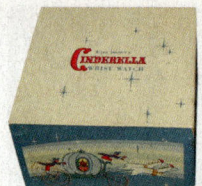 

(version in rectangular box)

☐ **CIN-10. "Cinderella" Wrist Watch With Slipper Display,**
1950. U.S. Time. 1" diameter watch with foil price sticker #30031 is attached to clear plastic slipper in 5" diameter by 3" deep cardboard box. Also came in rectangular box. A second variety pictures her on the dial.
Box (either) With Name Dial - **$100 $300 $600**
Box (either) With Portrait Dial - **$115 $330 $650**

CIN-11

☐ **CIN-11. "The Cinderella Magic Wand Book" English Hardcover,**
1950. Dean & Son Ltd. 7x10". 64 pages of story art with four 3-D photo pages featuring model scenes. 3-D "Magic Spectacles" included. - **$50 $100 $150**

CIN-12

☐ **CIN-12. "Cinderella" Catalin Plastic Pencil Sharpener,**
1950. 1-1/8" diameter. - **$25 $50 $75**

CIN-13

☐ **CIN-13. "Cinderella Railcar" With Original Box,**
1950. 8" tall handcar with tracks, key, and box. Made in England. Boxed - **$400 $800 $1500**

CINDERELLA

CIN-14

❑ **CIN-14. Cinderella Fan Card,**
c. 1950. Card is 7.25x9.25". - **$10 $20 $40**

CIN-15

❑ **CIN-15. "Cinderella Frame Tray Puzzle" With Slipcover,**
c. 1950. Whitman. 11.25x14.75".
With Cover - **$12 $25 $50**
No Cover - **$8 $20 $35**

CIN-16

❑ **CIN-16. "Bruno" The Dog Ceramic Figurine,**
c. 1950. American Pottery. 3" tall. - **$75 $150 $250**

CIN-17

❑ **CIN-17. Gus Ceramic Figurine,**
c. 1950. Shaw. 3.25" tall. - **$40 $75 $150**

CIN-18

❑ **CIN-18. Mama Mouse Ceramic Figurine,**
c. 1950. American Pottery. 3.25" tall. - **$75 $150 $225**

CIN-19

❑ **CIN-19. "Baby Mouse" Ceramic Figurine,**
c. 1950. Shaw. 2.25" tall. - **$75 $150 $225**

CIN-20

❑ **CIN-20. Jacques Figurine By American Pottery,**
c. 1950. Painted and glazed ceramic 3.5" tall. Back has foil sticker with character's name "Jacques." - **$50 $100 $175**

CIN-21

❑ **CIN-21. Cinderella Ceramic Planter,**
c. 1950. Shaw. 7.25" tall. - **$75 $150 $250**

CIN-22

❑ **CIN-22. Prince Charming Ceramic Planter,**
c. 1950. Shaw. 7.25" tall. - **$60 $125 $200**

CINDERELLA

CIN-23

CIN-24

❑ **CIN-23. "Cinderella Jewelry,"**
c. 1950. Stiff glossy display card is 3.25x3.75" and contains 2.25" long figural metal pin of Gus and Jacques holding onto clock. Carded - **$12 $25 $50**

❑ **CIN-24. "Cinderella Jewelry,"**
c. 1950s. Pair of 3.25x3.75" glossy stiff paper display cards containing two different 1.5" long or tall figural metal pins. Maker unknown. Each Carded - **$12 $25 $50**

CIN-25

CIN-26

❑ **CIN-25. "Cinderella" English China Lot,**
c. 1950. Lot of four figural pieces painted and glazed. "Fairy Godmother" pitcher is 3.75" in diameter and 6.5" tall, Two small pitchers each 3" tall and 2.25" tall creamer. Marked "Wheetman England."
Godmother - **$50 $100 $200**
Each Mouse - **$30 $60 $100**

❑ **CIN-26. "Cinderella" Dairy Product Glass Set,**
c. 1950. Each 4-5/8" tall from numbered series.
Each - **$3 $6 $12**

CIN-27

CIN-28

❑ **CIN-27. Cinderella Teapot,**
c. 1950. Teapot is 3.5x5.5x6" tall glazed ceramic with transfer images on each side. One is of Prince Charming dancing with Cinderella while the other is of a female mouse. Underside is marked "Western Germany" with incised "10133" and company mark. - **$40 $75 $135**

❑ **CIN-28. "Cinderella Apron" Premium Pattern,**
c. 1950. J. C. Penney. 7.5x10" folded size and opens to 30x40". One side has pattern and opposite side has Cinderella with story and additional Cinderella illustrations. - **$10 $20 $40**

CIN-29

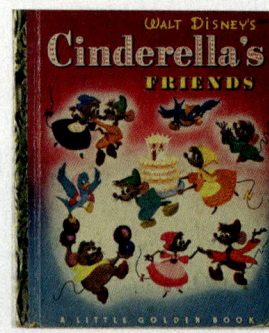

CIN-30

❑ **CIN-29. "Cinderella And The Magic Wand" Better Little Book,**
c. 1950. Whitman. Book #711-10. - **$10 $30 $65**

❑ **CIN-30. "Cinderella's Friends Little Golden Book,"**
c. 1950. Simon & Schuster. 6.75x8" with 28 pages. - **$10 $20 $35**

CINDERELLA

CIN-31

❏ **CIN-31. "Cinderella" English Card Game,** c. 1950. Pepys Games. 2.5x3.5x.75" deep box contains complete deck of 44 cards and instruction booklet. - **$50 $100 $200**

CIN-32

❏ **CIN-32. Cinderella Danish Hardcover Complete Card Album,** 1951. Premium by Rich's, likely candy or cookie product. 11x11" with 36 pages. 196 cards, each 1.75x2.75". Complete - **$50 $100 $165**

CIN-33

❏ **CIN-33. "Cinderella" German Game,** 1951. "Spiele-Schmidt." 11x15.5x1.5" deep box contains complete parts. Board is 15x21" with choice illustrations that tell the story of Cinderella. Other parts include six 1.25" tall hand-painted flat metal character playing pieces and cardboard play money coins. - **$75 $150 $275**

CIN-34

CIN-35

❏ **CIN-34. "Cinderella Wrist Watch",** 1958. Timex. 4.5x5.1.5" deep box contains watch with 1" diameter metal case. Box comes with plain cardboard slip cover. Inside of lid is an acetate image of Cinderella.
Near Mint Boxed - **$500**
Watch Only - **$25 $50 $100**

❏ **CIN-35. "Cinderella And Prince" Hanky,** 1950s. 8.5x9". Maker unknown. - **$10 $20 $35**

CIN-36

CIN-37

❏ **CIN-36. "Cinderella" Boxed Puzzle,** 1950s. Jaymar. Puzzle is 14x18.75 when assembled with title "The Slipper Fits." - **$10 $20 $30**

❏ **CIN-37. Bluebird Ceramic Figurine,** 1950s. Goebel. 3.75" tall. #DIS144. - **$100 $250 $400**

CIN-38

CINDERELLA

CIN-39

❏ **CIN-38. Gus Ceramic Figurine,**
1950s. Hagen-Renaker. 2.25" tall. - **$100 $200 $300**

❏ **CIN-39. Cinderella Book Cover,**
1950s. Issued by various bread companies. 11x17". - **$5 $12 $25**

CIN-40

CIN-41

❏ **CIN-40. Cinderella Cuban Picture Stamp Album,**
1950s. Issuer unknown. 9x11.5". 24 pages with 200 stamps. Complete - **$50 $100 $200**

❏ **CIN-41. "Cinderella" Charm Bracelet,**
1950s. Maker unknown. 6" long. Boxed - **$15 $30 $65**
No Box - **$10 $20 $30**

CIN-42

❏ **CIN-42. Cinderella And Prince Charming Wind-up,**
1950s. Irwin Corp. 3x3x5" tall hard plastic. This toy was sold titled as Cinderella or Prince Charming as well as the Royal Couple and came in several different color schemes. - **$30 $60 $100**

CIN-43

❏ **CIN-43. Cinderella Halloween Costume,**
1950s. Boxed. - **$50 $100 $250**

CIN-44

❏ **CIN-44. Jaq Pencil Sharpener,**
c. 1950s. .75x1.5x2.25" tall hard plastic with three dimensional figure of Jaq attached. - **$20 $40 $80**

CIN-45

❏ **CIN-45. Cinderella Watch Ceramic Figure,**
c. 1960. Timex. 5.25" tall. Also issued in plastic.
Ceramic - **$8 $12 $20**
Plastic - **$5 $10 $15**

CIN-46   CIN-47

❏ **CIN-46. "Cinderella Sticker Fun" Book,**
1965. Whitman. #2173. 8-3/8x12". Unused - **$10 $25 $60** Used - **$5 $15 $25**

❏ **CIN-47. "Cinderella" Soaky,**
1960s. Figure is 10.5" tall. - **$5 $12 $30**

CIN-48

CINDERELLA

CIN-49

❑ **CIN-48. Cinderella Rare Lady Head Vase,**
1960s. Ceramic figure is 3x4x5.5" tall painted and glazed. Other Disney "ladies" produced were Snow White, Sleeping Beauty and Mary Poppins. - **$125 $275 $400**

❑ **CIN-49. "Cinderella" Boxed Costume,**
c. 1960s. Ben Cooper. 8.25x11x2.75" deep box contains two-piece costume. Boxed - **$10 $20 $40**

CIN-50

❑ **CIN-50. "Cinderella Large Watch,"**
1960s. US Time. Near Mint Boxed - **$300**
Box Only - **$50 $100 $200**
Watch Only - **$25 $50 $100**

CIN-51

❑ **CIN-51. Cinderella Alarm Clock,**
c. 1960s. Phinney-Walker/West Germany, imported by Hamilton Watch Co. 3.75" tall metal. - **$30 $65 $100**

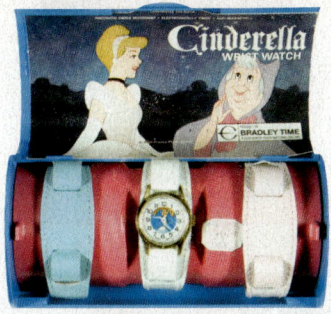

CIN-52

❑ **CIN-52. "Cinderella" Watch With Case,**
1973. Bradley. Near Mint Boxed - **$75**
Watch Only - **$15 $30 $50**

CIN-53   CIN-54

❑ **CIN-53. Cinderella Figurine,**
1970s. Painted and glazed ceramic 2.5x3x5.25" tall. - **$10 $20 $30**

❑ **CIN-54. Prince Charming Ceramic Figurine,**
1970s. Figure is 4" tall. - **$5 $12 $25**

CIN-55   CIN-56

❑ **CIN-55. Jaq Ceramic Figurine,**
1970s. Maker unknown. 3.5" tall. - **$5 $10 $20**

❑ **CIN-56. Gus Ceramic Figurine,**
1970s. Maker unknown. 2.5" tall. - **$5 $10 $20**

CIN-57   CIN-58

❑ **CIN-57. "Cinderella" Boxed Doll,**
1970s. Horsman. 7.75x10.75" box contains 8" tall doll from "Walt Disney's Classics" series. Near Mint Boxed - **$45**

❑ **CIN-58. Cinderella "Moving Picture Flip Book,"**
c. 1980. Merrimac Publishing Corp. 1.75x3". - **$5 $12 $20**

CIN-59

CIN-60

❑ **CIN-59. Autographed "Cinderella Limited Edition Serigraph,"**
1980s. Image is 7.5x8". Signed by Disney artist Marc Davis and has Walt Disney Co. seal. Near Mint - **$350**

❑ **CIN-60. Cinderella High Quality Print Signed By Marc Davis,**
1990. Disney Co. 7x7" image area. Limited issue. Mint As Issued - **$100**

CINDERELLA

CIN-61

CIN-62

CIN-65

❑ **CIN-61. "Cinderella Serigraph" Signed By Marc Davis,**
c. 1990. Disney Co. 8x8" acetate sheet in 16x20" mat. Edition of 9500. Mint As Issued - **$150**

❑ **CIN-62. Cinderella Charm Bracelet,**
1990s. Applause. 7" long. - **$5 $10 $15**

CIN-63

❑ **CIN-63. "Cinderella" Snow Globe,**
1990s. Has working clock on top. - **$90**

CIN-64

❑ **CIN-64. Brass Key Keepsake Cinderella Collection doll,**
2004. Porcelain collectible doll, 7.5 " inches high. - **$10**

❑ **CIN-65. Sparkle Princess Collection Cinderella doll,**
2005. Fashion doll with collectible ring, 11.5" tall. - **$12**

Clarabelle Cow

Clarabelle's first appearance came as a non-humanized cow in the first produced Mickey Mouse cartoon, *Plane Crazy* (1928). One could say that her early appearances are "udder" nonsense, as her udder is often the focal point of the humor involving her. In 1930's *The Barnyard Concert*, she was portrayed as a humanized figure for the first time. By 1931, her udder was being concealed under a dress. By then, she had become Minnie's best friend. She appeared as a major co-star in many shorts through the mid-1930s, and as an extra thereafter. She took a more important role in the comics, where she continues to feature as a major character today.

Clarabelle is often paired with Horace Horsecollar. He functions as her on-again, off-again boyfriend. While loyal to Horace, she's been known to occasionally date Goofy as well. One of her most memorable appearances occurs in *Mickey's Amateurs* (1937), where she appears as a piano virtuoso. Most recently, she was shown in the 2004 direct-to-video release, *The Three Musketeers*.

Clarabelle's image appears on a lot of merchandising, especially items dating to the 1930s. This includes books, magazines, cards and a bisque figure.

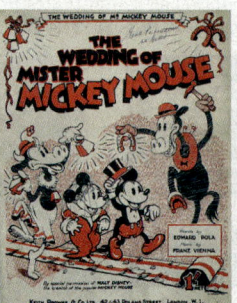

CLA-1

❑ **CLA-1. "The Wedding Of Mister Mickey Mouse" English Sheet Music,**
c. 1933. Keith Prowse & Co. Ltd. 9.75x12.25" with eight pages. - **$75 $150 $275**

CLA-2

❑ **CLA-2. "Clarabelle Cow" Store Display Standee,**
1934. Made By Old King Cole, distributed by Kay Kamen. Molded 'laminite' 11x15.5x1.5" deep. - **$500 $1000 $1600**

CLA-3

CLA-4

❑ **CLA-3. "Clarabelle Cow" Variety Glass,**
1936. Glass is 4.75" tall featuring the same image of Clarabelle that appears on the glass from the first dairy series of 1936 but the glass itself is like those used for the Disney Athletic Series of 1937. Has bulbous and ribbed bottom. The image is noticeably smaller than that of the dairy glass. - **$40 $75 $125**

❑ **CLA-4. "Clarabelle Cow" Framed Picture By Reliance,**
1930s. 4.25x5.75" framed with image printed on back of glass. - **$50 $100 $150**

CLA-5

❑ **CLA-5. Clarabelle Mug,**
1930s. Wade Heath Ware Co., England. 3" tall ceramic mug. - **$125 $250 $350**

DAVY CROCKETT

CLA-6

CLA-7

☐ **CLA-6. Clarabelle Cow and Horace Horsecollar Bisques,**
1930s. Japan. 5" tall. Each - $200 $400 $800

☐ **CLA-7. Clarabelle Cow and Horace Horsecollar Dolls,**
1930s. 27" tall. Unmarked, likely homemade possibly from Charlotte Clark McCall pattern. Each - $100 $200 $400

CLA-8

☐ **CLA-8. Horace Horsecollar And Clarabelle The Cow Dolls,**
1950s. Lars Of Italy. Each doll is about 6x7x19" tall. Almost entirely made of felt with stuffed bodies that have wire inserts in arms and legs for posing. Each has hard plastic eyes, Clarabelle has wood bead necklace and a purse attached to one arm. Production of dolls from 1950s into the 1970s. While these were licensed by Disney, they were not to be sold in the U.S.A. resulting in their rarity. Each - $600 $1200 $2500

Darby O'Gill and the Little People

Based on the stories of H.T. Kavanagh, this full-length, live-action feature was released in 1959. Darby is the caretaker at an Irish estate and he is trying to play matchmaker for his daughter. He has one particular young man in mind. Darby captures Brian, the King of the Leprechauns and he is naturally granted three wishes. His daughter almost loses her life in an accident, but Darby uses his wishes to save her. She is then married, and Darby ends up telling a lot of leprechaun tales.

The story was reputedly one of Disney's personal favorites and the film shows the care and effort everyone put into it. The special effects are done so well that, even today, they still amaze viewers. Directed by Robert Stevenson, the film features Albert Sharpe, Janet Munro and Jimmy O'Dea. The film is also famous for being one of the earliest screen appearances by Sean Connery. Fans still love to hear him sing. The film proved to be a durable success for Disney. It saw re-release in 1969 and 1977.

Merchandise included books and records.

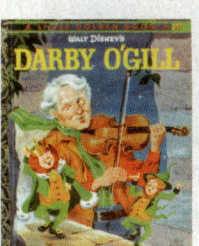

DAR-1   DAR-2

☐ **DAR-1. "Darby O'Gill Little Golden Book,"**
1959. 6.25x8" first printing by Golden Press. 24 pages. - $5 $15 $30

☐ **DAR-2. "Darby O'Gill And The Little People" Movie Comic Book,**
1970. Gold Key reprint of Four Color Comic #1024. - $5 $20 $60

Davy Crockett

Who would have thought that a frontier scout, bear and Indian fighter, who was also a congressman, statesman, and had died at the Alamo in 1836, would turn out to be one of the biggest success stories in the history of early television? When Davy Crockett's story was first shown on the *Disneyland* TV show in 1954, the country went crazy. The song *The Ballad of Davy Crockett* shot to the top of the charts. Overnight, almost every kid in America was wearing a coonskin cap, or at least trying to get his parents to buy them one.

Between 1954 and 1956, Davy Crockett starred in five one-hour episodes of the Walt Disney TV show. In order, they were *Davy Crockett, Indian Fighter*; *Davy Crockett Goes to Congress*; *Davy Crockett at the Alamo*; *Davy Crockett's Keelboat Race*; and finally *Davy Crockett and the River Pirates*. The television features were so incredibly popular that Disney edited the first three into a theatrical release titled *Davy Crockett, King of the Wild Frontier*. The TV episodes received an Emmy in 1956.

The actors who portrayed Davy and his friend George Russel, Fess Parker and Buddy Ebsen respectively, became stars. Disney knew he was going to use Ebsen from the start, but he was unsure about who could play Davy. The problem was solved when Fess Parker showed up to audition for the role. They knew they had their man. The national craze these shows spawned may be the best example you could ever find to demonstrate the incredible selling power of television. Disney eventually licensed over 500 products. He appears in *Four Color Comics* #631, 639, 664 and 671. *Dell Giants* lists *Davy Crockett, King of the Wild Frontier*.

Merchandise included the obvious coonskin cap, but with so many licensed and unlicensed items out there, it is almost impossible to keep track!

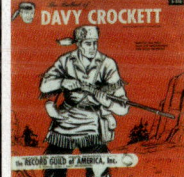

DVY-1

DVY-2

☐ **DVY-1. "The Ballad Of Davy Crockett" Record,**
1953. Record Guild of America, Inc. 45-rpm record features "The Ballad Of Davy Crockett (From The Walt Disney Production)." Backed with "Songs For Bronco Busters." - $10 $20 $45

☐ **DVY-2. "Walt Disney's The Ballad Of Davy Crockett" Premium Record,**
1954. Derby Peter Pan Peanut Butter. 7.5x7.5" mailing envelope serves as the sleeve and contains 78 rpm. - $15 $30 $55

DAVY CROCKETT

DVY-3

❑ **DVY-3. Davy Crockett Watch in Box,**
1954. WIth plastic gunpowder horn. Musical piece on top of horn that makes it blow is sometimes missing. Also has rawhide string that attaches to each end of the horn.
Complete - **$600**
Watch Only - **$35 $75 $150**

DVY-4

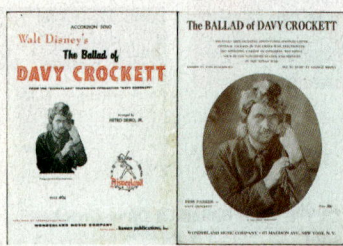

DVY-5

❑ **DVY-4. Davy Crockett Sheet Music,**
1954. Music is 9x12". - **$5 $15 $30**

❑ **DVY-5. "The Ballad Of Davy Crockett" Sheet Music,**
1954. Two From Wonderland Music Co. 9x12" folders with variation cover design. Each - **$5 $12 $20**

DVY-6

❑ **DVY-6. "Official Davy Crockett Indian Fighter Hat,"**
1955. Weathermac Corp. 9x13x2.75" deep box contains actual animal fur coonskin cap.
Box - **$100 $200 $300**
Hat - **$75 $150 $250**

DVY-7

❑ **DVY-7. "Davy Crockett King Of The Wild Frontier" Travel Case,**
1955. Neevel. 6x12x10.5" tall nice quality case constructed of wood and sturdy cardboard with simulated leather covering. Has flocking accent on lower half of Davy, teepee, bear, all text but name "Crockett." - **$50 $125 $215**

DVY-8

❑ **DVY-8. "Davy Crockett" Movie Poster,**
1955. Half-sheet is 22x28" stiff paper. - **$65 $125 $225**

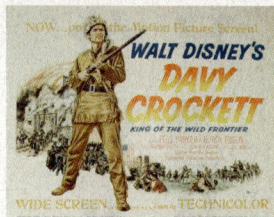

DAVY CROCKETT

DVY-9

☐ **DVY-9 "Davy Crockett King Of The Wild Frontier" Lobby Card Set,** 1955. Set of eight each 11x14" featuring various scenes from the film.
Set - **$200 $400 $600**

DVY-10

☐ **DVY-10. "Davy Crockett" Punch-Out Book,** 1955. Whitman. 10x14.75" with six pages. Un-Punched - **$20 $45 $85**

DVY-11

DVY-12

☐ **DVY-11. "Official Davy Crockett Frame-Tray Puzzle,"** 1955. Whitman. 11.5x15". - **$10 $20 $45**

☐ **DVY-12. Frame Tray Puzzle,** 1955. Jaymar. 9.75x12.75" **$12 $20 $40**

DVY-13

DVY-14

☐ **DVY-13. Frame Tray Puzzle,** 1955. Jaymar. 9.75x12.75" **$12 $20 $40**

☐ **DVY-14. "Official Davy Crockett" Frame Tray Puzzle,** 1955. Jaymar. 9.75x12.75". - **$15 $25 $40**

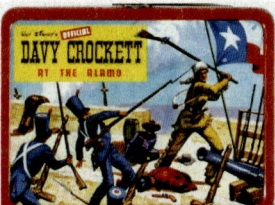

DVY-15

DVY-16

☐ **DVY-15. "Davy Crockett" Lunch Box,** 1955. Adco Liberty Corp. 7x9x4" deep metal. - **$125 $250 $800**

☐ **DVY-16. "Davy Crockett" Canadian Lunch Box,** 1955. Kruger Mfg. Co. Ltd. 7x9x4" deep metal. - **$175 $350 $1000**

DVY-17

☐ **DVY-17. "Davy Crockett" TV Tray,** 1955. Tin litho 12.5x17.25x1" deep. - **$50 $100 $160**

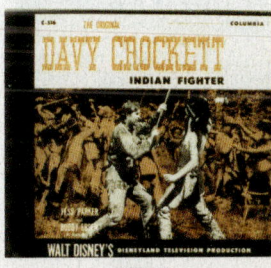

DVY-18

DAVY CROCKETT

DVY-19

☐ **DVY-18. "Davy Crockett Indian Fighter" Boxed Record Set,**
1955. Columbia. 10.25x11.75x.75" deep cardboard box with two 78 rpm records. From a series of three different, each featuring a different episode of the TV Show. This is Set C-518. Has episode which aired December 15, 1954. Each - **$35 $60 $100**

☐ **DVY-19. "Davy Crockett Indian Fighter" Record,**
1955. Columbia Records. 7x7" cardboard sleeve containing single 45 rpm two-part EP record B-2031 based on "Disneyland Television Production." - **$35 $60 $100**

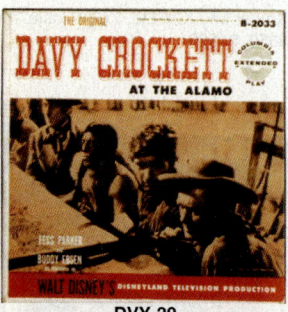

DVY-20

☐ **DVY-20. "Davy Crockett At The Alamo" Record,**
1955. Columbia Records. 7x7" cardboard sleeve containing single 45 rpm two-part EP record B-2033 based on "Disneyland Television Production." - **$35 $60 $100**

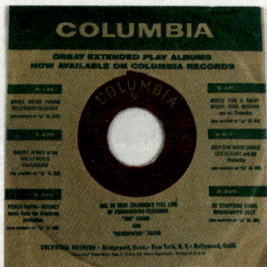

DVY-21

☐ **DVY-21. "Fess Parker As Davy Crockett" Record,**
1955. Columbia Records. 7x7" sleeve containing single 45 rpm record of "King Of The River/Yaller Yaller Gold" songs from "From Walt Disney's Disneyland TV Program." - **$12 $25 $45**

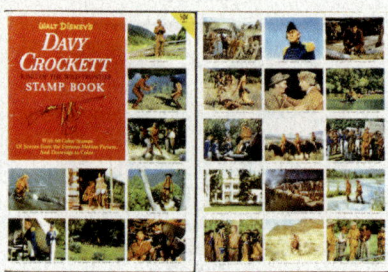

DVY-22

☐ **DVY-22. "Davy Crockett Stamp Book,"**
1955. Simon & Schuster. 8.25x10.75" with 32 pages. Inside front cover has stamp pages with gummed backs. Unused - **$15 $40 $90** Stamps Mounted - **$10 $25 $55**

DVY-23

☐ **DVY-23. "Davy Crockett Indian Fighter Brigade" Premium Club Kit,**
1955. Gimbel's of Philadelphia. Kit includes mailing envelope, 5x7" glossy fan picture, and 2.75x3.75 "Offishul" membership card. Complete - **$50 $100 $165**

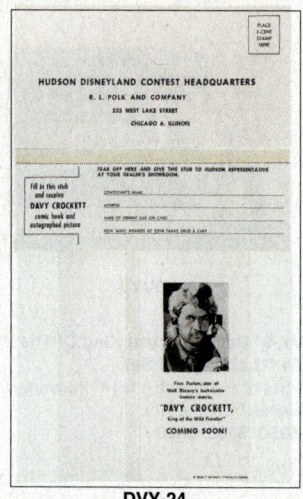

DVY-24

☐ **DVY-24. "Hudson Disneyland Contest" Folder Featuring Crockett,**
1955. Closed 6.5x7.25" mailer opening to 17" announcement for contest with grand prize of trip to Disneyland plus a new Hudson Hornet, Wasp or Rambler automobile. Other panels mention prizes of an "autographed" Fess Parker as Davy Crockett picture and Davy Crockett comic book obtained locally from Hudson dealer. - **$12 $25 $40**

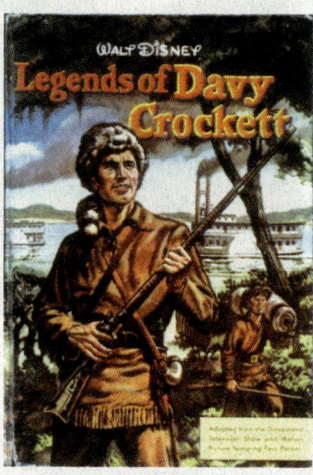

DVY-25

DAVY CROCKETT

❑ **DVY-25. "Legends Of Davy Crockett,"**
1955. Whitman. Hardcover measuring 5.5x7.75" with 288 pages and stories "Adapted From The Disneyland Television Show And Motion Picture." - **$15 $30 $60**

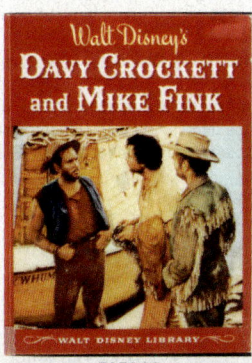
DVY-26

❑ **DVY-26. "Davy Crockett And Mike Fink" Hardcover,**
1955. Simon & Schuster. 8.5x11" with 48 pages. - **$20 $50 $80**

DVY-27

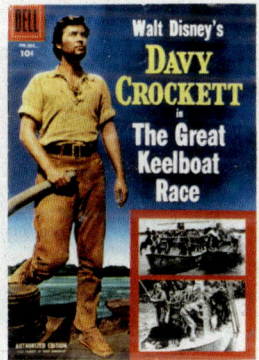
DVY-28

❑ **DVY-27. "Davy Crockett In The Raid At Piney Creek" Premium Comic Book,**
1955. Hudson Division Of American Motors. 5x7.25" with 16 pages. - **$10 $25 $60**

❑ **DVY-28. "Davy Crockett In The Great Keelboat Race" Comic Book,**
1955. Dell. Issue #664 from the Four Color Series. - **$20 $50 $230**

DVY-29

❑ **DVY-29. "Davy Crockett And The River Pirates" Comic Book,**
1955. Dell. Issue #671 from the Four Color Series. - **$20 $50 $230**

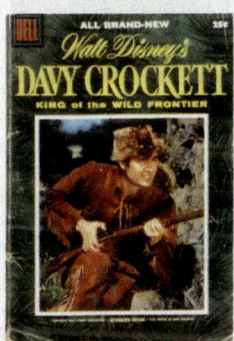
DVY-30

❑ **DVY-30. "Davy Crockett" First Issue Comic Book,**
1955. Dell. Issue #1 of Dell Giant with 96 pages. - **$20 $60 $360**

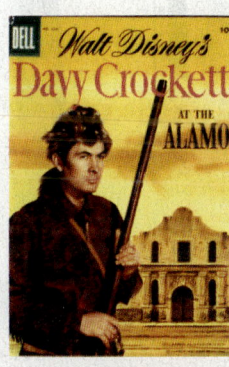
DVY-31

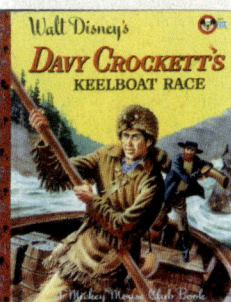
DVY-32

❑ **DVY-31. "Davy Crockett At The Alamo" Comic Book,**
1955. Dell Publishing Co. Four Color Series issue #639. - **$20 $50 $245**

❑ **DVY-32. "Davy Crockett Keelboat Race,"**
1955. Simon & Schuster. 6.75x8" designed like a Little Golden Book but marked "A Mickey Mouse Club Book." 24 pages. - **$12 $25 $45**

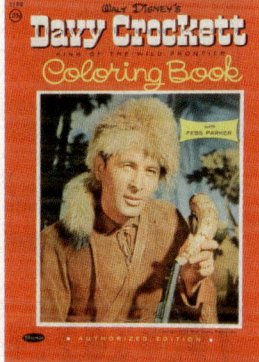

DVY-33

❑ **DVY-33. "Davy Crockett Coloring Book" With Cut-Out Coonskin Cap,**
1955. Whitman. 8.25x10.75". - **$20 $40 $100**

151

DAVY CROCKETT

DVY-34

DVY-37

❏ **DVY-39. Tru-Vue Film Card,**
1955. Card is 3.75x5.5" stereo views card "D-15 Pioneer" with full color Crockett TV film scenes. - **$8 $15 $25**

❏ **DVY-40. "Davy Crockett" Miniature Pocketknife,**
1955. Imperial. Knife is 2.25" long with hard plastic grips and variety with single retractable blade plus stationary hatchet blade. - **$40 $80 $135**

❏ **DVY-34. "Davy Crockett" Frontier Action Ring,**
1955. Karo Syrup. Dark green plastic ring holds brown and white flicker portrait of Davy holding and then aiming rifle to fire. Issued on a small display card. No Disney copyright but strong Fess Parker likeness.
Near Mint on Card - **$350**
Ring Only - **$50 $85 $165**

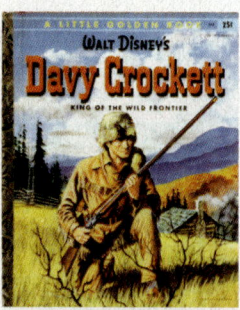

DVY-38

DVY-35

DVY-36

❏ **DVY-37. "Davy Crockett Rescue Race" Game,**
1955. Gabriel. 9.75x19.75x1.75" deep box contains board, spinner, cards, three dimensional Davy Crockett playing pieces and "Real Compass." - **$50 $125 $250**

❏ **DVY-38. "TV Guide" With Davy Crockett,**
1955. Vol. 3 #18, April 30. - **$35 $75 $150**

DVY-41

(rear view of chair)

DVY-39

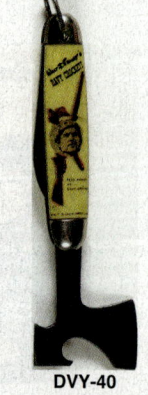

DVY-40

❏ **DVY-35. "Davy Crockett Little Golden Book,"**
1955. Simon & Schuster. 6.75x8" with 28 pages.
First Edition- **$8 $15 $30**
Others - **$3 $6 $10**

❏ **DVY-36. "Look" Magazine With Walt Disney/Davy Crockett,**
1955. Vol. 19 #15, July 26 is 10.5x13.25". - **$5 $10 $25**

❏ **DVY-41. "Davy Crockett" TV Chair,**
c. 1955. 13" diameter by 11" tall. Vinyl covered thick carboard with padded seat. - **$50 $100 $200**

DAVY CROCKETT

DVY-42

❑ **DVY-42. "Davy Crockett" Tool Kit,**
c. 1955. Liberty Steel Chest Corp. 6x16x3" deep metal case with an assortment of generic tools. - **$50 $110 $200**

DVY-43

DVY-44

DVY-45

❑ **DVY-43. "Walt Disney's Official Davy Crockett" Bowl,**
c. 1955. 2.5" deep and 5" diameter milk glass with various images around sides. - **$25 $50 $100**

❑ **DVY-44. "Davy Crockett" Childs Clothing Rack,**
c. 1955. 19x21x.5" thick die-cut pressed cardboard. Fess Parker portrait on the holster. - **$70 $150 $250**

❑ **DVY-45. "Davy Crockett Powder Horn,"**
c. 1955. 7" long plastic horn with original cord and illustrated box. Box - **$50 $100 $150**
Horn - **$50 $100 $150**

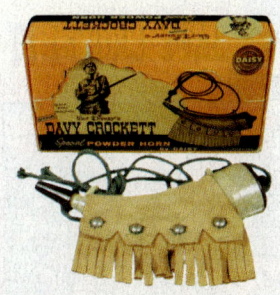

DVY-46

❑ **DVY-46. "Davy Crockett Special Powder Horn,"**
c. 1955. 7" long plastic horn with original cord, suede leather cover with metal stud and frindge trim. Illustrated box with die-cut lid.
Box - **$50 $100 $150**
Horn - **$50 $100 $150**

DVY-47

DVY-48

❑ **DVY-47. "Davy Crockett Push Puppet,"**
c.1955. Kohner Bros. 6" tall toy with original box. Near Mint Boxed - **$425**
Puppet Only - **$50 $100 $200**

❑ **DVY-48. "Davy Crockett" English Pinback Featuring Fess Parker,**
c. 1955. 1".- **$15 $35 $70**

DVY-49

❑ **DVY-49. "Davy Crockett" Belt With French Display Card,**
c. 1955. "La Veritable Gourde" 9.5x12.5" card and leatherette belt with 2x3.5" cast metal buckle. Belt has silk-screened designs including "Frontierland," silhouette images of Davy and Indians, text "Walt Disney's Davy Crockett." Silver buckle has same text plus raised rifle and powder horn design. Belt - **$15 $30 $50** Card - **$15 $30 $50**

DVY-50

DAVY CROCKETT

DVY-51

DVY-55

DVY-56

DVY-54

DVY-57

❑ **DVY-50 "Davy Crockett Braces,"** c. 1955. Stiff cardboard display is 5x12" and holds stretch fabric suspenders with chromed metal clips. - **$20 $40 $75**

❑ **DVY-51. "Davy Crockett Artcraft Magic Paint With Water Pictures" Boxed Set,** c. 1955. Artcraft Paper Products. 9.5x12.5x1" deep box contains complete set. Contents include thick diecut cardboard pieces covered by tiny paint dots, completed when water is applied. - **$25 $60 $125**

DVY-52

❑ **DVY-52. "Davy Crockett Balloon Toss-Up,"** c. 1955. Oak Rubber Co. 5.25x6.5" sealed with original shrink wrap. Object was to inflate the balloon and attach it to the feet so that when tossed in the air, it would then land on the feet. - **$20 $40 $65**

DVY-53

❑ **DVY-53. "Davy Crockett" Publicity Photos,** c. 1955. Each 8x10" glossy is complete with attached "ABC Television Photo" text sheet. Three are for "Davy Crockett Goes To Congress," one is "Davy Crockett, Indian Fighter." Each - **$10 $18 $30**

❑ **DVY-54. TV Publicity Photos,** c. 1955. Four 8x10" scenes from Disneyland show, each with "ABC Television Photo" caption sheet. Each - **$10 $18 $30**

❑ **DVY-55. "Davy Crockett Puzzle,"** c. 1955. Jaymar. 7.5x10.25x2.25" deep box contains puzzle titled "Defending The Fort" with colorful action scene. Assembled size is 14x19". - **$15 $30 $60**

❑ **DVY-56. "Davy Crockett" Bread End Label,** c. 1955. Waxed paper is 2.75x2.75" with text "Davy's Favorite Enriched Bread." Each - **$15 $30 $45**

DVY-58

❑ **DVY-57. "Davy Crockett Candies And Toy" Box,** c. 1955. Super Novelty Co. 2.5x3.75x1" deep empty box from series with punchout front and back panels. This is "In Congress" variety. Each - **$25 $75 $110**

❑ **DVY-58. "Davy Crockett Candies And Toy" Box,** c. 1955. Super Novelty Co. 2.5x3.75x1" deep empty box from series with punchout front and back panels. This is "At The Alamo" variety. Each - **$25 $75 $110**

DVY-59

DVY-60

DAVY CROCKETT

☐ **DVY-59. "Davy Crockett" Belgian Picture Card Album,**
c. 1955. Confectioner "De Beukelaer." 9x13" 64-page album with complete set of 125 thin paper picture cards. - **$50 $100 $160**

☐ **DVY-60. "Davy Crockett/Kit Carson" Lunch Box,**
c. 1955. Adco Liberty. 6.5x8.75x3.75" deep metal box version with red sides and color illustrations. Front has "Walt Disney's Official Davy Crockett At The Alamo" scene and reverse is "Kit Carson" and "Walt Disney's Frontierland." Top has small black and white portrait of Fess Parker and "An Official Disneyland Product." - **$60 $125 $275**

DVY-61

DVY-62

☐ **DVY-61. "Davy Crockett" Bread Label Clerk's Button,**
c. 1955. Celluloid is 2.25" with image made from a bread label and used by drivers and/or clerks to promote the product. - **$50 $100 $200**

☐ **DVY-62. "Davy Crockett" Premium Coonskin Cap,**
c. 1955. Peter Pan Bread, issued by various bread companies. 3.5x24.5" diecut stiff paper. Also issued with tail attachment. - **$10 $20 $40**

DVY-63

DVY-64

☐ **DVY-63. "Davy Crockett" Boxed English Soap Figure,**
c. 1955. Cusson. 3x6x2.5" deep box with 5" tall fully painted figural soap. - **$25 $50 $85**

☐ **DVY-64. "Star Cinemas Davy Crockett" Celluloid Button,**
c. 1955. United Kingdom. 1.25". - **$75 $125 $225**

DVY-65

DVY-66

☐ **DVY-65. "Fess Parker As Davy Crockett" Wash Mitt Hand Puppet,**
c. 1955. Terrycloth is 8x8.5". - **$20 $35 $60**

☐ **DVY-66. "Davy Crockett Toothbrush" On Card,**
c. 1955. Dupont. 3.25x6.25" stiff glossy paper card has attached 5" long hard plastic toothbrush. Carded - **$20 $40 $80**
Brush Only - **$10 $20 $30**

DVY-68

☐ **DVY-67. "Davy Crockett" Clothing Tags,**
c. 1955. Blue Bell Inc. Pair of 3x3.75" and 4.5x8" stiff paper attachments for jeans or other clothing, both picturing Fess Parker as Crockett. Each - **$12 $25 $40**

☐ **DVY-68. "Davy Crockett Indian Fighter" Party Plate,**
c. 1955. Plate measures 8.5x8.5" made of cardboard. - **$5 $15 $25**

DVY-69

DVY-70

☐ **DVY-69. "Davy Crockett/Fess Parker" Bath Towel And Wash Cloths,**
c. 1955. Cannon. 19x37" towel and pair of identical 10.5x12" wash cloths. Set - **$25 $60 $115**

☐ **DVY-70. "Davy Crockett" Charm Bracelet,**
c. 1955. Display card is 2.5x6.5" holding 5.5" long metal link bracelet with seven charms of framed glossy photo, Davy on horseback, Indian, knife, crossed rifles, Liberty Bell and bear. Near Mint Carded - **$100** Loose - **$15 $30 $60**

DVY-71

DAVY CROCKETT

DVY-72

❑ **DVY-71. "Davy Crockett" Cuff Links/Tie Bar,**
c. 1955. Display card measuring 3x3.25" contains goldtone metal frames with black and white Crockett photo insert under clear plastic cover. Cuff links are each 1" tall and tie bar is 1.75" long. Carded Set - **$25 $50 $80** Loose Set - **$15 $30 $60**

❑ **DVY-72. "Davy Crockett" Wallet,**
c. 1955. Fully opened size is 3.5x9" brown vinyl. Davy has simulated fur coonskin cap. Variety with both light and dark brown spots on cap. - **$10 $20 $40**

DVY-73

❑ **DVY-73. "Davy Crockett" Wallet,**
c. 1955. Fully opened size is 3.5x9" brown vinyl. Davy's simulated fur cap has just dark brown spots against white and his shirt and stockade fence and towers are not painted in a different shade of brown, rather in just the brown vinyl of the wallet itself. Also the green on the trees and bushes is a noticeably lighter shade. - **$10 $20 $40**

DVY-74

❑ **DVY-74. "Davy Crockett Ge-Tar",**
c. 1955. Mattel. 14" tall hard plastic guitar with original box. Crank mechanism activates music box. Guitar - **$25 $50 $100** Box - **$15 $40 $75**

DVY-75

❑ **DVY-75. "Walt Disney's Official Davy Crockett Guitar,"**
c. 1955. Peter Puppet Playthings. 12.5x25x2.5" box is designed as a carrying case containing 24.5" long guitar. Guitar is wood with tin neck plate and stiff cardboard sides. At top between tuning pegs is paper label with Davy Crockett portrait. Has attached shoulder cord as well as cord to hold pick which is same shape as guitar's body. Set includes a song book and instruction booklet. Boxed - **$100 $200 $400** Guitar Only - **$50 $100 $200**

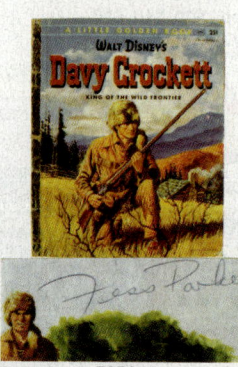
DVY-76

DVY-77

❑ **DVY-76. "Davy Crockett Little Golden Book" Signed By Fess Parker,**
c. 1955. Simon & Schuster. First printing 6.75x8" with 28 pages. The copyright page is boldly signed. Signed - **$25 $50 $100**

❑ **DVY-77. "Official Davy Crockett Frontier Bag" Boxed,**
c. 1955. National Leather Mfg. Co. Inc. 13x13x3.5" deep box contains nice quality bag to be used as a "School Bag/Utility Bag/Travel Bag." The bag is canvas with vinyl trim including fringes around three front sides, front flap is stiff embossed leatherette. Box - **$100 $200 $300** Bag - **$125 $250 $350**

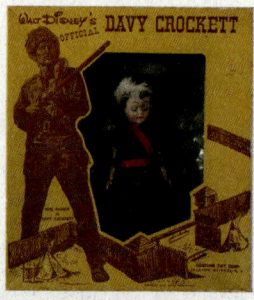
DVY-78

DAVY CROCKETT

DVY-79

◻ **DVY-78. "Davy Crockett" Boxed Doll,**
c. 1955. Fortune Toy Corp. 9.5x10.75x2" deep box with display window contains 7" tall hard plastic doll with movable arms and head, sleep eyes. - **$60 $125 $210**

◻ **DVY-79. "Davy Crockett At The Alamo" Playset,**
c. 1955. Marx. 11x23x3" deep box holding playset #3530 pictured on lid. - **$300 $600 $1200**

DVY-80

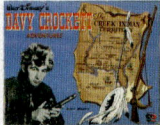
DVY-81

◻ **DVY-80. "Davy Crockett" Peace Pipe,**
c. 1955. Pipe is 11" long with wood body and plastic mouthpiece. - **$30 $65 $90**

◻ **DVY-81. "Davy Crockett Adventures" Game,**
c. 1955. Gardner Games. 10.25x13.5x1.5" deep box. - **$65 $125 $200**

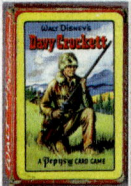
DVY-82

◻ **DVY-82. "Davy Crockett" English Card Game,**
c. 1955. Pepys. 2.5x3.5x.75" deep box contains complete deck of 44 cards and instruction booklet. - **$50 $125 $200**

DVY-83

◻ **DVY-83. "Davy Crockett Official Wagon Train" Boxed Marx Wind-Up,**
c. 1955. 1.5x14x2.75" tall toy with built-in key comes in box nicely illustrated on all panels. The toy consists of hard plastic horse-drawn stagecoach and three tin litho cars.
Box - **$35 $75 $150**
Toy - **$75 $150 $250**

DVY-84

◻ **DVY-84. "Davy Crockett Frontier Wagon" English Replica,**
c. 1955. Believed By Lesney. 2x7x3" tall cast metal free-wheeling covered wagon with movable hitch, four removable horses, removable driver, pair of cover braces that a fabric wagon cover slips over. - **$50 $115 $175**

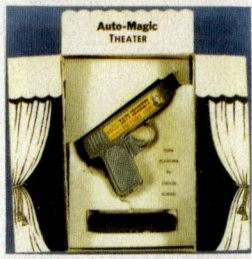

DVY-85

◻ **DVY-85. "Official Davy Crockett Auto-Magic Picture Gun,"**
c. 1955. Stephens Products Co. 7x9.25x2.75" deep box with 5.25" long cast metal gun and four 16mm filmstrips: three Davy, one "Little Hiawatha." - **$100 $200 $350**

DVY-86

◻ **DVY-86. "Davy Crockett Tru-Vue Film Card,"**
c. 1955. Card is 3.75x5.5" with photos from the TV show. "D-14/Indian Fighter." - **$8 $15 $25**

DAVY CROCKETT

DVY-87

❑ **DVY-87. "Davy Crockett Tru-Vue Film Card,"**
c. 1955. Card is 3.75x5.5" with photos from the TV show. "D-16/Battle Of The Alamo." - **$8 $15 $25**

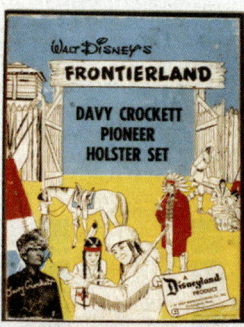

DVY-88

❑ **DVY-88. "Frontierland Davy Crockett Pioneer Holster Set,"**
c. 1955. L. M. Eddy Mfg. Co. 8.25x10x2" deep box. - **$100 $200 $325**

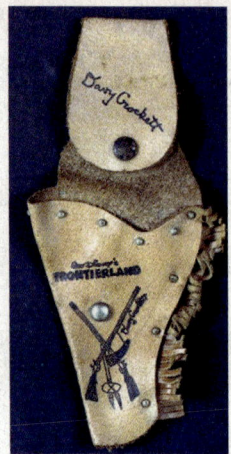

DVY-89

❑ **DVY-89. Crockett/Frontierland Holster,**
c. 1955. Leather single holster is 5x11" with design including Davy Crockett signature on belt flap with snap. Holster itself includes text "Walt Disney's Frontierland" and design with crossed rifles. - **$25 $50 $85**

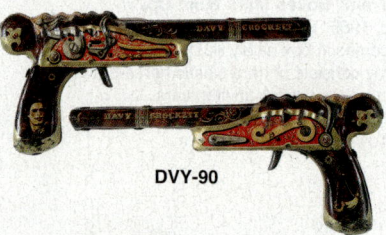

DVY-90

❑ **DVY-90. "Davy Crockett" Click Pistol,**
c. 1955. Marx. 10" long tin lithographed gun designed like flintlock pistol with ornate detailing plus marking, "Walt Disney Productions." - **$75 $150 $275**

DVY-91

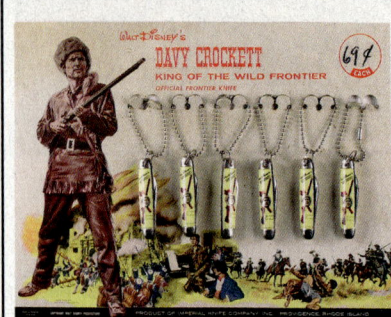

DVY-92

❑ **DVY-91. "Davy Crockett/King Of The Wild Frontier" Button With Knife,**
c. 1955. Button is 1.25" in diameter with attached orange ribbon holding a black leather sheath and small metal knife with plastic handle.
Button with knife - **$25 $50 $75**
Button only - **$15 $25 $50**

❑ **DVY-92. "Davy Crockett" Pocket Knife,**
c. 1955. Imperial Knife Co. 3.5" long. - **$25 $50 $90**

DAVY CROCKETT

DVY-93

❏ **DVY-93. "Davy Crockett" Pencil Case,**
c. 1955. Vinyl case is 4x8.5x1.5" deep with zippered closure along top edge. - **$12 $25 $50**

DVY-94

❏ **DVY-94. "Official Davy Crockett Frontierland Pencil Case,"**
c. 1955. 6.5x8.5" vinyl with attached shoulder strap. Contents include composition book and sealed pack containing assortment of pencils and a ruler. One pencil marked "Davy Crockett - King Of The Frontierland." Complete - **$35 $65 $125**

DVY-95

❏ **DVY-95. Crockett/Frontierland Pencil Case,**
c. 1955. Hassenfeld Bros. 4.25x8.75x1" deep paper-covered cardboard box with slide-out storage tray holding school supplies including supply of lead pencils marked "Davy Crockett- King Of The Wild Frontierland." - **$20 $40 $85**

DVY-96

❏ **DVY-96. "Davy Crockett Frontierland Pencil Case" Holster,**
c. 1955. Vinyl holster measures 4x7.5" with belt loop containing hard plastic gun-shaped pencil case. Holster - **$25 $50 $80** Pencil Case - **$10 $20 $40**

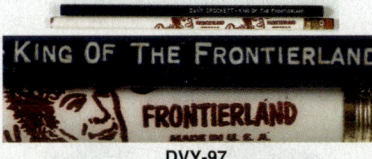

DVY-97

❏ **DVY-97. "Davy Crockett" Pencils,**
c. 1955. Two 7" or 7.5" long unsharpened lead pencils. Text is either "Davy Crockett-King Of The Frontierland" or "Davy Crockett Frontierland" with pair of portrait images. Each - **$5 $10 $15**

DVY-98

❏ **DVY-98. Leatherette Jacket,**
c. 1955. Store bought. TV merchandise. - **$75 $250 $475**

DVY-99

❏ **DVY-99. "Davy Crockett" Flintlock Pistol,**
c. 1955. Marx. 10.75" long plastic body and gold accents with name on one side of barrel. Has metal firing plate for caps. - **$35 $75 $160**

DVY-100

❏ **DVY-100. Davy Crockett Figure,**
c. 1955. Marx. 1-7/8" tall soft plastic issued with various 1950s Marx playsets. Underside reads "Official Davy Crockett As Portrayed By Fess Parker." - **$10 $20 $40**

159

DAVY CROCKETT

DVY-101

❏ **DVY-101. "Davy Crockett" Green Back Variety Gum Cards,**
1956. Topps. Set of 80, each 2-5/8x3.75". Second set "Series A." Set - **$200 $400 $800**

DVY-102

❏ **DVY-102. "Davy Crockett" Orange Back Variety Gum Card Set,**
1956. Topps. 80 cards, each 2.75x3.75". Set - **$120 $240 $320**

DVY-103

❏ **DVY-103. "Walt Disney Magazine,"**
1956. Volume 1, #3 from summer 1956 measures 8.25x11.5" with 44 pages. Shows Annette and Fess parker with "New Frontiers At Disneyland" article. - **$15 $35 $80**

DVY-104

❏ **DVY-104. "Davy Crockett" Reprint Comic Book,**
1963. Gold Key reprint copyright 1955. - **$20 $50 $230**

DVY-105

❏ **DVY-105. "Walt Disney's Three Adventures Of Davy Crockett" Record,**
1968. Disneyland. 12.25x12.25" cardboard cover contains 33-1/3 rpm. - **$10 $20 $45**

DVY-106

❏ **DVY-106. Davy Crockett Photo Signed By Fess Parker/Buddy Ebsen,**
1980s. Glossy photo is 8x10". - **$75 $150 $275**

DVY-107

❏ **DVY-107. "Davy Crockett Indian Fighter Hat" Photo Signed By Designer,**
2001. Publicity photo is 6x8" of packaging box for coonskin cap. Box design is by "Disney Legend" Al Konetzni. Bottom margin has notation "Orig. Photo/The Very First 'Davy' Item Made/Package Design" followed by Konetzni's signature. Mint - **$100**

DELL GIANT COMICS

Dell Giant Comics

Until 1949, almost all comics were held together by staples. Always looking for ways to expand their publishing business, Dell experimented with a new type of comic, one that had only been attempted a few times before, a square-bound book that could hold many more pages than the conventional comic.

For the first issue in this new approach to comic publishing, Dell went straight to one of their most reliable properties, Walt Disney. Titled *Christmas Parade*, the book sold for a quarter and was an immediate hit. The book had 132 pages, which made stapling almost impossible. The public loved the stories and the high number of pages. Shortly after *Christmas Parade* introduced the line, the page count was reduced to 100, but the public still loved the Giants. None of the *Dell Giants* published with Disney characters ever had ad pages, so they were a dream for comic readers of the day. Some issues were eventually printed using staples, but they are in the minority.

For the first ten years of publication, the *Dell Giants* were not sequentially numbered. They are only known by their title and the issue number of that title. As the collecting hobby grew, the different titles gradually became grouped together under the banner of *Dell Giants*. Since there was no cohesive numbering system for the books in the first ten years of their publication, we have listed the books in a strict chronological order. When a month of publication was not known, we have placed that title at the end of the calendar year. It is only fitting that the Disney run of Dell giants began with a Christmas Special in 1949 and ended in 1962 with another Christmas Special.

❑ Vacation Parade #1,
 July 1950. 132 pgs, Barks a. - **$82 $246 $1650**

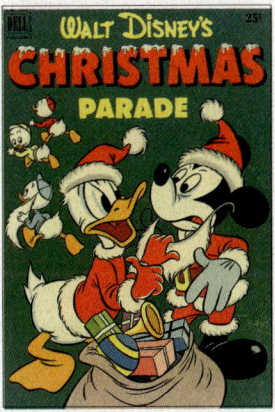

❑ Christmas Parade #3,
1951. 116 pgs. - **$13 $69 $230**

❑ Christmas Parade #2,
1950. 132 pgs, Barks-a. - **$40 $120 $800**

❑ Vacation Parade #3,
July 1952. - **$13 $39 $260**

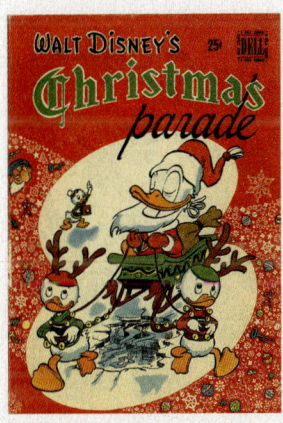

❑ Christmas Parade #1,
November 1949. 1st Dell Giant, 132 pgs, Barks-a. - **$55 $165 $1100**

❑ Vacation Parade #2,
July 1951. 116 pgs. - **$24 $72 $475**

❑ Silly Symphonies #1,
September 1952. - **$27 $81 $550**

DELL GIANT COMICS

❑ **Christmas Parade #4,**
1952. 100 pgs. - **$13 $69 $230**

❑ **Vacation Parade #5,**
July 1953. Becomes Picnic Party w/ #6. - **$13 $39 $260**

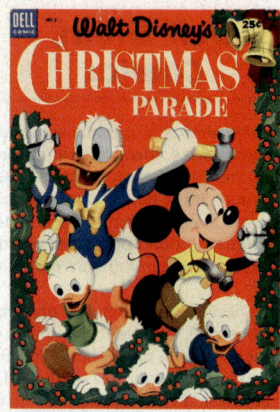

❑ **Christmas Parade #5,**
1953. - **$13 $69 $230**

❑ **Peter Pan Treasure Chest #1,**
January 1953. 54 pg movie adapt. 212 pgs total. - **$105 $315 $2100**

❑ **Mickey Mouse Birthday Party #1,**
September 1953. - **$29 $87 $585**

❑ **Donald Duck Fun Book #1,**
1953. - **$55 $165 $1100**

❑ **Vacation Parade #4,**
July 1953. - **$13 $39 $260**

❑ **Silly Symphonies #2,**
September 1953. Mickey Mouse in Sorcerer's Apprentice. - **$23 $69 $460**

❑ **Silly Symphonies #3,**
February 1954. - **$19 $57 $375**

DELL GIANT COMICS

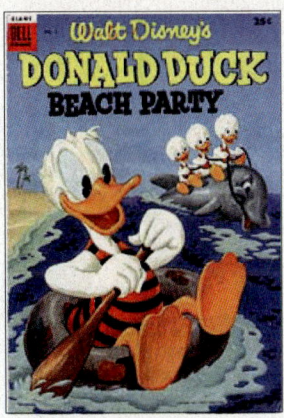
❏ **Donald Duck Beach Party #1,**
July 1954. - **$14 $42 $290**

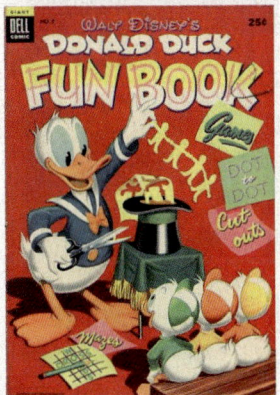
❏ **Donald Duck Fun Book #2,**
1954. - **$55 $165 $1100**

❏ **Picnic Party #6,**
July 1955. Formerly Vacation Parade. - **$11 $33 $220**

❏ **Silly Symphonies #4,**
August 1954. **$19 $57 $375**

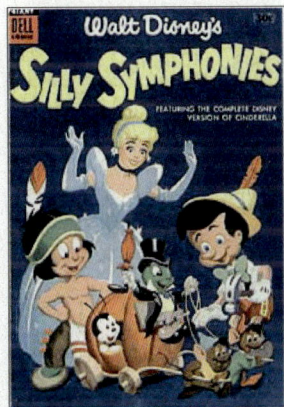
❏ **Silly Symphonies #5,**
February 1955. **$15 $45 $310**

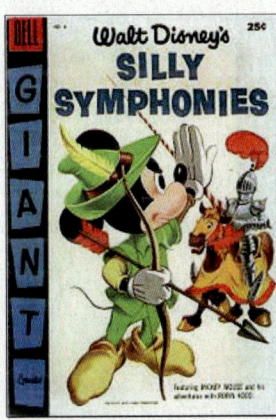
❏ **Silly Symphonies #6,**
August 1955. - **$15 $45 $310**

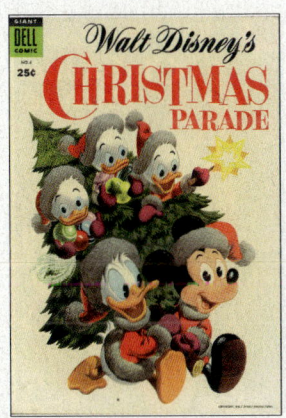
❏ **Christmas Parade #6,**
1954. - **$13 $69 $230**

❏ **Lady and the Tramp #1,**
June 1955. - **$15 $45 $310**

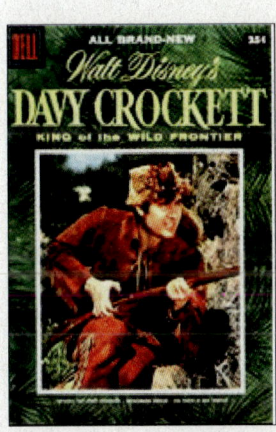
❏ **Davy Crockett, King of the Wild Frontier,**
September 1955. - **$18 $54 $360**

DELL GIANT COMICS

❑ **Donald Duck in Disneyland #1**,
September 1955. First Disneyland Dell Giant. - $14 $42 $275

❑ **Donald Duck Beach Party #2**,
1955.   Lady and the Tramp app.   - $10 $30 $210

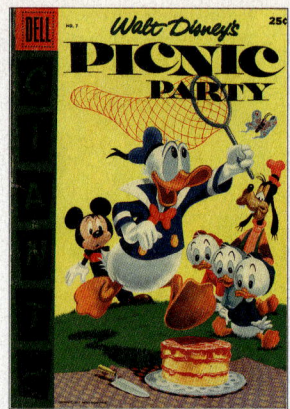

❑ **Picnic Party #7**,
June 1956. - $11 $33 $220

❑ **Mickey Mouse Club Parade #1**,
December 1955. - $21 $63 $425

❑ **Mickey Mouse in Fantasy Land #1**,
May 1956. - $12 $36 $240

❑ **Donald Duck Beach Party #3**,
1956. - $10 $30 $200

❑ **Christmas Parade #7**,
1955. - $13 $69 $230

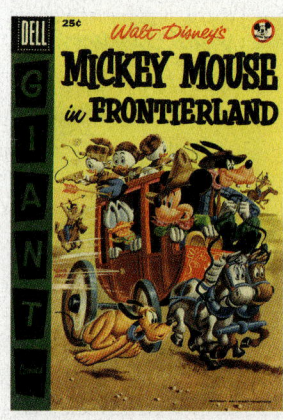

❑ **Mickey Mouse in Frontier Land #1**,
May 1956.   Mickey Mouse Club issue. - $12 $36 $240

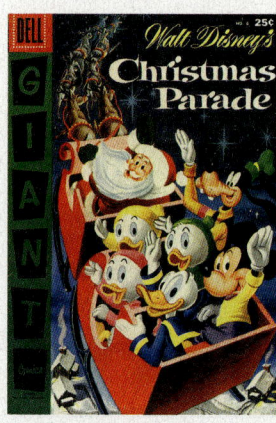

❑ **Christmas Parade #8**,
1956. Barks-a. - $20 $60 $410

DELL GIANT COMICS

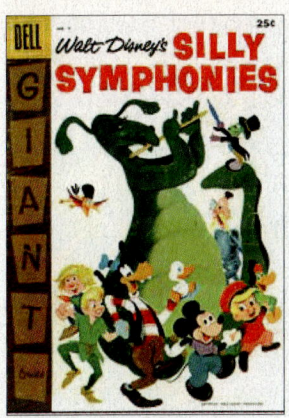
❏ **Silly Symphonies #7,**
February 1957. - **$15 $45 $310**

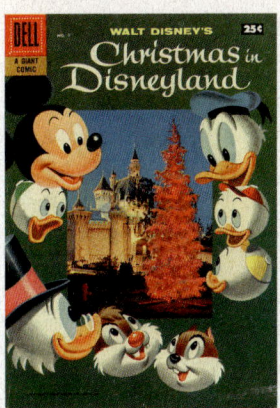
❏ **Christmas in Disneyland #1,**
December 1957. - **$24 $72 $475**

❏ **Silly Symphonies #8,**
February 1958. - **$15 $45 $310**

❏ **Picnic Party #8,**
July 1957. Barks-a. **$20 $60 $400**

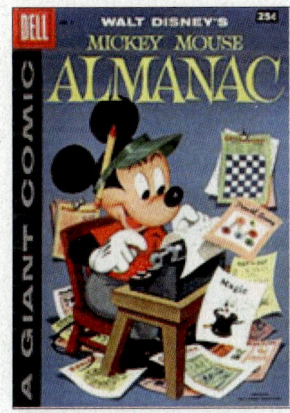
❏ **Mickey Mouse Almanac #1,**
December 1957. Barks-a. **$25 $75 $500**

❏ **Donald and Mickey in Disneyland #1,**
May 1958. - **$10 $30 $210**

❏ **Uncle Scrooge Goes to Disneyland #1,**
August 1957. Barks-a. - **$24 $144 $475**

❏ **Donald Duck Beach Party #4,**
1957. - **$10 $30 $200**

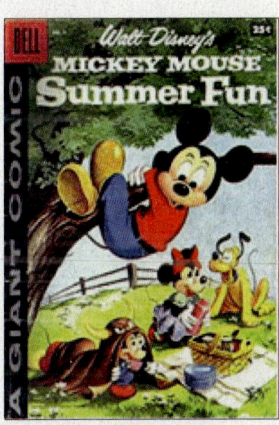
❏ **Mickey Mouse Summer Fun #1,**
August 1958. Becomes Summer Fun w/ #2. - **$12 $36 $240**

DELL GIANT COMICS

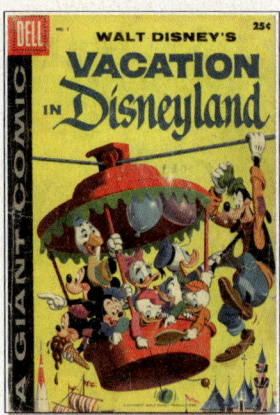

❏ **Vacation in Disneyland #1,**
August 1958. **$10 $30 $210**

❏ **Donald Duck Beach Party #5,**
1958. - $10 $30 $200

❏ **Sleeping Beauty #1,**
April 1959. **$25 $75 $500**

❏ **Huey, Dewey and Louie Back to School #1**
September 1958. - **$8 $24 $165**

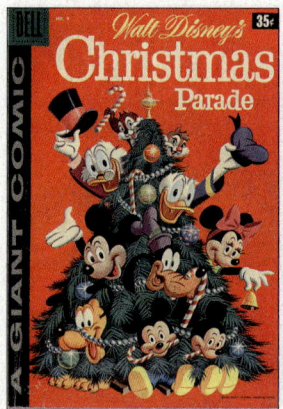

❏ **Christmas Parade #9,**
1958. Barks-a. - **$24 $72 $475.**

❏ **Donald Duck Beach Party #6,**
August 1959. 84 pgs, stapled. - **$7 $21 $150**

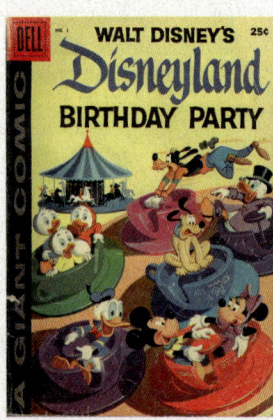

Disneyland Birthday Party #1,
October 1958. Barks-a. - **$24 $72 $475**

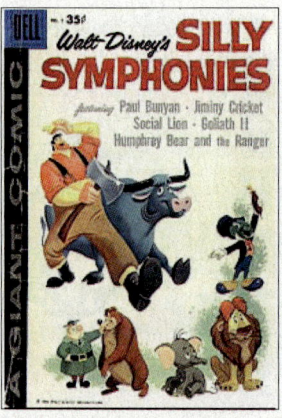

❏ **Silly Symphonies #9,**
February 1959. - **$14 $42 $290**

❏ **Summer Fun #2,**
August 1959. Formerly Mickey Mouse's, Barks-a. - **$24 $144 $475**

DELL GIANT COMICS

❏ **Huey, Dewey and Louie Back to School DG #22,**
October 1959. 84 pgs square binding begins.
$8 $24 $165.

❏ **Daisy Duck & Uncle Scrooge Picnic Time DG#33,**
September 1960. - $8 $24 $165

❏ **Walt Disney's Merry Christmas DG #39,**
December 1960. Cover based on pencil sketch by Barks. - $12 $36 $235

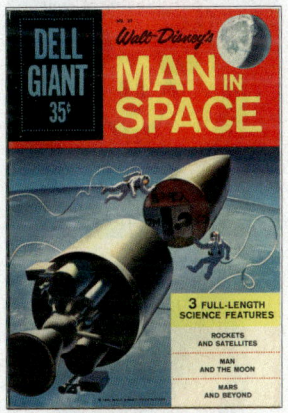

❏ **Walt Disney's Man in Space #1 DG#27,**
October 1959. 100 pgs. - $9 $27 $175

❏ **Huey, Dewey and Louie Back to School DG#35,**
October 1960. 1st app. of Daisy Duck's nieces. - $10 $30 $210.

❏ **Mickey and Donald in Vacationland DG#47,**
August 1961. - $8 $24 $155

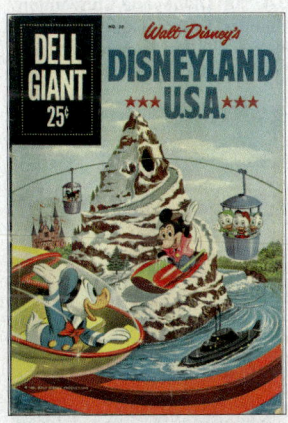

❏ **Disneyland USA (DG#30),**
June 1960. - $8 $24 $165

❏ **Uncle Donald and His Nephews Family Fun DG#38,**
November 1960. Cover art based on Barks pencil sketch. - $12 $36 $235

❏ **Daisy Duck and Uncle Scrooge Showboat DG#55,**
September 1961. - $8 $24 $165

DELL GIANT COMICS

❏ **Huey, Dewey and Louie Back to School DG#49,**
September 1961. - **$8 $24 $165**

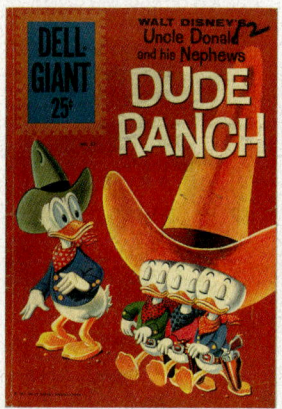

❏ **Uncle Donald and His Nephews Dude Ranch DG#52,**
November 1961. - **$7 $21 $145**

❏ **Donald Duck Merry Christmas DG#53,**
December 1962. - **$7 $21 $145**

Disneyana Convention

In 1992, The Walt Disney Company hosted its first convention designed solely for collectors of Disney items. Walt Disney World in Orlando, Florida hosted what would become, for a while, an annual event. Limited edition merchandise was made available to those who attended each convention. Special buttons and badges were given out as part of the arrival kit and each year featured a different theme. That theme was matched by a limited edition resin figure which was sold through a lottery drawing. All of this created instant collectibles which are highly sought on the secondary market.

DSC-1

❏ **DSC-1. "Steamboat Mickey" Figure,**
1990. First resin Convention figure produced, with only 600 made. Mickey is featured as the star of the 1928 cartoon *Steamboat Willie*. It sold out at the convention and is always in high demand in the secondary market because of it being the 1st in the series and the low number of figures produced. - **$1300**

DSC-2

❏ **DSC-2. "1st Convention" Pin on Card,**
1992. Pin is 1 1/2" high.
On original card - **$120**

DSC-3

❏ **DSC-3. First Disneyana Convention Button,**
1992. Limited issue for the historic first Disney-sponsored convention for collectors.
- **$5 $12 $25**

DSC-4

❏ **DSC-4. "1st Disneyana Convention" Boxed Limited Edition Collector's Plate,**
1992. Plate is 9.25" in diameter, limited to 500 pieces. Mint As Issued - **$100**

DSC-5

DISNEYANA CONVENTION

❑ **DSC-5. "1st Disneyana Convention Auction Catalog,"**
1992. Walt Disney World. 8.5x11" with 61 auction items. Limited distribution. - **$5 $15 $30**

DSC-6

❑ **DSC-6. "1st Disneyana Convention" Limited Edition Watch,**
1992. Limited Edition of 1500. Mint As Issued - **$220**

DSC-7

❑ **DSC-7. "Sorcerer's Apprentice" Figure,**
1993. Convention resin. Edition of 2,000. - **$275**

DSC-8

❑ **DSC-8. Mickey Mouse From "The Band Concert" Limited Edition Resin Figure,**
1993. Figure is 11.75" tall on 7x8.75x1.5" base. Edition of 1200. Mint As Issued - **$350**

DSC-9

❑ **DSC-9. "Official Disneyana Convention 1993" Boxed Limited Edition Watch,**
1993. Limited edition of 1800 for second Disneyana Convention. Mint As Issued - **$190**

DSC-10

❑ **DSC-10. "40th Anniversary of Disneyland",**
1994. Convention resin of Mickey and Minnie, limited to 1,500. - **$240**

DSC-11

❑ **DSC-11. "Official Disneyana Convention" Boxed Mickey As Sorcerer's Apprentice Sculpture,**
1994. Solid pewter figure is 4.75" tall. Limited edition of 2200. Mint As Issued - **$175**

DSC-12

DISNEYANA CONVENTION

DSC-13

❏ **DSC-12. "40 Years of Adventure" Pin,**
1995. On card. - **$35**

❏ **DSC-13. "40 Years of Adventure" Flicker Badge,**
1995. 4" diameter. - **$22**

DSC-14

❏ **DSC-14. "Mickey Mouse Club" Pin,**
1995. Limited edition pin promotes the anniversary of the show. On card. - **$22**

DSC-15

❏ **DSC-15 "Mickey Mouse Club" Figure,**
1995. Resin limited edition of 2,000. Sold out at the 1995 convention. - **$425**

DSC-16

❏ **DSC-16. "Brave Little Tailor" Figure,**
1996. Mickey Mouse featured in this limited resin figure of 1,500. Sold out at the 1996 convention. - **$450**

DSC-17

❏ **DSC-17. Carl Barks Signed Disneyana Convention Promo Card,**
1996. Card is 6.5x10.5". Mint As Issued - **$60**

DSC-18

❏ **DSC-18. "5th Convention" Pin on Card,**
1996. Theme of "Mickey and the Beanstalk." - **$25**

DSC-19

❏ **DSC-19. 1997 Official Pin,**
1997. Proclaims "I am a Convention Ear." 1 1/4" diameter. - **$30**

DSC-20

❏ **DSC-20. Disney Villains Pinback,**
1997. 4" diameter pinback with Convention theme. - **$25**

DSC-21

❏ **DSC-21. Villains Flicker Badge,**
1997. 4" diameter badge shows Chernobog from *Fantasia*. - **$25**

DISNEYANA CONVENTION

DSC-22

❏ **DSC-22. "Black Pete" Pin**, 1997. Promotes the Convention's Villain theme. - **$25**

DSC-23

❏ **DSC-23. "Peg Leg Pete" Figure**, 1997. Limited (1,000 made) resin figure of villain from cartoon *Steamboat Willie*. Sold out at the 1997 convention. - **$325**

DSC-24

❏ **DSC-24. "Carl Barks" Signed Baseball**, 1997. Signed at his birthday party in 1997 at the Disneyana convention. Mint - **$250**

DSC-25

❏ **DSC-25. Official Convention Pin**, 1998. 1 1/2" pin promotes "75 Years of Love and Laughter." - **$20**

DSC-26

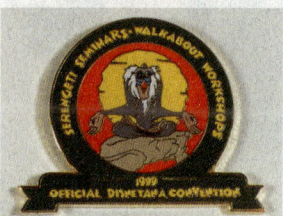

DSC-27

❏ **DSC-26. Safari Adventure Flicker Badge**, 1999. - **$10**

❏ **DSC-27. "Serengeti Seminars" Pin**, 1999. Special pin for those who attended Walkabout Workshops. Had *Lion King* theme. - **$10**

DSC-28

❏ **DSC-28. "The Pointer" Figure**, 1999. Mickey Mouse resin honoring the 1939 film *The Pointer*. Limited to 1,500. Sold out at the 1999 convention. - **$350**

DSC-29

DSC-30

DSC-31

❏ **DSC-29. "Mickey" Bean Figure**, 1999. With tag. 1999 Convention. - **$30**

❏ **DSC-30. "Minnie" Bean Figure**, 1999. With tag. 1999 Convention. - **$30**

❏ **DSC-31. "Mickey" Bean Figure**, 2000. With tag. 2000 Convention. - **$30**

DISNEYANA CONVENTION

DSC-32

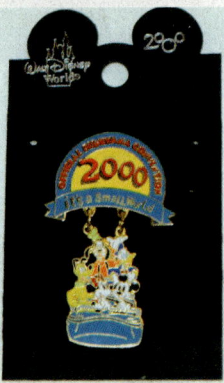

DSC-33

❏ **DSC-32. Convention Pin,**
2000. - **$45**

❏ **DSC-33. "It's a Small World" Badge With Pin Hanging,**
2000. On card. - **$45**

DSC-34

❏ **DSC-34 "It's a Small World" Resin Figure,**
2000. Only 1,000 made. - **$425**

DSC-35

DSC-36

❏ **DSC-35. California Adventure Pin Badge,**
2001. A Disney Family Reunion theme. - **$35**

❏ **DSC-36. Disneyana Pin,**
2001. Features shadow of Walt Disney in window telling Mickey to have fun at Walt's 100th Birthday Reunion Celebration. - **$35**

DSC-37

❏ **DSC-37. Promotional Plush,**
2001. Donald and his nephews take a ride to Walt's 100th Anniversary Reunion. Plush figures with tag. - **$65**

DSC-38

❏ **DSC-38. Pluto & Mickey Detectives,**
2002. Limited edition. - **$150**

Disneyland

"The Happiest Place on Earth" opened in Anaheim, California on July 17, 1955. The event was covered live by ABC-TV and it was hosted by Ronald Reagan and Art Linkletter. Less than a year earlier, in October 1954, the *Disneyland* TV show had also debuted on ABC-TV. Walt had been using the show to occasionally let the public know what the park would look like.

The struggle to build the park is well known. The original idea called for eight acres. By the time construction began, Walt had purchased a 160-acre orange grove. His vision included five distinct, individualized "lands" within the park. The visitor would enter through *Main Street USA* and from there they could visit *Frontierland*, *Adventureland*, *Fantasyland* and *Tomorrowland*.

The success of the park didn't happen overnight. There were problems on the park's opening day. Asphalt had been laid the night before and people were literally getting trapped on the pavement. The plumbers were on strike and there were very few working fountains. Those minor difficulties would have been okay, but on opening day, a fifteen day heat wave had temperatures reaching 110 degrees in the park itself and, as a result, the pavement was even hotter. In addition, over 28,000 people showed up. That would have been a great sign, except that many were brandishing counterfeit tickets.

Despite the initial problems, Disneyland started to grow. Within ten years the park could boast that fifty million people had visited. Walt visited the park often. He would greet people as they walked about and if they asked, he would sign autographs. Several of the animators took studios right above Main Street. Studio artists like Marc Davis and Herb Ryman had designed some of the parks major attractions.

In the 1950s and 60s, the Corner Art Store would sell matted animation cels for $1 or $2. Today, many of those cels are highly valued collectibles. Other collectibles include

DISNEYLAND

signs, tickets and virtually anything else connected with the park. The park continues to this day and Disney has built additional parks in Florida, Tokyo and Paris. The next city to gain a Disney Park will be Hong Kong.

Disneyland was featured in the following issues of *Four Color Comics* #716, 866 (both featuring *Tomorrowland*) and 1025. It was also spotlighted in the title of several issues of *Dell Giants*.

DSL-1

DSL-2

DSL-3

DSL-4

❑ **DSL-3. "Disneyland Coloring Book,"**
1955. Whitman. 8.25x10.75". 128 pages. - **$10 $25 $50**

❑ **DSL-4. Disneyland Opening Specialty Artwork,**
1955. Al Konetzni. 4.25x4.5" thin paper sheet mounted to a slightly larger 6.25x15.5" stiff white board. Unique - **$2000**

DSL-5

DSL-6

❑ **DSL-1. "Disneyland" Early Souvenir Spoon,**
1954. Bates And Klinke Inc. 4" long sterling spoon in original box. Spoon handle marked "Disneyland." Near Mint Boxed - **$80** Spoon Only - **$15 $25 $50**

❑ **DSL-2. "Disneyland Fun Box,"**
1955. Whitman. 9x11.75x1.5" deep box contains six 5.5x7.5" 24 page coloring books, crayons, 12 trading cards featuring Disney characters with text, 10x16" stiff cardboard sheet featuring 3 different games with unpunched playing pieces, 8x8.5x11" 32-page stamp book, two sheets of stamps (25 each) and a scrapbook. - **$50 $100 $160**

❑ **DSL-5. "Disneyland Frontierland" Frame Tray Puzzle Paper,**
1955. Whitman. 11.5x15" glossy paper sheet for frame tray puzzle that was never applied to puzzle. - **$10 $20 $45**

❑ **DSL-6. "Your Guide To Disneyland" Pamphlet,**
1955. Issued by "Bank Of America." 3.5x8" that opens to 13.5x16" with map of Disneyland. - **$10 $20 $40**

DSL-7

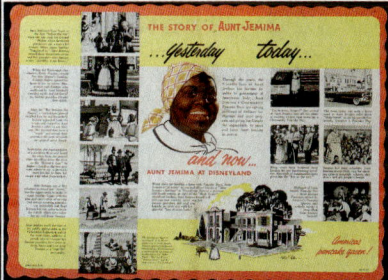

DSL-8

❑ **DSL-7. "Disneyland" Map And Ticket Paper,**
1955. Folder with map is 3.5x9" and opens to a total of 13.5" in length. Ticket paper is 5.5x8.5" and explains different ticket plans. Map - **$25 $50 $75** Paper - **$10 $15 $25**

❑ **DSL-8. "Aunt Jemima At Disneyland" Place Mat,**
1955. Slightly textured paper souvenir from Frontierland restaurant during the first year of Disneyland. - **$15 $30 $50**

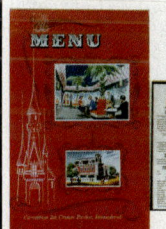

DSL-9

DISNEYLAND

DSL-10

❏ **DSL-9. "Carnation Ice Cream Parlor, Disneyland" Menus,**
1955. Two variety menus, first is 6.25x9.75" glossy stiff paper with text about Carnation in Disneyland. Second is 3x4.5" miniature replica which is a postcard mailer. Full Size - **$15 $30 $60** Miniature - **$10 $20 $30**

❏ **DSL-10. "Your Trip To Disneyland On Records,"**
1955. Mattel. 7.5x14.5" folder that opens to 42" contains set of five records with nice map of Disneyland. - **$40 $75 $150**

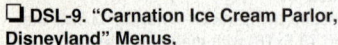

DSL-11

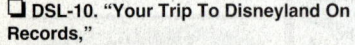

DSL-12

❏ **DSL-11. "Disneyland" First Guide,**
1955. Stiff glossy covers on 6x8.75" book with 20 pages. Contains artwork rather than real photos as park was still under construction when this was published. - **$50 $125 $200**

❏ **DSL-12. "Disneyland" First Year Guide Book,**
1955. Full color 6x8.75" glossy cover book with 24 pages of real photos. - **$40 $80 $175**

DSL-13

DSL-14

❏ **DSL-13. "Frontierland Game,"**
1955. Parker Brothers. 8x16x1.75" deep box contains board, spinner, four painted metal figural scout playing pieces, cardboard disks. - **$25 $60 $125**

❏ **DSL-14. "Disneyland,"**
1955. Souvenir letter 8.5x11" with 4x9.5" envelope. Letter describes Disneyland with color illustrations of various attractions. - **$30 $60 $110**

DSL-15

DSL-16

❏ **DSL-15. "Frontierland,"**
1955. Souvenir letter is 8.5x11" with 4x9.5" envelope. Paper is textured tan and features illustrations of Frontierland, Indians and rabbits dressed as cowboys. - **$35 $75 $135**

❏ **DSL-16. "Tomorrowland,"**
1955. Souvenir letter is 8.5x11" with 4x9.5" envelope. Letter features illustrations of TWA Rocket, spacemen, space vehicles and squid from 20,000 Leagues Under The Sea. - **$100 $200 $300**

DSL-17

DSL-18

DSL-19

❏ **DSL-17. "Disneyland" Postcard Folder,**
1955. Size is 3.75x6" but opens to total length of 29". 12 different photos. - **$20 $40 $65**

❏ **DSL-18. "Disneyland Pirate Ship Restaurant" Poster,**
1955. Chicken of the Sea. 24x62" poster. - **$100 $200 $300**

❏ **DSL-19. "Disneyland" Pennant,**
c. 1955. Felt 8.5x26.5" pennant shows Tinker Bell and castle. - **$15 $40 $80**

DSL-20

DSL-21

174

DISNEYLAND

❏ **DSL-20. "Carnation In Disneyland" Indian Headband,**
c. 1955. Thin cardboard measuring 3x9" which opens to 25" designed like Indian headband. - **$30 $50 $115**

❏ **DSL-21. Early Disneyland Area Motel Celluloid Button,**
c. 1955. 1.75" reading "I Stayed At The Viking Motel Near Disneyland Entrance." Reverse has covered tin back and horizontal pin. - **$15 $30 $50**

DSL-22

DSL-23

❏ **DSL-22. "Disneyland" Large Display,**
c. 1955. Dutch Boy. 8x32.5x18.5" tall diecut pop-up 3-D standee for paint store use with four different diecut cardboard pop-up pieces to give it a 3-D effect. - **$300 $750 $1250**

❏ **DSL-23. "Disneyland Christmas" Frame Tray Puzzle,**
1956. Whitman. 11.5x14.5". - **$12 $25 $45**

DSL-24

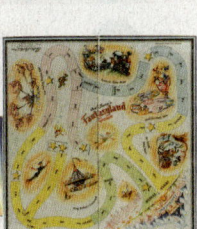
DSL-25

❏ **DSL-24. "Disneyland" Tickets,**
1956. Three tickets, each 2.5x5" for "Mark Twain," "Adult $2.50" and "Big 10 Book." Each - **$10 $20 $40**

❏ **DSL-25. "Fantasyland Game,"**
1956. Parker Brothers. 8x16x1.75" deep box contains board, ticket cards, die-cut cardboard stars. - **$30 $60 $110**

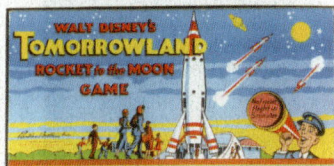
DSL-26

DSL-27

❏ **DSL-26. "Tomorrowland Rocket To The Moon Game,"**
1956. Parker Brothers. 7.5x16x1.75" box contains board with nice illustration of Tomorrowland, spinner, backdrop, four thick wood disks representing rocketships. - **$35 $65 $125**

❏ **DSL-27. "Disneyland" View-Master Set,**
1956. Envelope 4.5x4.5" contains set of 3 reels. - **$10 $20 $40**

DSL-28

DSL-29

❏ **DSL-28. "Disneyland Tom Sawyer Island" Map Folder,**
1957. Map is 4x9" and opens to total of 12". - **$50 $100 $150**

❏ **DSL-29. "Disneyland" First Lunch Box,**
1957. Aladdin. 7x8x4" deep metal. - **$125 $225 $400**

DSL-30

DSL-31

❏ **DSL-30. "Disneyland Hotel Child's Menu,"**
1957. Thin cardboard measuring 5x7" and opens to 21". One side has illustrations along with menu while opposite side has instructions for getting to Disneyland hotel. - **$50 $100 $200**

❏ **DSL-31. "1957 Disneyland Guide,"**
1957. Stiff paper cover. 28 pages of color photos and illustrations of park attractions. - **$40 $85 $185**

DISNEYLAND

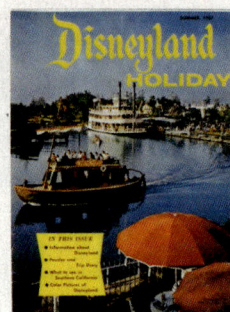

DSL-32

DSL-33

❑ **DSL-32. "Disneyland Holiday" Magazine,**
Summer 1957. Vol. 1 #2. 8.25x10.75" with 16 pages. - **$5 $10 $25**

❑ **DSL-33. "Disneyland" 1957 Home Movies Including Scene Of Walt Disney ,**
1957. Amateur film consists of two 8mm silent movies each on 3" diameter reel. Reel #1 begins with Disneyland Hotel sign and shows aerial park view from Sky Ride and various other attractions, a 15 second shot from about 30 feet away of Walt Disney standing by a bench. Reel #2 includes Riverboat, gunfight, burro rides, etc. and ends at Disneyland Hotel. Unique - **$125**

DSL-34

DSL-35

❑ **DSL-34. "Disneyland" Map,**
1958. Large 30x45" size showing overhead view of the park. - **$35 $75 $150**

❑ **DSL-35. "Walt Disney's Guide To Disneyland,"**
1958. Glossy paper guide is 8x11.5" with 28 pages. - **$25 $50 $90**

DSL-36

DSL-37

❑ **DSL-36. "Disneyland Red Wagon Inn" Menu,**
1959. Swift Co. 10.75x12" stiff glossy paper. - **$100 $200 $400**

❑ **DSL-37. "Disneyland" Drum Bank Featuring Dumbo,**
c. 1959. The sturdy cardboard drum bank with glossy paper labels is 5" diameter by 4" tall and attached to the top is a 3" tall painted composition figure of Dumbo. Underside has "Disneyland" logo and Disney copyright. - **$25 $50 $90**

DSL-38

DSL-39

❑ **DSL-38. "All Aboard For Disneyland" Oversized Mechanical Postcard,**
c. 1959. Postcard is 5.25x6.75" depiction of Donald Duck, Chip and Dale on Santa Fe train with diecut open window. Mechanical disk turns to change Donald's portrait to represent Adventureland, Fantasyland, Frontierland, Tomorrowland. - **$15 $30 $50**

❑ **DSL-39. "California" Souvenir Scarf Including Disneyland,**
1950s. Silk-like fabric scarf is 27x28" printed by image and name of various state tourist attractions including Mickey Mouse holding "Disneyland" sign at one corner. - **$6 $12 $20**

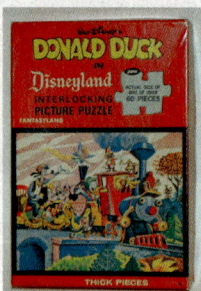

DSL-40

❑ **DSL-40. "Donald Duck in Disneyland" Puzzle,**
1950s. Boxed. 14" x 10". 1 of 3 different. Each - **$20 $40 $80**

DSL-41

DISNEYLAND

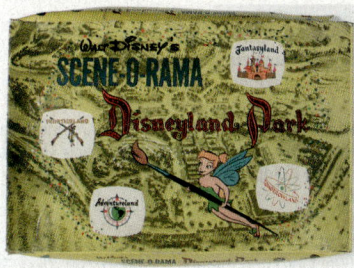

DSL-42

◻ DSL-41. "Walt Disney's Frontierland Logs" Boxed Set,
1950s. Halsam. #910, smallest of three available sets. 4.5x12x4.5" tall cardboard box. - **$40 $85**

◻ DSL-42. "Scene-O-Rama Disneyland Park" Paint Set,
1950s. Lido Toy Co. 14x21.5x2.5" deep boxed painting materials and large 13.5x18" molded thick white plastic "Picture Of Disneyland" with high relief design aerial view of the entire park to be painted and re-painted by washable paints in 16 colors. - **$30 $75 $125**

DSL-43

DSL-44

◻ DSL-43. "Disneyland" Pennant,
1950s. Felt fabric is 8.5x24" and accented by flocked images and 4" long streamers. - **$10 $20 $35**

◻ DSL-44. "Disneyland" Miniature Pennant,
1950s. Felt pennant is 4x8.75" with silk-screened design. - **$7 $15 $25**

DSL-45

DSL-46

◻ DSL-45. "Disneyland" Frame Tray Puzzles,
1950s. Jaymar. Each 9.75x12.75". One shows view of Fantasyland and the other shows Adventureland. Each - **$15 $25 $50**

◻ DSL-46. "Disneyland Hotel" Guest Soap,
1950s. Bar is 1.5x2.5x.5" thick of "Camay" soap in unopened wrapper including silhouette images of Sleeping Beauty's Castle and Monorail. - **$5 $12 $20**

DSL-47

DSL-48

◻ DSL-47. "Disneyland" Lamp,
1950s. Econolite Corp. Tin litho designed like a drum and measuring 6" diameter, 4" deep and 9.5" tall to top of socket. - **$45 $90 $175**

◻ DSL-48. "Disneyland" Decorative Wall Plate,
1950s. Plate is 9.5" diameter china. Reverse has "Disneyland" logo, "Japan" foil sticker, attached string for hanging. - **$10 $18 $35**

DSL-49

DSL-50

◻ DSL-49. "Fantasyland" Wall Plaque,
1950s. Painted and glazed ceramic is 8.5" diameter by 1.25" deep and centered by high relief image of Sleeping Beauty's castle. Reverse has "Disneyland" logo and copyright. - **$10 $20 $40**

◻ DSL-50. "Little Miss Disneyland" Boxed Charm Bracelet,
1950s. Metal link bracelet 5" long with five charms in 2x5.5x2" deep case. Includes Mickey, Tinkerbell, castle, stars.
Boxed - **$50 $100 $150**
Bracelet Only - **$25 $50 $75**

DISNEYLAND

DSL-51

DSL-52

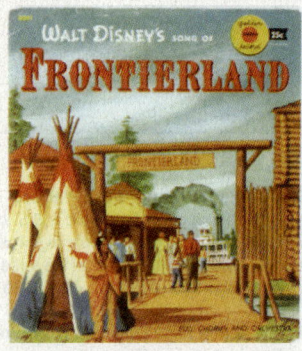

DSL-53

❑ **DSL-51. "Disneyland" Large Souvenir Plate,**
1950s. China plate is 8.5" in diameter with six illustrations of park attractions. - **$8 $15 $25**

❑ **DSL-52. "Disneyland" Salt & Pepper Set,**
1950s. "Japan" set of 2.25" tall bell-shaped ceramic shakers in original but generic box. Set - **$10 $20 $30**

❑ **DSL-53. "Walt Disney's Song Of Frontierland" Record,**
1950s. Little Golden Records. Paper sleeve contains 45 rpm record. - **$10 $20 $30**

DSL-54

❑ **DSL-54. "Disneyland Gloves" Store Display Box,**
1950s. Wells Lamont Corp. 8.5x11.5x3.75" deep box only originally containing assortment of "Disneyland Gloves." - **$15 $35 $60**

DSL-55

❑ **DSL-55. "Disneyland Souvenir Compact" With Box,**
1950s. 2.5x2.75x.5".deep compact with metal case comes in original illustrated box.
Box - **$20 $40 $60**
Compact - **$10 $20 $40**

DSL-56

DSL-57

❑ **DSL-56. "Official Driver's License For Richfield Autopia At Disneyland,"**
1950s. Stiff paper card measures 2.25x4" with area on back for owner information. Front text reads "This Certifies That The Undersigned Has Successfully Passed The Safe Driver's Test For Richfield Autopia At Disneyland." - **$20 $40 $80**

❑ **DSL-57. "Disneyland" Lighter,**
1950s. Chromed metal measuring .5x1.75x1.75" tall with inset metal plate showing castle design. - **$20 $40 $80**

DSL-58

DSL-59

❑ **DSL-58. "Disneyland Game,"**
1950s. Transogram. 9x17.5x1.75" deep box contains board, travel cards, spinner, 16 die-cut cardboard Disneyland characters. - **$25 $65 $125**

❑ **DSL-59. Australian "Fantasyland Game,"**
1950s. John Sands Pty. Ltd. 12x12x1.25" deep box. Comes with full color catalogue folder for this Australian company picturing games also produced by Milton Bradley including Cheyenne and The Rifleman. The board is 11.75x11.75. - **$35 $65 $100**

DSL-60

DISNEYLAND

DSL-61

❏ **DSL-60. "Disneyland Ferris Wheel" Wind-up,**
1950s. J. Chein & Co. 4.75x10.75x16.5" tall tin litho with built-in key. - **$165 $375 $800**

❏ **DSL-61. "Disneyland Tru-Vue" Set,**
1950s. Envelope is 4x5.75" and contains 3 "Fantasyland" film cards. - **$10 $20 $45**

DSL-62

DSL-63

❏ **DSL-62. "18 Pictures Of Disneyland" Miniature Camera,**
1950s. Hard plastic measuring 1x2x1.25" tall. Color photos can be viewed by looking through view finder and changed by pressing a small button. - **$35 $75 $125**

❏ **DSL-63. "Disneyland TV Magic Slate" In Packaging,**
1950s. Strathmore. 9.25x15" cardboard magic slate, complete with outer cardboard display cover with die-cut design. Packaged - **$65 $110 $175**
Loose - **$25 $65 $100**

DSL-64

DSL-65

❏ **DSL-64. "Disneyland Main Street U.S.A." Postcards,**
1950s. Five postcards from different late 1950s-early 1960s series including one oversized 3.5x11" "Panorama Card." Others are standard 3.5x5.5". Each - **$3 $6 $10**

❏ **DSL-65. "Disneyland" Ceramic Container,**
c. 1950s. High gloss finish on 2.75" diameter by 3.75" tall cylindrical container. - **$20 $40 $80**

DSL-66

❏ **DSL-66. "Disneyland" Full Size Tea Cup And Saucer,**
c. 1950s. China set 2" tall by 4" diameter cup and 6" diameter saucer. Has Disneyland name in gold. Inside of cup has illustration of Tinkerbell while saucer depicts castle. - **$20 $40 $80**

DSL-67

❏ **DSL-67. "Disneyland Eraser Set,"**
c. 1950s. Set of six erasers each featuring a Disneyland attraction. - **$30 $60 $90**

DSL-68

❏ **DSL-68. "Disneyland" Lunch Box,**
1960. Aladdin. 7x8x4" deep metal. - **$85 $175 $325**

DSL-69

❏ **DSL-69. "Disneyland" Thermos,**
1960. Aladdin. 6.5" tall metal showing Sleeping Beauty castle. This was for the second Disneyland box. - **$25 $50 $100**

DSL-70

179

DISNEYLAND

☐ **DSL-70. "Guide To Disneyland,"**
1960. Annual revised issue is 8x11.5" with 28 pages. - **$15 $30 $75**

DSL-71

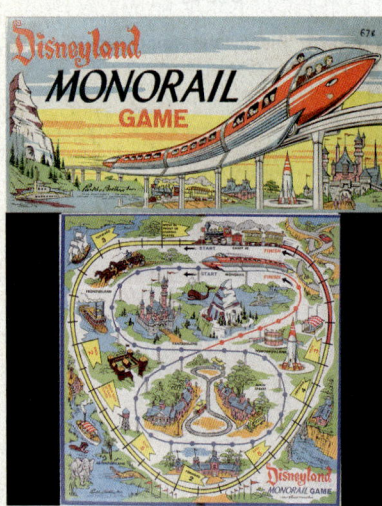

DSL-72

☐ **DSL-71. "Disneyland U.S.A." Comic Book,**
1960. Dell. Giant Comic #30 containing stories revolving around different park attractions. - **$8 $24 $165**

☐ **DSL-72. "Disneyland Monorail Game,"**
1960. Parker Brothers. 8x16x1.5" deep boxed playing pieces featuring 14.5" square playing board designed as aerial view of Disneyland with game routes of two "tracks," one for Casey Jr. and the other for the Monorail ride. - **$25 $60 $125**

DSL-73

☐ **DSL-73. "Disneyland Fantasyland" View-Master Reels,**
1960. Envelope is 4.5x4.5" and contains set of three reels. The diecut envelope was designed with "swing out" clear plastic sleeves for storage of the reels. - **$25 $50 $100**

DSL-74

DSL-75

☐ **DSL-74. "Disneyland" Silver Luster Keychain,**
c. 1960. 2" flexible chain and key loop joins 1.5" triangular-shaped heavy piece of metal depicting Fantasyland castle on front. Reverse shows Matterhorn, aerial cars, monorail and submarine. - **$8 $12 $20**

☐ **DSL-75. "Vacationland" Magazines,**
1961. Disneyland Inc. Quarterly publications Vol. 5 #2, Summer 1961 and Vol. 6 #1, Spring 1962. 20-24 pages. Each - **$5 $10 $15**

DSL-76

☐ **DSL-76. "Disneyland Hotel" Double Card Deck,**
c. 1961. Hard plastic case is 4x5x.5" deep and contains two complete card decks, each with 52 cards plus jokers. Each card back has same illustration of Monorail loading platform with "Disneyland Hotel" in background. - **$15 $30 $50**

DSL-77

☐ **DSL-77. "Disneyland" Map,**
1962. Map is 30x45" stiff paper. Original folded size is 8x15". - **$35 $75 $125**

DISNEYLAND

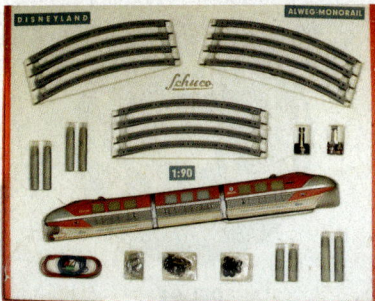

DSL-78

❏ **DSL-78. "Schuco Disneyland Alweg-Monorail" Boxed Set,**
1962. Schuco. 14.5x18.5x1.75" deep box contains complete and unused set #6633G and features a three-car monorail in red. A blue variety was also produced as well as a larger set #6333S that featured a four-car monorail and additional accessories. Box has styrofoam insert that holds the pieces in place and this includes Disneyland labels and embossed Schuco name. The tin lithograph and hard plastic monorail is 14" long and comes with 12 track sections, suspension posts, other small parts. Boxed - **$300 $600 $1500**

DSL-79

❏ **DSL-79. "Disneyland Punch-Out Book,"**
1963. Golden Press Inc. 7.5x13" with four pages. Un-punched - **$50 $100 $150**

DSL-80

❏ **DSL-80. "Guide To Disneyland,"**
1964. Annual revised issue is 8x11.5", 28 pages. - **$15 $35 $75**

DSL-81

❏ **DSL-81. "Disneyland Haunted House" Record,**
1964. Disneyland label. 12.25x12.25" album cover contains 33-1/3 rpm. Side 1 features ten stories with sound effects including "The Haunted House" and "The Martian Monsters" while Side 2 is a collection of sound effects including "Screams And Groans, A Collection Of Creaks," etc. Cover notes that the record is "Not Intended For Impressionable Young Children From Three To Eight." Front cover has sticker referring to insert "Added Bonus Inside...Spooky Party Hints." - **$15 $25 $50**

DSL-82

❏ **DSL-82. "Disneyland Sticker Fun" Book,**
1964. Whitman. 8.25x12" with sixteen pages. Unused - **$10 $20 $35**

DSL-83

❏ **DSL-83. "It's A Small World Souvenir Guide,"**
1964. 8.5x11" with stiff paper cover and 24 glossy pages. Copyright 1964 for New York World's Fair exhibit. This attraction did not debut at Disneyland until 1966. - **$20 $40 $60**

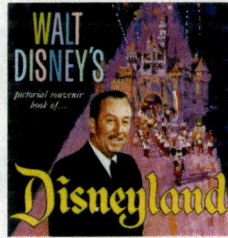

DSL-84

❏ **DSL-84. "Walt Disney's Pictorial Souvenir Book Of Disneyland,"**
1965. Book is 10.5x10.5" with 28 pages. - **$30 $60 $90**

DSL-85

DSL-86

DISNEYLAND

DSL-87

❑ **DSL-85. Disneyland "It's A Small World" Mug,**
c. 1966. Likely Enesco 3.75" tall painted and glazed ceramic depicting representative images from "Small World" exhibit titled on underside. - **$10 $18 $30**

❑ **DSL-86. "It's A Small World" Thermos,**
1968. Aladdin. Metal thermos 6.5" tall. - **$20 $40 $80**

❑ **DSL-87. "Disneyland It's A Small World" Lunch Box,**
1968. Aladdin. 7x9x4" deep vinyl. - **$50 $110 $175**

DSL-88

DSL-89

❑ **DSL-88. "Disneyland Guide,"**
1968. Book is 8.75x11.5" with 32 pages. - **$20 $40 $75**

❑ **DSL-89. "Disneyland" Hardcover,**
1969. Book measures 9.5x11.25" with 72 pages filled with great color photos of rides and attractions. - **$25 $50 $80**

DSL-90

DSL-91

❑ **DSL-90. "The Haunted Mansion" Boxed Film,**
1969. 3x3x.5" deep box contains Super 8mm color film. Film is on red plastic reel and about five minutes long. - **$10 $20 $45**

❑ **DSL-91. "Disneyland" Decorative Dish,**
c. 1969. Dish is 7.75" diameter by .75" deep ceramic picturing "Haunted Mansion, Monorail, Sleeping Beauty Castle, Jungle Cruise, Mark Twain." - **$5 $12 $20**

DSL-92

DSL-93

❑ **DSL-92. "Disneyland" Store Bags,**
1960s. Pair of 8.5x11.5" or 5.5x8" size and design variation paper bags for merchandise purchased at Disneyland shops. Each - **$1 $3 $5**

❑ **DSL-93. "Disneyland" Dumbo Figurine,**
1960s. Painted and glazed ceramic figure 2.5x3.5x3.5" tall with "Disneyland" on front. - **$10 $20 $40**

DSL-94

DSL-95

❑ **DSL-94. "Disneyland" Tray,**
1960s. Metal tray measuring 11" in diameter and 1-1/8" deep showing park attractions. - **$10 $20 $30**

❑ **DSL-95. "Disneyland Tray Gift,"**
1960s. "Houze Art." 4x4.75x.5" deep glass tray comes in original box. Boxed - **$10 $20 $35**

DSL-96

DISNEYLAND

❑ **DSL-96. "It's A Small World" Figure,**
1960s. A.D. Sutton & Sons, Inc. 3x3.5x7" tall vinyl figure from series. Depicts Chinese child playing a lute. Red felt shirt. - **$12 $25 $50**

DSL-97

DSL-98

❑ **DSL-97. "Tinker Bell" Disneyland Souvenir,**
1960s. Original plastic cylindrical container holds 3.25" tall bell. Boxed - **$25 $60 $100**
Bell Only - **$15 $40 $40**

❑ **DSL-98. "Disneyland Matterhorn Bobsleds" Large Sticker,**
1960s. 8x9" sticker sheet with 7x8" full color sticker of insignia-like design for this ride. Backing is marked "Fasson Fas Cal Marking Film." Unused - **$15 $35 $75**

DSL-99

DSL-100

❑ **DSL-99. "Disneyland Jeep,"**
1960s. Marx. 5x9.75x4.75" tall tin litho with rubber wheels. - **$75 $150 $250**

❑ **DSL-100. "Welcome To Disneyland" Brochure Maps,**
1960s. Four closed 3.5x9" folders, each opening to different aerial view of park. Earliest issue is 1956, followed by issues for 1964, 1968, 1974.
1956 - **$10 $20 $40**
1964-68 Each - **$2 $5 $10**
1974 - **$1 $3 $5**

DSL-101

DSL-102

❑ **DSL-101. Disneyland Mascots Oversized Cards,**
1960s. Birthday card folder is 8x14.75" picturing Goofy on front cover, and two 5.5x10.25" cards picturing Dopey and Donald Duck, both with blank reverse side. Each - **$4 $8 $15**

❑ **DSL-102. "Disneyland" Patch,**
1960s. 1.5x3.75" embroidered patch has "Disneyland" across center of simulated ribbon design. - **$6 $12 $20**

DSL-103

DSL-104

❑ **DSL-103. Disneyland "Mark Twain" Riverboat Replica Radio,**
1960s. "Made In Japan" 2.5x12x7.25" tall battery-operated hard plastic detailed replica with die cast metal paddle wheel, stamped brass railings, steel rod for mast, chimney pipes and pair of pewter smokestacks. - **$150 $300 $600**

❑ **DSL-104. "Tomorrowland Space Wheel Giant Motorized Action Toy,"**
1960s. AMF Wen Mack. Plastic replica assembly toy, then battery-operated, packaged in huge 23.5x23.5x5" deep illustrated box, including image of assembled toy. Complete with all parts and instructions. - **$50 $110 $225**

DSL-105

❑ **DSL-105. "Tomorrowland Rocket Ride Motorized Giant Action Toy,"**
1960s. AMF Wen Mack. Plastic replica assembly toy, then battery-operated, packaged in huge 23.5x23.5x5" deep illustrated box including image of assembled toy. Complete with all parts and instructions. - **$50 $110 $225**

DSL-106

DISNEYLAND

❑ **DSL-106. "A Day At Disneyland" Boxed Film,**
1960s. 5.25x5.25.5" deep box contains Super 8mm color film on red hard plastic reel. Underside includes a synopsis of the film and mentions "The Matterhorn-Pirates Of The Caribbean-Small World-Haunted Mansion." Film is probably about 10 minutes. - **$8 $15 $30**

DSL-107

DSL-108

❑ **DSL-107. "Disneyland Pencil Case,"**
1960s. "Japan" 3.5x7.5" vinyl-covered cardboard with snap closure top. - **$6 $12 $25**

❑ **DSL-108. "Disneyland" Squeak Postcards,**
1960s. Each 3.5x5.5" with illustrations on fronts and squeaker mechanism in center of each. Each - **$5 $10 $15**

DSL-109

DSL-110

DSL-111

❑ **DSL-109. "Disneyland Directors Guild Of America Inc. Special Guest" Button,**
1960s. 3.5" diameter. Limited issue. - **$5 $12 $25**

❑ **DSL-110. "Disneyland Pirates Of The Caribbean" Snow Globe Bottle,**
c. 1960s. Clear plastic bottle filled with liquid and sparkle pieces measuring 2x2.25x5" long. Inside has 4 attached pieces - two pirates dunking someone in a well, pirate ship, building and background scene. - **$50 $110 $200**

❑ **DSL-111. "Disneyland R.R." Oil Can,**
c. 1960s. L. M. Eddy Mfg. Co. 3" diameter by 12" tall metal can with text "Property Of Chief Engineer/Walt Disney's Disneyland R.R." - **$125 $225 $375**

DSL-112

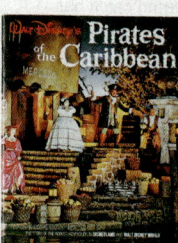

DSL-113

❑ **DSL-112. "Disneyland Host" Pin With Tinkerbell,**
c. 1970. 1-5/8x2-1/8" tall brass. Date specified is a guess, but we understand employees were assessed a high fee if pin was not returned when employment ended. - **$25 $50 $80**

❑ **DSL-113. "Pirates Of The Caribbean" Book,**
1974. Glossy paper souvenir is 9x10.75" and titled "The Story Of The Robust Adventure In Disneyland And Walt Disney World." 48 pages. - **$35 $75 $125**

DSL-114

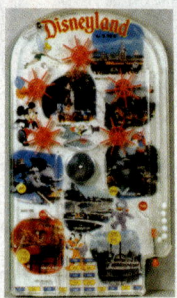

DSL-115

❑ **DSL-114. "Disneyland" Special Event Flyers,**
1970s. Issue is 5x7" for "Magic Holiday At Disneyland" Fri., Dec. 16, 1977 private party and 4.5x6" issue dated 12/70 for "New Year's Eve At Disneyland" celebration although denoting "Sold Out" status. Each - **$5 $10 $15**

❑ **DSL-115. "Disneyland Game" Large Boxed Bagatelle,**
1970s. Wolverine. 13.5x23.5x1.25" deep with clear plastic cover over tin litho back panel. Playing surface includes illustrations of Disney characters and park attractions. - **$15 $30 $60**

DSL-116

❑ **DSL-116. "Disneyland Construction" Workers Button,**
c. 1970s. 2.25" with serial number "887". Limited issue. - **$10 $20 $40**

184

DISNEYLAND

DSL-117

DSL-118

❏ **DSL-117. "Disneyland" Olympic Games Medal,**
1984. Summer Olympics. 4" long with ribbon, bar pin on back with attached 1.5" diameter cast metal medal. - **$10 $20 $40**

❏ **DSL-118. "Disneyland Splash Mountain" Employee Only Watch,**
1989. Dial is 1.25" diameter. Mint As Issued - **$150**

DSL-119

❏ **DSL-119. "Disneyland" Special Event Tickets,**
1980s. Three unused 2.5x7" admissions, one for Oct. 9, 1983 "Public Employees" party and other two for 1985 and 1986 events of CSEA (Calif. State Employees Assn.) Each Unused - **$3 $6 $10**

DSL-120

❏ **DSL-120. "Disneyland Hotel/Stromboli's Ristorante" Giant Ceramic Mug,**
1980s. Homer Laughlin China. 3.5" tall with 4.5" diameter Fiestaware. - **$20 $40 $70**

DSL-121

❏ **DSL-121. "Mickey's Toon Town" Employee Only Watch,**
1993. Watch is 1-3/8" in diameter and comes in 2.25x9.5" velvet pouch. Dial depicts "Jolly Trolley" with Disney characters. Reverse of case marked "Company D," "Grand Opening January 26, 1993." and 2750 sold only to Disney employees, each with incised serial number. Near Mint As Issued - **$115**

DSL-122

❏ **DSL-122. "The Magic Begins With People" Employee Only Watch,**
1993. Watch is 1.5" in diameter and comes in 2.25x9.5" velvet pouch. Dial shows color art of Disneyland castle with Mickey as Sorcerer's Apprentice. Reverse has "Company D" logo and "Disneyland Official Cast Member 1993." Limited edition of 750 each with incised serial number. Near Mint As Issued - **$135**

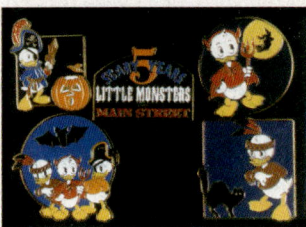

DSL-123

❏ **DSL-123. Disneyland Employee Only Donald's Nephews Enamel Pin,**
1994. Plastic case measuring 3.25x4.25x.75" deep holds set of five brass/enamel pins measuring 1" to 1.25" tall. Mint As Issued - **$60**

DSL-124

DSL-125

❏ **DSL-124. "Disneyland Matterhorn 35th Anniversary" Employee Watch,**
1994. Velvet pouch is 2.25x9.75" and contains employee-only limited edition wristwatch in 1.5" diameter metal case. Dial features illustration of the "Matterhorn" with date "1959-1994." Second hand disk that spins with image of Abominable Snowman. Produced and numbered individually in quantity of 1000. Mint As Issued - **$125**

❏ **DSL-125. "Disneyland 40th Anniversary Cookie Jar" Premium,**
1995. Nestle. 7x9x11" tall painted and glazed ceramic. Comes with "Certificate Of Limited Edition." Serially numbered on bottom from edition of 100,000. Mint As Issued - **$75**

DISNEYLAND

DSL-126

❑ **DSL-126. "Disneyland Riverfront Restaurant" Employee Only Watch With Pouch,**
1995. Velvet pouch is 2.25x9.5" holding award wristwatch produced and numbered serially for only 200 employees. Watch case is 1.5" diameter and dial face illustration is Three Caballeros in a boat with food and drinks. Text below is "Riverfront Restaurants Disneyland 40 Years 1995." Mint As Issued - **$85**

DSL-127

❑ **DSL-127. "Disneyland 40 Years Of Adventures" Employee Watch,**
1995. Wood presentation box is 3x3x2.5" deep and titled to include "Team Pride '95" on sliding lid over commemorative wristwatch for employees only. Watch case and dial have design of early compass including cutout points on the case rim. Text at center is in the style of Raiders of The Lost Ark film title reading "40 Years Of Adventures." On the crystal is "Disneyland" logo. The second hand image is Mickey swinging on a vine. Mint As Issued - **$150**

Disneyland Paris

With Tokyo Disneyland doing well, the company turned its attention to Europe as the next possible site to place a theme park. Spain was very seriously considered as a location. It had a lot going for it, especially the weather. However, when considering a map of Europe, Paris is much more centrally located. It also contained a large expanse of flat land that was just isolated enough for Disney's needs, while still a realistic distance from a populated area.

Once the choice of Paris was made, Disney approached the park with complete conviction. Having built three other parks, they were determined to not repeat earlier mistakes. However, once it was built, the park got off to a rocky start despite the detailed planning. It took several years to find its feet. One of the major changes made was that the original name of Euro Disney was changed to Disneyland Paris. This was done in order to distance the park from the initial difficulties of the first few years. In addition, the name change also helped align the park with the image of Paris as tourist location.

One standout feature of the park is the technical advancements behind many of its rides. Benefiting from the most modern technology available, the rides are the highlight for many visitors. The park continues to attract visitors from all over Europe as well as the rest of the world.

Merchandise includes items created especially for the Paris location.

DLP-1

❑ **DLP-1. "Disney Dollars" 10 Dollar Bill,**
2000. Commemorates the new Millennium. Near Mint - **$25**

DLP-2

❑ **DLP-2. Disneyland Paris Opening Day 1992 Commemorative Edition,**
July 2000. Part of the Walt Disney World Pin of the Month collection, this pin was released in July 2000 with a limited edition size of 15,000. - **$20**

DLP-3

❑ **DLP-3. Tinker Bell Fashion Doll,**
2000s. From Disneyland Paris. - **$35**

Disneyland TV Show

The first Disney TV show aired on ABC from October 27, 1954 to September 3, 1958. Shown on Wednesday nights, it was one of ABC-TV's earliest hits. The host was Walt himself and he proved to be as charming and comfortable on screen as he was off. Many people felt he came across as a member of the family and that is why he was welcomed into many living rooms week after week. The show gave the viewers everything from original programming, such as Davy Crockett, to Walt's vision for the Disneyland theme park.

In 1961, the show would switch networks to NBC. Walt wanted to take advantage of the technology for the then-new color television. Eventually, as the years passed, the show wound up being scheduled on all three major networks at different points in time. The family-oriented content of the show remained the same no matter what network it appeared on.

DTV-1

DTV-2

❑ **DTV-1. "TV Guide" With Disney Article,**
1954. Volume 2, #43 from October 23, 1954 Philadelphia edition. Features article on debut of Walt Disney TV show and opening of Disneyland. - **$20 $40 $85**

❑ **DTV-2. "Disneyland" TV Show Dairy Promotion Large Poster,**
1955. Poster is 19.5x58". - **$50 $100 $175**

Donald Duck, Daisy & Nephews

The world first saw the short-tempered Donald as a co-star in a 1934 cartoon. That cartoon, *The Wise Little Hen*, was one of Disney's popular *Silly Symphony* series of shorts. Several months later, Donald was featured again in *Orphans' Benefit* (1934) and with that appearance, was on his way to becoming a star in the Disney universe.

So many aspects of Donald's character stand out that it is hard to isolate the main reason for his popularity. Some feel his voice may be the reason they love him. That voice was provided by Clarence Nash, who somehow managed to combine a duck's quack with the complete destruction of the English language.

While Donald's speech may be almost unintelligible, the way he expressed himself wasn't. Donald's fits of temper and frustration were explosive; some would even say volcanic. This helped connect him to the audience, as every person watching could identify with his frustration, no matter the circumstance.

During World War II, Donald was the most popular cartoon character in America. His efforts to do the right thing and his unwillingness to take even the slightest amount of guff endeared him to a country engulfed in war. He appeared everywhere from films to comic strips to comic books. The comic books were so popular that a spin-off, *Uncle Scrooge*, was published in 1952. The title is still published today. Daisy Duck appears in *Four Color Comics* #600, and 659. She also had several other short-lived titles over the years.

Uncle Scrooge was created by a man who gave depth to Donald's personality, Carl Barks. He gave the comic book version of Donald a complete universe to operate in. By creating Duckburg and populating it with highly original characters such as Gladstone Gander and Gyro Gearloose, an identifiable humanity was added to almost every Duck story.

Many people saw in Donald a kind of "everyman" who simply cannot understand why things don't go his way. Even when everything is going wrong around him, Donald will not quit. He may not win, and often doesn't, but he never quits. When all the turmoil dies down, Donald often finds himself looking for a better understanding of what just happened. He may have made a mistake, or behaved inappropriately, but he is willing to admit it. His biggest problem may be that he cannot seem to understand why things go so easy for his friend Mickey, and yet, his life is one challenge after another.

Today, Donald is as popular as ever. He had a major role in the recent direct-to-video Disney release, *The Three Musketeers* (2004). He continues to be a top-selling comic book star around the world.

Over the years Donald has been merchandised on everything from orange juice to candy. There are plush toys, records, books, ceramics and figurines.

Donald Duck also has a solid extended family that has taken up residence inside the Duck mythology. Among the more well-known relatives are his nephews, Huey, Dewey and Louie. The nephews first appeared in a Donald Duck Sunday Page.

Carl Barks, drawing Donald for Walt Disney's Comics and Stories, began using them regularly. In 1961, Gold Key began publishing a *Huey, Dewey and Louie Junior Woodchucks* comic.

Daisy Duck is another part of Donald's extended family. She is clearly Donald's girlfriend. In early cartoon appearances, Donald did have a short relationship with a Duck named Donna, but many simply see her early appearances as a precursor to Daisy's actual arrival. Daisy's first appearance in an American newspaper strip was in November, 1940. A month later she appeared in a Sunday page. Daisy also has three nieces, April, May and June.

DDK-1

❏ **DDK-1. Original Donald Duck Model Sheet,**
The dedicated Donald Duck model sheet from *The Wise Little Hen* was most likely drawn in December 1933. While rough sketches of Donald may have been made before it, this was the all-important document that finalized the Duck's look for his first appearance on screen.

We don't know who drew the sheet itself, but before animation began, artist Clyde Geronimi modified Donald's tail on some copies of the sheet, giving it its modern feathery look rather than the bump-shape that was first drawn. Near Mint - **$26,500**

DDK-2

❏ **DDK-2. Pencil Drawing,**
1934. Animation paper is 9.5x12" centered by 1.75x2.75" early image of long-billed Donald. From the second Donald short, 'Orphan's Benefit' and No. "83" from a numbered sequence. - **$150 $300 $600**

DDK-3

❏ **DDK-3. Donald Duck Linen Book,**
1935. Whitman #978, 16 pgs. First book devoted to Donald Duck. Scarce in Near Mint, common in lower grades. - **$350 $1050 $3500**

DONALD DUCK, DAISY & NEPHEWS

DDK-4

DDK-5 (side view)

❑ **DDK-4. Donald Duck Snapshots Book,** 1935. Scrap picture book with hinges, in original box. Rare. - **$125 $250 $550**

❑ **DDK-5. Toothbrush Holder Figurine,** 1935. From S. Maw & Sons, London. This glazed ceramic item was one of the first Donald Duck toy figures. - **$300 $600 $1000**

DDK-8

❑ **DDK-8. "Donald Duck" Fun-E-Flex Figure,** c. 1935. 5" tall figure with wood body and poseable rubber-covered wire arms and neck.
Large 5" Size - **$500 $1000 $1500**
Small 3" Size - **$200 $400 $600**

DDK-5

DDK-6

❑ **DDK-6. Donald Duck Umbrella,** 1935. Produced by Louis Weiss Company. - **$80 $175 $350**

DDK-9

DDK-10

DDK-7

❑ **DDK-7. Celluloid Mickey And Donald In Rowboat,** c. 1935. Japan. Copyright Walt E. Disney. 5.75" long boat with Donald Duck with jointed arms rowing with Mickey Mouse in stern of boat. - **$200 $400 $850**

❑ **DDK-9. Semi-Flat Lead Figure,** c. 1935. Cast lead figure is 2.25" tall with raised details on both sides, either manufactured or from a home casting set. Detailing includes very long bill. - **$25 $50 $100**

❑ **DDK-10. Donald Duck Enamel On Brass Pin,** c. 1935. Reverse marked "W.D." 1 3/8" tall. - **$35 $85 $165**

DONALD DUCK, DAISY & NEPHEWS

DDK-11

❏ **DDK-11. "Wanna Fight" Cello. Button,**
c. 1935. Scarce. Image of exuberant long-billed Donald. - **$200 $450 $700**

❏ **DDK-12. Long-Billed Donald Doll,**
c. 1935. Knickerbocker. 5x5.5x8.5" tall painted composition large likeness with movable head and legs. - **$300 $650 $1200**

❏ **DDK-13. Donald Duck Carousel Large Size Celluloid Wind-Up,**
c. 1935. Japan. Borgfeldt #1316/3702. Copyright Walt E. Disney. Toy is 10.5" tall with celluloid figure of Donald under canopy with suspended figures of Mickey, Minnie, Donald and Pluto. - **$750 $1750 $3500**

❏ **DDK-15. Donald Duck Catalin Plastic Pencil Sharpener,**
c. 1935. 1-1/8x1-1/8" octagonal. - **$45 $100 $175**

DDK-12

DDK-16

DDK-14

DDK-17

❏ **DDK-14 "Walking Donald Duck" Boxed Wind-Up,**
c. 1935. Japan. Borgfeldt with copyright Walt E. Disney. Box is 2x2x3" tall. Celluloid Donald is 3.5" tall with metal feet. Right side of figure says "Donald Duck Walt Disney." Box - **$100 $250 $500** Toy - **$75 $200 $400**

❏ **DDK-16. Donald Duck Figurine,**
c. 1935. Carnival style figure- possibly a prototype for a German doll. Rare. - **$300 $800 $1200**

❏ **DDK-17. Donald Duck Figurine,**
c. 1935. Large-billed ceramic figure. Rare. - **$125 $275 $550**

DDK-13

DDK-15

DDK-18

DONALD DUCK, DAISY & NEPHEWS

❏ **DDK-18. "Donald Duck Jackets" Cello. Button,**
c. 1935. 1.5" or 1.125". Scarce. Norwich Knitting Co. - **$100 $200 $500**

DDK-19

❏ **DDK-19. Donald Duck Tape Measure,**
1936. Japanese. 3 1/2" tall celluloid. - **$250 $500 $1000**

DDK-20

❏ **DDK-20 Donald Duck Store Display Standee,**
1936. Made By Old King Cole, distributed by Kay Kamen. Molded 'laminite' 11x15.5x1.5" deep. - **$500 $1000 $2000**

DDK-21

❏ **DDK-21. "Walt Disney's Easter Parade By Fisher-Price" Boxed Set,**
1936. Box measures 4x16.25x1.75" deep and contains set of five-wheeled wood toys each with nice paper labels. Set #475. Each figure is 2.5" to 4" tall and includes Wee Bunny, Little Bunny, Big Bunny, Clara Cluck and Donald Duck. Near Mint Boxed - **$3000**
Box Only - **$300 $750 $1800**
Figure Set Only - **$200 $600 $1200**

DDK-22

❏ **DDK-22. "Fisher-Price" Donald Duck Wind-Up Toy,**
1936. Wooden toy with paper labels and built-in key measures 8.5x10x8.5" tall and numbered "358." Made only one year and known as "Donald Duck Back-Up." - **$1000 $2500 $4200**

DDK-23

❏ **DDK-23. "Dapper Donald Duck" Pull Toy,**
1936. Fisher-Price. 4x6.5x9" tall lithographed paper on wood toy including 7" height of Donald figure itself. This is the earliest version of Fisher-Price toy #460 introduced in 1936 and produced for two years. - **$500 $1000 $2000**

DDK-24

❏ **DDK-24. Standee For First Donald Duck Hardcover Book,**
1936. Diecut cardboard is 9.25x13.75" countertop display with cardboard easel on back. Issued to promote the 1936 Grosset & Dunlap book and features the same image of angry long-billed Donald that appears on the book's cover. Text reads "Every Boy's And Girl's Favorite Donald Duck/Profusely Illustrated By The Staff Of The Walt Disney Studios" and also notes purchase cost of 50 cents. **$2000 $4000 $8000**

DONALD DUCK, DAISY & NEPHEWS

DDK-25

DDK-28

❏ **DDK-25. Donald Duck Happy Face Trotter Fisher-Price Pull Toy,**
1936. Labeled #500. This item was produced as an Easter toy only. Yellow cart variety with rubber insert wings. - **$550 $1150 $2200**

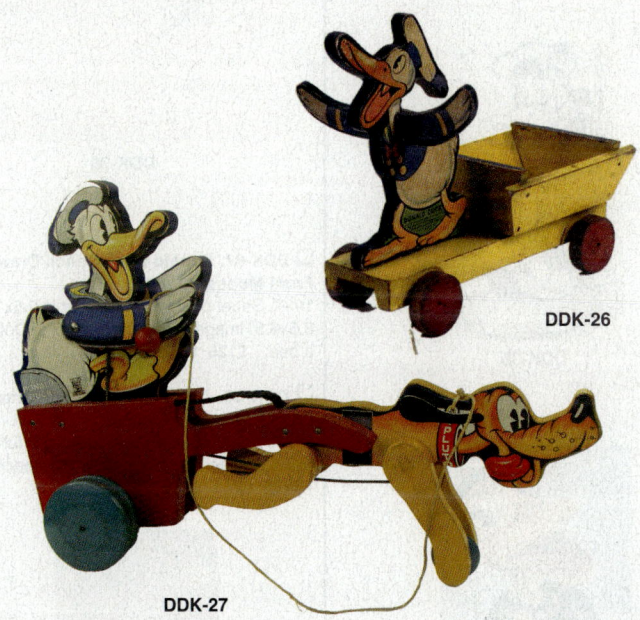

DDK-26

DDK-27

DDK-29

❏ **DDK-28. "Donald Duck Serenade" With Clara Cluck Flashlight,**
1936. U.S. Electric Mfg. Corp. 6-3/8" tall tin lithograph. - **$175 $325 $800**

❏ **DDK-29. Rare Donald Duck Plaster Lamp,**
1936. Soreng Manegold Co. Chicago. 5.25" diameter base by 11" tall with 7" figure of Donald. - **$1500 $3500 $7500**

DDK-30

❏ **DDK-26. "Donald Duck" English Pull Toy,**
1936. Chad Valley Ltd. Wooden toy virtually identical to Fisher-Price "Happy Face Trotter" #500 of same year. - **$500 $1000 $1750**

❏ **DDK-27. Donald Duck And Pluto Wooden Pull Toy,**
1936. Fisher-Price. #149. 9.5" tall, 15-3/8" long. Photo example is of the first off the assembly line. A whip in Donald's hand is missing because at beginning of production run it would not properly fit. - **$800 $1600 $3200**

DONALD DUCK, DAISY & NEPHEWS

❑ **DDK-30. "Donald Duck" Book,**
1936. Grosset & Dunlap. 9.5x10.5" hardcover, 36 pages, the first Donald hardcover. Story involves Donald and Mickey's nephews Morty and Monty.
Duct Jacket - **$500 $1000 $2000**
Book- **$100 $250 $400**

DDK-31

DDK-32

❑ **DDK-31. Donald Race Car Wind-Up,**
1936. Joseph Schneider Inc. 2x4x1.5" tall lithographed tin car with wooden hubs and rubber tires. A similar Mickey Mouse race car was also produced by this maker. - **$225 $525 $850**

❑ **DDK-32. "Donald Duck Hand Car" Wind-Up,**
1936. Lionel Corp. 3.5x10.5x6.75" tall tin toy designed as doghouse that contains composition figure of Pluto while attached to back is compo figure of Donald. Pluto's head is suspended and gravity moves it as toy operates. Includes 27" diameter circle of track. Originally sold for $1.25. Toy - **$500 $1100 $2200**
Box (not shown) - **$500 $1200 $1800**

DDK-33

❑ **DDK-33. "Donald Duck Rail Car" Printing Plate,**
1936. Lionel Corp. 2x2.75" reverse image copper plate with depiction ad for train toy based on Donald. - **$35 $65 $125**

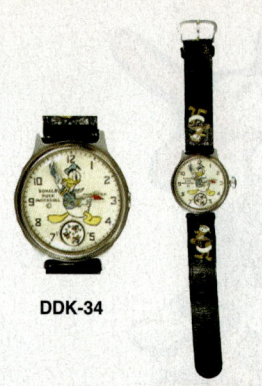

DDK-34

❑ **DDK-34. "Donald Duck Ingersoll" Wristwatch,**
1936. Total length of watch is 5.75" and dial is 1.25" in diameter. Each band has a .75" enameled metal Donald Duck. Three Small Mickey images on the second wheel.
Box (Not Shown) - **$500 $1000 $2000**
Watch - **$1000 $2000 $4000**

DDK-35

DDK-36

❑ **DDK-35. "Donald Duck" Glass,**
c. 1936. Glass is 4-3/8" tall. - **$25 $50 $80**

❑ **DDK-36. Large Donald Duck Doll,**
c. 1936. Krueger. 6.5x8x15.5" tall stuffed oilcloth with fabric hat, felt tongue and buttons. - **$375 $1000 $2200**

DDK-37

DDK-38

❑ **DDK-37. Donald Duck Pencil Drawing From Moose Hunters,**
1937. Sheet of animation paper is 9.5x12" with 5.5x6.5" image in lead/red pencil of Donald and a bee. - **$125 $250 $500**

❑ **DDK-38. Donald Duck Pencil Drawing From Lonesome Ghosts,**
1937. Sheet of animation paper is 9.5x12" with 3x3.5" image in lead pencil w/red pencil accent. - **$125 $250 $500**

DDK-39

DONALD DUCK, DAISY & NEPHEWS

❑ **DDK-39.** "Donald Duck" Musician Series Glass,
1937. Glass is 4.75" tall. - **$50 $100 $200**

❑ **DDK-41.** "Donald Duck Poster Paint Set,"
1937. Milton Bradley. 8.75x13x2" deep box set #4860. - **$75 $175 $350**

❑ **DDK-42.** Donald Duck and Clara Cluck Cut-Out Book,
1937. - **$500 $1500 $3000**

❑ **DDK-43.** "Donald Duck Paint And Crayon Box" With Book,
1937. Whitman. 9x14x1.25" boxed set #2175 comprised of boxed crayons, Donald Duck paint tablets, palette, water color brushes, water dish plus a 9x12" 96-page coloring book designed differently from other Whitman books due to the fact that it comes inside of a box. Variations include two 48-page sections, black and white art throughout including covers. - **$325 $650 $1250**

DDK-40

❑ **DDK-40.** Donald Duck Athletic Series Glass,
1937. Glass 4.25" tall. - **$50 $100 $200**

DDK-41

DDK-42

DDK-43

DDK-44

❑ **DDK-44.** Donald Duck Painted Glass Framed Picture,
1937. Reliance Picture Frame Co. 5.75x5.75" wood frame holds two glass sheets both with design painted on reverse of glass. Top sheet has border design with opening around 1.5x3" image of Donald. - **$60 $1250 $250**

DDK-45

❑ **DDK-45.** "Silly Symphony Featuring Donald Duck And His (Mis)Adventures" BLB,
1937. Whitman Big Little Book #1441. - **$35 $90 $175**

DONALD DUCK, DAISY & NEPHEWS

DDK-46

❏ **DDK-46. Donald Duck and Donna Duck Fisher-Price Pull Toy ,**
1937. The first Fisher-Price Disney toy to tie-in with a film. This is perhaps the most sought after of any of the early Fisher-Price toys. Extremely rare. Labeled #160 by the company. The film this toy promotes, "Don Donald," was Donald Duck's first solo feature. Donna Duck probably was the inspiration for Donald's next girl friend Daisy. - **$1250 $3100 $5350**

DDK-47

❏ **DDK-47. Donald Duck Angry Face Trotter Fisher-Price Pull Toy ,**
1937. Labeled #741 by the company. This item was produced as an Easter toy only. It is one of two "angry face Donald" toys, the other made in 1936. Both of these are extremely rare. The toy was sold without a box. - **$1550 $3600 $4600**

DDK-48

❏ **DDK-48. Donald Duck Pencil Drawing From The Fox Hunt,**
1937. Image is 4x5". From a numbered series and this is "163." - **$150 $275 $550**

DDK-49

❏ **DDK-49. Pencil Drawing,**
1937. Sheet of animation paper is 10x12" centered by 2.25x2.75" art of him trapped in some type of trick or illusion. Artist is Les Clark for segment in Magician Mickey film short. - **$125 $250 $500**

DDK-50

❏ **DDK-50. Pencil Drawing,**
1937. From Lonesome Ghosts. 10x12" sheet of animation paper centered by 3x3" image of Donald from 'Lonesome Ghosts' movie short. No. "542" from a numbered sequence. - **$125 $250 $500**

DDK-51

❏ **DDK-51. Pencil Drawing,**
1937. 10x12" sheet of animation paper with 3.5x4.5" image. From 'Magician Mickey' film short. No. "86" from a numbered series. - **$125 $250 $500**

DDK-52

DDK-53

❏ **DDK-52. Pencil Drawing From Magician Mickey,**
1937. 10x12" sheet of animation paper with 3x4.25" drawing in lead pencil just left of center. Full figure image of an angry Donald from 'Magician Mickey' short feature. No. "97" from a numbered sequence. - **$125 $250 $500**

❏ **DDK-53. Pencil Drawing,**
1937. Animation paper is 10x12" sheet with 3x4.5" image. For 'Lonesome Ghosts' short feature and No. "343" from a numbered sequence. - **$125 $250 $500**

DDK-54

DONALD DUCK, DAISY & NEPHEWS

DDK-55

❑ **DDK-54. "Donald Duck Has His Ups And Downs,"**
1937. Whitman. 8.5x9.5" stiff cover "Walt Disney Picture Storybook" #1077. 16 pages with both black and white and color illustrations. - **$200 $400 $600**

❑ **DDK-55. "Donald Duck Story Book" Hardcover,**
1937. Whitman. 8.5x11.5" with 48 pages. - **$75 $200 $400**

DDK-56

DDK-57

❑ **DDK-56. "Mickey Mouse/Donald Duck And All Their Pals" Book,**
1937. Whitman. 10.5x14.75" large hardcover #887 with 40 pages. Stories include Dippy The Goof, Mickey's Mistake, Hare And Hound, Bigger Badder Wolf, Three Little Wolves Go Swimming. - **$75 $185 $375**

❑ **DDK-57. "The Wise Little Hen" Book,**
1937. Whitman. 9.25x13" linen-like book #888 with 12 pages. Donald Duck's official debut was in the 1934 hardcover version of this title. - **$40 $80 $150**

DDK-58

DDK-59

❑ **DDK-58. "Donald Duck" Tablet,**
1937. Powers Paper Co. 5.5x9" school tablet. - **$30 $60 $125**

❑ **DDK-59. Pencil Drawing,**
c. 1937. 10x12" sheet of animation paper with 3x5" image, possibly from Magician Mickey. From a numbered sequence and this is "102-1/2." - **$100 $200 $400**

DDK-60

❑ **DDK-60. Donald And Donna Duck Container,**
c. 1937. English 6" diameter by 2" deep tin canister and lid "By Permission Walt Disney-Mickey Mouse, Ltd." Lid illustrtioan is Donald serenading Donna (later changed to Daisy) as they ride on the back of a donkey. This image is from the movie short, Don Donald, also the first and only appearance of Donna. - **$85 $175 $350**

DDK-61

❑ **DDK-61. Donald Duck Disney Studio Fan Card,**
c. 1937. Stiff paper card measures 7.25x9". Text is "Greetings To Helen" with large facsimile Walt Disney signature. - **$100 $175 $350**

DDK-62

❑ **DDK-62. "Donald Duck Express To Funland" English Book,**
c. 1937. Birn Brothers Ltd. 8x10" hardcover with 1.5" thickness from 124 stiff paper pages. - **$150 $300 $600**

DONALD DUCK, DAISY & NEPHEWS

DDK-63

DDK-66

❑ **DDK-63. "Donald's Ostrich" English Book,** c. 1937. Dean & Son Ltd. 7x9" cardboard covered, 64-page story with art in black and white on every page. - **$60 $135 $250**

DDK-64

DDK-65

❑ **DDK-64. Pencil Drawing,** 1938. 10x12" sheet of animation paper with 2x2.5" image in lead pencil just below center from 'Boat Builders' short. Image is Donald swinging an axe. No. "170" from numbered sequence. - **$65 $125 $200**

❑ **DDK-65. Donald Duck Easter Chick Cart Wooden Pull Toy,** 1938. Fisher-Price. Number 469. 8" tall by 10" long. Made for one year. - **$400 $800 $1600**

DDK-67

❑ **DDK-66. "Donald Duck" Lamp With Shade,** 1938. LaMode Studios. 4" diameter base by 9.5" tall with 5.75" figure of Donald. Has original paper label under base. Cardboard shade measures 6" tall and 8" diameter at bottom. Lamp - **$150 $300 $600** Shade - **$150 $300 $600**

❑ **DDK-67. "Donald Duck" Night Light,** 1938. LaMode Studios. 3x5.5x7.25" tall painted plaster. "Donald Duck" is incised on front edge of base. - **$300 $750 $1500**

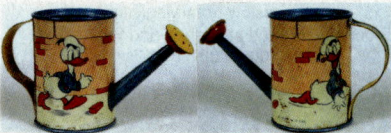

DDK-68

DDK-69

❑ **DDK-68. Sprinkling Can,** 1938. Ohio Art Co. 3" tall lithographed tin picturing two images of him walking and tripping over a brick. - **$150 $300 $600**

❑ **DDK-69. Donald Duck "Sunoco" Blotter,** 1938. Illustration of Donald in a car being pushed from the rear by a ram on 4x7.5" blotter. - **$30 $60 $125**

DDK-70

DDK-71

❑ **DDK-70. "Donald Duck Hunting For Trouble" Big Little Book,** 1938. Whitman. Big Little Book #1478 with front and back cover different portraits of him as a cowboy with mustache. - **$25 $80 $160**

❑ **DDK-71. "Donald Duck" Bookends,** 1938. LaMode Studios Inc. 4x4x7" tall painted plaster. Each - **$100 $200 $300**

DDK-72

DONALD DUCK, DAISY & NEPHEWS

DDK-73

❑ **DDK-72. "Story Of Donald Duck,"**
1938. Whitman. 5x5.5" hardcover #1066 from series of six different. 96 pages with black and white story art on nearly every other page. - $20 $40 $75

❑ **DDK-73. "Clock Cleaners" Walt Disney Picture Book,**
1938. Whitman. 9.25x12.25" linen-like paper book #947 with 12 pages. - $75 $150 $300

DDK-74

DDK-75

❑ **DDK-74. "Donald Duck" English Book,**
1938. Birn Brothers Ltd. 7.5x10" hardcover, 92 stiff paper pages in black and white. - $75 $150 $300

❑ **DDK-75. "Donald Duck's Party Game."**
1938. Parker Brothers. 9.75x19.25x2" deep box contains board, four die-cut Donald playing pieces, spinner with Donald pointer, 12 prize disks and instruction sheet. - $75 $160 $275

DDK-76

❑ **DDK-76. Talking Easter Card,**
1938. White & Wyckoff. 4.5" closed thick cardboard folder with front cover art of Donald in top hat and carrying cane plus flowers. Text includes "Donald Duck Has Recorded In A Way That's Novel And New, A Happy Easter Greeting Intended Just For You." Card is accompanied by plain mailing envelope plus second envelope containing parts and instruction for "The Card That Talks." Parts are a metal wire "tape" and metal ring assembling to produce "Happy Easter" audio greeting when slotted through the card and pulled. - $50 $100 $150

DDK-77

DDK-78

❑ **DDK-77. "Donald Duck" Sand Pail,**
1938. Ohio Art. Pail is 5" in diameter and 5" tall. - $200 $400 $650

❑ **DDK-78. "Donald Duck" Sand Pail With Shovel,**
1938. Ohio Art Co. Tin lithographed pail measures 3.5" in diameter and 3.25" tall. Pail - $100 $200 $325
Generic Shovel - $15 $30 $50

DDK-79

DDK-80

DDK-81

DONALD DUCK, DAISY & NEPHEWS

❑ **DDK-79. "Donald Duck" Sand Pail,**
1938. Ohio Art Co. 4.5" top diameter by 4" tall lithographed tin pail with carrying handle. - **$200 $400 $700**

❑ **DDK-80. "Donald Duck" Boxed Soap Figure,**
c. 1938. Lightfoot Schultz Co. 2.5x2.5x5.5" tall box contains 4.5" tall soap figure. Box **$25 $50 $100** Figure **$25 $50 $100**

❑ **DDK-81. Donald Duck Toy Telephone,**
c. 1938. N.N. Hill Brass Co. 7" tall candlestick phone with 3" tall thick die-cut cardboard Donald Duck. - **$700 $1500 $2500**

DDK-82

❑ **DDK-82. Donald And Others Tea Set Pieces,**
c. 1938. Ohio Art Co. Four lithographed tin pieces from larger original set, comprised of 5.5x7.5" tray, 4.25" diameter plate, two 2.5" diameter saucers. Pictured in total are Donald, Mickey and nephews, Clara Cluck. Tray - **$25 $50 $100**
Plate - **$10 $20 $30**
Saucer - **$5 $10 $15**

DDK-83

❑ **DDK-83. "Walt Disney's Fun Book" Australian Issue,**
c. 1938. Specialty Press Pty. Ltd. 8.25x11" stiff paper cover, 16 pages. Covers and contents are reprints from early issues of Mickey Mouse Magazine. Both front and back covers repeat Donald front cover art from earlier original magazine for April 1937. - **$75 $150 $350**

DDK-84

❑ **DDK-84. "Donald Duck/Ferdinand the Bull" Sand Pail,**
c. 1938. Unmarked but authorized Australian 6" top diameter by 5.5" tall lithographed tin pail with carrying handle. - **$175 $350 $700**

DDK-85

❑ **DDK-85. Donald Duck Oilcloth Doll,**
c. 1938. Richard G. Krueger. Collar and hat plume are felt. 16.25" tall. - **$550 $1600 $3600**

DDK-86

❑ **DDK-86. Donald Duck Band Leader Doll,**
c. 1938. Knickerbocker. 21" tall doll dressed in felt outfit with brass buttons, braid accent, leatherette belt with snap, plush hat with braid chin strap, and wood baton.
Doll- **$650 $1750 $4000**
Tag - **$50 $100 $150**

DDK-87

DDK-88

DONALD DUCK, DAISY & NEPHEWS

❑ **DDK-87. Donald Duck Catalin Plastic Pencil Sharpener,**
c. 1938. 1.75" tall. - **$40 $75 $135**

❑ **DDK-88. Donald Duck Drawing From The Hockey Champ,**
1939. Image is 3.25x4" and from a numbered sequence "67.". - **$100 $200 $375**

DDK-89

❑ **DDK-89. Donald Duck Pencil Drawing From Hockey Champ,**
1939. Image is 3.5x4.5". From a numbered sequence and this is "28.". - **$75 $175 $300**

DDK-90

❑ **DDK-90. Donald Duck Pencil Drawing From "Autograph Hound,"**
1939. Animation paper is 10x12" with 3x3.25" centered image. - **$100 $200 $400**

DDK-91

❑ **DDK-91. Donald Duck Pencil Drawing From Hockey Champ,**
1939. 10x12" sheet of animation paper with 3.5x5" image. - **$75 $175 $300**

DDK-92

❑ **DDK-92. Donald Duck Pocket Watch,**
1939. Ingersoll product. Box is blue with Donald pictured on the left holding the watch, showing it to a head shot of Mickey. Box is rare and watch is scarce. The plain back was released first, but because sales were slow, they added the Mickey decal to help sales.
Mickey Decal Back - **$700 $1800 $2750**
Plain Metal Back - **$650 $1750 $2500**
Box - **$300 $750 $1200**

DDK-93

DDK-94

❑ **DDK-93. "Walt Disney All Star Parade" Glass,**
1939. 4.25" tall tumbler with wrap-around illustration of Donald as troop leader and his nephews as Boy Scouts plus "Donna" Duck. One of the few items to picture "Donna" prior to her name change to Daisy. - **$25 $45 $75**

❑ **DDK-94. "Donald Duck 1939 Walt Disney All Star Parade" Glass Original Art,**
1939. 5.25x8.5" stiff poster board with pen and ink artwork for the glass from this series. All art is original with paste-on for the title "1939 Walt Disney All Star Parade." Reverse has ink stamp reading "Property Of Walt Disney Enterprises Not To Be Used Without Permission." Unique, Near Mint - **$325**

DDK-95

❑ **DDK-95. Tin Tray,**
1939. Ohio Art Co. 8x10x.5" deep lithographed tin serving tray centered by image of Donald as an extraordinarily busy chef. - **$125 $200 $350**

DDK-96

DONALD DUCK, DAISY & NEPHEWS

❑ DDK-96. "Donald Duck Dime Register Bank,"
1939. Measures 2.5x2.5x5/8" deep with text "Lookie What I Saved!" - **$200 $400 $800**

DDK-98

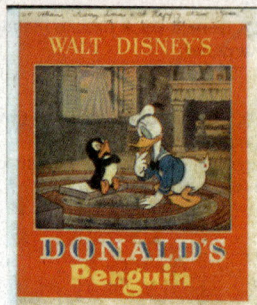

DDK-101

❑ DDK-101. "Donald's Penguin" Book,
1939. Shepherd & Newman Pty. Ltd. 6.5x7.25" Australian book with 12 pages. Color scenes on 4 inside pages. Many small illustrations throughout. - **$20 $40 $75**

DDK-99

❑ DDK-98. "Sunoco" Donald Duck Card,
1939. Card measuring 3.5x5.75" was sent as a reminder for recipient to prepare their car for the summer. Text reads "Now Is The Time" "To Change To Summer Oil And Grease." - **$25 $50 $100**

❑ DDK-99. "Donald Forgets To Duck,"
1939. Whitman. Better Little Book #1434. - **$25 $80 $160**

DDK-102

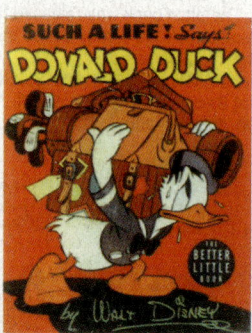

DDK-100

DDK-103

❑ DDK-102. "Donald Duck And His Nephews,"
1939. D.C. Heath & Co. 6.25x8.5" hardcover. 66 pages. - **$20 $45 $100**

DDK-97

❑ DDK-97. "Donald's Better Self" Premium Booklet,
1939. Whitman. 4x4.75" tall. Title was a 1938 short and booklet features a story based on this as well as a second Donald short "Sea Scouts." Back cover has imprint for York-Lancaster, PA shoe store "Newswanger's." - **$100 $200 $300**

❑ DDK-100. "Such A Life! Says: Donald Duck" Better Little Book,
1939. Whitman. Book #1404. - **$25 $85 $165**

❑ DDK-103. "Donald's Lucky Day" Book,
1939. Whitman. 9.5x11.5" horizontal format softcover #897 with 20 pages. - **$75 $165 $325**

DONALD DUCK, DAISY & NEPHEWS

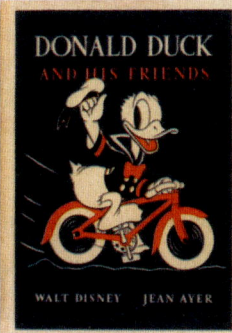
DDK-104

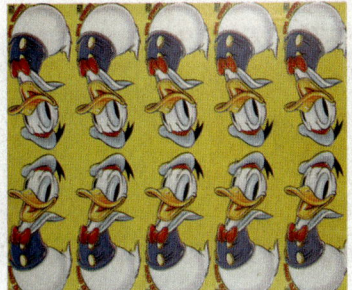
DDK-107

DDK-109

❏ **DDK-104. "Donald Duck And His Friends,"** 1939. D.C. Heath & Co. 6.25x8.5" with 102 pages. - **$15 $40 $85**

❏ **DDK-106. Mechanical Valentine,** 1939. 2.75x4.5" diecut thin cardboard. - **$10 $25 $50**

❏ **DDK-107. Struttin' Donald Duck Uncut Sheet For Push Toy,** 1939. Fisher-Price. 20x24" large glossy paper sheet mounted to thick cardboard. - **$100 $200 $400**

DDK-105

DDK-110

❏ **DDK-105. Donald Duck Valentine,** 1939. Stiff paper measuring 3.5x4.75". Mechanical design so that Donald's head can move slightly. - **$10 $25 $50**

❏ **DDK-109. Donald Duck "Nu-Blue Sunoco" Ink Blotter,** 1939. Blotter measures 4x7" with text "Here Ye!" - **$20 $50 $100**

❏ **DDK-110. "Donald Duck" Glass,** 1939. Illustration based on Donald's Lucky Day short. 4.75" tall. Poem reads "Donald Has A Package To Deliver At Any Cost, But He's Heading Into Wreckage-A Cat His Path Has Crossed." - **$30 $65 $120**

DDK-108

DDK-106

DDK-111

❏ **DDK-108. "Donald Duck In Sea Scouts" Australian Insert Movie Poster,** 1939. 14.25x40" paper poster for RKO Radio Pictures movie of 1937 although actually released in 1939. Poster is printed by Simmons Ltd. Litho, Sydney. - **$300 $750 $1500**

❏ **DDK-111. Donald Duck Still,** c. 1939. 8x10" glossy for the 1939 short 'Donald's Lucky Day.' **$12 $25 $40**

DONALD DUCK, DAISY & NEPHEWS

DDK-112

DDK-115

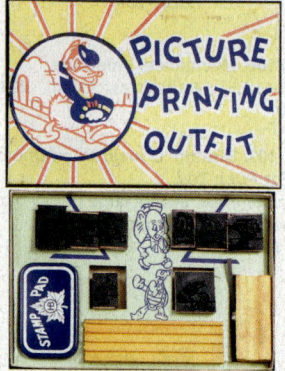

DDK-116

DDK-118

❑ **DDK-117. Donald Duck Silverware Holder Pull Toy,**
1930s. The International Silver Co. 2x4.5x5.25" tall die-cut thick cardboard with same image on each side and wooden wheels. - **$125 $250 $500**

❑ **DDK-118. "Donald Duck Man-Egg-Kins" Cut-Out Book,**
1930s. Paas Dye Co. 9x11.5" book wtih eight pages. Contains 20 cut-outs to be used to decorate Easter eggs. Each character consists of two pieces, a base that the egg sits on and a top piece with character's head and arms. - **$65 $125 $200**

DDK-113

DDK-119

❑ **DDK-115. "Donald Duck Art Stamp Picture Set,"**
1930s. Fulton Specialty Co. 10.25x12.25x1" deep box contains twelve 1.25x1.25" rubber ink stamps with wooden handles featuring characters, complete set of alphabet/number stamps and ink stamp pad. - **$100 $200 $400**

❑ **DDK-116. "Picture Printing Outfit" Canadian Set Boxed,**
1930s. H. Barnard Stamp & Stencil Co. Ltd. 5.5x8.25x1" deep boxed complete set of eight Disney character image ink stamp blocks and all related accessories. Stamp block images all differ for Donald (2), Toby Tortoise (3), Mickey Mouse, Elmer Elephant, Max Hare (one each). - **$40 $75 $135**

DDK-117

❑ **DDK-119. Donald Duck Decal Sheet,**
1930s. Palm Brothers Decalomania. Sheet of ten decals measuring 5.5x16.25". - **$50 $100 $150**

DDK-114

❑ **DDK-112. Donald Duck Soda Bottle,**
c. 1939. Rochester Bottling Co. 9.25" tall glass bottle. - **$100 $200 $400**

❑ **DDK-113. Cardboard Lubrication Reminder Postcard,**
c. 1939. Standard Oil Sons Inc. 3-3/8x5.5" stiff paper card. - **$20 $40 $70**

❑ **DDK-114. "Donald Duck" Sailor Hat,**
1930s. Child's cotton fabric hat measuring 7.5" in diameter and 1.5" deep. Headband has felt attachment with "Donald Duck" name and pair of irridescent streamers attached to back. - **$40 $85 $150**

DDK-120

DDK-121

DONALD DUCK, DAISY & NEPHEWS

☐ **DDK-120. Flag Bearer Bisque,**
1930s. "Made In Japan" 3.5" tall painted bisque figurine with rear incised number "S1333." - **$50 $100 $175**

☐ **DDK-121. Donald Duck With Bugle Bisque,**
1930s. Figure is 3" tall and has incised "S1334" on back. - **$30 $60 $100**

DDK-122   DDK-123

☐ **DDK-122. Donald Duck With Rifle Bisque,**
1930s. Figure is 3" tall and has incised "S1335" on back. - **$35 $75 $125**

☐ **DDK-123. Donald Duck With Sword Bisque,**
1930s. Figure is 3" tall and has incised "S1336" on reverse. - **$40 $90 $150**

DDK-124   DDK-125

☐ **DDK-124. Unusual Donald Duck Bisque Figure,**
1930s. Figure is 2-5/8" tall painted and glazed. Marked "Japan." - **$100 $200 $400**

☐ **DDK-125. Unusual Donald Duck Glazed Figure,**
1930s. Figure holding bass is 2.75" tall painted and glazed. Has incised "4" on back. - **$75 $150 $300**

DDK-126

☐ **DDK-126. Admiral Donald and Donald's Nephew Bisques,**
1930s. Nephew figure is 2" tall and was sometimes attached to candy package. Admiral figure is 3" tall. The two figures are companion pieces.
Donald's Nephew - **$25 $50 $80**
Admiral Donald - **$65 $130 $225**

DDK-127   DDK-128

☐ **DDK-127. Movable Arm Bisque Figurine,**
1930s. 5.5" tall. Borgfeldt & Co. bisque figure of Donald with movable arms. - **$500 $1000 $1500**

☐ **DDK-128. Donald With Concertina Bisque,**
1930s. "Japan" on foot underside. 2.5x3.5x4-3/8" tall. Larger of two sizes. - **$100 $215 $375**

DDK-129

☐ **DDK-129. Donald Duck With Concertina Figure,**
1930s. Japanese 4" tall painted bisque, the smaller of two sizes and depicted in yellow jacket rather than blue. Reverse has incised "S1131." - **$110 $225 $400**

DDK-130

☐ **DDK-130. Donald As Painter Figure,**
1930s. Painted bisque figurine is 2x2.5x4" tall. - **$400 $800 $1400**

DDK-131

DDK-132

☐ **DDK-131. Donald Duck 4 1/2" Bisque Figurine,**
1930s. Borgfeldt & Co. bisque figure of Donald. - **$125 $250 $400**

☐ **DDK-132. Donald Duck 4 1/2" Bisque Figurine,**
1930s. 4 1/2" tall Borgfeldt & Co. product. - **$110 $225 $400**

DONALD DUCK, DAISY & NEPHEWS

DDK-133

DDK-135

DDK-136

DDK-137

DDK-138

❑ **DDK-138 Long-Billed Double Figure Toothbrush Holder,** 1930s. Store item. - **$125 $400 $700**

DDK-139

❑ **DDK-139. Donald Duck Miniature Bisque,** 1930s. Figures is 1.75" tall. - **$15 $30 $75**

❑ **DDK-133. Donald Duck Bisque Figurine,** 1930s. 4" tall figure of Donald holding a mandolin. Marked "S1158". - **$200 $400 $700**

DDK-134

❑ **DDK-134. Double Figure Ashtray,** 1930s. Japanese-made glazed ceramic ashtray about 3.5" tall. - **$165 $525 $800**

❑ **DDK-135. Donald/Mickey/Minnie Bisque Toothbrush Holder,** 1930s. Measures 2.5x3.5x4.5" tall. Has incised "S1354" on reverse. - **$125 $250 $475**

❑ **DDK-136. Toothbrush Holder,** 1930s. 2x3x5" tall painted bisque featuring high-dimensional figure of long-billed Donald. - **$125 $275 $525**

❑ **DDK-137. Toothbrush Holder,** 1930s. "Made In Japan" 2x3x4.75" tall china depicting Donald walking and carrying a bowl with his head turned backwards. Reverse has small opening as made for wall mounting. - **$50 $100 $150**

DDK-140

DDK-141

DDK-142

DONALD DUCK, DAISY & NEPHEWS

☐ **DDK-140. Donald Duck Figure,**
1930s. "Japan" 3.25" tall painted bisque pose of head turned to the side and hands straight down by his sides. Reverse markings include incised "3." - **$35 $75 $115**

☐ **DDK-141. Donald On Scooter Figurine,**
1930s. Painted bisque is 3" tall. - **$50 $125 $165**

☐ **DDK-142. Donald On Kiddie Car Figurine,**
1930s. Painted bisque is 3" tall. - **$60 $135 $185**

DDK-143

☐ **DDK-143. Donald On Hobby Horse Figurine,**
1930s. Painted bisque is 3" tall. - **$75 $150 $225**

DDK-144

DDK-145

☐ **DDK-144. Donald in Canoe Bisque,**
1930s. "Japan" 1.25x3x2.25" tall painted bisque. - **$250 $525 $850**

☐ **DDK-145. Large Figurine,**
1930s. Unmarked but likely Italian. 4x5x6.5" tall painted and glazed ceramic. - **$50 $100 $200**

DDK-146

☐ **DDK-146. Plaster-Filled Celluloid Donald Duck,**
1930s. Figure is 3" tall. Underside is marked "Japan". - **$25 $50 $85**

DDK-147

DDK-148

☐ **DDK-147. Donald And Pluto Celluloid Novelty,**
1930s. "Japan" on 1x3.75" base under three-dimensional figures of 1.25" tall Donald and 1.25" long Pluto. Donald sits in a sleigh and holds string reins in one hand leading to Pluto as the sleigh puller. - **$100 $300 $600**

☐ **DDK-148. "Donald Duck" Celluloid Large Jointed Figure,**
1930s. "Japan" 3x3.5x5" tall figure with moveable arms and legs. - **$100 $200 $300**

DDK-149

☐ **DDK-149. Donald Duck Cowboy Jointed Composition Doll,**
1930s. Knickerbocker. 8.5" tall. - **$1000 $2000 $4000**

DONALD DUCK, DAISY & NEPHEWS

DDK-150

DDK-152

DDK-154

❏ **DDK-150. Donald Composition Doll,**
1930s. Knickerbocker Toy Co. 10" tall with velvet outfit. - **$800 $1600 $3200**

❏ **DDK-152. Fun-E-Flex Donald Duck On Sled,**
1930s. The wood sled is 2x6x.75" deep, seated Donald figure is 2.75" tall. Donald is wood with rubber-covered wire arms and legs. "Donald Duck" decal on chest. - **$250 $500 $1000**

❏ **DDK-154. Plaster Figure With Spring Body Parts,**
1930s. Figure is 5.5" tall painted torso with unpainted plaster hands and feet attached to wire springs. Top of head has metal loop for string attachment. No copyright and apparently used as a carnival prize. Matching Mickey and Minnie figures are also known.
- **$75 $150 $250**

DDK-151

DDK-153

DDK-155

❏ **DDK-151. Donald Duck Pattern Doll**
1930s. Large about 15" tall stuffed fabric doll. Produced from a pattern. - **$50 $100 $200**

❏ **DDK-153. Donald Duck Hard Rubber Figure,**
1930s. Seiberling Rubber Co. Figure measures 3.25x5x6" tall and has poseable head. - **$125 $250 $500**

❏ **DDK-155. Plaster Stauette,**
1930s. Unmarked 3x3.5x6" tall painted plaster likeness of long-billed Donald although depicted without his traditional hat. - **$50 $100 $225**

DDK-156

DONALD DUCK, DAISY & NEPHEWS

DDK-157

DDK-159

DDK-162

❏ **DDK-156. Cereal Bowl Premium,**
1930s. Post Cereals. 5.5" diameter x 1.5" deep hard plastic. Outer rim has raised alphabet and numerals. Underside is marked "Beetleware/Post's 40% Bran Flakes/Grape-Nuts Flakes." - **$12 $25 $580**

❏ **DDK-157. Donald Duck Milk Bottle,**
1930s. Bottle is 8.5" tall, one quart. Underside is marked "Duraglas." Has silk screened design on front and back. - **$100 $200 $300**

❏ **DDK-159. "Donald Duck Quack!" English Celluloid Button,**
1930s. 7/8". Photo example shows split in the celluloid. Bottom curl reads "By Permission Of Walt Disney-Mickey Mouse Ltd." - **$100 $200 $400**

DDK-160

❏ **DDK-160. "Donald Duck" Boxed Hair Brush,**
1930s. Hughes-Autograf Brush Co. Inc. 4x5.25x2" deep box contains 3.5" long dark wood brush with black bristles and attached top is aluminum panel with enameled paint design.
Box - **$50 $100 $200**
Brush - **$25 $50 $100**

DDK-161

❏ **DDK-161. Donald Duck Light Bulb,**
1930s. Tube-shaped glass bulb 4" tall with threaded brass socket that fits traditional bulb receptacle. Stamped metal filament figure of Donald is nicely detailed and glows a vivid pink.
Working - **$100 $200 $400**

❏ **DDK-162. Donald Duck Large Pillow,**
1930s. Pillow measures 16x17x3.5" deep. Front has nap with velvet-like finish and back is plain woven fabric. - **$100 $200 $300**

DDK-163

❏ **DDK-163. Figural Planter,**
1930s. "Japan" 3x4x5.5" tall china planter featuring highly dimensional image of Donald. - **$125 $275 $500**

DDK-158

❏ **DDK-158. Donald Duck Enameled Paint on Brass Pin In Rare Box,**
1930s. Brier Mfg. Co. 2.5x2.5x.5" deep box contains illustrated insert card holding 1.25" tall pin. From series of "Mickey Mouse Jewelry." Box - **$100 $200 $300** Pin - **$35 $75 $150**

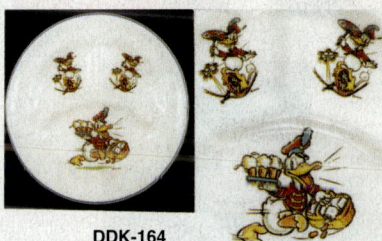

DDK-164

DONALD DUCK, DAISY & NEPHEWS

DDK-165

❏ **DDK-164. Child's Dish,**
1930s. Salem China Co. "Patriot" 8" diameter by 1" deep glazed china with three shallow divided sections. - **$50 $125 $250**

❏ **DDK-165. Ceramic Mug,**
1930s. Unmarked Salem China Co. 2.5" tall mug. - **$35 $65 $125**

DDK-166

❏ **DDK-166. European Container With Lid,**
1930s. Marbled bakelite-type plastic is 2.5" diameter by 1.25" tall. Threaded lid has raised image of long-billed Donald. Original content of small sponge that could be dampened to moisten postage stamps. - **$35 $75 $150**

DDK-167

DDK-168

❏ **DDK-167. Donald And Mickey Product Tin,**
1930s. Lithographed container 6" diameter by 2.25" deep with lid marked "By Permission Of Walt Disney (Mickey Mouse) Ltd." - **$100 $200 $375**

❏ **DDK-168. Figural Egg Cup,**
1930s. "Made In Japan." 1.75" diameter by 2.25" tall glazed china with high relief front image. - **$50 $100 $160**

DDK-169

❏ **DDK-169. "Donald Duck" Glass,**
1930s. "Bosco" chocolate beverage 3.25" tall tumbler with sponsor's name on reverse. - **$25 $50 $75**

DDK-170

DDK-171

❏ **DDK-170. "Donald Duck" Glass,**
1930s. Glass is 4.25" tall paint image tumbler from the scarcer of two dairy series. Image is Donald walking and waving his hands. More common image shows him with one hand raised to his head. - **$40 $75 $135**

❏ **DDK-171. "Donald" Duck Juice Glass,**
1930s. 3-3/8" tall. Believed to be Australian. - **$30 $60 $90**

DDK-172

❏ **DDK-172. Donald Duck English Teapot,**
1930s. Wade Heath England. 4.5x8x6.75" tall painted and glazed china. Arms are designed like handles and liquid is poured from Donald's open mouth. - **$250 $600 $1100**

DDK-173

208

DONALD DUCK, DAISY & NEPHEWS

DDK-174

DDK-176

❏ **DDK-173. Donald Duck China Tea Set,** 1930s. Complete set of 15 pieces including four each of saucers, cups, plates and then one teapot, creamer and sugar with original label "Toy Tea Set/Made In Japan." Each piece has Donald image. Underside of teapot is marked "Donald Duck" with Disney copyright. Near Mint Boxed **$1000**

❏ **DDK-174. "Joe Allen" Autographed Photo With Donald Duck Doll,** 1930s. Glossy sepiatone photo measures 7.25x9.75" with Joe Allen credited as "Lyric Tenor" at bottom. Inscription reads "To Walter, John, Joe And George - Thanks Fellows For Your Wonderful Cooperation - I'm Most Grateful! All Of You Are Swell - Sincerely Joe Allen." Also signed "Quacks! 'Donald Duck'." - **$20 $40 $65**

❏ **DDK-176. Cloth Doll,** 1930s. Unmarked but likely Richard G. Krueger. 6x7x13.5" tall stuffed fabric doll accented by oil-cloth head and legs, painted eyes, complete attached hat, separate collar piece tied around neck, four felt buttons on jacket. **$350 $1250 $3000**

DDK-175

DDK-177

DDK-178

❏ **DDK-175. Cloth Doll With Tag,** 1930s. Knickerbocker. 4.5x5.5x12" tall stuffed fabric body with felt beak, collar, bow tie and tail; oilcloth eyes and pair of buttons on jacket, separate removable hat. Attached to one arm is original 1.5x2" diecut cardboard string tag. One side of tag pictures Donald and opposite side has maker's logo.
Doll - **$250 $500 $1000**
Tag - **$50 $100 $150**

❏ **DDK-177. Donald Duck Plaster Ashtray,** 1930s. Overall size is 3.25x3.5x5" tall. Unmarked. - **$65 $125 $225**

❏ **DDK-178. "Donald Duck" Birthday Card,** 1930s. English card measures 3.25x5.5". From "Mickey Mouse Cut-Out Numeral" series. - **$15 $40 $75**

DDK-179

DDK-180

❏ **DDK-179. Sand Sieve,** 1930s. Ohio Art Co. 7.75" diameter by 2" deep lithographed tin sifter with attached carrying handle and complete wire mesh. - **$150 $300 $550**

❏ **DDK-180. "Bayard Donald" First Issue Animated Alarm Clock,** 1930s.. Bayard. 2x4.75x4.75" tall metal case. Donald's head moves as seconds tick. Made in France. - **$200 $400 $725**

DONALD DUCK, DAISY & NEPHEWS

DDK-181

❑ **DDK-181. Rare "Donald Duck" Boxed Celluloid Wind-Up Toy,**
1930s. Toy is 4.5x9.5x2.5" tall with built-in key marked "Made In Japan" and box is marked "Distributors- Geo. Borgfeldt Corp., New York." Has small inspection stamp on Donald's rear end. Box - **$300 $650 $1200**
Toy - **$500 $1600 $3200**

❑ **DDK-182. Celluloid Wind-Up Nodder,**
1930s. "TT" of Japan. 5.25" tall figure attached to circular domed, painted tin base, complete with instruction string tag. Separate celluloid head attaches to body by a ratchet and gear mechanism with attached rod counterweight. Underside of base has interior rubber band. When wound, Donald nods his head back and forth. - **$350 $775 $1300**

DDK-183

❑ **DDK-183. Donald Figure Wind-Up,**
1930s. Schuco. 2.5x4x6" tall toy with painted tin body plus felt outfit, hands and tail. Inside of mouth is a bellows mechanism to produce quacking sound. - **$325 $700 $1350**

DDK-182

DDK-184

❑ **DDK-184. Donald Duck Small Carousel With Original Box,**
1930s. Made In Japan. Celluloid figure is 7.5" tall on painted metal base. Box is 3.25x5.25x2.75" deep. Box - **$300 $600 $1200**
Toy - **$350 $650 $1300**

DDK-185

❑ **DDK-185. Donald Duck Small Carousel Wind-Up,**
1930s. 3.25" celluloid Donald with canopy of hanging balls. Sits on 2.5" long metal base. Jointed left shoulder. - **$400 $800 $1600**

DDK-186

❑ **DDK-186. Donald Duck Small Tricycle Wind-up,**
1930s. Made in Japan for the English market. Toy is 1.5x3.25x4" tall with celluloid figure of Donald that includes lower body comprised of fabric pants. Rear of vehicle has British flag fabric. - **$500 $1000 $1500**

DONALD DUCK, DAISY & NEPHEWS

DDK-187

❑ **DDK-187. "Donald Cyclist" Large Celluloid On Tin Tricycle Wind-up,**
1930s. Made in Japan for English market distributed by Paradise Novelty Co. Toy is 3.25x5.5x6.25" tall. Donald's upper body and feet are celluloid and his pants are fabric. Rear of vehicle has British flag fabric accent. Box - **$300 $600 $1200**
Toy - **$600 $1200 $1800**

DDK-189

❑ **DDK-189. "Donald Duck Shooting Game,"**
1930s. Chad Valley. Boxed English game measures 6x11x1" deep. Includes 3 colorful die-cut cardboard targets, thick metal wire gun and 3 wooden projectiles. - **$65 $135 $250**

DDK-191

❑ **DDK-191. Candy Container,**
1930s. "Made In Japan" Disney copyright 2.25" diameter by 5" tall stiff cardboard simulated wooden barrel topped by 2" tall celluloid figure of Donald from waist up. - **$150 $300 $600**

DDK-188

❑ **DDK-188. "Donald Duck On Trapeze" With Original Box,**
1930s. Made In Japan. Wind-up frame with celluloid Donald is 8.25" tall. Box is 6x9.25x2" deep. Box - **$300 $600 $1200**
Toy - **$200 $400 $800**

DDK-190

❑ **DDK-190. "Donald Duck Choo-Choo" Fisher-Price Pull Toy,**
c. 1930s. Toy measures 3.5x7.5x7" tall. Made of wood/cardboard with paper labels. Marked "465," although this variety is not pictured in the Fisher-Price price guide by Murray & Fox. Toy pictured in that book as "465" is a Teddy Choo-Choo and this toy has same base with an attached Donald Duck figure. - **$175 $350 $700**

DDK-192

❑ **DDK-192 Donald Duck Candy Container,**
1930s. Japan. 5.5" tall container consisting of celluloid figure depicting Donald holding a rifle mounted on a barrel-like cardboard container. - **$150 $300 $600**

DONALD DUCK, DAISY & NEPHEWS

DDK-193

❏ **DDK-193. Donald Duck Squeaker Toy,**
1930s. Rubber hardens over time, so toy is hard to find in high grade. - **$125 $300 $650**

DDK-194 (Box)

DDK-195

❏ **DDK-194. Donald Duck Celluloid Waddler With Box,**
1930s. Toy - **$375 $775 $1200**
Box - **$350 $500 $800**
Complete - **$650 $1275 $2000**

❏ **DDK-195. Large Donald Duck Quacking Celluloid Wind-Up,**
1930s. Japan. Donald is 8.5" tall.
- **$375 $775 $1200**

DDK-196

❏ **DDK-196. Donald Duck Large Celluloid Roly-Poly,**
1930s."Japan" 7" tall. Figure has movable arms.
- **$150 $300 $500**

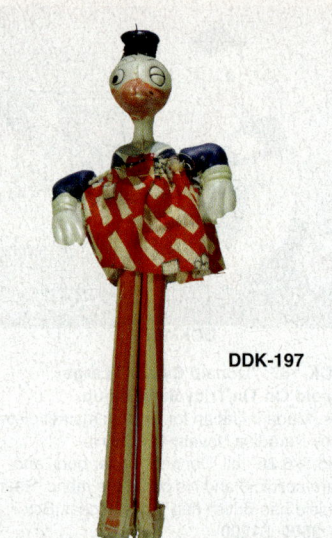

DDK-197

❏ **DDK-197. Donald Duck Party Favor,**
1930s. 6" tall celluloid, cloth, and cardboard.
- **$100 $200 $300**

DDK-198

❏ **DDK-198. Donald Duck Ceramic Tea Set With Figural Pieces Boxed,**
1930s. Japan. 7x10x3" deep box contains 7 piece set. Box has non-Disney graphics. Teapot is 4" tall. Set includes teapot, sugar, creamer, and matching pair of cups and saucers.
Near Mint Boxed - **$750**

DDK-194

DONALD DUCK, DAISY & NEPHEWS

DDK-199

◻ **DDK-199. Donald Duck Hanging Lapel Decorations On Card,**
c. 1930s. 7.5x10.5" cardboard display card with six pieces each 2" diameter.
Full Card - **$50 $100 $200**

DDK-200

◻ **DDK-200. Donald With Toothbrush Button,**
1930s. 1" unmarked but appears related to Kern County Health Dept. Mickey button.
- **$100 $200 $400**

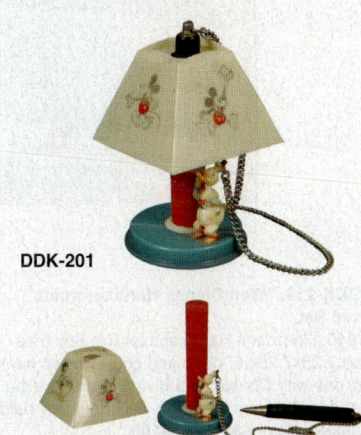

DDK-201

◻ **DDK-201. Donald Duck Celluloid Pencil Holder Designed As A Lamp,**
1930s. Japan. 3.25" tall. 1" tall Donald Figure attached to base. Shade features three images of Mickey and one of Donald. The center post holds a mechanical pencil which is attached to Donald's head by a chain. - **$150 $300 $500**

DDK-202

DDK-203

◻ **DDK-202. Donald Duck China Wall Pocket Planter,**
1930s. 5" tall. Incised text on reverse "Made In Japan/S1541." - **$250 $500 $1000**

◻ **DDK-203. Donald Duck Roly-Poly,**
1930s. 4" tall with Donald figure seated atop decorated ball. Interior has bell which rings as toy moves about. - **$75 $150 $275**

DDK-204

◻ **DDK-204. Donald Duck English Button,**
1930s. 1.25" "Granadier's Club" depicts Donald as an English Guard with a cork-popping rifle over his shoulder. - **$100 $200 $350**

DDK-205

◻ **DDK-205. "Donald Duck Archery" Boxed Target,**
1930s. Chad Valley, England. 11x13x1" deep box contains 10.5" diameter thick cardboard target. Photo example is missing gun and darts. Comes with three wood rods to stand upright.
Box - **$100 $175 $300**
Target - **$100 $175 $300**

DONALD DUCK, DAISY & NEPHEWS

DDK-206

❑ **DDK-206. Donald Duck Story Board Drawing,**
1940. 5 7/8"x7 7/8" full color art from a war time production. - **$100 $200 $400**

DDK-207

❑ **DDK-207. "Walt Disney Storybooks" Advertising Folder,**
1940. D.C. Heath & Co. Folder measures 6x9.25" and opens to 18x24". Used to advertise their series of eight books "For Use In Schools." - **$250 $500 $750**

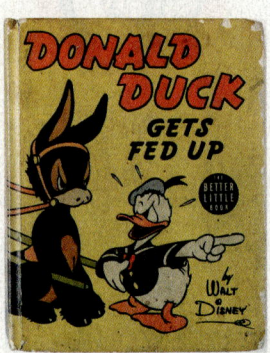

DDK-208

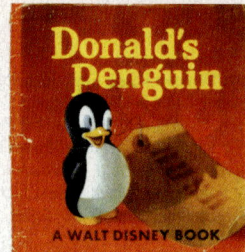

DDK-209

❑ **DDK-208. "Donald Duck Gets Fed Up" Big Better Little Book,**
1940. Whitman Better Little Book. #1462. - **$25 $80 $160**

❑ **DDK-209. "Donald's Penguin" Hardcover With Dust Jacket,**
1940. Garden City Publishing Co. Inc. 8.75x9.5" with 24 pages. Jacket - **$25 $100 $150** Book - **$75 $150 $250**

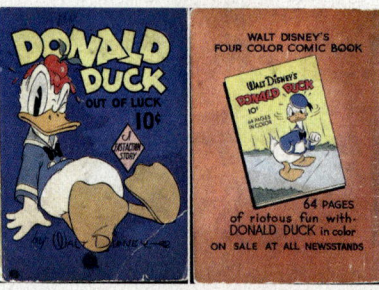

DDK-210

❑ **DDK-210. "Donald Duck Out Of Luck" Fast Action Book,**
1940. Dell Publishing Co. 4.5x5" format similar to a Whitman Big Little Book with 192 pages. - **$50 $125 $250**

DDK-211

❑ **DDK-211. "Liberty" Magazine With Classic Donald Cover,**
1940. 8.5x11.25" Volume 17, #43 from October 19, 1940. - **$25 $50 $125**

DDK-212

❑ **DDK-212. "Good Housekeeping" Magazine With Donald Page,**
1940. 8.5x11.5" monthly issue for March with full page color story titled "Donald's Elephant." Most issues of this magazine from 1934-1944 featured a Walt Disney story page. - **$5 $15 $30**

DDK-213

❑ **DDK-213. "Walt Disney Handkerchiefs" Boxed Set,**
c. 1940. Herrmann Handkerchief Co. Box measures 7.25x7.25x.5" deep and contains two hankies, one with Donald on a diving board and the other depicting him on swing. Box originally held 3 hankies. Box - **$35 $65 $100**
Each Hanky - **$15 $25 $40**

DONALD DUCK, DAISY & NEPHEWS

DDK-214

DDK-215

DDK-217

☐ **DDK-216. Donald Duck Courvoisier Galleries Print,** c. 1940. From a series of eight different. Art area is 8x10". - **$75 $125 $225**

☐ **DDK-217. Donald Duck Figurine,** c. 1940. Brayton's Laguna Pottery. 3.5x4x3.5" tall painted and glazed ceramic. - **$75 $150 $275**

DDK-218

☐ **DDK-218. Dell Comic Book Promo,** 1940. Used as postcard and promo flier. Card - **$50 $100 $175** Flier - **$75 $125 $250**

DDK-219

☐ **DDK-219. Donald Duck Plaster Statue,** c. 1940. Painted hollow plaster and measures 3.25x4.25x13.25" tall. - **$25 $50 $100**

DDK-220

☐ **DDK-220. The Wise Little Hen Argentinian Hardcover,** 1941. Coleccion Mis Cuentos. 7.25x10.75" foreign printing of the 1934 David McKay book. - **$100 $200 $300**

DDK-221

☐ **DDK-214. Donald Duck Studio Fan Card,** c. 1940. Stiff paper card measures 7-1/8x9" and has large facsimile Walt Disney signature. Same or Similar - **$30 $60 $100**

☐ **DDK-215. Movie Theater Original Art,** c. 1940. Runkle's Display Service. 14x22" stiff art board illustration in poster paint for a movie theater in Los Angeles. Large title at top reads "Donald Duck Cartoon" and art is signed by artist "Robert Runkle" with ink stamp name and address at bottom margin. Similar - **$200 $300 $600**

DDK-216

☐ **DDK-221. "Donald Duck Large Feature Comics #16,"** 1941. Dell Publishing Co. - **$484 $1452 $7500**

DDK-222

☐ **DDK-222. "Donald Duck Comic Paint Book,"** 1941. Dell Publishing Co. Issue #20 measuring 8.5x11.5" with 48 pages. Features reprints of Al Taliaferro Donald Duck comic strips. - **$516 $1548 $8000**

DONALD DUCK, DAISY & NEPHEWS

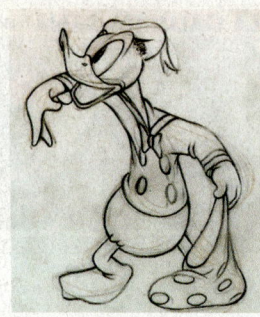
DDK-223

DDK-227

DDK-230

❑ DDK-229. "The Life Of Donald Duck" Book,
1941. Random House. 8.5x11.5" hardcover, 72 pages. Many illustrations from or based on various shorts. - **$75 $150 $375**

❑ DDK-230. "The Life Of Donald Duck" Australian Book,
1941. John Sands Pty. Ltd. 8.25x11" cardboard cover edition, 32 pages, an abbreviated version of the Random House hardcover, 72 pages. - **$65 $125 $275**

DDK-224

DDK-228

❑ DDK-223. Pencil Drawing,
1941. Animation paper is 10x12" centered by 3.5x4.5" full figure image of Donald looking upward and holding a sack. From 'Timber' short feature and No. "44" from a numbered sequence. - **$200 $400 $600**

❑ DDK-224. "Donald Duck Choo Choo" Fisher-Price Pull Toy,
1941. Wood toy with paper labels measures 3.5x8.5x7" tall. This toy is 1" shorter than the 1940 version. - **$125 $250 $400**

DDK-231

DDK-232

❑ DDK-227. "Donald Duck Sees Stars" Better Little Book,
1941. Whitman. Book #1422. - **$25 $80 $160**

❑ DDK-228. "Donald Duck Takes It On The Chin,"
1941. Dell. 4x5.5" "Fast Action Story" with 192 pages. - **$75 $150 $250**

DDK-225

DDK-226

DDK-229

❑ DDK-225 Strutter Donald Duck Pull Toy,
1941. Fisher-Price. Toy measures 4.5x11x10" tall. Wooden with paper labels. Toy is number #510. Produced for one year. - **$125 $250 $400**

❑ DDK-226 "Donald Duck Says Such Luck" Better Little Book,
1941. Whitman Book #1424. - **$25 $80 $160**

❑ DDK-231. Blotter Card,
1941. Nu Blue Sunoco. 4x7" illustration of him at a punching bag which strikes back. Text includes "Instant Response/Fastest Starting Gas We Ever Made." Unused local imprint band at bottom margin. - **$20 $40 $75**

❑ DDK-232. "Sunoco Oil" Blotter With Mickey And Donald,
c. 1941. Blotter measures 4x7". - **$30 $65 $125**

DONALD DUCK, DAISY & NEPHEWS

DDK-233

❑ **DDK-233. Opening Title Painting,**
1942. Used to introduce several of Donald's WWII-era cartoons. Ink, watercolor and airbrush on heavy paper. Unique - **$10,000**

DDK-234

DDK-235

❑ **DDK-234. Donald Gets Drafted Cel,**
1942. Courvoisier Galleries. 13x14.75" matted and painted 3.5x5" figure image on painted background of tent, grass accents, distant hills. Background has a "WD" symbol in circle at lower right. Reverse has an ink stamp copyright. - **$600 $1200 $1800**

❑ **DDK-235. "Donald Duck" With Cart Fisher-Price Pull Toy,**
1942. Wood toy with paper labels measures 4x10x8.5" tall and numbered "544." When pulled, arms move and clicking noise is produced. - **$100 $200 $400**

DDK-236

DDK-237

❑ **DDK-236. "Donald Duck Grapefruit And Orange Juice" Label,**
1942. Unused label measures 4.25x11". - **$30 $60 $110**

❑ **DDK-237. "Donald Duck Florida Orange Juice" Can,**
1942. Quart size 4.25" diameter by 7" tall tin canister in paper label wrapper with two differing illustrations. Reverse depicts Mickey and Pluto. - **$40 $75 $150**

DDK-238

❑ **DDK-238. "Donald Duck Grapefruit Juice" Can,**
1942. Quart size 4.25" diameter by 7" tall tin canister in paper label wrapper with two differing illustrations. Reverse depicts Mickey with juice text. - **$40 $75 $150**

DDK-239

❑ **DDK-239. "Donald Duck" Glass,**
1942. Glass is 4.75" tall from set of six. Reverse has four-line verse describing the scene. Each - **$30 $60 $90**

DDK-240

❑ **DDK-240. "Der Fuehrer's Face" Sheet Music,**
1942. Four page, 9x12" sheet music with words and music by Oliver Wallace for song from Disney film "Donald Duck In Nutzi Land." - **$25 $50 $100**

DONALD DUCK, DAISY & NEPHEWS

DDK-241

❏ **DDK-241 Metal Toys File Copy Catalogue Featuring Donald Duck,**
1942. Ohio Art Co. 8.5x11" eight-page full color catalogue on glossy paper for Spring-Summer season for "Lithographed Metal Toys" including sand sets, watering cans, sand pails, banks, beverage coasters. Donald items pictured include a watering can, two shovels and five sand pails. Banks include a baseball and figural tank. - **$30 $65 $125**

DDK-242

❏ **DDK-242. Donald "Sunoco" Blotter,**
1942. Blotter measures 3.75x6" and has small "Buy War Bonds" design. - **$20 $45 $90**

DDK-243

❏ **DDK-243. Donald Duck "Sunoco Oil" Blotter,**
1942. Blotter measures 3.75x6" and has printed "Buy War Bonds" logo. - **$35 $65 $100**

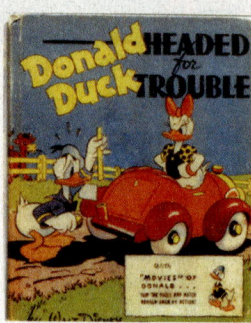

DDK-244

❏ **DDK-244. "Donald Duck Headed For Trouble" Better Little Book,**
1942. Whitman Better Little Book #1430 designed with "Flip Book" page upper corner illustrations plus story art. - **$25 $80 $160**

❏ **DDK-245 Pencil Drawing,**
c. 1942. Sheet of animation paper is 8.5x12" centered by 3.5x4" image of Donald. No. "269" from a numbered sequence. - **$80 $175 $300**

DDK-245

DDK-246

DDK-247

❏ **DDK-246. Donald Duck "Sunoco Oil" Ink Blotter,**
1943. Blotter measures 3.75x6-1/8" with text "Reinforced For Rationed Driving." - **$20 $50 $125**

❏ **DDK-247. "Donald Duck/Goodyear Tires" Premium Booklet,**
1943. Booklet measures 3.5x6" with 8 pages. Prepared by "Goodyear" printed with permission of "Look Magazine where this material appeared in the May 18, 1943 issue." - **$90 $150 $250**

DDK-248

DDK-249

DONALD DUCK, DAISY & NEPHEWS

❑ **DDK-248. "Donald Duck Off The Beam" Better Little Book,**
1943. Whitman Better Little Book. Book #1432. Pages have additional illustration at top right corner that shows Donald golfing when pages are flipped. Editions with and without flip pictures. - **$25 $80 $160**

❑ **DDK-249. Spanish Version Donald Duck Book,**
1943. Stiff glossy paper book measures 9.25x12.5" with 12 pages in Spanish text, but otherwise identical, except for back cover illustration to Whitman book #978 from 1935. - **$125 $300 $600**

DDK-250

DDK-251

❑ **DDK-250. "Walt Disney's Comics And Stories" Sears Giveaway,**
1943. K.K. Publications Inc. Measures 7.25x10.25" with 36 pages and includes a "Mickey Mouse Movie Wheel" cut-out. - **$50 $150 $625**

❑ **DDK-251. Donald Duck Birthday Card,**
1943. Hallmark Co. Closed 3.5 x 4.5" textured paper folder with front and inside greeting art. - **$20 $35 $60**

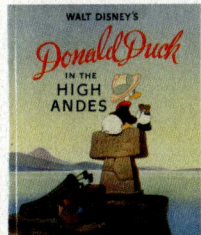 

DDK-252

❑ **DDK-52. "Donald Duck In The High Andes" Hardcover With Dust Jacket,**
1943. Grosset & Dunlap. 32 pages based on "Saludos Amigos."
Dust Jacket - **$50 $100 $200**
Book - **$50 $100 $200**

DDK-253

DDK-254

❑ **DDK-253. "Donald Duck Goes South American In 'Saludos Amigos'" Australian Folder Book,**
c. 1943. Colourtone Pty. Ltd. 6.5x14.25" cardboard book that opens to a length of 19.25". Contains a number of character cut-outs and interior is gray cardboard depicting scenes from the film. - **$50 $100 $160**

❑ **DDK-254. "America's Greatest Comics" Calendar Card With Donald And Others,**
1944. Chicago-Herald American. 8.5x11" Sunday newspaper comics promotion card with 12-month calender. - **$35 $75 $150**

DDK-255

❑ **DDK-255. War Bond Poster,**
1944. Scarce. - **$125 $250 $500**

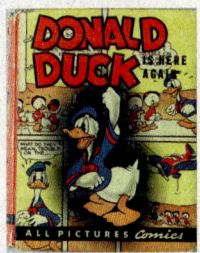
DDK-256

DDK-257

DONALD DUCK, DAISY & NEPHEWS

❑ **DDK-256. "Donald Duck Is Here Again" Better Little Book,**
1944. Whitman Better Little Book. #1484 in "All Pictures Comics" format of reprints from newspaper strips. - **$25 $80 $160**

❑ **DDK-257. "What Is Propaganda" War Department Education Manual,**
1944. American Historical Assn. 5x7.5", 48-page booklet from the "GI Round Table Series." Shows Donald on inside back cover reading newspaper "Daily Quack." - **$75 $150 $235**

DDK-258

❑ **DDK-258. "Donald Duck" Apron,**
1944. Canvas apron is 16x28" and image of Donald peeling potatoes at center is 8x9". Top reads "K.P. Duty" and he holds potato skin peeled into the word "Phooey." - **$35 $85 $190**

DDK-259

❑ **DDK-259. Donald Duck Christmas Card,**
1944. Hallmark. 5x5.75" card for "Husband." 8 pages with illustrations of Donald and Daisy throughout. - **$12 $25 $50**

DDK-260

(FRONT)

DDK-261
(BACK)

❑ **DDK-260. Christmas Card Booklet,**
1944. Hallmark, 4.75x4.75" folder opening to three inside double-panel pages. Art and text detail Donald's daily Christmas shopping adventures until too late to select a Christmas card. Text concludes "Oh Nuts! Merry Christmas Anyway!" along with P.S. message "I'll Send You A Purty Card Next Year." - **$25 $50 $75**

❑ **DDK-261. War Bond Promo Cardboard Stand-Up,**
1944. Scarce. - **$75 $200 $350**

DDK-262

❑ **DDK-262. "Sunoco" Donald Blotter,**
c. 1944. Blotter measures 3.75x6" and shows Donald driving his car through a large life preserver. - **$40 $85 $150**

DDK-263

DDK-264

❑ **DDK-263. "Donald Duck Up In The Air" Better Little Book,**
1945. Whitman. Book #1486. - **$30 $90 $180**

❑ **DDK-264. "Walt Disney's Comics And Stories" Christmas Subscription Card With Envelope,**
1945. Dell Publishing Co. 3.75x8.75" subscription card in envelope illustrated front and back.
Envelope - **$5 $15 $25**
Card - **$25 $50 $85**

DDK-265

DDK-266

DONALD DUCK, DAISY & NEPHEWS

❏ **DDK-265.** "Walt Disney Jigsaw Puzzle,"
c. 1945. Jaymar. 7x10x2" deep box contains complete puzzle from "Series No. 4" featuring characters from Three Caballeros. Puzzle is 14x22" when assembled. - **$15 $30 $65**

❏ **DDK-266.** "Walt Disney's Paint Book,"
1946. Whitman. 8.5x11" early post-WWII issue, 96 pages. Content is largely Mickey, Donald, Pluto and Goofy although also a number of other characters. - **$25 $60 $125**

DDK-267

DDK-268

❏ **DDK-267.** "Donald Duck Paint Box,"
1946. Transogram 3x8x.5" deep lithographed tin case containing original cardboard insert holding all paint tablets in place. - **$20 $40 $85**

❏ **DDK-268.** Donald Duck Pencil Drawing From Dumbbell Of The Yukon,
1946. Image is 3x3.75". From a numbered sequence and this is "73". - **$115 $225 $350**

DDK-269

DDK-270

❏ **DDK-269.** Donald Duck Pencil Drawing From "Dumbbell Of The Yukon,"
1946. Animation paper is 10x12" with large 6x7" image. No. "83" from a numbered sequence. - **$65 $150 $250**

❏ **DDK-270.** "Cheerios" Box With Disney Comic Book Offer,
1946. General Mills. 2.5x6.5x8.5" tall box advertises Disney pocket-size comic book sets listed as "W,X,Y and Z." Sets were obtained when order blank from top of package and 10-cents was sent in. - **$135 $275 $550**

DDK-271

DDK-272

❏ **DDK-271.** "Donald Duck And Ghost Morgan's Treasure" Better Little Book,
1946. Whitman. Book #1411 "All Picture Comics" featuring story art by Barks and Jack Hannah. - **$35 $95 $195**

❏ **DDK-272.** Donald Duck Easter Greeting Card,
1946. Hallmark. 5.25x6.25" card shows 13 different images of Donald. Comes with feather that was to be attached to diecut hole in hat. - **$15 $30 $60**

DDK-273

DDK-274

❏ **DDK-273.** Donald Duck "Missin' You" Card,
1946. Hallmark. Folded size is 4.75x4.75" with a total length of 18" when fully opened. Includes seven different illustrations of Donald. A Hallmark Rufftex Card. Verse ends with Donald exclaiming "Dammit!" - **$50 $100 $150**

❏ **DDK-274.** "Donald Duck Duet" Wind-Up,
1946. Marx. 4x7x10.5" tall lithographed tin toy with built-in key. - **$400 $900 $1500**

DONALD DUCK, DAISY & NEPHEWS

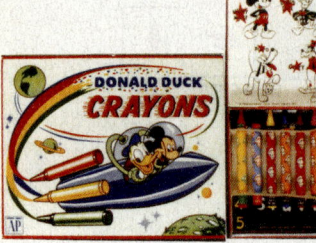
DDK-275

DDK-276

DDK-278

DDK-279

DDK-281

❏ **DDK-280. "The New Donald Duck Wrist Watch" Box Lid Proof Sheet,**
1947. U.S. Time. 5.5x9.5" glossy paper proof sheet. - **$50 $100 $200**

❏ **DDK-281. Donald Duck Wrist Watch in Box,**
1947. U.S. Time watch. Near Mint Boxed - **$1000**
Watch Only - **$100 $250 $500**

❏ **DDK-275. "Donald Duck Crayons" Tin,**
1947. Transogram 4.5x5.5x2.5" deep lithographed tin case with hinged lid. Inside lid pictures six characters. Set of ten crayons, each with Donald portrait label, is held in place by cardboard tray with illustration on reverse of Mickey and Donald at an easel holding illustration of Pluto. - **$30 $60 $110**

❏ **DDK-276. "Donald Duck And The Green Serpent" Better Little Book,**
1947. Whitman Better Little Book. #1432 in content format of comic panel on every page rather than text with illustrations. - **$30 $90 $180**

❏ **DDK-278 "Walt Disney's Comics And Stories" Subscription Postcard,**
1947. Card measures 3.5x5.5" and text reads "Yo Ho Ho And A Stick Of Gum, We've Set Our Course-To Your House We'll Come." - **$20 $50 $80**

❏ **DDK-279. Donald and Nephews Tree Ornament,**
1947. Stiff cardboard 6.25x6.75" with facsimile Walt Disney signature. - **$15 $30 $60**

DDK-282

DDK-277

❏ **DDK-277. "Walt Disney's Comics And Stories" Subscription Mailer With Donald,**
1947. Dell Publishing Co. 7.25x10.25" Four-page folder. Front and back art originally appeared on 1945 issues of this comic book. Original folded size is 3.5x7.5". - **$75 $130 $225**

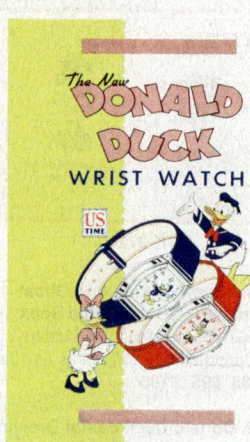
DDK-280

DDK-283

DONALD DUCK, DAISY & NEPHEWS

❏ **DDK-282. Daisy Duck Wristwatch,**
1947. US Time. 1.5" tall chromed metal case. This is the first female Disney character watch made. - **$110 $275 $550**

❏ **DDK-283. "Donald" Duck Figurine,**
c. 1947. American Pottery. 6.25" tall painted and glazed with foil label on one foot. - **$50 $100 $200**

DDK-286

DDK-284

DDK-285

DDK-287

❏ **DDK-284. Angry Donald Duck Figurine,**
c. 1947. Modern Ceramic Products of Sydney, Australia. 6" tall glazed ceramic. - **$60 $115 $175**

❏ **DDK-285. Angry Donald Duck Figurine From Mexico,**
c. 1947. 3.75" tall glazed ceramic. Marked "Mexico". - **$50 $100 $150**

❏ **DDK-286. Donald Duck Ceramic Figure,**
c. 1947. Zaccagnini. 5.5x7.5x9" tall beautifully painted and glazed ceramic with mark on underside for this Italian company. Has removable painted wood golf club. - **$1000 $2000 $3500**

❏ **DDK-287. Donald Duck Ceramic Figure,**
c. 1947. Zaccagnini. 5.5x7.5x9" tall beautifully painted and glazed ceramic with mark on underside for this Italian company. Has removable painted wood golf club. - **$1000 $2000 $3500**

DONALD DUCK, DAISY & NEPHEWS

DDK-288

❏ **DDK-289. Salt & Pepper Set,**
c. 1947. Leeds China Co. Matching pair of 3.25" tall glazed ceramic shakers with over-the-glaze paint. This is scarcer variety color set depicting Donald with orange bill and feet, blue bow tie, red buttons on jacket and black accents on sleeves. - **$20 $40 $100**

DDK-290

❏ **DDK-290. "Donald Duck" Cookie Jar By Leeds,**
c. 1947. 12" tall. - **$80 $175 $350**

DDK-291

DDK-292

❏ **DDK-291. Salt & Pepper Set,**
c. 1947. Leeds China Co. Matching pair of 3.25" tall glazed ceramic shakers with over-the-glaze paint. - **$20 $40 $100**

❏ **DDK-292. Figure Bank,**
c. 1947. Leeds China Co. 4x4x6" tall glazed ceramic with over-the-glaze paint. - **$25 $50 $85**

DDK-293

❏ **DDK-293. "Donald Duck" Lamp With Shade,**
c. 1947. Railley Corp. 9" tall. Cardboard shade measures 6.5" tall. Nautical theme shade with repeating images. Lamp - **$50 $100 $150** Shade - **$50 $100 $150**

DDK-294

❏ **DDK-294. Donald Duck Car,**
1947. Sun Rubber Company. Blue car variety. Scarce. - **$80 $175 $350**

DDK-295

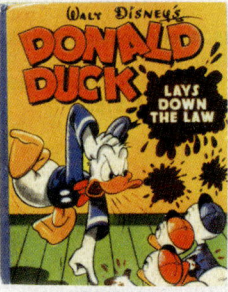

DDK-296

❏ **DDK-288. Donald Duck Ceramic Figure,**
c. 1947. Zaccagnini. 4.5x5.5x9" tall beautifully painted and glazed ceramic with mark on underside for this Italian company. Has removable painted wood golf club. - **$1000 $2000 $3500**

DDK-289

DONALD DUCK, DAISY & NEPHEWS

❏ **DDK-295. "Sunoco" Donald Blotter,**
1948. Blotter is 4x6.75" and shows illustration of him in car parked in front of "Nu-Blue Sunoco" gas pump. - **$25 $50 $100**

❏ **DDK-296. "Donald Duck Lays Down The Law" Better Little Book,**
1948. Whitman. Book #1449. - **$25 $80 $160**

DDK-297

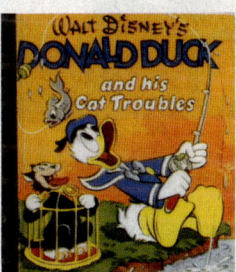
DDK-298

DDK-299

❏ **DDK-297. "Story Hour Series" Walt Disney Softcover Book,**
1948. Whitman. 4.5x6" with 32 pages titled "Donald Duck In Bringing Up The Boys." - **$15 $40 $75**

❏ **DDK-298. "Donald Duck And His Cat Troubles" Book,**
1948. Whitman. 5x5.5" hardcover from "845" series, 96 pages. - **$20 $50 $85**

❏ **DDK-299. "Donald Duck/Mickey Mouse Giant Crayons,"**
1949. Transogram. 4.25x6.25x.75" deep box contains set of 10 different color wax crayons. - **$15 $30 $70**

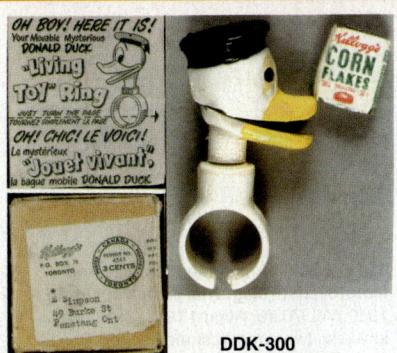
DDK-300

DDK-301

❏ **DDK-300 "Donald Duck 'Living Toy' Ring,"**
1949. Kellogg's. 2.25x2.25x1.5" mailing box holds 4x4.5", four-page instruction sheet, 2-1/8" hard plastic ring and small Corn Flakes cereal box magnet. Canadian issue with text on instruction sheet in French and English. Near Mint Boxed - **$600**
Ring And Magnet - **$100 $200 $350**

❏ **DDK-301. Donald Duck Living Toy Ring Radio Advertisement Record,**
1949. Kellogg's Pep. 12" diameter one-sided 78 rpm "Produced By Kenyon & Eckhardt/ Recorded By Radio Recorders Hollywood, California." Additional text "Donald Duck Pep Spot/October 17, 1949." Record features the voice of Donald as well as an announcer who describes in detail the Kellogg's Pep premium ring. - **$40 $75 $140**

DDK-302

DDK-303

❏ **DDK-302. "Donald Duck 'Living Toy' Ring" Newspaper Ad,**
1949. Clipped ad measuring 15.5x21.5" from Sunday newspaper comic section. - **$12 $25 $50**

❏ **DDK-303. "Donald Duck In Volcano Valley" Better Little Book,**
1949. Whitman. Book #1457. - **$25 $80 $160**

DDK-304

DDK-305

❏ **DDK-304. "Donald Duck And The Mystery Of The Double X" Better Little Book,**
1949. Whitman. "New" Better Little Book #705-10. - **$15 $40 $80**

❏ **DDK-305. "Walt Disney's Christmas Parade" Comic Book,**
1949. Dell Publishing Co. Issue #1 in "Giant" format, 80 pages. First 24-page story is by Carl Barks as is the last page. - **$55 $165 $1100**

DONALD DUCK, DAISY & NEPHEWS

DDK-306

DDK-307

❑ **DDK-306. "American Bicyclist And Motorcyclist" Magazine,**
1949. Shelby. Volume 70, #9 from September 1949. Features one-page ad for Donald Duck bicycle with photo of both boys' and girls' models plus Donald illustration. - **$10 $20 $30**

❑ **DDK-307. "American Bicyclist And Motorcyclist" Magazine With Donald Ad,**
1949. Vol. 70 #8, August 1949, 9x12" issue including two-page illustrated ad for "Shelby Donald Duck Bike." - **$10 $20 $35**

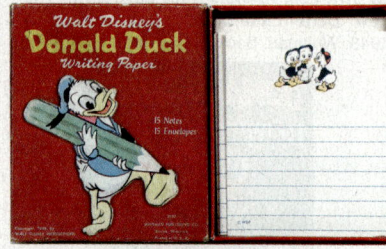

DDK-310

DDK-311

DDK-308

❑ **DDK-308. Donald Duck Boys Bike,**
1949. Shelby product features horn and Donald headlight. Bike is yellow with light blue highlights. Rare. - **$2500 $5000 $8000**

❑ **DDK-310. "Donald Duck Writing Paper" Boxed Set,**
1949. Whitman. 4.25x5x1" deep boxed original set of 15 folder sheets of 3.5x4.25" lined notepaper and 15 plain white envelopes. - **$15 $25 $50**

❑ **DDK-311. Donald Duck Figurine,**
c. 1949. American Pottery. 2x4.5x2.5" tall painted and glazed ceramic. Unmarked but by American Pottery. - **$50 $100 $175**

DDK-312

DDK-309

❑ **DDK-309. Donald Duck Girls Bike,**
1949. Shelby product features horn and Donald headlight. Bike is light blue with yellow highlights. Rare. - **$2300 $4700 $7500**

DONALD DUCK, DAISY & NEPHEWS

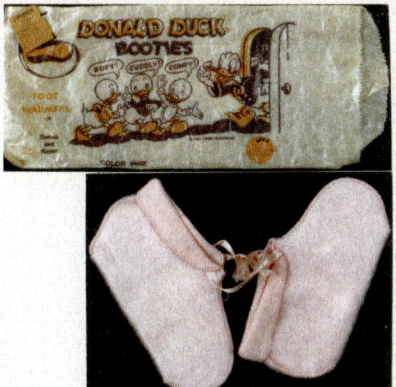

DDK-313

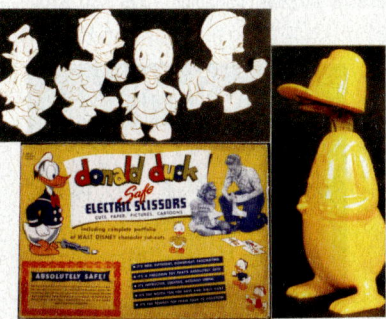

DDK-315

❏ **DDK-316. Daisy Duck Pencil Drawing,**
1940s. Image is 4x7" from a numbered sequence and this is "155." - **$75 $140 $250**

❏ **DDK-317. Jack-In-The-Box Toy,**
1940s. "Spear Product." 4.5x4.5x4.75" tall papered wooden box with latch front. Unlatching pops open the box lid and releases a pop-up Donald figure with composition head and fabric body over coil spring. - **$250 $500 $1000**

❏ **DDK-312. "Donald Duck" Pitcher,**
c. 1949. Leeds China Co. 4x4.5x6.5" tall painted and glazed china. Tail on back is designed like handle. - **$25 $50 $75**

❏ **DDK-313. "Donald Duck Booties" Envelope With Contents,**
1940s. 4x9.5" glassine envelope containing unworn "Size Medium" cotton/rayon fabric "Foot Warmers." Illustration on envelope is of Donald motioning his nephews to bed and they are depicted saying "Soft/Cuddly/Comfy." Booties are generic with no Donald designs. - **$15 $35 $65**

❏ **DDK-315. "Donald Duck Electric Scissors" Boxed Set,**
1940s. Universal Novelties Corp. 8x12x2.25" deep boxed complete set of figural scissors with electrical cord plus "Walt Disney Character Cut-Out Portfolio." The figural scissors are the first version in yellow hard plastic with attached electric cord. Donald's head is removable revealing thin metal scissor blades. Portfolio consists of sixteen different character images, each about 4.5" tall. - **$55 $110 $175**

DDK-316

DDK-314

❏ **DDK-314. Sylvania Radio Bulbs 18x28" Sign,**
1940s. Rare. This Version - **$1200 $3250 $5500**
Smaller Version (scarce) - **$300 $600 $1200**

DDK-317

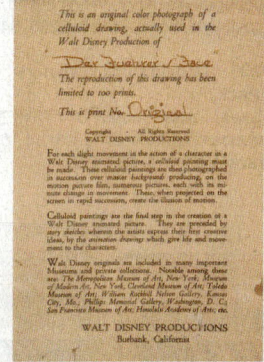

DDK-318

❏ **DDK-318. Disney Studios Donald Duck Original Publicity Cel Set-Up Signed By Walt Disney,**
1940s.15x15x1.5" deep frame with original cel. Clear acetate sheet over full color hand inked cutout cel of Donald mounted against prepared air brushed background. Lower right has a 3x5" area with bold inscription and signature of Walt Disney. Not from a cartoon. Used late 1940s - early 1950s for publicity and sometimes given to VIP guests at the studio.
Signed - **$1000 $2000 $4000**
Unsigned - **$500 $100 $1500**

DONALD DUCK, DAISY & NEPHEWS

DDK-319

DDK-320

❏ **DDK-321. "6 Puzzles By Walt Disney" Boxed Set,**
1940s. Ontex. 7x9.5x1.5" deep box contains six 6x8.75" puzzles. Canadian. - **$25 $50 $100**

DDK-322

❏ **DDK-322. "Donald Duck Meets The Seven Dwarfs Puzzle,"**
1940s. Ontex of Canada. 9.25x12.75x1" deep box. - **$25 $50 $90**

DDK-324

DDK-325

❏ **DDK-324. Donald Duck Figurine,**
1940s. Brayton Laguna Pottery. 3x3.5x6" tall painted and glazed ceramic. - **$75 $150 $250**

❏ **DDK-325. Mexican Figurine,**
1940s. Painted and glazed ceramic is 3x3.25x4" tall marked by Disney copyright and "Mexico" although identical pose but smaller size to figurine made by Shaw and American Pottery c. 1946. - **$40 $75 $135**

❏ **DDK-319. "Donald Duck" Xylophone Pull Toy,**
1940s. Fisher-Price. Large 6x11x13.25" wood toy with paper labels. #177. When pulled, Donald plays xylophone. - **$110 $225 $400**

❏ **DDK-320. "Donald Duck Transfers" English Pack,**
1940s. "Tower Press Product" of 4.75x6.25" diecut cardboard folder holding foldout 18" strip with 36 transfers. - **$15 $30 $50**

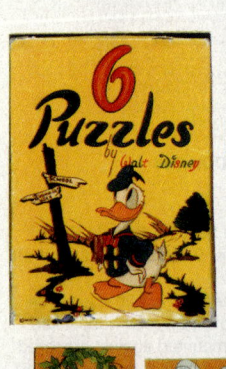

DDK-321

DDK-323

❏ **DDK-323. "Donald Duck" Figurine,**
1940s. Leeds China Co. 4x4.5x6.5" tall painted and glazed china. - **$50 $100 $160**

DDK-326

DONALD DUCK, DAISY & NEPHEWS

DDK-327

❑ **DDK-326. Louie Baseball Figurine,**
1940s. Shaw Pottery. 2.5" tall painted and glazed figurine from three-piece set depicting Donald's nephews playing baseball. Louie is depicted wearing catcher's mitt. Each - **$30 $60 $85**

❑ **DDK-327. Foreign Figurine,**
1940s. Unmarked but believed Portuguese 3.75x4x6.75" tall glazed ceramic with angry facial expression plus mitt hands formed and colored to suggest boxing gloves. - **$100 $200 $300**

DDK-328

DDK-329

❑ **DDK-328. Donald Duck Figural Pencil Sharpener,**
1940s. Unmarked cast metal. 1.5" long by 1.25" tall. Some maker also produced a Mickey and a Pluto. - **$40 $75 $125**

❑ **DDK-329. "Donald Duck/Joe Carioca" Turnabout Cookie Jar,**
1940s. Leeds China Co. 7x7x13" tall heavy glazed ceramic with over-the-glaze paint. Great two-in-one design depicting Donald on one side and Joe on the other. Incised text on underside reads "Donald Duck/Joe Carioca/Three Cabelleros" along with copyright. - **$60 $150 $300**

DDK-330

DDK-331

❑ **DDK-330. Plaster Carnival Statue,**
1940s. Painted hollow plaster figure is 4x4.5x13.5" tall, one of several known color variations. - **$15 $30 $50**

❑ **DDK-331. Plaster Figurine,**
1940s. "ITC" and Walt Disney copyrights 2.5x3x3.5" tall painted and glazed plaster image of Donald seated on tree stump. - **$25 $50 $100**

DDK-332

DDK-333

❑ **DDK-332. Donald Duck "Happiness Club" Australian Celluloid Button,**
1940s. Highly-domed 13/16" celluloid also reading "Arcadia Lidcombe Member." Various sponsor imprints. - **$75 $150 $225**

❑ **DDK-333. Movie Club Button,**
1940s. 13/16" Celluloid. Australian. - **$75 $150 $225**

DDK-334

❑ **DDK-334. Donald Figural Lamp,**
1940s. Leeds China Co. Over-the-glaze paint ceramic lamp measures 3.5x4.5x10.5" tall. - **$45 $85 $165**

DONALD DUCK, DAISY & NEPHEWS

DDK-335

DDK-338

DDK-341

❑ **DDK-335. "Donald Duck" Lamp,**
1940s. Unmarked but Leeds China Co. 5" bottom diameter by 7.25" tall ceramic over-the-glaze paint figural of him atop candlestick holder with arm wrapped around dripping candle. - **$100 $225 $350**

❑ **DDK-338. "Donald Duck" Wall Plaque,**
1940s. 4.5x5.5x.25" thick brown pressed wood with clear laminate cover over portrait picture. - **$20 $40 $65**

❑ **DDK-340. "Donald Duck ABC" Planter,**
1950. Unmarked but Leeds China Co. 3.5x6.5x5.5" tall painted and glazed ceramic. - **$25 $50 $80**

❑ **DDK-341. Donald As Cowboy Planter,**
1950. Leeds China Co. 3x7.25x6.5" tall. - **$35 $80 $135**

DDK-336

DDK-339

DDK-342

DDK-337

❑ **DDK-339. Donald As Cowboy Lamp Base,**
1950. Leeds China Co. 4x4x6.5" tall ceramic figural base with attached metal tube to bulb holder plus original cord. - **$50 $100 $175**

DDK-340

DDK-343

❑ **DDK-336. Donald Duck Glow-In-The Dark Picture,**
1940s. Wooden frame measures 8.75x10.75x5" deep and contains picture of Donald under glass. - **$15 $30 $50**

❑ **DDK-337. "Glow in the Dark" Picture,**
1940s. In a brown frame. - **$15 $30 $50**

❑ **DDK-342. Donald's Nephews Pin Set,**
1940s. Alpha-Craft. Set of three 3.75x4.5x.5" deep boxes, each holding 1.5" tall silvered brass figure pin on card individually naming each of the nephews. Each Boxed - **$5 $15 $30**

❑ **DDK-343. "Donald Duck" Glass,**
1940s. 4.5" tall tumbler featuring image of him and a bird amid flowers and grass. Reverse has four-line verse mentioning "Chocolate Milk Is Good." Probably late 1940s but possibly early 1950s. Also issued without verse. Verse - **$50 $85 $150** Without Verse - **$40 $75 $125**

DONALD DUCK, DAISY & NEPHEWS

DDK-344

DDK-345

DDK-347

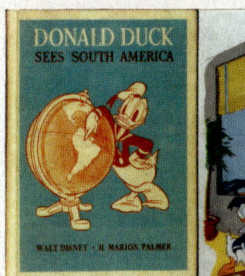

DDK-350

DDK-351

❏ DDK-347. "Walt Disney Character School Tablet" Sales Samples,
1940s. Pad of twelve 7.75x10" stiff paper tablet covers. Covers are mostly reprinted front covers of previous Walt Disney Comics and Stories comic books. Covers not shown in our photo are Donald w/flower, Donald and Mickey on a see-saw, Donald eating ice cream with Dopey, Donald and Mickey on sled, four involving Donald with one or all of his nephews in some type of antics. Set - **$75 $150 $275**

❏ DDK-344. Portrait Glass,
1940s. 5" tall clear tumbler with major single image of Donald plus bottom perimeter repeated raised images of Mickey Mouse, Donald and Pluto as if running around the glass. - **$25 $50 $75**

❏ DDK-345. Donald Duck China Tea Set,
1940s. Generic box measures 10x12x2.5" deep with complete 15-piece set and paper label with Disney copyright marked "Made In Occupied Japan." Each piece has image of Donald and set consists of: six 1" tall cups, six 3.5" diameter saucers, 2.25" tall creamer and sugar and 3.5" tall teapot. Near Mint Boxed - **$500**

DDK-346

❏ DDK-346. Oil Company Sticker,
1940s. Sunoco. 2.25x3" diecut sticker from series with stiff fabric backing issued by "Mystik Division-Chicago Show Ptg. Co." Front is "More Power Miles And Better Luck With Sunoco Oil-Says Donald Duck." Each - **$15 $35 $65**

DDK-348

DDK-349

❏ DDK-348. "America's Greatest Comics" Newspaper Promo Sign With Donald And Others,
1940s. Chicago Herald-American. Thin cardboard 10.5x14" hanger poster. - **$65 $125 $250**

❏ DDK-349. "Donald Duck Annual,"
1940s. Collins. 6.5x8.5x2" thick English hardcover with 124 pages. Features Donald and many other characters. - **$100 $200 $400**

❏ DDK-350. "Donald Duck Sees South America" Book,
1940s. D.C. Heath & Co. 6.25x8.5" hardcover with 144 pages from the educational "Walt Disney Storybooks" series and listed as the most advanced reader book in the series. Full color story art throughout plus additional small black and white illustrations at page corners. - **$20 $50 $100**

❏ DDK-351. "Donald Duck Annual" English Book,
1940s. Collins Ltd. 6.5x8.75" hardcover, 128 pages. Content is illustrated throughout with combination of text stories, comic panel stories, puzzle pages, plus single full color plate of Donald and nephews riding bicycles. - **$100 $200 $400**

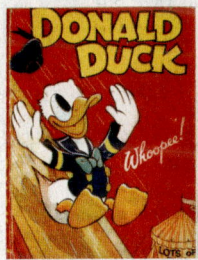

DDK-352

❏ DDK-352. "Donald Duck" English Book,
1940s. Collins, London & Glasgow. 7.25x9.5" hardcover, 128 pages. Content is assortment of illustrated stories, comic strip panel-style stories, full page illustrations, puzzle pages. Frontispiece art pictures Donald, Mickey and Minnie, Pluto. - **$100 $200 $400**

DONALD DUCK, DAISY & NEPHEWS

DDK-353

DDK-356

☐ **DDK-353. "School Days" Australian Book,**
1940s. John Sands Pty. Ltd. 7.5x11.5" 12-page book with cover and pages on stiff paper. - **$35 $65 $135**

DDK-354

DDK-355

☐ **DDK-354. Donald With Seven Dwarfs Premium Picture,**
1940s. Dell. 7.25x10.25" glossy paper picture comes in envlope with "K.K. Publications Inc., Poughkeepsie, New York" address. With Mailer - **$35 $65 $100** Picture Only - **$25 $50 $75**

☐ **DDK-355. Donald And Others Premium Pictures,**
1940s. Dell Publishing Co. Two 8 x 10" subscription premium prints. Each - **$25 $50 $75**

DDK-357

☐ **DDK-356. Donald And Others Premium Pictures,**
1940s. Dell Publishing Co. Two 8x10" subscription premium prints. Each - **$25 $50 $75**

☐ **DDK-357 Donald Duck Doll By Character Novelty Co.,**
1940s. Stuffed doll with velveteen/corduroy/felt body measures 5x6x12" tall. Doll has hat, bow tie and plastic buttons on jacket with stitched tag. - **$200 $400 $800**

DDK-358

DDK-359

☐ **DDK-358. English Holder,**
1940s. Potter & Moore/England. 1x1.5x1.5" tall hard plastic with high relief images on front of Donald and a nephew. Possibly to hold perfume bottle. - **$15 $30 $65**

☐ **DDK-359. "Donald Ducks' Hit The Jackpot" Canadian Game,**
1940s. Ontex Of Canada. 9.25x12.5x1" deep box containing game comprised of insert platform with attached spinner. Play money is used and instructions are on inner lid. - **$20 $40 $85**

DDK-360

DDK-361

DONALD DUCK, DAISY & NEPHEWS

❑ **DDK-360. Canadian Version Rubber Car,** 1940s. Sun Rubber Co. "Viceroy/Sunruco/Made In Canada" 2.5x6.5x3.5" tall. - **$40 $75 $175**

❑ **DDK-361. Donald With Nephews Wall Calendar,** 1940s. American Bedding Co. Thin cardboard calendar with scene titled "Bedtime" of Donald making sure his nephews are getting ready for bed. - **$60 $125 $225**

DDK-362

DDK-363

❑ **DDK-362. Donald Duck Wind-Up,** 1940s. Unmarked but made in France. Hollow composition with metal feet. 7.5" tall. - **$150 $300 $600**

❑ **DDK-363. Donald And Nephews Sand Pail,** 1940s. Ohio Art. 3.25" tall tin litho pail with handle. - **$115 $225 $325**

DDK-364

❑ **DDK-364. "Donald's Hockey Bowl,"** 1940s. Ontex. 6.75x11x2" deep box contains complete parts for this Canadian toy. Set consists of: target, red plastic hockey stick, and three marbles. Target shows Donald and nephews playing hockey on a frozen lake with snow-covered trees and mountains. - **$50 $100 $150**

DDK-365

❑ **DDK-365. Thermometer Plaque,** 1940s. Kemper-Thomas Co. 6x6x.25" thick ceramic tile painted image of Donald as bowler in unusual purple shirt. Text is bowling-related beneath image and attached glass working thermometer. Reverse is cardboard backing including list of four different "Walt Disney Designed Sportsmen Plaques." - **$15 $30 $75**

DDK-366

❑ **DDK-366 . Donald Duck Ceramic Tile Thermometer,** 1940s. Kemper-Thomas Company. 6x6x.25" thick tile with glass thermometer attached on right side with cardboard backing and text "Manufactured By The Kemper-Thomas Company." - **$15 $30 $75**

DDK-367

❑ **DDK-367. "Walt Disney Character School Tablet" With Donald Cover,** 1940s. 7.75x10" example from series that featured Walt Disney Comics and Stories. Cover art on tablet covers. Each - **$25 $50 $75**

DONALD DUCK, DAISY & NEPHEWS

DDK-368

❑ **DDK-368. "Donald Duck" Planter,**
1940s. Leeds China Co. 2.5x3.5x4.75" tall painted and glazed planter. - **$35 $65 $100**

DDK-370

DDK-372

❑ **DDK-372. Donald Duck Novelty Light Bulb,**
c. 1940s. 4" tall glass bulb has 1.5" tall inner die-cut filament figure of Donald.
Near Mint Working - **$350**

DDK-373

DDK-374

❑ **DDK-373. Donald Duck "Sunoco Blotter,"**
1940s. Illustration of Donald giving a "Quick Starting" award to a gas pump on 4x7" blotter. - **$25 $50 $100**

❑ **DDK-374. Donald/Sunoco "How's Your 'I.Q.'" Booklet,**
1940s. Booklet is 5x7" with 8 pages. Contents include questions and answers, advertisements and illustrations of characters throughout. - **$35 $80 $150**

DDK-371

DDK-369

❑❑ **DDK-369. Donald Duck Mexican Lamp,**
1940s. 9.5" tall to top of the socket. Painted plaster featuring an angry Donald with clenched fists. Same figurine was produced by Shaw. - **$65 $135 $250**

❑ **DDK-370. Angry Donald High School Button,**
1940s. 2.5". Reads "Stuyvesant Junior" likely from Bronx, New York and limited production. - **$100 $200 $350**

❑ **DDK-371. Donald Duck Doll,**
1940s. Charlotte Clark. 15" tall doll with velveteen stuffed body with cloth legs and beak, corduroy hat and jacket with mother-of-pearl buttons. - **$300 $600 $1200**

DDK-375

❑ **DDK-375. Donald Duck Push Puppet,**
1940s. - **$40 $805 $160**

DONALD DUCK, DAISY & NEPHEWS

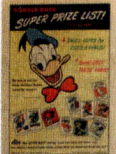

DDK-376

DDK-377

☐ **DDK-376. Ice Cream Premiums List With Donald And Others,**
1950. "Ice Cream Novelties." 7.5x10" four-page prize list. A number of these are Disney-related.
- $10 $20 $50

☐ **DDK-377. "Donald Duck Babysitter Golden Record,"**
1950. 6.75x7.5" paper sleeve contains yellow vinyl 78 rpm recording of "Donald Duck Babysitter/Mickey Mouse And Farmer Rush Rush." - $5 $12 $20

DDK-378

☐ **DDK-378. "Donald Duck's Toy Train" Little Golden Book,**
1950. Simon & Schuster. 6.5x8" with 28 pages. - $5 $15 $25

DDK-379

☐ **DDK-379. Donald Duck "Ducky Dubble" Club Member Button,**
1950. Also issued with imprint "Icy-Frost Twins."
- $135 $300 $800

DDK-380

☐ **DDK-380. "Icy-Frost Twins Club Of America" Member Button,**
1950. 1.25" blue on white cello with Donald accented in orange. - $275 $550 $1100

DDK-381

☐ **DDK-381. Beanie Premium,**
1950. "Icy-Frost Twins" 6" bottom diameter two-toned felt fabric accented by trim of third color. Two versions: green/orange or blue/gold. - $100 $200 $475

DDK-382

DDK-383

DDK-384

☐ **DDK-382. Icy-Frost Twins Cardboard Sign,**
1950. - $100 $250 $525

☐ **DDK-383. Ducky Dubble Cardboard Sign,**
1950. 13x13". - $125 $275 $550

☐ **DDK-384. Fudgi-Frost Cardboard Sign,**
1950. 13x13". - $125 $275 $550

DDK-385

DONALD DUCK, DAISY & NEPHEWS

❏ **DDK-385. Disney Studios Publicity Cel Set-Up With Donald,**
c. 1950. Clear acetate sheet is 9x10.75" over hand-inked cut-out cel of Donald mounted against hand-prepared air brushed background. This image was frequently used by the studio for publicity purposes but never appeared in any cartoon. These publicity cels were produced around the late 1940s-early 1950s and were sometimes given to special guests at the studio. - **$500 $1000 $1500**

DDK-386

❏ **DDK-386. Donald At Tiller Wheel Figurine,**
c. 1950. Unmarked but Australian 3x5.5x6.75" tall painted and glazed ceramic. - **$125 $250 $450**

DDK-387

DDK-388

❏ **DDK-387. "Donald Duck" Mechanical Greeting Card,**
c. 1950. Hallmark Co. 6.5x8.25" diecut stiff paper card from "Rock-N-Play Cards" series. - **$15 $30 $50**

❏ **DDK-388. Pencil Drawing,**
1951. Animation paper is 10x12" centered by 4x5" image of Donald. From 'Dude Duck' short feature and No. "9" from a numbered sequence. - **$300 $600 $1250**

DDK-389

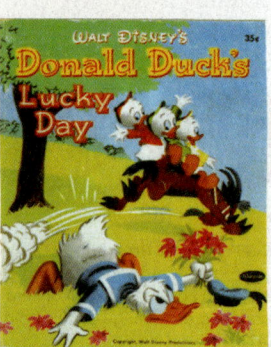
DDK-390

❏ **DDK-389. "Donald Duck And The Hidden Gold" Hardcover With Dust Jacket ,**
1951. Simon & Schuster. 5x7.25" with 80 pages. Color art throughout by main Donald Duck comic strip artist Al Taliaferro. Jacket Only - **$50 $100 $150** Book Only - **$15 $30 $60**

❏ **DDK-390. "Donald Duck's Lucky Day,"**
1951. Whitman. 5.5x6.25" with 28 pages from the "Tell-A-Tale" series. - **$10 $25 $40**

DDK-391

DDK-392

❏ **DDK-391. "Walt Disney's Comics And Stories" Subscription Mailer Folder,**
1951. Dell Publishing Co. 3.5x7" closed folder opening to 7x10" four-page promotion sheet. - **$65 $125 $200**

❏ **DDK-392. "Peter Pan Picture Puzzle" Bread Label Album,**
1952. 9x9" four-page folder issued by various bread companies and this example is for Donald Duck Bread. - **$12 $25 $50**

DDK-393

❏ **DDK-393. Donald As University Of Oregon Mascot Button,**
1952. 1-5/8". Limited distribution. - **$8 $15 $35**

DDK-394

DONALD DUCK, DAISY & NEPHEWS

DDK-395

❑ **DDK-394. "Donald Duck And The Wishing Star" Book,**
1952. Whitman. 7.25x8.25" hardcover from the "Cozy Corner Series", 24 pages with full color story art on every page. - **$10 $20 $40**

❑ **DDK-395. "Walt Disney's Comics And Stories" Christmas Gift Subscription Card and Envelope,**
1952. Stiff paper card measures 5x7" in original envelope. Mailer - **$10 $15 $25**
Card - **$40 $80 $150**

DDK-396

DDK-397

❑ **DDK-396. "Walt Disney's Comics And Stories" Subscription Mailer Folder With Donald And Others,**
1952. Four-page folder is 7x10". Front cover illustrates Santa Claus groomed by Mickey, Minnie, Donald and his nephews. Back cover is reprint of cover used on the January 1948 issue. - **$100 $200 $300**

❑ **DDK-397. "Donald Duck And Santa Claus" Book,**
1952. Simon & Schuster. 6.75x8" first edition Little Golden Book, 28 pages. - **$15 $25 $50**

DDK-398

❑ **DDK-398. "Walt Disney's Coloring Book,"**
1953. Whitman. 8x10.75" with 32 pages. - **$15 $30 $60**

DDK-399

❑ **DDK-399. Wheaties 12oz. Cereal Box Flat,**
1953. Has Donald Duck record on front and offer for Mouseketeers records on back.
Complete Box - **$50 $150 $300**
Cut-Out Record - **$5 $20 $40**

DDK-400

❑ **DDK-400. Donald Duck Story Board From "Canvas Back Duck,"**
1953. Paper is 6x8.25" with art covering nearly the entire sheet. - **$65 $150 $265**

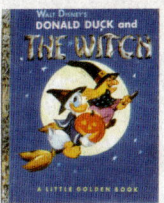
DDK-401

❑ **DDK-401. "Donald Duck And The Witch" Little Golden Book,**
1953. Simon & Schuster. 6.5x8" with 28 pages. - **$10 $20 $40**

DDK-402

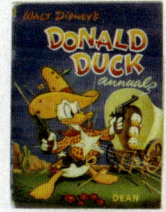

DDK-403

❑ **DDK-402. "Donald Duck" With Cart Fisher-Price Pull Toy,**
1954. Wood toy with paper labels measures 4.5x9x7.75" tall and numbered "605." When pulled, feet move and underside has mechanism to make quacking noise. - **$05 $150 $250**

❑ **DDK-403. "Donald Duck Annual" English Hardcover,**
1954. Dean & Son Ltd. 7.5x9.75" with 96 pages. Book contains numerous stories featuring Donald and other Disney characters. Has a two-page western theme gameboard "Donald Gets His Man." - **$65 $125 $225**

DONALD DUCK, DAISY & NEPHEWS

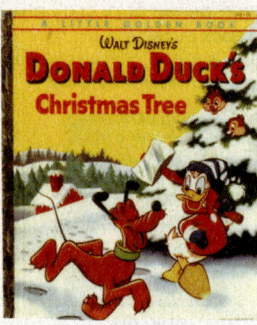

DDK-404

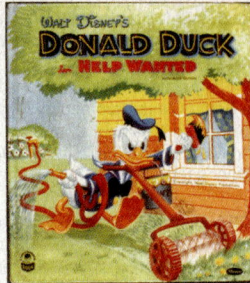

DDK-407

❏ **DDK-404. "Donald Duck's Christmas Tree" Book,**
1954. Simon & Schuster. 6.75x8" first edition Little Golden Book, 28 pages. - **$10 $20 $30**

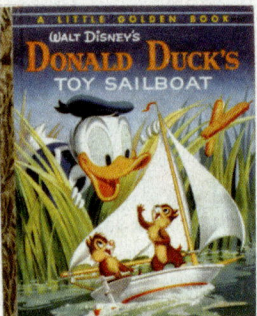

DDK-405

DDK-408

DDK-410

❏ **DDK-407. "Donald Duck In Help Wanted" Book,**
1955. Whitman. 7.5x8.25" "Cozy Corner Book," 16 pages. Story art involves Donald doing chores for Mr. Billy Goat, Granny Giraffe And Elephant Ellen. - **$10 $20 $30**

❏ **DDK-408. "Donald Duck In Disneyland Little Golden Book,"**
1955. Simon & Schuster. 6.75x8" with 28 pages showing Donald and nephews at various park attractions. - **$12 $25 $45**

❏ **DDK-409. "Donald Duck" Watch With Rare Box,**
1955. US Time 3.5x4x1.5" deep box with lid illustrations of Donald, Daisy and nephews. Inside of lid has separate attached diecut figure of Donald shown pointing at his wristwatch. Rarely found boxed. Box - **$125 $250 $500**
Watch - **$40 $85 $150**

❏ **DDK-410. Donald Duck English Cut-Out Books,**
c. 1955. Tower Press. Pair of 7x11.25" cardboard covered books titled "Donald Duck's Farm" and "Donald's Toyshop." Each has four full color cardboard pages of cut-outs plus related text story. Each - **$25 $50 $75**

DDK-406

DDK-409

DDK-411

❏ **DDK-405. "Donald Duck's Toy Sailboat" Book,**
1954. Simon & Schuster. 6.75x8" first edition printing Little Golden Book, 28 pages. - **$5 $10 $20**

❏ **DDK-406. "TV Guide" Store Sign With Donald,**
1954. Stiff cardboard sign measures 11x14". Text includes "Walt Disney In TV-Land" and advertises "October 23rd." - **$85 $165 $275**

DONALD DUCK, DAISY & NEPHEWS

☐ **DDK-411. Comic Character Candle With Donald And Others,**
c. 1955. "Christmas Greetings From King Features Syndicate" 4.25" diameter by 3.5" tall. Represented are Donald, Prince Valiant, Steve Canyon, Rip Kirby, Blondie & Dagwood, Henry & Henrietta, Buz Sawyer, Snuffy Smith, Beetle Bailey, Little Iodine, Jiggs & Maggie. Limited distribution, mainly sent to newspaper editors. - **$30 $60 $115**

DDK-412

☐ **DDK-412. "Ducky Dubble Prize List" With Donald And Others,**
1956. "Ice Cream Novelties." 5x7.25" 12-page booklet of prizes offered for popsicle bags redemption. Back cover includes information on the Donald Duck Ducky Dubble Club and pictures button, membership card and certificate. Contest prizes offered are generic, non-Disney. - **$25 $50 $75**

DDK-413

☐ **DDK-413. "Donald Duck Fudgi-Frost" Store Sign,**
1956. Fruit Products Corp. 7.25x17.75" glossy paper sign advertising frozen fudge treat. - **$50 $100 $185**

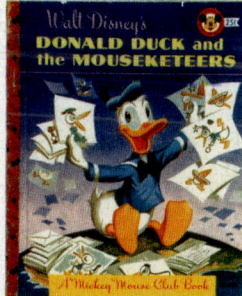
DDK-414

DDK-415

☐ **DDK-414. "Donald Duck And The Mouseketeers" Little Golden Book,**
1956. Simon & Schuster. 6.75x8" first printing edition also titled "Mickey Mouse Club Book." Content is 24-page illustrated story based on Disneyland television show "A Day In The Life Of Donald Duck." - **$10 $20 $40**

☐ **DDK-415. "Donald Duck Coloring Book,"**
1957. Whitman. 8x10.75" with 32 pages. - **$10 $20 $40**

DDK-416

☐ **DDK-416. Portrait Artwork Signed,**
1958. 9x13.25" sheet of stiff textured white paper with 5x8.5" portrait image in black marker by "Disney Legend" Al Konetzni, who then signed bottom margin with added "Hi From Donald Duck!" dated 1958. - **$25 $50 $75**

DDK-417

☐ **DDK-417. "Donald Duck Coloring Book",**
1958. Dell #206. Square bound book promotes The Mickey Mouse Club. Has pictures of Duck clan throughout. Odd size 11 1/4" x 6 1/2". Scarce. - **$50 $100 $300**

DDK-418

☐ **DDK-418. "Walt Disney's Comics And Stories" Shop Dummy For Gift Subscription Renewal Offer,**
1959. 10x14.25" layout unit leading to production of four-panel subscription renewal folder. Unit consists of two black and white sheets of base art and six acetate color separation overlays which have been attached back to back. Dummy was prepared for use by K.K. Publications Inc. Poughkeepsie, NY plant. As Made **$200**

DDK-419

DONALD DUCK, DAISY & NEPHEWS

❑ **DDK-419. "Walt Disney's Comics And Stories" Subscription Mailer Folder With Donald And Others,**
1959. Four-page folder is 7x10". - **$75 $150 $225**

DDK-420

DDK-421

❑ **DDK-420. "Donald Duck Disneyland Gloves,"**
1950s. Wells-Lamont Co. Pair of 6.25" long wool/nylon gloves. One glove has original "Disneyland Gloves" tag while the other has maker's fabric tag stitched inside. Near Mint - **$35**

❑ **DDK-421. Donald And Friends Handkerchief Pair,**
1950s. Two 8x8" fabric hankies. Each - **$5 $10 $15**

DDK-422

DDK-423

❑ **DDK-422. Donald Nephews Child's Shirt,**
1950s. Blue Bell Inc. Button-down cotton shirt, size 12, sealed in "Children's Disneyland Shirts" original cellophane packaging. Packaged - **$20 $40 $75**

❑ **DDK-423. Donald Duck Cel,**
1950s. Cel image is 5x5.5" depicting Donald in chef hat holding pair of spoons. Has gold foil "Art Corner At Disneyland" sticker. - **$115 $225 $450**

DDK-424

DDK-425

❑ **DDK-424. Donald Duck Art Corner Cel,**
1950s. Image is 4.25x5.5". "Walt Disney Productions" label is affixed to backing board. - **$100 $200 $400**

❑ **DDK-425. Donald Duck Cel,**
1950s. Image is 4x5.75". Cel has gold foil label. These were sold at Disneyland's Art Corner. - **$75 $175 $300**

DDK-426

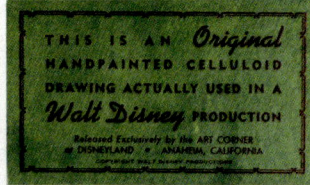

❑ **DDK-426. Donald Duck As Musketeer Cel,**
1950s. "Disneyland Art Corner." 6x8" image consisting of two separate acetate sheets, overprinted background sheet. Reverse has a label of certification of use in a Disney production. - **$115 $225 $450**

DONALD DUCK, DAISY & NEPHEWS

DDK-429

☐ **DDK-429. Donald Duck Bread Sign Art,**
1950s. Stiff art board measures 5.25x19.5" and promotes "Purity Made" bread. Text is "For My Little Friends! New Milk Improved Bread." Unique, Near Mint - **$1200**

DDK-427

☐ **DDK-427. Donald Duck And Nephew Cel,**
1950s. "Disneyland Art Corner." Overall 10x12" image consisting of three separate acetate sheets, overprinted background sheet, all attached to cardboard backing. Reverse has 2.5x4.25" foil label of certification of use in Disney production. - **$125 $250 $500**

DDK-430

DDK-428

☐ **DDK-428. Disneyland Original Art,**
1950s. 7 1/4" x 12" by the late Chet Marshall. Fine art shows scene of Donald Duck and commemorates his 1st appearance in *Wise Little Hen*. Used for a poster highlighting his performance in that film. Unique, Mint - **$3000**

☐ **DDK-430, Donald And Mickey Prototype Hand Puppets,**
1950s. Two 8x10.5" tall cloth hand covers with original art in watercolors on both front and back, depicting front and back of each character. Unique. Gordon Gold Archives. Pair Near Mint - **$850**

DONALD DUCK, DAISY & NEPHEWS

DDK-431

❏ **DDK-431. Dancing Figure Original Art Prototype,**
1950s. 11x22" stiff paper cut-out with art on front in tempera paint. Design is segmented body so when lifted in the air and moved up and down slightly, the body moves as if dancing. Hat has a pair of diecut holes for a string attachment. Unique prototype from Gordon Gold Archives. As Made - **$650**

DDK-432

DDK-433

❏ **DDK-432. "Donald Duck Orange Juice Action Toy" Puppet Lot With Original Art Prototype, Photostats, Photos,**
1950s. Total of nine pieces. Primary item is 5.5x10.5" prototype to create action toy puppet. Related pieces are puppet dummy sheets in pencil, store sign preliminary in pencil, four photostats and pair of glossy photos of the prototype. Gordon Gold Archives. Unique, Near Mint - **$400**

❏ **DDK-433. Donald Duck Original Art For Peter Pan Bread Label Album,**
1950s. 8x11" mounting board holding applied 6.75x10.25" tempera original art basis for back cover of four-page "Peter Pan Picture Puzzle" bread label album from 1952. Near Mint - **$275**

DDK-434

DDK-435

❏ **DDK-434. Concept Art For Donald Duck Figural Pencil Sharpener,**
1950s. "Product Concept" original art by "Disney Legend" designer Al Konetzni on 11x13" sheet of artist tracing paper. Near Mint - **$375**

❏ **DDK-435. Cel-Like Print,**
1950s. "Walt Disney Classics" 12x14" cardboard mat framing 7.25x9.25" glossy print under clear acetate. Mat reverse label certifies "This Artwork Has Been Authentically Reproduced From Selected Originals Used In A Walt Disney Productions." - **$25 $50 $80**

DDK-436

DDK-437

❏ **DDK-436. Mexican Gag Novelty,**
1950s. "Mexico" unauthorized. 1.25x3.5x2.5" tall wooden box ink-stamped on two sides by same Donald image and country of origin. Top of box has a panel that slides open. Object is to hand the box to an unsuspecting person and when the panel is slid open, a snake pops out with a pin in its open mouth to prick the victim. Snake has fabric-covered wire body and wooden head. - **$15 $30 $60**

❏ **DDK-437. Unusual Donald Duck Pull Toy,**
1950s. Wood train with rubber figure of Donald from waist up measuring 3x7x6" tall. Window decal on each side of cab and on the front is a Donald portrait decal. - **$50 $100 $200**

DDK-438

DONALD DUCK, DAISY & NEPHEWS

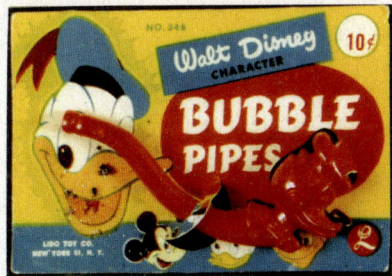

DDK-439

❏ **DDK-438. English Train Pull Toy,**
1950s. Generic 9.5x16x4" deep box contains set of four painted tin train pieces. Unmarked but English. Boxed - **$50 $100 $200**
Not Boxed - **$40 $80 $175**

❏ **DDK-439. "Walt Disney Character Bubble Pipes" Card With Donald Pipe,**
1950s. Lido Toy Co. 4x6" carded 4.25" long hard plastic figural Donald soap bubble pipe.
Carded - **$10 $20 $40**
Loose - **$5 $10 $20**

DDK-440

DDK-441

❏ **DDK-440. "Donald Duck Transfers" Book,**
1950s. Tower Press. 5x6.25" book opens to reveal a 2.5" wide strip that unfolds to 20" long. Strip tells tale of Donald and nephews going on an adventure involving air, land and sea. Marked "British Made." - **$15 $30 $60**

❏ **DDK-441. Donald's Nephews Wagon Decal,**
1950s. Radio Steel. 4.75x4.75" unused decal for toy wagon. Reverse is marked "Water-Dip Transfer Chicago Decalcomania Co." - **$10 $20 $40**

DDK-442

❏ **DDK-442. Donald Duck Ceramic Figurine,**
1950s. Beswick, England. 4" tall. Marked underneath with company mark. - **$100 $200 $400**

DDK-443

DDK-444

❏ **DDK-443. Dexterity Puzzle,**
1950s. Unmarked 2.5" diameter lithographed tin playing surface under clear plastic domed cover. - **$10 $20 $30**

❏ **DDK-444. Donald's Nephew Goebel Figurine,**
1950s. Goebel. Figure is 2x2.5x3.25" tall. Has foil sticker with name "Donald Duck" and underside has incised "DIS124" with full bee marking. - **$60 $125 $250**

DDK-445

DDK-446

DONALD DUCK, DAISY & NEPHEWS

☐ **DDK-445. "Donald Duck" Figurine,**
1950s. Goebel. Figure is on 2.75" diameter base and stands 4.25" tall. Underside has full bee marking and incised "DIS123." - **$100 $200 $300**

☐ **DDK-446. "Dewey" Figurine,**
1950s. Hagen-Renaker. 2x2.5" stiff paper card holds 1" tall painted and glazed figure. Card reads "Always 'Bats A Thousand' When It Comes To Playing Tricks On His 'Unca Donald' Duck." Near Mint Carded - **$165** No Card - **$25 $50 $115**

DDK-447

DDK-448

☐ **DDK-447. "Louie" Figurine,**
1950s. Hagen-Renaker. 2x2.5" stiff paper card holds 1" painted and glazed figure. Card reads "Will Probably 'Catch It' When Unca Donald Learns His Nephew 'Struck Out' At School." Near Mint Carded - **$165** No Card - **$25 $50 $115**

☐ **DDK-448. Guitarist Figurine,**
1950s. Shaw Pottery. 3" tall painted and glazed ceramic. - **$75 $150 $225**

DDK-449

☐ **DDK-449. Donald Duck Nephews Figurines,**
1950s. Unauthorized "Made In Japan" four china figurines, 3" to 3.25" tall. Each is likeness to Donald's nephews and all wear ball cap. Three are depicted with instruments of guitar, squeeze box, tambourines. The fourth holds a flower. Each - **$10 $20 $30**

DDK-450

☐ **DDK-450. "Donald Duck Bread" Countertop Standee,**
1950s. Die-cut cardboard measures 8.5x10.25" with easel back showing Donald holding loaf of "Donald Duck Bread." - **$60 $125 $225**

DDK-451

☐ **DDK-451. Donald Duck Bread Promotional Countertop Standee,**
1950s. NBC White Bread. 8x10" die-cut cardboard with easel on back. - **$60 $125 $225**

DDK-452

☐ **DDK-452. "Donald Duck Puppet" Punch-Out Premium,**
1950s. Stiff paper cut-out sheets with parts for assembly of 8" tall puppet. When assembled, puppet has movable mouth, eyes, arm and tail. Shows Donald holding "NBC" loaf of bread with Donald Duck bread label on one end. - **$20 $40 $75**

DDK-453

DONALD DUCK, DAISY & NEPHEWS

DDK-454

❑ **DDK-453. "Donald Duck" Bread Labels,** 1950s. NBC Bread. Each 2.75x3" from a set of 48 featuring American states. Each - **$3 $6 $10**

❑ **DDK-454. "Donald Duck Bread" Countertop Standees,** 1950s. Stiff cardboard standee measures 8x12". Has Donald Duck bread label on one end of loaf. Two shown. Each - **$60 $115 $185**

DDK-455

❑ **DDK-455. "Donald Duck" Bread Wrapper,** 1950s. Wax paper bread wrapper that measures 4x4x11" when wrapped around bread form. Issued by various bakeries. - **$20 $40 $80**

DDK-456

❑ **DDK-456. Donald Duck Bread Cardboard Banks,** 1950s. Regular and Wheat Blend versions. Each - **$25 $50 $100**

DDK-457

❑ **DDK-457. Donald And Cinderella Bread Company Book Cover,** 1950s. Sturdy paper is 11 x 17" unfolded. Published by J.M. Gaske, Baltimore, Md, for various bread companies. This example is "Hauswald's Bread." - **$8 $15 $25**

❑ **DDK-458. "Donald Duck" And Nephews Bread Labels,** 1950s. Twelve waxed paper labels from activities series, each 2.75x2.75". Each - **$2 $4 $10**

DDK-458

DDK-459

❑ **DDK-459. Bread Wrapper for Donald Duck Bread,** 1950s. McGavin Bread sponsor. Copyright Walt Disney Productions. Scarcer variety. - **$25 $50 $100**

DDK-460

❑ **DDK-460. "Donald Duck Bread" Pencil,** 1950s. Lead pencil is 6.75" long (sharpened from original length of 7.25") issued by various companies, and this example has imprint of "Ungles Baking Company." Additional text reads "Harvest Donald Duck Bread" plus image of bread loaf with Donald Duck wrapper and end label. - **$20 $40 $65**

DDK-461

DDK-462

❑ **DDK-461. "Donald Duck In Milk Chocolate" Candy Wrapper,** 1950s. Comet Candies Inc. 6.25x9" waxed paper wrapper. Features Donald holding sign reading "In Milk Chocolate." - **$20 $40 $80**

❑ **DDK-462. "Donald Duck 3 Minute Oats" Container,** 1950s. National Oats Co. 4" diameter by 7.25" tall cardboard container with wrap-around paper label. - **$100 $200 $400**

DONALD DUCK, DAISY & NEPHEWS

DDK-463

DDK-464

DDK-465

☐ DDK-463. "Donald Duck Frozen Orange Juice" Countertop Standee,
1950s. Stiff thick cardboard measuring 5.5x13" with glossy paper label on front. Text is "Each Can Makes 6 Glasses." - $100 $200 $300

☐ DDK-464. "Donald Duck Orange Juice" Proof Sheet,
1950s. Glossy paper sheet used to produce a countertop standee is 7.25x14". Gordon Gold Archives. - $30 $60 $115

☐ DDK-465. "Donald Duck Orange Juice" Store Sign,
1950s. Paper sign is 6.5x11.75". - $30 $65 $100

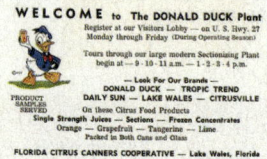

DDK-466

☐ DDK-466. "Donald Duck Plant" Promotional Card,
1950s. Stiff paper card is 3.25x5.5" issued by "Florida Citrus Canners Cooperative-Lake Wales, Florida." Text at top reads "Welcome To The Donald Duck Plant" and card notes registration information, times of tours, list of citrus food products and brands, "Product Samples Served" during tour. - $10 $20 $40

DDK-467

DDK-468

☐ DDK-467. "Donald Duck" Australian Lunch Tin,
1950s. "Fyna Foods Pty. Ltd." 5.5x8.5x3.5" deep lithographed tin container with pair of attached metal handles and latch on front. - $100 $200 $400

☐ DDK-468. "Donald Duck Tomato Ketchup,"
1950s. The Naas Corp. 8" tall glass bottle with colorful 2.25x2.25" label. - $20 $40 $75

DDK-469

☐ DDK-469. "Donald Duck Soft Drinks" Store Sign,
1950s. 10.5x21" paper sign. - $100 $200 $300

DDK-470

☐ DDK-470. "Donald Duck Beverages" Carrier With Bottles,
1950s. Cardboard carrier measures 5x7x7.5" tall and holds six 7.75" bottles with Donald portrait on each in blue and white. Canadian issue but text on carrier in both English and French. Underside is marked "Gair Company Canada Ltd." Carrier - $25 $50 $100 Each Bottle - $5 $10 $20

DDK-471

DDK-472

DONALD DUCK, DAISY & NEPHEWS

DDK-473

❏ **DDK-471. Donald Duck Beverage,**
1950s. Unopened with cap intact. - **$85**

❏ **DDK-472. "Donald Duck Beverages" Glass,**
1950s. Glass tumbler is 4" tall with slight tapering at lower third of body. - **$65 $125 $200**

❏ **DDK-473. "Donald Duck Cola" Large Standee,**
1950s. "Printed In Canada" 22x25.5" diecut cardboard standee with easel on reverse. - **$75 $200 $475** Smaller Version - **$50 $100 $200**

DDK-474

❏ **DDK-474. Donald Duck Soda Bottle Caps,**
1950s. 1.25" Metal caps with cork liner.
Cola Cap - **$5 $10 $20**
Ginger Ale Cap - **$10 $20 $40**

DDK-475

❏ **DDK-475. "Donald Duck Peanut Butter" Jar,**
1950s. Southeastern Foods Inc. Jar is 5" tall and label is 2x2.5". - **$20 $40 $70**

DDK-476

DDK-477

❏ **DDK-476. Donald Duck Beverage Hispanic Tray,**
1950s. Lithographed tin serving tray is 5x7x.25" deep and pictures bottle of orange flavored soda titled "Pascual/Fruta En Su Refresco." - **$20 $40 $60**

❏ **DDK-477. "Donald Duck Salted Peanuts" Bag,**
1950s. Flattened and unused "P.N." cellophane bag is 2.25x4.5". Reverse has Donald portrait and text "Packed In Holland For A.S.K.-Bolagen, Sweden." - **$5 $15 $30**

DDK-478

DDK-479

❏ **DDK-478. "Cafe Donald Duck" French Mini-Poster Ad,**
1950s. Poster is 5.25x8.25" paper titled in English but all other text in French, apparently offering an album for cards billed as his "Famous Adventures." - **$20 $40 $75**

❏ **DDK-479. "Donald Duck Chocolate Syrup" Can,**
1950s. Atlantic Syrup Refining Corp. 2.75" diameter x 4.5" tall lithographed tin can sealed without contents, probably for display purposes only. - **$20 $40 $75**

DDK-480

❏ **DDK-480 "Donald Duck Cheese Quackers" Sales Presentation Kit,**
1950s. Nabisco. 9.5 x 12.5 x 3" deep outer box containing 6" tall soft rubber figure of Donald and unopened 7.5" tall crackers box illustrated on three sides plus back panel of Donald and nephew baseball theme cut-outs. Box text mentions that Donald is "The Most Popular Fanciful Character The World Has Ever Known" with list of newspaper, comic book and film credits. - **$100 $200 $300**

DDK-481

DONALD DUCK, DAISY & NEPHEWS

DDK-482

DDK-481. "Donald The Bubble Duck,"
1950s. Morris Plastics Corp. 3x3x8" tall figure with soft plastic body and hard plastic head, feet and soda glass. Comes with small hard plastic ice cream scoop that contains "Magic Brew Bubble Powder." Glass was filled with powder and then when squeezed he would blow bubbles as his mouth opens and closes. Boxed - **$20 $40 $75** No Box - **$10 $20 $45**

DDK-482. Ceramic Toothbrush Holder,
1950s. Shaw Pottery. 4x7x4" tall painted and glazed ceramic slotted twice for toothbrushes plus opening for placement of a cup. Upright panel pictures a stern-looking Donald with word balloon "Hey You! Brush Your Teeth, Wash Your Face, Comb Your Hair." - **$75 $150 $250**

DDK-483

DDK-484

DDK-483. Wall Plaque,
1950s. Kemper-Thomas Co. 6x6x3/8" thick ceramic tile centered by 2x3.25" high relief pressed wood figure of Donald. - **$20 $40 $80**

DDK-484. Picnic Scene Bowl,
1950s. 6" diameter by 1.75" deep china with copyright on underside. - **$20 $40 $60**

DDK-485

DDK-486

DDK-485. Figural Egg Cup,
1950s. "Made In Japan" copyright 2.5x3x3.5" tall china depiction of Donald riding a scooter. - **$65 $125 $200**

DDK-486. Figural Egg Cup,
1950s. Unmarked Japanese 1.75" diameter by 2.5" tall glazed and over-glaze paint accents. - **$25 $50 $90**

DDK-487

DDK-488

DDK-487. Figural Italian Dish,
1950s. Zaccagnini Of Italy. 4x6x3.75" tall painted and glazed ceramic. - **$250 $500 $750**

DDK-488. Donald Duck Glass,
1950s. Glass measures 4-5/8" tall and text is "Doanld Duck Beverages" and "More! More! More!" - **$25 $50 $75**

DDK-489

DDK-489. "Donald/Daisy Duck" Glass,
1950s. From a set of four, each featuring two different Disney characters. Height is 4". - **$15 $30 $60**

DDK-490

DDK-490. Glass Tumbler,
1950s. 4-5/8" tall with front portrait and back text "Full/Going/Going/Gone." - **$100 $200 $300**

DONALD DUCK, DAISY & NEPHEWS

DDK-491   DDK-492

DDK-495

❏ **DDK-491. "Donald Duck" Glass,**
1950s. Probable product tumbler 4-3/8" tall with fluted bottom and same design repeated front and back. - **$50 $100 $150**

❏ **DDK-492. Donald Duck Glass,**
1950s. 5" tall tumbler with same silk screened image on each side. - **$35 $65 $120**

❏ **DDK-495. "Donald Duck Sunshine Straws,"**
1950s. Herz Mfg. Corp. 4x4.75x8.75" tall box with display window over original 100 generic white paper straws. - **$10 $20 $30**

❏ **DDK-497. Donald's Nephews & Three Little Pigs Juice Reamer,**
1950s. Limoges china. 4" diameter by 2.25" tall fruit squeezer marked on underside "License Walt Disney/Singer Limoges." - **$65 $125 $225**

DDK-498

❏ **DDK-498. "Donald Duck" Jar Bank,**
1950s. Nash-Underwood. 2.5" diameter by 4.75" tall glass jar with color label marked "Relish" and tin lid marked "Mustard." - **$35 $75 $165**

DDK-493

DDK-496

❏ **DDK-496. Donald Duck Beverage Hispanic Tray,**
1950s. 5x7x.75" deep lithographed tin serving tray picturing him as artist with fruit as his model for actual portrait done of a beautiful woman. Product title is "Pascual/Fruta En Su Refresco." - **$20 $40 $60**

DDK-494

DDK-497

❏ **DDK-493. "Donald Duck" Napkin,**
1950s. Folded 6.5x6.5" textured white paper with scalloped outer edges. - **$5 $10 $15**

❏ **DDK-494. Donald Duck Silver Plate Dish,**
1950s. Plate measures 8" diameter by 1" deep marked on the reverse "Horse Plate." No copyright but almost certainly authorized. - **$30 $60 $125**

DDK-499

DONALD DUCK, DAISY & NEPHEWS

DDK-500

❑ **DDK-499. Donald Duck Bank,**
1950s. Knickerbocker. 4x4.5x9" tall hard plastic. - **$25 $65 $100**

❑ **DDK-500. Donald & Others Mechanical Bank,**
1950s. J. Chein & Co. 3x6.5x3.5" tall lithographed tin designed as building marked "2nd National Duck Bank." The "Teller" window on front has Donald portrait and when locked into place, a tray representing his tongue sticks out. - **$75 $175 $325**

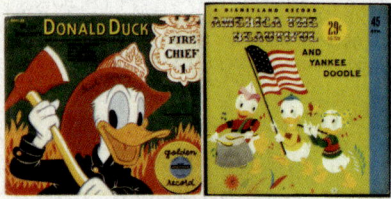

DDK-501

❑ **DDK-501. Donald And Nephews Records,**
1950s. Golden Record. Two 7x7.5" paper sleeves, one holding "Donald Duck Fire Chief" yellow vinyl 78 rpm. Second record is "Disneyland" 45 rpm copyright 1961, titled "America The Beautiful/Yankee Doodle." Each - **$5 $10 $20**

DDK-502

❑ **DDK-502. "Donald Duck Jams And Jellies" Cello Button,**
1950s. 1.25". - **$150 $300 $500**

DDK-503

❑ **DDK-503. "Donald Duck Jams Jellies" Litho Button,**
1950s. 1-1/8". - **$100 $200 $300**

DDK-504

❑ **DDK-504. "Member Of Donald Duck Club" English Candy Button,**
1950s. Jasco Ltd. 1.25". - **$75 $150 $300**

DDK-505

❑ **DDK-505. "I Eat Donald Duck Bread" Australian Cello Button,**
1950s. A. Patrick Pty. Ltd. Summer Hill. 1". - **$35 $65 $125**

DDK-506

DDK-507

❑ **DDK-506. Donald Duck Bread Cello Promotional Button,**
1950s. Text reads "Copyright Walt Disney Productions." A second version has additional text "Made In U.S.A." 2.25" worn by store clerks. Either version - **$100 $200 $300**

❑ **DDK-507. Plaster Bookends,**
1950s. Matching pair of painted solid plaster figural bookends, each 3x5x7.25" tall. Each - **$25 $50 $80**

DDK-508

❑ **DDK-508. "Donald's Day At The Farm" English Book,**
1950s. Birn Brothers Ltd. 8.75x12" linen paper softcover, 12 pages. - **$20 $40 $80**

DONALD DUCK, DAISY & NEPHEWS

DDK-509

❏ **DDK-509. Cloth Doll,**
1950s. Charlotte Clark. 4x4.5x8.5" tall stuffed fabric with stitched tag on left leg although picturing Mickey Mouse from same doll series. Detailing includes corduroy outfit, satin finish bill and legs, four mother-of-pearl buttons on jacket, oilcloth eyes, four string loops as his tail, underside feet felt covered. - **$200 $400 $700**

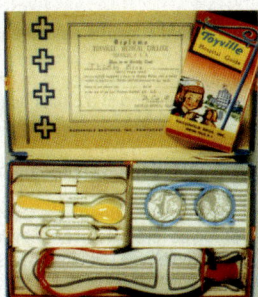

DDK-511

DDK-512

❏ **DDK-511. "Donald Duck Doctor Kit,"**
1950s. Hasbro. 5.5x9.75x2.25" deep cardboard box/carrying case with metal handle and latch. Content is generic medical toys of stethoscope, glasses, thermometer, spoon and tongue depressor plus a small color booklet "Toyville Hospital Guide." Inside of lid has facsimile medical college diploma. - **$50 $100 $175**

❏ **DDK-512. "Donald Duck" Squeaker Hand Puppet,**
1950s. Gund. 9" tall with soft vinyl head. - **$10 $20 $30**

DDK-514

❏ **DDK-513. Donald And His Nephews Ramp Walker,**
1950s. Marx. 3.5" long hard plastic figure. - **$20 $40 $75**

❏ **DDK-514. Donald Duck With Wheelbarrow Ramp Walker,**
1950s. Marx. Figure is 3" tall and made of hard plastic. - **$15 $30 $60**

DDK-515

❏ **DDK-515. "Donald Duck Camera,"**
1950s. Herbert George Co. 2.75x4.5x3" tall hard plastic camera in box with instruction folder. Front of camera has small metal plate with "Donald Duck" name while back panel has raised figures of Donald and his nephews. Box - **$50 $85 $1750**
Camera - **$25 $50 $100**

DDK-510

❏ **DDK-510. Cloth Figure,**
1950s. Lars Company. 23" cloth figure made in Italy. Only 10 produced. Near Mint - **$4000**

DDK-513

DDK-516

DONALD DUCK, DAISY & NEPHEWS

DDK-517

❏ **DDK-516. Figural Ashtray,**
1950s. Goebel. 3.25x3.75x3" tall painted and glazed ceramic featuring Donald pose of one hand on hip and the other raised as if waving. One of the first Goebel figures with incised "15" and earliest style foil sticker by maker. - **$100 $225 $425**

❏ **DDK-517. Comic Character Lighter With Donald And Others,**
1950s. King Features Syndicate promotional 2.25" tall cigarette lighter in original "Bowers Storm Master Lighter" box. Lighter is brushed silver finish with four characters shown on each side. Pictured are Donald, Popeye, Beetle Bailey, Snuffy Smith, Dagwood, Archie, Little Iodine, Jiggs. Limited issue, probably a give-away to newspaper editors. Box - **$5 $10 $15** Lighter - **$15 $30 $50**

DDK-518

DDK-519

❏ **DDK-518. Donald's Nephews Christmas Card,**
1950s. Gibson. 4x5" card that opens to reveal a Santa Claus outfit hanging in a closet along with bag of gifts. - **$8 $15 $25**

❏ **DDK-519. "Donald Duck Math-Magic Electric Quiz Game,"**
1950s. Jaymar. 8x10x1.5" deep box. Contents include: silver foil-covered insert board with pair of wires and light bulb plus set of six two-sided question/answer sheets and color insert card with blank areas for child to make his own questions/answers. - **$15 $40 $75**

DDK-520

DDK-521

❏ **DDK-520. Birthday Card,**
1950s. Hallmark. 4x4.75" slightly textured paper folder with diecut keyhole opening in front cover. - **$5 $15 $30**

❏ **DDK-521. "Growing With Donald Duck" Banner,**
1950s. Paragon Needlecraft. 11x37" fabric banner with original tag "Kit By Paragon Needlecraft." Has 36" long stiff paper tape measure stitched into right edge. - **$10 $20 $40**

DDK-522

❏ **DDK-522. "Louie" Watch,**
1950s. U.S. Time. 1-1/8x1.5" with chromed metal case. - **$75 $150 $300**

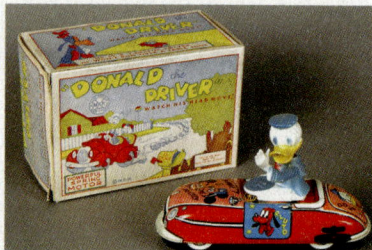

DDK-523

DDK-524

❏ **DDK-523. "Donald The Driver" Boxed Wind-Up,**
1950s. Marx. 6.5" long toy with built in key with nicely illustrated box. Has hard plastic Donald driver figure. Box - **$100 $200 $400** Toy - **$100 $200 $400**

❏ **DDK-524. "Donald Duck And His Nephews" Boxed Wind-Up,**
1950s. Marx. 11" long hard plastic toy with built-in key and nicely illustrated box.
Box - **$50 $100 $200**
Toy - **$50 $100 $200**

DONALD DUCK, DAISY & NEPHEWS

DDK-525

☐ **DDK-525. "Donald Duck In His Convertible" Boxed Car,**
1950s. Marx. Car is tin lithographed with separate removable celluloid figure of Donald from the waist up. Size is 2x5x2.25" tall. Marked on each side "Roadrunner" and includes image of Donald on the trunk. Has friction mechanism which also produces a siren sound. Box - **$200 $400 $600**
Car - **$200 $400 $600**

DDK-526

☐ **DDK-526. "Louie In His Dream Car" Boxed Car,**
1950s. Marx. Car is tin lithographed with separate removable celluloid figure of Louie from the waist up. 2.25x4.5x2.25" tall. Car is marked "Dream Car Disneyland Roadster" and has plastic windshield. Has friction mechanism which also produces a siren sound. Box - **$200 $400 $600**
Car - **$200 $400 $600**

DDK-527

☐ **DDK-527. "Donald Duck Wind-Up Animated Toy,"**
1950s. Reliable Plastic Co. Ltd., Canada. Boxed 4x5x6.5" tall plastic toy with built-in key.
Box - **$35 $65 $125**
Toy - **$50 $100 $200**

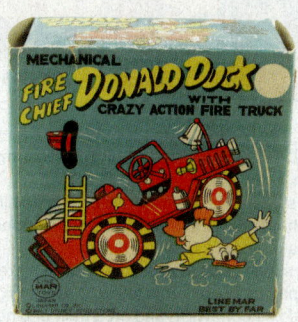

DDK-528

☐ **DDK-528. "Fire Chief Donald Duck With Crazy Action Fire Truck" Tin Litho Wind-Up,**
1950s. Line Mar. Number J-2564. Box is 3.5x5x5.5" tall. Toy is 7" long by 5.75" tall. Box - **$750 $1000 $1600**
Toy - **$500 $1000 $1600**

DDK-529

☐ **DDK-529. Donald Duck "Dipsy Car" Tin Litho Wind-Up,**
1950s. Line Mar. Number J-5173. Box is 5.5x5.75x3" deep, toy is 5.25" long and 5.75" tall. Box - **$100 $200 $400**
Toy - **$2500 $500 $700**

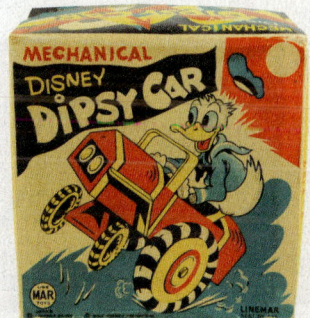

DONALD DUCK, DAISY & NEPHEWS

DDK-530

DDK-531

DDK-532

☐ **DDK-532. "Walt Disney's Rocking Chair" Boxed Wind-Up,**
1950s. Line Mar. Japan. Cello Donald sitting on 2.5x3.75" tin seat designed like Dumbo with string on front holding Pluto. Box - **$200 $400 $600**
Toy - **$250 $500 $1000**

☐ **DDK-531. Bobbing Head Donald Duck "Dipsy Car" Plastic And Tin Wind-Up,**
1950s. Line Mar. Number J-2137. Box is 5.5x5.75x3" deep, toy is 5.25" tall. Box - **$100 $200 $400**
Toy - **$200 $400 $600**

☐ **DDK-531. Donald Duck Wind-Up Tin Toy Tricycle,**
1950s. Line Mar. Number 257. 3-3/8" long, 3.75" tall with bell. - **$150 $300 $600**

DDK-533

☐ **DDK-533. Donald's Nephews Friction Train,**
1950s. Marx. 1.5x2.75x4" tall box containing 4" long hard plastic friction toy from a numbered series of "Plastic Disney Friction Toys." Illustrations of other character vehicles are on side panels of box. This toy is "2" depicting Donald's nephews in and on a train engine with their names in raised letters on each side. Each In Series Box - **$15 $30 $60**
Each In Series Toy - **$25 $50 $80**

DDK-534

☐ **DDK-534. "Disneyland Auto-Magic Picture Gun And Theater" Boxed Set,**
1950s. Stephens Products Co. 8x12x1" deep boxed complete set comprised of 6" long cast metal projector gun, seven insert film strips, "Going To The Movies" tickets for "Disneyland Theater," instruction sheet. One film is "Pluto In Trouble" and remaining films are generic interest as packaged. Outer box is designed to transform into a viewing screen as pictured on lid. - **$100 $200 $300**

DDK-535

DDK-536

☐ **DDK-535. "Donald Duck Magic Slate,"**
1950s. Strathmore Co. 8.5x13.5" diecut cardboard. - **$10 $20 $40**

☐ **DDK-536. "Donald Duck Note Paper For Children,"**
1950s. Content box is 6.5x8.75x.75" deep by unidentified maker containing set of 16 illustrated note sheets and 16 generic envelopes. - **$35 $65 $100**

DDK-537

DONALD DUCK, DAISY & NEPHEWS

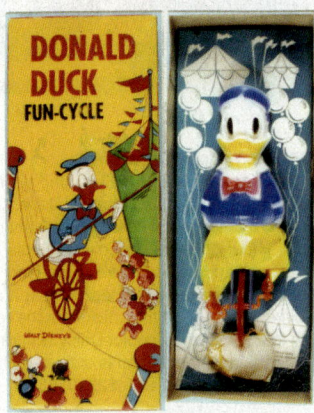
DDK-538

❑ **DDK-537. Mickey/Donald Ramp Walker,** 1950s. Marx. 4" long hard plastic figure. - **$30 $60 $110**

❑ **DDK-538. "Donald Duck Fun Cycle,"** 1950s. Empire. 7x18x3.5" deep box contains 11.5" tall Donald figure. A pair of metal balancing rods are attached to his hands and figure is placed on a string which has a pair of finger loops. Object is for two people to hold the string and have Donald travel back and forth on it. Box - **$10 $20 $30**
Toy - **$15 $30 $45**

DDK-539

❑ **DDK-539. "Donald Duck Wind-Up Toy,** 1950s. Donald on a scooter. Scarce. - **$300 $600 $1000**

DDK-540

❑ **DDK-540. Drummer Wind-Up Large Figure,** 1950s. Large figure by Marx. All plastic with tin-drum and metal sticks. - **$200 $400 $750**
Smaller figure by Line Mar. All tin.- **$200 $400 $750**
Box (Not Pictured) - **$100 $200 $300**

DDK-541

❑ **DDK-541. Donald Duck Celluloid Windup,** 1950s. Japan. 6" tall. Head moves up and down. - **$300 $600 $1200**

DDK-542

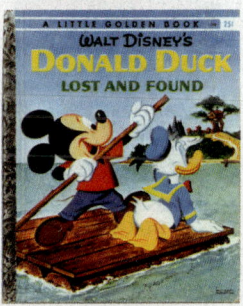
DDK-543

❑ **DDK-542. "Donald Duck's Adventure Little Golden Book,"** 1960. Golden Press. 6.75x8". 24 pages. Contest page at end of book "A Trip To Disneyland Contest." - **$10 $20 $40**

❑ **DDK-543. "Donald Duck Lost And Found,"** 1960. Golden Press. "Little Golden Book" 6.75x8" with 24 pages. - **$5 $12 $20**

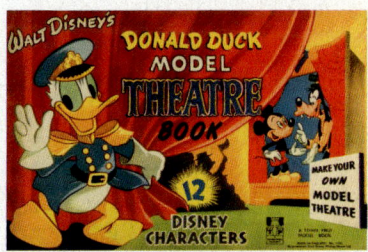
DDK-544

❑ **DDK-544. "Donald Duck Model Theatre Book,"** 1950s. Tower Press. 7x11" cardboard covers with four card stock pages of punch-outs and four paper pages of dialogue text for story "Donald Duck's Gold Mine." - **$50 $100 $200**

DDK-545

255

DONALD DUCK, DAISY & NEPHEWS

☐ **DDK-545. Donald Duck Ceramic Cookie Jar,**
1950s. Shaw. 11.5" tall and one of two different cookie jars produced. The other version depicts him holding his hat. - **$500 $1000 $2000**

DDK-546

☐ **DDK-546. "Donald Duck Pencil Sharpener" Example With Signed Sales Sheet,**
1960. 2.5x4x5" hard vinyl and cast metal figural sharpener created by "Disney Legend" designer Al Konetzni and marketed by Apsco Products Inc. Sharpener is accompanied by 8.5x11" retailer's sales sheet that includes image of the sharpener and notes it is "Just In Time For Last Minute Christmas Shoppers." Text also notes sharpener coincides to Donald's 25th anniversary and is available in pink or yellow.
Sharpener - **$25 $65 $100**
Autographed Sheet Near Mint - **$50**
Unsigned Sheet - **$5 $10 $20**

DDK-547

DDK-548

☐ **DDK-547. Donald & Others TV Tray,**
1961. 12.5x17.25" lithographed tin tray with pair of tubular retractable legs rising to height of 6.5". - **$15 $30 $60**

☐ **DDK-548. "Walt Disney's Comics And Stories" Subscription Mailer Folder With Donald And Others,**
1961. Four-page folder is 7x10". - **$50 $100 $150**

DDK-549

DDK-550

☐ **DDK-549. "Donald Duck Private Eye" Little Golden Book,**
1961. Golden Press. 6.75x8" stiff cover first printing edition. Story features Detective Donald disguising himself as Daisy, Grandma Duck and Scrooge. - **$25 $50 $100**

☐ **DDK-550. Donald Duck Cel,**
c. 1961. Image is 6x6.5". From a numbered sequence and this is "114." - **$75 $125 $250**

DDK-551

☐ **DDK-551. Donald Duck Chalkboard,**
1961. - **$25 $50 $100**
Ludwig Von Drake version - **$10 $20 $40**

DDK-552

☐ **DDK-552. "Happy Duck Car,"**
c. 1961. Ichiko. 3x7.5x2.25" tall tin lithographed friction Chevrolet by "Ichiko/Made In Japan" with pair of "I.K. 61" license plates. Shows eight duck characters, four of which strongly resemble Donald, Daisy and two nephews. There is another duck depiction designed with separate three-dimensional head that sticks out the rear window that is meant to depict Daisy with red bow in her hair. When friction is activated she moves up and down. - **$110 $2250 $375**

DDK-553

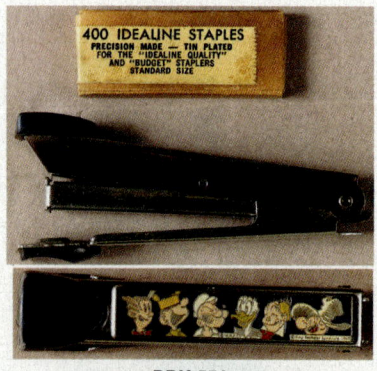

DDK-554

☐ **DDK-553. Donald Duck Still,**
1962. Glossy full figure image is 8x10". - **$5 $15 $25**

☐ **DDK-554. News Syndicate Comic Characters Stapler With Donald And Others,**
1962. King Features. Promotional 3-5/8" long chrome accent metal stapler with 5x2.5" enamel top art of Dagwood, Beetle Bailey, Popeye, Donald Duck, Jiggs and Snuffy Smith. Limited issue, mainly for newspaper editors. - **$25 $50 $85**

DONALD DUCK, DAISY & NEPHEWS

DDK-555

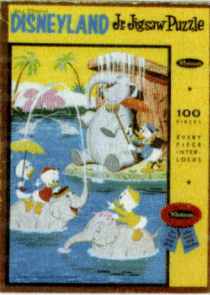

DDK-556

❏ **DDK-555. Italian Jointed Donald Duck Figure,**
c. 1962. Aradeanoa. 6.5x8x13" tall vinyl figure with movable head, arms and legs. - **$35 $65 $125**

❏ **DDK-556. "Disneyland Jr. Jigsaw Puzzle,"**
1963. Whitman. 8.5x11x1.5" deep box holds puzzle featuring Donald and his nephews giving baths to the elephants from Adventureland. - **$10 $18 $30**

DDK-557

DDK-558

❏ **DDK-557. "Donald Duck Bank Book,"**
1964. Ideal Toy Corporation. 4.5x6x1" thick hard plastic bank designed as replica book. - **$20 $40 $75**

❏ **DDK-558. "Walt Disney's Comics And Stories" Shop Dummy For Gift Subscription Renewal Offer,**
1964. Two pieces, each 7.25x10.25" leading to production of a two-sided subscription renewal offer paper. Each piece consists of paper sheet with printed base art plus three separate acetate cover separation overlays. Dummy was prepared for use by K. K. Publications Inc. Poughkeepsie, NY plant. As Made - **$165**

DDK-559

❏ **DDK-579. "Donald Duck" Australian Premium Comic Books,**
1964. Mobil Oil. Two 5x7.25" from a numbered weekly series, each 16 pages. These examples are #20 and #21, both featuring Carl Barks stories. "Spare The Rod" and "A Whale Of A Tale." Each - **$10 $20 $40**

DDK-560

❏ **DDK-560. "Donald Duck" Birthday Hat,**
c. 1964. 6x9x3.5" tall hat designed like his head. Main part is woven, starched white mesh. Front has a pair of google eyes and vinyl beak with squeaker mechanism. Attached to top is fabric patch with full figure image of Donald and a separate ribbon that reads "Happy Birthday Donald Duck." Probably issued in 1964 for his 30th birthday. - **$10 $20 $40**

DDK-561

❏ **DDK-561. Donald/Mickey/Minnie Hanky,**
1965. Cotton hanky is 7.5x7.5" with illustration of Donald nearly struck by a car with text "Don't Dawdle On A Busy Road" plus smaller illustrations of Mickey and Minnie with text "Mickey Mouse Safety First Hanky." - **$10 $20 $45**

DDK-562

DDK-563

DONALD DUCK, DAISY & NEPHEWS

❑ **DDK-562. Cereal Figural Container,**
1966. Nabisco Puppets Wheat Puffs. 4x5x9.5" tall soft plastic container depicting Donald as astronaut. Complete with tin lid base and also designed as bank with coin slot to be cut open on reverse. Uncut - **$10 $20 $40**
Cut - **$5 $10 $25**

❑ **DDK-563. Donald Duck "Patter Pillow",**
1967. Mattel. Talking cloth doll in box. - **$60 $120 $250**

DDK-564

DDK-565

DDK-566

❑ **DDK-564. Donald Nephews Cel,**
1960s. Image is 4.5x5". - **$50 $100 $175**

❑ **DDK-565. Donald Duck Production Cel,**
1960s. Image is 3x4". One corner marked "A109." - **$125 $250 $500**

❑ **DDK-566. "Donald Duck" Animation Cel,**
1960s. 9x12" cardboard matte with 6x9" cel. Depicts Donald behind treasure chest pointing to his tattered cap and holding a sign bearing his name. Sold at The Art Corner in Disneyland. - **$125 $250 $500**

DDK-567

DDK-568

❑ **DDK-567. Donald & Carioca Cel,**
1960s. "Art Corner At Disnesyland." 10x12" matted three acetate sheets forming 5x6.5" images of Donald and Jose Carioca on printed background sheet. - **$115 $225 $350**

❑ **DDK-568. "Disneyland" Donald Duck Bobbing Head,**
1960s. Painted composition figure 3x3x7" tall. Square base shows Disneyland name. - **$45 $85 $1250**

DDK-569

❑ **DDK-569. "Disneykin Play Sets" With Donald And Others,**
1960s. Marx. 1.5x6x3" tall display box containing set of five Disneykin figures and accessory pieces. Disneykins are Captain Hook, Goofy, Donald Duck, Daisy and Louie. Accessory pieces are boat, barrel, luggage, rope and post. Pieces are attached to insert platform designed like a dock against sky background. - **$25 $50 $85**

DDK-570

❑ **DDK-570. Donald Duck Spanish Valentine's Day Figure,**
1960s. Figure is 7" tall and made of hard vinyl attached to soft plastic base 4.5" diameter. Heart reads "Para (for) Daisy." - **$20 $40 $75**

DDK-571

❑ **DDK-571. "Donald Duck Orange Juice" Bottle,**
1960s. Large 64-ounce 4x4.5x9.5" tall glass bottle, complete with "Donald Duck" tin lid and foil label on front. - **$5 $15 $30**

DDK-572

DDK-573

DONALD DUCK, DAISY & NEPHEWS

❑ **DDK-572. Donald Duck Pez Dispenser,**
1960s. Figure is 4.5" tall. - **$10 $20 $40**

❑ **DDK-573. Donald Duck Soaky,**
1960s. Soft plastic container 7" tall. - **$10 $20 $35**

DDK-574

❑ **DDK-574. Italian Toothbrush,**
1960s. Paperino Giocoliere. 4.5" long hard plastic brush with 1.25" tall flat hard plastic figure of Donald attached to handle tip. Figure is designed to spin around. - **$10 $20 $40**

DDK-575

❑ **DDK-575. "Donald Duck Nitelite" On Card,**
1960s. General Electric. 3.25x5.5" blister display card holding 2.25" tall hard plastic figural plug-in night light. Carded - **$10 $20 $35**
Light Only - **$5 $10 $20**

DDK-576

❑ **DDK-576. Donald Duck Planter,**
1960s. Painted and glazed ceramic measuring 3.25x5.25x5.25" tall. Underside has 'Original Dan Brechner Exclusive' foil sticker and "WD-18." - **$50 $100 $150**

DDK-577

❑ **DDK-577. Bronzed Donald Duck Sprinkler With Production Photos,**
1960s. Unique bronzed version of 18" tall lawn sprinkler created by "Disney Legend" Al Konetzni, designer of many Disney merchandise items in the 1950s-1970s. Design features a figural Donald head topping a water shaft tube for insertion in lawn and coupling to water hose. It is accompanied by photo of contract signing for actual production. Unique - **$325**

DDK-578

DDK-579

❑ **DDK-578. Donald And Nephews Plate,**
1960s. "Original Dan Brechner Exclusive." 7.75" diameter glazed ceramic plate. Reverse has copyright, "WD-36" identification, plus maker's foil sticker. - **$15 $25 $40**

❑ **DDK-579. Donald's Nephews Salt & Pepper Set,**
1960s. "Japan" pair of 4" tall glazed ceramic shakers with over-the-glaze paint accents. - **$20 $40 $75**

DDK-580

DDK-581

❑ **DDK-580. Donald And Nephews TV Bank,**
1960s. Bank measures 3x6x5" tall. Has decal of Donald and nephews having picnic on TV screen. Underside marked "WD-23" with foil "Dan Brechner" sticker. - **$25 $50 $75**

❑ **DDK-581. Donald Duck Bank,**
1960s. Painted composition bank measures 3x5x5" tall. - **$25 $50 $75**

DDK-582

DONALD DUCK, DAISY & NEPHEWS

DDK-583

❑ **DDK-582. Donald Duck Bank,**
1960s. Painted composition bank measures 3.25x4x6" tall. - **$15 $30 $60**

❑ **DDK-583. Figure Bank,**
1960s. Painted composition is 3.5x3.5x5.75" tall, full figure image of Donald resting his head against one raised arm. Paper copyright sticker is under base with trap. - **$12 $20 $30**

DDK-584

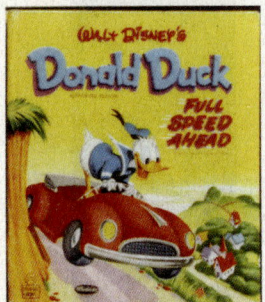

DDK-585

❑ **DDK-584. Figural Head Bank,**
1960s. Enesco. 3.5x5x5.5" tall glazed ceramic with over-the-glaze paint on hat, bow tie and bill. - **$30 $65 $115**

❑ **DDK-585. "Donald Duck Full Speed Ahead" Book,**
1960s. Whitman. 5.5x6.5" hardcover from "Tell-A-Tale" series, 28 pages. Copyright is 1953 but actual publication in the next decade. - **$5 $15 $25**

DDK-586

❑ **DDK-586. Donald Marionette Boxed,**
1960s. Pelham Puppets. 5x10x3.5" deep box containing 8.5" tall marionette made of composition, wood and hard plastic with cotton and felt outfit plus wood controller unit. Box - **$10 $20 $30**
Toy - **$20 $40 $70**

DDK-587

❑ **DDK-587. "Donald Duck" School Bag,**
1960s. Vinyl-covered canvas is 4x13x9" tall. Top left corner has small sticker mentioning entry blank included inside bag for a Disneyland trip sponsored by TWA. - **$25 $50 $80**

DDK-588

DDK-589

❑ **DDK-588. Donald's Nephew Squeaker Figure,**
1960s. "Made in Japan" with copyright 5x6x9" tall soft vinyl with movable head and inner squeaker mechanism. - **$10 $20 $40**

❑ **DDK-589. "Donald Duck Fun On Wheels,"**
1960s. Elm Toys. 1.75x2.25x1" deep box contains 1.5" tall hard plastic figure with gold foil tag. Boxed - **$20 $40 $60**
No Box - **$10 $20 $30**

DDK-590

❑ **DDK-590. "Donald Duck" Watch With Case,**
1960s. Bradley. Plastic case with clear lid holds watch with 1" diameter case. Case - **$10 $25 $40**
Watch - **$20 $40 $75**

DONALD DUCK, DAISY & NEPHEWS

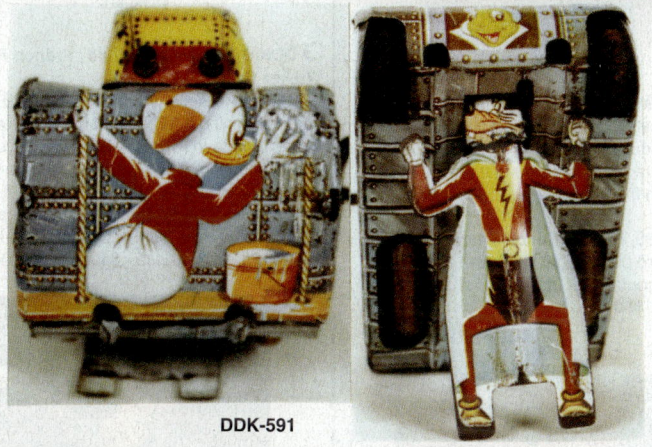

DDK-591

❏ **DDK-591. Donald Duck And Friends Turn-Over Tank Wind-Up,**
1960s. "Mexico" marked 2.25x4x3" tall lithographed tin toy with built-in key. Walt Disney Productions copyright and almost certainly made by Marx Toys for the Mexican market. Attached to underside is separate tin lithograph diecut figure of Goofy dressed in a super hero costume. - **$500 $1000 $1600**

DDK-592

❏ **DDK-592. Donald Duck Boxed Wind-Up Toys From Argentina,**
1960s. Mectoy. Two different sets. Each colorful box contains hard plastic "track" base and hard plastic wind-up car driven by a different character. First set is "50 Circo Donald." Box is 6.75x13.75x1.75" deep. The wind-up car is 1.25x2.5x2.5" tall and features one of Donald's nephews. Second set comes in 8.5x11.75x1.75" deep box and is "60 Donald Conductor." Each Box - **$20 $40 $60**   Each Toy - **$30 $60 $90**

DDK-593

❏ **DDK-593. Donald Duck Marx Friction Antique Automobile,**
1960s. Marx. 2x5x3" tall hard plastic with full figure of Donald driving "Stutz Bearcat." Underneath has Marx sticker. - **$20 $40 $75**

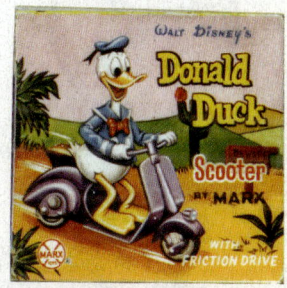

DDK-594

❏ **DDK-594. "Donald Duck Scooter" Boxed Friction Toy,**
1960s. Marx. Illustrated box containing 2x4.25x3.75" tall hard plastic replica of Donald seated on motorized scooter cart with revolving wheels to produce friction sound. Box - **$20 $40 $75**
Toy - **$35 $65 $115**

DONALD DUCK, DAISY & NEPHEWS

DDK-595

❑ **DDK-595. "Donald Duck" View-Master Set,** 1960s. 4.5x4.5" cover envelope with set of three reels in separate sleeve plus story booklet. Reels feature color photos of studio models for stories featuring Donald, Chip 'N Dale, Uncle Scrooge. - **$10 $20 $40**

DDK-596

DDK-597

❑ **DDK-596. Donald Duck Alarm Clock Distributed In France,** 1960s. Bayard. 5" tall with metal case. Donald's head moves as seconds tick. Made in France with limited U.S. distribution. - **$50 $125 $250**

❑ **DDK-597. Donald Duck Japanese Friction Racer,** 1960s. Masudaya, Japan. 12.5" long with tin litho body and large vinyl Donald Duck head. Features various images of Donald, Daisy, Pluto, Chip and Dale, and nephews with racing gear. - **$200 $400 $750**

DDK-598

DDK-599

❑ **DDK-598. Donald Duck Snow Dome,** 1960s. Plastic figure of Donald 3x4.5x5" tall holds round snow globe in his hands with small plastic figure of Pluto inside that moves back and forth in front of doghouse. - **$35 $65 $135**

❑ **DDK-599. Figural Pencil Sharpener,** 1960s. Hard plastic figure is 2x3x4.5" tall atop base that contains double pencil sharpener unit. - **$15 $30 $50**

DDK-600

❑ **DDK-600. Donald Duck Squeeze Toy,** c. 1960s. Soft vinyl figure measures 2x4.5x3" tall marked "Donald's Ice Cream." - **$30 $65 $100**

DDK-601

❑ **DDK-601. Donald Bendy Figure in Box,** c. 1960s. Near Mint Boxed - **$165**

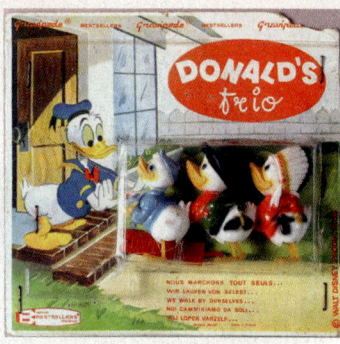
DDK-602

❑ **DDK-602. "Donald's Trio" French Ramp Walker Carded,** c. 1960s. Bestseller International. 6x6.25" blister card containing 3.25" long hard plastic ramp walker "Made In France." Toy depicts Donald's nephews, one holding bouquet of flowers, one as cowboy with gun, one as Indian chief with tomahawk. Attached by string is figural plastic weight depicting a stick of dynamite. Carded - **$65 $125 $175** Loose - **$40 $65 $100**

DDK-603

DDK-604

❑ **DDK-603. Figure On Base,** c. 1970. Multiple Toymakers. 1.75" tall hand-painted hard plastic figure on rectangular base similar to a Marx Disneykin but larger. Figure was included in various boxed toy sets by maker. - **$5 $10 $20**

DONALD DUCK, DAISY & NEPHEWS

❑ **DDK-604. "Donald Duck Mini-Puppet,"**
c. 1970. Kohner Bros. 2.75" tall hard plastic push puppet figure atop base with foil sticker. - **$10 $20 $35**

DDK-605

❑ **DDK-605. Donald Squeeze Toy,**
c. 1970. Marx. 7" tall. - **$10 $20 $40**

DDK-606

❑ **DDK-606. Donald And Nephews Music Box,**
1971. Anri. Large size with 6" diameter base by 6" tall. Nicely made wood with 3.5" tall carved Donald and each nephew is about 2" tall. Underside marked "Made In Italy By Anri" paper sticker that lists song title "Love Story." - **$60 $125 $250**

DDK-607

❑ **DDK-607. Donald Duck Music Box,**
1971. Anri. Small size with 3.5" diameter base by 5.25" tall. Has paper song label underneath "My Way." - **$50 $100 $200**

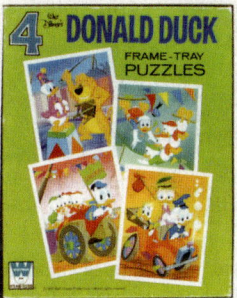

DDK-608

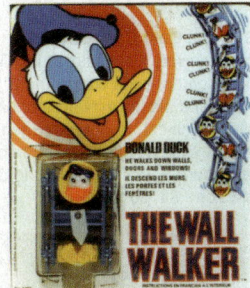

DDK-609

❑ **DDK-608. "Donald Duck Frame Tray Puzzles" Boxed Set,**
1972. Whitman. 8.25x10.25x1.5" deep boxed complete set of four puzzles. - **$10 $20 $35**

❑ **DDK-609. "Donald Duck The Wall Walker,"**
1972. Kenner. Card measures 8.25x9.5" and holds 3.25" tall figure. Canadian issue with text on card in English and French. Carded - **$15 $30 $50**

DDK-610

❑ **DDK-610. "Pull-Mee" Pull Toy,**
1973. Kohner Bros. 5.5x10x8.5" tall hard plastic car with mounted soft vinyl figure of Donald behind steering wheel. - **$8 $12 $25**

DDK-611

❑ **DDK-611. Donald Duck "Mechanical Wheelbarrow,"**
1973. Marx. 3x5.5x5" tall hard plastic toy with built-in key. When pushed along, Donald's legs rapidly move as if he is pushing the wheelbarrow. Box - **$15 $305 $50**
Toy - **$15 $50 $75**

DDK-612

DDK-613

❑ **DDK-612. "Donald Duck Costume,"**
1974. Ben Cooper. 8.25x11x3.5" deep box. Plastic mask and one-piece costume. Boxed - **$10 $20 $30**

❑ **DDK-613. "Mattel Chatter Chums/Donald Duck,"**
1976. Mattel. 6.5x11" display card contains 7" tall hard plastic figure of Donald with large head. Has pull string on back and figure says eight different phrases. Carded - **$25 $50 $100**
No Card - **$10 $25 $50**

DONALD DUCK, DAISY & NEPHEWS

DDK-614

DDK-615

DDK-616

DDK-617

❑ **DDK-616. "Donald Duck Tricky Trapeze,"** 1977. Gabriel. 2x3x5.25" tall hard plastic toy that spins and flips around when buttons on sides are pushed. - **$10 $20 $40**

❑ **DDK-617. Die Cast Cars Carded,** 1977. Azrak-Hamway International Inc. Three 3.75x5" blister cards, each containing 2" long die cast metal and plastic miniature of either dune buggy, sports car, or hot rod. Each has "Mickey Mouse Club" logo sticker on hood plus vinyl Donald figure from the waist up in driver's seat. Card Each - **$3 $6 $12**

DDK-618

❑ **DDK-618. "Daisy And Donald Paperdolls,"** 1978. Whitman. 10x13" with two inside pages of large punch-out dolls of Daisy and Donald as well as four glossy pages of paper outfits and accessories. - **$15 $30 $75**

DDK-619

❑ **DDK-619. "Donald Duck" Book With Dust Jacket,** 1979. Harmony Books. 8.5x11" hardcover, 256 pages. Content is an exceptional detailed authorized biography of "One Of Amereica's More Enduring Super Stars." - **$15 $30 $50**

DDK-620

❑ **DDK-620. Facial Belt Buckle,** 1970s. Unmarked but authorized 3x4" solid cast metal with bright luster finish plus high gloss enameled paint facial features. - **$10 $20 $40**

DDK-621

❑ **DDK-621. Metal Figure,** 1970s. Walt Disney Productions. Limited edition of 200. - **$150 $300 $475**

DDK-622

❑ **DDK-622. "Walt Disney World/Donald Duck" Hat,** 1970s. Designed like Donald's head and measures 7x10x4" tall. Made of starched white mesh and attached at top is fabric patch with Donald portrait, vinyl ribbon, google eyes and large vinyl beak with squeaker mechanism. - **$5 $15 $30**

❑ **DDK-614. "Donald Duck Stunt Scooter,"** 1976. Ahi. 1.5x6x8.75" tall blister card contains 4" tall gyro motorized hard plastic scooter with Donald figure. Package is designed to be converted into a stunt ramp. Near Mint Packaged - **$40**

❑ **DDK-615. "Donald Duck 1977 Annual,"** 1977. IPC Magazines Ltd. English hardcover "Fleetway Annual" measures 7.5x10.75" with 96 pages. Book is filled with comic book-style stories, puzzles, games, etc. - **$10 $20 $40**

DONALD DUCK, DAISY & NEPHEWS

DDK-623

■ **DDK-623. "Donald Duck Paint Box,"**
1970s. Page Of London. 5x10x.5" deep tin lithographed box with complete paint set. Marked "Made In England By Page Of London." - **$10 $18 $30**

DDK-624

■ **DDK-624. Animation Cel,**
1970s. 10.x12.5" acetate sheet centered by 5x6" painted image of Donald from the waist up holding a pair of drumsticks and turning his head to the side. From a Disney TV show and "D29" from a numbered sequence. - **$50 $75 $140**

DDK-625

■ **DDK-625. Walt Disney TV Show Cel With Pencil Drawing,**
1970s. Two 10.5x12.5" acetate sheets forming image of five characters. Minnie Mouse and Giro Gearloose image size is 4x6". Donald's three nephews image size is 4x4.75". Cels are from scene 8. Top sheet is for sequence "22" and this has images of Minnie and two nephews while second sheet is for sequence "24" with Giro and third nephew. Comes with lead pencil drawing on animation paper for sequence "24" featuring image of Giro and single nephew. - **$50 $100 $175**

DDK-626

DDK-627

■ **DDK-626. Bobbing Head Figure,**
1970s. "Walt Disney World" 3x3x6.5" tall painted composition with head mounted on a spring. - **$40 $75 $125**

■ **DDK-627. Fisherman Figurine,**
1970s. Painted bisque figure is 3x3x5.5" tall. - **$8 $15 $25**

DDK-628

DDK-629

■ **DDK-628. Golfer Mishap Figures,**
1970s. "Disney Gift-Ware." Two painted bisque figurines. One is 2.5x3x3" tall depiction of Donald reclining in the water beside his golf club. On top of head is lily pad with golf ball. Second is 4" tall depicting him about to take a swing. Each - **$8 $15 $25**

■ **DDK-629. Beach Theme Figurines,**
1970s. "Disney Gift-Ware." Two 4" tall painted bisque likenesses, both depicted in sea bathing suit. Each - **$5 $15 $25**

DDK-630

DDK-631

■ **DDK-630. "Donald Duck" Tagged Figure With Bag,**
1970s. Unmarked Dakin 7.5" tall poseable vinyl likeness in fabric shirt and bow tie, complete with diecut cardboard tag plus bag with carrying handle. Unmarked by maker as this is from the mid-1970s when Disney did its own distribution as "Walt Disney Distributing Co." Near Mint Bagged - **$40** Loose - **$10 $20 $30**

■ **DDK-631. Donald "Disney Dancers" Toy On Card,**
1970s. Monogram Products Inc. 6x8" blister card holding mechanical plastic toy on insert card titled "Showboat." Toy is a separate diecut plastic figure of Donald and an attached disk is turned causing the figure to move about as if dancing. Carded Near Mint - **$30**

DONALD DUCK, DAISY & NEPHEWS

DDK-632

❑ **DDK-632. Donald And Others Baked Goods Folders,**
1970s. Hostess Snacks. Two 9x12" glossy stiff paper retailer's sales brochures. One pictures Donald on front and opens to two large diecut flaps featuring Hostess products, comic books which featured Hostess ads, large image of Mickey, additional sales information papers. Second item is four-page folder featuring Goofy on front as a detective. Each - **$5 $10 $20**

DDK-633

DDK-634

❑ **DDK-633. "Donald Duck Pez Candy Dispenser Set,"**
1970s. 1.5x1.5x4.5" long unopened box containing inner boxed Donald Duck dispensers. These boxed dispensers were used in vending machines. While Donald is not pictured on the outer box, one end flap has text information. - **$20 $40 $80**

❑ **DDK-634. "Disney Comes Alive" Donald Toy,**
1970s. Kohner. 4.5x6x7" tall box contains 5.25" hard plastic toy. Inside of tub has simulated water and shark holding a bar of soap. When lever on front of tub is pushed back and forth it causes shark to move as Donald tries to strike him with his brush. Boxed - **$30 $60 $100** No Box - **$10 $20 $40**

DDK-635

DDK-636

❑ **DDK-635. "Donald Duck Fanciful Character Stool,"**
1970s. Gilbert & Ryan Inc. 17x24x3" deep box holds unassembled stool that measures 24" tall when assembled. Has vinyl-covered padded wood seat, wooden legs and chrome frame. Includes instruction sheet and envelope with screws and bolts. Near Mint Boxed - **$200** Stool Only - **$50 $100 $150**

❑ **DDK-636. "Donald Duck Paint-On Ceramic Bisque Plaque,"**
1970s. Leisuramics Inc. Boxed 10x12x1.5" deep unpainted white ceramic plaque in high relief design including simulated wood grain border. Boxed - **$10 $20 $35**

DDK-637

DDK-638

❑ **DDK-637. Figural Bank,**
1970s. PlayPal Plastics. 5x5.5x10.5" tall hard vinyl image of Donald sitting atop brick base. - **$10 $20 $35**

❑ **DDK-638. Figural Music Box,**
1970s. Schmid 3" diameter x 4.25" tall painted and glazed ceramic with over-the-glaze paint on shirt and hat. Underside has maker's foil label. Winds up to play "It's A Small World." - **$15 $25 $50**

DDK-639

DONALD DUCK, DAISY & NEPHEWS

❏ **DDK-639. Cloth Doll With Tag And Ribbon,**
1970s. "Stacee-Lee Originals/Commonwealth Toy & Novelty Co." 5x7x14" tall stuffed fabric with many felt accent pieces, both stitched tag and cardboard string tag. String tag has illustration of Mickey in a hot air balloon. Doll is formed in seated position. Attached to the bow tie is fabric ribbon naming him "Donald Duck." - **$15 $30 $60**

DDK-640

❏ **DDK-640. "Dancing Donald Duck" Boxed Doll,**
1970s. Hasbro Industries. 8.5x18x5.25" deep boxed 16.5" tall hard and soft vinyl doll in fabric outfit and hat. When the hands are squeezed, the legs move mechanically to simulate walking or dancing. Text on box reads "No Batteries Needed...Donald Runs On Love." Box - **$5 $15 $30**
Doll - **$10 $25 $50**

DDK-641

❏ **DDK-641. "Donald Duck" Hand Puppet,**
1970s. "Walt Disney Distributing Co." tagged 11" tall with hard vinyl head and fabric body. - **$5 $12 $20**

DDK-642

❏ **DDK-642. Donald Duck "Wind-Up Walking Toy,"**
1970s. Durham Industries Inc. 4.25" tall hard plastic figure with built-in key. Near Mint Carded - **$30**

DDK-643

❏ **DDK-643. "Talking Figure,"**
1970s. Mattel. 3.5x4.5x7" tall hard plastic figure with oversized head that moves when talking pull string on back is activated. Figure says several phrases in traditional voice. - **$10 $20 $40**

DDK-644

❏ **DDK-644. "Donald Duck Quartz Wall Clock,"**
1970s. Bradley Division Of Elgin. 8.25x27.25x1.75" deep box containing 25" long vinyl band centered by 6" diameter hard plastic case under clear plastic blister. Clock is designed like a giant wristwatch featuring illustration of Donald whose separate hands point at the numerals. Near Mint Boxed - **$150**
Clock Only - **$25 $50 $75**

DDK-645

DDK-646

❏ **DDK-645. Toy Watch,**
1970s. Plastic case is 1.25" in diameter with clear plastic cover over dial face Donald portrait. - **$5 $12 $20**

❏ **DDK-646. "Donald Duck" Boxed Schuco Wind-up,**
1970s. Toy is 2.25x3.75x6" tall in box with "Schuco" key. Toy vibrates around as Donald's mouth opens and closes. Box - **$50 $100 $200**
Toy - **$50 $100 $150**

DONALD DUCK, DAISY & NEPHEWS

DDK-647

DDK-648

❑ **DDK-647. "Donald Duck's Car" By Polistil,**
1970s. Made in Italy. Box measures 2.5x4.5x6.5" tall and contains 3.25" long die cast metal and plastic car. Has three dimensional rubber figure of Donald. Box - **$10 $20 $35** Car - **$15 $30 $65**

❑ **DDK-648. Donald Duck Figural Water Gun,**
1970s. Hard plastic three dimensional gun in the shape of Donald's body measures 4.5" long. - **$5 $15 $30**

DDK-649

DDK-650

❑ **DDK-649. Pencil Sharpener,**
1970s. Alco Products Inc. 1.5" diameter by 2.5" tall cylinder tin can. - **$15 $30 $50**

❑ **DDK-650. Donald And Daisy Duck Figurines,**
c. 1970s. Pair of 3" tall painted and glazed ceramic figurines. - **$8 $15 $25**

DDK-651   DDK-652

❑ **DDK-651. Donald Duck Jointed Figure,**
c. 1970s. Hollow soft plastic figure measures 4.5x5.9" tall. - **$15 $30 $60**

❑ **DDK-652. Donald Duck Necklace,**
c. 1970s. 1.75" tall solid cast metal figure with enamel paint on metal link chain. - **$6 $12 $25**

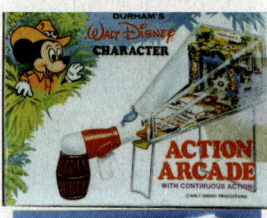
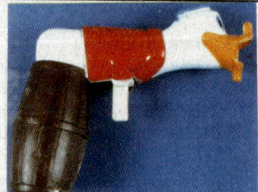

DDK-653

DDK-654

❑ **DDK-653. "Walt Disney Character Action Arcade,"**
c. 1970s. Durham. 5.5x8x4" deep box contains target with wire supports and has hard plastic 5" gun attached that depicts three dimensional image of Donald coming out of the barrel. Includes pack of bb's that are fired out of Donald's mouth. Boxed **$20 $40 $80** No Box **$10 $20 $40**

❑ **DDK-654. Donald Duck Carnival-type Statue,**
1980. - **$25 $50 $100**

DDK-655

DDK-656

❑ **DDK-655. "Donald Duck" Large Italian Deluxe Vehicle,**
1983. Burago, Italy. 7.5x14x16.5" tall box contains 9" long vehicle. Hood opens to reveal motor. Comes with removable soft plastic Donald figure. Box - **$20 $40 $75** Vehicle - **$55 $85 $175**

❑ **DDK-656. Donald Duck Cel,**
1984. Cel image is 4.25x6.5" from 50th birthday show. Accompanied by matching pencil drawing. Near Mint Pair - **$400**

DDK-657

268

DONALD DUCK, DAISY & NEPHEWS

DDK-658

DDK-661

DDK-664

❑ **DDK-657. Donald Duck Fishing Figurine,** 1984. Goebel. 3x5x4.5" tall. Underside is marked with Goebel name and artist's initials and date. - **$50 $100 $175**

❑ **DDK-658. Donald Duck "Merry Christmas 1984" Bisque Figurine,** 1984. Japan. Edition of 20,000. 6" diameter by 6" tall. Mint As Issued - **$200**

DDK-659

❑ **DDK-659. Donald Duck Goebel Figurine,** 1984. Base is 4.25" in diameter and figure is 3.25" tall. Underside has artist's initials and date. - **$30 $60 $100**

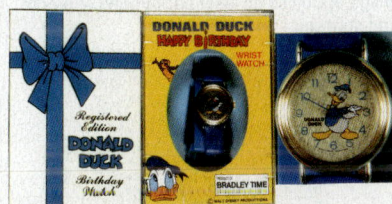

DDK-660

❑ **DDK-660. "Donald Duck Birthday Watch,"** 1984. Bradley Time. Box measures 3.75x5.25x2.5"deep and holds 1-1/8" watch with vinyl straps. Comes with warranty paper. Near Mint Boxed - **$135**
Watch Only - **$20 $40 $65**

❑ **DDK-661. Disneyworld Wood Figure,** 1984. Painted wood. - **$25 $50 $120**

DDK-662

❑ **DDK-662. "Donald Duck" Birthday Watches Store Display,** 1984. Bradley Time. 8.5x11" thick cardboard countertop standee with easel reverse. - **$10 $20 $45**

DDK-663

❑ **DDK-663. Donald Duck 50th Birthday Scene,** 1984. From Disney Capodimonte Collection. Sculpted by retired master Enzo Arzenton. Editon size 540. - **$3100**

❑ **DDK-664. "Donald Duck" Candle Holder,** 1980s. Royal Orleans. 3x4.5x4.25" tall painted bisque figural. Attached is "Disney Gift-Ware" cardboard string tag with Mickey illustration. - **$10 $20 $35**

DDK-665

❑ **DDK-665. Donald Duck German Souvenir Tray,** c. 1985. Tray is 4.25" diameter brass luster metal somewhat resembling ashtray except centered by 2.75" diameter aluminum disk. This has raised text around the rim in German for an outdoor walking or hiking group's 15th anniversary dates of 1970 and 1985. - **$20 $40 $60**

DDK-666

DONALD DUCK, DAISY & NEPHEWS

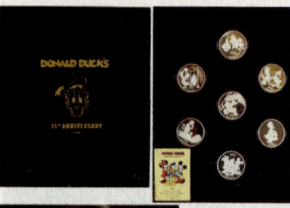

DDK-667

❑ **DDK-666. Large Donald Duck Stuffed Doll,**
1987. Stuffed plush/felt doll 11x14x21" tall wearing beret, vest and necktie. A Disneyland/Disney World limited issue. - **$20 $40 $75**

❑ **DDK-667. "Donald Duck's 55th Anniversary" Coin Proof Set Boxed,**
1989. Rareties Mint. "Rare Limited Edition" set of seven commemorative coins in celebration of "Donald Duck's 55th Anniversary." Each is 1.5" diameter .999 pure silver one troy ounce. Mint As Issued - **$160**

DDK-668

❑ **DDK-668. Donald Duck Figure,**
1980s. Capodimonte figure of Donald reading a comic. Produced in limited editon of 1,090. - **$475**

DDK-669

❑ **DDK-669. Donald Duck Cel With Matching Pencil Drawing,**
1980s. Cel image is 4.5x5.75", pencil image is same size. - **$60 $125 $235**

DDK-670

❑ **DDK-670. Donald Duck Cel With Matching Pencil Drawing,**
1980s. Image is 6x9.75". From a numbered sequence and this is number "17." - **$45 $90 $175**

DDK-671

DDK-672

DDK-673

❑ **DDK-671. Donald Duck Cel With Pencil Drawing From Disney Pops,**
1980s. Image is 5x7". From a numbered sequence and this is "D20." - **$100 $200 $400**

❑ **DDK-672. Minnie Mouse And Donald's Nephew Cel,**
1980s. Acetate sheet is 10.5x12.5" with character images left and right. Minnie is 4.5x7.5", nephew is 3x6". - **$50 $100 $150**

❑ **DDK-673. TV Program Cel With Matching Pencil Drawing,**
1980s. Pair of 10.5x12.5" acetate sheets combining to 3.25x6.25" Donald image against attached color laser background. - **$50 $125 $200**

DDK-674

❑ **DDK-674. Animation Cel,**
1980s. 10.5x12.5" acetate sheet with 6x6.5" cel image against laser background kitchen area for Epcot cartoon. Near Mint - **$135**

DDK-675

❑ **DDK-675. Animation Cel,**
1980s. 10.5x12.5" acetate sheet with 3.5x4" cel image of Donald on laser background of broom and doorway. - **$40 $75 $125**

DDK-676

DONALD DUCK, DAISY & NEPHEWS

◻ **DDK-676. Baby Daisy Duck Cel,**
1980s. 10.5x12.5" acetate sheet with 3.75x4.25" painted image of her riding a big wheel-type vehicle. From a Disney TV show and "11" from a numbered sequence. - **$40 $65 $125**

DDK-677

◻ **DDK-677. Animation Cel,**
1980s. 10.5x12.5" acetate sheet centered by 6x7" painted portrait. From a Disney TV show and "57" from a numbered sequence. - **$50 $75 $135**

DDK-678

◻ **DDK-678. Animation Cel,**
1980s. Acetate sheet is 10.5x12.5" with large 5x6" cel image of Donald from Disney TV show. No. "D13" from a numbered sequence. - **$35 $75 $125**

DDK-679

◻ **DDK-679. "Donald's Golf Game" Limited Edition Serigraph,**
1980s. Acetate sheet is 10.75x14" with 4.5x5.5" image of Donald as golfer. Has "Walt Disney Company" seal. Mint As Issued - **$100**

DDK-680

◻ **DDK-680. Donald's Nephews Painting,**
1980s. Stiff art board is 10.5x15.25" centered by 8x12.75" art in tempera paint with watercolor background. Hidden in the art are horseshoes, apparently some type of puzzle page in which these images were to be found. Margin notations indicate original use on page 115 of a 1983 Disneyland annual and then later used on page 8 of October 28 issue #88 of a Disneyland publication. This Or Similar - **$65 $125 $250**

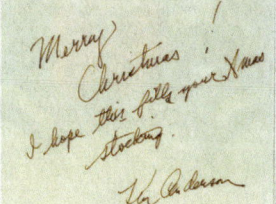
DDK-681

◻ **DDK-681. Animator Anderson Color Specialty Art With Handwritten Note,**
1980s. 8.5x10.75" stiff art board nearly filled by Ken Anderson Christmas art in pen and ink/colored crayon. Signed "Ken" at bottom in ink. Art is accompanied by 7.5x9.5" sheet with handwritten ink greeting "Merry Christmas! I hope this fills your Xmas stocking" and is signed in full. This art was commissioned by comic collector Charlie Roberts directly from Anderson, a top animator at the Disney Studios from the 1930s into the 1980s. Same Or Similar - **$250**

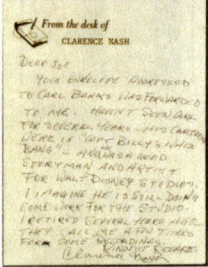
DDK-682

◻ **DDK-682. Nash (Voice Of Donald Duck) Handwritten Letter,**
1980s. 4x5" note paper imprinted at top "From The Desk Of Clarence Nash" followed by letter written in ballpoint pen by Nash, the voice of Donald from the character's beginning in Wise Little Hen, 1934. Nash was named a Disney Legend posthumously in 1992. Contents mostly refer to Carl Barks and he mentions "he was a good story man and artist for Walt Disney Studios." Nash also notes he recently retired but "they call me a few times for some recordings." Same Or Similar - **$100**

DDK-683

◻ **DDK-683. "Donald Duck Orange Juice" Premium Radio,**
1980s. Disney copyright boxed 3x4.5x1.25" deep hard plastic radio. - **$10 $20 $40**

DDK-684

◻ **DDK-684. Rubber Figures Set,**
1980s. Disney Park figures. Each - **$2 $4 $10** Bully-land figures handpainted with tags Each - **$5 $10 $25**

DONALD DUCK, DAISY & NEPHEWS

DDK-685

❑ **DDK-685. Disney English Flip Book "Activity Pack,"**
1980s. "Thumbflicks International Inc." 6.75x9" stiff paper book sealed in original plastic bag. Full title is "A Thumbflicks Activity Pack No. 1/2 Do-It-Yourself Moving Picture Flick Books." Content is 70 full color picture scenes from shorts to be cut apart and assembled into two different flip books. One is of Goofy as a carpenter, the other of Donald wrapped as a gift. Near Mint **$25**

DDK-686

❑ **DDK-686. Donald Duck Porcelain Figure,**
1991. 13" figure has felt clothing. Very limited by the Franklin Mint. - **$75 $150 $350**

DDK-687   DDK-688

❑ **DDK-687. Daisy Duck 13" Porcelain Doll,**
1991. Limited edition from the Franklin Mint. - **$75 $150 $275**

❑ **DDK-688. Dewey 9" Porcelain Figure,**
1991. Limited edition from the Franklin Mint. - **$40 $80 $175**

DDK-689   DDK-690

❑ **DDK-689. Huey 9" Porcelain Figure,**
1991. Limited edition from the Franklin Mint. - **$40 $80 $175**

❑ **DDK-690. Louie 9" Porcelain Figure,**
1991. Limited edition from the Franklin Mint. - **$40 $80 $175**

DDK-691

❑ **DDK-691. "Teddy Donald,"**
1993. Limited edition of 1,500, made by Steiff. Genuine mohair doll was sold in EPCOT Center during the 6th Annual Teddy Bear Convention at Walt Disney World. Near Mint - **$800**

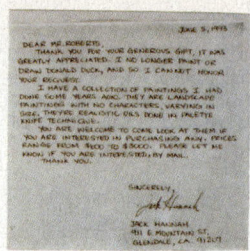

DDK-692

❑ **DDK-692. Animator Hannah Handwritten Letter,**
1993. 7.5x10.5" paper sheet with handwritten letter to comic art collector Charlie Roberts, signed in full and dated June 5, 1993. Hannah was the lead Donald Duck animator/director at Disney from the late 1930s into the 1940s. Eight of his cartoons were nominated for Academy Awards. Contents note that he no longer paints or draws Donald Duck so a request for such artwork could not be honored.
Same Or Similar - **$80**

DDK-693

❑ **DDK-693. Book-Burning Art With Donald And Goofy,**
c. 1993. Specialty pencil and ink art by Disney animator Bill Justice on 8.5x11" sheet centered by 4x10" image. Donald and Goofy are shown burning a pile of the anti-Disney book "Walt Disney Hollywood's Dark Prince" that was published in 1993. Art use was probably in a Disney in-house publication. Unique - **$265**

DDK-694

❑ **DDK-694. "Donald Duck" Limited Edition Wristwatch Boxed,**
1994. "Pedre." 3.75x5.75x1" deep boxed replica watch of unique prototype Ingersoll watch from 1935 but only discovered in 1990. Watch comes with certificate of authenticity detailing these facts. Issued to commemorate Donald's 60th birthday. Mint As Issued - **$125**

DONALD DUCK, DAISY & NEPHEWS

DDK-695

(CLOSED)

DDK-697 (OPEN)

DDK-699

☐ **DDK-699. Donald Duck Museum Exhibition German Poster,**
1995. Glossy paper is 23x33" for Donald's 60th anniversary. Text at bottom margin is German and issued for May 20-July 30. Donald Duck Exhibition at "Landesmusseum Mainz." - **$20** **$40** **$75**

☐ **DDK-695. "Sixty Years Quacking" Statue,**
1994. Fine English Bone China. Figure and base is 14" tall. Comes with small lithograph with a matching image from the Carl Barks painting "Hi, I'm Donald Duck." Limited editon of 100.
Editions no. 11-100 were issued at **$5300** each
Editions no. 1-10 were issued at higher prices. Price varies widely.

☐ **DDK-697. 60th Anniversary Watch,**
1994. Boxed - **$30** **$60** **$135**

DDK-700

DDK-696

DDK-698

☐ **DDK-696. Mechanical Moveable Christmas Figure,**
1994. Statue is 22" tall. - **$25** **$85** **$200**

☐ **DDK-698. "Admiral Duck" Statue,**
1995. From the Classic Disney Collection. Edition was retired in 1995. - **$285**

☐ **DDK-700. "Sheriff Of Bullet Valley" Limited Edition Bronze,**
1995. Signed by Carl Barks and sculptor P. Vought. Edition of 200, base signed in gold ink. 13" tall. Mint As Issued - **$3300**

DONALD DUCK, DAISY & NEPHEWS

DDK-701

DDK-703

❏ **DDK-705. "With Love From Daisy" Statue,** 1996. From the Classic Disney Collection. Edition was retired in 1996. - **$160**

DDK-706

❏ **DDK-701. Disneyana Convention Donald Duck Resin Limited Edition Display,** 1995. China. Edition of 2500 issued at September 6-10 convention. 6.25" wide by 6.5" tall. Mint As Issued - **$275**

❏ **DDK-703. "Three Caballeros" Statue,** 1996. From the Classic Disney Collection. Edition was retired in 1996. - **$250**

❏ **DDK-706. Donald Cookie Jar,** 1990s. - **$12 $25 $40**

DDK-704

DDK-707

DDK-702

❏ **DDK-704. "Mr. Duck Steps Out" Statue,** 1996. Donald and Daisy shown. From the Classic Disney Collection. Retired in 1996. Mint As Issued - **$900**

DDK-705

DDK-708

❏ **DDK-702. Donald Duck "Self Control" Metal Sculpture,** 1996. Designed by Bruce Lau. 6x9" base with 7.5" tall figure. Edition of 150 sold out at **$1800**. Mint As Issued - **$2000**

❏ **DDK-707. "Wise Little Hen" Figure,** 1997. Honors Donald Duck's debut cartoon. From the Classic Disney Collection. Golden Circle dealer event figure. 5 3/4" tall - **$340**

❏ **DDK-708. Armani 7" Figure,** 1998. Donald Duck holding an Armani briefcase. Limited edition made in Italy. - **$300**

DONALD DUCK, DAISY & NEPHEWS

DDK-709

❏ **DDK-709. Mechanical Christmas Figure,** 1998. Very large statue with Donald's usual look of Christmas cheer. - **$125**

❏ **DDK-710. Musical Doll with Key,** 1998. Plays "Ducktales" theme song. Commemorates "The Prince and the Pauper" movie. Porcelain head and feet. 15" tall - **$150**

❏ **DDK-711. Framed Pin Set,** 1999. Celebrates 65 Feisty Years with a framed set of 6 small pins and 1 large pin. Limited edition of 5000. - **$30 $75 $115**

DDK-710

DDK-712

❏ **DDK-712. Framed Pin Set,** 1999. Exclusive 3 pin set with Donald Duck model sheet. Framed in limited edition of 2,500. - **$25 $40 $65**

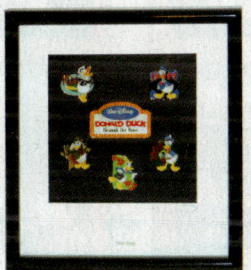

DDK-713

❏ **DDK-713. Framed Pin Set,** 1999. 65th Anniversary set of 6 pins in a 12" high frame with stamped matte. Third in the series and the hardest to find. Limited to 1,934, the year of Donald Duck's debut. - **$125**

DDK-714

DDK-711

❏ **DDK-714. 65th Anniversary Bisque,** 1999. Celebrates 65 Feisty Years as a movie star. Small figures of Donald represent appearances in successful cartoon features over 65 years. Sculpted by Bruce Lau. Limited to 2500. - **$200**

DDK-715

❏ **DDK-715. Anniversary Watch and Yo-Yo Set in Box,** 1999. Limited edition 65th Anniversary set includes a watch, yo-yo, pin and instructions. Complete - **$130**

DDK-716

❏ **DDK-716. "Donald's Better Self" Statues,** 1999. From the Classic Disney Collection. Commemorates the original 1938 cartoon. Set - **$650** Each figure - **$220**

DONALD DUCK, DAISY & NEPHEWS

DDK-717

❑ **DDK-717. Donald "On Ice" Statue,**
1999. From the Classic Disney Collection. Donald on skates - **$200**

DDK-718

❑ **DDK-718. Donald Duck Resin Figure on Base,**
1999. Commemorates 65th Anniversary. First few statues created had the date "1928" on the base. The error was corrected to "1934". Limited edition of 1,999. - **$325**

DDK-719

❑ **DDK-719. Donald Duck Pocket Watch with Resin Display Holder,**
1999. Limited edition 65th Anniversary pocket watch with chain displayed in a resin holder featuring the old and new Donald. Boxed - **$165**

DDK-720

❑ **DDK-720. Charm Bracelet ,**
1999. Disney Store exclusive. 65th Anniversary item boxed. 65 small duck figure charms on the bracelet. Silver and Gold editions produced. Each - **$300**

DDK-721

❑ **DDK-721. Magical Moments Pin Set,**
1999. Walt Disney Gallery exclusive. 65th Anniversary item. Set of 6 pins, each in a separate box. Each - **$10**
Set with boxes - **$60**

DDK-722

❑ **DDK-722. 65th Anniversary Ornate Clock,**
1999. Clock base has numerous images from Donald Duck's lengthy movie career. - **$350**

DDK-723

❑ **DDK-723. 65th Anniversary Marionette,**
1999. On stand. - **$165**

DDK-724

DONALD DUCK, DAISY & NEPHEWS

❏ **DDK-724. Mechanical Moveable Christmas Figure with Box,** 1996. Statue is 24" tall. - **$15 $65 $150**

DDK-725

❏ **DDK-725. "Donald's Drum Beat" Ceramic Figure on Base,** 1990s. From the Classic Collection. Mint As Issued - **$550**

DDK-726

❏ **DDK-726. "Dude For a Day" Statue,** 1990s. Created from Fine Bone China in a limited edition of 100. Issued with a matching, numbered lithograph. Original issue price **$7300**. Prices vary widely.

DDK-727

❏ **DDK-727. Donald Large Cookie Jar,** 1990s. By Treasure Craft. - **$15 $30 $50**

DDK-728

❏ **DDK-728. Donald Christmas Figure,** 1990s. Donald receives coal in his stocking for being a bad boy. This prototype was not produced for general distribution. Near Mint with tag - **$165**

DDK-729

❏ **DDK-729. Anniversary Figure with Pocketwatch,** 1990s. Limited edition of 2,500. With certificate, warranty and history booklets. - **$175**

DDK-730

❏ **DDK-730. Donald as The Duck Avenger Plush,** 1990s. - **$20**

DDK-731

❏ **DDK-731. Donald Blue Car With Wooden Chest,** 1990s. - **$115**

DDK-732

❏ **DDK-732. Donald Duck Fire Prevention Limited Issue Button,** 1990s. 2.25" Hancock School. - **$5 $12 $25**

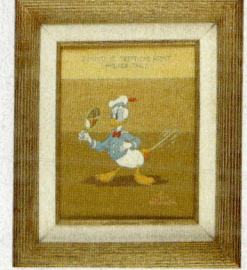
DDK-733

❏ **DDK-733. Donald Duck Oil Painting,** 1990s. 13x15" frame with 7.5x9.75" image of Donald looking into mirror with toilet bowl plunger stuck on his tail. Based on scene from 1936 short Moving Day. Painted by noted animator and director Jack Hannah. Unique - **$1250**

DDK-734

DDK-735

DONALD DUCK, DAISY & NEPHEWS

❏ **DDK-734. Embroidered Patch,**
1990s. Walt Disney Productions. - **$25**

❏ **DDK-735. Donald as Native American Bean Bag Figure,**
2000. - **$30**

DDK-736

DDK-737

❏ **DDK-736. Alarm Clock,**
2000. Stands on plastic duck feet. - **$40**

❏ **DDK-737. "Debonair Donald" Figure,**
2000. From Lenox. - **$175**

DDK-738

❏ **DDK-738. Donald Frontierland Plush,**
2000. - **$20**

DDK-739

❏ **DDK-739. Fire Brigade Donald,**
2000. Classic Collections. - **$200**

DDK-740

❏ **DDK-740. Chef Donald Sculpture,**
2001. 60th Anniversary event sculpture limited to 5,000. From the Classic Collection. 6 1/4" tall. - **$175**

DDK-741

DDK-742

❏ **DDK-741. Bobblehead Doll,**
2003. - **$20**

❏ **DDK-742. Bop Bag in Box,**
2004. - **$5**

DDK-743

❏ **DDK-743. Orphans' Benefit Commemorative Figure,**
2004. Limited edition of 6,000. From the Classic Collection. - **$100**

DDK-744

❏ **DDK-744. Swinging Hands Alarm Clock,**
2004. - **$30**

DDK-745

❏ **DDK-745. Donald Duck Watch,**
2004. - **$30**

DDK-746

❏ **DDK-746. Donald Figure on Green Base,**
2004. Limited edition large figure. - **$175**

DDK-747   **DDK-748**

❏ **DDK-747. Donald Daytona Die-Cut Car,**
2000s. - **$12**

❏ **DDK-748. Nascar Teddy Bear,**
2000s. - **$12**

DONALD DUCK COMICS

Donald Duck Comics

Dell Publishing did not start individually numbering Donald Duck Comics until issue #26 (Nov 52). Dell started the count late because they considered Donald's first 25 issues to have occurred in two other titles. First, Dell counted two issues of *Large Feature Comics* as part of the sequence. Next, they included *Four Color Comics* issue numbers, 4, 9, 29, 62, 108, 147, 159, 178, 186, 199, 203, 223, 238, 256, 263, 275, 308, 328, 339, 348, 367 and 408. Dell published the Donald title until issue #216. Whitman published the book from #217-245. Next, Gladstone published issues #246-307. Today, as of issue #308, Gemstone is publishing the book under the title *Donald Duck and Friends*. Gemstone also publishes a digest-format book titled *Donald Duck Adventures*. This book started with issue #1

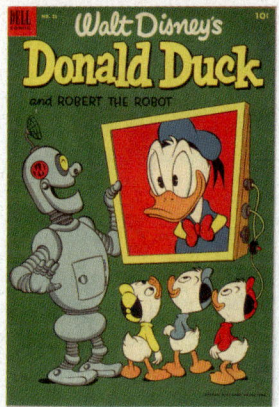
❑ Donald Duck #28,
March 1953. Barks-c. - $12 $36 $190

❑ Donald Duck #31,
September 1953. - $7 $21 $90

❑ Donald Duck #26,
November 1952. Barks-a. - $33 $99 $585

❑ Donald Duck #29,
May 1953. Barks-c. - $12 $36 $190

❑ Donald Duck #32,
November 1953. - $7 $21 $90

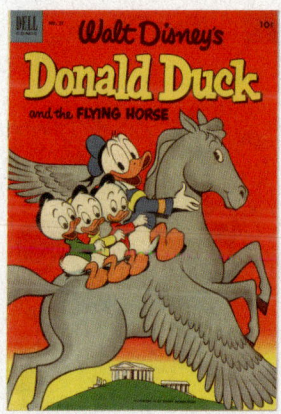
❑ Donald Duck #27,
January 1953. Barks-c. - $12 $36 $190

❑ Donald Duck #30,
July 1953. Barks-c. - $12 $36 $190

❑ Donald Duck #33,
January 1954. - $7 $21 $90

DONALD DUCK COMICS

☐ **Donald Duck #34,**
March 1954. - **$7 $21 $90**

☐ **Donald Duck #37,**
September 1954. - **$7 $21 $90**

☐ **Donald Duck #40,**
March 1955. - **$7 $21 $90**

☐ **Donald Duck #35,**
May 1954. - **$7 $21 $90**

☐ **Donald Duck #38,**
November 1954. - **$7 $21 $90**

☐ **Donald Duck #41,**
May 1955. - **$7 $21 $90**

☐ **Donald Duck #36,**
July 1954. - **$7 $21 $90**

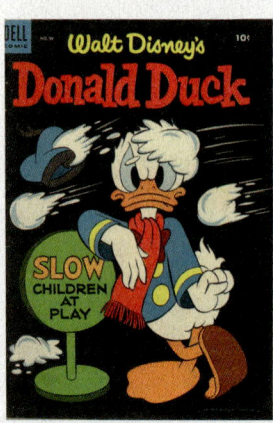

☐ **Donald Duck #39,**
January 1955. - **$7 $21 $90**

☐ **Donald Duck #42,**
July 1955. - **$7 $21 $90**

DONALD DUCK COMICS

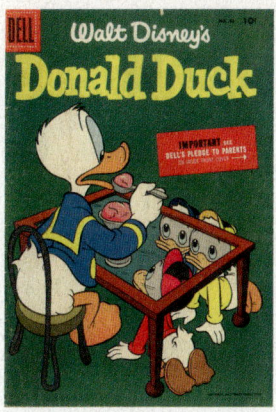

❏ **Donald Duck #43,**
September 1955. - **$7 $21 $90**

❏ **Donald Duck #46,**
March 1956. Barks-a. - **$20 $60 $325**

❏ **Donald Duck #49,**
September 1956. - **$7 $21 $90**

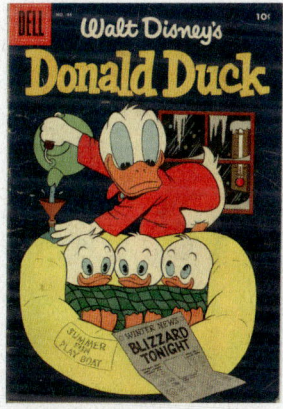

❏ **Donald Duck #44,**
November 1955. - **$7 $21 $90**

❏ **Donald Duck #47,**
May 1956. - **$7 $21 $90**

❏ **Donald Duck #50,**
November 1956. - **$7 $21 $90**

❏ **Donald Duck #45,**
January 1956. Barks-a. - **$14 $42 $225**

❏ **Donald Duck #48,**
July 1956. - **$7 $21 $90**

❏ **Donald Duck #51,**
January 1957. Barks-a. - **$8 $24 $95**

DONALD DUCK COMICS

❑ **Donald Duck #52,**
March 1957.   Barks-a. - **$14 $42 $230**

❑ **Donald Duck #55,**
September 1957. - **$7 $21 $80**

❑ **Donald Duck #58,**
March 1958. - **$7 $21 $80**

❑ **Donald Duck #53,**
May 1957. - **$7 $21 $80**

❑ **Donald Duck #56,**
November 1957. - **$7 $21 $80**

❑ **Donald Duck #59,**
May 1958. - **$7 $21 $80**

❑ **Donald Duck #54,**
July 1957.   Barks-a. - **$17 $51 $275**

❑ **Donald Duck #57,**
January 1958. - **$7 $21 $80**

❑ **Donald Duck #60,**
July 1958.   Barks-a. - **$17 $51 $275**

DONALD DUCK COMICS

❑ **Donald Duck #61,**
September 1958. - **$6 $18 $65**

❑ **Donald Duck #64,**
March 1959. - **$6 $18 $65**

❑ **Donald Duck #67,**
September 1959. - **$6 $18 $65**

❑ **Donald Duck #62,**
November 1958. - **$6 $18 $65**

❑ **Donald Duck #65,**
May 1959. - **$6 $18 $65**

❑ **Donald Duck #68,**
November 1959. Barks-a. - **$11 $33 $160**

❑ **Donald Duck #63,**
January 1959. - **$6 $18 $65**

❑ **Donald Duck #66,**
July 1959. - **$6 $18 $65**

❑ **Donald Duck #69,**
January 1960. - **$6 $18 $65**

DONALD DUCK COMICS

❑ **Donald Duck #70,**
March 1960. - **$6 $18 $65**

❑ **Donald Duck #73,**
September 1960. - **$6 $18 $65**

❑ **Donald Duck #76,**
March 1961. - **$6 $18 $65**

❑ **Donald Duck #71,**
May 1960. Barks-r. - **$6 $18 $70**

❑ **Donald Duck #74,**
November 1960. - **$6 $18 $65**

❑ **Donald Duck #77,**
May 1961. - **$6 $18 $65**

❑ **Donald Duck #72,**
July 1960. - **$6 $18 $65**

❑ **Donald Duck #75,**
January 1961. - **$6 $18 $65**

❑ **Donald Duck #78,**
July 1961. - **$6 $18 $65**

DONALD DUCK COMICS

❑ **Donald Duck #79,**
September 1961. Barks-a. - **$6 $18 $70**

❑ **Donald Duck #82,**
March 1962. - **$6 $18 $65**

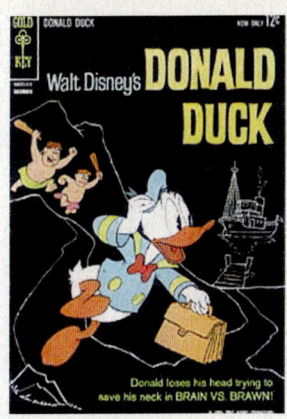

❑ **Donald Duck #85,**
December 1962. - **$6 $18 $65**

❑ **Donald Duck #80,**
November 1961. - **$6 $18 $65**

❑ **Donald Duck #83,**
June 1962. - **$6 $18 $65**

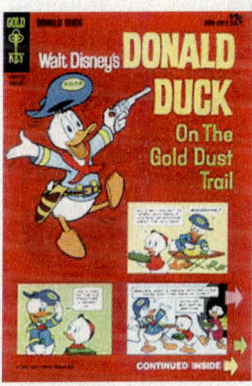

❑ **Donald Duck #86,**
February 1963. - **$6 $18 $65**

❑ **Donald Duck #81,**
January 1962. Barks-a. - **$6 $18 $70**

❑ **Donald Duck #84,**
September 1962. - **$6 $18 $65**

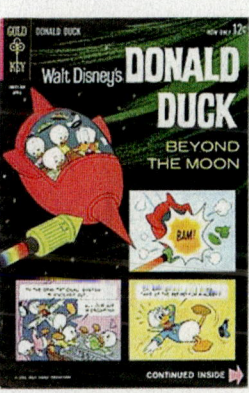

❑ **Donald Duck #87,**
April 1963. - **$6 $18 $65**

DONALD DUCK COMICS

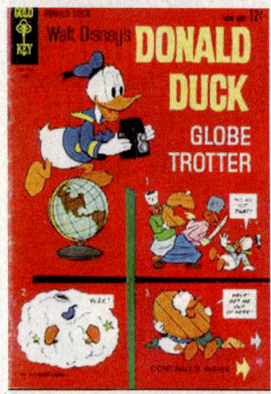

❏ **Donald Duck #88,**
June 1963. - **$6 $18 $65**

❏ **Donald Duck #91,**
November 1963. - **$6 $18 $65**

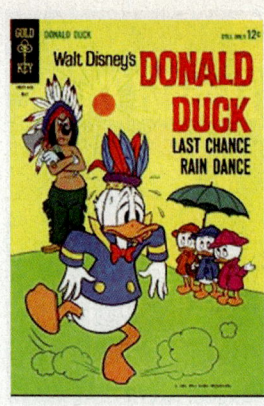

❏ **Donald Duck #94,**
May 1963. - **$6 $18 $65**

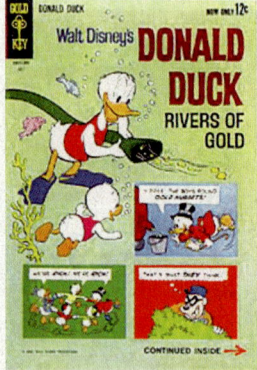

❏ **Donald Duck #89,**
July 1963. - **$6 $18 $65**

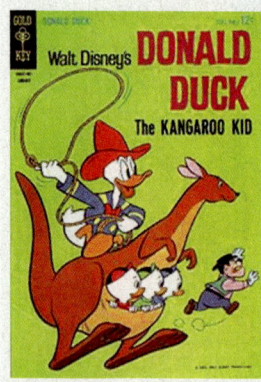

❏ **Donald Duck #92,**
January 1963. - **$6 $18 $65**

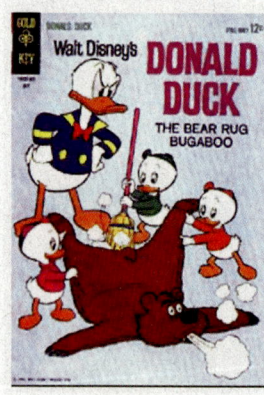

❏ **Donald Duck #95,**
July 1963. - **$6 $18 $65**

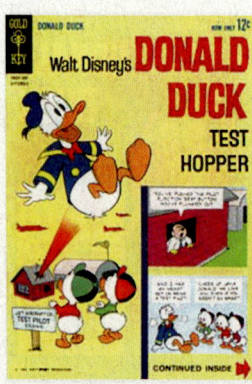

❏ **Donald Duck #90,**
September 1963. - **$6 $18 $65**

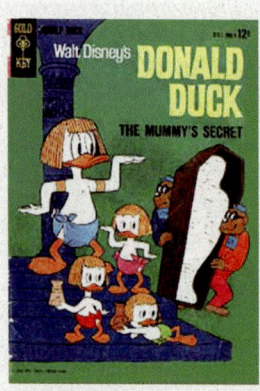

❏ **Donald Duck #93,**
March 1963. - **$6 $18 $65**

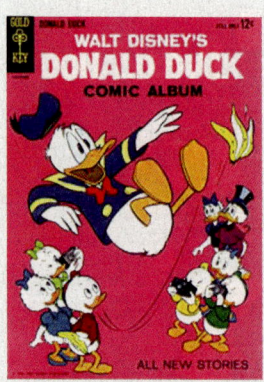

❏ **Donald Duck #96,**
September 1963. - **$6 $18 $65**

DUCKTALES

DuckTales

This animated television series ran in syndication from September 1987 until September 1992. It returned briefly in 1997. The stars of the show were Uncle Scrooge McDuck and his grand-nephews Huey, Dewey and Louie. Episodes largely revolved around Scrooge's quest for wealth, but others involved the nephews' trials in daily life or the travails of Launchpad McQuack. This accident-prone pilot was specifically created for the series.

Many fans consider the concept of *DuckTales* to have its origins in the world that Carl Barks created for the comics he'd written and drawn over the years. The show was a success for years and eventually led to a full length theatrical release, *DuckTales: the Movie - Treasure of the Lost Lamp* (1990).

Merchandise included books, stuffed animals, crayons, puzzles, figures and fast food tie-ins.

DKT-3

DKT-6

DKT-4

DKT-7

❑ **DKT-6. DuckTales Mexican Lunch Box,** 1980s. Vinyl 7x9x4" deep marked "Made In Mexico." - **$30 $75 $125**

❑ **DKT-7. "DuckTales" Framed Cel,** c. 1980s. 15x18" matted cel with 2.5x4" image of one of Donald's nephews on hand-painted background. - **$65 $125 $200**

❑ **DKT-3. Uncle Scrooge Cel,** 1980s. Acetate sheet is 9x10.5" with 3.5x5.25" image. #C-89 from a numbered sequence. - **$65 $125 $175**

❑ **DKT-4. Uncle Scrooge Cel,** 1980s. Acetate sheet is 10.5x12.5" with 3x4" image. #B-54 from a numbered sequence. Comes with laser printed background. - **$65 $125 $175**

DKT-1

DKT-5

DKT-8

DKT-2

❑ **DKT-1. Uncle Scrooge Cel,** 1980s. Acetate sheet is 9x10.5" with large 7x8" image. #A-5 from a numbered sequence with color laser background. - **$165 $275 $525**

❑ **DKT-2. Uncle Scrooge Cel,** 1980s. Acetate sheet 9x10.5". Image is 3.5x4.75". - **$75 $150 $225**

❑ **DKT-5. "Duck Tales" Cel Featuring Uncle Scrooge And Nephew,** 1980s. Pair of 9x10.5" acetate sheets each with cel image. Uncle Scrooge 3.5x5" and nephew is 2x3" has laser background depicting vault. - **$75 $135 $225**

DKT-9

DUCKTALES

❑ **DKT-8. Cereal Premium Disney TV Chracter Figurines,**
1993. Kellogg's. Complete set of 16 plastic figures 2" to 2.5" tall sealed in original mailing bag. Four each for four shows: DuckTales, Chip 'n' Dale Rescue Rangers, Gummi Bears and Tailspin. Near Mint Set - **$60**

❑ **DKT-9. "DuckTales" Button,**
1990s. Uncle Scrooge with Donald's nephews. 3". - **$1 $3 $6**

Dumbo

This is one of the most heartwarming films in the Disney catalog. A baby circus elephant is born with ears so big that he and his mother become objects of humiliation. When his mama tries to defend Dumbo from a taunting circus patron, she is locked up as a mad elephant and Dumbo must make do on his own.

One day, Timothy the Mouse helps him try to gain a foothold in life. The climax of this is that, with the help of some crows, Dumbo learns he can use his giant ears to fly. With that discovery, Dumbo's world suddenly changes.

This 1941 film followed two of the most expensive and taxing films that Disney had ever made, *Fantasia* and *Pinocchio* (both 1940). *Dumbo* may have cost less and taken less time, but it stands right next to those two as a true Disney classic. Many consider the scene where Dumbo's mother holds his trunk through the bars of her cage to be the most touching that Disney ever made.

Walt Disney's personal involvement in the project was less than usual. He was away in South America for twelve weeks and at the same time, he was also tied up with a strike that was happening at the studio. Even without his direct supervision, his animators came through for him with flying colors. *Dumbo* is arguably the most loved feature that Disney ever created. Directed by Ben Sharpsteen, the film was based on a story by Helen Aberson and Harold Pearl. Animators included Walt Kelly, Fred Moore, Art Babbitt and Wolfgang Reitherman.

The musical score by Oliver Wallace and Frank Churchill won an Academy Award. The crows' song sequence, *When I See an Elephant Fly* was animated by Ward Kimball. *Dumbo* was scheduled to be featured on the cover of *Time* magazine the week it was released, but, at the very last minute, the cover was changed due to the attack at Pearl Harbor.

Dumbo inspired numerous premiums and a broad range of licensed merchandise, with an emphasis on books and figurines. Dumbo appears in the following issues of *Four Color Comics*: # 17 (first series), 234 and 668 (two printings, different covers).

DUM-1

❑ **DUM-1. "Dumbo" Original Release Lobby Card,**
1941. Card is 11x14" featuring film scene of circus elephants performing. - **$100 $200 $350**

DUM-2

❑ **DUM-2. "Dumbo" Elaborate Movie Promotional Kit,**
1941. Elaborate brochure for the original release in three-sectioned die-cut folder opening to total size of 9x47". Each of the three separate sections of the folder contains a 12x17" publicity book on glossy paper, either 10 or 12 pages each. Total content includes pressbook of illustrations and photos, promotional items such as an autographed mail card, maps, "Publicity And Features" text and many scenes, "Advertisements" include variety of differnet ad mats in various sizes and styles. - **$215 $425 $650**

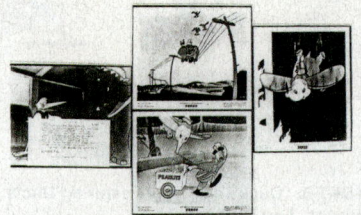

DUM-3

❑ **DUM-3. "Dumbo" Stills,**
1941. four glossy scene cards 8x10" for film's original release. Each - **$5 $12 $20**

DUM-4

❑ **DUM-4. "Dumbo" Stills,**
1941. Five glossy scene cards for film's original release. 8x10" based on his hallucination of pink elephants. Each - **$5 $12 $20**

DUM-5

❑ **DUM-5. Dumbo Pencil Drawing,**
1941. Animation paper is 10x12" with 6.5x7" image. Depicts Dumbo about to get the magic feather. - **$350 $750 $1400**

DUM-6

❑ **DUM-6. "Dumbo" Premium Coloring Book,**
1941. K.K. Publications. 5.5x8.5" issue, 48 pages. Every other page has illustration to be colored. Back cover has imprint of local sponsor "Weinberger Drugstore" and text explaining contest in which a completely colored book was to be turned in for a free ticket to "A Special Weinberger Performance Of The Grotto Circus." Issued by many companies including Weatherbird Shoes. Sixteen Pages, 9x10" - **$50 $150 $600**
Fifty-two Pages, 5.5x8.5" - **$30 $90 $300**

DUMBO

DUM-7

DUM-8

❏ **DUM-7. Mr. Stork Glazed Ceramic Figure,**
1941. Vernon Kilns. No. 42. 9" tall. - **$550 $1250 $2150**

❏ **DUM-8. Dumbo Glass,**
1941. 4-5/8" tall from rare set of six dairy promotion glasses. This features wrap-around scene of "The Five Black Crows" with four-line verse on the back. Top rim design includes additional character images. - **$75 $150 $225**

DUM-9

DUM-10

❏ **DUM-9. "Dumbo" Record Set,**
1941. RCA Victor. 10.5x12" stiff cardboard folder containing set of three 78rpm records "Recorded From The Sound Track Of The Film." - **$20 $40 $80**

❏ **DUM-10. "Dumbo Song Book,"**
1941. Whitman. 7.5x9.5" issue with 32 pages of lyrics to 100 songs including six from Dumbo, 36 from other Disney productions, other popular favorites. - **$15 $35 $90**

DUM-11   (detail)

DUM-12

❏ **DUM-11. "Dumbo Song Book" Newspaper Advertisement,**
1941. "Parker Quink" 10.5x14" clipped sponsorship ad from Sunday newspaper comic section. - **$5 $12 $20**

❏ **DUM-12. "Walt Disney's Dumbo,"**
1941. Western Printing and Lithographing Co. 9x10.25" softcover. 16 pages. Includes black and white and color and illustrations. Inside covers have black and white photos including seven of Walt Disney. - **$35 $80 $160**

DUM-13

❏ **DUM-13. "Dumbo Of The Circus,"**
1941. Garden City Publishing Co. 10x11.25" hardcover. 52 pages. - **$35 $80 $160**

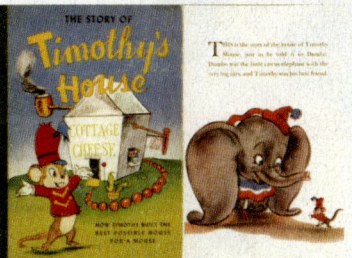

DUM-14

❏ **DUM-14. "The Story Of Timothy's House" Book,**
1941. Garden City Publishing Co./Western Printing. 6.75x9.5" hardcover, 28 illustrated story pages. - **$35 $75 $150**

DUM-15

❏ **DUM-15. "Dumbo The Flying Elephant" Comic Book,**
1941. Dell Publishing Co. Four Color Series I, Issue #17, the first comic book appearance of Dumbo. Also featured are Pluto and Brave Little Tailor stories. - **$185 $555 $3000**

DUMBO

DUM-16

☐ **DUM-16. "Coronet" Magazine With Dumbo Fold-Out,**
1941. December monthly issue of 5.25x7.5" family magazine featuring two-page fold-out for "Dumbo" with introduction by Walt Disney. Pictured are 12 film scenes. - **$10 $20 $40**

DUM-17

☐ **DUM-17. "Dumbo The Flying Elephant" Premium Version Book,**
1941. Whitman. 8x10.75" softcover, 32 pages. Back cover is imprinted for local sponsor "Fern Furniture Co." plus "Boys And Girls Bring Mother And Father With You To Dumbo's Toyland And Show Them What You Want Santa To Bring You." - **$50 $100 $200**

DUM-18

☐ **DUM-18. "Dumbo" Composition Doll,**
1941. Knickerbocker Toys. 8.5" tall painted compo likeness with movable head and trunk, satin-like fabric collar, starched felt ears, plastic movable eyes. Back of head has raised text "Dumbo" name and copyright. Collar has maker's stitched tag. - **$100 $200 $375**

DUM-19

☐ **DUM-19. "Dumbo" Planter,**
c. 1941. Painted ceramic, 4x5.5x3.5" tall unmarked but identical in design to a matching toothbrush holder which bears a Disney copyright. Back of piece has single opening to be used as a planter rather than segmented for toothbrushes. Planter - **$50 $100 $150**
Toothbrush Holder - **$65 $125 $175**

DUM-20

☐ **DUM-20. "Dumbo Weekly" Premium Publication Set With Cover,**
c. 1941. Diamond D-X Gasoline. 8.25x11" stiff paper two-hole binder cover containing complete set of eight numbered weekly issues distributed by local dealership service stations. Each issue is four pages featuring color art story that continues from issue to issue, "Dumbo's Midnight Adventure" plus puzzles and gags.
Folder - **$35 $100 $250**
First Issue - **$60 $25 $300**
Other Issues - **$25 $50 $100**

DUM-21

☐ **DUM-21. Timothy Mouse Doll,**
c. 1941. Character Novelty Company. 5x6x8" tall stuffed doll in seated position with stitched tag. Has corduroy and felt outfit. - **$70 $150 $275**

DUM-22

☐ **DUM-22. "Dumbo" English Card Game,**
c. 1941. Castell Brothers Ltd. 2.5x3.5x.75" deep boxed game from "Pepys Series" of complete 45 cards and instruction folder. - **$50 $100 $150**

290

DUMBO

DUM-23

❏ **DUM-23. Casey Jr. Catalin Plastic Pencil Sharpener,**
c. 1941. 1.75" tall. - **$35 $65 $135**

DUM-24

❏ **DUM-24. "Timothy Q. Mouse" Glass,**
1941. 4.75" tall with wrap-around design from set of 8 dairy promotion glasses.
Each - **$50 $100 $150**

DUM-25

❏ **DUM-25. "Dumbo The Acrobatic Elephant" Boxed Windup,**
1941. Marx. 4" tall tin windup.
Box - **$100 $200 $300**
Toy - **$100 $200 $300**

DUM-26

❏ **DUM-26. "Timothy Mouse" Catalin Plastic Pencil Sharpener,**
c. 1941. 1.75" tall. - **$40 $85 $165**

DUM-27

❏ **DUM-27. "Dumbo-The Story Of The Flying Elephant" Book,**
1942. Whitman. 10.25x11" stiff paper cover edition, 20 pages. - **$30 $75 $150**

DUM-28

❏ **DUM-28. "Liberty" Magazine With Disney Cover,**
1942. March 14 weekly 8.5x11.25" issue. Depicts characters filling out an income tax form that includes Walt Disney listed as a dependent. Cover was done for a corresponding income tax article in this issue although there is no other Disney reference. Income tax filing deadline in that era was March 15, extended in later years to April 15. - **$20 $40 $75**

DUM-29

❏ **DUM-29. Timothy Figurine,**
c. 1942. American Pottery. 2x2.75x5.5" tall painted and glazed ceramic version of figure originally produced by Vernon Kilns. - **$60 $125 $200**

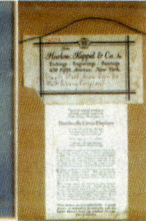

DUM-30

❏ **DUM-30. Original Framed Cel From "Dumbo, The Circus Elephant,"**
c. 1942. Image is 1.75x3". Has Courvoisier hand-painted background with small "WDP" in right corner and original paper label on back. Also has penciled number "56." - **$275 $550 $1150**

DUM-31 & 32

DUMBO

❏ **DUM-31. "D-X" Gasoline Station Cello. Button,** 1942. - **$15 $25 $40**

❏ **DUM-32. "D-X Dumbo Club" Member Card,** 1942. Diamond D-X Gasoline. Card includes chart to mark off first 16 copies of "Dumbo Weekly" obtained plus signature line for adult sponsor pledging a trial purchase of D-X products. - **$60 $125 $225**

DUM-33

(detail)

❏ **DUM-33. "Dumbo/D-X" Dealer's Promotional Sheet,** 1942. Diamond D-X Gas Stations. 12.5x19" glossy sheet showing station banners, posters and pennants. - **$35 $75 $125**

DUM-34

❏ **DUM-34. D-X Gasoline Mask,** 1942. Rare. - **$60 $165 $325**

DUM-35

❏ **DUM-35. "Dumbo" Toothbrush Holder,** c. 1942 Painted ceramic with matte finish is 3.5x5.5x3.75" tall by unidentified maker. Back has copyright, three openings for toothbrushes, small opening for wall mounting. Hat brim names him in raised lettering. Also issued as a planter. Toothbrush Holder - **$65 $125 $175** Planter - **$50 $100 $150**

DUM-36

❏ **DUM-36. Original Golden Book Art,** 1944. 7 3/4"x 17 1/2". Unique, Near Mint - **$2500**

DUM-37

DUM-38

❏ **DUM-37. Dumbo Salt & Pepper Set,** c. 1947. Leeds China Co. Pair of 3.25" tall over-the-glaze paint ceramic shakers. - **$10 $25 $45**

❏ **DUM-38. "Dumbo" With Timothy Planter,** c. 1949. Leeds China Co. 4.25x7.5x6.5" tall painted and glazed figural of Dumbo beside water barrel accented by high relief figure of Timothy who holds a feather. - **$30 $65 $100**

DUM-39

❏ **DUM-39. Dumbo Cermamic by Shaw,** 1940s. 3.75" tall with foil label. - **$50 $100 $150**

DUM-40

❏ **DUM-40. Australian Figurine,** 1940s. Modern Ceramic Products (MCP) Ltd. 2x2.5x3.5" tall painted and glazed image of Dumbo as newborn, complete with foil name sticker. - **$60 $125 $185**

DUM-41

DUMBO

DUM-42

❑ **DUM-41. Australian Figurine,**
1940s. Modern Ceramic Products (MCP) Ltd. 5x5x4.5" tall painted and glazed image of Dumbo sprawling, complete with foil name sticker. - **$50 $100 $150**

❑ **DUM-42. "Dumbo" Pitcher,**
1940s. Leeds China Co. 4x4.5x6" tall figural with his incised name on stomach, copyright on back. - **$15 $25 $50**

DUM-43

DUM-44

❑ **DUM-43. "Dumbo" Mask,**
1940s. Large 13x18" painted starched linen. Hat brim has "Dumbo" name ink stamp while reverse has stamped copyright. - **$40 $75 $140**

❑ **DUM-44. "Walt Disney Storybooks/Dumbo" Bookmark,**
1940s. D.C. Heath & Co. 4x7.5" die-cut stiff paper with text on each side promoting edition of "Dumbo Of The Circus" in the series of educational books by that publisher. - **$25 $50 $75**

DUM-45

❑ **DUM-45. "Dumbo" Catalin Plastic Pencil Sharpener,**
1940s. 1-1/8" with smooth outer edge. - **$25 $50 $115**

DUM-46

DUM-47

❑ **DUM-46. "Turnabout 4 In 1 Dumbo" Cookie Jar,**
1940s. Leeds China Co. 7x9x13" tall china with over-the-glaze paint. Has different images on each side. - **$65 $125 $250**

❑ **DUM-47. Dumbo Picture Puzzle,**
1950s. Jaymar. 7x10x1.5" deep boxed jigsaw puzzle assembling to 14x22" scene of him flying above circus tents. - **$25 $50 $75**

DUM-48

DUM-49

❑ **DUM-48. Dumbo Figurine,**
1950s. Goebel 3.5x4.25x4" tall figurine depicting Dumbo in crouched pose as if landing atop the circular base. Underside has maker markings including full bee and incised "63." - **$100 $175 $275**

❑ **DUM-49. "Dumbo" Large Size Figurine,**
1950s. Hagen-Renaker. 3x4x3.25" tall painted and glazed figurine with foil sticker for maker. - **$100 $250 $425**

DUM-50

DUMBO

DUM-51

□ **DUM-50. Timothy Figurine,**
1950s. Hagen-Renaker. 1.25" tall. - **$50 $125 $225**

□ **DUM-51. Dumbo Small Figurine,**
1950s. Hagen-Renaker. 1.25" tall painted and glazed miniature accented by tiny feather on tip of trunk (not on photo example). - **$75 $150 $250**

DUM-52

□ **DUM-52. Dumbo Character Bread Labels,**
1950s. Twelve 2.75" square waxed paper bread end labels from possibly larger set. Each - **$3 $6 $12**

DUM-54

□ **DUM-54. Egg Cup,**
1950s. "Made In Japan," 2x4x2.5" tall ceramic figural of Dumbo pulling wheeled cart which serves as egg cup. - **$50 $100 $150**

DUM-55

□ **DUM-55. Crows From Dumbo Salt & Pepper Set,**
1950s. "Japan" otherwise unmarked painted and glazed ceramic shaker replicas of 3" tall Dandy and 4" tall Preacher Crow. - **$75 $150 $250**

DUM-53

□ **DUM-53. "Casey Jr. The Disneyland Express" Wind-Up Train,**
1950s. Marx Toys. 2.5x12.75x3" deep box illustrated on all sides and containing 12.5" long toy with built-in key. Toy was made with several different single color hard plastic engines.
Box - **$50 $100 $150**
Toy - **$50 $100 $150**

DUM-56

□ **DUM-56. "Dumbo" Litho Button,**
1950s. From a set with "Donald Duck Peanut Butter" on back. 13/16". - **$12 $25 $40**

DUM-57

□ **DUM-57. "Tweak 'N Squeak" Doll,**
1950s. "Gund" tagged 5x9x13" tall stuffed plush doll designed to squeak when squeezed. - **$25 $50 $75**

DUM-58

DUMBO

☐ **DUM-58. Dumbo Bobbing Head,**
1960s. "Japan" 5.25" tall painted composition figure. No copyright but obviously Dumbo in traditional hat and collar. - **$35 $75 $135**

DUM-59

DUM-60

☐ **DUM-59. Dumbo Bowl,**
1960s. Westinghouse Melmac. 5.5" diameter by 1.75" deep hard plastic centered by image of him balancing ball on tip of trunk. - **$5 $12 $20**

☐ **DUM-60. "Dumbo Push Button Mini-Puppet,"**
1960s. Kohner Bros. 2.75" hard plastic figure with gold sticker on front. - **$15 $25 $50**

DUM-61

☐ **DUM-61. "Dumbo" Figure Toy With Bag,**
1970s. Unmarked Dakin 4x6.5x5.75" tall vinyl. Complete with cardboard tag plus plastic original carrying bag. Not marked Dakin as it is from the era when Disney did its own distribution marked "Walt Disney Distributing Co." Bag And Tag - **$3 $6 $10**
Figure Only - **$10 $20 $30**

DUM-62

DUM-63

☐ **DUM-62. "Dumbo" Doll,**
1970s. Regal Toy Ltd., Canada. 14" tall stuffed plush doll accented by felt fabric eyebrows and tongue plus plastic eyes. Die-cut name tag is attached to chest. - **$12 $25 $40**

☐ **DUM-63. Dumbo Figure,**
c. 1970s. 2x3x1.75" tall flexible soft vinyl figure by unidentified maker. - **$5 $10 $15**

DUM-64

☐ **DUM-64. "Dumbo" Limited Edition Serigraph Release,**
1980s. "Walt Disney Company" 10.75x14" acetate sheet centered by 5x9" image. Near Mint As Issued - **$135**

DUM-65

☐ **DUM-65. Dumbo Bronze Prototype,**
1989. Disney copyright. Only 5 made. Never produced by Disney for mass release. The 10x10" sculpture by artist Paul Vought is hand colored on a marble base. - **$4200**

DUM-66

DUM-67

☐ **DUM-66. Dumbo Bean Figure,**
1998. Applause product. With tag. - **$15**

☐ **DUM-67. Dumbo 8" Bean Figure,**
1998. Disney store exclusive. With tag. - **$10**

DUM-68

DUMBO

DUM-69

❑ **DUM-68. Dumbo Lunch Box,** 1999. With thermos. - **$45**

❑ **DUM-69. Dumbo Holiday Ornament,** 1999. With clown face; in box. - **$10 $20 $35**

DUM-70   DUM-71

❑ **DUM-70. Dumbo Keychain,** 2004. - **$10**

❑ **DUM-71. Dumbo & Timothy Bean Set,** 2004. Two figures in box. - **$35**

DUM-72

❑ **DUM-72. Dumbo & Timothy Figure,** 2004. Porcelain figure. - **$25**

Elmer Elephant

Elmer's story appeared in 1936 as part of Disney's *Silly Symphonies* cartoon series. In it, Elmer attends the birthday party of his girlfriend, Tillie Tiger, but he begins to find himself tormented by other animals that make fun of his long trunk. When he uses that much-maligned trunk to put out a fire in Tillie's Treehouse, he becomes a hero and the jungle bullies are quieted down.

The cartoon was very well received by the movie going public. Elmer convincingly goes through a series of complicated emotions, and the audience stays right with him. Critics see the cartoon as an important leap in Disney's ability to portray pathos through animation. Directed by Wilfred Jackson, the story idea came from Bianca Majolie. She did have some objections to the finished product. Her main concern was the amount of slapstick that had been added to the story in development. But since Majolie was a relatively new employee, with the added stigma of being a woman in the male-dominated story department, her objections went mostly unnoticed.

Elmer was one of the first characters to be merchandised after the runaway success of the *Three Little Pigs*. Store items include celluloid figures, (including one as a tape measure), several bisques and books.

ELM-1

ELM-2

❑ **ELM-1. Elmer Elephant Pencil Drawing,** 1936. Silly Symphonies #9 of a numbered sequence. 10x12" sheet wtih 3.5x4.75" image. - **$80 $140 $250**

❑ **ELM-2. "Elmer Elephant" Fisher Price Pull Toy,** 1936. Issued by itself as well as part of a boxed "Walt Disney's Carnival" set which included Mickey Mouse, Donald Duck and Pluto. 4" tall with paper label on each side of the wheeled wood figure. Elmer Only - **$60 $125 $200**

ELM-3   ELM-4

❑ **ELM-3. "Elmer Elephant" Hardcover,** 1936. David McKay Co. 6.5x7.5" with 48 pages. - **$75 $135 $300**

❑ **ELM-4. Elmer Elephant Bisque With Movable Arms,** c. 1936. Figure is 2.5x3x4.5" tall. Marked "Made In Japan" and has incised "S1407." - **$100 $150 $275**

ELM-5

ELM-6

ELMER ELEPHANT

❑ **ELM-5. Elmer Elephant Figure,**
c. 1936. Seiberling Latex Products Co. 3x4x5" tall hollow rubber figure with movable head. Most Examples subject to collapse and hardening of the rubber. - **$50 $100 $300**

❑ **ELM-6. "Elmer Elephant" Glass,**
c. 1937. 4.5" tall from the second dairy series. - **$15 $30 $50**

ELM-7

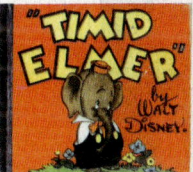
ELM-8

❑ **ELM-7. "Elmer Elephant Linen-Like" Book,**
1938. Whitman. Book #948. 9.25x12" with 12 pages. - **$40 $75 $175**

❑ **ELM-8. "Timid Elmer,"**
1939. Whitman, 5x5.5" hardcover. 64 pages. - **$25 $50 $100**

ELM-9   ELM-10

❑ **ELM-9. Elmer Elephant Miniature Bisque,**
1930s. Smallest size, 1.5" tall. Japan. - **$25 $50 $80**

❑ **ELM-10. Elmer Elephant Celluloid Figure,**
1930s. Celluloid figure 3x3.5x5" tall with movable arms, head and trunk. Japan. Disney copyright. - **$125 $250 $500**

ELM-11

ELM-12

❑ **ELM-11. Elmer Elephant Figural Celluloid Tape Measure,**
1930s. Made In Japan With Disney copyright. 2-3/8" tall with tape measure unit inside of body that pulls out from back bottom edge. - **$135 $250 $400**

❑ **ELM-12. "Elmer Elephant" Boxed Figural Soap,**
1930s. Lightfoot Schultz Co. 2.5x2.5x4.5" tall box contains 3.5" tall soap figure. Box - **$15 $25 $50**
Figure - **$25 $50 $75**

ELM-13

ELM-14

❑ **ELM-13. Elmer The Elephant Bisque Bank,**
1930s. Figure with movable trunk is 3x3.25x5" tall. Marked "Japan" with incised Disney copyright. - **$135 $250 $400**

❑ **ELM-14. Elmer Elephant Figural Celluloid Pencil Sharpener,**
1930s. Japan. 2.5" tall. - **$50 $100 $200**

ELM-15

❑ **ELM-15. "Elmer Elephant" Birthday Card,**
1930s. Die-cut card is 3.25x5.5" with Disney copyright. - **$25 $50 $75**

ELM-16

ELMER ELEPHANT

ELM-17

❑ **ELM-16. "Elmer The Elephant" Squeaker Doll,**
1940s. Stuffed doll 8.5" tall with plush-covered body, velveteen inner ears and feet, molded rubber face. Attached to neck is original cardboard tag. Japan. No Disney markings. - **$35 $65 $125**

❑ **ELM-17. Elmer Elephant And Tillie Tiger Ceramic Figurine,**
1950s. Goebel. Figure is 2.75x4.25x4.25" with "DIS101" on underside. - **$100 $175 $275**

EPCOT

Walt Disney's initial, personal dream for EPCOT was for it to become a self-sustaining entity. The city would house those that worked there as well as provide the utilities, stores, churches, entertainment and everything one would need. It was, in essence, Walt's vision of the city of the future.

EPCOT stands for "Experimental Prototype Community of Tomorrow," and it was actually one of the motivating ideas behind the conception of a second Disney theme park. Walt's personal utopian vision, first mentioned at a press conference in 1965, was intended to be the center of a new park. With Walt's passing, the central idea began to change over time.

The park finally opened on October 1, 1982. The end result was several steps removed from Walt's original vision. Rather than being the center of Walt Disney World, it is now simply is one of several parks that comprise Disney's vacation resort near Orlando, Florida. Like other Disney theme parks, EPCOT is composed of separate areas, each with a theme of its own: *Future World* and *World Showcase*.

EPCOT is more educational in nature than a regular Disney park, but many find it just as enjoyable an experience as anything else that Disney has built. The park was originally known as EPCOT Center, but over time that has shortened to simply EPCOT.

EPC-1

EPC-2

❑ **EPC-1. "EPCOT Center" Opening Day Commemorative Ticket,**
1982. 4x9" stiff bright silver foil cardboard envelope contains "Special Edition Commemorative Ticket." - **$12 $25 $50**

❑ **EPC-2. "Walt Disney World EPCOT Center" Under Construction/Grand Opening Items,**
1982. Twelve photos, letter, program, tickets and brochure. Similar Group - **$20 $40 $65**

EPC-3

EPC-4

❑ **EPC-3. Disney Studio Christmas Card,**
1982. Stiff paper 5.25x7.25" card. - **$5 $15 $25**

❑ **EPC-4. "EPCOT Center" Publicity Photos,**
1982. Lot of five 8x10" glossy photos. Each - **$1 $3 $5**

EPC-5

EPC-6

❑ **EPC-5. "Germany World Showcase/EPCOT Center" China Mug,**
1986. Reutter. 5.25" tall. - **$6 $12 $25**

❑ **EPC-6. Figment Ceramic Figurine,**
1980s. Painted and glazed 3" tall. Host character of the Journey Into Imagination at EPCOT. - **$10 $20 $30**

EPC-7

FANTASIA

EPC-8

❑ **EPC-7. Donald Duck Cel,**
1980s. EPCOT cartoon. 10.5x12.5" acetate sheet with 6x6.5" cel image. Comes with matching color laser bkg. Near Mint - **$135**

❑ **EPC-8. "EPCOT Center" 10th Anniversary Employee Only Watch,**
1992. Warranty card is marked "One of 3000." Mint As Issued - **$90**

Fantasia

This 1940 "Concert Feature" can be seen as the end result of Disney's earlier *Silly Symphonies* series. A fantastical combination of animation and classical music, *Fantasia* has eight distinct segments: *Toccata and Fugue in D Minor* (from the music of Bach), *The Nutcracker Suite* (Tchaikovsky), *The Rite of Spring* (Stravinsky), *The Sorcerer's Apprentice* (Dukas), *The Pastoral Symphony* (Beethoven), *Dance of the Hours* (Ponchielli), *Night on Bald Mountain* (Mussorgsky) and *Ave Maria* (Schubert).

The original plan was merely to produce a Silly Symphony based on *The Sorcerer's Apprentice*. However, Walt's vision for the project began to grow. He started to see that the film could be an organic entity, one that constantly evolved over time. With every theatrical re-release, segments of the film could be cut and new ones animated with new classical music choices. His dream would have to wait almost sixty years to be fulfilled.

The quality of animation may stand as the best ever done. Segments featuring Hop Low the dancing mushroom and Mickey Mouse as the Sorcerer's Apprentice still amaze audiences today. The music was conducted by Leopold Stokowski and performed by the Philadelphia Orchestra. The film was narrated by Deems Taylor.

The film was also a technological marvel. When first released, it used an early version of stereo called *Fantasound*. With the sound system so expensive to install, *Fantasia* opened in just fourteen theatres. It took time to achieve nationwide distribution. Still, the film was not a massive success. As a result of this, Walt was unable to realize his true vision of a new version being produced every few years..

The film was directed by Samuel Armstrong, James Algar, Bill Roberts, Paul Satterfield, Hamilton Luske, Jim Handley, Ford Beebe, T. Hee, Norm Ferguson and Wilfred Jackson. Animators included: Les Clark, Fred Moore, Preston Blair, Marvin Woodward, Riley Thompson, Cornett Wood, Cy Young and Bob Wickersham.

Fantasia had many re-releases, with Walt's vision finally coming close to realization in 1999 when a newly animated follow-up, *Fantasia/2000*, was released to theatres. It still carried Mickey Mouse's star-turn in *The Sorcerer's Apprentice* from the original film, but every other sequence of the film had been newly created, complete with new musical choices. A standout segment was the adaptation of Gershwin's *Rhapsody in Blue*. Animated in the style of artist Al Hirschfeld, critics praised its individualized appearance as a wonderful departure from the regular Disney animation style.

Fantasia merchandise includes figurines, china and jewelry. The image of Mickey as the Sorcerer's Apprentice has come to be instantly recognizable and that image has inspired a slew of merchandised items

FAN-1

❑ **FAN-1. Hippo Ballerina Character Model,**
c. 1938. 8" tall painted plaster figure over wire armature then mounted on 3.75" diameter base. Such models, known as maquettes, were produced in very limited numbers by Disney Studio's Character Model Department and most remained only in Disney archives. This example was produced for Ponchielli's Dance Of The Hours ballet segment of Fantasia. Underside has an inked "6" numeral, indicating at least six produced. - **$1500 $3000 $5000**

FAN-2

❑ **FAN-2. Disney Studio Animators Ben Ali Gator Model,**
c. 1938. Plaster on wire armature. 2.25" tall. - **$650 $1300 $2250**

FAN-3

❑ **FAN-3. Disney Studio Animators Hippo In Tutu Model,**
c. 1938. Plaster on wire armature. 2.25" tall. - **$550 $1100 $2000**

FANTASIA

FAN-4

❏ **FAN-4. Disney Studio Animators Elephanchine Model,**
c. 1938. Plaster on wire armature. 3" tall. - **$550 $1100 $2000**

FAN-5

❏ **FAN-5. Disney Studio Animators Ostrich Model,**
c. 1938. Plaster on wire armature. 2" tall. - **$550 $1100 $2000**

FAN-6

❏ **FAN-6. Fantasia Concept Pencil Drawing,** 1939. Outlined art area is 7.75x10.25" centered by closeup portrait of ostrich rendered in pencil. Reverse has Studio back stamp noting artist James Bodrero, sequence #10, sketch #836 and concept date July 11, 1939. Same Or Similar - **$300 $700 $1200**

FAN-7

❏ **FAN-7. Fantasia Concept Pencil Drawing,** 1939. Outlined art is 7.75x10.25" filled by colored pencil art of alligators going after elephants, hippos and an ostrich, all who flee in terror. Back stamp notes artist James Bodrero, sequence #10, sketch #265 and concept date July 5, 1939. Same Or Similar - **$300 $700 $1200**

FAN-8

❏ **FAN-8. Fantasia Concept Art,** 1939. Animation paper is 10x12" with watercolor art. Concept art from "Dance Of The Hours" by artist James Bodrero. - **$2000 $4000 $8500**

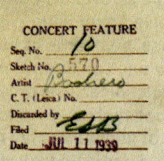

FAN-9

❏ **FAN-9. Fantasia Concept Art,** 1939. Animation paper is 10x12". Centered art is 6x6". Reverse of the sheet has studio back stamp noting artist James Bodrero, sequence #10, sketch #570, date of July 11 1939. - **$550 $1250 $2250**

FANTASIA

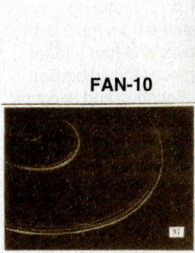

FAN-10

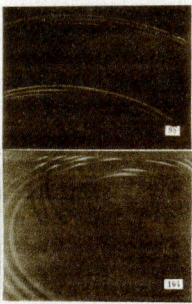

FAN-12

❏ **FAN-14. "Fantasia" Production Cel With Courvoisier Background,**
1940. 9x11.5" with 4.5x5.5" image. Features Mickey as the Sorcerer's Apprentice commanding the broom. - **$3000 $7500 $15000**

❏ **FAN-10. Fantasia Story Board Concept Art,**
1939. Three 5.25x7" stiff paper sheets with frontrace pastel art including images of water ripple areas. All three are from the Toccata and Fugue In D Minor sequence at beginning of the film. Each is from a numbered sequence with small number paste-on at lower right corner and these are 97, 98, 104. Each - **$30 $60 $115**

❏ **FAN-12. Sunflower Pencil Drawing From Fantasia,**
1939. Animation paper is 10x12" with 5.5x6" image. This character is a young black "servant" centaurette and was deemed politically incorrect. Starting with the 1960 theatrical re-release of the film, it was cut from the movie.
- **$200 $400 $650**

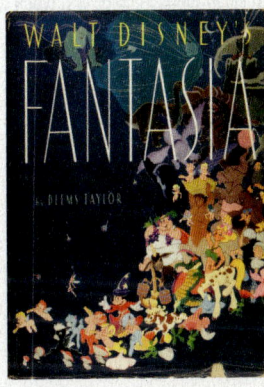

FAN-15

❏ **FAN-15. "Fantasia" Hardcover With Dust Jacket,**
1940. Simon and Schuster. 9.75x13" with 160 pages filled with text and art with many tipped-in plates.
Dust Jacket - **$100 $200 $400**
Book - **$100 $200 $400**

FAN-13

❏ **FAN-13. Fantasia Centaurette Large Pin,**
1940. 2.5" tall white metal pin. Reverse has copyright symbol and "WDP". - **$60 $125 $250**

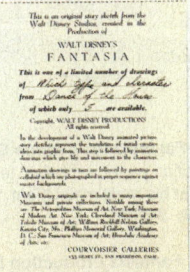

FAN-16

FAN-11

❏ **FAN-11. Exceptional Fantasia Concept Drawing Of Ben Ali Gator,**
1939. Animation paper is 10x12" with 7x9.5" image. Penciled number "429." - **$550 $1250 $2250**

FAN-14

❏ **FAN-16. "Dance Of The Hours From Fantasia" Book,**
1940. Harper & Brothers. 7x9.5" hardcover, 36 pages. - **$50 $100 $175**

FANTASIA

FAN-17

❏ **FAN-17. "The Nutcracker Suite" Hardcover,**
1940. Collins. 9x10.25" English edition. 72 pages with illustrations in color and black and white. - **$60 $125 $175**

FAN-18

❏ **FAN-18. Movie Theater Letter With Order Form,**
1940. "Fantasia" 8.5x11" letterhead with other designs including music notes, images of dancing Hyacinth Hippo, Pegasus, fauns, cupids; mushroom. These letters were sent to promote the showing of the film at local theaters accompanied by an order from for blank letterheads offered for local use. - **$10 $20 $40**

FAN-19

❏ **FAN-19. "The Nutcracker Suite From Fantasia,"**
1940. D. Davis And Co. Pty. Ltd. 9x11" Australian edition. 32 pages with both color and black and white illustrations. - **$50 $100 $150**

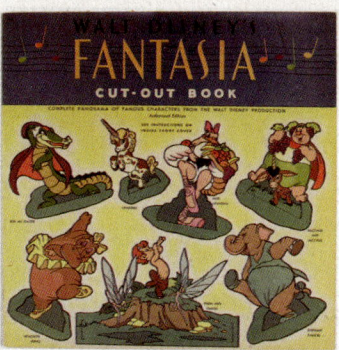

FAN-20

❏ **FAN-20. "Fantasia Cut-Out Book" With Politically Incorrect Character "Sunflower,"**
1940. Whitman. #950 is 13x13" featuring "Sunflower" which was deleted from the film by Disney. Has cardboard cover and four interior pages, all with punchout pieces including Ben Ali Gator, Mlle. Upanova, Bacchus and Jacchus, Hyacinth Hippo, Elephant Dancer, Baby Pegasus, Zeus, Malinda the Centaurette, Brudus the Centaur, Mickey as Sorcerer's Apprentice, others. Punchout of "Sunflower" depicts a young black centaurette eating a slice of watermelon. Un-Cut - **$600 $1200 $2150**

FAN-21

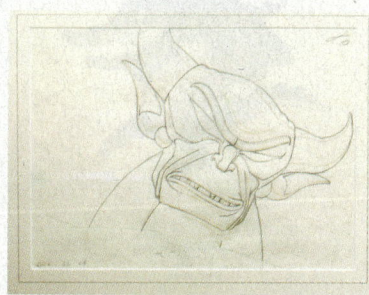

FAN-22

❏ **FAN-21. Fantasia Production Drawing,**
1940. Animation paper is 11x8.5" featuring Chernabog at his most malevolent moment. - **$300 $600 $1200**

❏ **FAN-22 . Fantasia Production Drawing,**
1940. Image is 9.5x8" featuring an extreme close-up Chernabog from the Night On Bald Mountain sequence. - **$300 $600 $1200**

FANTASIA

FAN-23

❑ **FAN-23. "Walt Disney Presents Fantasia" Movie Souvenir,**
1940. Western Printing Co. 9.5x12.5" softcover. Features color and black and white photos of Disney and other contributors to film. - **$25 $50 $100**

FAN-25

❑ **FAN-25. Fantasia Satyr Figurine,**
1940. Vernon Kilns U.S.A. 4" tall painted and glazed ceramic posed stretching and yawning. One of six different satyr figurines. Underside markings include incised "4" and copyright year. Each - **$100 $175 $300**

❑ **FAN-27. Fantasia Sprite Figurine,**
1940. Vernon Kilns U.S.A. 4.25" tall painted and glazed ceramic marked underneath by maker's name, incised "10" and copyright year. - **$75 $150 $275**

❑ **FAN-28. "Vernon Kilns" Sprite Figurine,**
1940. Vernon Kilns U.S.A. Painted and glazed 3.75" tall figurine. Marked "12." - **$75 $150 $275**

FAN-29

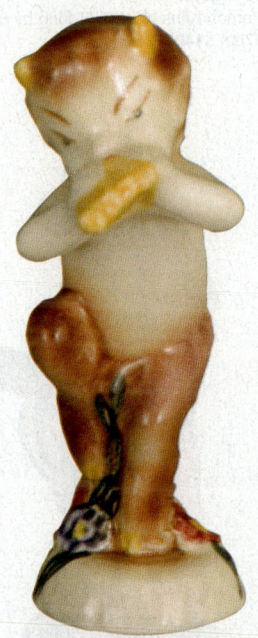

FAN-24

❑ **FAN-24. Fantasia Satyr Figurine,**
1940. Vernon Kilns U.S.A. 4.75" tall ceramic figurine posed playing the pan flute. One of six different satyr figurines. Marked underneath for maker with incised "3" and copyright year. - **$100 $175 $300**

FAN-26

❑ **FAN-26. Fantasia Sprite Figurine,**
1940. Vernon Kilns U.S.A. Painted and glazed 3.25" tall figurine. Marked "8". - **$100 $200 $300**

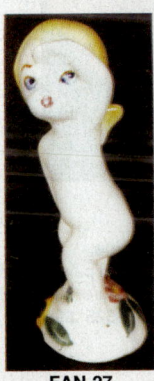 

FAN-27   FAN-28

FAN-30

❑ **FAN-29. Fantasia Gray Unicorn Figurine,**
1940. Vernon Kilns U.S.A. 5.25" tall painted and glazed ceramic figurine marked underneath for maker with incised "13" and copyright year. - **$150 $275 $475**

❑ **FAN-30. Fantasia Unicorn Figurine,**
1940. Vernon Kilns U.S.A. 5.25" tall ceramic figurine marked underneath for maker with incised "13" and copyright year. Variety done in black rather than gray. - **$75 $150 $275**

FANTASIA

FAN-31

❏ **FAN-31. Fantasia Unicorn Figurine,**
1940. Vernon Kilns U.S.A. 5.75" tall ceramic figurine marked underneath for maker with incised "15" and copyright year. - **$100 $200 $300**

FAN-32

❏ **FAN-32. Fantasia Black Pegasus Figurine,**
1940. Vernon Kilns U.S.A. 4.5" tall painted and glazed ceramic marked underneath by maker's name, incised number "19" and copyright year. - **$150 $250 $450**

FAN-33

❏ **FAN-33. Fantasia Gray Baby Pegasus Figurine,**
1940. Vernon Kilns U.S.A. 4.5" tall ceramic figurine marked underneath for maker with incised "19" and copyright year. Variety done in shades of gray rather than black. - **$150 $250 $450**

FAN-34

❏ **FAN-34. Fantasia Pegasus Figurine,**
1940. Vernon Kilns U.S.A. 5.75" tall painted and glazed ceramic marked underneath by maker's name, incised "21" and copyright year. - **$150 $250 $450**

FAN-35

❏ **FAN-35. Centaurette Figurine,**
1940. Vernon Kilns. 2.25x5x8" tall painted and glazed ceramic of Fantasia creature. Underside includes "22" marking. - **$275 $525 $900**

FAN-36

❏ **FAN-36. Nubian Centaurette Glazed Ceramic Figure,**
1940. Vernon Kilns No. 23. 5" long by 8" tall. - **$300 $700 $1400**

FAN-37

❏ **FAN-37. Fantasia Nubian Centaurette Figurine,**
1940. Vernon Klins. 7.5" tall painted and glazed ceramic figure. Underside includes makers name and incised "24" marking. - **$275 $525 $900**

FANTASIA

FAN-38

❑ **FAN-38. Elephant Figurine,**
1940. Vernon Kilns. 2.75x3.5x5.25" tall painted and glazed ceramic Fantasia creature in ballet pose, one of three different poses. Underside includes "27" marking. Each - **$150 $250 $400**

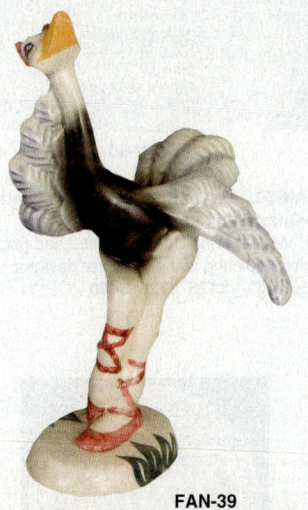

FAN-39

❑ **FAN-39. Fantasia Ostrich Figurine,**
1940. Vernon Kilns. 9" tall painted and glazed ceramic figure. One of three different ostrich figures. Marked underneath for maker with incised "28" and copyright year. - **$275 $525 $900**

FAN-40

❑ **FAN-40. Fantasia Centaur Figurine,**
1940. Vernon Kilns U.S.A. 2.5x6x10" tall painted and glazed ceramic depicting grape clusters held in each hand. This is the largest example from this series. Underside has Disney copyright and incised "31." - **$325 $825 $1500**

FAN-41

FAN-42

❑ **FAN-41. "Vernon Kilns" Hippo Figurine,**
1940. Vernon Kilns U.S.A. Painted and glazed ceramic 3x3x5" tall. Marked "34." - **$250 $500 $750**

❑ **FAN-42. Fantasia Goldfish Bowl,**
1940. Vernon Kilns. Painted and glazed ceramic 8" diameter by 5.5" tall. Underside includes "121 marking. - **$100 $200 $300**

FAN-43

❑ **FAN-43. Winged Nymph Bowl,**
1940. Vernon Kilns. 12" diameter x 2.5" tall painted and glazed ceramic with outer high relief design of five different winged nymphs along with leaves and flowers. Underside includes "122" marking. - **$65 $125 $250**

FAN-44

❑ **FAN-44. Fantasia Winged Nymph Vase,**
1940. Vernon Kilns U.S.A. 4.5" diameter by 7" tall painted and glazed ceramic with raised relief wrap-around design of two winged nymphs and flowers. Underside markings include #123 and copyright year. - **$100 $225 $350**

FANTASIA

FAN-45

❑ **FAN-45. Fantasia Winged Nymph Vase,**
1940. Vernon Kilns. 7" tall ceramic vase. Considered to be the more desirable full color variety rather than those issued in single solid color. Marked underneath for maker with incised "123" marking. - **$125 $250 $475**

FAN-46

❑ **FAN-46. Fantasia Satyr Bowl,**
1940. Vernon Kilns U.S.A. 7" diameter by 3.25" deep painted and glazed ceramic, the scarcer variety with fully painted design rather than single solid color. Perimeter is segmented into five panels of high relief satyr images, all in different poses including three shown playing pan flute. Underside markings include "124" and copyright year. Single Color - **$50 $85 $150**
Multicolor - **$125 $250 $450**

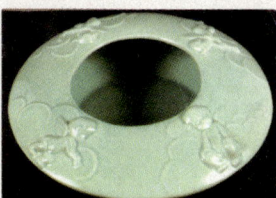

FAN-47

❑ **FAN-47. "Vernon Kilns" Sprite Bowl,**
1940. Vernon Kilns U.S.A. 10" diameter by 2.5" tall painted and glazed ceramic. Four different raised images of Sprite characters and clouds. Marked "125." - **$75 $150 $250**

FAN-48

❑ **FAN-48. Pegasus Vase,**
1940. Vernon Kilns. 4.5x11.5x7.75" tall glazed ceramic of Fantasia creature. Underside includes "127" marking.
Single Color Version - **$100 $200 $400**
Color Accented Version - **$300 $600 $1200**

FAN-49

❑ **FAN-49. Fantasia Goldfish Bowl By Vernon Kilns,**
1940. Painted and glazed ceramic 8" diameter by 5.5" tall. - **$200 $400 $800**

FAN-50

❑ **FAN-50. Vernon Kilns "Fantasia" Pattern One-Quart Pitcher,**
1940. Vernon Kilns U.S.A. Painted and glazed ceramic depicting leaf and flower designs. 5x6.5x7.25". - **$125 $225 $400**

FAN-51

FANTASIA

❏ **FAN-51. Vernon Kilns "Fantasia" Pattern Plate,**
1940. Vernon Kilns U.S.A. Design includes large image of Dew Drop Fairy in center of plate. 6-3/8" diameter. - **$65 $125 $200**

FAN-52

❏ **FAN-52. "Nutcracker" Tea Cups And Saucers,**
1940. Vernon Kilns. Painted and glazed ceramic set of four 6.5" diameter saucers and four 2" tall tea cups, all in design of fairies and/or flowers. Underside of each has "Nutcracker" marking and production year. Each Cup/Saucer - **$25 $50 $75**

FAN-53

❏ **FAN-53. "Flower Ballet" Plate,**
1940. Vernon Kilns. 9.5" diameter glazed ceramic from plate series in size and color variations. - **$35 $65 $110**

FAN-54

❏ **FAN-54. Hop Low Mushroom Salt & Pepper Set,**
1940. Vernon Kilns. Matched pair of 3.5" tall painted and glazed ceramic figurals. - **$40 $65 $125**

FAN-55

❏ **FAN-55. "Fantasia Autumn Ballet" Serving Plate,**
1940. Vernon Kilns U.S.A. Large 12.5" diameter painted and glazed ceramic in five colors. Design depicts flowers and leaves plus three different fairies. - **$75 $150 $225**

FAN-56

❏ **FAN-56. Fantasia Mushroom Bowl,**
1940. Vernon Kilns U.S.A. 7.25x12.25x2" deep painted and glazed ceramic with raised relief design on all sides including three mushrooms on one side and four on opposite side. Underside markings include #120 and copyright year. - **$50 $100 $150**

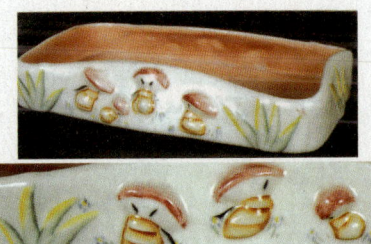

FAN-57

❏ **FAN-57. Fantasia Mushroom Bowl Multicolor Version,**
1940. Vernon Kilns U.S.A. 7.25x12.25x2" deep painted and glazed ceramic. Underside markings include #120 and copyright year. - **$100 $200 $300**

FAN-58

❏ **FAN-58. Fantasia Ostrich Ballerina Large Pin,**
1940. 2.5" tall white metal pin has fifteen rhinestone accents on the edges of her wings and rear. Her one wing is riveted to the body and is slightly movable as made. Reverse has copyright symbol and "WDP." - **$75 $150 $300**

FAN-59

❏ **FAN-59. "Pastoral From Fantasia" Book,**
1940. Harper & Brothers. 6.75x9.5" hardcover, 36 pages. - **$50 $80 $175**

FANTASIA

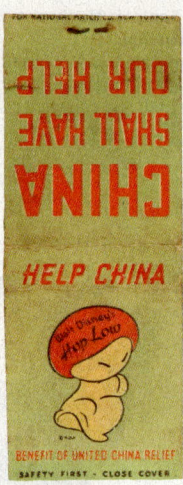

FAN-60

❏ **FAN-60. Fantasia Hop Low "Help China" Matchbook,**
1940. 1.5x4" open. Interior form to make monetary contribution to aid China against Japanese invasion. - **$15 $30 $60**

FAN-61

❏ **FAN-61. Fantasia Ostrich Pin On Card,**
c. 1940 Original 2.75x3.25" card holding 1" tall metal replica character pin without Disney marking but exact miniature likeness. Card is marked only "Styled For You/Made In U.S.A." and also apparently held a pair of matching earrings now missing. Card - **$3 $8 $15**
Pin - **$10 $20 $40**

FAN-62

❏ **FAN-62. "The Nutcracker Suite,"**
1943. Little, Brown And Co. 10.25x11.25" hardcover. 72 pages. - **$65 $135 $200**

FAN-63

FAN-64

❏ **FAN-63. "Walt Disney Cartoon Characters/Fantasia" Slide Set,**
1944. Craftman's Guild. 6.5x10" envelope containing complete set #4 of ten 2x2", 35mm mounted full color slides. - **$35 $60 $125**

❏ **FAN-64. "Fantasia" Lobby Card,**
1946. RKO Radio Pictures Inc. 11x14" title card for the film's first re-release. Features many of the film's most prominent characters including Mickey as Sorcerer's Apprentice, Mushroom Dancers, Centaurette, Mlle. Upanova, Bacchus and Jacchus, others. - **$100 $200 $325**

FAN-65

❏ **FAN-65. Fantasia Satyr Figurine,**
c. 1947. Zaccagnini. 7" tall figure playing flute while resting on a tree stump.
- **$300 $600 $1200**

FAN-66

FAN-67

FAN-68

❏ **FAN-66. Fantasia Wooden Display Plaques,**
1940s. Two approximately 9x12" raised relief images of Fantasia sequence characters centaurette carrying flowers followed by cupid blowing a horn, and Zeus rising from the clouds and holding a lightning bolt. Both are labeled on reverse. Each - **$125 $225 $425**

❏ **FAN-67. Fantasia Wooden Display Plaques,**
1940s. Two approximately 9x12" raised relief images of Fantasia sequence characters of faun riding on the back of a unicorn and cupid on the back of a baby Pegasus flying through the air. Both are labeled on reverse. Each - **$125 $225 $425**

❏ **FAN-68. Fantasia Wooden Display Plaques,**
1940s. Two approximately 9x12" raised relief images of Fantasia sequence characters of adult Pegasus flying through clouds and Apollo in his horse-drawn flying chariot. Both are labeled on reverse. Each - **$125 $225 $425**

FANTASIA

FAN-69

FAN-70

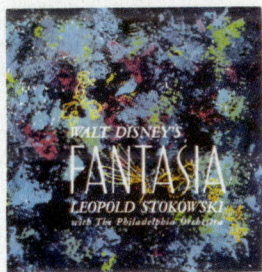

FAN-71

❏ **FAN-69. Fantasia Elephant Figurine,**
1940s. American Pottery. 5.25" tall glazed ceramic figurine which was originally produced by Vernon Kilns. Marked underneath "25". - **$50 $100 $200**

❏ **FAN-70. Fantasia Matchbox Showing Dew Drop Fairy,**
1940s. Made in Italy with WDP copyright. Wooden box with foil covering. 1x1-5/8x.5" deep. - **$10 $20 $50**

❏ **FAN-71. Record Album Order Form,**
1957. Glossy paper folder is 3.5x3.5" and opens to 13.5" long illustrated offer of LP three-record set with 24-page book issued as set "WDX101." Panels include three different full color film scenes, bluetone photo of Walt Disney. - **$4 $8 $15**

FAN-72

❏ **FAN-72. "Fantasia" Decorative Wall Plate,**
1950s. Plate is 4" in diameter china illustrating Bacchus and Jacchus surrounded by grapes and music notes plus four different satyrs. Reverse has Disneyland logo in triangular design plus text "In All The World Only At Disneyland...Inspired By Original Art From Fantasia." - **$35 $65 $125**

FAN-73

❏ **FAN-73. Fantasia Faun With Greek Column Two-Piece Figurine Set,**
1950s. Hagen-Renaker. 1.5" tall pieces. Depicts Faun playing a pan flute sitting atop column. Set - **$75 $150 $275**

FAN-74

❏ **FAN-74. Fantasia Unicorn Ceramic Figurine,**
1950s. Hagen-Renaker. Painted and glazed 2.75" tall figurine. - **$100 $200 $300**

FAN-75

❏ **FAN-75. Hippo Ballerina Figurine,**
1950s. Fantasia-inspired painted and glazed ceramic figure. 2x4x4.25" tall. - **$50 $100 $200**

FAN-76

❏ **FAN-76. Fantasia Ceramic Open Dish,**
1950s. Wade. 5.5x7.75x2.25" deep with three feet on underside. Features images of the Milkweed Ballet from the Nutcracker. - **$25 $50 $85**

FAN-77

FANTASIA

❏ **FAN-77. Fantasia Ceramic Vase,**
1950s. Wade. 6.75" tall painted and glazed ceramic. Features images of the Milkweed Ballet from the Nutcracker. - **$35 $60 $125**

FAN-78

❏ **FAN-78. "Fantasia" Deluxe Record Set With Program,**
1961. Buena Vista. 12.5x12.5" gatefold cover containing set of three 33-1/3rpm records re-issued from original 1957 release version. Bound in is 24-page program by Western Printing featuring color scenes from the film and corresponding text. - **$12 $25 $40**

FAN-79

❏ **FAN-79. "Walt Disney's Fantasia" Poster,**
1960s. Art by Bob Moore. 27x41". Includes images of most of the major characters. Designed to be colored. - **$30 $60 $100**

FAN-80

❏ **FAN-80. Hippo Ballerina Canadian Figurine,**
1960s. Canadian Pottery Ltd., Ontario. 4x4.5x7.25" tall glazed ceramic likeness variation with foil sticker, probably issued to coincide with re-release of Fantasia during psychedelic years of 1960s. - **$25 $50 $75**

FAN-81

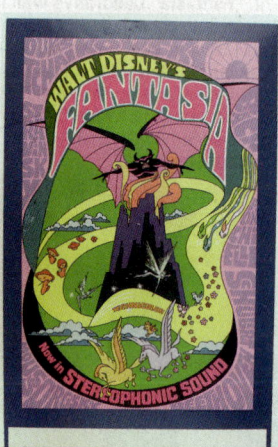

FAN-82

❏ **FAN-81. Baby Pegasus From Fantasia Figurine,**
c. 1960s. Wade Pottery. 1-5/8" tall glazed ceramic miniature. - **$35 $75 $125**

❏ **FAN-82. "Fantasia" Psychedelic Version Window Card,**
1970. Card is 14x22" on glossy card stock. Art was changed to reflect the times with obvious inspiration from Fillmore concert posters and Peter Max art. Art includes Chernabog prominently featured at center along with Family Pegasus, Mushroom Dancers, goldfish, Dewdrop Fairies. An image of Mickey's face is hidden at left corner. - **$30 $60 $125**

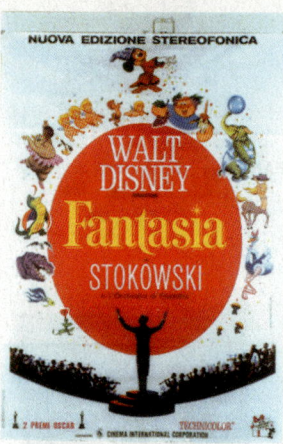

FAN-83

FAN-84

❏ **FAN-83. "Fantasia" Italian Movie Poster,**
1978. Poster is 39x55" and marked "Printed In Italy." Text is in Italian. - **$35 $75 $125**

❏ **FAN-84. Fantasia Mushroom Figurine,**
1985. Hagen-Renaker. .75" tall painted and glazed ceramic miniature. - **$20 $40 $75**

FAN-85

FANTASIA

FAN-86

❑ **FAN-85. Mickey Mouse Sorcerer Figurine,**
1985. Hagen-Renaker. 2.75" tall painted and glazed ceramic. - **$35 $75 $150**

❑ **FAN-86. Fantasia Broom Figure,**
1985. Hagen-Renaker. 2.5" tall painted and glazed ceramic. - **$15 $35 $60**

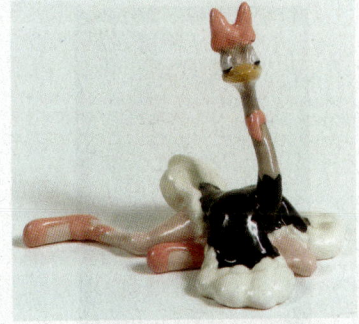

FAN-87

❑ **FAN-87. Fantasia Ostrich Figurine,**
1985. Hagen-Renaker. 3.25" tall painted and glazed ceramic. - **$50 $125 $250**

FAN-88

FAN-89

❑ **FAN-88. "Fantasia" Book Signed By Four Disney Animators,**
1987. Harry N. Abrams Inc. 9.5x12" hardcover with 224 pages. Opening pages are signed by film animators, Marc Davis, Frank Thomas, Ollie Johnston, Maurice Noble. - **$40 $80 $150**

❑ **FAN-89. "The Sorcerer's Apprentice" Candle Holder,**
1980s. "Royal Orleans Disney Gift-Ware." 3.75x4.5x5.25" tall bisque figural with cardboard string tag. - **$10 $20 $35**

FAN-90

FAN-91

❑ **FAN-90. "Fantasia" Italian Movie Poster,**
c. 1980s. Poster is 47x63". Text is in Italian. - **$40 $85 $150**

❑ **FAN-91. "Fantasia 50th Anniversary Commemorative Program,"**
1990. Glossy paper 11.25x13.5". - **$5 $10 $20**

FAN-92

❑ **FAN-92. "Fantasia Broom" Doll,**
1990. Disney-authorized 7x7x13" tall stuffed plush with three attached tags including one for the 1940-1990 50th anniversary of film's original release. - **$10 $20 $40**

FAN-93

❑ **FAN-93. Euro Disney Fantasia Restaurant China Dinnerware Set,**
1992. Royal Rego/Royal Porcelain. 56-piece set for a service of 6. Official dinnerware used by the "Fantasia" restaurant at Euro Disney. Not intended for retail sale. Near Mint- **$400**

FAN-94

FANTASIA

☐ **FAN-94. Centaurette Figure,**
1990s. From the Classic Collection. - **$225**

FAN-95

☐ **FAN-95. Fantasia Commemorative Audio/Visual Set,**
1990s. Item is 11.5x15x2" boxed "Walt Disney's Masterpiece Fantasia Deluxe Collector's Edition" comprised of fully restored Fantasia video with bonus tape "The Making Of A Masterpiece," commemorative lithograph, two compact disks of original soundtrack music, full color 16-page commemorative booklet and certificate of authenticity. Near Mint - **$100**

Ferdinand the Bull

Based on the 1936 Munro Leaf book which had been illustrated by Robert Lawson, the *Ferdinand the Bull* cartoon debuted in November 1938. The story begins with a peaceful and content Ferdinand who is happy to sit in a field and sniff flowers. After being stung by a bee and having a fit, however, he is mistaken for a fighting bull and taken to a bullring. Being such a peaceful bull, he refuses to fight and is taken back to the countryside.

The short won the Academy Award for Best Cartoon in 1938. Directed by Dick Rickard, it featured the animation of Ward Kimball, Jack Bradbury, Milt Kahl and Hamilton Luske. The film is especially notable for the appearance of many of the Disney animators in the cartoon. They even portray Walt himself.

Merchandise includes a jointed composition figure, a wind up toy, several bisques and books.

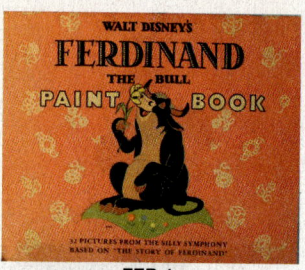

FER-1

FER-2

☐ **FER-1. "Ferdinand The Bull Paint Book,"**
1938. Whitman. Book #645. 8.25x13.75" with 32 pages. - **$25 $50 $110**

☐ **FER-2. Matador Pencil Drawing,**
1938. Sheet is 10x12" with 3.25x5.75" tall image. - **$125 $250 $425**

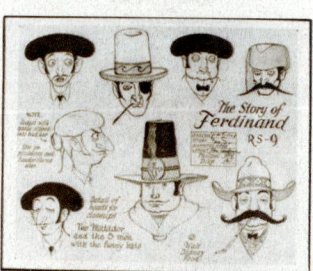

FER-3

FER-4

☐ **FER-3. "The Story Of Ferdinand" Model Sheet,**
1938. Printed sheet is 10x12.5 and numbered "RS-9." - **$10 $20 $40**

☐ **FER-4. "Ferdinand The Bull Cut-Outs,"**
1938. Whitman. Book #925. 10.5x16.25". Cardboard cover and three pages with a total of 20 punch-outs. - **$100 $225 $400**

FER-5

FER-6

☐ **FER-5. Matador Painted Composition Figure,**
1938. Crown Toy Co. 1.75x2.5x6" tall. - **$200 $400 $750**

☐ **FER-6. "Ferdinand's Mama" Glass,**
1938. Issued by various dairies. 4.5" tall. Premium from set of six. Each - **$20 $40 $60**

FERDINAND THE BULL

FER-7

FER-8

FER-9

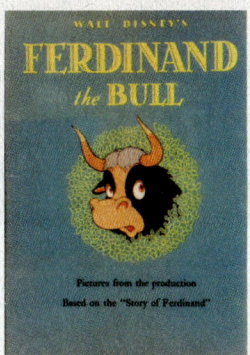
FER-10

❏ **FER-10. "Ferdinand The Bull,"**
1938. Whitman. 8x10.75" with 32 pages. - **$20** **$40** **$85**

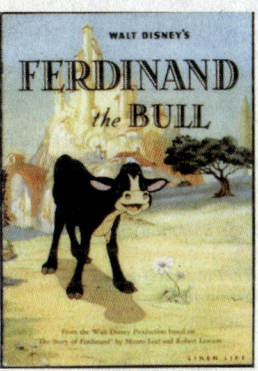
FER-11

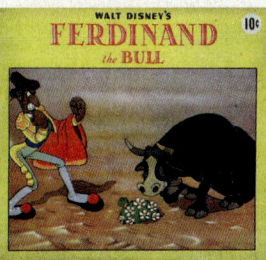
FER-12

FER-13

FER-14

❏ **FER-13. "Ferdinand The Bull" Hand Puppet,**
1938. Crown Toy Mfg. Co. 10" tall. - **$60** **$125** **$200**

❏ **FER-14. "Put The Tail On Ferdinand Party Game,"**
1938. Whitman. 7.75x10x1" deep box contains 19x26.5" paper sheet and 20 numbered tails. - **$45** **$85** **$165**

FER-15

FER-16

❏ **FER-7. Ferdinand The Bull Wall Plaque,**
1938. Maker unknown but believed by Kerk Guild Inc. 4.25x6x.25" thick wood. - **$25** **$50** **$90**

❏ **FER-8. "Ferdinand The Bull" Composition Wood Pin,**
1938. 1.75" tall. - **$30** **$60** **$125**

❏ **FER-9. "Ferdinand The Bull" Sheet Music,**
1938. ABC Music Corp. 9x12" with 4 pages. - **$20** **$30** **$50**

❏ **FER-11. "Ferdinand The Bull Linen-Like" Book,**
1938. Whitman. 8.75x12" with 12 pages. - **$25** **$50** **$90**

❏ **FER-12. "Ferdinand The Bull" Softcover,**
1938. Dell. 9.25x10" with 12 pages. - **$100** **$225** **$375**

❏ **FER-15. "Ferdinand The Bull Card Game,"**
1938. Whitman. 5x6.5" box with 35 cards plus instruction card. - **$35** **$75** **$135**

❏ **FER-16. "Ferdinand" Pop-Up Birthday Card,**
1938. White & Wyckoff. 5x5". - **$15** **$30** **$50**

FERDINAND THE BULL

FER-17

❑ **FER-17. "Ferdinand The Bull" Windup,**
1938. Marx. 6" tin. - **$125 $250 $500**

FER-18

❑ **FER-18. Ferdinand The Bull Ceramic Figurine,**
c. 1938 Brayton Laguna. 5x8.5x7" tall. Underside has Brayton/Disney foil sticker.
- **$150 $300 $500**

FER-19

FER-20

❑ **FER-19. Ferdinand's Mama Large Ceramic Figurine,**
c. 1938 Brayton Laguna. 4x9.5x5.75" tall. Underside has Brayton/Disney foil sticker.
- **$150 $300 $500**

❑ **FER-20. Ferdinand The Bull Mama Large Ceramic Figurine,**
c. 1938 Brayton Laguna. 4x9.5x5.75" tall. Figure and collar color variety. Underside has Brayton/Disney foil sticker. - **$150 $300 $500**

FER-21

FER-22

❑ **FER-21. Five Men In Funny Hats From Ferdinand Large Set,**
c. 1938. Brayton Laguna. Figures are all 8 to 10" tall with Brayton stickers on back.
Each - **$500 $1000 $1500**

❑ **FER-22. Picador/Toreador On Horse Back From Ferdinand,**
c. 1938. Brayton Laguna. 5x12x11.5" tall. Picador is holding lance and seated on horse. Toreador on swayback horse.
Each - **$600 $1200 $2000**

FER-23

❑ **FER-23. Ferdinand The Bull Dairy Premium Series Glass Set,**
c. 1938. 4.75" tall set of six which include Ferdinand as calf, Ferdinand The Bull, Ferdinand's Mama, Matador, La Senorita, and The Bee. Also issued as 4.5" tall set.
Each glass - **$20 $40 $60**

FER-24   FER-25

❑ **FER-24. Ferdinand Painted Plaster Statue.**
c. 1938. Maker unknown. 9" tall. Version without word "Bank" and no coin slot. - **$15 $30 $50**

❑ **FER-25. Ferdinand Painted Plaster "Bank,"**
c. 1938. Maker unknown. 8.5" tall. Coin slot on back of head. - **$20 $40 $75**

FER-26

❑ **FER-26. The Matador From Ferdinand Exceptional Doll,**
c. 1938. Maker unknown, but licensed. 19" tall. - **$800 $1600 $3200**

FERDINAND THE BULL

FER-27

❏ **FER-27. "Ferdinand" Glass,**
1939. Issued by various dairies. From the premium series of six different which came in two sizes. This is the smaller of the two sizes, 4.5". Each - **$20 $40 $60**

FER-28

FER-29

FER-30

❏ **FER-28. "Ferdinand 1939 Walt Disney All Star Parade" Glass,**
1939. Glass is 4.25" tall. - **$15 $25 $45**

❏ **FER-29. "Ferdinand's Chinese Checkers With The Bee,"**
1939. Parker Brothers. 13.5x17.5" box wtih 13x15" gameboard. Uses corks, not marbles. - **$75 $150 $275**

❏ **FER-30. "Ferdinand" Pull Toy,**
1939. Fisher-Price. 10" tall mostly wood pull toy #434. - **$300 $600 $1200**

FER-31

FER-32

❏ **FER-31. "Ferdinand" Bisque,**
1930s. Japan. 3" tall. - **$10 $20 $45**

❏ **FER-32. "Ferdinand" Seiberling Figure,**
1930s. Seiberling Latex Products. 3.75" tall. - **$35 $65 $175**

FER-33

❏ **FER-33. Ferdinand Ceramic Salt & Pepper Set,**
1930s. Each is 2.5" tall. No markings. - **$25 $40 $80**

FER-34

❏ **FER-34. "Ferdinand The Bull Golden Record,"**
1950. Sleeve is 6.75x7.5" and contains vinyl 78rpm. - **$5 $10 $15**

FER-35

❏ **FER-35. "Fierce Ferdinand The Bull" Boxed Wind-Up,**
1950s. Line Mar. 5.5" long bull with built in key.
Box - **$50 $100 $200**
Toy - **$150 $300 $450**

Finding Nemo

Without a doubt, *Finding Nemo* (2003) is one of the biggest successes in the history of animation. With *Toy Story* (1995), Pixar Animation had pioneered the use of computers in animation. In *Finding Nemo*, they may have reached an early high point. The computer animation for Nemo stands among the finest created. The characterizations are sharp, and the film bears repeated viewing for both adults and children.

In the film, a clownfish named Marlin has lost his son, Nemo, to a scuba diver. Setting out to find his son, no matter where he may be, Marlin travels the ocean while accompanied by a scatterbrained blue tang fish named Dory. Her presence proves to be both a help and a problem. Marlin deals with sharks, pelicans, jellyfish and just about any other type of undersea problem you can imagine.

FINDING NEMO

The film was directed by Lee Unkrich and Andrew Stanton; voice actors included Albert Brooks, Ellen DeGeneres, Willem Dafoe and Geoffrey Rush. The film won the Academy Award for Best Animated Film of 2003.

Merchandise covered the spectrum. It included books, an aquarium set, a View-Master set and fast food tie-ins among others.

FNO-3

❑ **FNO-3. "Finding Nemo" View-Master,** 2003. Viewer and 3 reels. NM - **$32**

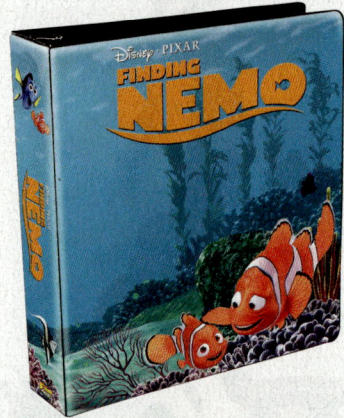

FNO-4

❑ **FNO-4. Binder for FilmCardz,** 2003. - **$20**

FNO-5

FNO-1

❑ **FNO-1. Box of FilmCardz Packs,** 2003. Artbox. Five cards per pack, were viewed using the Lighted FilmCardz Viewer. - **$110**

FNO-2

❑ **FNO-2. "Finding Nemo" Aquarium Gang Set,** 2003. Eight figures and accessories. NM - **$22**

❑ **FNO-5. Lighted FilmCardz Viewer,** 2003. - **$22**

FNO-6

❑ **FNO-6. Crush and Friends Water Globe,** 2003. Disney. Water globe on turtle figure. - **$110**

FNO-7

❑ **FNO-7. Fish Tank Snow Globe,** 2003. Disney. "Tiny Bubbles." - **$65**

FNO-8

❑ **FNO-8. Coral Reef Snow Globe,** 2003. Disney. "Over the waves." - **$100**

FLIP THE FROG

FNO-9

FNO-10

FNO-11

❑ **FNO-9. Bloat Toy,**
2003. From McDonald's. Toy lights up and squirts water. - **$5**

❑ **FNO-10. Nemo Bath Toy,**
2004. - **$5**

❑ **FNO-11. Dory Bath Toy,**
2004. - **$5**

Flip The Frog

Flip the Frog was the flagship creation of longtime Disney associate Ub Iwerks. Iwerks first met Walt Disney in 1919. They were both working at the Kansas City Film Ad Company. When Walt moved to Hollywood to open an animation studio, he brought Iwerks in as both a financial partner and the head animator. Iwerks was a very fast worker. Capable of more than just animation, he also worked on numerous scene backgrounds and poster designs. The earliest Mickey Mouse cartoons display his name in the opening credits. Iwerks also penciled the first three weeks of Mickey Mouse comic strip, which was launched in January, 1930.

In that same year, Iwerks left Disney to open his own studio. The first character he developed was Flip the Frog, a likeable loser in a rather adult, risqué pre-code cartoon world. The first released Flip cartoon, *Fiddlesticks* (1930), is also one of the first cartoons to have been produced in the then-new process of Technicolor. In all, Iwerks produced 37 Flip cartoons, but after several years of middling popularity, the character drifted out of favor with the general public. The next character Iwerks developed was Willie Whopper, a sort of boy Baron Munchausen, but Willie was even less successful than Flip.

The animation staff at Iwerks' studio included Chuck Jones, Virgil Ross, Al Eugster, Grim Natwick and Shamus Culhane. In 1940, Iwerks rejoined the Disney Studios team.

Merchandise for Flip has included ceramic planters, stuffed animals, a British comic annual and a coloring book.

FLP-1

❑ **FLP-1. "Flip The Frog" Doll By Dean's Rag Book Co,**
1930. 2.75x6x8.5" tall. Velveteen stuffed body with wire inserts in arms and legs for posing, checkered fabric bow tie, google eyes with felt eyelid accents. Underside of each foot has markings including company name, registration number and "Flip The Frog." - **$325 $625 $1250**

FLP-2

❑ **FLP-2. "Flip The Frog" English Doll,**
1930. Whyte, Ridsdale & Co. Ltd. 5" tall stuffed mohair with wire inserts for posing, felt hands and feet, glass eyes, fabric bow tie and mother-of-pearl buttons. - **$300 $500 $1000**

FLP-3

❑ **FLP-3. Flip The Frog English Doll,**
1930. 6.25" tall stuffed velveteen doll with felt hands, bakelite-like eyes, four mother-of-pearl pants buttons. Label reads: Trade Mark. Flip The Frog. By arrangement with Showman Films London. Regd. Design No. 757459.
- **$325 $550 $1100**

FLP-4

317

FLIP THE FROG

☐ **FLP-4. Flip The Frog Egg Timer,**
c. 1930, 3.75" tall timer with 3.25" tall ffigure. Base has incised registration number and the word "Foreign". - **$100 $225 $350**

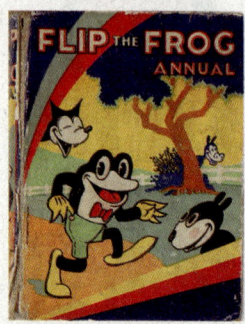

FLP-5

☐ **FLP-5. "Flip The Frog Annual" English Hardcover,**
1931. Dean & Son Ltd. Book is 6.5x8.75x2" thick with 124 pages. - **$150 $300 $800**

FLP-6

FLP-7

☐ **FLP-6. Ub Iwerks Personal Christmas Card Featuring Flip The Frog,**
1931. One-sided card is 4x6.5". Limited distribution. - **$115 $250 $500**

☐ **FLP-7. Flip The Frog Rare Composition Figure,**
c. 1931. Unmarked. 2.5x3.5x7" tall painted composition with movable arms. - **$525 $1050 $1600**

FLP-8

☐ **FLP-8. Flip The Frog Celluloid Figure With Movable Arms,**
c. 1931. 6.5" tall and "Made In Japan." - **$200 $400 $700**

FLP-9

FLP-10

☐ **FLP-9. "Flip The Frog Coloring Book,"**
1932. Saalfield. Book is 10.75x15.25" with 28 pages of both black and white illustratons to be colored plus full color example pictures. The 4/23/32 issue of trade magazine Motion Picture Herald mentions book's availablity from the publishers at 6.3 cents each for use as matinee premium. - **$60 $135 $300**

☐ **FLP-10. "Flip The Frog Four Picture Puzzles" Boxed Set,**
1932. Saalfield. Celebrity Productions Inc. 8.25x12x.5" deep box contains 5.75x8" puzzles. Titles are "Flip Returns From The Market, Blowing Bubbles, Winter Sport, Yum! Yum! Want A Bite!" - **$200 $400 $650**

FLIP THE FROG

FLP-11

FLP-13

FLP-14

FLP-17

FLP-18

FLP-12

FLP-15

FLP-16

FLP-19

❑ **FLP-11. Flip The Frog Tin Litho Clicker,**
c. 1932. Unmarked. 3-3/8" long. - **$60 $135 $250**

❑ **FLP-12. Flip The Frog Glazed Ceramic Candle Holder,**
c. 1932. United Kingdom. #8419. Designed to hold single birthday candle. 1.5" tall. - **$35 $60 $125**

❑ **FLP-13. Flip The Frog Glazed Ceramic Planter,**
c. 1932. Japan. 3x6.25x5.25" tall. Two versions.
Full Color - **$65 $135 $250**
Black And White - **$45 $70 $125**

❑ **FLP-14. Flip The Frog Glazed Ceramic Planter,**
c. 1932. Japan. 3x6.25x5.25" tall. Two versions.
Full Color - **$65 $135 $250**
Black And White - **$45 $70 $125**

❑ **FLP-15. Flip The Frog With Tuba Bisque,**
1930s. Figure is 3.5" tall and "Made In Japan." - **$50 $125 $215**

❑ **FLP-16. "Flip The Frog" Bisque,**
1930s. Figure is 5" tall. Japan. - **$100 $200 $325**

❑ **FLP-17. Flip The Frog With Clarinet Bisque,**
1930s. Figure is 3.5" tall. Japan. - **$50 $125 $215**

❑ **FLP-18. Flip The Frog Ceramic Planter,**
1930s. 2.5x3.5" tall and "Made In Japan." - **$40 $75 $125**

❑ **FLP-19. Flip The Frog Ceramic Planter,**
1930s. Figure is 2.25x4x3" tall and marked "Made In Japan." - **$25 $45 $90**

FLIP THE FROG

FLP-20

FLP-22

FLP-25

❏ **FLP-20. Flip The Frog Ceramic Planter,** 1930s. 2.5x4x3.75" tall. Japan. - **$25 $45 $90**

❏ **FLP-22. Flip The Frog Napkin Ring and Egg Timer,** 1930s. English. Napkin ring is 4" tall, Timer is 6" tall china. Each - **$40 $85 $135**

FLP-21

❏ **FLP-21. Flip The Frog Planter,** 1930s. Painted and glazed china marked "Made In Japan," 3x6.5x4.5" tall. - **$50 $100 $150**

FLP-23

FLP-26

❏ **FLP-25. Flip The Frog Ashtray,** 1930s. Painted and glazed ceramic. European issued and marked "Foreign," 2.5x4x3.25" tall. - **$65 $125 $250**

❏ **FLP-26. Flip The Frog Ashtrays,** 1930s. Pair of bakelite-like 2x4.5x.5" tall ashtrays with standing and seated figures. Unmarked but European. Each - **$45 $85 $150**

FLP-22

FLP-24

❏ **FLP-23. Flip The Frog Ceramic Ashtray,** 1930s. Figure is 2.5x2.75x3.25" tall. Japan. - **$75 $125 $225**

❏ **FLP-24. Flip The Frog Ceramic Ashtray,** 1930s. Figure is 2.5x5x3.25" tall. Japan. - **$100 $150 $250**

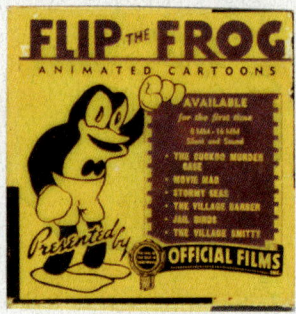
FLP-27

❏ **FLP-27. "Flip The Frog" Boxed Film,** 1940s. Official Films Inc. Box is 5x5x.5" deep and contains 8mm silent home movie. - **$10 $20 $40**

Four Color Comics

There were slightly over 1350 issues of *Dell Four Color Comics* published. However, the title featured an unlimited number of characters between the covers. One issue would feature Flash Gordon and the next one would feature Walt Disney's Bambi. This is because Dell contracted out the editorial content of their comics to a company named Western Publishing. Essentially, Dell supplied the money and approved the books to be published, but it was Western who made the arrangements with anyone who had characters they wanted to appear in comics. Western would also be responsible for the editorial content of each issue, including the creation of much of the comics content. Since many of the properties that Western was licensing, such as Oswald the Rabbit, Little Orphan Annie, or Wash Tubbs, couldn't support a monthly title on their own, the Four Color title became an anthology title that contained characters from many different companies. Once or twice a year, Dell and Western would meet. Western would bring a list of books they proposed. These would contain characters from many different licensees. Dell would agree to finance a certain number of issues for each character, regardless of whether it came from Disney or Walter Lantz. Western would then go back to their offices and determine when those choices would appear and also when these issues would come out on the newstand. We have isolated each Disney-related book that was published under the Four Color title. When they came out, Four Color Books were read by millions of children. They are seldom found in Near Mint condition which explains higher value in the top grade.

❏ Four Color Comics #13 (Series 1), June 1941. - $175 $525 $2700

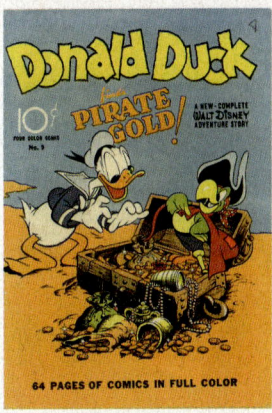
❏ Four Color Comics #9, October 1942. Barks-a. - $861 $2583 $15,500

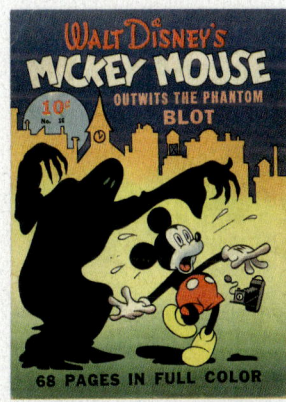
❏ Four Color Comics #16 (Series 1), April 1941. – GD - $1450   FN - $4260   VF - $14,200 none known to exist in NM

❏ Four Color Comics #12, April 1942. - $59 $177 $950

❏ Four Color Comics #4 (Series 1), February 1940. - $1000 $3000 $18,000

❏ Four Color Comics #17 (Series 1), May 1941. - $212 $636 $3200

❏ Four Color Comics #19, January 1943. - $49 $147 $885

FOUR COLOR COMICS

❑ **Four Color Comics #27,**
July 1943. - **$76 $224 $1525**

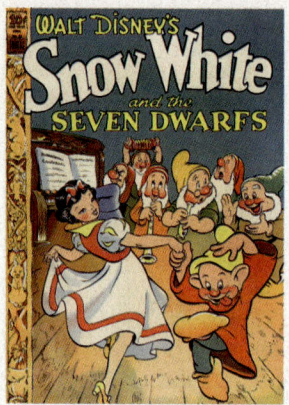

❑ **Four Color Comics #49,**
July 1944. - **$55 $165 $975**

❑ **Four Color Comics #79,**
August 1945. Mickey Mouse by Barks. - **$93 $279 $1850**

❑ **Four Color Comics #29,**
September 1943. Barks-a. - **$583 $1750 $10,500**

❑ **Four Color Comics #62,**
January 1945. Barks-a. - **$167 $501 $3500**

❑ **Four Color Comics #92,**
January 1946. Donald Duck by Kelly. - **$50 $150 $950**

❑ **Four Color Comics #30,**
October 1943. - **$56 $168 $875**

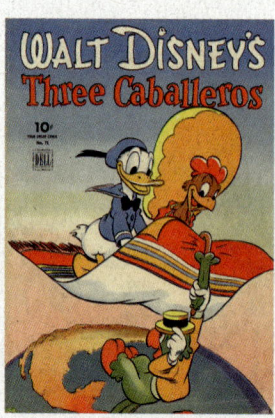

❑ **Four Color Comics #71,**
April 1945. Walt Kelly-a. - **$65 $195 $1300**

❑ **Four Color Comics #108,**
January 1946. Barks-a. - **$130 $390 $2600**

FOUR COLOR COMICS

❏ **Four Color Comics #116,**
August 1946. - **$27 $81 $410**

❏ **Four Color Comics #147.**
May 1947. Barks-a. – **$85 $255 $1700**

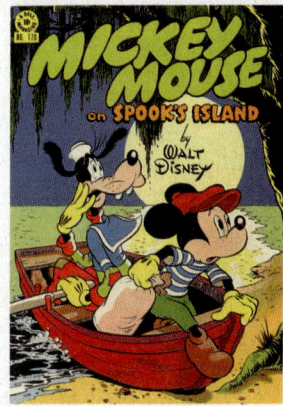

❏ **Four Color Comics #170,**
November 1947. - **$19 $57 $300**

❏ **Four Color Comics #129,**
December 1946. - **$29 $87 $450**

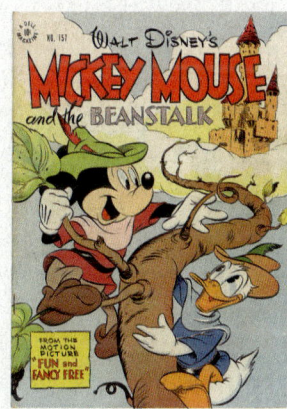

❏ **Four Color Comics #157,**
July 1947. - **$23 $68 $350**

❏ **Four Color Comics #178,**
December 1947. Barks-a. - **$105 $315 $2100**

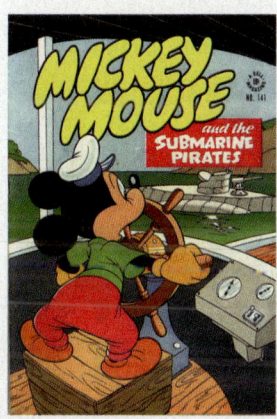

❏ **Four Color Comics #141,**
March 1947. - **$23 $68 $350**

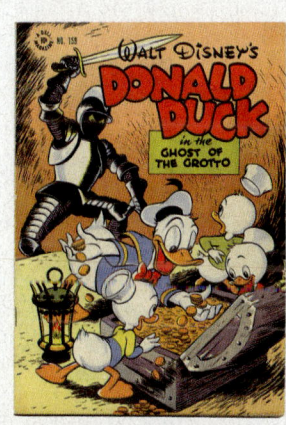

❏ **Four Color Comics #159,**
August 1947. Barks-a. - **$75 $225 $1500**

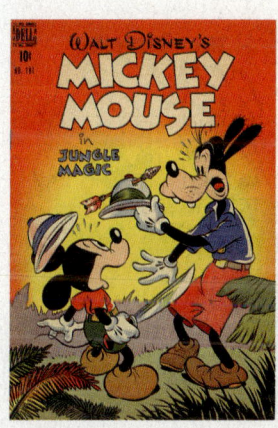

❏ **Four Color Comics #181,**
February 1948. - **$19 $57 $300**

FOUR COLOR COMICS

❏ **Four Color Comics #186,**
April 1948. - **$18 $54 $275**

❏ **Four Color Comics #199,**
October 1948. Barks-a. - **$69 $207 $1375**

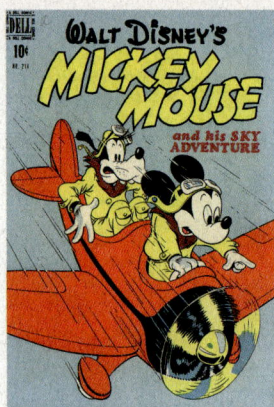

❏ **Four Color Comics #214,**
February 1949. - **$14 $42 $225**

❏ **Four Color Comics #189,**
June 1948. Barks-a. - **$63 $189 $1250**

❏ **Four Color Comics #203,**
December 1948. Barks-a. - **$50 $150 $950**

❏ **Four Color Comics #218,**
March 1949. - **$12 $36 $180**

❏ **Four Color Comics #194,**
August 1948. - **$19 $57 $300**

❏ **Four Color Comics #208,**
January 1949. - **$12 $36 $180**

❏ **Four Color Comics #223,**
April 1949. Barks-a. - **$65 $195 $1300**

FOUR COLOR COMICS

❏ **Four Color Comics #227,**
May 1949. - **$11** **$33** **$160**

❏ **Four Color Comics #238.**
August 1949. Barks-a. - **$50** **$150** **$950**

❏ **Four Color Comics #252,**
November 1949. - **$12** **$36** **$175**

❏ **Four Color Comics #231,**
June 1949. - **$14** **$42** **$225**

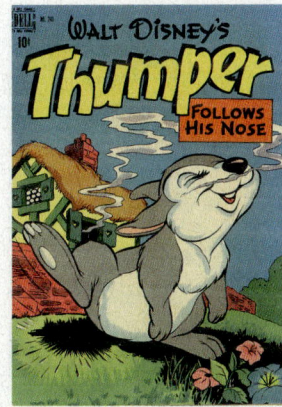

❏ **Four Color Comics #243.**
August 1949. Barks-a. - **$12** **$36** **$175**

❏ **Four Color Comics #256,**
December 1949. Barks-a. - **$41** **$123** **$725**

❏ **Four Color Comics #234,**
June 1949. - **$13** **$39** **$210**

❏ **Four Color Comics #248,**
October 1949. - **$14** **$42** **$225**

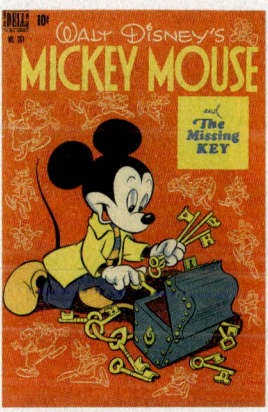

❏ **Four Color Comics #261,**
January 1950. - **$14** **$42** **$225**

FOUR COLOR COMICS

❑ **Four Color Comics #263,** February 1950. Barks-a. - **$41 $123 $700**

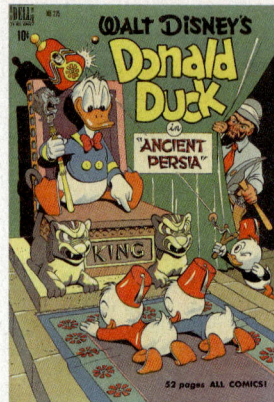

❑ **Four Color Comics #275,** May 1950. Barks-a. - **$40 $120 $675**

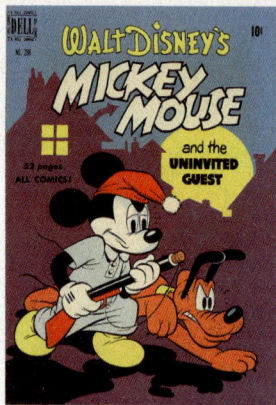

❑ **Four Color Comics #286,** August 1950. - **$11 $33 $160**

❑ **Four Color Comics #268,** March 1950. - **$14 $42 $215**

❑ **Four Color Comics #279,** June 1950. - **$11 $33 $160**

❑ **Four Color Comics #291,** September 1950. Barks-a. - **$40 $120 $675**

❑ **Four Color Comics #272,** April 1950. - **$13 $39 $200**

❑ **Four Color Comics #282,** July 1950. Barks-a. - **$40 $120 $675**

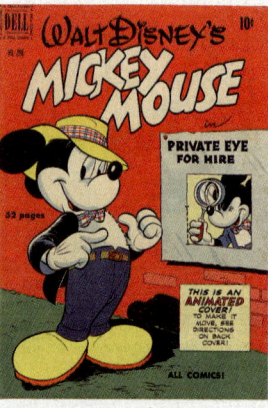

❑ **Four Color Comics #296,** October 1950. - **$11 $33 $160**

FOUR COLOR COMICS

❑ **Four Color Comics #300,** November 1950. Barks-a. - **$40** **$120** **$675**

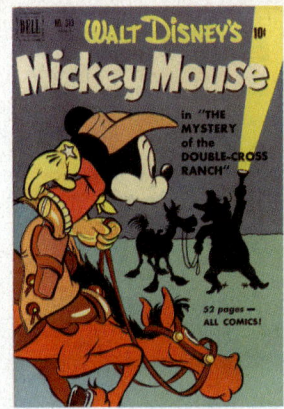

❑ **Four Color Comics #313,** February 1951. - **$10** **$30** **$135**

❑ **Four Color Comics #328,** May 1951. Barks-a. - **$38** **$114** **$650**

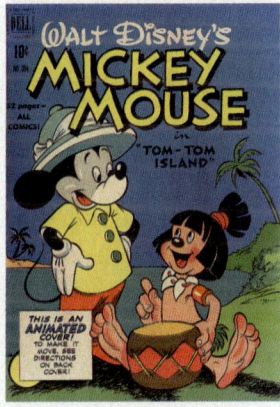

❑ **Four Color Comics #304,** December 1950. - **$10** **$30** **$135**

❑ **Four Color Comics #318,** March 1951. Barks-a. - **$38** **$114** **$640**

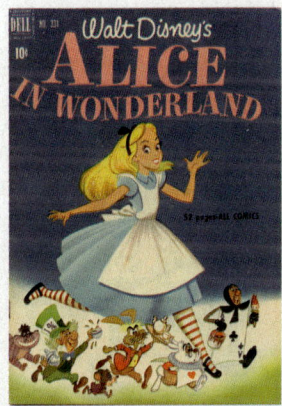

❑ **Four Color Comics #331,** May 1951. - **$16** **$48** **$245**

❑ **Four Color Comics #308,** January 1951. Barks-a. - **$38** **$114** **$640**

❑ **Four Color Comics #325,** April 1951. - **$10** **$30** **$135**

❑ **Four Color Comics #334,** June 1951. - **$10** **$30** **$135**

FOUR COLOR COMICS

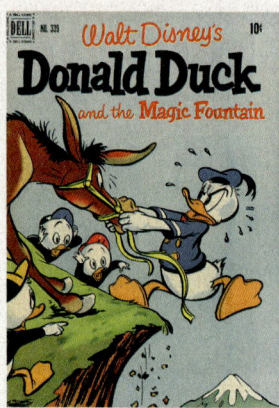
❏ **Four Color Comics #339,** July 1951. - **$11 $33 $160**

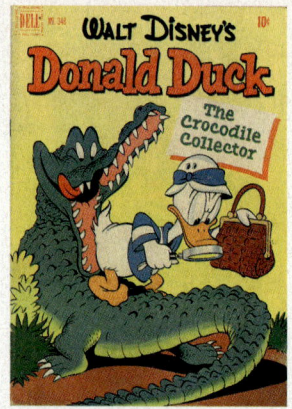
❏ **Four Color Comics #348,** September 1951. Barks-c. - **$19 $57 $300**

❏ **Four Color Comics #356,** November 1951. Barks-c. - **$19 $57 $300**

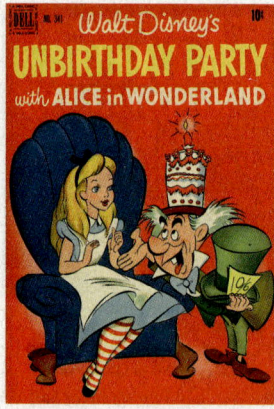
❏ **Four Color Comics #341,** July 1951. - **$16 $48 $245**

❏ **Four Color Comics #352,** October 1951. - **$9 $27 $115**

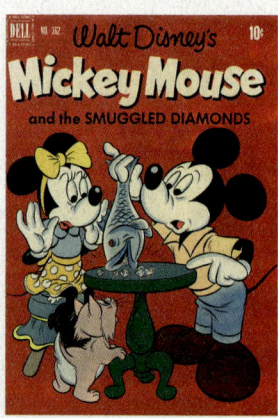
❏ **Four Color Comics #362,** December 1951. - **$9 $27 $115**

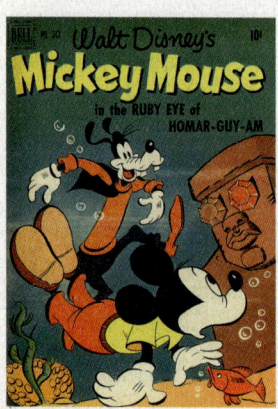
❏ **Four Color Comics #343,** August 1951. - **$9 $27 $115**

❏ **Four Color Comics #353,** November 1951. Barks-c. - **$10 $30 $140**

❏ **Four Color Comics #367,** January 1952. Barks-a. - **$31 $93 $525**

FOUR COLOR COMICS

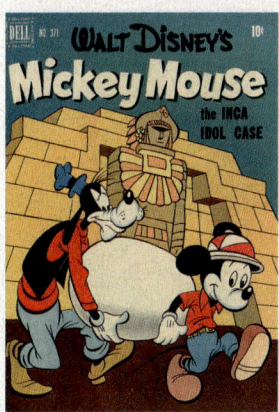
❏ **Four Color Comics #371,** February 1952. - **$9 $27 $115**

❏ **Four Color Comics #386,** March 1952. Uncle Scrooge Barks-a. - **$100 $300 $2000**

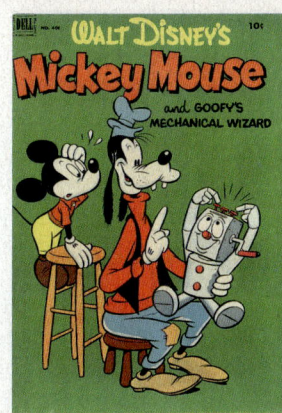
❏ **Four Color Comics #401,** June 1952. - **$7 $21 $90**

❏ **Four Color Comics #379,** March 1952. - **$11 $33 $160**

❏ **Four Color Comics #387,** April 1952. - **$9 $27 $115**

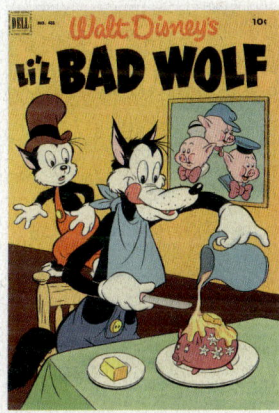
❏ **Four Color Comics #403,** June 1952. - **$8 $24 $105**

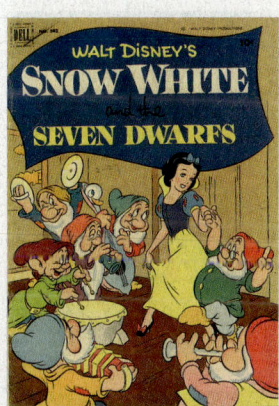
❏ **Four Color Comics #382,** March 1952. - **$11 $33 $160**

❏ **Four Color Comics #394,** May 1952. Barks-c. - **$19 $57 $300**

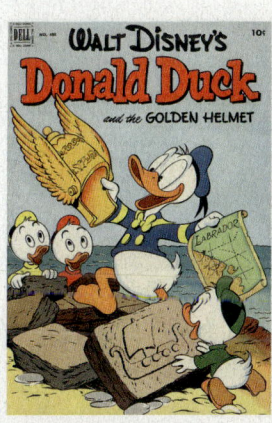
❏ **Four Color Comics #408,** July 1952. Barks-a. - **$31 $93 $525**

FOUR COLOR COMICS

❏ **Four Color Comics #411,**
August 1952. - **$7 $21 $90**

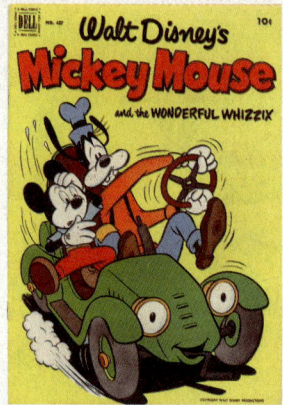

❏ **Four Color Comics #427,**
October 1952. - **$7 $21 $90**

❏ **Four Color Comics #442,**
December 1952. - **$12 $36 $165**

❏ **Four Color Comics #413,**
August 1952. - **$11 $33 $160**

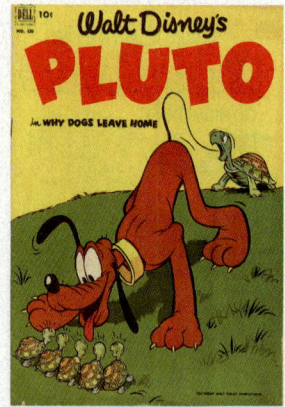

❏ **Four Color Comics #429,**
October 1952. - **$11 $33 $150**

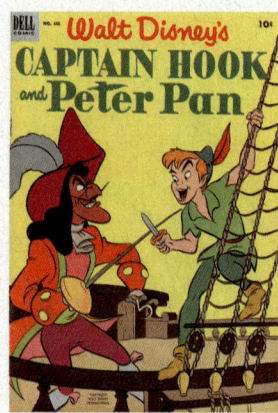

❏ **Four Color Comics #446,**
January 1953. - **$10 $30 $140**

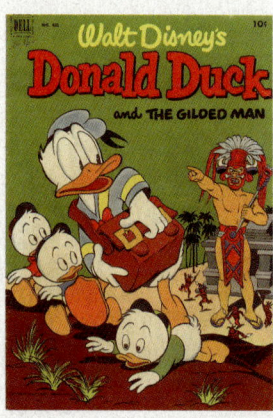

❏ **Four Color Comics #422,**
September 1952. Barks-a. - **$31 $93 $525**

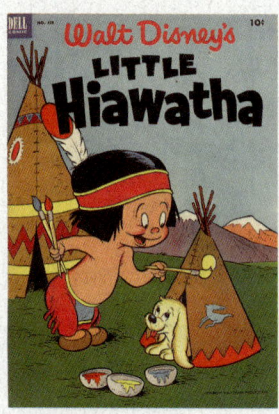

❏ **Four Color Comics #439,**
December 1952. - **$7 $21 $85**

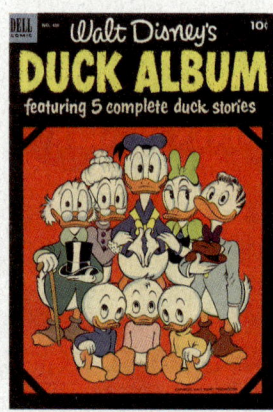

❏ **Four Color Comics #450,**
February 1953. Barks-c. - **$8 $24 $105**

FOUR COLOR COMICS

❑ **Four Color Comics #456,** March 1953. Barks-a. - **$55** **$165** **$1100**

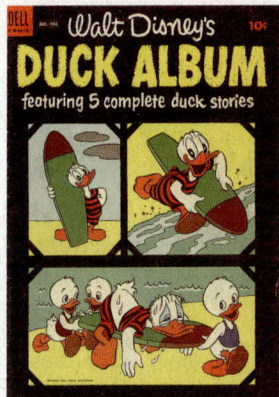
❑ **Four Color Comics #492,** August 1953. - **$7** **$21** **$80**

❑ **Four Color Comics #509,** October 1953. - **$7** **$21** **$90**

❑ **Four Color Comics #468,** May 1953. - **$13** **$39** **$195**

❑ **Four Color Comics #495,** September 1953. Uncle Scrooge by Barks. - **$44** **$132** **$800**

❑ **Four Color Comics #517,** November 1953. - **$11** **$33** **$160**

❑ **Four Color Comics #473,** June 1953. - **$6** **$18** **$65**

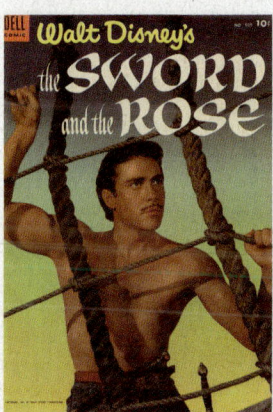
❑ **Four Color Comics #505,** October 1953. - **$10** **$30** **$130**

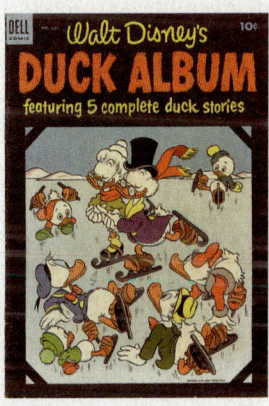
❑ **Four Color Comics #531,** January 1954. - **$7** **$21** **$80**

FOUR COLOR COMICS

❏ Four Color Comics #537,
February 1954. – **$5 $15 $60**

❏ Four Color Comics #545,
April 1954. - **$8 $24 $105**

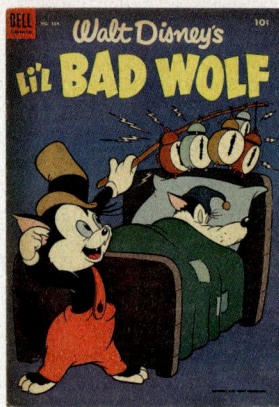
❏ Four Color Comics #564,
June 1954. - **$6 $18 $65**

❏ Four Color Comics #539,
March 1954. - **$4 $12 $50**

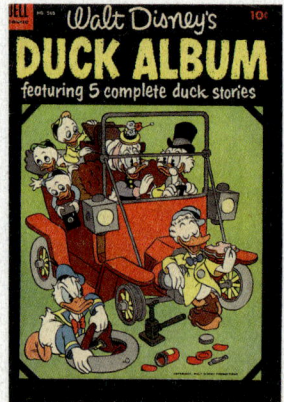
❏ Four Color Comics #560,
May 1954. - **$7 $21 $80**

❏ Four Color Comics #581,
August 1954. - **$7 $21 $80**

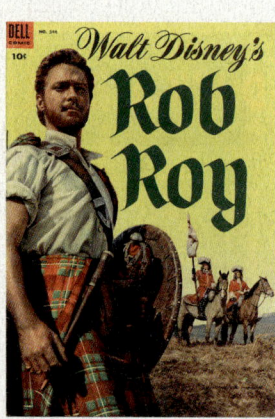
❏ Four Color Comics #544,
March 1954. - **$9 $27 $115**

❏ Four Color Comics #562,
May 1954. - **$8 $24 $105**

❏ Four Color Comics #586,
September 1954. - **$7 $21 $80**

FOUR COLOR COMICS

☐ Four Color Comics #595,
October 1954. - **$6 $18 $65**

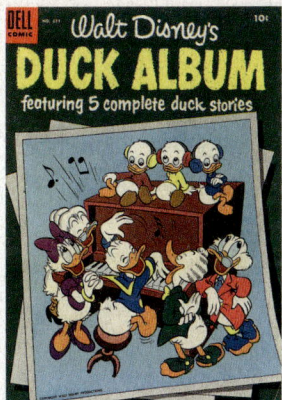

☐ Four Color Comics #611,
January 1955. - **$7 $21 $80**

☐ Four Color Comics #625,
April 1955. - **$7 $21 $90**

☐ Four Color Comics #600,
November 1954. - **$8 $24 $105**

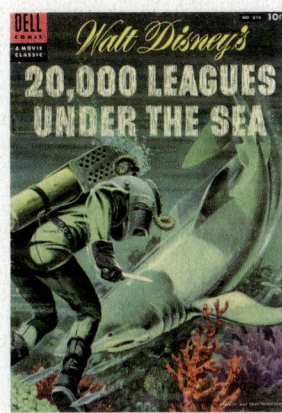

☐ Four Color Comics #614,
February 1955. - **$10 $30 $135**

☐ Four Color Comics #627,
May 1955. - **$8 $24 $105**

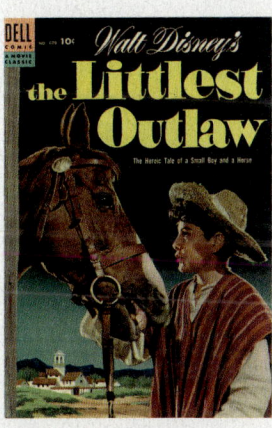

☐ Four Color Comics #609,
November 1954. - **$8 $24 $95**

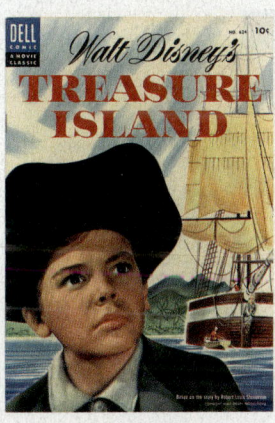

☐ Four Color Comics #624,
April 1955. - **$10 $30 $125**

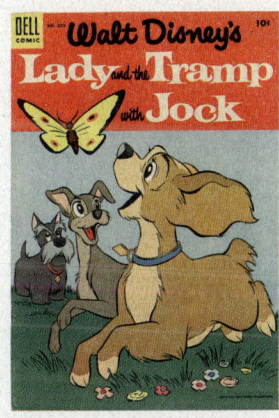

☐ Four Color Comics #629,
May 1955. - **$8 $24 $105**

FOUR COLOR COMICS

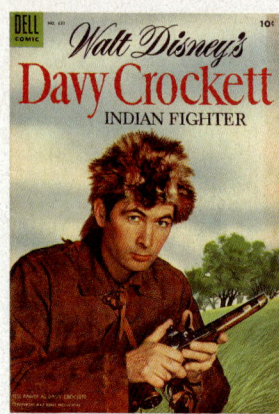

❏ Four Color Comics #631, May 1955. - **$21 $63 $320**

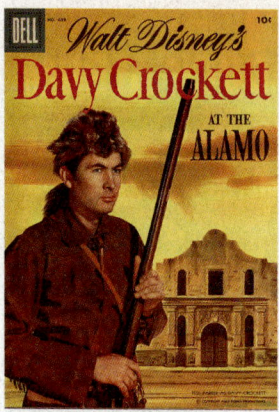

❏ Four Color Comics #639, July 1955. - **$17 $51 $260**

❏ Four Color Comics #658, November 1955. - **$8 $24 $105**

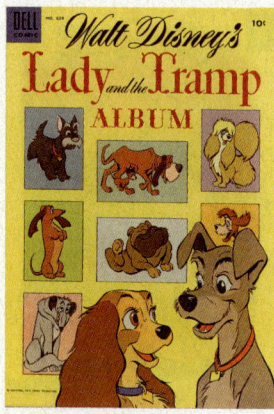

❏ Four Color Comics #634, June 1955. - **$6 $18 $70**

❏ Four Color Comics #649, September 1955. - **$7 $21 $80**

❏ Four Color Comics #659, November 1955. - **$7 $21 $80**

❏ Four Color Comics #636, July 1955. - **$7 $21 $80**

❏ Four Color Comics #654, October 1955. - **$6 $18 $65**

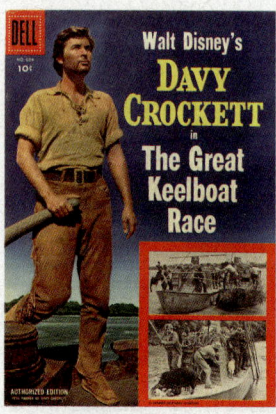

❏ Four Color Comics #664, November 1955. - **$16 $48 $245**

FOUR COLOR COMICS

❏ Four Color Comics #665, November 1955. - **$7 $21 $80**

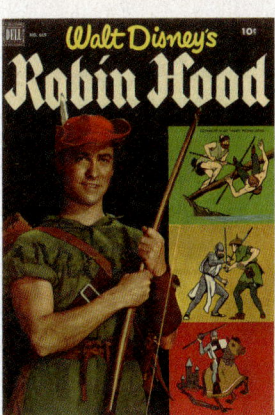
❏ Four Color Comics #669 (rprnt FC #413), December 1955. - **$7 $21 $80**

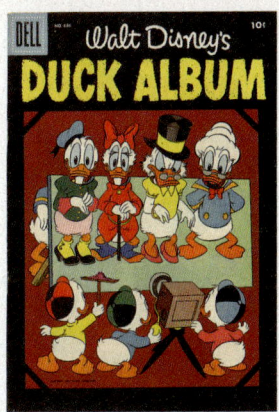
❏ Four Color Comics #686, March 1956. - **$7 $21 $80**

❏ Four Color Comics #668, December 1955. - **$11 $33 $155**

❏ Four Color Comics #671, December 1955. - **$16 $48 $245**

❏ Four Color Comics #693, April 1956. - **$10 $30 $130**

❏ Four Color Comics #668 (2nd prnt), December 1955. Timothy Mouse added to c. - **$8 $24 $100**

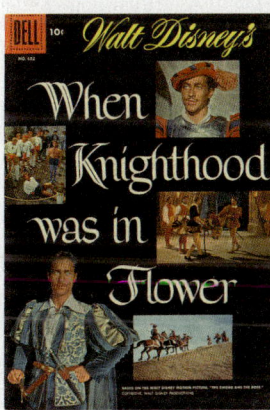
❏ Four Color Comics #682 (rprnt FC #505), November 1955. - **$8 $24 $105**

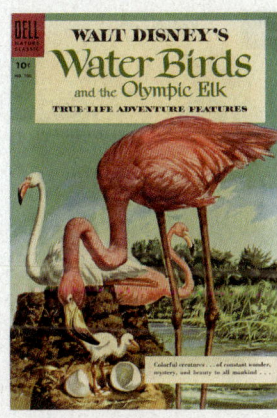
❏ Four Color Comics #700, April 1956. - **$6 $18 $75**

335

FOUR COLOR COMICS

❑ Four Color Comics #701, May 1956. - $10 $30 $130

❑ Four Color Comics #706, June 1956. - $7 $21 $80

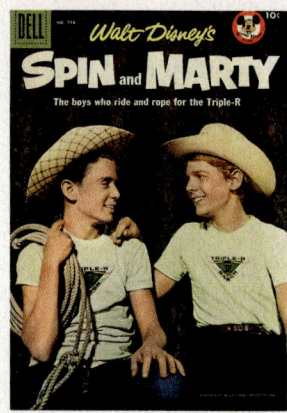

❑ Four Color Comics #714, June 1956. - $14 $42 $215

❑ Four Color Comics #702, May 1956. - $8 $24 $105

❑ Four Color Comics #707, July 1956. - $8 $24 $105

❑ Four Color Comics #716, August 1956. - $10 $30 $130

❑ Four Color Comics #703, May 1956. - $10 $30 $135

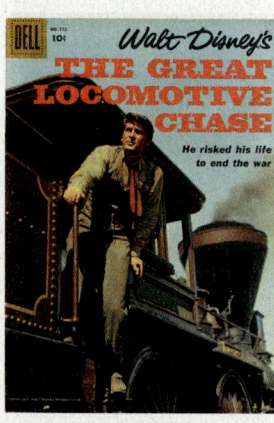

❑ Four Color Comics #712, July 1956. - $8 $24 $105

❑ Four Color Comics #726, September 1956. - $6 $18 $75

FOUR COLOR COMICS

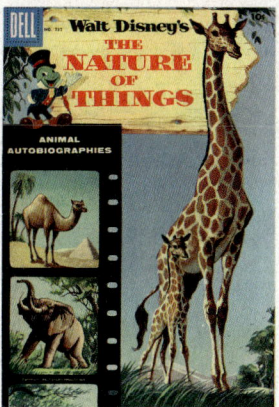

❏ **Four Color Comics #727,**
September 1956. - **$6 $18 $75**

❏ **Four Color Comics #743,**
November 1956. - **$7 $21 $80**

❏ **Four Color Comics #750,**
November 1956. - **$8 $24 $95**

❏ **Four Color Comics #736,**
October 1956. - **$6 $18 $65**

❏ **Four Color Comics #747,**
November 1956. - **$8 $24 $105**

❏ **Four Color Comics #758,**
December 1956. - **$6 $18 $75**

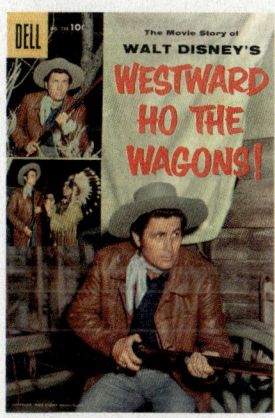

❏ **Four Color Comics #738,**
October 1956. - **$11 $33 $145**

❏ **Four Color Comics #749,**
November 1956. - **$6 $18 $70**

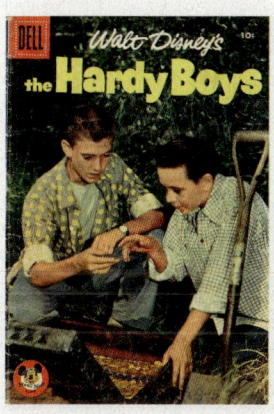

❏ **Four Color Comics #760,**
December 1956. - **$12 $36 $175**

FOUR COLOR COMICS

❏ Four Color Comics #763, January 1957. **- $9 $27 $115**

❏ Four Color Comics #782, March 1957. **- $6 $18 $75**

❏ Four Color Comics #795, May 1957. **- $8 $24 $95**

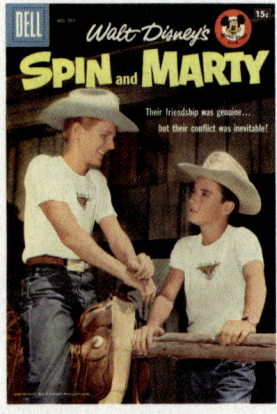

❏ Four Color Comics #767, February 1957. **- $10 $30 $140**

❏ Four Color Comics #786 partial r- FC #272 March 1957. **- $8 $24 $100**

❏ Four Color Comics #802, May 1957. **- $8 $24 $105**

❏ Four Color Comics #777, March 1957. **- $8 $24 $95**

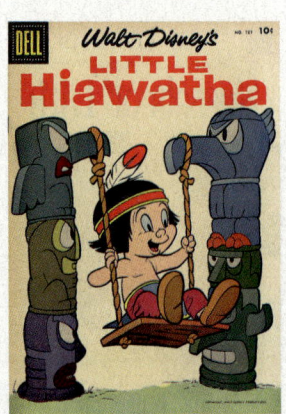

❏ Four Color Comics #787, April 1957. **- $6 $18 $65**

❏ Four Color Comics #806, June 1957. **- $8 $24 $95**

FOUR COLOR COMICS

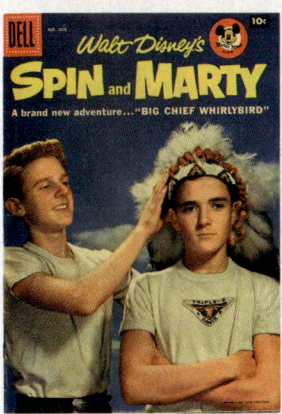
❑ **Four Color Comics #808,**
June 1957. - **$10** **$30** **$140**

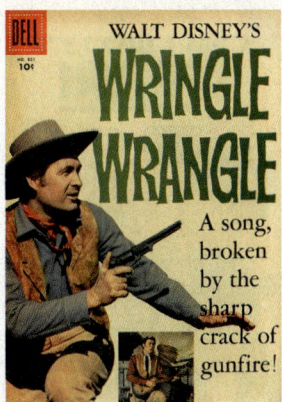
❑ **Four Color Comics #821,**
August 1957. - **$9** **$27** **$120**

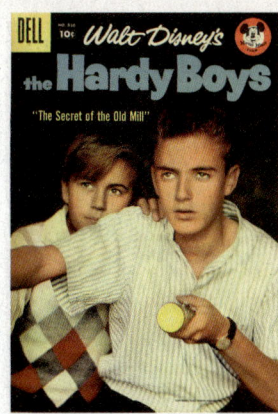
❑ **Four Color Comics #830,**
August 1957. - **$10** **$30** **$140**

❑ **Four Color Comics #814,**
July 1957. - **$6** **$18** **$75**

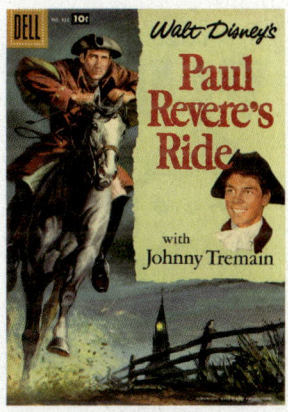
❑ **Four Color Comics #822,**
August 1957. - **$10** **$30** **$135**

❑ **Four Color Comics #833,**
September 1957. - **$8** **$24** **$95**

❑ **Four Color Comics #819,**
July 1957. - **$6** **$18** **$70**

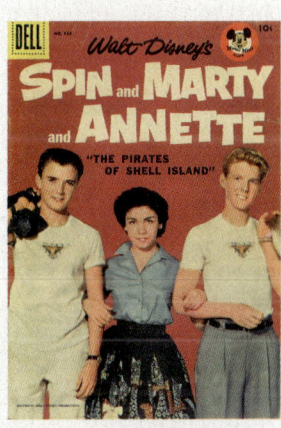
❑ **Four Color Comics #826,**
September 1957. - **$25** **$75** **$380**

❑ **Four Color Comics #836,**
September 1957. - **$8** **$24** **$105**

FOUR COLOR COMICS

❏ **Four Color Comics #840,**
September 1957. - **$6 $18 $75**

❏ **Four Color Comics #847,**
October 1957. - **$6 $18 $75**

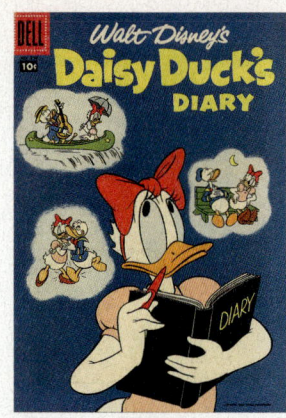

❏ **Four Color Comics #858,**
November 1957. - **$6 $18 $70**

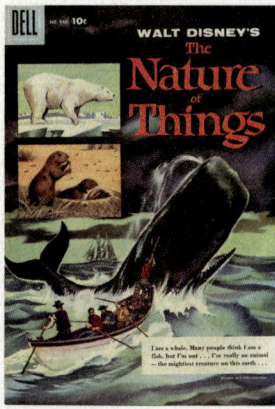

❏ **Four Color Comics #842,**
September 1957. - **$6 $18 $75**

❏ **Four Color Comics #853,**
October 1957. - **$6 $18 $65**

❏ **Four Color Comics #862,**
November 1957. - **$9 $27 $110**

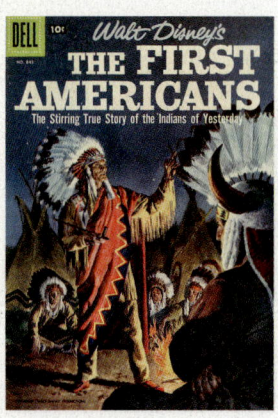

❏ **Four Color Comics #843,**
September 1957. - **$10 $30 $130**

❏ **Four Color Comics #857,**
November 1957. - **$8 $24 $105**

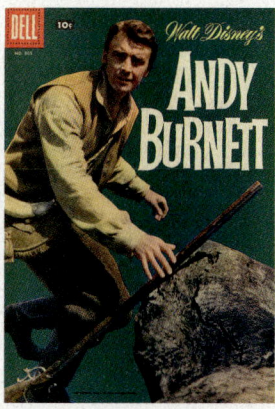

❏ **Four Color Comics #865,**
December 1957. - **$10 $30 $135**

FOUR COLOR COMICS

❑ **Four Color Comics #866,**
December 1957. - **$10** **$30** **$130**

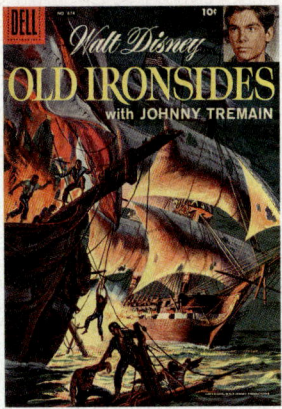

❑ **Four Color Comics #874,**
January 1958. - **$8** **$24** **$95**

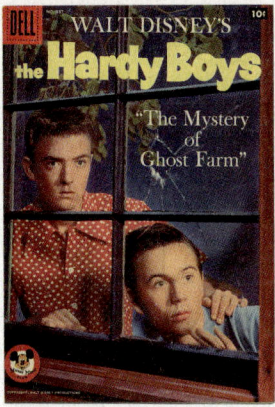

❑ **Four Color Comics #887,**
January 1958. - **$10** **$30** **$140**

❑ **Four Color Comics #869,**
January 1958. - **$6** **$18** **$75**

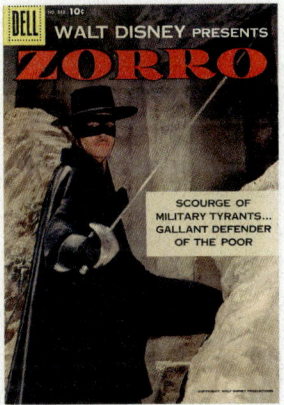

❑ **Four Color Comics #882,**
February 1958. 1st Disney Zorro issue. - **$17** **$51** **$260**

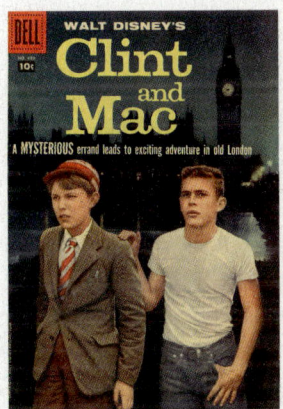

❑ **Four Color Comics #889,**
March 1958. - **$13** **$39** **$200**

❑ **Four Color Comics #873,**
January 1958. - **$6** **$18** **$75**

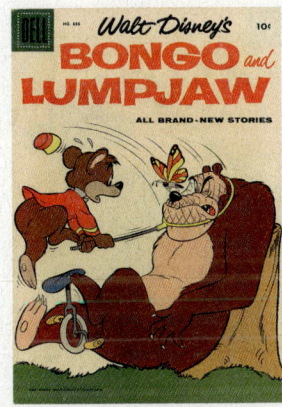

❑ **Four Color Comics #886,**
March 1958. - **$6** **$18** **$65**

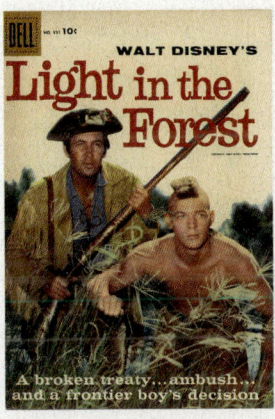

❑ **Four Color Comics #891,**
March 1958. - **$9** **$27** **$115**

FOUR COLOR COMICS

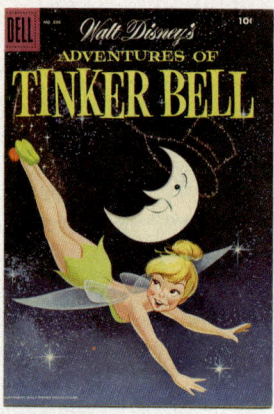

❑ **Four Color Comics #896,**
April 1958. - **$10 $30 $130**

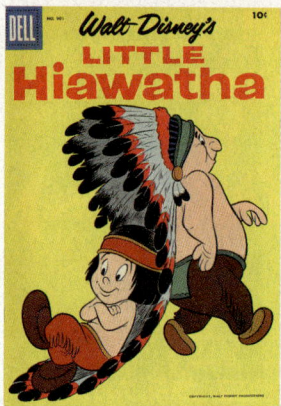

❑ **Four Color Comics #901,**
May 1958. - **$6 $18 $65**

❑ **Four Color Comics #926,**
August 1958. - **$5 $15 $60**

❑ **Four Color Comics #897,**
May 1958. - **$8 $24 $95**

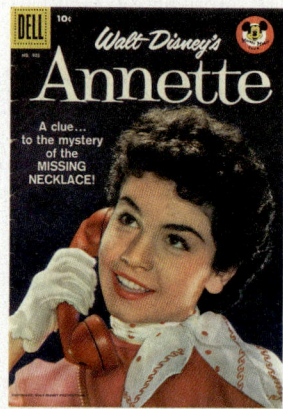

❑ **Four Color Comics #905,**
May 1958. - **$31 $93 $475**

❑ **Four Color Comics #933,**
September 1958. - **$13 $39 $195**

❑ **Four Color Comics #899,**
May 1958. - **$6 $18 $70**

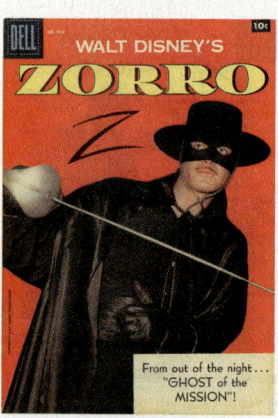

❑ **Four Color Comics #920,**
June 1958. - **$13 $39 $195**

❑ **Four Color Comics #941,**
October 1958. - **$5 $15 $60**

FOUR COLOR COMICS

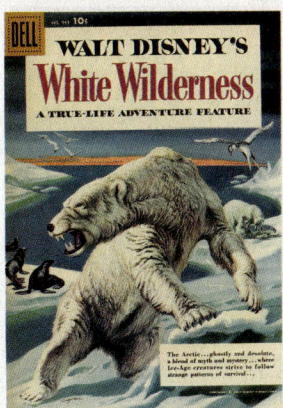
❏ **Four Color Comics #943,** October 1958. - **$8 $24 $95**

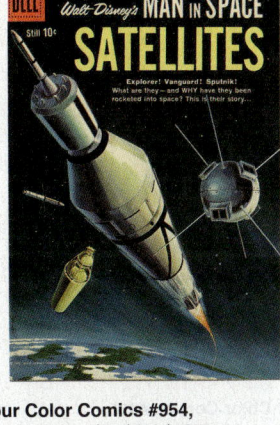
❏ **Four Color Comics #954,** February 1959. - **$8 $24 $105**

❏ **Four Color Comics #965,** January 1959. - **$6 $18 $65**

❏ **Four Color Comics #948,** November 1958. - **$6 $18 $70**

❏ **Four Color Comics #960,** December 1958. - **$13 $39 $195**

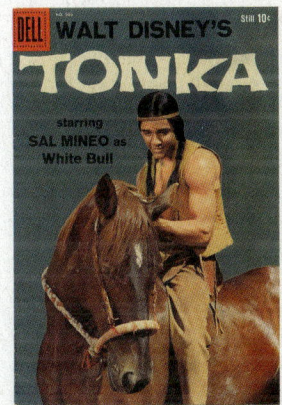
❏ **Four Color Comics #966,** January 1959. - **$10 $30 $130**

❏ **Four Color Comics #952,** November 1958. - **$6 $18 $70**

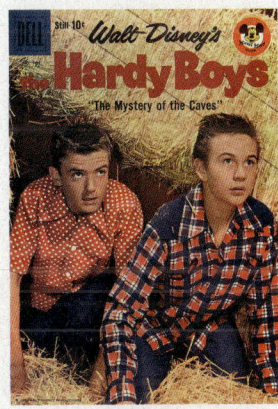
❏ **Four Color Comics #964,** January 1959. - **$10 $30 $140**

❏ **Four Color Comics #973,** May 1959. - **$12 $36 $180**

FOUR COLOR COMICS

❑ Four Color Comics #976,
March 1959. - $13 $39 $195

❑ Four Color Comics #985,
May 1959. - $9 $27 $115

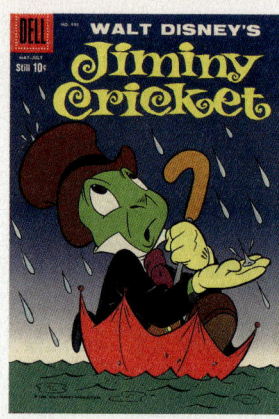

❑ Four Color Comics #989,
May 1959. - $8 $24 $95

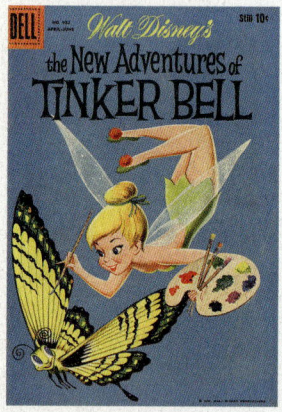

❑ Four Color Comics #982,
April 1959. - $9 $27 $120

❑ Four Color Comics #987,
July 1959. - $6 $18 $70

❑ Four Color Comics #995,
May 1959. - $7 $21 $90

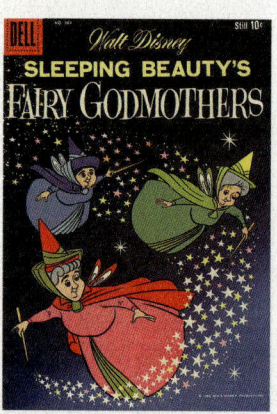

❑ Four Color Comics #984,
April 1959. - $10 $30 $130

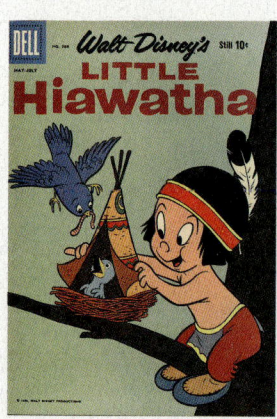

❑ Four Color Comics #988,
May 1959. - $6 $18 $65

❑ Four Color Comics #997,
June 1959. - $9 $27 $110

FOUR COLOR COMICS

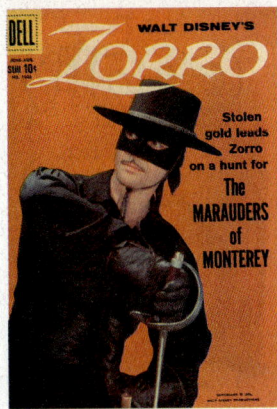
☐ **Four Color Comics #1003,** June 1959. - **$13 $39 $195**

☐ **Four Color Comics #1025,** August 1959. Barks-a. - **$19 $57 $280**

☐ **Four Color Comics #1039,** November 1959. - **$5 $15 $60**

☐ **Four Color Comics #1010,** July 1959. Barks-a. - **$14 $42 $215**

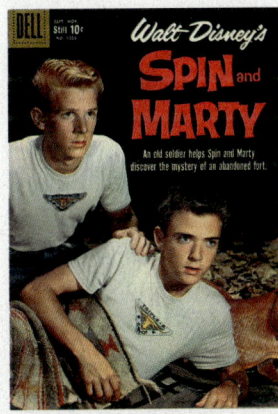
☐ **Four Color Comics #1026,** September 1959. - **$9 $27 $115**

☐ **Four Color Comics #1047,** November 1959. Barks-a. - **$19 $57 $290**

☐ **Four Color Comics #1024,** August 1959. - **$11 $33 $160**

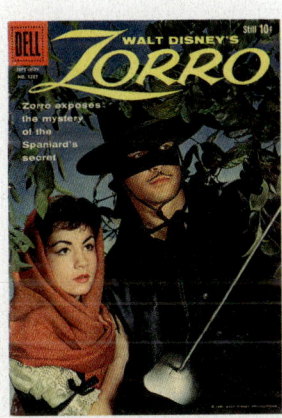
☐ **Four Color Comics #1037,** September 1959. - **$16 $48 $245**

☐ **Four Color Comics #1051,** August 1959. - **$10 $30 $135**

FOUR COLOR COMICS

❑ **Four Color Comics #1053,**
November 1959. - $6 $18 $70

❑ **Four Color Comics #1073,**
January 1960. Barks-a. - $14 $42 $215

❑ **Four Color Comics #1094,**
May 1960. - $6 $18 $70

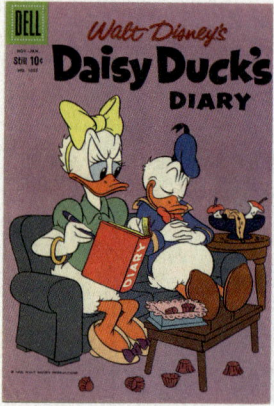

❑ **Four Color Comics #1055,**
November 1959. Barks-a. - $10 $30 $140

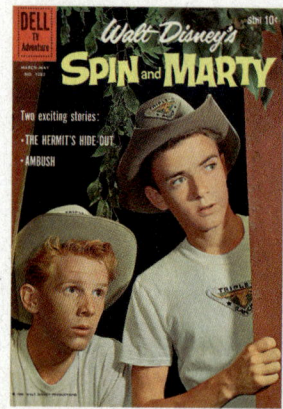

❑ **Four Color Comics #1082,**
March 1960. - $9 $27 $115

❑ **Four Color Comics #1095,**
April 1960. Barks-a. - $11 $33 $145

❑ **Four Color Comics #1057,**
November 1959. - $5 $15 $60

❑ **Four Color Comics #1092,**
March 1960. - $8 $24 $95

❑ **Four Color Comics #1099,**
May 1960. Barks-c. - $8 $24 $95

FOUR COLOR COMICS

❏ **Four Color Comics #1100,**
May 1960. - **$25 $75 $385**

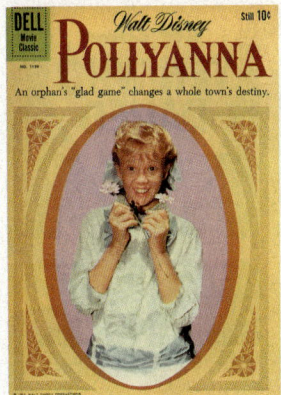
❏ **Four Color Comics #1129,**
August 1960. - **$9 $27 $115**

❏ **Four Color Comics #1143,**
November 1960. - **$5 $15 $60**

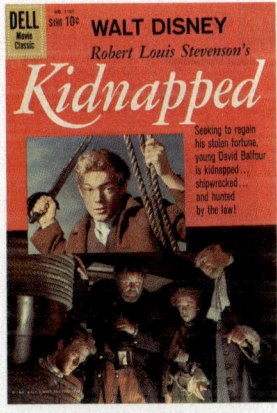
❏ **Four Color Comics #1101,**
May 1960. - **$8 $24 $95**

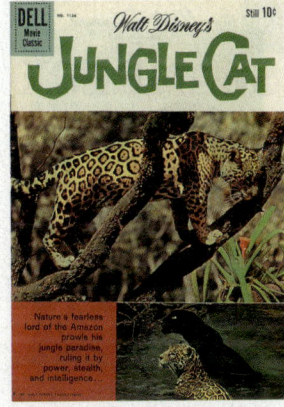
❏ **Four Color Comics #1136,**
November 1960. - **$8 $24 $95**

❏ **Four Color Comics #1149,**
November 1960. - **$6 $18 $70**

❏ **Four Color Comics #1109,**
August 1960. - **$15 $45 $230**

❏ **Four Color Comics #1140,**
October 1960. - **$8 $24 $95**

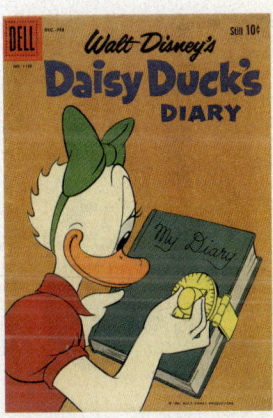
❏ **Four Color Comics #1150,**
December 1960. Barks-a. - **$10 $30 $140**

FOUR COLOR COMICS

☐ **Four Color Comics #1151,** November 1960. - **$5 $15 $60**

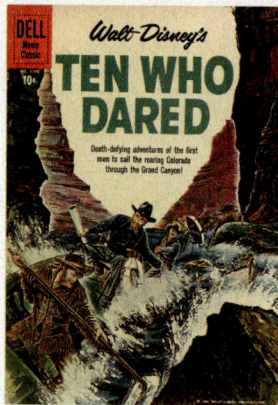

☐ **Four Color Comics #1178,** December 1960. - **$9 $27 $110**

☐ **Four Color Comics #1182,** May 1961. - **$6 $18 $65**

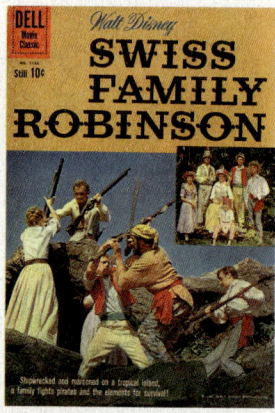

☐ **Four Color Comics #1156,** December 1960. - **$9 $27 $110**

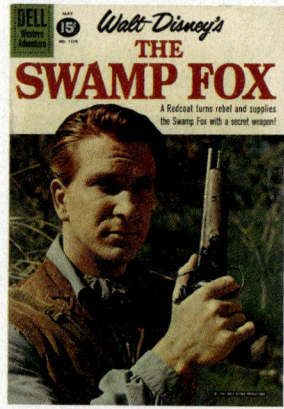

☐ **Four Color Comics #1179,** February 1961. - **$10 $30 $130**

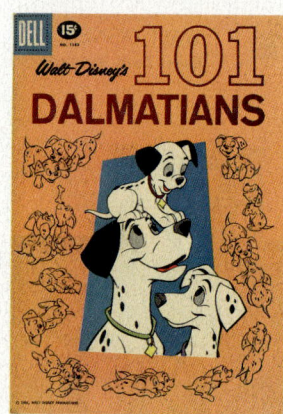

☐ **Four Color Comics #1183,** March 1961. - **$11 $33 $160**

☐ **Four Color Comics #1161,** February 1961. Barks-a. - **$14 $42 $215**

☐ **Four Color Comics #1181,** April 1961. - **$8 $24 $105**

☐ **Four Color Comics #1184,** May 1961. Barks-a. - **$11 $33 $145**

FOUR COLOR COMICS

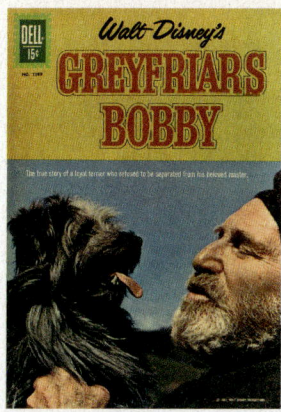
❏ Four Color Comics #1189,
November 1961. - **$8 $24 $105**

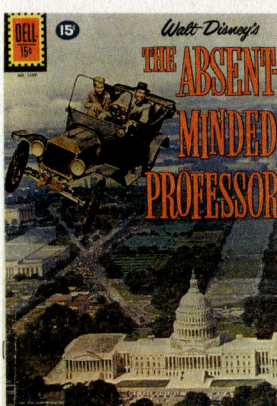
❏ Four Color Comics #1199,
April 1961. - **$9 $27 $120**

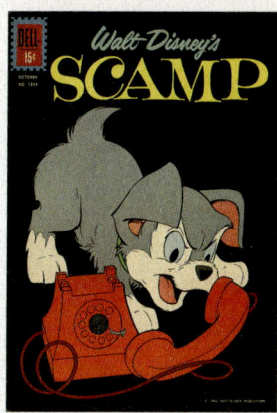
❏ Four Color Comics #1204,
July 1961. - **$5 $15 $60**

❏ Four Color Comics #1190,
November 1961. Barks-c. - **$9 $27 $120**

❏ Four Color Comics #1201,
August 1961. - **$6 $18 $70**

❏ Four Color Comics #1210,
August 1961. - **$10 $30 $140**

❏ Four Color Comics #1198, (rprnt of FC #1051),
February 1961. - **$8 $24 $95**

❏ Four Color Comics #1203,
March 1962. - **$6 $18 $75**

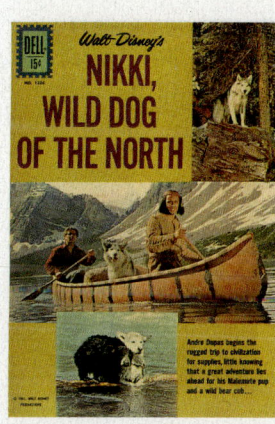
❏ Four Color Comics #1226,
September 1961. - **$6 $18 $75**

FOUR COLOR COMICS

❏ **Four Color Comics #1239,**
September 1961. Barks-c. - **$8 $24 $95**

❏ **Four Color Comics #1248,**
October 1961. - **$5 $15 $60**

❏ **Four Color Comics #1273,**
March 1962. - **$8 $24 $95**

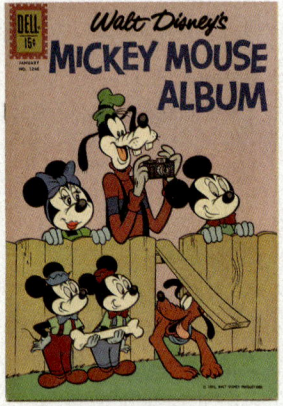
❏ **Four Color Comics #1246,**
November 1961. - **$5 $15 $60**

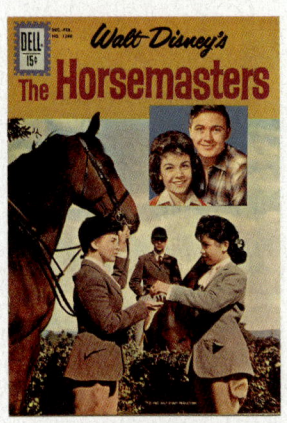
❏ **Four Color Comics #1260,**
November 1961. - **$14 $42 $215**

❏ **Four Color Comics #1279,**
January 1962. - **$6 $18 $65**

❏ **Four Color Comics #1247,**
November 1961. - **$6 $18 $70**

❏ **Four Color Comics #1267,**
November 1961. Barks-a. - **$9 $27 $110**

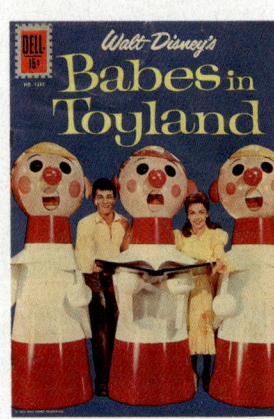
❏ **Four Color Comics #1282,**
January 1962. - **$15 $45 $230**

FUN AND FANCY FREE

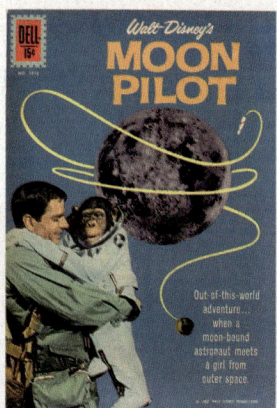

❏ Four Color Comics #1313, March 1962. - **$8 $24 $105**

❏ Gyro Gearloose 01329-207, May 1962. Likely intended to be published as Four Color Comics #1329. - **$7 $21 $80**

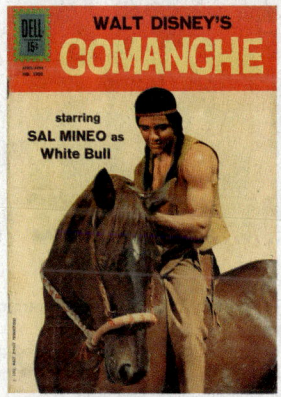

❏ Four Color Comics #1350, April 1962. - **$7 $21 $80**

The Fox and the Hound

Based on the 1967 book by Daniel Mannix, this full-length feature was released by Disney in July 1981. The picture centers on a bloodhound puppy who becomes friends with an orphaned fox cub. The film follows them as they get older and endure the trials and tribulations of growing apart. Finally, Copper the dog is now expected to hunt down his childhood friend the fox.

Veteran animators Frank Thomas and Ollie Johnston developed the main characters. What really makes this film important in the Disney canon is the influx of younger animators. Ironically, the film was delayed when some of those younger animators, such as Don Bluth and Gary Goldman, left to form their own company. By the time *The Fox and The Hound* was finished, the film had used twenty-four animators in total. Despite turmoil and delays, the film was a great success and even saw a theatrical re-release in 1988. The directors were Art Stevens, Ted Berman and Richard Rich. Vocal talent included Mickey Rooney, Kurt Russell, Corey Feldman and the great Pearl Bailey. The music from the film was a hit in its own right.

Merchandise included books, records and figures.

FOX-1

❏ FOX-1. "The Fox And The Hound" Cel, 1981. 12.5x16"cel with 5x6.5" image of Vixie. Also includes certificate of authenticity. Mint As Issued - **$325**

FOX-2

FOX-3

❏ FOX-2. Studio Christmas Card, 1981. Stiff glossy paper 5.25x7.75" card. - **$6 $15 $25**

❏ FOX-3. "Walt Disney Studios' Tiny Theater" Boxed Book Set, 1981. Golden Press. 2.5x5x8" tall sealed colorful box contains set of 12 miniature books, each 2x3". Similar to a 1950 set "Book Shelf Box." featuring some of the same titles while others have been changed to reflect current characters. Characters in this set are The Fox And The Hound, Mickey, Donald, Dumbo, Pablo the Penguin, Three Pigs, Pinocchio, Cinderella, Dopey, Bambi, Brer Rabbit, The Rescuers. - **$15 $30 $70**

Fun and Fancy Free

This feature-length film combined two featurettes. Neither was long enough to stand on its own as a full-length feature. The two, *Bongo* and *Mickey and the Beanstalk* are tied together by the narrative presence of Jiminy Cricket. Short live-action segments also appear, but the focus of the film is on the featurettes.

Jiminy introduces the *Bongo* cartoon by playing a Dinah Shore record. Later on, Jiminy is invited into the home of famed ventriloquist and radio star, Edgar Bergen. There, Jiminy meets Charlie McCarthy, Mortimer Snerd and Luana Patten. Bergen then begins to tell the story of Mickey and the Beanstalk as the cartoon begins to roll.

Mickey and the Beanstalk is one of the best examples of Disney using multiple-characters in a single cartoon. Joining Mickey are Goofy and Donald. With their respective personalities now imbedded in the audience's mind, they provide a thrilling and entertaining adventure together. Animators on the project included Ward Kimball, Les Clark and Fred Moore. The sequence marks a passing of the torch; partway through production, Walt Disney ceased to provide Mickey's voice, with sound effects man Jim MacDonald taking over.

Merchandise included books, records and sheet music. *Fun and Fancy Free* characters *Bongo* and *Lumpjaw* appear in *Four Color Comics* #706 and 886.

FUN AND FANCY FREE

FFF-1

❏ **FFF-1. Disney Studio Christmas Card,**
1947. Stiff paper card 7.25x8". - **$40 $80 $150**

FFF-2

FFF-3

❏ **FFF-2. "Fun And Fancy Free" Fan Card,**
1947. Stiff paper 7.25x9.25" two-sided card. - **$25 $50 $80**

❏ **FFF-3. "Fun And Fancy Free" Lobby Card,**
1947. RKO Pictures, Inc. Card is 11x14" original issue. Card #7 from set. - **$25 $55 $125**

FFF-4

❏ **FFF-4. "Mickey And The Beanstalk From Fun And Fancy Free" Book/ Record Set,**
1947. Capitol Records. 10.5x12" thick cardboad album cover from "Record Reader" series contains set of three 78 rpm records "Told By Johnny Mercer To Luana Patten And Bobby Driscoll." The bound-in, 40-page book includes photos of them, text and illustrations. - **$25 $50 $150**

FFF-5

❏ **FFF-5. "Fun And Fancy Free" Sheet Music,**
1947. Santly-Joy, Inc. 9x12". - **$10 $20 $50**

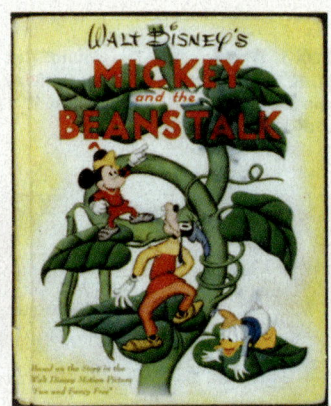
FFF-6

❏ **FFF-6. "Mickey And The Beanstalk" Hardcover,**
1947. Grosset & Dunlap. 7x8.25" with 32 pages. - **$40 $80 $175**

FFF-7

❏ **FFF-7. "The Rexall Magazine,"**
1947. Stiff paper 7.5x10" 16-page newsprint publication issued to customers of Rexall drugstores. Features a two-page article on the "Mickey And The Beanstalk" sequence of the Disney musical. - **$6 $15 $30**

FFF-8

❏ **FFF-8. Bongo And Lulubelle Ceramic Figurine,**
c. 1947. Figure is 1.75x3.75x4" tall marked "Made In Japan." Probably unauthorized but great likenesses. - **$25 $50 $85**

GOOFY

FFF-9

☐ **FFF-9. "Mickey And The Beanstalk Card Game,"**
c. 1947. Pepys. 2.5x3.5x.75" deep box contains English game of 44 cards plus 2.25x20.75" long beanstalk folder. - **$35 $75 $150**

Gnome-Mobile

Once again Disney turned to director Robert Stevenson to bring a live-action fantasy film to life. The cast may look a little familiar to the modern viewer, as Stevenson utilized the same two children that he had featured in *Mary Poppins* (1964), Mathew Garber and Karen Dotrice. Disney was hoping to capture the magic of *Poppins* once again by also featuring the creators of the *Poppins* musical score, Richard M. and Robert B. Sherman.

With Walter Brennan in a dual role, the film tells the story of a millionaire lumberman. Together with his grandchildren, he meets the last two known gnomes. They set off all together in the Gnome-Mobile, hoping to find some additional gnomes. The movie was taken from a story by Upton Sinclair. Stevenson excelled at directing family films like *The Gnome-Mobile* and he wasn't above including some wild slapstick.

Merchandise included books and records.

GNM-1

☐ **GNM-1. "Gnome-Mobile" Premium Action Toy,**
1967. Cains Potato Chips. 3.5x5.5" cellophane pack contains hard plastic toy from series of three different. Design on pack front shows the three toys "Gnome-Mobile," "Walking Gnome," "Tumbling Gnome." The example shown is the Gnome-Mobile. Each Loose - **$5 $10 $20** Near Mint Sealed - **$35**

GNM-2

☐ **GNM-2. "The Gnome-Mobile" Movie Poster,**
1976. 27x41" glossy full color re-release poster. - **$6 $12 $25**

Goofy

Goofy began his long history as an unnamed, bearded extra in the 1932 cartoon *Mickey's Revue*. His function in the cartoon was comedy relief. As Mickey's troupe performed on stage, Goofy sat in the audience and laughed. That laugh was supplied by animator and former circus clown Pinto Colvig. The laugh made the character instantly connect with the audience. It stood out so much that the character was swiftly reused in more major roles.

As time went on, Goofy became a regular in the Mickey Mouse comic strip where he was initially given the name Dippy Dawg. Animator Art Babbitt saw greater potential for the character and gave him more substantial screen time in the 1935 short *Mickey's Service Station*. With time, the character's design changed. He went from being an unclothed dog to a tall humanoid in sweater and long trousers. His name changed, too. Within Disney, Dippy was known from the start as "The Goof". By 1934, the moniker was being used publicly. In 1935, the new nickname Goofy began to be adopted. In 1939, the name change was complete with the cartoon release of *Goofy and Wilbur*.

From 1939 to 1966, Disney made forty-eight cartoons starring Goofy. During this time, his character underwent a bit of a metamorphosis. At first, he took the role of sportsman in the famous "How To" cartoons. That series of shorts focused on everyday activities like golfing or going to the gym. In the postwar years, Goofy became featured more as a suburban everyman. Eventually he acquired a son in *Fathers Are People* (1951). Much later, the son was named Max.

Throughout his career, Goofy also appeared in many cartoons with Mickey and Donald. They recently appeared together in the direct-to-video release *The Three Musketeers* (2004).

Merchandise for Goofy is extremely varied. Items include a Goofy watch that runs backwards. One of the bestselling items at the Disney theme parks is the Goofy hat, the brim of which simulates his nose. Goofy appears in *Four Color Comics* #468, 562, 627, 658, 702, 747, 802, 857, 899, 952, 987, 1053, 1094, 1149 and 1201.

GFY-1

GFY-2

☐ **GFY-1. Goofy Pencil Drawing From Mickey's Fire Brigade,**
1935. Sheet of animation paper is 9.5x12" with 7x10" multi-character action-packed image. Features Mickey Mouse, Donald Duck, Clarabelle Cow and Goofy. - **$200 $400 $600**

GOOFY

❑ **GFY-2. Mickey, Donald, And Goofy Pencil Drawing From Mickey's Fire Brigade,** 1935. Animation paper is 9.5x12" with 3.5x7" image of action sequence. - **$150 $300 $500**

GFY-3

❑ **GFY-3. Goofy Pencil Drawing From Mickey's Amateurs,** 1937. Sheet of animation paper is 9.5x12" with 5x7.5" image by Art Babbitt. - **$75 $150 $300**

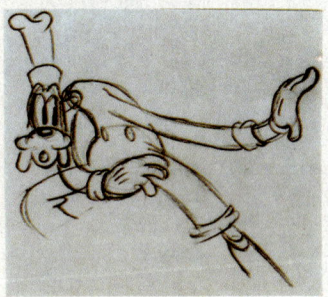
GFY-4

GFY-5

❑ **GFY-4. Pencil Drawing,** 1937. Animation paper is 10x12" centered by 4x5" image from 'Magician Mickey' cartoon short. No. "51" from a numbered sequence. - **$75 $150 $300**

❑ **GFY-5. One-Man Band Pencil Drawing,** 1937. Animation paper is 10x12" centered by 4.5x7.75" image of Goofy as multiple musician from 'Mickey's Amateurs' film short. No. "41" from a numbered sequence. - **$100 $200 $350**

GFY-6

GFY-7

❑ **GFY-6. "The Goof" Athletic Series Glass,** 1937. 5.5" tall from set of six Disney characters depicted playing sports. - **$110 $225 $325**

❑ **GFY-7. "Goof" Glass,** 1937. Painted image tumbler is 4" tall from set of glasses depicting Disney characters with musical instruments. - **$110 $225 $325**

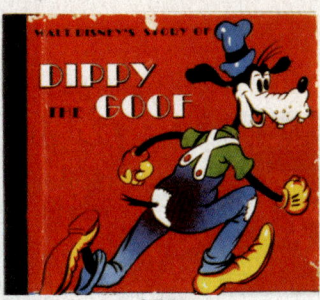
GFY-8

❑ **GFY-8. "Story Of Dippy The Goof" Book,** 1938. Whitman. 4.75x5.5" hardcover, 96 pages, from "1066" series based on various Disney characters. - **$25 $50 $75**

GFY-9

❑ **GFY-9. "Goofy And Wilbur 1939 Walt Disney All Star Parade" Glass,** 1939. Glass is 4.25" tall. - **$20 $40 $65**

GFY-10

❑ **GFY-10. Goofy "Sunoco Oil" Ink Blotter,** 1939. 4x7.25". - **$15 $30 $65**

GOOFY

GFY-11

GFY-12

❏ **GFY-13. "Goof" Glass,**
1930s. 4.25" tall with image in dark green of kneeling "Goof." Matching style to those from the dairy series although not part of that set. - **$30 $60 $100**

GFY-14

GFY-15

GFY-13

❏ **GFY-11. Oil Company Blotter Card,**
1939. Sunoco. "Winter Oil" 4x7" cardboard. - **$15 $30 $60**

❏ **GFY-12. Goofy Miniature Bisque,**
1930s. Smallest of only two 1930s Goofy bisques. 1-7/8" tall. Japan. - **$20 $35 $60**

GFY-16

❏ **GFY-14. Multi-Page Christmas Card,**
1946. Hallmark. 5x6" eight-page folder with Goofy situation art on each page. - **$15 $30 $50**

❏ **GFY-15. "Goofy's Paint Box,"**
1940s. Lithographed tin box is 2.5x6.25x.25" deep. Marked "Made In England." - **$35 $75 $135**

❏ **GFY-16. "How To Fish" Australian Movie Poster,**
1940s. Simmons Ltd. Lithograph, Sydney, 13.25x30" insert poster for 1942 short distributed by RKO Radio Pictures. - **$80 $165 $300**

GFY-17

❏ **GFY-17. "How To Ride A Horse" Publicity Photo,**
1940s. Photo is 8x10" glossy for cartoon film starring Goofy as equestrian hopeful. - **$8 $12 $25**

GFY-18

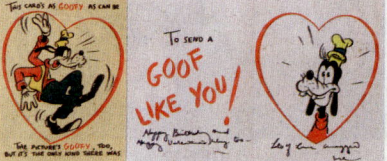

GFY-19

355

GOOFY

❏ **GFY-18. Goofy And Pluto Salt And Pepper Set,**
1940s. Painted and glazed ceramic shakers 2x4x4" tall with cork stoppers. Marked "Made In Japan" but no Disney markings. - **$25 $50 $80**

❏ **GFY-19. Greeting Card,**
1940s. "Hallmark Rufftex Card" 3.75x4.75" filament paper. - **$8 $15 $30**

GFY-20

❏ **GFY-20. Goofy Catalin Plastic Pencil Sharpener,**
1940s. 1" round. Scalloped edge style. - **$20 $40 $85**

GFY-21

GFY-22

❏ **GFY-21. Pencil Drawing,**
1950. Sheet of animation paper is 10x12" centered right by 4x5" drawing from 'Hold That Pose' cartoon. - **$100 $200 $300**

❏ **GFY-22. "Goofy Walking Gardener" Tin Wind-up,**
c. 1950. Marx, Made In England. Toy is 4.25x7.5x8.25" tall. Box is 7.75x8.25x4.25" deep. Box - **$60 $1250 $250**
Toy - **$110 $325 $650**

GFY-23

❏ **GFY-23. "Goofy Dots" Book,**
1953. Whitman. Pencil activity book, 8.25x10.75 with 128 pages. - **$8 $15 $30**

GFY-24

❏ **GFY-24. "Goofy And The Tiger Hunt" Book,**
1954. Whitman. 5.5x6.5" "Tell-A-Tale" hardcover, 28 pages. - **$8 $15 $30**

GFY-25

❏ **GFY-25. "Goofy Golf Cart" Concept Art,**
1957. Sheet of vellum paper is 7x9.5" centered by 5x7" drawing in colored pencils then signed by "Disney Legend" Al Konetzni, creator of numerous Disney toys and merchandise. Toy design is notated "Eccentric Action-Tilts Back/Spills Out Miniature Golf Clubs." Unique, Near Mint - **$225**

GFY-26

❏ **GFY-26. Mexican Oversized Lobby Card With Goofy,**
1950s. Card is 12.75x16.5" for compilation film of Disney movies Saludos Amigos and The Three Caballeros, newly released by RKO Radio Pictures under compilation title "Recuerdos de Walt Disney." - **$8 $15 $30**

GFY-27

❏ **GFY-27. Area Rug,**
1950s. Rug is 21x41" woven fabric. - **$40 $85 $150**

GOOFY

GFY-28

❏ **GFY-28. Goofy Unicyclist,**
1950s. Line Mar. "Made In Japan," 6" tin windup.
- **$125 $300 $600**

GFY-29

❏ **GFY-29. Goofy And Donald Duck Plate,**
1950s. Marx. 4" diameter china from tea set. Marx logo is on underside. - **$5 $10 $15**

GFY-30

❏ **GFY-30. "How To Draw Goofy/A Walt Disney Character Model Guide,"**
1950s. Spiral bound book is 8.5x11" with 16 one-sided pages plus stiff paper cover. Sold at The Art Corner at Disneyland. - **$20 $40 $80**

GFY-31

GFY-32

❏ **GFY-31. "Goofy" Hand Puppet,**
1950s. Gund. 10.25" tall with fabric body and soft vinyl head. - **$18 $35 $60**

❏ **GFY-32. Goofy Wind-Up,**
1950s. Marx. 3x4x8" tall hard plastic with built-in key. - **$35 $65 $125**

GFY-33

❏ **GFY-33. "Super Goof" Comic Book,**
1966. K.K. Publications Inc. Gold Key Comic #3 for month of May. - **$3 $10 $30**

GFY-34

GFY-35

❏ **GFY-34. Goofy Vinyl Figure,**
1968. Dakin. Poseable 8.5" tall. - **$10 $20 $40**

❏ **GFY-35. Poseable Figure,**
1960s. Marx. 7" tall figure with hard plastic body, vinyl-covered wire arms and legs for posing, fabric outfit. - **$15 $30 $50**

GOOFY

GFY-36

❑ **GFY-36. Candy Dispenser,**
1960s. Pez. 4.25" tall hard plastic figural variety with face that has removable teeth but molded nose. - **$25 $50 $85**

GFY-37

❑ **GFY-37. Push Puppets,**
1960s. Two elastic-jointed hard plastic figures on base with inner push plunger. Earlier is Kohner Bros. 3" tall "Mini-Puppet," 1960s. Second variety is Gabriel 5" tall, copyright 1977.
Kohner (3") - **$25 $50 $100**
Gabriel (5") - **$5 $10 $20**

GFY-38

GFY-39

❑ **GFY-38. Goofy Marx Friction Antique Automobile,**
1960s. 2x4x3.25" tall hard plastic toy by Marx. - **$15 $30 $60**

❑ **GFY-39. "Goofy The Sportcar Driver" Toy,**
1960s. Marx Elm Toys. 1.75" long hard plastic free-wheeling "M.G. Midget". Box - **$8 $12 $25**
Toy - **$10 $20 $40**

GFY-40

❑ **GFY-40. "Goofy The Old-Fashioned Car Driver" Toy,**
1960s. Marx Elm Toys. 1.5" long hard plastic free-wheeling "1910 Ford" holding vinyl upper torso of Goofy as driver. Complete with box and foil sticker. Box - **$8 $12 $25**
Toy - **$8 $15 $30**

GFY-41

❑ **GFY-41. "Disneyland" Goofy Giant Pencil,**
c. 1960s. Sharpened wood pencil is 14.75" long with four-colored tip. - **$6 $12 $25**

GFY-42

❑ **GFY-42. Goofy Head Bank,**
1971. Play Pal Plastics Inc. 5x9x10.5" tall molded hard vinyl. - **$10 $20 $40**

GFY-43

❑ **GFY-43. "Goofy Helbros" Backwards Watch,**
1972. Original issue which is scarce due to its short production run. 3.25x4.25x2" deep hard plastic case contains watch with 1.25" diameter metal case. Box And Related - **$50 $100 $200**
Watch Only - **$150 $300 $600**

GOOFY

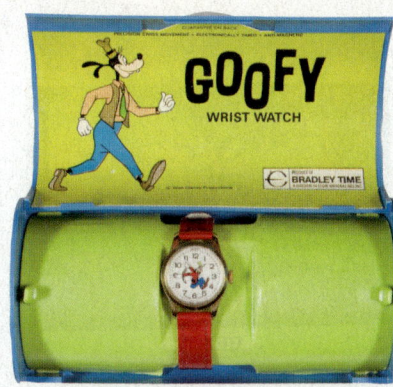

GFY-46

GFY-49

❏ **GFY-48. Goofy Cel,** 1970s. 10.5x12.5" with 3x6.25" image. Numbered "G23." - **$50 $100 $175**

❏ **GFY-49. Goofy And Mad Hatter Cel,** 1970s. Acetate sheet is 10.5x12.5" with large 7.5x9" painted image for Eastern Airlines animated TV ad. No. "G60" from a numbered sequence. - **$85 $150 $250**

GFY-44

❏ **GFY-46. "Tricky Trike" Toy Carded,** 1977. Gabriel. 5x8" display card holding 5" tall hard plastic tricycle toy. Carded - **$12 $25 $40**

GFY-47

GFY-50

❏ **GFY-44. "Goofy Bradley" Wrist Watch,** -1975. Bradley. 5.5" long hard plastic case. Contains 1" diameter metal case and vinyl band watch and insert card. Box - **$25 $50 $100** Watch - **$100 $200 $300**

❏ **GFY-47. Goofy And Mad Hatter Cel,** 1970s. 10.5x12.5" cel with 8.5x10" image from Eastern Airlines commerical. - **$75 $135 $200**

GFY-45

GFY-48

GFY-51

❏ **GFY-45. "Goofy Maxi-Puppet,"** 1975. 2x2.75x5.5" hard plastic figure attached to base by Gabriel. - **$10 $25 $45**

GOOFY

❑ **GFY-50. Goofy "Walt Disney World" Composition Bobbing Head,**
1970s. Figure is 2.5x2.5x7.5" tall marked "Japan." - **$25 $40 $100**

❑ **GFY-51. Drummer Figurine,**
1970s. Painted and glazed figure is 3" tall. - **$6 $12 $20**

GFY-52

GFY-54

GFY-56

❑ **GFY-56. Sport Goofy Cel,**
c. 1983. Acetate sheet is 10.5x12.5" with 3.5x5.5" cel image with laser background. No. "A-77" from a numbered sequence. Mint As Issued - **$140**

❑ **GFY-52. Dakin Poseable Figure Bagged,**
1970s. Painted vinyl figure is 8.75" tall with fabric outfit and cardboard tag. By Dakin although unmarked as issued in the mid-1970s when Disney was doing its own distribution marked "Walt Disney Distributing Co." Bag And Toy - **$5 $10 $15**
Figure Only - **$10 $20 $40**

❑ **GFY-53. Booklet And Postcard,**
c. 1980. Booklet is 4x9" from 1980 titled "Copyright Protection For Disney Works" with eight pages of related text and Goofy illustrations, plus 5x7" oversized postcard copyright 1979. Each - **$3 $6 $12**

❑ **GFY-54 "Sport Goofy" Lunch Box With Thermos,**
1983. 7x8x4" deep metal box with 6.5" plastic thermos by Aladdin. Box - **$15 $30 $60**
Bottle - **$10 $20 $35**

GFY-57

GFY-55

GFY-53

❑ **GFY-55. Italian Large Deluxe Vehicle Toy Boxed,**
1983. Burago of Italy. 7.5x14x6.25" deep illustrated box containing 10.5" long elaborately detailed diecast metal and plastic free-wheeling replica of antique automobile with vinyl Goofy figure as driver. Accessory piece is a trailer luggage cart. Short production run. Boxed - **$60 $125 $235**

GFY-58

THE GREMLINS

◻ **GFY-57. Goofy Figurine,**
1985. Goebel. 2.5x3.25x6.25" tall. - **$35 $65 $135**

◻ **GFY-58. Cel Painted Background,**
1980s. Acetate sheet is 10.5x12.5" with 5.5x6.5" painted image on hand-painted background of spaceship interior for a Disney TV show. Complete cel text is "Engines All Fire" if properly aligned on background. - **$100 $200 $325**

GFY-59

GFY-60

◻ **GFY-59. Goofy Serigraph,**
1980s. Acetate sheet is 10.75x14" centered by 5.5x6" painted image of him as golfer over laser background scene of fairway and trees. Art is replicated from 1944 short "How To Play Golf" and has "Walt Disney Company" authentication seal. Mint - **$65**

◻ **GFY-60. "Sport Goofy" Inflatable Figure,**
1980s. 7x15x16" tall inflatable vinyl figure of Goofy with "Magic Kingdom On Ice" logo sticker on back. - **$10 $25 $50**

GFY-61

◻ **GFY-61. "Goofy" Backward Watch,**
c. 1990. "Pedre" re-issue of 1972 wristwatch by Helbros. Dial image is Goofy whose hands run backward and point at the numerals which also appear in reverse order. Watch is battery-operated and comes in original Pedre 2x9.5" plastic display case. Mint Boxed - **$235**

GFY-62

◻ **GFY-62. Goofy As Roman Guard Ceramic Figure,**
1990s. China. 6.25" tall. - **$5 $10 $15**

GFY-63

GFY-64

◻ **GFY-63. Goofy Paddle Ball,**
2000. From Tootsietoy. - **$20**

◻ **GFY-64. Goofy Bobblehead,**
2003. - **$22**

The Gremlins

The World War II era was a fertile time for the invention of new myths, forms of slang, folklore and legends. Some of these new ideas spread quickly from one culture to another and than entered the language of the world. The idea of gremlins – small, trouble-making supernatural saboteurs – sounds enough like a traditional folklore trope that one might assume it came from the Brothers Grimm or a Russian fairy tale. In truth, gremlin lore first emerged in the British Royal Air Force. As conceived in pilots' imaginations, they were unseen little sprites who gathered their jollies specifically by sabotaging aircraft.

During the war Walt Disney got word of a book being written by children's author Roald Dahl, then an RAF pilot. Disney thought that the mischievous little creatures – who appeared to be more like fairies or leprechauns than trolls – might make a good subject for an animated feature. Disney bought a controlling interest in Dahl's project before the book was completed. Thanks to some very successful PR, the legend of gremlins spread throughout the United States.

Dahl's book centers on an RAF pilot named Gus. When Gus crash-lands, he meets a gremlin who adopts his name: Gremlin Gus. This opens the door to the world of the gremlins, sprites whose aircraft sabotage is explained as a defense of the grounds where their enchanted forest once stood. Female gremlins were called Fifinellas; genderless young gremlins were Widgets.

As Disney's planned feature film developed, its story was published in the December 1942 issue of Cosmopolitan. When Dahl's book followed the Cosmopolitan feature into print, the cover featured Disney's name in larger type than the author's. The look of the characters had been developed by Bill Justice, one of Disney's best animators. Justice also created most of the illustrations for the book.

Anticipating the release of its film in production, Disney made several attempts to establish a merchandising base for its gremlin characters, authorizing dolls, puppets and at least one puzzle. In addition, the Disney Gremlins were featured in a Look magazine Life Savers ad.

The next step was to bring the characters to comics. Western Publishing's first Disney gremlin tale, a dialogue-heavy six-page adaptation of Dahl's book, appeared in Dell's War Heroes 4 (April-June 1943), a non-Disney anthology title. From there, the Gremlins went on to a monthly two-page feature in Walt Disney's Comics and Stories. Initially drawn by Vivie Risto (WDC&S 33, June 1943), this series began as a talky, War Heroes-like Dahl adaptation; but one issue

THE GREMLINS

into the project, plans evidently changed. The new concept was to promote the single character of Gremlin Gus more than the film as a whole. This involved a new pantomime approach and a new artist, former Disney staffer Walt Kelly. Kelly produced a steady stream of dialogue-free stories with Gus and the Widgets from WDC&S 34 (1943) to 41 (1944). Kelly is better known today as the creator of the comic strip Pogo; nevertheless, his fans consider the Gremlin stories to be a high-water mark in his long career.

Unfortunately for Disney, their effort to promote gremlins was working too well; production of the feature film dragged, whereas advance publicity had created a fad that was already peaking. The public appeared to be going "gremlin-crazy" – but too soon to benefit a film that might still be one or two years away.

In addition, there were ownership problems with the concept of gremlins. Though Disney could trademark individual characters like Gremlin Gus, they could not register the word "gremlin" or keep gremlins from being used by other creative content producers. Count Basie had recorded a song called "Dance of the Gremlins," and there was even a short-lived, non-Disney gremlin newspaper comic strip. When Warner Brothers made two cartoons featuring gremlins (both directed by Bob Clampett), Disney's animation department dropped the idea of finishing its feature film.

From some perspectives, this was for the best; Dahl was unhappy with much of the Disney gremlin material that he saw. Dahl would find success on his own with the books Charlie and the Chocolate Factory and James and the Giant Peach, both of which were made into successful films – the latter by Disney.

With the success of Joe Danzi's 1984 Gremlins film and its 1990 sequel, many believed the original Dahl/Disney concept was dead. Almost everyone felt that the public would forever associate the concept with that live action adventure. It took an adventurous publisher to show the experts that they were wrong.

In 2006, Dark Horse Publishing – working closely with Disney – reprinted Dahl's original book, complete with a new introduction by Leonard Maltin. The new edition was a success, capturing the attention of both those who remembered the original and those who were too young to know that Disney's Gremlins had ever existed. In addition, Dark Horse has introduced a new series of figurines to commemorate Disney's Gremlins and plans to base a new comics mini-series around the sprites. The work of Dark Horse strives to be accurate to both Dahl's vision and the original Disney art that fans have grown to love.

❑ GRE-1. "The Gremlins" Hardcover With Dust Jacket,
1943. Random House. 9x11.25" with 56 pages.
Dust Jacket - **$100 $250 $500**
Book - **$100 $250 $500**

❑ GRE-2. Gremlins Glow-In-The-Dark Picture,
c. 1943. 8.75x10.75" original wood frame with glass over picture. Depicts female gremlin Fifinella with three babies known as Widgets.
- **$65 $135 $200**

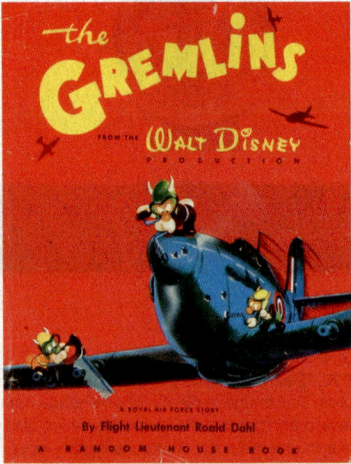

GRE-1

GRE-2

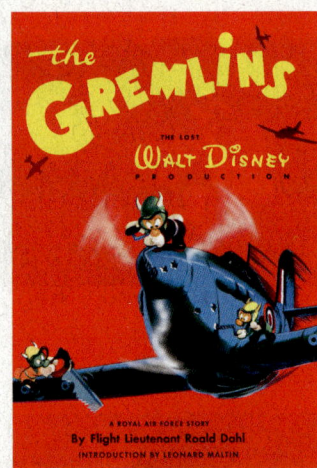

GRE-3

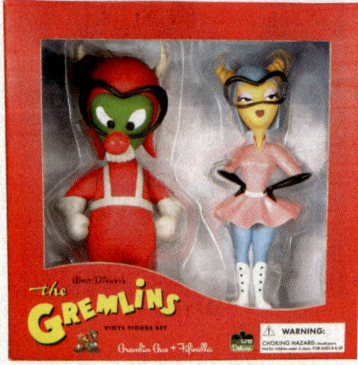

GRE-4

THE GREMLINS

GRE-7

☐ **GRE-3. Gremlins Hardcover Book,**
2006. Dark Horse. Reprints in slightly different format the 1943 Random House storybook. Can be easily identified against the original by size and notations ("From the Lost Walt Disney Production" and "Introduction by Leonard Maltin"). Launch point for Dark Horse's revival of The Gremlins. - **$13**

☐ **GRE-4. Gremlins Vinyl Figure Set,**
2006. Dark Horse. Two-pack of 7" vinyl figures features Gremlin Gus and Fifinella. - **$35**

GRE-5

GRE-8

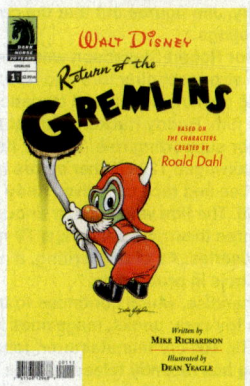

GRE-6

GRE-9

☐ **GRE-5. Gremlin with Pipe Statue,**
2007. Dark Horse. From the pages of the original Gremlins book, statue features Gremlin looking into a tobacco pipe. 3.5" tall. - **$45**

☐ **GRE-6. Return of the Gremlins #1,**
2007. Dark Horse. Written by Dark Horse Comics founder Mike Richardson and illustrated by Dean Yeagle, modern day sequel to the original Gremlins story. Published in comic book format. - **$3**

☐ **GRE-7. Gremlins Gus PVC Set,**
2006. Dark Horse. Roald Dahl and Walt Disney's Gremlins (1943) was never made, but the story survived. This set features lead character Gremlin Gus and two others. Produced by Gentle Giant Studios and issued by Dark Horse. - **$15**

☐ **GRE-8. Gremlins Jamface PVC Set,**
2006. Dark Horse. Features three Gremlins characters. - **$15**

☐ **GRE-9. Gremlins Rufus PVC Set,**
2006. Dark Horse. Features three Gremlins characters. - **$15**

HARDY BOYS, THE

The Hardy Boys

Based on the popular books first written by Leslie McFarlane (working under the pseudonym Franklin W. Dixon), two serialized Hardy Boys stories were featured on the *Mickey Mouse Club* TV show in 1956 and 1957. Tim Considine and Tommy Kirk starred as the brothers Frank and Joe Hardy. The first series, *The Mystery of Applegate Treasure*, ran for twenty episodes. It was based on the Hardy Boys book *The Tower Treasure*. The second series was original and not based on any pre-existing Hardy Boys book. Titled *The Mystery of Ghost Farm*, it ran fifteen episodes.

Merchandise included Dell comic books (Four Color Comics #760, 830, 887 and 964) and a premium doubloon ring that featured a secret compartment. It was available through Weather-Bird Shoes.

HDB-1

❑ **HDB-1. "Weather Bird Shoes" Premium Ring,** 1956. Plastic ring with inset silver luster medallion picturing Joe and Frank. Medallion pops out and underneath is a red on tan cardboard disk with one side showing the company logo while the opposite side has treasure directions. - **$40 $75 $150**

HDB-2

❑ **HDB-2. "Walt Disney's Mickey Mouse Club Magazine,"** 1957. Volume 2 #2 by Western Printing, 8.25x11.5". 42 pages. - **$12 $25 $50**

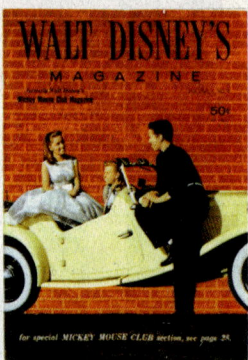

HDB-3

HDB-4

❑ **HDB-3. Walt Disney's Magazine,** 1957. Volume 2, #5 containing Hardy Boys story. - **$10 $20 $45**

❑ **HDB-4. "Hardy Boys Treasure Game,"** 1957. Parker Brothers. Board is 16.5x16.5" with colorful illustrations of the Hardy Boys investigating a case. Other parts include message cards and small die-cut cardboard pieces representing gold bags and doubloons in 9x17x1.5" deep box. - **$20 $65 $135**

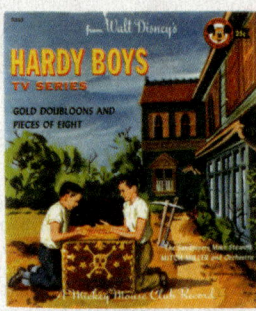

HDB-5

❑ **HDB-5. "Hardy Boys TV Series Record,** c. 1957. 6.75x7.5" paper sleeve with record marked "Simon & Schuster." - **$20 $40 $75**

Herbie the Love Bug

The Volkswagen with a mind of its own made its big screen debut in a full-length live-action feature that Disney released in March 1969. Race car driver Jim Douglas (Dean Jones) finds the Volkswagen and, with it, wins several races. However, the car will drive itself away when it feels unloved, which causes all kinds of problems. Eventually, Jim figures out that the car has actual feelings.

Director Robert Stevenson was one of Disney's strongest directors and he excelled at dealing with the action and slapstick that fuels the film. Buddy Hackett is a hoot in a very major supporting role. The car itself is a 1962 Volkswagen 1200. Other actors include Michele Lee and race car driver Andy Granatelli. The film was popular enough to spawn three theatrical sequels, a TV movie and a TV series. As of this writing, a new theatrical film is in production.

Merchandise, which continues to this day, includes toy cars, books, magazines and model kits. Toy car manufacturer Johnny Lightning has recently released three new cars based on the original Herbie.

HERCULES

HLB-1

❏ **HLB-1. "The Love Bug" Paper Plates,** 1968. Pair of unopened packs, each containing eight identical 9" diameter plastic-coated paper plates by Beach Products. Near Mint Sealed Pack **$25**
Single Loose Plate **$1 $2 $3**

HLB-2

HRC-3

Hercules

Taken from Greek mythology, but given a very modern twist, this 1997 animated feature is notable for its fast-paced dialogue and for numerous cultural references that dot the script. The story concept recasts Hercules as a parallel to modern sports stars, complete with promotional contracts and an agent, Phil the satyr. Though a mortal, Hercules has tremendous strength and must deal with characters based on the original Greek gods, including Hades. The climactic scene involves the Hydra and is the film's animation highlight.

Hades, as portrayed by James Woods, drew comparisons to Robin Williams' take on the genie in *Aladdin*. Since both characters were very fast talkers and had most of the best lines in each picture, some similarities were inevitable.

Directed by Ron Clements and John Musker, *Hercules*' animation was heavily influenced by British artist Gerald Scarfe, who was brought in as an advisor. Music was written by David Zippel and Alan Menken. Vocal talent included Tate Donovan, Danny DeVito, Susan Egan and Rip Taylor.

Merchandise included books, action figures and fast food tie-ins.

HRC-1

❏ **HRC-1. "Hercules" Cast & Crew Premier Sweatshirt,** 1997. "Lee Heavyweight" adult size. - **$50 $100 $150**

HRC-2

❏ **HRC-2. "Hercules" Cast & Crew Premier Items,** 1997. Four Pieces. Pair of 3.5x5" laminated passes. World Premiere 2.75x5" ticket stub. "Megamotion" boxed set of six flicker cards. Each - **$3 $6 $12**

❏ **HRC-3. Disney Movie Promo Badges Including Hercules,** 1997. Glossy die-cut 3x4" stiff cardboard with bar pin attachment on backs. Six different Hercules character badges include: Hercules, Megara, Hades, Phil, The Muses, Pain/Panic. Each Shown - **$1 $2 $3**

HRC-4

❏ **HRC-4. Hercules Figurine Gift Set,** 1997. Applause. Features Megara, Hercules, Pegasus, Phil, Pain and Panic, and Hades. - **$20**

HRC-5

HRC-6

HLB-3

❏ **HLB-2. "Scorpion" Replica Vehicle,** 1977. By Polistil. 5x7.5x8" tall box contains 5.5" tall die cast metal and plastic replica of Herbie's car companion "Scorpion." Based on the film Herbie Goes To Monte Carlo. Near Mint Boxed **$60** Unboxed **$8 $20 $30**

❏ **HLB-3. "Herbie" Replica Vehicle,** 1970s. By Polistil. 1.5x4x1.5" tall die cast metal and plastic. Has small lever on one side that is pressed to separate front and back halves of the car as it did in the film. - **$12 $35 $65**

HERCULES

❑ **HRC-5. Megara Vinyl Bank,**
1997. Disney. - **$12**

❑ **HRC-6. Baby Hercules Plush Doll,**
1997. Disney. Plush version of Hercules as a baby. - **$15**

HRC-7

HRC-8

❑ **HRC-7. Hercules Collectible Plate,**
1997. McDonald's. Hercules pictured on plate. - **$5**

❑ **HRC-8. Zeus Collectible Plate,**
1997. McDonald's. Zeus pictured on plate. - **$5**

HRC-9

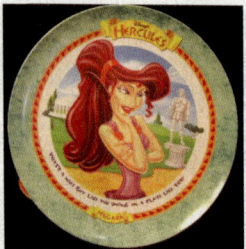
HRC-10

❑ **HRC-9. Pegasus Collectible Plate,**
1997. McDonald's. Pegasus pictured on plate. - **$5**

❑ **HRC-10. Megara Collectible Plate,**
1997. McDonald's. Megara pictured on plate. - **$5**

HRC-11

HRC-12

❑ **HRC-11. Phil Collectible Plate,**
1997. McDonald's. Phil pictured on plate. - **$5**

❑ **HRC-12. The Muses Collectible Plate,**
1997. McDonald's. The Muses pictured on plate. - **$5**

HRC-13

❑ **HRC-13. Hades Plush,**
1997. Disney Store. Plush version of Hades. - **$17**

HRC-14

❑ **HRC-14. Hades Signed Cel With Pencil Drawing,**
1990s. Acetate sheet is 10.5x12.5" with 6.5x9.5" image. Signed just above the character image in black Sharpie by James Woods who supplied the voice. "H-1" from a numbered series. Near Mint - **$210**

HRC-15

❑ **HRC-15. Hermex Signed Cel,**
1990s. 10.5x12.5" acetate sheet with 5x6" image. Signed at left center in Sharpie pen by Paul Schaffer who supplied the voice. Comes with laser background depicting forest scene and stone statue. #H-38 from a numbered sequence. Near Mint - **$135**

Horace Horsecollar

A cheerfully over-enthusiastic self-styled expert at everything, Horace made his first appearance in the 1929 Mickey Mouse cartoon *The Plowboy*. He appeared in twenty-five more shorts, but never starred in any shorts of his own. He was most often paired with Clarabelle Cow as a supporting player. His name is a perfect example of Disney's early penchant for alliteration.

Despite his low profile on screen, Horace was a major co-star in the Mickey Mouse newspaper strip, and as such was quite heavily merchandised during the strip's 1930s golden age.

Merchandise included magazines, books, cards and a bisque figure. As time went on, however, Horace's image disappeared from most marketing, leading to the popular belief that he had permanently been retired. That is not entirely true. Today, he continues to feature in dozens of Disney comic book stories, often headlining stories of his own.

HHC-3

HHC-6

❑ **HHC-6. Horace With Mickey "Express" Wagon Pull Toy,**
1930s. Fun-E-Flex. Wood toy about 3x6x4" tall accented by string reins and bristle tail on Horace. - **$775 $1600 $2650**

HHC-1

❑ **HHC-1. Mickey Mouse China Mug,**
c. 1931. Japan. Mug is 2.5" tall. Variety with location inscription as Canadian souvenir "Grand Falls, N.B." Image of Mickey riding Henry Horse taken from page 16 of 1931 book "The Adventures of Mickey Mouse." Henry later became Horace. Japan. - **$250 $500 $1000**

HHC-4

❑ **HHC-3. "Horace Horsecollar" Store Display Standee,**
1934. Made By Old King Cole, distributed by Kay Kamen. Molded 'laminite' 11x15.5x1.5" deep. - **$525 $1050 $1600**

❑ **HHC-4. "Horace Horsecollar" Musician Series Glass,**
1937. Glass is 4.25" tall. - **$75 $175 $250**

HHC-7

❑ **HHC-7. Horace Horsecollar Bisque,**
1930s. 3.5" tall. - **$40 $75 $135**

HHC-5

HHC-2

❑ **HHC-2. "Post Toasties Mickey Mouse Cut-Outs,"**
1934. Cardboard panel 8.5x12" consisting of complete back, right and left sides of a Post Toasties cereal box. Uncut - **$15 $25 $45**

❑ **HHC-5. Mickey Mouse/Horace Horsecollar Birthday Card,**
1938. Hallmark. 4.5x4.5" glossy slightly textured paper. - **$50 $100 $200**

HHC-8

❑ **HHC-8. Horace "Horse Collar" China Cup And Saucer,**
1930s. Patriot China. 2" tall cup and matching 5" diameter saucer. Cup - **$30 $65 $140** Saucer - **$15 $30 $60**

HORACE HORSECOLLAR

HHC-9   HHC-10

HHC-12

❏ **HHC-12. "Horace Horsecollar" Glass,**
1930s. Glass is 4-3/8" tall. - **$15 $30 $45**

HHC-13

❏ **HHC-13. "Horace Horsecollar" Glass,**
1930s. Glass is 4.25" tall. - **$50 $100 $150**

HHC-15

HHC-16

❏ **HHC-15. Horace Horsecollar Ashtray,**
1930s. 3x3x.5" china marked "Made In Bavaria."
- **$65 $125 $175**

❏ **HHC-16. Horace, Minnie, Mickey English Postcard,**
1930s. G. Delgado Ltd., London. 3.5x5.5". - **$15 $30 $65**

HHC-11

❏ **HHC-9. "Horace Horsecollar" Wood Jointed Figure,**
1930s. Fun-E-Flex. 6.5" with leather ears and bristle tail. - **$500 $1200 $2250**

❏ **HHC-10. Horace Horsecollar Bisque,**
1930s. Japan. 5" tall. - **$200 $400 $800**

❏ **HHC-11. Horace Horsecollar Doll,**
1930s. 27" tall. Unmarked, likely homemade possibly from Charlotte Clark McCall pattern.
- **$100 $200 $400**

HHC-14

❏ **HHC-14. Horace Horsecollar French Bank,**
1930s. 2.75x4.5x5.75" tall glazed ceramic unmarked but by French company Faiencerie d'Onnaing. - **$210 $425 $650**

HHC-17

❏ **HHC-17. Horace Horsecollar Doll,**
1950s. Lars of Italy. 6x7x19" tall. Stuffed doll made primarily of felt with wire inserts for posing. - **$600 $1200 $2500**

IN BEAVER VALLEY

The Hunchback of Notre Dame

Victor Hugo's original story was so dark and has such an adult theme that many people wondered what Disney was doing with the property. While Disney did sweeten the ending, the 1996 release remained fairly dark and somber. So much so that some complained it wasn't really appropriate for young children.

The lonely and disfigured Quasimodo is being mistreated by the evil Frollo, so he leaves the sanctuary of his bell tower at Notre Dame to wander the streets of Paris. There, he meets the beautiful Esmeralda who shows him kindness, possibly the first he has ever known. Sadly, Esmeralda loves Quasimodo's friend Phoebus. Eventually, Quasimodo sacrifices himself in order to help the two stay together.

The entire film has some of the most beautifully realized animation ever seen. The scenes of Paris are absolutely breathtaking and the choice of camera angles propels the story forward at all times. Directed by Gary Trousdale and Kirk Wise, the film included music from Stephen Schwartz and Alan Menken. They also wrote the hit song *Someday*. Vocal talent included Tom Hulce, Demi Moore, Kevin Kline and Tony Jay.

Merchandise included books, watches, premiums and fast food tie-ins.

HND-2

❏ **HND-2. "Sotheby's" Disney Art Auction Catalogue,**
1997. Full color 8.25x10.5" for "The Hunchback Of Notre Dame/James And The Giant Peach." - $3 $8 $15

HND-1

❏ **HND-1. "The Hunchback Of Notre Dame Cast And Crew World Premiere" Boxed Presentation,**
1996. Lucite display comes in box with title printed on the lid. Encased in display are two separate 35mm full color actual film frames, one from the opening title sequence, the other of the Huncback lifting Esmerelda over his head. Comes with 1.5x3.5" ticket stub for the New York premiere held at Ziegfeld Theater. MInt As Issued - $50

In Beaver Valley

Winner of the Academy Award for Best Two Reel Short Subject, this 1950 film was part of the Disney *True-Life Adventure* series. The series centered on presenting unusual facts about animals' lifestyles and, more generally, the natural world we live in. For many who saw the series, it was the first time that they were made aware of their own relation to nature and the planet we live on.

The film tells the story of a beaver sharing his space with other wildlife. It was directed by James Algar, narrated by Winston Hibler and photographed by Alfred Milotte. It was given a tremendous boost of popularity when it aired on the Disney TV show. Merchandise made specifically for this film was very minimal, but book spin-offs did appear.

IBV-1

❏ **IBV-1. "Walt Disney's True-Life Adventures" Book,**
1954. 5.5x6.5". Whitman "Tell-A-Tale" book with 28 pages. - $6 $15 $30

IBV-2

IBV-3

❏ **IBV-2. "Peter And The Wolf/Beaver Valley" Record,**
1950s. 6.75x7.5" two-sided sleeve contains yellow vinyl 78-rpm. Features "March From Peter And The Wolf/Jing-A-Ling Jing-A-Ling Theme Melody From Beaver Valley." - $10 $20 $35

❏ **IBV-3. Walt Disney Vintage Publicity Photos,**
1950s. Each 8x10". One photo depicts Walt with beaver from Beaver Valley movie, other two from mid-1960s believed related to "That Darn Cat" and "Monkeys Go Home." Each - $5 $10 $20

THE INCREDIBLES

The Incredibles

Disney released this Pixar computer animated feature in 2004. It tells the story of the family of superheroes named Parr. They are living in an era where the government has banned public superheroics due to a fear of lawsuits. Ironically, the family father, Bob Parr, formerly known as Mr. Incredible, now works at an insurance company. His wife Helen, once known as Elastigirl due to her ability to stretch to fantastic lengths, is now a stay-at-home mom. She has her hands full with daughter Violet, who can become invisible and project forcefields, and son Dash, who has the gift of super-speed. The illegality of using these superpowers presents a quandary when a seeming super-villain, Syndrome, plots to attack the Parrs' city with a deadly giant robot.

The film was created and directed by Brad Bird, also known for another fine modern animated film, *The Iron Giant* (1999). *The Incredibles* takes simple time-honored concepts, such as the existence of superheroes in a real world and turns them upside down. As with all Disney and Pixar productions, the vocal talent moves the success of the picture to another level. The actors include Craig T. Nelson, Holly Hunter, Sarah Vowell and Spencer Fox.

Merchandise created to accompany this film was tremendous. There were fast food tie-ins, charm bracelets, books, magazines, figurines, action figures and a host of other items.

INC-1

❏ **INC-1. Incredibile Car in Box,** 2004. With Mr. Incredible figure and bonus poster. - **$35**

INC-2

❏ **INC-2. Nesting Dolls in Pack,** 2004. Four figures. - **$30**

INC-3

❏ **INC-3. Incredibles View-Master Telescope & Projector,** 2004. Includes 3 View-Master reels. - **$30**

INC-4

❏ **INC-4. Frosted Flakes Cereal Box,** 2004. Promotes contest to win inflatable punching bag. - **$6**

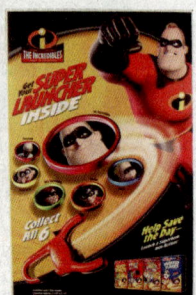
INC-5

❏ **INC-5. Frosted Flakes Cereal Box,** 2004. Promotes Super Launcher toy premium inside. - **$4**

INC-6

❏ **INC-6. Super Launcher Toy,** 2004. Premium from Frosted Flakes. Set of 6. Dash shown. - **$5**

INC-7

❏ **INC-7. Mr. Incredible Figure,** 2004. - **$160**

INC-8   INC-9   INC-10

❏ **INC-8. Mr. Incredible Pez Dispenser,** 2004. - **$3**

❏ **INC-9. Elastigirl Pez Dispenser,** 2004. - **$3**

❏ **INC-10. Dash Pez Dispenser,** 2004. - **$3**

James and the Giant Peach

A combination of live-action and stop-motion animation, this 1996 film came from the same team that had previously made *The Nightmare Before Christmas* (1993). It was produced by Tim Burton and Denise Di Novi and directed by Henry Selick.

Based on the book by Roald Dahl, the story centers on a child named James who is orphaned and is subsequently left to live with two cruel aunts. When his parents were alive, they had dreamed of visiting New York City with James. With that promise unfulfilled, James now dreams his days away. One day, through the accidental snack of a magical alligator tongue, he visits the interior of a giant peach. There, James meets a number of friendly, humanized and giant insects who decide to help him travel to New York. With the peach itself as the means of transportation, James's dream becomes fulfilled.

Brilliantly animated, the film celebrates the vanishing art of stop-motion animation. The vocal talent includes Joanna Lumley, Paul Terry, Richard Dreyfuss, Susan Sarandon and Jane Leeves. The five songs in the film were written by Randy Newman.

Merchandise included plush figures, dolls, books and fast food tie-ins.

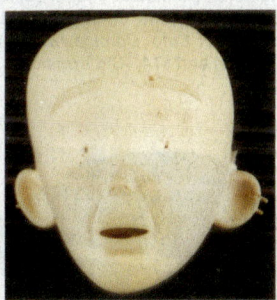

JAM-1

❏ **JAM-1. James And The Giant Peach Face Prop,**
1996. 2x3x3" tall soft flexible latex face prop which was placed over the mechanically operated figure's head. As Made - **$165**

JAM-2

❏ **JAM-2. James And The Giant Peach Movie Props,**
1996. 1.5x2.75x2" tall lot of three different resin face props used for different facial expressions of Spider Lady character. Each As Made - **$85**

JAM-3

❏ **JAM-3. James And The Giant Peach Movie Props,**
1996. Lot of four clear plastic boxes by "Amac Plastic Products Corp." Customized with labels depicting New York skyscrapers. Tops have customized sculptured rooftops. Each As Made - **$40**

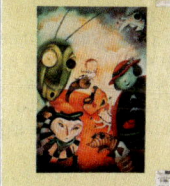 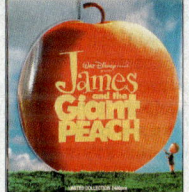

JAM-4

JAM-5

❏ **JAM-4. "James and the Giant Peach" Doll Set in Box,**
1996. Three dolls in the set. - **$65**

❏ **JAM-5. "James and the Giant Peach" Beanbag With Figures,**
1996. - **$40**

JAM-6

❏ **JAM-6. "James And The Giant Peach" Movie Promo Buttons,**
1996. Lot of six, possibly a set, each is rectangular 2x3" button. Each **$1 $3 $5**

JAM-7

❏ **JAM-7. "James And The Giant Peach" Original Story Book Art,**
1996. 18.5x23.5" elaborate wood frame with glass and double mats that has 8.5x13.5" area around art. Mixed media featuring 1" long image of James' head at center of spider web. Near Mint - **$1250**

JOHNNY APPLESEED

Johnny Appleseed

Originally released as a segment of the 1948 full-length feature *Melody Time*, the film was re-released as a short during Christmastime, 1955. It found even more popularity when it was shown on the Disney TV show.

Johnny himself, a humble soul who travels about planting apple trees, is based on the legends surrounding a real person; pioneer John Chapman (1774-ca. 1845). On screen, Johnny is voiced by Dennis Day, who brings a lot of charm to the role, especially when the character sings. The featurette was directed by Wilfred Jackson. Animators include Don Lusk, Eric Larson, Milt Kahl and Harvey Tombs. The sequence was written by Winston Hibler, Joe Rinaldi, Erdman Penner and Jesse March.

Merchandise includes books and records.

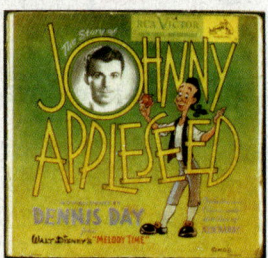

JNA-1

❑ **JNA-1. "The Story Of Johnny Appleseed" Record Set,**
1948. Stiff cardboard cover 10x11" contains three-record 78rpm set on the RCA Victor label. Dennis Day does all voices. - **$25 $50 $90**

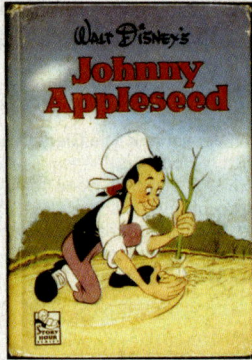

JNA-2

JNA-3

❑ **JNA-2. "Johnny Appleseed Story Hour Series" Book,**
1948. Whitman. 4.75x6.5" with 32 pages. - **$15 $30 $60**

❑ **JNA-3. "RCA Victor Record News" Featuring "Melody Time,"**
1948. Publication is 8.5x11" with 16 pages. Photo of Dennis Day and Roy Rogers. - **$15 $25 $45**

JNA-4

❑ **JNA-4. "Melody Time" Fan Card,**
c. 1948. Stiff paper card is 7.25x9.25". Pictures 12 characters from the film with their names at bottom margin. Includes Donald Duck, Jose Carioca, Johnny Appleseed, Pecos Bill, Little Toot and others. Has Walt Disney facsimile signature. - **$15 $30 $60**

JNA-5

❑ **JNA-5. "Johnny Appleseed" Boxed Squeaker Figure,**
1954. Box is 6.25x14.25x3.5" deep and contains 13.5" tall flexible rubber figure by Serugo. No Disney copyright. Box - **$10 $20 $40** Figure - **$15 $30 $60**

Johnny Tremain

This live-action 1957 film was based on the book by Esther Forbes. For many children, a viewing of *Johnny Tremain* marked the first time they could personally relate to the American Revolution. Set in Boston between 1773 and 1775, the story centers on a young apprentice silversmith who injures his hand. With his potential career ruined, Tremain gets in greater trouble when he finds himself accused of a crime he did not commit. With the help of Paul Revere and Josiah Quincy, the youth defends himself. Johnny eventually finds himself drawn into the Revolutionary War, as well as an exploration of human rights.

While *Johnny Tremain* was popular in its theatrical release, the film gained its greatest fame by being shown on the Disney TV show. The film was also made available for use in schools. Directed by Robert Stevenson, the film features Hal Stalmaster, Luana Patten, Jeff York and Sebastian Cabot.

Merchandise included books, costumes, premiums and records. Johnny Tremain appears in *Four Color Comics* #822 (Paul Revere's ride) and 874, (Old Ironsides movie).

JTR-1

❑ **JTR-1. "Johnny Tremain" Hat,**
1957. Benay Albee Novelty Co. 10.5x11x4" tall child's size large tricorn hat is formed and starched felt with vinyl trim. Attached to the front is a synthetic fabric patch with photo portrait of Hal Stalmaster as Tremain. - **$10 $20 $40**

THE JUNGLE BOOK

JTR-2

❏ **JTR-2. "Johnny Tremain" Lobby Card,** 1957. 11x14" glossy title card for original release. - **$10 $20 $40**

JTR-3

❏ **JTR-3. "Johnny Tremain" Record and Premium Coins,** 1957. "Golden Record" by Simon & Schuster "D344" 78 rpm in 6 3/4 x 7 1/2" sleeve. Silver plastic coins are 1 1/2" issued as cereal box insert. Each refers to "Sons Of Liberty" with rim hole as made, and owner placed these on a chain. Record - **$6 $12 $20** Each Coin - **$1 $3 $5**

JTR-4

❏ **JTR-4. "Walt Disney's Magazine,"** 1957. Volume 2, #4. This is the first issue in which the title was changed to just "Walt Disney's magazine." Cover photo is of Hal Stalmaster and Luana Patten from Johnny Tremain. Features article on Patten and an Uncle Scrooge story. - **$15 $30 $60**

JTR-5

❏ **JTR-5. Walt Disney Derringer Replica Promotion Cigarette Lighter,** 1950s. Lighter is 5.5" long heavy cast metal Derringer replica in black/bright brass luster and sitting on black wood base. Disney promo item from the collection of Disney legend Al Konetzni who created and designed many Disney merchandise items in the 1950s-1970s. Used to promote such 1950s films as Davy Crockett, Johnny Tremain and Zorro. Base has brass plate with "Walt Disney Productions" name in black. - **$15 $30 $50**

The Jungle Book

Rudyard Kipling's classic book came to vivid life in this 1967 full-length animated feature. The film begins with the young boy Mowgli being raised by wolves in the jungle. He is referred to as a "man-cub." As Mowgli gets older, he is forced to leave because the tiger Shere Khan has vowed to kill him. Mowgli desires nothing more than to stay with his jungle friends, Baloo the bear and Bagheera the panther, but the latter realizes Mowgli will ultimately have no choice but to leave. In time, Mowgli comes face-to-face with Shere Khan. With the help of his friends, he defeats the villain. When he meets the "girl-cub" Shanti, Mowgli must make a choice. Despite his inclination to stay wild, Mowgli decides to leave the jungle for a life in civilized society.

The Jungle Book was directed by Wolfgang Reitherman. Animators included Frank Thomas, Ollie Johnston, Milt Kahl and Eric Larson. Vocal talent included Phil Harris, Sebastian Cabot, Louie Prima and Sterling Holloway. The songs were by brothers Robert B. and Richard M. Sherman. The song *The Bare Necessities* was nominated for an Oscar. *The Jungle Book* was the last animated feature that was directly supervised by Walt Disney. The film has a rich history of re-release in theatres and on video.

Merchandise was extensive, especially for the time. Items included books, records, premium figures, salt and pepper shakers and ceramic figures.

JUN-1

❏ **JUN-1. Jungle Book Salt And Pepper Set,** 1964. Mowgli is 5.75" and baby elephant is 3.5" painted and glazed ceramic set with labels from "Calico Imports." - **$50 $125 $250**

JUN-2

❏ **JUN-2. Mowgli Figurine,** 1965. Enesco. 5.5" tall painted and glazed likeness on 2" diameter base. - **$15 $30 $60**

THE JUNGLE BOOK

JUN-3

❑ **JUN-3. Ziggy Rubber Figure Carded,**
1966. DMI Toys. 8x10" shrinkwrap display card holding 4" tall flexible figure of vulture character. Carded - **$6 $15 $25**

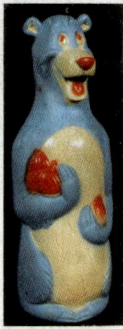

JUN-4

❑ **JUN-4. Baloo Soap Bottle,**
1966. Soaky 7" tall hard plastic from later series with hollow shell body to fit over a standard Soaky bottle. - **$8 $15 $25**

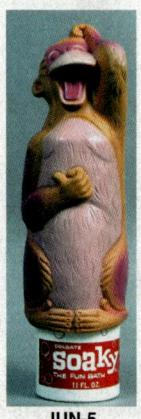

JUN-5

JUN-6

❑ **JUN-5. King Louie Soap Bottle,**
1966. Soaky 7.75" tall hard plastic from later series with hollow shell body to fit over a standard Soaky bottle. - **$10 $18 $30**

❑ **JUN-6. "Bagheera" Glass,**
1966. Tumbler is 6.5" tall with painted image #4 from set of six "Jungle Book" Canadian issue glasses. - **$12 $25 $40**

JUN-7

JUN-8

❑ **JUN-7. "Shere Khan" Glass,**
1966. Tumbler is 6.5" tall with painted image #2 from set of six "Jungle Book" Canadian issue glasses. - **$12 $25 $40**

❑ **JUN-8. "Baloo" Glass,**
1966. Tumbler is 6.5" tall with painted image #3 from set of six "Jungle Book" Canadian issue glasses. - **$12 $25 $40**

JUN-9

JUN-10

❑ **JUN-9. "Jungle Book Card Game,"**
1966. Edu-Cards. Complete set of 36 cards in 2x3x.5" deep box. - **$5 $10 $20**

❑ **JUN-10. "Jungle Book" View-Master Reels,**
1966. Envelope is 4.25" square and contains set of three stereo disks of color photo studio models accompanied by related story booklet. - **$8 $15 $25**

THE JUNGLE BOOK

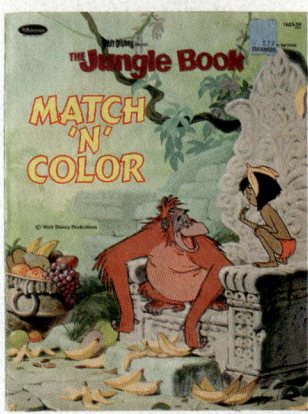

JUN-11

☐ **JUN-11. "The Jungle Book Match 'N' Color" Book,**
1967. Whitman. 8x10" with 128 pages. - **$10 $18 $30**

JUN-12

☐ **JUN-12. Jungle Book Animation Cel Set-Up Art,**
1967. Image is 4.5x4.75" with 17.5x9" background. Features Mowgli and King Louie. Background is a pan production background of the jungle temple. - **$1000 $2000 $4000**

JUN-13

☐ **JUN-13. "The Jungle Book" Movie Poster,**
1967. One-sheet poster is 27x41". - **$20 $40 $70**

JUN-14

☐ **JUN-14. "The Jungle Book" Movie Press Book,**
1967. Buena Vista. 11x14.75" with 32 pages. - **$15 $30 $60**

JUN-15

JUN-16

☐ **JUN-15. Cereal Premium Figures,**
1967. Nabisco Wheat Honeys. Complete box insert "Jungle Pals" set of six solid soft plastic figures each 2" to 3" tall/long. Each - **$3 $6 $12**

☐ **JUN-16. "Nabisco Wheat Honeys Jungle Pals" Box Flat With Premium Figure Set,**
1967. Flat is 13.5x18". Figures are 3" long or tall and include: Mowgli, Baloo, Buzzy, King Louie, Kaa and Bagheera. This is a file copy from Gordon Gold Archives. Near Mint Box - **$375** Near Mint Set - **$75**

JUN-17

☐ **JUN-17. Jungle Book Charm Bracelet,**
1967. Metal bracelet is 6.5" long with seven different three-dimensional cast metal charms: Mowgli, Girl, Baloo, Bagheera, Baby Elephant, Shere Khan, Vulture. - **$6 $12 $25**

JUN-18

☐ **JUN-18. Record/Book Set,**
1967. Gatefold 12.25x12.5" cardboard album cover containing 33-1/3 rpm on Disneyland label and bound-in 12-page story booklet with color art. - **$6 $12 $25**

THE JUNGLE BOOK

JUN-19

JUN-22

JUN-25

❑ **JUN-21. Jungle Book Baloo Concept Sketch,**
c. 1967. 12.5x17" with 6.5x8" image. - **$15 $30 $60**

❑ **JUN-22. Baloo Preliminary Sketch,**
c. 1967. Large animation sheet 12.5x17" centered by 8x8" image. - **$15 $30 $60**

❑ **JUN-25. King Louie Disneykin,**
c. 1967. Marx toys. 1.25" tall hand-painted hard plastic figure. - **$12 $25 $45**

JUN-20

JUN-23

JUN-26

❑ **JUN-19. Jungle Book Wind-Up,**
1967. Marx. 2.5x2.5x4.75" tall hard vinyl figure with built-in key of Bagheera. - **$10 $20 $40**

❑ **JUN-20. Jungle Book Mowgli Concept Sketch,**
c. 1967. 12.5x17" with 4x7.5" image. - **$25 $55 $80**

❑ **JUN-23. "The Jungle Book" Mexican Oversized Lobby Card,**
c. 1967. Spanish text card is 12.5x16.5", probably for the film's initial release. - **$5 $15 $25**

❑ **JUN-26. Baby Elephant From Jungle Book Disneykin,**
c. 1967. Marx toys. 1.25" hand-painted hard plastic. - **$12 $25 $45**

JUN-21

JUN-24

JUN-27

❑ **JUN-24. Bagheera Disneykin,**
c. 1967. Marx toys. 1" tall hand-painted hard plastic figure. - **$12 $25 $45**

❑ **JUN-27. Shere Kahn Disneykin,**
c. 1967. Marx toys. 1.5" hand-painted hard plastic figure. - **$10 $20 $40**

THE JUNGLE BOOK

JUN-28

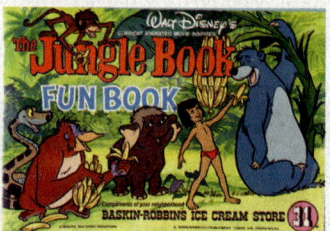

JUN-31

❏ **JUN-30. "Jungle Book" Lunch Box,** 1968. Aladdin. 7x8x4" deep embossed metal. - **$30 $65 $125**

❏ **JUN-31. "Jungle Book Fun Book" Premium,** 1978. Baskin-Robbins Ice Cream. 5.5x8" 24-page book of pictures to color, puzzles and games. - **$10 $20 $30**

JUN-34

❏ **JUN-33. King Louis Bisque,** c. 1970s. 2.5x4.5x5.25" tall. - **$15 $30 $60**

❏ **JUN-34. Jungle Book Surprise Egg Figure Set,** 1989. Set of 12 hand-painted hard plastic figures .75" to 1.5" tall. German by Ferrero Kinder. Set - **$25 $50 $100**

JUN-35

❏ **JUN-35. Jungle Book Bisque Figurine Set,** 1980s. Limited distribution. Sizes range from 2" tall to 6" long. Includes: Mowgli, Baloo, King Louie, Shere Khan. Each - **$8 $15 $30**

JUN-32

❏ **JUN-32. "The Jungle Book" Lobby Card Set,** 1970s. Buena-Vista Re-release. Set of eight 11x14" Set - **$40 $70 $120**

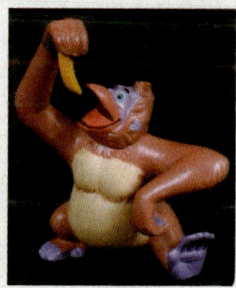

JUN-33

JUN-29

❏ **JUN-28. Mowgli Disneykin,** c. 1967. Marx. 1" tall hard plastic. - **$15 $30 $50**

❏ **JUN-29. Colonel Hathi Disneykin,** c. 1967. Marx. 2" tall hard plastic. - **$10 $20 $40**

JUN-30

JUN-36

❏ **JUN-36. King Louie & Baloo Bean Set,** 1990s. Mattel. Two figures in box. - **$20**

LADY AND THE TRAMP

Lady and the Tramp

This was the first Disney feature (1955) to be released in Cinemascope. Based on a short story by Ward Greene, the film is a wonderful tale of love. Two dogs from completely different backgrounds find each other and attempt to be together. Lady is a proper cocker spaniel from a good home and Tramp is a rail-yard dog of no particular pedigree.

The film contains one of the most memorable love scenes in animation history. Animated by Frank Thomas, the scene begins as Tramp invites Lady out to dinner at an Italian restaurant. While eating, they inadvertently find themselves sharing a single strand of spaghetti. Chewing it, they end up nose to nose and, with a just a second's hesitation, they kiss.

Other animators on the film include Milt Kahl, Ollie Johnston, Les Clark and Eric Larson. The film was directed by Wilfred Jackson, Clyde Geronimi and Hamilton Luske. Singer Peggy Lee voiced the Siamese cats Si and Am and the broken-down show dog Peg. As Peg, Lee sang *He's a Tramp*, a theme song she co-wrote herself. Lee also helped promote the film on the Disney TV show. Other vocal talent included Barbara Luddy and Larry Roberts.

Merchandise included premiums, figurines, dolls, books and records. In addition, the film also saw an unusual spin-off, the creation of a newspaper comic strip titled *Scamp*. It centered on the adventures of Lady's and Tramp's most mischievous puppy. The character of Scamp also starred in comic books and, more recently, a direct-to-video feature of his own *Lady and the Tramp 2: Scamp's Adventure*, (2001).

Lady and the Tramp, as well as characters from the film, appears in *Four Color Comics* #629, 634, 703, 777, 806, 833 and 1204. Many of these issues highlight Scamp. The film was also featured in a Dell Giant.

LAD-1

❏ LAD-1. "Lady And The Tramp Frame Tray Puzzle,"
1954. Whitman. 11.25x14.5". - **$12 $25 $40**

LAD-2

❏ LAD-2. "Lady And The Tramp Record-Reader" Set,
1954. Capitol. 7.5x8.5" thick cardboard cover contains 45 rpm record. Has bound-in, 20-page book. - **$10 $20 $40**

LAD-3

❏ LAD-3. Lady Pencil Drawings,
1955. Sheet of animation paper 12.5x15.5" with two images. - **$50 $100 $150**

LAD-4

❏ LAD-4. Lady Pencil Drawing,
1955. Animation paper is 12.5x15.5" with 4x4.75" image. #75 from a numbered sequence. - **$50 $100 $150**

LAD-5

❏ LAD-5. Lady and the Tramp Art Corner Animation Set-up Art,
1955. Image is 7.75x6.25" with 9.25x6.25" background. Art Corner was a shop located at Disneyland which offered original animation art for sale. - **$1000 $2000 $3000**

LAD-6

❏ LAD-6. Lady and the Tramp Art Corner Animation Set-up Art,
1955. Image is 4.5x5.25" with 16x11" background. The cel of Lady and also the pet store background are both production. - **$1500 $3000 $5000**

LAD-7

❏ LAD-7. Dachsie Ceramic Figurine,
1955. Shaw. 2" long. - **$35 $65 $100**

LADY AND THE TRAMP

LAD-8

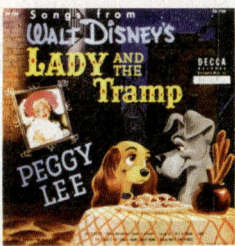

LAD-10

☐ **LAD-10. "Lady And The Tramp" Record Set,**
1955. Decca. 7x7" cardboard gate-fold cover contains pair of 45 rpm records. - **$12 $25 $50**

LAD-11

☐ **LAD-11. "Lady And The Tramp" Song Folio,**
1955. Hanson Publications Inc. 9x12" with 16 pages and stiff paper cover. - **$12 $25 $50**

LAD-12

☐ **LAD-12. "Scotch Tape/Lady And The Tramp" Premium Set With Promotional Material/Store Signs,**
1955. Lot consists of a 14.25x30" glossy poster, 8.5x11" four-page folder, two shelf signs, one 9.25x10.5" and one 3x14" and 8 thin molded plastic dog figures, each 2.5x3.5". From Sam and Gordon Gold Archives. Poster - **$110 $225 $325**
Folder - **$25 $50 $100**
Each Sign - **$15 $25 $50**
Figure Set - **$30 $60 $120**

LAD-13

LAD-14

☐ **LAD-8. "Pet Statuette" Cereal Premium Ad Proofs,**
1955. Kellogg's Rice Krispies. Two 9x15" advertising sheets for the 12 plastic miniature Lady and The Tramp figures packaged individually as box inserts. The color proof is for Sunday newspaper comic section, the other for grocery trade publications. Each - **$5 $12 $20**

LAD-9

☐ **LAD-9. Lady And The Tramp Cereal Premium Pet Statuettes,**
1955. Kellogg's Rice Krispies. Hard plastic figures, each about 2" tall. From a set of 12 issued one per box. Set consists of: Lady, Tramp, Trusty, Jock, Boris, Tuffy, Pedro, Daschie, Bull, Peg, Si and Am. Each - **$3 $5 $8**

☐ **LAD-13. "Lady And The Tramp" Fan Card,**
c. 1955. 8x10" on card stock. Text at bottom reads "Walt Disney's First All Cartoon Feature In Cinemascope." - **$20 $40 $65**

☐ **LAD-14. Jock Figurine,**
c. 1955. Shaw. Painted and glazed ceramic, 1.75" tall. - **$30 $60 $90**

LAD-15

LADY AND THE TRAMP

LAD-16

❏ **LAD-15. Lady And The Tramp Pictures,**
c. 1955. Pair of 8.75x10.75" wooden framed pictures. - **$10 $20 $40**

❏ **LAD-16. Lady Figurine,**
c. 1955. Shaw Pottery. 1.75" tall. - **$35 $65 $100**

LAD-17

❏ **LAD-17. "Lady And The Tramp" Figure Set On Card,**
c. 1955. Lido. 8.25x13" blister card contains complete set of 12 different three-dimensional figures 1.5" to 2" tall. These are identical to the premium versions that were included in boxes of Kellogg's Rice Krispies but these are in different colors and are soft plastic rather than hard plastic. Set of Lady, Tramp, Trusty, Jock, Boris, Toughy, Pedro, Dachsie, Bull, Peg, Si and Am.
Carded Set - **$30 $65 $110**
Each Loose - **$3 $5 $8**

LAD-18

❏ **LAD-18. "Lady And The Tramp/Dachsie" Glass,**
c. 1955. Clear glass with weighted bottom, 5.25" tall. - **$20 $50 $90**

LAD-19

❏ **LAD-19. "Lady And The Tramp" Vinyl Wallet,**
c. 1955. Wallet is 3.25x4.25". - **$20 $35 $65**

LAD-20

❏ **LAD-20. Lady Toy,**
c. 1955. Line Mar. 1.5x4.5x3" tall tin litho friction toy likeness of her holding a ball between front paws. - **$125 $250 $400**

LAD-21

❏ **LAD-21. Lady And The Tramp Spanish Postcards,**
1956. Lot of two 3.5x5.5" numbered 2 and 3. Each - **$5 $10 $15**

LAD-22

❏ **LAD-22. Lady And The Tramp German Market Goebel Figurines,**
1950s. Goebel. 2.5" tall Lady and Tramp is 3.25". Foil label with German text.
Lady - **$25 $50 $100**
Tramp - **$25 $50 $100**

LAD-23

❏ **LAD-23. Trusty Figurine,**
1950s. Hagen-Renaker. Painted and glazed ceramic, 2" tall. - **$30 $60 $100**

LAD-24

❏ **LAD-24. Tramp Figurine,**
1950s. Hagen-Renaker. Painted and glazed, .75x1.75x2.25" tall. - **$40 $75 $150**

LADY AND THE TRAMP

LAD-25

LAD-28

LAD-31

❑ **LAD-25. Lady And The Tramp Figurine of Ruffles,** 1950s. Hagen-Renaker. Painted and glazed, 1" tall. - **$25 $50 $75**

❑ **LAD-28. Jock Figurine,** 1950s. Hagen-Renaker. 1.25" tall. - **$30 $60 $100**

❑ **LAD-31. Lady And The Tramp Fabric Picture,** 1962. Fabric sheet is 8.25x10.5". - **$5 $15 $30**

LAD-26

LAD-29

LAD-32

LAD-33

❑ **LAD-26. "Lady And The Tramp/Ruffles" Ceramic Figurine On Display Card,** 1950s. Hagen-Renaker. .75" long on 2x2.5" card. On Card - **$35 $65 $100** Loose - **$25 $50 $75**

LAD-27

LAD-30

❑ **LAD-29. "Tramp" Hand Puppet,** 1950s. Gund Mfg. Co. 9.5" tall toy with soft vinyl head and fabric handcover body plus inner squeaker mechanism. - **$10 $20 $40**

❑ **LAD-30. Large Scamp Figurine,** 1961. Wade Porcelain. Marked "Wade Porcelain/Made In England." 2.25x4.25x3.75" tall. Produced from 1961-65, known as a "Blow-Up." - **$75 $150 $250**

❑ **LAD-27. Lady Figurine,** 1950s. Hagen-Renaker. 1.25" tall. - **$25 $45 $80**

❑ **LAD-32. Tramp Glazed Figurine,** 1960s. Figure is 3.5" tall. - **$10 $15 $25**

❑ **LAD-33. Si Or Am Figurine,** 1960s. Goebel. 2.75" tall painted and glazed ceramic of one of the two cat characters in Lady And The Tramp. Underside has incised "DIS 774" with stylized bee Goebel marking. - **$65 $125 $235**

LAD-34

LADY AND THE TRAMP

LAD-35

❑ **LAD-34. Jock Figurine,**
1960s. Probable Disneyland souvenir 3.5" tall painted and glazed ceramic with underside copyright. - **$8 $12 $25**

❑ **LAD-35. Jock Figurine,**
1960s. Probable Disneyland souvenir 4.25" tall painted and glazed ceramic with underside copyright. - **$10 $15 $30**

LAD-36

❑ **LAD-36. Disney Fun On Wheels,**
1960s. Marx. Cellophane-wrapped hard plastic figures with attached rubber wheels from set of 8. Pictured are Tramp, Lady, Brer Rabbit, Dumbo. Each Near Mint Wrapped - **$60** Each Unwrapped - **$10 $20 $40**

LAD-37

LAD-38

❑ **LAD-37. Scamp Figurine,**
1970s. Wade Pottery. 1.5" tall. - **$15 $30 $50**

❑ **LAD-38. Lady And The Tramp Dolls,**
1970s. Unmarked but by Dakin. Each about 2.25x4x5.5" tall stuffed felt. Each - **$10 $25 $50**

LAD-39

❑ **LAD-39. Serigraph Cel Signed,**
1980s. Acetate sheet 10.5x13.5" centered by 4.5x8" image. Signed by animator/designer Marc Davis. Mint, Signed - **$165**

LAD-40

❑ **LAD-40. Siamese Cats Cookie Jar,**
2004. Limited to 250. Mint As Issued - **$200**

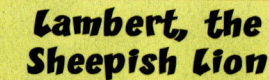

Lambert, the Sheepish Lion

Directed by Jack Hannah, this 1957 cartoon wound up being nominated for an Academy Award in the category of Best Short Subject Cartoons. The story starts when a stork accidentally delivers a baby lion cub to a flock of sheep. Since the cub is so markedly different, he is ostracized by the other sheep. However, things change when he defends them from an attacking wolf.

Animators who worked on the short include Eric Larson, Don Luske, John Lounsberry and Judge Whitaker. The story was narrated by Disney stalwart Sterling Holloway, who also reprised his role of the Messenger Stork from *Dumbo* (1942). Frequently rerun on TV for years, *Lambert* is one of the most fondly remembered 1950s Disney shorts.

Merchandise for the cartoon was minimal.

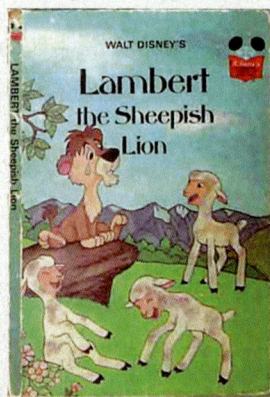
LAM-1

❑ **LAM-1. Lambert Story Book,**
1977. Random House publication, part of Disney's Wonderful World of Reading series. - **$5 $12 $25**

LAM-2

❑ **LAM-2. Lambert Pin,**
1990s. Part of astrological-themed set of 12 pins. Has raised section. NM - **$12**

LILO AND STITCH

The Legend of Sleepy Hollow

Originally released in 1949 as half of the feature *The Adventures of Ichabod and Mr. Toad* (see that listing for more details), this featurette is based on the timeless story by Washington Irving. Through repeated showings on the Disney TV show, the film continued to scare several generations over the years. It was also made available to many schools in the sixties.

LSH-1

❑ **LSH-1. Disney Studio Christmas Card,**
1948. Card is 7x8" on textured paper. On the card back are three separate illustrations for upcoming Disney films along with brief text. One image is of Ichabod Crane and Mr. Toad with film title noted as "Two Fabulous Characters" which was, of course, later changed to The Adventures Of Ichabod Crane and Mr. Toad. - $35 $65 $125

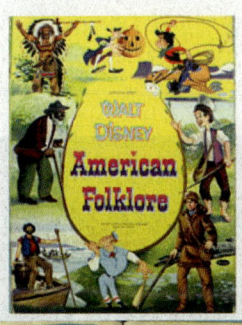

LSH-2

❑ **LSH-2. "Walt Disney American Folklore" Boxed Book,**
1956. Whitman. 8.5x11" hardcover comes in box which features the same artwork as the book's front cover. Book has 252 pages. Book spotlights nine different characters and most characters have multiple stories, book has 46 stories in total. Characters are Pecos Bill, Johnny Appleseed, Paul Bunyan, Uncle Remus, Casey at the Bat, Davy Crockett, Mike Fink, Hiawatha and Ichabod Crane. Box - $20 $35 $60
Book - $20 $40 $80

LSH-3

❑ **LSH-3. "Art Corner At Disneyland" Ichabod Crane Cel,**
1950s. 4.5x5.25 tall cel image of Ichabod Crane sniffing flower. - $125 $250 $500

Lilo and Stitch

A young Hawaiian girl is lonely, so she goes to the pound to find a pet. What she winds up with is actually an alien experiment gone awry. The creature, Stitch, has destructive tendencies which are only helped by his incredible strength and thick skin. He is in fact "Experiment 626," a test-tube life-form synthesized by a mad alien scientist. His home planet had dispatched him to an asteroid, but he escaped to Earth. Stitch's creator is released from jail and sent to retrieve him from Earth, only to find him gone. Meanwhile, Stitch is learning what it means to be part of a family, and for the first time in his life, feels he belongs somewhere.

Lilo and Stitch in essence takes the idea of Steven Spielberg's *E. T.* (1982) and turns everything upside down. It also tips its hat to *Star Trek* and *Star Wars* (1977). The film was directed by Dean DeBlois and Chris Sanders. Vocal talents include Daveigh Chase, Tia Carrere, Ving Rhames and David Ogden Stiers. Celebrated for its fine family values, the film led to a TV series and a direct-to-video sequel.

Merchandise was widespread and included books and records as well as plush dolls and figurines.

L&S-1

❑ **L&S-1. Lilo and Stitch Salt and Pepper Shakers,**
2002. From Walt Disney World. Hula Lilo and Stitch playing the guitar. - $30

L&S-2

❑ **L&S-2. Lilo in Hula Skirt Bobblehead,**
2002. From McDonald's. - $5

L&S-3

❑ **L&S-3. Lilo and Stitch Rockin Elvis Playset,**
2002. Hasbro. Stitch in full removable Elvis jumpsuit and Lilo in Hawaiian shirt. - $18

L&S-4

LILO AND STITCH

L&S-5

☐ **L&S-4. Stitch "King" Snow Globe,** 2002. Disney. Stitch posing as Elvis with guitar. - $60

☐ **L&S-5. Experiment 626 Snow Globe,** 2002. Disney. The origin of Stitch in snow globe form. - $60

L&S-6

☐ **L&S-6. Stitch as Elvis Bobblehead,** 2002. From McDonald's. - $6

L&S-7

☐ **L&S-7. Stitch Plush Doll,** 2002. From Walt Disney World. - $20

L&S-8

☐ **L&S-8. Lilo & Stitch Cereal Box,** 2002. Games and puzzles on back. - $5

L&S-9

☐ **L&S-9. Stitch Action Figure Doll,** 2002. In box. - $22

L&S-10   L&S-11

☐ **L&S-10. Lilo Bobblehead in Box,** 2002. - $18

☐ **L&S-11. Stitch Bobblehead in Box,** 2002. - $18

L&S-12

☐ **L&S-12. Stitch Cookie Jar,** 2004. - $55

The Lion King

A full-length 1994 animated feature, this movie was a tremendous hit. At the time of its release, some felt it was Disney's strongest film in over twenty years. The story centers around a lion cub named Simba. He is orphaned when his father, King Mufasa, is killed by his evil uncle Scar. In a twist, Scar convinces Simba that he is personally responsibly for his father's death and must now leave the Pride Lands in which they live. Growing to maturity in a distant savannah, Simba makes friends with Timon and Pumbaa, a meerkat and warthog, and together they live a relaxed existence. One day Nala, his female peer from the pride, shows up. She convinces Simba to return home and help stop the decay that Scar has caused. Simba returns, defeats Scar and takes his rightful place as king.

Directed by Robert Minkoff and Roger Allers, the film boasts an incredible cast and a stunning score. Vocal talent includes Jonathan Taylor Thomas, Mathew Broderick, Whoopi Goldberg, James Earl Jones and Jeremy Irons. Elton John and Tim Rice won Academy Awards for the song *Can You Feel The Love Tonight* and the score by Hans Zimmer also won for Best Musical Score.

Merchandise includes books, watches, video games, figures, plush toys and fast food tie-ins. Timon and Pumbaa later starred in a TV cartoon series of their own, engendering further merchandising spin-offs.

LIO-1

☐ **LIO-1. Employee Only Lion King Enamel Pin Set,** 1994. Set of three brass/enamel paint pins with needle post and clutch fasteners. Each is 1" to 1.25" tall. Includes Simba, Pumbaa and Timon. Mint As Issued - $45

THE LION KING

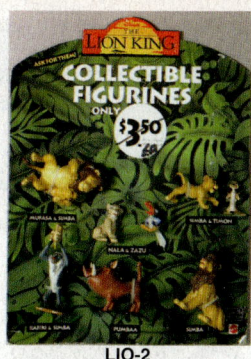
LIO-2

❏ **LIO-2. "The Lion King Collectible Figurines" Store Display,**
1994. Mattel. 12.5x16" thick cardboard display contains complete set of eight different PVC figures. Two figures feature two characters together, Mufasa with Simba and Rafiki with Simba. Others are: young and adult Simba, Nala, Zazu, Timon and Pumbaa. - **$15 $30 $60**

LIO-3

❏ **LIO-3. "The Lion King" Disney Employee Only Watch,**
1994. 2.25x9.5" velvet pouch contains 1-3/8" diameter watch in goldtone metal case. Leather watch strap has three "paw" prints. Image fades in and out as seconds tick. Reverse has "Company D" logo and serial number from limited edition of 1,750. Mint As Issued - **$135**

LIO-4

❏ **LIO-4. "The Lion King" Disney Employee Only Watch,**
1994. 1.75" watch in goldtone metal case with 2.75x2.75x3" wooden box. Reverse marked "Limited To 1750." Mint As Issued - **$160**

LIO-5

❏ **LIO-5. Pumbaa & Timon Music Box With Cookie Jar Head,**
1994. Made by Schmid. - **$115**

LIO-6

❏ **LIO-6. Pumbaa Pencil Drawing From The Lion King,**
1994. Animation paper is 12.5x17" with 7.5x8.5" image of Pumbaa singing "Hakuna Matata." - **$30 $60 $100**

LIO-7

❏ **LIO-7. "The Art Of The Lion King" Sotheby's Catalogue,**
1995. 8.25x10.5" catalogue for February 11, 1995 auction featuring 256 lots of art. - **$10 $25 $50**

LIO-8

❏ **LIO-8. Broadway Bean Bag Set,**
1998. From the Broadway Lion King set of 10. Simba shown with 2 tags - **$20**
Other 9 figures each - **$15**

LIO-9

THE LION KING

❑ **LIO-9. The Lion King Charm Bracelet,** 1990s. Metal link bracelet 7" long with five matching figural metal charms: Simba, Pumbaa, Timon, Raftiki and Zazu. - **$5 $10 $15**

LIO-10

❑ **LIO-10. Lion King "Video Day" Employee Only Watch,** 1990s. Valdawn. 2.25x9.5" velvet pouch with clear plastic window contains watch with 1x1.25" metal case. Marked "Video Day/Limited to 350." Pictures Rafiki holding baby Simba. Mint As Issued - **$85**

LIO-11

❑ **LIO-11. "Simba's Pride" Plush Doll Set,** 1990s. Three figures in box. - **$30**

LIO-12

❑ **LIO-12. Simba Plush Doll,** 2000s. Used as Toys-R-Us premium. Large doll. - **$55**

Little Hiawatha

Loosely based on the poem *The Song of Hiawatha* by Henry Wadsworth Longfellow, this 1937 short was released as part of Disney's Silly Symphonies series. Hiawatha wants to be a mighty hunter, but he ends up unable to make himself shoot the baby rabbit he tracks. They eventually become friends. All is not lost, as the other forest animals appreciate his kindness. The animals run to Hiawatha's rescue when he is attacked by a grizzly bear.

Directed by David Hand, the film also features music by Albert Hay Malotte and animation by Frank Thomas. This cartoon is acknowledged to be one of the best-looking that Disney had released up to that time. It's also remembered for the sheer number of times that toddler Hiawatha's breeches fall down, allowing him to accidentally "moon" the audience.

Merchandise was minimal; the character's appearances in comics were numerous. *Little Hiawatha* appears in Four Color Comics # 439, 787, 901, and 988. Aside from books, few dedicated licensed items appeared.

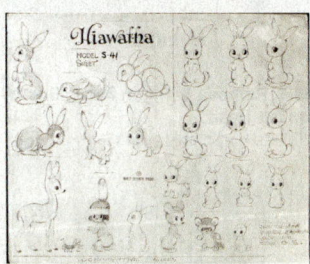
LTH-1

❑ **LTH-1. Little Hiawatha Model Sheet,** 1937. Vintage black and white photostatic model sheet is 12.5x15.5. From a numbered series marked "S-41." - **$25 $50 $85**

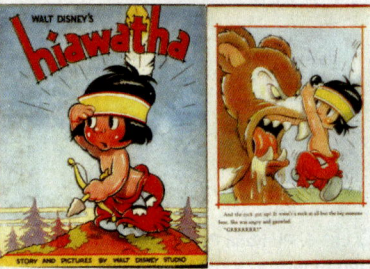
LTH-2

❑ **LTH-2. "Walt Disney's Hiawatha,"** 1937. 9.25x10.5" hardcover by David McKay Co. hardcover 9.25x10.5". 20 pages. - **$110 $225 $350**

LTH-3

LTH-4

❑ **LTH-3. "Mickey Mouse Presents Hiawatha's Paint Box,"** c. 1939. Lithographed tin box is 4.25x6.75x3/8" deep and marked "Made In England." - **$60 $125 $225**

❑ **LTH-4. Little Hiawatha Glazed Ceramic Cup,** 1930s. English By Wade Heath. Pictured is back of cup. Front has Pluto watching dancing brown rabbit with big red shoes. 2.75" diameter, 3" tall. - **$35 $65 $135**

LTH-5

LTH-6

THE LITTLE MERMAID

❑ **LTH-5. Little Hiawatha Button With Disney Copyright,**
1943. Philadelphia Badge. 2-1/8" button used by Philadelphia area high school graduating class. The upper left front edge has a small copyright symbol along with "Walt Disney Pro." Made in a very small quantity for graduating seniors who had a tradition in the Philadelphia area of producing buttons picturing comic characters. - **$55 $125 $225**

❑ **LTH-6. Ship Christmas Card With Little Hiawatha Insignia,**
1940s. Stiff white paper card is 4.25x5.5". Disney design with ship name "U.S.S. Winooski." - **$20 $40 $65**

LTH-7

❑ **LTH-7. Disney Designed Insignia Patch,**
1940s. 6x6.75" nice quality embroidered patch for 45th Pursuit Squadron. - **$125 $225 $350**

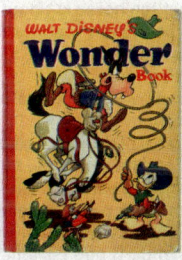 

LTH-8

❑ **LTH-8. "Walt Disney's Wonder Book" English Hardcover,**
c. 1951. The Sunshine Press. 8x10.75" with 60 pages. Many characters including Little Hiawatha. - **$30 $65 $135**

LTH-9

❑ **LTH-9. "Hiawatha Little Golden Book,"**
1953. 6.75x8" hardcover by Simon & Schuster, first printing with 28 pages. - **$12 $20 $40**

LTH-10

❑ **LTH-10. Painted Cover Rough To Dell Giant #5 "Silly Symphonies" Comic Book,**
1955. 5x7.25" with tempera and watercolor art showing front and back cover. Art attributed to Bob Grant. Excellent - **$650**

The Little Mermaid

Hans Christian Andersen's tale of a mermaid who is fascinated by the outside world was the first Disney feature (1989) in three decades to take its inspiration from a classic fairy tale. The last animated Disney film to use a fairy tale as its primary source was *Sleeping Beauty*. As early as the 1930s, Walt Disney had his eye on Andersen's story. At the time, he had asked illustrator Kay Nielsen to create some sketches for a prospective film version. When the modern-day production began, animators found the earlier sketches in studio vaults and used them for inspiration, leading to Nielsen's "visual development" credit on screen.

Young Ariel, the daughter of King Triton, longs to be human, especially after meeting Prince Eric. The sea witch, Ursula, wants to gain control of the undersea kingdom and convinces Ariel to give up her lovely voice in order to become human. Ursula also tricks Prince Eric, but Ariel and Eric work together to defeat her and save King Triton's domain.

Directed by Ron Clements and John Musker, *The Little Mermaid* features the voices of Jodi Benson, Pat Carroll, Christopher Daniel Barnes and Buddy Hackett. Alan Menken won an Academy Award for Best Musical Score and *Under the Sea* won for Best Song. The film inspired a TV cartoon series as well as direct-to-video sequel, *The Little Mermaid II: Return to the Sea* (2000).

Merchandise was widespread and included books, watches, figurines and fast food tie-ins.

LTM-1

❑ **LTM-1. Little Mermaid Ariel Concept Sketch,**
c. 1989. Actual sketch is 3.5x3.5". - **$25 $40 $80**

LTM-2

❑ **LTM-2. Multiple Key Cel Set-up with Original Background,**
c. 1989. Features Prince Eric. - **$2100**

LTM-3

❑ **LTM-3. Ariel The Little Mermaid Cel,**
1990s. Disney TV show. 10.5x13" acetate sheet with 2.5x3.75" image. - **$35 $65 $110**

LTM-4

THE LITTLE MERMAID

❏ **LTM-4. Sparkle Princess Collection Ariel Doll,**
2005. Fashion doll with collectible ring, 11 1/2 " tall. - **$12**

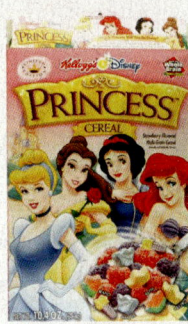

LTM-5

❏ **LTM-5. Kellogg's "Princess Cereal" Box,**
2000s. Features Ariel with Cinderella, Belle and Snow White. - **$6**

Little Toot

Based on a short story by early Disney animator Hardie Gramatky, *Little Toot* was originally part of the full length 1948 feature *Melody Time*. In 1954, it was released on its own as a theatrical short. A solid Disney piece, it is remembered by most for the title song sung by the Andrew Sisters.

In a world of humanized vehicles, a young tugboat named Little Toot is very mischievous and always in trouble. He finally makes his father, Big Toot, proud by rescuing an ocean liner from distress. The director was Clyde Geronomi. Animators included Eric Larson, Ollie Johnston, Bob Cannon and Rudy Larriva.

Little Toot merchandise includes records, books and a special figure designed for a Disneyana convention. Gramatky retained some rights to the character, so non-Disney Little Toot cartoons and merchandise have also appeared in recent years.

LTT-1

❏ **LTT-1. "Melody Time" Studio Fan Card,**
1948. Stiff paper card measures 7.25x9.25" with choice illustrations of characters from the "Full Length Musical Comedy." Illustrations include Donald Duck, Jose Carioca, Pecos Bill, Johnny Appleseed, Little Toot and others. - **$25 $45 $80**

LTT-2

❏ **LTT-2. Little Toot Ceramic Planter By Shaw,**
1948. Painted and glazed measuring 3x6.5x5" tall. Has incised "Toot" name on each side of front bow, back designed with small life boat and smokestack has opening. - **$300 $600 $1200**

LTT-3

❏ **LTT-3. "Melody Time" Record Set,**
1948. Glossy gatefold paper cover is 10x10.25" and contains two-record set on the RCA Victor label. Records feature "Little Toot, Bumble Boogie, Pecos Bill, Blue Shadows." Pecos is by Roy Rogers and The Sons of the Pioneers. - **$50 $100 $150**

LTT-4

❏ **LTT-4. "Little Toot" Record,**
1948. Gate-fold paper sleeve measures 10x10" and contains 78rpm on the Capitol label. Sleeve opens to reveal 11 numbered full color story illustrations with brief descriptive text. Back is an illustrated ad for Mickey and the Beanstalk and Uncle Remus record sets. - **$20 $40 $75**

LTT-5

❏ **LTT-5 "Little Toot Tugging & Tooting" Figure,**
2003. Classic Collection. - **$100**

The Littlest Outlaw

Disney filmed this 1955 full-length live-action feature entirely on location in Mexico. A young boy is in love with a general's horse. He steals the horse and then loses it. When he discovers that the horse is about to be killed in a bullring, he bravely rescues it. The general witnesses the rescue and rewards the boy with the horse.

The film was directed by Robert Gavaldon and adapted from a story by Larry Lansburgh, who also wrote Disney's screenplay with Bill Walsh. The film is notable for its authentic locales and appearance. The cast largely came from Mexico and included many non-actors. It includes Andrew Velasquez, Pedro Armendariz and Enriqueta Zazueta. It was also filmed in both Spanish and English. The film gained a lot of fans from its airing on the Disney TV Show.

Merchandise appears to have been limited to promotional posters, stills and *Four Color Comics* #609.

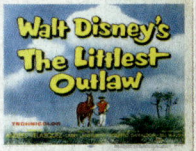 

LTO-1

LUDWIG VON DRAKE

☐ **LTO-1. "The Littlest Outlaw" Lobby Card Set,**
1955. Set of eight, each 11x14" for original release. Cards feature nice photo scene from the film and all but title card also have same inset illustrations of Pablito on left and bottom margins. Set - **$30 $60 $80**

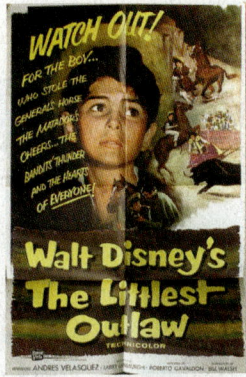

LTO-2

☐ **LTO-2. "The Littlest Outlaw" Movie Poster,**
1955. Poster is 27x41" for original release. Art features large portrait image of Pablito along with action scenes from the film. Original folded size is 10.5x13.75". - **$20 $40 $75**

LTO-3

☐ **LTO-3. "The Littlest Outlaw" Movie Stills Set,**
1955. Set of 24 for original release. Each is 8x10". All are different and most feature Littlest Outlaw Pablito. Each - **$1 $3 $5**

The Living Desert

This 1953 film was the first feature-length entry in the *True-Life Adventures* series. Prior to this title, Disney had been making similar films as featurettes. However, this one was sixty-nine minutes long and its length caused Disney to break away from their distributor at the time, RKO, in order to handle distribution on its own. RKO didn't think that anyone would pay for a full-length feature about desert creatures. The success of the film proved them wrong, very wrong. The film was a massive success for Disney and is a benchmark film in the history of real-life documentary film making. It was recognized with an Academy Award as Best Documentary Feature for the year.

While most people think of the desert as a barren, lifeless place, Disney showed the audience that it was actually a bustling part of the world that is inhabited by many different, interesting creatures. The film became a staple in many classrooms over the years.

Merchandise included books.

LIV-1

☐ **LIV-1. The Living Desert True-Life Adventure German Hardcover With Dust Jacket,**
1955. Printed in Germany 6.75x9" with 132 pages. Features full color photos throughout from the film. Dust jacket shows desert scene while back pictures this book and the matching Vanishing Prairie. Jacket - **$5 $10 $20**
Book - **$5 $15 $30**

Ludwig Von Drake

Donald Duck's eccentric Austrian uncle made his first appearance as the host of the 1961 season premiere of Walt Disney's new weekly television show. A staple of television since 1955, Disney's earlier shows had always been on ABC, but, at the time, that network lacked the technical requirements for the broadcast of a weekly color television show. Knowing the limitations of ABC, and anxious to take full advantage of the new color technology, Disney took his show over to NBC, who had the technical ability to give Disney what he wanted. This new, color version of the Disneyland show was re-titled *Walt Disney's Wonderful World of Color*. It appeared in September, 1961. That show was one of the earliest television shows to be broadcast in color.

On that very first show of the 1961 television season, Von Drake appeared for the first time and explained the principles of color itself. Throughout the show's run, Von Drake was primarily a host. He did not appear in the shorter cartoons that made up the body of each episode. But in the Donald Duck newspaper strips and comic books, Von Drake became a star. He was the first marketable Disney cartoon character to debut on television.

Von Drake's voice was done by Paul Frees, who also provided the voice of Boris Badenov (*Rocky and His Friends*, *The Bullwinkle Show*) and many other classic cartoon voices over the years. Von Drake's TV host career took him from strength to strength over several years. At one point, he replaced the original narrators of the film *Fun and Fancy Free*, Edgar Bergen and Charlie McCarthy, when the Disney TV show aired a special version (the original film was made in 1947).

Ludwig Von Drake merchandise includes a lunch box, several ceramic pieces and numerous books and comics.

LUD-1

☐ **LUD-1. "Professor Ludwig Von Drake Disneykin,"**
1961. Marx. 1.75x2.25x.75" deep box with die-cut display window contains 1.5" tall hand-painted hard plastic figure. Box - **$10 $20 $40**
Figure - **$35 $65 $110**

LUD-2

☐ **LUD-2. "Donald Duck/Ludwig Von Drake" Boxed Ceramic Salt & Pepper Set,**
1961. Dan Brechner. 4.5x5.5x2.5" deep box contains pair of 5" tall shakers.
Box - **$12 $25 $50**
Shakers - **$25 $50 $75**

LUDWIG VON DRAKE

LUD-3

❑ **LUD-3. "Ludwig Von Drake" Ceramic Mug,**
1961. Painted and glazed 3.5" tall with high relief image on front and marked "Japan." Also came in cardboard holder with Donald mug as an RCA premium. Ludwig Mug - **$5 $10 $20** Packaged Pair - **$15 $30 $60**

LUD-4

❑ **LUD-4. "Mickey Mouse Club Flan'l Fun Stick-ons Set,"**
1961. 8.5x13x1" deep box. By Standard Toykraft's. Fabric pieces of Ludwig, two nephews, Pluto and zoo animals to applied to felt-covered 8x9" board. - **$15 $30 $60**

LUD-5

❑ **LUD-5. "I'm Ludwig Von Drake" Sign,**
1961. Stiff die-cut paper sign 6.25x6.25". - **$15 $30 $50**

LUD-6

❑ **LUD-6. "Ludwig Von Drake Stickum Book,"**
1961. Golden Press Inc. 7.5x13" with eight pages and two sticker pages. Unused - **$10 $20 $40**

LUD-7

❑ **LUD-7. Ludwig Von Drake Squeaker Toy,**
1961. Dell. 7" tall molded soft vinyl. - **$10 $20 $40**

LUD-8

❑ **LUD-8. "Ludwig Von Drake Ball Toss Game,"**
1961. Transogram. 12x20x4.25" deep box. Designed with "Score-A-Matic Dial/Automatic Ball Return And Moving Eyes." Object is to throw the balls into the die-cut opening of Ludwig's hat to activate the different actions. - **$25 $50 $80**

LUD-9

❑ **LUD-9. "Walking Professor Von Drake" Boxed Line Mar Wind-up,**
1961. Tin lithographed toy is 2x2.75x6" tall in a box with illustrations of Ludwig on three panels. Walks forward when wound.
Box - **$100 $200 $300**
Toy - **$110 $225 $325**

LUD-10

MAKE MINE MUSIC

LUD-11

❑ **LUD-10. Walt Disney Characters Chalkboard,**
1961. Diamond H. Brand. 16x24" masonite. - **$10 $20 $40**

❑ **LUD-11. "Ludwig Von Drake In Disneyland" Thermos,**
1962. Aladdin. 6.5" tall metal thermos. - **$20 $40 $85**

LUD-12

❑ **LUD-12. "Ludwig Von Drake In Disneyland" Lunch Box,**
1962. Aladdin. 7x8x4" deep metal with embossed front panel. - **$65 $125 $200**

Make Mine Music

Disney's first post-World War II full-length animated release (1946) was comprised of ten music segments. The film is sometimes thought of as a "poor man's *Fantasia*", a reference to the 1940 classical music-themed Disney feature that preceded it. In the case of *Make Mine Music*, the music for this film comes from the more popular artists of the time. Dinah Shore, Benny Goodman and the Andrew Sisters all provide music for animated sequences.

Each segment of the film carries a different theme. The bobby-soxer era is remembered through *All the Cats Join In* and Sterling Holloway narrates a musical adaptation of the poem *Casey at the Bat*. The classics do receive some attention: two ballet dancers are the focus of *Two Silhouettes*, and Prokofiev's *Peter and The Wolf* shines as perhaps the best segment of the film. Other sequences include *The Whale Who Wanted to Sing at the Met*, *The Martins and the Coys*, *Blue Bayou*, and *Johnny Fedora and Alice Bluebonnet*. Directors for the segments include Ham Luske, Clyde Geronomi and Jack Kinney. Among the animators were Ward Kimball, Lex Clark, Mary Blair, Ollie Johnston, Fred Moore and Eric Larson. The music was overseen by Charles Wolcott. Several of the cartoons that comprised this feature were later released individually as theatrical features and others were shown as separate animated features on the Disney TV show. Some, like *Casey at the Bat*, experienced a second wave of popularity when shown on television.

Merchandise included books and records.

MAK-1

❑ **MAK-1. Pencil Drawing From All The Cats Join In Section Of Make Mine Music,**
1946. Animation paper is 10x12" with 3x4.5" image at center. - **$50 $100 $150**

MAK-2

❑ **MAK-2. "Make Mine Music!" Lobby Card Set,**
1946. RKO Radio Pictures Inc. Set of eight, each 11x14" for original release. Title card features Casey, teenagers and clarinet dancing atop piano keys. Other seven cards each feature choice art for a different segment of the film. Nice multi-character set. Set - **$250 $500 $850**

MAK-3

❑ **MAK-3. "Make Mine Music" Publicity Folio,**
1946. RKO Radio Pictures Inc. 8.5x14" with 59 black and white paper sheets with printing on front sides only. - **$20 $45 $85**

MAKE MINE MUSIC

MAK-4

❑ **MAK-4. "Baby Hep" Catalin Plastic Pencil Sharpener,**
1946. 1-3/8" from the series with scalloped outer edge. - **$25 $50 $80**

MAK-5

MAK-6

❑ **MAK-5. "Peter" Catalin Plastic Pencil Sharpener,**
1946. 1-1/8" from the series with scalloped outer edges. - **$30 $55 $90**

❑ **MAK-6. "Casey" Catalin Plastic Pencil Sharpener,**
1946. 1-1/8" from the series with scalloped outer $ **35 $60 $95**

MAK-7

❑ **MAK-7. "Peter And The Wolf" English Card Game,**
c. 1946. Pepys. 2.5x3.5x.75" deep box contains deck of 44 cards. As issued, front of box has title card mounted to it, reverse has additional art. - **$35 $75 $125**

MAK-8

MAK-9

❑ **MAK-8. "Walt Disney Character Pin" Pair From Make Mine Music,**
1940s. Alpha-Craft. Two 3.5x4" display cards, each with nice quality 2" figural metal pin with fastener on reverse. Each - **$15 $25 $40**

❑ **MAK-9. The Martins And The Coys Boxed Book Plates,**
1940s. Antioch Bookplate Co. 3.25x4.25x.5" deep box contains 40 unused glossy book plates with gummed reverses. - **$15 $30 $60**

Mary Poppins

The books of P. L. Travers served as the basis for this 1964 feature. A classic mixture of live action and animation, *Mary Poppins* has become one of Disney's most beloved films. Set in England, the story shows an ever-busy Mr. and Mrs. Banks having little time to spend on their unhappy children, Jane and Michael. In an attempt to deal with their children, the couple has gone through a succession of nannies. Out of the blue, the practically perfect Mary Poppins and her magic umbrella arrive at the Banks' home. Together with her friend, the chimney sweep Bert, Mary Poppins turns the house into a barrel of fun.

Directed by longtime Disney stalwart Robert Stevenson, the film has an incredible heart and projects such warmth that you cannot help but get caught up in it. The film may have the most perfect live-action cast that Disney ever assembled. Julie Andrews, Dick Van Dyke, David Tomlinson, Glynis Johns and Ed Wynn all shine in their respective roles, and the children, Mathew Garber and Karen Dotrice, are solid. The music was written by Richard M. and Robert B. Sherman. Several of the songs have entered the public consciousness, especially *Supercalifragilisticexpialidocious* (a word now so well-known that it is in this writer's spell-check!).

Mary Poppins was nominated for thirteen Academy Awards and won five. Best Actress went to Julie Andrews and Best Song went to *Chim Chim Cher-ee*. The film also won for Best Music Score, Best Film Editing and Best Visual Effects. The film was re-released theatrically in 1973 and 1980.

Merchandise was extensive. It included sheet music, books, records, Pez figures, vases and dolls.

MAR-1

❑ **MAR-1. "Mary Poppins Paperdoll Book,"**
1963 Whitman. Book is 7.25x15.75" with six pages, punch-out doll on back cover. Unpunched - **$12 $25 $40**

MAR-2

MARY POPPINS

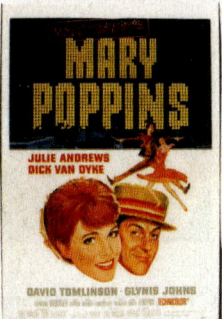

MAR-3

◻ **MAR-2. "Mary Poppins Sticker Fun,"**
1963. Whitman. 10.25x12" activity book with 12 pages. - **$8 $15 $30**

◻ **MAR-3. "Mary Poppins" Window Card,**
1964. Stiff paper card is 14x22". - **$25 $45 $85**

MAR-4

◻ **MAR-4. "Mary Poppins Frame Tray Puzzle,"**
1964. Whitman. 11.5x14.5". - **$8 $15 $25**

MAR-5

◻ **MAR-5. Mary Poppins Ceramic Head Vase,**
1964. Enesco. 3.5x4x5.25" tall. Photo example is missing umbrella handle above her hand. - **$75 $150 $250**

MAR-6   MAR-7

◻ **MAR-6. Mary Poppins Pop-Up Cereal Premium,**
1964. Nabisco Wheat and Rice Honeys 2.75x5" sealed cellophane pack containing hard plastic pieces on sprue frame for assembly of chimney toy with launching mechanism to propel 2.25" tall Mary figure holding umbrella. Issued in both red and blue for both Mary and Bert. Sealed - **$8 $15 $30**
Assembled - **$5 $10 $15**

◻ **MAR-7. Bert The Chimney Sweep Pop-Up Cereal Premium,**
1964. Nabisco Wheat And Rice Honeys. 2.75x5" sealed pack contains hard plastic pieces on sprue frame for assembly of mechanical toy of Bert holding broom. Issued in red or blue for Mary and Bert. Sealed - **$8 $15 $30**
Assembled - **$5 $10 $15**

MAR-8

◻ **MAR-8. Mary Poppins Dish Set,**
1964. Set of three hard plastic including: 3.75" tall cup, 5" diameter bowl and 7.25" diameter plate. Set - **$10 $20 $40**

MAR-9

MAR-10

◻ **MAR-9. Musical Teapot,**
1964. Enesco. 4x6.5x6" tall painted and glazed ceramic figural pot with removable lid, dimensional handle figure of Bert. Underside has metal musical mechanism that winds to chime tune "It's A Jolly Holiday." - **$75 $150 $250**

◻ **MAR-10. Musical Teapot,**
1964. Enesco. 3x6.5x5.5" tall painted and glazed ceramic with removable lid. Underside has metal musical mechanism that winds and plays "Chim Chim Cheree." - **$50 $100 $150**

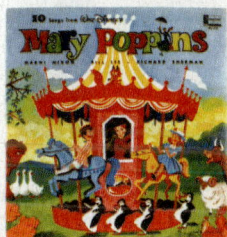

MAR-11

◻ **MAR-11. "Mary Poppins" Record,**
1964. Disneyland label. 12.25x12.25" cardboard album cover with 33-1/3 rpm record. - **$6 $12 $20**

MARY POPPINS

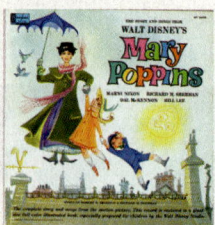
MAR-12

❑ **MAR-12. "Mary Poppins" Record/Book Set,**
1964. Cardboard gate-fold album cover is 12.25" square and contains "ST 3922", 33-1/3 rpm on Disneyland label of 11 songs from the motion picture. Bound-in, 10-page glossy paper book includes full color story art. - **$5 $12 $20**

MAR-13

❑ **MAR-13. "Mary Poppins Photo Album,"**
1964. Album with cardboard covers is 10.5x13.5x1.25" thick and covered by textured vinyl. 34 pages. - **$15 $30 $60**

MAR-14

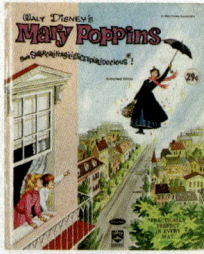
MAR-15

❑ **MAR-14. "Mary Poppins Photo Album,"**
1964. Album is 10.5x16x1.25" thick with sixty blank pages for mounting photographs, clippings, etc. Covers are lightly-textured vinyl over cardboard. - **$15 $30 $60**

❑ **MAR-15. "Mary Poppins" Book,**
1964. Whitman. 6.25x7.5" "Top Top Tales" hardcover, 28 pages. - **$5 $12 $20**

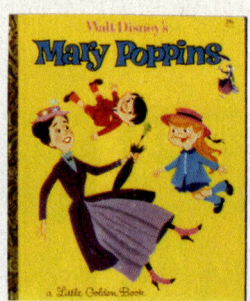
MAR-16

❑ **MAR-16. "Mary Poppins Little Golden Book,"**
1964. Golden Press. 6.75x8" first printing. 24 pages. - **$10 $18 $35**

MAR-17

❑ **MAR-17. "Mary Poppins" Hand Puppet,**
1964. Gund. 11" tall with fabric body and soft vinyl head. - **$25 $60 $110**

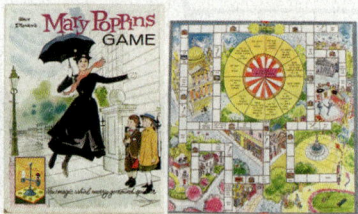
MAR-18

❑ **MAR-18. "Mary Poppins Game" Australian Version,**
1964. John Sands Pty. Ltd. 12.25x15.5x1.5" boxed authorized version of U.S. game by Whitman. Includes 15" square gameboard, " 3-D Merry-Go-Round Selector" for placement on the board, die-cut figures of Mary and Bert, instructions. - **$25 $45 $70**

MAR-19

❑ **MAR-19. "Mary Poppins Whirling Toy,"**
1964. Marx. 3.5x8x3" deep box contains 8" tall 3-D hard plastic wind-up toy with built-in key.
Box - **$25 $50 $75**
Toy - **$50 $100 $150**

MAR-20

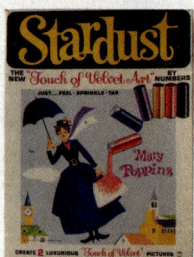
MAR-21

❑ **MAR-20. "Mary Poppins" View-Master Set,**
1964. Envelope is 4.5x4.5 and contains complete set of three reels with single inner sleeve and story booklet. - **$6 $12 $25**

❑ **MAR-21. "Mary Poppins Stardust" Paint Set,**
1965. Hasbro. Sealed box is 11x14.75x1.5" deep. - **$10 $20 $35**

MAR-22

MELODY TIME

❑ **MAR-22. Lunch Bottle,**
1965. Aladdin Industries. 7" tall metal thermos bottle with plastic cup, issued originally in companion metal lunch box. - **$15 $30 $60**

MAR-23

MAR-24

❑ **MAR-23. Lunch Box,**
1965. Aladdin Industries. 7x8x4" deep embossed metal with original "Property Of" sticker on front lower left. - **$50 $100 $200**

❑ **MAR-24. "Mary Poppins" Comic Book,**
1965. K.K. Publications Inc. Gold Key Movie Comic #10136-501. - **$5 $15 $60**

MAR-25

❑ **MAR-25. "Mary Poppins" Jump Rope" Prototype Art With Letter,**
1966. Three items from archives of Colorforms related to Disney-suggested toy believed never actually produced. Two 12x16" prototype design sheets in pencil and paint detail the proposed jumping rope and its advertising possibilities. Includes 8.5x11" letter from Louis Lispi, art director of Disney Character Merchandising Division dated Oct. 13 to Harry Kislevits, a Colorforms official. Unique, Near Mint - **$375**

MAR-26

❑ **MAR-26. "Mary Poppins" Vinyl Brunch Bag With Pair of Thermoses,**
1966. Aladdin. 4x8x8" tall with pair of 6.5" tall thermoses. First thermos is metal and came with both this brunch bag as well as the metal lunch box, second is plastic and was issued with vinyl lunch box. Bag - **$35 $65 $125**
Metal Bottle - **$15 $30 $60**
Plastic Bottle - **$15 $30 $50**

MAR-27

MAR-28

❑ **MAR-27. Mary Poppins Pez Dispenser,**
1960s. Has Disney copyright and is 4.5" tall. - **$200 $400 $700**

❑ **MAR-28. Mary Poppins Charm Bracelet,**
1960s. Metal link bracelet 6" long with six attached figural metal charms: Mary Poppins, Bert, carousel horse, carpet bag and opened and closed umbrellas. - **$10 $18 $30**

MAR-29

MAR-30

❑ **MAR-29. "Mary Poppins" Lunch Box With Thermos,**
1973. Aladdin. 7x9x4" deep vinyl box comes with 6.5" tall plastic thermos. Box - **$35 $75 $150** Bottle - **$15 $30 $50**

❑ **MAR-30. "Mary Poppins" Book,**
1973. Golden Press. 9.25x12.25" stiff covered 48-page storybook. - **$8 $12 $25**

Melody Time

This full-length 1947 feature was mostly animated, but included some brief live action segments as well. The most famous is *Johnny Appleseed*, but *Pecos Bill* comes in a close second. Other cartoons include *Little Toot*, *Blame it on the Samba* (with Donald Duck), *Once Upon a Wintertime*, *Bumble Boogie* and an adaptation of the Joyce Kilmer poem *Trees*. Direction was overseen by Wilfred Jackson and Clyde Geronimi. Animators include Ward Kimball, Milt Kahl, Ollie Johnston and Les Clark. Several of the component cartoons were later released theatrically as individual features. Several of the cartoons were also periodically featured on the Walt Disney TV show.

Original merchandise included sheet music, books and dolls. More recent items include an exclusive Disneyana Convention figure.

MELODY TIME

MEL-1

MEL-3

❑ **MEL-1. "Melody Time" Linen-Mounted Movie Poster,**
1948. RKO Radio Pictures, 40x60" for original release. - **$165 $325 $650**

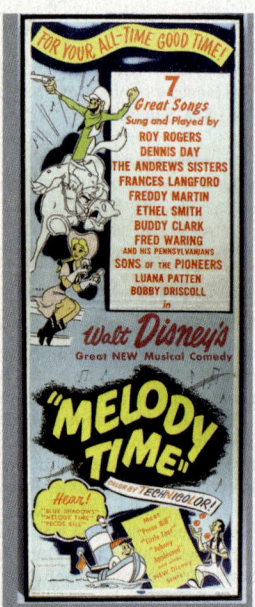

MEL-2

MEL-4

❑ **MEL-3. "Melody Time" Belgian Movie Poster,**
1948. RKO Radio Films. 14.5x18.75". - **$50 $100 $160**

❑ **MEL-4. Roy Rogers "Pecos Bill" Record Album,**
1948. RCA Victor. From the "Youth Series." 10x11" stiff covered album with inner sleeves holding set of three 78 rpm records. - **$25 $60 $110**

MEL-5

❑ **MEL-2. "Melody Time" Insert Poster,**
1948. RKO Radio Pictures Inc. 14x36" poster features image of Pecos Bill on Widowmaker, Slue Foot Sue, Little Toot, Johnny Appleseed. - **$60 $125 $250**

❑ **MEL-5. "Melody Time" Record Set,**
1948. RCA Victor. 10x10.25" glossy gatefold paper cover contains two-record set. Records feature "Little Toot, Bumble Boogie, Pecos Bill, Blue Shadows." Pecos is by Roy Rogers and The Sons Of The Pioneers. - **$50 $100 $150**

MEL-6

MEL-7

❑ **MEL-6. "RCA Victor Record News" Featuring "Melody Time,"**
1948. Publication #151 is 8.5x11" with 16 pages. - **$15 $25 $45**

❑ **MEL-7. "Melody Time" Promotional Movie Book,**
1948. RKO Radio Pictures. 5.25x8.5" "Handbook" with 45 pages. - **$25 $40 $80**

MEL-8

❑ **MEL-8. Walt Disney Film Rental Catalogue,**
1958. "Melody Time" front cover. 8.5x11" eight-page catalogue titled "1958-59 Catalogue Of Walt Disney 16mm Films." - **$10 $20 $35**

Mickey Mouse, Minnie & Nephews

Legend has it that Mickey Mouse was born over seventy-five years ago during a train trip from New York to Los Angeles. Among the many passengers on that train was Walt Disney. The trip out to New York had been a very hopeful journey for young Walt. However, the return trip was the exact opposite. When he began to scribble the beginnings of Mickey Mouse on a notepad, Walt was on his way home to California after receiving some very disturbing business news.

For the preceding year, Disney had been producing cartoons for film distributor Charles Mintz. Everyone of them had starred a Disney creation, Oswald the Lucky Rabbit. The cartoons were released through Universal and Mintz was operating as a middle-man. The visit to Mintz in New York was two-fold. Walt wanted to negotiate higher pay for a second season. He also intended to use the increase to improve the quality of the cartoons.

When Disney finally met with Mintz, Walt's vision for the future was dashed. He was told that there would be no increase. In fact, he had to instead accept a cut in pay or lose his control over the rabbit. It was revealed that Universal, not Disney was the actual owner of Oswald. In addition to that shocking news, Mintz had been given the authority to produce the shorts on his own if the need arose. In preparation for that very real possibility, Mintz had already been going behind Disney's back. He had already contracted with many of Disney's current animation staff so they could continue to produce the Oswald shorts without Walt.

After being given that incredible news, Disney made the decision to completely separate from Oswald. For all intents and purposes, he left Mintz's office unemployed. On the journey home, Disney came up with the beginnings of a character that would take over the licensing world.

The original Mickey was a series of ovals that somewhat resembled Oswald, but included a good amount of originality. What was new for the mouse, and what Walt gave to him, was an enthusiastic, adventurous, determined personality. The character would drive the action as opposed to reacting to it. The then recent solo flight of Charles Lindbergh across the Atlantic in his plane *The Spirit of St. Louis* was an obvious inspiration.

There was one last, very important characteristic that Walt provided, a voice. Mickey's vocals were supplied by Walt himself through 1946. Mickey's visual design was refined by Disney's longtime associate Ub Iwerks. The name of the mouse was originally going to be Mortimer, but, again according to legend, Disney's wife Lillian considered the name "too pompous." Walt knew to listen to his wife on this idea. Mortimer was out and the mouse's name was swapped for Mickey.

Mickey's screen debut came in 1928 with a silent cartoon titled *Plane Crazy*. The short was shown in May at a local theatre, but it did not achieve wide distribution. A second silent cartoon, *The Gallopin' Gaucho* (1928), was produced next, but it also was unable to get wide distribution.

Major film distributors were preparing to move into sound production, and another silent cartoon series simply did not interest them. Disney was aware of their objections and, with those objections in mind, prepared the next cartoon for sound.

When *Steamboat Willie* (1928), premiered at New York's Colony Theatre on November 18, audiences ran wild. There had been sound cartoons before *Steamboat Willie*, but no one had ever come close to the quality of Disney's new cartoon. Ironically, Mickey did not actually speak in *Willie*; a parrot is the only speaking character. Mickey and others merely grunt. It took another year for Mickey to actually speak in English. That occurred in *The Karnival Kid* (1929). That year also saw the debut of the first merchandise item to bear Mickey's likeness. It was a children's school tablet.

By 1930, Mickey was so well-known that Disney developed a comic strip featuring the character. Initially drawn by Iwerks, the strip was soon taken over by Floyd Gottfredson, who plotted it for fifteen years and drew it for forty-five. Gottfredson's plots were swashbuckling epics with a colorful interpretation of Mickey. His work made the strip an instant favorite. The vast majority of the Mickey children's books created during the thirties drew on the Gottfredson strip for plots, clip art, or both.

Four years after the fateful 1928 train ride, Walt Disney received a special Academy Award for the creation of Mickey Mouse. Within a few years, Mickey became the Disney company spokesman, and over time he increasingly came to be treated with the requisite respect. As a result, his screen personality lost some of its original edge. The smart-alecky, adventurous Mickey Mouse of the early days gradually became a squeaky-clean do-gooder. Over time, Disney creations such as Snow White and Donald Duck stole much of his thunder.

Nevertheless, Mickey remained a central figure at the core of Disney. Perhaps that's why, for recent TV cartoons, the studio has seen fit to restore some of Mickey's original funnier and more mischievous impulses. While he has undergone some minor physical changes over the years, the Mickey of today is essentially the same figure who rose to success in his early years; a scrappy little guy with a great big sense of adventure.

Mickey Mouse is the single most merchandised character in history.

Mickey's Nephews

Morty and Ferdie (the latter is sometimes spelled Ferdy), made their first appearance in the Mickey Mouse Sunday newspaper strip dated September 18, 1932. Their only animated cartoon appearance came in a 1934 Mickey Mouse short titled *Mickey's Steamroller*. Since then, they have only been active in the comics. The boys are patiently waiting for other opportunities to knock.

Merchandise exclusively depicting the two is limited, but they more frequently appear on items featuring multiple characters.

Minnie Mouse

She was with him from the beginning. Minnie appeared in *Steamboat Willie* (1928), Mickey's first cartoon with sound and the first to receive national distribution. Together with Mickey, Minnie appeared in 74 classic-era theatrical cartoons over the years. When visitors arrive at a Disney theme park, Minnie is always there to greet them and have her picture taken. Many of those visitors make a special effort to seek her out. For some, she is the best-loved character in the park.

Merchandise for Minnie isn't as extensive as it is for Mickey, but she does have her fair share. There have been dolls, books, records and many other items. In many European countries, Minnie is the star of her own long-running comic book title.

MKY-1

MICKEY MOUSE, MINNIE & NEPHEWS

☐ **MKY-1. Minnie Mouse Carrying Felix In Cages Lithographed Tin Wind-Up,**
1929. Made by Rogelio Sanchez, Spain with castle logo on left cage. 6-7/8" tall with electrical cord tail. Minnie has small points on ears and wears hobnail style shoes. Only a few known. Rare. - $8000 $12000 $35000

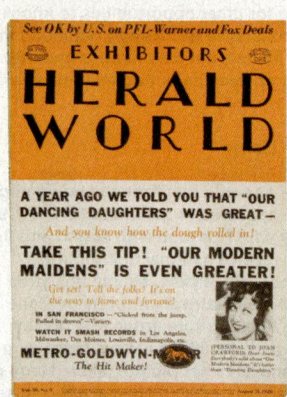

☐ **MKY-2. "Exhibitors Herald World" Featuring Mickey Mouse,**
1929. 9.25x12.25" Volume 96, No. 9 dated August 31,1929 issue. 82 pages with great 2-page ad for Mickey Mouse. - $100 $200 $300

MKY-2

MKY-3

☐ **MKY-3. "Mickey Mouse" Pencil Tablet,**
c. 1929. Tablet is 8x9.75" and .5" thick. From a series of several believed to be the first Disney items licensed, possibly as early as 1929. - $110 $225 $425

MKY-4

☐ **MKY-4. "The Cactus Kid" Pencil Drawing,**
1930. 9.5x12" sheet with 3.75x7" art, likely by Ub Iwerks, of Mickey with angry expression and Pegleg Pedro (Pete). - $550 $1100 $1850

MKY-5

☐ **MKY-5. "Mickey Mouse Club" Earliest Design Member's Celluloid Button,**
1930. The first movie club began January 11, 1930 at Fox Dome Theater in Ocean Park, California. The club idea came from theater manager Harry W. Woodin who in September 1929 received Disney's endorsement of his idea. Button is pictured on the membership application blank. 7/8" with small copyright symbol on the front. - $75 $125 $250

MKY-6

☐ **MKY-6. "Fox Mickey Mouse Club" Button,**
1930. 7/8". The first movie club began January 11, 1930 at Fox Dome Theater in Ocean Park, California. The club idea came from theater manager Harry W. Woodin who in September 1929 received Disney's endorsement of his idea. - $85 $150 $300

MKY-7

☐ **MKY-7. "Mickey Mouse Club" Washington State Earliest Design Club Button,**
1930. 7/8" button. No maker's name and no backpaper possibly as issued. - $85 $150 $300

MKY-8

☐ **MKY-8. Earliest Design Mickey Mouse Movie Club Officer Button,**
1930. From the earliest days of the west coast Mickey Mouse Clubs which began in 1930. Clubs elected officers from "Chief Mickey Mouse" on down and this button denotes the rank of "Courier." 2-3/16" button. - $500 $1500 $3500

MICKEY MOUSE, MINNIE & NEPHEWS

MKY-9

MKY-11

❏ **MKY-11. "Mickey Mouse Club" Second Design Member's Celluloid Button,**
1930. The first design was quickly replaced by Mickey image approved by Disney Studios. Copyright text was also added. 7/8" with Philadelphia Badge backpaper. Used briefly and replaced by designs 1.25" in size. - **$85 $135 $265**

MKY-12

❏ **MKY-12. "Mickey Mouse Club" Rare Imprint Celluloid Button,**
1930. Includes sponsor names of "Harris Family Theatre" and "Sears, Roebuck And Co." 7/8". - **$165 $325 $650**

MKY-13

❏ **MKY-13. Columbia Pictures Early Mickey Mouse Shorts Ad,**
1930. Ad is 11x14" neatly removed from a Columbia Pictures Promotional Productions yearbook. - **$20 $40 $75**

MKY-14

MKY-15

❏ **MKY-14. "Mickey Mouse" With French Horn Large Bisque,**
1930. Figure is 2.5x3x5-1/8" tall with string tail and paper label under feet. Has incised number on back "S36." - **$265 $525 $775**

❏ **MKY-15. "Minnie Mouse" With Violin Large Bisque,**
1930. Figure is 5.75" tall and has incised "S38" on back. - **$265 $525 $775**

❏ **MKY-9. "Mickey Mouse Movie Club" Campaign Folio,**
1930. 9x11.5" card stock cover holds a complete multi-page set of 8.5x11" single-sided sheets. Bound on left with brass clips so that pages can be easily removed. Folio filled with information and images detailing in every way, shape and form all aspects of the club. - **$500 $1200 $2000**

MKY-10

❏ **MKY-10. Mickey And Minnie On Motorcycle Tin Wind-Up,**
1930. Tipp & Co., Germany. 10" long. Immensely popular and very few known examples. - **$15000 $35000 $80000**

MICKEY MOUSE, MINNIE & NEPHEWS

MKY-16

❑ **MKY-16. "Mickey Mouse" Celluloid Figure,**
1930. Walter E. Disney. 2.25x2.75x5" tall with movable head and arms. String tail. - **$135 $275 $450**

MKY-17

MKY-18

❑ **MKY-17. "Minnie Mouse" Celluloid Figure,**
1930. Walter E. Disney. 2.25x2.75x5" tall with movable head and arms. String tail. - **$115 $250 $400**

❑ **MKY-18. "Mickey Mouse" Celluloid Novelty,**
1930. Base is 1x1.5" and has pair of attached 7/8" Mickey figures. Underside has label "Mickey Mouse." - **$65 $125 $250**

MKY-19

❑ **MKY-19. "Mickey Mouse" First American-Made Toy,**
1930. Wood with rope arms, leatherette ears and a stiff cord tail. When tail is pushed down, Mickey's head rises slightly. Designed by Disney artist Burton "Bert" Gillett for distribution by George Borgfeldt Corp. Label includes "c. 1928-1930 by Walter E. Disney Des. Pat. Apd For." 2.5x3x6.25" tall. - **$1000 $2000 $4000**

MKY-20

❑ **MKY-20. "Mickey Mouse" Wood Jointed Figure,**
1930. "Mickey Mouse/Walt E. Disney." 2x3x4.75" tall with flat disk hands to allow balancing in various positions. - **$225 $550 $1100**

MKY-21

❑ **MKY-21. "Official Mickey Mouse Song" English Sheet Music,**
1930. Lawrence Wright Music Co. 9.5x12.25" folder of words and music "Inspired By The Popular Mickey Mouse Sound Cartoons By Walter Disney For Ideal Films Ltd." Lyrics include "Dressed In Charlie Chaplin's Bags/One Night He'd A Glass Of Wine/Smiling Like The Prince Of Wales/Some Rat-Killing Stuff He Found." - **$55 $110 $165**

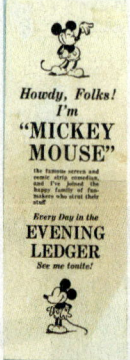

MKY-22

MKY-23

❑ **MKY-22. Theater Handout With Mickey Mouse Evening Ledger Ad,**
1930. Garrick Theater, Philadelphia. 3x8.5" with four pages for September 1. Ad is on back cover. - **$20 $35 $75**

❑ **MKY-23. The First "Mickey Mouse Book,"**
1930. Bibo and Lang. 9x12" with 16 pages. Includes pages 9-10, board game and playing pieces to cut out. Some issues have the Win Smith Mickey Mouse daily strips on page 8 and back cover. Complete - **$1200 $5400 $11000** Missing Pages - **$200 $800 $1500**

MICKEY MOUSE, MINNIE & NEPHEWS

MKY-24

MKY-26

❏ **MKY-24. "Mickey Mouse" Glazed China Ashtray,**
1930. Measures 3.25x5x2-7/8" tall. Underside has sticker "Mickey Mouse Copr 1928-1930 By Walter E. Disney." - **$125 $250 $500**

❏ **MKY-26. "The Mickey Mouse Quoit Game,"**
1930. Spears Games. Box is 7.5x11x1" deep with paper label playing surface in bottom along with wood block with slot to hold 5.5x9" cardboard Mickey figure. Also has three paper-covered cardboard rings. Object was to toss rings onto Mickey figure to land on various point value squares of insert. - **$125 $250 $450**

MKY-27

❏ **MKY-27. "Mickey Mouse" Hurdy Gurdy Tin Wind-up,**
1930. Probably Distler, Marked "Made In Germany." Dancing Minnie figure on the top is frequently replaced. Mickey has a spring tail. Toy is 6" long by 8" tall. - **$2500 $5000 $20000**

MKY-28

❏ **MKY-28. "Mickey The Musical Mouse" Lithographed Tin Toy,**
1930. Germany, for British import. 5.5" tall by 9.75" long with crank that moves the heads and operates music box on reverse. Front text "Regd. No. 508041 - All Rights Reserved, Germany, By Exclusive Arrangement With Ideal Films." Three versions with this considered the best. Minnie With Pram Version - **$12000 $20000 $30000**
Blue Background Dancing Mickey Version - **$10000 $17500 $20000**
Yellow Background Dancing Mickey Version - **$11000 $19000 $25000**

MKY-25

❏ **MKY-25. Mickey Mouse And Felix Litho Tin Sparkler,**
1930. Rogelio Sanchez, Spain marked "La Isla R.S." on front. 5" wide by 7" tall with action of them each bending over to light cigars on candle flame created by sparks that show through cellophane at flame center. No tail on Mickey as designed. Reproduced in the 1990s, Spain as a noisemaker but without any animation. - **$5000 $8000 $15000**

MICKEY MOUSE, MINNIE & NEPHEWS

MKY-29

❑ **MKY-29. Minnie Mouse Pushing Baby Felix In Pram Tin Lithographed Wind-Up,**
c. 1930. Rogelio Sanchez, Spain. Minnie is 6.5" tall with metal tail. Castle logo on her apron. 5.5" long stroller. Only several known. - **$12000 $20000 $35000**

❑ **MKY-31. "Mickey Mouse Slate Dancer" Litho Tin Toy,**
1930. German with only mark a registration number 508041. Two versions, each 3.5" wide by 6.5" tall, one with hand crank only and one with crank and fly wheel for use with a steam generator. Mickey's arms and legs move rapidly when activated. Also, a third version without the text and Mickey head image on back panel. Fly Wheel Version - **$8000 $14000 $20000**
Crank Only Version - **$6000 $12000 $18000**
No Text Version - **$4000 $8000 $12500**

MKY-32

MKY-30

MKY-31

❑ **MKY-30. Mickey Mouse With Moving Eyes And Mouth Lithographed Tin Wind-Up,**
1930. Germany for British import. 8-7/8" tall with rubber tail. Text on back "By Exclusive Arrangement With Ideal Films Ltd. Registered No. 508041." Among the rarest wind-ups. There is also a version without facial movement.
Moving Face - **$10000 $20000 $35000**
Non-Moving Face - **$5000 $10000 $17500**

❑ **MKY-32. "Mickey Mouse" Drumming Tin Litho Mechanical Toy,**
1930. Germany. There are four varieties. All are 6.5" tall with reverse plunger to activate. All show five-fingered gloves and all depict face positioned over his left shoulder. All drum heads are plain. Two versions show teeth, the example shown plus one with wide smile and teeth. Two versions without teeth showing are one with mouth open and one with mouth closed. All four came in plain generic box.
Version With Teeth - **$1000 $1800 $3000**
Version Without Teeth - **$600 $1000 $1500**

MICKEY MOUSE, MINNIE & NEPHEWS

MKY-33

MKY-35

MKY-36

MKY-38

MKY-39

❑ **MKY-33. Mickey Mouse With Saxophone And Cymbals Tin Mechanical Figure,** 1930. Made In Germany. 5.75" tall with reverse wire that activates arm and leg motion. Reverse has transparent decal with gray printing noting copyright by Ideal Films. - **$800 $1800 $3600**

MKY-34

❑ **MKY-34. English Photo Postcard,** 1930. "Fleetway Press Ltd." 3.5x5.5" postal with glossy front photo titled "Toy Soldier Display. Mickey Mouse Wipes Out The Toy Army." Photo is two adults wearing full Mickey Mouse costumes at a cannon while behind them are numerous men dressed as toy soldiers, all knocked to the ground. - **$15 $30 $60**

❑ **MKY-35. "Mickey Mouse" Pencil Tablet,** c. 1930. Tablet is 5.5x9". This is one of several cover styles and these tablets were the first pieces of Disney character merchandise ever produced. This example precedes those produced by Powers Paper Company under a license granted in 1931. - **$105 $215 $415**

❑ **MKY-36. "Mickey Mouse Club" Member's Celluloid Button,** c. 1930. Fox Hollywood Theatre. 1". - **$110 $165 $315**

MKY-37

❑ **MKY-37. "Aladdin-Tabor Mickey Mouse Club" Celluloid Button,** c. 1930. 1.25". Scarce imprint. - **$150 $350 $750**

❑ **MKY-38. "Mickey Mouse Club" Celluloid Button,** c. 1930. Western Badge & Button Co. 1.25". - **$50 $100 $160**

❑ **MKY-39. "Mickey Mouse Club" Celluloid Button,** c. 1930. Philadelphia Badge Co. 1.25". - **$50 $100 $160**

MKY-40

❑ **MKY-40. "Fox Park Plaza Theater Mickey Mouse Club" Celluloid Button,** c.1930. Philadelphia Badge Co. 1.25" shown with back paper. - **$55 $110 $165**

MKY-41

❑ **MKY-41. "Earle Mickey Mouse Club" Button,** c. 1930. Ed. H. Schlechter. 1.25". Likey issued only by Philadelphia theater that opened in 1924. - **$100 $200 $400**

MICKEY MOUSE, MINNIE & NEPHEWS

MKY-42

❑ **MKY-42. "Uptown Mickey Mouse Club" Celluloid Button,**
c. 1930. Philadelphia Badge Co. 1.25". Unusual for being serially number with rare sponsor imprint. - **$60 $125 $200**

MKY-43

❑ **MKY-43. "Hawaii Theatre Mickey Mouse Club" Button,**
c. 1930. 1.25". Presumably issued by the theater built in Honolulu in 1922, known as "Pride Of The Pacific." - **$60 $125 $200**

MKY-44

❑ **MKY-44. Mickey Mouse Movie Club "Sergt.-At-Arms" Celluloid Button,**
c. 1930. 2.25". Earliest movie clubs elected an officer slate headed by "Chief Mickey Mouse" and "Chief Minnie Mouse." Buttons were produced for those and other club officers plus "Master of Ceremonies," "Color Bearer," Song Leader" and "Chorus."
"Chief" Rank - **$1000 $3000 $6000**
Other Ranks - **$750 $2000 $4250**

MKY-45

❑ **MKY-45. "Courier" 2-1/8" Cello. Button,**
c. 1930. Cello button with back paper from set of club official buttons issued from the Mickey Mouse Club. Rare.
"Chief" Rank - **$1000 $3000 $6000**
Other Ranks - **$750 $2000 $4250**

MKY-46   MKY-47

❑ **MKY-46. Mickey Mouse Early Litho Button,**
c. 1930. Made by Western Theater Premium Co., LA. 13/16". - **$65 $125 $225**

❑ **MKY-47. Mickey Mouse Early Litho Button,**
c. 1930. Made by W&S Theater Premium Co., Pittsburgh, PA. 13/16". - **$65 $125 $225**

MKY-48

❑ **MKY-48. "Mickey Mouse Undies" Black And White Advertising Button,**
c. 1930. Philadelphia Badge Co. 7/8". Version has image of Mickey as used on the second design Mickey Mouse Club movie theater buttons. - **$100 $200 $400**

MKY-49

❑ **MKY-49. "Mickey Mouse Undies" Celluloid Button,**
c. 1930. Backpaper by maker Whitehead & Hoag, Newark. .5". - **$50 $100 $150**

MKY-50

❑ **MKY-50. "Mickey Mouse/Pluto The Pup" Bisque,**
c. 1930. Japan. 2.5x2.25x5.5" tall designed with movable arm holding fabric "leash." Incised number "S178". - **$200 $450 $800**

MKY-51

❑ **MKY-51. Minnie Mouse With Tambourine Bisque Figure,**
c. 1930. Unmarked. Likely German. 1-1/8" tall. - **$35 $65 $125**

MICKEY MOUSE, MINNIE & NEPHEWS

MKY-52

MKY-55

❏ **MKY-56. Mickey Mouse Early Metal Figure,**
c. 1930. Figure is 1x1x2-3/8" tall and made of cast lead. Marked "Walter E. Disney" underneath. Some figures also say "Design. Pat. Apld. For." A scarce figure and perhaps the earliest Mickey metal figural. - **$100 $250 $500**

❏ **MKY-57. "Mickey Mouse" Bulbous Head Bisque Toothbrush Holder,**
c. 1930. Holder is 2.75x3.25x5" tall designed with one movable arm and string tail.
- **$115 $225 $350**

❏ **MKY-52. "Mickey Mouse" Boxed Celluloid Novelty,**
c. 1930. Box is 1x4x1.75" tall and holds 3 figures each about 7/8" tall crossing a bridge. Box is marked "Made In Japan."
Box - **$115 $225 $350**
Figure - **$100 $200 $300**

❏ **MKY-55. Four Marching Mickeys Celluloid Novelty,**
c. 1930. Japan. 1-7/8" tall Mickey followed by three smaller Mickeys. Mounted on .75x4" base.
- **$100 $200 $400**

MKY-56   MKY-57

MKY-58

MKY-53

❏ **MKY-53. Celluloid Figure On Base,**
c. 1930. "Made In Japan" 1.25" tall. - **$100 $150 $200**

❏ **MKY-58. Minnie Bulbous Head Toothbrush Holder,**
c. 1930. "Japan" 2.5x3x5" tall painted bisque figure with string tail. No incised number.
- **$100 $200 $300**

MKY-54

MKY-59

❏ **MKY-54. Mickey Mouse Celluloid Place Card Holder,**
c. 1930. Base is 1.25x2" with two attached figures, one 1.5" and the other .75". Small house in back is celluloid. Underside has Disney copyright label. - **$150 $250 $500**

❏ **MKY-59. Mickey Mouse "Pull On His Ear" Lithographed Tin Bank,**
c. 1930. Saalheimer & Strauss, Germany. Text on back explains ear should be pulled to make tongue appear for coin placement and deposit. Side text "By Exclusive Arrangement With Ideal Films Ltd. Registered 508041." 2.25x3.5x7" tall. Four reverse design versions: Mickey with clasped hands, hands apart, pointing (version pictured), and playing accordion.
Each - **$10000 $15000 $25000**

MICKEY MOUSE, MINNIE & NEPHEWS

MKY-60

❏ **MKY-60. Mickey Mouse China Figural Vase,**
c. 1930. Crown Devon, England. 6" tall. Underside has incised number "578" and text "Reproduced With The Consent Of Walter E. Disney & Ideal Films Ltd." Also issued with match striker area.
Either version - **$1000 $2000 $3500**

MKY-62

❏ **MKY-62. "Mickey Mouse" Five-Fingered Celluloid Wind-Up,**
c. 1930. Germany by Rheinische Gummi Und Celluloid Fabrik Co. Figure is celluloid 6" tall with spring tail and flat tin ears that wiggle. Sticker under foot "Reproduced With The Consent Of Walter E. Disney And Ideal Films Ltd." Box is 3.5x6.5x2.5" deep. Box - **$500 $1000 $2000**
Toy - **$1000 $2500 $5000**

MKY-64

❏ **MKY-64. Mickey Mouse With Felix In Basket Tin Lithographed Mechanical Toy,**
c. 1930. Made by Rogelio Sanchez, Spain, marked "Ilsa." Photo example missing Mickey's cloth tail. 4.75" long with spring action that raises basket lid to allow Felix to pop up. - **$3000 $7500 $15000**

MKY-61

❏ **MKY-61. Mickey Mouse Charlotte Clark Large And Rare Doll,**
c. 1930. Velveteen-covered stuffed 8x19x21.5" doll with felt ears, oilcloth eyes, separate string whiskers and four plastic buttons on pants. Has a long 14" tail. Underside of one foot has bold marking "Walt Disney Mickey Mouse" plus design patent number. - **$1600 $3600 $7000**

MKY-63

❏ **MKY-63. Mickey Five-Fingered Walking Lithographed Tin Wind-Up,**
c. 1930. Commonly credited to Johann Distler, Germany. 2.25" wide by 9" tall with rubber tail. - **$3500 $8000 $15000**

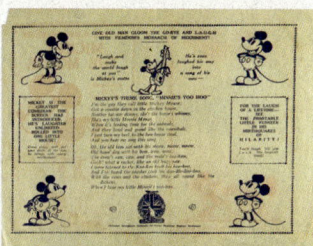

MKY-65

❏ **MKY-65. "Mickey The Mouse" Early Australian Movie Theater Hand-Out,**
c. 1930. 5.75x8.75" four page folder features numerous images of Mickey and related text along with "Mickey's Theme Song, Minnie's Yoo Hoo." Art by British artist Wilfred Haughton who drew the Mickey comics for the Mickey Mouse annual. - **$100 $200 $300**

MICKEY MOUSE, MINNIE & NEPHEWS

MKY-66

MKY-67

MKY-68

❏ **MKY-66. "Mickey Mouse" Flip Book,**
c. 1930. English by Flicker Productions Ltd. 2.25x3". Front cover reads "Mickey Mouse/Flicker No. 36/The Cheese Trap And Fatty Boy." Pages feature actual film scenes. - **$60 $125 $275**

❏ **MKY-67. "Mickey Mouse Coloring Book,"**
1931. Saalfield Publishing. 10.75x15.25". Book #871 with 28 pages. - **$100 $300 $800**

❏ **MKY-68. "Mickey Mouse Pictures To Paint" Book,**
1931. Saalfield. 9x10.5" softcover "No. 210" with 48 pages of illustrations by staff of Walt Disney Studios. Format is full color example pages and black/white identical pages to be colored. - **$125 $325 $850**

MKY-69

MKY-70

MKY-71

❏ **MKY-69. Walt Disney Studio Christmas Card,**
1931. Card is 5x7.5" closed with tipped-in paper sheet. - **$600 $1600 $3200**

❏ **MKY-70. Movie Exhibitor Magazine With Mickey Ad,**
1931. "Motion Picture Herald" 9.25x12.25" trade magazine issue for August 15 with eighty pages of articles, studio film ads, news features, plus two-page ad for "Mickey Mouse/Silly Symphonies" Columbia short features. - **$40 $65 $125**

❏ **MKY-71. Wood Jointed Figure With Lollipop Hands,**
1931. Figure is 3x6x7.25" tall complete with fabric-covered wire tail, pair of rubber-over-fabric ears, name decal on chest. Note: Yellow color is rare.
Red Figure - **$400 $800 $1500**
Yellow Figure - **$750 $1500 $2500**
Box - **$500 $1000 $1500**

MKY-72

❏ **MKY-72. Mickey/Minnie Fabric Pillow Cover,**
1931. Un-cut fabric sheet to be cut in half and then sewn together to form a pillow measures 16.5x34.5". Margin includes text "Mickey Mouse Series" and "98". - **$40 $75 $135**

MKY-73

❏ **MKY-73. Mickey/Minnie Fabric Pillow Cover,**
1931. Un-cut fabric sheet containing two halves that were to be sewn together to form a pillow and measures 16.5x34.5." Margin says "Mickey Mouse Series" and "97." - **$50 $100 $150**

MKY-74

❏ **MKY-74. "Mickey Mouse Handkerchiefs" Book,**
1931. Great Britain with Ideal Films and Disney copyright. 10x10.5" with six pages which likely held six hankies. Hanky art from Adventures of Mickey Mouse book. Book - **$100 $200 $400**
Each Hanky - **$15 $30 $60**

MICKEY MOUSE, MINNIE & NEPHEWS

MKY-75

MKY-77

MKY-78

MKY-79

❏ **MKY-79. "Mickey Mouse Storybook" Hardcover Version,**
1931. David McKay Co. 6x8.75" with 64 pages including black and white photos from early films. - **$125 $250 $500**

MKY-80

❏ **MKY-75. "Mickey Mouse Jazz Drummer" Mechanical Toy,**
1931. Nifty Co. 3x6.75" lithographed tin figure of Mickey with attached 1.5" diameter drum. German made. When lever on back is pushed down, this causes a pair of knobs inside the drum to spin rapidly and beat against the drum head which also moves up and down. Mickey's arms which are attached by rivets move up and down as if he is drumming with sticks. Specified as Nifty Toy #173 on top end of box.
Toy - **$800 $1800 $3000**
Box - **$500 $1200 $3500**

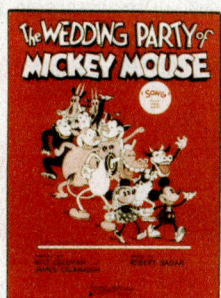

MKY-76

❏ **MKY-76. "The Wedding Party Of Mickey Mouse" Sheet Music,**
1931. Stasny Music Corp. 9x12" eight pages. - **$50 $100 $165**

❏ **MKY-77. "Mickey Mouse" First Newspaper Premium Picture Card,**
1931. Stiff paper card 3-3/8x5-3/8". Issued by various newspapers in May, 1931. Scene includes "Butch" in suit of armor. Historic and rare premium. - **$275 $550 $1100**

❏ **MKY-78. "Mickey Mouse Illustrated Movie Stories" Hardcover,**
1931. David McKay Co. 6.25x8.75" with 200 pages. Includes art taken from eleven of Mickey's earliest cartoons. Jacket - **$400 $800 $1600**
Book Only - **$250 $400 $850**
2" Red Slip-band With Instructions - **$100 $200 $300**

❏ **MKY-80. "Mickey Mouse Series No. 1" Reprint Book,**
1931. David McKay Co. 9.75x10" cardboard cover version with 48 pages of reprinted Floyd Gottfredson daily strips from 1930-1931 including the famous two-week sequence in which Mickey tries to commit suicide. - **$225 $650 $1500**

MKY-81

MICKEY MOUSE, MINNIE & NEPHEWS

MKY-82

◻ **MKY-81. "The Adventures Of Mickey Mouse Book 1,"**
1931. David McKay Co. 6.25x8.25" softcover with 32 pages. - **$100 $200 $400**

◻ **MKY-82. "The Adventures Of Mickey Mouse Book 1" Hardcover,**
1931. David McKay Co. 5.5x7.75" with 32 pages. Text refers to Clarabelle Cow as "Caroline" and to Horace Horsecollar as "Henry." The name "Donald Duck" designates a non-costumed generic duck. - **$125 $250 $500**

MKY-83

◻ **MKY-83. " The Adventures Of Mickey Mouse" Book Promotional Movie Theater Folder,**
1931. 6x9" glossy 4-page folder with images and various merchandise also includes an order form for classic Mickey book "The Adventures of Mickey Mouse." - **$200 $400 $800**

MKY-84

MKY-85

◻ **MKY-84. "Mickey Mouse" Sparkler,**
1931. By Nifty, distributed by Geo. Borgfeldt. 1.5x4x5.5" tall die-cut tin litho with spring plunger mechanism. Nifty Toy #174 on box. Beware of repro. boxes.
Box - **$250 $500 $1000**
Sparkler - **$200 $450 $750**

◻ **MKY-85. Mickey Mouse Iridescent Luster China Mug,**
c. 1931. Japan. 2.25" tall. Image near identical to front cover image of 1931 book "The Adventures of Mickey Mouse." - **$100 $200 $300**

MKY-86

◻ **MKY-86. Mickey In Santa Outfit Cello. Button,**
1931. Several imprints but usually "Meet Me At Hank's Toyland." - **$600 $850 $1850**

MKY-87

◻ **MKY-87. Mickey Mouse Theater Promo Cello Button,**
1931. Cello pinback with back paper. Rare. - **$600 $1050 $2100**

MICKEY MOUSE, MINNIE & NEPHEWS

MKY-88

❑ **MKY-88. Mickey Mouse Glazed Ceramic Napkin Ring,**
c. 1931. Comes in two sizes. 2-5/8" tall or 3-3/8" tall. Small - **$125 $250 $400**
Large - **$175 $350 $650**

MKY-89

❑ **MKY-89. Mickey Mouse Glazed Ceramic Napkin Holder,**
c. 1931. "Germany" on underside and "6567" on reverse. 4" tall. - **$200 $400 $775**

MKY-90

❑ **MKY-90. Mickey Mouse Figural China Condiment Jar,**
c 1931. German. 4" tall. Incised #2820. Depicts a five-fingered Mickey. - **$100 $200 $400**

MKY-91

❑ **MKY-91. "Fishin' Around Mickey Mouse Game,"**
c. 1931. English By Chad Valley Co. As noted on one side of game board "The Illustrations And Text Matter In This Game Were Taken From Mickey Mouse Movie Stories And Are Produced By Permission Of Dean & Son Ltd." - **$400 $800 $1350**

MKY-92

❑ **MKY-92. Mickey Pendant With Chain,**
c. 1931. Cohn and Rosenberger product. Black and green enameled pictured. Also comes in black with yellow. - **$50 $90 $150**

MKY-93

❑ **MKY-93. Mickey Classic Pose Silvered Brass Pin,**
c. 1931. 1" tall pin with silver finish and black and yellow enamel paint. - **$40 $80 $135**

MKY-94

❑ **MKY-94. Mickey Mouse Pencil Drawing From The Klondike Kid,**
1932. Sheet of animation paper is 9.5x12" with 2.5x4" image. #71 from a numbered sequence. - **$110 $225 $325**

MKY-95

MICKEY MOUSE, MINNIE & NEPHEWS

MKY-96

◻ **MKY-95. Walt Disney Studio Christmas Card,**
1932. Mailer card about 8x9" open. This example was sent to a theater in Allentown, PA. - **$500 $1000 $2000**

◻ **MKY-96. "Mickey Mouse Club" Rare Sweater Emblem,**
1932. Fisch & Co. 4.5" diameter felt. From an unknown theater in the Los Angeles area. - **$500 $1000 $1800**

MKY-97

◻ **MKY-97. Mickey Mouse Pull Toy By Steiff,**
1932. 4.5x7.25x8.5" tall toy consists of jointed Mickey figure attached to a four-wheel Irish mail which has heavy wire frame, wood seat and wheels. Metal button in ear, string whiskers, oil cloth eyes, fabric tail. Bellows in seat to squeak. - **$2500 $4500 $7750**

MKY-98

◻ **MKY-98. Fox Movie Theater Owner's Promo Booklet,**
1932. 4.5x6" with 16 pages. - **$30 $65 $110**

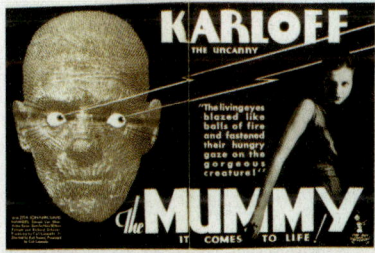
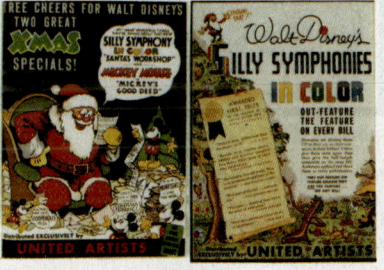

MKY-99

◻ **MKY-99. Movie Exhibitor Magazine With Mickey And Silly Symphonies,**
1932. "Motion Picture Herald." 9.25x12.25" December 17 weekly for movie theater owners, 76 pages. Content includes two-page ad for "Silly Symphony 'Santa's Workshop' And Mickey Mouse In 'Mickey's Good Deed'." Ad features Santa surrounded by four Mickeys reading mail sent to him. Another two-page ad introduces Boris Karloff as "The Mummy." - **$75 $150 $250**

MKY-100

◻ **MKY-100. Australian Movie Exhibitor Magazine Featuring Mickey Mouse And Silly Symphonies,**
1932. 10x12" Volume 13, No. 668 dated December 14, 1932 issue. Features 4-page full color insert for United Artists Mickey Mouse and Silly Symphonies shorts with artwork by Win Smith. - **$100 $200 $400**

MICKEY MOUSE, MINNIE & NEPHEWS

MKY-102

❑ **MKY-102. Mickey Mouse Early Glazed Ceramic Figure By Rosenthal,** 1932. Germany. About 4" tall. Likely the first figure produced. Incised #493. - **$1000 $2000 $3500**

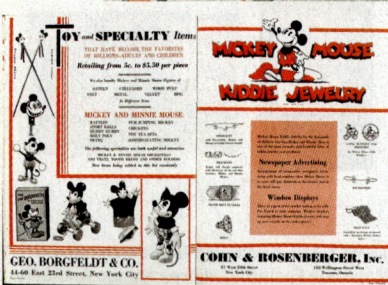

MKY-101

MKY-103

❑ **MKY-103. Mickey Mouse With Revolver Glazed Ceramic Figure By Rosenthal,** 1932. Germany. 3" tall. Incised #552. Rosenthal figures usually have a green and gold foil sticker under the base in German that translates to "Mickey Mouse Brings Luck To Your House." Rosenthal never distributed Disney items in the U.S.A. - **$750 $1500 $3000**

❑ **MKY-101. "Mickey Mouse And Silly Symphonies" Exceptional Film Exhibitor's Catalogue,** 1932. Book is 9x12" with 48 pages printed in limited run of around 15000 copies. Considered the first merchandise catalogue. Contents are black and white with great illustrations and photos. Attached to first page is reply postcard for theater owner stating their desire to run these features. - **$1500 $3500 $5250**

MICKEY MOUSE, MINNIE & NEPHEWS

MKY-104

MKY-106

❑ MKY-106. Mickey Mouse Playing Mandolin Glazed Ceramic Figure By Rosenthal, 1932. Germany. 3.25" tall. Incised #554. - $750 $1500 $3000

MKY-108

❑ MKY-108. Mickey Mouse Grinning Glazed Ceramic Figure By Rosenthal, 1932. Germany. 3.25" tall. Incised #551. - $650 $1350 $2750

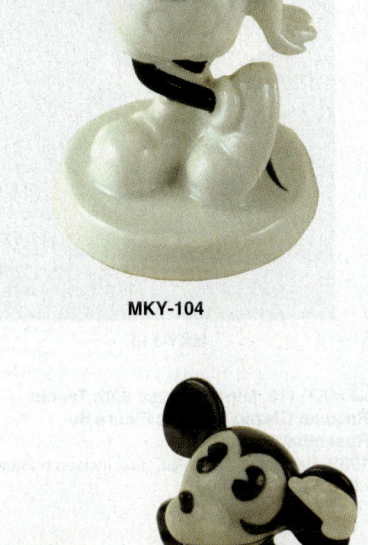

MKY-105

MKY-104

❑ MKY-104. Mickey Mouse Crossed Legs Glazed Ceramic Figure By Rosenthal, 1932. Germany. 3.5" tall. Incised #652. - $500 $1250 $2500

❑ MKY-105. Mickey Mouse Kicking Ball Glazed Ceramic Figure By Rosenthal, 1932. Germany. 3.5" tall. Incised #567. - $650 $1350 $2750

MKY-107

❑ MKY-107. Mickey Mouse Throwing Discus Glazed Ceramic Figure By Rosenthal, 1932. Germany. 3.25" tall. Incised #651. - $650 $1350 $2750

MKY-109

❑ MKY-109. Mickey Mouse With Saxophone Glazed Ceramic Figure By Rosenthal, 1932. Germany. About 3.5" tall. Incised #553. - $750 $1500 $3000

MICKEY MOUSE, MINNIE & NEPHEWS

MKY-110

❑ **MKY-110. Mickey Mouse Ball Toss Glazed Ceramic Figure By Rosenthal,** 1932. Germany. About 3.5" tall. Incised number. - **$750 $1500 $3000**

MKY-112

❑ **MKY-112. Minnie Mouse Bashful Pose Glazed Ceramic Figure By Rosenthal,** 1932. Germany. About 3.5" tall. Incised #556. - **$600 $1200 $1800**

MKY-113

❑ **MKY-113. Mickey Mouse On Ashtray Glazed Ceramic By Rosenthal,** 1932. Germany. About 3.5" diameter. Uncertain if with or without incised number. - **$600 $1200 $1800**

MKY-114

❑ **MKY-114. Mickey Mouse With Saxophone Glazed Ceramic Ashtray By Rosenthal,** 1932. Germany. 3.75x5.75" oval with 3" figure. No number. - **$750 $1500 $3000**

MKY-115

❑ **MKY-115. Minnie Mouse With Tennis Racquet Glazed Ceramic Figure By Rosenthal,** 1932. Germany. About 3.5" tall. Incised number. - **$750 $1500 $3000**

MKY-111

❑ **MKY-111. Minnie Mouse With Compact Glazed Ceramic Figure By Rosenthal,** 1932. Germany. About 3.5" tall. Incised #655. - **$750 $1500 $3000**

MKY-116

❑ **MKY-116. Mickey Mouse Hands On Hips Glazed Ceramic Figure By Rosenthal,** 1932. Germany. About 3.5" tall. Incised #550. - **$600 $1200 $1800**

MICKEY MOUSE, MINNIE & NEPHEWS

MKY-117

☐ **MKY-117. Mickey Mouse China Plate,**
1932. Rosenthal. 8.25" diameter depicts a happy Mickey Mouse image at center of plate. - **$100 $250 $500**

MKY-118

☐ **MKY-118. Mickey Mouse China Plate,**
1932. Rosenthal. 8.25" diameter depicts a puzzled Mickey Mouse image at center of plate. - **$100 $150 $500**

MKY-119

☐ **MKY-119. Mickey Mouse With Field Hockey Stick And Ball Glazed Ceramic Figure,**
1932. No markings. 1.25" tall. - **$65 $125 $185**

MKY-120

☐ **MKY-120. Mickey And Minnie Glazed Ceramic Salt & Pepper Set,**
1932. Marked "Germany." Mickey with incised number "6895." 2.5" tall. - **$125 $250 $400**

MKY-121

☐ **MKY-121. Pencil Drawing,**
1932. Animation paper is 9.5x12" centered by 4.5x5.5" image for 'Wayward Canary' film short. Depicted is Mickey poking his head through what appears to be a greenhouse framework with broken windows. No. "64" from a numbered sequence. - **$150 $250 $450**

MKY-122

☐ **MKY-122. Mickey Mouse Boxed Necklace,**
1932. Cohn & Rosenberger Inc. 2.75x5.25x.75" deep box contains nice quality necklace still attached to fabric-covered insert. Metal link necklace has three .5" tall silvered brass pendants with enameled paint.
Box - **$60 $135 $225**
Necklace - **$50 $100 $150**

MKY-123

☐ **MKY-123. "Mickey Mouse" Pillow Cover,**
1932. Vogue Needlecraft Co. #492 in series. 16x17.5". Unused - **$50 $100 $150** Neatly Stitched And Formed - **$25 $50 $75**

MKY-124

☐ **MKY-124. "Mickey Mouse" Pillow Pair,**
1932. Vogue Needlecraft. First is 16.5x18", #494, second is 15.5x16." Each Unused - **$50 $100 $150**
Each Used, Nicely Formed - **$25 $50 $75**

MICKEY MOUSE, MINNIE & NEPHEWS

MKY-125

❑ **MKY-125. "Mickey Mouse" Bracelet,**
1932. Cohn & Rosenberger. Silvered brass with 1.75" enamel Mickey figure. - **$40 $85 $200**

MKY-127

❑ **MKY-127. "Minnie" Mouse Child's Glass And Silver Beaded Necklace,**
1932. Likely By Cohn & Rosenberger. 6.75" long with 5/8" diameter glass pendant. - **$80 $165 $265**

MKY-130

❑ **MKY-130. Mickey Mouse Ring and Box,**
1932. Cohn & Rosenberger Inc. 1.25x1.25x1" deep cardboard box for enameled silver/brass Mickey Mouse ring pictured above.
Ring - **$300 $450 $900**
Box Only - **$100 $200 $300**

MKY-128

❑ **MKY-128. Minnie Mouse Bracelet With Charm,**
1932. 7/8" tall enamel paint on brass figure Minnie held on a child size 2.5" diameter brass link with green segments bracelet. - **$40 $75 $125**

MKY-131

❑ **MKY-131. Mickey Running Sterling And Enamel Pin,**
1932. 13/16" from jewelry series by Cohn & Rosenberger, New York City. - **$35 $75 $140**

MKY-129

❑ **MKY-129. Mickey & Minnie Enamel And Sterling Silver Child's Necklace,**
1932. Cohn & Rosenberger. 1" oval on 11" chain. Marked "Sterling." - **$65 $125 $200**

MKY-126

❑ **MKY-126. "Mickey/Minnie Mouse" Bangle Bracelet,**
1932. Cohn & Rosenberger. Silvered brass with enameled paint .5" wide and about 2.25" diameter. - **$125 $225 $425**

MKY-132

❑ **MKY-132. Mickey Mouse ABC Bowl,**
1932. Bavaria. 7.75" diameter by 1.5" deep. - **$125 $250 $450**

MICKEY MOUSE, MINNIE & NEPHEWS

MKY-133

MKY-136

❏ **MKY-136. Mickey/Minnie Mouse Ceramic Mug,**
1932. Mug is 3.5" tall. Marked on underside "Mickey Mouse/Copyright Walt E. Disney." Originally came as a set with bowl (previous item) and dish (following item.) - **$40 $85 $175**

MKY-139

❏ **MKY-139. "Mickey Mouse" China Cup And Saucer,**
1932. Bavaria. 2.5" tall cup and 4.75" diameter saucer. Both pieces have same company mark on underside that includes small Mickey image.
Cup - **$50 $75 $125**
Saucer - **$25 $50 $75**

MKY-134

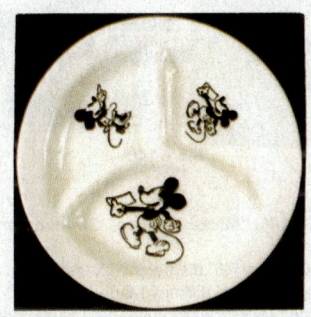

MKY-137

❏ **MKY-133. "Mickey Mouse" China Alphabet Bowl,**
1932. Bavaria. 8" diameter by 1.75" deep 1930s marked on underside "Walter E. Disney/Made In Bavaria" plus small full figure black, white and red Mickey image. Alphabet order error of "JI." - **$110 $240 $375**

❏ **MKY-134. "Mickey Mouse/Pluto The Pup" China Soup Bowl,**
1932. Bavarian. 7.5" diameter by 1.25" deep. - **$85 $175 $300**

❏ **MKY-137. Child's Partitioned Dish,**
1932. Dish is 7.5" diameter by 1" deep glazed ceramic segmented into three food sections. Reverse has copyright and name "Mickey Mouse." - **$75 $150 $300**

MKY-140

MKY-135

MKY-138

❏ **MKY-138. "Mickey Mouse China Creamer,**
1932. Bavaria. 3.5" tall. Incised #992. - **$100 $200 $300**

MKY-141

❏ **MKY-135. Mickey And Minnie Mouse Ceramic Bowl,**
1932. Krueger. 7" diameter by 1.75" deep. Reverse includes early copyright of "Walt E. Disney" as well as name "Mickey Mouse." - **$75 $150 $250**

❏ **MKY-140. "Mickey Mouse" China Sugar Bowl,**
1932. Bavaria. 4.5x6x3.25" tall. Underside has company markings plus small full figure image of Mickey and incised "590/3." Photo example missing lid. - **$135 $250 $400**

❏ **MKY-141. Minnie Mouse China Cup And Mickey Saucer,**
1932. Bavaria. 2.5" tall cup and 4.75" diameter saucer. Both pieces have company mark on underside that includes small Mickey image.
Cup - **$40 $65 $110**
Saucer - **$25 $50 $75**

MICKEY MOUSE, MINNIE & NEPHEWS

MKY-142

❏ **MKY-142. Mickey Mouse Mug,**
1932. Bavarian China. 3" tall. - **$50 $100 $200**

MKY-143

❏ **MKY-143. "Mickey Mouse" Bavaria German Cup,**
1932. China is 2.5" tall. - **$40 $65 $110**

MKY-144

❏ **MKY-144. "Mickey Mouse" German Large Plate,**
1932. China is 7.5" diameter with underside marking "Walter E. Disney/Made In Bavaria" plus small Mickey image. - **$100 $200 $325**

MKY-145

MKY-146

❏ **MKY-145. "Mickey Mouse" German Large Plate,**
1932. China is 7.5" diameter with underside marking "Walter E. Disney/Made In Bavaria" plus small Mickey walking image. - **$100 $200 $325**

❏ **MKY-146. "Mickey Mouse" Plate,**
1932. Bavarian, imported by Schumann, NYC. 6.25" diameter issue from chinaware series marked on underside by Mickey image and authorizations. - **$75 $175 $300**

MKY-147

❏ **MKY-147. "Mickey Mouse" Plate,**
1932. "Bavaria Schumann." 6.25" diameter issue from chinaware series marked on underside by Mickey image and authorizations. - **$75 $175 $300**

MKY-148

❏ **MKY-148. "Mickey Mouse" Plate,**
1932. "Bavaria Schumann." 6.25" diameter issue from series marked on underside by Mickey image and authorizations. - **$75 $175 $300**

MKY-149

MKY-150

❏ **MKY-149. "Mickey Mouse" Bavarian China Plate,**
1932. Plate is 6.25" in diameter and marked on reverse "Walter E. Disney/Made In Bavaria" with small Mickey image. - **$75 $175 $300**

❏ **MKY-150. "Mickey Mouse" Bavarian China Plate,**
1932. Plate is 6.25" in diameter and marked on reverse "Walter E. Disney/Made In Bavaria." - **$100 $200 $325**

MICKEY MOUSE, MINNIE & NEPHEWS

MKY-151

❏ **MKY-151. Mickey Mouse Glazed Ceramic Child's Tea Set By Rosenthal,**
1932. Set consists of six 1.25x7/8" deep cups and six 2-5/8" saucers, 3" tall teapot with lid, 1-5/8" tall sugar bowl with lid, 1-3/8" tall creamer and a ceramic serving tray. Set - **$3000 $7500 $15000**

MKY-152

MKY-153

❏ **MKY-152. Mesh Purse,**
1932. Mesh metal is 2.5x3.5" with enameled metal frame bar for the clasp closure. Attached to front by a pair of wire loops is a 1" tall metal diecut Mickey figure with painted accents. - **$200 $350 $550**

❏ **MKY-153. "1932-33 Art Needlework Specialty Shop" Catalogue With Mickey,**
1932. Issued by Frederick Herrschner Inc., Chicago. 8x11" with 68 pages. Shows many rare fabric items. - **$60 $135 $225**

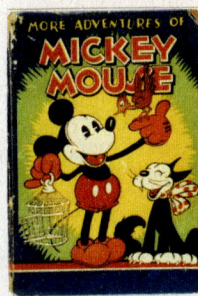

MKY-154

❏ **MKY-154. "More Adventures Of Mickey Mouse" English Book,**
1932. Dean & Son Ltd. 5.5x7.75" hardcover, 32 pages. Inside front and back covers feature full color map of town where Mickey lives. - **$100 $225 $550**

MKY-155

❏ **MKY-155. "Mickey Mouse Movie Stories" Book,**
1932. Musson Book Co. Ltd. "Second Canadian Edition" 6x8.75" clothbound hardcover, 190 pages. - **$100 $200 $375**

MICKEY MOUSE, MINNIE & NEPHEWS

MKY-156

❑ **MKY-156. "Mickey Mouse Book No. 2" Of Comic Strip Reprints,**
1932. David McKay Co. 9.75x10" cardboard cover book with 48 pages of reprinted 1931 daily strips by Floyd Gottfredson. - **$200 $600 $1200**

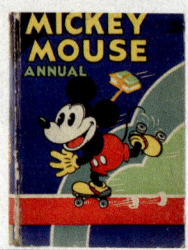

MKY-157

MKY-158

❑ **MKY-157. "Mickey Mouse Annual" Hardcover,**
1932. English by Dean & Son Ltd. 6.5x8.75x2" thick with 124 pages. - **$100 $250 $500**

❑ **MKY-158. Mickey And Minnie Book,**
1932. French by Hachette. 4.5x7" with 256 pages. - **$100 $225 $350**

MKY-159

❑ **MKY-159. "Movie Makers" Magazine With Mickey Mouse Film Ads,**
1932. 9x12" "Magazine Of The Amateur Cinema League Inc." - **$10 $20 $30**

MKY-160

❑ **MKY-160. Steiff Mickey Mouse Hand Puppet,**
1932. Velvet puppet 10" tall has sateen-covered hands, felt ears, oilcloth eyes and string whiskers. Came with ear button and cloth tag. There were two versions, this one shown with all black body and one with pants. With Tag And Button - **$400 $800 $1600**
With Tag Or Button - **$200 $500 $1000**
Without Tag And Button - **$100 $400 $800**

MKY-161

❑ **MKY-161. "Mickey Mouse" German Ashtray,**
1932. Bavarian China. 3x3x.5" deep. - **$50 $100 $150**

MKY-162

❑ **MKY-162. "Mickey Mouse" German Ashtray,**
1932. Bavarian China. 3x3x.5" deep. - **$50 $100 $150**

MKY-163

❑ **MKY-163. "Mickey Mouse" China Boxed Ashtray Set,**
1932. Bavaria. 7x7x.75" deep cardboard box with hinged lid contains set of four 3x3x.75" deep ashtrays. Underside of each ashtray has same markings which include small image of Mickey plus text "Mickey Mouse Authorized By Walter E. Disney/Made In Bavaria." Near Mint Boxed Set - **$750**

MICKEY MOUSE, MINNIE & NEPHEWS

MKY-164

MKY-165

❏ **MKY-164. "Mickey Mouse" Bavarian China Ashtray,**
1932. White china 3x3x.5". - **$50 $100 $150**

❏ **MKY-165. Minnie Mouse Ashtray,**
1932. White china 3x3x.5". - **$50 $100 $150**

MKY-166

MKY-167

❏ **MKY-166. Minnie Mouse Ashtray,**
1932. White china 3x3x.5". - **$50 $100 $150**

❏ **MKY-167. Minnie Mouse Bavarian China Ashtray,**
1932. China ashtray 3x3.5". - **$50 $100 $150**

MKY-168

❏ **MKY-168. Mickey Mouse China Ashtray,**
1932. Bavaria. 3x3x.75" deep. - **$50 $100 $150**

MKY-169

MKY-170

❏ **MKY-169. Mickey Mouse Get Well Card,**
1932. Hall Brothers. 4x5" paper card with scalloped edge. - **$25 $50 $80**

❏ **MKY-170. Mickey Mouse Calendar,**
1932. 6x11.75" die-cut stiff cardboard with attached complete 12-month calendar pad. - **$110 $225 $325**

MKY-171

❏ **MKY-171. "Mickey Mouse Home Movies" Promotion Material,**
1932. Lot of four pieces issued by "Hollywood Film Enterprises Inc," to store owners. Original envelope with Mickey/Minnie images is 4x9.5", a 12x18.5" sheet of paper designed like the front page of a newspaper titled "Cine Art Amateur Home Movies Vol. 1 No. 1," 8.5x11" letter typed on "Hollywood Film Enterprises" letterhead and a 3x8.5" sheet of pink paper with "Heading Correction" for the large "newspaper" sheet. As Issued - **$125 $250 $350**

MKY-172

❏ **MKY-172. Mickey Mouse In Bullet-Nose Car Bisque,**
c. 1932. 1.5" long. - **$135 $265 $525**

MICKEY MOUSE, MINNIE & NEPHEWS

MKY-173

MKY-174

MKY-175

MKY-176

❏ **MKY-176. Mickey Mouse In Chair German Metal Figure,**
c. 1932. Figure is 3-7/8" wide and 3.75" tall. - **$1000 $3000 $6000**

MKY-177

❏ **MKY-177. Mickey Mouse German Metal Figure,**
c. 1932. "Mickey Mouse" in lower relief text on one side, "Walt Disney" in lower relief text on other side. 4" wide, 3.25" tall. - **$650 $1300 $2150**

MKY-178

MKY-179

❏ **MKY-173. Mickey Mouse German Figure,**
c. 1932. Unmarked 2.75" tall with compressed paper body, heads, hands and feet plus pipe cleaner arms, legs and tail. - **$50 $100 $150**

❏ **MKY-174. Minnie German Figurine,**
c. 1932. "Deutschland" 1.75" tall china miniature. - **$40 $80 $150**

❏ **MKY-175. Mickey Mouse German Band China Figures,**
c. 1932. Set of six, each 2.25" tall. Incised numbers 4281 to 4286 consecutively. Each is a five fingered Mickey. Each - **$50 $100 $160**

❏ **MKY-178. Mickey Mouse With Umbrella German Metal Figure,**
c. 1932. Figure is 3.75" wide, 5" tall to top of umbrella. - **$800 $1500 $2500**

❏ **MKY-179. Mickey Mouse Metal Figure With Playing Card Suit Indicator,**
c. 1932. Germany. 'Book' pages flip to show card suits. A second version has Mickey with one arm bent down and one arm bent up. 3.25" tall by 4.25" wide. Either - **$1000 $2000 $3000**

MKY-180

MICKEY MOUSE, MINNIE & NEPHEWS

☐ **MKY-180. Mickey Mouse With Book Metal Figure,**
c. 1932. Germany. 3.5" tall. - **$800 $1500 $2500**

MKY-181

☐ **MKY-181. Mickey Mouse Metal Figure With Cigarette And Match Holders,**
c. 1932. Germany. 3.5" tall by 6" long. - **$1000 $2000 $3000**

MKY-182

MKY-183

☐ **MKY-182. Minnie Mouse Metal Figure Ashtray,**
c. 1932. Germany. 4.5" diameter by 5.25" tall. - **$800 $1500 $2500**

☐ **MKY-183. Minnie Mouse Metal Figure With Bell,**
c. 1932. Germany. 3.25" diameter by 5.75" tall. - **$1000 $2000 $3000**

MKY-184

☐ **MKY-184. Mickey Mouse Metal Figure Ashtray,**
c. 1932. Germany. 4.5" diameter by 5" tall. - **$850 $1600 $2750**

MKY-185

☐ **MKY-185. Mickey Mouse Metal German Astray With Floor Lamp,**
c. 1932. Metal Mickey is 3.5" tall on 3-1/8x4.75x5/8" metal base with 6" wire lamp at rear. Germany in black ink on underside. - **$1000 $2000 $3000**

MKY-186

☐ **MKY-186. Mickey Mouse Metal German Figure With Calendar On Lamppost,**
c. 1932. About 5.5" tall with paper calendar date sheets in holder. - **$1000 $2000 $3000**

MKY-187

☐ **MKY-187. Mickey Mouse Ceramic Bottle Stopper,**
c. 1932. Germany. 3-1/8" tall. Depicts Mickey with five fingers. - **$75 $150 $235**

MICKEY MOUSE, MINNIE & NEPHEWS

MKY-188

❑ **MKY-188. Large Mickey Mouse Candy Container,**
c. 1932. German. 6.25" tall painted composition figure stands atop cardboard candy box bottom platform which is 2.5" diameter by 1" tall. Underside of removable base has "Walter E. Disney" ink stamp plus German company name. - **$160 $275 $500**

MKY-189

MKY-190

❑ **MKY-189. Mickey Mouse Enameled Brass Comb Holder,**
c. 1932. Cohn & Rosenberger Inc. 1x4.5". - **$100 $150 $285**

❑ **MKY-190. Mickey/Minnie Fabric Pillow Cover Front,**
c. 1932. Unmarked 15x15.75" but item is known to be German-made. - **$125 $250 $500**

MKY-191

❑ **MKY-191. Mickey And Minnie Mouse Rug,**
c. 1932. Unmarked, likely German. 24x39". - **$85 $175 $350**

MKY-192

❑ **MKY-192. "Mickey Mouse" Compact,**
c. 1932. Cohn & Rosenberger. 1.5x1.75x3/8" deep chromed metal with enamel paint design on lid. - **$75 $150 $300**

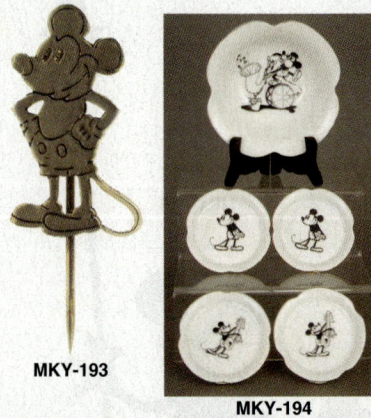

MKY-193   MKY-194

❑ **MKY-193. Mickey Mouse United Kingdom Stickpin,**
c. 1932. 1-1/8" tall silvered brass figure marked "All Rights Reserved." - **$40 $75 $135**

❑ **MKY-194. Mickey Mouse German China Bridge Set,**
c. 1932. "Koenigszelt Germany." Marked on underside of each piece. Set consists of 5.75" diameter by 1.75" deep dish and four 3.5" diameter individual serving plates, all have scalloped edges with bright gold trim. One example shown. Dish - **$200 $400 $750**
Each Plate - **$50 $100 $200**

MKY-195

MKY-196

❑ **MKY-195. "Mickey Mouse" Figural China Container,**
c. 1932. German. Marked "Foreign." 5.5" tall. Mickey has five fingers and his head serves as lid. - **$250 $500 $850**

❑ **MKY-196. Mickey And Minnie Glazed China Canister Set,**
c. 1932. Made In Japan. Nine pieces about 3" tall or smaller, most with lids, to hold various substances for kitchen use. Set - **$450 $900 $1800**

MKY-197

❑ **MKY-197. Child's Warming Dish,**
c. 1932. Bavarian China. 6" diameter by 2" deep bowl converted into a warming dish by mounting inside of a stainless steel container with American trademark "Excello" on underside. - **$100 $200 $400**

MICKEY MOUSE, MINNIE & NEPHEWS

MKY-198

MKY-199

MKY-200

❏ **MKY-198. Mickey Mouse China Egg Timer,**
c. 1932. Unmarked but likely German made. 3.75" tall. - **$250 $500 $800**

❏ **MKY-199. Mickey Mouse China Egg Timer,**
c. 1932. German. 3.5" tall overall. - **$115 $225 $400**

❏ **MKY-200. Mickey Mouse "30 Comics" Litho Button,**
c. 1932. Green Duck. 1-1/8". - **$125 $300 $600**

MKY-201

❏ **MKY-201. "Mickey Mouse Club" Button,**
c. 1932. Rim text copyright "1928-1930 By W.E. Disney." Kay Kamen backpaper. 1.25". - **$60 $115 $175**

MKY-202

❏ **MKY-202. "Mickey Mouse Club" Early Cello Button,**
c. 1932. 1/2". Likely produced by local theater owner using image from 1932 Exhibitor Campaign book. - **$200 $400 $650**

MKY-203

❏ **MKY-203. Mickey Mouse Stickpin,**
c. 1932. 1.5" tall tin die-cut in black and glossy silver luster. - **$25 $50 $85**

MKY-204

❏ **MKY-204. Mickey Mouse Mask,**
c. 1932. Germany. 8.5x9" pressed and formed paper mache. Inside of mask has ink stamps including name of "Walter E. Disney" as well as "Made In Germany." - **$135 $275 $450**

MKY-205

❏ **MKY-205. Mickey Mouse Vintage Homemade Adult Size Head Mask,**
c. 1932. 13x14.5x12.5". Paper mache and hand painted mask. - **$50 $100 $175**

MKY-206

❏ **MKY-206. Mickey Mouse Hand Puppet By Steiff,**
c. 1932. 10" tall velvetten puppet with stuffed head that has felt ears, oilcloth eyes and pair of string whiskers. Complete with small "Steiff" metal button in left ear. Front of pants are complete with pair of mother-of-pearl buttons. - **$750 $1500 $2500**

MICKEY MOUSE, MINNIE & NEPHEWS

MKY-207

❑ **MKY-207. Mickey Mouse Flat Figural Ceramic Ashtray,**
c. 1932. Germany. Incised under base #6584 and stamp "Germany" 5x5.25x2" deep. - **$250 $500 $1000**

MKY-208

❑ **MKY-208. Bagatelle Featuring Mickey Mouse And Felix The Cat,**
c. 1932. Italian by "Bottega Lithografica Muller And Brescia." 11.5x19.25x1.25" deep. - **$100 $200 $400**

MKY-209

❑ **MKY-209. Puzzle Set,**
1933. Features the whole gang, except Donald who didn't arrive until the following year. Four different puzzles. Each - **$50 $80 $150**

MKY-210

❑ **MKY-210. "The Art Of Mickey Mouse And His Creator Walt Disney" Booklet,**
1933. "College Art Assn." 5x6.5" eight-page glossy paper publication, probably issued for the first animation art exhibit. Contents include three Mickey short scenes, illustration of Mickey and Minnie ice skating, photo of Walt and Mickey. Film scene on back is from "Ye Olden Days." Text includes detailed information on Walt's career up to this point. - **$75 $135 $225**

MKY-211

❑ **MKY-211. Pencil Drawing,**
1933. Animation paper is 9.5x12" centered by 3x3.75" image for 'Puppy Love' cartoon short. No. "524" from a numbered sequence. - **$125 $250 $475**

MKY-212

❑ **MKY-212. Mickey And Minnie Mouse Pencil Drawing From Mickey's Mellerdrammer,**
1933. Animation paper is 9.5x12" with 4x6" image. Depicts Mickey in blackface as Uncle Tom and Minnie as Little Eva dancing. - **$150 $300 $550**

MKY-213

❑ **MKY-213. Ethnic Pencil Drawing,**
1933. Animation paper is 9.5x12" centered by 3x4.5" drawing for 'Mickey's Mellerdrammer' short. Mickey is depicted as African American caricature with black face, braided hair with bows, tattered outfit. Margin has "155/357," one being a sequence number. - **$150 $300 $550**

MKY-214

❑ **MKY-214. Minnie Mouse Pencil Drawing From Building A Building,**
1933. Sheet of animation paper is 9.5x12" with 2x3.5" image in lead/blue/red pencil. - **$125 $250 $400**

MKY-215

❑ **MKY-215. Mickey Mouse Pencil Drawing From Giant Land,**
1933. 9.5x12" sheet of animation paper with 2.75x2.75" image. "153" from a numbered sequence. - **$100 $200 $350**

MICKEY MOUSE, MINNIE & NEPHEWS

MKY-216

MKY-217

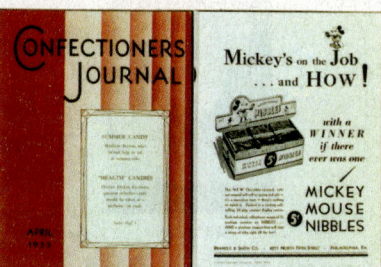

MKY-219

❑ MKY-218. "Confectioner's Journal" With Mickey Candy Ad,
1933. Ad is 8.5x11.5" in "The World's Oldest Candy Paper." Contains full page ad for "Mickey Mouse Nibbles" candy that includes photo with full display box. - $12 $30 $60

❑ MKY-219. "Confectioners Journal" With Mickey Mouse Ad,
1933. Volume 59, #699 from April 1, 1933 with 68 pages. Features a one-page ad for "Mickey Mouse Nibbles" including photo of candy display box picturing Mickey. - $12 $30 $60

MKY-220

❑ MKY-220. Mickey/Minnie Mouse Premium Masks With Envelope,
1933. Einson-Freeman Co. 10x12" brown envelope contains eight stiff paper masks, seven for Mickey and one for Minnie. Masks were given one per package in Quaker Crackles.
Envelope - $50 $100 $200
Mickey Mask - $35 $65 $135
Minnie Mask - $35 $65 $135

MKY-221

❑ MKY-216. Mickey Mouse Pencil Drawing "From The Mad Doctor,"
1933. Animation paper is 9.5x12" with 2.5x3" image. No. "71" from a numbered sequence. - $65 $125 $225

❑ MKY-217. "Lumar Mickey Mouse Jig-Saw" Boxed English Puzzle,
1933. Boxed puzzle is 6.5x9.5x1" deep titled "Mickey's Circus." Box underside has paper label for puzzle completion contest and a related leaflet entry form is enclosed. - $45 $85 $150

MKY-218

MKY-222

❑ MKY-221. "Wrights Mickey Mouse Biscuits" Wrapper,
1933. English by L. Wright & Son. 10x11.5" flattened wrapper was originally wrapped around a cardboard box. - $75 $150 $250

❑ MKY-222. "World Flight Of Mickey Mouse" Premium Game,
1933. Australian by John Sands Ltd./R.M. Osbourne Ltd. for Woodson's tea and "Anchor Brand Groceries." Also issued in USA.
Australian - $350 $650 $1000
USA - $600 $1200 $2000

MKY-223

❑ MKY-223. Mickey Mouse Wood Plaque,
1933. A Fine Art Picture. 4x5.5x.25" thick with image on front that is described on reverse as "Hand-Printed In Oil Colors/Washable." - $40 $75 $125

MICKEY MOUSE, MINNIE & NEPHEWS

MKY-224

❑ **MKY-224. Chicago World's Fair Bank,**
1933. Bank is 2.25x4.25x2" tall metal formed as replica chest overlaid by lightly embossed oilcloth fabric with brass-plated side panels. Oilcloth body is designed as a brick building. There are two versions of this bank and this world's fair variety has a number of differences to the standard "Mickey Mouse Bank." Text on top reads "Mickey And Minnie At The World's Fair" with images of them plus text "1933 Chicago 1934." - **$125 $250 $400**

MKY-225

❑ **MKY-225. Mickey Mouse Club Password Pinback,**
1933. The words and letters meant "Things are swell." Given away at clothing stores and theaters. This pinback was only produced for two months - January and February of 1933. - **$75 $175 $350**

MKY-226

❑ **MKY-226. "Mickey Mouse And Minnie's In Town" Sheet Music,**
1933. Irving Berlin Inc. 9x11.75" with eight pages. - **$35 $80 $135**

MKY-227

❑ **MKY-227. "Dream Of Mickey Mouse" Sheet Music,**
1933. Bach Music Co. 9.25x12.25" "Piano Solo." No Disney copyright, likely unauthorized. Does not feature studio art which is signed "C. Vaillant." - **$10 $25 $50**

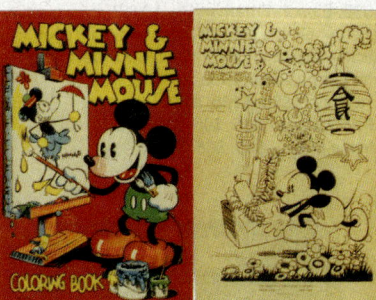

MKY-228

❑ **MKY-228. "Mickey & Minnie Mouse Coloring Book,"**
1933. Saalfield. 10.75x15.25" with 28 pages. Illustrations throughout by Disney Studio staff including 16 example pictures printed in full color. - **$85 $225 $450**

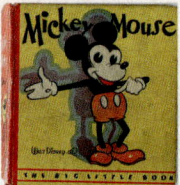 

MKY-229

❑ **MKY-229. "Mickey Mouse" First Big Little Book,**
1933. Whitman. Book #717. First ever Mickey Big Little Book with first edition cover design. This cover features a more primitive-looking Mickey on the front cover and has Walt Disney signature at lower left. - **$341 $1023 $2730**

MKY-230

❑ **MKY-230. "Mickey Mouse" First Big Little Book Variety,**
1933. Whitman. Big Little Book #717, the first Mickey Big Little Book but the second version as cover art was altered. On the first version Mickey has more of a rat-like appearance and illustration on back is Mickey and Minnie hugging. This cover has the classic Mickey image on front; on back he is depicted giving Minnie a flower. The first cover also had Walt's signature whereas it is removed on this edition. - **$175 $525 $1400**

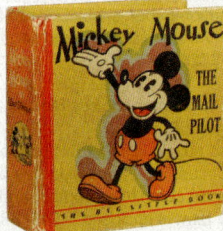

MKY-231

❑ **MKY-231. "Mickey Mouse The Mail Pilot" Rare Variety,**
1933. Whitman. Apparently Whitman was ready to publish Mickey's second story before new cover art was ready. This copy has cover from the first Mickey Big Little Book #717 (second edition) with the second title added to front cover. The back cover has black overprint of first story designation "No. 717" with "No. 731" printed next to it. - **$2500 $5000 $10000**

MICKEY MOUSE, MINNIE & NEPHEWS

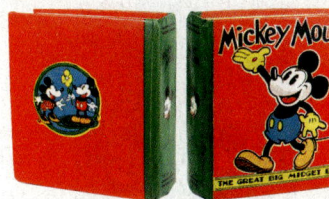

MKY-232

☐ **MKY-232. Mickey Mouse, The Great Big Midget Book,**
1933. England version of 1st book. Scarce. - **$200 $500 $1500**

MKY-233

☐ **MKY-233. "Mickey Mouse The Mail Pilot" Premium Big Little Book,**
1933. Whitman. (Un-numbered). Soft cover issued by American Oil Co. Also issued as standard hardcover Whitman #731. Either Version - **$39 $117 $270**

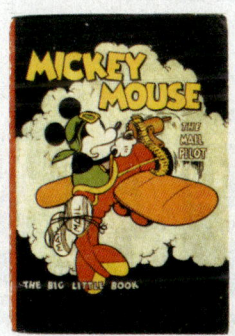

MKY-234

☐ **MKY-234. "Mickey Mouse The Mail Pilot" BLB,**
1933. Whitman. No number. Softcover version unusual format with size of 3.5x4.75" rather than 4x4" size. - **$39 $117 $270**

MKY-235

☐ **MKY-235. Correspondence/Publicity Material For "Mickey Mouse In The Mail Pilot,"**
1933. Lot of four papers, 8.5x11" relating to the 1933 short "The Mail Pilot." Includes letter from "United Artists Corp./Mickey Mouse Publicity," a one-page synopsis of the short, a "Special Notice To All Aviation Fans" paper that includes illustration of Mickey in an air battle and a typed letter from the "Autogiro Company of America." - **$50 $150 $250**

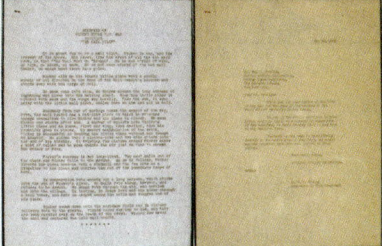

MKY-236

☐ **MKY-236. "Mickey Mouse Sails For Treasure Island" Big Little Book,**
1933. Whitman. Book #750. Also issued as un-numbered premium without ads or with Kolynos Dental Cream ad. Numbered Edition - **$49 $147 $345**
Un-numbered Edition - **$49 $147 $345**

MKY-237

☐ **MKY-237. "Mickey Mouse Sails For Treasure Island" English Book,**
1933. Dean & Son, England. "The Great Big Midget Book." - **$131 $393 $1050**

MKY-238

MKY-239

☐ **MKY-238. "Mickey Mouse Annual,"**
1933. The Musson Book Co. Ltd., Toronto 6.75x9x2" thick hardcover with 246 pages. - **$150 $300 $600**

☐ **MKY-239. "Mickey Mouse" Reprint Book,**
1933. Whitman. 8.5x10" edition #948 with dual copyright 1932-1933. Content is 34 pages of full color Sunday strip reprints. Cardboard covers have identical art front and back. A similar book was published by David McKay titled "Mickey Mouse Book No. 3." - **$150 $300 $600**

MICKEY MOUSE, MINNIE & NEPHEWS

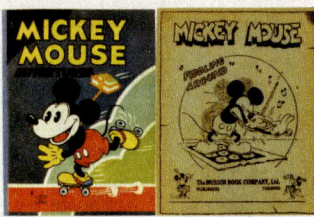

MKY-240

MKY-243

MKY-245

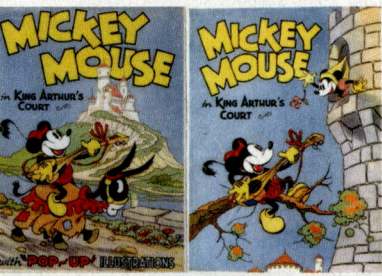

MKY-246

❑ **MKY-240. "Mickey Mouse Adventures" Canadian Book Condensed Version,** 1933. Musson Book Co. Ltd. 6.25x8.5" cardboard covered 36 pages. One page features four-panel story "Ear-Ear" in which Mickey tries to use his ear as a coin for a chocolate vending machine. - **$125 $250 $500**

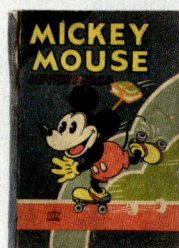

MKY-241

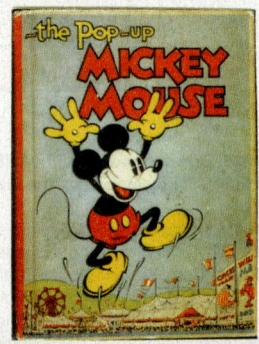

MKY-244

❑ **MKY-241. "Mickey Mouse Adventures" Standard Version Book,** 1933. Canadian by Musson Book Co. Ltd. 6.25x8.5" with 64 pages. - **$75 $150 $250**

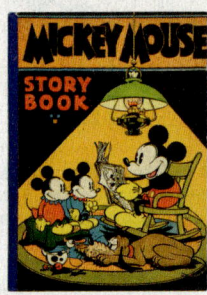

MKY-242

❑ **MKY-243. English Magazine With Mickey Mouse Contest,** 1933. Amalgamated Press Ltd. "Film Pictorial" 8.5x11.5" Vol. 4 #2 weekly issue for November 25. Content includes photo features on many U.S. movie stars plus a one-page "Mickey Mouse Cut-Out Puzzles" contest including four different numbered cut-outs of Mickey, each with slightly different body parts. Object was to make a complete Mickey figure using one or more of the cut-outs. Front cover has small Mickey image at top left corner pointing to title "New Mickey Mouse Contest: Money Prizes." - **$20 $40 $70**

❑ **MKY-244. "The Pop-Up Mickey Mouse,"** 1933. Blue Ribbon Books. 6.5x8.75" hardcover with 24 pages and three two-page full color pop-ups. - **$100 $300 $850**

❑ **MKY-245. "The Pop-Up Minnie Mouse" Hardcover,** 1933. Blue Ribbon Books Inc. 6.75x8.75" with 28 pages. - **$100 $300 $850**

❑ **MKY-246. "Mickey Mouse In King Arthur's Court With 'Pop-Up' Illustrations,"** 1933. Blue Ribbon Books. Hardcover with dust jacket. 7.5x9.5" with 48 stiff cardboard pages. Jacket - **$100 $250 $500**
Book - **$250 $525 $1500**

MKY-247

❑ **MKY-242. "Mickey Mouse Story Book" Canadian Printing,** 1933. Musson. 6.25x8.5" with 64 pages. Soft cover version. - **$60 $125 $200**

❑ **MKY-247. Mickey/Minnie Mouse Cut Out Doll Book,** 1933. Saalfield. 10x19.25" large format book featuring a cardstock cover and four pages. Outfits including cowboy and drum major for Mickey, Chinese costume and Dutch dress for Minnie. - **$500 $1000 $1500**

MICKEY MOUSE, MINNIE & NEPHEWS

MKY-249

❑ **MKY-249. Mickey Mouse Electric Clock,**
1933. Ingersoll. 4.5" square by 2.25" deep. Mickey's body revolves each minute. Paper band around three sides of the case. Clock - $400 $1000 $1800
Box With Pop-Up Mickey Flap - $650 $1300 $2100
Price Tag - $25 $50 $100

MKY-248

❑ **MKY-248. Mickey, Minnie and Pluto Marionettes,**
1933. Made By Hestwood Marionette Studio, Glendale Calif. Made of wood, composition and cloth. Each figure about 12". Each came in a yellowish fabric bag with drawstring.
"Bullocks Wilshire" Decorated Box - $300 $750 $1500
"Bullocks" Undecorated Black Box - $100 $200 $400
Mickey - $1000 $2000 $4000
Minnie - $800 $1750 $3500
Pluto - $600 $1500 $2500

MKY-250

❑ **MKY-250. First Variety of First "Mickey Mouse Ingersoll" Wristwatch,**
1933. Sold at Chicago World's Fair and distinguished from second variety introduced in the Fall, 1933 by: wider image of Mickey, different typeface for numerals, number "5" positioned above Mickey's knee on dial, Art Deco geometric design on bezel, wire lugs on case to hold either metal links or leather strap band.
Box (and Insert) with 1933 Exposition Logo Sticker - $500 $1500 $3000
Box (and Insert) without Sticker - $250 $500 $1000
Cardboard Strip with $2.75 price designated - $30 $60 $100
Guarantee Insert paper - $15 $25 $50
Watch with Metal or Leather Band - $400 $800 $1600

MKY-251

❑ **MKY-251. Mickey Mouse Ingersoll Silvered Brass Link Straps,**
1933. Two-piece strap 5.75" long has clasp and each piece consists of four links including a pair with Mickey image. For first watch. - $50 $100 $175

MKY-252

❑ **MKY-252. "Mickey Mouse Ingersoll" First English Watch,**
1933. 1-1/8" diameter with earliest Mickey image on the celluloid dial. The large image was later changed to the more traditional portrait with blush color on the face. - $1000 $2000 $3500

MICKEY MOUSE, MINNIE & NEPHEWS

MKY-253

MKY-254

❑ **MKY-254. "Mickey Mouse Ingersoll Pocketwatch" Complete Boxed Set,**
1933. Ingersoll. 2.5x4.75x.75" deep box contains complete and earliest issue. Box is scarcer style with large image of Mickey on lid and inside of lid rather than repeated pattern of small characters. Box has two-piece cardboard insert that holds the fob in place. The silvered brass fob with incised image of Mickey has black leather strap. Watch is earliest style with longer stem. Metal case has incised image of Mickey on back which matches design on the fob. Box Complete - **$325 $650 $1300**
Watch - **$325 $650 $1300**
Fob - **$50 $100 $200**

MKY-255

❑ **MKY-255. "Mickey Mouse Ingersoll Pocketwatch" Complete In Second Issue Box,**
1933. Ingersoll. 2.5x4.75x.75" deep box contains complete issue. Box has two-piece cardboard insert that holds fob in place. The silvered brass fob with incised image of Mickey has black leather strap.
Box Complete - **$250 $500 $1000**
Watch - **$300 $600 $1200**
Fob - **$50 $100 $200**

MKY-256

❑ **MKY-256. First English "Mickey Mouse Ingersoll" Pocket Watch,**
1933. Watch is 2" in diameter with silvered metal case. Second hand disk has three small Mickey images. - **$375 $800 $1500**

MKY-257

❑ **MKY-257. Mickey Mouse Musician Miniature Metal Figure,**
c. 1933. Unmarked. Likely Austrian. From a series known to include violinist, bass fiddle, bass drum. Each - **$125 $250 $500**

MKY-258

❑ **MKY-253. Second and Later Varieties of First Wrist Watch Design,**
Fall 1933 through 1939. Ingersoll. Re-designed 2.5x4.5x1" deep hinged lid box. To be complete, all versions through Spring/Summer 1935 contain box insert, cardboard strip with text specifying retail price and "Guarantee" paper. All versions were avalable with metal bands (seven links plus two with Mickey image) or leather bands with two metal die-cut Mickeys attached. Bands are now held to watch case by pins rather than wire lugs. Second variety (shown in photo) has same dial as Chicago World's Fair variety, but no designs on the bezel. The watch for 1934 has a newly designed dial with thinner Mickey, different typeface for the numerals and number "5" is below Mickey's knee. Beginning Fall 1935, the caption "Made in U.S.A." now appears on dial to the left of Mickey's pants. A larger blue box was introduced for Fall/Winter 1935 containing box insert, four-page guarantee folder and small slip telling dealer how to display the boxed watch. This watch design and box (with minor changes) were used through 1939, athough newly designed rectangular case watches were introduced in Spring 1937 (for girls) and Fall 1937 (for boys).
Second Variety Watch With Either Band - **$200 $400 $800**
Second Variety Box Complete - **$200 $400 $800**
Round 1935 - 1939 Watch With Either Band - **$150 $300 $600**
Blue 1935 - 1939 Box Complete - **$150 $300 $600**

MICKEY MOUSE, MINNIE & NEPHEWS

MKY-259

❑ **MKY-258. Mickey Camping Out Scene Reliance Art Glass Framed Picture,**
c. 1933. Reliance Picture Frame Co. 7.75x10.75" wood frame holding glass with bright enamel picture on reverse of glass. Titled "The Joys Of Camping." - **$150 $325 $600**

❑ **MKY-259. "Mickey Mouse Bank,"**
c. 1933. Zell Products Corp. 2.25x4.25x2" tall metal bank designed like a chest overlaid by lightly embossed oilcloth fabric with brass-plated side panels. This is the non-1933/1934 Chicago World's Fair variety with text "Mickey Mouse Bank Be Thrifty-Save Your Coins." - **$75 $150 $275**

MKY-260

❑ **MKY-260. Birthday Card,**
c. 1933. Hall Brothers Inc. Closed 4x4.25" folder card. - **$25 $50 $75**

MKY-261

❑ **MKY-261. "Sincerely Yours-Mickey Mouse" Celluloid Button,**
c. 1933. Button is 3.5". Worn by toy store employees. - **$300 $1250 $2500**

MKY-262

❑ **MKY-262. English Ingersoll Clock Variety,**
c. 1933. English version 2x4x4" tall wind-up clock differing in several aspects from its U.S. Ingersoll counterpart of same production era. Both have painted metal case but English version decal around one side across the top to opposite side has different images of Mickey, Minnie, Pluto, Horace, Clarabelle. English clock face design differs by a running pose by Mickey rather than standing pose. Similar pose variations are on the inset second timer wheel.
Clock - **$300 $600 $1200**
Box - **$300 $600 $1200**

MKY-263

MKY-264

❑ **MKY-263. Mickey Mouse Celluloid On Tin Litho Wind-Up Tricycle,**
c. 1933. Made in Japan. 4.5" Mickey on 5.5" long tricycle. - **$250 $500 $900**

❑ **MKY-264. "Mickey Mouse" Fountain Pen,**
c. 1933. Inkograph Company. Screw-on cap has pocket clip with "Mickey Mouse" name and around bottom edge are three decals, two of Mickey and one of Minnie. Body of pen has full figure Mickey decal and metal pen point has small Mickey portrait and copyright symbol. - **$50 $125 $250**

MKY-265

❑ **MKY-265. Mickey Mouse And Donald Duck Pencil Drawing From The Dognapper,**
1934. Animation paper is 9x12" with 4x4.5" image. #134 of a numbered sequence. - **$150 $300 $500**

MKY-266

❑ **MKY-266. Mickey's Steamroller Illustration Art,**
1934. 11.75x7.75" preliminary pencil art drawn in advance of pen and ink artwork used as publicity stills for this classic Disney short. - **$1000 $2000 $4000**

MICKEY MOUSE, MINNIE & NEPHEWS

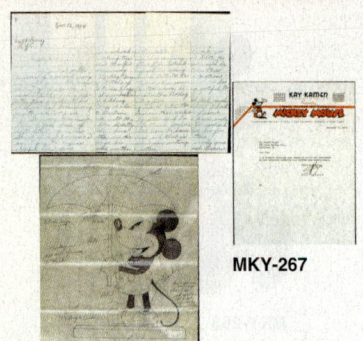

MKY-267

❑ **MKY-267. Lot Of Original Licensing Correspondence Including Kay Kamen Signed Letter,**
1934. Artists 4-page letter proposing a lamp design, sketch of lamp and refusal letter from Kamen. Unique Near Mint - **$450**

❑ **MKY-268. "Mickey Mouse Choral Top" With Box,**
1934. Box is 8.75" square holding very large tin lithographed top with 10" diameter by 11" tall. Top features great character images of Mickey, Minnie, Pluto, Three Little Pigs and Big Bad Wolf. Bottom half has text reading "Exclusively For Geo. Borgfeldt Corp./Made by Lackawanna Mfg. Co. Box - **$250 $600 $1100**
Top - **$200 $400 $700**

MKY-269

❑ **MKY-269. Film Directory Annual With Mickey And Others,**
1934. "Film Daily Production Guide and Directors Annual" 6x9.25" hardcover, 368 pages. Content overall is an encyclopedia of movie information including full-page Walt Disney ad with illustrations of Mickey and Minnie, smaller images of Silly Symphony characters, mention that cartoons will be in Technicolor "For The First Time." - **$35 $75 $125**

MKY-268

MKY-270

❑ **MKY-270. Mickey Mouse Metal English Car Mascot,**
1934. Desmo Corporation, England. 4.25" tall chromium with over-paint (displayed on plastic base). - **$2200 $4500 $8500**

MKY-271

❑ **MKY-271. Mickey And Minnie Metal English Car Mascot,**
1934. Desmo Corporation. Paint over chromium plating. Mickey is 4-3/8" tall, Minnie is 4-1/8" tall. Both are attached to 4.5" wide metal base which is mounted on a lucite base for display. - **$3000 $7500 $13000**

MICKEY MOUSE, MINNIE & NEPHEWS

MKY-272

❑ **MKY-272. "Post Toasties" Shipping Carton Panel With Mickey,**
1934. Panel is 14.75x16" with 4" tall image of Mickey plus his name below in large letters. Panel was cut from a carton of "Double-Crisp Corn Flakes." - **$30 $60 $100**

MKY-274

❑ **MKY-274. Mickey Mouse Jointed Wood Figure,**
1934. Made in Italy by Peri with Walter E. Disney copyright. 5-7/8" tall. - **$225 $450 $900**

MKY-275

❑ **MKY-275. "Folio Of Songs From Walt Disney's Famous Pictures Mickey Mouse And Silly Symphony,"**
1934. Irving Berlin Inc. 9x12" with 32 pages. Includes illustrations and words and music to eleven different songs. - **$60 $125 $250**

MKY-276

MKY-277

❑ **MKY-276. "Mickey Mouse Merchandise" First Catalogue,**
1934. Kay Kamen Inc. 9x12" With 76 pages of Disney licensee product photos and information. 25,000 produced. - **$2000 $3500 $6500**

❑ **MKY-277. Mickey Mouse Store Display Standee,**
1934. Made By Old King Cole, Distributed By Kay Kamen. Molded 'laminite' 11x15.5x1.5" deep. - **$550 $1050 $1700**

MKY-273

❑ **MKY-273. Mickey Mouse Glazed Ceramic Perfume Bottle,**
1934. 4" tall with removable hollow head and tin lithographed movable ears. Hole in nose for perfume. Missing rubber cover on back of head. Has 1934 Chicago World's Fair foil sticker. - **$200 $400 $800**

MKY-278

❑ **MKY-278. Minnie Mouse Store Display Standee,**
1934. Made By Old King Cole, distributed by Kay Kamen. Molded 'laminite' 11x15.5x1.5" deep. - **$500 $1000 $1500**

MICKEY MOUSE, MINNIE & NEPHEWS

MKY-279

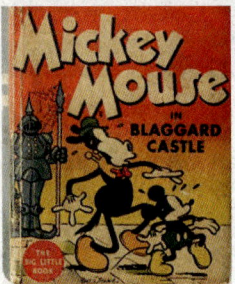

MKY-280

MKY-282

❏ **MKY-282.** "Mickey Mouse Stories,"
1934. David McKay Co. 6.25x8.5" stiff cover Book #2 with 62 pages. Has illustrations taken directly from Mickey's earliest cartoons including Pioneer Days, The Delivery Boy, The Castaway and The Moose Hunt. - **$75 $150 $350**

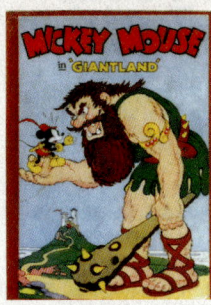

MKY-284

MKY-285

❏ **MKY-284.** "Mickey Mouse In 'Giant Land',"
1934. David McKay Co. 6.25x8.25 hardcover with 48 pages. - **$75 $150 $350**

❏ **MKY-285.** "Mickey Mouse Movie Stories Book 2" Hardcover,
1934. David McKay Co. 6.75x8.5" with 200 pages. Includes art taken from Mickey's earliest cartoons. - **$150 $300 $750**

❏ **MKY-279.** "Mickey Mouse The Detective" Big Little Book,
1934. Whitman. Book #1139. - **$36 $108 $250**

❏ **MKY-280.** "Mickey Mouse In Blaggard Castle" Big Little Book,
1934. Whitman. Book #726. - **$39 $117 $270**

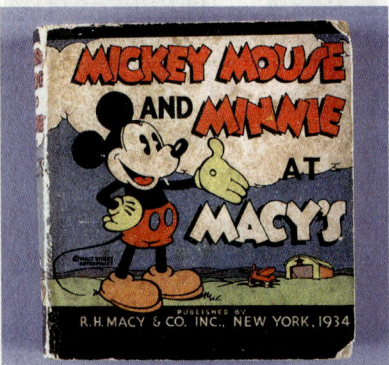

MKY-281

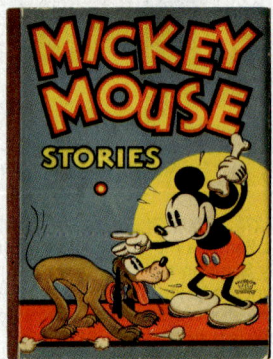

MKY-283

❏ **MKY-283.** "Mickey Mouse Stories" Canadian Printing,
1934. Musson. 6.25x8.5" with 56 pages. Soft cover version. - **$75 $150 $300**

❏ **MKY-281.** "Mickey Mouse And Minnie Mouse At Macy's" Premium Book,
1934. Whitman. No number. Christmas giveaway 3.25x3.5" softcover with 148 pages. - **$393 $1179 $3150**

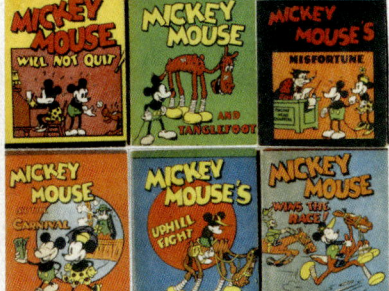

MKY-286

MICKEY MOUSE, MINNIE & NEPHEWS

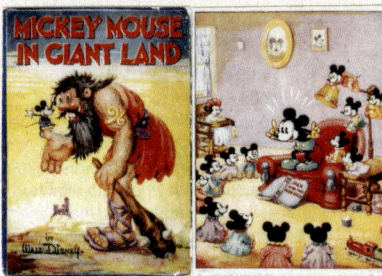
MKY-287

MKY-289

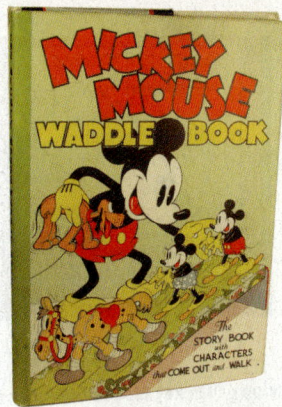

❏ **MKY-286. "Mickey Mouse Wee Little Books" Boxed Set,**
1934. Whitman. Set of six 3x3.5" books with 1.5x3.75x2" deep box. Each book has 40 pages.
Box - **$55 $125 $250**
Each Book - **$20 $40 $80**

❏ **MKY-287. "Mickey Mouse In Giant Land" English Hardcover,**
1934. William Collins Sons & Co. Ltd. 7.25x10" with 96 thick paper pages. - **$75 $150 $300**

❏ **MKY-289. "Mickey Mouse Waddle Book" Wrapper Strip,**
1934. Stiff paper band is 4.25x10.5" that originally went around the 1934 Waddle Book by Blue Ribbon Books. Band was usually disposed of and is extremely rare. - **$100 $300 $600**

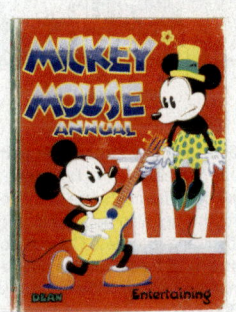

MKY-290

MKY-288

❏ **MKY-288. "Mickey Mouse Annual" English Hardcover,**
1934. Dean & Son Ltd. 6.5x8.5x2" thick with 124 thick paper pages. - **$100 $250 $500**

❏ **MKY-290. "Mickey Mouse Waddle Book" With Dust Jacket And Set Of Waddles,**
1934. Blue Ribbon Books. 7.75x10.25" hardcover with 28-page illustrated story and two instruction pages. Characters are designed to walk downward on a stiff paper ramp also included in the book but not pictured. Cover Slip Band - **$100 $300 $600**
Jacket Only - **$75 $200 $500**
Book Only - **$75 $200 $400**
Each Assembled Waddle - **$300 $600 $1000**
Each Unpunched Waddle - **$500 $1200 $4000**
Ramp - **$150 $250 $1000**
Near Mint, Complete - **$18500**

MICKEY MOUSE, MINNIE & NEPHEWS

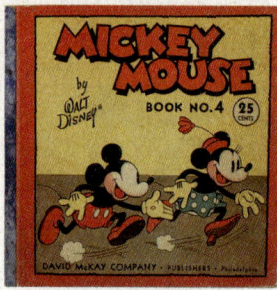

MKY-291

❏ **MKY-291. "Mickey Mouse Book No. 4" Early Reprint Book,**
1934. David McKay Co. 9.75x10" with 48 pages reprinting Floyd Gottfredson 1931 daily comic strips. - **$125 $500 $950**

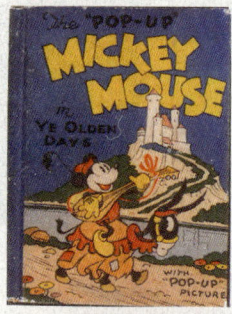

MKY-292

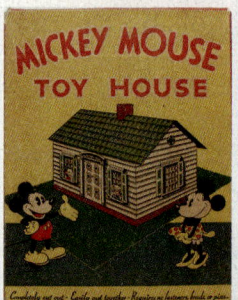

MKY-293

❏ **MKY-292. "The 'Pop-Up' Mickey Mouse In Ye Olden Days" Hardcover,**
1934. Blue Ribbon Press. 4x5" with 60 pages with a number of full page illustrations. Center has full color Mickey pop-up depicting him exiting a castle and preparing for a joust. - **$124 $372 $945**

❏ **MKY-293. "Mickey Mouse Toy House,"**
1934. O.B. Andrews Co. 13.25x17x.25" deep box holds parts for assembly of large cardboard house. - **$150 $275 $550**

MKY-294

MKY-295

❏ **MKY-294. "Mickey Mouse Animated Circus,"**
1934. Norwich Knitting Co. 4.5x5" cellophane envelope contains 19 cellophane strips, 10 featuring Disney characters and 9 featuring circus animals and a clown. - **$100 $200 $400**

❏ **MKY-295. "Mickey Mouse Circus Game,"**
1934. Marks Brothers Co. 9.5x20x2" box contains stiff cardboard panel that attaches to wood base of box bottom and separate cardboard panel with four 2.5x4.5" sections - two of Mickey and two of Minnie each with wood cup attached to top. Game also came with generic marbles and instruction sheet. Object was to place marble in top cup which caused panels to tip over dropping the ball down which strikes a bell before ball rolls into bottom insert to land in one of the various point value die-cut holes. - **$300 $600 $1200**

MKY-296

❏ **MKY-296. "Mickey Mouse" Activity Box,**
1934. Marks Brothers. 7.5x11x1" deep box contains a total of 12 items. Some of the images on the items in this set also appeared on other products by Marks Brothers Co. but we have never seen any of these images used in the manner that they are with this set. Boxed - **$250 $500 $1000**

MKY-297

❏ **MKY-297. Mickey Mouse Chinaware Sectional Plate,**
1934. Rare in high grade. Salem China Company. - **$50 $100 $350**

438

MICKEY MOUSE, MINNIE & NEPHEWS

MKY-298

MKY-301

MKY-303

☐ **MKY-298. "Mickey Mouse Hoop La Game,"**
1934. Marks Brothers Co. 10.75x18.5" thick die-cut cardboard. Comes with three generic rings. - **$225 $350 $700**

MKY-299

☐ **MKY-299. Mickey Mouse Greeting Cards,**
1934. Hall Brothers. First is 4x5" folder. Second is 4x4" folder. Each - **$20 $40 $60**

MKY-300

☐ **MKY-300. Mickey Mouse Emerson Radio,**
1934. Solid wood with pressed wood composition panels on four sides measures 5x7.25x7.25" tall. Front bottom has metal plate with raised text "Emerson Mickey Mouse." - **$750 $1500 $3000**

☐ **MKY-301. Mickey Mouse Painted Variety Radio,**
1934. Emerson. 5x7.25x7.25" tall solid wood radio with pressed wood composition panels on four sides. This painted version is much scarcer than the unpainted version. - **$1000 $2000 $3500**

MKY-302

☐ **MKY-302. Mickey Mouse Emerson Radio,**
1934. Emerson. 5.5x7.25x7.25" tall. Radio came in two different colors, black or cream. On the front at each corner are attached aluminum triangular pieces, each with different character image of Minnie, Pluto, Horace and Clarabelle. Bottom center attachment reads "Emerson Radio And Television" with Walt Disney copyright. Has aluminum grill plate depicting Mickey playing a bass. Back of radio has serial number plate. Cream - **$1000 $2000 $3000** Black - **$1250 $2500 $3500**

☐ **MKY-303. "Mickey Mouse Scatter Ball Game,"**
1934. Marks Brothers Co. 11.5x11.5x2" deep box contains cardboard insert playing surface with die-cut holes, a top and ten wooden balls. Balls are placed in the center and top is spun causing balls to scatter and land in holes with different point values. - **$125 $275 $575**

MKY-304

MKY-305

MICKEY MOUSE, MINNIE & NEPHEWS

❏ **MKY-304. "Mickey Mouse Bagatelle,"**
1934. Marks Brothers. 12x23.5x1" wood toy with paper label. - **$175 $400 $750**

❏ **MKY-305. "Mickey Mouse Ingersoll" English Wrist Watch,**
1934. Celluloid dial in 1.25" case. - **$550 $1100 $2200**

MKY-306

MKY-308

❏ **MKY-306. "Mickey Mouse" Second Version English Pocket Watch,**
1934. Ingersoll. 2" diameter silvered brass case with glass dial cover. - **$350 $650 $1100**

❏ **MKY-308. Minnie Mouse And Pram Tin Wind-Up,**
1934. Wells, England. 7" long lithographed tin with 3.5" composition Minnie. - **$800 $1500 $3500**
Box Marked #146 (not shown) - **$600 $1000 $3000**

MKY-309

❏ **MKY-309. "Mickey Mouse" Large Celluloid Wind-Up Boxed,**
1934. Made in Japan for U.S.A. distribution by George Borgfeldt. Known as 'Rambling Mickey.' 8" tall with wire tail. Box is 4.5x7.75x3.5" deep.
Box - **$300 $600 $1200**
Toy - **$500 $1000 $2000**

MKY-307

❏ **MKY-307. Mickey Mouse And Pram Tin Wind-Up,**
1934. Wells, England. 7" long lithographed tin with 3.5" composition Mickey. A second version has Mickey pushing the pram with his mouth.
Pictured Version - **$1000 $2000 $4000**
Second Version - **$1500 $2500 $4500**
Box Marked #146 (not shown) - **$500 $1000 $3000**

MICKEY MOUSE, MINNIE & NEPHEWS

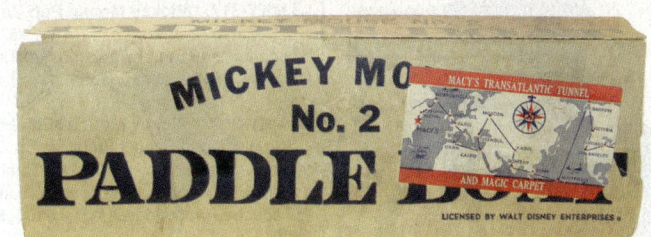

MKY-310

❏ **MKY-310. "Mickey Mouse No. 2 Paddle Boat" Boxed Tin Lithographed Wind-Up,**
1934. Licensed by Walt Disney Enterprises. Box is 2.25x4x12" long with "Macy's Transatlantic Tunnel And Magic Carpet" sticker on one side. 11.25" long wood boat has 2.25" tall Mickey Mouse holding 8.75" wide wire oars. Front has wire crank to activate Mickey as rower. Box - **$500 $1000 $1500**
Toy - **$1500 $3000 $4500**

MKY-311

❏ **MKY-311. Mickey Mouse Tricycle,**
1934. The Colson Co. Elyria, Ohio. 18x34x27" tall. Company was licensed for only one year. - **$900 $1800 $4250**

MKY-312

❏ **MKY-312. "Lionel Mickey Mouse Hand Car" Wind-Up,**
1934. Lionel Corporation. Box holds 27" diameter circle of track for the 2x7.5x5.5" tall metal car with 4.5" composition figures to travel on. Minnie has red wood hat. Both have rubber legs and rubber-coated wire tails. Car body in green or red versions. Box And Track - **$300 $600 $1300**
Hand Car - **$300 $650 $1300**

MKY-313

❏ **MKY-313. Mickey And Minnie Boxed Wind-Up "Playland" Toy,**
1934. Copyright Walt. Disney Enterprises Ltd. Borgfeldt. Box is 5.5x10.5x1.75" deep. Toy is 9" wide by 10.5" tall overall with thin cardboard canopy and pair of 3.5" celluloid figures. Mickey holds ring and Minnie has bell. Box - **$750 $1500 $3000**
Toy - **$1500 $2500 $4000**

MICKEY MOUSE, MINNIE & NEPHEWS

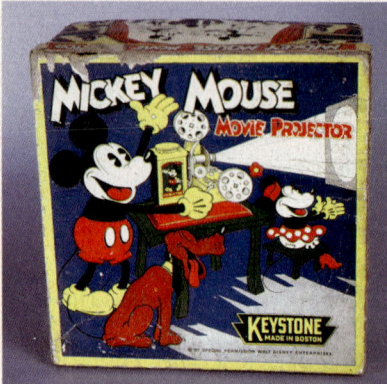

MKY-314

☐ **MKY-314. "Mickey Mouse Movie Projector,"**
1934. Keystone Mfg. Co., Boston. Large graphic box holds electrically operated 16mm projector to show "Mickey Mouse Cine Art Films" and others. Box lid served as screen. Box - **$400 $750 $1500**
Projector - **$250 $500 $1000**

MKY-315

☐ **MKY-315. "Mickey Mouse Soldier Set,"**
1934. Marks Brothers Co. 8.25x18.5x1" deep box contains eight 2.25x6" cardboard targets with wood bases. Four are of Mickey, four are of Donald. Both are depicted in soldier attire with rifles. Box included generic pop-rifle and corks.
Boxed Set - **$250 $500 $800**
Single Figure - **$15 $35 $50**

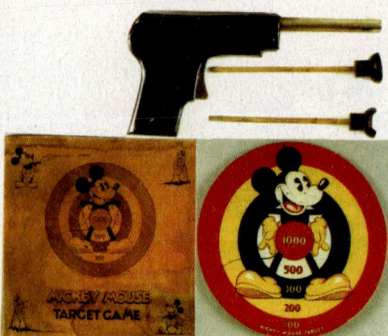

MKY-316

☐ **MKY-316. "Mickey Mouse Target Game" Boxed Set,**
1934. Marks Brothers. 18x18x1" deep box contains 17.5" diameter cardboard target (largest of two sizes issued by Marks), metal gun and pair of darts. Box - **$100 $200 $400**
Target - **$100 $200 $300**
Gun - **$10 $20 $50**

MKY-317

MKY-318

☐ **MKY-317. "Mickey Mouse Pop Game,"**
1934. Marks Brothers Co. 11x18x1.75" deep box contains graphic target and generic pop gun for corks. - **$150 $3050 $600**

☐ **MKY-318. "Mickey Mouse" Blackboard,**
1934. Richmond School Furniture Co. Thick masonite blackboard is 19.5x28". Total height of the piece from top of blackboard to bottom of the attached wood legs is 40". - **$100 $200 $400**

MKY-319

☐ **MKY-319. Mickey Mouse European Postcard,**
1934. 3.5x5.5". - **$15 $30 $50**

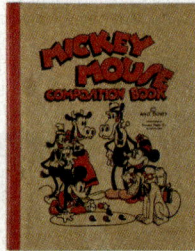

MKY-320

☐ **MKY-320. "Mickey Mouse Composition Book,"**
1934. Powers Paper Co. Book is 6.75x8.25". - **$20 $50 $75**

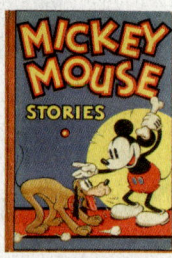

MKY-321

☐ **MKY-321. "Mickey Mouse Composition Book,"**
1934. Powers Paper Co. Book is 6.75x8.25". - **$20 $50 $75**

MICKEY MOUSE, MINNIE & NEPHEWS

MKY-322

❏ **MKY-322. Mickey/Minnie Large Wood Children's Clothing Rack,**
c. 1934. Kroehler. Figural piece consists of two wooden panels, each 16" wide by 42.5" tall. Image on outer surface of wood shows figures with arms raised as if to hold the bar that runs across top to hold clothing. At lower portion figures are separated by a slanted wooden board with raised edge intended to hold shoes. - **$300 $750 $1500**

MKY-323

❏ **MKY-323. Mickey And Minnie Riding Elephant Celluloid Wind-Up,**
c. 1934. Borgfeldt. 7.5" tall by 9.75" long. Elephant's head bobs and ears move. Elephant in orange or white versions. - **$1000 $2000 $4000**

MKY-324

❏ **MKY-324. Mickey And Minnie Mouse Theater Issued Variety Fan Cards,**
c. 1934. Local theater. Pair with identical text on back which reads "Mickey Mouse Presents The Big Bad Wolf And Walt Disney Presents Mickey Mouse In The Orphans' Benefit" with additional ad for non-Disney film The House of Rothschild plus text including "Now Playing At United Artists Theater Broadway At Ninth." Each - **$45 $85 $140**

MKY-325

MKY-326

❏ **MKY-325. "Mickey Mouse Toothbrush" With Card,**
c. 1934. Henry L. Hughes Co. Inc. 2.5x6" card holds 5.75" toothbrush, however the card is for the toothbrush variety that had a Mickey decal on the handle rather than this brush which has thick die-cut celluloid Mickey figure which were sold on larger cards. Card - **$50 $100 $200** Either Brush - **$35 $75 $150**

❏ **MKY-326. Mickey Mouse Cuff Bracelet,**
c. 1934. Cohn & Rosenberger. 1" wide by 2.25" diameter enamel paint on brass. Wrap-around design features two separate scenes. One of Mickey as hunter with rifle and Pluto by his side and the other a campfire scene of him and Minnie cooking over an open fire while behind them is tent and Pluto. - **$200 $400 $600**

MKY-327

❏ **MKY-327. Mickey Mouse Silver Plated Cup,**
c. 1934. International Silver Co. 1.75" tall with stamped-in image. From a set of six different. Each - **$40 $75 $135**

MKY-328

❏ **MKY-328. Minnie Mouse Silver Plated Cup,**
c. 1934. International Silver Co. 2.5" tall from a series of six different. Front has nice incised image of Minnie waving a hanky. Each - **$40 $75 $135**

MKY-329

MKY-330

443

MICKEY MOUSE, MINNIE & NEPHEWS

❑ **MKY-329. Mickey Mouse Silver Plated Cup,**
c. 1934. The International Silver Co. 2.5" tall. - **$40 $75 $135**

❑ **MKY-330. Mickey Mouse Napkin Ring,**
c. 1934. International Silver Co. .75" wide with 1.5" diameter. Silver plated. - **$30 $65 $125**

MKY-331

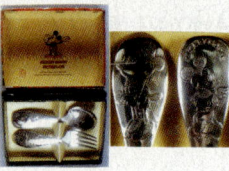

MKY-332

❑ **MKY-331. Mickey Mouse Silver Plated Child's Plate,**
c. 1934. International Silver Co. 7.5x9.25x1" deep. Side handle-like edges are for placement of utensils with incised text "My Mickey Mouse Fork/Spoon Goes Here." Reverse has small incised symbols and "8119." - **$60 $125 $200**

❑ **MKY-332. "Mickey Mouse" Boxed Utensils,**
c. 1934. International Silver Co. 3.5x5x2" deep box contains pair of 4.5" utensils, a Mickey spoon and Minnie fork. Box - **$50 $100 $200** Utensil Pair **$40 $65 $100**

MKY-333

❑ **MKY-333. Seiberling Retailers Catalogue/Sales Sheets Featuring Rare Disney Items,**
c. 1934. Seiberling Latex Products Co. Four items, each 8.5x10.75". Eight-page catalogue, two one-sided sale sheets and one two-sided sales sheet. Catalogue - **$100 $200 $300** Each Sales Sheet - **$25 $50 $100**

MKY-334

MKY-335

❑ **MKY-334. "Penney's For Back To School Needs" Celluloid Button,**
c. 1934. Backpaper by maker M. Pudlin Co. Inc. NYC. 7/8". - **$40 $65 $100**

❑ **MKY-335. "Pin The Tail On Mickey Party Game,"**
c. 1934. Marks Brothers Co. 8.25x10x.75" deep box contains 18x22" linen sheet. Photo example shows tails cut from sheet. Box - **$40 $60 $125** Uncut Sheet - **$30 $60 $100** Cut Sheet Complete - **$20 $40 $60**

MKY-336

❑ **MKY-336. "Mickey Mouse Composition Book,"**
c. 1934. Powers Paper Co. 6.5x8.25". Cover design depicts Mickey and Minnie sliding down a bannister for their breakfast. Photo example includes paste-in clippings. - **$40 $75 $135**

MKY-337

❑ **MKY-337. "The Story Of Mickey Mouse Big Big Book,"**
1935. Whitman. 7.25x9.25". Book #4062. - **$150 $450 $900**

MKY-338

MKY-339

❑ **MKY-338. "Another Mickey Mouse Coloring Book,"**
1935. Saalfield. 10.75x15.25" with 28 pages. Book #2110. One of the scarcest early coloring books. - **$250 $500 $1000**

❑ **MKY-339. "Another Mickey Mouse Coloring Book,"**
1935. Saalfield Publishing Co. 10.75x15" #295. Variety with 32 pages rather than 28 and all art in black and white rather than with some color illustration. - **$200 $400 $800**

MKY-340

MICKEY MOUSE, MINNIE & NEPHEWS

❑ **MKY-340. "Mickey Mouse Magic Movie Palette,"**
1935. Premium stiff paper card measures 5x8". Has small die-cut window at top and comes with attached disk with illustrations that can be turned to produce a "movie." Front reads "A Xmas Gift From Mickey Mouse." - **$100 $225 $400**

MKY-341

❑ **MKY-341. Pencil Drawing,**
1935. Animation paper is 9.5x12" centered by 2.75x3.25" image for 'Mickey's Man Friday' short. - **$125 $250 $400**

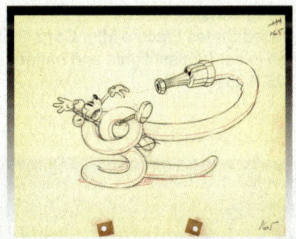

MKY-342

❑ **MKY-342. Mickey Mouse Pencil Drawing From Mickey's Garden,**
1935. Animation paper is 12x9.5" with 9x5.5" image. - **$250 $500 $1000**

MKY-343

MKY-344

❑ **MKY-343. Mickey Mouse Pencil Drawing From Mickey's Service Station,**
1935. 9.5x12" sheet of animation paper with 3.75x5.75" image. "64" from a numbered sequence. - **$200 $400 $750**

❑ **MKY-344. Mickey "Post Toasties Corn Flakes" Cereal Box,**
1935. Box is 2.5x7.5x11" tall with Mickey at lower right corner. Two side panels have cut-outs, one of "Minnie The Belle Of The Prairie" and one of "Mickey On Paint." Back of box features story of "Two-Gun Mickey, A Wild West Movie." - **$500 $1400 $2500**

MKY-345

❑ **MKY-345. Post Toasties Corn Flakes Mickey Mouse Picture Panel Set,**
1935. Set of six cards cut from box back panel. This set features stage production of "Uncle Tom's Cabin" performed by and involving Mickey, Minnie, Horace, Goofy and Pluto. Cut Set - **$25 $50 $100**

MKY-346

❑ **MKY-346. Post Toasties Corn Flakes Mickey Mouse Picture Panel Set,**
1935. Set of six cards cut from box back panel. This set is titled "Mickey's Kangaroo" and involves him boxing a baby kangaroo and its mother, other characters involved are Minnie and Pluto. Cut Set - **$25 $50 $100**

MKY-347

❑ **MKY-347. Post Toasties Corn Flakes Mickey Mouse Picture Panel Set,**
1935. Set of six cards cut from box back panel. This set is titled "Gulliver Mickey." Cut Set - **$25 $50 $100**

MKY-348

❑ **MKY-348. "Mickey Mouse Lunch Kit,"**
1935. Geuder, Paeschke & Frey Co., Milwaukee. 5x8x5" tall tin lithographed container and lid unit complete with separate inner tray and outer rigid wire carrying grips. - **$750 $1500 $3200**

MICKEY MOUSE, MINNIE & NEPHEWS

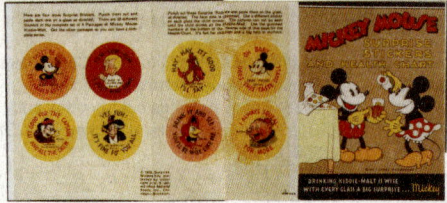

MKY-349

MKY-352

❑ **MKY-349. "Kiddie-Malt" Elaborate Sales Promotion Book With Accessories,**
1935. Remarkable and elaborate salesman's portfolio from archives of premium creators Sam and Gordon Gold. Design intent was to persuade storekeepers to purchase Kiddie-Malt, a product of National Foods Inc. Principal piece is an oversized 12x15" spiral-bound book with woodgrain design front cover accented by an inset foil reflective mirror and actual lock and key. 18 pages including slash pockets holding product photos, "Surprise Stickers" and 16x20" poster. - **$2250 $4500 $7500**

❑ **MKY-352. "Mickey Mouse Flashlight" Advertising Mailer,**
1935. United States Electric Mfg. Corp. 8.5x11" four-page folder for flashlights and batteries. - **$60 $125 $250**

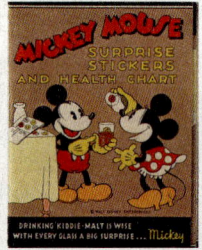

MKY-353

❑ **MKY-353. Mickey/Minnie Fabric Throw Rug,**
1935. Alexander Smith & Sons. 27x42" rug. - **$250 $500 $1200**

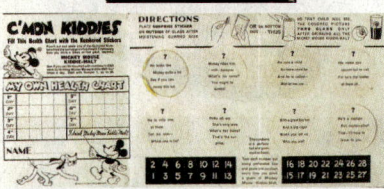

MKY-350

MKY-351

❑ **MKY-350. Premium Folder From Mickey Mouse Kiddie-Malt,**
1935. 4x5.5" with three panels containing total of eight characters on sixteen stickers. - **$125 $250 $500**

❑ **MKY-351. "Mickey Mouse Pocket Combs" Framed Ad,**
1935. American Hard Rubber Co. Ad is 8.75x11.75". - **$35 $65 $135**

MKY-354

MICKEY MOUSE, MINNIE & NEPHEWS

❏ **MKY-354. Mickey/Minnie/Donald Fabric Throw Rug,**
1935. Alexander Smith & Sons. 26x42" with company label on reverse. - **$250 $500 $1200**

MKY-355

MKY-356

❏ **MKY-355. Mickey Mouse Western Theme Rug With Pegleg Pete,**
1935. Alexander Smith & Sons. 27x43". - **$200 $400 $800**

❏ **MKY-356. Mickey Mouse With Donald Duck And Peter Pig Rug,**
1935. Alexander Smith & Sons. 27x43". - **$225 $450 $1000**

MKY-357

MKY-358

❏ **MKY-357. "Mickey Mouse" Framed Picture,**
1935. Reliance Art Glass. Number "D-110" in series. 4.25x5.75x3/8" deep wood frame. - **$60 $125 $165**

❏ **MKY-358. Wallpaper Section,**
1935. Canadian 10x19" single complete panel. - **$200 $400 $700**

MKY-359

❏ **MKY-359. Metal Figures Casting Set Boxed,**
1935. Home Foundry Manufacturing Co. Inc. 11x19x2" deep boxed set of casting molds for 2.5" tall figures of Mickey, Minnie, Pluto, Three Pigs. Accessories include electric casting ladle for molten lead, paint jars and brushes, four-page order blank/instruction folder. - **$300 $600 $1350**

MKY-360

MKY-361

❏ **MKY-360. "Popular Songs" With Mickey Mouse,**
1935. Volume 1, #4. Measures 8.5x11.5" with two pages of words and music for "What! No Mickey Mouse?" by Irving Caesar. - **$30 $60 $90**

❏ **MKY-361. "Mickey Mouse Magazine" Contest Folder With Mailing Envelope ,**
1935. "Didja Contest." Front of 8.5x11" folder has letter with prize mention for "Your Brilliant Entry In The Big Grin-Vention Contest." Mailer - **$25 $40 $65**
Folder - **$75 $125 $205**

MKY-362

❏ **MKY-362. "Mickey Mouse And The Bat Bandit" Big Little Book,**
1935. Whitman. Book #1153. - **$34 $102 $235**

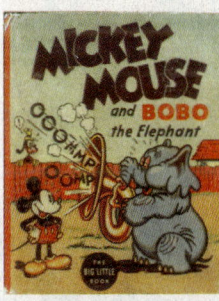
MKY-363

❏ **MKY-363. "Mickey Mouse And Bobo The Elephant,"**
1935. Whitman. Book #1160. - **$34 $102 $235**

MICKEY MOUSE, MINNIE & NEPHEWS

MKY-364

MKY-365

☐ **MKY-364. "Mickey Correo Aereo" Spanish Book,** 1935. Spanish reprint of the Big Little Book "Mickey Mouse The Mail Pilot" is 4.75x6.25" with 160 pages. - **$65 $125 $250**

☐ **MKY-365. "Mickey Mouse And The Magic Carpet" Premium Book,** 1935 Whitman. 3.5x4" designed like a Big Little Book with illustrations throughout. - **$90 $275 $600**

MKY-366

MKY-367

☐ **MKY-366. "Mickey Mouse Sails For Treasure Island" Premium Big Little Book,** 1935. Whitman. Big Little Book imprinted on back cover for sponsor "Kolynos Dental Cream." - **$49 $147 $345**

☐ **MKY-367. "Mickey Mouse And Minnie Mouse March To Macy's" Premium Book,** 1935. Whitman. No number. Christmas giveaway 3.5x3.5" softcover with 148 pages. - **$269 $807 $2150**

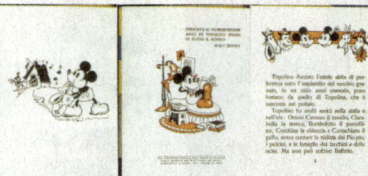

MKY-368

☐ **MKY-368. First Italian Mickey Mouse Book,** 1935. Grandi Piccoli Libri. 4.75x6" hardcover with 60 pages. All text is in Italian. - **$135 $275 $550**

MKY-369

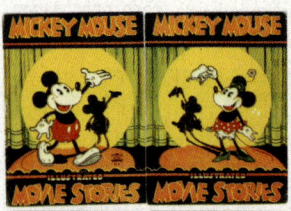 

MKY-370

☐ **MKY-369. "Mickey Mouse Annual,"** 1935. Dean & Son Ltd. 6.25x8.5x2" thick English hardcover with 124 pages. Has comic panel-style stories, text stories, a few puzzle and game pages including cut-out figure of Mickey riding Horace. - **$100 $250 $600**

☐ **MKY-370. "Mickey Mouse Illustrated Movie Stars" Canadian Hardcover,** 1935. Musson Book Co. Ltd. 6x8" with 40 pages featuring two cartoons "The Firefighters, The Cactus Kid." - **$125 $250 $400**

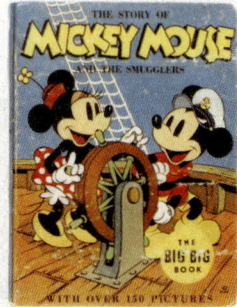

MKY-371

☐ **MKY-371. "The Story Of Mickey Mouse And The Smugglers" Big Big Book,** 1935. Whitman. Big Big Book #4062 with 320 pages and full page illustration on every other page. - **$180 $525 $1050**

MICKEY MOUSE, MINNIE & NEPHEWS

MKY-372

❑ **MKY-372. King Features Syndicate Christmas Card Folder To Media Customers,** 1935. Hallmark. 5.25x6.25" with nice quality filament paper cover and 24 full color pages of specialty comic strip character art and "Night Before Christmas" text. - **$200 $350 $650**

MKY-373

MKY-374

❑ **MKY-373. "Mickey Mouse Old Maid Cards,"** 1935. Whitman. 5x6.5x1" deep box contains deck of 35 cards, each 2.5x3.5". - **$30 $75 $150**

❑ **MKY-374. Mickey Mouse "Bridge Score Pad,"** 1935. Western Printing. 2.75x5" with stiff glossy paper front cover. - **$20 $40 $75**

 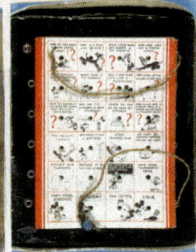

MKY-375

❑ **MKY-375. "Mickey Mouse Funny Facts/Answered By Electricity" Rare Toy,** 1935. Einson-Freeman Publishing Corp. 8.5x9.5x2.5" deep battery operated game designed like a large book. Playing area includes black cardboard insert with metal eyelets and pair of fabric-covered wires. Comes with three different two-sided question cards with images of Mickey, Minnie, Pluto, Horace and Clarabell. During play, card is placed on playing surface and one wire is placed on a question while the other is placed on the answer and if answer is correct a bulb was to light. - **$325 $800 $1750**

MKY-376

MKY-377

❑ **MKY-376. "Mickey Mouse" Birthday Card,** 1935. Hallmark. 3.5x4.5" glossy paper card. Inside text includes Mickey's name. - **$20 $40 $65**

❑ **MKY-377. Mickey Mouse Birthday Card,** 1935. Hallmark. 3.75x4.75" on glossy textured paper. - **$15 $25 $50**

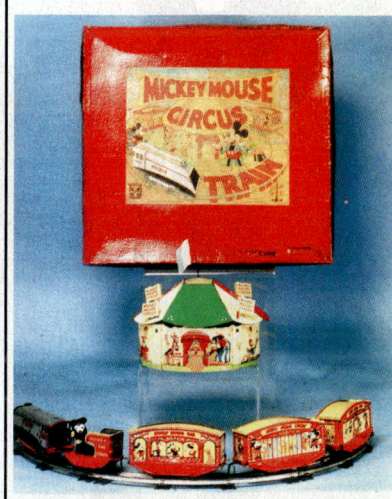

MKY-378

❑ **MKY-378. "Mickey Mouse Circus Train" Boxed Set,** 1935. A. Wells & Co. Ltd. England. By Permission Walt Disney Mickey Mouse, Ltd. Consists of wind-up locomotive, "Mickey The Stoker" coal car and three circus cars. Comes with lithographed tin circus tent accented by metal flags. Box is 17x19 by about 3.5" deep. Also issued in one or two car versions in smaller boxes and without the tent. Largest Boxed Set With Tent - **$3000 $6000 $12000**

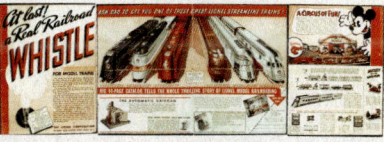

MKY-379

❑ **MKY-379. Promo Folder Featuring Mickey Train/Handcar,** 1935. Lionel Corp. 8.5x11" four-page glossy paper. - **$110 $225 $400**

MICKEY MOUSE, MINNIE & NEPHEWS

MKY-380

MICKEY MOUSE, MINNIE & NEPHEWS

❑ **MKY-380. "Lionel Mickey Mouse Circus Train,"**
1935. Lionel Corporation. 11.25x17x2.25" deep box holds wind-up gauge O Commodore Vanderbilt engine, tender with moving Mickey shoveling imaginary coal and 3 cars for length of about 30". Included are 84" of track, 5" Mickey circus barker composition figure, 8x18x15" tall paper tent, paper accessories of admission tickets, "To The Circus" sign, Mickey in truck and gasoline station. Complete Boxed Set - **$5000 $10000 $20000**
Engine - **$150 $300 $500**
Tender - **$250 $500 $1000**
Each Car - **$250 $500 $1000**
Barker - **$100 $250 $500**

MKY-383

❑ **MKY-383. "Mickey Mouse Safety Blocks" Set Boxed,**
c. 1935. Halsam Co. 5.5x9x1.75" deep boxed complete set of fifteen wood blocks, each 1.75" square. This set is one of eight different boxed sets by Halsam, containing anywhere from six to thirty blocks per set. - **$40 $80 $150**

MKY-381

❑ **MKY-381. Mickey Mouse Extends Invitation To Walter Merriam Pratt's Holiday Tea Party At Princess Hotel, Bermuda,**
1935. Five-piece group of paper items from founder of Dennison-Pratt Paper Co. and later president of Pratt Paper Co.
Group Near Mint - **$500**

MKY-384

MKY-382

❑ **MKY-382. Mickey Mouse Hairbrush And Comb Boxed Set,**
c. 1935. Henry L. Hughes Co. Inc. 4x5.5x1.5" deep box contains two-piece set of comb and brush. Box also includes a fabric lining.
Set - **$50 $75 $150**
Brush Only - **$25 $50 $100**

MKY-385

❑ **MKY-384. Mickey And Minnie Art Deco Tea Set,**
c. 1935. Faiencerie d'Onnaing, France. Teaset with twelve cups and saucers, creamer, covered sugar bowl and covered teapot. All with silver accents. - **$1250 $2500 $4000**

❑ **MKY-385. Mickey And Minnie Tea Set,**
c. 1935. Faiencerie d'Onnaing, France. Teaset with six cups and saucers, creamer, covered sugar bowl and covered 8" tall teapot. All with silver accents. - **$750 $1500 $2500**

MICKEY MOUSE, MINNIE & NEPHEWS

MKY-386

MKY-388

❏ **MKY-388. "Mickey Mouse Sneakers" Paper Production Sheet,**
c. 1935. 4-1/8x6-1/8" button maker's paper sheet with three complete images. Produced as a test printing prior to button production. Very Fine, likely unique - **$600**

MKY-391

❏ **MKY-391. "Mickey Mouse Hose" Celluloid Button,**
c. 1935. Backpaper by M. Pudlin Co. 7/8". - **$60 $100 $150**

❏ **MKY-386. "Mickey Mouse Undies" Box,**
c. 1935 or a few years earlier. 8.25x11.25x2" deep. Features various images of Mickey and Minnie. - **$150 $300 $600**

MKY-389

❏ **MKY-389. Mickey Mouse Converse Sneakers Celluloid Button,**
c.1935. 1.25" Kay Kamen Backpaper. - **$500 $1500 $3000**

MKY-392

❏ **MKY-392. "Mickey Mouse" Licensed Product Buttons,**
c. 1935. Issued as 1-1/8" litho (pictured) and 1-1/4" celluloid. Both issued with back paper reading "Mickey Mouse Gloves and Mittens."
Litho. - **$75 $175 $400**
Cello. - **$250 $750 $1500**

MKY-387

❏ **MKY-387. "Mickey Mouse Undies" Box,**
c. 1935. Box is 7.25x10.5x2.25" deep. Long-billed Donald on one end panel. - **$125 $275 $550**

MKY-390

❏ **MKY-390. "Gurd's Mickey Mouse Club" Celluloid Button,**
c. 1935. Issued by Canadian gingerale soda maker. 1.25". - **$250 $500 $1000**

MKY-393

❏ **MKY-393. "Minneapolis Morning Tribune Times-Tribune Movie Club Member" Button,**
c. 1935. Williamson Stamp Co. 1.25". The only 1930s button known showing both Mickey and Donald. - **$300 $600 $1000**

MICKEY MOUSE, MINNIE & NEPHEWS

MKY-394

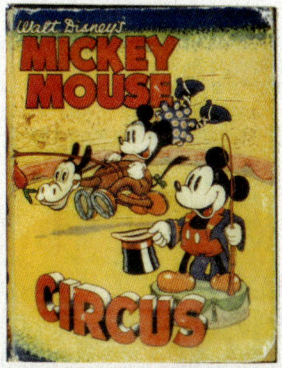

MKY-395

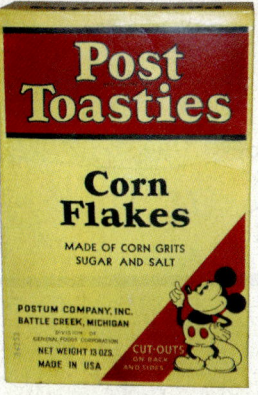

MKY-396

MKY-397

MKY-398

MKY-399

❏ **MKY-398. Mickey And Pluto Small Wind-Up Cart,**
c. 1935. Made In Japan. Celluloid figures with tin cart. Toy is 3.25" tall by 5" long. Paper label reads "By Permission Walt Disney." Pluto is missing one leg in the photo example. - **$300 $600 $1200**

❏ **MKY-399. "Mickey Mouse Jolly Cart" Boxed Wind-Up,**
c. 1935. Made in Japan for English market. Sold by Paradise Novelty Co. Celluloid figures with tin cart, 4" tall by 7.5" long. Box is 2.75x7.5x3.75" deep. Box - **$200 $400 $800** Toy - **$325 $650 $1300**

MKY-400

❏ **MKY-400. "Mickey Mouse Merchandise" Catalogue With Mailer,**
1936. Kay Kamen Ltd. Mailer - **$100 $200 $300**
Catalogue - **$750 $1500 $2500**

❏ **MKY-394. "A Handful Of Fun" Diecut Booklet,**
c. 1935. Eisendrath Glove Co. 5.25x7.75" stiff paper 12-page premium, die-cut throughout in the shape of Mickey's gloved hand. Content includes different image on every page. Gordon Gold Archives. - **$500 $1150 $2250**

❏ **MKY-395. "Mickey Mouse Circus" English Book,**
c. 1935. Birn Brothers Ltd. 8x10" hardcover, 124 stiff paper pages. - **$100 $200 $400**

❏ **MKY-396. Post Toasties Box,**
1935. Scarce. Mickey pictured on front. Several versions. Each Complete - **$500 $1400 $2500**
1934 box complete - **$1000 $2500 $3750**
Rare. Mickey pictured on front. Several versions. Few known to exist. "Mickey At The Circus" box back pictured above is from 1934.

❏ **MKY-397. "The First Step By Mickey Mouse" Bank,**
c. 1935. Automatic Recording Safe Company, 3.25x4.75x.75" deep metal bank designed like a book. - **$150 $325 $550**

MICKEY MOUSE, MINNIE & NEPHEWS

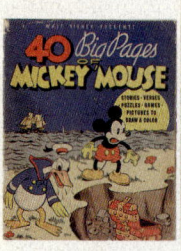 

MKY-401

☐ **MKY-401. "40 Big Pages Of Mickey Mouse,"**
1936. Whitman. Book #945. 10.25x12.5". Features "Stories, Verses, Puzzles, Games, Pictures To Draw & Color." - **$125 $300 $600**

MKY-402

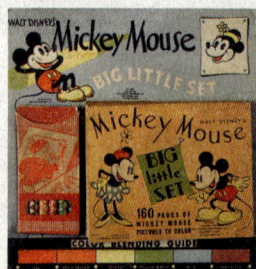

MKY-403

☐ **MKY-402. "Mickey Mouse Big Little Set,"**
1936. Whitman. 8.25x8.5" display card with attached 4x5.25" 160-page softcover book and box of crayons. Set #3059. Art is based on early Mickey cartoons. Set is usually missing crayons. Without Crayons - **$1000 $2000 $3500**
Add For Crayons - **$25 $50 $100**

☐ **MKY-403. "Mickey Mouse Big Big Box,"**
1936. Whitman. #2170. Box measures 8.75x12x2.5" deep and features a 5x5" tall separate die-cut cardboard Mickey figure attached to lid. 256 pages to color in format of seven signatures of 32 pages each. Set included crayons. - **$400 $800 $1350**

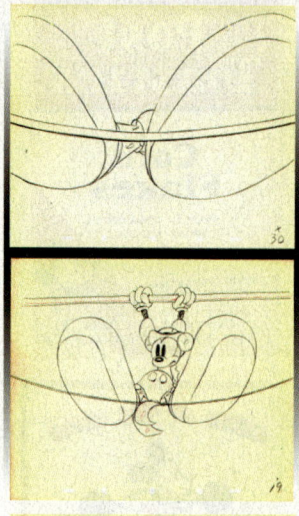

MKY-404

☐ **MKY-404. Mickey Mouse Pencil Drawings From Mickey's Circus,**
1936. Animation papers are 12x9.5" with three separate images measuring 12x6.25",12x7.5", and12x6.75". Group - **$300 $600 $1200**

MKY-405

☐ **MKY-405. Mickey Mouse Pencil Drawing From Mickey's Elephant,**
1936. Image is 2.5x3". From a numbered sequence and this is "59." - **$75 $150 $300**

MKY-406

☐ **MKY-406. Minnie Mouse Pencil Drawing From Mickey's Revival,**
1936. 10x12" sheet of animation paper with 2.5x4" image in lead pencil just left of center. #237 from a numbered sequence. - **$200 $350 $600**

MKY-407

MKY-408

☐ **MKY-407. "Mickey's Polo Team" Model Sheet Original,**
1936. Three-quarters of the sheet features different sketch designs and views of horses for Will Rogers, Jack Holt, Laurel & Hardy as well as Harpo Marx's ostrich. Bottom quarter features fully detailed images of Mickey, Goofy, Big Bad Wolf, Donald Duck riding horses/donkey. - **$250 $500 $800**

☐ **MKY-408. Mickey Mouse Pencil Drawing From "Alpine Climbers,"**
1936. Animation paper is 10x12" with 2.5x6" image. No. "87" from a numbered sequence. - **$75 $150 $300**

MICKEY MOUSE, MINNIE & NEPHEWS

MKY-409

MKY-410

❑ **MKY-409. Mickey And Minnie Mouse With Pluto Flashlight,**
1936. U.S. Electric Mfg. Co. Has text "Use Mickey Mouse Batteries." 6-1/8" tall. - **$200 $400 $900**

❑ **MKY-410. Mickey Figural Lamp,**
1936. Soreng-Manegold Co. 6" diameter painted plaster 6.25" tall to tip of upturned nose and 10.25" tall to top of bulb socket. Image is Mickey seated in armchair and holding a book. - **$500 $1000 $2150**

MKY-411

❑ **MKY-411. "Mickey Mouse Tool Chest,"**
1936. Hamilton Metal Products Co. 5.5x19x2.5" deep metal case, the largest of several by this maker, with carrying handle and latch for the hinged lid. Bottom edge has a 12" ruler decal. Sold with or without tools. - **$150 $300 $650**

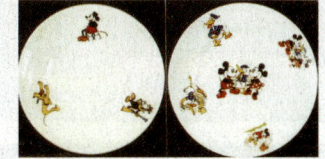

MKY-412

❑ **MKY-412. Mickey Mouse Ceramic Place Setting,**
1936. Sweden. 2" tall cup, 5" diameter saucer and 7-3/8" diameter plate. Cup - **$25 $50 $110**
Saucer - **$15 $30 $60**
Plate - **$25 $50 $110**

MKY-413

❑ **MKY-413. Mickey, Minnie, Pluto, Donald, Baby's Bowl,**
1936. Salem China Co. 7.75" diameter. - **$65 $140 $250**

MKY-414

❑ **MKY-414. Mickey & Others China Child's Divided Dish,**
1936. Unmarked but Salem China Co. 7.75" diameter by 1.5" deep. - **$65 $140 $250**

MKY-415

❑ **MKY-415. "Patriot China" Mickey Mouse Mug,**
1936. Salem China Co. 3" tall. - **$55 $120 $200**

MKY-416

❑ **MKY-416. Mickey Mouse Banjo,**
1936. Noble & Cooley Co. 20" long metal. - **$150 $300 $600**

MICKEY MOUSE, MINNIE & NEPHEWS

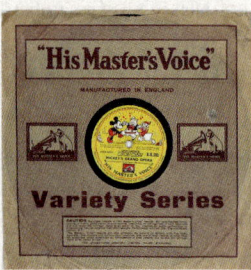

MKY-417

MKY-418

❏ **MKY-417. "Mickey Mouse" English Record,**
1936. His Master's Voice/Gramophone Co. Ltd. 10" diameter 78 rpm. Features "Mickey's Grand Opera/The Orphan's Benefit." - **$40 $75 $150**

❏ **MKY-418. "Mickey Mouse's Birthday Party" Sheet Music,**
1936. Music sheet is 9.25x12" with 4 pages. - **$40 $75 $150**

MKY-419

❏ **MKY-419. "Mickey Mouse's Birthday Party" Sheet Music,**
1936. Irving Berlin. 7x10.5". - **$50 $125 $225**

MKY-420

❏ **MKY-420. "Here Comes Mickey Mouse" Big Big Color Set,**
1936. Consists of 224 pages of pictures to color. Pages were reprinted from early Mickey Mouse related movie and strip reprints. With crayons. Rare. - **$425 $1275 $3400**

MKY-421

❏ **MKY-421. "Mickey Mouse Book for Coloring",**
1936. Fourth in a series of coloring books, but the first to be die-cut. Features early Mickey cartoons like *On Ice*, *Band Concert*, *The Pointer* and others. Has many great early pictures of Donald, Horace, Minnie, Tanglefoot, Pluto and the Goof. Usually found colored in. Book is 14" tall.- **$125 $275 $550**

MKY-422

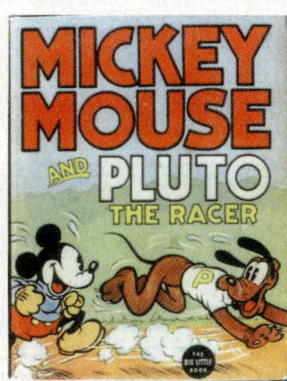

MKY-423

❏ **MKY-422. Catalogue With Classic Disney Merchandise,**
1936. "Morris Struhl Wholesalers Gifts /Novelties." 8x11" annual catalogue with photos and illustrations. Classic Mickey Mouse items include the Emerson radio, Ingersoll pocketwatch, wristwatch, alarm and electric clocks, movie projector, sunglasses display, flashlight and battery, thermometer, book bank and constipated Mickey novelty. - **$75 $150 $250**

❏ **MKY-423. "Mickey Mouse And Pluto The Racer" Big Little Book,**
1936. Whitman. Book #1128. - **$31 $93 $220**

MICKEY MOUSE, MINNIE & NEPHEWS

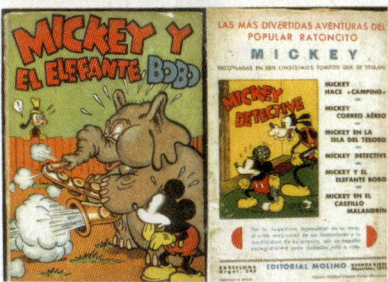

MKY-424

MKY-427

❑ **MKY-426.** "**Mickey Mouse Alphabet Book,**"
1936. Whitman. 6.75x9" with 32 pages. - **$125 $250 $500**

❑ **MKY-427.** '**Mickey Mouse Crusoe,**"
1936. Whitman. 7x9.5" with 72 pages. Includes black and white illustrations as well as one color plate. - **$75 $150 $300**

MKY-430

❑ **MKY-430.** "**A Mickey Mouse ABC Story**" **Hardcover,**
1936. Whitman. 7x9.25" with 32 stiff paper pages. Has single page devoted to each letter of the alphabet with art in a music theme of Mickey, Pluto, Donald, Silly Symphony characters, etc. playing musical instruments. - **$100 $200 $400**

❑ **MKY-424. Spanish Big Little Book Reprints,**
1936. Two Spanish reprints of Big Little Books Mickey Mouse and Bobo the Elephant and Mickey Mouse in Blaggard Castle. Each are 4.75x6.5" with 160 pages. Each - **$65 $125 $250**

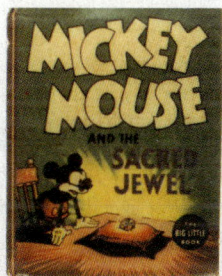

MKY-425

❑ **MKY-425.** "**Mickey Mouse And The Sacred Jewel**" **Big Little Book,**
1936. Whitman. Big Little Book #1187 with different art front and back cover. Latter depicts Mickey and Minnie riding a camel. - **$31 $93 $220**

MKY-426

MKY-428

MKY-429

❑ **MKY-428.** "**Mickey Mouse And Pluto The Pup**" **Hardcover,**
1936. Whitman. 7.25x9.75" with 68 pages. - **$75 $150 $300**

❑ **MKY-429.** "**The Mickey Mouse Fire Brigade**" **Hardcover With Dust Jacket,**
1936. Whitman. 7.25x10" with 68 pages. Jacket - **$25 $50 $100**
Book - **$50 $100 $250**

MKY-431

MKY-432

❑ **MKY-431.** "**Mickey Mouse In Pigmy Land,**"
1936. Whitman. 7.25x9.5" with 72 pages. - **$60 $135 $275**

❑ **MKY-432.** "**Mickey Mouse/A Stand-Out Book,**"
1936. Whitman. 7.25x8.25" hardcover, 32 pages. Title is derived from thick cardboard 5x5" die-cut figure applied on front cover. - **$75 $165 $350**

MICKEY MOUSE, MINNIE & NEPHEWS

MKY-433

❑ **MKY-433. "Mickey Mouse Annual" English Book,** 1936. Dean & Sons Ltd. 6.5x8" hardcover with 2" thickness from 128 stiff paper pages. - **$100 $200 $450**

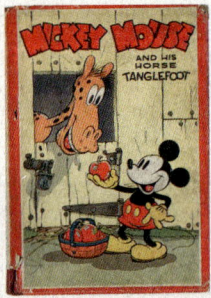

MKY-434

❑ **MKY-434. "Mickey Mouse And His Horse Tanglefoot" Hardcover With Dust Jacket,** 1936. David McKay Co. 6.5x8.75" with 60 pages. Rare with dust jacket. Jacket - **$100 $200 $400**
Book - **$165 $325 $900**

MKY-435

MKY-436

❑ **MKY-435. "Mickey Mouse Lights By Noma,"** 1936. Noma Electric Corp. Set consists of eight hard plastic bulb covers with decals and original bulbs. Box - **$75 $150 $300**
Lights - **$65 $125 $200**

❑ **MKY-436. "Mickey Mouse Playing Cards,"** 1936. Whitman Publishing Co. Complete miniature deck comes in 1.5x2.5x.75" deep box. - **$30 $60 $100**

MKY-437

MKY-438

❑ **MKY-437. Mickey Mouse Father's Day Card,** 1936. Hallmark. 4.25x5.25" glossy textured paper. - **$40 $75 $125**

❑ **MKY-438. Valentine Card,** 1936. Hallmark. 3.25x5" die-cut stiff paper folder. - **$25 $50 $75**

MKY-439

❑ **MKY-439. English "Ingersoll Mickey Mouse Pocket Watch" Box/Guarantee,** 1936. Empty box measuring 2.5x4.5x1" deep and originally contained the English pocket watch. Identical to American version but marked on inside "This Box Printed And Made In England." Photo example is missing insert that held watch in place. Comes with original 2x3" folded guarantee. - **$500 $1000 $2000**

MKY-440

❑ **MKY-440. Mickey Mouse Pull Toy,** c. 1936. N. N. Hill Brass Co. 5.5x9.5x14.25" tall with pair of steel wheels attached to thick die-cut wood figure which has two additional wooden wheels. Metal wheels originally had printed paper disks with Mickey images. - **$225 $450 $850**

MKY-441

❑ **MKY-441. Italian Mickey/Minnie Chocolate Bar Display Bin,** c. 1936. Cirio Topolino. Die-cut cardboard with flattened size of 15x19.5". - **$200 $400 $800**

458

MICKEY MOUSE, MINNIE & NEPHEWS

MKY-442

❏ **MKY-442. Italian Mickey/Minnie Chocolate Bar Promotional Pamphlet,**
c. 1936. - **$75 $150 $300**

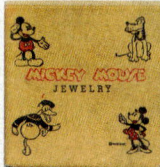 

MKY-443

❏ **MKY-443. "Mickey Mouse Jewelry" Boxed Pair of Pins,**
c. 1936. Brier Mfg. Co. 2.5x2.5x3/8" deep box contains pair of 1.25" tall enamel on brass pins.
Box - **$35 $65 $125**
Mickey - **$40 $75 $125**
Minnie - **$40 $75 $125**

MKY-444

❏ **MKY-444. Mickey And Minnie Mouse Wood Wall Plaques,**
c. 1936. Kerk Guild Inc. Each is 5x10.25x.25" thick. Originally sold in boxes marked "Mickey Mouse Art Gallery." Mickey - **$40 $75 $125**
Minnie - **$30 $65 $100**

MKY-445

MKY-446

❏ **MKY-445. Mickey Mouse Popcorn Popper,**
c. 1936. Ohio Art. 6.25" diameter by 3.75" tall lithographed tin. - **$125 $250 $500**

❏ **MKY-446. Toy Drum,**
c. 1936. Noble & Cooley Co. 6.5" diameter by 3.75" tall toy formed by painted wood body, stiff paper drum heads, painted tin rims, decorative stringing, plus a neck string possibly added. Mickey image on top drum head has "W.D. Ent." marking. - **$250 $500 $800**

MKY-448

❏ **MKY-448. "Mickey Mouse Racing Car" Boxed Wind-Up,**
c. 1936. Joseph Schneider. 4" long tin litho with nicely illustrated box. Box - **$250 $500 $1000**
Toy - **$250 $500 $1000**

MKY-447

❏ **MKY-447. "Mickey Mouse" Store Display Wall Sign,**
c. 1936. Old King Cole distributed by Kay Kamen. Molded 'laminate' in high relief about 24" across. - **$4000 $8000 $16000**

MICKEY MOUSE, MINNIE & NEPHEWS

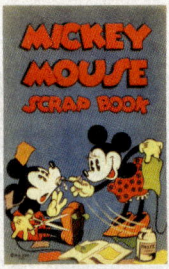

MKY-449

◻ **MKY-449. "Mickey Mouse Scrapbook,"**
c. 1936. Unmarked but by Whitman. 10.5x15.25". Unused - **$75 $150 $300**

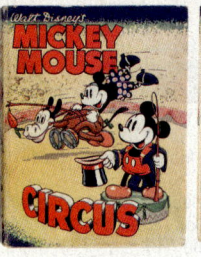 

MKY-450

◻ **MKY-450. "Mickey Mouse Circus" Rare English Hardcover,**
c. 1936. Birn Brothers Ltd. 8x10" by 1.25" thick with 124 pages and four color plates. - **$125 $250 $500**

MKY-451

◻ **MKY-451. Mickey Mouse Child's Scissors On Store Card,**
1937. Walt Disney Enterprises. Card is 3.5x6" with 3.25" metal scissors which have 5/8" die-cut tin Mickey figure. Card - **$100 $200 $400** Scissors - **$50 $150 $250**

MKY-452

◻ **MKY-452. "Mickey Mouse Annual" English Hardcover,**
1937. Dean & Son Ltd. 6.25x8.5x2". 128 pages features text stories and illustrations, comic panel stories, and several puzzles.
- **$125 $250 $500**

MKY-453

◻ **MKY-453. "A Walt Disney Paint Book,"**
1937. Whitman. 11x14" with 48 pages. - **$65 $125 $250**

MKY-454

◻ **MKY-454. Mickey Mouse Pencil Drawing From Lonesome Ghosts,**
1937. Image is 3.5x3.25" from a numbered sequence and this is "34." - **$85 $175 $350**

MKY-455

◻ **MKY-455. Movie Exhibitor Magazine With Mickey And Gene Autry,**
1937. "Motion Picture Herald." 9.25x12.25" September 18 weekly for movie theater owners, 108 pages. Content includes two-page ad for Walt Disney cartoons "Now Distributed By RKO-Radio Pictures" and "Mickey Hangs His Hat At RKO." Back of page includes illustration "Scene From Hawaiian Holiday" of Mickey and Minnie. Inside back cover ad is devoted to Gene Autry. - **$150 $300 $500**

MKY-456

◻ **MKY-456. Movie Exhibitor Magazine With Mickey And Others,**
1937. "Motion Picture Herald." 9.25x12.25" October 2 weekly for movie theater owners, 94 pages. Content includes two-page ad for Walt Disney/RKO. Front page features Mickey surrounded by photo portraits of other RKO stars, back of page includes list of films plus "Scene From Clock Cleaners" featuring Mickey and Donald. Other prominent movie ads are for Shirley Temple and Lone Ranger. - **$200 $400 $650**

MKY-457

MICKEY MOUSE, MINNIE & NEPHEWS

MKY-458

❑ **MKY-457. Movie Promo Blotter With Mickey,**
1937. Cardboard is 4x6.5" for "All Three Grand Hits On One Palace Program" movie triple feature. - **$25 $50 $85**

❑ **MKY-458. Mickey Mouse Globe Trotters Bread Company Store Sign,**
1937. Paper sign 10.5x23" with 1.5" vertical gummed left and right margins for window display. Illustrates May, 1937 issue of Mickey Mouse Magazine. - **$300 $600 $1200**

MKY-459

❑ **MKY-459. "Mickey Mouse" Globe Trotters Premium Picture,**
1937. Various bakeries and dairies. 4.75x5.75x5" deep wood frame contains 4x5" cardboard picture of Mickey. Back has partial label which reads "To My Dear Friend/For Completing Globe Trotter Map/Sincerely Mickey Mouse." - **$100 $200 $300**

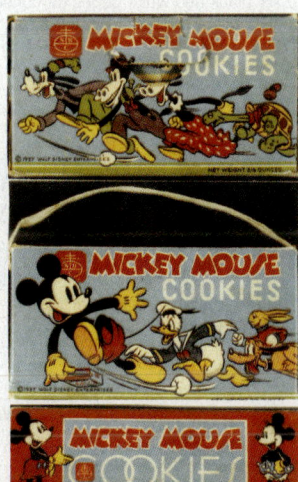

MKY-460

MKY-461

❑ **MKY-460. "Mickey Mouse Cookies" Box,**
1937. National Biscuit Co. 2x5x2.75" emptied box with string carrier. - **$100 $200 $375**

❑ **MKY-461. "Mickey Mouse Cookies" Store Window Sign,**
1937. National Biscuit Co. 9.5x12" glossy paper sign with .5" wide gummed strip on front top and bottom margins for window mounting. - **$600 $1200 $1800**

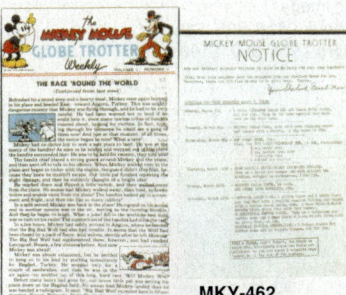

MKY-462

❑ **MKY-462. "The Mickey Mouse Globe Trotter Weekly,"**
1937. Volume 5, #5. Four-page publication 5x8.5" with continuing "Race 'Round The World" story. Each - **$25 $50 $75**

MKY-463

❑ **MKY-463. Walt Disney Characters "Pepsodent Paste & Powder" Store Display Sign,**
1937. Cardboard sign is 16x20". - **$300 $600 $1200**

MKY-464

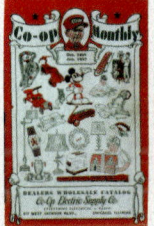 

MKY-465

❑ **MKY-464. "Minnie Mouse" As Tennis Player Glass,**
1937. Clear tumbler is 5.5" tall with fluted bottom from athletic series, also produced in smaller 4.75" height. - **$150 $300 $600**

❑ **MKY-465. "Co-Op Monthly Dealer's Wholesale Catalogue" With Mickey,**
1937. Co-Op Electric Supply Co. 5.75x8.75" catalogue featuring Mickey items such as Mickey wristwatch, child's rocker, pull toy, lamps. - **$75 $150 $250**

MKY-466

MICKEY MOUSE, MINNIE & NEPHEWS

❏ **MKY-466. "Playthings" Trade Publication Featuring Mickey Mouse,**
1937. Issue of "The National Magazine Of The Toy Trade" for May 1937 is 9x12" with 112 pages. Contents feature toy photos and ads. Includes special eight-page photo feature on the New York toy fair. - **$75 $150 $300**

MKY-467

❏ **MKY-467. "Mickey Mouse Drummer" Pull Toy,**
1937. Fisher-Price. 4x7.5x8.5" tall mostly wood pull toy #795. - **$300 $600 $1000**

MKY-468

❏ **MKY-468. "Mickey Mouse Ingersoll De-Luxe" Boxed Wrist Watch,**
1937. Box variety is 2.5x5x1.5" deep with sloped platform base.
Complete Box - **$400 $800 $1200**
Watch - **$200 $400 $800**

MKY-469

❏ **MKY-469. "Mickey Mouse Club" English Coronation Souvenir,**
1937. 7/8". Features issuer's name "County Cinemas" and bluetone photos of George VI and Queen Elizabeth. - **$100 $200 $400**

MKY-470

❏ **MKY-470. "Mickey Mouse Globe Trotters" Members Celluloid Button,**
1937. Imprints of various bakery and dairy companies. 1.25" with backpaper by M. Pudlin Co. or Kay Kamen Ltd. with Mickey extending left hand image.
Freihofer - **$15 $25 $45**
Others - **$25 $50 $100**

MKY-471

❏ **MKY-471. Mickey Mouse "Wesley's Bread" Button,**
1937. Kay Kamen Ltd. 1.25". Various sponsor imprints. - **$50 $100 $150**

MKY-472

❏ **MKY-472. "Mickey Mouse" The Atlanta Georgian's 1937 Silver Anniversary Button,**
1937. Roy Booker-Atlanta. 1 1/8" litho. from Southern newspaper button set which included other non-Disney characters. - **$200 $400 $800**

MKY-473

MKY-474

❏ **MKY-473. "Mickey Mouse Runs His Own Newspaper" Big Little Book,**
1937. Whitman. Book #1409. - **$25 $80 $165**

❏ **MKY-474. "Mickey Mouse And His Big Little Kit,"**
1937. Whitman. 4.5x6.5x1.5" deep box contains 384 4.25x6" black and white pages for construction of a customized Big Little Book. - **$200 $500 $1000**

MKY-475

❏ **MKY-475. "Mickey Mouse's Friends Wait For The County Fair,"**
1937. Whitman. 8.5x9.5" "Walt Disney Storybook" #883. 24 pages. - **$100 $200 $400**

MICKEY MOUSE, MINNIE & NEPHEWS

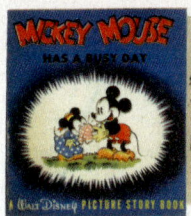

MKY-476

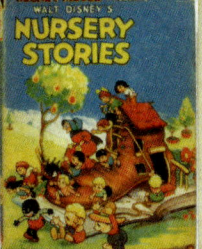

MKY-477

❏ **MKY-476.** "Mickey Mouse Has A Busy Day,"
1937. Whitman. Book #1077 from "Picture Storybook" series. - **$100 $200 $400**

❏ **MKY-477.** "Mickey Mouse Presents Walt Disney's Nursery Stories" Hardcover With Dust Jacket,
1937. Whitman. 6.5x9x1.5" thick with 212 pages of stories mostly related to nursery rhyme characters. The only reference to Mickey is the book's title. Jacket - **$15 $50 $100**
Book - **$25 $75 $150**

MKY-478

MKY-479

❏ **MKY-478.** "Mickey Mouse Annual" English Hardcover,
1937. Dean & Son Ltd. 6.5x8.5x2" thick with 124 thick stiff pages. Along with standard story pages, there is a two-page cut-out puzzle. - **$100 $200 $400**

❏ **MKY-479.** "Walt Disney Presents The Mickey Mouse Mother Goose" Hardcover,
1937. Whitman. 6.5x9x1.5" thick with 144 pages. Contents include numerous stories featuring Disney and nursery rhyme characters. - **$125 $250 $550**

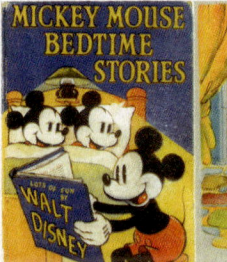

MKY-480

❏ **MKY-480.** "Mickey Mouse Bedtime Stories" English Book,
1937. William Collins Sons & Co. Ltd. 7.75x9.5" hardcover, 96 pages. - **$125 $250 $550**

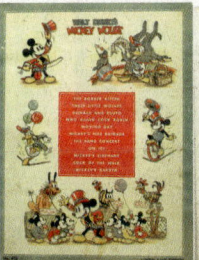

MKY-481

MKY-482

❏ **MKY-481.** "Walt Disney's Mickey Mouse Linen-Like" Book,
1937. Whitman. 9.75x12.5" with 12 pages. Contents are reprints of "Good Housekeeping" magazine pages. - **$65 $135 $250**

❏ **MKY-482.** "Walt Disney Silly Symphony Mickey's Magic Hat/Cookie Carnival" Book Abridged Version,
1937. Whitman. Book #1077. 8.5x9.5" with 16 pages rather than 24 pages in Whitman book #883 with the same title. - **$85 $175 $350**

MKY-483

❏ **MKY-483.** "Mickey Mouse Magazine" Gift Subscription Card,
1937. Stiff paper card is 4x5" sent to child notifying of one-year subscription to the magazine from mother and father. Card has inked "For/From" names on appropriate line. Mickey holds a copy of August 1937, Vol. 2 #11 issue with several other issues trailing behind the plane. - **$250 $600 $900**

MKY-484

MICKEY MOUSE, MINNIE & NEPHEWS

MKY-485

❑ **MKY-484. "Minnie Mouse" Oilcloth Doll,**
1937. Doll is 5x10.75" stuffed oilcloth with die-cut design and same Minnie image on both sides. - **$100 $200 $400**

❑ **MKY-485. "Mickey Mouse" Christmas Card,**
1937. Hall Bros. 4x5.25" stiff paper card with gold border designed like a movie screen. - **$75 $125 $225**

MKY-486

MKY-487

❑ **MKY-486. Mickey Mouse Christmas Card,**
1937. Hallmark. 3.5x4.5" card on parchment-like paper. - **$30 $60 $90**

❑ **MKY-487. Christmas Card,**
1937. Hallmark. 3x5.25" closed folder. - **$25 $50 $75**

MKY-488

❑ **MKY-488. Birthday Card,**
1937. Hallmark. Closed 3.25x5" folder card. - **$40 $75 $135**

MKY-489

MKY-490

❑ **MKY-489. Mickey Pencil Box With Donald And Nephews,**
1937. Textured paper-covered cardboard with snap closure lid is 2.5x8.25x1" deep. - **$50 $100 $160**

❑ **MKY-490. "Mickey's Inventions" Model Sheet,**
c. 1937. Copy sheet is 10x12.5" from the one original, distributed to various artists within the studio to guide them in drawing the character. There was never a short with title "Mickey's Inventions," likely revised to "Modern Inventions" of 1937, the first Donald Duck short. - **$25 $50 $115**

MKY-491

❑ **MKY-491. "County Mickey Mouse Club" English Enamel Pin,**
c. 1937. Die-cut Mickey with 1" octagonal border. - **$75 $150 $300**

MKY-492

❑ **MKY-492. Mickey Mouse China Cup/Egg Cup Boxed Set,**
c. 1937. "Limoges France." 4x6x3" deep original but generic pink box with hinged lid contains two-piece set consisting of 2.75" tall cup and 1.25" tall egg cup. Both pieces have gold stamp on underside "Licensed Walt Disney" as well as "Singer" name and Pegasus logo plus "Limoges France." Box - **$10 $20 $40**
Cup - **$75 $125 $225**
Egg Cup - **$75 $125 $225**

MICKEY MOUSE, MINNIE & NEPHEWS

MKY-493

❑ **MKY-493. Minnie Mouse Glass From Musical Note Series,**
c. 1937. 4.75" tall. - **$250 $500 $1000**

MKY-494

❑ **MKY-494. French Album Promoting Disney Premium Cards To Retailers,**
c. 1937. 6.25x9.25" with 24 pages. Reproduces 100 numbered cards from "Series A" set. - **$40 $85 $175**

MKY-495

❑ **MKY-495. Mickey Model Sheet,**
1938. 19x15" tall model sheet. - **$75 $150 $250**

MKY-496

❑ **MKY-496. "Mickey Mouse In Numberland" Activity Book,**
1938. Whitman. 8.25x11.25" #745 with 96 black and white pages. - **$60 $135 $275**

MKY-497

MKY-498

❑ **MKY-497. "Mickey Mouse Holiday Special" Publication,**
1938. English by Odhams Press Ltd. 9x12" with 64 pages. - **$75 $150 $300**

❑ **MKY-498. "Mickey Mouse Globe-Trotters" Door Hanger,**
1938. Die-cut 8x11.5" stiff paper. Bottom of piece is application card to be cut out and sent in for "Globe-Trotters Official Membership Button And World Map." - **$100 $200 $300**

MKY-499

❑ **MKY-499. "The Happy Homemakers Weekly/Mickey Mouse Travel Club News" Publications,**
1938. Various bakeries. Six consecutive issues, each 5.75x8" with four pages #3-#8. Each has one or two state-shaped cut-outs for mounting on map that details Mickey and Donald's journey across the USA. At least 22 known. Each - **$15 $25 $50**

MKY-500

MICKEY MOUSE, MINNIE & NEPHEWS

MKY-501

❑ **MKY-500. "Mickey Mouse Travel Club" Premium Map,**
1938. Mills Bakery and others. 16.5x24" for mounting cut-outs of states from folders titled "Happy Homemakers' Weekly." - **$100 $300 $650**

❑ **MKY-501. Mickey Mouse Chocolate Candy Bar Retailer's Folder,**
1938. Italian for "Topolino." 5.25x6.5", opens to 12x15.5". - **$40 $85 $175**

MKY-502

❑ **MKY-502. Mickey Mouse Chocolate Candy Box,**
1938. John F. Schoener Inc., Reading, PA. 5.5x11x4.25" deep. - **$75 $150 $300**

MKY-503

❑ **MKY-503. "Mickey Mouse" Lamp,**
1938. LaMode Studios. 4" diameter base and 9.5" tall. Mickey figure is 6.25" tall. - **$250 $500 $800**

MKY-504

❑ **MKY-504. Mickey Mouse Lamp Shade,**
1938. Doris Lamp Shades Co. Inc. 6" tall thin cardboard for use with LaMode Studios lamp. - **$400 $800 $1350**

MKY-505

❑ **MKY-505. Mickey & Minnie Mouse Wall Plaques,**
1938. Pair of 4x6" fiberboard with silk screened images. Each - **$20 $40 $60**

MKY-506

MKY-507

❑ **MKY-506. "Sunoco Oil" Disney Booklet,**
1938. Sun Oil Co. 4.75x7.25" booklet with 8 pages. - **$45 $90 $160**

❑ **MKY-507. "Marks Brothers Co. Games And Toys" 1938-1939 Catalogue,**
1938. Catalogue is 8.5x11" with 16 pages. On one page is the Mickey Mouse Target Game while on another page is Mickey Mouse Jack-In-The-Box and Piano with dancing figures. The final page of catalogue is devoted exclusively to Mickey and Snow White items. The Mickey items are Topple-Over Shooting Game, Rollem Bowling Game, Pin The Tail On The Mickey And Soldier. - **$65 $125 $250**

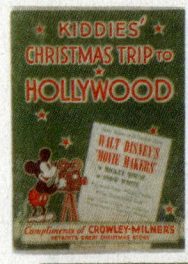 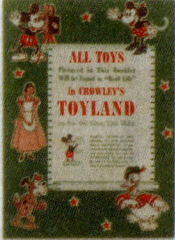

MKY-508

MICKEY MOUSE, MINNIE & NEPHEWS

❑ **MKY-508. "Kiddies' Christmas Trip To Hollywood" Premium Book,**
1938. Softcover 6x8" with 16 pages issued by Detroit department store. Story plus four full-page illustrations for four film sets including Snow White, Little Tailor, In The Nickel Of Time and Lonesome Ghosts. Also includes four pages of toys and related items. - **$125 $250 $500**

MKY-509

MKY-512

❑ **MKY-512. "Mickey Mouse/The Sheriff Of Nugget Gulch" Fast-Action Storybook,**
1938. Dell Publishing Co. 4x5.5" with 192 pages. Similar to Big Little Book with illustrations. - **$75 $150 $300**

MKY-514

❑ **MKY-514. "Mickey Mouse In The Race For Riches" Big Little Book,**
1938. Whitman. Book #1476. - **$30 $90 $210**

MKY-510

❑ **MKY-509. Disney Character Ink Blotter,**
1938. Sherwin Williams Co. of Canada. 3.5x8.75" with title "It's Time To Decorate." - **$100 $200 $300**

❑ **MKY-510. Mickey Mouse "Sunoco" Postcard,**
1938. Card is 3.5x5.5" with text "We Lubricated Your Car." - **$20 $40 $70**

MKY-511

❑ **MKY-511. Mickey Mouse Tenth Birthday Envelope,**
1938. 3.75x6.5" envelope. Has September 29, 1938 postmark from Los Angeles, California. - **$20 $40 $75**

MKY-513

❑ **MKY-513. Die Cut Standee,**
1938. From "The Mickey Mouse Theatre of the Air" program (NBC), sponsored by Pepsodent. 32" x 31". Rare. - **$2500 $5750 $8750**

MICKEY MOUSE, MINNIE & NEPHEWS

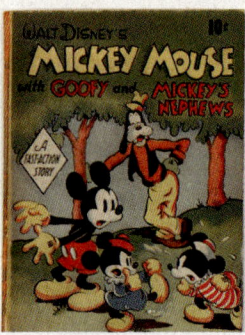
MKY-515

MKY-516

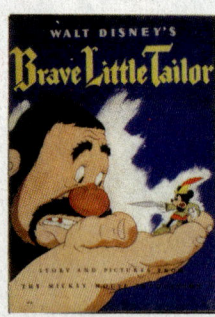
MKY-517

◻ **MKY-515. "Mickey Mouse With Goofy And Mickey's Nephews" Fast Action Storybook,** 1938. Dell. 4x5.25" softcover. Unusual variety with ads on both inside covers and back cover for Johnson Smith & Co. products. - **$100 $250 $400**

◻ **MKY-516. "Mickey Mouse Has A Party,"** 1938. Whitman. 7.25x10" with 48 pages. A "School Reader" book #798. Has thin cardboard covers. - **$75 $150 $300**

◻ **MKY-517. "Walt Disney's Brave Little Tailor,"** 1938. Whitman. 9.5x13" stiff cover with 24 pages. - **$60 $125 $250**

MKY-518

◻ **MKY-518. "A Mickey Mouse Alphabet/ABC" Book,** 1938. Whitman. 9.5x13" linen-like book with 16 pages of Disney characters representing different letters of the alphabet. - **$100 $225 $400**

MKY-519

◻ **MKY-519. "Mickey Mouse Annual" English Hardcover,** 1938. Dean & Son Ltd. 6.5x8.75x2" thick with 124 stiff paper pages. - **$100 $225 $500**

MKY-520

◻ **MKY-520. "Mickey's Hawaiian Holiday" English Hardcover,** 1938. Dean & Son Ltd. 7.2x9.75". 80 pages. - **$100 $200 $400**

MKY-521

◻ **MKY-521. Radio Magazine With Mickey,** 1938. "Radio Guide" 10.5x13.5" weekly for January 8 published by Regal Press Inc. Front cover pictures him at radio microphone and content includes half-page article about his radio debut, a 13-week series for NBC. Information on radio stars and programs such as "The Inside Story Of The Mae West-Charlie McCarthy Broadcast" with photos. - **$25 $50 $100**

MKY-522

◻ **MKY-522. Disney Characer Sand Pail,** 1938. Ohio Art. 8" tall with 8.25" diameter tin litho with attached carrying handle. - **$250 $500 $1000**

(BOX)

(DECAL ON BACK)

MKY-523

◻ **MKY-523. Mickey Mouse 'Lapel' Pocketwatch,** 1938. Ingersoll. 2"diameter. Reverse case features Mickey decal. Came with cord and brass button to fasten in lapel hole.
Box - **$400 $800 $1200**
Watch - **$500 $1000 $2000**
Cord - **$50 $100 $200**

MICKEY MOUSE, MINNIE & NEPHEWS

MKY-524

☐ **MKY-524. "Walt Disney Handkerchiefs" Boxed Set,**
c. 1938. Maker Unknown. 7x7x.25" deep box contains complete and unused set of three different fabric hankies. Boxed Set - **$75 $150 $250**

MKY-527

☐ **MKY-527. "Mickey Mouse" Celluloid Fan,**
c. 1938. Marked "Empire Made," likely Hong Kong and unauthorized. - **$35 $65 $100**

MKY-530

☐ **MKY-530. Mickey Mouse Composition Bank With Movable Head,**
c. 1938. Crown Toy Mfg. Co. 6" tall. - **$100 $200 $400**

MKY-525

MKY-528

☐ **MKY-525. Largest "Mickey Mouse Printing And Colouring Outfit,"**
c. 1938. English. A "Pingo" set by P.R.S. Co. Ltd. Box is 14.25x14.25x1.25" deep. This set has 27 different ink stamps ranging in size of 1x1.5" to 1.75x2.5". Four of the ink stamps are generic as issued and feature a tree, grass, house and light house. All of the others feature one or more Disney characters per stamp. Characters and number of different stamps per character are Pluto, Donald, Clarabelle and Horace each with one, Snow White 3, Three Little Pigs 4, Minnie Mouse 4, Mickey Mouse 8. - **$115 $250 $500**

☐ **MKY-528. Exceptional Walt Disney Character Rug With Tag,**
c. 1938. Large 21.5x45" rug with velvet-like nap. Has small tag marked "Made In Italy" and an additional 2.5x4" stiff paper tag with full color illustration of Snow White and four Dwarfs with text "By Permission Walt Disney." - **$250 $500 $1200**

MKY-531

☐ **MKY-531. "Mickey Mouse Toy Chest,"**
c.1938. 12x28" cardboard chest. Depicts various Disney characters on panels. - **$200 $400 $750**

MKY-526

MKY-529

MKY-532

☐ **MKY-526. "Mickey Mouse Paint Box,"**
c. 1938. Made In England. 2.5x6.25x.25" deep lithographed tin. - **$60 $125 $200**

☐ **MKY-529. "Mickey Mouse Weekly" Club Member Enamel On Brass Pin,**
c. 1938. United Kingdom. Issued by weekly publication. 1" with slogan "Mickey Mouse Chums." - **$65 $100 $225**

☐ **MKY-532. Disney Christmas Present Wrapping Paper,**
c. 1938. Department store large size roll paper 26" wide wrapped on a cardboard core 3.5" in diameter so that overall diameter is 6.5". Sold In 1997 Hake Auction #142 For $260.

MICKEY MOUSE, MINNIE & NEPHEWS

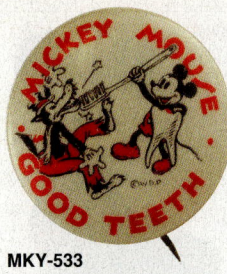

MKY-533

☐ **MKY-533. "Mickey Mouse Good Teeth" Celluloid Button,**
c. 1938. Button is 1.25" with backpaper "Distributed By The Bureau Of Public Relations American Dental Association 212 E. Superior St. Chicago, Ill." - **$60 $125 $185**

MKY-534

☐ **MKY-534. "Mickey Mouse Health Brigade" Pin,**
c. 1938. 1.25" tall die-cut brass pin. - **$100 $200 $300**

MKY-535

☐ **MKY-535. "Mickey's Fun Fair Card Game" Boxed Double Deck,**
c. 1938. Castell Brothers Ltd., England. .75x4.75x3.5" tall box contains two complete decks of cards and instruction book. Each deck consists of 44 cards, identical in design with only difference being the color of the card backs. - **$150 $300 $500**

MKY-536

MKY-537

☐ **MKY-536. Mickey Mouse Catalin Plastic Pencil Sharpener,**
c. 1938. 1.75" tall. - **$50 $100 $150**

☐ **MKY-537. English Squeaker Postcard,**
c. 1938. Valentine & Sons Ltd. 3.5x5.5" novelty card with inner mechanism that squeaks when pressed. - **$20 $40 $60**

MKY-538

☐ **MKY-538. "Hankyventures By Walt Disney" Book,**
1939. Playtime Hankies. 7x9" cardboard hanky book with eight pages. Hankies are incorporated as part of each page design. Complete - **$100 $200 $300**

MKY-539

☐ **MKY-539. "Mickey Mouse Magic Painting Book,"**
1939. Birn Brothers Ltd. 8.5x10.75" with 48 pages. Designed to be used with a wet brush to bring out color on pages. - **$175 $300 $600**

MKY-540

☐ **MKY-540. "Merry Christmas From Mickey Mouse,"**
1939. K. K. Publications Inc. 7x10" with 16 pages. Contents include illustrations, stories, puzzles, games, pictures to color, etc., much of which is Christmas related. - **$300 $1200 $3200**

MKY-541

☐ **MKY-541. Mickey Pencil Drawing From Society Dog Show,**
1939. Image is 3.25x4.75". From a numbered sequence and this is "43." - **$85 $175 $300**

MICKEY MOUSE, MINNIE & NEPHEWS

MKY-542

MKY-543

❏ **MKY-542. Minnie Pencil Drawing,**
1939. Animation paper is 10x12" centered by 3.5x4.5" image of her as a cook for 'Mickey's Surprise Party' film short. No. "6" from a numbered sequence. - **$65 $125 $200**

❏ **MKY-543. Mickey Mouse Pencil Drawing From Society Dog Show,**
1939. Sheet of animation paper is 10x12" with 4x7" image. #45 from a numbered sequence. - **$125 $250 $400**

MKY-544

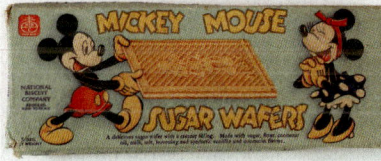
MKY-545

❏ **MKY-544. Fantasia Concept Sketch,**
1939. Image is 5x6.5". From a numbered sequence and this is "74." - **$200 $400 $600**

❏ **MKY-545. "Mickey Mouse Sugar Wafers" Box,**
1939. National Biscuit Co. 3x8x1" deep. - **$50 $100 $200**

MKY-546

❏ **MKY-546. "Walt Disney All Star Parade" Glass,**
1939. Clear tumbler is 4.75" with wrap-around illustration of Mickey, Minnie, Pluto and a parrot. From a "1939" dated series of glasses featuring various Disney characters. - **$20 $40 $60**

MKY-547

MKY-548

❏ **MKY-547. "Mickey Mouse Dime Register Bank,"**
1939. Lithographed tin bank is 2.75x2.75x.75" deep. - **$175 $300 $600**

❏ **MKY-548. Mickey/Minnie "Blue Sunoco" Ink Blotter,**
1939. Blotter is 4x7.25". - **$40 $80 $135**

MKY-549

❏ **MKY-549. "Mickey's And Donald's Race To Treasure Island" Premium Map,**
1939. Standard Oil Co. 19.5x27" map of United States. Has designated areas to paste pictures cut from "Travel Tykes Weekly." Reverse has text on obtaining stamps. - **$150 $300 $600**

MKY-550

❏ **MKY-550. "Travel Tykes Weekly" Premium Newspaper,**
1939. Standard Oil Co. Of California. 11.5x15" issue on newsprint paper. From series. Content of each includes puzzles, games, cartoons. Back cover has pair of numbered pictures to be mounted on the premium map "Mickey's And Donald's Race To Treasure Island," obtained separately. Each - **$10 $20 $50**

MKY-551

MICKEY MOUSE, MINNIE & NEPHEWS

MKY-552

MKY-555

MKY-558

❑ **MKY-551. Oil Change Reminder Postcard,** 1939. Sunoco. 3.5x5.5" depiction of Mickey as Pilgrim turkey hunter to illustrate season for changing automobile motor oil to winter grade. Reverse also has small Mickey image with ad text. - **$20 $50 $90**

❑ **MKY-552. Mickey Mouse Sign,** 1939. Sunoco. 19.75x28" cardboard with glossy outdoor protective coating. - **$200 $400 $800**

❑ **MKY-555. "Walt Disney's Storybooks,"** 1939. D.C. Heath & Co. 6.25x8.5" hardcover with 56 pages, designed for use in school. Title is "Here They Are." - **$35 $75 $150**

❑ **MKY-558. Religious Newspaper With Mickey Mouse Magazine Ad,** 1939. Complete 11x16.5" ad from "The Christian Science Monitor Weekly Magazine Section." Back cover has full color ad for "Mickey Mouse Magazine" with coupons for giving the magazine for a Christmas gift. - **$20 $40 $75**

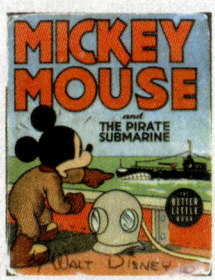

MKY-553

MKY-556

MKY-559

❑ **MKY-559. Mickey And Friends Get Well Card,** 1939. Hallmark. 3.75x4.75" on textured paper. Card opens to reveal large image of Donald with die-cut body that pops out slightly. - **$35 $75 $110**

MKY-554

MKY-557

MKY-560

❑ **MKY-553. "Mickey Mouse And The Pirate Submarine" Better Little Book,** 1939. Whitman. Book #1263. - **$25 $85 $165**

❑ **MKY-554. "Mickey Never Fails,"** 1939. D. C. Heath and Co. 6.25x8.5" hardcover with 108 pages including nice color throughout. - **$25 $50 $100**

❑ **MKY-556. "Mickey Mouse Annual" English Hardcover,** 1939. Dean & Son Ltd. 6.25x8.5x2" thick with 124 pages of comic-style stories. Also has one glossy color plate. - **$150 $350 $700**

❑ **MKY-557. "The Mickey Mouse Safety First Book,"** 1939. Dean & Son Ltd. Only issued in England. 7x9" with 62 pages. - **$135 $225 $450**

❑ **MKY-560. Mickey Mouse Valentine's Day Card,** 1939. Hallmark. 3x5" stiff paper card. - **$25 $50 $75**

MICKEY MOUSE, MINNIE & NEPHEWS

MKY-561

❑ **MKY-561. "Geo. Borgfeldt Corporation" Celluloid Calendar Card,**
1939. 2-1/8x4.75" two-sided. Text references Disney character toys. - **$20 $40 $75**

MKY-562

❑ **MKY-562. Cereal Box,**
1939. Mickey not on front. - **$200 $400 $700**

MKY-563

❑ **MKY-563. "Ingersoll Mickey Mouse Wristwatch" Box,**
1939. 3.75x6.75x1" deep box. - **$150 $300 $600**

MKY-564

❑ **MKY-564. Mickey Mouse Wristwatch Boxed,**
1939. Ingersoll. 4x6.75x1" deep box containing 1" wide chromed case watch with lady's style links band, one of four band styles offered. Dial is similar to the 1938 Ingersoll but on this version the Mickey second hand disk is replaced by conventional second hand with numerals and the case has fluted accents on sides.
Box Reading "New" - **$175 $350 $700**
Watch - **$150 $300 $600**

MKY-565

❑ **MKY-565. Gold Case Variety Wristwatch,**
1939. Ingersoll. First time Ingersoll offer of limited edition 14-karat gold plate "Goldtone" case watch for $1 more than the standard silvered brass case variety. Dial face has full figure image of Mickey whose hands point at the numerals. The second hand disk between Mickey's legs features numbers only. - **$175 $350 $700**

MKY-566

❑ **MKY-566. "Detective Adventures By Walt Disney" English Hardcover,**
c. 1939. Juvenile Ltd. Productions. 7.5x10.25" with 96 stiff paper pages. - **$75 $175 $350**

MKY-567

❑ **MKY-567. English Birthday Postcard,**
c. 1939. Valentine & Sons Ltd. 3.5x5.5" gloss stiff paper. - **$20 $40 $75**

MKY-568

❑ **MKY-568. English Birthday Postcard,**
c. 1939. Valentine & Sons Ltd. 3.5x5.5" gloss stiff paper. - **$20 $40 $75**

MKY-569

MKY-570

❑ **MKY-569. "Mickey Mouse Belt" Box,**
1930s. Hickok. 2x8x2" deep box. Bottom includes four different images of Mickey and two of Minnie. - **$75 $150 $275**

❑ **MKY-570. "Mickey Mouse" Child's Belt,**
1930s. Hickok Mfg. Co. Inc. 1.25x30" leather belt marked on reverse "Mickey Mouse Genuine Cowhide" with size "24." Entire front surface of belt has lightly ridged design with fourteen different images. - **$65 $150 $275**

MICKEY MOUSE, MINNIE & NEPHEWS

MKY-571

MKY-575

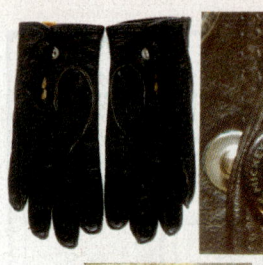

MKY-574. "**Mickey Mouse Hose**,"
1930s. Brier Mfg. Co. Satin-like socks. Size 8.5" with paper label. Shown with vintage generic Christmas box. - **$65 $100 $150**

❏ **MKY-575.** "**Converse Mickey Mouse Skoots**" **Boxed Sneakers,**
1930s. Box is 4.5x10.75x3.25" and contains pair of 9" long sneakers described on one side panel of box as "Misses' Patter White." Box - **$135 $250 $500**
Sneakers - **$65 $125 $250**

MKY-572

MKY-578

❏ **MKY-571.** "**Mickey Mouse**" **Clothing Buttons Carded,**
1930s. Brier Mfg. Co. 3x4.25" display card holding complete set of six figural plastic buttons. - **$30 $60 $125**

❏ **MKY-572.** "**Mickey Mouse Hose**" **Label,**
1930s. Thin paper label 1.75x4.25" that was originally attached to a pair of socks. Has gummed reverse. - **$20 $40 $65**

MKY-576

❏ **MKY-576.** "**Mickey Mouse Slippers**" **Empty Box,**
1930s. English, maker unknown. 3.25x7x2.75" deep. - **$200 $400 $750**

MKY-573

❏ **MKY-573.** "**Mickey Mouse Children's Hose Supporters**" **Empty Box,**
1930s. A. Stein & Co. 3.5x9x2.25" deep which originally held one dozen hose supporters. - **$125 $225 $450**

MKY-577

❏ **MKY-577.** Mickey Mouse Metal Shoe Horn,
1930s. Spanish with no Disney markings. 4" long. - **$75 $150 $300**

MKY-579

❏ **MKY-578.** "**Mickey Mouse**" **Child's Gloves,**
1930s. Rau F. Company, Prov. R.I. Size 4 gloves each 7.25" long. Outside snap closure. - **$35 $75 $150**

❏ **MKY-579.** "**Mickey Mouse**" **Child's Gloves,**
1930s. 6.5x10" with leather hands, cuffs are suede with matching fringe trim. Stitched to the front of each cuff is a 2.5x4.5" felt patch with silk screened design. - **$125 $250 $500**

MKY-574

MKY-580

MICKEY MOUSE, MINNIE & NEPHEWS

MKY-580. Mickey Mouse Child's Indian Headdress,
1930s. Unmarked but authorized. 3.5x11" with attached 11" long tail. - **$25 $50 $75**

MKY-581

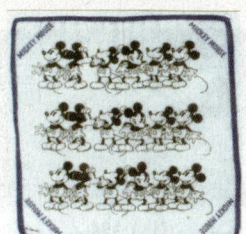
MKY-584

MKY-587

MKY-587. "Walt Disney Handkerchiefs,"
1930s. 7.25x7.25x3/8" deep box contains one 8.5x8.5" hanky of unknown original quantity. Box lid features Mickey, Minnie, Pluto, Donald and two nephews, Elmer Elephant and Dopey. Hanky features Dopey. Box - **$25 $50 $100**
Each Hanky - **$10 $20 $35**

MKY-585

MKY-582

MKY-584. "Mickey Mouse" Multiple Image Hanky,
1930s. Hanky is 9.5" square cotton in printed design of three repeated rows of six different Mickey images whose expression changes from happy to angry to sleepy to shocked. At each corner is his name. - **$35 $70 $115**

MKY-585. Baseball Theme Hanky,
1930s. Handkerchief is 11" square cotton. - **$25 $50 $75**

MKY-588

MKY-581. "Mickey Mouse Hankies" Boxed Set,
1930s. Box is 9x9.25x.25" deep and contains seven hankies. Each hanky features a different illustration of Mickey or Minnie along with name of each day of the week. Box - **$25 $50 $100**
Each Hanky - **$10 $20 $40**

MKY-582. Mickey/Donald Hanky,
1930s. 8.5x9" white cotton. - **$20 $40 $75**

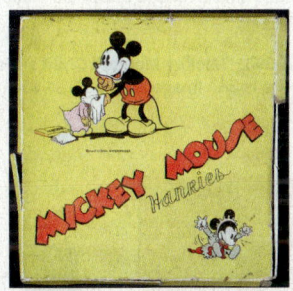

MKY-583

MKY-586

MKY-588. "Mickey Mouse" Hat,
1930s. Cotton twill hat 8x9" with celluloid visor. Outside has attached 7/8" button with brass rim and fabric center with Mickey image.
Hat - **$50 $100 $200**
Button - **$35 $75 $150**

MKY-589

MKY-589. Mickey Mouse Hat With Button,
1930s. 8x9" cotton twill hat with attached 7/8" diameter button that has brass rim and fabric center. Hat - **$35 $75 $150**
Button - **$35 $75 $150**

MKY-583. Mickey Hanky,
1930s. Herrmann Handkerchief Co. Inc. 7.5x8" cotton hanky with 1.75" long embroidered design. - **$10 $20 $40**

MKY-586. "Mickey Mouse Hankies" Boxed Set,
1930s. Herrmann Handkerchief Co. 7x7x.25" deep box contains set of three cotton hankies. Set - **$65 $125 $200**

475

MICKEY MOUSE, MINNIE & NEPHEWS

MKY-590

❏ **MKY-590. "Mickey Mouse Band-O" Hair Bow On Card,**
1930s. 5.5x8" display card holds silk-like hair bow with elastic band. - **$65 $150 $250**

MKY-591

❏ **MKY-591. "Mickey Mouse" French Shoe Polish Hat,**
1930s. Thin glossy paper hat measures 6x12". Text is in French. Each side has same design of Mickey shining his shoe to see his reflection along with can of shoe polish. - **$20 $40 $75**

MKY-592

❏ **MKY-592. "Mickey Mouse Comic Cookies" Premium Punch-Out Hat,**
1930s. Stiff paper sheet measures 8.25x13". When assembled, image of Mickey would appear on both sides. - **$100 $200 $350**

MKY-593

❏ **MKY-593. "Mickey Mouse Comic Cookies" Advertising Poster,**
1930s. 24x18" paper sign offering free hat. - **$300 $600 $1200**

MKY-594

❏ **MKY-594. "Mickey Mouse Tie Rack,"**
1930s. Rack is 5x8.75". Top has two hanging holes as made, front has attached wood bar for hanging ties. - **$100 $200 $300**

MKY-595

MKY-596

❏ **MKY-595. "Mickey Mouse Tie Rack,"**
1930s. Wooden rack 5x9" with large image of Mickey and smaller image of Donald. - **$65 $125 $250**

❏ **MKY-596. "Mickey Mouse" Child's Tie,**
1930s. Tie is 36". Image is 1.5x3.5". - **$30 $60 $100**

MKY-597

MKY-598

❏ **MKY-597. "Rodeo" Image Necktie,**
1930s. Child's fabric tie with overall 36" length. - **$30 $60 $100**

❏ **MKY-598. "Mickey Mouse" Child's Tie,**
1930s. Maker unknown. 43" long silk-like fabric. - **$20 $40 $75**

MKY-599

MKY-600

❏ **MKY-599. "Mickey Mouse Tie Rack,"**
1930s. Maker unknown. 4.25x9.5x.25" thick jig-sawed wood with silk screened design on front. - **$115 $250 $400**

❏ **MKY-600. Mickey/Minnie Umbrella,**
1930s. Japan. 19" long with diameter of about 23" constructed of wood handle and shaft with metal frame and silk-like synthetic fabric cover. - **$75 $150 $275**

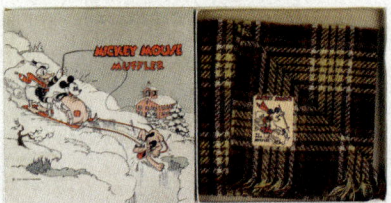

MICKEY MOUSE, MINNIE & NEPHEWS

MKY-601

MKY-604

MKY-607

MKY-605

◻ **MKY-607. "Mickey Mouse Undies" Sealed Pack,**
1930s. Sylcraft. 5x7.75" with single pair. Packaged - **$100 $200 $300**

◻ **MKY-604. Mickey Mouse Tie Clasp,**
1930s. Silvered brass 2" long with glass dome at center featuring reverse image with depth. - **$30 $65 $125**

◻ **MKY-605. "Mickey Mouse Undies" Clothing,**
1930s. Child's four fabric items believed comprising original set consisting of 10x21" sleeveless upper torso garment with button flap on back, size "6" panties, pair of elastic top ankle socks. Each piece is complete with small stitched fabric tag reading "Mickey Mouse Undies" although in two different styles. Group - **$100 $200 $350**

MKY-602

◻ **MKY-601. "Mickey Mouse Muffler" Boxed Scarf,**
1930s. Box is 9.5x9.5x.5" deep containing nice quality all wool "muffler," 8x38". Stitched to one corner of the muffler is 2x2.5" patch with image of Mickey skiing and Pluto running by his side. Box - **$115 $225 $350** Scarf - **$50 $100 $150**

◻ **MKY-602. "Mickey Mouse" Sweater,**
1930s. "Murrayknit" small child's wool sweater with body measuring 11x12". On breast pocket is 2x3" emboidered figural patch of Mickey. Stitched inside of collar is 1x1.25" tag for maker with Mickey image and word balloon that reads "It's All Wool." - **$50 $100 $200**

MKY-608

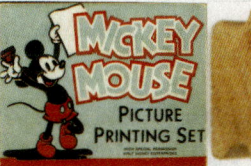

MKY-609

MKY-603

MKY-606

◻ **MKY-603. Mickey Mouse Baby Or Toddler Sweater,**
1930s. No tags, but authorized. Nice quality wool sweater. - **$50 $100 $200**

◻ **MKY-606. Child's Romper,**
1930s. One-piece cotton outfit measuring 13x18" overall. - **$35 $65 $125**

◻ **MKY-608. "Leader" Printing Set With Mickey Mouse Stamp Pad,**
1930s. Fulton Specialty Co. This is a generic stamp set although includes an official "Mickey Mouse Stamp Pad" with 1.25x2.25x3/8" deep tin case. Boxed - **$30 $75 $125** Pad Only - **$30 $75 $125**

◻ **MKY-609. "Mickey Mouse Picture Printing Set,"**
1930s. Canadian issue by H. Barnard Stamp & Stencil Co. Ltd. in 4.25x5.5x1" deep box. Set includes a single Mickey character ink stamp. All other contents are generic wood type holder, type line holder, metal tweezers, assortment of rubber letter and number stampers, tin lithograph stamp pad case with company logo. - **$50 $100 $150**

MICKEY MOUSE, MINNIE & NEPHEWS

MKY-610

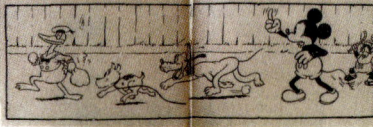

MKY-611

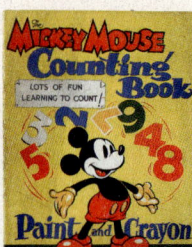

MKY-613

MKY-614

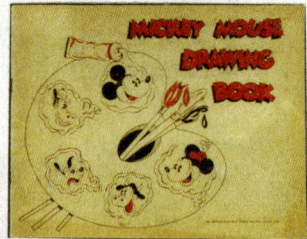

MKY-616

MKY-617

☐ **MKY-615. "Mickey Mouse Art Set,"**
1930s. Dixon. 8x13.25x.75" deep box contains six pictures to color, eight colored pencils, eraser, and pair of stencils of Mickey and Minnie. - **$150 $300 $600**

☐ **MKY-616. "Mickey Mouse Drawing Book,"**
1930s. Book is 8.5x11" with 28 blank pages. "Made In Great Britain." - **$25 $60 $120**

☐ **MKY-610. Picture Printing Set,**
1930s. Fulton Specialty Co. 8.5x11x1" deep boxed "Artistamp Picture Set No. 785" comprised of complete original 15 rubber ink stamps with wood grip handles. One stamp is scene of Mickey and Minnie from Steamboat Willie. - **$75 $175 $350**

☐ **MKY-611. Mickey Mouse Spanish Coloring Booklet,**
1930s. Booklet is 3x4.5" with 12 pages. Title is "El Juicio De Mickey." - **$15 $30 $50**

☐ **MKY-613. "The Mickey Mouse Counting Book/Paint And Crayon,"**
1930s. English by Collins Clear-Type Press. 10.5x13.5" with 32 pages. - **$125 $250 $500**

☐ **MKY-614. "Mickey Mouse Mystery Art Set,"**
1930s. Dixon. 8x11.5x5" deep cardboard unit comes with twelve colored pencils and 7x36" paper sheet with six different "Mystery Drawings," 3" wide illustrated cardboard band that slips over the "easel desk" and an eraser. Easel desk is corrugated cardboard and designed with a cardboard flap that is used to prop it up. - **$135 $275 $550**

MKY-612

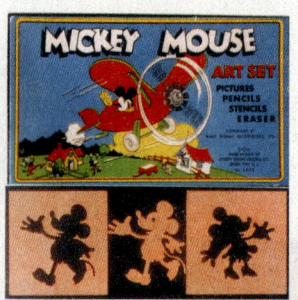

MKY-615

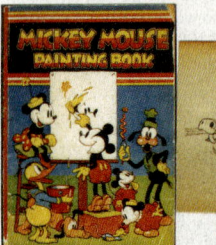

MKY-618

☐ **MKY-612. Mickey Mouse Spanish Coloring Booklet,**
1930s. 3x4.5" with 12 pages. Book #24 in series of 24 which came in five different sizes. Each - **$15 $30 $50**

☐ **MKY-617. "Mickey Mouse Pantograph,"**
1930s. Marks Brothers Co. 18x18x1.25" deep box contains 17.5" square pantograph board. Boxed - **$175 $350 $600**

☐ **MKY-618. "Mickey Mouse Painting Book,"**
1930s. Dean & Son, Ltd. 8.25x11.25" with 96 pages. Contains great full page illustrations from the earliest Disney cartoons. Title page is marked "For Color Guide See Any Copy Of The Mickey Mouse Weekly." - **$75 $150 $300**

MICKEY MOUSE, MINNIE & NEPHEWS

MKY-619

MKY-620

❏ **MKY-619. Mickey Mouse Label,**
1930s. Large 8x11.75" glossy label believed to be from The Netherlands, probably for a boxed paint set. - **$50 $100 $150**

❏ **MKY-620. "Mickey Mouse Poster Colour Painting Outfit,"**
1930s. English. 5.5x7.25x1.75" deep box contains complete amount of five glass bottles of paint plus brush. - **$60 $125 $200**

MKY-621

MKY-622

❏ **MKY-621. "Mickey Mouse Safety Blocks,"**
1930s. Halsam 4.25x4.25x1.25" deep box contains 9 wooden blocks. Two sides of each block have raised images of Mickey, Minnie or Pluto and other sides have animals or alphabet letters. One of eight different sets with six to thirty blocks per set. Boxed - **$35 $75 $150**

❏ **MKY-622. Mickey Mouse Puzzle Block Boxed Set,**
1930s. English by Chad Valley Co. Ltd. Set consists of fifteen wood blocks, each 1.5' square with full color paper labels on all sides to form six scenes. - **$150 $300 $600**

MKY-623

❏ **MKY-623. Mickey Mouse English Pull Toy,**
1930s. Chad Valley Toys. 2.5x3.5x8.75" tall overall. 5.5" tall thin wood figure of Mickey attached to circular wheel base. Figure has pair of separate arms attached to body by rubber strip and fits into slot of a thick wood disk. Disk is contained between pair of outer hard plastic circular sections. Front foot has small hole for string attachment to pull toy. - **$75 $150 $300**

MKY-624

❏ **MKY-624. Minnie Mouse On Scooter Pull Toy,**
1930s. Japan. 3.25" tall celluloid figure is attached to 4" long free-wheeling wood scooter. Attached to the front of the scooter is 19" long string with wood knob on the end. - **$500 $1000 $1500**

MKY-625

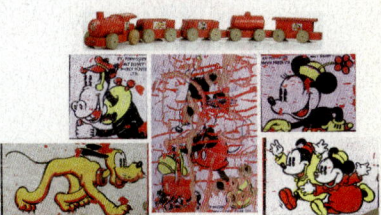
MKY-626

❏ **MKY-625. Mickey Mouse And Donald Duck In Boat Pull Toy,**
1930s. English by Chad Valley. 2.75x17x7.75" tall wooden. Photo example missing arms and/or oars. Complete - **$200 $400 $800**

❏ **MKY-626. Walt Disney Character Wood Train Pull Toy,**
1930s. Has Disney name but no maker; possibly Chad Valley. The engine is 3x7x3.5" tall, each of the four cars is 6.5" long. - **$125 $250 $500**

MKY-627

MICKEY MOUSE, MINNIE & NEPHEWS

❑ **MKY-627. "Mickey Mouse" Pull Toy,**
1930s. Fun-E-Flex. Free-wheeling painted wood car 3.5x11x2.5" tall with original pull string attached to front. Mickey figure 2.25" tall (missing hands in photo) fits in cylindrical opening above rear spare tire. - **$1000 $2000 $3750**

MKY-628

MKY-629

❑ **MKY-628. Mickey Mouse Decal Sheet,**
1930s. Italy. 3.5x10" sheet with four 2.25x3.25" decals. - **$10 $20 $40**

❑ **MKY-629. "Mickey Mouse Southern Dairies Ice Cream" Decal,**
1930s. "The Palm Brothers Decalomania Co." 4.25x4.25" unused decal. Reverse has maker's name with directions for transferring decal to glass. - **$50 $125 $250**

MKY-630

❑ **MKY-630. Mickey Mouse Southern Dairies Ice Cream Button,**
1930s. Parisian Novelty. 1.25". - **$200 $400 $800**

MKY-631

❑ **MKY-631. Mickey And Minnie Circus Pull Toy,**
1930s. By Nifty, distributed by Borgfeldt. Wooden figures swivel as platform moves. Has paper bellows on underside to create squeaking sound. Toy is 4.25x6x11" long. - **$300 $775 $1350**

MKY-632

❑ **MKY-632. Mickey Mouse Baby Rattle,**
1930s. Celluloid rattle is 3x5.75x1" thick with removable center compartment. No markings. - **$35 $65 $125**

MKY-633

MKY-634

❑ **MKY-633. "Mickey Mouse" Celluloid Baby Rattle,**
1930s. Marked "Made In Japan/Distributors: Geo. Borgfeldt Corp., New York." 8" long. - **$150 $300 $600**

❑ **MKY-634. Mickey Mouse Celluloid Roly Poly Toy,**
1930s. Toy has height of 3.5" including three-dimensional figure of Mickey with movable arms on top. - **$100 $225 $400**

MKY-635

❑ **MKY-635. Disney Character Top,**
1930s. Fritz Bueschel. 7" diameter by 6.5" tall tin litho with wood handle. - **$100 $200 $400**

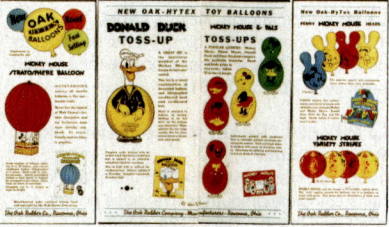

MKY-636

❑ **MKY-636. Disney Character Balloon Retailer's Catalogue Supplement Folder,**
1930s. Oak Rubber Co. 4x9" four-page glossy paper issued as a "Supplement To Catalogue No. 367." - **$35 $75 $135**

MKY-637

MICKEY MOUSE, MINNIE & NEPHEWS

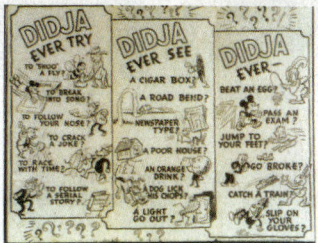

MKY-638

❏ MKY-637. "Mickey Mouse Balloon Novelty,"
1930s. Oak Rubber Co. Two-piece toy comprised of thick 5x7" die-cut cardboard base printed as pair of shoes to hold 6" tall balloon shaped as Mickey figure with large ears. - **$20 $50 $100**

❏ MKY-638. "Walt Disney Cut-Out Folder Book,"
1930s. Folder is 6.5x14.5" and opens to 19.25" long. Includes cut-outs for Mickey, Minnie, Goofy, Donna Duck, Dirty Bill and Big Bad Wolf along with accessories and outfits. - **$100 $225 $350**

MKY-639

❏ MKY-639. "Fire Chief Mickey Mouse" Dexterity Puzzle,
1930s. Cardboard frame puzzle 4x6x.75" deep with clear glass top. Has numerous small ball-bearings to be placed in die-cut holes on surface. At least four different. Each - **$65 $125 $200**

MKY-640

❏ MKY-640. Mickey Mouse With Harmonica Dexterity Puzzle,
1930s. "Made In Japan". 2.5x5" deep cardboard frame with glass cover. - **$60 $135 $200**

MKY-641

❏ MKY-641. "Mickey Mouse Picture Puzzles With Trays" Boxed Set,
1930s. Marks Bros. Co. 11x13.5x1.75" deep box with cellophane display window over complete set of four jigsaw puzzles. Each puzzle is 9.75x11.25" and nestles in individual cardboard tray when completed. The four trays are sized to nest within each other, smaller to larger, for storage in outer box. Near Mint Boxed Set - **$1750** Each Puzzle or Outer Box - **$100 $200 $350**

MKY-642

❏ MKY-642. French Jigsaw Puzzle Boxed,
1930s. "Vera" 6x6.75x.5" deep box containing complete wooden-piece puzzle assembling to 7x8.5". - **$65 $125 $225**

MKY-643

❏ MKY-643. Mickey Mouse/Three Little Pigs English Puzzle,
1930s. Chad Valley Co. Ltd. 7.25x9.25x.75" deep box contains puzzle with assembled size of 6x8" and consists of jigsawed wood pieces with paper label and same image as 1935 studio Christmas card. - **$100 $200 $400**

MKY-644

MKY-645

MICKEY MOUSE, MINNIE & NEPHEWS

❏ **MKY-644. "Mickey Mouse" Large Boxed Jigsaw Puzzle,**
1930s. English by Chad Valley Co. Ltd. Assembled size is 9.75x14". - **$75 $150 $250**

❏ **MKY-645. "Mickey Mouse" Boxed Puzzles,**
1930s. French "Les Pattences De Mickey Mouse." 9.25x14.5x1.25" deep box contains four jigsaw wood puzzles with full color paper labels, each 7x8.5". Set originally consisted of six. Complete - **$175 $250 $400**

MKY-646

❏ **MKY-646. "Mickey Mouse" With Horn Bisque,**
1930s. From musician set, 3.5" tall. Has incised "C73" on back. - **$35 $65 $135**

MKY-647

MKY-648

❏ **MKY-647. "Mickey Mouse" With Drum Bisque,**
1930s. From musician set, 3-3/8" tall. Has incised "C72" on back. - **$35 $65 $135**

❏ **MKY-648. "Minnie Mouse" With Concertina Bisque,**
1930s. Figure is 3-3/8" tall. Reverse has incised "C71." - **$30 $65 $100**

MKY-649

MKY-650

❏ **MKY-649. "Minnie Mouse" With Mandolin Bisque,**
1930s. Figure is 3.5" tall and has incised "C69" on back. - **$30 $65 $100**

❏ **MKY-650. "Mickey Mouse" With Banjo Large Bisque,**
1930s. Figure is 5.25" tall and has string tail. - **$135 $275 $475**

MKY-651

❏ **MKY-651. Mickey German Small Bisque,**
1930s. Figure of Mickey in boxing gloves is 1.25" tall. Incised on back is "Germany" with 4975. Issued with black paint accents. - **$75 $125 $225**

MKY-652

❏ **MKY-652. Mickey With Top Hat And Tuxedo Bisque,**
1930s. Figure is 4" tall. - **$200 $400 $800**

MKY-653

MKY-654

❏ **MKY-653. "Mickey Mouse" Bisque,**
1930s. Figure is 2.75" tall. - **$30 $65 $100**

❏ **MKY-654. "Minnie Mouse" Bisque,**
1930s. Figure is 2.75" marked "Made In Japan" with incised "S505." - **$25 $60 $80**

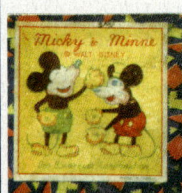
MKY-655

❏ **MKY-655. "Micky & Minne" (sic) Boxed Bisques,**
1930s. Geo. Borgfeldt Corp. 3x3x1.5" deep box holds pair of bisques 2.75" tall. Boxed - **$200 $400 $600**

MKY-656

MKY-657

MICKEY MOUSE, MINNIE & NEPHEWS

❏ **MKY-656. "Mickey Mouse" Large Bisque,**
1930s. Figure is 5.25" marked "Made In Japan" and has incised "A176" on back. - **$85 $175 $325**

❏ **MKY-657. "Minnie Mouse" Large Bisque,**
1930s. Figure is 5.25" marked "Made In Japan" and has incised "A177" on back. - **$85 $175 $325**

MKY-658

MKY-661

❏ **MKY-658. "Mickey Mouse" Conductor Bisque,**
1930s. Figure is 3.5" tall with movable arms. From set of six which included four musicians and Mickey with song book. No incised number. - **$125 $225 $400**

MKY-659   MKY-660

❏ **MKY-659. Mickey Singer Bisque,**
1930s. Figure is 3.25" tall with string tail. From set of six. - **$100 $200 $300**

❏ **MKY-660. Mickey With Saxophane Bisque,**
1930s. Figure is 3.25" tall with string tail. From set of six. - **$100 $200 $300**

❏ **MKY-661. Mickey With Drum Bisque,**
1930s. Figure is 3.25" tall with string tail. From set of six. - **$100 $200 $300**

❏ **MKY-662. Mickey And Minnie Unusual Bisque Figures,**
1930s. Figures are bisque with wire legs. Mickey is 3" tall and Minnie is 2-5/8" tall. Marked "Germany" under one foot of each and Mickey has incised "7759" on his rear. Each - **$100 $200 $400**

MKY-663

MKY-664   MKY-665

❏ **MKY-663. Mickey/Minnie Mouse German Bisque Band,**
1930s. Set of six, each marked "Germany." Three wear skirts and three wear pants. Each about 3" tall depicted with five fingers and playing a different instrument. Each - **$75 $150 $250**

❏ **MKY-664. "Minnie Mouse" Canadian Glazed Figure,**
1930s. Figure is 4" tall and marked "Made In Japan" and "S763." - **$65 $100 $200**

❏ **MKY-665. "Mickey Mouse" Canadian Glazed Ceramic Figure,**
1930s. Japan. 4" tall distributed in Canada only. Depicts Mickey playing a violin. - **$75 $125 $225**

MKY-666   MKY-667

❏ **MKY-666. Mickey Mouse Miniature Bisque,**
1930s. Japan. 1.5" tall smallest size of Mickey with one hand raised in the air. - **$25 $40 $75**

❏ **MKY-667. Soldier Mickey With Rifle Bisque,**
1930s. 3.25" tall with "S17" incised on back. - **$50 $100 $150**

MICKEY MOUSE, MINNIE & NEPHEWS

MKY-668

❏ **MKY-668. Officer Mickey Mouse With Saber Bisque,**
1930s. 3.25" tall with "S16" incised on back. - **$50 $100 $150**

MKY-669 MKY-670

❏ **MKY-669. Mickey Mouse Flag Bearer Bisque,**
1930s. 3.25" tall. #S15 from set of four. - **$50 $100 $150**

❏ **MKY-670. Minnie Mouse Nurse Bisque,**
1930s. 3.25" tall. #S18. - **$35 $65 $100**

MKY-671

❏ **MKY-671. "Mickey/Minnie Mouse" Seated Bisques,**
1930s. Pair of 3" tall figures in seated positions come with pair of chairs and table made of reed/wood with fabric covering. Set issued with a tiny china tea set not shown. Set - **$250 $500 $800**
Each Bisque - **$75 $150 $250**

MKY-672

MKY-673

❏ **MKY-672. Mickey Mouse Miniature Bisque,**
1930s. Japan. 1.75" tall. - **$30 $60 $100**

❏ **MKY-673. "Mickey/Minnie Mouse" Bisque Set,**
1930s. Japan. Matched 4" tall set. Mickey is #S1277, Minnie is #S1276. Each - **$40 $75 $125**

MKY-674

❏ **MKY-674. Mickey Mouse With Drum Large Bisque,**
1930s. Japanese large size 5.25" tall painted bisque likeness with label under base including Mickey and Disney names. - **$200 $400 $600**

MKY-675

❏ **MKY-675. "The Three Pals Mickey, Pluto, Minnie" Bisque Set With Box,**
1930s. 4.25" tall figures with box. "Made In Japan". Boxed set - **$200 $400 $600**

MKY-676 MKY-677

❏ **MKY-676. Minnie Figurine,**
1930s. "Made In Japan" 4.25" tall painted bisque pose holding umbrella and purse. Back has incised "S34" identification. - **$40 $75 $125**

❏ **MKY-677. Mickey With Cane Figure,**
1930s. "Made In Japan" 4.25" tall painted bisque pose with one hand on hip while the other holds a cane. Rear names him plus "S33" mold number. - **$40 $75 $125**

MICKEY MOUSE, MINNIE & NEPHEWS

MKY-678

MKY-681

MKY-682

MKY-686

❏ **MKY-678. Mickey And Minnie Mouse Figures,**
1930s. "Germany" matching pair of 1.75" tall painted bisques, each depicted with elongated snouts and wide smiles. Mickey - **$60 $125 $200**
Minnie - **$40 $100 $175**

❏ **MKY-681. "Mickey Mouse" Baseball Player Bisque,**
1930s. Japan. 3-3/8" tall from set of four depicting Mickey in various player positions. With glove and ball. Incised #S65. - **$100 $150 $250**

❏ **MKY-682. "Mickey Mouse" Baseball Player Bisque,**
1930s. Japan. 3-3/8" tall from set of four depicting Mickey in various player positions. In catcher's outfit. Incised #S67. - **$100 $150 $250**

❏ **MKY-686. Mickey Mouse Bisque Pin Cushion,**
1930s. "Made In Japan" 4.5" long with felt cushion. - **$200 $400 $800**

MKY-679

MKY-683

MKY-684

MKY-687

❏ **MKY-683. "Mickey Mouse" Baseball Player Bisque,**
1930s. Japan. 3-3/8" tall from set of four depicting Mickey in various player positions. With bat. Incised #S66. - **$100 $150 $250**

❏ **MKY-684. "Mickey Mouse" Playing French Horn Large Bisque,**
1930s. Japan. 5.25" tall. No incised number. - **$200 $400 $600**

❏ **MKY-687. Mickey Mouse And Santa Bisque,**
1930s. Unmarked, likely Japan. 1.25". - **$200 $350 $700**

MKY-680

MKY-685

MKY-688

❏ **MKY-679. "Mickey Mouse" Largest Size Bisque Figure,**
1930s. "Made In Japan" 8.5" tall painted bisque on 2.75" square base. Detailing includes two movable arms, string tail, incised name on base front. - **$400 $850 $1400**

❏ **MKY-680. Mickey Mouse Riding Pluto Bisque,**
1930s. Japan. 1x3x2.25" tall. - **$40 $90 $150**

❏ **MKY-685. "Mickey Mouse" Playing Accordion Large Bisque,**
1930s. Japan. 5.25" tall. No incised number. - **$200 $400 $600**

❏ **MKY-688. Mickey Mouse Bisque Figure,**
1930s. United Kingdom. Dean's Rag Book-style image incised with number that appears to be in the 500 series. 2" tall. - **$40 $65 $125**

MICKEY MOUSE, MINNIE & NEPHEWS

MKY-689

❏ **MKY-689. Minnie Mouse On Sled Bisque Figure,**
1930s. No markings. 1.5" tall. - **$100 $200 $350**

MKY-692

❏ **MKY-692. Mickey Mouse Celluloid Place Card Holder,**
1930s. Japan. 2.5" tall. All celluloid including die-cut Mickey. Has tube designed to hold a single flower. - **$100 $250 $500**

MKY-695

❏ **MKY-695. Minnie Mouse Celluloid Figure,**
1930s. Figure is 2.25" tall and is one of the character figures that dangle from the 1930s Mickey Mouse and Donald Duck Whirly-Gig celluloid wind-up toy. - **$50 $100 $150**

MKY-690

❏ **MKY-690. Mickey Mouse Stickpin Figure,**
1930s. Stiff molded spun paper body, pipe cleaner arms, legs and tail with die-cut ears figure is 2.75" tall. - **$50 $100 $150**

MKY-693

❏ **MKY-693. Mickey And Minnie Mouse Celluloid Place Card Holders,**
1930s. Unmarked. Mickey is 1.75" tall, Minnie is 2" tall. Both have small cello tab on back for card. Mickey - **$50 $85 $150**
Minnie - **$40 $65 $100**

MKY-696   MKY-697

❏ **MKY-696. Mickey Mouse Celluloid Figure,**
1930s. Japan. 3.75" tall holding a flag with raised text that reads "Yusho." Piece is unmarked but probably Japanese made for the European market. - **$65 $125 $200**

❏ **MKY-697. Minnie Celluloid Figure,**
1930s. Unmarked but probably Japanese 2.5x5.75x5.25" tall. - **$75 $150 $250**

MKY-691

❏ **MKY-691. Large "Mickey Mouse" Jointed Celluloid Figure,**
1930s. Figure is 2.75x3x6.25" tall, the largest of three sizes. Has raised name on chest and back is marked "Made In Japan." - **$300 $600 $1200**

MKY-694

❏ **MKY-694. Unusual Mickey Mouse Celluloid Figure,**
1930s. Figure is 2.25x2.75x4.25" tall. Eyes are attached to springs and when tapped vibrate feverishly. Marked "Made In Japan" with tax stamp under one foot. - **$100 $250 $500**

MKY-698

❏ **MKY-698 Mickey's Nephew Celluloid Figure,**
1930s. "Made In Japan". 5.25" tall. Depicts nephew in nightshirt and has movable head. Body contains granules so figure can be used as a rattle. - **$150 $350 $700**

MICKEY MOUSE, MINNIE & NEPHEWS

MKY-699   MKY-700   MKY-701

❏ **MKY-699. Mickey Mouse Plaster-Filled Celluloid Figure,**
1930s. "Foreign" marked on back. 5.5" tall. - **$125 $225 $350**

❏ **MKY-700. "Minnie Mouse" Large Jointed Celluloid Figure In Rarely Seen Blue Dress,**
1930s. Japan. 5-7/8" tall with movable arms and head. - **$150 $300 $600**

❏ **MKY-701. "Mickey Mouse" Celluloid Figure,**
1930s. Maker unknown. 5.75" tall. His name on chest, molded hands at waist and molded tail on reverse. - **$150 $300 $600**

MKY-702

❏ **MKY-702. Celluloid Mickey Mouse With Movable Head,**
1930s. Unmarked, likely Japanese. 3.5x3.5x4.5" tall. - **$250 $500 $900**

MKY-703

❏ **MKY-703. Mickey And Minnie Celluloid Squeaker Toys,**
1930s. Made In Japan. Mickey is 5.5" tall, Minnie is 6.25" tall. Each - **$200 $400 $800**

MKY-704

❏ **MKY-704. Mickey Mouse Celluloid Squeaker Figure,**
1930s. "Made In Japan". 6" tall. Celluloid body with felt pants with buttons and string tail. - **$250 $500 $1000**

MKY-705

❏ **MKY-705. Mickey Mouse In Bathing Suit Celluloid Figure/Rattle With Life Preserver,**
1930s. Japan. 4.25" tall figure with 3" diameter life preserver. Mickey filled with granules and serves as a rattle. - **$1000 $2000 $3500**

MKY-706

❏ **MKY-706. German China Mouse Band,**
1930s. Five different figures each 2.75" and marked "Germany." Gray with tan accents. Each - **$25 $50 $75**

MKY-707   MKY-708

❏ **MKY-707. Mickey Mouse Dean's Rag-Style China Figure,**
1930s. Figure is 2-1/8" tall. Back of base is marked "Reg." and underside has incised number. Made in Japan for the English market. - **$40 $65 $100**

❏ **MKY-708. Minnie Mouse Figurine,**
1930s. Germany. 1.75" tall china marked "Deutschland" under feet. She has one hand raised to her chin. - **$50 $100 $150**

MKY-709

❏ **MKY-709. Mickey Mouse Grinning Glazed Ceramic Figure,**
1930s. Looks identical to 3.5" porcelain figure by Rosenthal and has their incised #551, but this is 4" and glazed ceramic. Also has gold foil sticker in German that translates to "Mickey Mouse Brings Luck To The Home." - **$150 $300 $600**

MICKEY MOUSE, MINNIE & NEPHEWS

MKY-710

MKY-711

❏ **MKY-710. Mickey Mouse With Saxophone China Figurine,**
1930s. Germany. 3.25" tall. #6592. Each In Series - **$125 $250 $400**

❏ **MKY-711. Mickey Mouse In Chair English Ceramic Figurine,**
1930s. 2x2x3.75" tall marked on underside "British Maker." - **$100 $200 $325**

MKY-712

❏ **MKY-712. Mickey Mouse German Musician China Figurines,**
1930s. Each is 1.5" tall. Each - **$50 $100 $200**

MKY-713

❏ **MKY-713. Bath Salts Figural Container,**
1930s. "Imex Bath Crystals." 3x3x6.5" tall figure "Made In Japan" for English market. Reverse of base is simulated tree stump. Back has registration number and "By Special Permission Walt Disney Enterprises." - **$500 $1000 $1500**

MKY-714

❏ **MKY-714. Mickey Mouse China Band Figures,**
1930s. Japan. Unauthorized. Each is 6.5" to 7.5" tall. Each - **$25 $50 $75**

MKY-715

MKY-716

❏ **MKY-715. Mickey Mouse China Figural Bottle Stopper/Pourer,**
1930s. Germany. 3" tall. - **$60 $125 $200**

❏ **MKY-716. Mickey Mouse Large China Ashtray,**
1930s. Dutch by "Mosa Maastricht." 3.5x3.5x7.5" tall with five-fingered Mickey. - **$500 $1250 $2750**

MICKEY MOUSE, MINNIE & NEPHEWS

MKY-717

❑ **MKY-717. Mickey Mouse Golfer Tootbrush Holder Ceramic Figure,**
1930s. S. Maw Son & Sons. Ltd., London. 4" tall. - **$250 $550 $1000**

MKY-718

❑ **MKY-718. Mickey Mouse Seated Glazed Ceramic Figure,**
1930s. United Kingdom. Dean's Rag Book doll image marked "Foreign 2205." 1.25" tall. - **$35 $60 $90**

MKY-719

MKY-720

❑ **MKY-719. Mickey Mouse Standing Glazed Ceramic Figure,**
1930s. United Kingdom. Dean's Rag Book style image marked with number "8201." Stands 2.75" tall. - **$50 $75 $125**

❑ **MKY-720. Mickey Mouse Figural Ceramic Pitcher,**
1930s. Large size 4x7.5x6.75" tall painted and glazed ceramic. Incised markings underneath including number which appears to be "5028." - **$65 $135 $200**

MKY-721

❑ **MKY-721. Unauthorized Mickey Mouse Composition Figure,**
1930s. Figure is 4.25x4.75x10.25" tall composition. - **$50 $100 $150**

MKY-722   MKY-723

❑ **MKY-722. Mickey Mouse Painted Plaster Carnival Statue,**
1930s. 9.75" tall. - **$50 $100 $175**

❑ **MKY-723. "Mickey Mouse" Composition Ashtray Figure,**
1930s. 3.25" tall, originally stood on back base of ashtray. Complete - **$65 $125 $250**
Figure Only - **$35 $65 $100**

MKY-724

❑ **MKY-724. Minnie Compo/Wire Figure,**
1930s. Figure is 7.5" tall ornament dancer formed by painted composition body, hands and feet jointed by coil spring arms and legs. Top of head has metal loop for string or rubber band attachment. - **$150 $350 $600**

MICKEY MOUSE, MINNIE & NEPHEWS

MKY-725

❏ **MKY-725. "Mickey Mouse" Painted Lead Figure,**
1930s. Three-dimensional figure 2.5" tall with name on base. - **$125 $250 $400**

MKY-726

❏ **MKY-726. Mickey/Minnie/Pluto Painted Lead Figures,**
1930s. Set of three 2.25" tall semi-flat lead figures, all neatly painted as issued. Each - **$15 $30 $60**

MKY-727

❏ **MKY-727. Miniature Solid Bronze Mickey Mouse Figure,**
1930s. Vienna by Fritz Bermannwien with initials under base "FBW." 1.75" tall depicting a five-finger Mickey. - **$150 $300 $600**

MKY-728

❏ **MKY-728. Mickey Mouse Car Radiator Ornament,**
1930s, England. Maker unknown. 5.75" tall stamped brass originally finished in black paint and silver luster. Pair of long thin mounting wires on reverse. - **$150 $300 $600**

MKY-729

❏ **MKY-729. Mickey Mouse Playing Mandolin Pewter Figure,**
1930s. Figure is 1.75" tall. No markings. - **$165 $275 $550**

MKY-730

❏ **MKY-730. Mickey Mouse Cast Aluminum Doorstop,**
1930s. Maker unknown, three examples known to exist. Unusual design features include oversized shoes and, although his head is turned to the right, his ears remain in frontal view. One leg is slightly bent at the knee and his chest protrudes. 7" tall. - **$6000 $16000 $27500**

MICKEY MOUSE, MINNIE & NEPHEWS

MKY-731

❑ **MKY-731. Mickey Mouse Store Display Standee,**
1930s. Made By Old King Cole, Distributed By Kay Kamen. Molded 'laminite' 11x17.5x1.5" deep. - **$550 $1100 $1800**

MKY-732

❑ **MKY-732. Minnie Mouse Store Display Standee,**
1930s. Made By Old King Cole, Distributed By Kay Kamen. Molded 'laminite' 11x15.5x1.5" deep. - **$525 $1050 $1700**

MKY-733

❑ **MKY-733. "Mickey Mouse" Jumping Jack Fun-E-Flex Toy,**
1930s. George Borgfeldt. 12" tall wood toy which moves arms and legs when bellows are operated. - **$500 $1000 $2000**

MKY-734

❑ **MKY-734. Mickey, Minnie And Pluto Wood Sled,**
1930s. Fun-E-Flex. Toy is 1.75x4.25x10" long. - **$550 $1100 $2200**

MKY-735

MKY-736

❑ **MKY-735. Mickey And Minnie Fun-E-Flex Figures,**
1930s. Wooden figures with wire arms and legs measures 3.75" tall. Decals on chest. Each - **$50 $100 $150**

❑ **MKY-736. Miniature Mickey Mouse Figure,**
1930s. Painted wood figure 1.5" tall with wire tail and legs. Likely unauthorized. - **$25 $50 $100**

MKY-737

❑ **MKY-737. "Mickey Mouse Fun-E-Flex" Figure,**
1930s. Figure is 3x6.5x7" tall with wood body and metal cable arms and legs, cardboard ears and fabric-covered wire tail with wooden tip. Has Mickey decal on chest and Fun-E-Flex decal under foot. - **$200 $400 $800**

MKY-738

❑ **MKY-738. "Minnie Mouse Fun-E-Flex" Figure,**
1930s. Figure is 7" tall with metal cable arms and legs, fabric-covered wire tail with wooden tip, and cardboard ears. Has Minnie label on chest and Fun-E-Flex label under foot. Also issued with fabric skirt. - **$200 $400 $750**

MICKEY MOUSE, MINNIE & NEPHEWS

MKY-739

❑ **MKY-739. "Minnie Mouse" Medium Sized Wood Doll,**
1930s. Fun-E-Flex doll is 5" tall to the tip of her ears. Decal on chest. Designed with movable rubber-covered arms and movable head and midsection. Photo example is missing wooden hat. - **$100 $200 $400**

MKY-740

❑ **MKY-740. "Minnie Mouse" Largest Size Fun-E-Flex Figure,**
1930s. Figure is 2.75x6x7" tall. This large figure came in two varieties with either a painted skirt or as this figure has, a separate fabric skirt. Wood body with flexible sturdy metal arms and legs. Fabric Skirt - **$225 $425 $850**
Painted Skirt - **$200 $400 $750**

MKY-741

MKY-742

❑ **MKY-741. English Mickey Mouse Band Member Wood Figures,**
1930s. Each is 2.75" tall, similar in design to Dean's rag dolls. Each - **$50 $100 $150**

❑ **MKY-742. Mickey Mouse Small Wood Figure,**
1930s. Germany. 2.5" tall jointed figure with movable head, arms, legs and segmented tail. - **$50 $125 $250**

MKY-743

MKY-744

❑ **MKY-743. Mickey Mouse Folk Art Wood Flag Holder,**
1930s. Jigsawed wood Mickey is 12x16.5" and attached to wood base 8" diameter by 1" tall. Similar - **$50 $100 $150**

❑ **MKY-744. Mickey Mouse Folk Art Two-Sided Display Figure,**
1930s. Jigsawed plywood is 7x15". Maker is unknown. Similar - **$65 $125 $200**

MKY-745

MKY-746

❑ **MKY-745. Mickey Mouse Skier Articulated Wood Figure,**
1930s. Italian by Peri. 2.75" tall with 4" long skis. - **$200 $400 $600**

❑ **MKY-746. Unlicensed Mickey Mouse Wood Jointed Figure,**
1930s. Unmarked but by Jaymar. 5.75" tall with elastic string attached to head. This particular toy was never sold in a box. - **$50 $100 $165**

MKY-747

❑ **MKY-747. Boxed Mickey Mouse Wood Jointed Figure,**
1930s. "Patent Tokyo." 4" tall. Wooden body while arms, legs and tail are coated wire. Insert card 2x4" with images and Japanese text roughly translated to "Fun To Play With." Box Or Card Each - **$15 $30 $50** Figure - **$135 $275 $550**

MKY-748

❑ **MKY-748. Mickey Mouse Skiers Wood Jointed Pair,**
1930s. Unmarked but from Czechoslovakia. Identical 3" tall fully articulated figures with rubber tails. Each - **$25 $50 $75**

MICKEY MOUSE, MINNIE & NEPHEWS

MKY-749

❑ **MKY-749. Mickey Mouse On Scooters Wood Jointed Pair,**
1930s. Unmarked but from Czechoslovakia. 3" tall and 1.75" tall. Large - **$30 $60 $85**
Small - **$20 $40 $60**

MKY-750

❑ **MKY-750. Mickey Mouse Yarn Tool,**
1930s. Unmarked. 4.75" tall wooden. - **$25 $50 $100**

MKY-751

❑ **MKY-751. Unusual Wood/Metal Mickey Mouse Figure,**
1930s. Homemade. 1.5x4x4" tall with painted wood body parts and poseable metal rod arms and legs. Unique, Very Fine - **$200**

MKY-752

❑ **MKY-752. Unauthorized Mickey Plaster Figure,**
1930s. Solid plaster carnival statue 4.5x4x10.5" tall marked on back of one foot "Nunak." - **$25 $50 $75**

MKY-753   MKY-754

❑ **MKY-753. Mickey Mouse Painted Plaster Statue,**
1930s. Carnival statue 9.75" tall, the only one we know of which closely resembles 1930s studio images. Maker is unknown. - **$40 $75 $150**

❑ **MKY-754. Mickey Mouse German Bottle Stopper,**
1930s. 3.5" tall china marked "Allenegne." - **$40 $85 $150**

MKY-755

❑ **MKY-755. "Mickey Mouse" Bread Promotion Display Sign,**
1930s. 8x19.5" tri-fold die-cut cardboard. Advertises the premium scrapbook for collecting picture cards that were issued with loaves of bread. - **$250 $500 $1000**

MKY-756

❑ **MKY-756. "Mickey Mouse Bread" Store Sign,** 1930s. 9-7/8x16-3/4". Bottom has unused area for bakery imprint. - **$300 $750 $1200**

MKY-757

❑ **MKY-757. "Mickey Mouse Scrapbook" Advertising Paper,**
1930s. Waxed paper strip 2x9" that was part of a bread loaf packaging. - **$50 $125 $250**

MICKEY MOUSE, MINNIE & NEPHEWS

MKY-758

❏ **MKY-758. "Mickey Mouse Recipe Scrapbook,"**
1930s. Book is 4.25x6.25" with 48 pages. Issued by various bread companies. Inside has many character designs around recipe areas where picture cards were to be attached. Empty Book - **$50 $100 $150**

MKY-759

❏ **MKY-759. "Mickey Mouse Recipe Scrapbook" Display Sign,**
1930s. 6x9.75" die-cut cardboard with blank reverse. Depicts Mickey reading the scrapbook. - **$500 $1200 $1800**

MKY-760

❏ **MKY-760. "Mickey Mouse" Bread Picture Card Store Sign,**
1930s. Sign is 18x25". - **$675 $1500 $2400**

MKY-761

❏ **MKY-761. Mickey And Minnie Mouse Butter Nut Bread Store Sign,**
1930s. 10x17". - **$400 $800 $1200**

MKY-762

❏ **MKY-762. "Mickey Mouse" Bread Loaf Band,**
1930s. 2x19.5" complete waxed paper band with perforated top and bottom edges. - **$40 $100 $200**

MKY-763

❏ **MKY-763. Earliest Version "Mickey Mouse Scrapbook,"**
1930s. Armstrong's Bread. 4-1/8x7.25" album with 28 pages and 24 glued in superb color 3.25x5" paper pictures which illustrate a paragraph of text printed below the picture. See next item. Preceded similar but smaller "Recipe" album. Complete - **$325 $650 $1250**
Album Only - **$75 $150 $300**

MKY-764

❏ **MKY-764. Mickey Mouse Large Size Recipe Cards,**
1930s. Issued by various bakeries. Complete set of 24 stiff paper recipe cards, each 3.25x5". This is a totally different set than those mounted in previous item. Thus, there is an unknown 24-card album or, less likely, a 48-card album.
Each - **$10 $20 $35**

MICKEY MOUSE, MINNIE & NEPHEWS

MKY-765

❑ **MKY-765. Mickey Mouse Party Favor Candy Basket,**
1930s. Basket is 1x3.5x4" tall with diamond-shaped cardboard interior frame covered by crepe paper with thin rope handle. Attached to side is die-cut cardboard panel with Mickey image and cardboard panel for attendee's name. - **$15 $30 $60**

MKY-766

MKY-767

❑ **MKY-766. "Mickey Mouse Magic Show" Candy Wrapper,**
1930s. A. McLean & Son. 5x5" one-cent wrapper from a series of 24 different riddles. On this one, Donald is asking a question and the answer is to appear on the movie screen when wrapper is wet. - **$25 $50 $100**

❑ **MKY-767. Mickey Mouse Spanish Candy Cards,**
1930s. Maatller Chocolates. Set of 36, each 2.75x4.25", possibly issued one per candy bar and all 36 were to be assembled in order to tell a story with text on reverse. Each Card - **$5 $10 $20**

MKY-768

❑ **MKY-768. "Mickey Mouse Chocolate Bar" Candy Box,**
1930s. William Patterson Ltd., Canada. 1.5x4x1.25" deep waxed cardboard box originally held a "Caramel Nougat Chocolate Bar." Photo example ironically has mouse-chewed hole. - **$100 $200 $300**

MKY-769

❑ **MKY-769. Mickey Mouse Japanese Candy Tin,**
1930s. 2" diameter by 3/8" deep. Text translates to "Candy Ball." No Disney markings. - **$25 $50 $85**

MKY-770

❑ **MKY-770. Dutch Chocolate Tin,**
1930s. Lithographed tin canister with lid is 2.25" diameter by 4.75" tall. Design is circular brick building with total of thirteen windows and a door on front with simulated sign "Simon De Wit's Gestampte Muisjes" translating as Chocolate Mice. At each window is a totally different image of either Mickey or Minnie. An additional image of him on the lid is peeking out of a skylight window. - **$150 $375 $650**

MKY-771

❑ **MKY-771. Rare Mickey Mouse Picture Cards From Prague, Czechoslovakia,**
1930s. Large group of 41, each 1.75x2-3/8" glossy thin paper. Each is marked "Atlas Praha." Six feature Minnie Mouse. All others feature Mickey. Each - **$3 $6 $12**

MICKEY MOUSE, MINNIE & NEPHEWS

MKY-772

❑ **MKY-772. Mickey Mouse French Chocolate Card Set,**
1930s. Set of sixty each 1x2" card has black and white advertising "Chocolaterie Rubis Berbiers." Cards essentially feature just Mickey although one is of him with Minnie and another is of him washing Pluto. Each - **$3 $6 $12**

MKY-773

❑ **MKY-773. "Mickey Mouse" Complete Set of Licorice Flip Cards,**
1930s. Likely English or Australian issue. Giant Brand licorice. Set of 24 numbered cards, each 1-3/8"x2.5". Cards are designed to be held at bottom and flipped to view sequence. Set - **$200 $400 $600**

MKY-774

❑ **MKY-774. Mickey Mouse and Donald Duck General Foods Breakfast Cereal Display Sign,**
1930s. General Foods. 10x14" cardboard sign. - **$500 $1500 $2500**

MKY-775

❑ **MKY-775. "Post Toasties" Stationery,**
1930s. Paper is 8.5x11" with design at top advertising Post Toasties that feature "Mickey Mouse And Other Walt Disney Cut-outs On Back And Sides of Package." - **$55 $110 $225**

MKY-776

❑ **MKY-776. "Post Toasties" Box Back With Disney Cut-Outs,**
1930s. 7x9" back panel with eight different wearable cut-outs of belt buckle, bracelet, medals. Uncut - **$25 $40 $75**

MKY-777

MICKEY MOUSE, MINNIE & NEPHEWS

❏ **MKY-777. Mickey Mouse Boxed Plastic Cereal Bowl,**
1930s. No maker name, just "Cat. No. 705" on box. Box is 5.5x5.5x1.75" deep and bowl is 1.5" deep by 5.25" diameter. Box - **$65 $150 $250**
Bowl - **$25 $50 $75**

MKY-778

MKY-779

Back Cover Detail

❏ **MKY-778. "Mickey Mouse Picture Card Album" With Revised Cover Art,**
1930s. Gum Inc. Cover features more traditional looking Mickey Mouse image on the front. Version also has "Property" owner's name line at lower left. Album Only - **$100 $200 $400**

❏ **MKY-779. "Mickey Mouse Picture Card Album,"**
1930s. Volume 1, 6x10" for card series "No. 1 to No. 48." Has 16 pages for mounting cards. First version with primitive Mickey on front cover. - **$100 $200 $400**

MKY-780

MKY-781

❏ **MKY-780. "Mickey Mouse Picture Card Album" With Cards,**
1930s. Gum Inc. 6x10" 16-page album "Vol. 2" with complete set of 48 cards numbered 49-96. Album very fine, cards average fine to very fine. Set - **$2000**
Empty Album - **$125 $250 $500**

❏ **MKY-781. "Mickey Mouse With The Movie Stars" Gum Card,**
1930s. Gum Inc. 2.5x3-1/8" from second series #97-120. Card #100 showing Will Rogers. Each - **$75 $150 $300**

MKY-782

❏ **MKY-782. "Mickey Mouse" Canadian Gum Card,**
1930s. O-Pee-Chee Co. Ltd. Card #33, identical to American "Gum Inc." issue, except for company name on reverse. - **$15 $30 $50**

MKY-783

❏ **MKY-783. "Mickey Mouse Bubble Gum" Wrapper,**
1930s. Gum Inc. 5x7" waxed paper. Five character illustrations at top and includes ad for Mickey Mouse picture card album available with five wrappers and five cents. - **$60 $125 $250**

MKY-784

❏ **MKY-784. "Mickey Mouse Bubble Gum" Wrapper Variety,**
1930s. Gum Inc. 4.5x6" waxed paper design variation of character illustrations at top of just Minnie, Pluto and Horace rather than the five character variety that also featured Mickey and Clarabelle. This version also has thin blue border around center art and has no text "Save The Wrappers" which appears on the five-character variety. - **$100 $200 $350**

MICKEY MOUSE, MINNIE & NEPHEWS

MKY-785

MKY-788

MKY-791

❏ **MKY-785. "Mickey Mouse With The Movie Stars" Gum Card Wrapper,** 1933. Gum, Inc. 4.5x6" waxed paper. - **$150 $325 $650**

❏ **MKY-788. "Mickey Mouse" Drink Coaster,** 1930s. Coaster is 4.25" diameter with advertising for dairy glasses "Drink Meadow Gold Milk In 'Mickey Mouse Glasses,' They Come With Our Cottage Cheese." - **$25 $50 $85**

❏ **MKY-791. "Mickey Mouse Beverages" Hat,** 1930s. Felt 4.75x10.25" hat with same design on both sides. Band has designated areas for mounting the six different bottle caps, two per character that were issued with brass pins. - **$90 $175 $325**

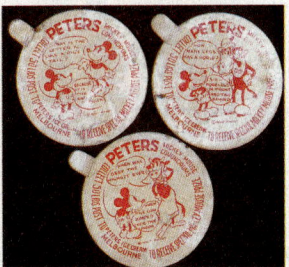

MKY-786

MKY-792

❏ **MKY-786. "Mickey Mouse" Ice Cream Cup Lids,** 1930s. Australian by "Peter's Ice Cream" Melbourne. Each is 2.25" diameter. 50 lids needed for prize. Each - **$25 $40 $75**

MKY-789

MKY-790

MKY-793

MKY-787

❏ **MKY-787. Spanish Comic Characters And Their Creators Cards,** 1930s. Lot of 12, each 1.75x2-3/8" thin paper from numbered set featuring large character image with inset circle featuring portrait of character's creator or person directly associated with them. Cards #1-4 feature Disney characters including Mickey, Minnie, Donald, Pluto. Also featured are Betty Boop, Popeye, Olive And Bluto, Henry, The Skipper and their creators plus two unknown. Major Characters - **$10 $20 $30**
Minor Characters - **$5 $10 $15**

❏ **MKY-789. Mickey Mouse Soda Bottle,** 1930s. 9.5" tall. 12 oz. Glass bottle. By Ludford Fruit Products Inc. Example shown likely missing a smaller label from bottle neck.
Complete - **$200 $350 $600**

❏ **MKY-790. "Rochester Healthful Beverages Minnie Mouse" Bottle,** 1930s. Heavy glass bottle is 9" tall with 2x2.5" silk screened label on front. - **$200 $325 $500**

❏ **MKY-792. Mickey Mouse Jam Jar/Bank,** 1930s. Clear glass jar with tin lid measures 2.5x2.5x6" tall. Came with paper label not shown on this example. Sides of jar have raised full figure images of Mickey, Minnie, Pluto and Horace. Lid has Mickey portrait with die-cut coin slot across his mouth. With Label - **$75 $150 $300** No Label - **$50 $100 $150**

❏ **MKY-793. Disney Characters Gelatin Mold,** 1930s. "Made In England" 6.5x7x3.25" deep five-sided aluminum mold with relief character images on outside of Mickey, Minnie, Pluto, Horace, Clarabelle. Top surface has different Mickey image. - **$100 $200 $300**

MICKEY MOUSE, MINNIE & NEPHEWS

MKY-794

❑ **MKY-794. "Mickey Mouse Cocoa" Australian Can,**
1930s. James Stedman-Henderson's Sweets Ltd., Sydney. 6" diameter by 2.5" deep tin lithographed "Sweetacres Cocoa" container with lid. - **$200 $400 $700**

MKY-795

❑ **MKY-795. Mickey Mouse Occupational Brass Badges,**
1930s. Each is 1-5/8" tall. Series includes "Aviation Dept.", "Fire Chief" (Mickey in fire truck), "Fire Dept." (Mickey with fire hose), "U.S. Navy" (Mickey with ship in background) and "Police Dept." Each - **$250 $500 $1000**

MKY-796

❑ **MKY-796. "Mickey Mouse Soap" Celluloid 1.25" Button,**
1930s. Reverse has union bug backstamp and name of maker Bastian Bros. with curl text "The Leo Hart Co. Rochester, N.Y." - **$1000 $3000 $5250**

MKY-797

❑ **MKY-797. "Mickey Mouse Club Safety First" Celluloid Button,**
1930s. Issuer Unknown. 7/8". - **$150 $400 $800**

MKY-798

❑ **MKY-798. "Mickey Mouse Evening Ledger Comics" Celluloid Button,**
1930s. Philadelphia newspaper issued set of 14 different characters, each 1.25" and including Minnie. Several backpaper designs. Mickey Or Minnie - **$250 $600 $100**

MKY-799

❑ **MKY-799. "Mickey Promotes "Boston Sunday Advertiser" Comic Section Button,**
1930s. 1 1/8" litho. - **$35 $65 $125**

MKY-800

❑ **MKY-800. Mickey Mouse "RKO Keith Kiddie Klub" Celluloid Button,**
1930s. Rare button from movie theater-sponsored club. 1.25". - **$300 $750 $1500**

MICKEY MOUSE, MINNIE & NEPHEWS

MKY-801

❑ **MKY-801. Mickey Mouse Australian Club Button,**
1930s. Vic Jensen, we believe a shoe retailer. The only 1930s button known to us, showing Mickey and Minnie full figure. - **$100 $200 $500**

MKY-804

❑ **MKY-804. "J.C. Penney Publix-Princess Mickey Mouse Club" Celluloid Button,**
1930s. No markings. 7/8". - **$50 $100 $150**

MKY-807

❑ **MKY-807. "Milk For Better Health Mickey Mouse" Button,**
1930s. Button is 3.5". Worn possibly by either an adult store clerk or milk truck driver.
- **$1000 $2000 $3500**

MKY-802

❑ **MKY-802. Mickey Mouse "Cameo" Celluloid Button,**
1930s. United Kingdom. 7/8". - **$60 $110 $200**

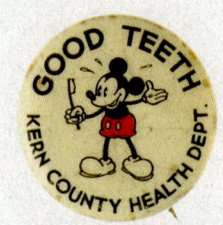

MKY-805

❑ **MKY-805. Mickey Mouse "Good Teeth" Button,**
1930s. Kern County, California Health Dept. 1" cello. - **$200 $400 $750**

MKY-808

❑ **MKY-808. Mickey, Minnie And Tanglefoot Washington Herald Newspaper Button,**
1930s. Parisian Novelty Co. 1.25". Button from set of 10 characters used to promote comic strips appearing in this newspaper.
- **$300 $600 $1250**

MKY-803

❑ **MKY-803. Mickey Mouse English Biscuits Button,**
1930s. 7/8". - **$75 $150 $300**

MKY-806

❑ **MKY-806. "Milk For Better Health Mickey Mouse" Celluloid Button,**
1930s. Backpaper by Pudlin Co. NYC. 1.25". - **$100 $250 $500**

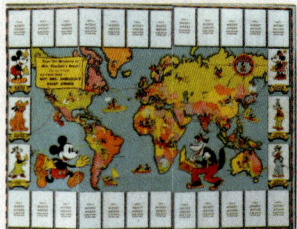

MICKEY MOUSE, MINNIE & NEPHEWS

MKY-809

❏ **MKY-809. "Mickey Mouse Globe Trotters Map,"**
1930s. Map is 20x26.5" and was issued by various bread companies. Comes with original envelope. Borders have designated areas for pasting pictures found on back covers of Mickey Mouse Globe Trotter weekly publications. Reverse has text on different countries and directions on the "Race 'Round The World" between Mickey and Wolf. Mailer - **$25 $50 $100**
Map - **$50 $125 $300**
Each Picture - **$5 $15 $25**

MKY-810

❏ **MKY-810. "Mickey Mouse" Rare Candy Premium Game From Amsterdam,**
1930s. Sickesz. 14.75x18.75" paper game board. Text is in Dutch with game play instructions at center. Game path has numbered circles and images of full figure Mickey, different candy bar products and three rather unusual images of Mickey in the mouth of a cat, Mickey in a mouse trap and Mickey drowning in a bucket of water. - **$400 $750 $1200**

MKY-811

❏ **MKY-811. Pocket Comb With Case,**
1930s. American Hard Rubber Co. 5" long comb in two-sided fabric-covered stiff cardboard case. One side of comb has lightly incised name "Mickey Mouse." - **$150 $250 $500**

MKY-812

❏ **MKY-812. Mickey Mouse Box Bottom,**
1930s. Henry L. Hughes Co. Inc. 3.25x5x1.5" deep box bottom only by makers of brushes, combs and toothbrushes. - **$50 $80 $135**

MKY-813

MKY-814

❏ **MKY-813. Hair Brush Boxed,**
1930s. "Made In England" 7.25" long brush in 2.25x7.75x1.25" deep box with hinged lid. Box inside and out has illustrations of Mickey and Minnie doing various types of yard work. Grip of brush is celluloid cover over metallic image. Box - **$75 $150 $250**
Brush - **$75 $150 $250**

❏ **MKY-814. "Mickey Mouse" Boxed Figural Soap,**
1930s. Lightfoot Schultz Co. 4.5" tall castile soap figure in box. Box - **$35 $75 $150**
Figure - **$30 $65 $125**

MKY-815

MKY-816

❏ **MKY-815. Mickey Mouse Soap Box,**
1930s. Rufino Ingles, Spanish. No Disney Markings. 3x4.5x1.5" deep box. - **$35 $60 $100**

❏ **MKY-816. "Mickey Mouse" Boxed Soap,**
1930s. Monogram Soap Co. 3x5.75x.75" deep box contains three bars. Boxed - **$85 $175 $350**

501

MICKEY MOUSE, MINNIE & NEPHEWS

MKY-817

☐ **MKY-817. Mickey/Minnie/Pluto Toothbrush Holder,**
1930s. Marked "Made In Japan" and 2x4x3.5" tall with incised "S335." - **$125 $250 $400**

MKY-818

☐ **MKY-818. Mickey Mouse And Pluto Bisque Toothbrush Holder,**
1930s. Figure is 4.25" tall. - **$125 $250 $400**

MKY-819

MKY-820

☐ **MKY-819. Mickey And Pluto Toothbrush Holder,**
1930s. Canadian version 2.25x4.4.75" tall glazed china. Back has incised "S870." - **$135 $275 $500**

☐ **MKY-820. Mickey English China Toothbrush Holder,**
1930s. Figure is 2x2.75x4" tall and marked underneath with Disney copyright, registration number and "Foreign." Made by Maw & Sons. - **$200 $425 $650**

MKY-821

☐ **MKY-821. "Mickey Mouse/Minnie Mouse" Bisque Toothbrush Holder,**
1930s. Holder is 1.75x3.25x4.5" tall with incised "C100" on back. - **$100 $200 $325**

MKY-822

☐ **MKY-822. "Mickey Mouse" Non-Movable Arm Toothbrush Holder,**
1930s. Bisque figure is 2.5x2.5x5.25" tall. Pedestal base is marked "Mickey Mouse" on front and "Made In Japan" on back. Has toothbrush opening on left side of body just above his hand and came with string tail. - **$350 $700 $1200**

MKY-823

MKY-824

☐ **MKY-823. "Minnie Mouse" Bisque Toothbrush Holder,**
1930s. Japan. 2.5x2.75x5" tall designed with one movable arm and the other arm serves as holder. - **$125 $250 $400**

☐ **MKY-824. Figural Toothbrush Holder,**
1930s. Unauthorized Japanese for Australian market. 2x2x5.25" tall painted china. - **$75 $150 $250**

MKY-825

☐ **MKY-825. "Mickey Mouse" Bisque Toothbrush Holder,**
1930s. Japan #A567. 4.5" tall. Back bottom of base also has copyright of Percy L. Crosby rather than Disney done in error as the company also produced Skippy bisques. - **$300 $600 $1250**

MICKEY MOUSE, MINNIE & NEPHEWS

MKY-826

MKY-829

MKY-830

MKY-833

❏ **MKY-826. Mickey Mouse Toothbrush Holder,**
1930s. English in Dean's Rag Book image style. Incised number on reverse "650611." - **$100 $200 $300**

❏ **MKY-829. "Mickey Mouse Razor Blade,"**
1930s. British Made. 1x1-7/8" paper wrapper contains actual razor blade authorized by Disney. - **$35 $60 $100**

❏ **MKY-830. Mickey Mouse Bisque Candle Holder,**
1930s. Item is 1-1/8" tall incised with "3761." Also came as Mickey seated with one hand resting on his feet. Each - **$35 $65 $125**

❏ **MKY-833. Mickey And Minnie Mouse Fabric,**
1930s. Cotton section 34x50" cut from a bolt. No copyright and maker is unknown but obviously studio-authorized artwork. Similar Size - **$50 $100 $150**

MKY-827

MKY-831

MKY-834

❏ **MKY-827. Long Soap Holder By Faiencerie d'Onnaing,**
1930s. France. 4x9.25" china designed to hold two soap bars. Also issued in "short version" to hold one soap bar. Long - **$150 $250 $450**
Short - **$125 $200 $350**

MKY-828

MKY-832

MKY-835

❏ **MKY-828. Boxed "Infant Mickey Mouse Baby Bottle,"**
1930s. Hot water bottle is 5x10" in 5.5x11.75x1.5" deep box. Maker is unknown.
Box - **$100 $200 $400**
Bottle - **$100 $200 $400**

❏ **MKY-831. "Mickey Mouse" Door Knocker,**
1930s. Unmarked but English .75x1.75x3.75" tall solid brass figural knocker with his name incised across bottom. - **$100 $200 $400**

❏ **MKY-832. Mickey Mouse Homemade Wood Doorstop,**
1930s. 5x13x3/8" thick jigsawed wood with attached wood wedge on back so the piece could be used as a doorstop. Same Or Similar - **$35 $75 $125**

❏ **MKY-834. Walt Disney Characters Fabric Panel,**
1930s. Maker unknown. 17x60". Similar Size - **$25 $50 $100**

❏ **MKY-835. Mickey Mouse Fireplace Fork,**
1930s. Unmarked but English 17.5" tall brass fork. - **$100 $200 $400**

MICKEY MOUSE, MINNIE & NEPHEWS

MKY-836

❑ **MKY-836. Mickey Mouse English Fireplace Brush,**
1930s. Brush is 7.5" tall with 2.5" figure of Mickey in brass. Reverse has incised registration number. - **$125 $250 $450**

MKY-837

❑ **MKY-837. Lamp Base,**
1930s. Soreng-Manegold Co. 5" diameter enameled metal 6.75" tall to top of electrical bulb socket. - **$60 $125 $250**

MKY-838

MKY-839

❑ **MKY-838. Mickey Mouse Ceramic Lamp,**
1930s. Mickey is 3x4x6.5" tall and stands atop 1" tall oval-shaped base. Believed English made for the Australian market. - **$100 $200 $300**

❑ **MKY-839. Mickey Mouse Wall Lamp,**
1930s. Maker unknown. 4x11x3/8" deep embossed tin lithograph. - **$225 $450 $750**

MKY-840

❑ **MKY-840. Mickey Mouse English Electric Space Heater,**
1930s. 12x12x5" deep. Made in England. Art Deco style heater. - **$500 $1500 $3000**

MKY-841

MKY-842

❑ **MKY-841. Mickey And Friends English Night Light Candle,**
1930s. Price's Patent Candle Co. Ltd. Of London. 1.75" diameter by 1.25" tall wax candle in wrap-around waxed paper design. - **$20 $45 $85**

❑ **MKY-842. Mickey Mouse Ceramic Candle Night Light Holder,**
1930s. Crown Devon, England. Unmarked. 2.5x5.5x4.5 tall. - **$250 $500 $800**

MKY-843

MICKEY MOUSE, MINNIE & NEPHEWS

❑ **MKY-843. Baseball Theme Pillow,**
1930s. Vogue Needlecraft Co. Inc. 15x16" cotton cover stuffed to 4" thickness with thread-stitched details. Unused - **$50 $100 $150**
Neatly Assembled - **$25 $50 $75**

MKY-844

MKY-845

❑ **MKY-844. Mickey And Minnie Mouse Rare Pillow Cover,**
1930s. Cover is 17x18" with top panel in velvet-like finish with thick nap. Great image of Mickey serenading Minnie. - **$85 $150 $250**

❑ **MKY-845. Mickey And Minnie Mouse Child's Potty,**
1930s. R.G.K./N.Y. Germany, initials are of are importer Richard G. Krueger. 3" tall with 5-5/8" top diameter enameled metal. - **$115 $235 $500**

MKY-846

❑ **MKY-846. Mickey Mouse Rug,**
1930s. Rug is 18.5x33". - **$65 $150 $300**

MKY-847

❑ **MKY-847. Mickey's Nephew With Funny Bunnies Rug,**
1930s. 19x34" fabric with velveteen nap and fringe trim along right and left side edges. Maker unknown. - **$50 $100 $175**

MKY-848

MKY-849

❑ **MKY-848. "Mickey Mouse Yarn Sewing Set,"**
1930s. Marks Brothers. 6.5x10.5x1.25" deep box contains complete set of six cards. Sewing cards are each 4x6.25". Boxed - **$135 $275 $550**

❑ **MKY-849. "Mickey Mouse" English Sweeper Toy,**
1930s. Wells-London. 4x6x1.5" tall tin lithograph with wood wheels. Top is three panels of scenes involving Mickey, Minnie, their nephews, semi-long billed Donald and Pluto, all involving a broom or the sweeper itself. Pictured example is missing the wood push rod and the metal bracket that held it. Complete - **$150 $300 $650**

MKY-850

MKY-851

❑ **MKY-850. English Whisk Brush,**
1930s. Brush is 3.5" tall painted white metal three-dimensional Mickey Mouse figure handle attached atop the brush for total height of 7.5". Marked registration number on rear leg is "75050." Figure is same image as Dean's used for rag dolls and depicts five fingers. Rear has a wire spring tail. - **$150 $300 $600**

❑ **MKY-851. "Mickey Mouse" Sweeper,**
1930s. Ohio Art. 4x6x2" tall tin litho with wood side panels and wood wheels. Came with red wood rod handle. - **$125 $250 $500**

MICKEY MOUSE, MINNIE & NEPHEWS

MKY-852

☐ **MKY-852. Mickey Mouse Bridge Table Cover,**
1930s. Maker unknown. 27x29" with small text "Bridge Lesson Broadcast." - **$35 $65 $135**

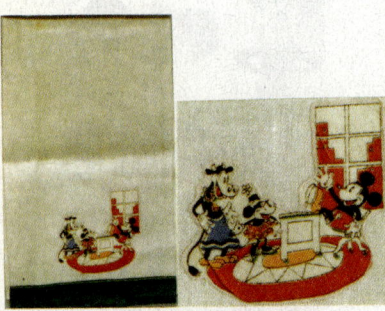

MKY-853

MKY-854

☐ **MKY-853. Tea Towel,**
1930s. Linen is 13.25x20.25" with single 3x3" die-cut fabric applique of Mickey leisurely seated at business desk to greet Minnie and Clarabelle. - **$30 $60 $125**

☐ **MKY-854. Mickey Mouse And Donald Duck Towel,**
1930s. Maker unknown. 17x24" terrycloth. - **$25 $50 $100**

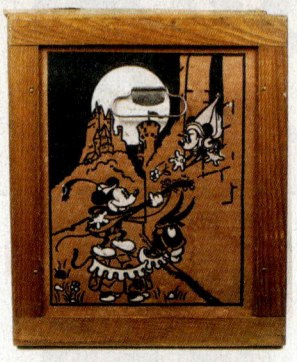

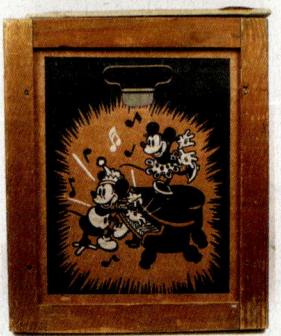

MKY-855

☐ **MKY-855. "Mickey Mouse Toy Chest And Children's Seat" Variety With Fabric-Covered Lid,**
1930s. Odora Co. 12.5x26.5x14.5" tall. Has wood frame with cardboard side panels, pair of metal carrying handles. Top is variety that has fabric covering and thin layer of padding over a wood board with cardboard panel on interior. Top depicts Mickey and Minnie holding a slate board with image of Pluto. - **$150 $300 $600**

MKY-856

☐ **MKY-856. "Mickey Mouse Toy Chest And Children's Seat" Variety With Cardboard Lid,**
1930s. Odora Co. 12.5x26.5x14.5" tall. This version has lid comprised of thick cardboard rather than fabric-covered wood. - **$125 $250 $500**

MKY-857

MKY-858

☐ **MKY-857. Walt Disney Character Wallpaper,**
1930s. Section measures 9.75x19.25". Similar Size - **$100 $200 $400**

☐ **MKY-858. "Mickey Mouse" Wash Tub,**
1930s. Ohio Art. 5.25" diameter by 2.25" deep lithographed tin. - **$75 $150 $300**

MICKEY MOUSE, MINNIE & NEPHEWS

MKY-859

❑ **MKY-859. "Mickey Mouse Washer,"**
1930s. Ohio Art Co. Child's tin lithographed toy washer is 5" diameter by 7.5" tall. - **$250 $500 $1000**

MKY-860

MKY-861

❑ **MKY-860. "Mickey Mouse" Sprinkling Can,**
1930s. Ohio Art. 4x8x6" tall lithographed tin. - **$175 $325 $650**

❑ **MKY-861. "Mickey Mouse Jewelry" Box,**
1930s. Empty box is 2.25x4x.5" deep originally containing some type of jewelry item. - **$50 $85 $165**

MKY-862

❑ **MKY-862. Mickey Mouse Bracelet,**
1930s. Unmarked, but authorized brass with image under domed glass. - **$60 $125 $175**

MKY-863

❑ **MKY-863. Mickey Mouse Italian Lapel Stud,**
1930s. F.M. Lorioli Castelli/Milano. 3/4" enamel on brass lapel stud with Mickey playing a concertina. - **$50 $100 $175**

MKY-864

❑ **MKY-864. Mickey Mouse Enamel On Gold Two-Sided Charm,**
1930s. Charm is 7/8" tall. - **$175 $350 $700**

MKY-865

❑ **MKY-865. Mickey And Minnie Mouse English Cinema Club Badge,**
1930s. 3/4x1" silvered brass badge for Kiddies 5 Star Club. - **$25 $50 $90**

MKY-866

❑ **MKY-866. Mickey Mouse European Enamel Pin,**
1930s. 1 1/8" tall. Features long nose and five fingered Mickey playing a banjo. - **$50 $100 $150**

MKY-867

❑ **MKY-867. "Mickey Mouse Club" Die-cut English Lapel Stud,**
1930s. Stud is 1.5" tall black enamel on silvered brass. - **$50 $100 $200**

MKY-868

❑ **MKY-868. Mickey Mouse Die-cut Tin Lithographed Mechanical Novelty Pin,**
1930s. Unmarked 1.5x2.25" with die-cut arm, rubber band and string which allows Mickey to remove his hat. - **$125 $275 $500**

MICKEY MOUSE, MINNIE & NEPHEWS

MKY-869

❑ **MKY-869. Mickey Mouse Tin Tab,**
1930s. Tab is 1.5" tall. Unmarked, believed to be English. - **$65 $150 $250**

MKY-872

❑ **MKY-872. "Mickey Mouse" Boxed Ring,**
1930s. Small 1x1x1" box contains adjustable brass ring with enamel paint. Reverse has small "WD" copyright. Box - **$100 $200 $400**
Ring - **$100 $200 $300**

MKY-875

❑ **MKY-875. Mickey And Minnie Celluloid Figures Bar Pin,**
1930s. English. .75" tall celluloid figures on bar pin. - **$20 $40 $65**

MKY-870

MKY-873

❑ **MKY-873. Mickey/Minnie Mouse Large Box For Jewelry,**
1930s. Cohn & Rosenberger Inc. 5x6.5x.75" deep cardboard box. Designed with three separate compartments. - **$75 $150 $250**

MKY-876

❑ **MKY-876. Mickey Mouse Sheet Music English Enamel And Brass Pin,**
1930s. 1.5" tall. Pin is titled "The Wedding of Mr. Mickey Mouse". - **$50 $100 $200**

MKY-871

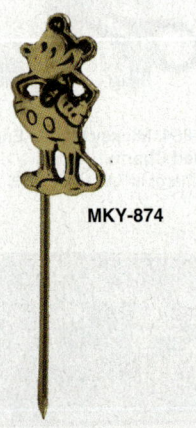

MKY-874

❑ **MKY-870. Mickey With Pluto Painted Composition Wood Pin,**
1930s. Pin is 1.5". - **$85 $175 $300**

❑ **MKY-871. Mickey Mouse With Umbrella Enamel On Brass Pin,**
1930s. No markings. 7/8" tall. - **$65 $125 $200**

❑ **MKY-874. Mickey Mouse Silvered Brass Stickpin,**
1930s. Figure is .75". - **$30 $60 $90**

MKY-877

❑ **MKY-877. Mickey Mouse Ceramic Bottle,**
1930s. Painted and glazed ceramic 3.25". Unmarked but European. - **$35 $65 $100**

MICKEY MOUSE, MINNIE & NEPHEWS

MKY-878   MKY-879

❏ **MKY-878. Mickey Mouse China Perfume Bottle**,
1930s. Container is 2"deep, 4" tall and 3.5" in diameter. No Disney markings and piece is marked "Made In Japan." - **$100 $200 $300**

❏ **MKY-879. Mickey Mouse Figural Glass Perfume Bottle**,
1930s. Made In France. Bottle is 2x2x5.25" tall with removable head. Has metal spring legs and long fabric tail. - **$275 $550 $1100**

MKY-880

MKY-881

❏ **MKY-880. "Mickey Mouse" Bavarian China Cereal Bowl**,
1930s. Bowl is 6" in diameter and 2" deep and has eleven images. Underside is marked "Made In Bavaria." - **$200 $400 $600**

❏ **MKY-881. "Minnie Mouse" Patriot China Bowl**,
1930s. Bowl is 6" in diameter by 1.5" deep and marked underneath with company name. - **$40 $75 $150**

MKY-882

❏ **MKY-882. Mickey & Minnie Mouse Child's Warming Dish**,
1930s. Marked on underside "Industria Argentina." 8" diameter by 2" deep. The ceramic bowl is mounted inside of a stainless steel container. Metal dish is complete with pair of finger loops and spout has screw cap. - **$65 $125 $200**

MKY-883

❏ **MKY-883. Mickey Cake Plates By Faiencerie d'Onnaing China Co. Of France**,
1930s. Serving plate is 11" and individual plates are 7.25". From a set of fifteen. Pictorial Mickey company trademark on reverse. Serving plate is captioned "Hop-La!" while other plates have "Walt Disney" and plate number. Most plates picture a circus theme. Serving Plate - **$100 $200 $400** Numbered Plates Each - **$35 $65 $125**

MKY-884

❏ **MKY-884. Mickey Dual Image Soup Bowl**,
1930s. Unmarked 8" diameter by 1.25" deep metal bowl centered by scene of two Mickeys finished in enameled paint accents with high gloss finish. - **$50 $100 $150**

MKY-885

❏ **MKY-885. Pitcher And Wash Basin By Faiencerie d'Onnaing**,
1930s. France. 9.75" tall pitcher and 4.25" tall by 13" diameter wash basin. About six sets are known including one in the Disney archives which years ago curator Dave Smith rescued from a movie set at the Disney Studio where it was about to be smashed as a meaningless movie prop. Pitcher - **$500 $1500 $2750** Basin - **$500 $1500 $2750**

MICKEY MOUSE, MINNIE & NEPHEWS

MKY-886

☐ **MKY-886. Disney Characters Cup And Saucer,**
1930s. 2.75" diameter cup and 5.25" diameter saucer. Cup - **$35 $65 $125**
Saucer - **$20 $40 $65**

MKY-887

☐ **MKY-887. Mickey And Friends Chinaware,**
1930s. Wadeheath of England. 6x6" octagonal plate and 1.75" tall tea cup picturing Mickey, 1.75" tea cup picturing Donald Duck, plus 1.25" tall open sugar bowl picturing "Baby Seal." Plate - **$30 $50 $85**
Each Cup - **$20 $35 $65**
Sugar - **$10 $20 $40**

MKY-888

☐ **MKY-888. Miniature Figural Teapot And Pitcher,**
1930s. Unmarked but Japanese pair of glazed ceramics. The teapot is 2x3.5x3" tall, pitcher is 2.25" tall. Mickey's head serves as the lid of the teapot and is removable while his right arm serves as the spout. Teapot - **$75 $150 $250**
Pitcher - **$50 $100 $150**

MKY-889

☐ **MKY-889. Mickey/Minnie Mouse China Creamer,**
1930s. French by Faiencerie d'Onnaing China Co. 3" tall #906 incised on underside. - **$65 $125 $200**

MKY-890

☐ **MKY-890. Mickey And Minnie Mouse China Condiment Set,**
1930s. English or German. 2.5x4.5x3.75" tall marked with registration number on underside "750611" plus second number of "11129." - **$600 $1200 $2400**

MKY-891

☐ **MKY-891. Mickey And Minnie Glazed Ceramic Condiment Set,**
1930s. Made in Japan. 4.5x4.5" tray holds 3.5" tall figures and 2" tall container with lid designed as cheese wheel. Example pictured missing generic ceramic condiment spoon. - **$500 $1000 $1500**

MKY-892

☐ **MKY-892. Mickey Mouse German China Condiment Set,**
1930s. Marked on underside "Deutchland." 3x4x3.75" tall. - **$200 $400 $700**

MICKEY MOUSE, MINNIE & NEPHEWS

MKY-893

❑ **MKY-893. Large Mickey/Minnie Foreign Tin,**
1930s. Lithographed tin with hinged lid measures 8.25x10x7"tall. Made in Belgium or France. - **$300 $600 $1200**

MKY-894

❑ **MKY-894. Mickey Mouse French Tin,**
1930s. Tin is 7" diameter by 1.75" deep with removable lid. Six different poses of Mickey and Minnie around sides. - **$100 $200 $300**

MKY-895

❑ **MKY-895. Mickey Mouse French Tin,**
1930s. Tin is 7" in diameter and 1.75" deep. Sides feature Pluto running. - **$100 $200 $300**

MKY-896

❑ **MKY-896. Mickey And Friends Canadian Container,**
1930s. "Concessionnaire Etab Molie/Montreuil." Rectangular 3x7.25x3" tall tin lithographed with single attached tin carrying handle. Pictured example is missing lid. Complete - **$125 $250 $525**

MKY-897

❑ **MKY-897. Mickey Mouse Tin,**
1930s. France. 5.5x6x2" deep hexagonal-shaped with hinged lid. Lid illustration of Mickey walking with nephew, side illustrations depict Mickey in different sports. - **$125 $250 $400**

MKY-898

❑ **MKY-898. Mickey Mouse Tin,**
1930s. Tin is 6.5" diameter by 2.25" deep with removable lid. Lid features Mickey, Minnie, Donald, Pluto, and Clarabell. - **$125 $250 $400**

MKY-899

❑ **MKY-899. Mickey Mouse/Pluto Gift Set Box,**
1930s. Seiberling Latex Products Co. 8x8.75x3" deep box only originally holding "Gift Set No. 2965" of Mickey and Pluto hard rubber figures. - **$85 $175 $300**

MICKEY MOUSE, MINNIE & NEPHEWS

MKY-900

❑ **MKY-900. Minnie Australian Tin,**
1930s. "W.D. Ent." 5x5.75x1" deep triangular tin. - **$125 $250 $475**

MKY-903

❑ **MKY-903. Mickey Mouse Mop Tin,**
1930s. Germany. 5x9.25x3.5" deep. No Disney markings. Photo example missing lid. Complete - **$125 $250 $400**

MKY-906

❑ **MKY-906. Mickey Mouse Enamelware Cup And Dish,**
1930s. Cup is 2" tall and dish is 7" in diameter, both marked "Made In Germany," Each - **$35 $65 $125**

MKY-901

❑ **MKY-901. Mickey Mouse China Jam Jar,**
1930s. Maws. 4.5" tall Mickey figure is attached to jar 3.75" tall with 2.75" diameter. Marked underneath with registration number and "By Special Permission Walt Disney Enterprises." Photo example missing lid. - **$200 $400 $700**

MKY-904

❑ **MKY-904. Mickey Mouse Head Ceramic Trinket Box,**
1930s. Japan, likely unauthorized. 3.5x3.5x2.5" tall. - **$100 $225 $350**

MKY-907

MKY-908

❑ **MKY-907. Unauthorized Mickey Mouse Egg Cup,**
1930s. Painted and glazed china 1.75x3.5x3.25" tall marked "Made In Japan." - **$20 $40 $75**

❑ **MKY-908. Mickey/Minnie Mouse Double-Sided French Ceramic Egg Cup,**
1930s. Faiencerie d'Onnaing. 1.75" diameter by 2-1/8" tall with recessed area on both top and bottom so either side could be used to hold egg. - **$125 $225 $350**

MKY-902

❑ **MKY-902. Minnie English Jam Jar,**
1930s. "Imex." 4.25" tall china figure and adjoining 3.75" tall jar for preserves. Pictured example underside has Disney markings and registration number. Photo example without lid. - **$175 $300 $600**

MKY-905

❑ **MKY-905. "Minnie Mouse" Patriot China Mug,**
1930s. Mug is 3" with text on underside including company name. - **$60 $125 $175**

MICKEY MOUSE, MINNIE & NEPHEWS

MKY-909

❑ **MKY-909. Mickey And Minnie French Egg Cup,**
1930s. "Faïencerie d'Onnaing Co. Of France." 2" top diameter by 2.25" tall glazed ceramic. - **$125 $225 $350**

MKY-910

❑ **MKY-910. Mickey Mouse Figural Egg Cup,**
1930s. Unmarked. 2.75" tall painted and glazed ceramic. Unusual full figure image depicting Mickey with his hands on hips, tail wraps around to the back. - **$65 $125 $200**

MKY-911

❑ **MKY-911. Minnie Mouse China Child's Divided Bowl,**
1930s. Bowl is 6.5" in diameter and 1.5" deep. Unmarked but probably by Salem China Co. - **$65 $125 $225**

MKY-912

❑ **MKY-912. Mickey, Minnie, And Donald Baby's English Bowl,**
1930s. Wadeheath. 6.75" diameter by 1.5" deep. - **$40 $85 $165**

MKY-913

❑ **MKY-913. Mickey Mouse Plastic Dish,**
1930s. Dish is 6" in diameter and 1" deep made of hard plastic. Unmarked with just a "Process Pat." number faintly stamped on underside. Identical in design and same image that appears on the "Beetleware" dishes used as Post's cereal premiums. - **$25 $50 $85**

MKY-914

❑ **MKY-914. Child's Italian Dish Set Boxed,**
1930s. "Laveno/Societa Ceramica/Italiana." 12.5x12.5x3.25" deep boxed complete set of eighteen glazed chinaware pieces comprised of soup tureen with lid, two serving dishes, three serving platters, six plates, six shallow soup bowls. Tallest is 3" tureen, flat pieces are 4" diameter or less. A total of seven different images depict Mickey, Minnie, occasional Pluto. Box pictures total of four different Mickey and Minnie dining activities. Box - **$200 $400 $600** China Set - **$300 $750 $1250**

MKY-915

❑ **MKY-915. Italian Ceramic Disney Miniature Tea Set,**
1930s. Laveno/Societa Ceramica/Italiano. Total of 28 pieces including four 1.25" tall teacups and four 2.75" diameter saucers (probably originally from set of six), six 3.25" diameter plates, six 3.25" diameter soup plates, 3.75" diameter round cake or serving plate, 3.5" long oval platter, 2.25" top diameter bowl and 3-1/8" top diameter either soup tureen or sugar bowl with lid, all about 1" tall. - **$500 $1000 $1500**

MKY-916

❑ **MKY-916. Candy Dish,**
1930s. "Made In Japan" 5.75" diameter by 1" deep china dish with attached arc wood handle rising 5" at center. - **$65 $150 $250**

MKY-917

MICKEY MOUSE, MINNIE & NEPHEWS

❑ **MKY-917. Mickey Mouse Enameled Metal Bowl,**
1930s. Probably European. 7.75" diameter by 1.25" deep bowl. Reverse has company mark of letters and numbers but not discernable. - **$20 $40 $75**

MKY-918

❑ **MKY-918. "Mickey Mouse Beetleware" Boxed Child's Dish Set,**
1930s. Bryant Electric Co. Of Bridgeport, Connecticut. 6x6x3.5" deep box contains complete three-piece hard plastic set consisting of 2.75" tall mug, 5.25" diameter bowl and 6" diameter child's feeding dish. Box - **$65 $150 $300** Each Piece - **$25 $50 $85**

MKY-919

MKY-920

❑ **MKY-919. "Mickey Mouse" Glass,**
1930s. Tumbler is 4.25" tall clear depicting him walking and waving above his name. Possible dairy glass although differing in size and design from known sets. - **$40 $75 $125**

❑ **MKY-920. German Mug,**
1930s. "Made In Germany/Richard G. Krueger Inc., N.Y." 3" tall glazed ceramic. - **$65 $125 $225**

MKY-921

MKY-922

❑ **MKY-921. Mickey Cute Unauthorized Mug,**
1930s. "Made In Japan" 2.75" tall glazed ceramic. - **$25 $50 $85**

❑ **MKY-922. Mickey Mouse Fleeing Tiger China Mug,**
1930s. Unmarked but similar to Paragon design. 3.75" tall. - **$60 $125 $200**

MKY-923

❑ **MKY-923. "Mickey Mouse and Pluto" English China Mug,**
1930s. Royal Paragon. 2.75" tall. - **$600 $1200 $1800**

MKY-924

❑ **MKY-924. Mickey/Minnie Mouse Napkin Rings,**
1930s. Pair of 2" diameter thick celluloid napkin rings each has attached hollow celluloid figure on front 2.25" tall. Marked "Made In England." Each - **$50 $100 $150**

MKY-925

❑ **MKY-925. Mickey Mouse Catalin Plastic Napkin Ring,**
1930s. 2.5x3x.5" thick with Mickey portrait decal on front. - **$50 $100 $175**

MKY-926

❑ **MKY-926. Figural Pitcher,**
1930s. "Made In Japan" 3.5x4.5x4.5" tall painted and glazed ceramic likeness of plump Mickey with curved tail as the handle and open mouth pouring spout. No Disney markings. - **$25 $50 $75**

514

MICKEY MOUSE, MINNIE & NEPHEWS

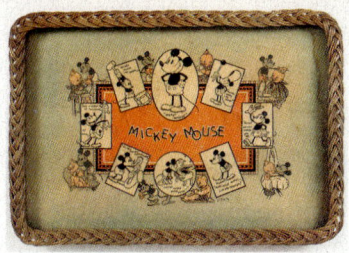

MKY-930

MKY-933

MKY-927

❑ **MKY-929. "Minnie Mouse" Plate,**
1930s. Plate is 6x6" and marked on reverse "Salem Heirloom" by Salem China Co., makers of Patriot China. - **$150 $300 $500**

❑ **MKY-930. Mickey & Minnie English China "Baby's Plate,"**
1930s. Royal Paragon China. Oval-shaped 5.75x8.25x1.25" deep glazed china plate marked underneath "Mickey Mouse Series." - **$400 $800 $1350**

❑ **MKY-933. "Mickey Mouse" Square Format Plate,**
1930s. Patriot China Co. 6.25x6.25" plate with company name in gold on reverse. Image of Mickey is 2.5" tall. - **$50 $100 $200**

MKY-934

❑ **MKY-927. "Mickey Mouse" Rare English Serving Tray,**
c. 1930s. St. Dunstan's Veterans Hospital, London. 12.5x18.25x1.5" deep celluloid over wood tray with woven wicker edge. Eight classic black and white images of Mickey, all with titles. In between these images are additional illustrations of him with Kewpie-like baby. Mickey is shown feeding, washing, snuggling and playing with baby. - **$300 $600 $1200**

MKY-931

❑ **MKY-931. Mickey Mouse Paragon China "Baby's Plate,"**
1930s. Paragon. 6.5x8.5x2" deep. Depicts scene of Mickey and Pluto hunting a moose. - **$500 $1000 $2000**

MKY-928

❑ **MKY-934. "Minnie Mouse" Square Format Plate,**
1930s. Patriot China Co. 6.25x6.25" plate with company name in gold on reverse. Image of Minnie is 3" tall. - **$40 $85 $175**

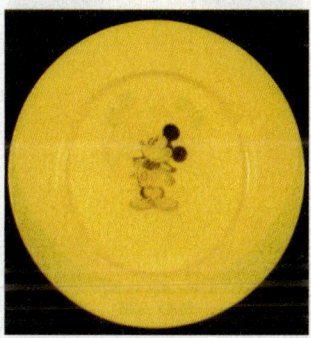

MKY-935

❑ **MKY-928. "Mickey Mouse/Pluto The Pup" Patriot China Plate,**
1930s. Patriot China. 7" diameter plate marked on reverse "Patriot China." - **$65 $125 $200**

MKY-929

MKY-932

❑ **MKY-932. "Mickey and Minnie Mouse" English China Sandwich Plate,**
1930s. Royal Paragon. 8.5" square. - **$600 $1200 $1800**

❑ **MKY-935. Mickey Mouse Child's Plate,**
1930s. Safetyware. 7" diameter hard plastic. Yellow/black variety. - **$25 $50 $85**

MICKEY MOUSE, MINNIE & NEPHEWS

MKY-936

MKY-937

MKY-939

❏ **MKY-939. "Mickey Mouse/Pluto" Ceramic Plate,**
1930s. Wade. English by Wadeheath Ware. 6" octagonal. - **$50 $85 $150**

MKY-940

MKY-942

MKY-943

❏ **MKY-942. Mickey And Minnie Ceramic Salt Shakers,**
1930s. Made in Japan. 3" tall. Set - **$150 $275 $425**

❏ **MKY-943. Mickey Mouse 4 Burner Gas Stove Enameled Metal Cover,**
1930s. Maker Unknown. 17x21x.5" deep burner cover for the top of an actual stove. - **$60 $125 $225**

❏ **MKY-936. Mickey Mouse Child's Plate,**
1930s. Safetyware. 7" diameter hard plastic. Pink variety. - **$25 $50 $85**

❏ **MKY-937. Mickey Mouse Boxing Theme China Plate,**
1930s. Australian. 6.25" diameter. - **$100 $250 $450**

MKY-938

MKY-941

MKY-944

❏ **MKY-940. Mickey Mouse Drummer China Shaker,**
1930s. Germany. 2x2x3.5". "6595" incised on back. - **$100 $200 $300**

❏ **MKY-941. Mickey Mouse China Salt & Pepper Set,**
1930s. Germany. Each 2.25" tall. #7733. - **$125 $250 $375**

❏ **MKY-938. China Mickey & Minnie "Happy Days" Plate,**
1930s. English by Paragon. 7" diameter. - **$125 $250 $500**

❏ **MKY-944. Mickey Mouse Boxed China Tea Set,**
1930s. 10x12.5x3" deep original but generic box containing 11 piece china set. - **$200 $400 $800**

MICKEY MOUSE, MINNIE & NEPHEWS

MKY-945

❑ **MKY-945. "Mickey And Minnie Mouse Toy Tea Set,"**
1930s. Geo. Borgfeldt Corp. 9.25x10.75x2.75" deep box with Mickey and Minnie images holds 15-piece china tea set. The cups, saucers and plates all have matching images - Minnie on fence, Mickey with balloons, Mickey playing hockey and Mickey with serving tray. Tray design also appears on creamer, sugar and teapot. Sugar and teapot have lids. Box only - **$100 $300 $600**
Set only - **$200 $400 $750**

MKY-946

❑ **MKY-946. Mickey Teapot,**
1930s. Wade Of England. Unmarked 3.5x6x3.5" tall painted and glazed ceramic pot and removable lid. - **$50 $100 $150**

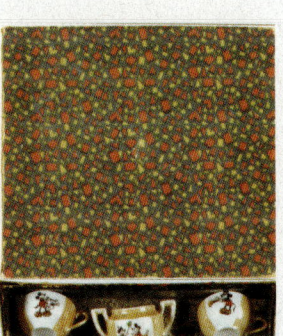

MKY-947

MKY-948

❑ **MKY-947. Near-Complete Japanese Toy Tea Set,**
1930s. "Made In Japan" 10.5x12.5x3" deep boxed with 21 original chinaware pieces comprised of teapot with lid, sugar bowl with lid, creamer, six cups, six saucers, six plates. Tallest piece is 3.5" teapot and each plate is 4.5" diameter, slightly larger than the saucers. Pictured in total are six different images of Mickey and Minnie. Box is original but generic pattern design. Complete Boxed - **$250 $450 $800**

❑ **MKY-948. Mickey/Minnie Mouse And Donald Duck Ceramic Teapot,**
1930s. England. Unmarked but believed to be by Wade. 3.5" tall. - **$50 $100 $150**

MKY-949

❑ **MKY-949. Mickey Mouse Scarce Variety Trivet,**
1930s. Trivet is 5.25" diameter by 2" tall scarce version in solid cast brass, usually found in cast iron. Cut-out design on top features large full figure image of Mickey surrounded by accent rays. Stands on three feet. Brass - **$100 $150 $275**
Iron - **$75 $135 $225**

MKY-950

❑ **MKY-950. Mickey And Minnie Mouse Tin Serving Tray,**
1930s. English. Happynak series No. 65. 3.5x6". - **$35 $60 $115**

MKY-951

❑ **MKY-951. "Mickey Mouse Silverplate" Boxed Utensil Set,**
1930s. International Silver Co. 4x8.5x1" deep box contains knife, fork and spoon ranging in size from 5.5" to 7.25". All have incised Mickey image and Mickey Mouse name. Box - **$50 $100 $200**
Each Utensil - **$15 $30 $50**

MKY-952

❑ **MKY-952. "Mickey/Minnie Mouse" Child's Fork And Spoon,**
1930s. Fairfield Silverplate. Each is 4.25" long.
Each - **$8 $15 $30**

517

MICKEY MOUSE, MINNIE & NEPHEWS

MKY-953

❑ **MKY-953. "Mickey Mouse" Fork,**
1930s. "Winthrop Silver Plate" 5.75" tall with design on handle of incised image of Mickey, his raised name and raised flower designs. - **$15 $30 $50**

MKY-956

❑ **MKY-956. Mickey Figure With Egg Timer,**
1930s. "Mickey Mouse/Foreign" 1.75x3x3.5" tall china figure with attached sand-filled glass timer that rotates manually. - **$200 $400 $600**

MKY-959

❑ **MKY-959. German Toothpick Holder,**
1930s. Figurine is 1.25x1.75x2.5" tall china. Underside has registration number. - **$75 $150 $250**

MKY-954

❑ **MKY-954. Mickey And Minnie Knife Rest,**
1930s. Unmarked but believed German 3.25x1.75" tall glazed ceramic figural of Mickey at one end holding a flower and Minnie at opposite end with hands clenched. - **$75 $150 $250**

MKY-957

❑ **MKY-957. Mickey Mouse China Egg Timer,**
1930s. 2.75" tall. Marked "Germany." - **$200 $400 $600**

MKY-960

❑ **MKY-960. "Mickey Mouse Treasure Chest" Bank,**
1930s. Japan. 2x3x2.5" tin litho. - **$175 $400 $800**

MKY-955

❑ **MKY-955. Mickey Mouse Silverware Caddy,**
1930s. William Rogers & Son. Two-piece unit comprised of thick layered painted cardboard while the base has wood wheels. 2x5.5x5.25" tall. - **$125 $250 $425**

MKY-958

❑ **MKY-958. Mickey Mouse China Egg Timer,**
1930s. 2.5" tall. Marked "Germany." Back back incised "2023." - **$50 $100 $175**

MKY-961

❑ **MKY-961. Mickey Mouse "Book" Bank With Key,**
1930s. Zell Products. 3x4.25x1" thick brass bank formed in image of book overlaid on covers by embossed oilcloth fabric. - **$75 $150 $225**

MICKEY MOUSE, MINNIE & NEPHEWS

MKY-962

MKY-963

MKY-965

❏ **MKY-962. "Mickey Mouse" Bee Hive Tin Bank,**
1930s. German by "Elbezet." 2.5" diameter by 3" tall lithographed tin. - **$100 $250 $500**

❏ **MKY-963. Mickey And Minnie Mouse Ceramic Banks,**
1930s. Faïencerie d'Onnaing. French. Each 6" tall. Underside of Minnie has company's mark while underside of Mickey has "Walt Disney" name. Mickey - **$175 $350 $600**
Minnie - **$150 $300 $500**

❏ **MKY-965. Mickey Mouse Cast Iron French Bank,**
1930s. Maker unknown. 4x6.5x9" tall. Original iron examples are scarce and boldly marked "Depose" on reverse. There are much more common cast aluminum versions of various quality, perhaps made by vocational school students in the 1930s.
Cast Iron - **$1000 $2500 $4250**
Aluminum - **$500 $1000 $2000**

MKY-966

MKY-967

MKY-964

❏ **MKY-964. Mickey Mouse Atop Drum Metal Bank,**
1930s. Maker unknown, likely French. 4.75" tall. - **$150 $300 $500**

❏ **MKY-966. Mickey Mouse Child's Purse,**
1930s. To the tip of the handle, purse is 4.25x7.5". Leatherette with metal snap closure. - **$35 $75 $150**

❏ **MKY-967. "Minnie And Mickey" Purse,**
1930s. Unmarked 3.5x6" leather coin purse with zippered top. - **$125 $250 $400**

MKY-968

❏ **MKY-968. "Minnie Mouse" Child's Purse,**
1930s. 4" tall. - **$200 $400 $600**

MKY-969

MICKEY MOUSE, MINNIE & NEPHEWS

☐ **MKY-969. Mickey And Minnie Mouse Mesh Purse,**
1930s. Whiting & Davis. 2.5x3.5" with enameled metal framework and mesh body, complete with attached chain link handle. - **$200 $400 $650**

MKY-970

☐ **MKY-970. Mickey And Minnie Metal Change Purse,**
1930s. Enamel on silvered brass purse is 2.25x2.25". - **$200 $400 $750**

MKY-971

☐ **MKY-971. Mickey And Minnie Wallet,**
1930s. Japan. 3x4" leather. Front has coin compartment with snap flap and wallet has attached snap closure. Reverse has clear plastic cover over owner's card. - **$65 $125 $200**

MKY-972

☐ **MKY-972. Mickey Mouse Makeup Kit,**
1930s. 4x3" tall with snap button, metal image of Mickey, and tassel. - **$50 $100 $200**

MKY-973

MKY-974

☐ **MKY-973. Mickey Mouse Bell,**
1930s. Three-dimensional painted cast metal figure of Mickey serving as handle attached to silvered metal bell. Mickey figure is 3" tall, total height is 4.75" with 2.5" diameter opening on bell bottom. Mickey is depicted in early 1930s English style featuring him with teeth and five fingers. A 2" coiled spring tail is on reverse. - **$150 $300 $600**

☐ **MKY-974. "Mickey/Minnie Mouse" Horn,**
1930s. Marks Brothers Co. 6.75" tall with paper label and wood mouthpiece. - **$75 $150 $275**

MKY-975

☐ **MKY-975. Mickey Mouse Drum,**
1930s. Ohio Art Co. 3.5" tall by 7" diameter tin litho. - **$100 $225 $450**

MKY-976

☐ **MKY-976. Mickey Mouse Drum,**
1930s. Ohio Art Co. 4.25" tall by 9" diameter tin litho. - **$125 $250 $550**

MKY-977

☐ **MKY-977. Mickey Mouse Drum,**
1930s. Ohio Art Co. 4.25" tall by 9" diameter tin litho. - **$100 $225 $450**

MICKEY MOUSE, MINNIE & NEPHEWS

MKY-978

❑ **MKY-978. "Mickey Mouse Drum Corps" Tin Drum,**
1930s. J. Chein & Co. 13" diameter by 5.5" deep. - **$800 $1750 $3000**

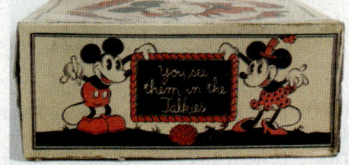

MKY-979

❑ **MKY-979. Box For Large "Mickey Mouse Drum,"**
1930s. Box says Nifty, but held 13" diameter drum marked J. Chein & Co. 13.25x13.5x5.5" deep box for "No. 171 Drum." - **$300 $600 $1200**

MKY-980

❑ **MKY-980. Czech Harmonica,**
1930s. "Made In Czechoslovakia" .75x1x4" long instrument formed by wood center reed bar between tin plate top and bottom. Top has incised name "Mickey Mouse Band" with copyright. - **$125 $250 $500**

MKY-981

❑ **MKY-981. Mickey Mouse Flute,**
1930s. "S.F.C./Made In Italy." 9.75" long lithographed tin. - **$125 $250 $500**

MKY-982

❑ **MKY-982. Mickey Mouse Child's Toy Saxophone,**
1930s. Czechoslovakia by "Haro." Imported by Borgfeldt. 16" long tin. Small "W.D." copyright. - **$150 $300 $600**

MKY-983

❑ **MKY-983. "Mickey Mouse" Wood Piano,**
1930s. Made in Japan with copyright "Walt Disney Enterprises, Ltd." 9x11x5.25" tall. - **$200 $500 $850**

MKY-984

MICKEY MOUSE, MINNIE & NEPHEWS

MKY-985

MKY-986

❑ **MKY-984. "Mickey Mouse Safe-Toy Music Box" For Projector,**
1930s. English by Ensign. 3.5" diameter by 2" deep tin with cardboard bottom panel, wrap-around paper label for use with Safe-Toy projector. - **$50 $100 $150**

❑ **MKY-985. "Mickey Mouse" Drum,**
1930s. Ohio Art. 6" diameter by 3.75" deep lithographed tin. Has string cross cord around body and stiff paper drumhead with thin mesh fabric covering. - **$150 $300 $600**

❑ **MKY-986. "Mickey Mouse Piano With Dancing Figures,"**
1930s. Marks Bros., Boston. Wood with cardboard figures that dance as keys are struck. Toy is 4.75x9.5x10.25" tall. Box is 5.5x9.75x10.75" tall. Box - **$300 $750 $1500**
Toy - **$500 $1250 $2200**

MKY-987

MKY-988

❑ **MKY-987. "Walt Disney Enterprises/Kay Kamen Incorporated" Sticker,**
1930s. 2.5" diameter sticker with gummed reverse. Used on Disney store displays produced by Old King Cole, available through Kay Kamen. - **$25 $50 $75**

❑ **MKY-988. "Mickey" Mouse French Product Folder,**
1930s. Folder is 4.25x7" and opens to 16" in length. Illustrations on both sides picture different shoe, metal and other polishes all of which feature Mickey containers or labels. Text is in French. - **$25 $50 $75**

MKY-989

❑ **MKY-989. Mickey English Camera Ad Folder,**
1930s. Ensign Ltd. Closed 4.25x5.25" fold-out opens to total size of 8.5x10.5". - **$25 $50 $90**

MKY-990

❑ **MKY-990. "Mickey Mouse Flexible Flyer" Sled Promo Folder,**
1930s. S.L. Allen & Co. Inc. 3.25x6.25" paper opening to 6.25x6.5". - **$100 $200 $400**

MICKEY MOUSE, MINNIE & NEPHEWS

MKY-991

☐ **MKY-991. Mickey Mouse Movie Club Pennant,**
1930s. 4x9" felt pennant attached to wood rod. An early movie club premium. - **$100 $200 $300**

MKY-992

MKY-993

☐ **MKY-992. Mickey "Sunoco Oil" Blotter,**
1930s. Blotter is 4x8.5". - **$30 $65 $100**

☐ **MKY-993. "Mickey Mouse/Thom McAn" Premium Flip Book,**
1930s. Book is 2.25x3" and features "Mickey Takes Minnie For A Ride" on one side and "The Boy In The Thom McAn's Wins" on the other. - **$100 $200 $400**

MKY-994

☐ **MKY-994. "Mickey Mouse Magic Slate,"**
1930s. 2.5x4". Issued as a premium with black and white label on reverse that reads "Compliments Of Mickey Mouse In Gold's Toyland." - **$65 $115 $175**

MKY-995

MKY-996

☐ **MKY-995. Comic Club Birthday Card With Mickey Mouse And Others,**
1930s. Washington Times Adventure Club. 4.25x5.5" stiff paper. Includes illustrations of Mickey Mouse, Popeye, Smitty, Little Annie Rooney and portrait believed to be Kit Carson. - **$25 $50 $85**

☐ **MKY-996. Mickey Premium Picture,**
1930s. "Congoleum Gold Seal Rugs." 9x12" stiff paper image of Mickey signing his name on wall within simulated wood frame. Text includes his name as spelled in various countries. - **$20 $40 $75**

MKY-997

☐ **MKY-997. Congoleum Gold Seal Rug Store Sign Featuring Minnie Mouse,**
1930s. 19.5" diameter die-cut cardboard sign noting 3 store prizes. - **$200 $400 $750**

MKY-998

☐ **MKY-998. "Mickey Mouse" Merchandise Box,**
1930s. Box is 2x5x5" and lid has repeated designs of Mickey and his name. Box designed like those used by International Silver Co. - **$50 $85 $150**

MKY-999

☐ **MKY-999. Mickey Mouse "Durkee's" Die-cut Sign,**
1930s. San Francisco. 3.5x6" stiff cardboard. - **$35 $65 $125**

MICKEY MOUSE, MINNIE & NEPHEWS

MKY-1000

☐ **MKY-1000. "Toytown" Sign With Mickey And Donald,**
1930s. Possibly Macy's. 7x11" two-sided sign on card stock. - **$100 $250 $400**

MKY-1001

☐ **MKY-1001. Mickey Mouse "Hallmark" Salesman's Announcement Card,**
1930s. Hallmark. 3.75x5" stiff paper with starched fabric flag attached sent by salesmen to their clientele to announce their upcoming arrival. - **$75 $150 $225**

MKY-1002

☐ **MKY-1002. "Mickey Mouse Pencil Box" Store Sign,**
1930s. Stiff cardboard sign measuring 5.5x7". - **$35 $65 $125**

MKY-1003

☐ **MKY-1003. "Mickey Mouse Pencil Box" Store Sign,**
1930s. Stiff cardboard sign measuring 3.5x5.5". - **$20 $40 $75**

MKY-1004

☐ **MKY-1004. "Mickey Mouse Pencil Boxes" Ad Card,**
1930s. Dixon. 4x5.25" die-cut cardboard card. - **$65 $125 $200**

MKY-1005

☐ **MKY-1005. European Cards,**
1930s. Seven examples including one believed Dutch 2.25x5.25" gift card picturing Mickey on bicycle. Other six are each 1.25x2-1/8" coated cardboard cards from a numbered series. Backs feature a four-line verse in both French and believed Dutch. Cards are #10, 16, 20, 25, 34, 39. Each - **$5 $12 $25**

MKY-1006

☐ **MKY-1006. "Mickey Mouse To Color And Draw Big Little Set,"**
1930s. Box is 3.75x5.25x1.5" deep and contains 320 two-sided picture pages to be colored. - **$125 $275 $550**

MKY-1007

☐ **MKY-1007. "The Princess Elizabeth Gift Book" With Disney Color Plates,**
1930s. Hodder & Stoughton of Great Britain 7.5x10" hardcover. 224 pages. Includes superb pair of double page multi-character illustrations. - **$100 $200 $400**

MICKEY MOUSE, MINNIE & NEPHEWS

MKY-1008

❏ **MKY-1008. "Mickey Mouse Bedtime Stories" English Hardcover,** 1930s. William Collins Sons & Co. Ltd. 7x9.5" with 96 stiff paper pages. - **$100 $200 $350**

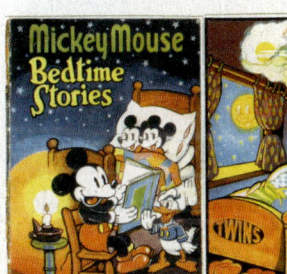

MKY-1009

MKY-1010

❏ **MKY-1009. "Mickey Mouse Bedtime Stories" English Softcover,** 1930s. Sunshine Press. 7.25x9.5" with 96 pages. - **$75 $150 $300**

❏ **MKY-1010. "Micky Maus" Promotional Advertising Flag For Magazines,** 1930s. Switzerland by Bollmann. 8.5x12" two-sided stiff paper. - **$50 $100 $150**

MKY-1011

❏ **MKY-1011. "Mickey Mouse On Tour" Book,** 1930s. English by Birn Brothers Ltd. 7x9.25" with 28 pages. - **$100 $225 $500**

MKY-1012

❏ **MKY-1012. "The Mickey Mouse Fun ABC" Book,** 1930s. English by London And Glascow. 7x9.25" with 28 pages. - **$100 $225 $500**

MKY-1013

❏ **MKY-1013. "Mickey Mouse Stories" Book,** 1930s. English by Dean & Son Ltd. 6x8.5" with 32 pages. - **$150 $350 $700**

MKY-1014

❏ **MKY-1014. "Mickey Mouse School Bag,"** 1930s. 11x11" velveteen-covered canvas. Maker is unknown. - **$75 $150 $250**

MICKEY MOUSE, MINNIE & NEPHEWS

MKY-1015

❑ **MKY-1015. Boxed "Minnie Mouse Costume,"**
1930s. Wornova Play Clothes, N.Y. Five-piece outfit in original 11x12x4" deep box. Box - **$50 $100 $200**
Costume - **$75 $150 $250**

MKY-1017

❑ **MKY-1017. Musical Band Leader Mickey Mouse Doll,**
1930s. Knickerbocker. 12" tall. Stuffed cloth body with felt ears, felt jacket with brass buttons and braid accents, oilcloth belt with brass snap, plush covered hat with braid chin strap, wood baton, composition feet, whiskers. Has inner music mechanism. - **$3000 $6000 $12000**

MKY-1019

❑ **MKY-1019. Cowboy Mickey Mouse Doll,**
1930s. Knickerbocker. 5x7.5x12" tall. Stuffed cloth body with felt ears, suede leather/wool chaps with metal studs, vest, composition feet, rubber tail, string whiskers, hat, neck scarf and metal guns. Photo example missing parts of outfit.- **$650 $1250 $2750**

MKY-1016

❑ **MKY-1016. Band Leader Mickey Mouse Doll,**
1930s. Knickerbocker. 25" tall. Stuffed cloth body with felt ears, felt jacket with brass buttons and braid accents, oilcloth belt with brass snap, plush covered hat with braid chin strap, composition feet, whiskers. - **$1000 $2000 $4000**

MKY-1018

❑ **MKY-1018. Cowboy Mickey Mouse 16" Tall Doll,**
1930s. Knickerbocker. Stuffed cloth body with felt ears, suede leather/wool chaps with metal studs, composition feet, rubber tail, string whiskers, hat, neck scarf and metal guns.
Doll - **$850 $1700 $4000**
Tag - **$50 $100 $200**

MKY-1020

❑ **MKY-1020. Mickey Mouse Cowboy Jointed Composition Doll,**
1930s. Knickerbocker. 10" tall. - **$1250 $2500 $5250**

MICKEY MOUSE, MINNIE & NEPHEWS

MKY-1021

❏ **MKY-1021. "Mickey Mouse Nursery Set, "**
1930s. Lines Bros. Ltd. England. 9.75x11.75x2.5" deep box contains five pieces of dollhouse furniture: wardrobe, bed, table, rocker and high chair. Box - **$50 $100 $200** Set of five - **$250 $500 $1000**

MKY-1022

❏ **MKY-1022. Mickey Mouse English Doll Bed,**
1930s. Wood-framed bed 10.5x20.5x10" tall. Has 4.5x5" Mickey decal on both headboard and footboard. Fabric covering features non-Disney characters. - **$150 $300 $500**

MKY-1023

❏ **MKY-1023. Mickey and Minnie Mouse English Doll Bed,**
1930s. 10.5x20x12" tall wood bed with fabric covering. - **$150 $300 $500**

MKY-1024

❏ **MKY-1024. Knickerbocker Mickey Mouse Stuffed Doll,**
1930s. Stuffed fabric doll 5x6.5x11.5" tall with felt ears, die-cut oilcloth eyes, string whiskers, four plastic buttons and gray rubber tail. Version with felt-covered cardboard feet rather than composition. - **$250 $500 $1000**

MKY-1025

❏ **MKY-1025. Minnie Mouse Doll,**
1930s. 10" tall Cloth and felt doll with paper tag. - **$250 $500 $1000**

MKY-1026

❏ **MKY-1026. Mickey Mouse Doll,**
1930s. Doll is 4x7x11.5" tall with satin-like covered body, felt ears, hands and shoes and cloth pants with plastic buttons. Has string whiskers, rubber tail and painted facial features. - **$275 $550 $1100**

MKY-1027

❏ **MKY-1027. Unusual Mickey Mouse Doll,**
1930s. 6x8.5x15" tall with composition head and arms, stuffed fabric body. Probably unauthorized. - **$75 $150 $300**

MICKEY MOUSE, MINNIE & NEPHEWS

MKY-1028

❑ **MKY-1028. Large Composition Mickey Mouse Doll,**
1930s. Knickerbocker. 4x5x9.25" tall painted composition with movable arms and head. - **$350 $750 $1500**

MKY-1029

❑ **MKY-1029. Australian Doll,**
1930s. "Joy-Toys Made In Australia." 4x7x11.5" tall early foreign stuffed fabric doll detailed by pie-eyes, felt ears, bow at neck, two buttons on trousers, stitched tag by maker. - **$400 $750 $1200**

MKY-1030

❑ **MKY-1030. Mickey Homemade Doll From Pattern,**
1930s. Large 7x11x18" tall stuffed fabric doll produced from a McCall's pattern. - **$50 $150 $300**

MKY-1031

❑ **MKY-1031. Minnie Mouse Doll,**
1930s. Unmarked, likely homemade. 12" tall. - **$25 $50 $100**

MKY-1032

❑ **MKY-1032. Mickey Mouse Medium Size Felt/Velveteen Doll,**
1930s. English by Deans Rag Book. 8" tall with wire inserts for posing. Registration number "730811" on neck. - **$200 $400 $675**

MKY-1033

❑ **MKY-1033. Mickey Mouse Jazzer Boxed Doll,**
1930s. Dean's Rag Book Company Ltd. 6" tall. Has wire attachment to reverse of doll and is designed to be mounted to a record player so that when the record is revolving the figure will dance. Includes 3x3.5" instruction sheet. - **$1000 $2000 $3000**

MKY-1034

❑ **MKY-1034. Minnie Mouse Medium Size Doll,**
1930s. Dean's Rag Book. England. 8" tall with tiny "730811" registration number on neck. - **$200 $450 $675**

MICKEY MOUSE, MINNIE & NEPHEWS

MKY-1035

MKY-1037

MKY-1039

❏ **MKY-1037. Mickey Mouse Largest Steiff Doll,**
1930s. Doll is 18". Near Mint With Metal Ear Button And Tag - **$10000**
With Button Or Tag - **$2000 $4000 $8000**
Without Button And Tag - **$1500 $3000 $6000**

❏ **MKY-1039. Minnie Mouse 9" Doll By Steiff,**
1930s. Near Mint With Ear Button And Tag - **$4500**
With Button Or Tag - **$800 $1750 $3500**
Without Button Or Tag - **$500 $1250 $2500**

MKY-1036

MKY-1038

MKY-1040

❏ **MKY-1035. Mickey Mouse Extremely Large Doll,**
1930s. English by Deans Rag Book. 22" tall mohair and velveteen with wire inserts for posing and a movable head. - **$300 $750 $1500**

❏ **MKY-1036. Minnie Mouse As Cowgirl Doll,**
1930s. Knickerbocker. 16.5" tall. Stuffed fabric body, felt ears, oilcloth eyes, separate string whiskers and painted composition shoes. Outfit consists of removable felt hat, neckerchief, leatherette skirt and wrist cuffs accented by metal studs. Underside of each foot has Knickerbocker label that includes small Mickey image. - **$80 $1600 $3750**

❏ **MKY-1038. Mickey Mouse 9" Doll By Steiff,**
1930s. Near Mint With Ear Button And Tag - **$5000**
With Button Or Tag - **$1000 $2000 $4000**
Without Button And Tag - **$750 $1500 $3000**

❏ **MKY-1040. Mickey Mouse 12" Doll By Charlotte Clark,**
1930s. - **$2000 $3500 $7500**

MICKEY MOUSE, MINNIE & NEPHEWS

MKY-1041

MKY-1043

❏ **MKY-1041. Minnie Mouse 18" Doll By Charlotte Clark,** 1930s. - **$2000 $3500 $7500**

❏ **MKY-1043. Mickey Mouse Blue Pants Doll,** 1930s. Borgfeldt. 10" tall. - **$750 $1500 $3000**

MKY-1045

MKY-1046

MKY-1042

MKY-1044

❏ **MKY-1042. Minnie Mouse 18" Doll By Charlotte Clark,** 1930s. - **$2000 $3500 $7500**

❏ **MKY-1044. Mickey Mouse Large 20" Heavy Velvet Doll,** 1930s. No markings. Tail is rubber coated wire. - **$1000 $2750 $4750**

❏ **MKY-1045. Minnie Mouse Large 20" Heavy Velvet Doll,** 1930s. No markings. Tail is rubber-coated wire. - **$850 $2250 $4250**

❏ **MKY-1046. Mickey Mouse 12" Doll By Steiff,** 1930s. Has white metal Steiff button in left ear. Walt Disney Mickey Mouse copyright under one foot. With Tag And Button - **$1250 $2600 $5250** With Tag Or Button - **$1100 $2100 $4250** Without Tag And Button - **$800 $1600 $3200**

MICKEY MOUSE, MINNIE & NEPHEWS

MKY-1047

MKY-1049

MKY-1051

❏ **MKY-1047. Mickey Mouse 12" Borgfeldt Doll,**
1930s. Underside of feet read "Walt Disney's Mickey Mouse Design Patent 82802 Geo. Borgfeldt & Co. New York." - **$1000 $2000 $4000**

❏ **MKY-1049. Minnie Mouse 15" Steiff Doll,**
1930s. Has ear button and tag as well as chest tag. Near Mint With All Tags - **$7500**
With Ear Or Chest Tag - **$1250 $2500 $4000**
Without Tags - **$1000 $2000 $3000**

❏ **MKY-1051. Easter Parade Minnie Mouse 16" Tall Doll,**
1930s. Knickerbocker. Stuffed cloth body with felt ears and composition shoes. Felt/cotton outfit includes hat with flower attachment, collar piece with flower attachment and bow on back, skirt with plastic buttons, bloomers.
- **$1500 $3000 $6000**

MKY-1048

MKY-1050

MKY-1052

❏ **MKY-1048. Mickey Mouse Large 18" Doll,**
1930s. No markings. - **$1200 $2500 $5000**

❏ **MKY-1050. Easter Parade Mickey Mouse Doll,**
1930s. Knickerbocker. 12.5" tall. Stuffed cloth body with felt ears and composition shoes. Elaborate outfit consists of jacket with plastic buttons, flower on lapel, ascot, starched felt hat.
- **$3000 $6000 $12000**
Tag - **$50 $100 $200**

❏ **MKY-1052. Easter Parade Minnie Mouse 12" Tall Knickerbocker Doll,**
1930s. Has rubber tail, composition shoes and string tag. Doll - **$800 $6500 $3500**
Tag - **$50 $100 $200**

MICKEY MOUSE, MINNIE & NEPHEWS

MKY-1053

MKY-1056

MKY-1059

❏ **MKY-1053. Minnie Mouse 15" Knickerbocker Doll,**
1930s. Variety with fabric shoes. Doll - **$500 $1200 $2500**
String Tag - **$50 $100 $200**

❏ **MKY-1059. "Mickey Mouse Garden Roller,"**
1930s. Maker unknown, likely English. Lithographed tin with overall size of 8.5x8.5x4.5" diameter of the roller. Meant to be filled with sand. - **$125 $275 $600**

MKY-1057

MKY-1060

MKY-1054

MKY-1055

❏ **MKY-1056. Unusual Mickey Mouse Celluloid Squeak Toy,**
1930s. 3.5" diameter by .5" thick circular body with small circular base and attached to the top is a 1.75" tall Mickey figure. Toy is designed so that the Mickey figure would pop up into the air about .5". - **$75 $150 $300**

❏ **MKY-1057. "Climbing Mickey Mouse" Boxed Toy,**
1930s. Dolly Toy Co. 5x9.5x2.25" deep boxed 9" tall diecut cardboard figure toy with wire tail plus length of string with wire finger loop on each end. When string is pulled tightly, Mickey moves up and down. Box - **$400 $800 $1250**
Toy - **$250 $500 $850**

MKY-1061

❏ **MKY-1060. Minnie And Pluto Ashtray,**
1930s. From a set of four designed as card game ashtrays. 3.25x4.25x3" tall. - **$100 $200 $350**

❏ **MKY-1061. "Mickey Mouse" Ashtray,**
1930s. Base resembling stone is 3.25x4x.5" deep with attached 3.25" tall composition figure. Complete - **$65 $125 $225** Figure Only - **$35 $65 $100**

❏ **MKY-1054. Mickey Mouse Hanging Marionette Composition Toy,**
1930s. Unmarked. Figure has painted composition head while body is covered by real animal fur, hands and feet are wood pegs. His body has size of 3.5x4.5x7" long with very long tail that is 7.5". Attached to the top of his head is a coil spring and attached to his arms and legs is string used to move these appendages. - **$125 $250 $500**

❏ **MKY-1055. Mickey Mouse Jack-In-The Box,**
1930s. Knickerbocker. 6x6.5x6.5" tall wood box with paper labels. Opens to reveal a pop-up Mickey Mouse head 5" tall. - **$1000 $2000 $3000**

MKY-1058

❏ **MKY-1058. Mickey Mouse Wood Walking Toy,**
1930s. Unmarked but licensed. 13.75" tall with 19.5" black wood rod that fits into hole on back. - **$85 $175 $350**

MKY-1062

532

MICKEY MOUSE, MINNIE & NEPHEWS

MKY-1063

❑ **MKY-1062. Mickey Mouse Cigarette Holder/Ashtray,**
1930s. Marked "Made In Japan" china ashtray 2.5x4.5x2.5" tall. No Disney copyright. - **$50 $100 $200**

❑ **MKY-1063. Mickey Mouse Drummer China Ashtray,**
1930s. Japan. 3x5x3" tall. - **$100 $175 $300**

MKY-1064

❑ **MKY-1064. Mickey And Friends Figural Ashtray,**
1930s. "Made In Japan" circular 3" diameter by 3" tall china bowl tray with high relief figures of Mickey with tuba, Minnie with guitar, Pluto. Bottom edge of base has their incised names and copyright. Believed made for Canadian market. - **$150 $300 $550**

MKY-1065

MKY-1066

❑ **MKY-1065. Mickey Mouse High Quality Glass Ashtray,**
1930s. Maker Unknown. 3.5". - **$75 $150 $300**

❑ **MKY-1066. Minnie Mouse Bavarian China Cigarette Holder,**
1930s. White china piece is 1.5x3.25x2.5" tall and marked "Made In Bavaria." - **$125 $250 $400**

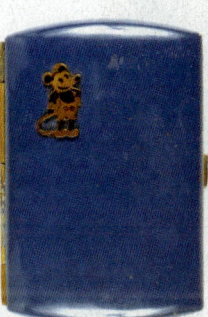
MKY-1067

❑ **MKY-1067. Mickey Mouse Cigarette Case,**
1930s. Likely English. 2.5x3.25x.5" deep enameled metal. Designed with spring-loaded opening mechanism with push button on right side. - **$100 $225 $350**

MKY-1068

❑ **MKY-1068. English Mickey Mouse Christmas Card,**
1930s. Valentine & Sons. 4x5.25" paper accordion-fold card that opens to 10.5". - **$20 $40 $70**

MKY-1069

MKY-1070

❑ **MKY-1069. English Mickey Mouse Christmas Card,**
1930s. Valentine & Sons. 4x5.25" stiff paper accordion-fold card that opens to 10.5". - **$20 $40 $70**

❑ **MKY-1070. English Birthday Card,**
1930s. G. Delgado Ltd. Closed 4.25x4.25" folder card on parchment-like paper. - **$25 $50 $80**

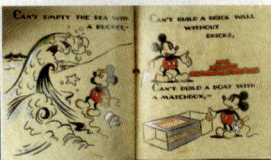

MKY-1071

MKY-1072

MICKEY MOUSE, MINNIE & NEPHEWS

❏ **MKY-1071. Mickey Mouse Christmas Card,**
1930s. Hallmark. 5.25x5.25" eight-page card including cover on parchment-like paper. - **$50 $100 $150**

❏ **MKY-1072. Mickey Mouse English Christmas Card,**
1930s. G. Delgado Ltd. 5x5". - **$25 $50 $80**

MKY-1073

❏ **MKY-1073. Mickey Mouse Celluloid Ornament,**
1930s. Three-dimensional figure of Mickey is 3.25" tall with string attachment on back to be used as Christmas ornament. - **$25 $50 $100**

MKY-1074

MKY-1075

❏ **MKY-1074. Minnie Celluloid Ornament,**
1930s. "Made In England" 2.25x2.5x3.75" tall with string loop at back of head for hanging. - **$50 $125 $200**

❏ **MKY-1075. Minnie Mouse Pair Of Wooden Ornaments,**
1930s. Unmarked. Each 4" tall. Wood body with leather fabric and rubber over wire accents. Each - **$25 $50 $75**

MKY-1076

❏ **MKY-1076. Mickey Mouse Christmas Decoration,**
1930s. Japan. 4x7x4.25" tall pressed and formed painted cardboard decoration with 1.75" tall painted composition and wire figure. - **$50 $85 $175**

MKY-1077

❏ **MKY-1077. Mickey Mouse And House Christmas Decoration,**
1930s. Japan. Mickey Mouse bisque is 1" at front door of 3.5" tall corrugated cardboard house. Both are attached to 3.25x5.25x.5" deep die-cut cardboard base. - **$40 $80 $150**

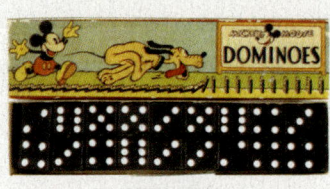

MKY-1078

MKY-1079

❏ **MKY-1078. "Mickey Mouse Dominos,"**
1930s. Halsam. 2x8.5x1" deep box contains wood dominos. - **$65 $135 $250**

❏ **MKY-1079. "Mickey Mouse/Minnie Mouse Score Pad Tally" Lot,**
1930s. Lot of four, each 2.25x4.5" with stiff paper covers and string attachments with tassels. Each - **$12 $25 $40**

MKY-1080

❏ **MKY-1080. "Mickey Mouse Ludo" English Game,**
1930s. Chad Valley Co. 6x11x1" deep box. - **$100 $200 $400**

MICKEY MOUSE, MINNIE & NEPHEWS

MKY-1081

❑ **MKY-1081. Mickey/Pluto Humor Sentiment Card,**
1930s. Hall Brothers Inc. 3.5x4.5" on textured paper. Inside shows them dejected with a rain cloud over Pluto's head. - **$25 $50 $75**

MKY-1082

❑ **MKY-1082. Mickey Mouse Get Well Card,**
1930s. Card is 4.25x5.25" textured paper. Probably unauthorized. - **$20 $40 $65**

MKY-1083

❑ **MKY-1083. Mickey Mouse Birthday Card,**
1930s. Hall Brothers Inc. 4x5" on glossy textured paper. - **$25 $50 $75**

MKY-1084

❑ **MKY-1084. Mickey Mouse "Easter" Card,**
1930s. Hall Brothers. 4.75x6" one-sided card. - **$35 $65 $110**

MKY-1085

❑ **MKY-1085. Mickey Mouse Birthday Card,**
1930s. Hallmark. 4x5" card on tan textured paper. - **$30 $60 $90**

MKY-1086

❑ **MKY-1086. Mickey Mouse Die-cut Birthday Card,**
1930s. Hallmark. 4.5x4.5" stiff paper card with Mickey holding die-cut birthday cake. Inside has stove with slot for cake to be inserted. - **$30 $60 $90**

MKY-1087

MKY-1088

❑ **MKY-1087. Mickey Mouse Easter Card,**
1930s. Hall Brothers Inc. Card is 3.75x6.5". Inside text mentions Mickey and includes a small illustration of him. - **$20 $40 $65**

❑ **MKY-1088. "Mickey Mouse" Birthday Card,**
1930s. Hallmark. 3.5x4.5" diecut stiff paper. - **$35 $65 $100**

MKY-1089

MKY-1090

❑ **MKY-1089. Mickey Mouse Get Well Card,**
1930s. Hallmark. 4x5" die-cut on glossy linen-like paper. Pair of die-cut flaps on front. - **$25 $50 $75**

❑ **MKY-1090. Mickey Mouse Missing You Card,**
1930s. Hall Brothers Inc. Folded size is 4.75x5.75" and opens a total of four times revealing a different illustration each time for a total size of 18.5x22.5". - **$35 $75 $150**

MICKEY MOUSE, MINNIE & NEPHEWS

MKY-1091

❏ **MKY-1091. "Mickey Mouse" English Birthday Card,**
1930s. G. Delgado Ltd., London. 4x4" on parchment-like paper. - **$30 $60 $100**

MKY-1092

MKY-1093

❏ **MKY-1092. Get Well Card,**
1930s. Hall Brothers Inc. Closed 3.5x3.5" folder card picturing Mickey three times with verse for "Little Shut-In." - **$20 $45 $70**

❏ **MKY-1093. Minnie "Happy Easter" Card,**
1930s. Hall Brothers. 5x6" die-cut stiff paper. - **$30 $60 $100**

MKY-1094

❏ **MKY-1094. Mickey English Birthday Card,**
1930s. Valentine & Sons Ltd. 3.5x5.5" die-cut stiff paper "Mickey Mouse Cut-Out Numeral" card. - **$10 $20 $35**

MKY-1095

❏ **MKY-1095. Mickey Mouse Christmas Gift Tag,**
1930s. Dennison. 3.5x3.5" stiff paper which opens. - **$20 $40 $65**

MKY-1096

❏ **MKY-1096. Minnie Mouse Boxed Gift Stickers,**
1930s. Hall Brothers. 2x2-3/8x3/8" deep box with slip cover bearing example of contents. Contained unknown quantity. Empty Box - **$25 $50 $85**

MKY-1097

MKY-1098

❏ **MKY-1097. "Mickey Mouse" Birthday Card,**
1930s. Hall Brothers. 4.25x4.5" die-cut stiff paper. - **$25 $45 $75**

❏ **MKY-1098. "Mickey/Minnie Mouse" Birthday Card,**
1930s. Hallmark. 4.5x4.5". - **$25 $45 $75**

MKY-1099

MKY-1100

MICKEY MOUSE, MINNIE & NEPHEWS

❑ **MKY-1099. Mickey Mouse Multi Page Birthday Card,**
1930s. Hall Brothers Inc. 5.5x6.5" with eight pages. - **$50 $100 $150**

❑ **MKY-1100. "Mickey Mouse Baby's First Birthday" Card,**
1930s. Hall Brothers. 3.5x4.5". - **$35 $65 $100**

MKY-1101

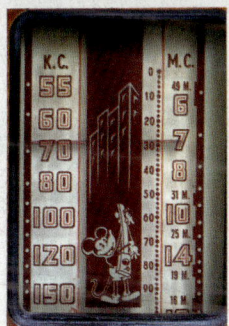

MKY-1102

❑ **MKY-1101. "Mickey" Argentine Radio Front,**
1930s. Heavy cast brass 6x6" originally attached to front of radio. Has "Mickey" name on lower right corner. - **$100 $200 $300**

❑ **MKY-1102. Mickey Mouse Radio,**
1930s. Industria Argentina. 7x13x8.75" tall lacquered wood. - **$500 $1000 $1500**

MKY-1103

❑ **MKY-1103. Mickey Mouse Silver Plate Prototype Radio,**
1930s. "Wm. Rogers & Son." 4.25x8.75x6.5" tall. This radio is a prototype and we know of only two others and as far as we know, it was never put into production. - **$2500 $5000 $7500**

MKY-1104

❑ **MKY-1104. Mickey Mouse Valentine's Day Card,**
1930s. Hall Brothers Inc. 5x6" stiff brown paper card that opens a total of four times revealing a different illustration each time for a total of 19x23". - **$50 $100 $150**

MKY-1105

MKY-1106

❑ **MKY-1105. Mickey Mouse Pop-Up Valentine's Day Card,**
1930s. Hall Brothers Inc. 4.75x4.75" on glossy textured paper. - **$100 $250 $400**

❑ **MKY-1106. Minnie Valentine,**
1930s. Hall Brothers Inc. 5x6" die-cut stiff paper card image of her with key unlocking a heart-shaped lock. Text is "You Have The Key To My Heart Valentine." - **$30 $60 $100**

MKY-1107

MICKEY MOUSE, MINNIE & NEPHEWS

MKY-1108

❏ **MKY-1107. Mickey Valentine,**
1930s. Hall Brothers Inc. 4.75x5.75" die-cut stiff paper. - **$35 $70 $125**

❏ **MKY-1108. "Mickey Mouse" Sand Sieve,**
1930s. Ohio Art Co. 8" diameter by 2" deep. Nice beach-related scenes around sides of Mickey, Minnie, Pluto, Horace and Clarabelle. - **$100 $200 $400**

MKY-1109

❏ **MKY-1109. Mickey Mouse "Atlantic City" Sand Pail,**
1930s. Ohio Art. 4.25" tall lithographed tin pail with handle. - **$250 $500 $1000**

MKY-1110

MKY-1111

❏ **MKY-1110. Mickey Mouse Sand Pail,**
1930s. Ohio Art. 5.5" diameter lithographed tin pail with handle. - **$300 $600 $1200**

❏ **MKY-1111. "Mickey Mouse" Sand Pail Shovel,**
1930s. Ohio Art. 1.5x6" long lithographed tin shovel. - **$100 $200 $300**

MKY-1112

❏ **MKY-1112. Mickey Sand Pail With Shovel,**
1930s. Ohio Art. 3.25" tall lithographed tin pail. Pail - **$175 $350 $600** Generic Shovel - **$15 $30 $50**

MKY-1113

❏ **MKY-1113. Mickey Mouse Sand Pail,**
1930s. Ohio Art Co. 4.25" tall by 4.25" diameter tin litho. - **$200 $400 $800**

MKY-1114

MKY-1115

❏ **MKY-1114. Disney Embossed Tin Litho Sand Pail,**
1930s. Ohio Art Co. 6" tall by 5.75" top diameter. Green Water Verision - **$300 $750 $1250** Yellow Water Verision - **$400 $900 $1500**

❏ **MKY-1115. English Sand Pail,**
1930s. "Happynak Seaside Pail No. 12" tin lithographed pail 6.25" tall by 7" top diameter with attached metal carrying bail. - **$125 $250 $400**

MKY-1116

MKY-1117

❏ **MKY-1116. Mickey And Friends Sand Pail,**
1930s. Ohio Art Co. 8" top diameter by 8" tall tin lithographed with wrap-around beach scene. - **$250 $500 $1000**

❏ **MKY-1117. "Mickey's Garden" Sand Pail,**
1930s. Ohio Art Co. 5.25" top diameter by 5" tall lithographed tin. - **$175 $350 $600**

MKY-1118

❏ **MKY-1118. "Mickey Mouse Picnic" Sand Pail,**
1930s. Ohio Art Co. 7" tall with narrow flared-out base. - **$500 $1200 $2200**

MICKEY MOUSE, MINNIE & NEPHEWS

MKY-1119

❑ **MKY-1119. "Happynak" Mickey Mouse Sand Pail,**
1930s. Great Britain. 4.5" tall tin litho. - **$125 $225 $375**

❑ **MKY-1121. Large Sand Pail Featuring Unauthorized Likenesses Of Mickey, Minnie, And Krazy Kat,**
1930s. Marked "Made in U.S.A." 8" tall tin litho. - **$300 $600 $1000**

❑ **MKY-1122. Mickey And Minnie Mouse Sand Shovel,**
1930s. Ohio Art. 4.25x5" tin litho. - **$125 $250 $500**

MKY-1120

❑ **MKY-1120. Mickey Mouse Sand Pail,**
1930s. English. Happynak Seaside Pail No. 7. Lithographed tin pail is 4.25". - **$100 $200 $300**

MKY-1123

❑ **MKY-1123. "Mickey Mouse" Sled,**
1930s. Sled toy is 6x18x29" long formed by steel frame and runners plus wood top panels, side rails and steering bar. Underside of center slat includes text "Mickey Mouse No. 80/Made By S.L. Allen & Co. Manufacturers Of The Flexible Flyer Sled." Top of steering bar has "Mickey Mouse" name decal. - **$150 $300 $750**

MKY-1125

❑ **MKY-1125. "Mickey Mouse" Alarm Clock Boxed,**
1930s. Bayard. "Made In France" wind-up alarm in 5x5x3" deep box. Lid side panels picture a sequence of four events related to Mickey and his morning use of the clock. Clock is 4.75" diameter by 2" deep in enameled metal case. Dial face has separate diecut pointer hands and separate diecut tin head that nods as seconds tick. This is an original issue by Bayard, which re-issued this and other character clocks in the 1960s. Box - **$300 $750 $1300** Clock - **$250 $500 $800**

MKY-1124

❑ **MKY-1124. "Mickey" French Ring Toss Game,**
1930s. "Jeux-Spear." 6.75x8.5x1" deep boxed skill toy game for up to four players. A 4x6.5" die-cut cardboard Mickey figure with paper label inserts into a wood stand. - **$125 $250 $450**

MKY-1121   MKY-1122

MKY-1126

❑ **MKY-1126. "Mickey Mouse" Celluloid Nodder With Box,**
1930s. "Made In Japan" 7" tall. Swinging pendulum rubber-band operating mechanism.
Box - **$100 $200 $400**
Nodder - **$200 $400 $800**

MICKEY MOUSE, MINNIE & NEPHEWS

MKY-1127

MKY-1127. Street Vendor Wind-Up,
1930s. Lithographed figure is 5.75" tall with built-in key on back. Marked "Made In Germany." When wound, monkeys swing back and forth as vendor raises and lowers his arm and his eyes move. - **$300 $600 $1200**

MKY-1128

MKY-1128. "Mickey Mouse" Tin Litho Clickers,
1930s. 1.5" tall tin litho. Six different each featuring Mickey with a different musical instrument. Each - **$35 $65 $125**

MKY-1129

MKY-1130

MKY-1129. Mickey Mouse Wind-Up,
1930s. Schuco, Germany. 4" tall. Velveteen-covered body. Does somersaults when wound. - **$150 $250 $500**

MKY-1130. Minnie Mouse Small Carousel Wind-Up,
1930s. Made In Japan. 7.5" tall with celluloid figure on painted metal base.
Toy - **$500 $1000 $1650**
Box - **$200 $500 $1000**

MKY-1131

MKY-1131. Mickey Mouse Small Carousel With Original Box,
1930s. Made In Japan. 7.5" tall with celluloid figure on painted metal base. Box is 3.5x5.5x2.75" deep. Box - **$300 $600 $1200**
Toy - **$600 $1200 $1800**

MKY-1132

MKY-1132. "Mickey Mouse As Cowboy On Pluto" Celluloid Wind-Up,
1930s. Made In Japan. Celluloid figures, plus paper hat on Mickey, on wood base. Toy is 8" long by 7.5" tall. Box is 5.5x8.25x2.5" deep. Box - **$750 $1500 $2500**
Toy - **$1200 $2500 $4250**

MKY-1133

MKY-1134

MKY-1133. Mickey And Minnie See-Saw In Original Box,
1930s. Made In Japan. Toy is 5" tall by 6" wide with celluloid figures on painted metal base. Operates by means of pendulum and wind-up rubberband mechanism. Box is 2.5x2.5x2.75" deep. Box - **$200 $400 $600**
Toy - **$300 $750 $1250**

MKY-1134. Mickey And Minnie See-Saw With Overhead Umbrella,
1930s. Made In Japan. Toy stands 7.5" tall. - **$750 $1300 $2000**

MICKEY MOUSE, MINNIE & NEPHEWS

MKY-1135

❑ **MKY-1135. "Mickey & Minnie Mouse Motoring" Wind-Up,**
1930s. Made In Japan. Toy is 2.25" tall by 5.5" long with celluloid figures on painted tin three-wheeled vehicle. Box is 4.75x5.5x2.75" deep.
Box - **$350 $700 $1400**
Toy - **$325 $650 $1350**

MKY-1136

❑ **MKY-1136. Donald Duck And Minnie Mouse Celluloid Wind-Up,**
1930s. Japan. 2x5x4.75" tall. - **$1000 $2000 $3000**

MKY-1137

❑ **MKY-1137. Celluloid "Mickey Mouse Whirligig" On Ball Wind-up,**
1930s. Made In Japan. Celluloid toy is 9.5" tall on small wooden base. Box is 2.5x2.75x8" tall.
Box - **$400 $800 $1600**
Toy - **$400 $800 $1600**

MKY-1138

❑ **MKY-1138. "Mickey Mouse And Minnie Mouse As Acrobats" Boxed Wind-Up,**
1930s. Nifty toy distributed by Borgfeldt. Box is 6.25x13x1.75" deep. Toy consists of 12.5" wire rods with pair of 5" cello figures. Box - **$400 $800 $1200**
Toy - **$200 $400 $800**

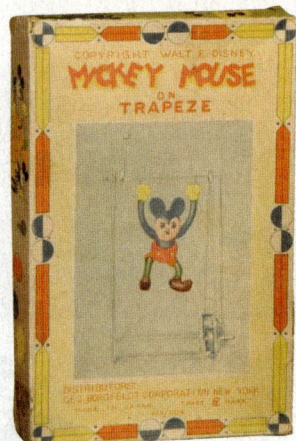

MKY-1139

❑ **MKY-1139. "Mickey Mouse On Trapeze" Boxed Wind-Up,**
1930s. Japan. Distributed by Borgfeldt. Mickey celluloid is 4" tall with 6.5" tall trapeze.
Box - **$200 $400 $800**
Toy - **$150 $300 $600**

MKY-1140

❑ **MKY-1140. "Mickey & Minnie Acrobat" Boxed Wind-Up,**
1930s. 8" tall with celluloid figures. Marked "Australia". Box - **$200 $400 $800**
Toy - **$200 $400 $800**

MICKEY MOUSE, MINNIE & NEPHEWS

MKY-1141

❑ **MKY-1141. "Mickey & Pluto Runabout" Boxed Wind-Up,**
1930s. Borgfeldt. Made In Japan. Walt E. Disney. Box is 5x7.5x3" deep. Toy is 2.5x9x4.5" tall. Box - **$300 $600 $1200**
Toy - **$450 $900 $1500**

MKY-1142

❑ **MKY-1142. "Mickey & Pluto" Wind-Up Toy With Box,**
1930s. Borgfeldt. 8" long.
Box - **$300 $600 $1200**
Toy - **$450 $900 $1500**

MKY-1143

❑ **MKY-1143. Mickey Mouse Felt Figure In Wind-Up Car,**
1930s. Schuco, Germany. Copyright Walt E. Disney. 3.75" long by 4.5" tall to top of ball. - **$1500 $3000 $6000**

MKY-1144

❑ **MKY-1144. Mickey Mouse Carousel Toy Wind-Up,**
1930s. Wheeled tin base holds 5.75" celluloid Mickey. Eight celluloid rods hold celluloid balls and dimensional celluloid figures of Mickey, Minnie, Donald and Pluto. Toy - **$800 $2000 $3750**
Box (Not Shown) - **$1000 $2000 $4000**

MKY-1145

❑ **MKY-1145. "Mickey Mouse On Rocking Horse" Boxed Wind-Up,**
1930s. Mickey 4.5" celluloid on wood horse and base 3.5x5.75x7.75" long. Box is 6.75x7.75x3.5" deep. Box - **$1000 $2000 $3000**
Toy - **$1000 $2000 $3000**

MICKEY MOUSE, MINNIE & NEPHEWS

MKY-1146

☐ **MKY-1146. Mickey Mouse Riding Horse Celluloid Wind-Up,**
1930s. 6" tall. "Marked Made In Japan". - $600 $1200 $2250

MKY-1147

☐ **MKY-1147. Mickey Mouse Cowboy Celluloid On Wooden Horse,**
1930s. Figure (probably missing stiff paper cowboy hat) is 4.75" on jointed horse 4.75" tall by 7" long. - $600 $1200 $2500

MKY-1148

☐ **MKY-1148. Minnie Mouse And Elmer Dancing Celluloid Wind-Up,**
1930s. Japan. 3.75" tall. Box not shown. Box - $1500 $2500 $4000
Toy - $1200 $2150 $3250

MKY-1149

☐ **MKY-1149. "Crawling Mickey Mouse" Celuloid Toy With Original Box,**
1930s. Paradise Novelty. 5" tall.
Box - $500 $1000 $2000
Toy - $500 $1000 $2000

MKY-1150

☐ **MKY-1150. Acrobat Toy,**
1930s. Action toy featuring small 1.75" tall celluloid Mickey figure attached to thin metal trapeze unit with overall size of 1.75" wide by 3.5" tall. - $125 $275 $550

MKY-1151

☐ **MKY-1151. "Mickey Mouse" Flip Book,**
1930s. Moviescope Corp. 1.75x2.5" with title "Mickey Mouse In Actual Motion Pictures (Series A)." Mickey is playing piano on page fronts, page backs depict Mickey and Minnie dancing. - $100 $200 $325

MKY-1152

☐ **MKY-1152. "Mickey Mouse In Actual Motion Pictures" Flip Book,**
1930s. Moviescope Corp. 1.75x2.25" "Series D". - $100 $200 $325

MICKEY MOUSE, MINNIE & NEPHEWS

MKY-1153

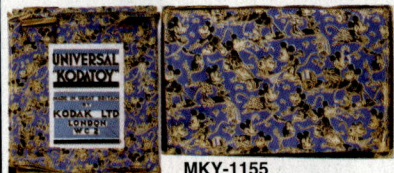

MKY-1155

MKY-1156

❏ **MKY-1153. "Mickey Mouse" Boxed Films,**
1930s. Keystone Mfg. Co. Each box is 3.75x3.75x1" deep with 16mm black and white film. Films are loops, not on reels, designed to be projected as "Continuous Show." Includes "1050 Oh Suzannah, 1054 To The Rescue, 1055 The Covered Wagon." Each - **$15 $25 $50**

❏ **MKY-1155. Mickey English Boxed Projector,**
1930s. "Kodak Ltd., London." 8.5x12x13" tall boxed electrical 16mm film projector and accessories. Entire box except label area has repeated images of Mickey and Minnie doing various types of yard work. Boxed - **$200 $400 $600**

❏ **MKY-1156. "Mickey Mouse Safe-Toy Cinema" Boxed Electric Film Projector,**
1930s. English By Ensign. 9x10x5" deep illustrated box contains 3x9x6.5" tall metal projector and 9mm film. Box - **$250 $500 $800**
Projector - **$115 $225 $400**
Boxed Film - **$12 $25 $50**

MKY-1157

❏ **MKY-1157. "Mickey Mouse Lantern Slides" English Set,**
1930s. Ensign Ltd., London. 3.5x3.5x1.25" deep boxed single complete set from a series of ten different Mickey sets listed on one side of box label. This example is set "G/The Delivery Boy," consisting of eight different slides produced by arrangement from "The Mickey Mouse Movie Stories Published By Dean & Son Ltd." Slides are comprised of a pair of glass plates with heavy cellophane sheet sandwiched between them and black paper border seal around edges of glass. - **$40 $80 $160**

MKY-1154

❏ **MKY-1154. "Mickey Mouse Movie Jecktor" With Films,**
1930s. The Movie Jecktor Co. 10x10x5" tall tin projector in box comes with original cord with special adapter and original bulb. Has decal of Mickey on top. Boxed paper films on wooden spools included both Disney and non-Disney titles. Box - **$125 $250 $500**
Projector - **$115 $225 $400**
Boxed Disney Film - **$12 $25 $50**

MICKEY MOUSE, MINNIE & NEPHEWS

MKY-1158

❑ **MKY-1158. "Cine Mickey" Boxed Movie Projector,**
1930s. Made in France. 6.5x9.25x2.25" deep box with paper label on the lid contains 4x6.5x4" tall projector. Boxed - **$150 $300 $550**

MKY-1159

❑ **MKY-1159. Mickey Mouse Flicker Picture Card,**
1930s. 2.25x3" cardboard cover with oval opening. Features image of Mickey using a punching bag. - **$40 $65 $125**

MKY-1160   MKY-1161

❑ **MKY-1160. "Mickey Mouse" Pocketknife,**
1930s. Knife is 2.75" long with celluloid grips and single metal blade. One Blade - **$75 $150 $300**
Two Blade Version - **$100 $175 $350**

❑ **MKY-1161. Mickey Mouse Four-Blade Pocket Knife,**
1930s. Imperial. 3.75" long. - **$85 $200 $400**

MKY-1162

MKY-1163

❑ **MKY-1162. Mickey Mouse English Target,**
1930s. Chad Valley Co. 10.5" diameter thick cardboard. - **$75 $150 $300**

❑ **MKY-1163. "Mickey Mouse Quoits" Target,**
1930s. Thick wood 18.25" square English toy by Chad Valley Co. Ltd. Board has paper cover target design of Mickey Mouse holding bullseye, also used on circular target boards by this maker. This target is for "Quoits" ring-tossing and has thirteen hook pegs extending outward. - **$150 $300 $600**

MKY-1164

❑ **MKY-1164. "Mickey Mouse Thermometer" Variety,**
1930s. Character Art Manufacturing Co. 3.5" diameter by .75" deep metal frame with tin litho thermometer insert. Round case variety rather than octagon. - **$200 $400 $600**

MKY-1165

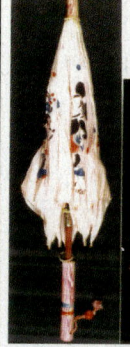 

MKY-1166

❑ **MKY-1165. Thermometer Plaque,**
1930s. Steel frame is 3.25x3.25x.75" deep pressed with tin lithograph thermometer insert under glass. - **$125 $275 $550**

❑ **MKY-1166. Mickey Mouse Umbrella,**
1930s. Authorized "Made In Japan" parasol with 19.5" long wood shaft, inner metal struts, and silk-like fabric cover opening to 24" diameter. - **$100 $200 $300**

MKY-1167

❑ **MKY-1167. Mailing Envelope,**
1930s. Paper envelope is 4.75x6.5" unidentified for original content but believed to be the mailer for Mickey Mouse Recipe Scrapbook. - **$12 $25 $40**

MICKEY MOUSE, MINNIE & NEPHEWS

MKY-1168

❑ **MKY-1168. "Mickey Mouse Composition Book,"**
1930s. Powers Paper Co. 6.75x8.25". Stiff brown paper cover has design on front of Mickey and Minnie carrying books. - **$30 $65 $135**

MKY-1169

❑ **MKY-1169. "Dixon's Mickey Mouse Map Of The United States,"**
1930s. Dixon. 9.75x14.25" came with larger version pencil boxes which had pull-out drawers. - **$30 $60 $125**

MKY-1170

❑ **MKY-1170. "Mickey Mouse" Pencil Box,**
1930s. Dixon. Box is 4x8.25x.75" with snap closure lid. - **$50 $100 $150**

MKY-1171

MKY-1172

❑ **MKY-1171. "Mickey Mouse" Pencil Box With "Mickey Mouse" Contents,**
1930s. Dixon. 6x8.75x.75"deep. Inside has images of Mickey, Minnie and Pluto and also includes 1.75" diameter gold tin "Dixon Saving Bank," an eraser with image of Mickey, pencil and 8" wooden ruler. With Contents - **$100 $200 $300**
Box Only - **$50 $100 $150**

❑ **MKY-1172. "Mickey Mouse" Pencil Box,**
1930s. Dixon. 5.5x10.5x1" deep stiff cardboard box. Interior has repeated images of Mickey, Minnie and Pluto. - **$50 $100 $150**

MKY-1173

❑ **MKY-1173. "Mickey Mouse Parade" Pencil Box With Complete Contents,**
1930s. Dixon. 5.75x10.75x1.25" deep stiff cardboard box. Both top and bottom have different scenes of Mickey and friends in band motif. Has metal snap closure with paper lining featuring repeated Disney character images. Has separate storage tray that holds 9.75x14" "Dixon's Mickey Mouse Map Of The United States." Also includes wooden Mickey ruler, protractor colored pencil. Box - **$50 $100 $150**
Map - **$30 $60 $125**
Ruler - **$10 $15 $25**

MKY-1174

❑ **MKY-1174. Mickey Mouse Figural Pencil Box Varieties,**
1930s. Dixon 5x8.5x.5" thick. Usual variety has a cream background. Rare variety has an orange background.
Cream Version - **$100 $250 $400**
Orange Version - **$150 $350 $550**

MKY-1175

❑ **MKY-1175. Minnie Mouse Figural Pencil Box,**
1930s. Dixon #2761. 5.75x8.5x.5" thick. - **$125 $225 $400**

546

MICKEY MOUSE, MINNIE & NEPHEWS

MKY-1176

MKY-1177

❏ **MKY-1176. "Mickey Mouse Dixon Student Set,"**
1930s. Box is 4x8.5x.5" deep and numbered "3102." Includes ruler with Mickey images, pencil with "Mickey Mouse" name, eraser with Mickey image. Box Only - **$40 $75 $125** Ruler, Pencil, Eraser Each - **$10 $15 $25**

❏ **MKY-1177. "Mickey Mouse" Pencil Box,**
1930s. Dixon. 3.5x8x.75" deep paper-covered cardboard with snap closure on top of lid. Front illustration is Mickey with bow and arrows shooting at apple on Donald's head. - **$50 $100 $150**

MKY-1178

❏ **MKY-1178. "Mickey Mouse" Pencil Box,**
1930s. Dixon. 4.25x8.25x.5" deep paper-covered cardboard. - **$60 $120 $175**

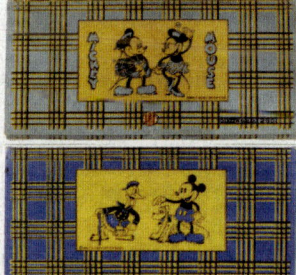

MKY-1179

❏ **MKY-1179. "Mickey Mouse" Pencil Box,**
1930s. Dixon. 4x8.75x.75" deep cardboard box. - **$50 $100 $150**

MKY-1180

MKY-1181

❏ **MKY-1180. Mickey Mouse Figural Pencil Box,**
1930s. Dixon. 3.25x8.25x5" deep box with stiff cardboard side panels plus die-cut thin cardboard front and back panels. - **$300 $600 $1000**

❏ **MKY-1181. "Mickey Mouse" Pencil Box,**
1930s. Dixon. 5.75x9x1.25" deep slightly textured paper-covered cardboard box with snap closure. - **$75 $150 $250**

MKY-1182

MKY-1183

❏ **MKY-1182. "Mickey Mouse" Pencil Box,**
1930s. Dixon. 5x8.5x.75" deep cardboard box with textured paper covering. - **$75 $150 $250**

❏ **MKY-1183. "Mickey Mouse" Pencil Box,**
1930s. Dixon. 6x10.5x1.25" deep textured paper over cardboard box #2918 with snap closure. - **$65 $125 $200**

MKY-1184

❏ **MKY-1184. "Mickey Mouse" Pencil Box With Original Contents,**
1930s. Dixon. 4.5x9.75x2" deep textured paper-covered cardboard box with snap closure and inner two slide-out storage trays. - **$75 $150 $250**

MKY-1185

MICKEY MOUSE, MINNIE & NEPHEWS

MKY-1186

❏ **MKY-1185. Figural Compo Pencil Box,**
1930s. Dixon. 5.5x8.5x1.25" deep painted composition box #2770 with details in high relief on both sides. Cardboard storage tray slides out from top of the box. - **$250 $450 $800**

❏ **MKY-1186. "Mickey Mouse" Vertical Format Pencil Box,**
1930s. Dixon. 5.25x8.75x.75" deep. - **$85 $150 $300**

MKY-1187

❏ **MKY-1187. Mickey/Minnie Mouse Wood Pencil Boxes,**
1930s. Unmarked, but obviously studio artwork. Each is 2.75x8x1.25" deep. Each - **$25 $50 $100**

MKY-1188

❏ **MKY-1188. "Mickey Mouse" Pencil Box,**
1930s. Dixon #2525. 5x8.5x1.25" deep textured paper-covered cardboard box with snap closure. Lid features circus theme illustration with Mickey as ringmaster, Donald riding a seal while dangling a fish in front of its face. Complete With Contents - **$85 $175 $325**
Without Contents - **$50 $125 $250**

MKY-1189

❏ **MKY-1189. "Mickey Mouse/Donald Duck" Pencil Box,**
1930s. Dixon. 4.5x8.5x.75" deep cardboard box with textured paper covering. - **$85 $150 $300**

MKY-1190

❏ **MKY-1190. "Mickey Mouse" Pencil Box,**
1930s. Dixon, 5x8.5x.75" deep textured paper-covered cardboard box with label on lid. Label notes "Weston's Crackerettes" and box was apparently issued as a premium for them. - **$100 $200 $400**

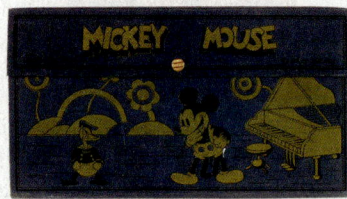

MKY-1191

❏ **MKY-1191. "Mickey Mouse" Pencil Box With Ruler,**
1930s. Dixon. 5.75x10.5x1.25" deep textured paper-covered cardboard pencil box with snap closure. This box is #" 2714." Box - **$40 $75 $150**
Ruler - **$10 $15 $25**

MKY-1192

❏ **MKY-1192. Mickey Mouse Full Color Pencil Box,**
1930s. "Made in Japan." 9" long. Depicts Mickey and his nephews, Clarabell, and Donald Duck. - **$100 $200 $400**

MKY-1193

MKY-1194

❏ **MKY-1193. Mickey Moving Head Celluloid Pencil Holder,**
1930s. Base is 1.75" in diameter by 3" tall with celluloid figure of Mickey. Attached to front of base is crescent-shaped celluloid piece which may serve as a rest for pencil. - **$150 $300 $550**

❏ **MKY-1194. Mickey Mouse Pencil Holder,**
1930s. Dixon. 1.25x2.25x4.75" tall painted composition. - **$100 $200 $350**

MICKEY MOUSE, MINNIE & NEPHEWS

MKY-1195

❏ **MKY-1195. Mickey Pencil Holder,** 1930s. Unmarked but Spanish 3.75x4.25x1.5" deep painted jigsawed wood figure with attachment on back designed to hold twelve pencils. - **$100 $200 $300**

MKY-1196

MKY-1197

❏ **MKY-1196. Minnie Pencil Holder,** 1930s. Unmarked but Spanish 3.75x4.25x1.5" deep painted jigsawed wood figure with attachment on back designed to hold twelve pencils. - **$100 $200 $300**

❏ **MKY-1197. Mickey Mouse Pencil Holder,** 1930s. Spanish. 3.75" diameter by 5.25" tall painted wood. - **$125 $250 $400**

MKY-1198

❏ **MKY-1198. Minnie Mouse Pencil Holder,** 1930s. Spanish. 3x5.5x5.75" tall painted wood. - **$100 $200 $300**

MKY-1199

❏ **MKY-1199. Mickey Mouse Figural Pencil Sharpener,** 1930s. Celluloid 2.75" tall sharpener. - **$175 $300**

MKY-1200

❏ **MKY-1200. "Mickey Mouse" Classic Pose Catalin Plastic Pencil Sharpener,** 1930s. 1 1/8" diameter. - **$125 $250 $500**

MKY-1201

❏ **MKY-1201. Mickey Mouse Catalin Plastic Pencil Sharpener,** 1930s. One of about eight different designs picturing Mickey or Minnie. 1-1/8x1-1/8" square with beveled corners. Each - **$65 $125 $175**

MKY-1202

❏ **MKY-1202. Minnie Mouse Catalin Plastic Pencil Sharpener,** 1930s. 1-1/8" octagon. - **$50 $100 $150**

MKY-1203

❏ **MKY-1203. "Mickey Mouse Colored Pencils,"** 1930s. Dixon. 2.5x5.3/8" deep box contains set of eight pencils. - **$100 $225 $325**

MICKEY MOUSE, MINNIE & NEPHEWS

MKY-1204   MKY-1205

MKY-1207

MKY-1210

❏ **MKY-1204. "Mickey Mouse" Mechanical Pencil,**
1930s. Inkograph Co. 5.25" long with cast metal Mickey head on top plus brass pocket clip. - **$60 $125 $175**

❏ **MKY-1205. "Mickey Mouse Ever-Lasting Soft" True Lead Pencil,**
1930s. "Made In England" Disney copyright 5.5" long solid lead (no wood) pencil with enameled paint covering and silkscreen design including small Mickey image. - **$30 $60 $100**

MKY-1208

❏ **MKY-1207. Mickey English Postcards,**
1930s. Valentine & Sons Ltd. Two, each 3.5x5.5" with hand-colored images, raised border designs and glossy fronts. Each - **$8 $15 $30**

❏ **MKY-1208. Mickey English Postcards,**
1930s. Valentine & Sons Ltd. Two 3.5x5.5", one with scalloped border and the other with raised border. - **$8 $15 $30**

❏ **MKY-1210. Mickey Mouse English Postcards,**
1930s. Inter-Art Co. Each is 3x5.5". Series #7087, 7088. Each - **$10 $20 $40**

MKY-1211

MKY-1212

MKY-1206

❏ **MKY-1206. Hand-Colored French Mickey Postcard,**
1930s. Card is 3.75x5.25" with text underneath "Bonne Annee." - **$15 $25 $45**

MKY-1209

❏ **MKY-1209. "Micky-Maus" German Postcard,**
1930s. Stiff glossy paper card 3.5x5.5". - **$35 $75 $125**

❏ **MKY-1211. Mickey Mouse English Postcards,**
1930s. Woolstone Bros. Each is 3x5.5". Series #512, 517. Each **$10 $20 $40**

❏ **MKY-1212. "Mickey Mouse" English Postcard,**
1930s. G. Delgado Ltd., London. 3.5x5.5". Title is "We're In Luck's Way Down Here." - **$20 $40 $65**

MKY-1213

550

MICKEY MOUSE, MINNIE & NEPHEWS

MKY-1214

□ **MKY-1213. "Mickey Mouse" English Postcard,**
1930s. G. Delgado Ltd., London. 3.5x5.5". Title is "I Am Glad To Say That We Are 'Jogging Along' As Usual." - **$20 $40 $65**

□ **MKY-1214. "Mickey Mouse" English Postcard,**
1930s. G. Delgado Ltd., London. 3.5x5.5". Title is "Little Man You've Had A Bee'sy Day." - **$20 $40 $65**

MKY-1215

□ **MKY-1215. German Postcard,**
1930s. Glossy art depiction is 3.5x5.5". - **$25 $50 $75**

MKY-1216

MKY-1217

□ **MKY-1216. English Postcards,**
1930s. "Inter-Art Company." Four 3x5.5" unused postcards from a numbered series. These examples are 7095-"You're Such A Comfort To Me," 7094-"Now Where Is That Billy Cat?," 7091-"Here's Something To Tickle You," 7085-"I Like What You Like-And You Like What I Like." Each - **$10 $20 $40**

□ **MKY-1217. German Postcard,**
1930s. Vertical format card is 3.5x5.5" published for the French market. Front has slightly raised gold text "Bonne Annee," translating literally to Maid Year, apparently for a first anniversary. - **$20 $40 $75**

MKY-1218

□ **MKY-1218. "Walt Disney" European Postcard,**
1930s. Unmarked. 4-1/8x5.75". Glossy front and blank back. Walt holds 1932 achievement certificate from Academy of Motion Picture Arts and Sciences. - **$10 $20 $40**

MKY-1219

□ **MKY-1219. Mickey Mouse Foreign Postcard,**
1930s. Likely Netherlands. 3.5x5.5" with winter scene on the front plus text "Haad Uut Aastat." - **$20 $40 $65**

MKY-1220

MKY-1221

□ **MKY-1220. "Mickey Mouse" Stationery,**
1930s Powers Paper Co. 6.5x9.5x1" deep box with 24 sheets of paper and 24 envelopes. Boxed - **$100 $200 $300**

□ **MKY-1221. "Mickey Mouse" Composition Book,**
1930s. "Hilroy Series No. 3520" school tablet with 32 lined pages. - **$25 $60 $100**

MICKEY MOUSE, MINNIE & NEPHEWS

MKY-1222

❏ **MKY-1222.** "Mickey Mouse" Composition Books,
1930s. Hilroy. Each is 7x9.25" Series #3520. Each - **$25 $60 $100**

MKY-1223

❏ **MKY-1223.** Mickey Mouse Birthday Card,
1930s. English by Wm. E. Coutts Co. Ltd. 4x4.25". - **$20 $40 $60**

MKY-1224

❏ **MKY-1224.** Mickey Mouse English Christmas Card,
c. 1930s. Valentine & Sons Ltd. 4.5x4.5" stiff paper. - **$20 $30 $45**

MKY-1225

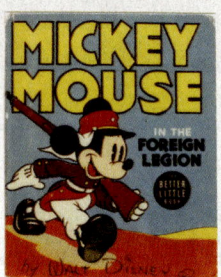

MKY-1226

❏ **MKY-1225.** Mickey "Sunoco" Blotter,
1940. Blotter is 4x6.75". - **$50 $100 $150**

❏ **MKY-1226.** "Mickey Mouse In The Foreign Legion" Better Little Book,
1940. Whitman. Better Little Book #1428. - **$30 $90 $210**

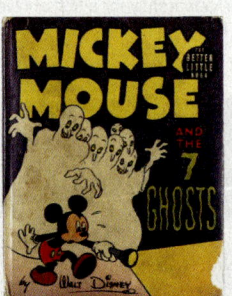

MKY-1227

❏ **MKY-1227.** "Mickey Mouse And The 7 Ghosts" Better Little Book,
1940. Whitman. Book #1475. - **$30 $90 $210**

MKY-1228

❏ **MKY-1228.** "Walt Disney's Wild West" English Hardcover,
1940. Juvenile Productions Ltd. 8x10x1.25" thick with 128 pages. Has two full color plates. - **$115 $225 $400**

MKY-1229

MKY-1230

❏ **MKY-1229.** "Mickey Mouse Annual" English Hardcover,
1940. Book is 6.25x8.5x2" thick with 124 pages. Among the scarcest of pre-war annuals. - **$300 $600 $1000**

❏ **MKY-1230.** "Mickey Mouse Weekly" Example English Newspaper,
1940. Volume 5, #232 is 10.5x14" with 8 pages. Original run began February 8, 1936 and continued into the 1950s. Typical Example Pre-1950 - **$10 $15 $30**
1950's Example - **$5 $8 $12**

MKY-1231

❏ **MKY-1231.** Fuel Oil Blotter Card,
c. 1940. "Sunheat Furnace Oil." 3.25x6" cardboard. - **$100 $200 $300**

MICKEY MOUSE, MINNIE & NEPHEWS

MKY-1232

❏ **MKY-1232. "Walt Disney's Ski-Jump Target Game,"**
1940. American Toy Works. 13.25x19.5x2" deep box. Cardboard target board is 13x18.5" with paper label on front. Came with gun and darts. - **$175 $350 $700**

MKY-1233

❏ **MKY-1233. "Mickey Mouse Drummer" Pull Toy,**
1941. Fisher-Price. 4x7.5x8.5" tall mostly wood pull toy #476, first introduced in 1941 for five years. - **$100 $200 $350**

MKY-1234

❏ **MKY-1234. Mickey Mouse Pencil Drawing From Canine Caddie,**
1941. 10x12" sheet of animation paper with 4x5" image. "4" from a numbered sequence.
- **$125 $250 $500**

MKY-1235

553

MICKEY MOUSE, MINNIE & NEPHEWS

❏ **MKY-1235.** "Mickey Mouse Annual" Hardcover,
1941. English by Dean & Son Ltd. 6.25x8.5x1.75" thick with 128 pages. - **$100 $200 $400**

MKY-1236

❏ **MKY-1236.** Mickey "Sunoco Oil" Ink Blotter,
1942. Blotter is 3.5x6". - **$35 $65 $100**

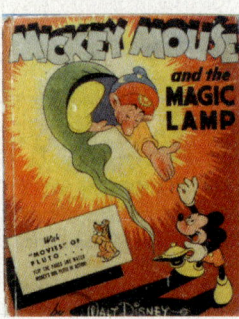

MKY-1237

❏ **MKY-1237.** "Mickey Mouse And The Magic Lamp" Better Little Book,
1942. Whitman. Book #1429. - **$30 $90 $210**

MKY-1238

❏ **MKY-1238.** "Mickey Mouse And Pluto,"
1942. Dell Publishing Co. 4x5.5" with 192 pages. - **$50 $100 $200**

MKY-1239

MKY-1240

❏ **MKY-1239.** "Mickey Mouse Annual" English Book,
1942. Dean & Son Ltd. 6.5x8.5" hardcover with 1.5" thickness from 192 stiff paper pages. - **$125 $250 $500**

❏ **MKY-1240.** "Walt Disney Character Plaks,"
c. 1942. Youngstown Pressed Steel Co. Five 11x14.5" envelopes containing rigid cardboard parts for assembling and coloring dimensional wall plaques picturing Mickey, Donald, Bambi, Thumper, Flower plus Pluto, not shown by example photo. Completed plaques are each 10.5x14". Mickey and Donald Each In Envelope - **$20 $30 $75** Others in Envelope - **$15 $25 $50**

MKY-1241

MKY-1242

❏ **MKY-1241.** "Minnie Shows You The Way To A Lustron Cold Permanent" Beautician Instruction Book,
1943. Spiral bound hardcover 9x11.5" with 20 pages for "Professional Visual Training Guide" with illustrations by Walt Disney. - **$100 $200 $350**

❏ **MKY-1242.** "Mickey Mouse And The Dude Ranch Bandit" Better Big Little Book,
1943. Whitman. Better Little Book #1471 version with 352 pages and back cover text on yellow background with list of other Big Little Books. Last two pages also list additional Big Little Book titles. - **$25 $75 $150**

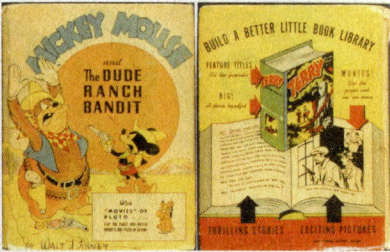

MKY-1243

❏ **MKY-1243.** "Mickey Mouse And The Dude Ranch Bandit" Better Big Little Book,
1943. Whitman. Better Little Book #1471 version with 432 pages. Back cover has color ad for Better Little Books. - **$30 $90 $210**

MICKEY MOUSE, MINNIE & NEPHEWS

MKY-1244

MKY-1245

MKY-1246

MKY-1247

❑ **MKY-1244.** "Mickey Mouse Annual" English Hardcover,
1943. Dean & Son Ltd. 6.5x8.75x1.5" thick with 192 pages. - **$100 $200 $350**

❑ **MKY-1245.** "Mickey Mouse On The Cave-Man Island" Better Little Book,
1944. Whitman. Book #1499. - **$27 $81 $190**

❑ **MKY-1246.** "Mickey Mouse Annual,"
1944. Dean & Sons Ltd. English hardcover 6.5x8.5" with 192 pages. - **$200 $400 $750**

❑ **MKY-1247.** "Mickey Sees The U.S.A." Hardcover.
1944. D. C. Heath & Co. 6.25x8.25" with 144 pages. From "Walt Disney Storybooks" educational series and this is one of the more advanced reader books. - **$25 $50 $100**

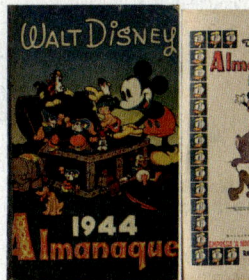

MKY-1248

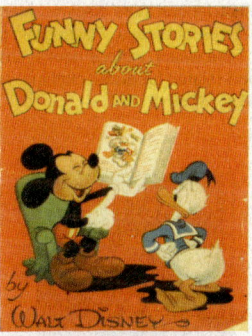

MKY-1249

❑ **MKY-1248.** "Walt Disney 1944 Almanaque" Brazilian Hardcover,
1944. Book is 8.25x13.5" with 104 pages based on Disney shorts and other stories. - **$100 $200 $350**

❑ **MKY-1249.** "Funny Stories About Donald And Mickey By Walt Disney,"
1945. Whitman. 8.25x10.75" with 128 pages. - **$30 $60 $125**

MKY-1250

MKY-1251

❑ **MKY-1250.** "Mickey Mouse Annual"
English Hardcover,
1945. Dean & Son Ltd. 6.5x8.5x1.25" thick with 192 pages. - **$125 $250 $400**

❑ **MKY-1251.** "Western Family" Magazine With Mickey Thanksgiving Cover,
1945. Measures 8.5x11.25" with 32 pages. - **$10 $20 $40**

MKY-1252

❑ **MKY-1252.** "Mickey Mouse And The 'Lectro Box'" Better Little Book,
1946. Whitman. Book #1413. - **$19 $57 $135**

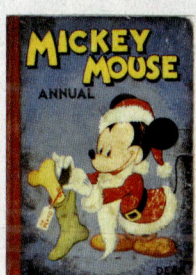

MKY-1253

❑ **MKY-1253.** "Mickey Mouse Annual" English Hardcover,
1946. Dean & Son Ltd. 6.5x8.5x1.25" thick with 192 pages. - **$75 $150 $300**

MICKEY MOUSE, MINNIE & NEPHEWS

MKY-1254

❏ **MKY-1254. Mickey Mouse Wristwatch Boxed,**
1946. Kelton/US Time. 2x9.5x1" deep cardboard box with hinge lid containing watch in 1x1.5" 10K gold-plated case with original leather straps plus packaging leaflet and original $12.50 price tag. Dial features separate die-cut tin Mickey head and hands which point at the numerals. His head is on a post and designed to rotate with hour hand. This is the version with all twelve numerals and no Kelton name on the dial, the first post-WWII Mickey watch produced. Box - **$50 $100 $200**
Watch - **$250 $600 $1200**

MKY-1255

❏ **MKY-1255. Willie The Giant Pencil Drawing.** 1947. Animation paper is 10x12" with large 7x9" image from "Mickey And The Beanstalk". - **$60 $125 $225**

MKY-1256

❏ **MKY-1256. "Mickey And The Beanstalk" Record Set,**
1947. Set comes in 10.5x12" album containing three 78-rpm records on the Capitol label. Has 40-page booklet bound inside. - **$25 $50 $100**

MKY-1257

❏ **MKY-1257. "Walt Disney Character Merchandise 1947-1948" Retailer's Catalogue,**
1947. 9x12" with glossy stiff paper covers and 100 pages featuring black and white photographs. Items include American Pottery figurines, Ben Cooper costumes, Fisher-Price pull toys, Gund stuffed dolls, Jaymar puzzles, Leeds China items, various store displays, Marx wind-up toys, Sun Rubber toys, Transogram paint sets, US Time watch, various books, sheet music, food-related products, clothing, much more. - **$325 $650 $1200**

MKY-1258

MKY-1259

❏ **MKY-1258. "Mickey Mouse And The Lazy Daisy Mystery" Better Little Book,**
1947. Whitman. Book #1433. - **$20 $55 $110**

❏ **MKY-1259. "Mickey Mouse Annual" English Hardcover,**
1947. Dean & Son Ltd. 7.75x10" with 128 pages including full color plate of Mickey, Minnie, Goofy and Pluto. - **$25 $50 $100**

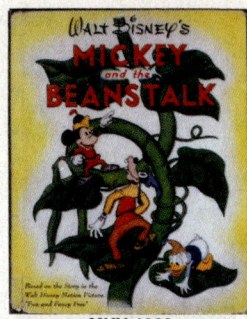

MKY-1260

❏ **MKY-1260. "Mickey And The Beanstalk" Hardcover,**
1947. Grosset & Dunlap. 7x8.25" with 32 pages. - **$75 $150 $300**

MKY-1261

❏ **MKY-1261. Mickey Mouse Silver Bowl,**
1947. International Sterling silver children's bowl. - **$75 $225 $350**

MKY-1262

MICKEY MOUSE, MINNIE & NEPHEWS

❑ **MKY-1262.** "Mickey Mouse Library Of Games,"
1947. Russell Mfg. Co. 2x5.75x2.5" tall open box with foil label on the front contains complete set of six individually boxed card games. - **$75 $200 $325**

MKY-1263

MKY-1264

❑ **MKY-1263.** "Mickey Mouse Alarm Clock,"
1947. Ingersoll/U.S. Time 4.75x4.75x3.25" tall box contains 4.5" alarm clock. Comes with generic guarantee paper plus original $2.95 price tag. Box - **$100 $200 $400**
Clock - **$100 $200 $400**

❑ **MKY-1264.** Mickey Mouse Wristwatch,
1947. U. S. Time 1x1.5" silvered metal case marked "Ingersoll/U.S. Time." Has original red leather straps. - **$60 $125 $175**

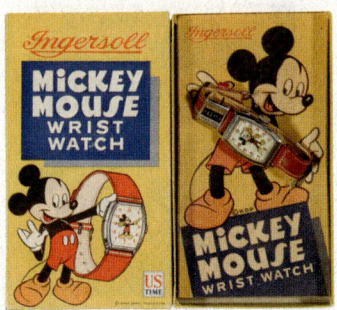
MKY-1265

❑ **MKY-1265.** "Mickey Mouse Wristwatch" Box,
1947. U.S. Time. 4x7x1" deep box with nicely illustrated insert. - **$75 $150 $300**

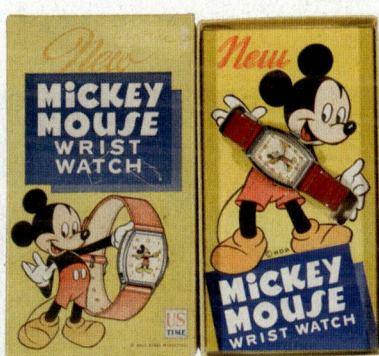
MKY-1266

❑ **MKY-1266.** "Mickey Mouse" Boxed Wrist Watch Variety.
1947. US Time. 4x7x1" deep box with variety text. The word "New" replaces "Ingersoll" on both box and insert. Box - **$100 $200 $400**

MKY-1267

❑ **MKY-1267.** Mickey Mouse And Donald Duck Molded Soap Heads,
c. 1947. Kerk Guild Inc. Each is 3" tall with original 12" long string loop attachment. Each - **$10 $20 $35**

MKY-1268

MKY-1269

❑ **MKY-1268.** "Mickey Mouse" Ceramic Cookie Jar,
c. 1947. Leeds China Co. 5.5x8x11.75" tall Mickey with flowers between his feet. Rare, few known. - **$600 $1250 $2250**

❑ **MKY-1269.** Mickey Mouse Ceramic Bank,
c. 1947. Leeds China Co. 3x4.5x6.5" tall with over-the-glaze paint accents. - **$25 $50 $90**

MKY-1270

❑ **MKY-1270.** "Ritz Theatre Mickey Mouse Club" Button,
c. 1947. 7/8". Uses same image that appears on the 1947 alarm clock by Ingersoll/U.S. Time. - **$100 $225 $350**

MICKEY MOUSE, MINNIE & NEPHEWS

MKY-1271

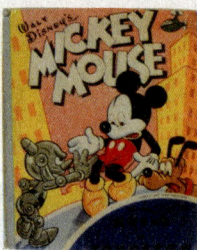

MKY-1272

❏ **MKY-1271.** "Mickey Mouse's Summer Vacation" Premium Book,
1948. Whitman. 4.5x6.25" softcover version from "Story Hour Series," 32 pages. This version was given away with subscriptions to Walt Disney's Comics and Stories. - **$10 $20 $40**

❏ **MKY-1272.** "Mickey Mouse In The World Of Tomorrow" Better Little Book,
1948. Whitman. Book #1444. - **$31 $93 $220**

MKY-1273

❏ **MKY-1273.** "Mickey Mouse And The Desert Palace" Better Little Book,
1948. Whitman. Book #1451. - **$19 $57 $135**

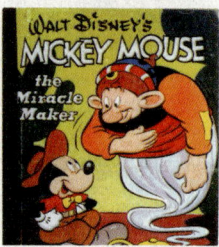

MKY-1274

MKY-1275

❏ **MKY-1274.** "Mickey Mouse The Miracle Maker,"
1948. Whitman. 5.25x5.25" hardcover book from "845" series. - **$20 $50 $100**

❏ **MKY-1275.** "Mickey Mouse And The Boy Thursday,"
1948. Whitman. From series #845. - **$20 $50 $100**

MKY-1276

❏ **MKY-1276.** "Mickey Mouse Annual" English Book,
1948. Dean & Son Ltd. 7.75x9.75" hardcover, 128 pages. - **$30 $60 $110**

MKY-1277

❏ **MKY-1277.** "Mickey And The Beanstalk" Hardcover Premium Issue Book,
1948. Whitman. 5x6.75" with 32 pages from the "Story Hour Series." Comes with original mailing envelope with illustration of Mickey as Santa marked "Do Not Open Until Christmas." Given as premium for subscription to Walt Disney's Comics & Stories. Mailer - **$15 $25 $40** Book - **$10 $25 $60**

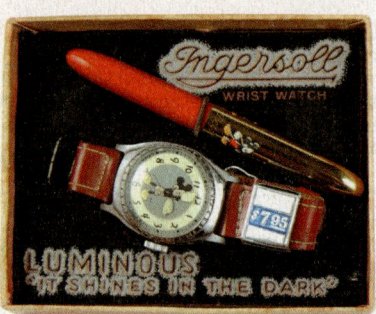

MKY-1278

MKY-1279

❏ **MKY-1278.** Mickey Mouse Luminous Wristwatch,
1948. Ingersoll (U.S. Time). 3.25x4.25x1" deep box with 3.75" long ballpoint pen which has Mickey decal on cap. One of ten in Mickey's 20th birthday series. Birthday theme lid not shown. Boxed - **$250 $700 $1350** Watch Only - **$125 $275 $550**

❏ **MKY-1279.** Mickey And Friends Blotters.
1948. Arlington Trust Co. Lot of four, each 3.75x9". Each - **$5 $15 $25**

MKY-1280

MICKEY MOUSE, MINNIE & NEPHEWS

MKY-1281

☐ **MKY-1280. Minnie Mouse Pencil Drawing From Pluto's Sweater,**
1949. Animation paper is 10x12" with 4.5" image. #3 from a numbered sequence. - **$65 $125 $275**

☐ **MKY-1281. "Mickey Mouse Choo-Choo" Fisher-Price Pull Toy,**
1949. Toy is wood with paper labels measuring 3.5x8.75x7" tall. Toy is #485. - **$75 $150 $275**

MKY-1282

☐ **MKY-1282. "Mickey Mouse And The Stolen Jewels" Better Little Book,**
1949. Whitman. Book #1464. - **$20 $75 $150**

MKY-1283

MKY-1284

☐ **MKY-1283. "Mickey Mouse Annual" English Book,**
1949. Dean & Son Ltd. 7.25x9.75" hardcover, 128 pages. - **$30 $60 $110**

☐ **MKY-1284. Boxed "Mickey Mouse Alarm Clock,"**
1949. Ingersoll/U.S. Time. 2x4x4.5" tall clock with ivory colored plastic case. Box - **$100 $200 $400**
Clock - **$85 $175 $350**

MKY-1285

☐ **MKY-1285. Mickey Mouse Timepieces Ad,**
c. 1949. Ingersoll. Two-page advertisement from magazine totaling 14" tall by 20" wide. - **$5 $10 $15**

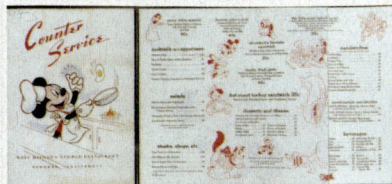

MKY-1286

☐ **MKY-1286. "Walt Disney's Studio Restaurant" Menu,**
1940s. 9.25x12.5" stiff paper. - **$75 $150 $250**

MKY-1287

☐ **MKY-1287. "Walt Disney Character Jewelry" Charm Bracelet On Card,**
1940s. Nemo. 3x8.25" die-cut cardboard display card contains 6" long bracelet with five different three-dimensional hard plastic charms .75" to 1" tall. Card - **$5 $15 $30**
Bracelet - **$10 $20 $40**

MKY-1288

MKY-1289

☐ **MKY-1288. "Walt Disney Character Alphabet" Boxed Set,**
1940s. Plane Facts Co. 12x13.25x1" deep box contains two unpunched thick cardboard sheets with 44 punch-out letters for Disney characters and a block of wood where letters can be placed to spell out words. - **$40 $75 $140**

☐ **MKY-1289. "Mickey Mouse Hingees,"**
1940s. Envelope is 7.5x11.5 and contains unpunched sheet of characters Mickey, Minnie, Donald Pluto and Goofy. - **$35 $75 $150**

MICKEY MOUSE, MINNIE & NEPHEWS

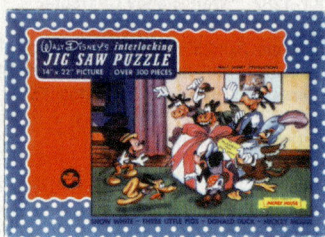

MKY-1290

MKY-1291

MKY-1292

MKY-1293

❏ **MKY-1293. Mickey Pencil Drawing,**
1940s. Animation paper 10x12" with 2.75x4.25" image of Mickey." No. "12" from a numbered sequence. Thought to be for never released jungle theme short with Mickey and Goofy. - **$100 $200 $300**

MKY-1294

❏ **MKY-1294. Minnie Mouse Mexican Ceramic Figurine,**
1940s. 2.5x3x4-3/8" tall similar to the 6.25" tall figurine by Shaw. "Made In Mexico" sticker and foot underside has Disney copyright and Mexico mark. - **$50 $85 $165**

MKY-1295

❏ **MKY-1295. Minnie Mouse Figurine,**
c. 1940s. 7.75" tall painted and glazed ceramic marked "Mexico". Underside marked "21".
- **$50 $100 $200**

MKY-1296

❏ **MKY-1296. Mickey As Santa Planter,**
1940s. Unmarked but Leeds China Co. 3.5x6x6" tall glazed ceramic with over-the-glaze paint on face, outfit, sleigh. - **$35 $75 $125**

MKY-1297

❏ **MKY-1297. "Ingersoll" Mickey And Donald Complete Ring Display,**
1940s. Countertop display 8.25x11" with easel back contains twelve sterling silver rings. Ring tops and bands are in various shapes with various designs. Near Mint Complete - **$1200**
Display Card - **$75 $150 $300**
Each Ring - **$25 $40 $75**

MKY-1298

❏ **MKY-1290. "Walt Disney Jigsaw Puzzle,"**
1940s. Jaymar. 7x10x2" box holds puzzle that measures 14x22" when assembled. - **$15 $30 $50**

❏ **MKY-1291. "Walt Disney's Puzzle Rhymes/Jack And Jill" With Mickey And Minnie Mouse,**
1940s. Canadian by Ontex. 6.5x9.25x1" deep box contains complete three puzzle set. - **$25 $50 $75**

❏ **MKY-1292. "Walt Disney's Parade" Boxed Puzzle,**
1940s. Canadian by Ontex. 6.5x18.75x1" deep box contains complete single puzzle. - **$20 $40 $65**

❏ **MKY-1298. "Turnabout Mickey & Minnie Mouse" Cookie Jar,**
1940s. Leeds China Co. 7x7x13" tall with over-the-glaze paint. - **$125 $225 $400**

MICKEY MOUSE, MINNIE & NEPHEWS

MKY-1299

❑ **MKY-1299. "Disney Playtime Plastics For The Nursery" Dish Set,**
1940s. John Dickinson & Co. Ltd. 9x15x3.5" deep box contains Gadeware Plastics English set. This is "Set No. 2." Pieces with decals are: Egg cup, small beaker with Mickey, large mug with Elmer, servette ring with Goofy, spoon with Thumper, pusher with Fifer Pig and feeding bowl with Pinocchio. - **$60 $125 $175**

MKY-1300

MKY-1301

❑ **MKY-1300. Advertising Blotter,**
1940s. Cardboard is 4x9" with action scene printed at right angle to imprint for a local heavy machinery handler company. Scene title is "It's An Ill Wind." - **$12 $25 $40**

❑ **MKY-1301. "Walt Disney's Wonder Book" English Hardcover,**
1940s. Mardon Sons & Hall Ltd. 8x10.5" with 80 pages. - **$25 $50 $110**

MKY-1302

❑ **MKY-1302. "Mickey's Very First Book" English Book,**
1940s. Wm. Collins Sons & Co. Ltd. 7.25x9.75" hardcover, 44 pages. Content includes 26 alphabet pages with one letter per page featuring 1930s art including pie-eyed Mickey and other early characters, all with different musical instruments or band-related images. Rest of book is stories and art featuring early 1940s Mickey. End paper design depicts Goofy watching Donald chase after Pluto. - **$250 $500 $800**

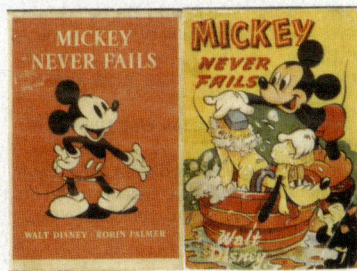

MKY-1303

❑ **MKY-1303. "Mickey Never Fails" Book Varieties,**
1940s. Two variations under same title but different publishers and a decade apart. Earlier 1939 original edition is 6.25x8.5" hardcover from "Walt Disney Storybooks" series by D.C. Heath & Co., 102 pages. Second 1949 edition is English by London and Glasgow, also 102 pages. Story is identical throughout between the two, and both have same full color story art. Difference is cover art of portrait on 1939 version opposed to full color group scene on front and back on 1949 version. Earlier - **$25 $50 $100**
Later - **$20 $40 $90**

MKY-1304

❑ **MKY-1304. "Mickey's Wonder Book" English Hardcover,**
1940s. William Collins Son & Co. Ltd. 8.5x10.75" clothbound edition, 76 pages. - **$20 $40 $85**

MKY-1305

❑ **MKY-1305. "Walt Disney Designed Ash Tray Set,"**
1940s. Kemper-Thomas Co. 4.75x14x1" deep box contains three different clear glass ashtrays, each 4.5x4.5x1" deep. Box - **$30 $60 $100**
Each Tray - **$20 $40 $80**

MKY-1306

561

MICKEY MOUSE, MINNIE & NEPHEWS

MKY-1307

☐ **MKY-1306. "Walt Disney's Jigsaw Lotto,"**
1940s. Jaymar. 7x10x1" deep boxed game. - $10 $20 $40

☐ **MKY-1307. "Journey Through Disneyland" Canadian Game,**
1940s. Ontex Of Canada. 10.75x17.75x1.5" deep boxed game featuring 16x20" railroad route game board plus spinner card and six generic pawns. Board art also relates to Disney film scenes. - $65 $110 $165

MKY-1308

☐ **MKY-1308. Mickey Mouse Trapeze Toy,**
1940s. 8" tall wood frame with 4" long Mickey figure comprised of wood arms and legs, die-cut cardboard body with paper label on each side. This 1940s version is scarcer than the 1930s version. - $50 $100 $150

MKY-1309

MKY-1310

☐ **MKY-1309. "The Disney Derby" Game,**
1940s. Australian by Metal-Wood Repetitions Co., Sidney. 10x10x2.25" deep box contains complete game. Boxed - $65 $125 $225

☐ **MKY-1310. Australian Walt Disney Birthday Cards,**
1940s. Lot of six different die-cut paper cards, each with separate die-cut attachment on front that folds down for three-dimensional effect. Each - $6 $12 $20

MKY-1311

☐ **MKY-1311. "Mickey Mouse Viewer" English Boxed Set,**
1940s. 2.5x2.75x1.5" deep box contains 2.5" long hard plastic viewer and smaller box containing full color "Film Shots." Each is cut frame of actual 35mm full color film. - $40 $60 $100

MKY-1312

☐ **MKY-1312. "Mickey Mouse Viewer" With Boxed Filmstrips,**
1940s. Craftsmen's Guild. 3" long marbled plastic viewer comes with 3.5x5.25" ad paper/order form and eight 1.75x1.75x.75" deep individually boxed filmstrips. Each is a 16mm strip with "16 Scenes Comprising A Complete Condensed Version Of A Famous Disney Picture" and feature actual film scenes. Films are 1 Brave Little Tailor, 2 Three Little Pigs, 4 Chicken Little, 6 The Ugly Duckling, 7 The Grasshopper And The Ants, 9 The Golden Touch, 10 Little Hiawatha, 11 The Pointer (Pluto). Paper - $8 $15 $25
Viewer - $10 $25 $50
Each Box Film - $6 $12 $20

MKY-1313

☐ **MKY-1313. "Mickey Mouse Movie Fun" Boxed Set,**
1940s. Mastercraft Toy Co. Inc. Consists of black metal "Animator" (zoetrope) which is 4" tall with 7" diameter, complete with wood handle that attaches on underside. The "Animator" is designed with die-cut slots around outer edge and has embossed title "Mickey Mouse Movie-Fun." Ten 2x22" strips are inserted in animator to view movie. Five are Disney: Mickey, Donald, Pluto, Bambi and Pinocchio. Five are non-Disney. Boxed - $125 $250 $400

MICKEY MOUSE, MINNIE & NEPHEWS

MKY-1314

☐ **MKY-1314. Mickey Mouse Catalin Plastic Pencil Sharpener,**
1940s. 1" in diameter. - **$40 $65 $100**

MKY-1315

☐ **MKY-1315. "Mickey Mouse" Folder Like Book,**
1940s. Australian. 6.5x14.25" on card stock with three panels which open to length of 19.5". Titled "Mickey's Musical ABC." - **$25 $50 $100**

MKY-1316

☐ **MKY-1316. Mickey And Minnie Dolls By Gund,**
1940s. Pair of matching dolls each 4.5x8x14.5" tall with plush bodies, rubber faces, hands and shoes and felt ears with red bows at neck. Mickey has felt pants and Minnie has bow in her hair, cotton skirt and panties. Each - **$115 $225 $400**

MKY-1317

☐ **MKY-1317. Mickey Mouse On Train Pencil Sharpener,**
1940s. Item is 1.25" long by 1.25" tall painted white metal. Two similar issued with Donald and Pluto. - **$40 $75 $150**

MKY-1318

☐ **MKY-1318. Mickey Mouse Cookies Box,**
1940s. National Biscuit Co. Box is 5" long with a fabric carrying strap. Mickey pictured on back, Minnie and Pluto on sides. - **$125 $250 $400**

MKY-1319

☐ **MKY-1319. Walt Disney Character Frame Tray Puzzles,**
1950. Jaymar. Each is 8.5x11" with four-line poem describing illustration. Each - **$5 $10 $15**

☐ **MKY-1320. Mickey And Donald Duck Golden Record,**
1950. Simon & Schuster. 6.75x7.5" paper sleeve containing 78 rpm yellow vinyl record. - **$6 $12 $20**

MKY-1320

MKY-1321

☐ **MKY-1321. "Playthings November 1950,"**
1950. Volume 48, #11 with 186 pages of toys. Mickey as Santa cover. - **$25 $50 $100**

MKY-1322

MKY-1323

563

MICKEY MOUSE, MINNIE & NEPHEWS

❑ **MKY-1322. "Wheaties Walt Disney Comic Books" Order Form,**
1950. Two-sided paper is 6x6" and issued to promote 1950-1951 premium comic books. - **$6 $12 $25**

❑ **MKY-1323. "Mickey Mouse On The Haunted Island" Better Little Book,**
1950. Whitman. "New Better Little Book" with 3.25x5.5" format, #708-10. - **$15 $45 $85**

MKY-1324

❑ **MKY-1324. "Walt Disney's Hanky Clock,"**
c. 1950. English-made 7.5x7.5" die-cut stiff paper clock-shaped folder designed to hold a hanky. Front has a pair of diecut clock hands. - **$40 $75 $135**

MKY-1325

❑ **MKY-1325. Disney Characters Jell-O Comic Molds Original Art Prototype Sign,**
c. 1950. 12x17" sheet of crescent art board with diecut design and art done in tempera paint. From Gordon Gold Archives. Unique, Very Good - **$525**

MKY-1326

❑ **MKY-1326. Mickey Mouse Glass Figure,**
c. 1950. Occupied Japan. 3.75" tall. - **$25 $50 $75**

MKY-1327

❑ **MKY-1327. "Mickey Crazy Car" With Box,**
c. 1950. Celluloid figure in 4" long tin car with box. "Made In Japan". Box - **$200 $400 $800** Toy - **$500 $1000 $1500**

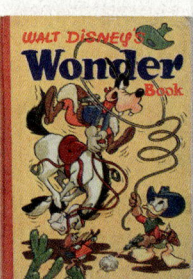

MKY-1328

❑ **MKY-1328. "Walt Disney's Wonder Book" Hardcover,**
c. 1951. English by The Sunshine Press. 8x10.75" with 60 pages. - **$20 $40 $75**

MKY-1329

MKY-1330

❑ **MKY-1329. "Mickey Mouse Paint Box,"**
1952. Transogram. 4.5x5.75x.5" deep tin litho with hinged lid. - **$10 $20 $40**

❑ **MKY-1330. "Mickey Mouse Wristwatch" Variety Box,**
1952. US Time. 3x4.25x5" tall display box in rectangular format, the scarcer variation of two designs also offered in oval box format. Sleeve removes to reveal 4.5" tall diecut Mickey figure with slotted hands for strap of watch originally held. Box Only - **$200 $400 $600**

MKY-1331

❑ **MKY-1331. "Mickey Mouse Ingersoll/U.S. Time" Watch With Rare Packaging ,**
1952. Cardboard presentation box is 3.75x5x5.5" tall with die-cut insert containing watch with 7/8" diameter chromed metal case.
Box - **$175 $375 $550**
Watch - **$35 $65 $100**

MICKEY MOUSE, MINNIE & NEPHEWS

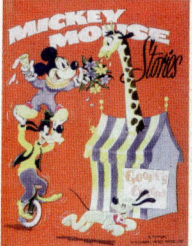 

MKY-1332

❏ **MKY-1332. "Mickey Mouse Stories" Book,**
1952. English by Dean & Son Ltd. 7.5x9.75" with 44 pages. - **$20 $40 $80**

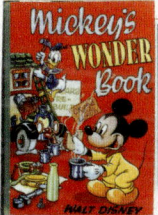  

MKY-1333

 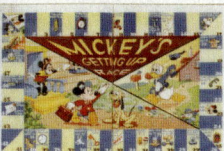

MKY-1334

❏ **MKY-1333. "Mickey's Wonder Book" English Hardcover,**
c. 1952. Collins. 8x10.75" with 80 pages. - **$20 $40 $80**

❏ **MKY-1334. "Mickey Mouse Annual" English Book,**
1953. Dean & Son Ltd. 7.5x9.75" hardcover, 96 pages. - **$25 $50 $100**

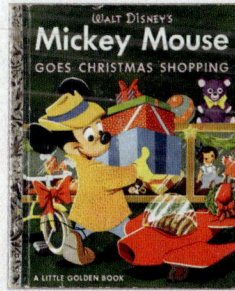

MKY-1335

MKY-1336

❏ **MKY-1335. "Mickey Mouse Goes Christmas Shopping Little Golden Book,"**
1953. Simon & Schuster. 6.5x8" with 28 pages. - **$10 $20 $35**

❏ **MKY-1336. "Tempo" Magazine With Mickey,**
1953. Volume 1, #14. 4.25x6" featuring four-page article titled "The Mouse Who Made Millions" with several pictures of Mickey and one of Walt Disney. - **$10 $20 $35**

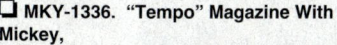

MKY-1337

❏ **MKY-1337. "Walt Disney Stories" Tru-Vue Film Card Set,**
1953. 4x5.75" envelope contains complete set of three "DA-1" series cards for Mickey, Donald and Pluto. Set - **$8 $15 $25**

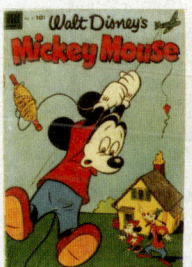 

MKY-1338

MKY-1339

❏ **MKY-1338. Comic Book Cover Concept Art And Actual Comic Book,**
c. 1953. Animation paper is 10x12" centered by 7.5x8" pencil art. For "Mickey Mouse" comic book #31 from 1953 by Dell Publishing Co. Art Unique, Very Fine - **$350**

❏ **MKY-1339. "Cheerios" With Disney 3-D Comic Books,**
1954. Box flat is 13.25x20.5" and advertises the three different sets of 3-D comics that were issued one per package. There were eight comics per set. One side panel lists all 24 titles and front of box has attached pair of 3-D glasses to be cut out. Gordon Gold Archives. Box - **$125 $250 $450**

MKY-1340

❏ **MKY-1340. "Mickey Mouse" Thermos,**
1954. Adco-Liberty. 8.25" tall metal and red plastic cup. - **$250 $600 $1100**

MICKEY MOUSE, MINNIE & NEPHEWS

MKY-1341

☐ **MKY-1341. "Mickey Mouse/Donald Duck" Lunch Box,**
1954. Adco-Liberty Mfg. Corp. 6.5x8.75x3.75" metal box with illustrations on front and back while band has character portraits. - **$100 $250 $500**

MKY-1342

MKY-1343

☐ **MKY-1342. "Mickey Mouse Annual" English Book,**
1954. Dean & Son Ltd. 7.5x9.75" hardcover, 96 pages. - **$25 $50 $80**

☐ **MKY-1343. "Mousegetar" Concept Art,**
c. 1954. Art is 7x13" in pencil by "Disney Legend" toy designer Al Konetzni. Image is titled "Mickey Mouse Ukulele" and was the genesis of toys that came to be produced by Mattel as the Mousegetar and Mousegetar Junior. Original design shows body of ukulele in the shape of Mickey's head. Unique, Fine - **$1100**

MKY-1344

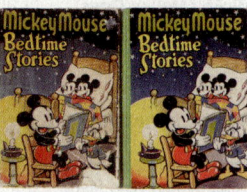

MKY-1345

☐ **MKY-1344. "Mousegetar/Mousegetar Junior" Publicity Photos,**
c. 1954. Pair of glossy photos are 6x8.5" and 7.5x9.5" for final production models of plastic guitars produced by Mattel and originally developed by "Disney Legend" toy designer Al Konetzni. Each - **$10 $20 $30**

☐ **MKY-1345. "Mickey Mouse Bedtime Stories" Hardcover With Dust Jacket,**
c. 1954. English by The Sunshine Press. 6.75x9.75". Later edition with 96 pages on glossy paper. Jacket - **$15 $30 $60**
Book - **$50 $125 $225**

MKY-1346

☐ **MKY-1346. "Walt Disney's Sketch A Graph Paint Book,"**
1955. Ohio Art Co. and Whitman. 8x10.75" with 64 pages. - **$15 $30 $60**

MKY-1347

☐ **MKY-1347. Mickey And Friends Candy Box Prototype,**
1955. Original art in ink and color pencil by "Disney Legend" toy designer Al Konetzni consisting of two thin paper sheets, each 6.5x13.5" and overlaid. Nearly the entire top sheet is the proposed box's front, right and left side panels. Mickey is depicted as the store owner pointing to his open door for Donald and his nephews, Minnie, Goofy and Pluto. Sign above awning reads "Mickey Mouse Candy Store" and simulated poster on the wall reads "Try Donald Duck Ice Cream." Unique, Fine - **$1850**

MKY-1348

☐ **MKY-1348. "Mickey Mouse School House" Concept Art,**
1955. Art is 7x9" original in pencil by "Disney Legend" toy designer Al Konetzni for play building to house small character figures and schoolroom accessories. Mickey is pictured as school bell ringer for Pinocchio, Donald Duck and nephews, Minnie, Pluto, Goofy. Unique, Near Mint - **$350**

MKY-1349

MICKEY MOUSE, MINNIE & NEPHEWS

❑ **MKY-1349. "Walt Disney Character My First Game,"**
1955. Gabriel, 9.25x14.25x1.25" deep box. - **$10 $20 $35**

MKY-1350

MKY-1351

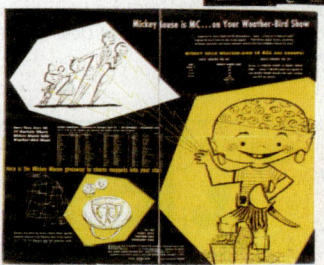
MKY-1350

❑ **MKY-1350. "Walt Disney Cartooning Card" Set,**
1956. Set of eighteen numbered stiff paper cards, each 2.25x3.5". Maker unknown. Set - **$180 $360 $540**

❑ **MKY-1351. "Mickey Mouse/Weather-Bird Shoes" Promotional Folder,**
1956. Glossy folder is 8.5x11" and opens to 17x22" with various text and illustrations relating to the Weather-Bird Shoes campaign on the Mickey Mouse Club TV show. - **$20 $40 $75**

MKY-1352

MKY-1353

❑ **MKY-1352. "Mickey Mouse Circus Cheerios" Box,**
1957. Flattened box is 9x10.5". Ad on front and back for "Mickey Mouse Circus Wiggle Picture Badge" along with six different "Wiggle Pictures." - **$100 $250 $500**

❑ **MKY-1353. "Walt Disney/Cheerios" Premium Flicker Set,**
1957. Vari-Vue. 3.5x5.5" mailing envelope contains complete seven-piece premium. Has thin molded plastic badge with opening to hold one of six different flasher inserts. Near Mint Set - **$350**
Badge Only - **$40 $75 $150**
Each Insert - **$10 $20 $30**

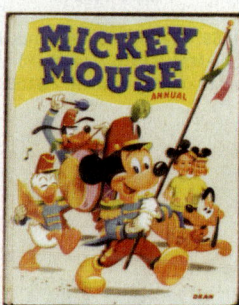
MKY-1354

❑ **MKY-1354. "Mickey Mouse Annual" English Hardcover,**
1957. Dean & Son Ltd. 8.25x10" with 80 pages. - **$20 $40 $85**

MKY-1355

❑ **MKY-1355. Mickey Mouse Concept Art For Pull Toy,**
1958. Gong Bell. 12.5x17.5". Three separate art panels glued to a sheet of tissue paper. For a wood pull/riding toy. Art is by Al Konetzni, long-time Disney toy designer. Unique - **$275**

MKY-1356

❑ **MKY-1356. "Minnie Mouse" Boxed Timex Watch With Figure,**
1958. U.S. Time. 4x4.5x5.75" tall box with top that lifts off to reveal display with attached 5" tall hard plastic figure and watch.
Near Mint Boxed - **$250**
Figure Only - **$12 $25 $40**
Watch Only - **$30 $60 $90**

MKY-1357

❑ **MKY-1357. "Mickey Mouse" Boxed Timex Watch With Figure,**
1958. U.S. Time. 4x4.5x5.75" tall box with top that lifts off to reveal display with attached 5" tall hard plastic figure and watch. Near Mint Boxed - **$350**
Figure Only - **$10 $20 $40**
Watch Only - **$30 $60 $90**

MICKEY MOUSE, MINNIE & NEPHEWS

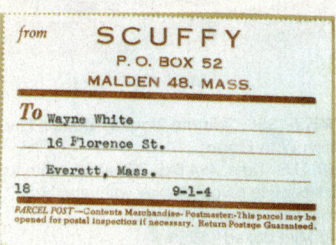

❏ **MKY-1358. "Scuffy" Premium Prints With Original Product,**
c. 1958. Three different 11.5x14.5" prints with original envelope and bottle of shoe polish in original box. Prints are of Mickey and Donald as they appeared in "Fun And Fancy Free," Snow White and dwarfs with forest animals and picnic scene of "Mickey And His Pals" featuring many Disney characters.
Box With Polish - **$20 $40 $75**
Print Set - **$45 $90 $150**

MKY-1359

❏ **MKY-1359. Minnie Mouse Wind-Up,**
c. 1958. Line Mar. 3.5x5x7" tall tin litho with fabric attached to knitting needles. - **$150 $300 $600**

MKY-1360

MKY-1361

❏ **MKY-1360. Mickey Mouse Pencil Drawing,**
1959. Image is 3x6". - **$65 $125 $250**

❏ **MKY-1361. Mickey Mouse French Magazines Bound Book,**
1959. Hardcover 9x12" "Le Journel De Mickey Album No. 16" from a series of bound runs of weekly publication. This volume contains #360-377. Each weekly has 24 pages so book totals 432 pages. Each issue features a combination of Disney and non-Disney stories and features plus comic book-style stories. - **$50 $100 $150**

MKY-1362

❏ **MKY-1362. "Mickey Mouse Shoes,"**
1950s. Trimfoot Co. 4.5x8x3" deep box contains pair of original but generic "Baby Deer" shoes. Boxed - **$35 $75 $150**

MKY-1363

MKY-1364

❏ **MKY-1363. "Mickey Mouse Kiddie Hankies,"**
1950s. Box is 8.25x8.25x.25" and likely held three 8x8" hankies. Box - **$15 $30 $60**
Each Hanky - **$5 $10 $20**

❏ **MKY-1364. Mickey Mouse Hankies,**
1950s. Each is 8.5x8.5" cotton. Maker is unknown. Each - **$5 $10 $20**

MKY-1358

MICKEY MOUSE, MINNIE & NEPHEWS

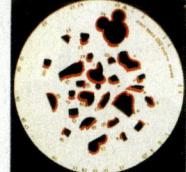

MKY-1365

◻ **MKY-1365. "Walt Disney's Book Of Puzzle Discs,"**
1950s. English 7.5x8.5" stencil activity book #1 by Williams, Ellis & Co. Ltd. with circular stiff paper cover and four paper pages of drawing guide discs plus blank paper sheets. Object is to place a disc on top of one of the supplied pieces of paper and draw the body outlines one at a time in numerical order turning the wheel as needed to complete the image. Discs images are Mickey, Donald, Fifer Pig, Snow White. - **$20 $40 $75**

MKY-1366

◻ **MKY-1366. Disney Character Fan Card,**
1950s. 8-1/8x10-1/8" stiff paper. - **$10 $20 $40**

MKY-1367

◻ **MKY-1367. "Mickey Mouse Bouncing Ball Target Game" Prototype Box Lid,**
1950s. Konetzni. Original art in ink and color pencil by "Disney Legend" toy designer Al Konetzni on 11x11.75" paper centered by images of a bouncing ball going across the box text, Mickey image at lower left, "Club" emblem at top right. Bottom margin is signed by Konetzni. Unique, Fine - **$225**

MKY-1368

MKY-1369

◻ **MKY-1368. Puzzle Prototype,**
1950s. Paper sheet is 5x8" with pen and ink watercolor art for proposed appliance company jigsaw puzzle premium, probably GE. Image is Mickey fishing although a "No Fishing" sign is behind him. Bottom right corner is an inset image of a stove. Comes with separate acetate sheet of hand-done black outlines of the puzzle pieces which can be placed over top of the art thus showing how completed puzzle would look. Gordon Gold Archives. Unique, Near Mint - **$375**

◻ **MKY-1369. "Mickey Mouse Nestled Rattle Blocks,"**
1950s. Gabriel. Set of five cardboard blocks with paper labels. Largest is 5x5x5.5" while smallest is 3x3x4". - **$10 $20 $40**

MKY-1370

◻ **MKY-1370. "Disneyland Ark" English Punch-Out Set,**
1950s. Williams, Ellis & Co. Ltd. Set consists of three colorful thin cardboard sheets with original 3.5x6.25" illustrated paper band used to hold the sheets together. A total of 29 different punch-outs representing 33 different characters. - **$25 $60 $110**

MKY-1371

MKY-1372

◻ **MKY-1371. Mickey "The 3-Dimensional Jigsaw Puzzle,"**
1950s. Jaymar. 9.75x11.25x2" deep box. Puzzle is 18x18" when assembled and titled "Mickey Mouse-High Diver." Came with 3-D glasses. - **$25 $50 $85**

◻ **MKY-1372. "Mickey Mouse" As Hunter,**
1950s. Goebel. 3.5" tall. Log has foil sticker and "Mickey Mouse" name. Underside has incised "78" and full bee marking. - **$100 $200 $300**

MICKEY MOUSE, MINNIE & NEPHEWS

MKY-1373

❏ **MKY-1373. Bandleader Mickey Mouse Ceramic Figurine,**
1950s. Hagen-Renaker. 1.75" tall. - **$60 $125 $200**

MKY-1374

❏ **MKY-1374. Mickey Mouse Small Ceramic Figurine,**
1950s. Shaw. 2" tall. - **$40 $75 $125**

MKY-1375

❏ **MKY-1375. Mickey Mouse with Hat Ceramic Figure,**
1950s. Shaw. 2-5/8" tall. - **$40 $75 $125**

MKY-1376

❏ **MKY-1376. Mickey Mouse Cereamic Potty For Boys,**
1950s. 6" diameter by 5" deep. By Shaw Company. Given as gift from Walt Disney to new parents. - **$500 $1000 $2000**

MKY-1377

❏ **MKY-1377. Mickey Mouse Cereamic Potty For Girls,**
1950s. 6" diameter by 5" deep. By Shaw Company. Given as gift from Walt Disney to new parents. - **$1000 $2000 $3000**

MKY-1378

❏ **MKY-1378. Mickey Mouse Ceramic Figurine,**
1950s. Beswick, England. 3.75" tall. Marked underneath with company mark. - **$150 $300 $500**

MKY-1379

❏ **MKY-1379. Minnie Mouse Ceramic Figurine,**
1950s. Beswick, England. 4.25" tall. Marked underneath with company mark. - **$150 $300 $500**

MKY-1380

❏ **MKY-1380. Marx Disney Character Figures,**
1950s. Lot of five plastic figures 1.5" to 2" tall. Sold individually as well as included with Marx playset. Each - **$3 $6 $12**

MICKEY MOUSE, MINNIE & NEPHEWS

MKY-1381

❑ **MKY-1381. Minnie Mouse Rubber Figure,**
1950s. Goebel. 2.5x3.75x6" tall pliable hollow rubber figure is totally unmarked. - **$25 $50 $85**

MKY-1382

❑ **MKY-1382. Mickey Mouse Candy Container/Ornament,**
1950s. Germany. 2x2.5x4.5" tall pressed and formed figure with removable head. - **$10 $20 $40**

MKY-1383

❑ **MKY-1383. "Mickey Mouse Sugar Babies" Candy Box,**
1950s. Empty box 5.75x9x2.75" that contained 24 packages of candy prices a 5 cents each. - **$20 $40 $75**

MKY-1384

MKY-1385

❑ **MKY-1384. "Comet Candies Inc." Retailers Sales Sheet,**
1950s. Old Dominion Candy Corp. 8.5x11" one-sided sheet. Includes "Mickey Mouse Rave Chocolate Covered Coconut" candy bars as well as "Walt Disney Animated Chocolate," a boxed set of four figural candies of Mickey, Minnie, Donald and Pluto. - **$15 $30 $50**

❑ **MKY-1385. "Mickey Mouse Cookies" Box,**
1950s. Nabisco. 1.75x5x2.75" tall box with front and back panels showing Mickey and Donald while sides are Pluto and Minnie. Top flap is Mickey and Minnie. - **$100 $200 $300**

MKY-1386

❑ **MKY-1386. "Mickey Mouse Cookies" Box,**
1950s. National Biscuits Co. 2x5x2.5" tall cardboard with original string carrier. - **$100 $200 $300**

MKY-1387

❑ **MKY-1387. Disney Character Birthday Party Kit,**
1950s. Rendoll Paper Corp. 9.5x15.25x1" deep illustrated box containing complete, elaborate set of "Over 40 Complete Pieces For 8 Kiddies." Set includes eight colorful stiff paper punch-out party hats and candy baskets, each featuring a different character of Mickey, Minnie, Donald, Daisy, Pluto, Goofy, Dumbo, Pinocchio. Other parts include "Pin The Ear On Pluto" game with eight ears that were to be cut out. - **$25 $50 $75**

MKY-1388

❑ **MKY-1388. "Mickey Mouse" Planter,**
1950s. Leeds. 3x7x7" tall painted and glazed china depicting Mickey in cowboy outfit. - **$20 $50 $80**

MICKEY MOUSE, MINNIE & NEPHEWS

MKY-1389

MKY-1390

❑ **MKY-1389. "Disney Candles" Set Boxed,**
1950s. "Made In Japan" 4.25x10x2" deep boxed complete set of 4" tall figural painted wax candles of Mickey, Minnie, Donald, Daisy, Pluto. Boxed - **$15 $30 $65**

❑ **MKY-1390. Disney Characters Ceiling Lamp Boxed,**
1950s. "Globe Product." 13x13x9.5" deep boxed complete ceiling light fixture of 11" diameter painted aluminum mounting base and 8" diameter by 3.25" deep frosted glass bulb cover shade with paint images on inner side.
Box - **$5 $15 $25**
Fixture - **$50 $100 $150**

MKY-1391

❑ **MKY-1391. "Mickey Mouse Magic Milk Pump,"**
1950s. Morris Plastics Corp. 3.5x3.5x11" tall box contains 11" soft plastic pump designed to be attached to a bottle and pressed down to dispense milk. Plastic top section has raised image of Mickey flexing his muscles.
Box - **$10 $15 $30**
Pump - **$10 $15 $30**

MKY-1392

MKY-1393

❑ **MKY-1392. Mickey And Thumper Rug,**
1950s. Woven fabric rug is 21.5x41" with fringe trim on right and left margins. - **$40 $75 $135**

❑ **MKY-1393. Mickey Mouse As Hunter Goebel Vase,**
1950s. Figure is 2.75x4.5.25" tall and has full bee marking with incised "DIS 75." - **$100 $225 $350**

MKY-1394

❑ **MKY-1394. Mickey Mouse Boxed (2) Wallpaper Border,**
1950s. United Wallpaper Inc./Trimz Co. Each roll is 12' long. Each with very similar design. Each Boxed - **$15 $30 $60**

MKY-1395

❑ **MKY-1395. Mickeypops Club Button,**
1950s. 1.25" button issued by English candy maker. - **$100 $200 $300**

MKY-1396

❑ **MKY-1396. Mickey Mouse Key Chain On Display Card,**
1950s. Maker unknown. 2.25x3.75" card contains 1.25" tall three-dimensional hard plastic Mickey Mouse head with attached brass key chain. Card has small WDP copyright. Additional text including misspelled name reads "Micky Mouse Key Chain/I Stick Out My Tongue." When back plunger is pushed Mickey's nose and tongue extend as ears move forward. Carded - **$25 $50 $75**

MKY-1397

MICKEY MOUSE, MINNIE & NEPHEWS

MKY-1398

MKY-1403

❑ MKY-1397. "Walt Disney Character Party Baskets,"
1950s. Best Hobby Kits. Five 3.5" tall hard plastic baskets in different colors. Packaged - **$10 $20 $40**

❑ MKY-1398. "Walt Disney Character Cookie Cutters,"
1950s. Loma Plastics Inc. 4.5x10x1.25" deep box contains complete set of four figural hard plastic cookie cutters, each 4" tall in different color. Includes Mickey, Minnie, Pluto and Donald. Box - **$10 $20 $40**
Cutters Each - **$3 $6 $12**

MKY-1401

MKY-1399

❑ MKY-1401. "Mickey Mouse's Savings House Bank,"
1950s. Tin litho bank from "The State Savings Bank Of Victoria, Australia." Underside has metal trap. - **$60 $115 $165**

❑ MKY-1403. Birthday Musical Cake Plate,
1950s. Authorized "Japan" 7.25" diameter by 1.25" tall tin lithographed plate on wind-up mechanism with on/off switch. - **$25 $40 $65**

MKY-1404

❑ MKY-1404. Birthday Revolving Carousel,
1950s. Authorized "Made In Japan" tin lithographed cake decoration on 4" diameter base by 8.5" tall. Base has holders for six candles. Heat from lighted candles causes suspended die-cut metal character figures to revolve slowly while brushing against two metal bell caps to produce delicate chime tones. - **$40 $75 $125**

MKY-1400

MKY-1402

MKY-1405

❑ MKY-1399. "Disneyland/Beswick" Ceramic Mug,
1950s. 3" tall. Underside marked "Made In England Expressly For Disneyland By Beswick." - **$25 $45 $75**

❑ MKY-1400. "Mickey Mouse Sunshine Straws,"
1950s. American Sel-Kap Corp. 3.75x8.75x1" deep box contains complete amount of 100 multicolored straws. - **$8 $15 $30**

❑ MKY-1402. "Disneyland Melody Player" Musical Toy,
1950s. J. Chein & Co. 6.x7.5x6.5" tall tin litho. Paper rolls inserted and music produced by cranking. - **$100 $175 $275**

❑ MKY-1405. "Mickey Mouse And Pluto 6 In 1 Record Album,"
1950s. RCA Victor. 7.5x7.5" storybook record sleeve contains 45 rpm. - **$25 $50 $85**

MICKEY MOUSE, MINNIE & NEPHEWS

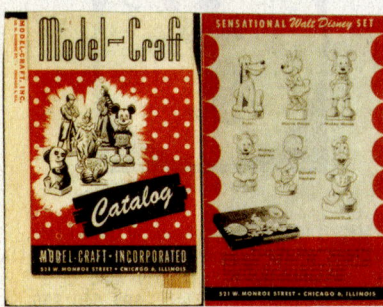

MKY-1406

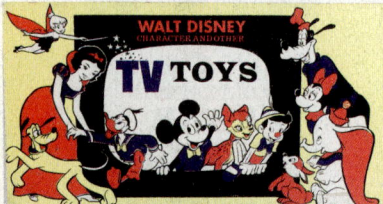

MKY-1407

❑ **MKY-1406. Models Catalogue With Mickey And Others,**
1950s. "Model-Craft." 5.5x8.5" catalogue with original mailing envelope. Content is 32 pages devoted to plaster casting sets for various themes but including a Disney set picturing Mickey, Minnie, Donald, Donald's nephew, Mickey's nephew, Pluto. Mailer - **$3 $8 $12** Catalogue - **$10 $20 $30**

❑ **MKY-1407. "Walt Disney Character And Other TV Toys" Store Sign,**
1950s. Sign is 9.5x18x.25" thick cardboard with same design repeated front and back. - **$25 $50 $75**

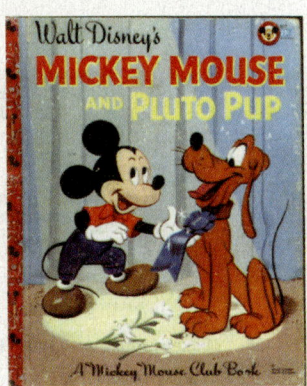

MKY-1408

MKY-1409

❑ **MKY-1408. "Mickey Mouse And Pluto Pup,"**
1950s. Simon & Schuster. 6.75x8" with 28 pages. Same as Little Golden Book but this is second edition "Mickey Mouse Club Book." - **$10 $20 $40**

❑ **MKY-1409. Large Doll House With Disney Character Room,**
1950s. Marx. 8x25x16" tall tin litho. Interior features room depicting wallpaper of Mickey, Minnie and nephews, Donald and his nephews, Pluto and Goofy. Floor shows Donald and corner portraits of Mickey and Donald. - **$60 $125 $250**

MKY-1410

❑ **MKY-1410. "Walt Disney's Television Playhouse" Playset,**
1950s. Marx. 11x28.5x3" deep box contains set #4349. Has complete set of hard plastic accessories including banquet table, two-story house front, fireman's safety net, treasure map, 38 soft plastic figures 1.25" to 2.25" tall. Includes Snow White and The Seven Dwarfs, five Alice characters, five Pinocchio characters, four Dumbo characters, Mickey, Minnie and nephews, Donald, Daisy and nephews, Pluto. - **$200 $400 $800**

MKY-1411

❑ **MKY-1411. Large Mickey As Clown Squeeze Toy,**
1950s. Soft vinyl figure 10.5" tall made by "Viceroy/Made In Canada." - **$15 $30 $60**

MKY-1412

MKY-1413

MICKEY MOUSE, MINNIE & NEPHEWS

❑ **MKY-1412. Mickey Mouse Ramp Walker,**
1950s. Marx. 3.25" tall hard plastic. - **$15 $30 $60**

❑ **MKY-1413. Minnie Mouse With Stroller Ramp Walker,**
1950s. Marx. 3" tall hard plastic. - **$20 $40 $70**

MKY-1414

MKY-1415

❑ **MKY-1414. Mickey And Donald Ramp Walker,**
1950s. Marx. 4" long hard plastic. - **$35 $65 $110**

❑ **MKY-1415. Mickey/Minnie Ramp Walker,**
1950s. Marx. 3" tall hard plastic. - **$35 $65 $110**

MKY-1416

❑ **MKY-1416. Hunter Mickey With Pluto Ramp Walker,**
1950s. Marx. 3.25" hard plastic. - **$25 $50 $100**

MKY-1417

MKY-1418

❑ **MKY-1417. "Mickey And Minnie Mouse In Rumba Rhythm" Magnetic Toy,**
1950s. Masco Corp. 1x1.5x2" deep box contains pair of 1.5" tall plastic figures attached to magnet bases. - **$12 $25 $45**

❑ **MKY-1418. Christmas Card,**
1950s. Gibson. Closed 4x5" folder card. - **$5 $10 $15**

MKY-1419

❑ **MKY-1419. Mickey Mouse Figural Christmas Ornament,**
1950s. 2.5x4.25" two-sided embossed diecut tin. Maker unknown. - **$6 $12 $20**

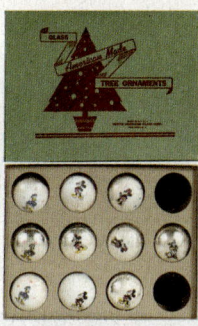
MKY-1420

❑ **MKY-1420. Walt Disney Characters Boxed Christmas Balls,**
1950s. American Glass Corp. 7.5x10x2.5" deep cardboard box has twelve glass ball tree ornaments. Complete Boxed - **$40 $75 $150**

MKY-1421

MKY-1422

❑ **MKY-1421. English Pop-Up Game Board,**
1950s. Chad Valley Co. Ltd. Stand-up board only from amusement park themed game. Board assembles to 10x12x9.5" tall and has cardboard easel on reverse of upright panel. Pop-up elements include game path and staircase. - **$20 $40 $75**

❑ **MKY-1422. "Mickey Mouse 2 Transistor Radio,"**
1950s. Hard plastic figural radio measures 5x5x1" deep. Has thin metal Mickey image on front. Ears serve as on/off knobs. Small sticker on reverse "Gabriel Industries/Japan." - **$30 $60 $100**

MICKEY MOUSE, MINNIE & NEPHEWS

MKY-1423

MKY-1424

❑ **MKY-1423. Mickey And Friends Sand Pail,** 1950s. Chein. 5.25" tall lithographed tin with carrying handle. - **$60 $125 $235**

❑ **MKY-1424. Mickey Mouse Sand Pail,** 1950s. Chein & Co. 5.25" tall by 5" diameter with attached handle. - **$60 $125 $235**

MKY-1425

❑ **MKY-1425. "Mickey Mouse Sand Set,"** 1950s. Eldon. 5x6x17.5" set includes soft plastic bucket, sprinkling can, shovel and sand mold attached to cardboard insert and wrapped in yellow string mesh "beach bag." - **$10 $20 $40**

MKY-1426

❑ **MKY-1426. "Mickey Mouse Sand Set,"** 1950s. Eldon. 5x6x17.5" with soft plastic sprinkling can, bucket, shovel, rake, scoop and red string mesh "beach bag." - **$10 $20 $40**

MKY-1427

❑ **MKY-1427. Disney Characters Australian Pail,** 1950s. "A Willow Production." 6.75" top diameter by 6" tall tin lithographed sand pail with wrap-around beach scene involving Mickey, Donald and his nephews, Pluto, Goofy. - **$100 $200 $300**

MKY-1428

❑ **MKY-1428. "Mickey The Magician" Battery Operated Boxed Toy,** 1950s. Line Mar. Lithographed tin with felt cape and starched felt hat. 10" tall on 5-3/8x7" base. Mickey reveals and then makes disappear a tin chick. Box is 6.75x10.5x7.5" deep. Box - **$150 $300 $600**
Toy - **$300 $600 $1200**

MICKEY MOUSE, MINNIE & NEPHEWS

MKY-1429

❑ **MKY-1429. "Walt Disney Friction Delivery Wagon" Boxed Toy,**
1950s. Line Mar. 2.5x5x4.25" toy consists of tin lithographed three-wheeled wagon with attached figure of Mickey who has tin lithographed body and feet, celluloid head and legs.
Box - **$110 $225 $350**
Toy - **$110 $225 $350**

MKY-1430

❑ **MKY-1430. "Line Mar Toys" Disney Friction Airplane,**
1950s. Tin lithographed toy 6x7.5x2" tall. Sides have images of Mickey while Pluto appears on tail fins. Wings have illustrations of Pluto, Goofy and Donald. - **$250 $500 $1000**

MKY-1431

❑ **MKY-1431. Mickey Friction Motorcycle By Line Mar,**
1950s. Marx. Toy is 1.25x3.5x3" tall. - **$100 $200 $400**

MKY-1432

MKY-1433

❑ **MKY-1432. Mickey Mouse Friction Truck,**
1950s. Marx. Hard plastic truck measures 1.75x3.75x2.75" tall. Unmarked. - **$30 $65 $100**

❑ **MKY-1433. "Whirling Tail Mickey Mouse" Boxed Wind-Up,**
1950s. Line Mar. 2x2.75x5.5" tall toy with built-in key. Box - **$125 $250 $500**
Toy - **$125 $250 $500**

MKY-1434

❑ **MKY-1434. "Mickey The Driver" Boxed Wind-up,**
1950s. Marx. 3x7x4.25" tall lithographed tin with built-in key. Box - **$200 $400 $650**
Toy - **$150 $250 $450**

MKY-1435

❑ **MKY-1435. "Mickey Mouse" Dipsy Car Wind-up,**
1950s. Marx. Version with 3.5x5.5x5.75" tall lithographed tin car with hard plastic Mickey. Box - **$200 $400 $650**
Toy - **$150 $250 $450**

MICKEY MOUSE, MINNIE & NEPHEWS

MKY-1436

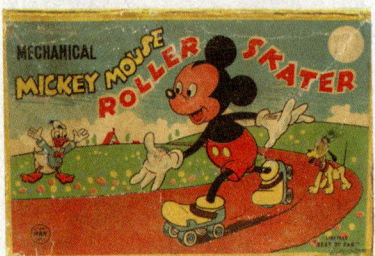

❑ **MKY-1436. "Mickey Mouse Roller Skater" Boxed Wind-Up,**
1950s. Line Mar. Box is 4.5x6.75x2.5" deep. Tin figure is 6-3/8" tall with fabric pants and rubber ears. Box - $250 $500 $800
Toy - $250 $500 $800

MKY-1437

❑ **MKY-1437. "Disney Parade Roadster" Boxed Wind-Up Car,**
1950s. Marx. 4.75x11.5x3.25" deep box contains 11" long car with built-in key. Box - $200 $400 $650
Toy - $200 $400 $850

MKY-1438

❑ **MKY-1438. "Mickey Mouse Mouseketeers Moving Van" Friction Powered,**
1950s. Line Mar. 15" long tin toy with box.
Box - $200 $400 $800
Toy - $300 $500 $1000

MKY-1439

❑ **MKY-1439. "Disneyland" Marx Wind-Up Train,**
1950s. Toy is 1.5x12.5x2.5" tall. Engine has built-in wind-up key. Engine made either of single color plastic or illustrated litho. tin.
Plastic engine - $40 $80 $135
Litho. Tin engine - $50 $100 $150

MKY-1440

❑ **MKY-1440. "Mickey Mouse Express" Windup,**
1950s. Line Mar. 9" tin. Box - $75 $150 $250
Toy - $75 $150 $250

MKY-1441

❑ **MKY-1441. "Marx" Wind-Up Mickey Mouse Tricycle,**
1950s. Lithographed tin toy is 2.5x3.5x3.5" tall. - $100 $225 $325

MKY-1442

❑ **MKY-1442. Mickey Mouse On Scooter Wind-Up By Line Mar Toys,**
1950s. Marx. Lithographed tin 2.5x3.5x4.25" tall. When wound, toy travels in a circle. - $250 $600 $1000

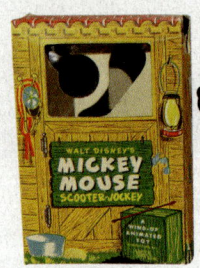

MKY-1443

❑ **MKY-1443. "Mickey Mouse Scooter Jockey" With Original Box,**
1950s. Marco. 7" tall plastic toy.
Box - $25 $50 $75
Toy - $35 $75 $125

MICKEY MOUSE, MINNIE & NEPHEWS

MKY-1444

❑ **MKY-1444. "Minnie Mouse" Twisti Dancer With Box,**
1950s. Schuco. 4" tin toy. Box - **$50 $100 $200** Toy - **$100 $200 $300**

MKY-1445

MKY-1446

❑ **MKY-1445. "Mickey's Air Mail" Airplane,**
1950s. Hard rubber vehicle 5x6.25x3.5" tall with three-dimensional figure of Mickey. Rare color variety and Canadian version by "Sunruco." Has raised "Mickey's Air Mail" on each side. - **$75 $150 $250**

❑ **MKY-1446. "Mickey Mouse The Old Fashioned Car Driver,"**
1950s. Elm Toys. 2" long free-wheeling hard plastic "Stutz Bearcat" comes in colorful box. Box - **$10 $20 $30**
Car - **$10 $20 $30**

MKY-1447

❑ **MKY-1447. Mickey And Minnie Mouse With Street Organ Metal Figure Set,**
1950s. Sacul, England. 1.75" tall figures of Mickey and Minnie and 2.25" tall free-wheeling street organ. When organ is cranked it produces musical notes. - **$115 $250 $400**

MKY-1448

❑ **MKY-1448. "A Walt Disney Flip Book" Featuring Mickey,**
1950s. Disneyland Art Corner. 3x3.5" featuring illustrations of Mickey as a cowboy performing tricks with his lasso. - **$10 $20 $30**

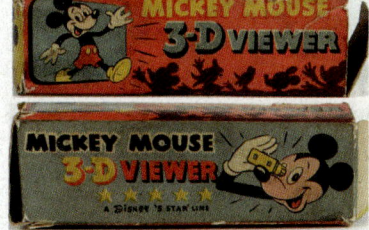

MKY-1449

MKY-1450

❑ **MKY-1449. "Mickey Mouse 3D Viewer" Set,**
1950s. English by Martin Lucas Ltd. 2x5.5x1.75" tall box contains 4" long hard plastic viewer and includes raised image of Mickey holding "3-D" sign. Comes with 1x5.5" full color cardboard sleeve containing one of two full color filmstrips titled "Mickey's Picnic." Boxed Viewer - **$40 $75 $125** Boxed Strip - **$10 $20 $30**

❑ **MKY-1450. "Mickey Mouse School Tablet,"**
1950s. Tablet 8x10" by ample 1" thick. - **$15 $25 $45**

MICKEY MOUSE, MINNIE & NEPHEWS

MKY-1451

☐ **MKY-1451. Mickey Mouse Desk Letter Holder,**
c. 1960. MPFL Co. 1.25x4x4" tall solid brass with high relief design. - **$12 $25 $45**

MKY-1452

☐ **MKY-1452. "Mickey Mouse World Reporter Kit" Complete Premium,**
1961. "Vicks Medi-Trating Cough Syrup." 7x10" mailing envelope contains complete 3-piece kit consisting of 1.75" button, 2.5x3.5" World Reporter Press Card, 25.75x35" map by Rand McNally. Button - **$30 $65 $125**
Card - **$10 $20 $35**
Mailer - **$10 $20 $35**
Map - **$25 $50 $85**

MKY-1453

☐ **MKY-1453. "Mickey Mouse Annual" English Hardcover,**
1961. Dean & Son Ltd. 8x10" with 96 pages. - **$20 $50 $90**

MKY-1454

MKY-1455

☐ **MKY-1454. Mickey And Donald Floating Soap Raft,**
c. 1961. Dell. 5x6.5x4.25" tall soft vinyl squeaker toy. - **$15 $30 $50**

☐ **MKY-1455. "Mickey Mouse" Ceramic Figurine,**
1963. Dan Brechner. 5" tall with "WD 25" under base. - **$15 $30 $60**

MKY-1456

MKY-1457

☐ **MKY-1456. "Mickey Mouse And Friends Kaboodle Kit,"**
1963. 7x9x4" deep vinyl lunch box. Maker unknown. - **$75 $150 $275**

☐ **MKY-1457. "Mickey And The Beanstalk" Record,**
1963. Disneyland label 12.25x12.25" cardboard album cover containing 33-1/3 rpm recording. - **$5 $10 $20**

MKY-1458

☐ **MKY-1458. "Mickey Mouse Bank Book,"**
1964. Ideal Toy Corp. 4.5x6x1" deep hard plastic designed like a book. - **$20 $40 $75**

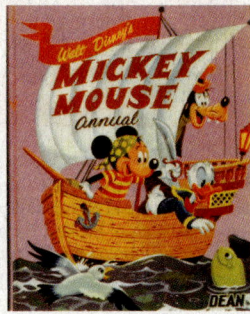

MKY-1459

☐ **MKY-1459. "Mickey Mouse Annual" English Book,**
1964. Dean & Son Ltd. 8x10.25" hardcover, 96 pages. - **$20 $40 $80**

MICKEY MOUSE, MINNIE & NEPHEWS

MKY-1460

MKY-1462

MKY-1465

☐ **MKY-1460. Mickey Mouse Drawing By Andy Engman With Autograph,**
c. 1965. 12.5x15.5" sheet with 7x13.5" illustration of Mickey in tuxedo raising a glass of champagne. Engman was the president of Walt Disney Animation from 1949-1966. - **$75 $150 $250**

☐ **MKY-1462. Mickey Mouse 3-D Picture,**
1966. W.C. Jones Publishing Co. 10.5x13.5" plastic. - **$20 $40 $60**

MKY-1463

MKY-1464

MKY-1466

MKY-1467

☐ **MKY-1463. Mickey Mouse 3-D Picture,**
1966. W. C. Jones Publishing Co. 8x10" rigid plastic. - **$12 $25 $40**

☐ **MKY-1464. Australian Rugby Tray With Disney Characters,**
1966. "Walt Disney Productions." Licensed 12" diameter by .75" deep tin lithographed "Rugby Tour Souvenir Tray" picturing rugby game between "Black Petes" and "Beagle Boys." Goofy is shown scoring a goal and Mickey is pictured as referee. - **$20 $40 $70**

☐ **MKY-1465. "Mickey Mouse Kookie Kamper,"**
1966. Multiple Toymakers. 4x13.5x7" tall boxed 6" long "Putt Putt Motor Sound" friction camper vehicle. Box - **$10 $20 $40**
Toy - **$20 $40 $80**

☐ **MKY-1466. Mickey "Bendiface" Toy,**
1967. Lakeside Toys. 6x9" blister card containing 5" tall bendable foam rubber face. Reverse of face has open slot/holes for placement of fingers to change his facial expressions. Near Mint Boxed - **$30**

☐ **MKY-1467. Boy Scout "World Jamboree" Song Booklet,**
1967. 7Up. 4x6.75" with 32 pages issued for the 12th World Jamboree held in Idaho. - **$5 $12 $20**

MKY-1461

☐ **MKY-1461. "Nabisco Puppets Wheat Puffs Cereal" Container,**
1966. 4.5x5x9.5" tall soft plastic. Also designed as a bank with coin slot on back. - **$10 $20 $40**

MICKEY MOUSE, MINNIE & NEPHEWS

MKY-1468

❑ **MKY-1468. Disney College Homecoming Ashtray,**
1967. 4x4.75" smoked glass. Issue for University of Pittsburgh. - **$10 $20 $30**

MKY-1470

❑ **MKY-1470. Mickey Mouse 40th Birthday Publicity Stills,**
1968. Each is 8x10". Each - **$3 $6 $10**

MKY-1472

❑ **MKY-1472. Mickey Mouse 40th Birthday Sculpture By Ernest Trova,**
1968. From a numbered edition of fifty originally sold for $350 each by Ernest Trova, noted contemporary sculptor and collector of Disneyana. Has a 4" diameter and height of 3.5". Sterling silver with embossed text and enameled metal Mickey figural appliques. Four segments with repeated text around rims reading "Mickey Mouse/Empire Builder/1928-1968." Includes 12 Mickey appliques, each 1" tall. Two segments have cut-out image. Stamped-in edition number. Sits atop small black plastic base. Mint As Issued - **$1300**

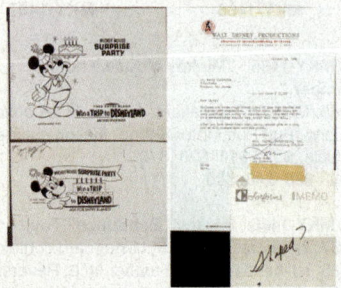

MKY-1469

❑ **MKY-1469. "Mickey Mouse Surprise Party" Production Letter And Photostats,"**
1968. Colorforms archives. Four items relating to "Free Trips To Disneyland Sweepstakes Promotion." Group - **$25 $50 $75**

MKY-1471

❑ **MKY-1471. Mickey Mouse Gumball Machine Bank,**
1968. Hasbro. 4x4.5x9" tall hard plastic. Box - **$5 $15 $30** Bank - **$5 $15 $30**

MKY-1473

❑ **MKY-1473. Mickey Mouse 40th Birthday/GE Nitelite Press Release,**
1968. 8.25x10.75" paper with attached 8x10" glossy photo. The "Picture Caption" text notes the discussion of "Mickey Mouse's 40th Birthday And GE's Mickey Mouse Nitelite Line At The National Hardware Show" between account executive Al Konetzni and GE employee. - **$15 $30 $50**

MICKEY MOUSE, MINNIE & NEPHEWS

MKY-1474

❑ **MKY-1474. "American Heritage" Hardcover Magazine,**
1968. 8.5x11" with 112 pages for April. Feature article for Mickey's 40th birthday. - **$10 $20 $30**

MKY-1475

❑ **MKY-1475. Mickey Mouse "Magnetic Buckle Belt" Display,**
c. 1968. Pyramid Belt Co. 11x12.5" die-cut cardboard. Complete - **$35 $60 $100**

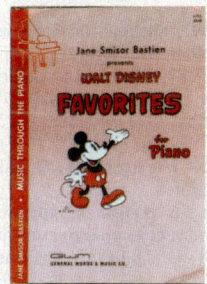

MKY-1476

MKY-1477

❑ **MKY-1476. "Walt Disney Favorites For Piano" Song Folio,**
1969. Bourne Co. 9x12" with 16 pages. Lyrics and music for The Three Little Pigs, Lullaby Land, Pinocchio and Snow White along with several character illustrations. - **$20 $40 $60**

❑ **MKY-1477. Disney Cartoons Song Folio,**
1969. Bourne Co. 9x12" compilation titled in full, "Song Highlights From Walt Disney's Famous Cartoons/Mickey Mouse And Silly Symphony," 60 pages. Content is reprint collection of 1930s material including 19 songs. Cover art is 1930s style, picturing different Mickey image front and back. - **$20 $40 $75**

MKY-1478

❑ **MKY-1478. "Walt Disney Character Firefighters" Lunch Box With Thermos,**
c. 1969 Aladdin Industries Inc. 7x9x4.25" deep. Underside has three-panel cartoon of safety tips with Donald and his nephews. Thermos is 6.75".
Box - **$55 $110 $225**
Bottle - **$20 $40 $80**

MKY-1479

❑ **MKY-1479. "Parade Of Values" Shelf Display,**
c. 1969. Nabisco. Thin 6x8" flexible die-cut plastic sheet with overhang figure of Mickey as band drummer that wobbles when sheet is mounted on shelf edge. - **$10 $20 $35**

MKY-1480

❑ **MKY-1480. Shoe Holder With Slippers,**
1960s. Soft vinyl hanger rack is 8x35" reinforced by cardboard inserts top and bottom depicting Mickey's head and feet. Center section is elongated body designed to pocket three pairs of shoes and/or slippers. Child's slipper sets of Mickey and Donald are likely not original to the holder. Holder - **$10 $20 $40**
Slipper Sets Each - **$5 $10 $20**

MKY-1481

MKY-1482

MICKEY MOUSE, MINNIE & NEPHEWS

❑ **MKY-1481. "Walt Disney Studios" Licensee Character Guide,**
1960s. 8.5x11" with stiff paper cover plus 12 slightly textured paper sheets. Eleven have character designs, the twelfth has copyright information. - **$30 $60 $90**

❑ **MKY-1482. Daily Comic Strip Original Art Autographed By Gottfredson,**
1960s. Sheet is 6.25x19". Publication date indicated is January 30, 1967. Same or Similar - **$200 $400 $600**

MKY-1483

❑ **MKY-1483. Concept Art For "Mickey Umbrella,"**
1960s. Paper is 7x9" sheet of tracing paper with inked art, text and signature by Al Konetzni, "Disney Legend" toy and merchandise designer. At center is 3x3.25" sketch of an umbrella with entire top designed like Mickey Mouse's hand. Text below this is "Mickey Umbrella/Rain Or Shine-Mickey's Hand Will Captivate Crowds Wherever It Is Exposed/Crowds-Sporting Events- Around The World. Mass & Single Photos." Art was for Disney park use. Unique, Near Mint - **$60**

MKY-1484

❑ **MKY-1484. Al Konetzni Concept Art For Disney "School Bus Book,"**
1960s. Sheet of paper measuring 5.25x5.25" mounted to slightly larger 7x7.25" art board featuring art in lead and colored pencil. Unique, Near Mint - **$110**

MKY-1485

❑ **MKY-1485. "Mousekamagic" Prototype Item,**
1960s. Hand-made prototype measures 1x3" by Al Konetzni, long-time Disney toy designer. Outer sleeve is thin cardboard plus separate die-cut Mickey head image. Also has separate cardboard insert with die-cut diamond opening around drawing of Donald Duck. Object was to hold left end and pull on right to see Donald and then reverse and reinsert to see Mickey. Unique, Very Fine - **$85**

MKY-1486

❑ **MKY-1486. Mickey Hair Clip,**
1960s. 1.5" brass clip with enameled and silvered brass Mickey at center. - **$8 $12 $25**

MKY-1487

❑ **MKY-1487. Mickey Mouse Plaster Crib Toy,**
1960s. Enesco. 4" tall. - **$8 $12 $25**

MKY-1488

❑ **MKY-1488. Mickey Mouse Nodder,**
1960s. Marx. 2.25" tall hard plastic figure. - **$10 $20 $35**

MKY-1489

MKY-1490

❑ **MKY-1489. "Mickey And His Friends" Publicity Folder With Photos,**
1960s. Buena Vista Distribution Co. Inc. 8.5x11" folder contains six different 6.75x9.25" glossy publicity photos. - **$20 $40 $65**

❑ **MKY-1490. Mickey Mouse/Donald Duck Poseable Figures,**
1960s. Marx. 5.5" tall figures with hard plastic bodies plus vinyl-covered wire arms and legs for posing. Each wears a fabric outfit. Each **$8 $15 $30**

MICKEY MOUSE, MINNIE & NEPHEWS

MKY-1491

MKY-1492

MKY-1494

MKY-1495

MKY-1497

❑ **MKY-1497. "Walt Disney Character Ex-Pan-Dees Sponge Toy,"**
1960s. James. 11x12x1" deep box contains printed sponge cut-out pieces to form six different "Expanding Characters" for Mickey, Minnie, Donald, Daisy, Pluto and Goofy. Boxed - **$5 $15 $30**

❑ **MKY-1491. Mickey Figurine,**
1960s. Japanese 6.25" tall painted and glazed ceramic. - **$10 $20 $30**

❑ **MKY-1492. Mickey With Goofy And Pluto Ceramic Figurines,**
1960s. Dan Brechner. 1.5x4x5.25" tall Mickey attached by a pair of metal link chains to 3.75" tall Goofy and 2.5" tall Pluto. - **$50 $100 $150**

❑ **MKY-1494. Disney Characters South American Lunch Box,**
1960s. "El Trigal/Uruguay." 3.5x9x3.5" deep metal box designed like suitcase with simulated travel stickers on all sides for Disney characters, different hotels, cruise ships, airlines, e.g. "Grand Mickey Hotel, Pluto Airlines." - **$85 $175 $350**

❑ **MKY-1495. "Mickey And The Band Leader" Soaky,**
1960s. Soft vinyl body and hard vinyl head figure is 9.5" tall. - **$10 $20 $40**

MKY-1498

MKY-1493

MKY-1496

MKY-1499

❑ **MKY-1493. Mickey Mouse Figurine,**
1960s. Painted and glazed ceramic figure 2.25x3x4.75" tall. Has foil "Enesco" sticker. - **$10 $20 $30**

❑ **MKY-1496. "Soaky" Picture Sheet With Soap Bars,**
1960s. Picture sheet is 12x12" and three bars of soap are each 1.5x2" with picture to cut and mount. Map - **$12 $25 $50**
Each Uncut Wrapper - **$2 $4 $8**

❑ **MKY-1498. "Mickey Mouse" Ceramic Lamp Base,**
1960s. Dan Brechner. 8" tall. Socket rod gone from photo example. - **$45 $90 $160**

❑ **MKY-1499. Mickey Mouse Planter,**
1960s. Painted and glazed ceramic 5.25x6.5x4.25" tall. Underside has copyright and "Japan." - **$25 $50 $75**

MICKEY MOUSE, MINNIE & NEPHEWS

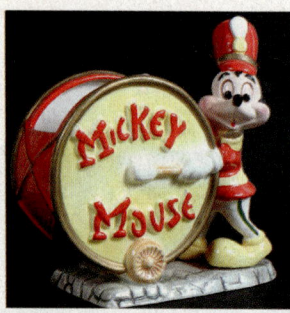

MKY-1500

MKY-1501

❏ **MKY-1500. "Mickey Mouse" Ceramic Planter,**
1960s. Unmarked. Likely by Enesco. 6" tall. - **$15 $30 $60**

❏ **MKY-1501. "Mickey Mouse Planter,"**
1960s. Painted and glazed ceramic 3.25x5.5x5" tall comes in cardboard box with color label on lid "An Original Dan Brechner Exclusive." Box - **$15 $25 $50**
Planter - **$25 $50 $80**

MKY-1502

❏ **MKY-1502. Mickey Mouse Rug,**
1960s. Rug is 20.5x36" fabric with thick cotton nap centered by large image of mod Mickey without name or text. - **$15 $30 $60**

MKY-1503

MKY-1504

❏ **MKY-1503. Mickey Mouse Ceramic Cookie Jar,**
1960s. Enesco. 7.5x12.5x8.25" tall. Unusual design with large pair of die-cut vinyl ears attached to his head. - **$100 $200 $300**

❏ **MKY-1504. Mickey/Minnie Ceramic Mug,**
1960s. Enesco. 4.5" tall. - **$15 $35 $60**

MKY-1505

❏ **MKY-1505. "Disney Cartoon Mug,"**
1960s. Eagle Products. 3.5" tall hard plastic. - **$8 $15 $25**

MKY-1506

❏ **MKY-1506. "Mickey Mouse" Ceramic Salt & Pepper Set,**
1960s. Painted and glazed figures are 4.75" tall. One has foil sticker on reverse "Original Dan Brechner Exclusive." - **$20 $45 $85**

MKY-1507

MKY-1508

❏ **MKY-1507. "Mickey/Minnie Mouse" Ceramic Salt & Pepper Set,**
1960s. Dan Brechner. Each is 5.25" tall. Ink stamp number on underside "WD-52." - **$30 $60 $100**

❏ **MKY-1508. Mickey And Minnie Salt & Pepper Set,**
1960s. Painted and glazed 4" tall shakers on 2x4x2.5" wooden bench. Complete with stopper, foil copyright sticker and small "Japan" sticker. - **$50 $100 $150**

MKY-1509

MICKEY MOUSE, MINNIE & NEPHEWS

MKY-1510

MKY-1512

MKY-1515

❑ **MKY-1515. "Walt Disney Christmas Parade Giant Comic,"**
1960s. Gold Key Series. Issue #5 featuring reprints copyright 1949, 1950, 1952. Has 24-page Christmas story by Carl Barks. - **$8 $25 $95**

❑ **MKY-1509. Mickey Mouse Composition Bank,**
1960s. 3x4x6" tall. - **$10 $20 $40**

❑ **MKY-1510. French Disney Character Bank,**
1960s. Bank is 2.5x5x5.25" tall and lithographed tin. Underside has Disney name and manufacturer "Gulliver-Lyon/Made In France." - **$65 $125 $225**

❑ **MKY-1512. "Mickey Mouse" Record Player,**
1960s. Unit is 9x14x5.5" deep with plastic case and carrying handle. Case opens to turntable and figural plastic tone arm in the shape of Mickey's arm and hand with his index finger pointing forward. Canadian issue from the "Sears Electronics" line made for Simpsons-Sears, Toronto, Canada. - **$75 $150 $225**

MKY-1513

MKY-1514

MKY-1511

❑ **MKY-1511. Mickey and Minnie English Button,**
1960s. 2.25". - **$20 $40 $90**

❑ **MKY-1513. "Mickey Mouse" Premium Picture,**
1960s. 5x7" glossy stiff paper featuring the classic official Mickey Mouse 25th birthday portrait by John Hench from 1953. Reverse is marked "Compliments Of Your Mickey Mouse Shoe Dealer" with inked stamp imprint for Wyandotte, Michigan store. - **$10 $20 $40**

❑ **MKY-1514. Mickey Mouse Ceramic Bookends,**
1960s. Dan Brechner. "WD19." Each is 4.5" tall. Set - **$35 $65 $125**

MKY-1516

❑ **MKY-1516. "Mickey Mouse Springees" Boxed Band Set,**
1960s. Multiple Toymakers. The unusual 4" tall figures have hard plastic bodies with wire arms and legs for posing, bodies are in a variety of colors and each plays a different instrument. Boxed - **$20 $35 $60**

MKY-1517

❑ **MKY-1517. "Mickey's Haunted House" Game With Original Box,**
1960s. 15x22" wood with glass cover battery operated game. Box - **$20 $40 $65**
Toy - **$25 $50 $100**

MICKEY MOUSE, MINNIE & NEPHEWS

MKY-1518

MKY-1520

MKY-1523

❏ **MKY-1518. Mickey Mouse Bobbing Head Figure,**
1960s. Japan. 6" tall painted composition. - **$20 $40 $60**

❏ **MKY-1520. Mickey "Rolykins" Figure Toy,**
1960s. Marx. Boxed 1.25" tall hard plastic figure with ball bearing insert and foil sticker.
Box - **$2 $4 $8**
Toy - **$3 $6 $12**

❏ **MKY-1523. Mickey Figure With Inset Clock,**
1960s. Case is 2.5x3.75x6.25" tall molded hard vinyl holding metal alarm clock unit with glow-in-dark accents. Clock face is marked "West-Germany/Alarm" but no company indicated. Back of base has Disney copyright. - **$15 $30 $65**

MKY-1519

MKY-1521

MKY-1524

❏ **MKY-1519. Minnie Mouse Marionette,**
1960s. Pelham. 10" tall with painted composition head, hands and feet, wood segment arms and legs, fabric dress. - **$25 $50 $100**

MKY-1520 (Box)

MKY-1522

MKY-1525

❏ **MKY-1521. Mickey Mouse Alarm Clock Distributed In France,**
1960s. Bayard. 2x4.5x4.75" tall in metal case. Mickey's head nods as seconds tick. U.S. version has dark red case while this French version is pink. Each Version - **$50 $100 $200**

❏ **MKY-1522. "Bradley Mickey Mouse" Clock,**
1960s. 2x4.25x4.5" tall metal case. - **$20 $40 $80**

❏ **MKY-1524. "Disney Busy Boy" German Alarm Clock,**
1960s. "Hamilton/Made In Germany." 2.5x5x7" tall metal cased wind-up clock topped by 2" tall painted solid vinyl figures of Mickey and Minnie. - **$40 $75 $150**

❏ **MKY-1525. "Mickey Mouse" Watch,**
1960s. Helbros. 1.25x1.5" metal case with matching metal expansion bands. - **$20 $40 $75**

MICKEY MOUSE, MINNIE & NEPHEWS

MKY-1526

❑ **MKY-1526. "Acrobatic Clown" Mickey Mouse Trapeze Toy,**
1960s. Kohner, 4.5x7" bag contains 5" tall hard plastic toy. Near Mint Bagged - **$75**
Loose - **$10 $20 $40**

MKY-1527

❑ **MKY-1527. "Mickey And Donald Magic Slate,"**
1960s. Watkins-Strathmore Co. 8.5x13.75" die-cut cardboard with plastic stylus. - **$5 $15 $30**

MKY-1528

❑ **MKY-1528. "Minnie" Mouse Ceramic Pencil Holder,**
1960s. Likely by Enesco. 3x4x4.5" tall. - **$15 $30 $60**

MKY-1529

❑ **MKY-1529. Mickey Mouse French Sand Pail,**
c. 1960s. Virojanglor Paris. 5" tall tin litho with vintage 1930s style graphics. - **$50 $125 $250**

MKY-1530

❑ **MKY-1530. "I've Been To Disney Village At Donaldson's" Button,**
c. 1960s. 3" diameter. Rim curl has Disney copyright and maker name "Wendell's Mpls." - **$10 $25 $50**

MKY-1531

MKY-1532

❑ **MKY-1531. "Mickey & Pluto Joggers" Prototype Watch,**
1970. Designed by "Disney Legend" Al Konetzni. 1.25" diameter chromed metal case, leather straps. - Unique, Near Mint - **$350**

❑ **MKY-1532. Floyd Gottfredson Large Framed Specialty Art,**
1970. The India ink and watercolor art covers nearly the entire 10.75x14" sheet and was done in 1970 while Gottfredson was still at Disney Studio doing the Mickey Mouse daily strip. Unique, Mint As Made - **$4250**

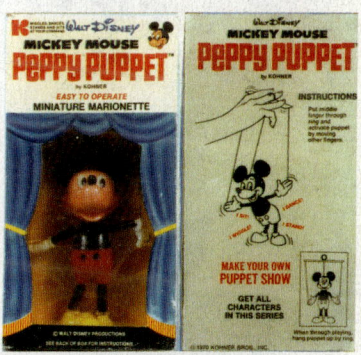

MKY-1533

❑ **MKY-1533. "Mickey Mouse Peppy Puppet,"**
1970. Kohner Bros. Inc. 4.25x8x2" box contains 4" hard plastic "Miniature Marionette."
Box - **$20 $50 $75**
Toy - **$15 $30 $50**

MICKEY MOUSE, MINNIE & NEPHEWS

MKY-1534

❑ **MKY-1534. Al Konetzni Personally Owned Watches With Handwritten Note,**
1970. Both have 1.25" diameter goldtone metal cases, leather straps. First watch is a one-of-a-kind made for his retirement in 1980 and second was given to him by Bradley in 1970, registered edition 0047.
Retirement watch - Unique, Near Mint - **$125**
Bradley watch - **$15 $25 $50**

MKY-1535

❑ **MKY-1535. "Marx Mickey Mouse Little Big Wheel Battery Operated" Toy,**
1970. Boxed 5x9.5x7" tall hard plastic toy depicting Mickey in Big Wheel. Includes illustrated 8.5x11" paper sheet advertising Big Wheel and Krazy Kar by Marx. Box - **$10 $20 $40**
Toy - **$20 $40 $65**

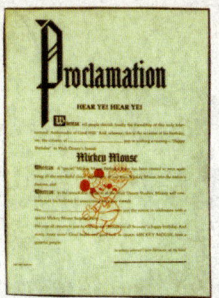

MKY-1536

MKY-1537

❑ **MKY-1536. Birthday Proclamation,**
c. 1970. Parchment-like paper is 8.5x11.75" centered by background image of Mickey wearing birthday hat and holding a birthday cake. Text is legal document style and includes mention of a birthday show. Has designated lines for original recipient to fill in information. - **$8 $15 $25**

❑ **MKY-1537. "Mickey Mouse 1932" Daily Strip Reprint Book,**
1971. Italy. 7.75x13.75" with 140 pages. English text. - **$20 $40 $75**

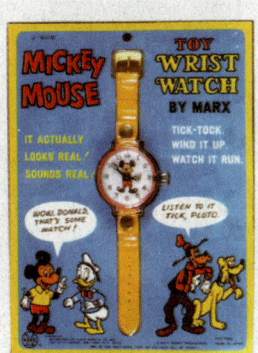

MKY-1538

❑ **MKY-1538. "Mickey Mouse" Toy Wristwatch By Marx,**
1971. Blister card is 7x9" and contains hard plastic watch with vinyl straps. Watch produces a "tick-tock" sound as hands move.
Carded - **$15 $30 $60**
Loose - **$5 $15 $30**

MKY-1539

❑ **MKY-1539. "Mod Mickey" Miniature Souvenir Frying Pan,**
c. 1971. John Wright who only had a Disney license for one year. 3.25x4.5x.5" deep cast iron. - **$10 $20 $40**

MKY-1540

❑ **MKY-1540. Grateful Dead/Mickey Mouse-Related "Mickey And The Daylites" Concert Poster,**
1972. 14x20" stiff paper poster for December 17, concert featuring Mickey and The Daylites (Mickey Hart, percussionist of The Grateful Dead) and Batucaje Music of Brazil at Pyramid Pins, Garberville, California. Art is by Kelly. First and only printing. - **$35 $65 $125**

MICKEY MOUSE, MINNIE & NEPHEWS

MKY-1541

MKY-1544

MKY-1546

❏ **MKY-1541. "Walt Disney Characters Unscrambler Slide Rule Action,**
1972. Marx. 7.5x12" blister card contains 3.5x11" hard plastic picture puzzle featuring eight Disney characters with bodies divided into three sections. Attached is frame to be placed over one character image and the different sliding sections are then moved to form a complete character image. Near Mint Carded - **$30**

❏ **MKY-1544. "Mickey Mouse Scooter" By Marx,**
1972. Boxed hard plastic friction toy 2.5x4.25x4" tall. Scooter includes three-dimensional figure of Mickey. Box - **$10 $20 $30**
Toy - **$15 $30 $50**

❏ **MKY-1546. Mickey And Minnie Boxed Watch/Pocket Watch,**
c. 1972 Photorific Products, Inc. (Unauthorized.) 4x9.5x1.75" deep box has clear plastic lid, black cardboard bottom. Timepiece is 2" diameter pocket watch which can be also be used as a wristwatch mounted on 1.5" wide black band. Pocket watch snaps into place or can be taken off and comes with metal pocket watch chain. Dial features a 1930s style image of pie-eyed Mickey and Minnie with Mickey playing a banjo and Minnie singing. Watch is attached to red felt-covered insert. Comes with instruction/guarantee card. Limited production.
Mint Boxed - **$600**
Loose - **$100 $200 $350**

MKY-1542

❏ **MKY-1542. Mickey Mouse And Tinker Bell Figures,**
1972. Marx. Pair of solid soft plastic figures with 6" tall Mickey and 5.25" tall Tinker Bell.
Each - **$3 $6 $12**

MKY-1545

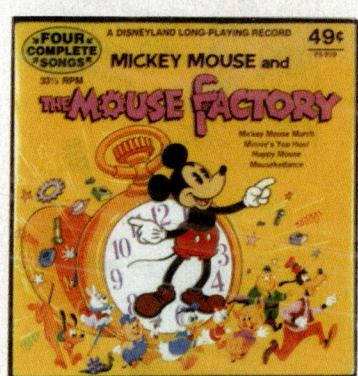

MKY-1543

❏ **MKY-1543. "Mickey Mouse And The Mouse Factory" Record,**
1972. Sleeve is 7x7" picturing numerous characters and contains 33-1/3 rpm record on Disneyland label. - **$6 $12 $25**

❏ **MKY-1545. Mickey And Minnie Mouse Boxed Watch/Pocket Watch,**
c. 1972. Photorific Products, Inc. (Unauthorized.) 4x9.5x1.75" deep box has clear plastic lid, black cardboard bottom. Timepiece is 2" diameter pocket watch which can also be used as wristwatch mounted on 1.5" wide black leather band. Pocket watch snaps into place or can be taken off and comes with metal pocket watch chain. Dial features a 1930s style image of pie-eyed Mickey and Minnie embracing with hearts floating above their heads. Watch is attached to red felt-covered insert. Comes with instruction/guarantee card. Limited production.
Mint Boxed - **$1000**
Loose - **$250 $500 $750**

MKY-1547

❏ **MKY-1547. "Mickey Mouse" Unlicensed Pocketwatch,**
c. 1972. Fantasy creation by Al Horne, one of the early dealers in character collectibles, designed as 1930s pocketwatch with silvered metal case and image on dial of pie-eyed Mickey playing piano. Watch is created as actual timepiece rather than toy. - **$100 $200 $300**

MICKEY MOUSE, MINNIE & NEPHEWS

MKY-1548

MKY-1549

❑ **MKY-1548. Mickey Mouse Toy Watch,**
1973. Marx. Child's toy watch with glow-in-the-dark dial. - **$8 $15 $30**

❑ **MKY-1549. Konetzni Mock Magazine Cover Original Art,**
1973. Vellum paper sheet is 8.5x11" with art in pencil, watercolor and ink by Joseph Haboush, a member of Disney character merchandise Art Dept. Image is simulated "Time" magazine cover with banner across title "Super Salesman," and featuring a portrait of Al Konetzni wearing Mickey Mouse ears hat. Art was a surprise presentation to "Disney Legend" toy designer Konetzni. Unique, Near Mint - **$250**

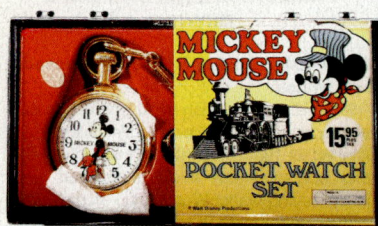

MKY-1550

❑ **MKY-1550. Mickey Mouse Pocket Watch,**
1973. In plastic box with advertising overlay Train pictured on back of case. Bradley. Complete - **$30 $100 $250**

MKY-1551

❑ **MKY-1551. "Schmid" First Issue Christmas Collector Plate,**
1973. 7.5" diameter decorative china. Reverse text includes "The Disney Family Collector Series/Limited First Edition." - **$100 $200 $350**

MKY-1552

❑ **MKY-1552. Mickey Mouse "School/Utility" Bags,**
1974. Al Nyman & Son Inc. Each is 8x12" nylon with carrying handle and snap closure plus tag and address card. Each Near Mint - **$20**

MKY-1553

❑ **MKY-1553. "The Best Of Walt Disney Comics 1934 To 1952" Complete Display,**
1974. Western Publishing. 16x25x3" deep cardboard countertop display contains complete amount of 24 reprint books each 8x10.5". Featuring reprints from 1934, 1944, 1947, and 1952 including Mickey Mouse And The Bat Bandit Of Inferno Gulch, comic reprints including the first issue of Uncle Scrooge plus stories from Four Color Comics #62, 159, and 178. Near Mint - **$500**

MKY-1554

MKY-1555

MICKEY MOUSE, MINNIE & NEPHEWS

❏ **MKY-1554. Minnie Art,**
c. 1974. Foam core is 9x12" sheet with original art in ink and colored marker by "Disney Legend" toy designer Al Konetzni. Near Mint - **$115**

❏ **MKY-1555. Mickey Toy Concept Art,**
c. 1974. Paper sheet is 9x10.5" centered by 5x6" original art in ink and wash by "Disney Legend" toy designer Al Konetzni. Depiction is Mickey Mouse three-wheeled riding toy chained to a fire hydrant. Art is signed by Konetzni. Unique, Near Mint - **$115**

MKY-1556

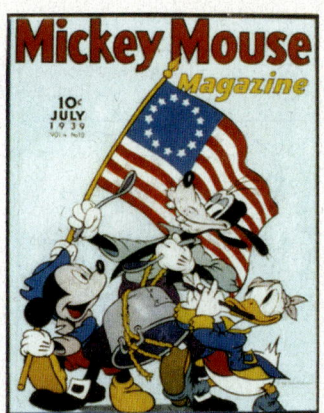
MKY-1558

MKY-1561

❏ **MKY-1558. "Spirit Of '76" Puzzle,**
1976. Hallmark Cards. 11x14x1.5" deep box contains puzzle by Springbok Editions. When assembled 17.5x23.5". Near Mint - **$20**

❏ **MKY-1561. "Mickey Mouse Seed Shop" Display Board,**
1976. Board is 17x17x3" deep diecut cardboard which sat atop display bin containing variety of garden seed packs. Attached to front is separate diecut piece of Minnie plus two examples of the row markers that were part of each seed package. - **$35 $75 $125**

MKY-1559

MKY-1557

MKY-1560

MKY-1562

❏ **MKY-1556. "Mickey Mouse Cookbook" Hardcover,**
1975. Golden Press. 8.25x11.25" with 94 pages. Filled with great color illustrations on every page of Disney characters preparing food with corresponding recipes including "Peter Pan's Pasta, Bambi's Garden Salad, Wonderland Pancakes," etc. - **$5 $15 $20**

❏ **MKY-1557. Gottfredson Autographed Photo,**
c. 1975. Photo is 5x5" of Floyd Gottfredson, the main Mickey Mouse newspaper daily strip artist in earlier years. - **$30 $60 $85**

❏ **MKY-1559. Spirit Of '76 Patriotic Figurine,**
1976. Bisque is 4x9.5x6.75" tall painted depiction of Mickey, Goofy and Donald as symbolic patriots, complete with separate bisque flag on metal rod. Issued only for 1976, the year of U.S. Bicentennial celebration. - **$110 $225 $325**

❏ **MKY-1560. "America On Parade" Mug,**
1976. 4" tall milk glass. - **$10 $20 $30**

❏ **MKY-1562. Mickey Mouse Seeds,**
1976. Colorforms. Nine example packets with attached die-cut plastic hanger measures 3.5x9". Each is marked "Packed For 1977." Packets are for Radish, Carrot, Tomato, Cucumber, Pumpkin, Beans, Lettuce, Daisy, Zinnia. These and others hung from store display rack. Each - **$4 $8 $12**

MICKEY MOUSE, MINNIE & NEPHEWS

MKY-1563

MKY-1566

MKY-1567

❏ **MKY-1566. Walt Disney Bicentennial Sand Pail,**
1976. 5.5" tall by 7" diameter soft plastic pail with handle marked "Made In Italy By Suci For Worcester Toy Corp." - **$10 $20 $40**

❏ **MKY-1567. Mickey Mouse Bicentennial Pocket Watch,**
1976. Bradley. 3.5x4.5x1" deep plastic display case with plastic storage tray containing 2" diameter pocket watch with individual serial number. Boxed - **$40 $75 $140**
Watch Only - **$20 $40 $85**

MKY-1565

❏ **MKY-1565. "The Mickey Mouse Phone" Boxed Push-Button Version,**
1976. Large hard plastic phone is 8.5x8.5x15" tall and comes in box with color photo of this phone on four side panels. American Telecommunications Corp. Box design includes word balloon above each phone image reading "Hey Minnie It's For You." Phone is designed with 12" tall Mickey figure in classic 1930s style with pie-cut eyes and attached to the base which has wood grain design on side. This is the push-button variety, also issued as a rotary phone. Box - **$35 $65 $100**
Telephone - **$35 $65 $100**

MKY-1564

❏ **MKY-1563. "Mickey Mouse Seed Shop" Publicity Photos,**
1976. Two 8x10" glossies sponsored by Colorforms. Each - **$3 $6 $12**

❏ **MKY-1564. "The Mickey Mouse Phone,"**
1976. American Telecommunications Corp. 15" tall hard plastic. Rotary dial version, also issued with push button numbers. Each - **$35 $65 $100**

MKY-1568

❏ **MKY-1568. Disney's America On Parade Magic Slate,"**
1976. Whitman. 8.5x13.5" die-cut cardboard slate. Has plastic stylus. Near Mint - **$30**

MICKEY MOUSE, MINNIE & NEPHEWS

MKY-1569

❏ **MKY-1569. "Walt Disney's America On Parade" Lunch Box With Thermos,**
c. 1976. Aladdin Industries. 7x8x4" deep metal box and 6.5" tall plastic thermos. Box - **$25 $55 $110**
Bottle - **$10 $20 $30**

MKY-1570

MKY-1571

❏ **MKY-1570. Disney Legend Al Konetzni Lunch Box Presentation Publicity Photo,**
c. 1976. 7.5x9.5" glossy of Konetzni plus Aladdin Industries Vice President and National Sales Manager. Konetzni is being presented with a plaque noting 9,000,000 units sold of the Disney School Bus lunch box which he designed. Unique, Fine - **$200**

❏ **MKY-1571. Disney Spirit Of '76 Product Sticker,**
c. 1976. Glossy sticker is 9.5x12.5". Sticker backing has ink stamp "Ariston Inc., Hillside, New Jersey." Near Mint - **$25**

MKY-1572

❏ **MKY-1572. "Disco Mickey Watch" Boxed Set By Bradley,**
1977. Bradley. 8.25x8.75x1" deep box. Set comes with a 45rpm record featuring the songs "Disco Mouse/Walking The Dog." Two-sided record sleeve features 1930s style art of Mickey and Minnie dancing. Watch has animated hands. Boxed Near Mint - **$100**
Watch only - **$15 $30 $50**

MKY-1573

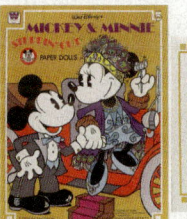 

MKY-1574

❏ **MKY-1573. "Mickey Mouse Fifty Happy Years" Autographed Book,**
1977. Harmony Books. 8.5x10.75" softcover 256-page "Official Birthday Book." Title page of this example is autographed by Floyd Gottfredson and page 22 by Ward Kimball, both early Mickey artists. - **$30 $60 $90**

❏ **MKY-1574. "Mickey & Minnie Steppin' Out Paperdolls,"**
1977. Whitman. 10x12.75". - **$10 $20 $40**

MKY-1575

❏ **MKY-1575. "NSDA Convention Anaheim, California 1977" Painted Glass Bottle,**
1977. Bottle is 9.5" tall and issued for National Soft Drink Assn. convention. - **$10 $20 $40**

MKY-1576

MKY-1577

❏ **MKY-1576. "Mickey Mouse Nostalgic Radio,"**
1977. Made in China for Canadian Company. Lidco. 12x13x9" deep colorful box contains exceptionally well made electric radio nearly identical in every way to the classic 1930s radio by Emerson. Near Mint Boxed As Issued - **$425**

❏ **MKY-1577. "Mickey Mouse Die-Cast" Vehicles,**
1977. Azrak-Hamway. Four 4x5" blister cards each containing 2.25" long die cast metal vehicle with three dimensional figure of Mickey. Each Near Mint Carded - **$12**

MICKEY MOUSE, MINNIE & NEPHEWS

MKY-1578

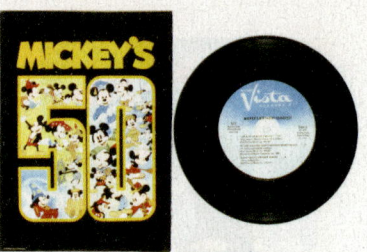

MKY-1581

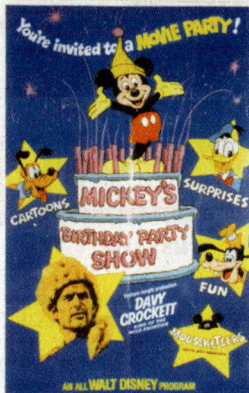

MKY-1583

❑ **MKY-1578. "Tricky Trike" Toy Carded,**
1977. Gabriel Toys. 5x8" display card holding 5" tall painted hard plastic action toy.
Carded - **$10 $20 $35**
Toy Only - **$5 $10 $15**

❑ **MKY-1580. "Mickey Mouse Magic Glow Fun House,"**
1978. Colorforms. 12.5x16x1" deep box holds set consisting of 5x12x16" pop-up fun house with three different floors with great interior illustrations intended to be used with lamp. All other lights are turned out and lamp is placed behind house which then reveals images hidden in the artwork such as ghosts, skeletons, Mickey and Minnie. Also comes with two large sheets of accessories. - **$25 $50 $115**

❑ **MKY-1581. "Mickey's 50" Birthday Publicity Kit,**
1978. Glossy stiff paper folder 9x11.75" contains three different press releases on "Walt Disney Productions" stationery, a promo 45 rpm record and Volume 13, #4 Sept-Nov 1978 issue of Disney News magazine. - **$20 $40 $85**

❑ **MKY-1582. "Mickey Mouse" Comic Strip Reprint Book Signed,**
1978. Abbeyville Press Inc. 9.75x13.25" hardcover with 204 pages, featuring full color reprints of Mickey Mouse 1930s comic strips by Floyd Gottfresdson. His inked autographed greeting and signature is on blank fly leaf page to collector friend Charlie Roberts. Signed - **$25 $50 $75**
Unsigned - **$5 $10 $15**

❑ **MKY-1583. "Mickey's Birthday Party Show" Movie Poster,**
1978. Poster is 27x41" glossy one-sheet for feature length film celebrating Mickey's 50th birthday. - **$15 $30 $50**

MKY-1579

❑ **MKY-1579. Commemorative 50th Birthday Belt,**
1978. Pyramid Belt Co. 2x7.5x2" deep boxed leather belt with brass buckle raised relief image of Mickey holding boxed gift. Near Mint Boxed - **$35**

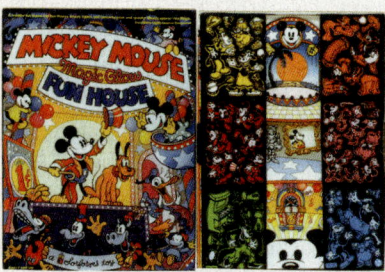

MKY-1580

MKY-1582

MKY-1584

❑ **MKY-1584. Mickey 50th Anniversary German Movie Poster,**
1978. Poster is 23.5x33" paper with text in both German and English including "Fox-MGM Technicolor" and "Walt Disney Cartoon Jubilee." - **$20 $40 $75**

MICKEY MOUSE, MINNIE & NEPHEWS

MKY-1585

MKY-1586

❏ **MKY-1585. Mickey 50th Anniversary German Movie Poster,**
1978. Poster is 23.5x33" paper with text in both English and German, apparently issued for an anniversary compilation cartoon film. - **$20 $40 $75**

❏ **MKY-1586. "Mickey's Birthday Party Show" Publicity Book,**
1978. Book is 9x12" with 16 pages. Issued for NBC-TV special. - **$12 $25 $50**

MKY-1587

❏ **MKY-1587. "Mickey's Birthday Songfest" Folio,**
1978. Folio is 9x12" stiff paper covered issue for Mickey's 50th birthday, 36 pages. - **$10 $20 $35**

MKY-1588

❏ **MKY-1588. Birthday Card Mobile,**
1978. Montgomery Ward. 6x10" closed stiff paper card opening to 18" of die-cut character punch-outs of Mickey, Donald, Pluto and Goofy to be assembled into a "Fun-Time Mobile." Card refers to Mickey's 50th birthday and also mentions that a special gift was available if card was brought to a Mongomery Ward store. - **$10 $20 $30**

MKY-1589

MKY-1590

❏ **MKY-1589. "Mickey Mouse: The First Fifty Years" Exhibition Booklet,**
1978. 8x8" with 16 pages. - **$10 $20 $40**

❏ **MKY-1590. "LIFE" Magazine,**
1978. Issue for Mickey's 50th birthday. Inside has 3-page article emphasizing then current projects such as Black Cauldron and The Fox And The Hound. - **$10 $20 $40**

MKY-1591

❏ **MKY-1591. "Mickey Mouse Commemorative Watch,"**
1978. Bradley. Box is 2.5x5.5x.75" deep and contains goldtone watch issued for 50th birthday. Comes with small registration form and is numbered with incised "37235" on reverse.
Box - **$10 $20 $30**
Watch - **$15 $30 $50**

MKY-1592

❏ **MKY-1592. Mickey Mouse Visible Mechanism Wind-Up,**
1978. Gabriel. 3x4x9.25" tall hard plastic that walks forward when wound and also has manually movable arms. - **$30 $60 $100**

MICKEY MOUSE, MINNIE & NEPHEWS

MKY-1593

☐ **MKY-1593. Mickey's 50th Birthday First Day Covers,**
1978. Each is 3.5x6.5" with individual hand-inked edition number on reverse. - **$6 $12 $20**

MKY-1594

☐ **MKY-1594. "Mickey Mouse" Girl's Wristwatch,**
c. 1978. Bradley. 3x6x2.5" tall hard plastic display case with hinged lid over 1" diameter gold-tone metal case watch with vinyl straps. Case - **$10 $20 $30**
Watch - **$20 $40 $70**

MKY-1595

☐ **MKY-1595. "Minnie Mouse Wrist Watch" Set,**
c. 1978. Bradley. Hard plastic case with hinged lid contains set consisting of 1" diameter metal case watch and three different bands.
Boxed Near Mint - **$100**
Watch only - **$20 $40 $60**

MKY-1596

☐ **MKY-1596. "Disney's World On Ice" Original Design Art,**
1979. Vellum paper sheet is 10.25x12.25" with inked original art by "Disney Legend" toy designer Al Konetzni. Depicted is Mickey in disco outfit wearing roller skates under title. Unique, Near Mint - **$85**

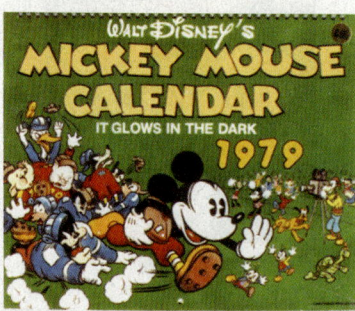

MKY-1597

☐ **MKY-1597. "Mickey Mouse Glow-In-Dark Calendar,"**
1979. 10.5x13" spiral-bound on stiff glossy paper. Each month features a large full color action scene with Disney characters. Front and each picture page has areas designed to glow in the dark. - **$5 $10 $25**

MKY-1598

☐ **MKY-1598. Stockbroker's Necktie,**
1970s. Cervantes. Silk/polyester blend tie with 4.5x5" stitched image of Mickey painting a rising line on a monthly report graph. - **$5 $15 $30**

MKY-1599

MKY-1600

☐ **MKY-1599. "Mickey Math Educational Ruler,"**
1970s. Walt Disney Distributing Co. 3.25x15x.5" deep box contains large hard plastic ruler. Can be used for addition, subtraction, division and other mathematical problems. Near Mint Boxed - **$20**

☐ **MKY-1600. "Mickey Mouse Pop-Up Playset,"**
1970s. Colorforms. 12.5x16x1" deep box with pop-up scene that opens to 11" height depicts Mickey, Minnie, nephews, Pluto, Horace and Clarabelle. Includes accessory pieces including instruments and party items. - **$25 $50 $110**

MICKEY MOUSE, MINNIE & NEPHEWS

MKY-1601

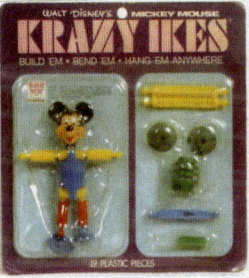

MKY-1602

MKY-1604

MKY-1605

❏ **MKY-1604. Mickey Mouse Cel From Eastern Airlines Commercial,** 1970s. Image is 2x3.75". - **$40 $75 $125**

❏ **MKY-1605. Baby Mickey Mouse Cel,** 1970s. Acetate sheet is 10.5x12.5" with 4x6" painted side view of him crawling and reaching forward. No. 29 from a numbered series for a Disney TV show. Near Mint - **$115**

MKY-1606

❏ **MKY-1606. Minnie Mouse Cel,** 1970s. Acetate sheet is 10.5x12.5" with 5x5.25" painted image. No. "37" from a numbered sequence for a Disney TV show. Near Mint - **$115**

MKY-1607

❏ **MKY-1607. Newspaper Comic Strip Signed By Gottfredson,** 1970s. Strip is 3x12.5" vintage complete four-panel comic for August 26, 1933 neatly removed from a newspaper. Title is "The Big Chance" and depicts Mickey receiving a letter and rushing to tell Minnie that "They're Gonna Let Tanglefoot Run In Th' Big Race." Third and fourth panels have signature "To Charles Roberts Best Wishes Floyd Gottfredson." Gottfredson was the artist on the Mickey Mouse comic strip from 1930 until his retirement in 1975. Same Or Similar - **$30 $60 $90**

❏ **MKY-1601. "Tricky Mickey Magic Colorforms,"** 1970s. Colorforms. 10x16x1" deep box. Insert board has cardboard disk with wooden knob to turn. Complete with accessories and booklet. - **$12 $25 $50**

❏ **MKY-1602. "Mickey Mouse Krazy Ikes" Kit Carded,** 1970s. Whitman. 9x9.5" blister card holding figure building parts set for 4.5" tall Mickey figure. Carded - **$5 $10 $20**

MKY-1603

❏ **MKY-1603. Minnie Mouse Cel,** 1970s. Image is 6.5x7". - **$65 $125 $175**

MKY-1608

❏ **MKY-1608. Mickey Mouse Jack In The Box Toy,** 1970s. Carnival Toys Inc. 5.75x5.75x5.75" tall tin lithographed toy. When crank is turned, "Pop Goes The Weasel" plays and a figure of Mickey pops out. He has hard plastic head and fabric body. - **$40 $70 $140**

MKY-1609

MKY-1610

MKY-1611

MICKEY MOUSE, MINNIE & NEPHEWS

❏ **MKY-1609. Mickey Mouse 3-D Puzzle,**
1970s. 9.5x11.5" deep plastic frame holds 3-D style puzzle picture with figural plastic pieces of Mickey. Has small magnets on reverse to hold them to the tin sheet underneath. - **$8 $15 $25**

❏ **MKY-1610. Mickey And Minnie Porcelain Figurines,**
1970s. MIckey is 2.25" tall and Minnie is 2.75". Over-the-glaze paint. Unmarked. Each - **$6 $12 $20**

❏ **MKY-1611. Mickey And Minnie Ceramic Figurines,**
1970s. 4" tall pair with additional over-the-glaze paint. Pair - **$12 $25 $40**

MKY-1612

MKY-1613

❏ **MKY-1612. Walt Disney Character Bendables,**
1970s. Durham Industries Inc. Three 5x8.5" blister cards each containing 4.5" tall rubber figure. Included are Donald, Mickey and Pinocchio. Each Carded -**$6 $12 $20**

❏ **MKY-1613. "Minnie Mouse" Figure by Dakin,**
1970s. Dakin. 7.75" tall poseable vinyl figure with cardboard tag. Came in plastic bag. Near Mint Bagged With Tag - **$50**
Figure Only - **$10 $20 $35**

MKY-1614

MKY-1615

❏ **MKY-1614. "Mickey Mouse" Toothbrush Holder,**
1970s. Painted and glazed ceramic 2.25x5x4.75" tall. - **$15 $30 $60**

❏ **MKY-1615. "Mickey Mouse" Dakin With Bag,**
1970s. 7.75" tall poseable vinyl complete with cardboard tag. With Bag & Tag - **$20 $40 $60**
Figure Only - **$12 $25 $40**

MKY-1616

❏ **MKY-1616. Giant Santa Mickey Pepsi-Cola Premium Doll,**
1970s. Animal Fair. 34" tall stuffed plush with hard plastic eyes and felt belt with vinyl buckle. Marked "Made For The Pepsi-Cola Company" with Disney copyright. We believe these were issued one per store to be used for promotional display. - **$35 $75 $135**

MKY-1617

❏ **MKY-1617. "Mickey Mouse Hallmark Candle,"**
1970s. 4x4.5x7.25" tall painted figural. - **$5 $10 $15**

MKY-1618

MKY-1619

❏ **MKY-1618. "Happy Birthday" Mickey Mouse Party Plates,**
1970s. Beach Products. 9" diameter sealed set of eight paper plates. Near Mint Sealed - **$15**

❏ **MKY-1619. "Mickey Mouse Sew-Ons,"**
1970s. Colorforms. 8x12.5x1" deep boxed set designated on lid as Canadian version. - **$12 $25 $40**

MKY-1620

❏ **MKY-1620. "Battery Operated Minnie Mouse Sewing Machine,"**
1970s. Ahi. 4.5x9x6.5" tall hard plastic.
Box - **$10 $20 $30**
Toy - **$20 $40 $70**

MKY-1621

MICKEY MOUSE, MINNIE & NEPHEWS

MKY-1622

▢ **MKY-1621. Minnie Wall Plaque,**
1970s. "Futuristic Products." 5x6x.5" deep wood plaque with scalloped edge design and high gloss finish over portrait decal. - **$10 $20 $35**

▢ **MKY-1622. "Paint-on Plaque,"**
1970s. Leisuramics Inc. 10x12.5x1.25" deep box holds unpainted white bisque high relief design. Near Mint Boxed - **$25**

MKY-1623

▢ **MKY-1623. "Mickey And Minnie Mouse" Trash Can,**
1970s. Cheinco. 7.5x10x13" tall tin lithograph waste container. - **$15 $30 $60**

MKY-1624

▢ **MKY-1624. Mickey Mouse Faux Watch Bracelet,**
1970s. Strap is 1" wide by 9" long with attached 1.25" diameter die-cast metal simulated watch dial. - **$12 $25 $50**

MKY-1625

MKY-1626

▢ **MKY-1625. "Mickey Mouse" Retro Cuff Links,**
1970s. Hickok. Pair of 1.25x2" figural cast metal cuff links attached to original cardboard holder with string tag, "Authorized Limited Edition From The Original 1934 Dies Out Of The Hickok Archives." Carded - **$10 $20 $35**

▢ **MKY-1626. Mickey Mouse & Others Frying Pan/Pot,**
1970s. Japan. Tin litho pieces including pot with removable lid 3.5" diameter by 2" deep and frying pan 4.5" diameter by 1" deep. Near Mint - **$15**

MKY-1627

MKY-1628

▢ **MKY-1627. Child's Feeding Dish,**
1970s. "Japan" 5.25x9.25x.75" deep china dish compartmentalized into food area and cup holder space. - **$10 $20 $30**

▢ **MKY-1628. Mickey Mouse Telephone Mug,**
1970s. Heavy clear glass 5.5" tall has small Bell Telephone Co. logo. - **$20 $40 $75**

MKY-1629

▢ **MKY-1629. "Mickey's Spaceship,"**
1970s. Eagle Affiliates. 8.5" tall hard plastic mug held by cardboard wrapper strap within unopened original shrinkwrap. Near Mint Packaged - **$30**

MKY-1630

▢ **MKY-1630. "Mickey Mouse" Bank,**
1970s. Animal Toys Plus Inc. 8.5" tall by 4" diameter hard vinyl bank. One hand is designed to hold a coin and the arm is movable for placing coin in bank. - **$15 $30 $60**

MKY-1631

▢ **MKY-1631. Mickey Mouse Bank,**
1970s. Hard vinyl with one movable arm and head. 6.5" tall. - **$10 $20 $40**

MICKEY MOUSE, MINNIE & NEPHEWS

MKY-1632

❏ **MKY-1632. Minnie Mouse Bank,**
1970s. Glazed composition with over-the-glaze paint bank 4x4.5x4" tall. - **$10 $20 $40**

MKY-1633

MKY-1634

❏ **MKY-1633. "Walt Disney Ceramic Greenware Figure Maker,"**
1970s. Jaymar. 11.5x16x3" deep box contains casting molds and accessories for Mickey, Minnie, Donald and Pluto. Near Mint Boxed - **$25**

❏ **MKY-1634. Mickey Mouse Coin-Sorting Bank,**
1970s. 1.5x5x7" tall hard plastic. Back of bank is clear plastic so coin sorting mechanism can be viewed. - **$10 $20 $40**

MKY-1635

MKY-1636

❏ **MKY-1635. Mickey Mouse Large Plaster Bust Bank,**
1970s. Unmarked. 7x9x11.5" tall painted plaster depicting Mickey's head atop a block of swiss cheese. Coin slot is on top of head, back of base has plastic trap. - **$12 $25 $50**

❏ **MKY-1636. "Mickey Mouse Play Money Set,"**
1970s. Kingsway. 8.5x11.5" blister card includes play money with character portraits, credit and I.D. cards featuring Mickey portrait and castle illustration, vinyl wallet and plastic money clip, both depicting Uncle Scrooge plus five plastic coins with raised Mickey portrait/castle. Carded - **$5 $15 $30**

MKY-1637

❏ **MKY-1637. Mickey/Minnie Mouse Purse,**
1970s. Disney Fashion Parade by Lanco. 5x6x1.5" deep vinyl with shoulder strap. - **$8 $15 $30**

MKY-1638

MKY-1639

❏ **MKY-1638. English Bicycle Bell Attachment,**
1970s. "C.J. Adie & Nephew Ltd." 2" diameter by 1.75" tall chromed metal. - **$10 $20 $40**

❏ **MKY-1639. "Mickey Mouse Guitar,"**
1970s. Carnival Toy. 6x17" display card holds 15" tall hard plastic guitar. Carded - **$15 $30 $60**

MKY-1640

MICKEY MOUSE, MINNIE & NEPHEWS

☐ **MKY-1640. "Walt Disney Character Appliques By Streamline" Store Display,** 1970s. Large 8x16x34" tall display with metal frame and pair of revolving columns with top die-cut attachment being thick mason board with thin cardboard covering. - **$50 $100 $200**

MKY-1641

☐ **MKY-1641. "Le Journal De Mickey" Huge Outdoor Advertising Banner,** 1970s. French. 36x79" vinyl-coated fabric for outdoor use to promote publication. - **$30 $60 $125**

MKY-1642

MKY-1643

☐ **MKY-1642. "Le Journal De Mickey" Huge Outdoor Advertising Banner,** 1970s. French. 27.5x112" vinyl-coated fabric for outdoor use to promote publication. - **$30 $60 $125**

☐ **MKY-1643. Disney Characters "Musical Collectibles" Promotion Figurine,** 1970s. Schmid. 2x5.5x3.75" tall painted and glazed ceramic store display. - **$10 $20 $45**

MKY-1644

☐ **MKY-1644. "Minnie Mouse Rag Doll,"** 1970s. 5x9.5x1" deep box holds 7.5" tall stuffed rag doll. Back of box pictures matching Mickey doll. Near Mint Boxed - **$50**

MKY-1645

☐ **MKY-1645. Mickey Mouse "Wind-Up 'Walking' Toy,"** 1970s. Durham Industries Inc. 6x9" die-cut blister card contains 4" tall hard plastic figure with built-in key. Near Mint Carded - **$20**

MKY-1646

MKY-1647

☐ **MKY-1646. "Mickey Mouse/Donald Duck Disney Dancer,"** 1970s. Gabriel. Each is 2.5x3.5x1" deep hard plastic. Each has a die-cut plastic jointed figure attached to backdrop by a wheel which is spun causing figure to move about as if dancing. Each - **$6 $12 $20**

☐ **MKY-1647. Walt Disney Characters Kaleidoscope,** 1970s. Hallmark. 9" long. - **$20 $40 $65**

MKY-1648

☐ **MKY-1648. "Mickey Mouse Sing-A-Long Radio,"** 1970s. "Concept 2000." Boxed 5x7.5x9" tall hard plastic three-dimensional replica of band wagon topped by vinyl figures of Mickey as bandleader with accordian, Donald with guitar, Pluto as singer, plus small removable microphone for "Sing-A-Long" use. Box - **$5 $10 $20** Radio - **$15 $30 $50**

MKY-1649

☐ **MKY-1649. "Mickey Mouse Sing-A-Long Radio,"** 1970s. Simpsons-Sears Ltd. Toronto. 3x8.5x6.5" tall hard plastic battery operated. Boxed - **$15 $30 $50**

MICKEY MOUSE, MINNIE & NEPHEWS

MKY-1650

MKY-1651

❑ **MKY-1652. "Mickey Mouse Watch,"** 1970s. Bradley. 2x3x3" deep plastic display case contains watch with 1" diameter metal case. Mickey's head nods as seconds tick. Near Mint Boxed - **$70**

MKY-1653

❑ **MKY-1653. Minnie Wristwatch,** 1970s. Bradley. 1.25" diameter chromed metal case with dial illustration of Minnie whose hands point at the numerals. Leather strap has images of Mickey. - **$45 $75 $125**

MKY-1654

MKY-1655

❑ **MKY-1650. "Mickey Mouse Talking Alarm Clock,"** 1970s. Bradley Time. 4.5x5.25x8.75" tall hard plastic clock in box. Attached to top is hard vinyl figure of Mickey from waist up depicted as engineer. Box - **$10 $20 $30** Clock - **$10 $20 $30**

❑ **MKY-1651. "Teach 'N' Play Clock,"** 1970s. Illco. 8x11.5x3.5" deep display box containing 8" tall Mickey figural hard plastic with inset wind-up toy clock. Near Mint Boxed - **$35**

MKY-1652

❑ **MKY-1654. "Windup Climbing Mickey Mouse" Boxed Fireman Toy,** 1970s. Durham. 4x5x11" tall box contains hard plastic toy with built-in key. Toy consists of 9" tall Mickey as fireman figure plus base with two-piece ladder that extends to height of 17". Mickey climbs to the top of the ladder and then slides down. Box - **$25 $50 $75** Toy - **$40 $65 $100**

❑ **MKY-1655. "Mickey Mouse's Car" By Polistil,** 1970s. Box is 2.5x4.5x6.5" tall and contains 3.75" long cast metal and plastic car. Car has three-dimensional rubber figure of Mickey. Box - **$10 $20 $30** Toy - **$20 $40 $60**

MKY-1656

❑ **MKY-1656. "Mickey Mouse Radio Control Camper Van,"** 1970s. Boxed 4x10.5x5.25" tall hard plastic battery toy with separate hand-held remote control unit. Box - **$10 $20 $35** Toy - **$20 $40 $75**

MKY-1657

❑ **MKY-1657. "The Wonderful World Of Disney" Snow Dome,** 1970s. Hard plastic 3.25x4x2.5" tall with clear front view three-dimensional figures of Mickey and Minnie with Sleeping Beauty's castle. - **$20 $40 $60**

MICKEY MOUSE, MINNIE & NEPHEWS

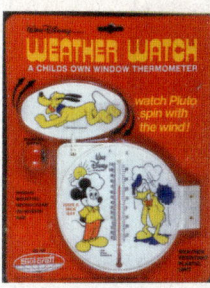

MKY-1658

MKY-1659

❏ MKY-1658. "Walt Disney Character Weather Watch,"
1970s. Skil-Craft. 10x12.5" blister card contains hard plastic "Child Window Thermometer." Near Mint Carded - **$30**

❏ MKY-1659. Mickey Mouse Figural Pencil Sharpener,
1970s. Hard plastic 4.75" tall. - **$10 $20 $30**

MKY-1660

MKY-1661

❏ MKY-1660. "Mickey Mouse Good Grooming Club" Set,
c. 1970s. The Dep Corp. 8x8.5x2" deep box holds two 7.5" soft plastic figural containers, one bottle is "Mickey Mouse Shampoo" and the other is "Donald Duck Lotion." Near Mint Boxed - **$45**

❏ MKY-1661. Mickey Mouse Lamp,
c. 1970s. Wis-Ton, Canada. Large 9" tall soft vinyl Mickey figure attached to 5.25" diameter vinyl base with total height of 14". - **$15 $25 $45**

MKY-1662

❏ MKY-1662. Minnie Mouse/Three Little Pigs Wall Plaques or Trivets,
c. 1970s. Cast aluminum, one of Minnie and one of the Three Pigs. Each has hanging hole at top center. Each - **$10 $15 $25**

MKY-1663

MKY-1664

❏ MKY-1663. Minnie Mouse Bank,
c. 1970s. Painted and glazed ceramic bank 4x4x5.75" tall and complete with trap. - **$20 $40 $60**

❏ MKY-1664. "Mickey Mouse Pocketwatch,"
c. 1970s. Bradley Time. 2" diameter hard plastic watch in box. Box - **$5 $15 $25** Watch - **$15 $30 $50**

MKY-1665

❏ MKY-1665. "Mickey Mouse" Wristwatch,
c. 1970s. Bradley. 1-1/8" square silvered metal case. Has unusual one-piece silvered metal bracelet-style wrist strap. - **$20 $40 $65**

MKY-1666

MKY-1667

MICKEY MOUSE, MINNIE & NEPHEWS

❏ **MKY-1666. Mickey Mouse As Sorcerer's Apprentice Carved Wood Figure,** c. 1980. Limited edition by Anri of Italy. 3.5" tall. - **$55 $110 $160**

❏ **MKY-1667. "Mickey & Minnie Mouse Doctor And Nurse Playset" By Colorforms,** 1981. Includes colorful background board depicting doctor's office and two oversized sheets of die-cut vinyl characters and accessories. - **$12 $25 $45**

MKY-1668

❏ **MKY-1668. Mickey Mouse Lever-Action Car,** 1981. Modern Toys. 3x4x3.25" tall tin lithographed and plastic car with three-dimensional vinyl figure of Mickey with movable head. Right side of car has small lever that when pulled back and released causes the car to speed forward. - **$10 $20 $35**

MKY-1669

❏ **MKY-1669. World On Ice Banner With Mickey,** c. 1981. Large 30.5x61" rubberized vinyl banner, believed for first year of World On Ice performances and used as show promotion, not as souvenir item. - **$25 $50 $110**

MKY-1670

MKY-1671

❏ **MKY-1670. "The Disney Channel" Salesman's Promotional Folder,** 1982. 10x14" on stiff glossy paper issued to promote upcoming The Disney Channel which began broadcasting in April 1983. - **$5 $10 $20**

❏ **MKY-1671. "The Rescuers/Mickey's Christmas Carol" Lobby Card Set With Envelope,** 1983. Set of eight 11x14" stiff glossy paper for double-feature release. Set - **$10 $20 $40**

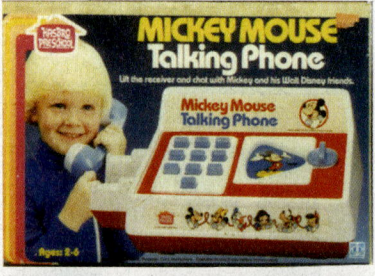

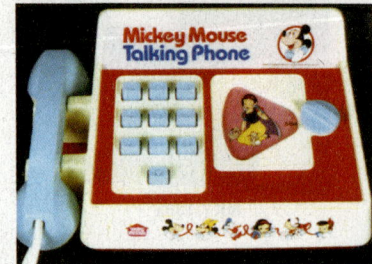
MKY-1672

❏ **MKY-1672. "Mickey Mouse Talking Phone,"** 1983. Hasbro. 8x12.5x6" deep box contains battery operated hard plastic phone. Phone has rubber tube cord. Top of unit has viewing screen and knob is used to change character image. Each image has matching character voice activated when certain button combination is pressed. Near Mint Boxed - **$55**

MKY-1673

❏ **MKY-1673. Mickey Mouse Wrist Watch Original Concept Art,** 1983. 14x17" paper sheet with large art done in pencil and colored marker featuring Mickey on watch dial. Art was produced for Bradley. Unique, Excellent. - **$200**

MKY-1674

MICKEY MOUSE, MINNIE & NEPHEWS

☐ **MKY-1674. Disney Christmas Collector Plates,**
1985. Schmid. First china plate is 7.5" limited to 20,000, second 1986 plate is 8.5" limited to 25,000. Each - **$5 $10 $15**

MKY-1675

☐ **MKY-1675. Mickey Animator Kimball Letter With Drawings,**
1986. Two-page 8.5x11" typewritten letter by Mickey Mouse legendary animator Ward Kimball from c. 1934 onward. Letter is to English book publisher and Disney historian Justin Knowles and recalls many events from Kimball's close and often amusing involvement with Mickey through five decades. Letter is on photocopy vintage Disney letterheads of the 1930s. Second page includes actual pencil drawings by Kimball of Mickey, Donald, Goofy, Pluto. Unique, Very Fine - **$450**

MKY-1676

☐ **MKY-1676. "Cooking With Mickey Around Our World,"**
1986. Has 292 pages of "Walt Disney World's Most Requested Recipes" divided into twelve sections, each with tabbed divider page featuring Mickey as chef illustrations. - **$10 $20 $40**

MKY-1677

☐ **MKY-1677. "Mickey Mouse 60th Anniversary Limited Edition Commemorative Serigraph,"**
1988. Image is 8x10" from the short "Nifty Nineties." Comes with laser background. Mint As Issued - **$225**

MKY-1678

☐ **MKY-1678. Mickey Mouse Cel,**
1988. Cel image of Mickey is 3x4" and second cel image is of three small butterflies. Shown with pencil drawing. - **$65 $125 $250**

MKY-1679

☐ **MKY-1679. "Mickey's 60th Birthday" Boxed Bisque,**
1988. Disneyland/Disney World. 4.5" tall. Plain generic box. Cost $45. Mint As Issued - **$60**

MKY-1680

MKY-1681

☐ **MKY-1680. "Mickey Mouse 60th Anniversary" Metal Figurine Boxed Set,**
1988. Pixi. 3.5x4.25x1.75" deep box contains three painted lead figures by French company. From a series and this is "Disney Memory/60th Anniversary." Comes with illustrated certificate card stamped with collection name and stock #4604 as well as inked edition "121." Figures are Walt, a chair and Mickey. Mint As Issued - **$225**

☐ **MKY-1681. "Steamboat Willie" 60-Year Commemorative Medal,**
1988. Rarities Mint Inc. 1.5" diameter .999 silver troy ounce commemoration for Mickey's first appearance in 1928 in "Steamboat Willie" short. Reverse has "Mickey's Sixty" official logo. Medal is displayed in 4.5x6.5x1" deep velveteen covered box with logo lid. Mint As Issued - **$45**

MKY-1682

☐ **MKY-1682. "Mickey Is Sixty!" Commemorative Magazine With Cel Insert,**
1988. Time Inc. 8x10.75" specialty publication comprised of 64 pages in full color supplemented by "Exclusive Disney Animation Art" cel of Mickey as Sorcerer's Apprentice. Cover art is by Andy Warhol and content includes contributions by Ray Bradbury, George Lucas, Stephen Spielberg, Jimmy Carter, many others. - **$5 $10 $25**

MICKEY MOUSE, MINNIE & NEPHEWS

MKY-1683

❑ **MKY-1683. "Mickey's Sixtieth Birthday" Sculpture,**
1988. From the Disney Capodimonte Collection by retired sculptor Enzo Arzenton. Edition size of 192. - **$2500**

MKY-1684

❑ **MKY-1684. Disney M-G-M Grand Opening Cel,**
1989. Hand-painted animation cel is 5.5x5.5" produced in limited edition only for opening day of Disney M-G-M Studios theme park. Mint As Issued - **$240**

MKY-1685

❑ **MKY-1685. German Figure Set,**
c. 1989. "Ferrero Kinder." Set of eleven different hand-painted hard plastic figures, each about 1.5" tall. All are similar to Disneykins of the 1960s but are much more detailed. Set includes two different Mickeys, Minnie, the nephews, Goofy, Pluto, Beagle Boys, Black Pete and police officer. Set is accompanied by 1.5x4.5" paper with illustration of the figures plus their names in German. Set - **$30 $60 $120**

MKY-1686

MKY-1687

❑ **MKY-1686. "Mickey Lunch Kit" Figural Lunch Box,**
c. 1989. Aladdin. 9x10.5x9.5" tall hard plastic with 6" tall plastic thermos. Box - **$5 $10 $40**
Bottle - **$5 $10 $40**

❑ **MKY-1687. Mickey Mouse Cel,**
1980s. Image is 5.25x7". From a 1980s TV appearance. - **$100 $200 $300**

MKY-1688

MKY-1689

MICKEY MOUSE, MINNIE & NEPHEWS

❏ **MKY-1688. Minnie Mouse And Donald's Nephew Cel,**
1980s. Image of Minnie is 4.5x7.5", nephew is 3x6". From a Disney Pops commercial. - **$60** **$115** **$165**

❏ **MKY-1689. Mickey Mouse Cel,**
1980s. 10.5x12.5" acetate sheet has 5x7" image. #6/52 from a numbered sequence. - **$50** **$100** **$150**

MKY-1690

❏ **MKY-1690. Mickey Mouse Cel,**
1980s. 10.5x12.5" acetate sheet with 3.25x4.25" hand-inked cel image. - **$50** **$100** **$150**

MKY-1691

❏ **MKY-1691. Mickey And Pluto Serigraph Cel,**
1980s. Matted and framed individual images combined into 5x9.5" dual image from 1939 cartoon short, "The Pointer." Reverse of frame has label notation of limited edition of 9500 pieces by "Walt Disney Productions." Mint As Issued - **$185**

MKY-1692

❏ **MKY-1692. Wizard Of Id/Mickey Mouse Sketch,**
1980s. Paper is 3.5x8.5" with 3x3" inked art by Brant Parker, creator of Wizard of Id comic strip and a former Disney artist. Unique, Near Mint - **$160**

MKY-1693

MKY-1694

❏ **MKY-1693. Carl Barks Signed Mickey Mouse Print,**
1980s. 9x11" image size. Limited edition of 174. Mint As Issued - **$300**

❏ **MKY-1694. "Mouskamania Puzzle,"**
1980s. Hallmark Cards Inc. Springbok 11.5x11.5x2" deep boxed 1000-piece jigsaw puzzle assembling to 24x30" color photo scene of exceptional vintage 1930s Mickey collection of Disney collector Bernard Shine. - **$10** **$20** **$30**

MKY-1695

MKY-1696

❏ **MKY-1695. "Walt Disney Schmid" Store Display Figurine,**
1980s. Schmid. 2.5x5.25x6" painted and glazed ceramic. - **$10** **$20** **$40**

❏ **MKY-1696. Mickey Mouse Band Leader Miniature Metal Figure,**
1980s. Detailed but only 1" tall. Sold briefly at Disneyland. - **$60** **$125** **$225**

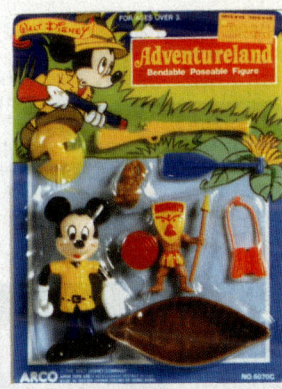
MKY-1697

❏ **MKY-1697. Mickey "Adventureland" Poseable Figure,**
1980s. Arco Toys Ltd./Mattel. 8.5x11" blister card packaged set of 4.5" tall flexible bendy Mickey as jungle explorer plus accessory pieces of pith helmet, rifle, boat and oar, binoculars, monkey, smaller bendy of a witch doctor. Carded Near Mint - **$25**

MICKEY MOUSE, MINNIE & NEPHEWS

MKY-1698

MKY-1699

MKY-1700

❏ **MKY-1698. Mickey Mouse Conductor Limited Edition Wooden Figure,**
1980s. Anri of Italy. Number 12 in club series limited to 5000. 4.75" tall. - **$55 $135 $215**

❏ **MKY-1699. Mickey Mouse Riding Butterfly Enamel On Brass Jewelry By Wendy Gell,**
1980s. Beautifully crafted 1.25x2.25" piece of jewelry with hinged circular clip on reverse rather than a pin. - **$12 $25 $50**

❏ **MKY-1700. Mickey As Chef Salt & Pepper Set,**
1980s. Large pair of 4.5" tall glazed ceramic matched shakers. - **$8 $15 $25**

MKY-1701

❏ **MKY-1701. Figure Bank,**
1980s. Leonard Of Japan. 3.5x3.5x5.25" tall cast metal figural finished in silver luster depicting Mickey in tuxedo holding his hat and sitting atop a suitcase. Foil sticker on underside, complete with trap. - **$10 $20 $30**

MKY-1702

MKY-1703

❏ **MKY-1702. "Disney Video Cassettes" Promotional Clock,**
1980s. 10.25" diameter by 1.5" deep battery operated hard plastic. Issued on a promotional basis to video store owners. - **$20 $40 $80**

❏ **MKY-1703. "Disney" Video Store Promo Clock,**
1980s. 14.5" diameter by 1.5" deep hard plastic issued on a promotional basis to video store owners. - **$10 $20 $40**

MKY-1704

❏ **MKY-1704. "Mickey's Corn Popper" Battery Operated Toy,**
c. 1980s. Illco. 3.5x8x6.5" tall hard plastic. Mickey pushes the cart around with bump-and-go action as his head moves. Inside lights and balls pop around as the song "It's A Small World" is played. - **$12 $25 $50**

MKY-1705

❏ **MKY-1705. "Pelham Puppets" Mickey Mouse Store Display Marionette,**
c. 1980s. Exceptionally large Mickey marionette with attached wood hand control unit. Mickey is 10x10x25.5" tall with composition body, felt ears and shirt, cloth pants and black flexible rubber legs. Control unit has metal plate marked "Pelham Puppets/Made In England." Production of these displays was quite limited. - **$250 $500 $750**

MKY-1706

MICKEY MOUSE, MINNIE & NEPHEWS

MKY-1707

◻ **MKY-1706. The Sorcerer's Apprentice Pencil Drawing,**
1990. Image of Mickey is 4.5x4.5" and broom is 2.5x5.5". Has penciled signature and date "Ken Anderson '90." Anderson began his career in 1934 as art director to many films including Snow White and The Pastoral Symphony section of Fantasia. - **$250 $500 $750**

◻ **MKY-1707. "Mickey's Holiday Treasures" Troy Ounce Of Silver,**
1990. Rarities Mint. 1.5" diameter. Limited edition of 10,000 with individual proof number. Mint - **$35**

MKY-1708

◻ **MKY-1708. "Disney Collectible Classic Charlotte Clark Dolls" Boxed Reproductions,**
1990. Limited editions of 10,000 by Applause. Each 16" tall. Includes numbered certificate. Each Boxed - **$25 $50 $75**

MKY-1709

◻ **MKY-1709. German Museum Disney Exhibition Catalogue,**
1991. Catalogue is 7.75x8.5" with 208 pages, about 1,000 copies published for a Disney Expo at the Film Museum of Potsdam, Germany. All in German, plus many photos covering German-issued Disney items and a history of Disney in Germany from 1927-1945. Sixteen full color pages show merchandise of rare toys and porcelain figurines including Rosenthals. - **$40 $80 $150**

MKY-1710

◻ **MKY-1710. "Minnie on the Beach" Figure,**
1993. Very unusual Capodiamonte figure; a sold out edition of only 197. - **$675**

MKY-1711   MKY-1712

◻ **MKY-1711. "The Disney Channel" Promotional Champagne Bottle,**
1993. 12" tall clear glass filled with jellybeans. Near Mint - **$35**

◻ **MKY-1712. "Through The Mirror" Bronze Sculpture,**
1996. Limited edition of 200. Sculpted by Paul Vought. Signed by Carl Barks.
Mint As Issued - **$500**

MKY-1713

◻ **MKY-1713. Bob Mackie Collectible Millenium Minnie Mouse Doll,**
1999. This limited edition doll marks the debut of Minnie Mouse Fashion dolls. Mint As Issued - **$115**

MKY-1714

◻ **MKY-1714. Mickey Mouse Cel From The Disney Channel's Mouse Works,**
1999. Acetate sheet is 10.5x12.5" with 3.5x3.75" image. Mint As Issued - **$110**

MICKEY MOUSE, MINNIE & NEPHEWS

MKY-1715

❏ **MKY-1715. "Mr. Mouse Takes A Trip" Serigraph,**
1990s. Image is 4.25x8" with Walt Disney Co. seal. From a limited edition of 9,500 pieces. Mint As Issued - **$150**

MKY-1716

❏ **MKY-1716. Mickey And Minnie Serigraph,**
1990s. Acetate sheet is 10.75x14" with 6x6.5" image of Minnie covering Mickey's face with lipstick kisses, based on the 1939 "Mickey's Surprise Party" short. Background is color laser scene. Limited edition with "Walt Disney Company" seal at bottom right. Near Mint As Issued - **$125**

MKY-1717

❏ **MKY-1717. Mickey And Minnie Serigraph,**
1990s. Acetate sheet is 10.75x14" with 5.5x7" cel image of Mickey and Minnie skating based on the 1935 "On Ice" short. Background is color laser depiction of frozen lake waters. Limited edition with "Walt Disney Company" seal at bottom right. Near Mint As Issued - **$125**

MKY-1718

❏ **MKY-1718. Mickey With Donald's Nephews Cel,**
1990s. Mouse Works TV. Cel consisting of four 10x12" acetate sheets, each with different character image for combined image of 4x5.5" on color laser background. Near Mint - **$175**

MKY-1719

MKY-1720

❏ **MKY-1719. Mickey Animation Cel,**
1990s. Acetate sheet is 10.5x12" with 3x4.75" full figure painted image. Laser background sheet. Near Mint - **$275**

❏ **MKY-1720. Mickey And Minnie As Roman Citizens Ceramic Figures,**
1990s. China. Sold at Caesar's Palace Casino, Las Vegas. Each 5" tall. Each - **$5 $10 $15**

MKY-1721

❏ **MKY-1721. "Mickey & Minnie" Creamer/Sugar Set,**
1990s. Painted and glazed ceramic set 4.25" tall. - **$10 $25 $50**

612

MICKEY MOUSE, MINNIE & NEPHEWS

MKY-1722

☐ **MKY-1722. "Mickey/Minnie Japanese Candy Tin,"**
1990s. Lithographed tin container 6x10.75x1.5" deep. Contains two layers of taffy with each piece wrapped in identical wrapper depicting Mickey with guitar and Minnie holding umbrella. Lid is marked "Milaoshu/Tang." Near Mint As Issued - **$50**

MKY-1723

☐ **MKY-1723. Mickey Wristwatch Retro Re-Issue Boxed,**
1990s. "Pedre." Reproduction of the first Ingersoll watch from 1933 in 2.5x4.5x1.75" deep box with hinged lid. Mint As Issued - **$215**

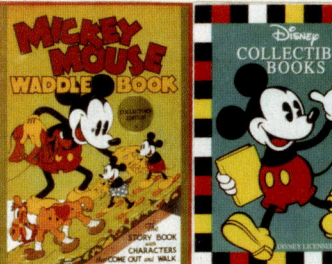

MKY-1724

☐ **MKY-1724. "Mickey Mouse Waddle Book Collector's Edition" Set,**
1990s. Applewood Books. 8.25x11x1" deep boxed limited edition and authorized exact reproduction of the 1934 "Mickey Mouse Waddle Book" published originally by Blue Ribbon Books. The Applewood edition includes an extra set of punch-out waddle characters Mickey, Minnie, Pluto and Tanglefoot plus folder for other "Disney Collectibles Books." Reproduction publication was limited to 1,000 copies at original $70 purchase price each. Mint As Issued - **$90**

MKY-1725

MKY-1726

☐ **MKY-1725. "Mickey's Busy Book,"**
1990s. Book is 6.5x7.25" with eight pages. Near Mint - **$12**

☐ **MKY-1726. Fantasia Limited Edition Sericel,**
1990s. Image is 5x6.75". Limited edition of 5000 with "The Walt Disney Company/Sericel Certified" seal. Mint As Issued - **$250**

MKY-1727

☐ **MKY-1727. "Lenox Bandleader Mickey" Ornament Inspired By Macy's Parade Balloon,**
2000. Box is 4x4x6.25" and contains quality clear glass ornament issued for the 2000 Macy's Thanksgiving Day Parade. This is the first in a series. Displays NYC landmarks including World Trade Center. Mint As Issued - **$80**

MKY-1728

☐ **MKY-1728. Very Victorian Minnie Mouse Collectible Doll,**
2000. From the Minnie Mouse Fashion doll collection. Mint As Issued - **$60**

MICKEY MOUSE, MINNIE & NEPHEWS

MKY-1729

☐ **MKY-1729. Rice Krispies Cereal Box,** 2000. Promotes Mini Bobble Head inside. - **$12**

MKY-1730

☐ **MKY-1730. Mickey Mini Bobble,** 2004. Premium from Rice Krispies box. - **$8**

MKY-1731

☐ **MKY-1731. Mickey Mini Bobble,** 2004. - **$20**

MKY-1732

☐ **MKY-1732. Mickey Mouse Monopoly Game,** 2004. Mint As Issued - **$35**

MKY-1733

MKY-1734

☐ **MKY-1733. Mickey Plush Keyring,** 2004. - **$5**

☐ **MKY-1734. Mickey Keyring,** 2004. - **$5**

MKY-1735

MKY-1736

☐ **MKY-1735. Mickey Keyring,** 2004. - **$5**

☐ **MKY-1736. Minnie Keyring,** 2004. - **$5**

MICKEY MOUSE COMICS

Mickey Mouse Comics

Dell Publishing started Mickey's own self-titled book with issue # 28 (Dec 51). They considered his previous appearances in *Four Color Comics* as the early part of his book's run. Those issues are: *Four Color Comics* #16, 27, 79, 116, 141, 170, 181, 194, 214, 231, 248, 261, 268, 279, 286, 296, 304, 313, 325, 334, 343, 352, 362, 371, 387, 401, 411, and 427. His title was published by Dell/Gold Key from issues #28-204. Whitman published issues #204-218. Gladstone published the title from #219-256. Gemstone started their run with issue #257 Gemstone also publishes a digest-format book *Mickey Mouse Adventures*. It started fresh with issue #1.

❏ Mickey Mouse #30,
April 1953. - $6 $18 $70

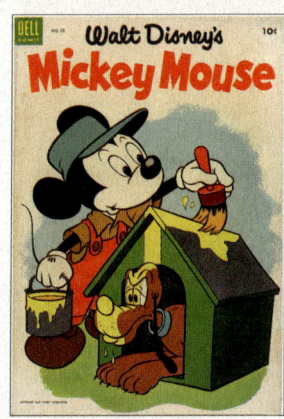
❏ Mickey Mouse #33,
October 1953. - $6 $18 $70

❏ Mickey Mouse #28,
December 1952. - $6 $18 $70

❏ Mickey Mouse #31,
June 1953. - $6 $18 $70

❏ Mickey Mouse #34,
February 1954. - $6 $18 $70

❏ Mickey Mouse #29,
February 1953. - $6 $18 $70

❏ Mickey Mouse #32,
August 1953. - $6 $18 $70

❏ Mickey Mouse #35,
April 1954. - $5 $15 $60

MICKEY MOUSE COMICS

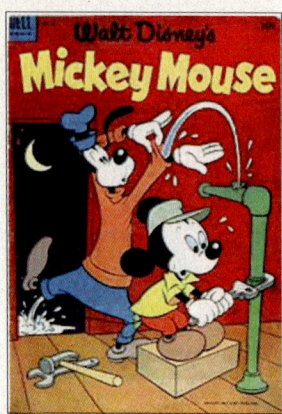

❏ **Mickey Mouse #36,**
June 1954. - $5 $15 $60

❏ **Mickey Mouse #39,**
December 1954. - $5 $15 $60

❏ **Mickey Mouse #42,**
June 1955. - $5 $15 $60

❏ **Mickey Mouse #37,**
August 1954. - $5 $15 $60

❏ **Mickey Mouse #40,**
February 1955. - $5 $15 $60

❏ **Mickey Mouse #43,**
August 1955. - $5 $15 $60

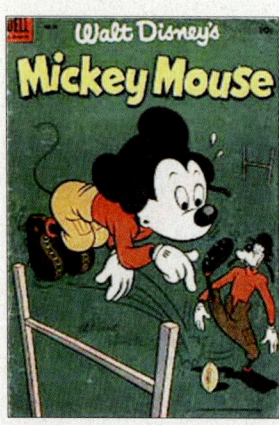

❏ **Mickey Mouse #38,**
October 1954. - $5 $15 $60

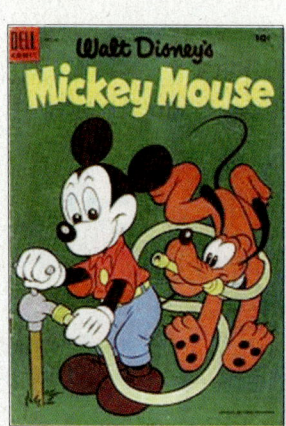

❏ **Mickey Mouse #41,**
April 1955. - $5 $15 $60

❏ **Mickey Mouse #44,**
October 1955. - $5 $15 $60

MICKEY MOUSE COMICS

☐ Mickey Mouse #45,
December 1955. - $5 $15 $60

☐ Mickey Mouse #48,
June 1956. - $5 $15 $60

☐ Mickey Mouse #51,
December 1956. - $4 $12 $45

☐ Mickey Mouse #46,
February 1956. - $5 $15 $60

☐ Mickey Mouse #49,
August 1956. - $5 $15 $60

☐ Mickey Mouse #52,
February 1957. - $4 $12 $45

☐ Mickey Mouse #47,
April 1956. - $5 $15 $60

☐ Mickey Mouse #50,
October 1956. - $5 $15 $60

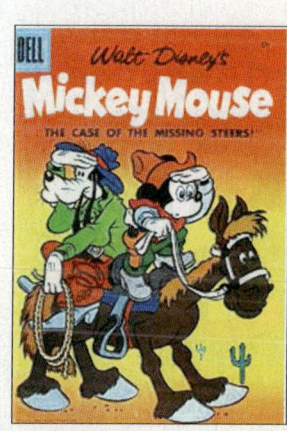
☐ Mickey Mouse #53,
April 1957. - $4 $12 $45

MICKEY MOUSE COMICS

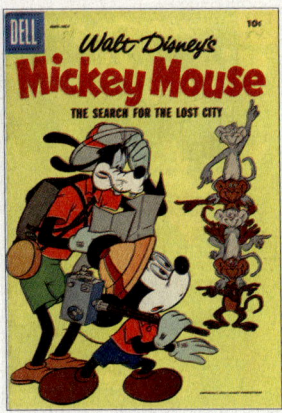
❏ **Mickey Mouse #54,**
June 1957. - $4 $12 $45

❏ **Mickey Mouse #57,**
December 1957. - $4 $12 $45

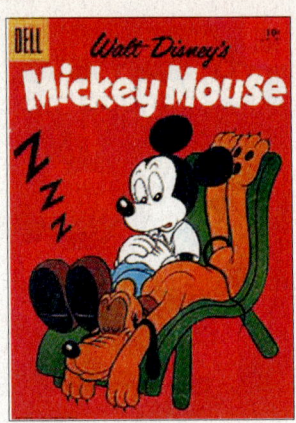
❏ **Mickey Mouse #60,**
June 1957. - $3 $10 $45

❏ **Mickey Mouse #55,**
August 1957. - $4 $12 $45

❏ **Mickey Mouse #58,**
February 1958. - $4 $12 $45

❏ **Mickey Mouse #61,**
August 1958. - $3 $10 $45

❏ **Mickey Mouse #56,**
October 1957. - $4 $12 $45

❏ **Mickey Mouse #59,**
April 1958. - $4 $12 $45

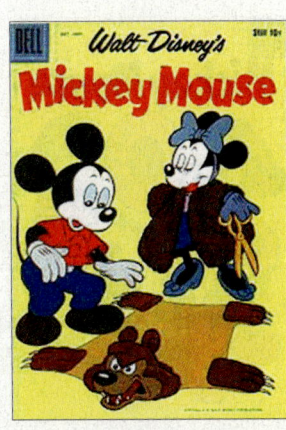
❏ **Mickey Mouse #62,**
October 1958. - $3 $10 $45

Mickey Mouse Club (TV)

On October 3, 1955, the ABC television network televised the first episode of *The Mickey Mouse Club*. Scheduled as an afternoon program from Monday though Friday, the show was hosted by a group of children who were just about the same age as the target audience. These hosts were known as Mouseketeers. Within a few months they became household names. Some of the more memorable Mouseketeers were Cheryl Holdridge, Cubby O'Brien, Karen Pendleton, Tommy Kirk, Darlene Gillespie and Annette Funicello. Different segments showed them singing and dancing, introducing guests, appearing in skits and generally just having fun.

The concept for the club was not a new one. Mickey Mouse Clubs were first organized as a theatrical promotion in 1929. The lodge-like club meetings were also a way for theatres to bring in an increased number of children during sparsely attended hours. The clubs also doubled as a way to advertise and promote cartoons by Disney.

Years later, the advent of TV created a massive need for programming. As TV networks began to expand their broadcast day to include afternoons and mornings, this became especially true. More importantly, it created a need for programming that could be directed to the primary audience watching during that specific time period.

ABC, a relatively new network and a distant third to NBC and CBS at the time, singled out children as a desirable afternoon target group. With that in mind, network executives decided to give a revived and largely reinvented Mickey Mouse Club a chance.

Adult members, called Mooseketeers, were also featured on the show. They appeared to be riding herd over their younger counterparts. Guitar-playing Jimmie Dodd wrote many of the show's songs. Animator and comics writer Roy Williams offered drawing lessons. *The Mickey Mouse Club* also featured several different segments. *Mousekartoon Time* would feature early Disney cartoons. The Mickey Mouse Club Newsreel presented international human interest pieces. The show also featured adventure serials, such as *Spin and Marty*, *The Hardy Boys*, *Annette*, and *Corky and White Shadow*. The serial aspect of these features assured that kids would tune in the next day.

Kids who watched *The Mickey Mouse Club* were encouraged to wear the official Mouseketeer hat. This was essentially a round, black beanie cap with really big Mickey ears attached.

Originally broadcast as a one-hour series, *The Mickey Mouse Club* was later cut down to a half-hour. It was syndicated in that form from 1962-65 and again in 1975. The club concept has experienced several reinventions over the past few years. An all-new series, *The New Mickey Mouse Club*, appeared in 1977-78. Still another incarnation, called both *Mickey Mouse Club* and the shorter *MMC*, appeared on the Disney Channel from 1989-93. This most recent series is best known for having been the first television series to feature Britney Spears.

Merchandise connected to the show's variations included hats, books and records, and the "Mousegetar," a toy version of Jimmie Dodd's guitar. Several characters and episodic series taken from the *Mickey Mouse Club* appear in *Four Color Comics*. # 70 showcases *Corky and White Shadow*. Issues #714, 767, 808, 826, 1026 and 1082 all feature *Spin and Marty*. *The Hardy Boys* can be seen in #760, 830, 887 and 964,

MMC-2

MMC-1

MMC-3

❏ **MMC-2. "Mousegetar Jr.",**
1955. Mattel 5.25x14x1.75" deep illustrated display box containing 13.5" tall hard plastic toy guitar operated by crank but detailed by four nylon strings, tuning keys plus shoulder strap. This "Jr" version is the smaller of two Mousegetars produced. Box - **$15 $30 $60** Guitar - **$35 $65 $125**

❏ **MMC-3. "Walt Disney's Fun With Music From Many Lands" Sealed Record ,**
1955. Stiff paper sleeve is 7x7" and contains 45rpm "Official Mickey Mouse Club" record #53 from the "DBR" series. - **$20 $40 $65**

❏ **MMC-1. "Mickey Mouse Club Animation Kit" Elaborate Prototype,**
1954. Unique design crafted by "Disney Legend" toy designer Al Konetzni consisting of total four cardboard or paper parts varying in size from 3x5" up to largest 8.25x11" prototype instruction sheet. Parts are combined with string to form a "Spinning Mobile" whereby creating a moving animation image of Mickey, referred to as "Ani-Mates." Prototype was created for "Ipana's premium or for other uses of animation twirl idea." Unique, Very Fine - **$375**

MMC-4

MICKEY MOUSE CLUB (TV)

❏ **MMC-4. "Jiminy Cricket" Record Of Mickey Mouse Club Songs,**
1955. Am-Par Record Corp. 7.25x7.25" paper sleeve containing "DBR56" 45rpm record on "Official Mickey Mouse Club" label. Jiminy Cricket is the singing voice of five Mickey Mouse Club songs. - **$6 $12 $25**

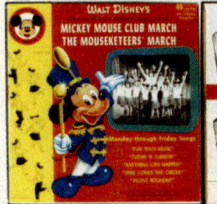 

MMC-5

MMC-6

❏ **MMC-5. "Official Mickey Mouse Club Songs" Record,**
1955. Am-Par Record Corp. 7x7" cardboard sleeve holding "DBR50" black vinyl version 45rpm including songs "Mickey Mouse Club March/The Mouseketeers' March" featuring voices of Jimmy Dodd, The Mouseketeers, Mickey, Donald, Jiminy Cricket. - **$12 $25 $50**

❏ **MMC-6. "Fun With Music Vol. 1" Record,**
1955. Simon & Schuster. 10x10" cardboard sleeve containing single 78 rpm "Official Mickey Mouse Club" orange vinyl record #DBR51. Songs are by Jimmy Dodd and Mouseketeers. - **$20 $40 $65**

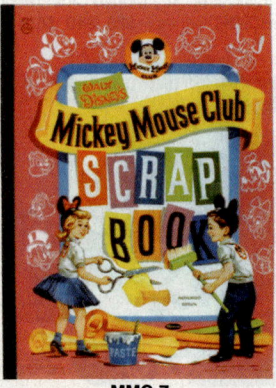

MMC-7

❏ **MMC-7. "Mickey Mouse Club Scrapbook,"**
1955. Whitman. 10.25x13.5" hardcover album with 72 blank pages. - **$10 $20 $50**

MMC-8

❏ **MMC-8. "Mouseketeer Write-On Cloth Doll" Concept Art Signed,**
1956. 9.75x11" tracing paper sheet with art plus notations by "Disney Legend" Al Konetzni. Notations include "Mouseketeer Write-On Cloth Doll With Liquid Lead Pencil Attached" and "Join The Mouseketters/Write Your Name On Me." Konetzni signed both in 1956 and recently. Unique, Fine - **$165**

MMC-9

MMC-10

❏ **MMC-9. Jimmy Dodd Signed Letter On Club Stationery With Related Papers,**
1956. 8.5x11" sheet of "Mickey Mouse Club Mouseketeers" letterhead with typewritten letter dated Nov. 9 signed personally "Jimmy Dodd." Letter is to American Broadcasting Co. and refers to TV ad jingles created by Dodd. Accompanying papers list past and future dated uses of jingles. Signed Letter - **$40 $75 $135**

❏ **MMC-10. Retailer's Sales Sheet With Mickey Mouse Club Items,**
1956. Mattel. 8.5x11" four-page "Spring" issue folder with cover page printed front and back by club logos plus items including Mousegetar, Mousegetar Jr., Mickey Mouse Club and Disneyland Musical Maps, Mousekartooner. - **$12 $25 $45**

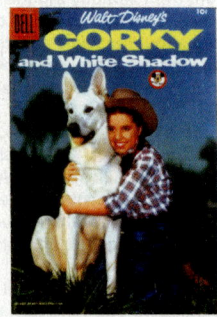

MMC-11

❏ **MMC-11. "Walt Disney's Corky And White Shadow" Comic Book,**
1956. Dell Publishing Co. Comic #707. - **$8 $24 $82**

MMC-12

❏ **MMC-12. "Mickey Mouse Club Magazine," First Issue,**
1956. Western Printing Co. 8.25x11.25" Volume 1 #1 "Winter" issue with 44 pages of articles, stories, puzzles, photos and illustrations. - **$65 $125 $225**

MMC-13

MICKEY MOUSE CLUB (TV)

❏ **MMC-13.** "Mickey Mouse Club Magazine,"
1956. Western Printing Co. 8.25x11.5" Volume 1 #4 "Fall" issue with 44 pages. - **$25 $50 $100**

MMC-14

❏ **MMC-14.** "Walt Disney's Mickey Mouse Club Magazine,"
1956. Western Printing. Volume 2, #1 from December 1956. 8x25x11.5". 42 pages. - **$30 $60 $125**

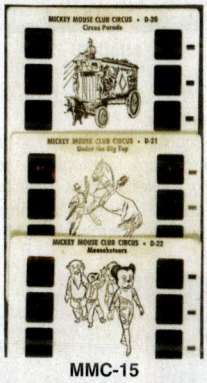
MMC-15

❏ **MMC-15.** "Mickey Mouse Club Circus" Film Card Set,
1956. Tru-Vue complete set D-20-22 of three 3.5x5.5" color photo stereo view cards titled "Circus Parade, Under The Big Top, Mouseketeers." Photos include Mouseketeers at Disneyland and performing in the circus. Set - **$15 $25 $40**

MMC-16

❏ **MMC-16.** "Mickey Mouse Club Fun Box,"
1957. Whitman. 9.25x11.75x1.5" boxed extensive set of storybooks, scrapbook with blank pages, stamp book with stamp blocks, two frame tray puzzles, coloring books, crayons, game sheet. - **$40 $65 $120**

MMC-17

❏ **MMC-17.** "Mouseketeer Cut-Outs,"
1957. Whitman. 10.5x12" with pocket storage areas. Dolls are of Cubby and Karen with outfits and accessories. Uncut - **$25 $65 $135**

MMC-18

❏ **MMC-18.** "Official Mouseclubouse Treasury Bank,"
1957. Mattel. 5.5x8x6.5" tall clubhouse-designed bank comes in nicely illustrated box. One side panel of box has photo including Jimmy Dodd and Annette. Bank is mostly tin lithographed with hard plastic front door, roof and barrel chimney. Top of roof has coin slot, front door opens by means of a key. Comes with pair of these specially designed 1.5" tall hard plastic keys featuring the head of Mickey Mouse.
Box - **$25 $50 $125**
Bank - **$100 $200 $300**
Each Key - **$5 $10 $25**

MMC-19

MMC-20

❏ **MMC-19.** "Mickey Mouse Club" Frame Tray Puzzle,
1957. Whitman. 11.5x14.5" inlay scene of county fair pig judging outside of the clubhouse. - **$5 $15 $30**

❏ **MMC-20.** "27 New Songs From The Mickey Mouse Club TV Show" Record,
1957. Cardboard album cover is 12.25x12.25" and contains 33-1/3rpm "Official Mickey Mouse Club" single record. Back cover also pictures Mouseketeers plus Annette individually. - **$65 $125 $200**

621

MICKEY MOUSE CLUB (TV)

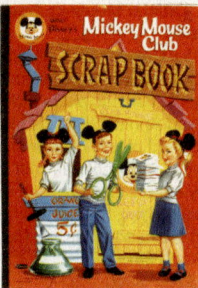
MMC-21

☐ **MMC-21. "Mickey Mouse Club Scrap Book,"**
1957. Whitman. 10x13.5" with sixty blank paper pages. - **$8 $12 $40**

MMC-22

☐ **MMC-22. Toy Retailer's Catalogue With Mickey Mouse Club Emphasis,**
1957. Pressman Toy Corp. 8.5x11" softcover 35th anniversary annual, 36 pages. Content features total of 20 Mickey Mouse Club items pictured and described including art and craft sets, carded toys of beauty, medical and barber nature, plus games. - **$12 $25 $40**

MMC-23

☐ **MMC-23. Mickey Mouse Club/Disney Character Belts,**
1950s. Three illustrated vinyl belts, each on 4x13.5" die-cut display card that also includes punch-out character figures. Each Carded - **$10 $20 $30**

MMC-24

☐ **MMC-24. "Mickey Mouse Club Mouseketeers" Unusual Figural Hat,**
1950s. Benay-Albee. 6.5x7.5x3" deep felt fabric designed to be worn on back of the head for a Mickey face image when viewed rearwards. Front image is skull cap with mouse ears. Attached to the top front of hat is synthetic fabric patch with Mouse Club logo. Reverse of hat is a pair of black and white metal and plastic google eyes, raised mouth area with red felt tongue, black wood ball nose. - **$15 $30 $60**

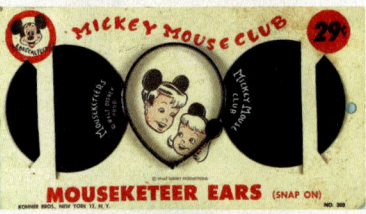
MMC-25

☐ **MMC-25. "Mouseketeer Ears,"**
1950s. Kohner Brothers. 6.75x12.5" display card holding "Mickey Mouse Club" hard plastic "Snap-On" unit to resemble Mouseketeer hat.
Card - **$8 $15 $30**
Ears - **$5 $12 $20**

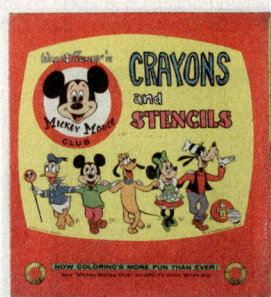

MMC-26

☐ **MMC-26. "Mickey Mouse Club Crayons And Stencils" Set,**
1950s. Transogram. 12x12.5x1.25" boxed set of four cardboard character stencils of Mickey, Donald, Pluto, Tinkerbell plus blank coloring sheets, pre-printed character coloring sheets, crayons and crayon sharpener. - **$35 $60 $100**

MMC-27

☐ **MMC-27. "Mattel Mousekartooner" Drawing Toy Boxed,**
1950s. Mattel. 9x15x1.5" deep illustrated display box holding 9x14x1" deep tin litho and plastic device aid for drawing pictures, mostly Disney characters. Box - **$15 $30 $50**
Toy - **$12 $25 $40**

MMC-28

MICKEY MOUSE CLUB (TV)

❑ **MMC-28. "Walt Disney Character Paint Set,"**
1950s. Transogram. 13x16.5x1.5" boxed extensive assortment of figural paint tablets plus crayons, poster paint containers and other activity materials. Segment of stencils is overlaid by Mickey Mouse Club logo paper. - **$35 $65 $110**

MMC-29

❑ **MMC-29. "Walt Disney's Mickey Mouse Club Magazine" Lay-Out Board,**
1950s. Western Printing 8.5x10.5" stiff white paper sheet used to produce envelopes for the magazine. Unique, Near Mint - **$55**

MMC-30

❑ **MMC-30. Mickey Mouse Concept Art For Pull Toy,**
1950s. Original art by "Disney Legend" toy designer Al Konetzni for wooden pull or riding toy produced by Gong Bell in 1958. Overall size is 12.5x17.5" comprised of three separate panels. Art is pencil and crayon. Depicted are front, side and rear of "Studio Bus." One panel has hand-lettered "Mickey Mouse Club Stars" which was changed to "Walt Disney Stars" on the finished product. Mickey is drawn as the bus driver. Unique, Fine - **$775**

MMC-31

❑ **MMC-31. Mickey Mouse Club Miniature Magic Slate Prototype,**
1950s. Unique design by "Disney Legend" toy designer Al Konetzni of 3x3.25" die-cut stiff cardboard photo applied of Roy Williams standing next to a simulated framed canvas centered by magic slate. Unique, Very Fine - **$200**

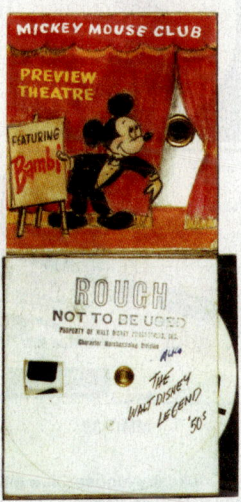

MMC-32

❑ **MMC-32. "Mickey Mouse Club Preview Theater" View-Master Prototype Item,**
1950s. Unique design by "Disney Legend" toy designer Al Konetzni of full-dimensioned 3.25x3.75x1.5" deep cardboard viewer for View-Master stereo view reel. Unique, Very Fine - **$200**

MMC-33

❑ **MMC-33. Mickey Mouse Club Mailer Folder/Premium Photos,**
1950s. 4x7.75" folder and opens to reveal club certificate and membership card. The folder was sent to acknowledge a subscription to the club magazine. Three 5x7" photos include cast photo of the Mouseketeers in their western outfits, Spin and Marty, and Ipana Toothpaste character Bucky Beaver. - **$60 $120 $200**

MMC-34

MMC-35

❑ **MMC-34. Mickey Mouse Club Publicity Photo,**
1950s. Glossy photo is 8x10" of cardboard clubhouse, three children each wearing "Mouseketeer" hat. One boy also holds club member booklet. - **$8 $12 $25**

❑ **MMC-35. Mouseketeers With Donald Duck Publicity Still,**
1950s. 8x10" glossy of 11 Mouseketeers wearing their personalized shirts and Mickey ear hats watching cartoon image of Donald, also wearing ear hat. - **$15 $30 $60**

MICKEY MOUSE CLUB (TV)

❑ **MMC-37. "Mickey Mouse Candy And Toy" Box,**
1950s. Super Novelty Candy Co. 2.5x3.75x1" "Candy And Toy" box. Front panel is simulated TV screen with punch-out "Mickey Mouse Club Official Emblem." Back panel is punch-out card for Captain Hook. All side panels feature different character portraits. Each In Series - **$15 $25 $50**

MMC-40

❑ **MMC-38. "Mickey Mouse Club" Store Poster,**
1950s. Welch's large 9.75x45" horizontal format paper promoting sponsor products and "Walt Disney's Mickey Mouse Club/ABC-TV." - **$50 $85 $150**

MMC-38

❑ **MMC-40. "Mickey Mouse Club Surprise" Store Premium Lot,**
1950s. Pillsbury. Three items associated to premiums offered by either "Fudge Brownie Mix" or "Chocolate Chip Cookie Mix." Lot includes 18x24" paper sign "Watch Mickey Mouse Club On ABC-TV," 4.25x11" perforated sheet of 5 shelf stickers for pricing of Pillsbury products, "Pinocchio" 3" patch is one of 12 "Surprise" patches offered as box insert premiums. From Gordon Gold Archives. Sign - **$55 $110 $175**
Sticker Sheet - **$3 $5 $15**
Each Patch - **$5 $10 $20**

MMC-36

❑ **MMC-36. Mickey Mouse Club Authentic Cast Member Outfit,**
1950s. L. M. Eddy Mfg. Worn by Mouseketeer John Joseph 'Jay-Jay' Solari every Friday for 'Talent Roundup Day. Unique, same or similar - **$1000 $2000 $3000**

MMC-39

MMC-41

MMC-37

❑ **MMC-39. "Mickey Mouse Club Magic Patch" Box Flat With Patch,**
1950s. Pillsbury Fudge Brownie Mix. 9.25x12.25" complete box flat with back panel illustrated text for set of twelve club patches packaged individually as box insert premiums. Accompanied by "Goofy" peel-off 3" diameter patch. Gordon Gold Archives. Box Flat Near Mint - **$85**
Each Patch - **$5 $10 $20**

❑ **MMC-41. "Mickey Mouse Club Magic Kit" Premium,**
1950s. Mars Candy. 8.5x10.5" mailing envelope contains pair of 8x20" sheets with punch-out parts for mechanical figures based on Dumbo, Chip and Dale, Lady and Tramp, Tinkerbell, Three Little Pigs. Mailer - **$6 $12 $25**
Un-Punched Sheets - **$20 $40 $65**

MICKEY MOUSE CLUB (TV)

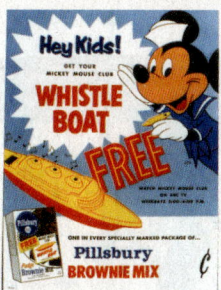

MMC-42

❑ **MMC-42. "Mickey Mouse Club Whistle Boat" Store Sign,**
1950s. Pillsbury Fudge Brownie Mix. 17x22" glossy paper poster for boat toy premium packaged as box insert. Text mentions "Mickey Mouse Club TV Show." From Gordon Gold Archives. - **$65 $125 $200**

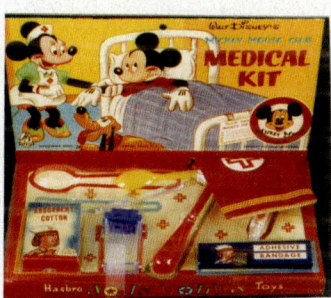

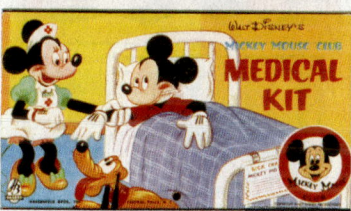

MMC-43

❑ **MMC-43. "Mickey Mouse Club Medical Kit",**
1950s. Hasbro. 5x9x1 deep box with lid that opens to blister pack containing set of generic medical and first aid accessories. Box lid illustration of Minnie as a nurse taking Mickey's temperature is repeated on inner lid. - **$40 $65 $120**

MMC-44

❑ **MMC-44. "Mickey Mouse Club Brush-Up Kit,"**
1950s. Dupont. 7.5x8x2" deep box with display window for set contained in 6x7x2" deep hard plastic storage unit designed as Mickey Mouse Clubhouse. Front opens to reveal storage slots/hooks for comb, nail brush and 5" long toothbrush with three-dimensional Mickey head on end of handle. Box includes character cut-outs on the back to be hung from the clubhouse.
Box - **$10 $20 $40**
Unit - **$20 $40 $60**

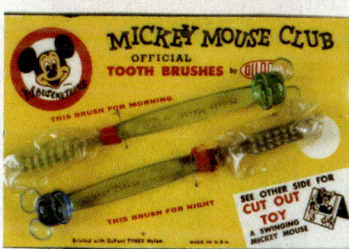

MMC-45

❑ **MMC-45. "Mickey Mouse Club Official Toothbrushes,"**
1950s. Dupont. 4x6.25" display card holding two 5" long transparent hard plastic brushes, each topped at handle end by a 3-D Mickey head. Card back is a cut-out Mickey on swing toy that also features illustrations of Donald and nephews. Carded - **$15 $30 $60**

MMC-46

❑ **MMC-46. "Mickey Mouse Club" Lamp,**
1950s. Econolite Corp. 6" diameter by 4" deep tin litho lamp base 11" tall to top of socket. Base image is drum with illustration repeated front and back. - **$40 $70 $135**

MMC-47

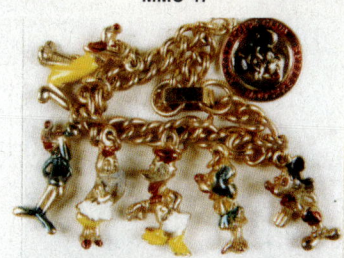

MMC-48

❑ **MMC-47. "Mickey Mouse Club TV Bulb And Nite-Lite,"**
1950s. Solar Electric Corp. 3x3x6.5" display box with cellophane window over illustrated 6" tall electrical bulb. One panel of box pictures Mickey as bandleader to be cut out and placed on the bulb when in use. Boxed - **$20 $40 $75**

❑ **MMC-48. "Mickey Mouse Club" Charm Bracelet,**
1950s. Metal link bracelet suspending seven figural metal charms with paint accents. Depicted are Mickey, Minnie, Donald, Daisy, Goofy, Pluto and an embossed "Mickey Mouse Club Mouseketeers" logo disk. - **$15 $30 $50**

MICKEY MOUSE CLUB (TV)

MMC-49

❏ **MMC-49. "Mickey Mouse Club" TV Tray,**
1950s. Lithographed tin tray is 12.5x17.25x.75" deep picturing clubhouse and activities of Mickey, Chip & Dale, Pluto, Jiminy, Goofy. Designs around rim edges include club logo, pair of Mouseketeers and small image of the Mousegetar. - **$25 $50 $90**

MMC-50

❏ **MMC-50. Mickey Mouse & Donald Duck Wallet,**
1950s. Closed 3.25x4.25" vinyl with wrap-around design depicting "Mickey Mouse Clubhouse" with "The Mouseketeers" door on front panel. Beside the door is raised relief plastic Donald. - **$15 $30 $60**

MMC-51

❏ **MMC-51. "Mousegetar,"**
1950s. Mattel. 9x24x2.75" deep cardboard box contains 23" long hard plastic guitar and 5.5x8.5" instruction/song book.
Box - **$30 $65 $125**
Guitar - **$55 $110 $165**

MMC-52

❏ **MMC-52. "Disneyland Musical Pin-Up,"**
1950s. The Dolly Toy Co. 4.5x6.25x9" tall musical and lighted toy in box depicts the Mickey Mouse Club building. A rare Mickey Mouse Club item. Box - **$25 $50 $100**
Toy - **$100 $200 $300**

MMC-53

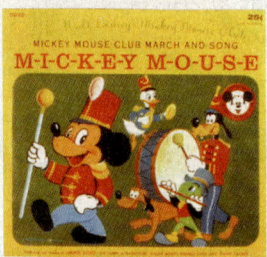
MMC-54

❏ **MMC-53. "Songs From Mickey Mouse Club" Record,**
1950s. Simon & Schuster. 6.75x7.5" paper sleeve with single 78 rpm record. - **$8 $15 $25**

❏ **MMC-54. "Mickey Mouse Club" Record,**
1950s. Simon & Schuster. 6.75x7.5" paper sleeve contains 78 rpm orange vinyl record "Official Mickey Mouse Club Song" and "Official Mickey Mouse Club March." - **$10 $18 $30**

MMC-55

❏ **MMC-55. "Mickey Mouse Club" Record,**
1950s. Simon & Schuster. 6.75x7.5" paper sleeve with single 78 rpm orange vinyl record of "Mickey Mouse Club Pledge" and "Sho-Jo-Ji (Japanese Play Song)." - **$8 $15 $25**

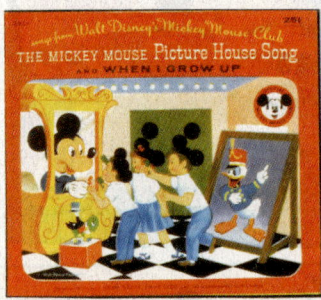

MMC-56

MICKEY MOUSE CLUB (TV)

MMC-57

❏ **MMC-56. Mickey Mouse Club/Mouseketeer Records,**
1950s. Two 6.75x7.5" sleeves, each holding single 78 rpm orange vinyl record. One is "Official Mickey Mouse Club" release. Second is a premium issued by General Mills from a series of four different "Mouseketeer Records." Sleeve also serves as mailing envelope. Club - **$8 $15 $25**
General Mills Each - **$10 $20 $30**

❏ **MMC-57. "Official Mouseketeer Badge" In Display Bag,**
1950s. Dan Brechner Co. Header card on 4x5.5" bag holding 3.5" diameter lithographed tin authorized badge. Bag - **$10 $20 $30**
Badge - **$20 $50 $85**

MMC-58

❏ **MMC-58. "Mickey Mouse Club" Mouseketeer Dolls,**
1950s. Unmarked but made by Hungerford companion pair of 11.75" tall jointed vinyl boy and girl doll. Each wears mouse ears hat over molded hair plus painted outfit with raised "Club" logo on chest centered by Mickey portrait. Each - **$30 $60 $125**

MMC-59

❏ **MMC-59. Mouseketeer Doll,**
1950s. Scarce. Mickey Mouse Club. Store bought marionette on roller skates. - **$100 $250 $400**

MMC-60

❏ **MMC-60. Donald Duck Boxed Ring,**
1950s. "Mouseketeers" issue in box.
Box. - **$25 $50 $100**
Ring - **$25 $50 $100**

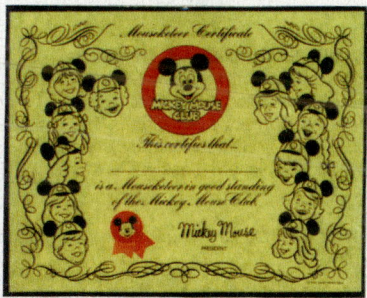

MMC-61

❏ **MMC-61. "Mickey Mouse Club Mouseketeer Certificate,"**
1950s. 8.5x11" parchment-like paper with design elements of club logo, portrait illustrations of Mouseketeers, Mickey Mouse seal and his facsimile signature to certify "That... (name) Is A Mouseketeer In Good Standing Of The Mickey Mouse Club." Scarce design variety. - **$75 $150 $300**

MMC-62

❏ **MMC-62. "Mickey Mouse Club Loony-Kins" Set Boxed,**
1950s. Hasbro. 11.5x15x1.5" illustrated display box contains complete set of hard plastic head and torso parts plus pipe cleaner arms and legs for assembly of Mickey, Minnie, Goofy, Pluto figures. Also includes 6.5x8" clubhouse front plastic tray with modeling-type clay insert to serve as "Clubhouse Lawn." Figures were to be placed on "lawn" and bent into desired positions. - **$40 $75 $125**

MICKEY MOUSE CLUB (TV)

MMC-63

❑ **MMC-63. "Mickey Mouse Club" Stroller,**
1950s. Adco Liberty. 10x15x19.5" tall all tin lithographed. Seat has wrap-around design on the outside depicting Disney characters marching with pennants reading "Mickey Mouse Club/Donald Duck." - **$70 $150 $250**

MMC-64

❑ **MMC-64. "Mickey Mouse Club" ID Card/Certificate,**
1950s. Two stiff glossy paper items. Identification card is 2.25x4" with club logo on front side. Reverse includes additional logo plus typed name and serial number of original recipient on appropriate lines, plus a designated area where recipient's picture could be pasted. The certificate is 4x7.75" featuring simulated Mickey portrait seal and facsimile signatures of him and Walt Disney. Typed name and serial number matches the ID card. Each - **$10 $20 $40**

MMC-65

MMC-66

❑ **MMC-65. "Mouseketeer Certificate,"**
1950s. Parchment-like paper 8.5x11" with text "This Certifies That" (blank line) "Is A Mouseketeer In Good Standing Of The Mickey Mouse Club." Included is Mickey facsimile signature noting him as "President." - **$15 $30 $50**

❑ **MMC-66. "Mickey Mouse Club" Certificate Variety,**
1950s. Certificate is tan stiff paper 8.5x11", unlike parchment variety. - **$12 $25 $40**

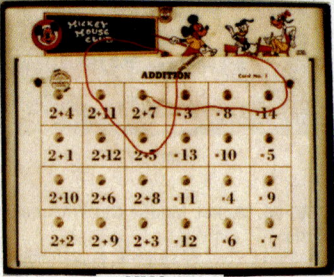

MMC-67

❑ **MMC-67. "Mickey Mouse Club Magic Adder" Educational Toy,**
1950s. Jacmar. 8x10x2" deep boxed battery-operated quiz game designed to light small bulb by touching correct answer by pointer wire. Comes with complete set of question and answer cards, six of which are two-sided with math problems. - **$15 $30 $60**

MMC-68

❑ **MMC-68. "Mickey Mouse Club Mouseketeers" Patch,**
1950s. Synthetic fabric patch is 2.75" in diameter with paper backing. - **$30 $60 $110**

MMC-69

MICKEY MOUSE CLUB (TV)

❏ **MMC-69. Mickey Mouse Club Membership Card,**
1950s. Stiff paper 2x3.5" "Official" card sponsored by a Milwaukee TV station and local kids' TV show host and his ventriloquist dummy shown wearing Mouseketeers hat. Back of card lists club rules. - **$20 $45 $75**

MMC-71

❏ **MMC-71. "Mickey Mouse Club" English Member's Pin,**
1950s. 1" silvered brass with enamel paint. - **$20 $40 $75**

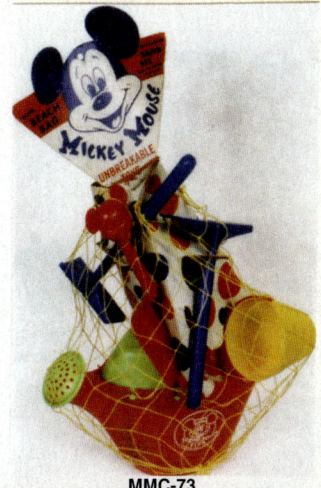

MMC-73

❏ **MMC-73. "Mickey Mouse Sand Set,"**
1950s. Eldon. 5x6x17.5" set consisting of soft plastic large sprinkling can, small bucket, rake and scoop, shovel, plus cardboard insert, all wrapped inside string mesh "beach bag." Sprinkling can has "Mouse Club" logo and shovel has mIckey face on end of handle. - **$10 $20 $40**

MMC-70

MMC-72

MMC-74

❏ **MMC-70. "Mickey Mouse Roller Skates,"**
1950s. Globe-Union Inc. 3x9x4.5" tall box contains complete set. Sides feature image of Mickey roller skating, top pictures the badge which is included with set. Each roller skate is 2.5x7x3.5" deep with metal body and wheels, leather straps and flaps which cover the toes and feature Mickey portrait and name. Top of heels also have Mickey portrait sticker. 1.25x2.25" tin lithographed tab featuring "Mouseketeers" Mickey portrait logo plus title "Safety Skater Badge." Near Mint Boxed With Tab - **$300**
Skates Only - $50 $100 $150
Tab Only - $12 $25 $50

❏ **MMC-72. "Mickey Mouse Sand Set,"**
1950s. Eldon. 5x6x17.5" set consisting of soft plastic large bucket, sprinkling can, shovel, sand mold with attached cardboard insert, all wrapped inside a string mesh "beach bag." Bucket and can have "Mickey Mouse Club" logo, mold is of Mickey's face and handle of shovel has raised Mickey face as well. - **$10 $20 $40**

❏ **MMC-74. "Mickey Mouse Club Newsreel" Boxed Set With Shipping Carton ,**
1950s. Mattel. 12.5x13.5x10" carton originally holding six boxed sets, each comprised of 9" tall hard plastic projector, cardboard insert "Screen," pair of black and white film slides, 6" diameter 45rpm record in illustrated sleeve, instruction paper/order form for additional filmstrips. Filmstrip/record enclosed titles are "Touchdown Mickey/Dance Of The Leopard Boys" from series A. Set is contained in 4.5x6x9.5" photo lid box . Shipping Carton - **$20 $35 $60**
Boxed Toy - **$40 $85 $150**

MICKEY MOUSE CLUB (TV)

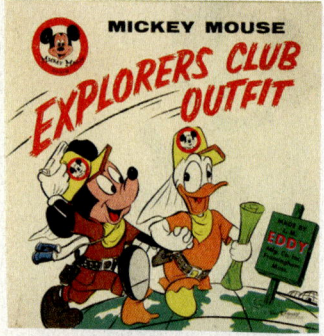

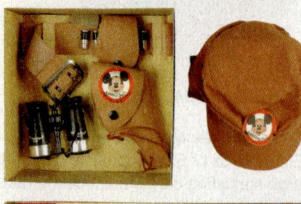

MMC-75

❏ **MMC-75. "Mickey Mouse Explorers Club Outfit" Boxed Set,**
1950s. L.M. Eddy. 10x10x4" deep box contains set including a 5" long "Champ" cast metal cap gun by Hubley, metal binoculars, simulated leather belt with wood bullets and holster, fabric Legionnaire-style hat and "Mickey Mouse Explorers Club" badge. - **$75 $150 $250**
Badge Only - **$15 $30 $50**

❏ **MMC-76. "Mickey Mouse Club" Gun And Holster Adventure Set,**
1950s. Leslie-Henry Co. 11x12" display card with clear plastic cover over eight-piece set of 8" long cast metal and plastic generic cowboy cap gun in leather holster with pair of "Mickey Mouse Club" logos including one in a star badge design. Other pieces are non-Disney generic tin badge, plastic whistle, canteen, telescope, compass, vinyl belt. Carded - **$50 $100 $175**

MMC-77

❏ **MMC-77. Oversized Postcard,**
1950s. Postcard is 5x7" of glossy thick cardboard picturing Jimmy Dodd, Roy Williams, 14 Mouseketeers, all identified by name. - **$35 $75 $125**

MMC-78

MMC-76

❏ **MMC-78. "Mouseketeer Fan Club Typewriter" Boxed Toy,**
1950s. T. Cohn Inc. 7.5x11x5" deep box with carrying handle contains very nicely detailed and actual working tin lithographed typewriter. Design includes simulated keys and pair of Mouse Club logos. At center is the letter wheel and typing bar. As you type the carriage moves. Comes with 7.5x9.5" two-sided black, white and red sheet that includes detailed instructions. Box - **$30 $60 $100**
Toy - **$50 $100 $150**

MMC-79

❏ **MMC-79. "Mickey's Mousekebank,"**
1960. Australia. Lithographed tin 3.5x3.5x4" tall bank. Wall panels include terms "Saving Bee" and "Thrifty Saving Bee," Uncle Scrooge, name of local sponsor. Underside has trap with key. - **$40 $80 $125**

MMC-80

MICKEY MOUSE CLUB (TV)

☐ **MMC-80. "Mousegetar Jr." Boxed Set,**
c. 1960. Marx. 20" tall hard plastic guitar with accessories including sealed bag containing picks and steel bar, four different song sheets, and instructions. Only one string as made.
Box - **$20 $40 $65**
Toy - **$25 $50 $100**

MMC-81

☐ **MMC-81. "Mickey Mouse Club Card Game Set,"**
1961. Russell Mfg. Co. 7.75x16x1.5" deep boxed set of five individually boxed card deck games held in slotted insert platform. Three are the same small-size card decks found in the Library of Games set and these are for Mickey, Donald and Pinocchio. The other two are standard-size card deck games for Pinocchio and Ludwig Von Drake. - **$25 $45 $75**

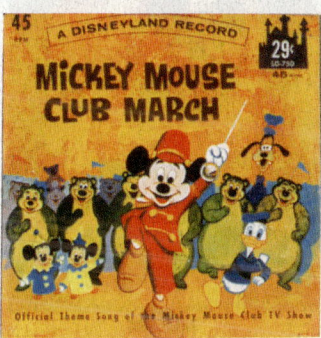

MMC-82

☐ **MMC-82. "Mickey Mouse Club March" 45-RPM Record,**
1962. Theme song 45-rpm record in 7x7" stiff paper sleeve with Disneyland label. - **$8 $15 $30**

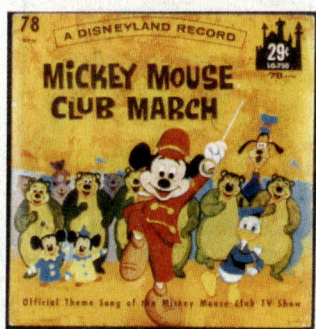

MMC-83

☐ **MMC-83. "Mickey Mouse Club March 78-RPM Record,"**
1962. Disneyland label 7x7" paper sleeve containing 6" diameter 78-rpm vinyl record of titles Mickey Mouse Club March and Club Song. - **$8 $15 $30**

MMC-84

MMC-85

☐ **MMC-84. "Mickey Mouse Club" Lunch Box,**
1963. Aladdin Industries. 7x8x4" deep embossed metal. Design includes "Mickey Mouse Club ID Card" area for owner's identification. - **$40 $75 $125**

☐ **MMC-85. "Mickey Mouse Club" Thermos,**
1963. Aladdin Industries. 6.5" tall metal thermos. - **$25 $50 $85**

MMC-86

MMC-87

☐ **MMC-86. "Pillsbury/Mickey Mouse Club" Store Shelf Hanger,**
1960s. Fully opened, hanger is 6x21.5" stiff paper with same design on each half. Advertises club balloons free in chocolate chip cookie mix boxes. Gordon Gold Archives. - **$35 $75 $150**

☐ **MMC-87. "Pillsbury/Mickey Mouse Club" Store Shelf Hanger,**
1960s. Fully opened, hanger is 6x21.5". Advertises a Mickey Mouse Club "Magic" patch available free in boxes of Pillsbury Fudge Brownie Mix. Gordon Gold Archives. - **$35 $75 $150**

MMC-88

☐ **MMC-88. "Mouseketeer" Soap Bottle,**
1960s. Soaky 9.75" tall container with soft plastic body and hard plastic head. - **$10 $20 $45**

631

MICKEY MOUSE CLUB (TV)

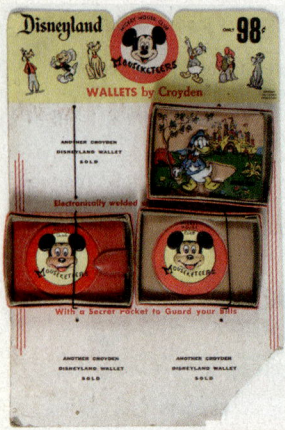

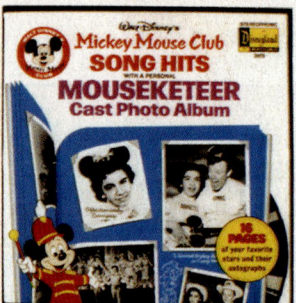

MMC-91

MMC-93

MMC-89

❑ **MMC-93. "Mickey Mouse Club Puzzle,"**
1970s. Jaymar. 8.5x13x1.5" deep boxed jigsaw puzzle titled "Mobile Home" and assembling to 13x18" scene based on the 1937 short "Mickey's Trailer." - **$5 $12 $20**

❑ **MMC-89. Mickey Mouse Club/Disneyland Wallets Display,**
1960s. Croyden Co. 10.25x15.25" display holding three of six original vinyl wallet variations, each individually boxed. Two are "Mouse Club" theme and third variety is Disneyland theme. Each contains "Mouseketeers Membership Card" I.D. card and a single piece of "Disneyland Play Money." Display - **$35 $65 $125**
Each Wallet - **$12 $25 $50**

MMC-92

MMC-94

MMC-90

❑ **MMC-91. "Mickey Mouse Club Song Hits With A Personal Mouseketeer Cast Photo Album" LP,**
1975. Commemorative 12.25x12.25" gate-fold album cover containing 33-1/3rpm record on the Disneyland label. Cover includes photos from the 1950s show, an inner bound-in 16-page glossy paper "Photo Album" with additional cast member photos and portraits with facsimile signatures. - **$12 $25 $45**

❑ **MMC-92. "Mickey Mouse Club" Lunch Box With Bottle,**
1976. Aladdin Industries. 7x8x4" deep embossed metal box and companion 6.5" tall thermos with plastic cup. Box - **$25 $50 $100**
Bottle - **$10 $20 $35**

❑ **MMC-94. "Mickey Mouse Club Mug,"**
1970s. "Eagle-Div. of APL" 4.5" bottom diameter by 5.5" tall plastic. - **$8 $15 $25**

❑ **MMC-90. "Mickey Mouse Club" Foot Stool,**
c. 1960s. 13" diameter by 10" tall. Has vinyl-covered top featuring the club logo and attached are four wood legs. - **$25 $50 $80**

MICKEY MOUSE CLUB (TV)

MMC-95

MMC-97

MMC-98

❑ **MMC-95. "Mickey Mouse Club Official Mouseketeer Doll" Boxed,**
1970s. Horsman. 8.5x11.5x3" display box containing 9' tall poseable vinyl doll detailed by sleep eyes, rooted hair, fabric outfit and thin plastic Mouseketeer hat. Boxed - **$20 $40 $75**

❑ **MMC-97. Mickey Mouse Bagatelle,**
1970s. Wolverine Mfg. Co. Marble shooter game 10x15.5x1" deep formed by clear plastic cover over tin litho bottom panel. - **$10 $20 $40**

❑ **MMC-98. "Mickey Mouse Club" Limited Edition Watch,**
1995. Wooden box measuring 4x8.5x1.25" deep holds 1.25" diameter watch with leather straps. Case is marked "This Watch Commemorates The 40th Anniversary Of The Mickey Mouse Club 1955-1995/Limited Edition of 5000 Pieces." Mint As Issued - **$140**

MMC-96

MMC-99

❑ **MMC-96. "Mickey Mouse Club Catch The Mouse Color A Deck,"**
1970s. Russell Mfg. Co. 6.25x8" blister card holding boxed deck of cards for game similar to "Old Maid" plus set of five crayons to color the cards. - **$5 $10 $20**

❑ **MMC-99. "Mickey Mouse Club" Resin,**
2000. Limited edition from Disney Store shows Donald ringing a gong. - **$95**

Mickey Mouse Clubs

The Fox Dome Theatre in Ocean Park, California was one of the first theatres to sponsor a Mickey Mouse Club. The club was originally thought of as a publicity stunt. However, the idea of theatrical clubs was soon sponsored directly by Disney and they proved to be a very viable marketing tool. At the height of the craze in 1932, Mickey Mouse Clubs had over a million members. Considering that the country was going through a depression of historic size and had a population of 124 million people, that million is an amazing statistic.

Mickey Mouse Clubs would typically gather on Saturdays. Children would meet at theatres, watch cartoons and hold meetings. The meetings were managed by youthful elected officials who were known as the Chief Mickey Mouse and the Chief Minnie Mouse. The Mickey Mouse Club craze eventually lost steam, but it came back full force in the fifties when TV recycled the concept.

Merchandise included premiums distributed at the events.

MCS-1

❏ **MCS-1. "Mickey Mouse Club" Movie Theater Handout Sheet Music,**
1930. Walter E. Disney. 7x9" four-page music. - **$40 $70 $135**

MCS-2

❏ **MCS-2. "Mickey Mouse" Movie Theater Club Felt Beanie,**
c. 1930. Two-tone beanie shown lying flat in photo and as such, size is 5x8.5". On one of the four sections is 2.5" tall silk-screened full figure image of Mickey with facsimile signature and inscription "Yours Truly." - **$135 $275 $450**

MCS-3

❏ **MCS-3. "Mickey Mouse Club" Movie Theater "Free Show" Hand-Out,**
c. 1930. Newsprint paper is 7.5x11". - **$30 $60 $115**

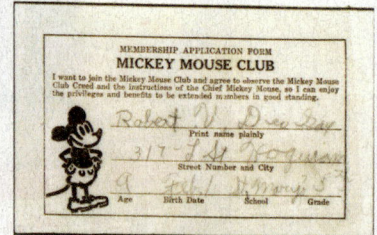

MCS-4

❏ **MCS-4. "Mickey Mouse Club Membership Application Form,"**
c. 1930. Various theaters. 3.25x5.25" paper sheet. - **$40 $85 $150**

MCS-5

MCS-6

❏ **MCS-5. "Mickey Mouse Club" Movie Theater Card,**
c. 1930. Various theaters. 2.25x3.75" stiff paper. - **$45 $90 $160**

❏ **MCS-6. "Mickey Mouse Club" Movie Theater Membership Card,**
c. 1930. 2.25x3.75" stiff paper card for "Fox Mt. Baker Theater, Bellingham, Washington" with individual issue number of "1298." Card has inked name of original recipient plus inked stamp name of "Chief Mickey Mouse," probably that of the theater owner. Also on front is a small image of Mickey wearing a badge while on the back is the "Club Creed." - **$40 $85 $150**

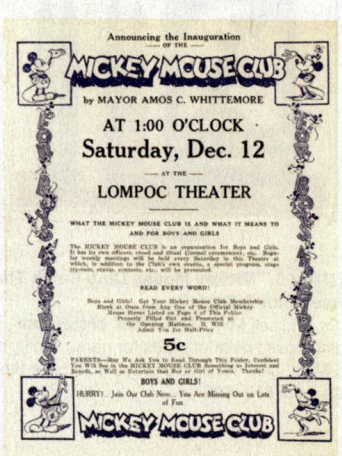

MICKEY MOUSE CLUBS

MCS-8

◻ **MCS-8. "Mickey Mouse Saturday Matinee Club Membership Card,"**
1935. 4x4.5" card stock. Text reads "Get The Date Stamped On This Card Every Saturday Matinee And You'll Receive A Mickey Mouse Magazine Absolutely Free-Every Month." Top left corner notes "For Christmas Issue." - **$65 $125 $200**

MCS-9

◻ **MCS-9. Mickey Mouse Movie Theater Club English Membership Card,**
1936. Regal Golders Green theater chain. 3.25x4.75" cardstock. Includes ink stamp signature by "Chief Mickey Mouse." - **$65 $150 $250**

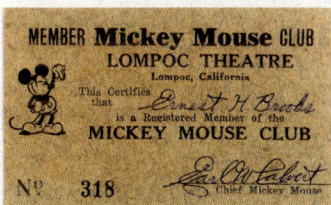

MCS-7

MCS-10

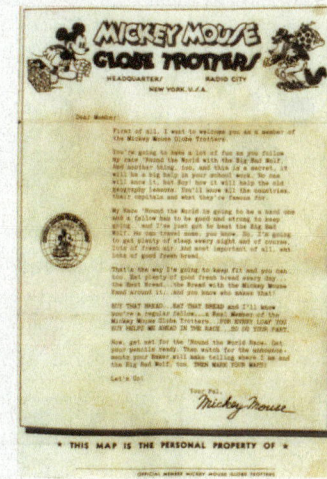

MCS-11

◻ **MCS-7. Early "Mickey Mouse Club" Lot,**
1931. Lompoc Theater Of California. Three pieces. First is 7x9.25" four-page folder promoting the club. Title on front reads "Announcing The Inauguration Of The Mickey Mouse Club By Mayor Amos C. Whittemore." Second item is 7x9" four-page "Mickey Mouse Theme Song" sheet music. Third item is the 2.25x3.75" club card on stiff filament paper. Front has individual issue number "318" and has inked name of recipient and "Chief Mickey Mouse," most likely the theater owner. Folder - **$100 $250 $500**
Music - **$40 $70 $135**
Card - **$45 $90 $160**

◻ **MCS-10. Mickey Mouse Club Envelope,**
c. 1937. Pevely Dairy. 5x7". - **$15 $30 $50**

◻ **MCS-11. "Mickey Mouse Globe Trotters 'Round The World Race" Premium Map With Envelope,**
1937. Various bread companies. Envelope is 6.75x10.5", map has fully opened size of 20x26". Has spaces to mount 2x3" paper pictures distributed by sponsor. Envelope - **$25 $50 $100**
Map - **$50 $100 $200**
Each Picture - **$5 $15 $25**

MICKEY MOUSE CLUBS

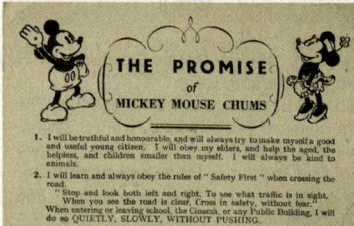

MCS-13

❑ **MCS-13. "Mickey Mouse Chums" English Membership Card,**
c. 1938. Weekly club. 3.5x4.75" two-sided stiff paper card with individual registration number came with matching enamel badge. - **$100 $200 $300**

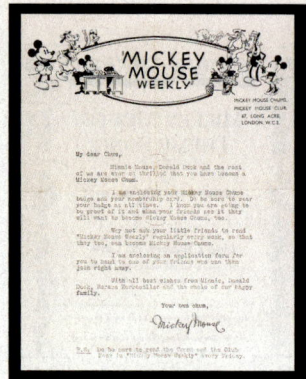

MCS-15

❑ **MCS-15. "Mickey Mouse Chums" English Club Letter,**
c. 1938. Weekly publication club. 8x10" letter from Mickey welcoming new club member.
- **$50 $100 $150**

MCS-16

❑ **MCS-16. "Mickey Mouse Club" Movie Theater Birthday Card,**
1930s. Palace Theater Hilo Hawaii. 3x5" stiff paper card with mailing envelope. - **$40 $75 $125**

MCS-12

❑ **MCS-12. "Mickey Mouse Travel Club News" Premium,**
1938. Issue #10 is a 5.75x8", four-page weekly publication issued by various bread companies. Has pair of cut out states to be applied to a premium map. 22 issues in series with Mickey & Donald going around the country. Each - **$25 $50**

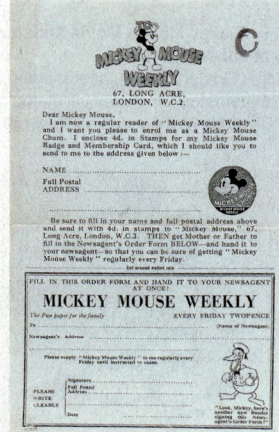

MCS-14

❑ **MCS-14. "Mickey Mouse Chums" English Enrollment Form,**
c. 1938. Weekly publication club. 5x8" enrollment form.
- **$50 $100 $150**

MCS-17

❑ **MCS-17. "Mickey Mouse Christmas Club Official Membership Card,"**
1930s. Canton, Ohio radio station. Oversized membership card is 3-3/8x5". - **$50 $100 $150**

MODERN PINBACKS

Modern Pinbacks

Quality collectible pins have been available through the Walt Disney Company and its themed resorts for decades. They have depicted favorite characters and movies, as well as special events. However, in October 1999 during the Millennium Celebration, the concept of Disney Pin Trading was introduced. This was a new venture designed to promote goodwill between guests and cast members alike. Pins could be purchased throughout all the Disney theme parks and resorts, although EPCOT was considered the host park for the celebration. Cast members donned lanyards displaying many different Disney pins. Guests were encouraged to purchase Disney pins and to trade with any cast member wearing a lanyard. Many of the pins worn on these lanyards were not offered for retail sale and could only be traded for. Pin trading was originally expected to last only as long as the Millennium Celebration itself. Due to its popularity with both children and adults alike, Disney Pin Trading has now become a tradition. With thousands of unique pins to choose from, there is something of interest for every collector. Pins are either open edition or limited edition. Limited edition pins have the edition size stamped on the back. Older pins are eventually retired to make room for new pins. Some of the newer Disney pins feature dangles, sliding parts, hinges, three-dimensional effects or they may even be interactive with attractions in certain theme parks. Occasionally, a mystery pin is introduced. These pins are put into circulation without prior announcement of where and when they will be sold. In addition to the pins made for purchase by the general public, cast member exclusive pins are also created. Only cast members of the Walt Disney Company may purchase these pins. Special events are held each year for collectors and fans of Disney pins. Each event features its own theme as well as event exclusive pins. The perceived value of each pin is subjective. What makes one pin more desirable than another is up to each individual collector. Therefore the rule of thumb is to collect what you like.
*Thanks to Vince Gredone for his photos which grace these pages

Cast Member Service Awards

MPB-1

MPB-2

❑ **MPB-1. 1 Year Service Award,**
This pin was given to cast members in recognition of their first service anniversary. It features Mickey Mouse as Steamboat Willie. This pin had been retired. - **$15**

❑ **MPB-2. 5 Year Service Award,**
This pin was given to cast members in recognition of their fifth service anniversary. It has been retired and replaced with a version featuring Pluto. - **$20**

MPB-3

❑ **MPB-3. 10 Year Service Award,**
This pin was given to cast members in recognition of their tenth service anniversary. This pin has been retired. - **$50**

MPB-4

❑ **MPB-4. Guest Service Fanatic 25,**
2001. Featuring Tinker Bell, this pin was given to Disney MGM Studios cast members after receiving 25 guest fanatic cards for excellent service. It has a limited edition size of 300, but not all of them are in circulation. - **$80**

MPB-5

MPB-6

❑ **MPB-5. Guest Service Fanatic 50,**
2001. Featuring Tinker Bell, this pin was given to Disney MGM Studios cast members after receiving 50 guest fanatic cards for excellent service. The limited edition size is unknown. - **$80**

❑ **MPB-6. Guest Service Fanatic 75,**
2001. Featuring Jiminy Cricket, this pin was given to Disney MGM Studios cast members after receiving 75 guest fanatic cards for excellent service. The limited edition size is unknown. - **$80**

MPB-7

MPB-8

❑ **MPB-7. Guest Service Fanatic 100,**
2001. Featuring Jiminy Cricket, this pin was given to Disney MGM Studios cast members after receiving 100 guest fanatic cards for excellent service. The limited edition size is unknown. - **$80**

❑ **MPB-8. Disney Catalog Cover Series #1 - Buzz cover,**
October 2002. One in the series of a three-pin set featuring the Disney Catalog covers. - **$9**

MODERN PINBACKS

MPB-9

MPB-10

❑ **MPB-9. Disney Catalog Cover Series #1 - Tinker Bell cover,**
October 2002. One in the series of a three-pin set featuring the Disney Catalog covers. - **$16**

❑ **MPB-10. Disney Catalog Cover Series #1 - Mickey & Minnie cover,**
October 2002. One in the series of a three-pin set featuring the Disney Catalog covers. - **$9**

Conventions & Special Events

MPB-11   MPB-12

❑ **MPB-11. Disney Special Activities,**
Early 1990s. This cast member pin was given out to celebrity guests, VIP tours, and to VIP tour guides. - **$40**

❑ **MPB-12. Goon Squad,**
1997. This pin was used as a security pass by cast members for the 1997 Disneyana Convention. It features the evil Maleficent's goons. - **$140**

MPB-13

MPB-14

MPB-15

❑ **MPB-13. EPCOT Food & Wine Festival 2000 Chef Hat,**
2000. This Walt Disney World event-only pin has a limited edition size of 5200. **$7**

❑ **MPB-14. EPCOT Flower & Garden Festival 2000,**
2000. This Walt Disney World event-only dangle pin has a limited edition size of 5500. - **$9**

❑ **MPB-15. Swan Boat,**
May 2001. This event only pin was released at the Countdown to Disney's Pin Celebration event. It has a limited edition size of 1000. - **$25**

MPB-16

MPB-17

❑ **MPB-16. Mickey Golfing,**
July 1, 2001. This event only pin was released during the Walt Disney World Resort pin event held at the Contemporary Resort on July 1, 2001. It has a limited edition size of 1000. - **$15**

❑ **MPB-17. Mickey Mouse Pin Celebration 2001,**
September 2001. This pin was part of a gift set given to attendees at a breakfast during the Pin Celebration event. It has a limited edition size of 500. - **$25**

MPB-18

MPB-19

MPB-20

❑ **MPB-18. Bamboo Mickey,**
2001. This three-dimensional pin event only pin was released during the 2001 Animal Kingdom event. It has a limited edition size of 1000. - **$25**

❑ **MPB-19. Epcot Flower & Garden Festival 2001 Flowerpot,**
2001. This Walt Disney World event-only pin comes packaged in a clear-topped plastic flowerpot. Limited edition of 5000. - **$10**

❑ **MPB-20. EPCOT Flower & Garden Festival 2002 Mickey & Minnie,**
2002. This Walt Disney World event-only dangle pin has a limited edition size of 5000. - **$12**

MODERN PINBACKS

MPB-21

MPB-22

MPB-23

MPB-24

❑ **MPB-24. Disneyana 2002 Mr. Toad,**
2002. This Walt Disney World event-only pin was given to attendees and has a limited edition size of 2000. - **$20**

MPB-25

❑ **MPB-25. Disneyana Mystery Boxed Set 2002,**
2002. This Walt Disney World event-only boxed set of three pins has a limited edition size of 750. It comes in a door shaped box with the conventions logo on the front. - **$150**

MPB-26

MPB-27

❑ **MPB-26. 27th Festival of the Masters Mixed Media Mickey,**
November 2002. This Walt Disney World event-only pin has a limited edition size of 2500. - **$12**

❑ **MPB-27. EPCOT Food & Wine Festival 2004 Boxed Set,**
2004. This set of three event-only pins from Walt Disney World has a limited edition size of 750. **$65**

MPB-28

MPB-29

❑ **MPB-21. Teddy Bear & Doll Convention 2002 Xmas Tree,**
2002. This Walt Disney World event-only pin was a gift with the purchase of a limited edition teddy bear. The pin is limited edition, but the lot size is unknown. - **$12**

❑ **MPB-22. Disneyana M. Mouse Private Ear 2002,**
2002. This Walt Disney World event-only pin has a limited edition size of 2500. - **$20**

❑ **MPB-23. Disneyana M. Mouse 2002,**
2002. This Walt Disney World dangle event-only pin has a limited edition size of 2500. **$20**

❑ **MPB-28. EPCOT Food & Wine Festival 2004 Chef Goofy,**
2004. This Walt Disney World event-only pin has a limited edition size of 3500. - **$14**

❑ **MPB-29. EPCOT Food & Wine Festival 2004 Chip & Dale,**
2004. This Walt Disney World event-only pin has a limited edition size of 3500. **$14**

MODERN PINBACKS

MPB-30

❏ **MPB-30. EPCOT Food & Wine Festival 2004 Pumba & Timon,**
2004. This Walt Disney World event-only pin has a limited edition size of 3000. - **$14**

MPB-31

MPB-32

❏ **MPB-31. EPCOT Food & Wine Festival 2004 Snow White,**
2004. This Walt Disney World event-only pin has a limited edition size of 3500. - **$14**

❏ **MPB-32. Family Pin Gathering 2004 Mickey & Minnie Kissing,**
2004. This Walt Disney World event-only pin has a limited edition size of 1200. - **$20**

MPB-33

❏ **MPB-33. Family Pin Gathering 2004 Going Home,**
2004. This Walt Disney World dangle event-only pin has a limited edition size of 1000. - **$16**

MPB-34

❏ **MPB-34. Family Pin Gathering 2004 Jiminy Cricket,**
2004. This Walt Disney World event-only pin has a limited edition size of 1000. - **$16**

MPB-35　　MPB-36

❏ **MPB-35. Family Pin Gathering 2004 Peter Pan,**
2004. This Walt Disney World spinning event-only pin has a limited edition size of 750. - **$16**

❏ **MPB-36. 999 Happy Haunts A Ghoulish Gathering,**
November 2004. This Walt Disney World three-dimensional event-only pin has a limited edition size of 2000. - **$12**

MPB-37　　MPB-38

❏ **MPB-37. 999 Happy Haunts Red Cup,**
November 2004. This Walt Disney World event-only pin was given to attendees and has a limited edition size of 1300. - **$14**

❏ **MPB-38. The Uninvited Guest,**
2004. This Walt Disney World event-only pin was part of a gift item given to attendees of the 2004 999 Happy Haunts event. It features Stitch as a gargoyle and has a limited edition size of 500. - **$80**

Disney Cruise Line

MPB-39　　MPB-40

❏ **MPB-39. Castaway Club,**
1998. This Disney Cruise Line pin is given to repeat cruisers known as Castaway Club members. - **$7**

❏ **MPB-40. Chip & Dale,**
1998. Originally available only aboard the Disney Magic or Disney Wonder, this pin has been retired. - **$7**

MPB-41　　MPB-42

MPB-43

❏ **MPB-41. DCL Bahamas Stamp Night,**
1998. Originally available only aboard the Disney Magic or Disney Wonder, this pin has been retired. - **$5**

❏ **MPB-42. DCL Mickey Ears Starry Night,**
1999. This three-dimensional pin is available only aboard the Disney Magic or Disney Wonder. - **$9**

❏ **MPB-43. Disney Wonder-Gold Stamp,**
2000. Originally available only aboard the Disney Magic or Disney Wonder, this pin has been retired. - **$7**

MODERN PINBACKS

MPB-44

MPB-45

MPB-46

❏ **MPB-44. Disney Magic - Pewter Stamp,**
2000. Originally available only aboard the Disney Magic or Disney Wonder, this pin has been retired. - **$7**

❏ **MPB-45. Disney Magic 2nd Anniversary,**
2000. Commemorating the second anniversary of the Disney Magic's first voyage, July 30, 1998. The dangle pin was available only onboard and has been retired. - **$6**

❏ **MPB-46. Common Grounds,**
2000. Originally available only aboard the Disney Magic or Disney Wonder, this pin has been retired. Pin depicts a teen coffee shop that has since been replaced with The Stack. - **$5**

MPB-47   MPB-48

❏ **MPB-47. Parrot Cay,**
2000. Originally available only aboard the Disney Magic or Disney Wonder, this pin has been retired. Pin depicts one of the three main restaurants on board the Disney ships. - **$5**

❏ **MPB-48. Animator's Palate,**
2000. Originally available only aboard the Disney Magic or Disney Wonder, this pin has been retired. Pin depicts one of the three main restaurants on the Disney ships. It changes color when in contact with body heat, similar to a mood ring. - **$5**

MPB-49   MPB-50

MPB-51

❏ **MPB-49. Lumiere's,**
2000. Originally available only aboard the Disney Magic or Disney Wonder, this pin has been retired. Pin depicts the Beauty and the Beast inspired restaurant aboard the Disney Magic. - **$5**

❏ **MPB-50. Palo,**
2000. Originally available only aboard the Disney Magic or Disney Wonder, this pin has been retired. This dangle pin depicts the adults only restaurant aboard the Disney ships. - **$5**

❏ **MPB-51. Helmsman Mickey,**
2000. This pin is a Disney Cruise Line cast member exclusive which has been retired. - **$7**

MPB-52   MPB-53

❏ **MPB-52. Poolside Mickey,**
This Disney Cruise Line pin was released during a special event cruise and had a limited edition size of only 500. - **$100**

❏ **MPB-53. Disney Dreams,**
2000. Available only aboard the Disney Magic or Disney Wonder, this pin depicts the amazing stage show performed on board. - **$7**

MPB-54   MPB-55

MPB-56

❏ **MPB-54. Hercules the Muse-ical,**
2000. Originally available only aboard the Disney Magic or Disney Wonder, this pin has been retired. This dangle pin depicts the Hercules inspired stage show performed on board. - **$7**

❏ **MPB-55. DCL July 4th 2001,**
July 2001. Released aboard the Disney Magic and Wonder to commemorate the holiday, its limited edition size is unknown. - **$15**

❏ **MPB-56. Castaway Cay Mickey & Minnie Beach,**
September 2001. This pin depicts Mickey and Minnie sunning themselves on Disney's private island of Castaway Cay. The pin is sold only on the island or aboard the Disney Magic or Wonder. - **$6**

MODERN PINBACKS

MPB-57

MPB-58

MPB-61

MPB-62

MPB-64

MPB-65

❏ **MPB-57. DCL Logo 2001,**
2001. Released and available only aboard the Disney Magic or Wonder. - **$7**

❏ **MPB-58. DCL Burnt Duck,**
2001. This pin depicting a very sunburned Donald Duck can be purchased only aboard the Disney Magic or Wonder. - **$7**

❏ **MPB-61. Mickey & Minnie Fresh Catch,**
2002. This dangle pin depicts Mickey and Minnie fishing on Disney's private island of Castaway Cay. The pin was sold only on the island or aboard the Disney Magic or Wonder and has been retired. - **$7**

❏ **MPB-62. Donald Flying to Castaway Cay,**
2003. This dangle pin with rotating propellers was released only aboard the Disney Magic or Wonder. - **$20**

❏ **MPB-64. DCL 2004 Capt. Mickey & Sailor Goofy,**
October 2004. Available only aboard the Disney Magic or Wonder, this pin has a limited edition size of 1500. - **$10**

❏ **MPB-65. Captain's Choice DCL,**
November 2004. Part of the Captain's Choice series, this three-dimensional pin has a limited edition size of 1000. The pin is sold only aboard the Disney Magic or Wonder. - **$12**

MPB-59

MPB-60

MPB-63

MPB-66

MPB-67

❏ **MPB-59. Shipmates,**
March 2002. Available only on board the Disney Magic or Disney Wonder. - **$10**

❏ **MPB-60. DCL Slider,**
September 2002. Available only on board the Disney Magic or Wonder, this pin features a sliding cruise ship. - **$7**

❏ **MPB-63. DCL Fab 4 ,**
2003. This 4 pin set recreates the four buoys found ashore on Disney Cruise Line's private island of Castaway Cay. The set has been retired. - **$12**

❏ **MPB-66. DCL Mickey Minnie Heart,**
November 2004. Pin depicting part of a mural found onboard the Disney Magic and Wonder. This pin is available only onboard one of the two Disney ships. - **$7**

❏ **MPB-67. Golden Mickeys,**
2004. Available only aboard the Disney Magic or Disney Wonder, this pin depicts the newest stage show performed on board. - **$9**

MODERN PINBACKS

Donald Duck

MPB-68

MPB-69

MPB-70

MPB-71

MPB-72

❏ **MPB-68. My First Donald Pin,**
July 2000. This now retired Walt Disney World pin was originally available only in combination with a special purchase. The edition was limited, but the lot size is unknown. - **$20**

❏ **MPB-69. Donald Hot Air Balloon,**
August 2000. Dangle pin from Walt Disney World. Limited edition size of 7500. - **$20**

❏ **MPB-70. Donald On The Attack,**
2000. A Magical Moments limited edition pin celebrating Donald Duck's 65th birthday. Limited edition size of 15,000. - **$10**

❏ **MPB-71. Proud Donald Duck,**
2000. A Magical Moments limited edition pin celebrating Donald Duck's 65th birthday. Limited edition size of 15,000. - **$10**

❏ **MPB-72. Mad Donald Mystery,**
2000. This is the fourth mystery pin released in Walt Disney World. It has a limited edition size of only 500 and each pin is individually numbered. - **$120**

MPB-73

MPB-74

❏ **MPB-73. Huey - Red,**
2000. Originally available at various Disney resorts and theme parks, this pin is now retired. - **$5**

❏ **MPB-74. Dewey - Blue,**
2000. Originally available at various Disney resorts and theme parks, this pin is now retired. - **$5**

MPB-75

MPB-76

MPB-77

❏ **MPB-75. Louie - Green,**
2000. Originally available at various Disney resorts and theme parks, this pin is now retired. - **$5**

❏ **MPB-76. Daisy Duck,**
2000. Walt Disney World pin featuring Donald Duck's girlfriend. This pin is now retired. - **$6**

❏ **MPB-77. Wet Paint Donald,**
January 31, 2001. This highly sought after limited edition mystery pin was only available at the Magic Kingdom in Walt Disney World. It has a limited edition size of 1000. - **$150**

MODERN PINBACKS

MPB-78

MPB-79

MPB-82

MPB-83

MPB-84

MPB-85

MPB-86

MPB-87

❏ **MPB-78. Marching Band Donald with Trumpet,**
February 2001. Originally available at the Disneyland and Disney's California Adventure theme parks, this pin is now retired. - **$6**

❏ **MPB-79. Tourist Donald,**
2001. Originally available at the Disneyland and Disney's California Adventure theme parks, this pin is now retired. - **$6**

MPB-80   MPB-81

❏ **MPB-80. Uncle Scrooge with Cane,**
2001. Walt Disney World pin featuring Donald Duck's uncle. This pin is now retired. - **$10**

❏ **MPB-81. Uncle Scrooge & Gold Coins,**
2001. Walt Disney World pin featuring Donald Duck's uncle and his beloved gold. This pin is now retired. - **$10**

❏ **MPB-82. Donald Kodak Share the Magic Pin #4,**
June 2002. This now retired Walt Disney World pin was originally available only in combination with a special purchase. The edition was limited, but the lot size is unknown. - **$10**

❏ **MPB-83. Donald Pin Trading Center,**
August 2002. This dangle pin was released to commemorate the grand opening of the Pin Traders Station in Walt Disney World's Downtown Disney on August 4, 2002. Limited Edition size of 2000. - **$20**

❏ **MPB-84. I Conquered the World Donald,**
August 2002. Part of the "I Conquered the World Pin Pursuit" in Walt Disney World. - **$6**

❏ **MPB-85. Duckosaurus,**
August 2002. A surprise release pin from Walt Disney World's Animal Kingdom. Limited edition size of 1000. - **$30**

❏ **MPB-86. Donald Bad Boy,**
September 2003. Walt Disney World pin featuring Donald with devil horns. - **$15**

❏ **MPB-87. Donald Duck,**
2004. Available at Walt Disney World and Disneyland as part of the Real Mickey series. DLR in February 2004, WDW in July 2004. - **$6**

MODERN PINBACKS

Fab Five and Friends

MPB-88

MPB-89

MPB-90

MPB-91

MPB-92

MPB-93

MPB-94

MPB-95

MPB-96

MPB-97

MPB-98

MPB-99

❑ **MPB-88. Fab Five First Day of 2000,** January 2000. Walt Disney World pin to commemorate the first day of 2000. This is an error pin, notice the misspelling of January. While a lot size of 5000 was produced, due to the error, only about 1500 are in actual circulation. - **$25**

❑ **MPB-89. Fab 4 Pirate's Jail Scene,** March 2000. This is the silver version (a gold version was done as well) of the pin given to attendees of the 2nd annual Walt Disney Art Classics Convention in March 2000. It features the Fab 4 recreating the famous jail scene from the Pirates of the Caribbean ride. It has a limited edition size of 1500. - **$140**

❑ **MPB-90. Art of Disney Vintage Mickey Doll,** 2000. Available in Walt Disney World's EPCOT at the Art of Disney store. This pin has been retired. - **$6**

❑ **MPB-91. Art of Disney Vintage Minnie Doll,** 2000. Available in Walt Disney World's EPCOT at the Art of Disney store. This pin has been retired. - **$6**

❑ **MPB-92. Art of Disney Vintage Donald Doll,** 2000. Available in Walt Disney World's EPCOT at the Art of Disney store. This pin has been retired. - **$10**

❑ **MPB-93. Art of Disney Vintage Pluto Doll,** 2000. Available in Walt Disney World's EPCOT at the Art of Disney store. This pin has been retired. - **$6**

❑ **MPB-94. Mickey, Minnie, Goofy Puzzle Set,** 2000. Each pin was part of a three piece puzzle set available in Walt Disney World and Disneyland. All three pins have been retired.
Mickey - **$5**
Minnie - **$5**
Goofy- This is an error pin, notice Goofy's green face and missing ears. - **$5**

❑ **MPB-95. Mickey and the Gang 2001,** 2001. This retired pin was first made available in Disneyland, and later in the Japan Disney stores. **$6**

❑ **MPB-96. Foot and Hand Prints Mickey,** August 2002. A surprise release pin featuring rubber feet in Free D, a patented term for the three dimensional effect on the pin. Limited edition size of 1000. - **$20**

❑ **MPB-97. Foot and Hand Prints Minnie,** August 2002. A surprise release pin featuring rubber feet in Free D, a patented term for the three dimensional effect on the pin. Limited edition size of 1000. - **$20**

❑ **MPB-98. Foot and Hand Prints Donald,** August 2002. A surprise release pin featuring rubber feet in Free D, a patented term for the three dimensional effect on the pin. Limited edition size of 1000. - **$20**

❑ **MPB-99. Foot and Hand Prints Daisy,** August 2002. A surprise release pin featuring rubber feet in Free D, a patented term for the three dimensional effect on the pin. Limited edition size of 1000. - **$20**

MODERN PINBACKS

MPB-100

MPB-103

MPB-106

❏ **MPB-100. Foot and Hand Prints Goofy,**
August 2002. A surprise release pin featuring rubber feet in Free D, a patented term for the three dimensional effect on the pin. Limited edition size of 1000. - **$20**

❏ **MPB-103. Railroad Surprise Linking Set Pluto Pin,**
September 2002. Part of a series of 6 interlocking train pins, released as surprise pins at various locations in Walt Disney World. Limited edition size of 1000. - **$20**

❏ **MPB-106. Railroad Surprise Linking Set Huey, Dewey, Louie Pin,**
September 2002. Part of a series of 6 interlocking train pins, released as surprise pins at various locations in Walt Disney World. Limited edition size of 1000. - **$20**

MPB-101

MPB-104

MPB-107

MPB-102

MPB-105

MPB-108

❏ **MPB-101. Railroad Surprise Linking Set Mickey Pin,**
September 2002. Part of a series of 6 interlocking train pins, released as surprise pins at various locations in Walt Disney World. Limited edition size of 1000. - **$20**

❏ **MPB-102. Railroad Surprise Linking Set Minnie Pin,**
September 2002. Part of a series of 6 interlocking train pins, released as surprise pins at various locations in Walt Disney World. Limited edition size of 1000. - **$20**

❏ **MPB-104. Railroad Surprise Linking Set Goofy Pin,**
September 2002. Part of a series of 6 interlocking train pins, released as surprise pins at various locations in Walt Disney World. Limited edition size of 1000. - **$20**

❏ **MPB-105. Railroad Surprise Linking Set Donald & Daisy Pin,**
September 2002. Part of a series of 6 interlocking train pins, released as surprise pins at various locations in Walt Disney World. Limited edition size of 1000. - **$20**

❏ **MPB-107. Wanna Trade Chip & Dale,**
February 2003. A surprise release pin from the Walt Disney World resort hotel, Disney's Wilderness Lodge. Limited edition size of 1000. - **$20**

❏ **MPB-108. Mickey & Minnie Photo booth pull-down,**
July 2003. Walt Disney World pin featuring a pull-down photo strip. - **$10**

MODERN PINBACKS

Goofy and Pluto

MPB-109

MPB-110

MPB-111

MPB-112

MPB-113

MPB-114

MPB-115

MPB-116

MPB-117

MPB-118

MPB-119

❑ **MPB-109. Mickey, Donald, & Goofy Summer Vacation 2003**, 2003. Part of the Summer Vacations 2003 pin series, available at Walt Disney World's Contemporary Resort. This is a limited edition pin, however the lot size is unknown. - **$8**

❑ **MPB-110. Three Chefs**, November 2004. This Walt Disney World pin was a surprise release featuring Mickey, Donald, and Goofy as chefs. Limited edition of 1000. - **$20**

❑ **MPB-111. Fab 4 2005**, December 2004. Part of Walt Disney World's 2005 collection, featuring Mickey, Donald, Goofy, and Pluto. - **$9**

❑ **MPB-112. Goofy Laughing**, 1999. A petite sized pin, now retired. - **$6**

❑ **MPB-113. Goofy Face**, 1999. Originally available at various Disney resorts and theme parks, this pin is now retired. - **$6**

❑ **MPB-114. Mini Pin Goofy Waving**, 1999. Originally available at Disneyland and Disney's California Adventure theme parks, this pin is only 7/8" high x 1/2" wide. This pin has been retired. - **$8**

❑ **MPB-115 Goofy 45 Signature Series**, January 2000. Part of the 45th Anniversary Signature series available at Disneyland and Disney's California Adventure theme parks. This pin has been retired. - **$7**

❑ **MPB-116. Pluto 70th Anniversary,** December 2000. This mystery dangle pin was only available on December 1, 2000 at the World of Disney store in Downtown Disney. It has a limited edition size of 1000. - **$40**

❑ **MPB-117. Pluto Sitting with Blue Collar,** 2000. Originally available at various Disney resorts and theme parks, this pin is now retired. - **$6**

❑ **MPB-118. Rubber Goofy Head,** 2000. Pin made of rubber from Walt Disney World. This pin has been retired. - **$4**

❑ **MPB-119. Mini Pluto,** 2000. This pin from Walt Disney World was sold as part of a set that came on a safari hat. The pin is now retired. - **$8**

MODERN PINBACKS

MPB-120

MPB-121

MPB-122

MPB-123

MPB-124

MPB-125

MPB-126

MPB-127

MPB-128

MPB-129

❏ **MPB-123. Pluto Rubber Hockey Puck,** June 2002. Part of the Sports Series, this pin features a three-dimensional rubber puck that is referred to by the Disney Company as Free D. - **$8**

❏ **MPB-124. Pluto Share the Magic #6,** July 2002. Featuring Pluto and Tinker bell, this now retired Walt Disney World pin was originally available only in combination with a special purchase. - **$7**

❏ **MPB-125. Goofy Pin Traders Official Website,** August 2002. This dangle pin was released to commemorate the grand opening of the Pin Traders Station in Walt Disney World's Downtown Disney on August 4, 2002. Limited Edition size of 2000. - **$11**

❏ **MPB-120. Goofy Golfing,** 2000. Released originally at Walt Disney World as an open rack pin in 2000. Now this pin is part of the 2004 lanyard series. - **$5**

❏ **MPB-121. Goofy Balloon,** March 2001. A cast member exclusive pin from Walt Disney World. - **$5**

❏ **MPB-122. Goofy's Son, Max,** 2001. Originally available at Walt Disney World as part of the Canine series, this pin has been retired. - **$7**

❏ **MPB-126. Goofy with Wilbur, 2 pin set,** September 2002. Available only at the Walt Disney World "Search for Imagination Pin Event", this set has a limited edition size of 2000. - **$12**

❏ **MPB-127. Goofy Grape Soda Bottle Cap,** February 25, 2003. Part of the Soda Pop pin series from Walt Disney World. - **$6**

❏ **MPB-128. Pluto Disney Tails' Grand Opening,** July 2004. A surprise release pin to commemorate the Grand Opening of Disney Tail's in Walt Disney World's Downtown Disney. Limited edition size of 500. - **$15**

❏ **MPB-129. Goofy's Candy Co.,** August 2004. Walt Disney World surprise release pin. Limited edition size of 1000. - **$8**

MODERN PINBACKS

Holidays and Special Occasions

MPB-130

MPB-131

❏ **MPB-130. Happy New Year 2000 Fab 4,** 2000. Disneyland and Disney's California Adventure holiday pin featuring Mickey, Donald, Goofy, and Pluto. Limited edition size of 2000. - **$15**

❏ **MPB-131. Happy New Year 2000 Mickey,** 2000. Walt Disney World holiday pin featuring Mickey Mouse in a party hat. Limited edition size of 20,000. - **$10**

MPB-132

❏ **MPB-132. Happy Valentine's Day 2000,** February 2000. This Walt Disney World pin has a limited edition size of 20,000. - **$8**

MPB-133

❏ **MPB-133. Happy St Patrick's Day 2000,** March 2000. Walt Disney World holiday pin featuring Mickey dressed as a Leprechaun. Limited edition size of 7500. - **$10**

MPB-134

MPB-135

❏ **MPB-134. Pooh as Easter Bunny,** April 2000. Released in Walt Disney World, this pin has a limited edition size of 20,000. - **$7**

❏ **MPB-135. Earth Day 2000 Jiminy Cricket,** April 2000. This Walt Disney World pin celebrates Earth Day and has a limited edition size of 10,000. - **$8**

MPB-136

❏ **MPB-136. Graduation Mickey in Purple,** 2000. This Walt Disney World pin has a limited edition size of 20,000. - **$6**

MPB-137   MPB-138

❏ **MPB-137. Happy Mother's Day 2000 Perdita,** 2000. This Walt Disney World pin fits together like a puzzle with the Happy Father's Day 2000 pin. It is limited edition, but the lot size is unknown. - **$8**

❏ **MPB-138. Happy Father's Day 2000 Pongo,** 2000. This Walt Disney World pin fits together with the Happy Mother's Day 2000 pin. Limited edition size of 5000. - **$8**

MPB-139

❏ **MPB-139. Graduation Pooh in Blue,** 2000. This Walt Disney World pin has a limited edition size of 20,000. - **$6**

MODERN PINBACKS

MPB-140

MPB-141

MPB-140. 4th of July EPCOT Mickey 2000,
July 2000. This Walt Disney World three-dimensional pin was part of a series of 4th of July pins, one for each theme park .Limited edition size of 10,000. - **$10**

MPB-141. 4th of July Magic Kingdom Minnie 2000,
July 2000. This Walt Disney World three-dimensional pin was part of a series of 4th of July pins, one for each theme park .Limited edition size of 10,000. - **$10**

MPB-142

MPB-143

❑ **MPB-142. 4th of July Disney MGM Studios Goofy 2000,**
July 2000. This Walt Disney World three–dimensional pin was part of a series of 4th of July pins, one for each theme park .Limited edition size of 10,000. - **$15**

❑ **MPB-143. 4th of July Animal Kingdom Donald 2000,**
July 2000. This Walt Disney World three-dimensional pin was part of a series of 4th of July pins, one for each theme park .Limited edition size of 10,000. - **$15**

MPB-144

MPB-145

❑ **MPB-144. 4th of July 2000 Mickey on Firecracker,**
July 2000. This Walt Disney World features Mickey dressed as Uncle Sam. This holiday pin had a limited edition size of 10,000. - **$15**

❑ **MPB-145. Halloween Pooh as Jack O'Lantern,**
October 2000. One of four pins in the Walt Disney World 2000 Halloween series. Limited edition size of 1200. - **$15**

MPB-146

MPB-147

❑ **MPB-146. Halloween Eeyore as Dinosaur,**
October 2000. One of four pins in the Walt Disney World 2000 Halloween series. Limited edition size of 1200. - **$15**

❑ **MPB-147. Halloween Tigger as Mad Scientist,**
October 2000. One of four pins in the Walt Disney World 2000 Halloween series. Limited edition size of 1200. - **$15**

MPB-148

MPB-149

MODERN PINBACKS

MPB-150

MPB-153

MPB-156

MPB-157

☐ **MPB-148. Halloween Mickey as Scarecrow,**
October 2000. One of four pins in the Walt Disney World 2000 Halloween series. Limited edition size of 1200. - **$15**

☐ **MPB-149. Happy Halloween 2002 Mickey Trick or Treat Series,**
October 2000. Part of a special series from Walt Disney World, this pin has a limited edition size of 1500. - **$15**

☐ **MPB-150. Mickey & Minnie Thanksgiving 2000,**
2000. This Walt Disney World holiday pin has a limited edition size of 7500. - **$20**

MPB-151

MPB-152

MPB-154

MPB-155

☐ **MPB-153. Happy Birthday Mickey & Minnie,**
January 2001. This pin celebrating birthday's with Mickey and Minnie was available at Walt Disney World. - **$5**

☐ **MPB-154. Happy New Year 2001 Fab 4,**
2001. Walt Disney World holiday pin featuring Mickey, Donald, Goofy, and Pluto. Limited edition size of 15000. - **$10**

☐ **MPB-155. Inauguration 2001,**
2001. This pin was created in honor of George W. Bush's inauguration. It has a limited edition size of 1000. - **$110**

☐ **MPB-156. Tigger Painting Easter Eggs,**
April 2001. This 2 pin set was released in Disneyland and Disney's California Adventure and has a limited edition size of 2400. - **$12**

☐ **MPB-157. Disney's California Adventure Easter 2001 - Mickey in Egg,**
April 2001. Released in Disneyland and Disney's California Adventure, this pin features an Easter egg that opens to reveal Mickey Mouse. Limited edition size of 2400. - **$10**

MPB-158

MPB-159

☐ **MPB-151. Grad Night 2000,**
2000. This event-only Disneyland and Disney's California Adventure pin was available only during Grad Nights. Limited edition size of 2000. - **$6**

☐ **MPB-152. Spring Break 2000 Fab 3,**
2000. This Disney pin features Mickey, Donald, and Goofy and has a limited edition size of 10,000. - **$15**

☐ **MPB-158. Happy Earth Day 2001 Jiminy Cricket,**
April 2001. Released in Disneyland and Disney's California Adventure to celebrate Earth Day. - **$7**

☐ **MPB-159. Graduation Minnie 2001,**
2001. This three-dimensional Walt Disney World pin has a limited edition size of 5000. - **$6**

MODERN PINBACKS

MPB-160

MPB-161

MPB-164

❑ **MPB-162. July 4, 2001 Mickey's Retreat,**
July 2001. This three-dimensional holiday pin was a Walt Disney World cast member exclusive. Limited edition size of 3000. **$8**

❑ **MPB-163. Mickey Happy Thanksgiving 2001,**
2001. This Walt Disney World pin features Pilgrim Mickey and a pop-up bird holding a sign. Limited edition size of 7500. - **$10**

❑ **MPB-164. Thanksgiving Pooh as Pilgrim,**
November 2001. One of three in the 2001 Walt Disney World Thanksgiving series. Limited edition size of 3500. - **$9**

MPB-165

MPB-166

❑ **MPB-165. Thanksgiving Eeyore as Turkey,**
November 2001. One of three in the 2001 Walt Disney World Thanksgiving series. Limited edition size of 3500. - **$9**

❑ **MPB-166. Thanksgiving Tigger as Native American,**
November 2001. One of three in the 2001 Walt Disney World Thanksgiving series. Limited edition size of 3500. - **$9**

❑ **MPB-160. Graduation Mickey 2001,**
2001. This three-dimensional Walt Disney World pin has a limited edition size of 5000. - **$6**

❑ **MPB-161. 4th of July Light Up Minnie as Lady Liberty,**
July 2001. This Walt Disney World pin features an on/off switch on the back and a torch that lights up. Limited edition size of 7500. - **$8**

MPB-162

MPB-163

MPB-167

MPB-168

MPB-169

❑ **MPB-167. Happy Holidays Castle Light,**
November 23, 2001. This Walt Disney World pin features an on/off switch on the back and light up fireworks. - **$16**

❑ **MPB-168. April Fool's Day 2002 Goofy & Mickey,**
April 2002. This pin is part of the Disney Store's 12 Months of Magic series. - **$5**

❑ **MPB-169. Canada Dominion Day July 10, 2002,**
July 2002. After discovering following production was completed that Canadians no longer celebrate this day, this pin was never sold in Disney theme parks. It has been circulated through other venues and has a limited edition size of 4500. - **$8**

MODERN PINBACKS

MPB-170

MPB-171

◻ **MPB-170. Pooh Class of 2002 Graduation Cap,**
2002. Originally sold as part of the graduation frame and pin set from the Disney Catalog. - **$6**

◻ **MPB-171. Mickey's Very Merry Christmas Party 2002,**
December 2002. Released in Walt Disney World this pin features Tinker Bell atop a Christmas ornament. It is number 8 in a series of party pins and has a limited edition size of 2500. - **$18**

MPB-172

MPB-173

◻ **MPB-172. Tinker Bell Happy Holidays 2002,**
2002. Released in Disneyland and Disney's California Adventure in 2002, this pin is hinged and opens to reveal a festive Tinker Bell and a Happy Holidays message. This larger pin (1 1/2 ", opens to 3") has a limited edition size of 3500. **$16**

◻ **MPB-173. EPCOT Happy Holidays 2002,**
2002. This Walt Disney World dangle pin features Santa Mickey, Donald, and Goofy. Limited edition size of 5000. - **$12**

MPB-174

MPB-175

MPB-176

◻ **MPB-174. 4th of July Ariel with Scuttle with Fireworks,**
July 2003. This Walt Disney World pin is first in the Fireworks and Fanfare series. It was a surprise release and has a limited edition size of 1000. - **$20**

◻ **MPB-175. 4th of July Dumbo with Sparkler,**
July 2003. This Walt Disney World pin is second in the Fireworks and Fanfare series. It was a surprise release and has a limited edition size of 1000. - **$20**

◻ **MPB-176. 4th of July Pooh & Friends Fireworks,**
July 2003. This Walt Disney World pin is fourth in the Fireworks and Fanfare series. It was a surprise release and has a limited edition size of 1000. - **$20**

MPB-177

MPB-178

◻ **MPB-177. Mickey & Minnie USA Hot Air Balloon,**
August 2003. This Walt Disney World slider pin was a surprise release. It is #3 in the Fanfare and Fireworks series. While a limited edition size of 1000 was produced, only 500 ever made it into circulation. - **$30**

◻ **MPB-178. Happy Anniversary Mickey & Minnie,**
August 2003. This pin celebrating anniversaries with Mickey and Minnie was available at Walt Disney World. - **$6**

MPB-179

◻ **MPB-179. First Day of Winter Cruella,**
December 2003. This Walt Disney World pin commemorates the first day of winter. - **$10**

MODERN PINBACKS

MPB-180

MPB-184

MPB-188

❑ **MPB-180. Merry Christmas 2003 Peter Pan & Wendy Mistletoe,**
December 2003. Released in Walt Disney World, this limited edition dangle pin of 2500 features a jealous Tinker bell pulling Wendy's hair. It was part of the 2003 Mistletoe series. - **$14**

MPB-181

MPB-185

MPB-189

❑ **MPB-184. Chip & Dale Easter 2004,**
April 2004. Part of the Easter Finest series, this pin was released at Walt Disney World. Limited edition of 1500. - **$12**

❑ **MPB-185. Fall 2004 Stitch with Apples,**
2004. This Walt Disney World pin was a surprise release and is one of four in the Stitch Fall series. Limited edition size of 1000. - **$10**

MPB-182

MPB-186

MPB-190

MPB-183

MPB-187

❑ **MPB-181. DCL Valentine's Day 2004,**
February 2004. This three-dimensional pin from the Disney Cruise Line has a limited edition size of 1000. - **$12**

❑ **MPB-182. Stitch Easter Basket,**
April 2004. This Walt Disney World pin was a surprise release. Limited edition of 1000. - **$14**

❑ **MPB-183. WDW Tinker Bell Easter Egg,**
April 2004. This Walt Disney World pin was a surprise release. Limited edition of 1000. - **$14**

❑ **MPB-186. Fall 2004 Stitch with Pumpkins,**
2004. This Walt Disney World pin was a surprise release and is one of four in the Stitch Fall series. Limited edition size of 1000. - **$10**

❑ **MPB-187. Fall 2004 Stitch with Leaves,**
2004. This Walt Disney World pin was a surprise release and is one of four in the Stitch Fall series. Limited edition size of 1000. - **$10**

❑ **MPB-188. Fall 2004 Stitch with Corn,**
2004. This Walt Disney World pin was a surprise release and is one of four in the Stitch Fall series. Limited edition size of 1000. - **$10**

❑ **MPB-189. DCL Thanksgiving 2004 Mickey & Pluto,**
November 2004. Available only aboard the Disney Magic or Wonder, this three-dimensional pin has a limited edition size of 1000. - **$11**

❑ **MPB-190. Chip & Dale Winter 2004,**
2004. The first pin in the Walt Disney World Winter Surprise series. This surprise release pin has a limited edition size of 1000. - **$10**

MODERN PINBACKS

Mickey Mouse

MPB-191

MPB-192

MPB-193

MPB-194

MPB-195

MPB-196

MPB-197

MPB-198

MPB-199

❑ **MPB-191. Plane Crazy,**
October 1999. The first pin in Mickey Filmstrip series from Walt Disney World. Limited edition of 1200. (all pins in this series were released late 1999, early 2000-exact dates unknown) **$100**

❑ **MPB-192. Mail Pilot,**
Late 1999-early 2000. The second pin in Mickey Filmstrip series from Walt Disney World. Limited edition of 1200. - **$80**

❑ **MPB-193. Band Concert,**
Late 1999-early 2000. The third pin in Mickey Filmstrip series from Walt Disney World. Limited edition of 1200. - **$40**

❑ **MPB-194. Polo Team,**
Late 1999-early 2000. The fourth pin in Mickey Filmstrip series from Walt Disney World. Limited edition of 1200. - **$40**

❑ **MPB-195. Lonesome Ghosts,**
Late 1999-early 2000. The fifth pin in Mickey Filmstrip series from Walt Disney World. Limited edition of 1200. - **$40**

❑ **MPB-196. The Pointer,**
Late 1999-early 2000. The sixth pin in Mickey Filmstrip series from Walt Disney World. Limited edition of 1200. - **$40**

❑ **MPB-197. Nifty Nineties,**
Late 1999-early 2000. The seventh pin in Mickey Filmstrip series from Walt Disney World. Limited edition of 1200. - **$40**

❑ **MPB-198. Symphony Hour,**
Late 1999-early 2000. The eighth pin in Mickey Filmstrip series from Walt Disney World. Limited edition of 1200. - **$40**

❑ **MPB-199. Fun and Fancy Free,**
Late 1999-early 2000. The ninth pin in Mickey Filmstrip series from Walt Disney World. Limited edition of 1200. - **$40**

MODERN PINBACKS

MPB-200

MPB-201

☐ **MPB-200. The Simple Things,**
Late 1999-early 2000. The tenth pin in Mickey Filmstrip series from Walt Disney World. Limited edition of 1200. - **$40**

☐ **MPB-201. Mickey's Christmas Carol,**
Late 1999-early 2000. The eleventh pin in Mickey Filmstrip series from Walt Disney World. Limited edition of 1200. - **$40**

MPB-202

☐ **MPB-202. Mouseworks,**
Late 1999-early 2000. The twelfth pin in Mickey Filmstrip series from Walt Disney World. Limited edition of 1200. - **$40**

MPB-203

☐ **MPB-203. WDW 100 Years Countdown Series #5,**
1999. Pin featuring Walt's first merchandise item, a school tablet with Mickey Mouse on the front. Limited edition of 5000. - **$15**

MPB-204

MPB-205

MPB-206

☐ **MPB-204. Mickey Mouse Club 2000,**
July 2000. Walt Disney World pin featuring band leader Mickey Mouse. Limited edition size of 10,000. - **$9**

☐ **MPB-205. Mickey Hot Air Balloon,**
August 2000. Dangle pin from Walt Disney World. Limited edition of 10,000. - **$15**

☐ **MPB-206. Mickey for President,**
November 2000. This is a highly sought after pin released in Walt Disney World. It has a limited edition size of 1000. - **$140**

MPB-207

MPB-208

☐ **MPB-207. Castle Grey/Black with Mickey Profile,**
2000. This mystery pin has a limited edition size of only 500 and each pin is individually numbered. - **$40**

☐ **MPB-208. Mickey & Minnie Pin Trading set,**
February 2001. Originally sold on a starter lanyard from Walt Disney World, this set is now retired. - **$25**

MPB-209

☐ **MPB-209. Mickey Surfing,**
July 2001. This pin is part of the mystery series from Walt Disney World. This pin has a limited edition size of 1000. - **$15**

MODERN PINBACKS

MPB-210

MPB-211

❏ **MPB-210. Chubby-faced Mickey,**
July 2002. Cast lanyard series pin available for trade only from cast members. - **$6**

❏ **MPB-211. Inner-tube Mickey,**
July 2002. Cast lanyard series pin available for trade only from cast members. - **$6**

MPB-212

MPB-213

❏ **MPB-212. Mickey 75 Years Randy Noble,**
September 2002. Pin is from a framed set of pins with a limited edition size of only 12. - **$75**

❏ **MPB-213. Sleeping Mickey,**
November 2002. Cast lanyard series pin available for trade only from cast members. - **$6**

MPB-214

MPB-215

❏ **MPB-214. Mickey Monorail Pilot,**
July 2003. Walt Disney World cast exclusive, surprise release pin. Limited edition of 500. - **$12**

❏ **MPB-215. Snowboarding Mickey,**
July 2003. Part of a 4 pin series of Walt Disney World Extreme Sports. - **$9**

MPB-216

❏ **MPB-216. Mickey Red Star,**
December 2003. Walt Disney World pin features on/off switch on the back and flashing light. - **$10**

MPB-217

MPB-218

❏ **MPB-217. Mickey Dragon #3,**
May 2004. Third in a series of surprise release pins from Walt Disney World. Limited edition of 500. - **$11**

❏ **MPB-218. Mickey Mouse World's Best,**
June 2004. Walt Disney World surprise release pin featuring vintage Mickey Mouse. Limited Edition of 1000. - **$10**

Millennium Pins

MPB-219

❏ **MPB-219. 2000 Celebrate the Future Hand in Hand with Dancers,**
September 1999. This pin was released during the 2000 Millennium Celebration in Walt Disney World. It was sold in hotel gift shops, but not in the theme parks. It was also given to guests at Walt Disney World resorts when they booked a vacation package. This pin has been retired. - **$5**

MODERN PINBACKS

MPB-220

MPB-221

MPB-223

❑ **MPB-223. 2000 Art of Disney - Black,** December 1999. This black background pin was released during the 2000 Millennium Celebration in Walt Disney World. The pin has since been retired. - **$8**

MPB-224

❑ **MPB-220. Silver Celebrate the Future Hand in Hand on Card,** October 1999. This pin features Mickey holding a child's hand and was a gift from Walt Disney World president Al Weiss to cast members only during the millennium celebration. - **$7**

❑ **MPB-221. 2000 Celebrate the Future Hand in Hand with Dancers - Square, Black Version,** October 1999. This pin was released during the 2000 Millennium Celebration in Walt Disney World. It was sold during pin weekends and given to concierge guests of Walt Disney World hotels. The pin has since been retired. - **$5**

MPB-222

MPB-225

❑ **MPB-224. Pin Trading Walt Disney World,** 1999. This is the Official Pin Trading pin from Walt Disney World. This cast member pin is considered to be one of the ultimate pins for any pin trader. It is limited edition, but the lot size is not known. It has been estimated to be around 5000. - **$120**

❑ **MPB-225. 2000 Mickey I Was There,** 2000. This pin was released during the 2000 Millennium Celebration in Walt Disney World. The pin has since been retired. - **$8**

MPB-226

MPB-227

❑ **MPB-226. 2000 Fab 3 Celebrate the Future Hand in Hand,** 2000. This pin featuring Mickey, Donald and Goofy was released during the 2000 Millennium Celebration in Walt Disney World. The pin has since been retired. - **$5**

❑ **MPB-227. World Showcase Millennium Banner,** 2000. This pin is the second in the mystery pin series from Walt Disney World. It has a limited edition size of 1000. - **$40**

MPB-228

❑ **MPB-228. 2000 Fab 4 Boxed Set,** 2000. This boxed set features Mickey, Donald, Goofy and Pluto. It is limited edition but the lot size is unknown. - **$45**

❑ **MPB-222. Millennium Village Gifts to the World,** December 1999. This dangle pin was released during the 2000 Millennium Celebration in Walt Disney World. The pin has since been retired. - **$16**

MODERN PINBACKS

MPB-229

MPB-232

❑ **MPB-232. Rubber Minnie Mouse Head,** 2000. This rubber recreation of Minnie's face has been retired. - **$4**

MPB-235

MPB-230

MPB-236

❑ **MPB-229. Pin Trading Disneyland,** February 2000. This pin trading pin was only available to Disneyland Annual Passholders. Limited edition of 10,000. - **$9**

❑ **MPB-230. Pin Trading Merchandise,** August 2000. This cast member only pin from Walt Disney World has a limited edition size of 5000. - **$12**

MPB-233

MPB-234

❑ **MPB-235. Minnie Mouse Birthstone Series - March,** 2001. Available at both Walt Disney World and Disneyland. - **$4**

❑ **MPB-236. Minnie Mouse Birthstone Series - April,** 2001. Available at both Walt Disney World and Disneyland. - **$4**

Minnie Mouse

MPB-231

MPB-237

❑ **MPB-231. Small Minnie Mouse,** 1999. Pin features a rare Minnie with white face and a solid red dress, minus the traditional dots. This pin had been retired. - **$6**

❑ **MPB-233. Minnie Mouse Birthstone Series - January,** 2001. Available at both Walt Disney World and Disneyland. - **$4**

❑ **MPB-234. Minnie Mouse Birthstone Series - February,** 2001. Available at both Walt Disney World and Disneyland. - **$4**

❑ **MPB-237. Minnie Mouse Birthstone Series - May,** 2001. Available at both Walt Disney World and Disneyland. - **$4**

MODERN PINBACKS

MPB-238

MPB-241

MPB-244

❏ **MPB-238. Minnie Mouse Birthstone Series - June,** 2001. Available at both Walt Disney World and Disneyland. - $4

❏ **MPB-244. Minnie Mouse Birthstone Series - December,** 2001. Available at both Walt Disney World and Disneyland. - $4

MPB-242

MPB-239

MPB-245

❏ **MPB-241. Minnie Mouse Birthstone Series - September,** 2001. Available at both Walt Disney World and Disneyland. - $4

❏ **MPB-242. Minnie Mouse Birthstone Series - October,** 2001. Available at both Walt Disney World and Disneyland. - $4

MPB-240

MPB-243

MPB-246

❏ **MPB-239. Minnie Mouse Birthstone Series - July,** 2001. Available at both Walt Disney World and Disneyland. - $4

❏ **MPB-240. Minnie Mouse Birthstone Series - August,** 2001. Available at both Walt Disney World and Disneyland. - $4

❏ **MPB-243. Minnie Mouse Birthstone Series - November,** 2001. Available at both Walt Disney World and Disneyland. - $4

❏ **MPB-245. Minnie in Blue Dress,** January 2001. Available at Disneyland and Disney's California Adventure theme parks, featuring a very well dressed Minnie Mouse. - $6

❏ **MPB-246. Carmen Miranda Minnie,** January 2001. Available at Disneyland and Disney's California Adventure theme parks, featuring Minnie as Carmen Miranda. - $6

MODERN PINBACKS

Movie Characters

MPB-247

MPB-248

MPB-249

MPB-250

MPB-251

MPB-252

MPB-253

MPB-254

❑ **MPB-253. Duchess,**
1999. This Disney pin has been retired. - $6

❑ **MPB-254. O'Malley,**
1999. This Disney pin has been retired. - $6

MPB-255

MPB-256

❑ **MPB-247. Minnie Born to Shop,**
March 2001. Limited Edition of 1000. event-only pin released March 22, 2001 in Downtown Disney at the first Walt Disney World Pin event. - $10

❑ **MPB-248. Sugar Plum Fairy Minnie,**
December 2001. Walt Disney World pin from the 2001 Holiday season. Limited edition size of 3500. - $10

❑ **MPB-249. Hula Minnie,**
June 2002. Cast lanyard series pin available for trade only from cast members. - $6

❑ **MPB-250. Minnie Pin Traders,**
August 2002. This dangle pin was released to commemorate the grand opening of the Pin Traders Station in Walt Disney World's Downtown Disney on August 4, 2002. Limited Edition size of 2000. - $20

❑ **MPB-251. Minnie with Fifi,**
September 2002. Available only at the Walt Disney World "Search for Imagination Pin Event". Limited edition size of 2000. - $10

❑ **MPB-252. Minnie as Tinker Bell,**
September 2003. Part of the Princess series from Walt Disney World. - $8

❑ **MPB-255. Marie,**
1999. This Disney pin has been retired. - $6

❑ **MPB-256. Berlioz - grey,**
1999. This is the corrected version of this pin showing Berlioz with grey fur, not orange. - $6

MODERN PINBACKS

MPB-257

MPB-258

MPB-259

❏ **MPB-257. Toulouse - grey,**
1999. This pin is an error. Toulouse should be orange, not grey. - **$8**

❏ **MPB-258. Berlioz - orange,**
1999. This is an error pin. Berlioz should be grey, not orange. - **$8**

❏ **MPB-259. Toulouse - orange,**
1999. This is the corrected version of this pin showing Toulouse with orange fur, not grey. - **$6**

MPB-260

MPB-261

❏ **MPB-260. Toy Story 1995 Buzz & Woody,**
December 1999. This pin is #21 in the Disney Store "Countdown to the Millennium" collection and has been retired. - **$5**

❏ **MPB-261. Toy Story 2 Woody & Jessie,**
December 1999. This pin is #15 in the Disney Store "Countdown to the Millennium" collection and has been retired. - **$5**

MPB-262

MPB-263

MPB-264

❏ **MPB-262. Flubber,**
2000. This highly sought after pin is the third mystery pin released at Walt Disney World. It has a limited edition size of only 500 and each pin is individually numbered. - **$150**

❏ **MPB-263. Jiminy Cricket Official Conscience,**
2001. This pin was originally available at Disneyland and Disney's California Adventure. It has been retired. - **$8**

❏ **MPB-264. Fox & The Hound 3D Celebrating 20 Years,**
July 2001. This three-dimensional Walt Disney World pin was released to commemorate the twentieth anniversary of the film's release. Limited edition of 3500. - **$9**

MPB-265

MPB-266

❏ **MPB-265. Elliott the Dragon Tic Tac Toe,**
October 2001. This surprise release pin from Walt Disney World has a limited edition size of 1000. - **$15**

❏ **MPB-266. Jessie,**
April 2002. This pin is part of the Disney Store's "12 Months of Magic" series. - **$5**

MPB-267

MPB-268

❏ **MPB-267. Stitch Alien Surf,**
June 2002. This three-dimensional pin is available at both Walt Disney World and Disneyland Resort. - **$7**

❏ **MPB-268. Slinky Dog,**
July 2002. This Walt Disney World pin features a real spring in the dog's midsection. - **$8**

MODERN PINBACKS

MPB-269

MPB-272

MPB-276

❏ **MPB-269. Boo,**
September 2002. This Disney pin features Boo from the Disney Pixar film, Monsters Inc. - **$7**

MPB-270

MPB-273

MPB-277

❏ **MPB-272. Friends Series - Dumbo,**
March 2003. This surprise release pin from Walt Disney World is part of the Friends series and has a limited edition size of 1000. - **$15**

❏ **MPB-273. Friends Series - Flounder,**
April 2003. This surprise release pin from Walt Disney World is part of the Friends series and has a limited edition size of 1000. - **$15**

MPB-271

MPB-274

MPB-275

MPB-278

❏ **MPB-276. Lilo with Fish,**
June 2003. This is the Walt Disney World version of this pin. A similar pin, except for the eye color of the fish, was released in Disneyland Paris. - **$6**

❏ **MPB-270. Flounder & Sebastian,**
September 2002. This spinning Walt Disney World pin was released during the Search for Imagination Pin event at Epcot. Limited edition of 3500. - **$9**

❏ **MPB-271. Cheshire Cat Weird & Wacky,**
2002. This colorful pin is available at Walt Disney World. - **$7**

❏ **MPB-274. Friends Series - Bambi,**
April 2003. This surprise release pin from Walt Disney World is part of the Friends series and has a limited edition size of 1000. - **$15**

❏ **MPB-275. Friends Series - Pinocchio,**
April 2003. This surprise release pin from Walt Disney World is part of the Friends series and has a limited edition size of 1000. - **$15**

❏ **MPB-277. Stitch with Ducklings,**
July 2003. This open stock Walt Disney World pin was released in July 2003. - **$6**

❏ **MPB-278. Dumbo with Moving Ears,**
October 2003. This three-dimensional pin features moveable ears and is available at both Walt Disney World and the Disneyland Resort. - **$11**

MODERN PINBACKS

MPB-279

MPB-280

Princesses & Heroines

MPB-283

❏ **MPB-283. Snow White Dancing,**
1987. This Disney pin has been retired. - **$6-8**

MPB-286

MPB-287

❏ **MPB-279. Robin Hood 30th Anniversary,**
November 2003. This Walt Disney World pin was created to commemorate the thirtieth anniversary of the movie's release in 1973. Limited edition of 2500. - **$11**

❏ **MPB-280. Mickey's Christmas Carol,**
December 2003. This is the last pin in the Walt Disney World "75 Years of Mickey" series. The pin resembles a frame and features a stand up, easel back. Limited edition of 3000. - **$14**

MPB-284

MPB-285

❏ **MPB-286. Cinderella with Blue Dress Holding Skirts,**
1999. This Disneyland and Disney's California Adventure pin has been retired. - **$9**

❏ **MPB-287. Ariel - Small,**
1999. This small Disney pin features two pin backs. It is limited edition, but the lot size is unknown. - **$10**

MPB-281

MPB-282

❏ **MPB-281. Summer 2004 Nemo,**
July 2004. This is the first in a series of four surprise "Summer Nemo" pins from Walt Disney World. Limited edition of 1000. - **$8**

❏ **MPB-282. Doc "I dig a Good Trade" Surprise,**
September 2004. This surprise release pin from Walt Disney World is part of the Friends series and has a limited edition size of 1000. - **$11**

❏ **MPB-284. Megara,**
June 1997. Part of a series of promotional pins, this pin came with a movie ticket to a sneak preview showing of Hercules in June, 1997. Although it is limited edition, the lot size is unknown. - **$9**

❏ **MPB-285. Cinderella with White Gloves - Small,**
1999. Several versions of this pin has been produced over the years. The date and origin can be determined by reading the back of the pin. The oldest version was produced in Taiwan over ten years ago, while a 2004 version can be found on cast member lanyards. - **$7**

MPB-288

MPB-289

❏ **MPB-288. Mulan,**
1999. This Walt Disney World pin features Mulan in front of a blue screen. It has been retired. - **$7**

❏ **MPB-289. Cinderella DLR 50th Anniversary Celebration,**
February 2000. This Disneyland event-only pin came in a velvet lined box. Limited edition of 1950, the debut year of the Cinderella movie. - **$15**

MODERN PINBACKS

MPB-290

MPB-293

MPB-296

MPB-293

MPB-297

❏ **MPB-293. 10th Anniversary Beauty & The Beast,**
2001. This Walt Disney World pin is hinged, and lights up. Limited edition of 5000. - $25

MPB-291

MPB-294

❏ **MPB-296. Aurora - Blue Dress,**
2001. This Walt Disney World pin has been retired. - $10

❏ **MPB-297. Aurora Blue Dress Holding Skirts,**
2001. This Walt Disney World pin is considered to be an error due to the missing sleeves on her gown, however a corrected version has never been produced. - $7

MPB-292

MPB-295

MPB-298

❏ **MPB-290. Snow White with Flowers,**
2000. This Walt Disney World pin has been retired. - $7

❏ **MPB-291. Cinderella & Fairy Godmother,**
January 2001. Part of the Memorable Moments collection released in 2001, this two-pin set has been retired. - $15

❏ **MPB-292. Cinderella Hinged Coach Boxed Set,**
June 14, 2001. Countdown to Disney Pin Celebration. This Walt Disney World boxed set was released during the Magic Kingdom Pin Event on June 14, 2001. Limited edition of 3500. - $45

❏ **MPB-294. Belle in Red Dress,**
2001. This pin is sold in both Walt Disney World and the Disneyland Resort. - $7

❏ **MPB-295. Belle - Yellow Dress,**
2001. This Walt Disney World pin has been retired. - $7

❏ **MPB-298. Sparkling Princess Jasmine,**
June 2002. This sparkle pin is available from both Walt Disney World and the Disneyland Resort. - $7

MODERN PINBACKS

MPB-299

MPB-302

MPB-305

❏ **MPB-305. Kissing in Frame - Ariel & Eric,**
December 2003. This pin is part of a series of three-dimensional pins sold in both Walt Disney World and the Disneyland Resort. - **$10**

❏ **MPB-299. Sparkling Princess Ariel,**
June 2002. This sparkle pin is available from both Walt Disney World and the Disneyland Resort. - **$7**

MPB-303

MPB-300

❏ **MPB-302. Meg and Hercules in Pink Heart,**
September 2002. This pin is part of the Walt Disney World cast member lanyard series and was available for trade only. - **$7**

❏ **MPB-303. Cinderella Surrounded by Roses,**
June 2003. This surprise release pin from Walt Disney World has a limited edition size of 1000. - **$9**

MPB-306

MPB-304

MPB-307

MPB-301

❏ **MPB-300. Sparkling Princess Aurora,**
June 2002. This sparkle pin is available from both Walt Disney World and the Disneyland Resort. - **$7**

❏ **MPB-301. Esmeralda,**
June 2002. This Walt Disney World pin features Esmeralda with a dangle hoop earring. - **$8**

❏ **MPB-304. Kissing in Frame - Cinderella & Prince,**
December 2003. This pin is part of a series of three-dimensional pins sold in both Walt Disney World and the Disneyland Resort. - **$10**

❏ **MPB-306. Kissing in Frame - Aurora & Phillip,**
December 2003. This pin is part of a series of three-dimensional pins sold in both Walt Disney World and the Disneyland Resort. - **$10**

❏ **MPB-307. Kissing in Frame - Jasmine & Aladdin,**
December 2003. This pin is part of a series of three-dimensional pins sold in both Walt Disney World and the Disneyland Resort. - **$10**

MODERN PINBACKS

MPB-308

MPB-309

MPB-311

MPB-312

MPB-314

❑ **MPB-314. 3D Aurora,**
June 2004. This surprise release pin from Walt Disney World has a limited edition size of 1000. - $15

❑ **MPB-311. Blue Portrait Cinderella Surprise Pin,**
February 2004. This pin was presented to attendees of the Walt Disney World "This Is Love" event. It is marked on the back as a surprise pin and has a limited edition size of 1000. - $15

❑ **MPB-312. Pink portrait Aurora Surprise Pin,**
February 2004. This surprise release pin from Walt Disney World has a limited edition size of 1000. - $15

MPB-315

❑ **MPB-308. Disney Film Storybook Pin Series- Snow White,**
2003. Available from the Disney catalog, this hinged pin is the first in the Storybook Series. - $25

❑ **MPB-309. Disney Film Storybook Pin Series- Sleeping Beauty,**
2003. Available from the Disney catalog, this hinged pin is fourth in the Storybook Series. - $25

MPB-310

❑ **MPB-310. Disney Film Storybook Pin Series- Cinderella,**
2003. Available from the Disney catalog, this hinged pin seventh in the Storybook Series. - $40

MPB-313

❑ **MPB-313. 3D Ariel,**
June 2004. This surprise release pin from Walt Disney World has a limited edition size of 1000. - $15

MPB-316

❑ **MPB-315. 3D Cinderella,**
July 2004. This surprise release pin from Walt Disney World has a limited edition size of 1000. - $15

❑ **MPB-316. 3D Belle,**
July 2004. This surprise release pin from Walt Disney World has a limited edition size of 1000. - $15

MODERN PINBACKS

MPB-317

MPB-318

MPB-321

❏ **MPB-319. Happily Ever After - Belle & Prince,**
August 2004. This pin is part of a series of three-dimensional pins from Walt Disney World. - $12

❏ **MPB-320. Happily Ever After - Cinderella & Prince,**
August 2004. This pin is part of a series of three-dimensional pins from Walt Disney World. - $12

❏ **MPB-321. Happily Ever After - Aurora & Phillip,**
August 2004. This pin is part of a series of three-dimensional pins from Walt Disney World. - $12

❏ **MPB-317. Happily Ever After - Jasmine & Aladdin,**
August 2004. This pin is part of a series of three-dimensional pins from Walt Disney World. - $12

❏ **MPB-318. Happily Ever After - Ariel & Eric,**
August 2004. This pin is part of a series of three-dimensional pins from Walt Disney World. - $12

-Theme Parks - All

MPB-322

MPB-319

MPB-323

❏ **MPB-322. Earful Tower,**
1990. This Walt Disney World pin recreates the Disney MGM Studios landmark Earful Tower. - $6

❏ **MPB-323. Cast Member Safari,**
1998. This Walt Disney World was a cast member exclusive. This pin has been retired. - $5

MPB-320

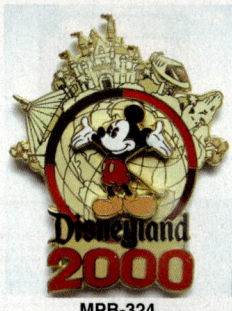

MPB-324

MPB-325

❏ **MPB-324. Disneyland 2000 Logo,**
November 1999. Featuring Mickey on a globe surrounded by Disneyland attractions, this pin has a limited edition size of 2000. - $80

❏ **MPB-325. Mickey Hands on Face in Front of Castle,**
1999. This Walt Disney World pin has been retired. - $5

MPB-326

MPB-327

MODERN PINBACKS

❑ **MPB-326. Animal Kingdom Safari Set - Mickey,**
1999. One of four Safari pins from Walt Disney World's Animal Kingdom. This pin has been retired. - **$8**

❑ **MPB-327. Animal Kingdom Safari Set - Minnie,**
1999. One of four Safari pins from Walt Disney World's Animal Kingdom. This pin has been retired. - **$7**

MPB-328

MPB-329

❑ **MPB-328. Animal Kingdom Safari Set - Pooh,**
1999. One of four Safari pins from Walt Disney World's Animal Kingdom. This pin has been retired. - **$10**

❑ **MPB-329. Animal Kingdom Safari Set - Tigger,**
1999. One of four Safari pins from Walt Disney World's Animal Kingdom. This pin has been retired. - **$7**

MPB-330

MPB-331

❑ **MPB-330. Alien Encounter,**
1999. This Walt Disney World pin has been retired, and the attraction that inspired it has now been replaced by the more kid-friendly attraction- Stitch's Great Escape. - **$6**

❑ **MPB-331. Tree of Life with 3D Animals,**
1999. This three-dimensional Walt Disney World Animal Kingdom pin features a dragon, elephant and rhino. The pin has been retired. - **$6**

MPB-332

MPB-333

❑ **MPB-332. Mickey with Film Clapboard,**
1999. Blue Background. This Walt Disney World pin has been retired. - **$6**

❑ **MPB-333. The Walt Disney Studios with Mickey,**
1999. This Walt Disney World pin is said to be the first pin featuring the name Walt Disney Studios, rather than Disney MGM Studios. - **$6**

MPB-334

MPB-335

❑ **MPB-334. Epcot 2000 Spaceship Earth with Wand,**
1999. This pin has since been retired. - **$7**

❑ **MPB-335. Epcot World in White Mickey Gloved Hands,**
1999. This pin has since been retired. - **$6**

MPB-336

❑ **MPB-336. Tokyo Pirates of the Caribbean Sword,**
1999. This Tokyo Disneyland pin has been retired. - **$7**

MODERN PINBACKS

MPB-337

MPB-338

❏ **MPB-337. Tokyo Pirates of the Caribbean Skeleton,**
1999. This Tokyo Disneyland pin has been retired. - **$8**

❏ **MPB-338. Tokyo Pirates of the Caribbean Skull,**
1999. This Tokyo Disneyland pin has been retired. - **$14**

MPB-339

MPB-340

❏ **MPB-339. Disney MGM Opening Day 1989 Commemorative Edition,**
May 1, 2000. Released as part of the Walt Disney World Pin of the Month collection. Limited edition of 15,000. - **$8**

❏ **MPB-340. Pirates of The Caribbean,**
May 2000. This Disneyland event-only boxed pin has a limited edition size of 1967. - **$25**

MPB-341

MPB-342

❏ **MPB-341. 3D Autopia Donald,**
June 2000. This three-dimensional Disneyland and Disney's California Adventure pin has been retired. - **$12**

❏ **MPB-342. 3D Autopia Pluto,**
June 2000. This three-dimensional Disneyland and Disney's California Adventure pin has been retired. - **$11**

MPB-343

❏ **MPB-343. Disneyland Paris Opening Day 1992 Commemorative Edition,**
July 2000. Part of the Walt Disney World Pin of the Month collection, this pin was released in July 2000 with a limited edition size of 15,000. - **$15**

MPB-344

❏ **MPB-344. Roger Rabbit's Car Toon Spin with 3D Cab,**
Fall 2000. This three-dimensional Disneyland and Disney's California Adventure pin has been retired. - **$11**

MPB-345

MPB-346

❏ **MPB-345. Tokyo Disney Resort Opening Day 1983 Commemorative Edition,**
2000. Part of the Walt Disney World Pin of the Month 2000 series, this pin has a limited edition size of 15,000. - **$15**

❏ **MPB-346. Tokyo Disney Sea Grand Opening Fall 2001,**
Fall 2000. This Disney pin announcing the opening of Disney Sea in Tokyo has been retired. - **$6**

MODERN PINBACKS

MPB-347

MPB-348

MPB-349

❏ **MPB-347. Theme Parks of WDW Four Pin Set,**
November 2000. This four pin set featuring each of the four Walt Disney World theme parks has been retired. - $12

MPB-350

MPB-351

MPB-352

MPB-353

❏ **MPB-350. 3D Goofy's Bounce House with Bouncing Goofy,**
December 2000. This three-dimensional Disneyland and Disney's California Adventure pin has been retired. - $12

❏ **MPB-351. Animal Kingdom Opening Day 1998, Commemorative Edition,**
2000. Part of the Walt Disney World Pin of the Month 2000 series, this pin has a limited edition size of 3000. $9

❏ **MPB-352. Animal Kingdom 2000 - Green Background with Animals,**
2000. This Walt Disney World dangle pin featuring Animal Kindgom has been retired. - $7

❏ **MPB-353. AK 2000,**
2000. This Walt Disney World four pin set featuring Animal Kindgom has been retired. - $12

MPB-354

MPB-355

MPB-356

❏ **MPB-348. 3D Space Mountain Mickey, Donald, Goofy,**
December 2000. This three-dimensional Disneyland and Disney's California Adventure pin has been retired. - $12

❏ **MPB-349. 3D Goofy's House with Goofy,**
December 2000. This three-dimensional Disneyland and Disney's California Adventure pin has been retired. - $14

❏ **MPB-354. 3D It's a Small World,**
2000. This three-dimensional Disneyland and Disney's California Adventure pin has been retired. - $14

❏ **MPB-355. 3D Jungle Cruise with Fab 3,**
2000. This three-dimensional Disneyland and Disney's California Adventure pin has been retired. - $14

❏ **MPB-356. 2000 Director Mickey,**
2000. This Walt Disney World pin has been retired. - $9

MODERN PINBACKS

MPB-357

MPB-358

MPB-361

❏ **MPB-359. Muppet Vision 3D,**
2000. Features the Muppets theme park attraction found in Walt Disney World and Disney's California Adventure. This pin has been retired. - **$6**

❏ **MPB-360. Rockin Roller Coaster Mickey,**
2000. This Walt Disney World pin features the Aerosmith inspired roller coaster attraction in Disney MGM Studios. It has been retired. - **$5**

❏ **MPB-361. Black/White Castle with Mickey Profile,**
2000. This Walt Disney World pin has been retired. - **$8**

MPB-364

MPB-365

❏ **MPB-357. Disney MGM Theme Park Mickey with Lion,**
2000. This Walt Disney World pin has been retired. - **$7**

❏ **MPB-358. On With The Show 2000,**
2000. This Walt Disney World pin has been retired. - **$8**

MPB-359

MPB-362

MPB-363

❏ **MPB-362. Magic Kingdom Opening Day 1971 Commemorative Edition,**
2000. Part of the Walt Disney World Pin of the Month 2000 series, this pin has a limited edition size of 5000. - **$9**

❏ **MPB-363. Dumbo E Ticket,**
2000. Part of a series of five pins from Walt Disney World, this pin has a limited edition size of 2000. - **$25**

❏ **MPB-364. Pirates of the Caribbean E Ticket,**
2000. Part of a series of five pins from Walt Disney World, this pin has a limited edition size of 2000. - **$35**

❏ **MPB-365. Splash Mountain E Ticket,**
2000. Part of a series of five pins from Walt Disney World, this pin has a limited edition size of 5000. - **$10**

MPB-366

MPB-360

❏ **MPB-366. Haunted Mansion E Ticket,**
2000. Part of a series of five pins from Walt Disney World, this pin has a limited edition size of 3000. - **$35**

MODERN PINBACKS

MPB-367

❑ **MPB-367. It's a Small World E Ticket,** 2000. Part of a series of five pins from Walt Disney World, this pin has a limited edition size of 1000. - **$30**

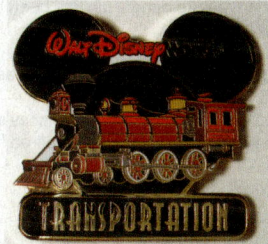

MPB-368

MPB-369

MPB-370

❑ **MPB-368. Transportation Series Train,** 2000. Part of a series of four pins from Walt Disney World, this pin has a limited edition size of 5000. - **$15**

❑ **MPB-369. Transportation Series Tram,** 2000. Part of a series of four pins from Walt Disney World, this pin has a limited edition size of 5000. - **$15**

❑ **MPB-370. Transportation Series Bus,** 2000. Part of a series of four pins from Walt Disney World, this pin has a limited edition size of 5000. - **$15**

MPB-371

MPB-372

❑ **MPB-371. Transportation Series London Bus,** 2000. Part of a series of four pins from Walt Disney World, this pin has a limited edition size of 5000. - **$15**

❑ **MPB-372. EPCOT Pin Trading Mickey,** 2000. This pin's limited edition size is unknown. - **$7**

MPB-373

❑ **MPB-373. EPCOT Mickey Circle Surrounded by Flags,** 2000. This pin has since been retired. - **$6**

MPB-374

MPB-375

❑ **MPB-374. EPCOT Figment,** 2000. This Walt Disney World pin features the loveable character, Figment, originally from Epcot's Journey Into Imagination attraction. - **$6**

❑ **MPB-375. EPCOT Opening Day 1982 Commemorative Edition,** 2000. Part of the Walt Disney World Pin of the Month 2000 series, this pin has a limited edition size of 5000. - **$7**

MPB-376

❑ **MPB-376. EPCOT Spinner with Flags,** 2000. This spinner pin features the flags from each of the countries represented in World Showcase. - **$10**

MODERN PINBACKS

MPB-377

MPB-380

MPB-384

❑ **MPB-377. Partners Bronze Dangle 1955-2000,**
2000. This dangle Disneyland and Disney's California Adventure pin has been retired. - $10

MPB-378

MPB-381

❑ **MPB-382. Sun Logo,**
February 2001. This three-dimensional Disneyland and Disney's California Adventure pin has been retired. - $7

❑ **MPB-383. Disneyland Resort Monorail with Fab 5,**
March 2001. This Disneyland and Disney's California Adventure dangle pin has been retired. - $7

❑ **MPB-384. Disneyland Resort Compass Style Pin,**
March 2001. This Disneyland and Disney's California Adventure pin has been retired. - $11

❑ **MPB-380. 3D Space Mountain Mickey,**
January 2001. This three-dimensional Disneyland and Disney's California Adventure pin has been retired. - $12

❑ **MPB-381. 3D Donald's Boat with Donald,**
January 2001. This three-dimensional Disneyland and Disney's California Adventure pin has been retired. - $12

MPB-385

MPB-379

MPB-382

MPB-386

MPB-383

❑ **MPB-378. 2000 Minnie with Butterfly On Finger,**
2000. This Disneyland and Disney's California Adventure pin has been retired. - $9

❑ **MPB-379. 3D Matterhorn,**
January 2001. This three-dimensional Disneyland and Disney's California Adventure pin has been retired. - $12

❑ **MPB-385. Animal Kingdom Pin Club,**
April 2001. This pin was awarded to cast members only. It features a white rhino. Although the limited edition size is unknown, it is believed to be somewhere between 300-500. - $60

❑ **MPB-386. Disneyland Paris Bon Jour Daisy,**
August 9, 2001. This pin was part of the Passport to our World event-only set from Walt Disney World. - $7

MODERN PINBACKS

MPB-387

MPB-388

❏ MPB-387. Sleeping Beauty's Castle with Fireworks Tinker bell Slider,
September 2001. This large (3 1/16 ") Disneyland and Disney's California Adventure pin features a sliding Tinker Bell and has limited edition size of 2400. - **$20**

❏ MPB-388. Tower of Terror Mickey,
November 2001. This Walt Disney World dangle pin has a limited edition size of 5000. - **$20**

MPB-389

MPB-390

❏ MPB-389. AK 2001 Tiger Dangle,
2001. This Walt Disney World dangle pin featuring Animal Kindgom has been retired. - **$8**

❏ MPB-390. Sorcerer Hat 100 years of Magic,
2001. This Walt Disney World pin commemorates the 100 years of Magic celebration. - **$9**

MPB-391

MPB-392

❏ MPB-391. Magic Kingdom Pin Celebration August 2001,
2001. From the June 14th 2001 Countdown Event at Magic Kingdom in Walt Disney World, this event's only dangle pin has limited edition size of 2500. - **$10**

❏ MPB-392. Large Castle with 3D Disneyland Sign,
2001. This large (2 1/2 ") Disneyland and Disney's California Adventure pin features three-dimensional words at the bottom and has been retired. - **$10**

MPB-393

❏ MPB-393. Mickey & Minnie on Dumbo,
2001. This Disneyland and Disney's California Adventure pin has been retired. - **$10**

MPB-394

❏ MPB-394. Disneyland Character Logo Sign,
2001. This Disneyland and Disney's California Adventure pin has been retired. - **$9**

MPB-395

MPB-396

❏ MPB-395. Disneyland Resort Blue 3D Logo,
2001. This Disneyland and Disney's California Adventure pin has been retired. - **$6**

❏ MPB-396. Disneyland Resort Adult Admission Ticket,
2001. This Disneyland and Disney's California Adventure pin is part of the "Disneyland 45th Anniversary" series. The pin has been retired. - **$8**

MODERN PINBACKS

MPB-397

MPB-398

❏ **MPB-397. Paradise Pier Red with Dangle,**
2001. This Disneyland and Disney's California Adventure pin has been retired. - **$10**

❏ **MPB-398. Paradise Pier White with 3 Dangles,**
2001. This Disneyland and Disney's California Adventure pin has been retired. - **$10**

MPB-399

MPB-400

MPB-401

❏ **MPB-399. Grizzly Peak with Fab 4,**
2001. This Disneyland and Disney's California Adventure pin has been retired. - **$7**

❏ **MPB-400. Everything Under the Sun,**
2001. This Disneyland and Disney's California Adventure pin has been retired. - **$7**

❏ **MPB-401. Purple Dinosaur Jack with Sunglasses,**
2001. This three-dimensional Disneyland and Disney's California Adventure pin has been retired. - **$7**

MPB-402

MPB-403

❏ **MPB-402. California State,**
2001. This three-dimensional Disneyland and Disney's California Adventure pin has been retired. - **$7**

❏ **MPB-403. Disney's California Adventure Hibiscus,**
2001. This Disneyland and Disney's California Adventure pin has been retired. - **$7**

MPB-404

MPB-405

❏ **MPB-404. Disney's California Adventure Fuzzy Bear,**
2001. This Disneyland and Disney's California Adventure pin features a fuzzy and furry feeling bear. The pin has been retired. - **$8**

❏ **MPB-405. Disney's California Adventure Surfboard,**
2001. This Disneyland and Disney's California Adventure pin has been retired. - **$7**

MPB-406

MPB-407

MODERN PINBACKS

❏ **MPB-406. Grizzly River Rapids Bear with Raft,**
2001. This Disneyland and Disney's California Adventure pin has been retired. - $7

❏ **MPB-407. Disney's California Adventure Monorail,**
2001. This Disneyland and Disney's California Adventure slider pin has been retired. - $8

MPB-408

MPB-409

MPB-410

❏ **MPB-408. Hollywood Backlot,**
2001. This Disneyland and Disney's California Adventure pin has a cartoon like style. The pin has been retired. - $6

❏ **MPB-409. Produce Orange Crate,**
2001. This Disneyland and Disney's California Adventure pin has been retired. - $7

❏ **MPB-410. Condor Flats Large Version,**
2001. This Disneyland and Disney's California Adventure pin is a larger version of a similar style pin. The pin has been retired. - $7

MPB-411

MPB-412

❏ **MPB-411. Mickey Surf Co.,**
2001. This Disneyland and Disney's California Adventure pin features Mickey Mouse in his surfer duds. - $7

❏ **MPB-412. Minnie Surf Co.,**
2001. This Disneyland and Disney's California Adventure pin features Minnie Mouse in her surfer duds. - $7

MPB-413

MPB-414

MPB-415

❏ **MPB-413. Paradise Pier Surfboards Fab 4,**
2001. This Disneyland and Disney's California Adventure pin features Mickey, Donald, Goofy and Pluto. This pin has been retired. - $7

❏ **MPB-414. Surfboard Series Goofy,**
2001. Part of the Disney's California Adventure "Established 2001 Surfboard Series", this pin has been retired. - $7

❏ **MPB-415. Surfboard Series Pluto,**
2001. Part of the Disney's California Adventure "Established 2001 Surfboard Series", this pin has been retired. - $7

MPB-416

MPB-417

❏ **MPB-416. Surfboard Series Donald,**
2001. Part of the Disney's California Adventure "Established 2001 Surfboard Series", this pin has been retired. - $7

❏ **MPB-417. Surfboard Series Mickey,**
2001. Part of the Disney's California Adventure "Established 2001 Surfboard Series", this pin has been retired. - $7

MODERN PINBACKS

MPB-418

MPB-419

❑ **MPB-418. Surfboard Series Minnie,**
2001. Part of the Disney's California Adventure "Established 2001 Surfboard Series", this pin has been retired. - $7

❑ **MPB-419. Surfboard Series Daisy,**
2001. Part of the Disney's California Adventure "Established 2001 Surfboard Series", this pin has been retired. - $7

MPB-420

MPB-421

❑ **MPB-420. Carousel Seahorse,**
2001. This pin is part of the King Triton's Jeweled Carousel series from Disney's California Adventure. The pin has been retired. - $7

❑ **MPB-421. Carousel Otter,**
2001. This pin is part of the King Triton's Jeweled Carousel series from Disney's California Adventure. The pin has been retired. - $7

MPB-422

MPB-423

MPB-424

❑ **MPB-422. Carousel Fish - Purple,**
2001. This pin is part of the King Triton's Jeweled Carousel series from Disney's California Adventure. The pin has been retired. - $7

❑ **MPB-423. Carousel Whale,**
2001. This pin is part of the King Triton's Jeweled Carousel series from Disney's California Adventure. The pin has been retired. - $7

❑ **MPB-424. Carousel Seal,**
2001. This pin is part of the King Triton's Jeweled Carousel series from Disney's California Adventure. The pin has been retired. - $7

MPB-425

MPB-426

❑ **MPB-425. Carousel Fish,**
2001. This pin is part of the King Triton's Jeweled Carousel series from Disney's California Adventure. The pin has been retired. - $7

❑ **MPB-426. Carousel Dolphin,**
2001. This pin is part of the King Triton's Jeweled Carousel series from Disney's California Adventure. The pin has been retired. - $7

MPB-427

MPB-428

MODERN PINBACKS

❑ **MPB-427. Sorcerer Mickey with Tinker Bell - Where the Magic Lives,**
May 2002. This Disneyland Resort pin features a sliding Tinker Bell. - **$9**

❑ **MPB-428. Phone a Complete Stranger,**
February 2002. This Walt Disney World pin inspired by the *Who Wants to be a Millionaire?* Attraction features an actual ringing telephone. - **$16**

❑ **MPB-430. EPCOT Figment Artist Choice,**
September 22, 2002. This Walt Disney World spinner pins was released during the Search For Imagination Pin Event. Limited edition of 3500. - **$10**

❑ **MPB-431. Fab 4 Rockin Roller Coaster,**
2002. This slider pin features Mickey, Donald, Goofy and Pluto riding the Aerosmith inspired roller coaster attraction in Disney MGM Studios. - **$12**

MPB-434

MPB-429

MPB-432

MPB-435

❑ **MPB-429. EPCOT Figment in Imagine Hot Air Balloon,**
July 2002. This Walt Disney World dangle pin has a limited edition size of 5000. - **$12**

❑ **MPB-432. Haunted Mansion Doom Buggy,**
June 2003. This Walt Disney World pin features Mickey and Goofy riding in a Doom Buggy. The coffin lifts up to expose a ghostly hand. - **$10**

MPB-430

MPB-433

MPB-436

❑ **MPB-434. Annual Passholder Animal Kingdom 2003,**
2003. Available in Walt Disney World, this pin was sold only to annual passholders and celebrates 75 years with Mickey. - **$7**

❑ **MPB-435. Minnie Red Carpet Light Up,**
March 2004. Part of the Disney MGM Studios Lights, Camera, Pins series, this light up, event-only pin has a limited edition size of 750. - **$14**

❑ **MPB-436. Rockin Roller Coaster Guitar Pick,**
2004. This Walt Disney World pin features the Aerosmith inspired roller coaster attraction in Disney MGM Studios. - **$7**

MPB-431

❑ **MPB-433. Pewter Castle with Blue Sparkle Background,**
August 2003. This Walt Disney World three-dimensional pin features a pewter Cinderella's Castle and a glitter background. - **$9**

MODERN PINBACKS

Tinker Bell & Fairies

MPB-437

MPB-438

MPB-441

MPB-442

MPB-443

MPB-444

MPB-445

❑ **MPB-437. Tinker Bell Sparkle Wings Sassy,**
November 2000. A 2 pin set featuring Tinker Bell with sparkle wings from Disneyland. This set has been retired. - **$9**

❑ **MPB-438. Tinker Bell Sparkle Wings Spoiled,**
November 2000. A 2 pin set featuring Tinker Bell with sparkle wings from Disneyland. This set has been retired. - **$9**

MPB-439

MPB-440

❑ **MPB-439. Tinker Bell Sparkle Wings Naughty,**
November 2000. A 2 pin set featuring Tinker Bell with sparkle wings from Disneyland. This set has been retired. - **$9**

❑ **MPB-440. Tinker Bell Sparkle Wings Glancing Over Shoulder,**
2000. Available at Disneyland, this glitter wings pin has been retired. - **$8**

❑ **MPB-441. Tinker Bell Sparkle Wings on Flower,**
2000. Available at Disneyland, this glitter wings pin has been retired. - **$8**

❑ **MPB-442. Tinker Bell Sparkle Wings Kneeling,**
2000. Available at Disneyland, this glitter wings pin has been retired. - **$8**

❑ **MPB-443. Tinker Bell Sparkle Wings on Inkwell,**
2000. Available at Disneyland, this glitter wings pin has been retired. - **$8**

❑ **MPB-444. Tinker bell Sparkle Wings Whispering,**
2000. Available at Disneyland, this glitter wings pin has been retired. - **$8**

❑ **MPB-445. Tinker Bell Sparkle Wings on Mirror,**
2000. Available at Disneyland, this glitter wings pin has been retired. - **$8**

MPB-446

MPB-447

MODERN PINBACKS

❏ **MPB-446. Cast Member Spot Award,**
2000. Walt Disney World managers give this pin as a spot award to cast members for exhibiting exceptional service. - **$7**

❏ **MPB-447. WDW Magic Delivery 2000 Tinker Bell,**
2000. This pin was made available to Magic Kingdom Club members through a special promotion. The edition size is limited, but unknown. - **$10**

MPB-448

MPB-449

❏ **MPB-448. Fairy Godmother,**
2000. Available at Disneyland and Disney's California Adventure, this pin has been retired. - **$6**

❏ **MPB-449. Blue Fairy with Dangle Star Wand,**
2000. Originally available at Walt Disney World and Disneyland, this pin has been retired. - **$7**

MPB-450

MPB-451

MPB-452

❏ **MPB-450. Flora,**
2000. Originally available at Walt Disney World and Disneyland, this pin has been retired. - **$6**

❏ **MPB-451. Fauna,**
2000. Originally available at Walt Disney World and Disneyland, this pin has been retired. - **$6**

❏ **MPB-452. Merryweather,**
2000. Originally available at Walt Disney World and Disneyland, this pin has been retired. - **$6**

MPB-453

MPB-454

❏ **MPB-453. Neverland and Night Sky on Card,**
April 2001. Oversized Tinker Bell pin on card available from the Japan Disney Stores. Limited Edition size of 10,000. - **$10**

❏ **MPB-454. Tinker Bell Sparkle Wings on Spool,**
2001. Available at Disneyland, this glitter wings pin has been retired. - **$8**

MPB-455

MPB-456

❏ **MPB-455. Pixie License Plate,**
September 2002. Cast lanyard series pin available for trade only from cast members. - **$9**

❏ **MPB-456. Disney Ambassador Tinker bell,**
December 2002. Part of the Walt Disney World Ambassadors series. This pin acknowledges Tokyo Disneyland. - **$7**

MODERN PINBACKS

MPB-457

❏ **MPB-457. Pixie Power Sparkle Pin,**
2002. Available in Walt Disney World and Disneyland, this pin features Tinker Bell on a blue sparkle background. - **$7**

MPB-458

MPB-459

❏ **MPB-458. Pixie Room,**
May 2003. Available at Disneyland and Disney's California Adventure, this pin features Tinker Bell and a fictional "wings" joint called the Pixie Room. - **$7**

❏ **MPB-459. Tinker Bell Compact,**
June 2003. Part of the Sparkle Compact series from Walt Disney World, this pin opens to reveal a mirror and an image of Tinker Bell. - **$10**

MPB-460

❏ **MPB-460. Peter Pan holding Wendy with Tinker Bell,**
August 2003. Available as part of the Mickey's Super Star Pin Trading Team Event in Walt Disney World. This was a surprise release pin, the first of three in the Fantasy Frame Series. Limited edition size of 1000. - **$15**

MPB-461

MPB-462

❏ **MPB-461. Mood Subject to Change,**
September 2003. Pin featuring Tinker Bell from Walt Disney World. - **$7**

❏ **MPB-462. Tinker bell Naughty List,**
November 2003. Released at the Disney MGM Studios in Walt Disney World. Limited edition size of 3000. - **$10**

MPB-463

MPB-464

MPB-465

❏ **MPB-463. Think Tink,**
2003. This dangle pin was released as a part of Tinker bell Tuesdays in 2003. - **$9**

❏ **MPB-464. Tinker bell Portrait,**
2003. Part of the Princess Portrait series at both Walt Disney World and Disneyland. - **$5**

❏ **MPB-465. Purple Monochromatic Tinker Bell,**
February 2004. A surprise release pin from the Disney MGM Studios in Walt Disney World. Limited edition size of 1000. - **$12**

MODERN PINBACKS

MPB-466

MPB-467

❏ **MPB-466. Tinker Bell Spring Surprise - Disney's MGM Studios,**
May 2004. Part of a series of surprise pins released at Walt Disney World, one for each theme park. Limited edition size of 1000. - **$10**

❏ **MPB-467. Tinker Bell Spring Surprise - Epcot,**
May 2004. Part of a series of surprise pins released at Walt Disney World, one for each theme park. Limited edition size of 1000. - **$10**

MPB-468

MPB-469

❏ **MPB-468. Tinker Bell Spring Surprise - Disney's Animal Kingdom,**
May 2004. Part of a series of surprise pins released at Walt Disney World, one for each theme park. Limited edition size of 1000. - **$10**

❏ **MPB-469. Tinker Bell Spring Surprise - Magic Kingdom,**
May 2004. Part of a series of surprise pins released at Walt Disney World, one for each theme park. Limited edition size of 1000. - **$10**

MPB-470

❏ **MPB-470. Denim Tinker Bell Blowing Kisses,**
June 2004. A three dimensional pin featuring denim and embroidery from Walt Disney World. - **$9**

MPB-471

MPB-472

❏ **MPB-471. Modern Tinker Bell,**
October 2004. Part of the Modern collection available at Walt Disney World. - **$5**

❏ **MPB-472. 50 Years of Disney on TV Tinker Bell,**
October 2004. Pin commemorating five decades of Disney on television from Walt Disney World. Limited edition size of 2000. - **$9**

MPB-473

MPB-474

❏ **MPB-473. Tinker Bell Sparkling Flutter Wings,**
2004. Featuring sparkling wings that actual flutter, this pin was available at Walt Disney World and Disneyland. - **$10**

❏ **MPB-474. DVC Members are Magical 2004,**
2004. Available to Disney Vacation Club members only, it is the first in a series of Members are Magical pins. - **$7**

Villains

MPB-475

❏ **MPB-475. WDW Fantasmic Hat Pin Set: Sorcerer Mickey,**
1999. Pin was sold as part of a 4 pin set on a Fantasmic hat in Walt Disney World. This pin glows in the dark and has been retired. - **$8**

MODERN PINBACKS

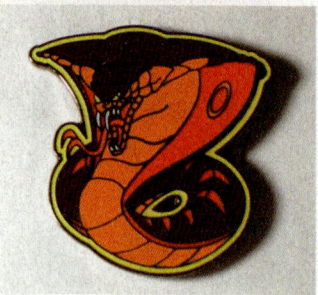

MPB-476

MPB-479

MPB-482

❏ **MPB-476. WDW Fantasmic Hat Pin Set: Jafar the Snake,**
1999. Pin was sold as part of a 4 pin set on a Fantasmic hat in Walt Disney World. This pin glows in the dark and has been retired. **$7**

MPB-477

MPB-480

MPB-483

❏ **MPB-479. Ursula,**
1999. This pin was part of a framed set of six Villains pins. Limited edition size of 1000. - **$7**

❏ **MPB-480. Framed Witch,**
2000. This pin was sold at both Walt Disney World and Disneyland and is part of a series of villain pins framed by the Magic Mirror. - **$7**

❏ **MPB-482. Framed Chernabog,**
2000. This pin was sold at both Walt Disney World and Disneyland and is part of a series of villain pins framed by the Magic Mirror. - **$7**

❏ **MPB-483. Hades Boss's Day 2002,**
October 15, 2002. From Walt Disney World, this pin is three-dimensional and features Hades and bobbling Pain and Panic. Limited edition size of 3500. - **$7**

MPB-478

MPB-481

MPB-484

❏ **MPB-477. WDW Fantasmic Hat Pin Set: Hades,**
1999. Pin was sold as part of a 4 pin set on a Fantasmic hat in Walt Disney World. This pin glows in the dark and has been retired. - **$7**

❏ **MPB-478. WDW Fantasmic Hat Pin Set: Cruella,**
1999. Pin was sold as part of a 4 pin set on a Fantasmic hat in Walt Disney World. This pin glows in the dark and has been retired. **$7**

❏ **MPB-481. Framed Capt. Hook,**
2000. This pin was sold at both Walt Disney World and Disneyland and is part of a series of villain pins framed by the Magic Mirror. - **$7**

❏ **MPB-484. Ursula,**
September 2003. A surprise release pin from Walt Disney World. Limited edition size of 1000. - **$7**

MODERN PINBACKS

MPB-485

❑ **MPB-485. Maleficent Being Bad Just Comes Naturally,**
February 2004. Available from Walt Disney World, this pin features the evil fairy from Sleeping Beauty. - **$7**

MPB-486

MPB-487

❑ **MPB-486. Jafar Being Bad,**
April 2004. This pin was sold at both Walt Disney World and Disneyland and is part of the Being Bad series of villain pins. - **$7**

❑ **MPB-487. Chernabog Being Bad,**
April 2004. This pin was sold at both Walt Disney World and Disneyland and is part of the Being Bad series of villain pins. - **$7**

MPB-488

MPB-489

❑ **MPB-488. Maleficent Being Bad,**
April 2004. This pin was sold at both Walt Disney World and Disneyland and is part of the Being Bad series of villain pins. - **$7**

❑ **MPB-489. Hades Being Bad,**
April 2004. This pin was sold at both Walt Disney World and Disneyland and is part of the Being Bad series of villain pins. - **$7**

MPB-490

❑ **MPB-490. Hinged Villains,**
December 2004. This Walt Disney World pin is hinged, and opens wide to display Chernabog, along with Scar, Jafar, Captain Hook, Hades and Gaston. - **$15**

MPB-491

❑ **MPB-491. Framed Maleficent,**
2004. This pin was sold at both Walt Disney World and Disneyland and is part of a series of villain pins framed by the Magic Mirror. - **$7**

Wedding Pins

MPB-492

❑ **MPB-492. Mickey Proposes to Minnie,**
2000. This pin depicts Mickey proposing to his sweetheart, Minnie. It was available at various Disney theme parks. - **$6**

MPB-493 MPB-494

❑ **MPB-493. Minnie Bride with Bouquet,**
April 2000. This pin depicting Minnie with a heart-shaped bouquet was available at Disneyland and Disney's California Adventure. This pin has been retired. - **$7**

❑ **MPB-494. Mickey Groom with Ring,**
April 2000. This Disney pin depicting Mickey with a diamond ring in hand, has been retired. - **$7**

MODERN PINBACKS

MPB-495

MPB-496

MPB-499

MPB-500

Winnie the Pooh & Friends

MPB-503

❏ **MPB-495. WDW 2000 Wedding Cinderella & Prince,**
July 2000. Part of the Wedding series of pins released at Walt Disney World in 2000. It has a limited edition of 5000. - **$10**

❏ **MPB-496. WDW 2000 Wedding Jasmine & Aladdin,**
July 2000. Part of the Wedding series of pins released at Walt Disney World in 2000. It has a limited edition of 5000. - **$10**

❏ **MPB-499. Disney's Fairy Tale Weddings,**
April 2001. Released in Disneyland and Disney's California Adventure, this pin has been retired. - **$7**

❏ **MPB-500. WDW Wedding Mickey & Minnie,**
2001. This Walt Disney World pin depicts the happy couple on their big day and had a limited edition size of 5000. - **$10**

MPB-501

MPB-504

❏ **MPB-503. Tigger with Black Nose,**
1999. This Walt Disney World pin features Tigger with a black nose, similar the costumed Tiggers found in Disney theme parks. - **$5**

❏ **MPB-504. Rubber Head Pooh,**
2000. This Walt Disney World pin is made of rubber material rather than the traditional metal. - **$5**

MPB-497

MPB-498

MPB-502

MPB-505

MPB-506

❏ **MPB-497. WDW 2000 Wedding Ariel & Eric,**
July 2000. Part of the Wedding series of pins released at Walt Disney World in 2000. It has a limited edition of 5000. - **$10**

❏ **MPB-498. WDW 2000 Wedding Donald & Daisy,**
July 2000. Part of the Wedding series of pins released at Walt Disney World in 2000. It has a limited edition of 5000. - **$10**

❏ **MPB-501. Minnie Bride,**
2002. Available at Walt Disney World this pin depicts Minnie as a bride with a stained glass border. - **$8**

❏ **MPB-502. Mickey Bridegroom,**
2002. Available at Walt Disney World this pin depicts Mickey as a bridegroom with a stained glass border. - **$8**

❏ **MPB-505. Tiny Piglet,**
2000. Originally available at Walt Disney World, this pin has been retired. - **$6**

❏ **MPB-506. Tiny Tigger,**
2000. Originally available at Walt Disney World, this pin has been retired. - **$6**

MODERN PINBACKS

MPB-507

MPB-508

❑ **MPB-507. Tiny Eeyore,**
2000. Originally available at Walt Disney World, this pin has been retired. - **$6**

❑ **MPB-508. Tigger with Pink Nose,**
2000. This Walt Disney World pin features Tigger with a pink nose, similar to Tigger in the Winnie the Pooh movies. This pin has been retired. - **$6**

MPB-509

MPB-510

❑ **MPB-509. Pooh with Flowers in Blue Diamond,**
2000. Originally part of a promotional Hallmark pin set, this pin has been retired. - **$6**

❑ **MPB-510. Piglet with Flowers in Yellow Diamond,**
2000. Originally part of a promotional Hallmark pin set, this pin has been retired. - **$6**

MPB-511

MPB-512

MPB-513

❑ **MPB-511. Tigger Puzzle Piece,**
2000. Part of a three-piece puzzle set sold in Walt Disney World. The set has been retired. - **$6**

❑ **MPB-512. Pooh Puzzle Piece,**
2000. Part of a three-piece puzzle set sold in Walt Disney World. The set has been retired. - **$6**

❑ **MPB-513. Eeyore Puzzle Piece,**
2000. Part of a three-piece puzzle set sold in Walt Disney World. The set has been retired. - **$6**

MPB-514

MPB-515

❑ **MPB-514. Eeyore Autumn Breeze,**
2000. Part of the Walt Disney World Seasons series, this pin has a limited edition size of 5000. - **$10**

❑ **MPB-515. Piglet Giggling,**
August 2001. This Walt Disney World features a Piglet belly laughing. - **$6**

MPB-516

MPB-517

❑ **MPB-516. Eeyore with Pink Bow Tail,**
2001. This Walt Disney World pin was also sold in a variation with a white nose and tail bow. - **$6**

❑ **MPB-517. Tigger Spring Is In The Air,**
2001. Part of the Walt Disney World Seasons series, this pin has a limited edition size of 5000. - **$10**

MODERN PINBACKS

MPB-518

MPB-521

MPB-524

❑ **MPB-518. Piglet Lazy Days,**
2001. Part of the Walt Disney World Seasons series, this pin has a limited edition size of 5000. - **$10**

MPB-519

MPB-522

MPB-525

❑ **MPB-524. Chubby Cub Pooh,**
2002. Available from various Disney sources, this pin features Pooh and his chubby tummy. - **$6**

❑ **MPB-525. "Give me a minute" Pooh & Rabbit,**
March 2003. Part of the "Wanna Trade?" Series, this surprise release pin is from Walt Disney World. Limited edition size of 1000. - **$12**

MPB-520

MPB-523

❑ **MPB-521. Tigger in Frame with Pink Nose,**
2001. Originally available in Walt Disney World, this pin has been retired. - **$9**

❑ **MPB-522. T is for Tigger,**
2001. Part of a series of Disney alphabet pins. - **$9**

❑ **MPB-523. Tigger & Rabbit "Tradin?",**
June 23, 2002. Part of the "Wanna Trade?" Series, this pin was released in Walt Disney World during the Mickey's Pin Trading Night event. Limited edition size of 2500. - **$15**

MPB-526

❑ **MPB-519. Piglet Sleeping on Flowers,**
2001. Originally available in Disneyland and Disney's California Adventure as part of the Summer Fun series, this pin has been retired. - **$7**

❑ **MPB-520. Pooh Holding Flower Pot,**
2001. Originally available in Disneyland and Disney's California Adventure as part of the Summer Fun series, this pin has been retired. - **$7**

❑ **MPB-526. Piglet's Pork Chop Karate,**
March 2004. A surprise release pin from Walt Disney World. Limited edition size of 1000. - **$10**

MULTI-CHARACTER

Mulan

After years of adapting European folk and fairy tales, as well as the occasional American myth, Disney went outside its normal sphere of influence and in 1998 adapted a tale from Chinese folklore. A girl named Fa Mulan wants to be the perfect daughter, but always feels she is letting her parents down. When her father is called to battle, she decides to take his place. Dressing like a man, she joins the Chinese army. Her good intentions bring a guardian dragon named Mushu to life to "watch over" her. Sadly, Mushu does more harm than good and the two of them are banished. In the end, though, Mulan's positive spirit wins out and helps her defeat the Hun warriors, bringing honor to her home.

The full length animated feature was directed by Tony Bancroft and Barry Cook. Vocal actors included Ming-Na Wen, Lea Salonga, B.D. Wong, Donny Osmond and Eddie Murphy. The music was written by David Zippel, Mathew Wilder and Jerry Goldsmith. The film is notable for its portrayal of a strong female character.

Mulan also marked one of the last times that Disney would approach an animated film with a Broadway sensibility. That is to say with characters singing about their feelings and emotions rather than discussing them in plain, conversational speech.

Merchandise for the film was extensive. It included dolls, books, compact discs, food products and fast food tie-ins.

MUL-2

❏ **MUL-2. Mulan Pinback,**
1999. This Walt Disney World pin features Mulan in front of a blue screen. It has been retired. - **$8**

Multi-character

The most famous and durable team in Disney history consists of Mickey, Donald and Goofy. Over the years they have teamed up together in cartoons, books, comics and television. However, they are not the only team in the Disney universe. As a company, Disney has never had a problem mixing and matching its stars in any number of combinations. The core characters of the Disney universe were frequently shown as friends and peers, gathering in whatever number a story required. One of the best early examples comes in the classic Mickey Mouse cartoon *The Band Concert* (1935). Though Mickey was the star, his band and its onlookers included numerous other residents of Disney's cartoon village. These included Goofy, Clarabelle Cow, Horace Horsecollar, Peter Pig, and Donald Duck just to name a few.

Disney comics continue the tradition of community to this day, with Mickey's town of Mouseton and Donald's Duckburg positioned next to each other. It is easy to see Mickey sitting in his living room and imagine that Donald lives just a few miles away. According to the continuity established in the comics, he actually does.

The Duckburg supporting cast features a high number of characters originally created for comics. The most famous of these were originated by Carl Barks (see separate entry). Known to fans as the "Duck Man", Barks is famous for his many additions to duck mythology.

Over the years, Disney characters have appeared together on a variety of merchandise. This merchandising policy seems to have been in place from the very beginning. Early examples include Mickey and Minnie dolls and bisque figures being sold as sets. Today, the theme parks have replaced the five and ten cent stores that used to sell items to the public. In addition, the advent of the Disney collector has created a market for all sorts of highly individualistic and esoteric "team-up" collectibles. Some of these items include dioramas, figurines, prints, and lithographs portraying multiple characters on adventures together.

MLT-1

❏ **MLT-1. Disney Character Spanish Pitcher,**
1936. 9" tall glass pitcher with wrap around character images matching those from 1936 second dairy series glasses. - **$100 $200 $300**

MLT-2

❏ **MLT-2. "Mickey Mouse, Donald Duck And All Their Pals,"**
1937. Whitman. #887. 40 pages. - **$110 $225 $450**

MLT-3

MUL-1

❏ **MUL-1. Mulan and Father Snow Globe,**
1998. Disney. Rotating action with Mulan and her father. - **$60**

MULTI-CHARACTER

❏ **MLT-3. "Toytown" Newspaper Mailer,**
1938. Mailer is 11.5x17.5" with 8 pages featuring toys mostly as black and white illustrations. - **$25 $50 $80**

MLT-4

❏ **MLT-4. "Tinkersand Pictures Mickey Mouse Series,"**
1938. Toy Tinkers Inc., Walt Disney Enterprises. Box is 6-5/8x12-3/8x1-3/8" deep. - **$75 $175 $350**

MLT-5

❏ **MLT-5. "Disneyland American Safety Blocks,"**
c. 1938. Halsam. 4.25x4.25x1.25" deep box contains set of nine wood blocks. Sides of blocks have designs in red and blue including letters and generic images, mostly of animals/vehicles. Boxed - **$40 $80 $150**

MLT-6

❏ **MLT-6. Disney Character Milk Bottle,**
c. 1938. Various dairies. 7.25" tall pint bottle with silk screened design on each side. Front has image of cow head followed by name "McDonald Farm Wakefield, Massachusetts." Reverse text reads "This Is The Way To Spend The Day-We Drink Our Milk Then Run And Play!" - **$100 $200 $400**

MLT-7

❏ **MLT-7 Disney Character Glass Shade For Dairy Company,**
c. 1938. Various dairies. 8" tall and 10" diameter. Milk glass with silkscreen designs. Has image of cow head followed by name "McDonald Farm Wakefield, Massachusetts." Reverse text reads "This Is The Way To Spend The Day-We Drink Our Milk Then Run And Play!" - **$200 $400 $800**

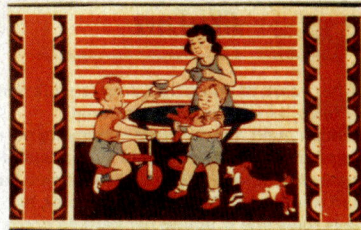

MLT-8

❏ **MLT-8. Disney Character Children's Tea Set,**
c. 1938. Ohio Art Co. 5x9x2" deep box containing smaller quantity but complete and unused six-piece tin lithographed set consisting of teapot with lid, two cups, two saucers, one plate. Boxed - **$200 $400 $800**

MLT-9

MULTI-CHARACTER

MLT-10

◻ **MLT-11. Mickey Mouse/Silly Symphony Characters Tea Set,**
1930s. Group of seven china pieces. Unmarked but similar to sets done by Wade of England. Group - **$85 $175 $280**

MLT-12

◻ **MLT-9. Disney Character Children's Tea Set,**
c. 1938. Ohio Art Co. Larger quantity version complete 23-piece lithographed tin tea set consisting of teapot with lid, six cups, six saucers, six plates, sugar bowl, cream pitcher, two serving trays. Set - **$350 $600 $1200**

◻ **MLT-10. Walt Disney Film Exhibitors Campaign Book,**
c. 1939. Stiff cover spiral-bound book detailing Walt Disney film campaign just after Snow White and just before Pinocchio. 16 pages. Has large fold-out detailing the next eighteen Disney shorts to be released starting with Brave Little Tailor in Sept. 23, 1938 through The Pointer in Sept. 1, 1939. 9.25x12.25" **$225 $450 $800**

MLT-11

MLT-13

◻ **MLT-12. "Walt Disney's Family Album" English Sticker Book,**
1930s. Juvenile Productions Ltd., London. 8.75x11.25" cardboard covered, 16 stiff paper pages book supplemented by two bound pages of gummed-back Disney character stickers to be cut out. Complete - **$150 $300 $550**

◻ **MLT-13. "Old King Cole & Stensgaard" Promo Folder For Store Displays/Signs,**
1930s. Opens to 23.5x34" includes display plaques, signs and posters for purchase by store owners. - **$300 $650 $1000**

MLT-14

◻ **MLT-14. "Walt Disney's Merbabies And Other Stories,"**
1930s. Hardcover 8.25x11". 28 pages. Printed in Australia by John Sands Pty. Ltd., Sydney. - **$50 $100 $200**

691

MULTI-CHARACTER

MLT-15

❑ **MLT-15. Walt Disney Multi-Character Embossed Sand Pail,**
1930s. Ohio Art. Lithographed tin pail is 5.75" tall with 6" diameter top. Has attached carrying handle. Green Water Version - **$300 $750 $1250** Yellow Water Version - **$400 $900 $1500**

MLT-16

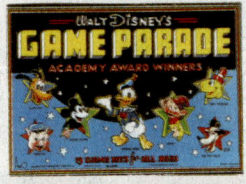

MLT-17

❑ **MLT-16. "The Walt Disney Parade" Book,**
1940. Garden City Publishing Co. 8.5x11.25" hardcover, 176 pages. Content is eight different full-length stories separated by six additional two-page stories. - **$50 $125 $225**

❑ **MLT-17. "Walt Disney's Game Parade,"**
1940. American Toy Works. 13.25x19.25x2" deep box holds parts for numerous games. - **$125 $250 $500**

MLT-18

MLT-19

❑ **MLT-18. "The Victory March/The Mystery Of The Treasure Chest" Mechanical Book,**
1942. Random House. 8x10" spiral-bound hardcover, 10 pages. Mechanical features are wheels to turn, segments to lift, cardboard slides to move in and out as part of the story in which the Big Bad Wolf steals Donald's treasure chest which contains something "to help us win the war!" - **$250 $500 $850**

❑ **MLT-19. "National AAU Track And Field Championships" Program,**
1942. 9x12" program with 148 pages for event to "Benefit Army Emergency Relief" held June 19-20 at Randall's Island Stadium, New York. Disney cover depicts six characters. - **$40 $90 $165**

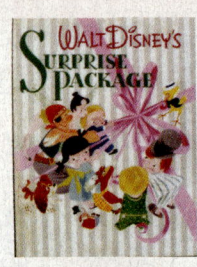

MLT-20

❑ **MLT-20. "Walt Disney's Surprise Package" Book,**
1944. Simon & Schuster. 10.25x13" hardcover, 92 pages. Content is twelve illustrated stories, several of which went on to become full-length animated features including Alice in Wonderland, Peter Pan, Lady From Lady and the Tramp. Other stories include Brer Rabbit, Peter and the Wolf. - **$45 $85 $175**

MLT-21

❑ **MLT-21. "Walt Disney's Paint Book,"**
1946. Whitman. 8.5x11" with 96 pages featuring Mickey, Donald and others. - **$25 $50 $100**

MULTI-CHARACTER

MLT-22

❑ **MLT-22. "Instrument Flight Rules" Poster Featuring Disney Characters,**
c. 1946. British Air Forces. 20x30" poster. Top text reads "You Must Use Instrument Flight Rules Under These Conditions…" and beneath this are three different panel scenes for "Proximity, Visibility, Density." These feature Disney characters in different types of aircraft plus word balloons featuring related text. Bottom margin has text "Air Traffic Service" plus insignia of British and Army Air Forces. Additional text reads "Printed For H.M. Stationery Office By S.S. Offset Ltd. B'ham." - **$110 $225 $450**

MLT-23

MLT-24

❑ **MLT-23. "Mickey Mouse Annual,"**
1947. Dean & Son Ltd. English hardcover 7.75x10". 128 pages. - **$25 $50 $110**

❑ **MLT-24. "Walt Disney's Comics And Stories" Subscription Mailer,**
1947. Opened size of four-page folder is 7.25x10.25". Front cover art originally appeared on 1945 issues of this comic including Vol. 5 #10 Spirit of '76 design featuirng Mickey, Donald and Dopey. Back cover art of Donald originally appeared on front cover of Vol. 5 #11. - **$75 $150 $225**

MLT-25

MLT-26

❑ **MLT-25. "Pictorial Review" With Disney Covers,**
1949. Pittsburgh Sun-Telegraph. Three newspaper supplements with Disney covers. Each 11x15". Nov. 20, 1949 with Mickey and Donald Thanksgiving illustration, Nov. 18, 1951 with Snow White And Seven Dwarfs Thanksgiving cover, Dec. 23, 1962 with Christmas cover of Mickey, Donald, Goofy and Pluto singing caroles. Each - **$25 $50 $100**

❑ **MLT-26. Disney Italian Candy Card Set,**
c. 1949. Ferraro Chocolate complete set of 100 numbered paper cards, each 1-5/8x2-1/8" illustrated on fronts with text on backs. First 50 cards are full figure character illustrations and the second 50 are illustrations based on scenes from a number of Disney films. Rare as a complete set, since we believe cards were distributed one per candy bar. Set - **$600**
Each - **$1 $3 $6**

MLT-27

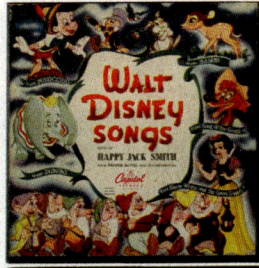

MLT-28

❑ **MLT-27. "Walt Disney Character Jewelry" Charm Bracelet Carded,**
1940s. Nemo Co. 3x8.25" display card holding 6" long metal link bracelet suspending five three-dimensional hard plastic painted 1" charms for Mickey, Donald, Pluto, Pinocchio, Snow White. Card - **$12 $25 $50** Bracelet - **$15 $30 $60**

❑ **MLT-28. "Walt Disney Songs" Record Set,**
1940s. Capitol Records. 7.5x7.5x.5" deep boxed "CCF3057" set of three 45 rpm records totaling twelve songs from movies Snow White, Pinocchio, Dumbo, Bambi, Song of the South. - **$25 $50 $75**

MLT-29

❑ **MLT-29. "A Walt Disney Picture Storybook,"**
1940s. Ayers and James Pty. Ltd., Sydney 9.5x10" Australian book. 12 pages. - **$30 $60 $100**

MULTI-CHARACTER

MLT-30

MLT-30. "The Disney Gang 'At The Circus'" Premium Picture,
1940s. Dell. 10.25x14.5" glossy paper sheet showing many Disney characters in circus theme. - **$30 $60 $125**

MLT-31. "The Tiny Golden Library,"
1950. Golden Press. 6.25x12x2.25" deep simulated wood-grain box contains set of 36 hardcover books each 2x3". Each book has a 16 page story with color illustrations. - **$100 $200 $300**

MLT-32. Marx Toys Character Figures Artwork,
c. 1950. 18x21" mat has pentagon-shaped opening of 13.5x17". Features character designs of Marx soft plastic figures that were sold individually on large displays. Ten different designs, each 3" in diameter for - Peter Pan, Alice, Snow White, Donald, Mickey, Dumbo for Disney and Dick Tracy, Li'l Abner, Orphan Annie, Sandy. Custom matted. Unique, Near Mint - **$1300**

MLT-31

MLT-32

MLT-33

MLT-33. "Walt Disney's Comics And Stories" Subscription Mailer Folder,
1951. Dell Publishing Co. Glossy paper 3.5x7" folder opening to 7x10". - **$65 $125 $200**

MLT-34

MLT-34. Club Membership Card,
1952. - **$25 $50 $110**

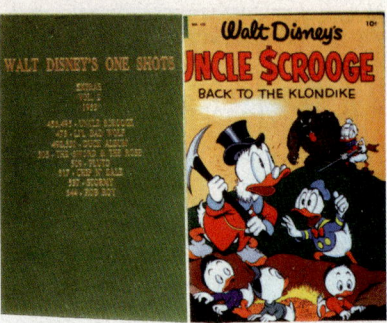

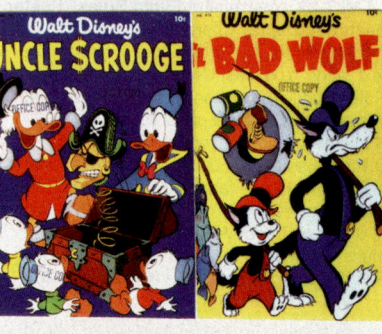

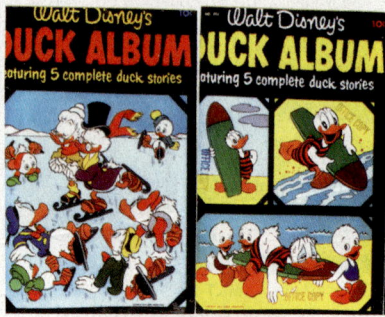

MLT-35

MLT-35. "Walt Disney's One Shots" Dell File Copy Bound Comics,
1953. Hardcover 7.25x10.25" with ten bound-in comics. Titles and issue numbers are: #456, 495, Uncle Scrooge; #473, Li'l Bad Wolf; #429, 531 Duck Album; #505, The Sword And The Rose; #509, Pluto; #517, Chip 'N' Dale; #537, Stormy; #544 Rob Roy. - **$75 $120 $250**

MULTI-CHARACTER

MLT-36

☐ **MLT-36. "Walt Disney Stories" Film Card Set,**
1953. Tru-Vue. 4x5.75" slipcase envelope holding three-card "DA-1" set of stereo views for Mickey, Donald, Pluto adventures. - **$5 $12 $20**

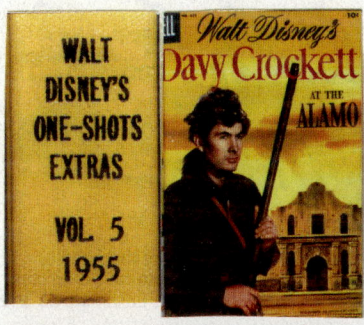

MLT-37

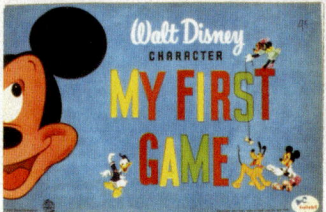

MLT-38

☐ **MLT-37. "Walt Disney's One-Shots Extras" Dell File Copy Bound Comics ,**
1955. Hardcover 7.25x10.25" with twelve bound-in comics. "Vol. 5, 1955." Titles and issue numbers are: "Chip 'N' Dale #636, Davy Crockett At The Alamo #639, Duck Album #649, Pluto #654, Goofy #658, Daisy Duck's Diary #659, Davy Crockett In The Great Keelboat Race #664, The African Lion #665, Chip 'N' Dale #4, Dumbo #668, Robin Hood #669, Davy Crockett & The River Pirates #671." - **$120 $240 $360**

☐ **MLT-38. "Walt Disney Character/My First Game,"**
1955. Gabriel Toys. 9.25x14.25x1.25" deep boxed game featuring gameboard illustrating houses of Mickey, Minnie, Pluto, Donald plus a quantity of wooden sticks. - **$10 $20 $35**

MLT-39

☐ **MLT-39. Mickey Mouse And His Pals Plastic Rings,**
1956. Sugar Jets cereal. Peter Pan example from set of eight: Mickey, Minnie, Donald, Pluto, Snow White, Pinocchio, Dumbo, Peter Pan. Each - **$15 $25 $75**

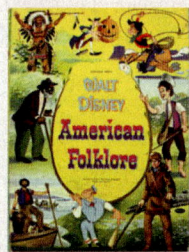

MLT-40

☐ **MLT-40. "Walt Disney American Folklore" Book,**
1956. Whitman. 8.5x11.5" hardcover with 252 pages of 46 illustrated stories. Book is contained in a box. Box - **$15 $30 $60** Book - **$20 $40 $85**

MLT-41

☐ **MLT-41. Mickey Mouse And Donald Duck Wall Planters,**
c. 1956. Shaw. Matching set each 2.5x7x5.5" tall painted and glazed ceramic with Shaw foil copyright sticker on right side edge. Back of each planter has a hole as made for wall mounting if desired or could be set on a shelf. Each - **$75 $135 $250**

MULTI-CHARACTER

MLT-42

☐ **MLT-42. "Action Valentines From Disneyland" Box Set,**
1957. Includes 24 cards, envelopes and two teacher cards. - **$75 $125 $250**

MLT-43

☐ **MLT-43. 3D Wiggle Picture Display,**
1957. Cheerios Cereal. Thin plastic badge pictures Cheerio Kid. Center of circus tent design is open to hold one of six different Disney character flasher pictures. Offered as a set.
Badge Only - **$40 $75 $150**
Each Flasher - **$10 $20 $30**

MLT-44

MLT-45

☐ **MLT-44. "Walt Disney The Art Of Animation," Hardcover,**
1958. Simon & Schuster. By Bob Thomas. 188 pages. Filled with much text, black and white and color illustrations and photos of Disney art and artists. Jacket - **$12 $25 $40**
Book - **$30 $60 $100**

☐ **MLT-45. "Drawing Guide" Folders,**
1950s. Probable set of five 8.5x12" four-page folder guides showing "Construction And Proportions, Expressions, Action Lines" and final steps for drawing Disney characters. Set - **$25 $50 $100**

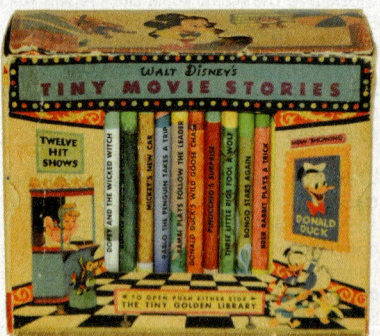

(Back)   (Front)

MLT-46

☐ **MLT-46. Tiny Golden Books Library Set,**
1950s. "Tiny Golden Theater" box holds 12 tiny Golden Library books. - **$75 $150 $225**

MLT-47

☐ **MLT-47. Disney Character "Joinies,"**
1950s. Five thin cardboard 4x5" sheets, each with punch-out body parts. Un-punched Each - **$3 $6 $12**

MLT-48

☐ **MLT-48. Bread Loaf Wrapper Labels,**
1950s. Complete set of 48 die-cut waxed paper end labels, each 2.75x2.75". Each - **$3 $6 $12**

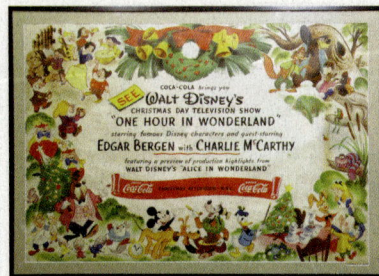

MLT-49

MLT-50

696

MULTI-CHARACTER

❑ **MLT-49. Walt Disney Coca-Cola Christmas Day Television Show Poster,**
1950s. 59x41" featuring many of the classic Disney characters. - **$250 $500 $1000**

❑ **MLT-50. Toothpaste Advertising Slick,**
1950s. Listerine Toothpaste. 7.5x10.5 glossy paper, probably from a salesman's binder and possibly only the left half of original. Inset illustration is store display containing "Listerine Toothpaste With Walt Disney Character Heads." When toothpaste was used up the heads, which serve as caps, were removed and placed on bodies to make statues of Mickey, Donald, Pluto, Brer Rabbit. - **$6 $15 $25**

MLT-53

MLT-51

❑ **MLT-51. Birthday Party Kit,**
1950s. Rendoll Paper Corp. 9.5x15x1" deep boxed elaborate party kit set of "Over 40 Complete Pieces For 8 Kiddies." Pieces are based on eight Disney popular characters and include hats, candy baskets, placemats, invitations, napkins, party game. Boxed - **$20 $40 $60**

❑ **MLT-53. "Disneyland Roller Coaster Wind-up Toy,"**
1950s. Chein. 8.25x19.5x9.5" tall with built-in key. - **$125 $275 $500**

MLT-54

MLT-55

MLT-52

❑ **MLT-54. Disney Character Boxed "Musical Top" By Chein,**
1950s. Tin lithographed top with wooden handle has diameter of 7" and height of 6.5", comes in original but non-Disney box. Box - **$25 $50 $75** Toy - **$35 $75 $150**

❑ **MLT-55. "Walt Disney Character Lites" Boxed Christmas Tree Light Bulbs,**
1950s. Paramount. 5.25x7.5x1" deep box with display window contains set of eight different 2.5" tall figural glass light bulbs. Bulbs are Mickey, Minnie, Donald, Pluto, Pinocchio, Jiminy Cricket, Pig and Dwarf. Boxed - **$35 $75 $125**

❑ **MLT-52. "Marx Walt Disney Mechanical Train Set,"**
1950s. Marx Toys. Train platform is 13x21.5x2.5" tall with two tin lithographed tunnels attached. Has plastic signal tower and gate. Train is 1.5x11x1.5" tall with hard plastic engine and built-in key. Also has two lithographed tin cars. Box - **$25 $50 $100** Toy - **$200 $400 $800**

MULTI-CHARACTER

MLT-56

❑ **MLT-56. Disney Characters Bowl,**
1950s. Unmarked. 6" diameter by 2" deep glazed ceramic centered by group of characters. - $8 $15 $25

MLT-57

❑ **MLT-57. "How To Draw And Color Book,"**
1960. Whitman. Large format 11.25x13.25" instruction guide with 80 pages illustrating how to draw Disney characters. - $25 $45 $75

MLT-58

❑ **MLT-58. "Disney Land Friction Van Trailer" Boxed Truck By Line Mar,**
c. 1960. 4x9x3" deep box with nicely illustrated lid contains two-piece tin lithographed truck consisting of cab and van trailer with size of 3x12x3.75" tall. Early 1960s from a series of trucks produced by Line Mar which also included Snow White and The Three Little Pigs. Box - $150 $300 $500
Toy - $300 $600 $1000

MLT-59

❑ **MLT-59. "Walt Disney Cookie Bus" Boxed Cookie Jar,**
1961. Dan Brechner. 4.5x10.25x5.5" tall painted and glazed ceramic in original box. Decorated with decals at all windows showing different Disney characters along with decals for "Walt Disney/Cookie Bus" on each side. Back of bus has license plate reading "Disneyland U.S.A." Underside has Brechner foil sticker. Box - $50 $100 $150
Jar - $200 $400 $700

MLT-60

MLT-61

❑ **MLT-60. "The Hunting Instinct" Mexican Oversized Lobby Card,**
c. 1961. 12.75x16.75" Spanish text card for compilation film comprised of various hunting-related Disney cartoon shorts involving multiple characters. - $5 $12 $20

❑ **MLT-61. Comic Characters Stapler With Donald Duck And Others,**
1962. King Features Syndicate. Newspaper comics promotional 3.5" long chrome accent metal stapler with .5x2.5" enamel top art of Donald, Dagwood, Beetle Bailey, Popeye, Jiggs, Snuffy Smith. Copyright below Donald reads "W.D.P." Limited issue, mainly for newspaper editors. - $25 $50 $80

MLT-62

❑ **MLT-62. "Walt Disney's Treasury/21 Best-Loved Stories" Book,**
1963 Golden Press. 10x13" Giant Golden Book hardcover 13th edition printing of original 1953 edition. Content is 140 pages of illustrated stories based on many different popular characters. - $25 $45 $75

MLT-63

MULTI-CHARACTER

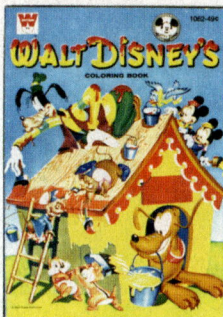

MLT-64

☐ **MLT-63. "Walt Disney's Happiest Songs" Sign,**
1967. 12x17" stiff cardboard two-sided sign with fold line at top for use as easel or string hanger. Promotes the record album issued as a $1.00 premium by Gulf Oil. - **$25 $50 $75**

☐ **MLT-64. "Walt Disney's Coloring Book,"**
1969. Western Publishing Co. 8x11" with 60 pages of multi-character scenes. - **$15 $25 $50**

MLT-65

☐ **MLT-65. Disney "School Bus Book" Concept Art,**
1960s. 5.25" square paper with art by "Disney Legend" Al Konetzni. Signed by him with his added notations "Orig. Rough Cover For Children's Book '60s" and "School Bus Book/Drive Carefully." Unique, Near Mint - **$125**

MLT-66

☐ **MLT-66. "Disneykins By Marx" Gift Box Set,**
1960s. Marx. 10x12.5x1.5" deep box with 34 Disneykins. - **$200 $450 $750**

MLT-67

☐ **MLT-67. "Disneykings" Near-Set Boxed,**
1960s. Marx. 9.5x11x1.5" display box with cellophane window over 19 of 20 plastic hand-painted figures 1.25" to 2.75" tall. Missing is the "Dewey" figure. Complete - **$150 $300 $600**

MLT-68

☐ **MLT-68. "Disneykins No. 3 Collection,"**
1960s. Marx. 6x7.5" display bag with header card title for set of eight individually boxed hand-painted hard plastic Disneykin figures. From a series of four numbered sets in this style of packaging. Each Set - **$200 $400 $750**

MLT-69

☐ **MLT-69. "Disneykins No. 4 Collection,"**
1960s. Marx. 6x7.5" display bag with header card title for set of eight individually boxed hand-painted hard plastic Disneykin figures. From a series of four numbered sets in this style of packaging. Each Set - **$200 $400 $750**

MLT-70

MLT-71

☐ **MLT-70. "Disneykins" Figures Individually Boxed,**
1960s. Marx. Fourteen different hand-painted hard plastic miniatures 1.5" tall or less, each in individual box. From a set of eighteen. Each - **$5 $10 $15**

☐ **MLT-71. "Disneykins Set B" Figures,**
1960s. Marx. Boxed set of 24 hard plastic 1.5" tall or less hand-painted miniatures designated Set B, an apparent special issue. Boxed - **$125 $250 $400**

MULTI-CHARACTER

MLT-72

❏ **MLT-72. "Marx Disneykins" Six-Scene Boxed Set,**
1960s. 8x9.5x1" deep box contains six different scenes which were also offered in individual "TV Scenes" boxes. Each scene is 2.25x2.5" with different background illustration and each is numbered. These are scenes #7-12 and feature Pinocchio with Figaro, Snow White with table and two stools, Daisy Duck with nephew, Minnie Mouse with refrigerator, Alice with dog house and water pump, Dopey with two beds. Boxed Set - **$85 $175 $300**

MLT-73

❏ **MLT-73. Disney School Bus Variety Thermos,**
1960s. Aladdin Industries. 6.5" tall metal lunch bottle with plastic cup, companion to the classic domed metal school bus lunch box, although produced in more than one variation. This one shows school as brown, non-brick building, trees above bus, flag pole on school roof, no boy and dog at back of building. - **$20 $35 $60**

MLT-74

❏ **MLT-74. "Walt Disney's School Bus" Spanish Variation,**
1960s. "Payva." 7x9x4.5" deep metal domed version of the U.S. classic version by Aladdin Industries. Difference of Spanish box is depiction of character getting off the bus as Fiddler Pig rather than Jiminy Cricket. - **$75 $150 $300**

MLT-75

❏ **MLT-75. "Walt Disney School Bus" Lunch Box,**
1960s. Aladdin Industries. 7x9x4.5" deep metal domed box designed by "Disney Legend" Al Konetzni. Yellow version shown, also issued as orange version in 1961. Yellow - **$30 $60 $125**
Orange - **$40 $75 $150**

❏ **MLT-76. Walt Disney Records,**
1960s. Group of five 45 rpm records, all on the Disneyland label and each in 7x7" colorful paper sleeve. All are from "LG (Little Gem)" series. Each - **$3 $6 $12**

MLT-76

MLT-77

MLT-78

❏ **MLT-77. Comic Characters Pencil Cup With Donald Duck And Others,**
1960s. King Features Syndicate. Newspaper comics promotional 2.25" diameter by 3.5" tall plastic segmented inside for pencils and pens. Other pictured characters are Snuffy Smith, Steve Canyon, Hi, Beetle Bailey, Archie, Blondie. Limited issue, mainly for newspaper editors. - **$35 $65 $110**

❏ **MLT-78. "Walt Disney's Rolykins By Marx,"**
1960s. Marx. 6.5x8" blister card contains set of six 1.5" tall hand-painted hard plastic figures.
Carded Near Mint - **$90**
Each Loose - **$3 $6 $12**

MLT-79

❏ **MLT-79. "Pip Squeek" Figures,**
1970. Louis Marx & Co. Three boxed 4" tall vinyl figures of Mickey, Goofy, Donald, each with accordian-like body designed to squeak when head is squeezed. Each Boxed - **$10 $20 $40**

MLT-80

MULTI-CHARACTER

❑ **MLT-80. Promtional Sign for "Wonderful World Of Disney Magazine,"**
1970. With Pinocchio. - **$30 $60 $115**

MLT-81

❑ **MLT-81. "Wonderful World Of Disney" Magazines,**
1970. Gulf. Group of four 8.5x11". Volume 1, issues 2 and 4 and Volume 2, issues 1 and 2. Each - **$2 $4 $8**

MLT-82

❑ **MLT-82. "Disneyland Magazine" First Issue,**
1972. Fawcett Publication. 10.25x12.5", 16 pages. - **$12 $30 $75**

MLT-83

❑ **MLT-83. "Disneyland Magazine,"**
1972. Fawcett Publication. Issue #2. 10.25x12.5". - **$8 $20 $50**

MLT-84

❑ **MLT-84. "Disneyana: Walt Disney Collectibles" Book With Dust Jacket ,**
1974. Hawthorn Books. 9x11" hardcover classic reference authored by Cecil Munsey, 400 pages with illustrated dust jacket. Content includes historical text and hundreds of photos of early Disney merchandise mostly taken from Kay Kamen published catalogues. Jacket - **$8 $15 $25**
Book - **$25 $60 $110**

MLT-85

❑ **MLT-85. "The Art Of Walt Disney,"**
1975. Abrams. "New Concise Edition" hardcover with dust jacket. 9x11.5". 160 pages. Book details the history of Disney art "From Mickey Mouse To The Magic Kingdoms." - **$10 $20 $40**

MLT-86

❑ **MLT-86. "Disney Checkers,"**
1977. Whitman. 8.5x16.5x1.5" boxed set of 16.25" square checkerboard bordered by Disney characters, punch-out sheet of more than seven character marker pieces for game play plus plastic slotted bases for standing the character markers. - **$8 $15 $30**

MLT-87

MLT-88

MULTI-CHARACTER

◻ **MLT-87. Mickey Mouse Jack-In-The-Box-Toy,**
1970s. Carnival Toys Inc. 5.75x5.75x5.75" tall lithographed tin box. Plays "Pop Goes The Weasel" and when finished, Mickey with hard plastic head and fabric-covered body pops out. - **$40 $70 $140**

◻ **MLT-88. Rubber "Disney-Kins" Carded,**
1970s. Durham Industries. Probable set of three 4.75x7" blister cards each holding 2" tall soft flexible figure of Donald, Goofy, Mickey. Distributed by Woolworth Co. stores. Each Carded - **$3 $6 $12**

MLT-89

◻ **MLT-89. "Tell-A-Tale Storytime Playset,"**
1980. Whitman. 6.5x11.5x1.25" deep boxed set of six "Tell-A-Tale" 5x5x6.5" hardcovers. Also packaged are related character punch-out sheets for finger puppets plus cardboard scenery board for each. Boxed - **$5 $12 $25**

MLT-90

MLT-91

◻ **MLT-90. Disney Character Miniature Wood Figures Display,**
c. 1980. Anri, Italy. 3.75x6x9" tall with ten figures: Mickey (2); Pluto; Minnie; Donald (2); Goofy (2); Pinocchio (2). Display - **$25 $50 $125**
Each Figure - **$25 $50 $85**

◻ **MLT-91. Disney Employee Only "Serigraph Cel,"**
1992. Created exclusively for "The Walt Disney Company Team Members" as a fund raiser for California Institute Of The Arts and includes certificate of authenticity. 10.5x13". Mint As Issued - **$215**

MLT-92

◻ **MLT-92. "Villains" Snow Globe,**
1999. Features all the nasty Disney character crew. - **$90**

MLT-93

◻ **MLT-93. Disney Princess Walkie Talkies Two-Piece Play Set,**
2004. - **$10**

MLT-94   **MLT-95**

◻ **MLT-94. Disney Princess Gift Set,**
2004. Has notepad, pencils, journal and phone book. - **$8**

◻ **MLT-95. Disney Princess Digital Watch,**
2004. With vinyl wristband and matching mini hair clips. - **$15**

MLT-96

◻ **MLT-96. Disney Princess Book Block,**
2004. Featuring 12 board books with storage box. - **$12**

MLT-97

THE NIGHTMARE BEFORE CHRISTMAS

❏ **MLT-97. Disney Princess Deluxe Glamour Case,**
2004. Set with real makeup, nail polish and play earrings. - **$12**

MLT-98

❏ **MLT-98. Disney Nesting Dolls,**
2004. Set of five dolls. - **$30**

MLT-99

❏ **MLT-99. Disney Robot Figures,**
2004. Set of five mini-robots. - **$25**

The Nightmare Before Christmas

Based on an extended poem by filmmaker Tim Burton, this 1993 film is one of the finest examples of stop-motion animation ever seen. The story elements may be a bit scary for the very youngest, but the film plays against those very elements in order to get its story told.

Jack Skellington is the Pumpkin King and he is tired of the same old routine that surrounds Christmas. As ruler of Halloween Town, he takes it upon himself to provide a change of direction. After kidnapping Santa Claus, he sets out to take over Christmas himself. With the help of his assistants, Lock, Shock and Barrel, he builds some presents which he thinks will charm children. Unfortunately, the gifts are unintentionally quite fiendish. When Jack sees how everyone reacts to his gifts, he changes his plans, ultimately saving Santa from the evil Oogie Boogie. Finally Jack restores a more traditional Christmas for the residents of Halloween Town.

Directed by Henry Selick, the film featured the vocal talents of Chris Sarandon, Catherine O'Hara, Glenn Shadix and William Hickey. The film was helped immensely by the soundtrack provided by Danny Elfman, who also provided the singing voice of Jack.

Merchandise was extensive and collectible spin-offs continue to this day. Among the items were dolls, books, CDs and many other items including a set of figurines posing the movie's heroes in a coffin.

NBX-1

❏ **NBX-1. "The Nightmare Before Christmas" Burger King Watch Display,**
1993. Burger King Corp. 35x56" diecut cardboard standee with easel reverse. - **$55 $110 $165**

NBX-2

❏ **NBX-2. "Nightmare Before Christmas" Mayor Bank,**
1993. Schmid. Painted and glazed ceramic. Near Mint Boxed - **$135**

NBX-3

NBX-4

❏ **NBX-3. "Nightmare Before Christmas" Wallet Cards,**
1993. Touchstone Pictures. Four thick plastic cards, each 2x3.25". Cards are of Jack, Zero, Sally, Lock, Shock & Barrel. Each - **$3 $6 $10**

❏ **NBX-4. "Nightmare Before Christmas" Mayor Music Box,**
1993. Schmid. 4x4.5x7" tall painted and glazed ceramic bank plays "What's This?" from the film. Body rotates in one direction while head rotates in opposite direction. Near Mint Boxed - **$275**

THE NIGHTMARE BEFORE CHRISTMAS

NBX-5

NBX-6

NBX-8

NBX-9

NBX-10

❑ **NBX-10. "Nightmare Before Christmas" Watch,**
1993 Timex. 3.5x9.5" blister pack containing plastic and vinyl wristwatch copyrighted by Touchstone Pictures. Insert card includes illustration of spiral hill against moon background plus pumpkins. Watch has figural Jack Skellington head which lifts up to reveal digital time. Near Mint Carded - **$30**

❑ **NBX-5. "Nightmare Before Christmas" Applause Dealer's Catalogue,**
1993. Applause. 9x12". 12 pages. Shows dolls, PVC figures, mugs, etc. - **$30 $60 $115**

❑ **NBX-6. "Nightmare Before Christmas Jack Skellington" Action Figure,**
1993. Hasbro. 7.75x11.5" blister card containing 9" tall poseable figure with tombstone base and pumpkin. Carded - **$35 $60 $110**

NBX-7

NBX-11

❑ **NBX-8. "Nightmare Before Christmas Jack Skellington And Zero" Boxed Dolls,**
1993. Hasbro. 18.5" tall box with display window over 17" tall Jack and 6" long Zero. Jack is a talking figure activated by pressing a button on his chest to produce either a "Fiendish Laugh" or one of four comments, "Merry Christmas/Eureka/Fantastic/Perfect." Near Mint Boxed - **$165**

❑ **NBX-9. "Nightmare Before Christmas Electronic Video Game,"**
1993. Tiger Electronics. 7x11.5" blister pack holding insert paper and 4x5" hard plastic handheld video game copyright by Touchstone Pictures. Carded - **$10 $20 $40**

❑ **NBX-11. "Tim Burton's Nightmare Before Christmas" Limited Edition "Indiglo" Watch In Coffin Box,**
1993. 3.5x7.5x1" deep coffin-shaped cardboard box contains nice quality watch with 1.25" diameter metal case. Sold exclusively through Disneyland in 1993. Box lid has recessed image of Jack Skellington with his arms crossed over his chest. This image really only shows up in reflected light. Watch dial features additional image of Jack, back of case includes limited edition text and individual number of "1478/2000." Watch is designed with "Indiglo Night-Light Pusher" button that illuminates the dial. Mint As Issued - **$275**

❑ **NBX-7. "Nightmare Before Christmas Jack As Santa" Action Figure,**
1993. Hasbro. 7.75x11.5" blister card containing 9" tall poseable figure with removable hat and beard, tombstone base and gift. Carded - **$25 $50 $85**

THE NIGHTMARE BEFORE CHRISTMAS

NBX-12

❏ **NBX-12. "Nightmare Before Christmas" Disney Employee Watch,**
1993. "Company D." 2.5x9.5" velvet pouch containing 1.5" diameter wristwatch in metal case. Dial face is silhouette image of Jack on hilltop and the second hand disk depicts Zero. Front of pouch has Halloween Town landscape while inside pocket features Jack Skellington's Theory of Christmas. Limited edition issue of 750. Mint As Issued - **$275**

❏ **NBX-13. "Nightmare Before Christmas" Premium Watches Set Boxed,**
1993. Burger King set of four wristwatches, each in 1.25" diameter plastic case with vinyl straps. Each comes in box with different colored simulated ribbon accent design. Watch names as printed on box flaps are "Halloween Town, Christmas Town, Pumpkins, Bats And Cats." Each Mint Boxed - **$10**

❏ **NBX-14. "Nightmare Before Christmas" Boxed Watch,**
1993. Timex 2.5x2.5x3.5" boxed display stand holding 1" diameter child's watch in plastic case with elastic expansion bands. Crystal features black lines representing a window pane while dial illustration is of Lock, Shock and Barrel. Near Mint Boxed - **$75**

NBX-13

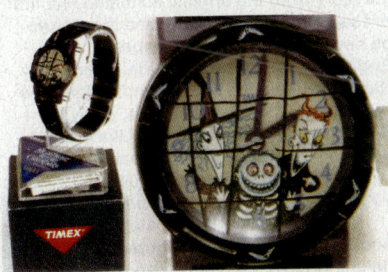
NBX-14

NBX-15

❏ **NBX-15. "The Nightmare Before Christmas" Employee Only Watch,**
c. 1995. Company D. 2.5x9.5" pouch contains 1.25" diameter watch. Sold only to Disney employees and from a limited edition of 750. Mint As Issued - **$225**

NBX-16

❏ **NBX-16. The Nightmare Before Christmas Zero Charger Plate,**
1996. 16" diameter by 3" deep heavy high quality porcelain. Limited edition of only 50 pieces. Sold exclusively through Art Of Disney Gallery. Mint As Issued - **$350**

NBX-17

❏ **NBX-17. The Nightmare Before Christmas Oogie Boogie Charger Plate,**
1997. 16" diameter by 3" deep heavy high quality porcelain. Limited edition of only 75 pieces. Sold exclusively through Art Of Disney Gallery. Mint As Issued - **$350**

NIKKI, WILD DOG OF THE NORTH

Nikki, Wild Dog of the North

Based on the book *Nomads of the North* by James Oliver Curwood, this full-color live-action feature was released in July, 1961. The pup Nikki becomes separated from his master. He grows up into a strong animal, but a mean hunter captures him and turns him into a fighting dog. Through a series of events, he is reunited with his original master. Directed by Jack Couffer and Dan Haldane; the film stars Jean Couto and Emile Genest.

Merchandise was very limited.

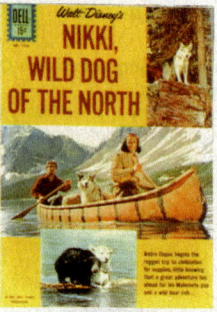

NIK-1

❑ NIK-1. Four-Color Comic #1226, 1961. - $8 $20 $60

Old Yeller

This full color live-action 1957 release still resonates with anyone who saw it as a child. It contains one of the most heart-wrenching scenes in the entire Disney canon. Set in 1860s Texas, the film centers on the Coates family; Old Yeller is a mongrel dog who becomes their pet and then a member of the family. After being bitten by an infected wolf, however, Yeller tragically has to be put down by the Coates son, Travis.

Actors include Fess Parker, Dorothy McGuire, Tommy Kirk and Kevin Corcoran. Directed by Robert Stevenson, *Old Yeller* was based on the book by Fred Gipson. A favorite among theatre-goers, the film saw theatrical re-release in 1965 and 1974. Since then, it has been a powerful seller in the video market.

Merchandise was limited. Old Yeller can be seen in *Four Color Comics* #869.

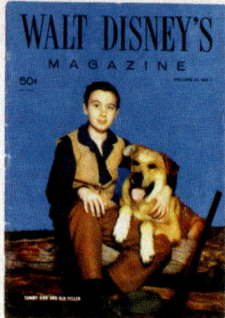

OLD-1

❑ OLD-1. "Walt Disney Magazine," 1957. Volume 3, #1. Cover photo is of Tommy Kirk and Old Yeller. Issue features a two-page story by Kirk. - $15 $30 $60

OLD-2

OLD-3

❑ OLD-2. "Old Yeller" Record, 1958. Mickey Mouse Club Records. 7x7" stiff paper sleeve contains 45 rpm release. - $10 $20 $30

❑ OLD-3. "Old Yeller Big Golden Book," 1958. Golden Press, 9.5x12.25". 28 pages. - $25 $50 $110

One Hundred and One Dalmatians

The film represented a shift from the classic, textured, luxurious look of Disney films into a more modern style sensibility. Taking advantage of a technological breakthrough called the Xerox process, animators were now able to mechanically transfer their drawings to cels. This sped up the production considerably, eliminating as it did the need for ink artists to handle such tracing. Considering that this particular film contained multiple spotted dogs in every scene, the tracing would have been a very expensive and time-consuming chore.

Based on the book by Dodie Smith, the full-length animated feature was released in January, 1961. A lonely songwriter named Roger Radcliffe owns a dalmatian named Pongo. One day, while out for a walk, Pongo meets a dalmatian named Perdita and Roger meets her owner, Anita. When Roger and Anita marry, the dalmatians have no complaints. Perdita gives birth to fifteen puppies. This attracts the attention of Cruella De Vil, who wishes to use the puppies to make a dalmatian fur coat. She begins kidnapping puppies across the countryside. Pongo and Perdita track down the stolen puppies and rescue every single one of them. The Radcliffe family winds up planning to build a dalmatian plantation. This will serve as a home to the newly recovered hundred and one dalmatians.

Directed by Wolfgang Reitherman, Hamilton Luske and Clyde Geronimi, the movie featured songs by Mel Levin. Animators on the project include Marc Davis, Frank Thomas, Ollie Johnston, Milt Kahl and Eric Larson. The film was a massive hit and saw re-release in 1969, 1979, 1985 and finally in 1991. Vocal talent included Rod Taylor, Lisa Daniels, Cate Bauer, Ben Wright and Lucille Bliss. The film inspired a live-action re-make in 1996.

With the advances being made in the technology of film-making, Disney felt that a live-action version of one of their most consistent successes might be feasible. Taking the story from the original animated film first released in 1961, Disney filmed the picture on seven separate sound stages in England's Shepperton Studios. Directed by Stephen Herek, the live-action film featured actors Glen Close, Jeff Daniels, Joley Richardson and Hugh Laurie. Like the original, the film proved to be a great success. It inspired a direct-to-video sequel *101 Dalmatians II, Patch's London Adventure*.

Merchandise for both features included books, records, ceramic figures, fast-food tie-ins, figures, doll, books and records.

ONE HUNDRED AND ONE DALMATIANS

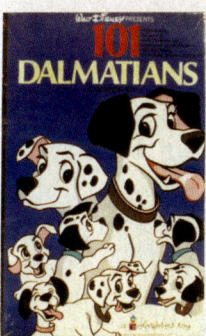

ONE-1

ONE-5

ONE-7

❑ ONE-1. "101 Dalmatians" Colorforms, 1959. Box is 8x12.5x1" deep. - **$15 $30 $60**

ONE-2

❑ ONE-4. Lucy Goose From 101 Dalmatians Cel,
1961. Gray cardboard mat 12x14" has 8x10" opening around 6x6.25" cel image. Souvenir from The Art Corner at Disneyland. - **$60 $125 $200**

❑ ONE-5. 101 Dalmatians Original Art By Al Konetzni,
1961. 4x7" tracing paper with 3x5.25" image of Pongo and pup for potential merchandise. Unique, Fine - **$60**

ONE-8

❑ ONE-7. "Lucky" From 101 Dalmatians Puzzle,
1961. Wood frame tray puzzle is 7.5x8.5x.25" thick. - **$6 $12 $20**

❑ ONE-8. 101 Dalmatians Ceramic Figurines,
1961. Enesco. Group of seven including 4.25" tall Perdita and six pups, each about 2.25" tall including five different and one duplicate.
Perdita - **$12 $25 $50**
Each Pup - **$6 $12 $20**

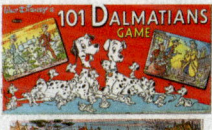

ONE-3

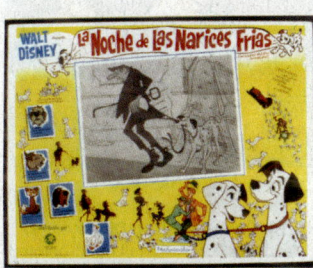

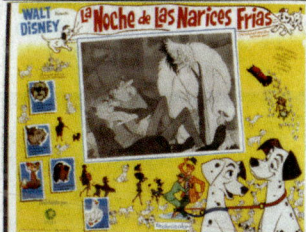

ONE-6

ONE-9

❑ ONE-2. "Songs From 101 Dalmatians" Record,
1960. Disneyland label. 7x7" stiff paper sleeve contains 45 rpm. - **$8 $15 $25**

❑ ONE-3. "101 Dalmatians Game,"
1960. Whitman. 8x15.5x1.5" deep box. - **$20 $35 $60**

ONE-4

❑ ONE-6. 101 Dalmatians Oversized Mexican Lobby Cards,
1961. Group of two, each 12.5x16.5". Each - **$5 $15 $25**

❑ ONE-9. "Jolly" Dalmatian Pup Ceramic Figurine,
1961. Enesco. From a series of at least ten, 2.5x5x3.5" tall. - **$20 $45 $75**

ONE HUNDRED AND ONE DALMATIANS

ONE-10

❑ **ONE-10. 101 Dalmatians Pup Ceramic Figurine,**
1961. Enesco. From a series of at least ten, 3x4.5x4" tall. - **$20 $45 $75**

ONE-11

❑ **ONE-13. "101 Dalmatians" View-Master Set,**
1961. Envelope is 4.5x4.5" and contains complete set of three reels with single inner sleeve and booklet. - **$10 $20 $45**

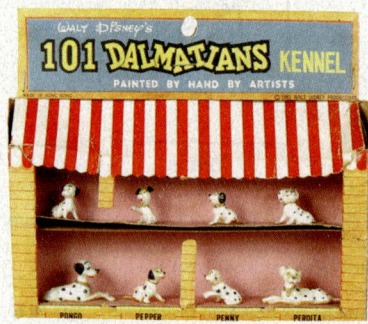

ONE-14

❑ **ONE-14. "101 Dalmations Kennel" Disneykin Boxed Set,**
1961. Marx. 7x8x1.25" deep box contains complete set of eight hand-painted plastic figures each about .75" tall. - **$50 $100 $200**

ONE-15

❑ **ONE-15. Dalmatian Pup Disneykins,**
1961. Marx toys. Two .75" tall hand-painted plastic figures of Patch and Lucky. Each - **$5 $10 $20**

ONE-16

❑ **ONE-16. 101 Dalmatians "Lucky Pup" Charm Bracelet,**
c. 1961. Case is 2x5.75x.25" deep and contains metal link bracelet with four attached painted figural charms of Pongo plus three identical pups. Boxed - **$10 $20 $40**

ONE-17

❑ **ONE-17. Pongo English Figurine,**
1960s. 2.5x3x3.75" tall painted high quality plaster with foil sticker "Crown Staffordshire Fine Art Figurines/England/Hand Painted." - **$100 $200 $300**

ONE-18

❑ **ONE-18. "Pongo Mini-Puppet,"**
1960s. Kohner Bros. Hard plastic push puppet 2.5" tall. - **$20 $40 $60**

ONE-12

❑ **ONE-11. "101 Dalmatians In Story And Song" Record,**
1961. Disneyland label. 12.25x12.25" cardboard album cover contains 33-1/3 rpm. - **$8 $12 $25**

❑ **ONE-12. "Lucky" From 101 Dalmatians Squeeze Toy,**
1961. Dell. 3.5x4x6.75" tall soft vinyl. - **$10 $20 $30**

ONE-13

ONE-19

❑ **ONE-19. 101 Dalmatians Puffy Stickers,**
c. 1970s. 9x11.5" sheet of vinyl stickers in clear plastic package. Packaged - **$5 $10 $20**

OSWALD, THE LUCKY RABBIT

ONE-20

❑ **ONE-20. 101 Dalmatians Serigraph Cel,** 1990s. Acetate sheet is 11x14" with 6x9.5" image depicting Perdita and three pups. One of the first four Disney sericels ever produced, only 250 were made. Mint As Issued - **$175**

Oswald, the Lucky Rabbit

- Between May, 1927 and August, 1928, Disney's animation studio produced 26 films featuring a slick, enthusiastic rabbit named Oswald. He was Disney's first featured cartoon character that had been developed specifically for a starring role. The series' financial backer was film producer Charles Mintz and the shorts were released by Universal.

With each Oswald cartoon Disney made, the quality of the animation took a leap forward. But it did come at a price. Within a year, production costs became troublesome. Disney visited Mintz to apply for a higher per-film budget. To the great amazement of Disney, Mintz instead told him that he was to cut production costs by twenty percent. Mintz also pointed out that Universal owned the character of Oswald. Should Disney not accept the budget cut, Mintz could produce the series without him. In preparation for this possibility, Mintz had already contracted with many of Disney's staffers behind Disney's back.

Disney made the decision to separate from Oswald; on the train trip home from his meeting with Mintz, he created Mickey Mouse.

As for Oswald himself, Universal eventually reassigned control of the character to former Bray studio animator Walter Lantz. Lantz's studio made more than a hundred Oswald shorts, but took the ill-advised decision to make the character's design cuter and simplify his formerly mischievous personality. By the late 1930s, Oswald had lost his ability to function in complex cartoons. In 1943, he made his final starring appearance on-screen.

This was not the end for the character, however. In 1942, when Lantz characters became the stars of Dell publishing's *New Funnies* comic book, Oswald immediately began to feature in stories of his own. Through the 1960s, the rabbit regularly appeared in Lantz comics titles. Only in the 1970s did he pretty much vanish from sight.

Today, the character has recently made a comeback in Japan. Thanks to new merchandise and reruns of his original cartoons on Japan's Cartoon Network, Oswald is again a recognizable figure in some households.

OSW-1

❑ **OSW-1. "Oswald The Lucky Rabbit" Earliest Known Disney-Related Button,** 1927. 7/8". Used to promote the cartoons Disney produced for Universal Pictures. - **$1000 $2000 $4000**

OSW-2

OSW-3

❑ **OSW-2. "Universal Weekly" With Oswald,** 1927. Volume 25, #20 with 40 pages is 8x10.5", Limited distribution to movie theater exhibitors.- **$35 $60 $125**

❑ **OSW-3. "Universal Weekly" With Oswald,** 1927. Volume 26, #2 with 40 pages is 8x10.5". - **$35 $60 $125**

OSW-4

❑ **OSW-4. "Universal Weekly" With Oswald,** 1927. Volume 26, #13 with 40 pages is 8x10.5". **$35 $60 $125**

OSW-5

❑ **OSW-5. "Universal Weekly" With Oswald,** 1927. Volume 26, #16 with 40 pages is 8.5x10.5". - **$35 $60 $125**

OSW-6

OSW-7

OSWALD, THE LUCKY RABBIT

❏ **OSW-6** "Universal Weekly" With Oswald, 1927. Volume 26, #17 with 40 pages is 8x10.5".
- **$50 $100 $150**

❏ **OSW-7.** "Universal Weekly" With Oswald, 1927. Volume 26, #18 with 40 pages is 8x10.5".
- **$35 $60 $125**

OSW-8

❏ **OSW-8** "Howdy Folks,"
c. 1927. Oswald The Luck Rabbit one sheet
- **$7000 to $15,000**

OSW-9

❏ **OSW-9.** "Universal Oswald," The Lucky Rabbit Of The Movies Stencil Set, 1928. Universal Toy & Novelty Co. N.Y. One of the very earliest items of Disney character merchandise and possibly the earliest Disney-related "toy." Complete set comes in 6.5x8.5x.75" deep box with six different images of Oswald which are identical to the set of six stencils included with this set. Stencils are each 4.5x5.5" on stiff cardboard and come with set of six glossy paper sheets. - **$150 $300 $600**

OSW-10

❏ **OSW-10.** "Oswald The Lucky Rabbit" Movie Club Button,
c. 1928. 7/8" with club member's serial number.
- **$75 $150 $300**

OSW-11

❏ **OSW-11.** "Oswald" Celluloid Crib Toy, 1931. "Oswald Copr. Universal Pictures/An Irwin Product." 6.75" tall with celluloid body, wood ball hands and feet, felt ears. Attached to top of head is string loop for hanging. - **$75 $150 $250**

OSW-12

❏ **OSW-12.** Early "Oswald" Doll,
1931. Universal Pictures Corp. 2.5x6.5x14.5" tall stuffed felt doll. - **$175 $325 $650**

OSW-13

OSW-14

❏ **OSW-13.** Early "Oswald" Color Variety Doll,
1931. "Oswald Copyrighted Universal Pictures Corp./An Irwin Product." 2.5x6.5x14.5" tall stuffed felt doll with additional terrycloth material on front lower half of body. Face has printed design as well as a separate felt nose. The other pictured example has body entirely in red felt whereas this body is primarily orange with red felt ears. - **$175 $325 $650**

❏ **OSW-14.** "Oswald" Windup Doll,
1931. Doll is 5x8x16.5" tall and has built-in key and stitched to the shirt is fabric ribbon which serves as his belt and reads "Oswald/Copyrighted Universal Picture Corp." Has velveteen face while rest of fabric-covered body is cloth and felt. Has leatherette shoes with strings. When wound, rocks back and forth as it slowly moves itself forward. - **$325 $650 $1200**

PECOS BILL

OSW-15

☐ **OSW-15. Oswald The Lucky Rabbit Doll By Dean's Rag Book Co.,**
1931. 2.5x3x7.5" tall doll. Has velveteen stuffed body with five fingered felt hands, glass eyes and string whiskers attached at nose. Attached to the doll and apparently as issued is a backpack held in place by string around neck and ribbon belt. - **$300 $600 $1200**

OSW-16

☐ **OSW-16. "Oswald The Lucky Rabbit" Large Size Doll By Dean's Rag Book Co.,**
c. 1931. England. 5x7x20.5" tall to the tips of his ears. Doll has stuffed velveteen body with felt ears, glass eyes and nose, round "cotton tail." Printed facial features include Dean's trademark toothy grin. The head is movable. Small lettering on one side of head reads "Oswald The Lucky Rabbit" while on opposite side text includes registration number. Underside of each foot has company mark and "Oswald" name. - **$1600 $3200 $5500**

Pecos Bill

Originally part of the 1948 feature *Melody Time*, *Pecos Bill* was released on its own as a short in 1955. Combining live action and animation, the story has Roy Rogers entertaining Luana Patten and Bobby Driscoll with music and a tall tale.

Baby Bill falls out of a wagon heading out west and as a result, is raised by coyotes. When he grows up, Bill saves the life of a horse named Widowmaker and also romances the beautiful Slue Foot Sue. Every bit the figure of outrageous legend, Bill can roll a cigarette while riding a cyclone; he can lasso a rain cloud from California to stop a drought, and he shoots out all the stars in the sky over Texas in order to make Texas the Lone Star State.

Merchandise included books, records, a Marx mechanical toy and a limited edition statue.

PEC-1

☐ **PEC-1. "Melody Time" Fan Card,**
c. 1948. Disney Studios 7.25x9.25" stiff paper picturing and naming twelve characters from the film. - **$25 $50 $80**

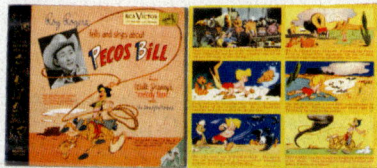

PEC-2

☐ **PEC-2. "Roy Rogers Tells And Sings About Pecos Bill" Record Album Set,**
c. 1948. RCA Victor Little Nipper Series Y-389 rigid cardboard album holding set of three 78rpm records. - **$30 $65 $90**

PEC-3

☐ **PEC-3. Pecos Bill Boxed Wind-Up,**
c. 1948. Line Mar. 10" tall hard plastic toy with built-in key. Box - **$75 $150 $250**
Toy - **$75 $150 $250**

PEC-4

☐ **PEC-4. RCA Christmas Records Promo Game With Mailer,**
c. 1952. "Little Nipper RCA Victor" Christmas greeting mail envelope holding stiff paper gameboard opening to 7.5x13.5" including punch-out markers. Playing surface has metal spinner needle plus cartoon image of TV popular characters available on RCA recordings. Depictions include Pecos Bill, Roy Rogers, Howdy Doody, Tom Corbett, Miss Frances of Ding Dong School. Reverse pictures total of 20 record covers.
Mailer - **$5 $12 $25**
Game - **$60 $135 $225**

PEC-5

☐ **PEC-5. "Pecos Bill Art Corner Souvenir" Animation Wheel,**
1950s. "Souvenir Of Disneyland" and "Magic Movies From The Art Corner" bagged 11" diameter slotted cardboard wheel repeating illustrations of him on his horse Widowmaker and firing his gun. User spins wheel on a wooden rod while facing a mirror to produce animated illusion from the slotted design. - **$50 $100 $150**

PECOS BILL

PEC-6

Pegleg Pete

He is known by many names. Among them are Bootleg Pete, Putrid Pete, Black Pete and Big Bad Pete. Surprisingly, this villainous character is actually Disney's longest-lived animated creation. His first appearance came as early as *Alice Solves the Puzzle* (1925). Part of the early Alice Comedies, his heroic nemesis in that short was Julius the Cat. Pete went on to appear in the Oswald Rabbit shorts, then appeared as Mickey Mouse's foil in *Steamboat Willie* (1928), the first Mickey cartoon released to general distribution.

Pete originally appeared as a bear, but became a cat to take on Mickey Mouse. He has remained a cat to this day. Pete gradually lost his pegleg, but he has continued to torment Mickey, Donald and Goofy in films and comics throughout the years. In 2004, he appeared in the direct-to-video release *The Three Musketeers*.

Merchandise featuring Pete is limited.

PEG-3

❑ **PEG-2. Post Toasties Corn Flakes Mickey Mouse Picture Panel Set,**
1935. Complete set of six numbered story panels 2.5x3", all neatly cut from back panel of Post cereal box. Set is The Dognapper and features Mickey, Donald, Minnie and her Pekinese who was kidnapped by Pegleg Pete. Cut Set - **$30** **$50** **$100**

❑ **PEG-3. "Mickey Mouse Ludo" English Game,**
1930s. Chad Valley. The insturctions are printed on inside of lid but box also comes with separate small instruction sheet. Box is 6x11x1" deep. The stiff cardboard gameboard is 10.5x10.5" with choice full color linen-like label. Game path has action illustrations featuring Mickey as well as single images of Pluto, Pegleg Pete and Patricia Pig. - **$100** **$200** **$400**

PEG-1

❑ **PEG-1. "The Cactus Kid" Pencil Drawing,**
1930. Image is 3.75x7", on 9.5x12" sheet. Art is likely by Ub Iwerks. - **$600** **$1200** **$2000**

PEG-2

Perri

Part of the *True-Life Adventure* series, this 1957 film stands out as the only episode in the series to be adapted from a work of fiction. Shot in Utah and Wyoming, the film is based on a story by the author of *Bambi*, Felix Salten.

Perri is a young pine squirrel whose father gives his life for her. She grows up encountering predators; eventually, she falls in love. Walt Disney's nephew Roy E. Disney served as a cameraman on the project. From there, he moved through producing TV programs and today is a respected film producer in his own right.

Merchandise for Perri is limited. Perri can be seen in *Four Color Comics* #847, and theatrical posters are known to exist.

PEC-7

❑ **PEC-6. "Pecos Bill" Statue,**
1990s. From the Disney Classic collection. Limited to 10,462. - **$600**

❑ **PEC-7. "Slue Foot Sue" Statue,**
1990s. From the Disney Classic collection. - **$600**

PETE'S DRAGON

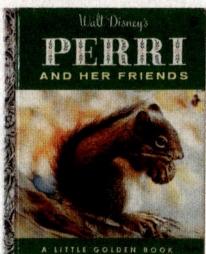

PER-1

❏ **PER-1. "Perri And Her Friends Little Golden Book,"**
1956. Simon & Schuster. Has 24 pages. - **$10 $20 $40**

PER-2

❏ **PER-2. "Perri" The Squirrel, By Steiff.**
c. 1957. This is the larger of two sizes, 3x5x6" tall. Complete with cardboard tag, fabric tag and button in ear. - **$30 $60 $125**

PER-3

PER-4

❏ **PER-3. "Perri" Record,**
1958. Mickey Mouse Club Records. 7x7" stiff paper sleeve contains 45rpm # "DBR-72." Record features three songs from the film "Sung By Jimmie Dodd And Darlene Gillespie." - **$5 $15 $25**

❏ **PER-4. "Steiff" Catalogues,**
1959. Two in full color, each 6x8.25". Second catalogue is from 1961. Both picture numerous bears and other small and large plush animals, hand puppets, etc. Both include Bambi and Perri. Each - **$10 $20 $30**

Pete's Dragon

A combination of live-action and animation, this full-length feature opened in December, 1977. Based on a story by Seton Miller and S.S. Field, the film is set in Maine. An orphaned youngster, Pete is accompanied on his travels by his somewhat clumsy animated dragon friend, Elliott. Pete winds up living with a lighthouse keeper and his grown daughter. A crooked salesman, Dr. Terminus, decides to try and kidnap the animated dragon. The kidnapping doesn't go as smoothly as he had planned. At the film's climax, the lighthouse's lamp goes out in the midst of a great storm, but Elliott uses his flame to rekindle the lamp and save a ship from crashing.

Ken Anderson was the film's animation director and he also created the dragon Elliott. The film itself was directed by Don Chaffey. The cast includes notables such as Shelly Winters, Sean Marshall, Helen Reddy, Mickey Rooney, Red Buttons and Jim Backus. Charlie Callas was the voice of the dragon Elliott. The songs were by Al Kasha and Joel Hirschorn.

Merchandise included figures, books and records.

PDR-1

❏ **PDR-1. Studio Christmas Card,**
1977. Stiff textured paper card 5.25x7.25" with full color art. Card opens to reveal Pete's Dragon Elliott pulling Santa's sleigh with text "Elliott, In Place Of Eight Tiny Reindeer." - **$20 $40 $60**

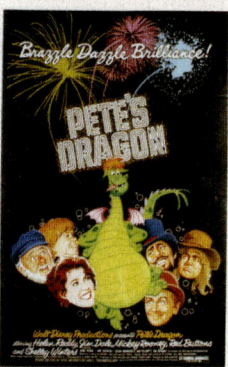

PDR-2

PDR-3

❏ **PDR-2. "Pete's Dragon" Movie Poster,**
1977. Glossy 27x41" full color one-sheet for original release. - **$20 $35 $70**

❏ **PDR-3. "Pete's Dragon" Book/Record,**
c. 1977. Disneyland label. 7.25x7.25", 24-page storybook with flap on inside back cover that holds the 45rpm record. - **$5 $10 $15**

PDR-4

❏ **PDR-4. "The Magical Music Of Walt Disney" Boxed Record Set,**
1978. Ovation Records. Cardboard slipcase contains complete set of four 33-1/3rpm records and 48 page booklet featuring "50 Years Of Original Motion Picture Soundtracks." The four record set features music, dialogue and special effects from films beginning with Steamboat Willie, 1928 through Pete's Dragon, 1977. - **$25 $50 $90**

PETE'S DRAGON

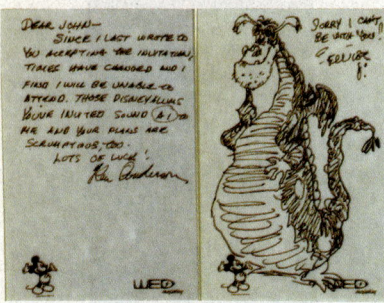

PDR-5

❑ **PDR-5. Ken Anderson Handwritten Letter And Pete's Dragon Sketch,**
c. 1990. Ken Anderson was a Disney animator from the mid-1930s on, helped design parts of both parks and is the creator/designer of Elliott. Two 5.5x8.5" black and white sheets of "WED Imagineering" stationery with small printed Mickey image at lower left. One is a handwritten letter in black fountain pen signed in full. Second sheet has black fountain pen sketch of Elliott and includes text "Sorry I Can't Be With You Elliott." Unique Near Mint - **$175**

Peter Pan

The eternally popular story of the boy who wouldn't grow up was written by Sir James M. Barrie in 1904. Walt Disney and his brother Roy had seen a roadshow version in their youth and Walt had actually appeared as Peter in a school play. As early as 1935, Walt attempted to start production on an animated adaptation of the story. Production on the property wouldn't fully come together for many years. Animation production would not begin until 1949 and the film would not see release until February, 1953.

Just as the children of the Darling Family are going to bed, they receive a visit from Peter Pan. He convinces them to come with him to his mystical home called Never Land. With the help of Tinker Bell's pixie dust, the Darlings fly over England to Never Land. Once there, they have adventures fighting Captain Hook and meeting the Lost Boys.

It has been rumored that actress Marilyn Monroe was the inspiration for Tinker Bell, Peter's pixie friend. In truth, character designer Marc Davis actually used actress Margaret Terry as the model. During the earliest theatrical productions, women were cast in the role of Peter Pan, a tradition that continues on stage to this day. Disney's film was the first major production in which Peter was played by a boy; actor Bobby Driscoll served as the live model for Peter and he also provided his voice in the film. Other voices used were Kathryn Beaumont and the immortal Hans Conried as Hook.

Directing animators included Ward Kimball, Milt Kahl, Marc Davis, Frank Thomas and Wolfgang Reitherman.

Merchandise included one obvious tie-in, collectible character coaster lids sealing jars of Peter Pan peanut butter. Store items included Hagen-Renaker figures, puzzles, comic books and premium items. Peter Pan appears in *Four Color Comics* #442 and 926. A 54 page adaptation of the film itself can be found in the 200 page Dell Giant *Peter Pan*.

PPN-1

❑ **PPN-1. "Peter Pan" Concept Art,**
c. 1950. 8x10 5/8" watercolor and ink by noted artist David Hall. Unique - **$4000**

PPN-2

❑ **PPN-2. "Peter Pan" Concept Art,**
c. 1950. 6x8" watercolor and ink by noted artist David Hall. Unique - **$5000**

PPN-3

❑ **PPN-3. "Peter Pan Coloring Book,"**
1952. Whitman. 8x10.75" with 128 pages. - **$20 $40 $75**

PPN-4

PPN-5

❑ **PPN-4. "Peter Pan Coloring Book,"**
1952. Whitman. 8.5x11" with 32 pages. - **$15 $30 $60**

❑ **PPN-5. Peter Pan Coloring Book Artwork,**
1952. Whitman. 10x12" sheet of paper with 6.5x8.5" art image from Whitman coloring book. Same Or Similar - **$25 $50 $85**

PPN-6

❑ **PPN-6. "Peter Pan Picture Puzzle" Complete Bread Premium Picture Album,**
1952. Donald Duck Bread. 9x9" four-page folder with 24 mounted cut-outs from bread labels. Complete - **$50 $100 $150** Album Only - **$10 $20 $35**

PETER PAN

PPN-7

❏ **PPN-7. "Peter Pan Golden Record,"**
1952. Simon & Schuster. 6.5x7.5" paper sleeve containing yellow 78 rpm. - **$5 $12 $20**

PPN-8

PPN-9

❏ **PPN-8. Storybook Album,**
1952. RCA Victor. "Little Nipper" 7.5x7.5" cardboard spiral-bound album cover containing WY-4001 set of two yellow vinyl 45 rpm song records sung by film's original cast. Cover has bound-in, 24 page illustrated storybook. - **$10 $20 $40**

❏ **PPN-9. "Weather Bird Shoes Presents Peter Pan Hat" Premium,**
1952. Stiff paper cut-out sheet is 13.5x18". Uncut - **$20 $40 $80**

PPN-10

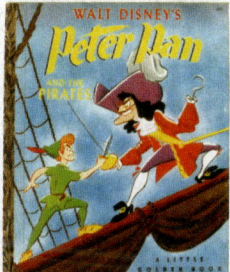

PPN-11

❏ **PPN-10. "Peter Pan" Book,**
1952. Whitman. 7.5x8.25 "Cozy Corner" hardcover, 24 pages. - **$12 $25 $50**

❏ **PPN-11. "Peter Pan And The Pirates Little Golden Book,"**
1952. Simon & Schuster. 6.75x8" with 28 pages. First printing. - **$10 $20 $40**

PPN-12

❏ **PPN-12. Nana Cel,**
1953. Image is 5x5.5". - **$125 $300 $475**

PPN-13

PPN-14

❏ **PPN-13. George Darling Cel From Peter Pan,**
1953. Image is 7x8". - **$75 $150 $300**

❏ **PPN-14. Studio Fan Picture,**
1953. 8x10" glossy thin cardboard issue for the film's initial release. - **$10 $20 $30**

PPN-15

❏ **PPN-15. Movie Still,**
1953. 8x10" glossy for Peter Pan film release. - **$12 $25 $40**

PPN-16

PETER PAN

❏ **PPN-16. "Peter Pan" Press Book,**
1953. Stiff paper 12x18" cover and 20 glossy pages comes with separate "Part 2" 20 page campaign book. Gordon Gold Archives. - **$100 $200 $425**

PPN-17

PPN-18

PPN-19

PPN-20

❏ **PPN-17. Michael Ceramic Figurine,**
1953. Shaw. 1.5" tall. - **$65 $125 $200**

❏ **PPN-18. Nana Ceramic Figurine.**
1953. Shaw. Figure is 2" tall. - **$75 $150 $250**

❏ **PPN-19. Peter Pan Ceramic Figurine,**
1953. Shaw. 3.25" tall. - **$100 $200 $300**

❏ **PPN-20. Wendy Ceramic Figurine,**
1953 Shaw. 3.25" tall. - **$90 $180 $275**

PPN-21

❏ **PPN-21. Tinker Bell Glazed Ceramic Figurine,**
1950s. Shaw. 2" tall issued with die-cut celluloid-like wings, typically missing. Incomplete - **$50 $85 $175**
Complete - **$100 $200 $300**

PPN-22

❏ **PPN-22. "Admiral Television Studio Featuring Walt Disney's Peter Pan" Premium,**
1953. Envelope is 15.5x16.5" and contains 50 piece punch-out set with 32 page script book. Unpunched - **$60 $125 $175**

PPN-23

PPN-24

PETER PAN

❏ **PPN-23. "Peter Pan Souvenir Caps" Ad,**
1953. 14.5x21.5" complete single page from newspaper Sunday comic section with bottom third of one side ad for Peter Pan Peanut Butter series of sixteen different lithographed tin "Souvenir Cap" lids. - **$5 $8 $12**

❏ **PPN-24. "Peter Pan Peanut Butter" Store Sign,**
1953. 11x14" paper announcement "Now Get Your Walt Disney Originals/See Walt Disney's Movie 'Peter Pan' In Technicolor." Peanut Butter was issued with lithographed tin lids featuring various characters. - **$40 $70 $125**

PPN-25

❏ **PPN-25. Peter Pan Peanut Butter Lids,**
1953. Nine different from a set of sixteen. 3" in diameter. Each - **$8 $15 $25**

PPN-26

❏ **PPN-26. Clerk's Peter Pan Premium Promo Button,**
1953. 1.5" litho. - **$15 $30 $60**

PPN-27

❏ **PPN-27. "Peter Pan" Soap,**
1953. Colgate-Palmolive-Peet Co. 1x2x3" long glossy paper wrapped "Newest Beauty Bar With Chlorophyll." - **$3 $6 $12**

PPN-28

PPN-29

❏ **PPN-28. "Peter Pan" Premium Map,**
1953. Colgate-Palmolive. 18x24" textured paper. Text mentions "Peter Pan Beauty Bar." - **$100 $200 $400**

❏ **PPN-29. Indian Chief Standee,**
1953. Admiral Television. 14.5x17.5" die-cut paper on cardboard figure with easel back, one of several different Peter Pan character standees issued to promote Admiral sales. Bottom margin text is "See Walt Disney's Peter Pan At Your Movie Theater." - **$65 $135 $240**

PPN-30

❏ **PPN-30. "Peter Pan" Costume,**
1953. Ben Cooper 8x10.5x3.5" deep "Walt Disney" display box with cellophane window over costume of starched linen mask and fabric outfit comprised of separate vest and trousers. Boxed - **$125 $200 $300**

PPN-31

❏ **PPN-31. "Peter Pan" German Toy Watch,**
1953. 2.25x7.75" display card contains child's toy watch with tin case and vinyl straps. Carded - **$10 $20 $30**

PETER PAN

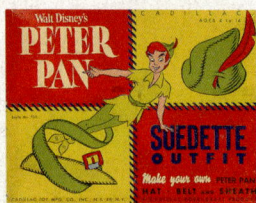

PPN-32

❏ **PPN-32. "Peter Pan" Suedette Outfit,** 1953. 2.25x7.75" display card contains child's toy watch with tin case and vinyl straps. Carded - **$10 $20 $30**

PPN-33

❏ **PPN-33. "Walt Disney Tinker Bells" Toy,** c. 1953. Peter Puppet Playthings. Base is 11x16x2" deep with eight metal bells attached at top along with a 6" long three-dimensional hard plastic Tinker Bell figure. Total height is 5.5". - **$110 $225 $350**

PPN-34

PPN-35

❏ **PPN-34. "Peter Pan" Dual Purpose Advertising Sign,** c. 1953. 11x14" stiff cardboard halved by ads for "Little Golden Books/Records" available for 25 cents "Now On Sale Here" and the Disney movie showing at local "RKO Keith Memorial" theater. - **$20 $40 $70**

❏ **PPN-35. "Peter Pan" English Hardcover,** c. 1953. The Sunshine Press. 8.25x10.25" with 60 pages. - **$30 $60 $110**

PPN-36

❏ **PPN-36. "Disneyland Electric Quiz,"** c.1955. Jaymar. 8x10x2" deep box contains complete battery operated quiz game. - **$15 $30 $50**

PPN-37

❏ **PPN-37. "The Walt Disney Illustrated Peter Pan & Wendy,"** 1958. Brockhampton Press English hardcover 5.5x7.5". 132 pages. Contains six beautiful color plates. Jacket - **$10 $20 $40** Book - **$30 $80 $160**

PPN-38

❏ **PPN-38. Peter Pan Ceramic Planter,** 1950s. Leeds. 4" tall painted and glazed. - **$25 $50 $100**

PPN-39

❏ **PPN-39. Nana Figurine,** 1950s. Hagen-Renaker. 1.5" tall. - **$75 $125 $200**

PPN-40

PPN-41

PETER PAN

❏ **PPN-40. Peter Pan Figurine,**
1950s. Hagen-Renaker. 1.75" tall. - **$100 $200 $300**

❏ **PPN-41. Mermaid Figurine,**
1950s. Hagen-Renaker. 2" tall. Blonde hair variety, also issued as redhead. Each - **$100 $200 $300**

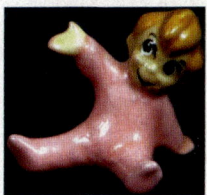
PPN-42

❏ **PPN-42. Michael Figurine,**
1950s. Hagen-Renaker. 1" tall. - **$65 $110 $175**

PPN-43

❏ **PPN-43. Michael's Teddy Bear Figurine,**
1950s. Hagen-Renaker. Tiny 5/8" tall painted and glazed ceramic with foil sticker on underside. Miniature size is in appropriate scale to the Michael figurine by same maker. - **$50 $100 $150**

PPN-44

❏ **PPN-44. Spanish "Peter Pan" Book,**
1950s. Editorial Vilcar, Barcelona. 6.5x9.5" with stiff cardboard cover. 16 pages. Cover has removable red hat feather and red sword. - **$50 $100 $150**

PPN-45

❏ **PPN-45. "Peter Pan" Doll,**
1950s. Gund. 2.5x5.5x6" tall with stuffed plush body and soft vinyl head. - **$20 $40 $75**

PPN-46

PPN-47

❏ **PPN-46. "Peter Pan And Tinker Bell Dolls" Set,**
1950s. Duchess Doll Corp. 9.5x10.75x2.25" deep display box with cellophane window over pair of 7.5" tall hard plastic dolls, detailed by sleep eyes, life-like hair, fabric outfits. Tinker Bell has satin-like wings. Peter Pan has hat with feather plus metal miniature sword. Boxed - **$50 $100 $150**

❏ **PPN-47. Captain Hook Marionette,**
1950s. Peter Puppet Playthings. 16.5" tall figure has painted composition head, hand and legs with cotton/felt outfit and attached cardboard hand control unit. One hand is a wire hook. - **$60 $125 $200**

PPN-48

PPN-49

❏ **PPN-48. "Peter Pan Push Button Puppet,"**
1950s. Kohner Bros. 4.25" tall figure atop plastic base comes in illustrated box. Box - **$25 $50 $100** Puppet - **$50 $100 $200**

❏ **PPN-49. "Wendy" Hand Puppet,**
1950s. Gund Mfg. Co. 9" tall toy with soft vinyl head, fabric handcover body with stitched tag. Interior of fabric has squeaker mechanism. - **$15 $30 $50**

PETER PAN

PPN-50

❑ **PPN-50. Squeaker Doll,**
1950s. Sun Rubber Co. 9.75" tall pliable soft rubber youthful likeness. - **$25 $50 $75**

PPN-51

PPN-52

❑ **PPN-51. Tinker Bell Night Light,**
c. 1961. Enesco. 3x4x4" tall painted and glazed ceramic complete with original electric cord, bulb socket and bulb, foil sticker, separate paper sticker "WDE-195." Lighting emits from the Lost Boys tree behind her image. - **$50 $100 $150**

❑ **PPN-52. 3-D Picture,**
1966. W.C. Jones Publishing Co. Thick plastic 8x10" dimensional illusion scene of Peter flying in front of the Jolly Roger with Captain Hook on boat's stern. - **$8 $15 $25**

PPN-53

❑ **PPN-53. Christmas Poster With Tinker Bell,**
1967. Gulf Oil Corp. Large 28x42" poster "To Be Posted During December 1967 At All Gulf Stations." - **$60 $125 $175**

PPN-54

❑ **PPN-54. "Peter Pan" Thermos,**
1969. Aladdin. 6.5" tall plastic for vinyl lunch box. - **$12 $25 $40**

PPN-55

❑ **PPN-55. "Peter Pan" Lunch Box,**
1969. Aladdin Industries. 7x8.75x3.5" deep soft vinyl. - **$50 $85 $150**

PPN-56

❑ **PPN-56. "Tinker Bell" Lunch Box,**
1969. Aladdin Industries. 7x9x4" deep soft vinyl. - **$65 $125 $200**

PPN-57

❑ **PPN-57. "Peter Pan Games" Premium,**
1969. Hunt-Wesson Foods. 7.5x15" mailing envelope containing glossy stiff cardboard game folder that opens to 14.5x20". Two of the three folder panels are gameboard, third perforated panel is a set of cards. Mailer - **$5 $10 $15** Game - **$35 $60 $100**

PPN-58

❑ **PPN-58. "John" Canadian Glass,**
1969. 6-3/8" tall paint image tumbler #1 from Canadian numbered set of six featuring Peter Pan characters. Each - **$30 $60 $100**

PETER PAN

PPN-59   PPN-60

❏ **PPN-59. Tinker Bell Candy Dispenser,**
1960s. Pez. 4.25" tall plastic dispenser variety with white hair. - **$65 $135 $225**

❏ **PPN-60. Captain Hook Candy Dispenser,**
1960s. Pez. 4.25" hard plastic. - **$25 $50 $80**

PPN-63

❏ **PPN-63. "Jolly Roger" Model Kit,**
1981. Revell Plastics. 7.5x11x2" boxed unopened plastic parts for assembly of "Peter Pan's Pirate Ship." Box marking includes "Made And Printed In Germany" although instruction sheet text is in English. Boxed - **$10 $20 $30**

PPN-66

❏ **PPN-65. Tinker Bell Snow Globe,**
1999. With mushrooms and flowers, plays "You Can Fly!". - **$35**

❏ **PPN-66. Signed "Peter Pan Limited Edition Serigraph,"**
c. 1990s. Image of Peter Pan and Captain Hook is 7.5x11.5" with "Walt Disney Company" seal and signed by animator Marc Davis. Near Mint - **$350**

PPN-61

❏ **PPN-61. Tinker Bell Figurine,**
1960s. Enesco. 1.5" tall. - **$60 $150 $240**

(CLOSED)   PPN-64   (OPEN)

❏ **PPN-64. Neverland Music Box,**
1998. From the Disney store, plays "You Can Fly!". - **$40**

PPN-67

❏ **PPN-67. Tinker Bell Doll,**
2000. Part of Peter Pan ornament series. - **$30**

PPN-62

PPN-65

❏ **PPN-62. Peter Pan Doll,**
1960s. Madame Alexander 14" tall plastic and vinyl doll detailed by sleep eyes, rooted life-like hair, felt hat, jacket and shoes; stretch fabric pants, simulated leather belt with snap-on back. Jacket has stitched tag, hat is complete with feather attachment. - **$25 $50 $100**

PPN-68

PETER PAN

PPN-69

PPN-71

PPN-74

❑ **PPN-68. Tinker Bell Photo Holder,** 2000. With Cinderella's Castle from Walt Disney World. - **$20**

❑ **PPN-69. Tinker Bell Snow Globe,** 2000. With jewelry and perfume bottles, plays "You Can Fly!". - **$35**

❑ **PPN-71. Tinker Bell Water Globe,** 2003. Comes with jewelry box, plays "You Can Fly!" - **$35**

PPN-72

❑ **PPN-72. Tinker Bell Lamp,** 2003. From the Disney store. - **$75**

❑ **PPN-74. Tinker Bell Fashion Doll,** 2000s. From Disneyland Paris. - **$35**

PPN-75

PPN-76

PPN-70

❑ **PPN-70. Tinker Bell "Spirit of Neverland" Fashion Doll,** 2002. Doll stands 11 1/2" tall. - **$30**

PPN-73

❑ **PPN-73. Tinker Bell Character Statuette,** 2006. Master Replicas. From Walt Disney Showcase Collection series. Porcelain figure is 25" tall with 12x17x2.5" base. - **$275**

❑ **PPN-75. Tinker Bell Figure,** 2000s. - **$75**

❑ **PPN-76. Tinker Bell Cookie Jar,** 2000s. - **$100**

Pinocchio

A classic among classics, Disney's second full-length animated film (1940) was based on Italian author Carlo Collodi's story of a young marionette who wishes to be a real boy. Written in serial form in the 1880s, the story was translated into English in 1892. The marionette's adventures are amazing. Pinocchio is kidnapped by the puppeteer Stromboli; gets in trouble with bad boy Lampwick, and then rescues father Geppetto from the belly of Monstro the Whale. Thanks to Pinocchio's good deeds, the Blue Fairy grants his wish to become human.

Disney altered some elements of the original story. In Collodi's original version, Pinocchio ignores the cricket who attempts to lecture him, finally squashing him like the bug he is. The Disney feature lets the cricket live to become a real hero. For all his hard work as Pinocchio's conscience, Jiminy Cricket was awarded an Official Conscience Medal by the Blue Fairy. Jiminy would go on to an illustrious career in other Disney films.

An early problem with *Pinocchio*'s production was that the puppet couldn't seem to carry the film on his own. This was solved by creating the strongest supporting cast ever seen in a Disney picture. Characters from this film include Figaro the kitten, Cleo the goldfish, the Coachman, the Blue Fairy and the famous Fox and Cat, "Honest" John Worthington Foulfellow and Gideon.

The film was directed by Hamilton Luske and Ben Sharpsteen. The look of the film was based on the art of children's illustrator Gustav Tenggren. Noted animator Ward Kimball developed the look and feel of Jiminy Cricket. The music was composed by Leigh Harline, Ned Washington and Paul Smith. The picture won two Academy Awards, both for music: *When You Wish Upon a Star* won for Best Song, while the film as a whole won for Best Scoring of an Original Picture. Vocal talent included Dickie Jones, Christian Rub, Cliff Edwards and Mel Blanc. The film is tied with *Snow White* (1937) as the motion picture to have been re-released the greatest number of times.

Merchandise was extensive. It began in 1939, the year before the film's release, and included a variety of figural items, toys by the Marx Company, books, dolls and other products. Pinocchio, as well as characters from the Pinocchio family, appear in *Four Color Comics* #92, 252, 545, 701, 750, 795, 886, 897, 982, 989 and 1203. Some issues contain partial reprints of earlier issues. Pinocchio is considered a true Disney classic and items related to it are still being manufactured today.

PIN-1

❑ **PIN-1. "Pinocchio Art Stamp Picture Set,"** 1939. F.S. Co. 6.75x13x1" deep boxed complete set of seven different character ink stamps with wood handle, generic tin stamp pad and tablet. - **$85 $165 $375**

PIN-2

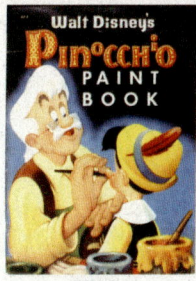
PIN-3

❑ **PIN-2. "Pinocchio Art Stamp Picture Set,"** 1939. Fulton Specialty Co. 11x17x1" deep box contains set "No. 495." Has set of ink stamps featuring thirteen different characters, standard tin stamp pad. Comes with twelve illustrated black and white sheets, each 7.5x9.5" and a single full color sheet to be used as a guide. There is a 5x7" instruction sheet. - **$110 $225 $450**

❑ **PIN-3. "Pinocchio Paint Book,"** 1939. Whitman. 11x15" book #573 with 48 pages including an eight-page "Story of Pinocchio." - **$50 $100 $200**

PIN-4

PIN-5

❑ **PIN-4. Geppetto And Figaro Pencil Sketch,** 1939. Animation paper is 8.25x8.75" centered by 5.5x7" story concept sketch. Bottom margin of sheet has "Original WDP" ink stamp. - **$225 $425 $700**

❑ **PIN-5. Pinocchio Story Sketch Original Art With Label,** 1939. Courvoisier Galleries. Animation paper is 8.25x8.75" with 5.5x7" image. Has "Original WDP" ink stamp. - **$300 $600 $1000**

PINOCCHIO

PIN-6

❏ **PIN-6. Pinocchio Pencil Drawing,**
1939. Animation paper is 10x12" with 4x4.5" image. Depicts Pinocchio as the Blue Fairy brings him to life. - **$250 $500 $1000**

PIN-7

❏ **PIN-7. "Pinocchio" Story Board Art,**
1939. 8.75x11" pencil drawing. - **$350 $650 $1300**

PIN-8

❏ **PIN-8. "Pinocchio" Production Drawing,**
1939. 10x12" paper with color artwork. - **$350 $650 $1300**

PIN-9

❏ **PIN-9. Figaro Pencil Drawing,**
1939. Image is 3x5" on animation paper. - **$40 $75 $150**

PIN-10

❏ **PIN-10. Gideon Pencil Drawing,**
1939. Sheet of 10x12" animation paper centered by 7x7.5" image for Red Lobster Inn scene from movie depicting him smoking a cigar and covering his mouth. - **$65 $125 $225**

PIN-11

❏ **PIN-11. Stromboli Pencil Drawing,**
1939. Animation paper is 12.5x15.5" with 4x7" image. - **$100 $200 $400**

PIN-12

❏ **PIN-12. Pinocchio Story Board,**
1939. Mat is 11x14" tan cardboard and has 7x8.5" opening around the art which is done on animation paper. Title at top "A Sock On The Nose." Depicts Lampwick throwing a punch while Pinocchio stands in front of him pointing. Image of Pinocchio was done on a separate 3.5x4.5" sheet. - **$250 $450 $750**

PIN-13

❏ **PIN-13. Pinocchio And Jiminy Cricket Original Art,**
1939. Thick 8x14" sheet of art board with two images done in ink and watercolor. Pinocchio image is 3x3.5" and Jiminy is 1.5x1.75". Pencil text at bottom includes "F.A.3716" plus date of December 8, 1939, prior to the film's release date of February 7, 1940. Reverse has ink stamp reading "Property Of Walt Disney Productions/Not To Be Used Without Permission." Unique, Near Mint - **$400**

PINOCCHIO

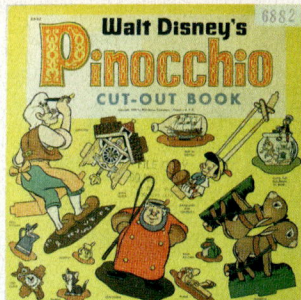

PIN-14

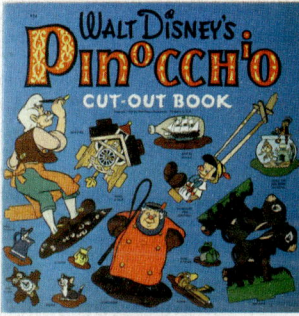

PIN-15

PIN-17

PIN-20

❑ **PIN-14. "Pinocchio Cut-Out Book,"** 1939. Whitman. 13x13" stiff cover book #6882. Uncut - **$150 $300 $650**

❑ **PIN-15 "Pinocchio Cut-Out Book" Variety,** 1939. Whitman. 13x13" book #974 in cardboard rather than stiff paper cover. Other cover variations are title in different lettering, cover art color differences in comparison to similar edition #6882 published same year. Uncut - **$165 $325 $675**

❑ **PIN-17. "Pinocchio Circus" Premium,** 1939. Envelope measuring 9.5x10.5" holds 10x20" paper sheet with circus tent, ticket booth, elephant, lion and sideshow marquee, 8.5x10" "Ringmaster Guide," 8.75x9" "Ringmaster" hat, 3.5x5.5" ringmaster's certificate and 2x5.5" sheet with printing including name of bread company and mention of "60 Characters" found in bread loaves. Issued by various bread companies. Set - **$115 $225 $350**

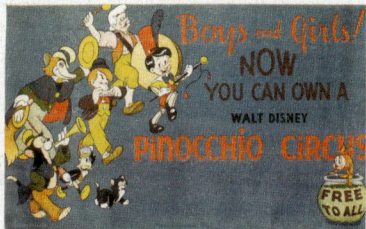

PIN-18

❑ **PIN-18. "Pinocchio Circus" Linen Sign,** 1939. 32x51" sign used to promote this premium campaign that enlisted various bread companies. - **$750 $1500 $2500**

PIN-16

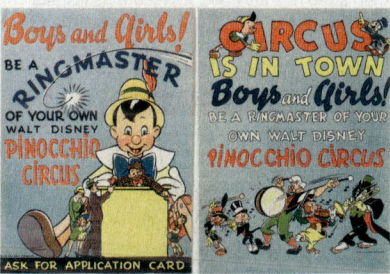

PIN-19

❑ **PIN-16. "Pinocchio Picture Puzzles" Boxed Set,**
1939. Whitman. 8.5x10.25x1" boxed pair of jigsaw puzzles, each assembling to 8.5x10" movie scene. Set - **$35 $70 $125**

❑ **PIN-19. "Pinocchio Circus" Store Signs,** 1939. Two 6x8" stiff paper promotion ads for elaborate premium sponsored by various bread companies. Pinocchio ticket booth with text at bottom margin "Ask For Application Card." The other sign includes illustrations of Pinocchio characters playing instruments with Pinocchio as the bandleader. Each - **$40 $75 $125**

❑ **PIN-20. "Pinocchio" Bread Wrapper,** 1939. Wax paper sheet 16x17" localized for "Waldensian's Screen Twist" bread. - **$25 $50 $80**

PINOCCHIO

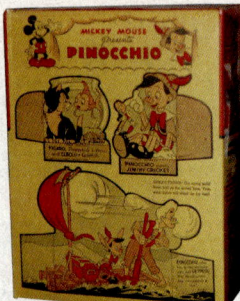

PIN-24

PIN-27

❑ **PIN-23. "Jiminy Cricket" Store Sign,**
1939. Sign is 6x18" glossy paper advertising "Monstro Soda." - **$75 $150 $275**

❑ **PIN-24. Pinocchio Store Sign And Related Premium Book,**
1939. Cocomalt items pair of 10.25x16" paper sign and 8.5x11.25" premium book advertised by the sign. Book has 48 pages. Inside back cover is Cocomalt illustrated ad. Sign depicts book's front cover in its actual size. Bottom margin offers free copy of book for Cocomalt purchase with product cost to be filled in by the local retailer. Sign - **$75 $150 $275**
Book - **$12 $20 $50**

❑ **PIN-26. "Pinocchio Children's Writing Paper,"**
1939. Whitman. Closed 5.25x7.5" cardboard folder opening to 15.5" width containing 4x5.5" lined paper sheets individually picturing Pinocchio, Jiminy Cricket, Figaro or Foulfellow, plus plain envelope for each. - **$30 $60 $90**

❑ **PIN-27. Figaro And Cleo Saucer,**
1939. Ohio Art Co. Lithographed tin 2.5" diameter saucer from toy tea set, featuring Figaro climbing Cleo's fish bowl as Cleo jumps up and out of the water. - **$5 $12 $25**

PIN-25

PIN-28

❑ **PIN-25. Pinocchio Characters Soap Set Boxed,**
1939. Lightfoot Schultz Co. Set of five castile soap figures, 3.5" tall or less, in 6.75x8.5x2.5" deep cardboard box designed as book with cover that opens from right side. Soap figures have some color paint detailing as made and Cleo soap has attached rope cord as issued. Inner cover has text "Story of Pinocchio" and inner box has cardboard partitions to separate the figures. Boxed - **$100 $200 $350**

PIN-21

❑ **PIN-21. Post Toasties Box,**
1939. Various boxes with cut-outs. Series was issued prior to movie's release. Each Complete - **$250 $500 $1000**

PIN-22

❑ **PIN-22. "Pinocchio Lids" Store Sign,**
1939. Glossy paper sign 6.25x17.75". - **$75 $150 $275**

PIN-23

PIN-26

PIN-29

726

PINOCCHIO

☐ **PIN-28. "Pinocchio" Menu,**
1939. Stiff paper folder is 5x6.75" and issued for various department store restaurants. This example has imprint on inside for Philadelphia, Pa. store "Strawbridge & Clothier." - **$30 $60 $110**

☐ **PIN-29. Pinocchio Riding Turtle Figure Bank,**
1939. Crown Toy Manufacturing Co. 6.5" tall painted composition. - **$200 $400 $650**

PIN-30

☐ **PIN-30. "Jiminy Cricket" Bank,**
1939. Crown Toy Co. Inc. 2.75x3x6" tall painted composition bank with metal trap and key. - **$75 $140 $275**

PIN-31

☐ **PIN-31. "Pinocchio" Sheet Music,**
1939. Irving Berlin Inc. Five 9x12" folders, each with identical front cover except for title. A total of seven different titles were issued in this series. Each - **$5 $12 $40**

PIN-32

☐ **PIN-32. "Give A Little Whistle" Song Folio,**
1939. Irving Berlin Inc. 7x10.5" glossy paper cover containing 14 different loose folio sheets for ensemble performance by fifteen different instruments. - **$15 $35 $60**

PIN-33

☐ **PIN-33. "Pinocchio Good Teeth Certificate,"**
1939. American Dental Assn. 4x9" paper certification with text "Pinocchio Presents This Good Teeth Certificate To/Assisted By: Jiminy Cricket The Lord High Keeper Of The Knowledge Of Right And Wrong." - **$35 $75 $140**

PIN-34

☐ **PIN-34. Pinocchio "Good Teeth" Button,**
1939. American Dental Association. 1.25". - **$65 $160 $250**

PIN-35

☐ **PIN-35. "Pinocchio" Ring Toss Toy,**
1939. De-Ward Novelty Co. 6x9.5x3/8" thick wood toy with paper label on each side. Attached by string is a cardboard ring that is to be flipped up onto his nose. Also seen stamped "Visit Sears Toyland." - **$50 $100 $200**

PIN-36

☐ **PIN-36. "Pinocchio's Christmas Party" Premium Book,**
1939. Issued by various department stores. 8x10.75" with 16 pages. One scene shows Pinocchio characters gathered around a tree along with toys including Seiberling figures of Mickey and Donald. - **$30 $60 $120**

PIN-37

☐ **PIN-37. "Pinocchio School Tablet" Premium,**
1939. Tablet is 8x10" lined paper. Various local sponsors and this example is imprinted "Head Of The Class Values-Read's Dept. Store-Reading, Pa." - **$20 $40 $80**

PINOCCHIO

PIN-38

❏ **PIN-38. "Pinocchio Masks" Store Sign,**
1939. Gillette. 9x24" glossy paper window display with gummed right and left margins. - **$150 $300 $550**

PIN-40

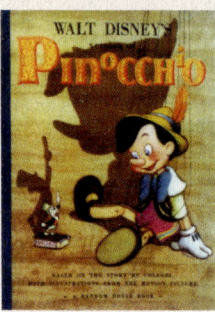

PIN-43

❏ **PIN-43. "Pinocchio" Hardcover With Dust Jacket,**
1939. Random House. 8.5x11.25" with 72 pages including a special Monstro insert. Jacket - **$10 $20 $50**
Book - **$25 $50 $110**

PIN-39

PIN-41

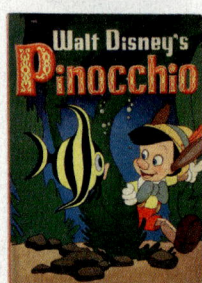

PIN-44

❏ **PIN-39. "Pinocchio Masks" Set With Envelope,**
1939. Gillette sent earlier 10x11.75" envelope containing mail premium set of five die-cut stiff paper masks. Each mask is about 9x10" and set consists of Pinocchio, Geppetto, Jiminy Cricket, Figaro and Cleo. Envelope text notes that two masks were available free with five Gillette Blue Blades, five were available with ten blades. Back of each has illustrated Gillette text plus side tabs holding rubber band as issued.
Envelope - **$8 $15 $25**
Each Mask - **$10 $20 $30**

❏ **PIN-40&41. "Pinocchio/Figaro And Cleo" Old King Cole Store Displays,**
1939. Old King Cole Inc. Matched pair of painted composition displays with high relief design. Pinocchio is 13.5x24x3" deep while Figaro and Cleo is 12.5x18x3" deep. Base front has simulated carved wood design with raised character name(s) and recessed text "From Walt Disney's Pinocchio." Each - **$325 $650 $1100**

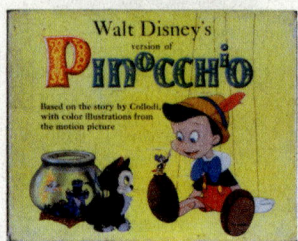

PIN-42

❏ **PIN-42. "Pinocchio" Hardcover**
1939. Grosset & Dunlap. 7x9" with 48 pages. - **$25 $50 $100**

PIN-45

❏ **PIN-44. "Pinocchio" Book,**
1939. Whitman. 8.5x11.5" softcover #709 with 96 pages. - **$20 $40 $85**

❏ **PIN-45. "Pinocchio Doll Cutouts" Book,**
1939. Whitman. Large 11x16.75" book #935 with card stock covers and six paper pages. Pinocchio cut-outs include face with long nose plus a donkey disguise. - **$215 $425 $800**

PINOCCHIO

PIN-46

❑ **PIN-46. "Pinocchio Puppet Show,"**
1939. Whitman. 10.5x15.5x1.25" deep box holds a four-piece backdrop, eight different characters each with a long handle showing their name, two cardboard flaps with assembly instructions and two different play scripts. - **$85 $175 $300**

PIN-47

❑ **PIN-47. "Pinocchio Game,"**
1939. Parker Brothers. 9.75x19.25x1.75" deep box contains gameboard, four large wood cone-shaped pieces representing "noses," two decks (16 each) of instruction and puzzle cards and instruction sheet. - **$60 $125 $225**

PIN-48

PIN-49

❑ **PIN-48. "Pinocchio The Merry Puppet Game,"**
1939. Milton Bradley. 9.5x19.25x1.75" deep box contains board, deck of cards, spinner and 100 die-cut cardboard gold pieces with foil covering. - **$80 $160 $275**

❑ **PIN-49. "Pin The Nose On Pinocchio" Game,**
1939. Parker Brothers. 15.5x20x1" deep boxed party game comprised of thick cardboard 14.75x17" portrait with string hanger plus original nine 4.5" long wooden needle nose pieces, each with suction cup for adherence. - **$100 $200 $300**

PIN-50

PIN-51

❑ **PIN-50. "Pinocchio Playing Card Game,"**
1939. Whitman. 5x6.5x1" deep boxed complete deck of 35 playing cards plus instruction card. - **$20 $40 $80**

❑ **PIN-51. Pinocchio Mechanical Valentines,**
1939. Two 3x5", one picturing Pinocchio and the other Foulfellow. Each - **$10 $20 $30**

PIN-52

❑ **PIN-52. Pinocchio Mechanical Valentine,**
1939. Large 6.25x7" card with attached tab to move Pinocchio and Jiminy. - **$10 $20 $40**

PIN-53

PIN-54

❑ **PIN-53. Large Mechanical Pinocchio Valentine,**
1939. Die-cut cardboard measuring 6.25x7.5". One donkey can be moved by a small tab. - **$15 $30 $60**

❑ **PIN-54. "Jiminy Cricket" Mechanical Valentine,**
1939. Die-cut stiff paper card 3x5.25" tall. - **$10 $20 $40**

PINOCCHIO

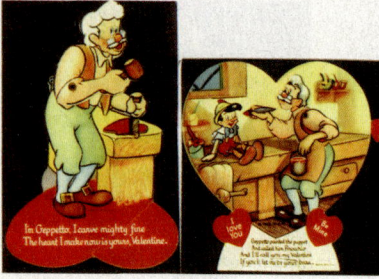

PIN-55

❑ **PIN-55. Pinocchio/Geppetto Mechanical Valentines,**
1939. Two examples from die-cut thin cardboard set. One is 3.25x5" of Geppetto and other is 5x5" heart-shaped. Each - **$10 $20 $30**

PIN-56

❑ **PIN-56. "Cleo" Mechanical Valentine,**
1939. Die-cut stiff paper Valentine is 3x5.75". - **$12 $25 $50**

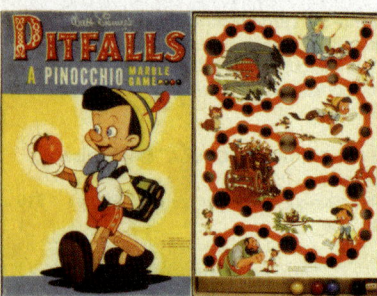

PIN-57

PIN-58

❑ **PIN-57. "Pitfalls - A Pinocchio Marble Game,"**
1939. Whitman. 7.5x11x1" boxed insert playing board. - **$40 $75 $125**

❑ **PIN-58. "Pinocchio The Acrobat" Marx Wind-Up,**
1939. Marx. Lithographed tin toy with built-in key measures 2x11x17" tall. Pinocchio figure is 7" tall. Base which includes many character illustrations rocks back and forth as Pinocchio sways back and forth. - **$200 $400 $750**

PIN-59

PIN-60

❑ **PIN-59. "Pinocchio" Marx Wind-Up,**
1939. Marx. 2.5x2.5x8.5" lithographed tin toy with built-in key. Pinocchio rocks back and forth as his eyes move. - **$150 $300 $600**

❑ **PIN-60. "Figaro" Wind-Up,**
1939. Marx. 2x4.5x2.75" tall tin lithographed toy. When key is wound Figaro travels around short distances and tumbles over flipping himself upright with his tail.
Box (Not Shown) - **$35 $65 $125**
Toy - **$50 $100 $200**

PIN-61

❑ **PIN-61. "Pinocchio Express" Pull Toy,**
1939. Fisher-Price. 11x10" tall paper on wood pull toy #720. - **$150 $300 $600**

PIN-62

❑ **PIN-62. "Plucky Pinocchio" Pull Toy,**
1939. Fisher-Price. 11x10" tall paper on wood pull toy #494. - **$150 $300 $600**

PINOCCHIO

PIN-63

PIN-64

PIN-66

❑ **PIN-66. "Pinocchio" Australian Premium Story Booklet,**
c. 1939. Colgate-Palmolive. 5x7" with 16 pages. Pictures Jiminy on back cover. - **$20 $35 $70**

PIN-67

❑ **PIN-67. Pinocchio and Jiminy Sand Shovel,**
c. 1939. Unmarked but Spanish 3.5x5" tin lithographed blade attached to 13" long wood rod handle. - **$65 $135 $225**

PIN-69

PIN-70

PIN-71

❑ **PIN-63. "Pinocchio" French Metal Figure Set Boxed,**
c. 1939. "Le Gouet Philippe." 5x5x2" deep box with Disney authorization containing set of four painted solid cast aluminum figures of 4.75" tall Geppetto, 3.5" Pinocchio, 2.5" Figaro, 2" Jiminy Cricket. - **$250 $500 $750**

❑ **PIN-64. "Pinocchio" Ice Cream Cup Lid,**
c. 1939. "Fudgee Cup." 2.75" diameter waxed cardboard sponsored by "Erie County Milk Assn." - **$15 $30 $50**

PIN-65

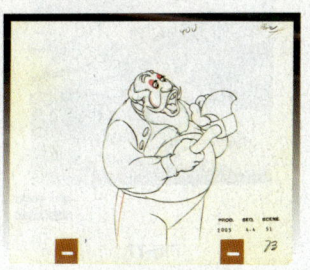

PIN-68

❑ **PIN-65. "Pinocchio Glasses" Window Sign,**
c. 1939. Sign measures 8.25x23.75" and advertises glasses available with purchase of "Calox Mouth-Wash." - **$75 $150 $250**

❑ **PIN-68. Stromboli Pencil Drawing,**
1940. Image 5.75x7.25" on animation paper. - **$100 $200 $400**

❑ **PIN-69. Coachman Pencil Drawing,**
1940. 8.5x5" on animation paper. - **$150 $300 $600**

❑ **PIN-70. Cleo and Bubble Effects Animation Set-Up Art,**
1940. Courvoisier. Image is 1.5x1.25" and background is 3.5x3" with original mat.
- **$500 $1000 $2000**

❑ **PIN-71. Gideon and Honest John Animation Set-Up Art,**
1940. Courvoisier. Image is 9.25x12.25". Cels are applied to a simple colored background and complete with Courvoisier certificate.
- **$600 $1200 $2000**

PINOCCHIO

PIN-72

□ **PIN-72. Pinocchio Characters Paint Books Set,**
1940. Whitman. Complete set of six 8.5x11.25" stiff paper cover books, each 24 pages. Each - $15 $30 $60

PIN-73

□ **PIN-73. "Liberty" Magazine With Pinocchio Cover,**
1940. Volume 17, #9 measures 8.5x11.5". - $15 $30 $60

PIN-74

□ **PIN-74. Pinocchio Print Set Matted,**
1940. Courvoisier Galleries. Set of four, each in 13x15" vintage stiff cardboard mat with paper trim around outer edge to simulate frame. Each mat is centered by 8.5x10.5" opening filled by paper print. Each print has "WDP" copyright. Each - $50 $100 $150

PIN-75

□ **PIN-75. "Pinocchio" Movie Herald,**
1940. Closed 6x9" paper folder publicizing original release of movie, described on front cover, "The Last Word In Screen Magic By The Man Who Gave You Snow White." Back cover is imprinted by local theater information. - $15 $30 $60

PIN-76

PIN-77

□ **PIN-76. "Pinocchio" Original Release Lobby Card,**
1940. Card is 11x14" featuring film scene of the Coachman, Foulfellow and Gideon gathered around a table. - $100 $200 $300

□ **PIN-77. "Pinocchio" Original Release Lobby Card,**
1940. Card is 11x14" featuring film scene of Pinocchio as donkey boy underwater with rock tied around his tail and fish swimming by. - $110 $225 $350

PIN-78

□ **PIN-78. "Pinocchio" Movie Theater Standee,**
1940. Thick cardboard 9x18" tall countertop display for original movie release. - $85 $175 $300

PIN-79

□ **PIN-79. "Pinocchio" Insert From English Movie Exhibitor's Publication,**
1940. "Kinematograph Weekly." 10.75x16.75" issue for March 21 with same size large format four-page fold-out insert for Pinocchio movie. - $35 $75 $150

PIN-80

□ **PIN-80. "Pinocchio" Boxed Bisque Figurine Set,**
1940. Set of 6 figures. Marked "Made In Japan." Complete With Box - $250 $500 $850

PINOCCHIO

PIN-81

PIN-82

❑ **PIN-81. Pinocchio Figurine,**
1940. National Porcelain Co. Figure is 3" tall. Issued in white or light green. - **$10 $20 $40**

❑ **PIN-82. Jiminy Cricket Figure,**
1940. National Porcelain Co. Figure is 3" tall. Issued in white or light green. - **$10 $20 $40**

PIN-83

PIN-84

❑ **PIN-83 Foulfellow Figurine,**
1940. National Porcelain Co. Figure is 3" tall. Issued in white or light green. - **$10 $20 $40**

❑ **PIN-84. Gideon Figurine,**
1940. National Porcelain Co. Figure is 2.5" tall. Issued in white or light green. - **$10 $20 $40**

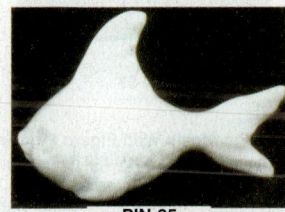
PIN-85

❑ **PIN-85. Cleo Figurine,**
1940. National Porcelain Co. Inc. 2.5" long glazed china figure. Scarcest of the series. Issued in white or light green. - **$25 $50 $100**

PIN-86

❑ **PIN-86. Pinocchio Rare Figurine Set,**
1940. National Porcelain Company. Set of eight painted and glazed figures consisting of Pinocchio, Geppetto, Jiminy, Foulfellow, Gideon, Figaro, Cleo and donkey. Size ranges from 2" for Cleo to 3.5" Pinocchio. More commonly seen in white or light green and much more common in those colors. Each - **$75 $125 $200**

PIN-87

❑ **PIN-87. The Coachman Cookie Jar,**
1940. Brayton Laguna. 6x8x8.75" tall painted and glazed ceramic. - **$1200 $2500 $4500**

PIN-88

❑ **PIN-88. Figaro In Bed Figure,**
1940. Brayton's Laguna Pottery. 4.25x6.5x6" tall painted and glazed ceramic. - **$700 $2000 $3250**

PIN-89

❑ **PIN-89. Figaro Figurine,**
1940. Brayton's Laguna Pottery. 2x4x3.25" painted and glazed ceramic. - **$75 $125 $225**

PIN-90

❑ **PIN-90. Geppetto Figurine,**
1940. Brayton Laguna. 3x4.5x5.75" tall painted and glazed ceramic pensive pose sitting atop a chest. - **$650 $1300 $2250**

PINOCCHIO

PIN-91

PIN-93

PIN-94

PIN-96

❏ **PIN-96. Pinocchio Ceramic Figurine,** 1940s. Brayton Laguna. 5.75" tall. Underside includes name "Geppetto Pottery." - **$175 $350 $675**

❏ **PIN-91. Geppetto Figurine,** 1940. Brayton Laguna. 8" tall painted and glazed ceramic. Depicts Geppetto with a contemplative pose with one hand raised to his chin. - **$300 $600 $1000**

❏ **PIN-93. Figaro Figurine,** 1940. Brayton Laguna. 2.25x2.25x3.5" tall painted and glazed ceramic. - **$85 $150 $250**

❏ **PIN-94. "Figaro" Figurine,** 1940. Brayton Laguna. Figurine is 2x4.5x3.5" tall painted and glazed ceramic. Underside has "Geppetto Pottery" marking. - **$100 $200 $300**

PIN-92

PIN-95

PIN-97

❏ **PIN-92. Figaro Figurine,** 1940. Brayton Laguna. 2.5x4.25x3.75" tall painted and glazed figurine with underside mark "Geppetto Pottery." - **$85 $150 $250**

❏ **PIN-95 Pinocchio Seated Figurine,** 1940 Brayton Laguna. 3x3x4.25" tall beautifully painted and glazed ceramic. - **$200 $400 $800**

❏ **PIN-97. Pinocchio With Figaro Figurine,** 1940. Brayton Laguna. 4.25" tall painted and glazed ceramic. Marked underneath with "Geppetto Pottery" mark. - **$225 $450 $850**

PINOCCHIO

PIN-98

PIN-100

PIN-102

❏ **PIN-102. Pinocchio Plaque,**
1940. Multi Products. Five different scenes in two formats. Scarce in high grade.
3.5x6" plaque - **$90 $150 $350**
3.5x4" plaque - **$100 $175 $375**

❏ **PIN-98. Jiminy Cricket Figurine,**
1940. Brayton Laguna. 3" tall painted and glazed ceramic. Depicts Jiminy with one hand raised in the air. - **$200 $400 $600**

❏ **PIN-100. "Pinocchio" Multi Products Figure,**
1940. 2.25x2.5x7.5" tall wood composition figure. - **$100 $200 $400**

PIN-103

❏ **PIN-103. Pinocchio Plaque,**
1940. Multi Products. Five different scenes in two formats. Scarce in high grade.
3.5x6" plaque - **$90 $150 $350**
3.5x4" plaque - **$100 $175 $375**

PIN-99

❏ **PIN-99. Honest John Figurine,**
1940. Brayton Laguna. 3.5x6x6.25" tall. - **$600 $1200 $2200**

PIN-101

❏ **PIN-101. "Jiminy Cricket" Multi Products Figure,**
1940. Wood composition figure measures 2.25x2.5x7.5". - **$100 $200 $400**

PIN-104

❏ **PIN-104. Pinocchio Characters Wall Plaque,**
1940. Multi Products. Five different scenes in two formats. Scarce in high grade.
3.5x6" plaque - **$90 $150 $350**
3.5x4" plaque - **$100 $175 $375**

PINOCCHIO

PIN-105   PIN-106

❑ **PIN-105. "Honest John" Medium Size Figure,**
1940. Multi Products. 2x2.25x4.25" tall composition wood from scarce size series. - **$100 $200 $300**

❑ **PIN-106. "Lampwick" Medium Size Figure,**
1940. Multi Products. 1.25x1.5x3.5" tall composition wood from scarce size series. - **$125 $250 $400**

PIN-107

❑ **PIN-107. "Giddy" (Gideon) Medium Size Figure,**
1940. Multi Products. 1.5x2x3" tall composition wood from scarce size series. - **$100 $200 $300**

PIN-108

❑ **PIN-108. Jiminy Cricket Figurine,**
1940. Painted plaster figurine is 1.5x1.75x3.25" tall and marked on back of base "WDP" with dated copyright. Rear has unusual design of closed insect wings. - **$45 $85 $150**

PIN-109   PIN-110

❑ **PIN-109. Figaro 6" Figure,**
1940. Store item by Multi Products, Chicago. - **$40 $110 $225**

❑ **PIN-110. Geppetto Sitting 6" Figure,**
1940. Store item by Multi Products, Chicago. - **$65 $115 $225**

PIN-111   PIN-112

❑ **PIN-111. Geppetto Standing 6" Figure,**
1940. Store item by Multi Products, Chicago. - **$40 $90 $145**

❑ **PIN-112. Giddy 6" Figure,**
1940. Store item by Multi Products, Chicago. - **$50 $100 $175**

PIN-113

❑ **PIN-113. Honest John 7" Figure,**
1940. Store item by Multi Products, Chicago. Large 7" size. Scarce. - **$100 $250 $400**

PIN-114

❑ **PIN-114. Jiminy Cricket 6" Figure,**
1940. Store item by Multi Products, Chicago. - **$50 $125 $250**

PIN-115

PINOCCHIO

☐ **PIN-115. Lampwick 6" Figure,**
1940. Store item by Multi Products, Chicago. - $50 $100 $175

PIN-116

PIN-117

☐ **PIN-116. Giddy 2" Figure,**
1940. Store item by Multi Products, Chicago. - $40 $110 $200

☐ **PIN-117. Lampwick 2" Figure,**
1940. Store item by Multi Products, Chicago. - $40 $110 $200

PIN-118

PIN-119

☐ **PIN-118. Figaro 1-1/4" Figure,**
1940. Store item by Multi Products, Chicago. - $40 $125 $250

☐ **PIN-119. Geppetto 2" Figure,**
1940. Store item by Multi Products, Chicago. - $40 $110 $200

PIN-120

PIN-121   PIN-122

☐ **PIN-120. Pinocchio 2" Figure,**
1940. Store item by Multi Products, Chicago. - $50 $125 $250

☐ **PIN-121. Honest John 2" Figure,**
1940. Store item by Multi Products, Chicago. Scarce. - $100 $200 $350

☐ **PIN-122. Jiminy Cricket 2" Figure,**
1940. Store item by Multi Products, Chicago. - $50 $125 $225

PIN-123

☐ **PIN-123. "Pinocchio Poster Stamps," With Envelope,**
1940. Independent Grocers Alliances (IGA). Premium of 3.75x5.25" descriptive envelope containing block of four perforated and numbered sticker stamps for placement in IGA 16 page album booklet obtained separately. - $15 $30 $60

PIN-124

☐ **PIN-124. "Pinocchio" English Picture Card Album,**
1940. Dean & Son Ltd. 8.25x10.5". Issued by "De Beukelaer's Chocolate Wafers & Crispies/ The Watford Biscuit Company Limited." 24 pages containing set of 125 picture cards each 2x2.75". Album Complete - $65 $125 $250

PIN-125

PIN-126

☐ **PIN-125. "Pinocchio" Wood Figure,**
1940. Wood painted figure is 4x4x9.25" tall likeness with two movable arms. Label under foot with Disney copyright and Geo. Borgfeldt name. - $40 $70 $125

☐ **PIN-126. "Pinocchio" Candy Bar Wrapper,**
1940. Schutter Candy Co. 3.5x7.25" waxed paper sheet offering mail premium of "Jiminy Cricket Official Conscience Medal." Text describes the medal including "Exactly Like The Blue Fairy Gave Jiminy Cricket." The brass badge medal was available for five Pinocchio wrappers and ten cents. Wrapper - $35 $60 $110
Medal Badge - $75 $150 $300

PIN-127

PINOCCHIO

❏ **PIN-127. "Pinocchio Chewing Gum" Full Pack,**
1940. Dietz Gum Co. 1x2.75x.5" paper wrapper around complete original quantity of five gum sticks, each in silver foil wrapping. Cover wrapper has different image front and back. Latter includes gum-related verse also serving as a coupon for prizes. - **$55 $115 $175**

PIN-128

❏ **PIN-128. "Pinocchio Candy Bar" Countertop Display Box,**
1940. Schutter Candy Co. 7x10.25x3.5" deep box which originally contained twenty-four candy bars. - **$150 $275 $600**

PIN-129

❏ **PIN-129. "Pinocchio Poster Stamps" Set With Booklet,**
1940. Independent Grocers Alliance (IGA) Premium of 5x7" 16 page album booklet and complete set of 32 sticker stamps printed in perforated blocks. Inside back cover lists IGA products to be purchased for acquisition of stamp strips individually. Complete set tells the Pinocchio movie story. Complete - **$35 $75 $150**

PIN-130

❏ **PIN-130. "Pinocchio" First Issue Record Set,**
1940. RCA Victor. Thick cardboard 10.25x11.75" album containing 78 rpm three-record set #P18 "The Original Soundtrack Of Pinocchio." Front cover of this first edition has diecut design with illustrations inside covers. Second 1940 edition without die-cut and illustrations. First - **$40 $75 $150** Second - **$25 $50 $85**

PIN-131

❏ **PIN-131. "Pinocchio" Lamp With Shade,**
1940. Multi Products. Composition wood figural base featuring 5" tall Pinocchio figure in front of metal wiring tubular post leading to bulb socket and support for stiff cardboard shade 6.5" bottom diameter by 6" tall. Lamp - **$100 $200 $300**
Shade - **$100 $200 $300**

PIN-132

PIN-133

❏ **PIN-132. Figaro-Like Planter,**
1940. China planter 3.25x5x4" tall marked underneath "Made in Japan/Hand Painted." - **$35 $65 $110**

❏ **PIN-133. "Geppetto/Lampwick" Bowl,**
1940. Clear glass bowl 4.75" in diameter by 2.25" tall. - **$20 $40 $75**

PIN-134

❏ **PIN-134. "Pinocchio" Glass Bowl,**
1940. Libbey. 2.25" tall with 4.75" diameter. - **$25 $50 $100**

PIN-135

738

PINOCCHIO

PIN-136

❑ **PIN-135. Pinocchio Tin Canister,**
1940. Lithographed tin canister measures 5" diameter by 6.5" tall. Has attached carrying handle and removable lid. - **$85 $175 $300**

❑ **PIN-136. Figaro Cookie Jar,**
1940. Painted and glazed ceramic measuring 8x9.5x10.25" tall. Unmarked, but resembles product of Geppetto Pottery. - **$125 $250 $500**

PIN-137

PIN-138

❑ **PIN-137. "Pinocchio" Dairy Glasses Folder,**
1940. Folder is 3.25x6.25" and opens to 20". Advertises "12 Tumblers Filled With Creamed Cottage Cheese." Issued by various dairies. - **$40 $75 $150**

❑ **PIN-138. "Pinocchio" Glass,**
1940. 4 3/8" tall. Front features Pinocchio surrounded by portraits of other characters, back has poem. - **$50 $100 $150**

PIN-139

❑ **PIN-139. "Pinocchio" Rare Boxed Set Of Glasses,**
1940. Box is 10x17.5x3" deep containing complete set of twelve glasses, each 4.25" tall. Glasses feature character images in a wide variety of colors with four-line verse. Glasses are Pinocchio, Jiminy Cricket, Monstro, Blue Fairy, Figaro, Foulfellow, Cleo, Stromboli, Gideon, Coachman, Lampwick and Geppetto. Near Mint Boxed - **$600**
Each Glass - **$10 $20 $35**

PIN-140

PIN-141

❑ **PIN-140. Figaro Pitcher,**
1940. Painted and glazed ceramic pitcher 4.5" tall. Marked underneath "Geppetto Pottery." - **$200 $400 $600**

❑ **PIN-141. Figaro Salt & Pepper Set,**
1940. National Porcelain Co. Inc. Each figure is 2-3/8" tall. - **$50 $100 $150**

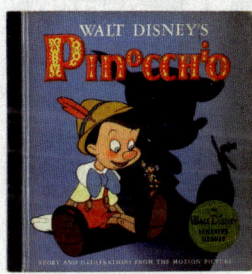

PIN-142

❑ **PIN-142. "Pinocchio" Book,**
1940. Whitman. 7x7" hardcover, 24 pages. Front cover includes series title "The Walt Disney Children's Library." - **$30 $60 $100**

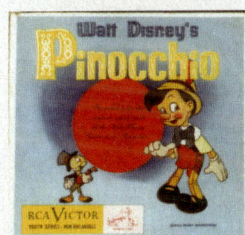

PIN-143

PIN-144

PINOCCHIO

❑ **PIN-143. "Pinocchio" Second Edition Record Set,**
1940. RCA Victor. 10.25x11.25" stiff cardboard cover contains set of three 78 rpm records featuring the film's original cast. - **$25 $50 $85**

❑ **PIN-144. "Pinocchio Song Hit Folio,"**
1940. Allan & Co. Pty. Ltd. 9x12" with 16 pages Australian issued and features seven songs including "When You Wish Upon A Star." - **$15 $25 $45**

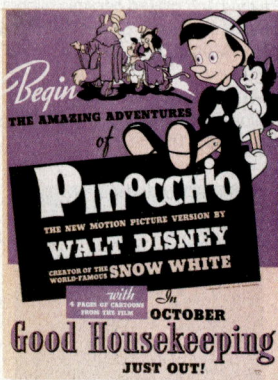
PIN-145

❑ **PIN-145. "Pinocchio" Good Housekeeping Appearance Promotional Sign,**
1940. 10.5X13.5" cardstock. Promotes the appearance of "4 Pages of Cartoons From The Film" in the October issue. - **$250 $500 $1000**

PIN-146

PIN-147

❑ **PIN-146. Pinocchio Premium Button,**
1940. Button is 1.25". - **$15 $30 $60**

❑ **PIN-147. Pinocchio Premium Button,**
1940. Button is 7/8". - **$50 $100 $200**

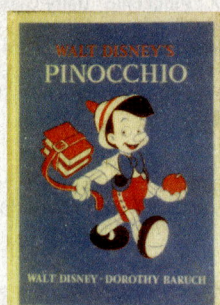
PIN-148

PIN-149

❑ **PIN-148. "Pinocchio,"**
1940. D.C. Heath and Co. 6.25x8" hardcover from "Walt Disney Storybooks" with 96 pages. - **$20 $45 $85**

❑ **PIN-149. "Pinocchio Linen-Like Book,"**
1940. Whitman. 7.25x8" with 12 pages. Sometimes used as a premium with sponsor ink stamp. - **$30 $65 $125**

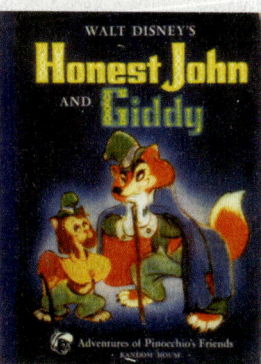
PIN-150

❑ **PIN-150. "Honest John And Giddy" Hardcover,**
1940. Random House. 7x9" book with 28 pages. "Adventures Of Pinocchio's Friends." - **$50 $100 $200**

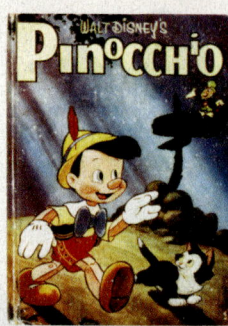
PIN-151

PIN-152

❑ **PIN-151. "Pinocchio" English Book,**
1940. Dean & Son Ltd. 7.5x10.25" hardcover. - **$30 $65 $125**

❑ **PIN-152. "Pinocchio Picture Storybook" English Book,**
1940. William Collins, Sons & Co. 8.25x11" softcover, 32 pages. - **$25 $50 $100**

PIN-153

❑ **PIN-153 "Figaro" Jointed Composition Doll,**
1940. Knickerbocker. 5x7x7" tall. Complete with cardboard string tag. - **$150 $300 $600**

PINOCCHIO

PIN-154

■ **PIN-154. "Jiminy Cricket" Jointed Composition Doll,**
1940. Knickerbocker. 3x5.5x9.5" tall painted composition doll with movable head and arms. Has fabric jacket but photo example is missing hat. - **$200 $400 $700**

■ **PIN-155. Composition Doll,**
1940. Knickerbocker. 4x4.5x10.5" tall with movable arms and head, completed by original felt/cotton outfit with pair of plastic buttons on front, bow at neck, matching felt hat with feather and chin strap. - **$200 $400 $700**

■ **PIN-156. Composition Doll,**
1940. Crown Co. 4x4x9.25" tall painted likeness with two movable arms. - **$65 $125 $200**

PIN-158

■ **PIN-158. "Pinocchio Doll" Boxed,**
1940. Ideal Toy Corp. 3.25x7.5x3" deep illustrated box containing 7.75" tall doll formed by wood jointed body and painted composition head plus accents of oilcloth collar and felt fabric bow tie. Chest has name decal. Box - **$85 $150 $300** Doll - **$65 $125 $250**

PIN-155

PIN-157

■ **PIN-157. "Jiminy Crickett" Wood Jointed Doll,**
1940s. Ideal Toy Corp. 8.5" tall complette with fabric collar/bow and hat brim. Wood jointed body with wood umbrella. - **$125 $250 $450**

PIN-159

PIN-156

PIN-160

PINOCCHIO

☐ **PIN-159. "Pinocchio" Largest Size Doll By Ideal,**
1940. 7x10x19" tall composition and wood doll with felt hat and bow tie. Hat has chin strap and attached feather. Composition head often develops surface cracks and numerous examples are restored with various degrees of skill. - **$300 $750 $1500**

☐ **PIN-160. "Pinocchio" Sand Pail,**
1940. Ohio Art. 4.25" tall and 4.5" in diameter with attached carrying handle. - **$225 $450 $700**

PIN-164

☐ **PIN-164. "Pinocchio" Clothing Hanger,**
c. 1940. Thick wood hanger measures 5x11x.25" with decal of Pinocchio on front. - **$10 $20 $40**

PIN-168

☐ **PIN-167. "Pinocchio Souvenir Program,"**
c. 1940. English release program measures 8.25x11.25" with 16 pages. - **$50 $100 $150**

☐ **PIN-168. Pinocchio Italian Baby Rattle,**
c. 1940. "Licenza Walt Disney's." 6.5" tall shaker toy including 2" diameter celluloid cylinder under clear wrapper. Rattle produces musical sounds when shaken. - **$30 $65 $125**

PIN-161

☐ **PIN-161. "Figaro" Pen Holder,**
1940. Multi Products. Composition wood base depicting figural tree stump with leaves and featuring 3" tall figure. Attached to the stump is metal and plastic swivel pen holder holding generic but believed original 7.5" long two-tone plastic fountain pen. - **$100 $200 $300**

PIN-165   PIN-166

☐ **PIN-165. Pinocchio Largest Bisque Figure,**
c. 1940. "Japan" 2x2.5x5.5" tall painted bisque with copyright, the largest and scarcest size from series of Japanese bisques. - **$35 $60 $125**

☐ **PIN-166. Celluloid Pinocchio Figure,**
c. 1940. Figure is 2x2.25x5.5" marked on reverse "Made In Japan" and small diamond-shaped logo "GM." - **$100 $200 $300**

PIN-169

☐ **PIN-169. Figaro Figurine,**
c. 1940. Grindley Ware. 1.75x3.75x3" tall painted and glazed figurine with label for "Grindley Ware Manufactured In Sebring, Ohio." - **$65 $125 $185**

PIN-162

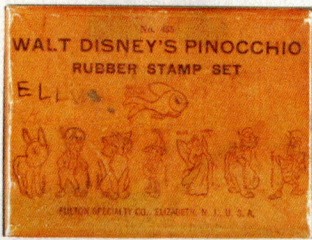

PIN-163

☐ **PIN-162. "Pinocchio" Hat,**
c. 1940. Hat is about 8" in diameter and 4.5" tall and has a chin strap. - **$20 $50 $80**

☐ **PIN-163. "Pinocchio Rubber Stamp Set,"**
c. 1940. Fulton Specialty Co. 2x3.75x.5" deep boxed complete set of eight rubber stamps and generic ink pad. - **$30 $60 $90**

PIN-167

PIN-170

☐ **PIN-170. Stromboli Japanese Figurine,**
c. 1940. "Japan" painted and glazed ceramic likeness 4.75" tall on 2.75" diameter base. One of the few figural pieces for this character. - **$30 $65 $125**

742

PINOCCHIO

PIN-171

🔲 **PIN-171. "Pinocchio" GE Promo Giveway Figure,**
c. 1940. Multi Products. 1.75x1.75x5" tall wood composition figure with label under base that reads "Pinocchio & Mickey And All The Other Members Of Walt Disney's Family Now Work In The New Walt Disney Studios Air Conditioned By General Electric." - **$65 $125 $250**

PIN-172

PIN-173

🔲 **PIN-172. Pinocchio Pleasure Island "Donkey" Figure,**
c. 1940. Seiberling. 4" tall hollow rubber figure. - **$50 $100 $250**

🔲 **PIN-173. "Pinocchio" Figure,**
c. 1940. Seiberling. 1.75x2.25x6" tall rubber figure with squeaker but rubber typically hardens and becomes un-squeezeable. - **$60 $125 $275**

PIN-174

PIN-175

🔲 **PIN-174. Pinocchio Plaster Statue,**
c. 1940. Painted plaster figure measures 3.25x3.5x10". No Disney copyright. - **$20 $40 $75**

🔲 **PIN-175. Figaro Planter,**
c. 1940. American Bisque. Unmarked 3.5x8x5.5" tall painted and glazed heavy ceramic. - **$25 $50 $75**

PIN-176

🔲 **PIN-176. Figaro Pitcher,**
c. 1940. American Bisque. Large 8x8.5x8" tall glazed ceramic. - **$40 $75 $150**

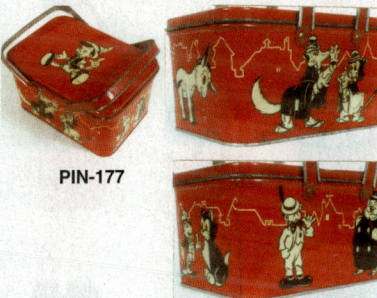

PIN-177

🔲 **PIN-177. Pinocchio Lunch Pail,**
c. 1940. Lithographed tin measuring 5.25x7.75x4" tall with removable lid, carrying handles and inner storage tray. - **$85 $175 $300**

PIN-178

🔲 **PIN-178. "Pinocchio" Premium Spoon With Papers,**
c. 1940. Royal Desserts. 5.5" spoon in original mailing envelope with 7x7" remnant of order form offering matching set of fork and knife available for fifty cents and three package fronts. Spoon is marked "Duchess Silver Plate" and handle has raised images and names of Pinocchio and donkey. Mailer - **$5 $10 $15** Form - **$8 $15 $25** Spoon - **$5 $15 $25** Knife Or Fork - **$10 $25 $40**

PIN-179

🔲 **PIN-179. Jiminy Cricket English Toothbrush Holder,**
c. 1940. Maw of London. 3.25" tall high quality china. - **$150 $300 $500**

PIN-180

🔲 **PIN-180. Geppetto Toothbrush Holder,**
c. 1940. Maw of London. High quality and exceptional china figure 1.75x2x3.5" tall of him holding a paint brush. - **$150 $300 $600**

PIN-181

🔲 **PIN-181. "Pinocchio" English Card Game,**
c. 1940. "Pepys Series" 2.5x3.5x.75" boxed complete deck of 45 cards and instruction folder. - **$40 $85 $150**

PINOCCHIO

PIN-182

❑ **PIN-182. Figaro Planter,**
c. 1940. Unmarked 3x5.5x4.5" tall painted and glazed ceramic. - **$30 $60 $90**

PIN-183

PIN-184

❑ **PIN-183. Salt & Pepper Set,**
c. 1940. "Hand Painted Japan" pair of 4.75" tall glazed china shakers without copyright but precise likenesses. - **$30 $60 $90**

❑ **PIN-184. Jiminy Cricket Motor Oil Sticker,**
c. 1940. Sunoco. 1.75x3.25" die-cut image of him wearing his Good Conscience medal with text "For More Power, Says Jiminy Cricket Sunoco Oil - That's The Ticket!" Reverse fabric backing includes blank area for local sponsor imprint. One of a small set. Each - **$12 $25 $50**

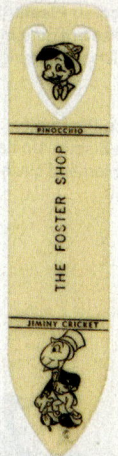
PIN-185

❑ **PIN-185. "Pinocchio/Jiminy Cricket" Bookmark,**
c. 1940. Thin celluloid 1.25x5". Center has imprint for a local sponsor, "The Foster Shop." - **$12 $25 $50**

PIN-186

PIN-187

❑ **PIN-186. Trio Of Pinocchio Dolls,**
c. 1940. Three color varieties of the same doll, each 4x7x19" tall. Marked "Made In Belgium." Each has stuffed felt body with felt/synthetic fabric clothes and celluloid faces. Some came with feather in hat. Each - **$25 $50 $85**

❑ **PIN-187. "Pinocchio Race Game,"**
c. 1940. Chad Valley Co. English game in 10x15x1.75" deep box. Content features 14.5" square playing board plus generic but original four disk markers, dice set and dice cup in addition to instructions insert. - **$75 $150 $250**

PIN-188

❑ **PIN-188. "Pinocchio" Boxed French Wind-Up,**
c. 1940. Les Jouets Creation Paris. 3.5x3.5x8.5" tall box contains 7.5" tall painted composition wind-up with built-in key. Toy rocks side-to-side as it moves forward. Box - **$50 $100 $200** Toy - **$125 $250 $500**

PIN-189

PINOCCHIO

☐ **PIN-189. Pinocchio Characters Spanish Cards,**
c. 1940. Unmarked but possible premium insert cards from numbered set of believed 240 total cards. Each is 2.25x3" with movie illustration on front. Reverse text describes the pictured scene and tells the story of Pinocchio in numerical order. Each - **$2 $4 $6**

PIN-190

☐ **PIN-190. "Pinocchio" Catalin Plastic Pencil Sharpener,**
c. 1940. 1.75" tall. - **$40 $75 $135**

PIN-191

☐ **PIN-191. "Jiminy Crickett" Catalin Plastic Pencil Sharpener,**
1940. 1.75" tall. - **$45 $90 $150**

PIN-192

☐ **PIN-192. "Lampwick" Catalin Plastic Pencil Sharpener,**
1940. 1.75" tall. - **$40 $75 $135**

PIN-193

☐ **PIN-193. Cleo Catalin Plastic Pencil Sharpener,**
1940s. 1.75" long. - **$125 $250 $500**

PIN-194

☐ **PIN-194. "Pinocchio" Italian Postcard Set,**
c. 1940. Saiga Press/Genova. Complete set of 12 cards, each 4x5.75", in original slipcase wrapper picturing long-nosed Pinocchio. Each card has scene from the movie plus single line description of scene in Italian. Set - **$40 $75 $150**

PIN-195

☐ **PIN-195. "Pinocchio" Exceptional Color French Postcard Set,**
c. 1940. Set of 24 cards, each 3.5x5.5" and numbered 1-24 with text describing scene in French following the story from beginning to end with all major characters. Set - **$75 $150 $300**

PIN-196

PIN-197

☐ **PIN-196. Pinocchio Figurine,**
1946. Figure is 3x3.25x6.25" tall painted and glazed ceramic. Produced by both American Pottery and Shaw. - **$100 $200 $400**

☐ **PIN-197. "Figaro" Figurine,**
1946. American Pottery Co. 2x4x3.5" tall painted and glazed ceramic figure with foil sticker on underside. - **$50 $100 $150**

PIN-198

☐ **PIN-198. "Pinocchio" Song Folio,**
1946. Decca Records. 5.5x8.5" glossy paper 8 page brochure of lyrics to eight songs from record set A-424. - **$10 $20 $30**

PINOCCHIO

PIN-199

❑ **PIN-199. Pinocchio As Donkey Boy Ceramic Figure,**
c. 1947. Zaccagnini. 7.75" tall. Underside has mark for this Italian company. - **$500 $1000 $2000**

❑ **PIN-200. Stromboli Italian Figure,**
c. 1947. "Zaccagnini." Impressively large 6x7x10" tall painted and glazed ceramic with company markings under feet including "Made In Italy/W 80." Photo example missing a moustache tip. - **$600 $1200 $2500**

PIN-201

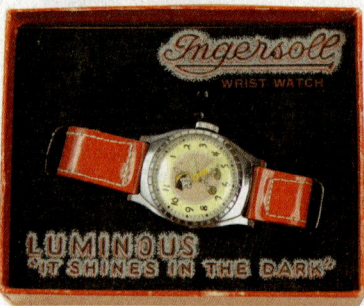

PIN-202

❑ **PIN-201. Pinocchio Watch,**
1948. U.S. Time. Issue from character series of ten wristwatches in 1948 to celebrate Mickey Mouse's 20th birthday. Dial face portrait is within 1-1/8" diameter chromed metal case. - **$50 $125 $250**

❑ **PIN-202. Pinocchio Luminous Wristwatch,**
1948. Ingersoll (U.S. Time) 3.25x4.25x1" deep box. One of ten in Mickey's 20th birthday series. Birthday theme lid and ballpoint pen not shown.
Boxed - **$200 $600 $1000**
Watch Only - **$65 $150 $300**

PIN-203

PIN-200

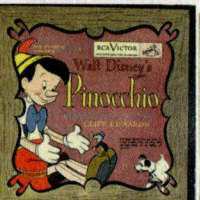 

PIN-204

❑ **PIN-203. "Pinocchio Storybook Album,"**
1949. RCA Victor. 10.5x12" stiff cardboard cover contains set of two 78 rpm records and a bound in 24 page storybook. - **$20 $40 $75**

❑ **PIN-204. "Pinocchio" Storybook And Record Album,**
1949. RCA Victor. "Little Nipper Series" 7.5x7.5" cardboard cover containing pair of yellow vinyl 45 rpm records and bound-in 24 page book. Set is WY 385. - **$15 $30 $50**

PIN-205

❑ **PIN-205. Pinocchio Characters Handkerchief,**
1940s. Hanky is 9.5" square cotton with Disney copyright. - **$15 $30 $50**

PIN-206

PINOCCHIO

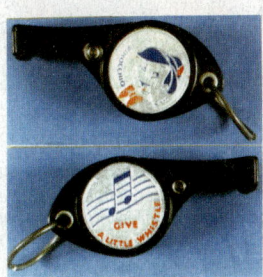

PIN-207

❑ **PIN-206. "Walt Disney Puzzle Pinocchio Series,"**
1940s. Ontex of Canada. 6.75x9.25x1" deep box contains three puzzles. - **$25 $50 $75**

❑ **PIN-207. "Pinocchio" Whistle,**
1940s. Hard plastic 2" whistle with metal hanging loop has foil sticker on each side, one showing Pinocchio portrait and the other with music note and text "Give A Little Whistle." - **$12 $25 $50**

PIN-208

❑ **PIN-200. "United Fund Campaign Award" Jiminy Cricket Figure,**
1940s. Multi Products. 2.25x3x5.25" tall wood composition figure with sticker marked "United Fund Campaign Award." Includes color accents. - **$50 $75 $150**

PIN-209

❑ **PIN-209. Jiminy Cricket United Fund Figure,**
1940s. Unmarked. Multi Products 2.25x3x5.5" tall composition wood version without color painted accents. Foil sticker on base denotes "United Fund Campaign Award." Single Color - **$30 $60 $90** Color Accents - **$50 $75 $150**

PIN-210

PIN-211

❑ **PIN-210. "Pinocchio" Carnival Statue,**
1940s. Figure is 4.5x5x14" tall painted chalk plaster. - **$40 $75 $125**

❑ **PIN-211. Pinocchio Rug,**
1940s. Woven 21x41" rug with fringe on left and right side depicting Pinocchio, Figaro, Jiminy, Cleo and sea horses. - **$50 $100 $150**

PIN-212

❑ **PIN-212. "Coo-Ees Pinocchio Boys Club" Australian Pin,**
1940s. 1-1/8" enamel paint on aluminum. - **$25 $50 $100**

PIN-213

❑ **PIN-213. "Mazda Pinocchio Disneylights" English Boxed Set,**
1940s. British Thomson-Houston Co. Ltd. 9.5x16.5x2" deep boxed strand of tree bulbs, one of five different sets. This set is comprised of complete twelve hard plastic bulb shades finished in total of eight different decals of Pinocchio characters and/or film scenes. Boxed - **$125 $250 $400**

PINOCCHIO

PIN-214

PIN-215

❑ **PIN-214. Pinocchio Pin Cushion Wall Plaque,**
1940s. Canadian issue 4.5x11" layered cardboard with separate diecut figure of Pinocchio as schoolboy. Rest of plaque has wood grain design with text "Pins Are Scarce You Must Admit, So Pick Them Up And Do Your Bit." At bottom center is fabric-covered pin cushion. Cardboard hanger attachment on reverse is marked "Made By Associated Advertising Toronto for British Canadian Sales." - **$30 $60 $100**

❑ **PIN-215. Figure Bank,**
1940s. Crown Mfg. Co. 2.75x3x5.75" tall painted composition. - **$75 $140 $275**

PIN-216

❑ **PIN-216. Pinocchio Largest Character Glasses Set,**
1940s. Complete set of twelve tumblers issued as part of 12-week dairy promotion. This is the largest size set produced for this purpose. Cleo glass is 4.75" tall and others are various fractions shorter as issued. Each has full figure character image in a single color with reverse four-line poem describing that character. Depicted are Pinocchio, Jiminy Cricket, Stromboli, Blue Fairy, Monstro, Coachman, Cleo, Figaro, Lampwick, Gideon, Geppetto, Foulfellow. Each - **$12 $25 $40**

PIN-217

❑ **PIN-217. "Pinocchio" Dutch Picture Album,**
1940s. "Margriet" of Amsterdam. 8x10.75" hardcover with all text in Dutch, probably published early post-World War II. Content is 28 pages with complete set of 80 numbered picture sheets mounted in place. Pictures are either 1.25x2.5" or 4.5x6", all picturing movie scenes. Complete - **$75 $150 $250**

PIN-218

❑ **PIN-218. Pinocchio Bookplates,**
1940s. Antioch Bookplate Co. 2.75x3.75" sealed pack of twenty identical paper bookplates plus one example from another pack. Packaged set pictures Pinocchio and Jiminy Cricket. Single version pictures Jiminy wearing his Official Conscience medal. Each Sheet - **$2 $4 $6**

PIN-219

PIN-220

❑ **PIN-219. "Pinocho" Cuban Cards Album,**
1940s. "Colecciones Nogueiras." 9x12" hardcover 20 page album containing complete numbered set of 200 cards. Each card is 2x2.75". Complete - **$100 $200 $300**

❑ **PIN-220. "Pinocchio Jigsaw Puzzle,"**
c. 1940s. Jaymar. 7x10x1.75" box holds "Series No. 3" puzzle. When assembled, size is 14x22" and features Pinocchio, Geppetto, Jiminy and Mastro. - **$25 $50 $85**

PIN-221

❑ **PIN-221. Cleo Squeeze Toy,**
c. 1940s. The Sun Rubber Co. 4.5" tall soft rubber figure. - **$30 $55 $100**

PIN-222

PIN-223

PINOCCHIO

❑ **PIN-222. Cereal Box With Mask,**
c. 1950. Wheaties. Emptied but complete and fully formed 2.25x6.5x8.5" tall 8-oz. box. Back panel features mask of Pinocchio from a set of eight. Other seven pictured on one side panel are Mickey Mouse, Bambi, Dumbo, Brer Rabbit, Donald Duck, Cinderella, Lucifer. Opposite side panel is an ad for Walt Disney comic books available as premiums from General Mills. - **$65 $125 $225**

❑ **PIN-223. Tell The Truth Ring,**
1954. Weather-Bird Shoes. Brass with rubber nose. - **$250 $500 $800**

PIN-224

❑ **PIN-224. "Pinocchio Ring" Ad,**
1954. Weather-Bird Shoes. Sunday comic page 10.75x15.25" with full page ad for the "Tell The Truth" ring. - **$10 $20 $35**

PIN-225

❑ **PIN-225. Jiminy Cricket Straw Clickers With Envelope,**
1958. Baker's Instant Chocolate Flavor Mix 3x9" mail premium envelope containing set of 1.5" tall figural hard plastic clickers and four 8" long plastic straws. Premium mailing includes insert paper offering Jiminy Cricket "Official Mickey Mouse Club" record for fifty cents and foil label from Baker's product box. Complete - **$25 $50 $80**

PIN-226

❑ **PIN-226. "Jiminy Cricket Dancing Puppet" Premium With Membership Card,**
1958. Baker's Instant Chocolate Drink. 4x5" envelope contains 9" tall die-cut Jiminy figure and 2.25x3.5" membership card. Puppet is designed with two tiny holes on hat where string is to be attached to suspend the figure.
Envelope - **$5 $15 $25**
Puppet - **$20 $30 $60**
Card - **$5 $15 $25**

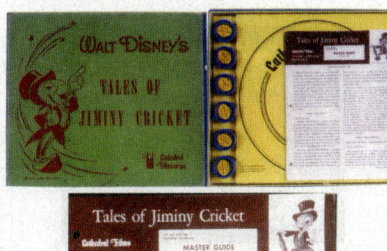
PIN-227

❑ **PIN-227. "Walt Disney's Tales Of Jiminy Cricket" Filmstrip And Record Boxed Sets,**
1959. Cathedral Films, Inc. Three boxed sets each measuring 12.75x14.5x1.5" deep and marked Series 1, 2, 3. Each box contains six numbered filmstrips and three 33-rpm records plus a master guide and individual four-page "Teacher's Study Guide And Manual." - **$75 $125 $200**

PIN-228

❑ **PIN-228 "Pinocchio" Button Printer's Block,**
1950s. Wood block is 4.25x6.5x1" deep with attached metal printing plate featuring six identical reverse button images to produce 1.5" "I've Seen 'Pinocchio' At Hudson's" Detroit department store button. - **$15 $30 $60**

PIN-229

❑ **PIN-229. Pinocchio Characters Handkerchief,**
1950s. Hanky is 8.25" square cotton. - **$8 $15 $25**

PIN-230

❑ **PIN-230. Pinocchio Ceramic Figurine,**
1950s. Beswick, England. 4" tall. Marked underneath with company mark. - **$100 $200 $400**

PIN-231

❑ **PIN-231. "Jiminy Cricket" With Cigar Figurine,**
1950s. Beswick. 4" tall painted and glazed ceramic. - **$125 $250 $400**

PIN-232

PINOCCHIO

❏ **PIN-232. Honest John Figurine,**
1950s. Goebel. Figure is 3x3.25x7.75" tall with foil label and full bee marking. - **$65 $125 $250**

PIN-233   PIN-234

❏ **PIN-233. "Pinocchio" Figurine,**
1950s. Goebel. 4.25" tall figure. Foil sticker underneath and full bee marking. - **$150 $300 $450**

❏ **PIN-234. Gideon Figurine,**
1950s. Goebel. 2.5x3x4.75" tall. - **$150 $300 $450**

PIN-235

PIN-236

❏ **PIN-235. Figaro Figurine,**
1950s. Goebel. 2.5x4x3.75" tall glazed ceramic. Underside has maker markings including full bee and incised "58." - **$75 $150 $250**

❏ **PIN-236. Seated Figurine,**
1950s. Goebel. 2.25x3x3.75" tall glazed ceramic pose. Underside has various maker markings including full bee and incised "DIS 99." - **$75 $150 $250**

PIN-237

PIN-238

❏ **PIN-237. Jiminy Cricket & Others Lunch Pail,**
1950s. General Steel Ware. 5x7.25x4.25" tall tin lithographed box with hinged lid and pair of tin carrying handles. Illustrations are Jiminy and Donald Duck's nephews with safety theme "Stop, Look, Listen." - **$115 $225 $500**

❏ **PIN-238. "Jiminy Cricket" Flicker Eye Premium Mug,**
1950s. Baker's Instant Chocolate. 3.75" tall hard plastic mug. - **$10 $20 $35**

PIN-239

PIN-240

❏ **PIN-239 "Figaro" Salt & Pepper Set,**
1950s. Goebel, Pepper shaker is 2.5" tall and basket salt shaker is 2" diameter by 1.25" tall. Has foil sticker and full bee marking with incised "DIS 138 A/B." - **$100 $200 $300**

❏ **PIN-240. Figaro Bank By Hagen-Renaker,**
1950s. 3.5x4.5x5.5" tall large ceramic with coin slot in mouth and underside opening covered by gold and black foil company label. - **$125 $250 $400**

PINOCCHIO

PIN-241

PIN-242

❑ PIN-243. "Pinocchio" Litho Button From Set,
1950s. From Disney character set with "Donald Duck Peanut Butter" on reverse. 13/16". - **$12 $25 $40**

PIN-244

❑ PIN-241. "Jiminy Cricket/Mickey Mouse Club" Record,
1950s. Paper sleeve is 6.75x7.5" and contains 78 rpm "Official Mickey Mouse Club" record. - **$6 $12 $20**

❑ PIN-242. "Pinocchio Souvenir Album" Song Folio,
1950s. Bourne Inc. 9x12" music and lyrics songbook copyright 1945 but a 1950s re-issue. Content is 40 pages comprised of ten different songs from the film plus three pages of film scenes. - **$20 $40 $75**

❑ PIN-244. Jiminy Cricket Safety Award Button,
1950s. 1.5". Issued by N. Olmsted Police. - **$20 $40 $65**

PIN-245

❑ PIN-245. "Pinocchio Mask And Puppet" Sheet,
1950s. "First National Stores." Premium 10x16" stiff paper sheet with large cut-out Pinocchio mask and 7" tall cut-out full figure puppet parts. These assemble to a Pinocchio figure who sticks out his tongue and holds a slingshot. Uncut - **$15 $30 $60**

PIN-243

PIN-246

PIN-247

❑ PIN-246. "Walt Disney's Pinocchio And The Blue Fairy Dolls,"
1950s. The Duchess Doll Corp. 9.5x10.75x2" deep box holds pair of 7" tall hard plastic dolls with movable arms and sleep eyes. Pinocchio has silk-like shirt, felt hat and pants, vest, feather in hat and vinyl book bag. Blue Fairy has silk-like dress with shawl, wings, magic wand with paper star and tiara. Boxed - **$35 $75 $125**

❑ PIN-247. Hand Puppets,
1950s. Gund-tagged two variations, both with vinyl heads and fabric bodies. Taller 11" has print of full body plus an inner squeaker mechanism. Second 9.5" version has plaid fabric handcover without squeaker as made. Each - **$12 $25 $40**

PINOCCHIO

PIN-248

☐ **PIN-248. "Walking Pinocchio" Boxed Linemar Wind-Up,**
1950s. 5.75" tall tin litho toy with built-in key comes in original box. Rubber nose. Walks forward. Near Mint - **$700 $850 $1100**

PIN-249

☐ **PIN-249. Jiminy Cricket Ramp Walker,**
1950s. Marx. 3" tall hard plastic. - **$15 $30 $60**

PIN-250

☐ **PIN-250. Jiminy Cricket Pencil Sharpener With Flicker Eyes,**
1950s. Apsco Products Inc. 2.5x4.5x5" tall boxed 4" tall hard plastic figural head with applied eye disks that flutter by movement. Box is marked "Donald Duck's Home Pencil Sharpener With Moving Eyes" and features Donald illustrations on all sides as well as the Donald sharpener; however, box also notes "This Box Contains A Jiminy Cricket." Enclosed hardware is metal crank handle and base with attachment screws. Box - **$15 $30 $50**
Sharpener - **$15 $30 $60**

PIN-251

PIN-252

☐ **PIN-251. "Pinocchio" Record In "Magic Mirror" Album,**
1960. Disneyland series 12.25x12.25" cardboard gatefold cover with oval diecut opening around detail from inner cover of 10 page storybook based on original movie. Enclosed 33-1/3 rpm single record of "The Complete Story, All The Songs And The Music." - **$5 $12 $20**

☐ **PIN-252. "Pinocchio's Christmas Story" Newspaper Sign,**
1961. Boston Globe. 10x16" cardboard sign announcing "A Great New Christmas Entertainment-Pinocchio's Christmas Story By Walt Disney...Now In...The Boston Globe." - **$75 $150 $250**

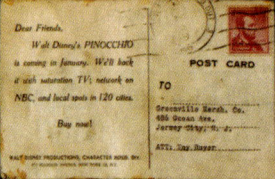

PIN-253

☐ **PIN-253. "Pinocchio Disneykin" Promotional Postcard,**
1961. Stiff paper postcard is 3.5x5.5" with plastic blister attachment over printed bird cage image holding carded 1.25" Disneykin. Reverse includes mention of the Pinocchio film which was to be shown on NBC and has typed mailing address to "Toy Buyer" of "Greenville Mech. Co." in New Jersey. Carded - **$35 $75 $150**

PIN-254

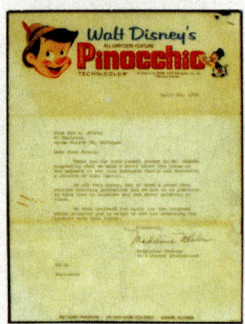

PIN-255

PINOCCHIO

❑ **PIN-254. "Colorforms Pinocchio Toys And Games" Store Sign,**
1962. Sign is 7x24". - **$20 $40 $80**

❑ **PIN-255. "Pinocchio" Letterhead With Jackie Robinson Reference,**
1962. Official "Walt Disney Productions" 8.5x11" stationery sheet. Typed message is dated April 25, 1962 thanking sender for suggesting a story "about the lives of the members of the Jack Robinson family" to be turned into a movie. Signed in ink by "Madeleine Wheeler" although no Disney job title indicated. Unique, Near Mint - **$60**

❑ **PIN-257. "Pinocchio Game,"**
1962. Whitman. 8.25x15.5x1.5" deep boxed game comprised of tri-fold game board opening to 15x23", insert platform with spinner and instructions, ten "Wishing Star" cards with character images. - **$12 $25 $50**

PIN-256

❑ **PIN-256. Pinocchio Musical Stuffed Doll,**
1962. Gund. 11" tall. - **$25 $65 $150**

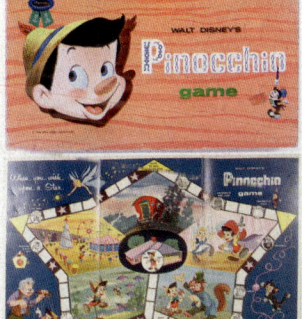

PIN-257

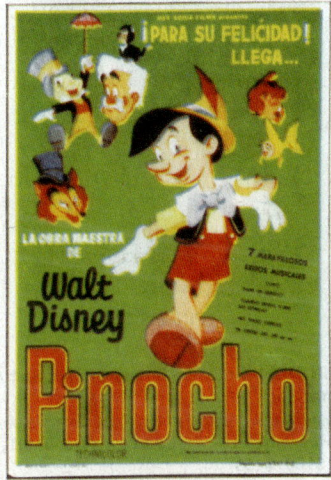

PIN-258

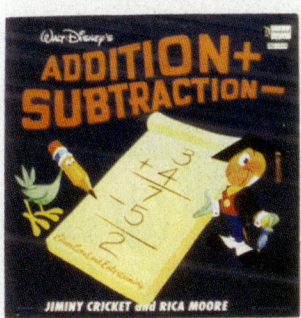

PIN-259

❑ **PIN-258. "Pinocchio" Movie Spanish Herald,**
1963. Paper sheet is 4.5x6" printed in Spain for 1963 re-release. - **$5 $10 $15**

❑ **PIN-259. "Addition And Subtraction" Record With Jiminy Cricket,**
1963. "Disneyland" issue 12.25x12.25" cardboard album cover containing 33-1/3 rpm. - **$6 $12 $20**

PIN-260

PIN-261

❑ **PIN-260. "Pinocchio Bayard" Boxed Alarm Clock,**
1964. "Made In France" 2x3.5x4.75" tall clock with metal case comes in standard "Bayard" box. Box - **$10 $15 $25**
Clock - **$40 $75 $135**

❑ **PIN-261. "Disneykin TV Scenes,"**
1960s. Marx. 1x3x3" tall box with display window is designed like a TV set with wood grain design. Content is miniature figures of Pinocchio and Jiminy Cricket against backdrop of "Carpenter Shop." - **$20 $40 $60**

753

PINOCCHIO

PIN-262

PIN-263

◻ **PIN-262. Pinocchio Soap Bottle,**
1960s. "Soaky" 9.75" tall empty container with soft plastic body and hard plastic head. This bottle came in three varieties and this is version with solid red body. Each - **$10 $25 $50**

◻ **PIN-263. "Jiminy Cricket" Glass,**
1960s. Decal from series of Disney characters distributed in Cheerios to be applies as kids desired, in this case a generic glass.. - **$5 $10 $20**

PIN-264

◻ **PIN-264. "Jiminy Cricket Pez Dispenser" In Box,**
1960s. Box contains 4.25" tall figure. Box - **$50 $100 $150**
Dispenser - **$40 $75 $125**

PIN-265

◻ **PIN-265. Pinocchio/Jiminy Cricket Salt & Pepper Set,**
1960s. Pair of painted and glazed ceramic shakers. Pinocchio is 3.5" tall and Jiminy is 4" tall. - **$50 $100 $150**

PIN-266

◻ **PIN-266. Pinocchio Bust Bank,**
1960s. Enesco. 4x4.5x5.5" tall painted composition with foil "Savings Bank" on side and "Enesco" sticker on bottom. - **$20 $40 $80**

PIN-267

PIN-268

◻ **PIN-267. "Anri" Pinocchio Music Box,**
1960s. Hand-carved and painted wood. Plays "Give A Little Whistle." - **$50 $85 $175**

◻ **PIN-268. "Disneyland/Pinocchio Mini-Flex Playset,"**
1960s. Lakeside Toys. 2.25x7.5x2.75" deep box contains small flexible figures of Pinocchio, Geppetto and Jiminy, table, chair, stool and insert depicting Geppetto's workshop. - **$25 $50 $100**

PIN-269

PINOCCHIO

PIN-270

PIN-273

❑ PIN-275. Jiminy Cricket On Mouseketeers Ears Original Painting,
c. 1970. 9.75x17.25" artboard with painted image 7x13.5". Art was for a double-page spread in a book by Golden Press. Unique, Near Mint - **$350**

❑ PIN-269. "Pinocchio/Jiminy Cricket Mini Puppet,"
1960s. Kohner. Pair of 2.75" tall hard plastic push puppets each with foil sticker on front. Each - **$10 $20 $35**

❑ PIN-272. "Pinocchio" Pencil Case,
1960s. Case is 5x8.5" vinyl. - **$8 $12 $20**

❑ PIN-273. Pinocchio Character Cereal Premium Figures,
c. 1960s. Plastic figures, each 1.75" tall which can be placed on the edge of cereal bowl or spoon handle. Each - **$5 $10 $15**

PIN-276

❑ PIN-270. "Jiminy Cricket" Hand Puppet,
1960s. Gund. 11" tall toy comprised of soft vinyl head, full figure printed fabric handcover body with stitched maker's tag, interior squeaker mechanism. - **$15 $30 $50**

PIN-274

❑ PIN-276. Pinocchio/Jiminy Cricket Figures,
1971. Marx. Two soft vinyl figures. Pinocchio is 5.75" tall and Jiminy is 4.25" tall. - **$5 $10 $15**

PIN-271

❑ PIN-274. Pinocchio Wood Jointed Advertising Figure,
c. 1960s. European figure measures 6" tall and marked "Pinotex" with Disney copyright on back. - **$15 $30 $50**

PIN-277

❑ PIN-271. Figaro Tin Toy,
1960s. Marked "Made In Japan" 7.5" long similar to version marked "Line Mar." Tail is pushed down and released to make Figaro roll forward. Rubber ears. - **$50 $100 $150**

PIN-272

PIN-275

PIN-278

PINOCCHIO

❑ **PIN-277 "Pinocchio" Lunch Box And Thermos,**
c. 1971. Aladdin Industries. 7x8x4" deep metal box and 6.5" plastic thermos.
Box - **$25 $50 $100**
Bottle - **$10 $20 $40**

❑ **PIN-278. Pinocchio Tea Cup Music Box Prototype Art,**
c. 1977. Original double-matted 7x8" pencil, ink and watercolor illustration by "Disney Legend" designer Al Konetzni for proposed music box featuring Pinocchio seated in tea cup. Unique, Near Mint - **$325**

PIN-279

PIN-280

❑ **PIN-279. "Pinocchio Pop Pal,"**
1970s. Kohner. 2.5x3x3" tall hard plastic push button toy. When pushed, lid opens to reveal a three-dimensional hard plastic figure of Pinocchio from the shoulders up as a squeaking noise is made. - **$10 $15 $25**

❑ **PIN-280. "Bendables" Figure,**
1970s. Durham Industries. 5x8.5" blister card containing 4.75" tall rubber figure with wire inserts for posing. Near Mint Carded - **$25**

PIN-281

❑ **PIN-281. "Pinocchio" Figure With Bag,**
1970s. Unmarked Dakin. 8.25"tall poseable vinyl figure in fabric outfit complete with die-cut gold cardboard tag in clear plastic bag with carrying handle. By Dakin although unmarked as issued in the mid-1970s when Disney did its own distribution marked "Walt Disney Distributing Co."
Near Mint Bagged - **$75**
Figure Only - **$10 $20 $40**

PIN-282

❑ **PIN-282. "Pinocchio in Geppetto's Workshop" Sculpture,**
1984. Disney Capodimonte by master sculptor Enzo Arzenton. Edition 391. - **$3000**

PIN-283

❑ **PIN-283. Coachman & Jiminy Cricket Pencil Drawing,**
1980s. Sheet of animation paper is 10.5x13" with 4.5x6.5" concept sketch for production of a book. - **$50 $125 $200**

❑ **PIN-284. "Pinocchio" Limited Edition Serigraph,**
1980s. "Walt Disney Company." 10.75x14" acetate sheet centered by 4.5x9.25" image. Mint As Issued - **$140**

PIN-284

PIN-285

PINOCCHIO

❏ **PIN-285 "Pinocchio" Video Release Display,**
1980s. "The Classics" home video series thin countertop display with easel on back. Top of display is separate cardboard piece that extends forward from the background. Attached to this is a die-cut jointed figure of Pinocchio with string attachments so figure moves if tapped. - **$15 $25 $40**

PIN-288

❏ **PIN-288. "Pinocchio" Home Video Banner Poster,**
1992. Large horizontal format 11x60" stiff paper with review quote from Los Angeles Times "The Most Perfect Animated Feature Walt Disney Produced" plus "Available For The Last Time This Century." - **$10 $20 $35**

PIN-286

❏ **PIN-286. "Pinocchio Golden Book,"**
1980s. Western Publishing Co. 8.25x11" with 20 pages and 1953 copyright. - **$5 $10 $15**

PIN-289

❏ **PIN-289. Jiminy Cricket "Safety Award" Disney Employee Watch,**
1994. Metal case is 1.25" in diameter with dial face portrait plus citation text "1993 Shops Services/Safety Award Accident Free In '93." Issued only for Disney employee recipients. Mint As Issued - **$90**

PIN-291

❏ **PIN-291. Disney Artist Promotional Pin,**
2000. - **$40**

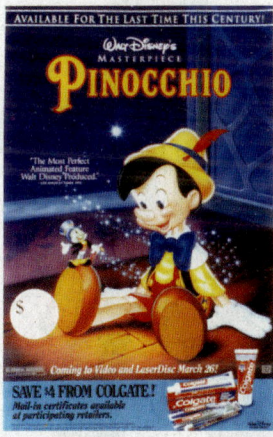
PIN-287

❏ **PIN-287. "Pinocchio" Home Video Promotional Poster,**
1993. Colgate. 26x40" glossy paper store poster advertising the Pinocchio video cassette and laser disk "Coming March 26." Ad at bottom for $4 mail-in rebate with expiration date of 1993. - **$10 $20 $40**

PIN-290

❏ **PIN-290. Jiminy Cricket Earth Day Button,**
1996. 2" square. - **$3 $6 $12**

PIN-292

❏ **PIN-292. Pinocchio Water Globe,**
2000. - **$75**

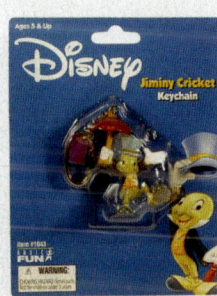
PIN-293

❏ **PIN-293. Jiminy Cricket Keychain,**
2004. - **$6**

PIRATES OF THE CARIBBEAN

Pirates of the Caribbean

Normally, merchandising is an effective way to increase public awareness of a movie or book. *Pirates of The Caribbean* effectively turned that concept on it's head, and did it with spectacular results! In the evolution of the Pirates of the Caribbean, they were first imagined to be a wax museum of famous pirates in Disneyland. As technology of the early theme parks grew, it eventually became a ride at Disneyland in California. Opening in 1967, PoC also had the distinction of being the very last ride created with input from Walt himself. A success from the word go, the ride became a staple feature of Disney theme parks around the world.

When word of a movie based on the original ride became public knowledge in 2002, almost everyone wrote it off as a cheap way for Disney to generate publicity for their theme parks. Disney had the last laugh as the film, *Pirates of the Caribbean: Curse of the Black Pearl*, went on to become one of the highest grossing films ever.

The combination of sharp writing, incredible special effects and the acting skills of Johnny Depp (Best Actor nomination in the 76th Academy Awards for his work as Captain Jack Sparrow), Geoffrey Rush. Keira Knightly and others paid off for both Disney and the audience. The film brought in over $625 Million world wide and spawned two sequels. Released in 2006 *Pirates of the Caribbean: Dead Man's Chest* became the fastest film to ever reach $1 Billion worldwide. DVD sales for both films were also record-setters.

Scheduled for release in May 2007, *Pirates of the Caribbean: At the World's End* is sure to follow in the successful steps of the first two films.

Merchandising for the films was widespread and a big success. In addition to updating all the theme parks rides to include storylines and the new characters, Disney published books, coloring books, action figures, dolls, statues, clothing, stamps, posters and many, many other items.

POC-1   POC-2

❑ **POC-1. Pirates of the Caribbean Jack Sparrow Mini-Bust,**
2005. Jack Sparrow, 6 1/2" tall, 2,500 pieces. - **$45**

❑ **POC-2. Pirates of the Caribbean Captain Barbossa Mini-Bust,**
2005. Captain Barbossa, 6 1/2" tall, 2,500. - **$45**

POC-3

❑ **POC-3. Pirates of the Caribbean 15-inch Jack Sparrow Stature,**
2006. Captain Jack Sparrow 15" hand-painted resin statue, 1,000 pieces. Painted. - **$155**

POC-4

❑ **POC-4. Pirates of the Caribbean Action Figure Set,**
2005. 7" tall action figures. Series includes Captain Jack Sparrow, Will Turner, Captain Barbossa, and a Skeleton Pirate. Each - **$12**

POC-5

❑ **POC-5. Pirates of the Caribbean Action Figure Box Set,**
2005. Boxed set features the zombie versions of Captain Jack Sparrow and Captain Barbossa, two complete diorama bases that form one large scene with Mayan treasure chest. Can connect and interact with the figures from Series I and II to form a massive display. - **$30**

POC-6

❑ **POC-6. Pirates of the Caribbean 18-inch Talking Jack Sparrow Action Figure,**
2006. Captain Jack Sparrow, 18" tall, with pistol, sword, and compass and a removable hat. Motion activated sound chip plays actual movie dialogue. - **$45**

Pluto

Pluto debuted as a nameless prison bloodhound in Mickey Mouse's 1930 cartoon *The Chain Gang*. Later that year he appeared as Minnie's dog Rover in *The Picnic*. Starting with *The Moose Hunt* (1931), he was known under his most famous moniker.

Pluto went on to star in two Silly Symphonies and forty-eight of his own shorts while still co-starring in frequent Mickey cartoons. While most animals in Mickey's world were humanized, Pluto had only one human attribute, the ability to speak, and lost that ability less than a year into his career. For the vast majority of his appearances on screen, Pluto would be featured as a "real" dog in a world of anthropomorphic mice and ducks. Pluto's bark was supplied by the same man who did Goofy's voice, Pinto Colvig. Later on, Pluto's vocals were provided by Jim MacDonald.

A star in the Disney universe, Pluto has long been featured on merchandise such as figurines, books, toys and dolls. He appears in *Four Color Comics* #509, 537, 595, 654, 736, 853, 941, 1039, 1143 and 1248. Pluto also appears in *Large Feature Comics* (series 2) # 7. It is the first comic book work by Carl Barks.

PLU-2

❑ **PLU-2. "Pluto's Nightmare" Model Sheet,** 1935. Sheet is 12x15" vintage photostatic copy for cartoon short that was renamed "Pluto's Judgement Day" for its release. Sheet is numbered "U.M. 35" and pictures nineteen cat characters including Uncle Tom Cat, Lawn Mower Cat, Topsy Cat, Steam-Roller Cat, Midget Cat, Dog-Shock Victim. - **$25 $50 $85**

PLU-5

PLU-6

❑ **PLU-5. "Pluto" Glass,** 1936. Tumbler is 4-3/8" tall painted image from first dairy series picturing Disney characters. - **$20 $40 $60**

❑ **PLU-6. "Mickey Mouse And Pluto The Racer" Big Little Book,** 1936. Whitman. Book #1128. - **$30 $90 $175**

PLU-3

PLU-1

❑ **PLU-1. "Pluto" Store Display Standee,** 1934. Made By Old King Cole, distributed by Kay Kamen. Molded 'laminite' 11x15.5x1.5" deep. - **$375 $750 $11500**

PLU-4

❑ **PLU-3. Pluto Enamel On Brass Pin,** c. 1935. Marked "W.D." on back. 1.25" long. - **$40 $85 $150**

❑ **PLU-4. "Pop-Up Kritter" Toy,** 1936. Fisher-Price. Wood mechanical toy #440, 2.5x11.5x5.5" tall to tip of tail. Detailing includes oilcloth ears. Body parts are joined by stringing and move variously by pair of metal finger loops extending from the paddle board base. - **$40 $85 $215**

PLU-7

PLUTO

❑ **PLU-7. Pluto Flea Bath Battery Operated Night Light With Mickey And Minnie,** c. 1936. Unmarked. 4" tall tin lithograph designed like flashlight has attached 4.5" thin cardboard shade. Column holds batteries. - **$300 $650 $1300**

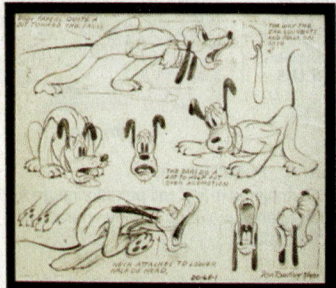
PLU-8

❑ **PLU-8. Pluto Model Sheet,** 1937. 19x15" tall model sheet. - **$75 $150 $250**

PLU-9

PLU-10

❑ **PLU-9. Pluto Pencil Drawing From "Pluto's Quin-Puplets,"** 1937. Animation paper is 9.75x12" with centered 3.25x7.5" image. No. "259" from a numbered sequence. - **$65 $150 $250**

❑ **PLU-10. "Pluto" Glass With Copyright Date,** 1937. Tumbler is 4.25" tall with paint image of Pluto striking a large bass drum with beater attached to his tail as he steps on the bulb of a horn. Wrap-around design is small music notes. - **$75 $150 $250**

PLU-11

❑ **PLU-11. "Pluto The Pup" Book,** 1937. Whitman. 9.25x12.75" publication #894 with stiff linen-like cover and pages. - **$65 $125 $250**

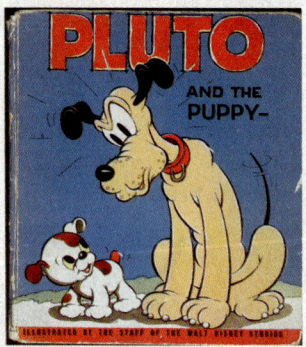
PLU-12

❑ **PLU-12. "Pluto And The Puppy" Book,** 1937. Grosset & Dunlap. 9.5x10.5" hardcover with 36 pages. - **$50 $100 $200**

PLU-13

PLU-14

❑ **PLU-13. Pluto Pencil Drawing,** c. 1937. Animation paper is centered by 6.5x7" frontal view image in pencil. Drawing is "190" from a numbered sequence. - **$65 $150 $250**

❑ **PLU-14. "Pluto" Glass,** c. 1937. "W.D. Ent." 4.75" tumbler with paint image of Pluto with eyes closed and mouth wide open belting out a song. In front of him is a music stand. A similar Donald version is known. - **$75 $150 $250**

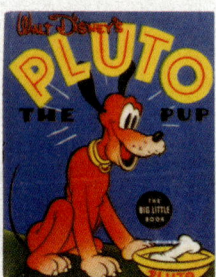
PLU-15

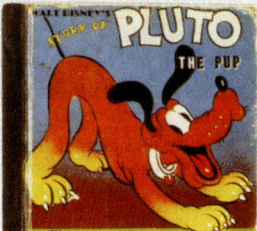
PLU-16

❑ **PLU-15. "Pluto The Pup,"** 1938. Whitman. Big Little Book #1467. - **$15 $50 $100**

❑ **PLU-16. "Story Of Pluto The Pup" Book,** 1938. Whitman. 4.75x5.5" hardcover from "1066" series of character books, 96 pages. - **$20 $40 $75**

PLUTO

PLU-17

❏ **PLU-17. Pluto Marionette,**
c. 1938. Madame Alexander 3.5x8x6" tall composition marionette complete with fabric collar, fabric-covered rubber tail, original wood hand control unit. These marionettes were sold individually but also issued through the Mickey Mouse Magazine as a theater contest prize. - **$160 $325 $55 0**

PLU-18

PLU-19

❏ **PLU-18. Pencil Drawing,**
1939. Animation paper is 10x12" centered by 6x7" image of a cowering Pluto before a scowling judge from scene in cartoon short "Society Dog Show." No. "21" from a numbered sequence. - **$115 $225 $350**

❏ **PLU-19. Pluto "RPM Motor Oil" Card,**
1939. Stiff paper card measuring 3.5x5.5". - **$20 $40 $80**

PLU-20

❏ **PLU-20. "Mother Pluto" Book,**
1939. Whitman. 5x5.5" hardcover from "1058" character series, 64 pages. - **$20 $40 $75**

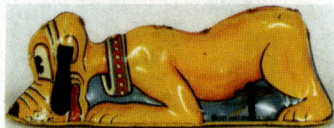

PLU-21

❏ **PLU-21. Pluto Wind-Up,**
1939. Marx Toys. 2.5x8x2.75" tall lithographed tin with built-in key. Pictured example is missing thin rubber tail. - **$75 $175 $375**

PLU-22

PLU-23

❏ **PLU-22. "Pluto The Pup" Seated Figure,**
1930s. "Made In Japan." 2.25" tall painted bisque with incised name on one side of body plus copyright. This is the smaller version of two known size variations. - **$20 $40 $85**

❏ **PLU-23. "Pluto The Pup" Seated Figure,**
1930s. "Made In Japan." 2.75" tall painted bisque with incised name on one side of body plus copyright. This is the larger version of two known size variations. - **$15 $35 $75**

PLU-24

PLU-25

❏ **PLU-24. Pluto Rubber Figure,**
1930s. Seiberling Rubber Co. 3.5" long by 2" tall painted solid hard rubber in scarcer red version rather than the brown variety. Example shown is missing rubber tail and tiny nose tip. Red - **$30 $60 $125**
Brown - **$25 $45 $100**

❏ **PLU-25. "Pluto The Pup" Fun-E-Flex Figure,**
1930s. Wood body with rubber-covered wire legs and felt ears measuring 1.75x2.75x7.5" long. - **$60 $125 $225**

PLU-26

❏ **PLU-26. "Pluto The Pup" Fun-E-Flex Figure With Doghouse,**
1930s. 3.5" long Pluto with blue collar variety rather than standard red. Complete with felt ears and cord tail. 3.75" tall wood doghouse and with metal chain that attaches Pluto to doghouse. - **$125 $250 $400**

PLU-27

❏ **PLU-27. Pluto China Toothbrush Holder Or Vase,**
1930s. Unmarked but likely English 1.5x3.25x3.75" tall seated figural with hollowed body. - **$65 $110 $175**

PLUTO

PLU-28

PLU-29

PLU-31

❑ **PLU-31. Pluto French Ceramic Bank,**
1930s. Faiencerie d' Onnaing. 5.5" tall. Depicts Pluto holding a bone and he is white with black spots. - **$100 $200 $400**

PLU-32

❑ **PLU-32. Pluto Doll By Dean's Rag Book,**
1930s. England. 5.5" tall by 12" long in velveteen with leather collar. - **$150 $300 $600**

PLU-34

❑ **PLU-34. Large Pluto Doll,**
1930s. 12" straw filled doll with plush fur. - **$50 $100 $200**

PLU-35

❑ **PLU-28. "Pluto The Pup" Framed Glass Picture,**
1930s. Reliance Picture Frame Co. 4.25x5.75" original wood frame holding reverse glass painted portrait with name. Reverse is cardboard backing with text about the character series produced by Reliance. - **$30 $60 $100**

❑ **PLU-29. Pluto As "Wild Lion" Plaque,**
1930s. Plaque is 4.5x5x.25" thick wood titled on reverse "A Fine Art Picture" by unidentified maker although process is termed "Hand-Printed In Oil Colors/Washable." Image is from a cartoon depicting him as a chained lion behind title sign "Wild Lion." - **$25 $50 $85**

PLU-30

❑ **PLU-30. "Pluto The Pup/Mickey Mouse" Plate,**
1930s. Salem China Co. 7" diameter plate. - **$60 $110 $165**

PLU-33

❑ **PLU-33. Pluto Doll By Charlotte Clark,**
1930s. Seated figure about 15" tall. Primarily corduroy fabric with felt accents. - **$1000 $2000 $4000**

PLU-36

❑ **PLU-35. Pluto Catalin Plastic Pencil Sharpener,**
1930s. Octagonal shape. 1-1/8x1-1/8". - **$50 $100 $150**

❑ **PLU-36. Pluto Pencil Drawing,**
c. 1930s. Image is 3.5x4.5". From a numbered series and this is number "16." - **$100 $200 $300**

PLUTO

PLU-37

❑ **PLU-37. Pluto Figurine,**
1940. Brayton Laguna. 3.75x6x3.25" tall painted and glazed ceramic. - **$40 $80 $135**

PLU-40

❑ **PLU-40. Pluto Animation Set-Up Art,**
c. 1940. Image is 2.75x3" with 8.5x7" background. - **$300 $600 $1200**

PLU-43

❑ **PLU-43. Pluto Pencil Drawing,**
c. 1942. Paper is centered by 3.5x4.25" image, #36 from a numbered sequence. - **$50 $100 $150**

PLU-38

❑ **PLU-38. Pluto Figurine,**
1940. Brayton Laguna. 3.75x3.5x6.75" tall painted and glazed ceramic. - **$35 $75 $125**

PLU-41

❑ **PLU-41. "Mickey Mouse And Pluto,"**
1942. Dell Publishing Co. 4x5.5" "Fast-Action Story" with 192 pages. - **$50 $150 $300**

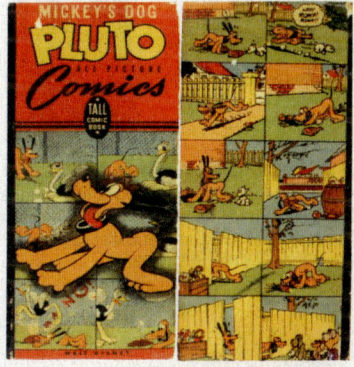

PLU-44

❑ **PLU-44. "Mickey's Dog Pluto All Picture Comics/Tall Comic Book,"**
1943. Whitman. 3.75x8.5" hardcover, 188 pages comprised entirely of a comic strip panel story in black and white. - **$40 $110 $215**

PLU-39

❑ **PLU-39. Pluto "Sunoco Oil" Blotter,**
c. 1940. Blotter is 4x7.5". "Flows..Even Below Zero." - **$40 $75 $125**

PLU-42

❑ **PLU-42. Birthday Card With Hitler Reference,**
1942. Hallmark. 4.5x5.25" elaborate design eight-page booklet card. Pluto is pictured on every other page and each facing page has a die-cut lift-up. Text under the birthday gift is "A Rat That's Known As Hitler And Though The Box Looks Good, The Little Gift That Ticks Inside Will Blow Him Where It Should." - **$20 $40 $60**

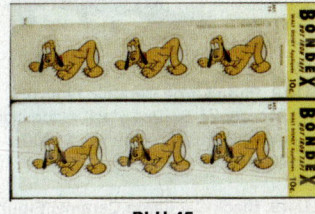

PLU-45

❑ **PLU-45. Pluto "Hot Iron Tape,"**
1946. Bondex Industrial Tape Corp. Two identical 1.75x7" long fabric iron-on "Walt Disney Appliques" attached to display card. Each - **$8 $12 $20**

PLUTO

PLU-46

❑ **PLU-46. Salt & Pepper Set,**
1947. Leeds China Co. Matched pair of 3" tall glazed ceramic shakers with over-the-glaze paint accents. - **$15 $30 $50**

PLU-47

❑ **PLU-47. Large Stuffed Pluto Doll,**
1947. Doll is 6x12x11" tall in velvet-like material with felt eyes, ears, nose and tongue plus patches on paws and a red leather collar. Similar to doll by Gund. - **$100 $200 $300**

PLU-48

PLU-49

❑ **PLU-48. Pluto Large Ceramic Figure,**
c. 1947. Zaccagnini. 6x12x4.5" tall. Underside has mark for this Italian company. - **$1000 $2000 $4000**

❑ **PLU-49. Black Cat Large Ceramic Figure,**
c. 1947. Zaccagnini. 5.25x10.25x8" tall. Companion piece to Pluto figure. Cat appeared in various cartoon shorts and with Pluto in comic strips as well as the Good Housekeeping adaptation of "Lend A Paw." Underside has mark for this Italian company. - **$750 $1500 $3000**

PLU-50

PLU-51

❑ **PLU-50. Pluto Luminous Wristwatch,**
1948. Ingersoll (U.S. Time). One of ten in Mickey's 20th birthday series. Birthday theme lid and ballpoint pen not shown. Boxed - **$200 $600 $1000**
Watch Only - **$65 $150 $300**

❑ **PLU-51. Pluto Figurine,**
1949. American Pottery. 5x6x3.75" tall. - **$50 $100 $150**

PLU-52

❑ **PLU-52. Figural Planter,**
c. 1949. Leeds China Co. 3.5x7x6.5" tall. - **$20 $40 $65**

PLU-53

PLU-54

❑ **PLU-53. "Pluto Pencils" Display Card,**
c. 1949. Hassenfeld Bros. 5x10" card only originally holding three lead pencils. Text includes "Pluto Says Cut Me Out For Your Scrapbook Or Pin Me Up." Card - **$10 $20 $35**

❑ **PLU-54. Pluto Pencil Drawing,**
1940s. Image is 3.25x3.25 in lead pencil. Art is "51" from a numbered sequence. - **$50 $100 $150**

PLU-55

❑ **PLU-55. "Pluto The Sleep-Walker" Movie Australian Poster,**
1940s. Simmons Litho Ltd., Sydney. 12.75x30" stiff paper insert poster for release of 1942 short distributed by RKO Radio Pictures. - **$85 $175 $300**

PLUTO

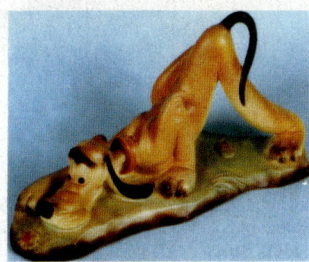

PLU-56

◻ **PLU-56 Pluto English Figurine,**
1940s. Leonardi Ltd., England. 3.5x10x5" tall painted plaster figural. Underside names maker "By Permission Of Walt Disney/Mickey Mouse Ltd." Reverse edge of base has incised "W/13." - **$100 $250 $450**

PLU-59

◻ **PLU-59. "Pluto" Catalin Plastic Pencil Sharpener,**
1940s. 1.5" with scalloped edge. - **$30 $60 $100**

PLU-62

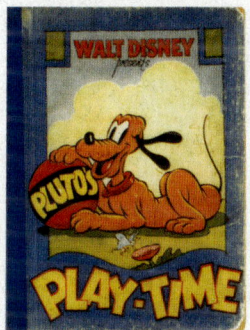

PLU-57

PLU-60

PLU-63

◻ **PLU-62. "Pluto Autograph Hound" Concept Art,**
1955. Paper is centered by 4x5" Pluto image. Art and text in colored pencil is by Al Konetzni, "Disney Legend" toy designer. Illustration is design for Pluto doll to be autographed by pencil attached to his tail. Unique, Near Mint - **$175**

◻ **PLU-63. Pencil Drawing For Disneyland Flip Book,**
1955. 7.25x10.25 animation paper centered by 3.5x5.5" image in pencil and crayon under zipa-tone shading. Artist is Ralph Kent. Book - **$5 $10 $20**
Art - **$25 $50 $85**

PLU-58

◻ **PLU-57. "Pluto's Play-Time" English Book,**
1940s. Juvenile Productions Ltd. 7.5x10.25" hardcover, 96 pages. Content combines text stories with illustrations and comic book-style stories, all featuring Pluto along with Mickey, Goofy, Donald. - **$50 $100 $175**

◻ **PLU-58. "Pluto" Catalin Plastic Pencil Sharpener,**
1940s. 1" from series with smooth round edges. - **$25 $50 $90**

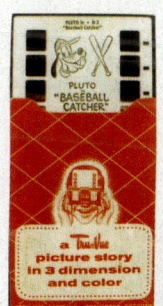

PLU-61

◻ **PLU-60. Pluto With Doghouse Pencil Sharpener,**
c. 1950. Painted white metal 1-1/8" tall. - **$35 $65 $125**

◻ **PLU-61. "Pluto In Baseball Catcher" Stereo View Card,**
1953. Tru-Vue 3.75x5.5" slipcase envelope holding color photos view card of studio models. - **$5 $10 $15**

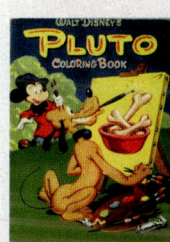

PLU-64

◻ **PLU-64. "Pluto Coloring Book" Australian,**
1956. Golden Press, Sydney. 8x10.25" cardboard covered book #218 with 16 pages. - **$25 $50 $80**

PLUTO

PLU-65

❑ **PLU-65. "Disneyland Gloves" With Pluto,** 1950s. Wells Lamont Co. 7" long wool/nylon gloves attached at top by maker's tag. Each glove top has puffy felt fabric portrait patch plus his name in hand-lettered inking. With Tag - **$10 $20 $40** Without Tag - **$8 $15 $25**

PLU-66

PLU-67

❑ **PLU-66. Pluto Figurine,** 1950s. Shaw. 1.5x2.25x1.75" tall painted and glazed ceramic. - **$50 $100 $150**

❑ **PLU-67. Incense Burner Figure,** 1950s. Goebel. 3x5x5.75" tall painted and glazed ceramic with wire and bulb holder with bulb to heat a drop of liquid incense to perfume the air. Figure has seven vent holes for scent release. Goebel and "DIS149" markings. - **$75 $150 $250**

PLU-68

❑ **PLU-68. Pluto English China Figurine,** 1950s. Beswick. 3.75" tall. - **$100 $200 $300**

PLU-69

PLU-70

❑ **PLU-69. Seated Pose Figure,** 1950s. Unmarked but likely Italian 3.5x4x6.5" tall painted and glazed ceramic by Zaccagnini. - **$300 $600 $1000**

❑ **PLU-70. Pluto Flashlight,** 1950s. 1x1x5" long hard plastic three-dimensional figural without maker or licensee markings. Complete unit of removable end cap holding plunger button, bulb and coil spring. - **$20 $40 $75**

PLU-71

❑ **PLU-71. Boxed Line Mar "Pluto Lantern,"** 1950s. Lantern is 3.25x3.5x6.75" tall figural battery operated in box illustrated on all sides. Lantern is mostly tin lithographed with glass midsection containing a light bulb. Eyes are plastic, tongue, tail and ears are rubber. Ears are attached to wire carrying handle. Body lights and light is also visible through the plastic eyes. Box - **$50 $150 $275** Lantern - **$50 $100 $150**

PLUTO

PLU-72

PLU-73

❏ **PLU-72. Egg Cup Figural,**
1950s. "Made In Japan." 1.75x3.75x2.5" tall. - **$65 $125 $185**

❏ **PLU-73. "Pluto/Goofy" Glass,**
1950s. Drinking tumbler is 5" tall with single image of each character from set of four glasses, each also featuring two different character images. - **$15 $30 $50**

PLU-74

❏ **PLU-74. Hand Puppet,**
1950s. Gund Mfg. Co. 11" tall full figure puppet formed by plush-covered body with stitched tag, vinyl head and feet plus interal squeaker mechanism. - **$20 $35 $65**

PLU-75

❏ **PLU-75. "Pluto" Boxed Push Puppet,**
1950s. Kohner. 2.25" diameter plastic base by 5" tall with illustrated box. Box lid has ink stamp "Pluto No. 131." Box - **$12 $25 $50**
Toy - **$30 $50 $90**

PLU-76

PLU-77

❏ **PLU-76. Ramp Walker,**
1950s. Marx. 4.25" long hard plastic with movable legs. - **$20 $40 $80**

❏ **PLU-77. "Walt Disney's Pluto Electric Clock,"**
1950s. Allied Mfg. Co. Ltd. Box holds hard plastic clock measuring 4x5x9.5" tall. Has glow-in-dark eyes and bones that serve as clock's hands. Box - **$60 $125 $200**
Clock - **$115 $225 $400**

PLU-78

PLU-79

PLUTO

- **PLU-78. "Line Mar" Pluto Pulling Cart Friction Toy,**
1950s. Line Mar. 2.5x8.75x5" tall lithographed tin. Pluto is accented by a separate tin tongue that hangs out of his mouth and a rubber tail. - **$200 $400 $600**

- **PLU-79. Pluto On Tricycle Wind-Up,**
1950s. Line Mar. 2x4x3.5" toy with built-in key. - **$75 $150 $250**

PLU-80

- **PLU-80. Pluto "Battery Operated Disney Acrobat" Boxed Toy,**
1950s. Line Mar. Toy is 1.5x7x9.5" tall tin litho with attached 4.5" tall figure.
Box - **$50 $10 $200**
Toy - **$100 $200 $300**

PLU-81

- **PLU-81. Pluto The Drum Major Wind-Up,**
1950s. Line Mar. 3x3x6.25" tall lithographed tin toy with built-in key. Winding causes toy to rock back and forth, shake both arms, blow the horn in mouth. Figure is accented by rubber tail. Box - **$125 $250 $500**
Toy - **$200 $400 $600**

PLU-82

- **PLU-82. Party Pluto Musical Toy,**
1950s. Marx. 5x5x10" tall mostly hard plastic wind-up depicting him wearing top hat, horn in mouth and holding a pair of metal bells. Figure is detailed by original rubber ears and tail. Built-in key produces rocking movement back and forth as the bells shake. Internal bellows mechanism produces a horn sound. - **$85 $150 $250**

PLU-83

- **PLU-83. "Whirling Tail Pluto" Boxed Wind-Up,**
1950s. Marx. 5.5" hard plastic toy with wire tail and built-in key. Box - **$25 $50 $100**
Toy - **$25 $50 $100**

PLU-84

- **PLU-84. "Pluto And Goofy" Windup Set With Box,**
1950s. Line Mar. 5" tall tin windups.
Box - **$150 $300 $600**
Each Loose - **$100 $200 $400**

PLU-85

- **PLU-85. Pluto Wind-Up Car By Marx,**
1950s. 2x5x2" tall hard plastic with built-in key. - **$35 $75 $125**

PLU-86

- **PLU-86. Pluto Friction Toy,**
c. 1960. Hong Kong 2.5x7x2.5" tall hard plastic figural without Disney markings but obvious likeness of Pluto. When pushed, friction mechanism turns inner rod wheels causing outer legs to move as if running. - **$20 $40 $75**

PLU-87

- **PLU-87. Pluto French Alarm Clock,**
1960s. Bayard. 2x4.5x4.75 tall in metal case. Pluto's head moves as seconds tick. Made in France with limited U.S. distribution. - **$60 $125 $200**

PLUTO

PLU-88

PLU-92

❏ **PLU-88. Bobbing Head Figure,**
1960s. "Made In Japan" 5.75" tall painted composition with spring-mounted head, felt fabric ears. Rear has foil sticker with copyright. - **$20 $40 $80**

❏ **PLU-91. "Pluto" Candle,**
1960s. Figural wax candle 1.5x2x3.5" tall. - **$10 $20 $35**

❏ **PLU-92. Figural Wooden Bank,**
1960s. Unmarked but believed European creation, entirely wood painted body except for pair of felt ears and a string tail. Coin slot is on his back, underside has metal padlock and key that fits through a pair of metal loops. His body is threaded at the neck and comes apart to remove coins. - **$35 $60 $100**

PLU-89

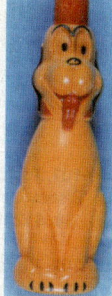

PLU-90

PLU-94

❏ **PLU-89. Nodder Figure,**
1960s. Marx. Original plastic bag holding 2.5" long plastic Pluto with separate but jointed head that nods. - **$10 $20 $30**

❏ **PLU-90. Pluto Soaky,**
1960s. Bottle is 8.5" tall. - **$5 $10 $20**

PLU-91

PLU-93

❏ **PLU-93. "Pluto" Squeaker Hand Puppet,**
1960s. Gund 10.5" tall likeness with molded soft vinyl head and printed fabric handcover body. Complete with stitched tag by maker and squeaker mechanism attached to inside of body. - **$10 $20 $40**

❏ **PLU-94. "Pluto" Squeaker Hand Puppet,**
1960s. Gund 4x5x6.5" boxed 9" likeness with molded soft vinyl head and internal squeaker mechanism, stitched tag by maker. Box - **$10 $20 $40**
Puppet - **$10 $20 $40**

PLUTO

PLU-95

❏ **PLU-95. Pluto Squeak Toy,**
1960s. Japanese large 4x9x9" tall vinyl figure. - **$20 $40 $65**

PLU-96

❏ **PLU-96. "Pluto" Boxed Sports Car,**
1960s. Elm Toys. 1.5x2x1" deep "Mercedes Benz" with "30" on hood and three dimensional figure of Pluto from the waist up. Box - **$5 $10 $20**
Car - **$10 $20 $40**

PLU-97

❏ **PLU-97. "Pluto The Old-Fashioned Car Driver" Toy,**
1960s. Marx subsidiary Elm Toys boxed 1.5" long hard plastic free-wheeling miniature "1910 Studebaker." Box - **$5 $10 $20**
Car - **$8 $15 $30**

PLU-98

❏ **PLU-98. "Pluto The Sport Car Driver" Toy,**
1960s. Marx subsidiary Elm Toys boxed 2" long hard plastic free-wheeling miniature "Cunningham." Box - **$5 $10 $20**
Car - **$10 $20 $40**

PLU-99

❏ **PLU-99. Battery Operated Pluto,**
1960s. Frankonia, Japan. 10.5" long toy with original box. Toy is plush covered with tin litho and rubber pieces including dog collar w/his name and bee attached to nose.
Box - **$25 $50 $100**
Toy - **$25 $50 $100**

PLU-100

❏ **PLU-100. "Pluto Pop Pal" Toy,**
1970s. Kohner Bros. 2.5x3x3" tall hard plastic replica of doghouse. When front button is pushed, roof pops up to release a three-dimensional upper torso figure of Pluto as a squeaking noise is produced. - **$10 $20 $35**

PLU-101

PLU-102

❏ **PLU-101. Pluto Figure,**
1970s. "Disney Gift-Ware." 3.5" tall painted bisque. - **$8 $12 $20**

❏ **PLU-102. Pluto Figurine,**
1970s. Licensed Japanese small 2.5" tall painted and glazed ceramic with some over-the-glaze paint accents. - **$8 $15 $25**

PLU-103

❏ **PLU-103. Pluto Figurine,**
1970s. Unmarked 1.5x5x2.5" tall painted and glazed likeness with over-the-glaze accent paint. - **$8 $15 $25**

770

POCAHONTAS

PLU-104

PLU-105

❏ **PLU-106. Pencil Sharpener Figure,**
1970s. Alco Products Inc. 3.5x7.5" display card holding 3.5" tall hard plastic figural sharpener. Carded - **$8 $15 $25**

PLU-107

❏ **PLU-107. Pluto English Oversized Postcard,**
1970s. F.J. Warren Ltd. "Dufex" card 4x6". Front has reflective foil accent with color image against bright sunburst design background. - **$3 $5 $10**

Pocahontas

In an unusual move for Disney, this full-length 1995 animated feature was not based on a book or fairy tale. Instead, it was based, albeit loosely, on historical fact. Set in Jamestown, Virginia during the 1600s, the film tells the story of the daughter of the chief of the Powhatan tribe. She is unsure of what her future holds. When she meets the English captain John Smith, they fall in love. Unfortunately, other settlers, and their governor, Ratcliffe, believe that the Indians are withholding gold from them.

One settler kills an Indian brave and John Smith takes the blame. He is condemned to death. Pocahontas pleads for his life and he is spared. However, he is wounded by an attack from the enraged Ratcliffe and ends up having to return to England for treatment. Pocahontas comes to realize that she has helped the settlers and the Indians live together peacefully.

Directed by Eric Goldberg and Mike Gabriel, the film included vocal performances by Irene Bedard, Judy Kahn, Mel Gibson and David Ogden Stiers among others. Academy Awards went to Stephen Schwartz and Alan Mencken for Best Song and to Mencken for Best Score.

Merchandise included books, records, premiums and fast-food tie-ins.

❏ **PLU-104. Pluto And Doghouse Bank,**
1970s. Animal Toys Plus. Inc. 8.5" tall hard vinyl figural on 4" diameter base. Figure has single movable arm to hold a coin before dropping into slotted roof. Base has sticker "I'm A Bank With Movable Arm." - **$10 $20 $40**

❏ **PLU-105. Bean Bag Doll,**
1970s. Doll is 3x6x5.5" tall plump fabric bean-filled and weighted body detailed by plastic disk feet and soft vinyl head that squeaks when squeezed. With Tag - **$10 $20 $35**

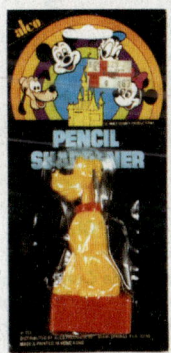

PLU-106

PLU-108

❏ **PLU-108. Pluto Bobblehead,**
2003. Hand painted figure on base. - **$20**

POC-1

POCAHONTAS

❏ **POC-1. "Pocahontas/The Premiere In The Park" VIP Shirt And Pass,**
1995. Pullover shirt and admission pass for invited attendee to the June 10 premiere of the film held at "The Great Lawn, Central Park," N.Y. Shirt also has "City Of New York Parks & Recreation" logo on one sleeve. Laminated card pass pictures her and has attached neck cord and pocket clip. Reverse includes serial number of issue. Shirt - $5 $10 $20
Pass - $5 $10 $20

POC-2

POC-3

❏ **POC-2. WDCC Pocahontas Statue,**
1995. Walt Disney Collector's Club. "Listen with Your Heart" tribute series. - $250

❏ **POC-3. Meeko Plush,**
1995. Disney. Plush Doll. - $20

POC-4

❏ **POC-4. Pocahontas Colors of the Wind Snow Globe,**
1995. Disney. Snow globe with Pocahontas and John Smith holding hands. - $60

POC-5

❏ **POC-5. Pocahontas and Meeko Snow Globe,**
1995. Disney. Pocahontas and Meeko in canoe. "Just Around the River Bend." - $60

Pollyanna

This 1960 live-action film starred famous adolescent actress Hayley Mills in her first of what would become several major roles for Disney. Based on the 1913 book by Eleanor Porter, the story has the cheerful orphan Pollyanna bringing hope and a positive outlook to a New England town. During the early days of cinema, the story had been made into a film for Mary Pickford. Disney's version, written and directed by David Swift, is one of the finest live action films in the Disney catalog.

Exceptional acting may be the main reason for *Pollyanna*'s success. Hayley Mills won a special Oscar for the film, and she clearly deserved it; this is one of the finest performances ever created by a child actor. Other actors featured in the film include Agnes Moorehead, Jane Wyman, Kevin Corcoran, Richard Egan and Donald Crisp.

Merchandise included books and records.

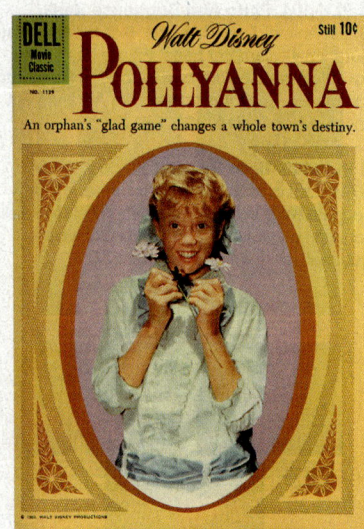

POL-1

❏ **POL-1. Pollyanna Comic Book,**
August 1960. Dell's Four Color Comics #1129. - $9 $27 $115

Pop-Up Books

Although mechanical or movable books of various types had been published in large numbers since the 1800s, Blue Ribbon Publishing adopted the actual term "Pop-Up" and utilized Disney characters and fairy tale stories in their movable books. It was designer and master marketer Sam Gold who pioneered the effort at Blue Ribbon with the production of the *Mickey Mouse Waddle Book*, for which Gold arranged the licensing of Mickey and signed Disney to handle the artistic chores. He then secured the rights to the likes of Buck Rogers, Little Orphan Annie and Tarzan, spearheading an entire line of "Pop-Up" volumes starring these and many other popular comic characters. Blue Ribbon released several numbered and unnumbered series in the "Pop-Up" format.

BACK COVER

POP-1

FRONT COVER

INTERIOR POP-UPS

☐ **POP-1. The "Pop-Up" Mickey Mouse,**
1933. Blue Ribbon Press. 34 pgs., 6 1/2" x 9", 75 cents, hard-c. Artist: Floyd Gottfredson. Three Pop-Up pictures..
- $100 $300 $850

POP-UP BOOKS

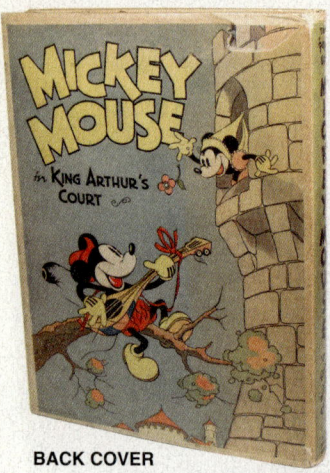
BACK COVER

POP-2

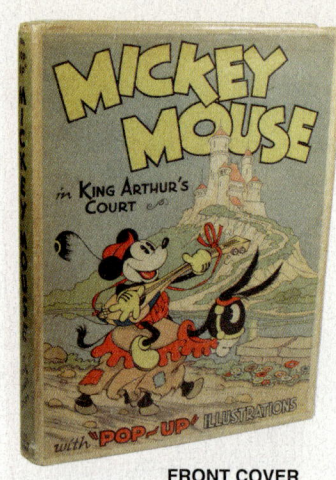
FRONT COVER

☐ **POP-2. The "Pop-Up" Mickey Mouse In King Arthur's Court,**
1933. Blue Ribbon Press. 56 pgs., 7 1/2" x 9 1/4", $2 hard-c with dustjacket. Artist: Floyd Gottfredson. 4 Pop-Up pictures.
Jacket - **$100 $250 $500**
Book - **$250 $525 $1500**

INTERIOR POP-UPS

774

POP-UP BOOKS

☐ **POP-3. The "Pop-Up" Minnie Mouse,** 1933. Blue Ribbon Press. 36 pgs., 6 1/2" x 9, 75 cents hard-c. Artist: Floyd Gottfredson. Three Pop-Up pictures. - **$100 $300 $850**

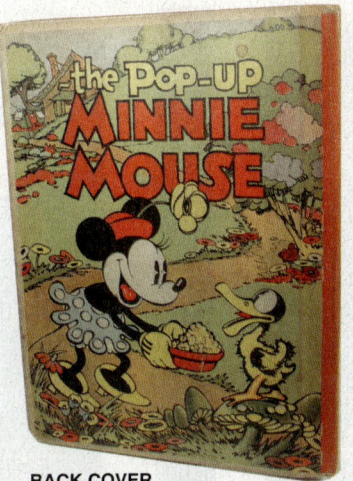
BACK COVER

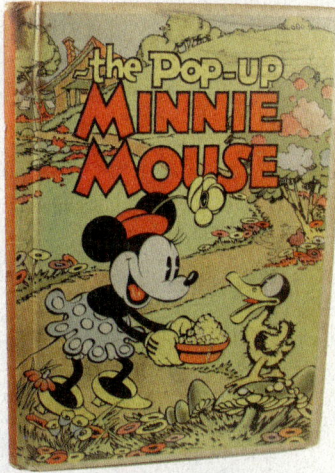
FRONT COVER

POP-3

INTERIOR POP-UPS

POP-UP BOOKS

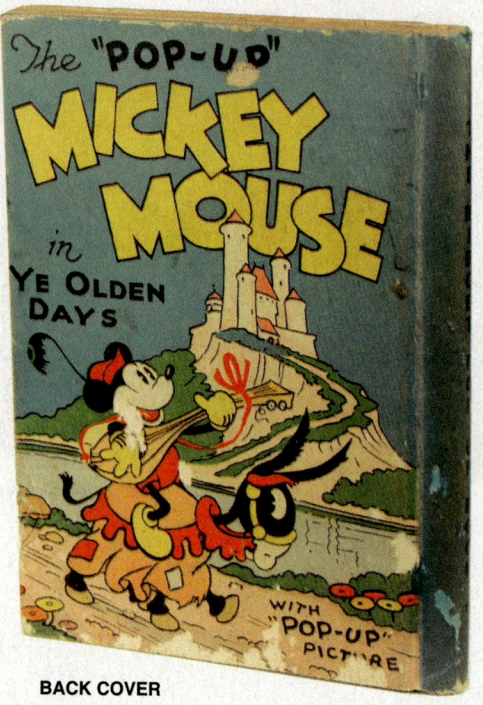

BACK COVER

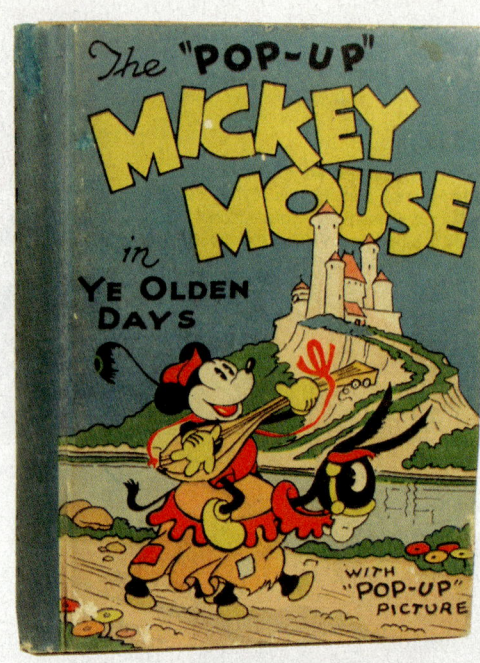

FRONT COVER

POP-4

☐ **POP-4. The "Pop-Up" Mickey Mouse in "Ye Olden Days,"** 1934. Blue Ribbon Press #101. 62 pgs. The Midget Pop-Up Book. Artist: Floyd Gottfredson.
One Pop-Up picture in the center of book. - $200 $400 $1200

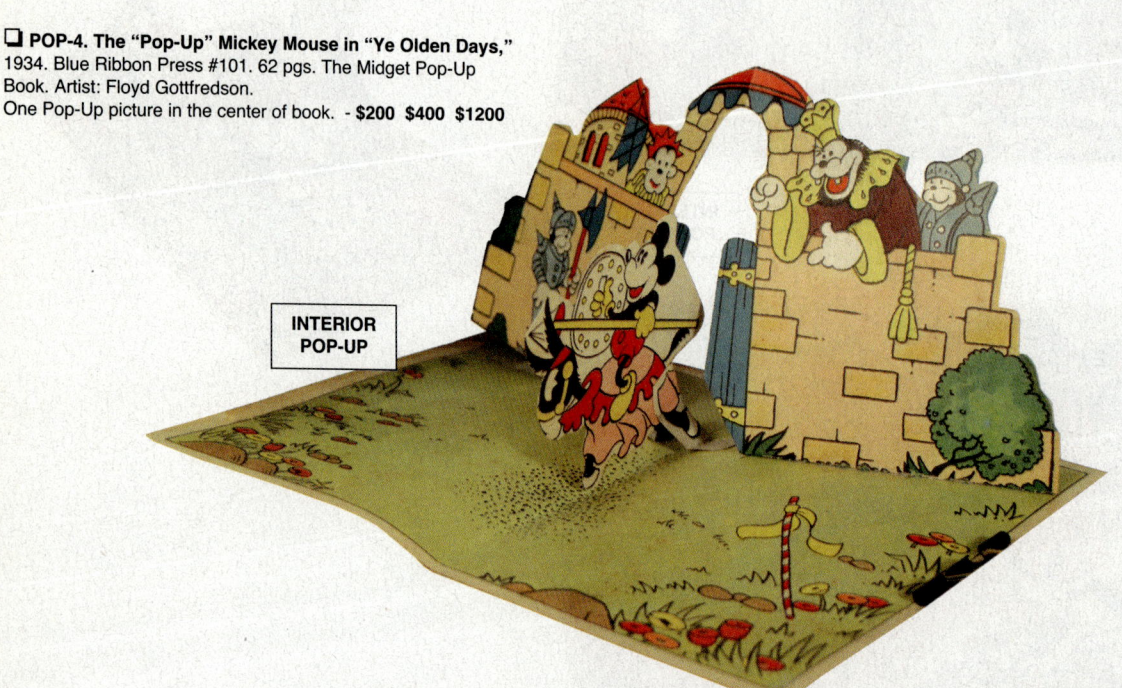

INTERIOR POP-UP

POSTERS

Posters

From the lobbies of grand movie theaters when going to the pictures was a major family event, to the homes of enthusiasts happy to relive the memories of those bygone times, posters are one of the most cherished and sought-after collectibles. In this section we present some of the amazing examples of movie posters produced to promote and celebrate Disney productions from the 1920s to the present day.

❑ POS-1. "Alice Gets in Dutch," 1924. One sheet. - **$10,000 to $15,000**

❑ POS-4. "The Cactus Kid," 1930. Mickey Mouse stock one sheet with title. - **$20,000 to $35,000**

❑ POS-7. "The Bears and the Bees," 1932. Silly Symphony one sheet. - **$8,000 to $12,000**

❑ POS-2. "Alice in the Jungle," 1925. One sheet. - **$16,000 to $25,000**

❑ POS-5. "The Musical Farmer," 1932. Columbia Pictures Corp., New York, NY. - **$40,000 to $60,000**

❑ POS-8. "The Klondike Kid," 1932. Mickey Mouse one sheet. - **$60,000 to $80,000**

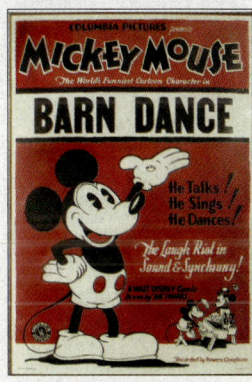

❑ POS-3. "Barn Dance," 1929. Mickey Mouse stock one sheet with title. - **$25,000 to $40,000**

❑ POS-6. "Mickey's Nightmare," 1932. Mickey one-sheet. - **$60,000 to $80,000**

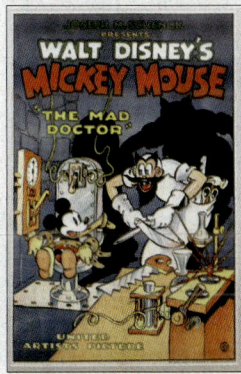

❑ POS-9. "The Mad Doctor," 1932. Mickey Mouse one sheet. - **$90,000 to $140,000**

POSTERS

❏ POS-10. "Mickey's Good Deed,"
1932. Mickey Mouse one sheet. - **$70,000 to $90,000**

❏ POS-13. "Silly Symphony,"
1934. Stock with 'Donald' image one sheet. - **$6,000 to $10,000**

❏ POS-16. "Hiawatha,"
1937. Silly Symphony, 40" x 60." Large silkscreen on heavy paper. - **$40,000 to $60,000**

❏ POS-11. "Just Dogs,"
1932. Silly Symphony one sheet. - **$25,000 to $35,000**

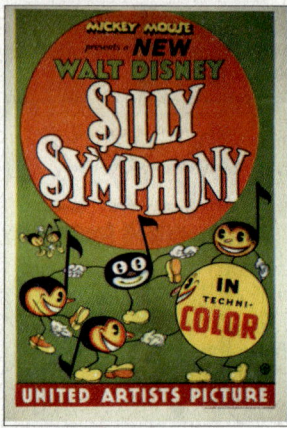

❏ POS-14. "Silly Symphony,"
1934. One sheet. - **$6,000 to $8,000**

❏ POS-17 "Magician Mickey,"
1937. Mickey Mouse, 40" x 60." Large silkscreen on heavy paper. - **$60,000 to $80,000**

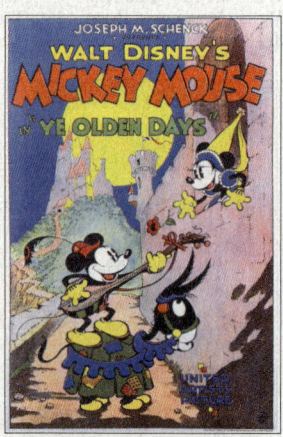

❏ POS-12. "Ye Olden Days,"
1933. Mickey Mouse one sheet. - **$70,000 to $100,000**

❏ POS-15. "Mickey Mouse,"
1934. Stock one sheet, no 'Now in Color' at top. - **$15,000 to $20,000**

❏ POS-18. "Snow White,"
1937. One sheet with Tenggren art, style B. - **$15,000 to $25,000**

POSTERS

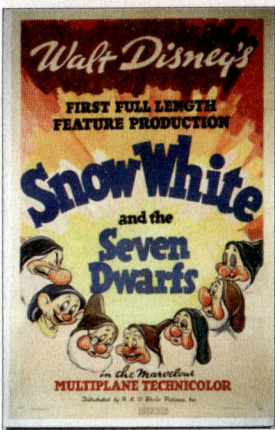

❏ **POS-19. "Snow White,"**
1937. (Dwarfs image) One sheet, style A. - **$5,000 to $8,000**

❏ **POS-20. "Snow White,"**
1937. (Scary Forest) One sheet, style C. - **$20,000 to $30,000**

❏ **POS-21. "Brave Little Tailor,"**
1938. Mickey Mouse one sheet. - **$15,000 to $25,000**

❏ **POS-22. "Ferdinand the Bull,"**
1938. Silly Symphony one sheet. - **$8,000 to $15,000**

❏ **POS-23. "Merbabies,"**
1938. Silly Symphony one sheet. - **$8,000 to 12,000**

❏ **POS-24. "Society Dog Show,"**
1939. Mickey Mouse one sheet. - **$15,000 to $20,000**

❏ **POS-25. "The Practical Pig,"**
1939. Silly Symphony one sheet. - **$10,000 to $15,000**

❏ **POS-26. "Donald's Lucky Day,"**
1939. Donald Duck one sheet. - **$15,000 to $20,000**

❏ **POS-27. "Sea Scouts,"**
1939. Donald Duck one sheet. - **$10,000 to $15,000**

POSTERS

❏ **POS-28.** "Beach Picnic,"
1939. Donald Duck one sheet. - **$15,000 to $20,000**

❏ **POS-31.** "Donald's Cousin Gus,"
1939. Donald Duck one sheet. RKO Radio Pictures. - **$18,000 to $25,000**

❏ **POS-34.** "Donald's Dog Laundry,"
1940. Donald Duck one sheet. - **$12,000 to $15,000**

❏ **POS-29.** "Goofy and Wilbur,"
1939. Goofy one sheet. - **$15,000 to $20,000**

❏ **POS-32.** "Officer Duck,"
1939. Donald Duck one sheet. - **$8,000 to $12,000**

❏ **POS-35.** "Mr. Duck Steps Out,"
1940. Donald Duck one sheet. RKO Radio Pictures. - **$20,000 to $30,000**

❏ **POS-30.** "Hockey Champ,"
1939. Donald Duck one sheet. - **$18,000 to $25,000**

❏ **POS-33.** "The Riveter,"
1940. Donald Duck one sheet. - **$12,000 to $18,000**

❏ **POS-36.** "Bone Trouble,"
1940. Pluto one sheet. - **$6,000 to $10,000**

POSTERS

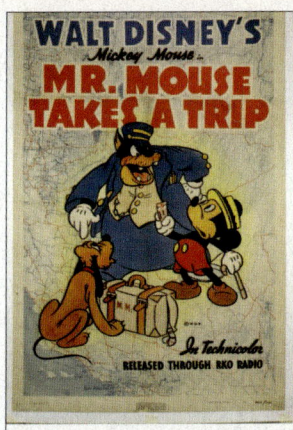

❏ **POS-37. "Mr. Mouse Takes a Trip,"**
1940. Mickey Mouse one sheet. - **$10,000 to $15,000**

❏ **POS-40. "Goofy's Glider,"**
1940. Goofy one sheet. - **$5,000 to $7,000**

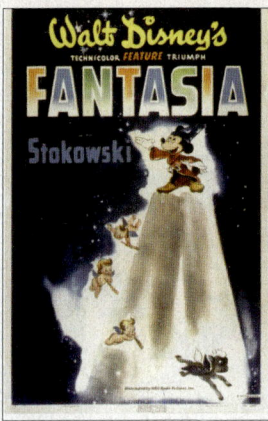

❏ **POS-43. "Fantasia,"**
1940. One sheet (Mickey Mouse on mountain). - **$10,000 to $15,000**

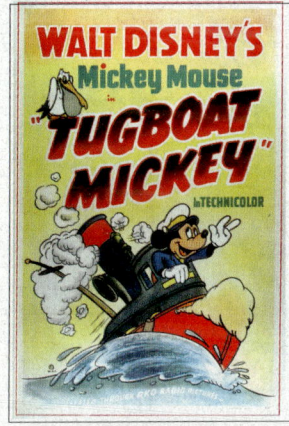

❏ **POS-38. "Tugboat Mickey,"**
1940. RKO Radio Pictures. - **$8,000 to $10,000**

❏ **POS-41. "Pinocchio,"**
1940. One sheet (Jiminy on foot). - **$5,000 to $8,000**

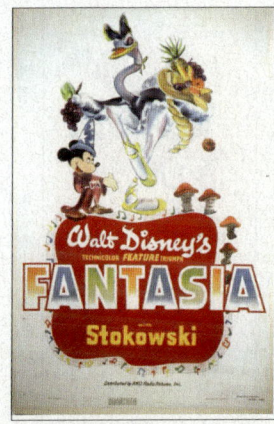

❏ **POS-44. "Fantasia,"**
1940. One sheet (with Ostrich). - **$8,000 to $10,000**

❏ **POS-39. "Fire Chief,"**
1940. RKO Radio Pictures. - **$15,000 to $25,000**

❏ **POS-42. "Pinocchio,"**
1940. One sheet (holding sign). - **$6,000 to $9,000**

❏ **POS-45. "Dumbo,"**
1941. One sheet. - **$8,000 to $12,000**

POSTERS

❑ **POS-46. "Dumbo,"**
1941. One sheet. - **$8,000 to $12,000**

❑ **POS-49. "Donald's Camera,"**
1941. RKO Radio Pictures. - **$4,000 to $6,000**

❑ **POS-52. "Bambi,"**
1942. - **$1,500 to $3,000**

❑ **POS-47. "Dumbo,"**
1941. Three sheet. - **$8,000 to $12,000**

❑ **POS-50. "The Reluctant Dragon,"**
1941. - **$2,400 to $3,600**

❑ **POS-53. "Bambi,"**
1942. - **$1,500 to $3,000**

❑ **POS-48. "Chef Donald,"**
1941. RKO Radio Pictures. - **$4,000 to $6,000**

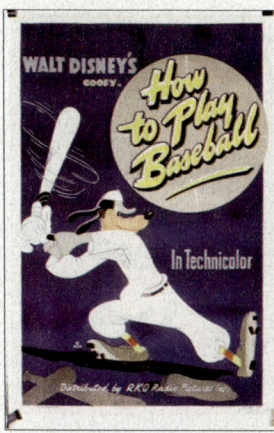

❑ **POS-51. "How to Play Baseball,"**
1942. Goofy one sheet. - **$10,000 to $15,000**

❑ **POS-54. "Der Fuehrer's Face,"**
1943. Donald Duck one sheet. - **$7,000 to $10,000**

POSTERS

❏ POS-55. "Saludos Amigos,"
1943. - **$2,000 to $5,000**

❏ POS-58. "The Trail of Donald Duck,"
1948. RKO Radio Pictures. - **$1,000 to $2,000**

❏ POS-61. "Cinderella,"
1950. - **$750 to $1,500**

❏ POS-56. "No Sail,"
1945. RKO Radio Pictures. - **$1,500 to $3,000**

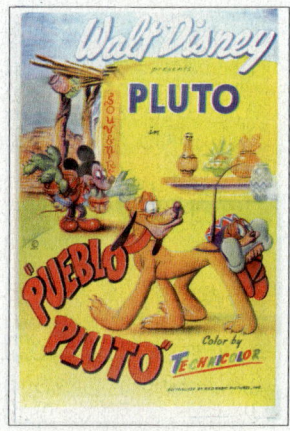

❏ POS-59. "Pueblo Pluto,"
1949. - **$500 to $1,000**

❏ POS-62. "Alice in Wonderland,"
1951. - **$1,000 to $2,000**

❏ POS-57. "Song of the South,"
1946. - **$1,000 to $2,000**

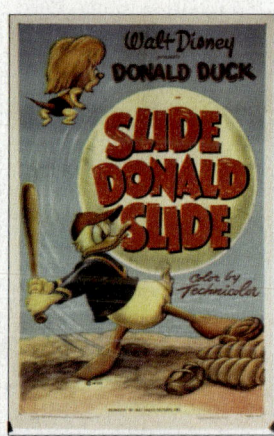

❏ POS-60. "Slide Donald Slide,"
1949. - **$3,000 to $4,500**

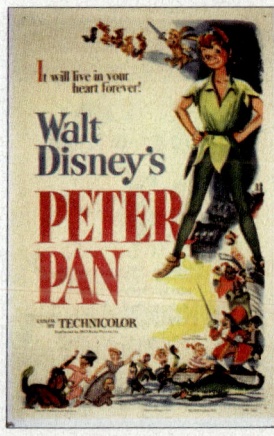

❏ POS-63. "Peter Pan,"
1953. - **$500 to $1,000**

POSTERS

❏ **POS-64. "Lady and the Tramp,"**
1955. - **$500 to $1,000**

❏ **POS-67. "The Sword in the Stone,"**
1963. - **$300 to $600**

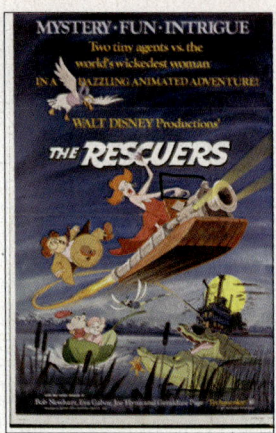

❏ **POS-70. "The Rescuers,"**
1977. - **$50 to $100**

❏ **POS-65. "Sleeping Beauty,"**
1959. - **$500 to $1,000**

❏ **POS-68. "The Jungle Book,"**
1967. - **$300 to $500**

❏ **POS-71. "The Fox and the Hound,"**
1981. - **$50 to $100**

❏ **POS-66. "One Hundred and One Dalmatians,"**
1961. - **$500 to $1,000**

❏ **POS-69. "Robin Hood,"**
1973. - **$50 to $100**

❏ **POS-72. "The Black Cauldron,"**
1985. - **$50 to $100**

POSTERS

❏ POS-73. "The Great Mouse Detective,"
1986. - $50 to $100

❏ POS-76. "Beauty and the Beast,"
1991. - $50 to $100

❏ POS-79. "Aladdin,"
1992. - $50 to $100

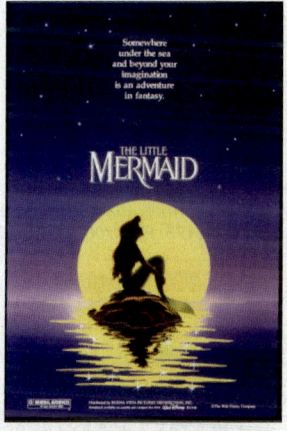
❏ POS-74. "The Little Mermaid,"
1989. - $75 to $150

❏ POS-77. "Beauty and the Beast,"
1991. - $50 to $100

❏ POS-80. "The Lion King,"
1994. - $50 to $150

❏ POS-75. "The Little Mermaid,"
1989. - $75 to $150

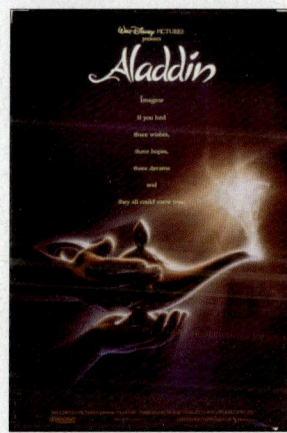
❏ POS-78 "Aladdin,"
1992. - $50 to $100

❏ POS-81."The Lion King,"
1994. - $50 to $150

PROMOTIONAL COMICS

Promotional Comics

Promotional or giveaway comics have been produced for over 70 years and used to sell and promote various products, events, and also give social commentary. The Walt Disney Company has been prolific in the use of these "free" wonders with examples ranging from shoe store giveaways, cereal, ice cream, the dangers of electricity, and more. The background of the company and the ability to use known characters that are loved by generations gives them a strong ability to have their characters be a spokesperson for the many products and services over the years.

Promotional comics today are not only distributed as stand-alone giveaways, but are also included with video games, action figures, limited edition DVD's, and as mail-away premiums from product manufacturers. The availability of the promotional comics as well as the rarity of others has spawned a collecting area of their own. The examples found here are just some of the numerous examples of these "free" wonders and some of the fascinating products they promote. SPECIAL NOTE: We have included the complete run of *Mickey Mouse Magazine* here, as the series began as promotional books initially (see below).

❏ **Mickey Mouse Magazine Vol. 1 No. 1,** 1933. Kamen-Blair giveaway issued by different dairies and leading stores through local theaters. - **GD-$540 FN-$2160 VF-$6500**

❏ **Mickey Mouse Magazine Vol. 1 No. 2,** 1933. Kamen-Blair dairy and theater giveaway. - **GD-$225 FN-$900 VF-$1750**

❏ **Mickey Mouse Magazine Vol. 1 No. 3,** 1933. Kamen-Blair dairy and theater giveaway. - **GD-$225 FN-$900 VF-$1750**

❏ **Mickey Mouse Magazine Vol. 1 No. 4,** 1933. Walt Disney Prods. (dairy and theater giveaway). - **GD-$225 FN-$900 VF-$1750**

❏ **Mickey Mouse Magazine Vol. 1 No. 5,** 1933. Walt Disney Prods. (dairy and theater giveaway). - **GD-$175 FN-$700 VF-$1350**

❏ **Mickey Mouse Magazine Vol. 1 No. 6,** 1933. Walt Disney Prods. (dairy and theater giveaway). - **GD-$175 FN-$700 VF-$1350**

❏ **Mickey Mouse Magazine Vol. 1 No. 7,** 1933. Walt Disney Prods. (dairy and theater giveaway). - **GD-$175 FN-$700 VF-$1350**

❏ **Mickey Mouse Magazine Vol. 1 No. 8,** 1933. Walt Disney Prods. (dairy and theater giveaway). - **GD-$175 FN-$700 VF-$1350**

❏ **Mickey Mouse Magazine Vol. 1 No. 9,** 1933. Walt Disney Prods. (dairy and theater giveaway). - **GD-$175 FN-$700 VF-$1350**

❏ **Mickey Mouse Magazine Vol. 1 No. 1,** 1933. Walt Disney Productions (Mills giveaway issued by different dairies). - **$240 $960 $2700**

PROMOTIONAL COMICS

❏ **Mickey Mouse Magazine Vol. 1 No. 2,** 1933. Walt Disney Productions (Mills giveaway issued by different dairies). - $80 $320 $900

❏ **Mickey Mouse Magazine Vol.1 No. 6,** 1934. Walt Disney Productions (Mills giveaway issued by different dairies). - $80 $320 $900

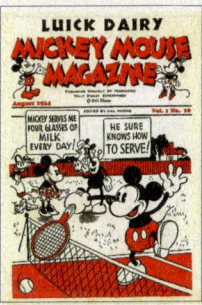
❏ **Mickey Mouse Magazine Vol. 1 No. 10,** 1934. Walt Disney Productions (Mills giveaway issued by different dairies). - $80 $320 $900

❏ **Mickey Mouse Magazine Vol. 1 No. 3,** 1934. Walt Disney Productions (Mills giveaway issued by different dairies). - $80 $320 $900

❏ **Mickey Mouse Magazine Vol. 1 No. 7,** 1934. Walt Disney Productions (Mills giveaway issued by different dairies). - $80 $320 $900

❏ **Mickey Mouse Magazine Vol. 1 No. 11,** 1934. Walt Disney Productions (Mills giveaway issued by different dairies). - $80 $320 $900

❏ **Mickey Mouse Magazine Vol. 1 No. 4,** 1934. Walt Disney Productions (Mills giveaway issued by different dairies). - $80 $320 $900

❏ **Mickey Mouse Magazine Vol. 1 No. 8,** 1934. Walt Disney Productions (Mills giveaway issued by different dairies). - $80 $320 $900

❏ **Mickey Mouse Magazine Vol. 1 No. 12,** 1934. Walt Disney Productions (Mills giveaway issued by different dairies). - $80 $320 $900

❏ **Mickey Mouse Magazine Vol. 1 No. 5,** 1934. Walt Disney Productions (Mills giveaway issued by different dairies). - $80 $320 $900

❏ **Mickey Mouse Magazine Vol. 1 No. 9,** 1934. Walt Disney Productions (Mills giveaway issued by different dairies). - $80 $320 $900

❏ **Mickey Mouse Magazine Vol. 2 No. 1,** 1934. Walt Disney Productions (Mills giveaway issued by different dairies). - $55 $192 $600

PROMOTIONAL COMICS

❏ **Mickey Mouse Magazine Vol. 2 No. 2,** 1934. Walt Disney Productions (Mills giveaway issued by different dairies). - **$55 $192 $600**

❏ **Mickey Mouse Magazine Vol. 2 No. 6,** 1935. Walt Disney Productions (Mills giveaway issued by different dairies). - **$55 $192 $600**

❏ **Mickey Mouse Magazine Vol. 2 No. 10,** 1935. Walt Disney Productions (Mills giveaway issued by different dairies). - **$55 $192 $600**

❏ **Mickey Mouse Magazine Vol. 2 No. 3,** 1935. Walt Disney Productions (Mills giveaway issued by different dairies). - **$55 $192 $600**

❏ **Mickey Mouse Magazine Vol. 2 No. 7,** 1935. Walt Disney Productions (Mills giveaway issued by different dairies). - **$55 $192 $600**

❏ **Mickey Mouse Magazine Vol. 2 No. 11,** 1935. Walt Disney Productions (Mills giveaway issued by different dairies). - **$55 $192 $600**

❏ **Mickey Mouse Magazine Vol. 2 No. 4,** 1935. Walt Disney Productions (Mills giveaway issued by different dairies). - **$55 $192 $600**

❏ **Mickey Mouse Magazine Vol. 2 No. 8,** 1935. Walt Disney Productions (Mills giveaway issued by different dairies). - **$55 $192 $600**

❏ **Mickey Mouse Magazine Vol. 2 No. 12,** 1935. Walt Disney Productions (Mills giveaway issued by different dairies). - **$55 $192 $600**

❏ **Mickey Mouse Magazine Vol. 2 No. 5,** 1935. Walt Disney Prods. 1st app. of Donald Duck in sailor outfit on-c (Mills giveaway issued by different dairies). - **$96 $288 $1350**

❏ **Mickey Mouse Magazine Vol. 2 No. 9,** 1935. Walt Disney Productions (Mills giveaway issued by different dairies). - **$55 $192 $600**

❏ **Mickey Mouse Magazine Vol.1 #1,** 1935. (Large size, 13-1/4x10-1/4"; 25 cents) Contains puzzles, games, cels, stories & comics. - **GD-$1325 FN-$3975 VF/NM-$17500**

PROMOTIONAL COMICS

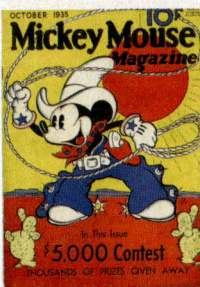

❏ **Mickey Mouse Magazine Vol. 1 #2,** 1935. (Size change, 11-1/2x8-1/2"; 10/35; 10¢ price) High quality paper begins; Messmer-a. - GD-$247 FN-$741 VF-$2100

❏ **Mickey Mouse Magazine Vol. 1 #6,** 1936. 36 pg. Issues begin; Donald becomes editor. - GD-$124 FN-$372 VF-$1050

❏ **Mickey Mouse Magazine Vol. 1 #10,** 1936. - GD-$118 FN-$354 VF-$1000

❏ **Mickey Mouse Magazine Vol. 1 #3,** 1935. Messmer-a. - GD-$129 FN-$387 VF-$1100

❏ **Mickey Mouse Magazine Vol. 1 #7,** 1936. - GD-$124 FN-$372 VF-$1050

❏ **Mickey Mouse Magazine Vol. 1 #11,** 1936. 1st Pluto/Mickey-c; Donald fires himself and appoints Mickey as editor. - GD-$118 FN-$354 VF-$1000

❏ **Mickey Mouse Magazine Vol. 1 #4,** 1935. Messmer-a. - GD-$129 FN-$387 VF-$1100

❏ **Mickey Mouse Magazine Vol. 1 #8,** 1936. 2nd Donald solo-c. - GD-$124 FN-$372 VF-$1050

❏ **Mickey Mouse Magazine Vol. 1 #12,** 1936. - GD-$118 FN-$354 VF-$1000

❏ **Mickey Mouse Magazine Vol. 1 #5,** 1936. 1st Donald Duck solo-c; 2nd cover app. ever; last 44 pg. & high quality paper issue. - GD-$224 FN-$672 VF-$1900

❏ **Mickey Mouse Magazine Vol. 1 #9,** 1936. 1st Mickey/Minnie-c. - GD-$124 FN-$372 VF-$1050

❏ **Mickey Mouse Magazine Vol. 2 #1,** 1936. - GD-$118 FN-$354 VF-$1000

PROMOTIONAL COMICS

❏ **Mickey Mouse Magazine Vol. 2 #2,** 1936. - **GD-$118 FN-$354 VF-$1000**

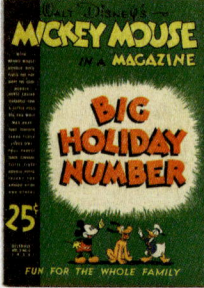

❏ **Mickey Mouse Magazine Vol. 2 #3,** 1936. Special 100 pg. Christmas issue (25 cents); Messmer-a; Donald becomes editor of Wise Quacks. - **GD-$400 FN-$1200 VF-$3400**

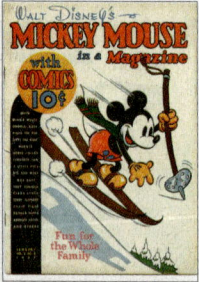

❏ **Mickey Mouse Magazine Vol. 2 #4,** 1936. Mickey Mouse Comics & Roy Ranger (adventure strip) begin; both end V2 #9, Messmer-a. - **GD-$98 FN-$294 VF-$835**

❏ **Mickey Mouse Magazine Vol. 2 #5,** 1937. Ted True (adventure strip, ends V2 #9) & Silly Symphony Comics (ends V3 #3) begin. - **$53 $159 $710**

❏ **Mickey Mouse Magazine Vol. 2 #6,** 1937. 1st solo Minnie-c. Mickey Movies cut-out in issue. - **$53 $159 $710**

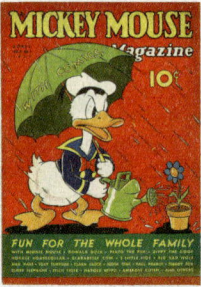

❏ **Mickey Mouse Magazine Vol. 2 #7,** 1937. Mickey Movies cut-out in issue. - **$53 $159 $710**

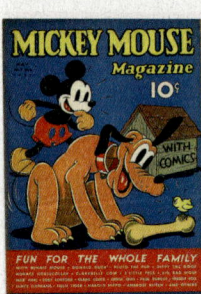

❏ **Mickey Mouse Magazine Vol. 2 #8,** 1937. Mickey Movies cut-out in issue. - **$53 $159 $710**

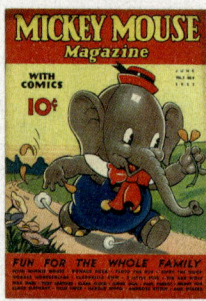

❏ **Mickey Mouse Magazine Vol. 2 #9,** 1937. Mickey Movies cut-out in issue. - **$53 $159 $710**

❏ **Mickey Mouse Magazine Vol. 2 #10,** 1937. 1st full color issue; Mickey Mouse (by Gottfredson; ends V3 #12) & Silly Symphony (ends V3 #3). - **$79 $237 $1100**

❏ **Mickey Mouse Magazine Vol. 2 #11,** 1937. - **$51 $153 $685**

❏ **Mickey Mouse Magazine Vol. 2 #12,** 1937. - **$51 $153 $685**

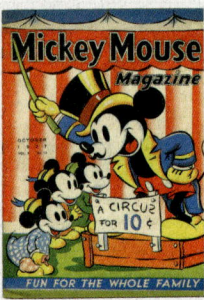

❏ **Mickey Mouse Magazine Vol. 2 #13,** 1937. Hiawatha-c & feature story. (Please note that there is no Vol. 3 #1) - **$51 $153 $685**

PROMOTIONAL COMICS

❏ **Mickey Mouse Magazine Vol. 3 #2,** 1937. Big Bad Wolf Halloween-c. - **$59 $177 $825**

❏ **Mickey Mouse Magazine Vol. 3 #6,** 1938. Snow White serial ends; Lonesome Ghosts app. - **$59 $177 $825**

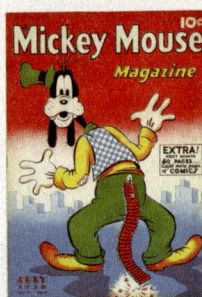

❏ **Mickey Mouse Magazine Vol. 3 #10,** 1938. 1st solo Goofy-c. - **$47 $141 $635**

❏ **Mickey Mouse Magazine Vol. 3 #3,** 1937. (12/37) 1st app. Snow White & The Seven Dwarfs (before release of movie) (possibly 1st in print); Mickey X-Mas-c. - **$107 $321 $1500**

❏ **Mickey Mouse Magazine Vol. 3 #7,** 1938. Seven Dwarfs Easter-c. - **$55 $165 $760**

❏ **Mickey Mouse Magazine Vol. 3 #11,** 1938. (44 pgs; 8 more pgs. color added). Mickey the Sheriff serial begins. - **$51 $153 $685**

❏ **Mickey Mouse Magazine Vol. 3 #4,** 1938. (1/38) Snow White & The Seven Dwarfs serial begins (on stands before release of movie). - **$88 $264 $1225**

❏ **Mickey Mouse Magazine Vol. 3 #8,** 1938. - **$47 $141 $635**

❏ **Mickey Mouse Magazine Vol. 3 #12,** 1938. - **$51 $153 $685**

❏ **Mickey Mouse Magazine Vol. 3 #5,** 1938. 1st Snow White & Seven Dwarfs-c (St. Valentine's Day). - **$107 $321 $1500**

❏ **Mickey Mouse Magazine Vol. 3 #9,** 1938. Dopey-c. - **$47 $141 $635**

❏ **Mickey Mouse Magazine Vol. 4 #1,** 1938. Brave Little Tailor-c/feature story, nominated for Academy Award. - **$50 $150 $685**

PROMOTIONAL COMICS

❑ **Mickey Mouse Magazine Vol. 4 #2,** 1938. (44 pgs.) 1st Huey, Dewey, & Louie-c. - **$53 $159 $710**

❑ **Mickey Mouse Magazine Vol. 4 #7,** 1939. (No #6, two #7s, please note date: 3/39) The Ugly Duckling-c/feature story, Academy Award winner. - **$51 $153 $685**

❑ **Mickey Mouse Magazine Vol. 4 #10,** 1939. Classic July 4th drum & fife-c; last Donald Sunday-r. - **$61 $183 $860**

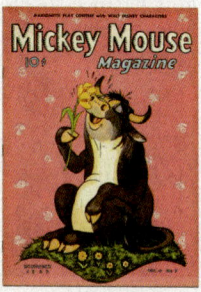

❑ **Mickey Mouse Magazine Vol. 4 #3,** 1938. Ferdinand The Bull-c/feature story, Academy Award winner. - **$51 $153 $685**

❑ **Mickey Mouse Magazine Vol. 4 #7,** 1939. (4/39) Goofy & Wilbur The Grasshopper classic-c/feature story from 1st Goofy solo cartoon movie. - **$50 $150 $650**

❑ **Mickey Mouse Magazine Vol. 4 #11,** 1939. 1st slick-c; last over-sized issue. - **$41 $141 $635**

❑ **Mickey Mouse Magazine Vol. 4 #4,** 1939. Spotty, Mother Pluto strip-r begin, end V4 #8. - **$47 $141 $635**

❑ **Mickey Mouse Magazine Vol. 4 #8,** 1939. Big Bad Wolf-c from Practical Pig movie poster; Practical Pig feature. - **$50 $150 $650**

❑ **Mickey Mouse Magazine Vol. 4 #12,** 1939. (9/39; format change, 10-1/4x8-1/4") 1st full color, cover to cover issue; Donald's Penguin-c/feature story. - **$55 $165 $765**

❑ **Mickey Mouse Magazine Vol. 4 #5,** 1939. St. Valentine's day-c. 1st Pluto solo-c. - **$54 $162 $725**

❑ **Mickey Mouse Magazine Vol. 4 #9,** 1939. Donald Duck & Mickey Mouse Sunday-r begin; The Pointer feature. - **$50 $150 $650**

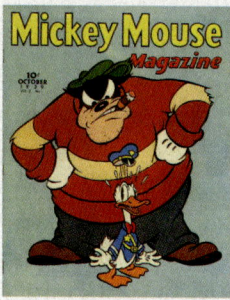

❑ **Mickey Mouse Magazine Vol. 5 #1,** 1939. Black Pete-c; Officer Duck-c/feature story; Autograph Hound feature. - **$55 $165 $750**

PROMOTIONAL COMICS

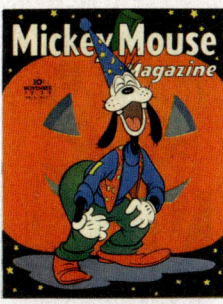

❑ **Mickey Mouse Magazine Vol. 5 #2,** 1939. Goofy-c; 1st brief app. Pinocchio. - $70 $210 $985

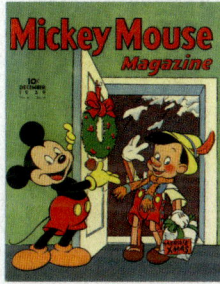

❑ **Mickey Mouse Magazine Vol. 5 #3,** 1939. (12/39) Pinocchio Christmas-c (Before movie release). 1st app. Jiminy Cricket; Pinocchio serial begins. - $82 $246 $1150

❑ **Mickey Mouse Magazine Vol. 5 #4,** 1940. - $55 $165 $750

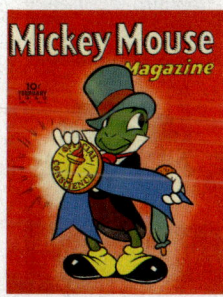

❑ **Mickey Mouse Magazine Vol. 5 #5,** 1940. Jiminy Cricket-c; Pinocchio serial ends; Donald's Dog Laundry. - $55 $165 $750

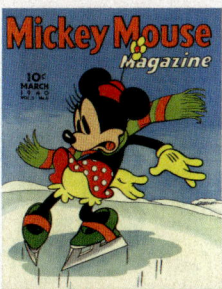

❑ **Mickey Mouse Magazine Vol. 5 #6,** 1940. Tugboat Mickey feature; Rip Van Winkle feature begins, ends V5 #8. - $54 $162 $725

❑ **Mickey Mouse Magazine Vol. 5 #7,** 1940. 2nd Huey, Dewey & Louie-c. - $54 $162 $725

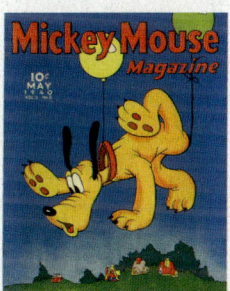

❑ **Mickey Mouse Magazine Vol. 5 #8,** 1940. Last magazine size issue; 2nd solo Pluto-c; Figaro & Cleo feature story. - $55 $165 $750

❑ **Mickey Mouse Magazine Vol. 5 #9,** 1940. (6/40; change to comic book size) Jiminy Crickey feature story; Donald-c & Sunday-r begin. - $59 $177 $825

❑ **Mickey Mouse Magazine Vol. 5 #10,** 1940. Special Independence Day issue. - $59 $177 $825

❑ **Mickey Mouse Magazine Vol. 5 #11,** 1940. Hawaiian Holiday & Mickey's Trailer feature stories; last 36 pg. issue. - $59 $177 $825

❑ **Mickey Mouse Magazine Vol. 5 #12,** 1940. (Format change) The transition issue (68 pgs.) becoming a comic book. With only a title change to follow, Walt Disney's Comics & Stories #1 with the next issue. - $453 $1359 $7700

❑ **Mickey Mouse Magazine Mailer Envelope,** 1937. 14x10 fi" subscription mailer which features Mickey carrying Mickey Mouse Magazine Vol. 2 #10. - $59 $177 $825

PROMOTIONAL COMICS

❏ **Merry Christmas From Mickey Mouse,**
1939. K.K. Publications 16 pgs. (Shoe store giveaway) Donald Duck & Pluto app.; text with (Rare), c-reprint/Mickey Mouse Mag. V3 #3 (12/37) . - **$257 $771 $3600**

❏ **Donald And Mickey Merry Christmas,**
1943. Donald Duck-r/WDC&S #32 by Carl Barks. - **$75 $225 $1050**

❏ **Donald And Mickey Merry Christmas,**
1944. Donald Duck-r/WDC&S #35 by Carl Barks. - **$71 $213 $1000**

❏ **Donald Duck,**
1944. K.K. Publications (Christmas giveaway, paper-c 16 pgs.) Kelly cover reprint. - **$84 $252 $1175**

❏ **Donald And Mickey Merry Christmas,**
1945. "Donald Duck's Best Christmas," 8 pgs. Carl Barks. - **$107 $327 $1525**

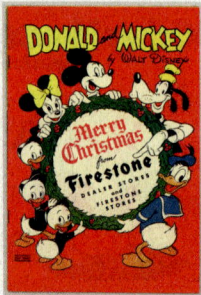

❏ **Donald And Mickey Merry Christmas,**
1946. Donald Duck in "Santa's Stormy Visit," 8 pgs. Carl Barks. - **$73 $219 $1025**

❏ **Donald And Mickey Merry Christmas,**
1947. Donald Duck in "Three Good Little Ducks," 8 pgs. Carl Barks . - **$73 $219 $1025**

❏ **Donald And Mickey Merry Christmas,**
1948. Donald Duck in "Toyland," 8 pgs. Carl Barks. - **$73 $219 $1025**

❏ **Donald And Mickey Merry Christmas,**
1949. Donald Duck in "New Toys," 8 pgs. Barks. - **$68 $204 $950**

❏ **Walt Disney's Comics & Stories,**
1943. Walt Disney Productions (36 pgs.) (Dept. store X-mas giveaway) X-mas-c with Donald & the boys; Donald Duck by Jack Hannah; Thumper by Ken Hultgren . - **$48 $144 $650**

❏ **March of Comics #4,**
1947. K.K. Publications Donald Duck by Carl Barks, "Maharajah Donald," 28 pgs. Kelly-c. - **$700 $2100 $9000**

❏ **March of Comics #8,**
1947. K.K. Publications Mickey Mouse, 32 pgs. - **$46 $138 $625**

PROMOTIONAL COMICS

❏ **March of Comics #20,**
1948. K.K. Publications Donald Duck by Carl Barks, "Darkest Africa," 22 pgs.; Kelly-c. - **$300 $900 $4800**

❏ **March of Comics #27,**
1948. K.K. Publications Mickey Mouse; r/in M.M #240. - **$37 $111 $440**

❏ **March of Comics #41,**
1949. K.K. Publications Donald Duck by Carl Barks, "Race to the South Seas," 22 pgs.; Kelly-c. - **$300 $900 $4800**

❏ **March of Comics #45,**
1949. K.K. Publications Mickey Mouse. - **$28 $84 $330**

❏ **March of Comics #56,**
1950. K.K. Publications Donald Duck; not by Barks; Barks art on back-c. - **$29 $87 $350**

❏ **March of Comics #60,**
1950. K.K. Publications Mickey Mouse. - **$27 $81 $320**

❏ **March of Comics #69,**
1951. K.K. Publications Donald Duck; Barks-a on back-c. - **$23 $69 $275**

❏ **March of Comics #74,**
1951. K.K. Publications Mickey Mouse. - **$21 $63 $245**

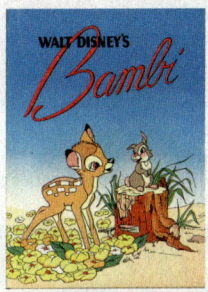

❏ **Bambi,**
1941. K.K. Publications Horlick's Malted Milk & various toy stores; text & pictures; most copies mailed out with store stickers on-c. - **$40 $120 $525**

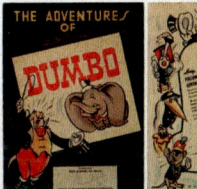

❏ **Dumbo Weekly Binder,**
1942. (Binder for premium books supplied by Diamond D-X Gas Stations). - **$475**

❏ **Dumbo Weekly,**
1942. (Premium supplied by Diamond D-X Gas Stations) #1. - **$64 $182 $900**

❏ **Cheerios Premiums,**
1947. W1 Donald Duck & the Pirates (pocket size, 32 pgs.). - **$11 $33 $105**

❏ **Cheerios Premiums,**
1947. W2 Bucky Bug & the Cannibal King (pocket size, 32 pgs.). - **$7 $21 $55**

795

PROMOTIONAL COMICS

❏ **Cheerios Premiums,**
1947. W3 Pluto Joins the F.B.I. (pocket size, 32 pgs.). - **$7** **$21** **$55**

❏ **Cheerios Premiums,**
1947. W4 Mickey Mouse & the Haunted House (pocket size, 32 pgs.). - **$8** **$24** **$65**

❏ **Cheerios Premiums,**
1947. X1 Donald Duck, Counter Spy (pocket size, 32 pgs.). - **$11** **$33** **$105**

❏ **Cheerios Premiums,**
1947. X2 Goofy Lost in the Desert (pocket size, 32 pgs.). - **$7** **$21** **$55**

❏ **Cheerios Premiums,**
1947. X3 Br'er Rabbit Outwits Br'er Fox (pocket size, 32 pgs.). - **$7** **$21** **$55**

❏ **Cheerios Premiums,**
1947. X4 Mickey Mouse at the Rodeo (pocket size, 32 pgs.). - **$8** **$24** **$65**

(U.S. version back cover)

(Canadian version back cover)

❏ **Cheerios Premiums,**
1947. Y1 Donald Duck's Atom Bomb by Carl Barks. Disney had banned reprinting this book until 1992. Canadian edition has different back cover (pocket size, 32 pgs.). - **$86** **$258** **$1200**

❏ **Cheerios Premiums,**
1947. Y2 Br'er Rabbit's Secret (pocket size, 32 pgs.). - **$7** **$21** **$55**

❏ **Cheerios Premiums,**
1947. Y3 Dumbo & the Circus Mystery (pocket size, 32 pgs.). - **$7** **$21** **$55**

❏ **Cheerios Premiums,**
1947. Y4 Mickey Mouse Meets the Wizard (pocket size, 32 pgs.). - **$8** **$24** **$65**

❏ **Cheerios Premiums,**
1947. Z1 Donald Duck Pilots a Jet Plane (not by Barks) (pocket size, 32 pgs.). - **$11** **$33** **$105**

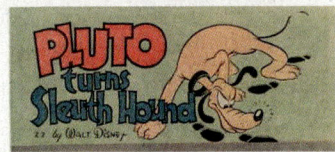

❏ **Cheerios Premiums,**
1947. Z2 Pluto Turns Sleuth Hound (pocket size, 32 pgs.). - **$7** **$21** **$55**

❏ **Cheerios Premiums,**
1947. Z3 The Seven Dwarfs & The Enchanted Mtn. (pocket size, 32 pgs.). - **$8** **$24** **$65**

❏ **Cheerios Premiums,**
1947. Z4 Mickey Mouse's Secret Room (pocket size, 32 pgs.). - **$8** **$24** **$65**

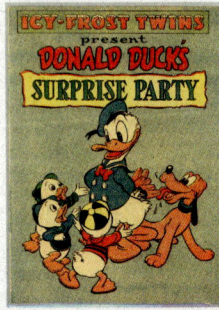

❏ **Donald Duck's Surprise Party,**
1948. Walt Disney Productions (16 pgs) (Giveaway for Icy Twins Ice Cream Bars) nn- (Rare) -Kelly-c/a. - **$300** **$900** **$3600**

PROMOTIONAL COMICS

❏ "Wheaties" Box With "Walt Disney Comic Books" Ad,
1950. 32 comics offered 1950-1951. Complete Box - **$125** **$375** **$500**

❏ Wheaties,
1950. A-1 Mickey Mouse & the Disappearing Island; (pocket-size, 32 pgs.). - **$7** **$21** **$55**

❏ Wheaties,
1950. A-2 Grandma Duck, Homespun Detective; (pocket-size, 32 pgs.). - **$7** **$21** **$50**

❏ Wheaties,
1950. A-3 Donald Duck and the Haunted Jewels; (pocket-size, 32 pgs.). - **$9** **$27** **$85**

❏ Wheaties,
1950. A-4 Donald Duck and the Giant Ape; (pocket-size, 32 pgs.). - **$9** **$27** **$85**

❏ Wheaties,
1950. A-5 Mickey Mouse, Roving Reporter; (pocket-size, 32 pgs.). - **$7** **$21** **$55**

❏ Wheaties,
1950. A-6 Li'l Bad Wolf, Forest Ranger; (pocket-size, 32 pgs.). - **$7** **$21** **$50**

❏ Wheaties,
1950. A-7 Goofy Tightrope Acrobat; (pocket-size, 32 pgs.). - **$7** **$21** **$50**

❏ Wheaties,
1950. A-8 Pluto and the Bogus Money; (pocket-size, 32 pgs.). - **$7** **$21** **$50**

❏ Wheaties,
1950. B-1 Mickey Mouse and the Pharaoh's Curse; (pocket-size, 32 pgs.). - **$8** **$24** **$60**

❏ Wheaties,
1950. B-2 Pluto, Canine Cowpoke; (pocket-size, 32 pgs.). - **$7** **$21** **$50**

❏ Wheaties,
1950. B-3 Donald Duck and the Buccaneers; (pocket-size, 32 pgs.). - **$9** **$27** **$85**

❏ Wheaties,
1950. B-4 Mickey Mouse and the Mystery Sea Monster; (pocket-size, 32 pgs.). - **$8** **$24** **$60**

❏ Wheaties,
1950. B-5 Li'l Bad Wolf in the Hollow Tree Hideout; (pocket-size, 32 pgs.). - **$7** **$21** **$50**

❏ Wheaties,
1950. B-6 Donald Duck, Trail Blazer; (pocket-size, 32 pgs.). - **$9** **$27** **$85**

❏ Wheaties,
1950. B-7 Goofy and the Gangsters; (pocket-size, 32 pgs.). - **$7** **$21** **$50**

❏ Wheaties,
1950. B-8 Donald Duck, Klondike Kid; (pocket-size, 32 pgs.). - **$9** **$27** **$85**

❏ Wheaties,
1951. C-1 Donald Duck and the Inca Idol; (pocket-size, 32 pgs.). - **$9** **$27** **$85**

❏ Wheaties,
1951. C-2 Mickey Mouse and the Magic Mountain; (pocket-size, 32 pgs.). - **$7** **$21** **$50**

❏ Wheaties,
1951. C-3 Li'l Bad Wolf, Fire Fighter; (pocket-size, 32 pgs.). - **$7** **$21** **$50**

PROMOTIONAL COMICS

❏ **Wheaties,**
1951. C-4 Gus and Jaq Save The Ship; (pocket-size, 32 pgs.). - **$7 $21 $50**

❏ **Wheaties,**
1951. C-5 Donald Duck in the Lost Lakes; (pocket-size, 32 pgs.). - **$9 $27 $85**

❏ **Wheaties,**
1951. C-6 Mickey Mouse and the Stagecoach Bandits; (pocket-size, 32 pgs.). - **$8 $24 $60**

❏ **Wheaties,**
1951. C-7 Goofy, Big Game Hunter; (pocket-size, 32 pgs.). - **$7 $21 $50**

❏ **Wheaties,**
1951. C-8 Donald Duck, Deep-sea Diver; (pocket-size, 32 pgs.). - **$9 $27 $85**

❏ **Wheaties,**
1951. D-1 Donald Duck in Indian Country; (pocket-size, 32 pgs.). - **$9 $27 $85**

❏ **Wheaties,**
1951. D-2 Mickey Mouse and the Abandoned Mine; (pocket-size, 32 pgs.). - **$8 $24 $60**

❏ **Wheaties,**
1951. D-3 Pluto and the Mysterious Package; (pocket-size, 32 pgs.). - **$7 $21 $50**

❏ **Wheaties,**
1951. D-4 Brer Rabbit's Sunken Treasure; (pocket-size, 32 pgs.). - **$7 $21 $50**

❏ **Wheaties,**
1951. D-5 Donald Duck, Mighty Mystic; (pocket-size, 32 pgs.). - **$9 $27 $85**

❏ **Wheaties,**
1951. D-6 Mickey Mouse and the Medicine Man; (pocket-size, 32 pgs.). - **$8 $24 $60**

❏ **Wheaties,**
1951. D-7 Lil's Bad Wolf and the Secret of the Woods; (pocket-size, 32 pgs.). - **$7 $21 $50**

❏ **Wheaties,**
1951. D-8 Minnie Mouse, Girl Explorer; (pocket-size, 32 pgs.). - **$7 $21 $50**

❏ **Kite Fun Book,**
1953. Pinocchio Learns About Kites, Pacific Gas & Electric Co. - **$43 $129 $575**

❏ **Kite Fun Book,**
1954. Donald Duck Tells About Kites-Fla. Power, P.G.&E. issue -7th page redrawn changing middle 3 panels to show P.G.&E. in story line; (All Barks-a) Scarce . - **$214 $642 $3000**

❏ **Kite Fun Book,**
1954. Donald Duck Tells About Kites-Fla. Power, S.C.E. & version with label issues -Barks pencils -8 pgs.; inks -7 pgs. (Rare). - **$300 $900 $3800**

❏ **Kite Fun Book,**
1955. Brer Rabbit in "A Kite Tail" Southern California Edison Company (16 pgs 5x7-1/4"). - **$29 $87 $340**

PROMOTIONAL COMICS

❑ **A New Adventure Of Walt Disney's Snow White And The Seven Dwarfs,**
1952. Bendix Washing Machines: (32 pgs., 5x7-1/4"). - **$11 $33 $110**

❑ **Robin Hood (New Adventures of...),**
1952. Walt Disney Productions (Flour giveaways, 5x7-1/4", 36 pgs.) "New Adventures of Robin Hood", "Ghosts of Wylea Castle", & "The Miller's Ransom" each… - **$5 $15 $35**

❑ **New Adventures Of Peter Pan,**
1953. Western Publishing Co. (5-7-1/4", 36 pgs.) (Admiral giveaway). - **$14 $42 $140**

❑ **Cheerios 3-D Giveaways,**
1954. (Set 1) 1-Donald Duck and Uncle Scrooge, The Firefighters; (pocket size, 32 pgs.). - **$9 $27 $85**

❑ **Cheerios 3-D Giveaways,**
1954. (Set 1) 2-Mickey Mouse and Goofy, Pirate Plunder; (pocket size, 32 pgs.). - **$9 $27 $85**

❑ **Cheerios 3-D Giveaways,**
1954. (Set 1) 3-Donald's Nephews, The Fabulous Inventors; (pocket size, 32 pgs.). - **$9 $27 $85**

❑ **Cheerios 3-D Giveaways,**
1954. (Set 1) 4-Mickey Mouse, Secret of the Ming Vase; (pocket size, 32 pgs.). - **$9 $27 $75**

❑ **Cheerios 3-D Giveaways,**
1954. (Set 1) 5-Donald Duck The Seafarers; (pocket size, 32 pgs.). - **$9 $27 $85**

❑ **Cheerios 3-D Giveaways,**
1954. (Set 1) 6-Mickey Mouse, Moaning Mountain; (pocket size, 32 pgs.). - **$9 $27 $75**

❑ **Cheerios 3-D Giveaways,**
1954. (Set 1) 7-Donald Duck, Apache Gold; (pocket size, 32 pgs.). - **$9 $27 $85**

❑ **Cheerios 3-D Giveaways,**
1954. (Set 1) 8-Mickey Mouse, Flight to Nowhere; (pocket size, 32 pgs.). - **$9 $27 $75**

❑ **Cheerios 3-D Giveaways,**
1954. (Set 2) 1-Donald Duck, Treasure of Timbuktu; (pocket size, 32 pgs.). - **$9 $27 $85**

❑ **Cheerios 3-D Giveaways,**
1954. (Set 2) 2-Mickey Mouse & Pluto, Operation China; (pocket size, 32 pgs.). - **$9 $27 $75**

❑ **Cheerios 3-D Giveaways,**
1954. (Set 2) 3-Donald Duck in the Magic Cows; (pocket size, 32 pgs.). - **$9 $27 $85**

❑ **Cheerios 3-D Giveaways,**
1954. (Set 2) 4-Mickey Mouse & Goofy, Kid Kokonut; (pocket size, 32 pgs.). - **$9 $27 $75**

❑ **Cheerios 3-D Giveaways,**
1954. (Set 2) 5-Donald Duck, Mystery Ship; (pocket size, 32 pgs.). - **$9 $27 $85**

❑ **Cheerios 3-D Giveaways,**
1954. (Set 2) 6-Mickey Mouse, Phantom Sheriff; (pocket size, 32 pgs.). - **$9 $27 $75**

❑ **Cheerios 3-D Giveaways,**
1954. (Set 2) 7-Donald Duck, Circus Adventures; (pocket size, 32 pgs.). - **$9 $27 $85**

❑ **Cheerios 3-D Giveaways,**
1954. (Set 2) 8-Mickey Mouse, Arctic Explorers; (pocket size, 32 pgs.). - **$9 $27 $75**

❑ **Cheerios 3-D Giveaways,**
1954. (Set 3) 1-Donald Duck & Witch Hazel; (pocket size, 32 pgs.). - **$9 $27 $85**

PROMOTIONAL COMICS

❏ **Cheerios 3-D Giveaways,**
1954. (Set 3) 2-Mickey Mouse in Darkest Africa; (pocket size, 32 pgs.). - **$9 $27 $75**

❏ **Cheerios 3-D Giveaways,**
1954. (Set 3) 3-Donald Duck & Uncle Scrooge, Timber Trouble; (pocket size, 32 pgs.). - **$9 $27 $85**

❏ **Cheerios 3-D Giveaways,**
1954. (Set 3) 4-Mickey Mouse, Rajah's Rescue; (pocket size, 32 pgs.). - **$9 $27 $75**

❏ **Cheerios 3-D Giveaways,**
1954. (Set 3) 5-Donald Duck in Robot Reporter; (pocket size, 32 pgs.). - **$9 $27 $85**

❏ **Cheerios 3-D Giveaways,**
1954. (Set 3) 6-Mickey Mouse, Slumbering Sleuth; (pocket size, 32 pgs.). - **$9 $27 $75**

❏ **Cheerios 3-D Giveaways,**
1954. (Set 3) 7-Donald Duck in the Foreign Legion; (pocket size, 32 pgs.). - **$9 $27 $85**

❏ **Cheerios 3-D Giveaways,**
1954. (Set 3) 8-Mickey Mouse, Airwalking Wonder; (pocket size, 32 pgs.). - **$9 $27 $75**

❏ **Brer Rabbit In "Ice Cream For The Party",**
1955. American Dairy Assoc. (5x7-1/4", 16pgs., soft-c) (Scarce). - **$38 $114 $450**

❏ **Cinderella In "Fairest Of The Fair",**
1955. American Dairy Assoc. (5x7-1/4", 16 pgs., soft-c). - **$10 $30 $90**

❏ **Davy Crockett In the Raid at Piney Creek,**
1955. Walt Disney Prod.: (16 pgs., 5x7-1/4", photo-c) -American Motors giveaway. - **$8 $24 $60**

❏ **Lady and the Tramp In "Butter Late Than Never",**
1955. American Dairy Assoc. 16 pgs 5x7-1/4", soft-c. - **$10 $30 $90**

❏ **Snow White And The Seven Dwarfs In "Milky Way",**
1955. American Dairy Assoc. (16 pgs., 5x7-1/4") - **$10 $30 $100**

❏ **Movie Classics,**
1956. Bambi #3; Reprints Four Color #186. - **$4 $12 $48**

❏ **Snow White And The Seven Dwarfs,**
1958. Western Publishing Co. (16 pgs, 5x7-1/4") "Mystery of the Missing Magic." - **$8 $24 $65**

❏ **Frito-Lay Giveaway,**
1962. Donald Duck "Plotting Picnickers". - **$6 $18 $70**

❏ **Frito-Lay Giveaway,**
1962. Ludwig Von Drake "Fish Stampede". - **$4 $12 $40**

❏ **Frito-Lay Giveaway,**
1962. Mickey Mouse and Goofy "Bicep Bungle". - **$4 $12 $45**

❏ **Donald Duck In "The Litterbug",**
1963. Keep America Beautiful: 1963 (5x7-1/4", 16 pgs., soft-c). - **$4 $12 $50**

THE RELUCTANT DRAGON

The Reluctant Dragon

Combining live action with animation was a Disney trademark since the studio's earliest days. In this 1941 film, the mixture takes place under the aegis of a studio tour. The broad storyline has noted humorist Robert Benchley and his wife visiting Disney's studio to suggest that Walt use Kenneth Grahame's short story, *The Reluctant Dragon*, for a cartoon.

Benchley wanders around the studio and runs into various members of the staff: animator Ward Kimball, voice actor Clarence Nash and even Walt Disney himself. Cartoon segments include *Baby Weems*, *How to Ride a Horse*, *The Reluctant Dragon*, a Donald Duck sequence drawn on *Old MacDonald Duck* (1941) and a sequence with Casey Jr, the circus train from *Dumbo* (1941). With so many different cartoons and live segments in the picture, *The Reluctant Dragon* required the services of six directors. The acting and vocal talent included Benchley, Nash, Kimball, Jimmy Luske, Frances Gifford and others.

The merchandise for this feature was limited. *The Reluctant Dragon* appears in *Four Color Comics* (first series) #13

REL-1

☐ **REL-1. Disney Studio Christmas Card With Reluctant Dragon And Others,**
1940. Stiff textured paper 5.5x6" closed fold-out card with front cover Fantasia fairy "Greetings." Card opens once to reveal fairy spelling out "From Walt Disney" and opens one final time for total length of 22" illustration of numerous characters from Fantasia plus Reluctant Dragon, Donald, Minnie, Goofy, Pinocchio, Snow White and Dopey singing Christmas carols . - **$65 $140 $225**

REL-2

☐ **REL-2. Baby Weems Ceramic Figurine,**
1941. Vernon Kilns U.S.A. Painted and glazed 6" tall figurine. Marked "37". - **$60 $125 $200**

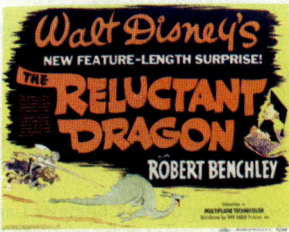

REL-3

☐ **REL-3. "The Reluctant Dragon" Lobby Card Set,**
1941. RKO Radio Pictures Inc. Set of eight, each 11x14" for original release. Title card features images of the Reluctant Dragon and Baby Weems. Four additional cards feature scenes/art from the Reluctant Dragon, two feature Baby Weems and one is a behind-the-scenes photo. Set - **$325 $700 $1250**

REL-4

REL-5

☐ **REL-4. "The Reluctant Dragon" Sheet Music,**
1941. Broadcast Music Inc. 9x12" four-page folder. - **$20 $35 $65**

☐ **REL-5. "The Reluctant Dragon" Book,**
1941. Garden City Publishing Co. 9.25x10.75" hardcover, 72 pages. - **$70 $140 $300**

REL-6

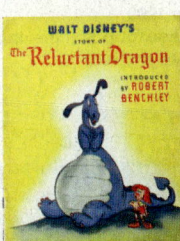

REL-7

☐ **REL-6. "Walt Disney's Reluctant Dragon" Comic Book,**
1941. Dell Publishing Co. Four Color Comic #13. Content includes photos related to movie release plus comic book stories also involving Goofy, Baby Weems, Donald Duck, Mickey Mouse in "The Sorcerer's Apprentice From Fantasia." - **$150 $450 $2500**

☐ **REL-7. "The Reluctant Dragon" Australian Book,**
1940s. Cardboard covered 8.5x10.75" condensed version of original 1941 version (72 pages) published by Garden City Co. This condensed edition is 32 pages. - **$40 $85 $165**

THE RESCUERS

The Rescuers

Adapted from the Margery Sharp books *Miss Bianca* and *The Rescuers*, this 1977 full-length animated feature took four years to make. It was worth the work, as the film turned out to be Disney's most profitable picture in a long time. Some reviewers called it the best film that Disney had produced since *Mary Poppins* (1964). A staff of over 250 worked on *The Rescuers*. Forty of them were .strictly animators.

In the film, the evil Madame Medusa has kidnapped an orphan named Penny, with plans to use her to get her hands on a diamond. Penny sends for help by using a message in a bottle for help. That bottle is found by the International Rescue Aid Society. The IRAS is a group of mice located in the basement of the UN. Soon rescuers Bianca and Bernard are off to rescue Penny. The mice are aided by a cat named Rufus, Orville, a bird of the Albatross Air Charter Service, and Evinrude the dragonfly.

The film was directed by John Lounsbury, Wolfgang Reitherman and Art Stevens. Animators included Frank Thomas, Ollie Johnston, Milt Kahl and Don Bluth. Among the vocal talent were Eva Gabor, Geraldine Page, Bob Newhart and Jim Jordan (of *Fibber McGee and Molly* radio fame). The music was composed by Carol Connors, Sammy Fain and Ayn Robbins. The song *Someone's Waiting for You* was nominated for an Academy Award.

Ultimately, *The Rescuers* was so successful that it inspired Disney's first sequel: *The Rescuers Down Under*, which was released theatrically in 1990.

Merchandise for both films included books, puzzles and records.

RES-1

❑ **RES-1. "The Rescuers" Lunch Box And Thermos,**
1971. Aladdin Industries. 7x8x4" deep metal box and 6.5" plastic thermos. (Thermos not shown)
Box - **$12 $25 $85**
Bottle - **$10 $20 $40**

RES-2

❑ **RES-2. Disney Studio Christmas Card,**
1976. Stiff glossy paper folder card 6x9". Front cover pictures Christmas ornament topped by Mickey at the hanger loop. Front top half of card opens vertically to add images of Santa hat and beard, Mickey, Donald, Pluto, Goofy and characters from The Rescuers. Card reverse has calendar for 1977. - **$20 $40 $70**

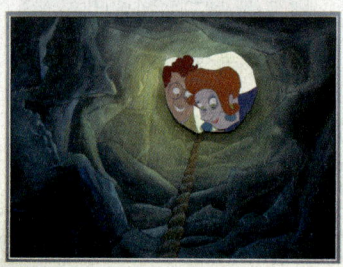

RES-3

❑ **RES-3. The Rescuers Animation Cel Set-Up,**
1977. Image is 4x3.5" with 14.25x10.75" background. A key set-up from this film featuring the world's largest diamond. - **$500 $1000 $2000**

RES-4

❑ **RES-4. "The Rescuers" Studio Fan Card,**
1977. Glossy stiff paper 5x7" replica of the film's movie poster. - **$5 $10 $15**

RES-5

❑ **RES-5. "The Rescuers" Pressbook And Ad Pad,**
1977. Two 10.5x14" glossy paper publicity aids for movie release. Pressbook is 24 pages. The "Program Facilities Ad Pad" consists of 13 one-sided stapled sheets of ad designs, theater flags, banners and "Disney Feline Stars Contest." Pressbook - **$15 $30 $50**
Ad Pad - **$3 $5 $10**

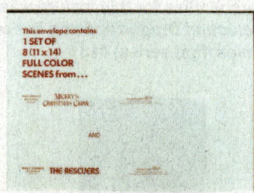

RES-6

❑ **RES-6. "The Rescuers/Mickey's Christmas Carol" Movies Re-Release Lobby Card Set With Envelope,**
1983. Set of eight 11x14" stiff glossy paper lobby cards in mailer envelope for double feature re-release of both movies. Title card art is for both films. Three cards are devoted to the Rescuers and remaining four to Christmas Carol. Set - **$12 $25 $40**

ROBIN HOOD

RES-7

❑ **RES-7. "The Rescuers/Mickey's Christmas Carol" Movie Re-Release Poster,** 1983. Stiff glossy 14x36" paper insert poster for double feature re-release of both movies. Header text is "A Dickens Of A Package For This Holiday Season" and art includes single Rescuer scene, three different scenes from Christmas Carol. - **$5 $12 $25**

Robin Hood

Disney combined two sources when making this 1973 full-length animated feature. They referenced their own 1952 live-action film, *The Story of Robin Hood*. In addition, they also consulted the twelfth-century legend of Reynard the Fox. Since all the characters in this film were to be played by animals, the Legend of Reynard was appropriate source material.

Robin Hood and Maid Marion are foxes, Little John is a bear, King Richard and Prince John are lions, Friar Tuck is a badger and Allan-a-Dale, who also functions as the narrator, is a rooster. In a series of swashbuckling adventures, Robin and his band defeat the evil Prince John and give their loot to the community. In the end, Robin marries Maid Marian.

Walt Disney had been looking at the Reynard the Fox stories since the thirties, but had concerns over the central character's lack of heroic qualities. Attaching an animal cast to the story of Robin Hood became a way to utilize many aspects of the aborted Reynard film.

Because *Robin Hood* shares some vocal talent with Disney's *Jungle Book* (1967), especially with Phil Harris voicing a bear character in each film, many people see more similarities between the two movies than there really are.

Robin Hood was directed by Wolfgang Reitherman. Animators who worked on the project include Frank Thomas, Ollie Johnston, Milt Kahl and John Lounsbury. Vocal talent includes Roger Miller, Peter Ustinov, Terry-Thomas, Andy Devine, George Lindsey and Pat Buttram.

The vocal work of talent such as Miller, Buttram (Mr. Haney on *Green Acres*), and Lindsey (better known as Goober on *The Andy Griffith Show*), tends to give the film a bit more of a "down-home" feel than other Disney features. The music was composed by Roger Miller, Johnny Mercer, Floyd Huddleston and George Bruns. The song *Love* was nominated for an Academy Award. The film was re-released in 1982 and has since seen numerous video releases.

Merchandise included books and records.

ROB-1

❑ **ROB-1. Robin Hood Animation Cel Set-Up Art,**
1973. Image is 10.5x8.5" with 16.25x10" background. Art features Robin Hood and Little John in disguise stealing his highness's gold. - **$500 $1000 $2000**

ROB-2

❑ **ROB-2. "Robin Hood Things-To-Do Book,"**
1973. Whitman. Book is 10.25x12" with 16 numbered pages. Has a number of character punchout figures plus finger puppets, castle and throne. Numbered pages have large simulated framed pictures and illustrated story scenes. Book also features several pages of cut-out masks. - **$10 $20 $30**

ROB-3

ROB-4

❑ **ROB-3. Studio Christmas Card,**
1973. Stiff paper card 6x9.25". Front has die-cut window around illustration that appears on inside of Prince John decorating a Christmas tree inside of his carriage. Front of card has scored margin panel along right edge so card can be folded to give it a dimensional design. - **$12 $25 $40**

❑ **ROB-4. "Robin Hood" Canadian Lunch Box,**
1973. Aladdin. 7.5x8x4" deep, Canadian issue only by Aladdin Industries Products of Canada. - **$20 $40 $65**

ROB-5

ROBIN HOOD

❑ **ROB-5. "Robin Hood Game,"**
1973. Parker Brothers, 8.74x17x1.5" deep box. - **$10 $20 $40**

ROB-6

❑ **ROB-6. "Robin Hood" Certificate,**
1973. Stiff paper is 11x14" proclamation for "An Honorary Member In The Fellowship Of Robin Hood And His Merry Menagerie." Includes facsimile signature of Robin as "Proprietor Of Good Things From Walt Disney Productions." - **$15 $25 $40**

ROB-7

❑ **ROB-7. Figural Water Gun,**
1973. Marx. 5.5x7x3" deep well-illustrated box containing 6.5" tall hard plastic figure gun with oversized head on small body that serves as the grip with trigger. Box - **$10 $20 $35**
Gun - **$10 $20 $35**

ROB-8

❑ **ROB-8. Canadian Robin Hood Cereal Premium Figures,**
c. 1973. Set of six 2.25" tall solid soft plastic figures c. 1973. Issuer is unknown but Canadian cereal box premiums. Set consists of Robin Hood, Maid Marian, Little John, Prince John, Friar Tuck and Sir Hiss. Each **$5 $10 $15**

Robin Hood, The Story of...

The time-honored story of Robin of Sherwood was made into one of Disney's first full-length, live-action features in 1952. King Richard leaves England to fight in the crusades and his brother tries to seize the throne. With the help of Maid Marian, Robin Hood and his band of Merry Men step in and save the crown. The king returns, makes Robin Earl of Locksley and gives him permission to marry Marian.

Filmed in England, *The Story of Robin Hood* was directed by Ken Annakin. The cast includes Richard Todd, Joan Rice, Peter Finch, Hubert Gregg and Patrick Barr. Many people consider this film the inspiration for a mid-1950s Robin Hood TV show which starred Richard Greene, though Disney was not involved in that production.

Merchandise included comic books (*Four Color Comics* #669) but was otherwise extremely limited.

RHS-1

❑ **RHS-1. "Walt Disney's Story Of Robin Hood" Store Sign,**
1952. Stiff paper sign advertising "Robin Hood Flour." 9.5x17". - **$35 $65 $110**

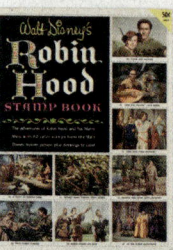
RHS-2

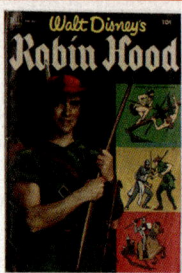
RHS-3

❑ **RHS-2. "Robin Hood Stamp Book,"**
1955. Simon & Schuster. 8.25x10.75" with 32 pages and set of 60 full color photo stamps mounted throughout. Book With Stamps - **$12 $25 $40**
Book with Unmounted Stamps - **$15 $35 $60**

❑ **RHS-3. "Robin Hood" Comic Book,**
1955. Dell. Book #669 from the Dell Four-Color series. - **$7 $21 $80**

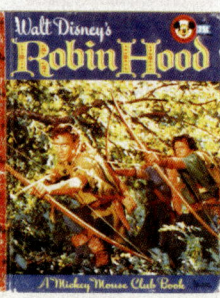
RHS-4

❑ **RHS-4. "Walt Disney's Robin Hood,"**
c. 1955. Book is 6.75x8" from "Mickey Mouse Club Books" series by Simon & Schuster with 24 pages. - **$10 $20 $35**

The Rocketeer

Source material for this 1991 sci-fi film was a successful comic book character created by Dave Stevens. Set in the 1930s, the action finds air race pilot Cliff Secord and his partner, Peevey, inventing a rocket pack which allows a man to fly. Cliff is helped by his girlfriend Jenny as thieves try to steal the rocket pack.

The *Rocketeer* comic had been a huge success. Stevens, a terrific artist, used 1950's pinup model Bettie Page as inspiration for his portrayal of the Jenny character. She was actually called Betty (sic) in Stevens' original comics. The sudden notoriety provided by Stevens' work propelled Page, at the time a recluse, back into the spotlight of modern-day fandom. This helped cement her status as a cultural icon.

The Rocketeer was not as big a box office success as Disney had hoped. Still, it was a strong feature that boasted a terrific cast and a wonderful look that stayed true to the feel of the thirties. It was directed by Joe Johnston. The cast includes Billy Campbell, Jennifer Connelly, Alan Arkin, Timothy Dalton and Paul Sorvino.

Promotional items include a Rocketeer "Thrill Club" badge and a watch. There were also statues, books, posters and figures.

ROC-1

☐ **ROC-1. "The Rocketeer" Movie Poster,** c. 1991. One-sheet poster 27x41" on heavy glossy paper. - **$12 $25 $45**

ROC-2

☐ **ROC-2. "Rocketeer" Employee Only Watch,** c. 1991. 1.5" diameter metal case with text on reverse "All Of Los Angeles Is Buzzing/Who Is The Rocketeer" with small Rocketeer image. Has incised edition number "406" from only 1500 produced. Mint As Issued - **$135**

ROC-3

☐ **ROC-3. "The Rocketeer" Resin Statue,** 1999. Sculpted by Kent Melton. 1,000 produced. There are also 50 bronze editions created a few years earlier. The resin version comes with a colorful box, but the bronze version does not.
Resin - **$165**
Bronze - **$2750**

Saludos Amigos

Set in South America and combining live action with animation, *Saludos Amigos* was one of two features that Disney made at the request of the Office of Inter-American Affairs. The idea was that to promote goodwill with Latin America, Walt and a crew of Disney staffers would visit the region and create a travelogue linking four cartoon sequences. At forty-two minutes, it is considerably shorter than other Disney animated features, but the studio still considers it part of their main canon. *Saludos Amigos* premiered in Rio de Janeiro in August, 1942 and in America in February, 1943.

The film's cartoon sequences are *Lake Titicaca,* featuring Donald Duck in the Andes; *Pedro,* a young airplane who learns the mail route from his father; *El Gaucho Goofy,* with Texas cowboy Goofy learning to be a gaucho; *Aquarela do Brasil,* featuring Donald's first meeting with the parrot José (or Joe) Carioca. José, who teaches Donald the samba, would become one of Disney's most popular 1940s cartoon characters.

Sequence directors included Ham Luske, Wilfred Jackson, Jack King and Bill Roberts. Animators include Ward Kimball, Fred Moore, Milt Neil, Milt Kahl and Wolfgang Reitherman. Vocal talent featured Clarence Nash, Pinto Colvig, Jose Oliveria and Fred Shields as the narrator. *Saludos Amigos* received Academy Award nominations for Best Sound, Best Scoring of a Musical Picture, and Best Song, *Saludos Amigos*. It was re-released theatrically in 1949.

Saludos Amigos merchandise included ceramic figures, books and records. Outside of the film, José Carioca became a popular character in comics. He was particularly loved in Brazil. There, he is still treated as one of Disney's leading lights.

SAL-1

☐ **SAL-1. "Saludos Amigos" Window Card,** c. 1942. 14x22" stiff cardboard from RKO Radio Pictures Inc. Top is usually blank to allow handwritten addition of local theatre name and/or show times. - **$85 $165 $325**

SALUDOS AMIGOS

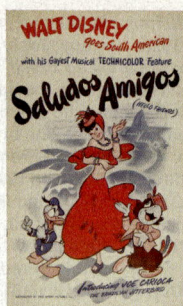

SAL-2

❑ **SAL-2. "Saludos Amigos" Movie Pressbook,**
c. 1942. RKO Radio Pictures Inc. 11x17" 24 page book with extensive advertising images, merchandise, poster designs, and related materials. - **$60 $125 $200**

SAL-3

❑ **SAL-3. "Pedro" Hardover, With Dust Jacket,**
1943. Grosset & Dunlap. 6.75x8.25" with 32 pages. Jacket - **$10 $25 $60**
Book - **$25 $50 $100**

SAL-4

❑ **SAL-4. Jose Carioca Pencil Drawing From Three Caballeros,**
1945. 4.25x5.75" image number "24." - **$50 $125 $225**

SAL-5

❑ **SAL-5. Three Caballeros Musical Toy,**
c. 1945. 3" diameter by 2.5" tall marked "Made In France/Autor. Walt Disney." - **$150 $300 $500**

SAL-6

❑ **SAL-6. Joe Carioca Figurine,**
c. 1946. 2.5x3.5x5.75 tall painted and glazed ceramic. American Pottery or Shaw. - **$50 $100 $150**

SAL-7

❑ **SAL-7. Saludos Amigos Brazilian Picture Album,**
c. 1960. Album is 9x12.5" with 40 pages, all text in Portugese. Contains complete set of 294 glossy 2.25x2.75" thin paper pictures. Complete - **$75 $150 $250**

SAL-8

❑ **SAL-8. Pedro Statue,**
2003. From the Classic Collection. - **$125**

The Shaggy Dog

A teenager speaks the magic words he finds on an amulet ("In Canis Corpore Transmuto") and finds himself magically changed into a big, clumsy sheepdog. This full-length, black-and-white 1959 feature proved to be one of Disney's strongest and longest lasting concepts. It inspired a theatrical sequel, *The Shaggy D. A.* (1976); a made-for-TV movie, *The Return of the Shaggy Dog* (1987); and a TV remake of the original film in 1994. The original film is also scheduled to be once again remade for theatres in 2005.

The original film was directed by Charles Barton and adapted from the novel *The Hound of Florence*, written by the author of *Bambi*, Felix Salten. The *Shaggy Dog* cast included Tommy Kirk, Kevin Corcoran, Annette Funicello and Fred MacMurray.

The Shaggy Dog appears in *Four Color Comics* #985. There are four known covers, each with a different photo. Each one still has the same content.

SHA-3

❏ **SHA-3. "The Shaggy Dog" Wallet,**
1959. Features "Furry" logo. - **$10 $18 $30**

SHA-6

❏ **SHA-6. "Walt Disney's Magazine,"**
1959. Vol. 4, #3 has cover photo with Roberta Shore and Shaggy Dog. Features include two-page Shaggy dog article and Part 1 of a Zorro story featuring Annette. - **$20 $50 $100**

SHA-1

SHA-4

❏ **SHA-1. Shaggy Dog Doll,**
1959. Gund. 14" tall stuffed plush doll with complete felt outfit and 3" diameter cardboard string tag. Doll - **$50 $100 $200**
Tag - **$12 $25 $50**

❏ **SHA-4. "The Shaggy Dog" Book/Comic Book,**
1959. Golden Press. Book is 6x9" with 60 pages. Comic is issue #985 of Dell Four Color series. Book - **$8 $12 $20**
Comic - **$10 $25 $115**

SHA-7

❏ **SHA-7. "The Shaggy D.A." Button,**
1976. 4" button with slogan "Win With Wilby."
- **$8 $15 $25**

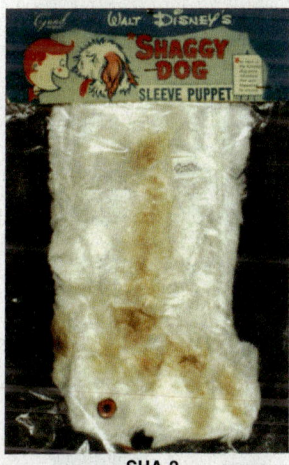

SHA-2

SHA-5

SHA-8

❏ **SHA-2. "Shaggy Dog Sleeve Puppet,"**
1959. Gund. 9x13.5" display bag contains 10" long plush puppet. Packaged - **$12 $25 $45**

❏ **SHA-5. "The Shaggy Dog Little Golden Book,"**
1959. Golden Press. 6.75x8" first printing. - **$6 $12 $20**

❏ **SHA-8. Tommy Kirk Autographed Photo,**
c. 1980s. Glossy 8x10" black and white reprint of an original still from "The Shaggy Dog." Boldly signed in black Sharpie "To John Good Luck Always Tommy Kirk." - **$10 $20 $30**

SILLY SYMPHONIES

Silly Symphonies

Between 1929 and 1939, Disney released 75 animated shorts under this umbrella title. There is a slight disagreement over who had the idea first, famed musician Carl Stalling or Walt. Several historians feel that the idea for Silly Symphonies seemed to generate from Stalling. Tired of having to tailor his music to the pre-planned actions of animated mice, he yearned to work on a series where music took the lead role and animation followed.

Regardless of the origin, Disney and Stalling worked together and came up with a series that not only was a decade-long success, but proved to be a great way for the animators to improve their skills. The series featured Disney's first use of a multi-plane camera. The studio's first color cartoon short was a Silly Symphony. Animators used the series to learn how to animate realistic human and animal figures which is a skill that proved essential to the success of *Snow White* (1937).

Notable cartoons in this series included *Three Little Pigs* (1933), *The Tortoise and the Hare* (1935), *Elmer Elephant* (1936) and *The Ugly Duckling* (1939), (itself a remake of a 1931 Silly Symphony). One of Disney's most important characters, Donald Duck, made his debut in the 1934 Symphony, *The Wise Little Hen*. Disney's first color cartoon, *Flowers and Trees* (1932), won an Academy Award. Over the years, six other Symphonies were also honored by the Academy.

Merchandise depended on the popularity of the individual cartoon. *Three Little Pigs* and *The Tortoise and the Hare* saw everything from plush animals to books and games, whereas other cartoons received little, if any, merchandising. *Silly Symphonies* ran for nine issues of *Dell Giants*. Various characters from the series were also featured in Four Color Comics. *Little Hiawatha* appears in Four Color Comics # 439, 787, 901, and 988. The Three Little Pigs appeared in *Four Color Comics* issue #218. The character of Li'l Bad Wolf appears in # 403, 473 and 564. As a series, the cartoons are featured in books and Disney-related magazines.

SIL-1

❑ **SIL-1. "Motion Picture Herald" With Silly Symphonies,**
1931. August 15 weekly 9.25x12.25" issue of movie exhibitor magazine for movie theater owners, 80 pages. Includes two-page ad for "Mickey Mouse/Silly Symphonies" Columbia short features with illustration of Mickey playing a one-stringed instrument and singing "Sing A Song Of Quickpence-A Pocketful Of Dough!" - **$50 $100 $150**

SIL-2

❑ **SIL-2. Silly Symphonies Witch Pencil Drawing From Babes In The Woods,**
1932. Art on 9.5x12" sheet of animation paper with 3.5x4.25" image in lead pencil. No. 122 from a numbered sequence. - **$100 $200 $300**

SIL-3

❑ **SIL-3. Silly Symphony Spanish Coloring Books,**
c. 1932. "Editorial Molino, Barcelona." 8.5x11.75" Book #2, "Babes In The Woods" and Book #4, "King Neptune" from the "Grande" largest size series of 24 Disney coloring books in five different series. Format is 16 pages. Each - **$20 $40 $80**

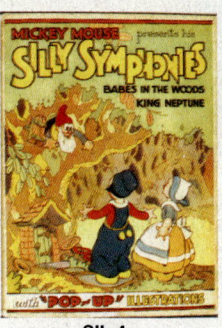
SIL-4

❑ **SIL-4. "Silly Symphonies" Pop-Up Book With Dust Jacket,**
1933. Blue Ribbon Books. 7.5x10" hardcover with 48 stiff cardboard pages plus four full color pop-up inserts. Full title is "Mickey Mouse Presents His Silly Symphonies/Babes In The Woods/King Neptune." Jacket - **$50 $150 $300** Book - **$150 $325 $900**

SIL-5

❑ **SIL-5. "Silly Symphonies" English Pop-Up Book,**
c. 1933. Dean & Son Ltd. 7.5x9.75" hardcover with 48 illustrated story pages interspersed by four pop-up "Scenic Illustrations." Book is essentially the same as U.S. version by Blue Ribbon Books copyright 1933. - **$150 $275 $450**

SIL-6

SILLY SYMPHONIES

☐ **SIL-6.** "Walt Disney's Mickey Mouse And Silly Symphony" Picture Disk Record Set With Sleeves, 1934. RCA Victor Records. Each two-sided 78 rpm picture disc is 7" diameter, in numbered inner sleeve along with outer sleeve. The records are #224 Who's Afraid Of The Big Bad Wolf Parts 1 and 2, #225 In A Silly Symphony/Mickey Mouse And Minnie's In Town, #226 Lullaby Land Of Nowhere/Dance Of The Boogie Men. Set In Sleeves - **$700 $1400 $2300** Outer Sleeve - **$50 $100 $200**
#224 Only - **$200 $400 $700**
#225 Only - **$300 $600 $900**
#226 Only - **$150 $300 $500**

SIL-9

☐ **SIL-9.** "Santa's Workshop From A Walt Disney Silly Symphony" English Book, 1934. Wm. Collins Sons Ltd. 6.75x9.25" hardcover, 128 pages. - **$150 $300 $600**

SIL-11

☐ **SIL-11.** "Father Noah's Ark From A Walt Disney Silly Symphony," 1934. Birn Brothers Ltd. England. 5x6.5" hardcover. 124 pages. - **$100 $200 $400**

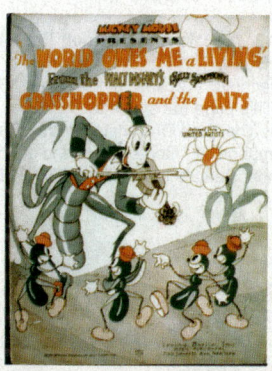

SIL-7

SIL-8

☐ **SIL-7.** "Silly Symphony Grasshopper And The Ants" Sheet Music, 1934. Irving Berlin Inc. 9.25x12" eight-page folio. - **$20 $40 $100**

☐ **SIL-8.** "Folio Of Songs From Walt Disney's Famous Pictures Mickey Mouse And Silly Symphony," 1934. Irving Berlin, Inc. 9x12" songbook, 32 pages. Each page has character illustrations and/or film scenes for 11 corresponding songs. - **$25 $50 $125**

SIL-10

☐ **SIL-10.** "Peculiar Penguins From A Walt Disney Silly Symphony" Book, 1934. David McKay Co. 6.25x8.25" hardcover, 52 pages. - **$50 $100 $200**

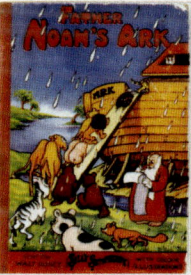

SIL-12

☐ **SIL-12.** "Mickey Mouse Presents Father Noah's Ark/A Silly Symphony" English Book, c. 1934. Birn Brothers Ltd. 7.25x9.5" hardcover, 128 pages. - **$200 $400 $700**

SILLY SYMPHONIES

SIL-13

SIL-13. Silly Symphony Primary Boy Sailor Toy Pencil Drawing,
1935. Art from 'Broken Toys' short on 10x12" sheet of animation paper with 2.25x4" image mostly in lead pencil. - **$60 $125 $175**

SIL-14

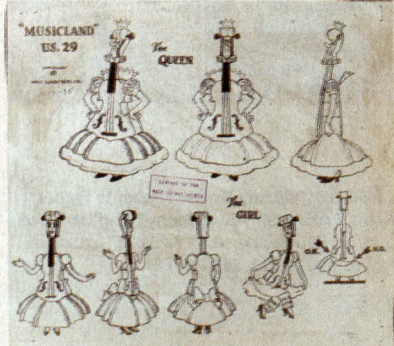

SIL-15

❑ **SIL-14. Robber Kitten Pencil Drawing,**
1935. Animation paper is 9.5x12" centered by 4x5.5" image of title character from Silly Symphony cartoon short. No. "52" from a numbered sequence. - **$75 $125 $200**

❑ **SIL-15. "Musicland" Model Sheet,**
1935. Sheet is 11.25x13" original photostatic copy for Silly Symphony short. Image is different views of two of the string instrument characters, Queen and Girl. Sheet is "U.S. 29" stamped "Library Of The Walt Disney Studio." - **$25 $50 $75**

SIL-16

❑ **SIL-16. "Mickey Mouse Presents Walt Disney's Silly Symphony 'Music Land'" Publicity Mailer,**
1935. United Artists Corp. 6x9.25" folder designed as pressbook with text about the film including synopsis, illustrations, movie poster, ad designs, mention of upcoming Silly Symphony feature "Three Orphan Kittens." - **$65 $135 $200**

SIL-17

SIL-18

❑ **SIL-17. "The Robber Kitten,"**
1935. Whitman Publishing Co. Hardcover, 9x10". 40 pages with dust jacket. Jacket - **$25 $40 $75** Book - **$40 $75 $175**

❑ **SIL-18. "Les Jouets De Noel" French Disney Book,**
1935. Hachette. 7.25x9.25" hardcover, 48 pages. Title page translates as "Mickey Presents The Toys Of Christmas/Walt Disney Silly Symphonies." Content is based on the 1932 short, Santa's Workshop. - **$65 $125 $200**

SIL-19

❑ **SIL-19. "The Tortoise And The Hare" Book,**
1935. Whitman. 8.75x9.75" hardcover with 40 pages. - **$40 $75 $175**

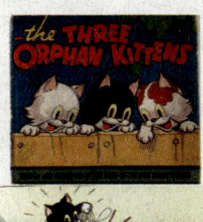

SIL-20

❑ **SIL-20. "The Three Orphan Kittens" Book,**
1935. David McKay Co. 9x10" hardcover from series of Silly Symphony books. Content is 48 pages. - **$40 $75 $175**

SILLY SYMPHONIES

 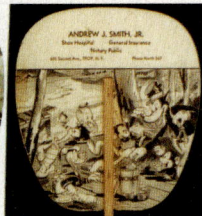

SIL-21

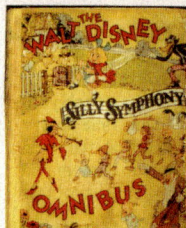 

SIL-24

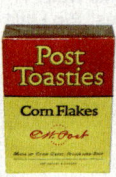 

SIL-26

SIL-22

❑ **SIL-21. "Silly Symphony" Premium Fan,**
c. 1935. Die-cut 8.25x14" stiff cardboard with front color scene of picnic attended by Big Bad Wolf, Tortoise & Hare, Elmer Elephant, Donald Duck, two monkeys plus background penguin diving off a dock and Three Pigs in a rowboat. Sponsor's name on reverse. - **$20 $40 $65**

❑ **SIL-22. "Rainbow Color" Art Glass Picture Featuring Silly Symphonies Funny Bunnies,**
c. 1935 Reliance Picture Frame Co. 7.75x10.75" wood framed reverse painted glass scene. - **$65 $125 $200**

SIL-23

❑ **SIL-23. "Sandman Of Lullaby Land" Silly Symphonies Art Glass Picture,**
c. 1935 Reliance Picture Frame Co. 7.75x10.75" wood framed reverse painted glass scene. - **$65 $125 $200**

❑ **SIL-24. "The Walt Disney Silly Symphony Omnibus" Rare English Book,**
c. 1935. Henderson and Spalding Ltd. 7.5x9.75" hardcover comprised of three stories, "The Pied Piper, Lullaby Land, Little Red Riding Hood (And The Big Bad Wolf)." Each story has front illustration, title pages, list of illustrations as if it was a separate book so effect is three separate books bound in a single binding. Each story has about 70 pages with illustrations, many in full color as well as full page or double-page size. - **$500 $1000 $1600**

SIL-25

❑ **SIL-25. Silly Symphony "Ninna Nanna" Italian Coloring Booklet,**
1936. A. Mondadori. 4.75x6" booklet No. 9 with 16 stiff paper pages and glossy cover. Content is based on the Silly Symphony Lullaby Land and features picture pages to be colored next to full color example pages. - **$30 $50 $100**

❑ **SIL-26. Post Toasties Cereal Box with Movie Promo,**
1936. Promotes the Walt Disney Silly Symphony "Cock O' The Walk" on back and the Melvin Purvis Junior G-Man Corps and Badge on side. - **$300 $600 $1000**

SIL-27 SIL-28

❑ **SIL-27. Silly Symphony Abner The Country Mouse Pencil Drawing,**
1936. 'Country Cousin' film short art on 10x12" sheet of animation paper centered by 3.5x4.25" image in three lead pencil accents. No. 80 from a numbered sequence. - **$60 $110 $165**

❑ **SIL-28. "Silly Symphonies Joy-A-Teers" Flashlight With Elmer Elephant And Tillie,**
1936. U.S. Electric Mfg. Co. 6.5" tall lithographed tin. - **$125 $275 $700**

SIL-29

SILLY SYMPHONIES

❑ **SIL-29. "Mickey Mouse Presents Walt Disney's Silly Symphonies Stories" Big Little Book,**
1936. Whitman. Book #1111 featuring Donald Duck, Peter Pig, Benny Bird and Bucky Bug all pictured on front cover. - **$40 $110 $215**

SIL-30

❑ **SIL-30. "Tobie Tortoise" Glass,**
c. 1936. From the second dairy series. 4.25" tall. - **$50 $100 $200**

SIL-31

SIL-32

❑ **SIL-31. Toby Tortoise English Toothbrush Holder,**
c. 1936. Maw & Sons. 2x2.5x4.25" tall painted and glazed ceramic figural of him wearing boxing gloves as he appeared in the 1936 short "Toby Tortoise Returns." Underside markings are Disney copyright, registration number and "Foreign." One of the very few figurals for this character. - **$150 $300 $575**

❑ **SIL-32. "Silly Symphony Annual" English Book,**
1937. Wm. Collins & Son Ltd. 8.25x11" hardcover, 96 pages. Content includes a two-page "Meet Uncle Walt" illustrated biography feature plus text stories with illustrations, comic panel stories, puzzles, games, cut-outs, coloring pages. - **$135 $275 $550**

SIL-33

SIL-34

❑ **SIL-33. Silly Symphony Concept Storyboard,**
c. 1937. Sheet of animation paper is 10x12" with cartoon concept art in lead pencil that fills nearly the entire sheet. Circus scene depicts "Flea Circus" tent with ticket barker out front. Running from the tent are a pair of male and female fleas as an elephant turns his head to watch the action. - **$100 $175 $300**

❑ **SIL-34. Merbabies Pencil Drawing,**
1938. Art is 3x6" showing six different Merbaby images. - **$65 $125 $200**

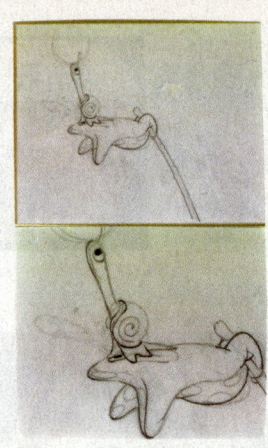

SIL-35

SIL-36

SIL-37

❑ **SIL-35. Pencil Drawing From Merbabies,**
1938. Image is 5x7". - **$50 $85 $125**

❑ **SIL-36. Pencil Drawing From Merbabies,**
1938. Art shows six starfish images each about 1.5" long or tall along with two starfish depicted with snails on them. - **$50 $85 $125**

❑ **SIL-37. Silly Symphonies Mother Goose Goes Hollywood Pencil Drawing,**
1938. Art for cartoon featuring famous movie stars. 10x12" sheet of animation paper has 2.5x3.25" image in lead pencil of Cab Calloway bursting through an opening. No. 323 from a numbered sequence. - **$85 $165 $250**

SILLY SYMPHONIES

SIL-38

❑ **SIL-38. "Mother Goose Goes Hollywood" Silly Symphony Model Sheet,**
1938. Original photostatic copy 11x14" model sheet on glossy paper for Silly Symphony short featuring movie stars as Mother Goose characters. Sheet is "RS-6" and includes Three Men In A Tub portrayed by Charles Laughton, Spencer Tracy, Freddie Bartholomew. - **$50 $100 $150**

SIL-39

❑ **SIL-39. Eddie Cantor Pencil Drawing,**
1938. Animation paper is 10x12" centered by 2x4" image of popular radio and movie entertainer. Art is from 'Mother Goose Goes Hollywood' Silly Symphony cartoon which featured movie stars caricatured as nursery rhyme characters. No. "58" from a numbered sequence. - **$85 $165 $250**

SIL-40

❑ **SIL-40. Eddie Cantor Pencil Drawing,**
1938. Animation paper is 10x12" centered by 2.5x5.5" image of popular radio and movie entertainer. Art is from 'Mother Goose Goes Hollywood' Silly Symphony cartoon which featured movie stars caricatured as nursery rhyme characters. No. "46" from a numbered sequence. - **$85 $165 $250**

SIL-41

❑ **SIL-41. Hugh Herbert Pencil Drawing,**
1938. Animation paper is 10x12" centered by 5x5.75" image of movie actor and possibly radio entertainer. Art is from 'Mother Goose Goes Hollywood' Silly Symphony cartoon which featured movie stars caricatured as nursery rhyme characters. No. "35" from a numbered sequence. - **$75 $150 $225**

SIL-42

❑ **SIL-42. Silly Symphony The Moth And The Flame Advertising Poster,**
1938. Walt Disney Enterprises. 20x30" glossy paper ad for Larvex insecticide issued the same year as the Silly Symphonies short "The Moth And The Flame" and featuring characters from that film. Illustration is of a living room being destroyed by 11 cartoon moths with text, "Will The Moths Enjoy Your Vacation? Don't Take Chances? Moth-Proof Your Clothes, Furniture, Rugs With Larvex." Reverse top and bottom margins are fitted by thin wood strips for hanging. - **$275 $550 $1100**

SIL-43

❑ **SIL-43. "Toby Tortoise And The Hare,"**
1938. Whitman. Linen-like book 9.5x12.25". 12 pages. - **$50 $125 $250**

SIL-44

❑ **SIL-44. Toby Tortoise And The Hare Linen-Like Book Argentinian Printing,**
1938. Libreria Hachette. 9.5x12.5" foreign printing of Whitman book No. 928 from 1938. - **$25 $50 $125**

SILLY SYMPHONIES

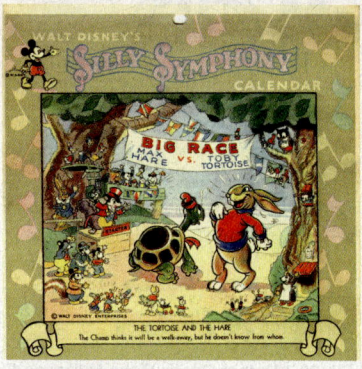

SIL-47

❑ **SIL-47. "Walt Disney's Silly Symphony Calendar,"**
1938. Brown & Bigelow. 9x16.5" 12 pages. Each page has full color illustration. Cover scene shows a scene from "The Tortoise and the Hare" which was pulled from a Good Housekeeping page. - **$135 $275 $550**

SIL-45

❑ **SIL-45. Shuffled Symphonies Card Game,**
1938. From England. 45 cards of different Disney characters. - **$50 $150 $250**

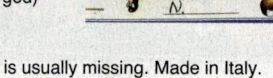

(Snow White tag enlarged)

SIL-46

❑ **SIL-46. Tortoise and "Bunny" Hare Rug,**
1938. Blue or bronze with Snow White tag on back. Tag is usually missing. Made in Italy.
Rug - **$50 $175 $375**
Rug with Snow White tag - **$75 $225 $475**

SIL-48

❑ **SIL-48. Tortoise And The Hare Australian Bank,**
c. 1938. 8" tall with 1.5" diameter cardboard tube. - **$50 $100 $200**

814

SILLY SYMPHONIES

SIL-49

❑ **SIL-49. "Toby Tortoise And The Hare" Australian Book,**
c. 1938. Ayers & James Pty. Ltd., Sydney. 7x9.25" softcover with 12 stiff paper pages, patterned after 1938 Whitman linen-like book #928. - **$35 $65 $125**

SIL-50

❑ **SIL-50. "The MerBabies" Post Card,**
c. 1938. Valentine & Sons Ltd. 3.5x5.5" English post card titled "The Merbabies' Deep-Sea Frolics." - **$15 $30 $50**

SIL-51

SIL-52

❑ **SIL-51. Wally Walrus And Penguins Glass,**
1939. 4.25" tall. - **$30 $60 $100**

❑ **SIL-52. "The Ugly Duckling" Glass,**
1939. Tumbler is 4.75" tall from 1939 "Walt Disney All Star Parade" series. - **$12 $25 $40**

SIL-53

❑ **SIL-53. "The Greedy Pig And Colt 1939 Walt Disney All Star Parade Glass,"**
1939. Glass is 4.25" tall with nice wrap-around art. - **$40 $75 $125**

SIL-54

❑ **SIL-54. "Silly Symphony Lights" Set With Three Little Pigs & Others,**
1930s. Noma Electric Corp. 6.25x16.25x2" deep boxed electrical strand set of hard plastic bulb shades, each finished by wrap-around decal. Each shade has different decal and five shades depict Pigs/Wolves. Remaining three depict Silly Symphony characters Tortoise and Hare, Cock Robin, Orphan Kitten. Box lid and side panel art is Christmas theme with Three Pigs, Big Bad Wolf, Three Little Wolves, Clara Cluck, Tillie, Elmer and Robber Kitten. Box interior has insert with large flip-up top panel with same art that appears on lid. Box - **$100 $200 $325**
Lights Complete - **$50 $100 $225**

SIL-55

❑ **SIL-55. Silly Symphonies Baby Rattle,**
1930s. Noma Electric Corp. 3.5" tall baby rattle constructed of two hard plastic light bulb shades glued together with particles added inside to make noise when shaken. Attached to rattle is cord that runs through a pair of wood balls used to tighten the cord around baby's wrist or other object. Depicted by decals are Elmer, Tillie, Clara Cluck, Cock Robin, Robert Kitten, Orphan Kitten. - **$20 $40 $65**

SIL-56

❑ **SIL-56. Canadian Cereal Box With Silly Symphonies,**
1930s. Canadian Postum Co. Ltd. 3x6.5x8.5" tall "Post Sugar-Crisp Corn Flakes" box with text in both English and French. Back panel has four-frame story about a boxing match between Toby Tortoise and Max Hare. Side panels include text "Mickey Mouse Toys And Games Or 'Movies' On Every Box By Walt Disney." - **$125 $250 $500**

SIL-57

815

SILLY SYMPHONIES

SIL-58

SIL-60

❑ **SIL-57. "Baby Mustn't Touch" Glass Picture,**
1930s. Reliance Picture Frame Co. 7.75x10.75" original wood frame around glass scene formed by painted image on reverse of glass then backed by cardboard. Reverse text indicates #D-120 from a series and also includes "Mickey Mouse And His Pals Of The Famous Silly Symphonies Are Always Ready To Brighten Your Home" and "Hand Processed Enamels Right On The Glass." - **$75 $150 $250**

❑ **SIL-58. "Water Babies' Circus And Other Stories" Book,**
1930s. D.C. Heath & Co. 6.25x8.5" hardcover from the educational "Walt Disney Storybooks" series. Content is 78 illustrated pages comprising four stories titled Snow White's Friends, The Hungry Bears, Beaver and His Brothers, Water Babies' Circus. - **$20 $40 $75**

SIL-59

❑ **SIL-59. "Water Babies' Circus" Book Art,**
c. 1940. Acetate sheet overlays combining to 7.75x12.5" and an art area of 3.5x5.5". Top sheet has black printed outline art, second sheet has the full color painted art. Original art for page 57 of "Water Babies' Circus And Other Stories" 1940 hardcover by D.C. Heath & Co. - **$60 $125 $175**

❑ **SIL-60. "Walt Disney Calendar" Premium,**
1942. Morrell's Hams. 8.25x14.5" 12-page monthly wall calendar with 8x8.5" superb color scene for each month above descriptive text and small character illustrations. Scene titles, from January to December are "The Three Little Pigs, Society Dog Show, The Ugly Duckling, The Funny Little Bunnies, Donald's Golf Game, Farm Yard Symphony, Brave Little Tailor, The Band Concert, The Grasshopper And The Ants, The Old Mill, Pinocchio, Snow White And The Seven Dwarfs." Bottom margins have illustrated Morrell ads. - **$125 $275 $550**

SIL-61

SIL-62

❑ **SIL-61. "Ugly Duckling" English Book With Silly Symphony,**
c. 1944. Collins Clear-Type Press. 7.25x10" hardcover, 60 pages. Content is multi-character despite the book's singular title reference to only the opening story. This is followed by five pages featuring Silly Symphony characters. Third and final story is "The Three Golden Keys By Mickey Mouse" and features him and Minnie, Donald, King Neptune. - **$75 $150 $250**

❑ **SIL-62. "The Ugly Duckling" Australian Book,**
c. 1944. Collins, Glasgow & London. 6.5x7.25" stiff paper 12-page story. - **$12 $25 $40**

SIL-63

❑ **SIL-63. Ugly Duckling Coloring Book,**
1945. Spanish title and text 6.75x9.25" stiff paper-covered 16 pages. - **$10 $20 $30**

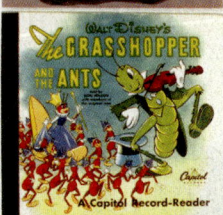

SIL-64

SIL-65

SILLY SYMPHONIES

❏ **SIL-64. "The Grasshopper And The Ants" Book/Record Set,**
1949. Capitol Records. 7.5x8.5" cardboard cover containing "Record-Reader" set #CBXF comprised of two 45 rpm records and bound-in story booklet with forty pages. - **$20 $35 $65**

❏ **SIL-65. "Winken, Blinken And Nod" Multiplane Painting,**
1940s. Frame is 8x8.75x1.75" deep original painted composition surrounding three-dimensional scene formed by two layers of glass over painted cardboard background. This is #6 in a series produced by Courvoisier Galleries for sale as representations of the Disney art form. - **$125 $225 $350**

SIL-66

❏ **SIL-66. "Bunnies In Bed" Multiplane Painting,**
1940s. Frame is 8x8.5x1.5" deep original painted composition surrounding three-dimensional scene formed by two layers of glass over painted cardboard background. This is #7 in a series produced by Courvoisier Galleries for sale as representations of the Disney art form. - **$125 $225 $350**

SIL-67

❏ **SIL-67. "The Tortoise And The Hare" Puzzle,**
1940s. Jaymar. 7x10x2" deep box. - **$12 $25 $40**

SIL-68

❏ **SIL-68. "The Ugly Duckling" Puzzle,**
1940s. Jaymar. 7x10x1.75" deep boxed jigsaw puzzle from "Series No. 3." - **$15 $30 $60**

SIL-69

❏ **SIL-69. Water Babies Thermometer Plaque,**
1940s. Kemper-Thomas Co. 6x6x.25" thick ceramic tile. - **$15 $30 $50**

SIL-70

❏ **SIL-70. Painted Cover Rough To Dell Giant #5 "Silly Symphonies" Comic Book Cover Art,**
1955. Rough is 5x7.25" for front and back cover of Dell Giant issue #5 for February. Art is tempera and watercolor, attributed to Bob Grant. A total of 21 characters are pictured. Unique, Near Mint - **$650**

SIL-71

❏ **SIL-71. "Silly Symphonies" Comic Books,**
1950s. Dell Giant consecutive issues #1-8 from total of nine under this title published 1952-1958. Each is 96 pages of comic stories for many different Disney characters, films, etc. along with several puzzle and game pages and cut-outs. First - **$30 $80 $550**
Others Each - **$15 $50 $325**

SIL-72

❏ **SIL-72. "The Tortoise and the Hare" Movie Figures,**
2000. Two figures from the Disney Classic collection. Each - **$110**

Sleeping Beauty

This 1959 film was created during one of the most active periods in Walt Disney's career. Disneyland had opened but still drew a lot of his time. There was a weekly network television show. Than, there was also the money side of the business that demanded constant attention. Still, Walt Disney was an animator at heart. He knew that the prevailing feeling of the day was that Disney films had become old-fashioned. Especially in light of the recent success that UPA Studios was having with their experimental and highly stylized approach to the art of animation. The advances made by UPA had caused critics to hold them up as the leading example of animation excellence. UPA may have had the critic's eye and ear, but they did not have Walt Disney's drive for perfection and incredible sense of detail. In order to make the story of *Sleeping Beauty* into the greatest animation film of all-time, Disney started by bringing in his top artists.

Marc Davis, John Lounsbery, Milt Kahl, Eric Cleworth, Frank Thomas, Ollie Johnston and John Sibley were each allowed to do many more tests and pencils than would have been normally allowed for a big budget animation film. Disney also allowed the artists and animators extra time to clearly refine and detail many points of the film. Often, the top-level animators found themselves doing detailed work on in-between scenes that would have normally been a bit more rushed. This extra time, combined with the use of his top animators on assignments that might have usually been relegated to someone else, allowed a highly individualistic sense of style to come through to the final production. Another positive aspect was the additional time used for deepening the characterizations of the film's animated cast. The film developed more advanced characters that were fuller in personality and scope than previous animated films had seen. No matter what the artists and animators did, it still had to get by Walt's unrelenting eye for detail. It was this drive for perfection on the film that almost brought his studio to bankruptcy.

The final budget approached six million dollars. In the end, it was all worth the time and extra cost because the film quite possibly saved the studio. Some felt for all its forward-looking animation and the lushness of the final production, it was still a good old-fashioned Disney fairy tale. In fact, some went as far as to say it was actually *Snow White and the Seven Dwarfs* retold. One of the hidden facts about *Sleeping Beauty* is that it did in fact incorporate a few scenes that had originally been planned for Snow White over twenty years earlier. Those scenes had been cut from the film before it had actually been animated. Released in 70MM widescreen, with a six-track sound mix, the film was an incredible success and returned Disney to the number one spot in the world of animation. Many movie-goers actually saw the film in 35mm with a stereo mix. This was still very innovative for the time. Today, the technical achievements, as well as the leaps in detailed characterizations, are echoed in modern Disney films such as *The Little Mermaid* and *Beauty and the Beast*. The story adaptation for the film was from the version written by Charles Perrault and published in his 1697 book, *Stories or Tales from Times Past, with Morals: Tales of Mother Goose*. It was adapted for the screen by Erdman Penner. Vocal talent included Mary Costa as Princess Aurora/Briar Rose, Bill Shirley as Prince Phillip, and Eleanor Audley as the magnificent Maleficent. The Three Fairy Godmothers became stars in their own right. The musical adaptation of Tchaikovsky's *Sleeping Beauty Ballet* was arranged by George Burns. The background music used Tchaikovsky's ballet as a reference point. The original ballad, *Once Upon a Dream,* stands out as one of the finest musical moments in a Disney animated feature. The supervising director on the film was Clyde Geronimi.

Merchandise includes figurines, records, magazines, ceramics by both Hagen-Renaker, plastic Disneykins by Marx toys and dolls. *Sleeping Beauty*, as well as characters from the film, appears in *Four Color Comics* #973 and 984.

SLE-1

❏ **SLE-1. Sleeping Beauty "Disney Time" Alarm Clock,**
1957. Clock is 2.5x4x4.25" tall hard plastic marked on back "Made Exclusively For Phinney-Walker In Japan." Back of clock is transparent green so inner mechanism is visible. - **$40 $75 $125**

SLE-2

SLE-3

❏ **SLE-2. "Sleeping Beauty " Glass,**
1958. Clear glass is 5" tall with weighted bottom from set of six. Each - **$15 $30 $50**

❏ **SLE-3. "Sleeping Beauty" Canadian Glass,**
1958. Glass is 5" tall tumbler #2 from numbered series. Each - **$15 $30 $50**

SLE-4

❏ **SLE-4. "Sleeping Beauty Dolls With Magic Stay-On Dresses" Boxed Set,**
1958. Whitman. 8.25x15.5x1" deep box includes crayons and plastic scissors. Uncut - **$40 $85 $150**

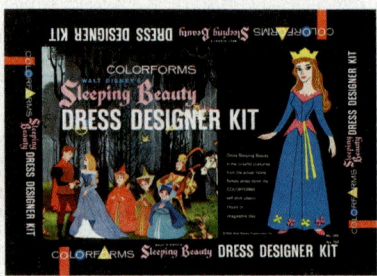

SLE-5

❏ **SLE-5. "Sleeping Beauty Dress Designer Kit" Box Proof,**
1959. Colorforms 11.25x16.25" glossy paper proof for merchandise item box lid. Proof is that company's archives copy. - **$20 $40 $75**

SLEEPING BEAUTY

SLE-6

SLE-10

❑ **SLE-10. Sleeping Beauty Animation Cel Set-Up Art,**
1959. Image is 8.75x6" with 11x10.75" background. Art features Flora, one of the three good fairies who mentors Briar Rose. - **$600 $1200 $2500**

SLE-13

SLE-14

❑ **SLE-6. Autographed Sleeping Beauty Cel,**
1959. 12.5x14" with 3.25x5.5" image signed by Frank Thomas, Ollie Johnston and Marc Davis. Near Mint - **$550**

SLE-7

SLE-8

❑ **SLE-7. Prince Phillip Pencil Drawing From Sleeping Beauty,**
1959. Large sheet of animation paper is 12.5x15.5" with 2.5x7" full figure image. #174 from a numbered sequence. - **$40 $65 $115**

❑ **SLE-8. Briar Rose Pencil Drawing,**
1959. Animation paper is 12.5x15.5" oversized centered by large 4.5x7" rear image of Sleeping Beauty movie character. No. "60" from a numbered sequence. - **$40 $65 $115**

SLE-9

❑ **SLE-9. "Sleeping Beauty" Disney Concept Art,**
1959. 6x15" tempera painting. By noted artist Eyvind Earle. Unique, Same or Similar - **$2150 $4250 $8500**

SLE-11

❑ **SLE-11. Sleeping Beauty Concept Art,**
1959. Image is 14.25x6.25" featuring the wicked dark fairy Maleficent who has transformed into a dragon. Painted by Disney artist Eyvind Earle. Unique, Same or Similar - **$2500 $5000 $10000**

SLE-12

❑ **SLE-12. Sleeping Beauty Briar Rose Concept Art,**
1959. Image is 13.75x6.25" featuring Briar Rose in the forest with a flower basket. Painted by Disney artist Eyvind Earle. Unique, Same or Similar - **$2000 $4000 $8000**

❑ **SLE-13. Sleeping Beauty Oversized Mexican Lobby Cards,**
1959. Two each 12.5x16.5". - **$10 $20 $30**

❑ **SLE-14. "Sleeping Beauty" Boxed Puzzle,**
1959. Jaymar. 7x10x2" deep box contains "Triple Thick" puzzle titled "The Wicked Fairy's Gift." - **$8 $15 $30**

SLE-15

❑ **SLE-15. "Sleeping Beauty" Boxed Puzzle,**
1959. Jaymar. Box is 7x10x2" deep and contains "Triple Thick" puzzle titled "A Gown For Briar Rose." - **$8 $15 $30**

SLEEPING BEAUTY

SLE-16

❑ **SLE-16. "Sleeping Beauty" Prince Philip Ring,**
1959. Bright silver luster plastic base with aqua blue shield on top with words "Truth Virtue." Shield has small raised piece with an open area holding a 7/8" long miniature removable sword in bright silver luster. - **$20 $40 $75**

SLE-17

❑ **SLE-17. Sleeping Beauty Canadian Lunch Box,**
1959. General Steel Wares. 7x8x4" deep metal. - **$125 $300 $600**

SLE-18

❑ **SLE-18. "Sleeping Beauty" Canadian Lunch Pail,**
1959. General Steel Wares. 4.5x7x4.5" tall tin lithographed. - **$115 $275 $575**

SLE-19

❑ **SLE-19. "Sleeping Beauty Castle" Punch-Out Premium Set,**
1959. Hills Brothers Coffee. 13.5x23.5x.5" deep plain cardboard mailing box contains complete and unused set. Four different stiff paper punch-out sheets, each with overall size of 13x39.5". Includes: Princess Aurora, Prince Phillip, The Fairy Godmothers, King Stefan, King Hubert, Maleficent, knights, guards, etc. Accessory pieces including catapult, spinning wheel, crib, table, etc. Each figure is about 2.5" tall. Unpunched - **$35 $75 $135**

SLE-20

❑ **SLE-20. "Sleeping Beauty Golden Record,"**
1959. Stiff paper sleeve 7x7.75" contains 45 rpm black vinyl record. - **$5 $12 $20**

SLE-21

❑ **SLE-21. "Sleeping Beauty" Song Folio,**
1959. Walt Disney Music Co. 9x12" with 32 pages. - **$15 $35 $65**

❑ **SLE-22. "Sleeping Beauty" Un-cut Decal Sheet,**
1959. Unused sheet is 6.5x12.5". - **$15 $30 $50**

SLE-22

SLE-23

❑ **SLE-23. "Sleeping Beauty Infants' And Children's Catalogue,"**
1959. Disney Character Merchandising Division "Fall and Winter" 8.5x11" catalogue of stapled 11 two-sided glossy paper sheets. Pictured, described and priced are numerous Sleeping Beauty merchandise items including Prince Phillip hat, crib mattress, doll car-bed, costumes, doll, night light, crib mobile, handkerchiefs, clothing items. Catalogue is from the archives of "Disney Legend" Al Konetzni, creator of numerous Disney toys and merchandise items. - **$35 $65 $110**

SLE-25

SLE-24 SLE-26

820

SLEEPING BEAUTY

❑ **SLE-24. "Sleeping Beauty Lite-Up Magic Wand,"**
1959. Bantamlite Inc. 4x19.5" display card holds 16" long hard plastic wand. Carded - **$15 $30 $60**

❑ **SLE-25. Fairy Godmother Merryweather Figurine,**
c. 1959. Hagen-Renaker. 1.75" tall. - **$50 $100 $150**

❑ **SLE-26. Fairy Godmother Fauna Figurine,**
c. 1959. Hagen-Renaker. 2.25" tall. - **$50 $100 $150**

SLE-27

❑ **SLE-27. Flora From Sleeping Beauty Ceramic Figurine,**
c. 1959. Hagen-Renaker. 2.25" tall. - **$50 $100 $150**

SLE-28   SLE-29

❑ **SLE-28. King Hubert From Sleeping Beauty Figurine,**
c. 1959. Hagen-Renaker. 2-1/8" tall. - **$65 $125 $250**

❑ **SLE-29. Queen From Sleeping Beauty Figurine,**
c. 1959. Hagen-Renaker. 2-3/8" tall. - **$75 $150 $250**

SLE-30

❑ **SLE-30. Prince Phillip From Sleeping Beauty Figurine,**
c. 1959. Hagen-Renaker. 2.75" tall glazed ceramic. - **$75 $150 $250**

SLE-31

❑ **SLE-31. "Maleficent" Hand Puppet,**
c. 1959. Gund Mfg. Co. 11" tall toy formed by soft vinyl head and fabric handcover body with stitched tag and inner squeaker mechanism. - **$45 $85 $150**

SLE-32

❑ **SLE-32. "Sleeping Beauty Game,"**
c. 1959. Parker Brothers. 10.25x17x1.5" deep box containing game consisting of 16.5" square playing board, four spinner cards, illustrated playing cards deck, plastic sticks representing "wands." - **$12 $25 $50**

SLE-33

❑ **SLE-33. Maleficent Glazed Ceramic Figure By Hagen-Renaker,**
c. 1959. 2.5" tall. One of the scarcest in their series. - **$300 $600 $1000**

SLE-34

❑ **SLE-34. Danish Sleeping Beauty Premium Hardcover Card Album,**
1960. Issued by Rich's. 10.5x11.5" with 34 pages. 187 spaces for cards. Album Only - **$12 $25 $40**

SLE-35

❑ **SLE-35. "Sleeping Beauty" Record,**
1963. Disneyland label. 12.25x12.25" cardboard album cover contains 33-1/3 rpm. - **$5 $10 $15**

SLEEPING BEAUTY

SLE-36

SLE-37

SLE-38 SLE-39

❏ SLE-36. Sleeping Beauty Disneykin,
1960s. Marx. 1.5" tall hand-painted hard plastic figure. - **$15 $30 $60**

❏ SLE-37. "New Disneykins TV Scenes" Sleeping Beauty Set,
1960s. Marx. 1x3.25x2.75" tall box with display window contains pair of 1.5" tall hand-painted hard plastic figures. - **$50 $100 $160**

❏ SLE-38. "Prince Charming" Boxed Second Series Disneykin,
1960s. Marx. 1x1.5x2.25" tall window display box contains hand-painted hard plastic figure. Boxed - **$25 $50 $100**
Loose - **$10 $20 40**

❏ SLE-39. "Flora" Boxed Second Series Disneykin,
1960s. Marx. 1x1.5x2.25" tall window box with hand-painted hard plastic figure. Boxed - **$25 $50 $100**
Loose - **$10 $20 $40**

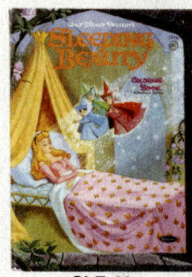

SLE-40

❏ SLE-40. "Sleeping Beauty Coloring Book,"
1970. Whitman. 8x10.75" has 128 pages. - **$12 $25 $40**

SLE-41

SLE-42

❏ SLE-41. "Sleeping Beauty" Vinyl Lunch Box With Thermos,
1970. Aladdin. 7x9x4" deep vinyl box comes with 6.5" tall plastic thermos. Box - **$65 $125 $200** Bottle - **$15 $30 $60**

❏ SLE-42. "Sleeping Beauty" Doll Boxed,
1977. Effanbee. 8x18x4" deep display box with cellophane window over 14" tall poseable vinyl doll from Disney series commissioned to Effanbee. Boxed - **$15 $30 $50**

SLE-43

❏ SLE-43. Sleeping Beauty Sericel,
c. 1990s. 11x14" with 7x10" image and laser background. Limited edition of 5000 with "The Walt Disney Company/Sericel Certified" seal. Mint As Issued - **$165**

SLE-44

❏ SLE-44. Brass Key Keepsake Collection Sleeping Beauty doll,
2004. Porcelain collectible doll, 7 1/2 " inches high. - **$10**

SLE-45

❏ SLE-45. Sparkle Princess Collection Sleeping Beauty doll,
2005. Fashion doll with collectible ring, 11 1/2 " tall. - **$12**

SNOW WHITE AND THE SEVEN DWARFS

Snow White and the Seven Dwarfs

At the height of the Depression, Walt Disney staked his entire life's savings on a single idea: that a full-length animated feature would be able to capture the public's attention. Originally budgeted at a half million dollars, which at the time was already an astronomical sum, the feature, released December 21, 1937, eventually cost $1.4 million dollars.

Years earlier, in his newsboy days, Walt Disney had seen a silent screen version of *Snow White* that featured the actress Marguerite Clark. Memories of the film stayed with him for years. When it came time to make a feature cartoon, the fairy tale by the brothers Grimm was his first choice for a subject. There are many reasons for the success of the film, but primary among them is the quality of the animation, which, almost seventy years later, is still stunning. Other reasons include the fully-fleshed-out supporting cast as well as the memorable music.

Few of Disney's villains can match the evil of Snow White's wicked stepmother. Jealous because her magic mirror has proclaimed Snow White as the fairest in the land, the stepmother wants her killed. Knowing she is in danger, Snow White flees and, lost in the forest, is taken in by seven dwarfs.

The decision to give each of the dwarves a distinctive personality was one of the biggest reasons for the movie's success. Their scenes are among the film's highlights. The scenes with the stepmother are as close to evil as Disney will ever get.

When the film was released in England, censors initially found it too scary for children. Viewers under sixteen had to be accompanied by an adult.

Supervising director was David Hand. Animators included Grim Natwick, Gustaf Tenggren, Ward Kimball, Fred Moore, Frank Thomas and Charles Philippi. Background artists for the incredibly lush and detailed cartoon included Samuel Armstrong, Claude Coats and Maurice Noble.

Vocal talent included Adriana Caselotti (Snow White), Harry Stockwell, Lucille LaVerne, Billy Gilbert, Pinto Colvig (also known as the voice of Goofy) and Stuart Buchanan. Music was by Frank Churchill, Leigh Harline and Paul Smith. In 1939, *Snow White* received a special Academy Award consisting of one full-sized Oscar and seven smaller ones. The film was theatrically reissued eight times. Although eventually outpaced by *Gone With the Wind* (1939), *Snow White* was for some time the most financially successful film ever made.

Merchandise was phenomenal in scope and quality. There were records, sheet music, figures, dolls and hundreds of other items. Characters from *Snow White and the Seven Dwarfs* also appear in the following issues of *Four Color Comics*: #19, 49, 227 and 382.

SNW-1

❑ **SNW-1. Early Snow White Storyboard Featuring Sleepy,**
c. 1934. 5.25x7.5" trimmed sheet of animation paper with 4x5.75" image. - **$250 $500 $1000**

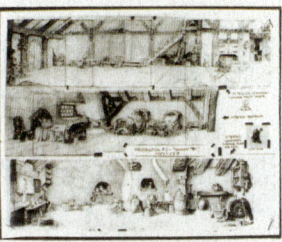

SNW-2

❑ **SNW-2. "Snow White" Vintage Photostat Production Sheet,**
1936. Sheet is 11x14" paper depiction of three different interior views of the cottage including bedroom and downstairs. Photostats were provided to studio artists as a design guide. - **$35 $65 $100**

SNW-3

❑ **SNW-3. Bashful Model Sheet,**
1936. Sheet is 10x12" reproduced from the one original and distributed to various artists within the studio as a guide in drawing the character. This is "Sheet 1" of full figure and facial images with notations. - **$35 $65 $100**

SNW-4

SNW-5

❑ **SNW-4. Sleepy Animation Set-Up Art,**
1937. Courvoisier. Image is 4.25x4" and background is 8x8" studio prepared woodgrain image. - **$500 $1000 $2000**

❑ **SNW-5. Snow White Animation Set-Up Art,**
1937. Image is 8.25x8.25" production cels with 15.5x11" reproduction background. - **$2000 $4000 $7000**

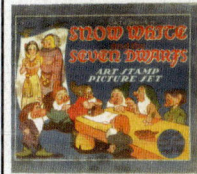

SNW-6

❑ **SNW-6. "Snow White And The Seven Dwarfs Art Stamp Picture Set,"**
1937. Set of eight with an ink pad marked "Butler Brothers." Box is 7x8.25x.75" deep. - **$65 $125 $225**

SNW-7

SNOW WHITE AND THE SEVEN DWARFS

❑ **SNW-7. Snow White Pencil Drawing,** 1937. Animation paper is 10x12" with 3.5x6" image from a numbered sequence. - **$250 $500 $1000**

SNW-8

SNW-9

❑ **SNW-8. Bashful Pencil Drawing From Snow White,** 1937. Image is 2.5x4.75" from a numbered sequence and this is "374." - **$100 $200 $350**

❑ **SNW-9. Witch Pencil Drawing,** 1937. Animation paper is 10x12" with 5.5x5" image. - **$400 $800 $1600**

SNW-10

❑ **SNW-10. Witch Pencil Drawing From Snow White,** 1937. Image is 7.25x5.25". Reverse features a studio stamp. - **$250 $500 $850**

SNW-11

❑ **SNW-11. Witch Pencil Drawing From Snow White,** 1937. Image is 5x6". Attached to reverse is certificate from "Gallery Lainzberg, Cedar Rapids, Iowa" which describes this as an original animation drawing from Snow White, 1937 and notes animator "Norman Ferguson." - **$200 $450 $750**

SNW-12

❑ **SNW-12. Doc Pencil Drawing From Snow White,** 1937. Image is 4x6.5". From a numbered sequence and this is "163." - **$100 $200 $300**

SNW-13

❑ **SNW-13. Sneezy Pencil Drawing,** 1937. Animation paper sheet 10x12" with 3.5x4.5" preliminary rough image for Snow White movie. Rough sketch is attributed to Disney artist Bill Tytla. No. "105" from a numbered sequence. - **$65 $135 $200**

SNW-14

❑ **SNW-14. Doc Pencil Drawing,** 1937. Animation paper is 10x12" with 3.5x6.5" image for Snow White movie. No. "213" from a numbered sequence. - **$75 $175 $300**

SNW-15

❑ **SNW-15. Sneezy Pencil Drawing,** 1937. Animation paper is 12.5x15.5" oversized centered by 3.5x4.75" image for Snow White movie. No. "276" from a numbered sequence. - **$75 $175 $300**

SNW-16

SNOW WHITE AND THE SEVEN DWARFS

SNW-17

SNW-20

SNW-21

SNW-24

❏ **SNW-16. Happy Pencil Drawing,**
1937. Animation paper is 10x12" centered by 4x6" image for Snow White movie. No. "64" from a numbered sequence. - **$65 $135 $200**

❏ **SNW-17. Sleepy Pencil Drawing,**
1937. Animation paper is 10x12" centered by 5x6" image for Snow White movie. No. "R-33" from a numbered sequence. - **$75 $175 $300**

❏ **SNW-20. Sneezy Pencil Drawing,**
1937. Animation paper is 10x12" centered by 2x4.25" image for Snow White movie. No. "24" from a numbered sequence. - **$75 $175 $300**

❏ **SNW-21. Bashful Pencil Drawing,**
1937. Animation paper is 10x12" centered by 2.5x4.25" image for Snow White movie. No. "94" from a numbered sequence. - **$75 $175 $300**

SNW-18

SNW-22

❏ **SNW-24. "Snow White And The Seven Dwarfs" World Premier Movie Program,**
1937. 10x13" oversized textured paper cover holds glossy paper program with pages that are 9x11". 24 pages with four-page center insert on silver foil paper. Insert notes the world premier at Carthay Circle Theater Los Angeles. Front cover has die-cut opening around full color art that was used for the one-sheet poster. Dated December 31, 1937. - **$250 $500 $900**

❏ **SNW-22. Doc Pencil Drawing From Snow White,**
1937. Image is 4x5". From a numbered sequence and this is "47." - **$75 $175 $300**

SNW-19

SNW-23

SNW-25

❏ **SNW-18. Happy Pencil Drawing,**
1937. Animation paper is 10x12" centered by 4x4.25" image for Snow White movie. No. "54" from a numbered sequence. - **$75 $175 $300**

❏ **SNW-19. Sneezy Pencil Drawing,**
1937. Animation paper is 10x12" with 3x4.5" image for Snow White movie. No. "82" from a numbered sequence. - **$75 $175 $300**

❏ **SNW-23. "Sneezy" Large Decal,**
1937. Colorful, unused "Decal Transfer Decoration For Walls." Reverse includes instructions. - **$15 $30 $50**

❏ **SNW-25. "The Playgoer" Magazine With Snow White Movie Premiere,**
1937. "The Magazine In The Theater" issued for the film's premiere at the Carthay Circle Theater, Los Angeles, California. Contains "Disneygrams" which are brief facts and statements about the film scattered throughout.
Program - **$35 $75 $125**
Ticket Stub - **$10 $20 $30**

825

SNOW WHITE AND THE SEVEN DWARFS

SNW-26

❏ **SNW-26. "Snow White And The Seven Dwarfs" Promotional Book Issued By Good Housekeeping Magazine,**
1937. Hearst Magazines Inc. 9x12.5" book with original mailing envelope. Book has stiff paper covers and includes sixteen pages of text story with art illustrated by Gustaf Tenggren.
Mailer - **$35 $75 $125**
Book - **$65 $150 $250**

SNW-27

❏ **SNW-27. "Snow White And The Seven Dwarfs" Original Pressbook,**
1937. 12x18.25". 44 pages of promotional material, photos, advertising, and images of classic promotional items and artwork.
- **$600 $1200 $2000**

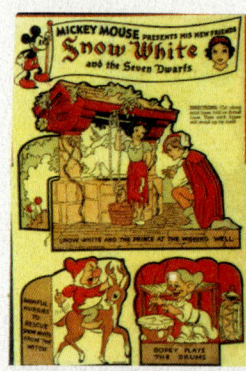

SNW-28

SNW-29

❏ **SNW-28. "Snow White" Post Toasties Box Back,**
1937. Cardboard panel 7.5x10.5" with three different cut-outs of Snow White, the Prince, Bashful and Dopey. - **$10 $20 $40**

❏ **SNW-29. "Snow White" Mask,**
1937. Einson-Freeman Co. Inc. 7.75x8.25. Issued by Proctor & Gamble, various bread companies, and others. - **$30 $60 $125**

SNW-30

SNW-31

❏ **SNW-30. "Doc" Mask,**
1937. Einson Freeman Co. Inc. 9.25x11". Issued by various bread companies. - **$25 $55 $110**

❏ **SNW-31. "Grumpy" Mask,**
1937. Einson Freeman Co. Inc. 9.25x13.25". Issued by various bread companies. - **$25 $55 $110**

SNW-32

❏ **SNW-32. "The Witch" Mask,**
1937. Einson Freeman Co. Inc. 8x10.25". Issued by various bread companies. - **$30 $60 $125**

SNOW WHITE AND THE SEVEN DWARFS

SNW-33

SNW-34

SNW-36

❏ **SNW-36. "Snow White" Sheet Music,**
1937. Irving Berlin Inc. 9x12" folder of words and music for song "Someday My Prince Will Come." Front has inset list of twelve different songs available in the Snow White series. Each - **$5 $15 $35**

SNW-37

❏ **SNW-37. "Snow White Children's Album" English Song Folio,**
1937. Chappell & Co. Ltd. 8.5x11" Softcover published under Irving Berlin Inc. copyright. Content is 20 pages of words and music for eight songs. - **$15 $30 $65**

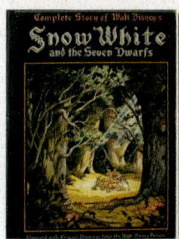 

SNW-39

❏ **SNW-39. "Complete Story Of Walt Disney's Snow White And The Seven Dwarfs" Deluxe Edition Book,**
1937. Grosset & Dunlap. 9.75x12.5" hardcover with 80 pages, the largest size of all vintage Snow White books with most pages and most expensive when originally issued. This first edition features "The Complete Story" with choice art on every page in either black and white or full color "Original Drawings From The Walt Disney Picture." - **$100 $200 $400**

SNW-40

❏ **SNW-33. Fabric Bows Display Card,**
1937. "Stark Product." Thin cardboard 5.5x7.75" illustrated card slotted twice at center to hold pair of bows. Card With Bows - **$25 $50 $80**
Card Only - **$15 $30 $50**

❏ **SNW-34. "Snow White/Doc" Serving Plate,**
1937. "Made In Japan." 6" diameter china. - **$20 $40 $75**

SNW-35

SNW-38

SNW-41

❏ **SNW-40. "Photoplay Studies" With Snow White,**
1937. Volume 3, #10 with 20 pages. Features several different articles on the film. - **$25 $50 $150**

❏ **SNW-41. Walt Disney & Dwarfs Cover Article,**
1937. Time magazine 8x25x11.5" weekly issue for Dec. 27 with cover photo of Disney at desk displyaing set of studio models for the Seven Dwarfs. Three-page article titled "Mouse And Man" reviews Walt Disney and his films. - **$25 $50 $75**

❏ **SNW-35. "Snow White" Boxed Tea Set,**
1937. W.D. Enterprises. 10x12x2.75" deep box holds 22-piece china tea set marked "Made In Japan." Tea cups are 1.25" tall, saucers are 3.5" in diameter, creamer and sugar are 2.5" tall, teapot is 4" tall, plates are 4-3/8" in diameter an large serving plate is 6" in diameter. - **$200 $400 $800**

❏ **SNW-38. "Snow White And The Seven Dwarfs" Premium Game,**
1937. Tek. Gameboard is 14.5x17.75". Originally attached to gameboard was perforated cardboard sheet containing instructions and 34 game pieces. Complete - **$60 $125 $250**
Board Only - **$35 $75 $125**

SNOW WHITE AND THE SEVEN DWARFS

SNW-42

☐ **SNW-42. "Snow White" Ideal Doll With Tag,**
1937. Ideal Novelty And Toy Co. 3x6.5x15.5" tall stuffed cloth doll with starched linen face and life-like hair. Front of bottom edge of dress has Snow White name, dwarfs and forest animal images but faded in photo example. Has cardboard tag with character illustrations on front and text on reverse. Doll - **$100 $250 $450** Tag - **$30 $60 $100**

SNW-43

☐ **SNW-43. "Snow White" Canadian Magic Doll,**
1937. Somerville Paper Boxes. 9x13.5" cardboard folder with 11" tall die-cut cardboard doll. - **$100 $200 $325**

SNW-44

☐ **SNW-44. "The Game Of Snow White And The Seven Dwarfs,"**
1937. Milton Bradley. 9.5x19.1.75" deep box contains board, instruction booklet, text story booklet, numerous wood playing pieces representing characters, poison apple and two box inserts picturing Snow White and Dwarfs. - **$85 $175 $350**

SNW-45

SNW-46

☐ **SNW-45. Toy Jacks Set Carded,**
1937. United States Lock & Hardware Co. 5x7" illustrated display card holding original complete set of flexible rubber ball and eight metal jack stars in metallic colors. - **$50 $100 $150**

☐ **SNW-46. "Snow White And The Seven Dwarfs" Pencil Box,**
1937. Dixon. 4x8.5x1.25" deep textured paper-covered cardboard with snap closure lid. Interior has paper covering with repeated photos of Seiberling Disney figures. This version includes a drawer tray beneath the top storage compartment tray. - **$65 $125 $185**

SNW-47

☐ **SNW-47. "Doc" Stationery Boxed,**
1937. Box is 3.5x5.75x1.25" deep containing original set of ten paper sheets and envelopes. - **$25 $50 $85**

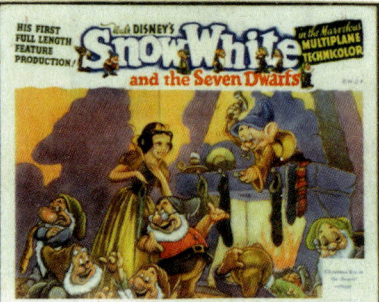

SNW-48

☐ **SNW-48. Special Release Lobby Card December,**
1937. Card is standard 11x14" and has Christmas theme showing Seven Dwarfs and Snow White hanging stockings. - **$325 $650 $1100**

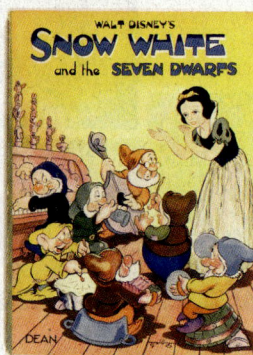

SNW-49

☐ **SNW-49. "Snow White And The Seven Dwarfs" English Softcover,**
c. 1937. Dean & Son Ltd. 8.25x11" with 64 pages in black and white and story art on every page including a number of full page illustrations. - **$60 $125 $250**

SNOW WHITE AND THE SEVEN DWARFS

SNW-50

❏ SNW-50. "Snow White" Sand Pail, 1938. Ohio Art. 4.25" tall and 4.25" in diameter. - **$150 $300 $600**

SNW-51

❏ SNW-51. Pictorial Sprinkling Can, 1938. Ohio Art Co. Large size 5x10x9" tall lithographed tin. - **$175 $300 $600**

SNW-52

❏ SNW-52. Dopey Wind-Up, 1938. Marx. 2.5x2.75x8" tall lithographed tin toy with built-in key. - **$150 $300 $550**

SNW-53

❏ SNW-53. Snow White Mechanical Valentine, 1938. Cardboard is 5.25x5.25" diecut with tab action. - **$12 $25 $45**

SNW-54

❏ SNW-54. Snow White Mechanical Valentine, 1938. Cardboard is 5.25x5.25" diecut with tab action. - **$12 $25 $45**

SNW-55

❏ SNW-55. Dwarfs Mechanical Valentine, 1938. Die-cut glossy 4.75x8.5" card depiction of Dwarfs outside their cottage. - **$12 $25 $45**

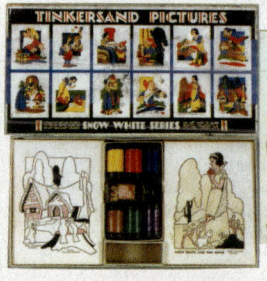

❏ SNW-56. "Snow White Tinkersand Pictures," 1938. The Toy Tinkers Inc. 8.5x17x1.75" deep box contains tubes of colored sand, cement bottle, 12 different 6.25x8.25" stiff cardboard pictures with partial designs, the rest of which was to be painted with cement and then covered with sand, test card and a four-page catalogue. - **$60 $140 $275**

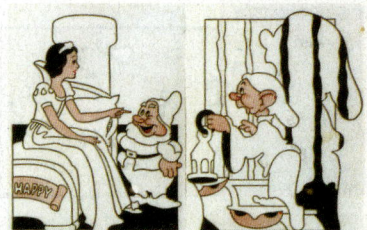

SNW-56

SNW-57

❏ SNW-57. "Snow White And The Seven Dwarfs Bagatelle," 1938. Chad Valley Co. 8.5x19x1" deep boxed English set. Box insert serves as bagatelle game with wood spring plunger unit and tin frames across surface where 4 wooden balls are to land to score points. - **$85 $175 $350**

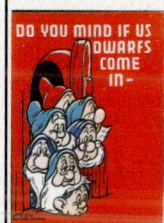

SNW-58

❏ SNW-58. Snow White Birthday Card, 1938. White & Wyckoff 4.25x5". Card opens to reveal dwarfs in single file wishing Snow White a happy birthday. - **$10 $20 $40**

SNOW WHITE AND THE SEVEN DWARFS

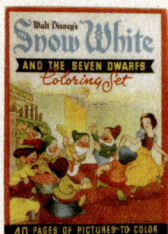

SNW-59

SNW-60

SNW-61

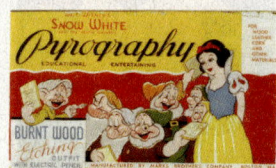

SNW-62

❏ **SNW-62. "Pyrography" Wood Burning Set,**
1938. Marks Brothers Co. 8.75x15.25x1.25" deep boxed set comprised of etching tool "Electric Pencil" with electrical cord plus five thick wood pre-printed pictures, 5x7" or smaller. Pictures of this set have been completed and neatly painted. - **$125 $225 $450**

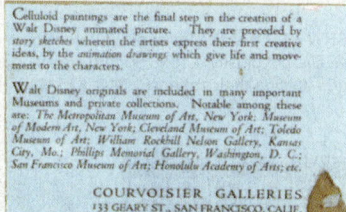

SNW-63

❏ **SNW-59. "Snow White And The Seven Dwarfs Coloring Set,"**
1938. Whitman. 8x11x1" deep boxed complete set of "40 Pages Of Pictures To Color" and a generic box of crayons. Set consists of two 20-page paint books with single story panel to be colored on each page. - **$35 $75 $150**

❏ **SNW-60. "Snow White And The Seven Dwarfs Paint Book,"**
1938. Whitman. Book #696 with 40 pages. 10.75x15". - **$50 $125 $250**

❏ **SNW-61. "Animals From Snow White Paint Book,"**
1938. Whitman. Oversized 10.5x14.75" edition #606 with 40 pages. - **$40 $85 $175**

❏ **SNW-63. Grumpy Framed Cel From "Courvoisier Galleries,"**
1938. Image is 4x4.5" and has hand-done background. Back has Courvoisier Galleries label. - **$600 $1100 $2250**

SNW-64

❏ **SNW-64. "Snow White And The Seven Dwarfs" Baby Rattle,**
1938. Completely celluloid shaker toy totaling 6" length by 2.25" diameter hollowed cylinder. - **$100 $200 $300**

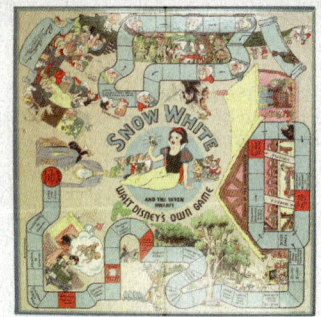

SNW-65

830

SNOW WHITE AND THE SEVEN DWARFS

☐ SNW-65. "Snow White And The Seven Dwarfs" Game, 1938. Parker Brothers. 9.5x18.75x1.75" deep box. Gameboard is 18x18" with great illustrations of Snow White characters and scenes. - $75 $150 $275

SNW-66

SNW-68

☐ SNW-66. "Dopey's Bean Bag Game," 1938. Parker Brothers. 14.5x23.5x1.25" deep boxed complete skill game comprised of thick cardboard 13x22.5" target board holed three times, pair of slotted wood base pieces and four fabric-covered bean bags. - $75 $150 $300

☐ SNW-68. "Snow White And The Seven Dwarfs Blowing Bubbles" Boxed Set, 1938. Milton Bradley. 9x14x1.5" deep box contains pair of washcloths, cardboard storage tray with illustrations of the Dwarfs, soap bars, two metal trays and a pair of wooden pipes. - $50 $125 $250

☐ SNW-69. "Snow White And The Seven Dwarfs" Movie Theater Giveaway Picture, 1938. Stiff paper 8x10". Reverse advertises film's debut at the "Garden Theatre, Frackville." - $10 $25 $40

☐ SNW-70. Snow White Polish Movie Herald, 1938. Paper herald 3x4.5" opens to 11.75" long with small "RKO Radio Films" logo. Text is in Polish. - $25 $50 $80

SNW-71

☐ SNW-71. "Snow White And The Seven Dwarfs" Radio City Music Hall Souvenir Program, 1938. Program is 6.75x9" with 16 pages. This is Volume 2, #4 spotlighting the film's appearance. Contains five Snow White-related ads including "The Seven Dwarfs Visit Rockefeller Center Skating Pond." - $20 $40 $80

SNW-67

SNW-69

☐ SNW-67. Snow White Pull Toy, 1938. N.N. Hill Brass Co. 5x11x8.5" tall. Base is metal with attached bells and wooden wheels. Figure is wooden with paper labels depicting Snow White on horseback with Prince, Dopey, Doc, Grumpy and animals. When pulled, piece rocks back and forth and small metal attachments on front strike the bells. - $325 $650 $1300

SNW-72

☐ SNW-72. "Snow White And The Seven Dwarfs Cut-Out Book," 1938. Whitman. 13x13". Includes punch-outs of Snow White, Seven Dwarfs, Prince, Queen, animals and cottage with accessories. Store item but also used as Little Orphan Annie 1938 premium from Ovaltine. Unpunched - $150 $300 $600
Annie Mailer - $50 $100 $150

SNW-70

SNOW WHITE AND THE SEVEN DWARFS

SNW-73

❑ **SNW-73. "Snow White And The Seven Dwarfs Paperdolls,"**
1938. Whitman. 12x17" envelope holds 11.75x17" doll book. Item did sell as a retail item printed in blue, as well as a Little Orphan Annie premium printed in red, plus 3.5x5" insert slip explaining "This even more expensive book" was sent as a replacement due to depleted supply of original 1938 Christmas premium by Ovaltine. Includes six pages of uncut clothing for Snow White and all Dwarfs. Christmas Insert - **$25 $50 $125**
Unpunched Book - **$300 $750 $1600**
Mailer - **$50 $100 $150**

SNW-74

❑ **SNW-74. "Masks Of The Seven Dwarfs And Snow White" Punch-Out Book,**
1938. Whitman. 10.5x10.75" in book format consisting of eight stiff paper sheets with punch-out masks of all Seven Dwarfs and Snow White. Book #990. Un-Punched - **$300 $600 $1100**

SNW-75

❑ **SNW-75. "Snow White And The Seven Dwarfs Picture Puzzle,"**
1938. Whitman. Box is 7.75x10.5x1" deep and contains two puzzles, one showing Snow White in forest with huntsman and the other the dwarfs at a dining table. - **$50 $100 $200**

 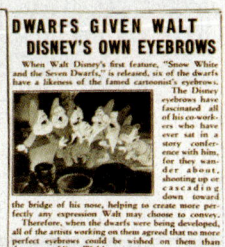

SNW-76

❑ **SNW-76. Dwarfs "Eyebrows" Article,**
1938. "RKO Newsette" a 6.5x9" four-page movie theater giveaway for week of Jan. 14, 1938, prior to national release of Snow White movie. Inside article, "Dwarfs Given Walt Disney's Own Eyebrows" refers to Walt's eyebrows as the inspiration for six of the Dwarfs and is illustrated by example film scene. - **$15 $30 $50**

SNW-77

❑ **SNW-77. "Snow White" Armour Meat Products Countertop Standups,**
1938. 6x10.5" Snow White with all seven dwarfs and 6x7" individual standups featuring Doc and Happy. Each - **$40 $75 $125**

SNW-78

SNW-79

❑ **SNW-78 "Sleepy" Large Bisque,**
1938. Figure is 4-7/8" tall. From set of seven plus Snow White. Each - **$30 $60 $90**
Snow White (about 6") - **$40 $75 $135**

❑ **SNW-79. "Snow White And The Seven Dwarfs" Figures Set Boxed,**
1938. Box is 5x9x1.5" deep containing complete set of eight painted bisques marked "Japan." Box label is marked "Distributors Geo. Borgfeldt Corp., New York." Snow White is 3.5" tall and Dwarfs are each about 2.5" tall. Boxed - **$225 $400 $650**
Each Loose - **$15 $30 $50**

SNOW WHITE AND THE SEVEN DWARFS

SNW-80

☐ **SNW-80. "Snow White And Seven Dwarf" Bisque Set With Box,**
1938. "Made In Japan". 5" tall Snow White and 4" tall Dwarf figures. Boxed - **$250 $500 $750** Each Loose - **$20 $40 $60**

SNW-81   SNW-82

☐ **SNW-81. Fawn From Snow White Figurine,**
1938. Brayton Laguna. 2.25x4.5x6.25" tall painted and glazed ceramic, the smaller of two versions from series by this maker of figurines depicting Snow White, Dwarfs, forest animals.
Small - **$50 $100 $150**
Large - **$75 $125 $200**

☐ **SNW-82. Squirrel From Snow White Figurine,**
1938. Brayton Laguna. 3.5" tall ceramic. - **$75 $125 $200**

SNW-83

☐ **SNW-83. Seven Dwarfs Metal Figure Set,**
1938. Lincoln Logs. Complete set of seven painted cast metal figures, 3.5 to 3.75" tall. Front of each has Dwarf's name in raised lettering, backs have company name, copyright and individual number 1-7. Each - **$65 $125 $200**

SNW-84

☐ **SNW-84. Rubber Figures Set,**
1938. Seiberling Rubber Co. Complete set of painted solid latex Dwarfs, each 5.5" to 6" tall plus 8" tall painted Snow White figure that rarely survives due to hollowed thin latex body casting. Snow White figure (not to scale in photo) additionally has moveable head and arms as made.
Snow White - **$100 $300 $1000**
Each Dwarf - **$25 $50 $100**

SNW-85

☐ **SNW-85. "Snow White And The Seven Dwarfs Candy" Bag,**
1938. Paper bag is 3.75x7.5". - **$12 $25 $40**

SNW-86

☐ **SNW-86. "Snow White And The Seven Dwarfs" Candy Box,**
1938. Consolidated Biscuit Company. 5x8x1" deep box. Contained 7 Dwarf "Pops" and one "Snow White Pop." Empty box - **$100 $225 $450**

SNW-87

☐ **SNW-87. Cuban Chocolate Premium Card Album,**
1938. Spanish text 7.5x12" stiff paper album of 16 pages containing complete set of 100 full color numbered thin paper stock cards, each 2.25x3" and neatly mounted on appropriate numbered spots. Set consists of individual character cards for Snow White and each Dwarf. Remaining cards are scene illustrations with Spanish text relating the story. - **$100 $200 $300**

SNW-88

☐ **SNW-88. "Snow White And The Seven Dwarfs Cereal Bowl" Newspaper Advertisement,**
1938. General Foods' Huskies Cereal. 11x15.5" half-page ad clipped from Sunday comics section. Ad includes illustration of milk glass bowl offered by mail for one box top and 10 cents. - **$8 $15 $25**

SNW-89

☐ **SNW-89. "Snow White Chewing Gum" Wrapper,**
1938. Dietz Gum Co. 2.75x2.75" paper wrapper with Snow White and Dwarf illustrations. - **$25 $50 $100**

SNW-90

☐ **SNW-90. "Snow White And The Seven Dwarfs Sealtest Ice Cream" Store Sign,**
1938. Glossy paper sign measures 11x35.25" and reads "Playing Here All Summer/ Sponsoring Sealtest Velvet Brand Ice Cream." - **$150 $300 $550**

SNOW WHITE AND THE SEVEN DWARFS

SNW-91

SNW-94

SNW-96

❑ **SNW-91. Snow White & Dwarfs Wrapper Set,**
1938. Consolidated Biscuit Co. Set of eight waxed paper sheets comprised of 6.5x9" Snow White wrapper and seven individual Dwarf wrappers, each 4.5x5.25". Each has name and flavor below illustration and Snow White also has a five cent price printing. Others have no price indicated. Set - **$160 $240 $400**

❑ **SNW-93. Sleepy Beanie,**
1938. - **$30 $75 $150**

❑ **SNW-94. Snow White Paddle,**
1938. Rare. Kraft premium. - **$50 $100 $200**

❑ **SNW-96. Grape-Nuts Cereal Sign,**
1938. Scarce. - **$250 $500 $1000**

SNW-92

SNW-97

❑ **SNW-92. Boxed Cut-Outs By Whitman,**
1938. Store item. Unused Near Mint - **$300** Boxed and Cut - **$50 $100 $150**

SNW-95

SNW-98

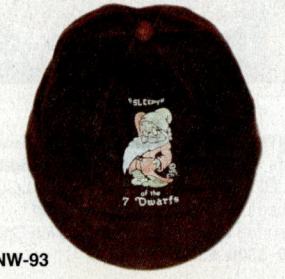

SNW-93

❑ **SNW-95. "Snow White" Promo Poster,**
1938. Rare. 28" x 22". - **$300 $600 $1200**

❑ **SNW-97. Bracelet - Painted,**
1938. Small figure charms of Snow White and the Seven Dwarfs. Store bought. - **$40 $75 $150**

❑ **SNW-98. "Jingle Book" for Stickers,**
1938. Black and white cover and contents. Rare. - **$75 $150 $275**

SNOW WHITE AND THE SEVEN DWARFS

SNW-99

☐ **SNW-99. Stickers for Black and White Issue of "Jingle Book,"**
1938. Birds Sticker - **$10 $20 $40**
Others Each - **$25 $50 $75**

SNW-100

☐ **SNW-100. Snow White Bread Issued Jingle Strips,**
1938. Seven from a set of 24. Each waxed paper strip is 2x4.5". Each features four line verse. Each - **$10 $25 $40**

SNW-101

☐ **SNW-101. "Snow White Jingle Book" Premium,**
1938. Booklet measuring 4.25x5.5" with 16 pages issued by various bread companies containing character scenes and 24 jingles with last line left blank to be filled in by owner. - **$20 $40 $80**

SNW-102

☐ **SNW-102. "Snow White Jingle Club" Application Postcard,**
1938. 5.5x3.5" postcard with reverse mentioning a baking company from Wausau, Wisconsin. - **$75 $150 $250**

SNW-103

☐ **SNW-103. "Snow White Jingle Club Member" Button,**
1938. Kay Kamen backpaper. 1.25". - **$12 $25 $45**

SNW-104

☐ **SNW-104. Snow White And The Seven Dwarfs Button,**
1938. Button is 3.5". Likely worn by either theatre employees or toy department clerk. - **$350 $700 $1200**

SNW-105

☐ **SNW-105. "Snow White Jingle Club" Application,**
1938. Two-sided paper sheet 4.25x7" with application form on reverse. - **$20 $40 $75**

SNW-106

☐ **SNW-106. "Grumpy & Dopey" Hair Brush,**
1938. Hughes-Autograf Brush Co. Inc. 2x3.5x1.5" dark brown wood brush with aluminum panel top that has enamel paint accents. - **$30 $60 $90**

SNW-107   SNW-108

☐ **SNW-107. Snow White China Toothbrush Holder,**
1938. Painted and glazed holder 2.25x2.75x6" tall and marked "Genuine Walt Disney Copyright/Foreign." Distributed by Maw of England. - **$65 $125 $175**

☐ **SNW-108. Sneezy English Toothbrush Holder,**
1938. Maw Ltd. 2.5x2.5x4" tall china figural from Dwarf toothbrush set marked on underside "Genuine Walt Disney Copyright/Foreign." Rear of body has open area for toothbrush storage. Each - **$40 $70 $125**

SNOW WHITE AND THE SEVEN DWARFS

SNW-109

❏ SNW-109. "Moving Picture Machine" Envelope,
1938. Pepsodent 8.75x13.25" mailing envelope for premium punch-out sheets of assembly parts for cardboard mechanical viewer. Design includes illustration of assembled machine with Snow White, Seven Dwarfs, Donald Duck. - **$35 $65 $100**

SNW-110

❏ SNW-110. "Moving Picture Machine" Premium,
1938. Pepsodent 2x7.5x7" tall assembled cardboard premium with simulated gears and dials, portraits of Snow White and Seven Dwarfs, Mickey, Minnie and Donald. Has complete set of 56 pictures. One side shows Mickey and Donald performing on stage while opposite side is Snow White dancing with Dwarfs. Crank on one side is turned to view the pictures through the top die-cut eye piece. Bottom panel includes assembly instructions, illustrations of Pepsodent products.
Assembled - **$135 $275 $450**
Unpunched - **$175 $400 $700**

SNW-111   SNW-112

❏ SNW-111. "Doc" Lamp,
1938. LaMode Studios. 9.5 tall and base is 4" in diameter. Doc is 6" tall. - **$100 $200 $350**

❏ SNW-112. "Grumpy" Lamp,
1938. LaMode Studios. Lamp is 9" tall and has 4" diameter base. Grumpy is 6" tall. - **$100 $200 $350**

SNW-113

❏ SNW-113. "Dopey" And Others Lamp With Shade,
1938. "La Mode Studios" painted plaster figural lamp base with cardboard original pictorial shade totaling 14" assembled height. Base is 4" diameter with 6.5" tall Dopey figure. Shade image is Dopey covering his mouth, having swallowed soap, and around him are soap bubbles. Each Dwarf Lamp - **$100 $200 $350**
Snow White Lamp - **$75 $150 $300**
Each Shade - **$150 $300 $550**

SNW-114

❏ SNW-114. "Snow White" Lamp With Shade,
1938. LaMode Studios. Figural painted plaster lamp is 3x3.5x7.25" tall to the top of Snow White, 9.75" tall to top of socket. Underside has original paper label with company name and Disney copyright. The glossy thin cardboard shade has bottom diameter of 8" and height of 5.75". Features image of Snow White with Dwarfs who show her their hands.
Lamp - **$75 $150 $300**
Shade - **$150 $300 $550**

SNW-115

❏ SNW-115. "Happy" Unusual English Lamp With Fabric Shade,
1938. Lamp is 6x6x7.25" tall to the top of Happy, 9.75" tall to the top of socket. Has square wood base with high relief painted plaster top. Front edge of his feet have incised name "Happy" while back has Disney copyright. Shade has six panels. Height of 8" with base diameter of 10" and is fabric-covered with tassel fringe. Lamp - **$75 $150 $250**
Shade - **$75 $150 $250**

SNOW WHITE AND THE SEVEN DWARFS

SNW-116

❑ **SNW-116. "Snow White" Night Light,**
1938. LaMode Studios Inc. 5x6.5x9" tall solid painted plaster. Wishing well holds light bulb, and a translucent glass covers the top of the well. Complete - **$225 $350 $600**
Missing Glass Cover - **$175 $300 $500**

SNW-117

❑ **SNW-117. "Dopey" Figural Night Light,**
1938. LaMode Studios. 5x6x8.5" tall solid painted plaster. Drum has a small recessed inner rim where a translucent glass insert covered the interior light bulb. Complete - **$200 $300 $500**
Missing Glass Cover - **$150 $250 $400**

SNW-118

❑ **SNW-118. Dopey & Others Night Light,**
1938. Micro-Lite Co. 5" tall battery-operated light on 3.5" diameter painted tin base. Diecut cardboard Dopey figure is mounted beside battery compartment cylinder finished in tin sheet wrap-around picturing Snow White in bed surrounded by the Dwarfs including three of them holding lighted candles. From a "Kiddy-Lites" series of three, also including similar lights for Mickey Mouse and Donald Duck. - **$115 $225 $350**

SNW-119

SNW-120

❑ **SNW-119. "Snow White" And Dwarfs Musical Notes Glasses,**
1938. 4.75" tall from that year's second dairy series issued in two heights. Each glass is this set has character image on front with music notes that wrap around to a verse on the back referring to that particular character. Each, Either Size - **$45 $85 $150**

❑ **SNW-120. Doc & Bashful Salt & Pepper Set,**
1938. Painted and glazed ceramic set each about 2.5" tall and marked "Foreign" on bottom. - **$35 $65 $125**

SNW-121

❑ **SNW-121. Baby Fork And Spoon With Character Images,**
1938. International Silver Co./Rogers Brothers. 4" long silverplate matched pair. Front of each handle has raised image of Snow White at top followed by descending full figures of Bashful, Sneezy and Doc. Back of each handle has raised images of Grumpy, Happy, Dopey and Sleepy. Each - **$5 $15 $25**

SNW-122

❑ **SNW-122. "Dopey" Bank,**
1938. Crown Toy Mfg. Co. Inc. 3x3.5x7.75" tall painted plaster used as a carnival prize. - **$40 $85 $175**

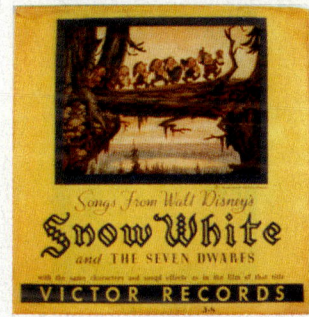

SNW-123

❑ **SNW-123. Movie Soundtrack First Record Set,**
1938. Victor Records. 10.5x10.75" envelope-style sleeve containing complete set of three 78 rpm records, believed to be the first-ever U.S. movie feature soundtrack album. Song titles are Whistle While You Work, I'm Wishing, One Song, With A Smile And A Song, Dig-A-Dig-Dig, Heigh-Ho, Some Day My Prince Will Come, Dwarfs' Yodel Song. - **$75 $150 $300**

SNOW WHITE AND THE SEVEN DWARFS

SNW-124

❑ **SNW-124. Dime Register Bank,**
1938. Walt Disney Enterprises. 2.5x2.5x.75" deep tin lithographed mechanical register bank. - **$65 $150 $300**

SNW-125

❑ **SNW-125. "Snow White Childrens Album,"**
1938. Chappell & Co. Ltd. 8.5x10.75" English song folio with 20 pages including illustrations. - **$20 $40 $75**

SNW-126

SNW-127

❑ **SNW-126. "Snow White And The Seven Dwarfs" Souvenir Song Album,**
1938. Folio is 8.75x11.75" with 52 pages. Features words and music to nine of the film's songs. This is the version with illustrated margin design on every page depicting forest with cottage and castle. - **$25 $50 $90**

❑ **SNW-127. "Snow White And The Seven Dwarfs" Souvenir Song Album,**
1938. Folio is 8.75x11.75" with 52 pages featuring nine of the film's songs. This is the version with plain margins throughout. - **$20 $40 $70**

SNW-128

SNW-129

❑ **SNW-128. "Toytown" Newspaper With Snow White Cover,**
1938. Eight page 11.25x17.5" newsprint double folio advertising flier designed for local imprint of a "Toytown" store. Front cover has invitation text to store by Snow White, Dwarfs and other Disney characters. Front also includes illustration ad for "Seven Dwarfs Fruit Drops." Content includes illustrated ad for Snow White boxed bisque figure set and numerous other Disney or non-Disney character toys and games. - **$25 $50 $85**

❑ **SNW-129. "Snow White And Seven Dwarfs" Flower Bulb Premium,**
1938. B.T. Babbitt Inc. 2.25x4x.75" deep box held crocus bulbs. Includes small instruction folder, unused order form for additional bulbs, small plain cardboard tube and white tissue paper sheet that was wrapped around bulbs. - **$30 $60 $90**

SNW-130

❑ **SNW-130. Doc Window Sign,**
1938. Unmarked but possibly Armour Meats 10.5x20.5" paper sign. - **$25 $50 $80**

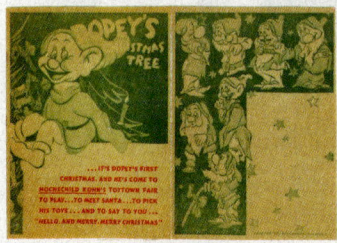

SNW-131

SNW-132

❑ **SNW-131. "Dopey's Christmas Tree" Premium Book,**
1938. Book is 8.5x11.25" with 16 pages. Issued by various department stores. - **$35 $65 $150**

❑ **SNW-132. Mechanical Valentine Set,**
1938. Eight die-cut stiff paper cards with tab for movement activity such as Sleepy playing accordion. Each - **$10 $20 $30**

SNW-133

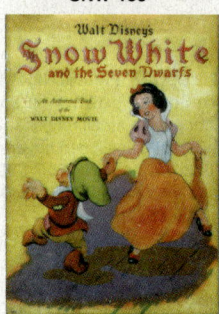

SNW-134

❑ **SNW-133. "Snow White And The Seven Dwarfs" Big Little Book,**
1938. Whitman. Book #1460. - **$30 $85 $165**

❑ **SNW-134. "Snow White And The Seven Dwarfs,"**
1938. Whitman. 9.5x13" book #925 with 16 pages. - **$25 $50 $125**

SNOW WHITE AND THE SEVEN DWARFS

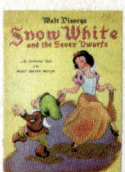 

SNW-135

❑ **SNW-135. "Snow White And The Seven Dwarfs" Variety Book,**
1938. Whitman. 9.5x13" edition #925 variety on stiff paper rather than otherwise identical linen-like paper version. Content is 16 pages. - **$40 $70 $150**

SNW-136

❑ **SNW-136. "Snow White And The Seven Dwarfs,"**
1938. K.K. Publications Inc. 9.25x10" with 12 pages. - **$30 $75 $150**

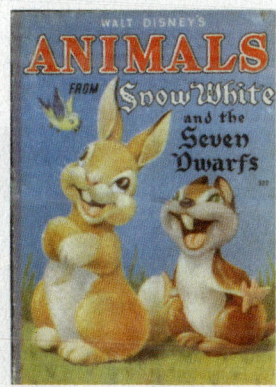

SNW-137

❑ **SNW-137. "Animals From Snow White And The Seven Dwarfs,"**
1938. Whitman. 8.75x12" with 12 pages. - **$30 $60 $125**

SNW-138

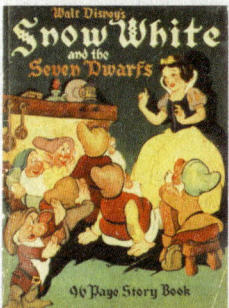

SNW-139

❑ **SNW-138. "Snow White And The Seven Dwarfs" Hardcover,**
1938. Grosset & Dunlap. 7.25x9" with 40 pages. About half of illustrations are done by Gustaf Tenggren who was one of the art directors on the Snow White film. - **$35 $75 $175**

❑ **SNW-139. "Snow White And The Seven Dwarfs" Book,**
1938. Whitman. 8.5x11.25" stiff cover book, 96 pages. Contents includes story art in black/white on almost every page. Back cover has different Dwarfs illustration from front. - **$20 $40 $90**

SNW-140

❑ **SNW-140. "Forest Friends From Snow White And The Seven Dwarfs" Book With Dust Jacket,**
1938. Grosset & Dunlap. 7.25x9.25" hardcover, 28 pages. Jacket - **$15 $30 $60**
Book - **$50 $100 $150**

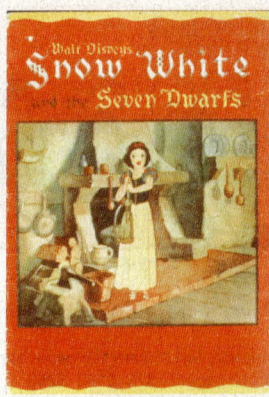

SNW-141

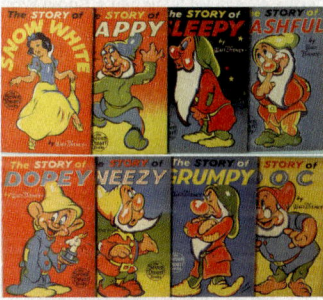

SNW-142

❑ **SNW-141. "Snow White And The Seven Dwarfs" Book,**
1938. Whitman. 8.75x12.25" linen-like book #927 consisting of twelve pages of full color film scenes. - **$45 $85 $175**

❑ **SNW-142. Snow White And Seven Dwarfs Books Set,**
1938. Whitman. "1044" set each titled "The Story Of" followed by individual character name. Each is 7.5x11" cardboard covered 24 pages. Each - **$50 $100 $275**

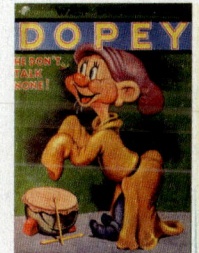 

SNW-143

SNOW WHITE AND THE SEVEN DWARFS

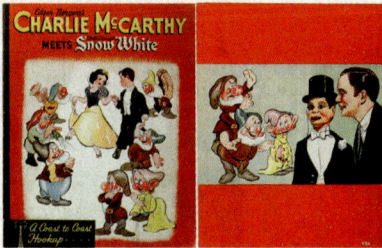

SNW-144

❏ **SNW-143. "Dopey He Don't Talk None" Book,**
1938. Whitman. 9x12" linen-like paper book #955 with 12 pages. - **$75 $150 $250**

❏ **SNW-144. "Edgar Bergen's Charlie McCarthy Meets Walt Disney's Snow White" Book,**
1938. Whitman. 9.5x11.5" softcover #986 with 24-page illustrated story. - **$65 $135 $250**

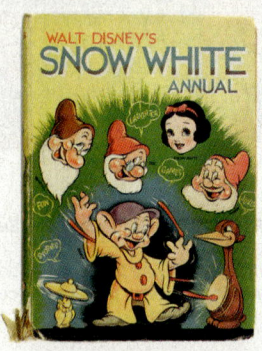

SNW-145

SNW-145

❏ **SNW-145. "Snow White Annual" English Hardcover,**
1938. Dean & Son Ltd. 7.75x10.5" by 1.25" thick with 160 pages. Has full color frontispiece. Dwarf portraits appear on the spine. - **$200 $300 $600**

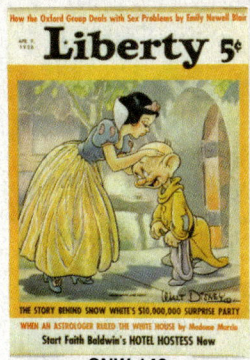

SNW-146

❏ **SNW-146. "Liberty" With Snow White Cover,**
1938. Volume 15, #15 is 8.5x11.5" with 16 pages. Features two-page article on Snow White film. - **$25 $50 $85**

SNW-147

❏ **SNW-147. Doll Tag,**
1938. Knickerbocker Toy Co. Inc. 2" diameter stiff paper string tag for stuffed cloth doll. - **$25 $50 $85**

SNW-148

❏ **SNW-148. "Grumpy" Mask,**
1938. Apon Noveltly Co. 8x10x3" deep formed and starched linen. - **$15 $30 $60**

SNW-149

SNW-150

❏ **SNW-149. Christmas Ornaments Boxed Set,**
1938. "Doubl-glo" 9.5x12x2" deep boxed complete set of eight 3.5" tall painted blown glass figural ornaments, the first Snow White set produced. Each ornament is complete with metal cap and wire hanger loop. Box - **$100 $200 $300**
Each ornament - **$10 $20 $30**

❏ **SNW-150. "Snow White And The Seven Dwarfs" English Card Game,**
1938. Castell Brothers Ltd. "Pepys Series" boxed complete deck of 45 cards plus instruction booklet. - **$40 $85 $150**

SNW-151   SNW-152

❏ **SNW-151. Dwarfs From Snow White Tie,**
c. 1938. Tie is 37" long with Dwarf illustrations, music notes and words "Hi-Ho." - **$10 $20 $40**

SNOW WHITE AND THE SEVEN DWARFS

❏ **SNW-152. "Dopey Of The 7 Dwarfs" Child's Tie,**
c. 1938. Silk-like fabric necktie with 2.5" tall silk-screened image. - **$15 $30 $50**

SNW-153

❏ **SNW-153. "Snow White Paint Box,"**
c. 1938. "Made In England" 4x9.75x5" deep tin litho with hinged and segmented lid scene. - **$30 $65 $125**

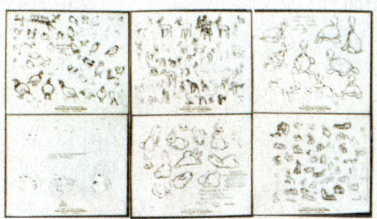
SNW-154

❏ **SNW-154. "Snow White" Model Sheet Publicity Photos,**
c. 1938. Six including Prince, turtle, deer, birds and bunnies. Each is 8.25x10". Each - **$10 $15 $25**

SNW-155

SNW-156

❏ **SNW-155. Bashful Celluloid Rattle,**
c. 1938. Rattle is 5.5" tall. Marked on back "Licenza Walt Disney." - **$20 $40 $80**

❏ **SNW-156. Snow White Celluloid Baby Rattle,**
c. 1938. Maker unknown but known Italian figure toy 8.5" tall overall including 4.5" painted hollow cello body. Handle is also cello with loop attached at bottom. - **$20 $40 $80**

SNW-157

❏ **SNW-157. Dopey Minature Bisque,**
c. 1938. Figure is 1-5/8" tall and was used as a cake decoration. - **$10 $20 $40**

SNW-158

SNW-159

❏ **SNW-158. Snow White Bisque Candy Pack,**
c. 1938. Figure is 2.75" tall and still attached to cellophane-wrapped candy pack tied together with fabric bow. Has pair of cardboard disk inserts with candy between and underside of disk is marked "Candy Crafters Toypaks." - **$65 $135 $225**

❏ **SNW-159. Snow White Figurine,**
c. 1938. Unmarked 2.25" tall painted small bisque in unusual pose of hands tugging on the front of her dress rather than folded in front of her chest. Underside has tiny hole that had a wire attachment for use as a cake decoration. - **$20 $40 $75**

SNW-160

❏ **SNW-160. Snow White And Seven Dwarfs Musician Bisque Set,**
c. 1938. Set features 4" tall Snow White and Dwarfs are 2.5", each depicted playing a different instrument. Set - **$200 $400 $650**

SNW-161

SNW-162

❏ **SNW-161. Snow White And The Seven Dwarfs Musician Large Size Bisque Set,**
c. 1938. This is the largest and rarest Snow White bisque set from Japan and consists of 6.5" tall Snow White, the Dwarfs are each about 4.25" tall. A similar but small musician set was produced. Each - **$100 $150 $200**

❏ **SNW-162. Snow White And The Seven Dwarfs Plaster-Filled Celluloid Figurine Set,**
c. 1938. Set consists of 5.25" Snow White and Seven Dwarfs are 3.25". Set - **$120 $240 $400**

SNOW WHITE AND THE SEVEN DWARFS

SNW-163

❑ **SNW-163. Celluloid Figure Set,**
c. 1938. Complete set of eight painted hollow figures, each marked on back either "Foreign" or "Celluloid/Foreign." Snow White is 6.25" tall, Dwarfs are 5.25 to 5.5" tall. Snow White is depicted holding a bird in one hand. Set - **$200 $320 $480**

❑ **SNW-164 "Happy" Celluloid And Plaster Figure With Label,**
c. 1938. Japanese 4.5" tall plaster-filled cello with both Disney copyright and label on back. - **$25 $50 $75**

❑ **SNW-165. Snow White Celluloid Figure,**
c. 1938. Unmarked but known Italian 2x2.5x6.25" tall painted cello likeness. - **$20 $40 $80**

SNW-165

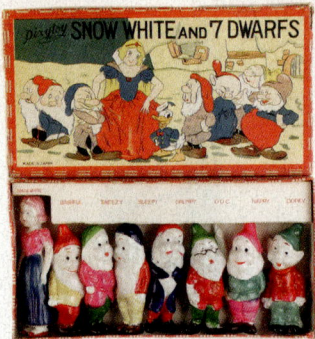

SNW-166

❑ **SNW-166. "Snow White And The Seven Dwarfs" Boxed Celluloid Figure Set ,**
c. 1938. Box is 3.75x7.5x1" deep and contains set of eight celluloid figures. Box is marked "Pixytoy Made In Japan." Snow White stands 3.25" tall while the Dwarfs are each about 2.75". Box insert includes each character's name for placement in the box. Boxed Set - **$100 $225 $350**

SNW-167

❑ **SNW-167. Snow White Celluloid Rattle Figure,**
c. 1938. 4.25" tall unmarked but Italian-made. Figure is on a circular base and stands independently. - **$25 $50 $100**

SNW-168

❑ **SNW-168. "Dopey" English Wind-Up,**
c. 1938. 5.25" tall tin litho toy with original box. No manufacturer indicated but box notes both a Dopey and a Happy toy produced.
Box - **$65 $125 $200**
Toy - **$100 $200 $300**

SNW-169

❑ **SNW-169. Sleepy Italian Figurine,**
c. 1938. "Laccouprini." Unknown if artist or company name 2x3x4" tall painted and glazed heavy ceramic depicting plump Sleepy. - **$30 $65 $100**

SNW-170

❑ **SNW-170. "Dopey And Grumpy Painted Plaster Statue,**
c. 1938. 8" tall solid plaster depicting a large mushroom between the two characters. Unmarked. - **$50 $100 $200**

SNW-171

SNOW WHITE AND THE SEVEN DWARFS

SNW-172

❑ **SNW-171. Snow White And Dwarfs English Figures,**
c. 1938. Britains Ltd. seven from set of eight painted lead figures comprised of 2.25" tall Snow White and Seven Dwarfs, each about 1.75" tall. Photo is missing Happy figure. Snow White - **$40 $75 $150**
Each Dwarf - **$15 $30 $50**

❑ **SNW-172. Snow White And Dwarfs Painted Composition Figures,**
c. 1938. Seven figures with 6.75" Snow White and Dwarfs are each 5.5" tall. Photo of six Dwarf figures pictures only three different of seven in set. Snow White - **$50 $100 $150**
Each Dwarf - **$15 $25 $40**

SNW-173

❑ **SNW-173. Snow White Seiberling Rubber Standups,**
c. 1938. Five of eight die-cut thin rubber figures consisting of Snow White 3.5" tall and Bashful, Grumpy, Sneezy and Sleepy, each 3.25". All have full color decals and rubber base. Each - **$15 $25 $40**

SNW-174

❑ **SNW-174. Seven Dwarfs Wood Standups,**
c. 1938. Twelve pieces of jigsawed wood figures with paper labels. Included are 7 Dwarfs, one piece with 2 Dwarfs sawing, one piece with 3 Dwarfs assembling pieces of wood, 2 deer and one tree. English made. Each - **$10 $20 $30**

SNW-175

❑ **SNW-175. Snow White And Seven Dwarfs Wood Standups,**
c. 1938. Eight jigsawed wood figures including Snow White and each of 7 Dwarfs. Each - **$10 $20 $30**

SNW-176

❑ **SNW-176. Snow White And The Seven Dwarfs Exceptional Figurine Set By Leonardi,**
c. 1938. G. Leonardi. Set of eight painted solid plaster figures. Snow White is 4.5x7x12" tall, Dwarfs are each about 3.5x3.5x7.5" tall. Each piece has company mark and Disney name, this is incised on Snow White and stamped on underside of each Dwarf. Snow White - **$150 $300 $600**
Each Dwarf - **$75 $125 $200**

SNW-177

❑ **SNW-177. "Walt Disney's Seven Dwarfs" Candy Box,**
c. 1938. Box is 3x6x1" deep and contained "Curtiss Candy Drops From Toytown." Side panels have portraits of all dwarfs while underside has a cut-out of Bashful. - **$50 $100 $200**

SNW-178

❑ **SNW-178. "Walt Disney's Seven Dwarfs" Candy Box With Wrapper Set,**
c. 1938. Curtiss Candy Co. 3x6x1" deep box and complete set of seven candy wrappers originally holding rolls of candy drops. Each roll featured a different flavored candy and different Dwarf wrappers are keyed by a single color to represent that candy's flavor. Box lid has diecut image of Doc. The underside panel features instructions to "Make Your Own Dwarf Cut-Outs" with example cut-out of Bashful. Object was to paste the wrappers to sheets of "heavy paper" and then cut them out. Box - **$50 $100 $200**
Each Wrapper - **$12 $25 $50**

SNOW WHITE AND THE SEVEN DWARFS

SNW-179

SNW-180

❏ **SNW-179. Snow White Series Glasses Ad Paper,**
c. 1938. Two-sided 3.25x5.75" glossy paper advertising set of eight glasses that were issued with cottage cheese by various dairies. - **$15 $30 $60**

❏ **SNW-180. "Snow White/Dopey" Bosco Glasses,**
c. 1938. Each 3.25" tall. - **$15 $30 $50**

SNW-181

❏ **SNW-181 "Bashful/Sleepy" Bosco Glasses,**
c. 1938. Each 3.25" tall. - **$15 $30 $50**

SNW-182

❏ **SNW-182. Snow White Premium Poster Stamps,**
c. 1938. Perforated sheet with 8 stamps 4.75x6.5" reads "Compliments Of Armour And Co. And Your Dealer" for placement in booklet.
Stamp Sheet - **$10 $20 $40**
Booklet (not shown) - **$20 $40 $75**

SNW-183   SNW-184

❏ **SNW-183. "Happy" Bisque Toothbrush Holder,**
c. 1938. Painted bisque figure 1.25x1.75x3.5" tall marked "Japan." - **$75 $150 $300**

❏ **SNW-184. Sneezy Toothbrush Holder,**
c. 1938. Unmarked 1x2x2.5" tall painted and glazed ceamic depiction of him in pre-sneeze facial expression. - **$65 $110 $175**

SNW-185

❏ **SNW-185 Happy Toothbrush Holder,**
c. 1938. Unmarked but probable English 2.75x3.5x5.5" tall painted and glazed depiction of him with arms bent and connected to his waist forming loops for placement of two toothbrushes. Front of base has a rest for tube of toothpaste. - **$75 $150 $250**

SNW-186

❏ **SNW-186. Grumpy Planter,**
c. 1938. "Made In Japan" with copyright 2x3.5x3.75" tall painted and glazed ceramic. - **$15 $30 $50**

SNW-187

❏ **SNW-187. "Sleepy/Dopey" Toothbrush Holder,**
c. 1938. Painted bisque figure is 2x3.5x3.5" tall of larger Sleepy in seated position next to smaller standing Dopey who holds a saw. Behind them is a wood fence with two tree stump posts that serve as individual toothbrush holder. - **$150 $300 $550**

SNW-188

❏ **SNW-188. Dopey English Lamp Base,**
c. 1938. Painted solid plaster figural of him in front of tree trunk. Overall height is 9" to top of socket with 3.75" diameter base. - **$100 $200 $300**

SNOW WHITE AND THE SEVEN DWARFS

SNW-189

☐ **SNW-189. Rare Bashful Ceramic Mirror Holder,**
c. 1938. Possibly by Maw & Sons, England. Painted and glazed ceramic figure is 3x3.75x4.25". Attached behind him is mirror holder. - **$60 $125 $250**

SNW-190

☐ **SNW-190. Dopey China Bookend,**
c. 1938. Maw of London, 4.5" tall featuring same style figure that was produced as a toothbrush holder. Underside has Disney copyright and incised number "7776". Set of Two - **$100 $200 $300**

SNW-191

☐ **SNW-191. Snow White Rug,**
c. 1938. Rug is 21.5x44" with velveteen nap and fringe trim. - **$65 $165 $350**

SNW-192

☐ **SNW-192. Snow White Table Cover,**
c. 1938. Unmarked other than "EJS" 46x51" printed cotton cloth centered by 10" diameter illustration of Queen, Witch, Magic Mirror, well, forest animals. Larger border illustrations are six different scenes of Snow White and/or related story characters or events. Example photo shows four details. - **$50 $100 $150**

SNW-193

☐ **SNW-193. "Dopey" Linen Dish Towel,**
c. 1938. Pure linen 12.5x19.5" towel with bottom center 2x4" embroidered design. Above this is original 1.25x1.75" paper label. With Label - **$25 $50 $75** Towel Only - **$15 $30 $50**

SNW-194

☐ **SNW-194. Snow White And Seven Dwarfs Framed Pictures,**
c. 1938. Set of eight, each 4x5". Reverse has cardboard hanger. Set - **$40 $80 $160**

SNW-195

☐ **SNW-195. "I'm Grumpy" And "I'm Doc" Framed Pictures,**
c. 1938. Two "W.D. Ent." embossed character images in original matching 5.5x7" wood frames. A set exists of seven identical but non-embossed Dwarf pictures, also framed identically. Embossed Each - **$10 $20 $30**
Non-Embossed Each - **$8 $15 $25**

SNW-196

☐ **SNW-196. Figural Wall Plaques Set,**
c. 1938. Complete eight die-cut stiff cardboard wall hangers. Snow White is 3.5x8.5" and Dwarfs are each about 3.5x5.5". Set - **$80 $120 $240**

SNW-197

☐ **SNW-197. Snow White And The Seven Dwarfs Charms,**
c. 1938. Set of eight celluloid charms. Snow White is 1-1/8" and Dwarfs are .75". Each Dwarf has raised name on reverse along with "Japan" but Snow White is unmarked. Set - **$35 $65 $100**

SNOW WHITE AND THE SEVEN DWARFS

SNW-198

❏ **SNW-198 Snow White And The Seven Dwarfs Charm Bracelet,**
c. 1938. Brass link bracelet 6.5" long holds eight .5" to .75" charms with enamel paint. Also attached to one end is a .5" diameter brass disk with raised "Union Station" building from Kansas City, MO. - **$75 $150 $250**

SNW-199

❏ **SNW-199. "Snow White And The Seven Dwarfs" Bowl,**
c. 1938. Possible dairy premium 4.75" top diameter x 2.25" tall clear glass. - **$40 $80 $150**

SNW-200

❏ **SNW-200. Sneezy Swedish Cup And Saucer,**
c. 1938. Rostrand of Sweden. 2" tall porcelain cup with matching 4.25" diameter saucer. - **$20 $40 $80**

SNW-201

❏ **SNW-201. Snow White Large Biscuit Tin From Belgium,**
c. 1938. 8x13x2.5" deep tin litho. Front is designed with lock. - **$100 $200 $350**

SNW-202

❏ **SNW-202. "Snow White" Large Belgian Tin,**
c. 1938. Container is 8x13x2.5" deep marked "Made In Belgium." Illustration of Prince, Dwarfs and forest animals gathered around Snow White's casket. Sides show additional scenes from the film. - **$115 $250 $400**

SNW-203

❏ **SNW-203. English Tin,**
c. 1938. "Mickey Mouse Ltd." 5x5.25x2.5" tall litho tin container and lid. Snow White and/or Dwarfs are pictured on all outer surfaces except bottom. - **$150 $300 $500**

SNW-204

❏ **SNW-204. Bunny From Snow White Egg Cup,**
c. 1938. "Made In Japan" with Disney copyright 2x4x2.75" tall china figurine. - **$40 $75 $150**

SNW-205

846

SNOW WHITE AND THE SEVEN DWARFS

❑ **SNW-205. "Snow White And The Seven Dwarfs" Glass Pitcher,**
c. 1938. 9.5" tall with wrap-around design in blue and white. - **$125 $250 $500**

SNW-206

❑ **SNW-206. Snow White And The Seven Dwarfs Pitcher,**
c. 1938. 9.5" tall clear glass. Wrap-around design with Snow White and the Seven Dwarfs. Issued in a variety of colors. - **$125 $250 $500**

SNW-207

❑ **SNW-207. "Snow White And The Seven Dwarfs" Boxed Set Of Glasses,**
c. 1938. Libbey. 10x11.5x3" deep box contains set of eight glasses each 4-5/8" tall. Glasses are a two-color variety. Box lid features large portrait of Snow White surrounded by smaller portraits of the dwarfs. Box - **$125 $250 $500**
Each Glass - **$50 $100 $150**

SNW-208

❑ **SNW-208. Decal Glasses Set,**
c. 1938. Set of eight 4" tall tumblers, each with character image and name single decal plus "W.D." copyright. Scarce set rarely found collectively or individually with decal(s) in original condition. Each - **$65 $125 $175**

SNW-209

❑ **SNW-209. "Dopey" English Mug,**
c. 1938. "Wadeheath By Permission Walt Disney England." 3" tall ceramic. - **$50 $100 $150**

SNW-210

❑ **SNW-210. Snow White Musical Variety Ceramic Pitcher,**
c. 1938. Wadeheath. 9" tall large and impressive beautifully painted and glazed pitcher. Features Snow White, the Seven Dwarfs, and their cottage. This variety is the rare musical variety with built-in music box. - **$600 $1200 $2500**

SNW-211

SNOW WHITE AND THE SEVEN DWARFS

❏ **SNW-211. Snow White And The Seven Dwarfs Pair Of Pitchers,**
c. 1938. Wade Heath England. Painted and glazed ceramic with high relief wrap-around designs and figural handles. Larger pitcher of characters with castle and cottage is 9" tall with top diameter of 5.5", base diameter of 4". Smaller pitcher is 3.75" tall. Large - **$100 $200 $300**
Small - **$45 $90 $140**

SNW-212   SNW-213

❏ **SNW-212. Snow White Ceramic Jam Jar,**
c. 1938. Wadeheath. 3.25" glazed ceramic with high relief designs with removable lid. - **$60 $125 $175**

❏ **SNW-213. Snow White Ceramic Toast Rack,**
c. 1938. Wadeheath. 4x8.5" ceramic base with attached metal rack 3.25" tall. Has raised images of Dopey and squirrels. - **$75 $150 $200**

SNW-214

SNW-215

❏ **SNW-214. "Sneezy" Figural Bank,**
c. 1938. Japanese 2.25x4x3.75" tall painted bisque of him standing next to a simulated cash register detailed by a raised bell image plus small window openings. Top of register has incised "$150 yen" and his name incised on front edge of his stocking cap. Coin slot is in back, underside has trap. - **$125 $250 $450**

❏ **SNW-215. "Snow White And The 7 Dwarfs" Purse,**
c. 1938. 4.5x5" celluloid over cardboard handbag with leatherette sides and accent trim, metal top frame with metal clasp and chain handle. - **$50 $100 $150**

SNW-216

❏ **SNW-216. Dopey Music Box,**
c. 1938. Music box is 2.5x5x6.25" tall painted wood frame holding pressed cardboard front panel with slightly raised portrait and title, "I'm Dopey." Reverse built-in key activates tune "Whistle While You Work." - **$75 $135 $225**

SNW-217

❏ **SNW-217. Paper Portraits Premium Sheet,**
c. 1938. "Kinney's Shoe Store." 7.5x8" uncut paper set of eight character images, each with different four-line descriptive verse. Sheet reverse has sponsor's stamped name. A similar set is known for recipe cards with recipe and bakery imprint on reverse. Each - **$35 $65 $115**

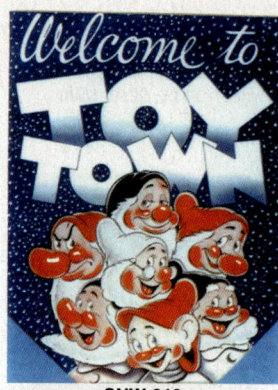

SNW-218

SNW-219

❏ **SNW-218. "Welcome To Toy Town" Paper Store Sign,**
c. 1938. Single 18x25" sheet that was originally two sheets with same design on each side and joined at top to be hung over a display cord and viewed from either side. Single Sheet - **$100 $200 $300**
Double Sheet - **$200 $400 $600**

❏ **SNW-219. Spanish Snow White Card Sign,**
c. 1938. Sign is 8x15" with text in Spanish advertising a collection of "Walt Disney" cards and album. - **$30 $60 $90**

SNW-220

SNOW WHITE AND THE SEVEN DWARFS

❑ **SNW-220. "Snow White And The Seven Dwarfs" Premium Booklet,**
c. 1938. Palmolive Soap. 4.75x7.25" softcover Australian premium, 16 pages. - **$65 $135 $225**

SNW-221

❑ **SNW-221. "The House Of The Seven Dwarfs" Dean's Cut-Out Book,**
c. 1938. English. 9.5x13" with glossy cardboard covers with cut-outs on inside and two additional cut-out sheets. Features cottage, characters and animals. Uncut - **$300 $600 $1200**

SNW-222

SNW-223

❑ **SNW-222. "Sneezy" Krueger Doll,**
c. 1938. Stuffed doll 4x6x13" has leatherette-covered body, painted starched linen face and life-like beard. Has stitched tag by R.G. Krueger. One of seven. Each - **$75 $150 $275**

❑ **SNW-223. Happy Doll,**
c. 1938. Unmarked Knickerbocker 5x10x14" tall stuffed cloth doll including starched, painted fabric stuffed head completed by life-like beard. Body cover outfit plus hat are velveteen. One of seven. Each - **$60 $125 $225**

SNW-224

SNW-225

❑ **SNW-224. "Dopey" Doll,**
c. 1938. Ideal Toy Corp. Unmarked 15" tall stuffed cloth doll with starched and painted linen face plus outfit combining felt, oilcloth, leatherette belt with metal buckle. One of seven. Each - **$60 $125 $225**

❑ **SNW-225. "Dopey" Doll,**
c. 1938. Madame Alexander. 3x6x14" tall (to peak of cap) stuffed fabric doll with painted composition head. Detailing includes felt jacket with single button, leatherette belt with button, stitched tag with Dopey and Madame Alexander names. Each Dwarf - **$60 $125 $225**

SNW-226

SNW-227

❑ **SNW-226. Snow White And Others English Birthday Card,**
c. 1938. Valentine & Sons Ltd. Closed 4.5x5.75" folder card. Cover art with Walt Disney facsimile signature. - **$20 $40 $60**

❑ **SNW-227. Snow White & Dwarfs Norwegian Pail,**
c. 1938. Pail is 4" top diameter by 4" tall lithographed tin with attached wire bail carrier. Text is Norwegian except part of Disney copyright in English. Title text is "Stabburmat Pa Alle Fat," translation unknown but most likely some type of product, possibly lard. - **$225 $450 $800**

SNW-228

❑ **SNW-228. "Bashful" Celluloid Wind-Up Nodder,**
c. 1938. Figure is 5.75" and mounted to a 2.5" diameter painted tin base. Separate head is mounted to a nodding mechanism with an attached counterweight. When rubber band is wound, his head nods back and forth. Marked on back "Made In Japan" plus Disney copyright. - **$200 $400 $800**

SNW-229

849

SNOW WHITE AND THE SEVEN DWARFS

SNW-230

SNW-233

SNW-234

SNW-236

❏ **SNW-229. Lantern Slides English Set Boxed,**
c. 1938. Ensign Ltd. 4.5x5.5x.5" deep boxed set of six 1.5x5.25" rigid glass slides. Each slide features six numbered scenes that combine in order to tell the story of Snow White. - **$40 $75 $125**

❏ **SNW-230. Snow White & Dwarfs Umbrella,**
c. 1938. Disney. Copyrighted parasol 19" long that opens to 24" diameter silk-like synthetic fabric. - **$65 $135 $175**

SNW-231

SNW-232

❏ **SNW-231. Dwarfs Pencil Case,**
c. 1938. Case is 3.75x8" felt-covered canvas fabric with silk screen design on front. - **$20 $40 $80**

❏ **SNW-232. "Happy" Celluloid Pencil Sharpener Figure,**
c. 1938. 2.5" tall three dimensional figure with metal rim marked "Made In Japan." - **$75 $150 $250**

❏ **SNW-233. "Snow White" Catalin Plastic Pencil Sharpener,**
c. 1938. Sharpener is 1.75" tall. - **$45 $80 $115**

❏ **SNW-234. Snow White French Postcards,**
c. 1938. Nine from a set of twenty-five 3.5x5.5" cards. Each depicts a different scene from film with text in French at bottom. Each - **$8 $12 $20**

SNW-235

❏ **SNW-235. "The Great Walt Disney Festival Of Hits" Australian Brochure,**
1939. RKO. "Greater Union Theaters" 9.75x12" four-page brochure for "Festival" of five Disney film features "Combined In One Big Feast Of Glorious Entertainment." Films are Snow White, Ferdinand, The Ugly Duckling, The Practical Pig, Donald's Lucky Day. Brochure opens to additional different images for the five features with Snow White prominently featured as "Hit No. 1" at center. - **$40 $85 $150**

❏ **SNW-236. "Snow White And The Seven Dwarfs Guards Of The Magic Forest" Complete Bread Label Picture,**
1939. Large 17.5x20" picture issued by various bread companies. Front is titled "Guards Of The Magic Forest". There are 36 different cut-out paste-ons of Snow White, Seven Dwarfs, Prince, Witch, Huntsman and forest animals. Reverse has text plus facsimile letter that includes facsimile signatures of Snow White and all seven dwarfs. Complete - **$200 $400 $750**

SNW-237

❏ **SNW-237. "Walt Disney Characters Embroidery Set,"**
1939. Standard Toykraft Products Inc. Box is 9.75x13.5x1.25" deep and contains six fabric hankies plus thread and scissors. Five hankies measure 5.5x6" while the Snow White hanky is 8x8.5". Also comes with postcard with illustration of all characters in set to be colored and sent "To Your Friends." - **$65 $140 $225**

SNOW WHITE AND THE SEVEN DWARFS

SNW-238

SNW-239

❏ **SNW-238. "1939 Walt Disney All Star Parade" Glass,**
1939. Glass is 4.75". - **$15 $30 $60**

❏ **SNW-239. "Snow White And The Seven Dwarfs" Glass,**
c. 1939. Tumbler is 4.25" tall with wrap-around illustration of all eight characters. Design is same as the 'Walt Disney All Star Parade' glass but without the title banner around the top. - **$35 $60 $100**

SNW-240

SNW-241

❏ **SNW-240. Snow White & Dwarfs Radio,**
1939. Emerson. 5.5x7.25x7.5" tall wooden case. Front has raised high relief images of Snow White and all Dwarfs against background of cottage and large shuttered window. Tuning and volume knobs are simulated acorns. A simulated jewel on Snow White's dress lights when radio is turned on. - **$825 $1650 $3250**

❏ **SNW-241. Dopey Dwarf Pull Toy,**
1939. Fisher-Price. 9" tall paper on wood pull toy #770. - **$350 $700 $1400**

SNW-242

SNW-243

❏ **SNW-242. Snow White And Dwarfs Original Art,**
c. 1939. Believed English 4x6" art in ink and watercolor on 7x7" paper sheet. Situation image is Snow White in broken-down automobile being pushed by the Dwarfs who sweat profusely. License plate reads "7 D." Bottom corner has "TB 39." Unique, Fine - **$85**

❏ **SNW-243. "Dopey Says Get It At The Hecht Co." Cello Button,**
c. 1939. Likely from Baltimore-Washington area department store chain. 1.25". - **$135 $275 $550**

SNW-244

SNW-245

❏ **SNW-244. "Happy" Large Display Figure,**
c. 1939. Painted composition hollow figure is 12x19x23" tall, probably a Christmas store display and most likely by Old King Cole. Edge of one shoe has Walt Disney copyright. Right hand lies flat and probably held an item for display. - **$300 $600 $1000**

❏ **SNW-245. "Snow White Magic Mirror" English Book With 3-D Insert,**
c. 1939. Dean & Son Ltd. 7x10" hardcover published as premium "Specially For Stephenson Bros. Ltd." with Stephenson Furniture Polish ad on final page. Content is 60 pages with black and white story art on nearly every page plus six glossy paper pages of 3-D photo scenes featuring studio models, described as "Stereoscopic Scenes That Enable You To See Into The Distance With A Wonderful Real-Life Effect." A pair of original "Magic Spectacles" 3-D viewer glasses are held by inside front cover attached pocket. - **$100 $200 $325**

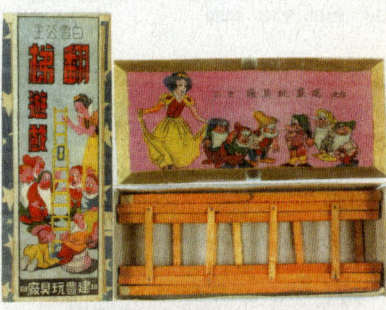

SNW-246

❏ **SNW-246. Snow White Japanese Tumbling Toy,**
1930s. Box is 4x9.5x1" deep and contains toy with 3x7x.25" thick wood base and ladder that unfolds to 26". Wooden block picturing Dopey tumbles down the rungs. Boxed - **$50 $125 $250**

SNW-247

❏ **SNW-247. Snow White Carnival Statue,**
1930s. Hollow plaster 4x5x14" tall figure. - **$20 $50 $110**

SNOW WHITE AND THE SEVEN DWARFS

SNW-248

SNW-251

SNW-253

❏ **SNW-248. Snow White And The Seven Dwarfs Ceramic Figurine Set,**
c. 1930s. Figures are painted and glazed ceramic. Snow White is 8.5" tall and each dwarf is 4.5" tall. Snow White and Dopey are marked "Lota Chile" and others are marked just "Lota". Set - **$160 $240 $480**

❏ **SNW-250. "Snow White And Seven Dwarfs" Record Set,**
1944. Decca. Four 78-rpm records in 10.5x12" sleeve. Features "Selections From Walt Disney's Feature Production." - **$30 $60 $115**

❏ **SNW-251. Snow White And Seven Dwarfs Figurine Set,**
1946. Evan K. Shaw. Set of eight painted and glazed ceramic figures. Snow White is 4.5x5.5x8.75" tall, Dwarfs are 5.5" to 6" tall with foil stickers. Snow White - **$100 $200 $300** Each Dwarf - **$50 $100 $150**

❏ **SNW-253. Snow White Boxed Watch,**
1947. US Time. Box - **$300 $600 $1200** Watch **$150 $300 $500**

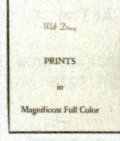

SNW-252

❏ **SNW-252. "Walt Disney Prints" With Folder,**
1947. New York Graphics Society. Folder is 12.5x14.25" and contains set of 4 prints each 11.5x13.5", two for Snow White and two for Bambi. These were available in three different sizes and could be ordered with special frames. Folder - **$25 $40 $75**
Set - **$50 $100 $200**

SNW-254

SNW-249

❏ **SNW-249. Movie Re-Release Lobby Cards,**
1943. RKO Radio Pictures. Pair of 11x14" examples from eight-card set for the film's first re-release. Each - **$40 $75 $150**

SNW-250

SNW-255

SNOW WHITE AND THE SEVEN DWARFS

☐ **SNW-254. Snow White Italian Large Figure,**
c. 1947. "Zaccagnini" large 5x5.25x10" tall painted and glazed ceramic marked underneath with company name as well as "W1." This company signed a contract with Disney in 1947 which lasted for about ten years although all example figures are quite scarce. - **$300 $600 $1200**

☐ **SNW-255. Snow White Italian Ceramic Smaller Figurine By Zaccagnini,**
c. 1947. Figure is 3x4x7" tall painted and glazed ceramic. Has company markings on underside including their full name, made in Italy and "W1." - **$225 $450 $750**

SNW-256   SNW-257

☐ **SNW-256. Bashful Figurine,**
c. 1947. Zaccagnini. 3.75" tall and marked "W2." - **$100 $200 $300**

☐ **SNW-257. Doc Figurine,**
c. 1947. Zaccagnini. 5.75" tall and marked "W6." - **$125 $250 $350**

SNW-258

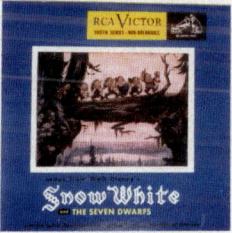
SNW-259

☐ **SNW-258. Dopey Lamp Base,**
c. 1947. Shaw Pottery. 5.75x6x8.25" tall painted and glazed ceramic made for Railley Corp. Image includes lantern held in one hand. This example has bulb socket bolted to the top of his head, possibly a replacement for original metal rod. - **$100 $200 $300**

☐ **SNW-259. "Snow White And The Seven Dwarfs" Record Set,**
1949. RCA Victor. Set of three 78-rpm records in 10.25x11" sleeve. Records feature "Same Characters And Sound Effects As In The Film." - **$30 $60 $100**

SNW-260

SNW-261

☐ **SNW-260. Snow White Movie Songs Record Pair,**
1949. Two 6" diameter 78 rpm records, one from 1949 and the second from 1962, both in 6.5x7.5" paper sleeve. Earlier is Little Golden Record on yellow vinyl of songs "Whistle While You Work" and "Snow White In The Cottage." Second record is on Disneyland label for "The Walking Song" and "Whistle While You Work."
First - **$8 $12 $20**
Second - **$4 $8 $12**

☐ **SNW-261. Snow White Figurine,**
c. 1949. Leeds China Co. 3x4x6.5" tall painted and glazed china. - **$25 $50 $75**

SNW-262

SNW-263

☐ **SNW-262. Dopey Planter,**
c. 1949. Leeds China Co. 4x6x6" tall painted and glazed china. - **$25 $50 $75**

☐ **SNW-263. Snow White Bank,**
c. 1949. Leeds China Co. 3x4x6.5" tall painted and glazed ceramic. - **$30 $60 $90**

SNW-264

☐ **SNW-264. Character Blocks,**
1940s. Four from larger set of wooden play blocks, each 1.25" square. Front and back of each have raised character name and design is single color. Other four sides of each block have either alphabet letter or animal illustration. Each - **$2 $4 $6**

SNW-265

SNW-266

SNOW WHITE AND THE SEVEN DWARFS

SNW-267

☐ **SNW-265. Snow White Dwarfs Pins,**
1940s. Group of five, each about 1.75" tall thin molded plastic with high relief detailed images. Five of almost certain set of eight. Pins are Dopey, Grumpy, Sleepy, Bashful and Sneezy. All have a bar pin on reverse. Dopey has a solid flat back while others have hollow backs. The original collector acquired these five over a 20-year period. Two came from France and Belgium, other three from England. No markings. Each - **$10 $20 $40**

☐ **SNW-266. Dwarf Figurines,**
1940s. Unmarked trio of painted and glazed ceramics, each about 4" tall, depicting Sneezy, Dopey, Sleepy. Back of each figure has small unpainted square area with character's name. Each - **$15 $30 $60**

☐ **SNW-267. "Walt Disney's Snow White" Theater Production Herald,**
1940s. Paper sheet measures 7x8.5" for a "Baltimore Actors' Theater Production" at the "Ford's Theater." - **$10 $20 $40**

SNW-268

SNW-269

SNW-270

☐ **SNW-268. Snow White Carnival Statue,**
1940s. Figure is 4x5.5x14.5" tall painted chalkware plaster, one example from a wide variety of finish colors then accented by glitter sparkles. - **$20 $40 $65**

☐ **SNW-269. Bashful Norwegian Figure,**
1940s. 6" tall figure which is same size and pose as figurine by American Pottery/Shaw; however, it is painted plaster rather than glazed ceramic. Underside has sticker noting "Made in Norway." - **$50 $100 $165**

☐ **SNW-270. "Snow White" Planter,**
1940s. Leeds China Co. 3x6x6.5" painted and glazed china. - **$20 $40 $65**

SNW-271

☐ **SNW-271. "Mazda Show White And The Seven Dwarfs Disneylights" Boxed English Set,**
1940s. British Thomson-Houston Co. Ltd. 9.5x16.5x2" deep illustrated box containing complete electrical strand set of 12 hard plastic bulb shades. Some decals are repeated for a total of eight different images. - **$100 $200 $400**

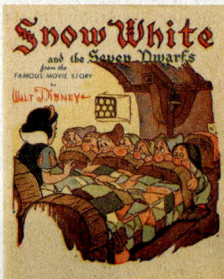

SNW-272

☐ **SNW-272. "Snow White And The Seven Dwarfs" Australian Book,**
1940s. Shepherd & Newman Pty. Ltd. 6.5x7.5" softcover with twelve stiff paper pages. - **$20 $40 $75**

SNW-273

☐ **SNW-273. "Snow White Ingersoll" Wristwatch With Specially Designed Box,**
1950. Ingersoll/US Time. 4.25x5.5x1.5" deep oval box contains 7/8" chromed metal case watch with red fabric straps. Bottom of box has plastic insert designed to represent magic mirror. Box With Insert - **$200 $400 $650** Watch - **$15 $40 $100**

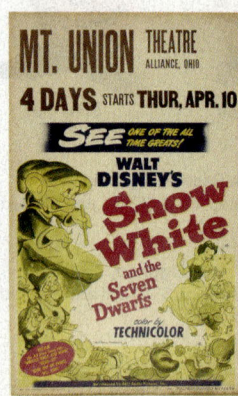

SNW-274

☐ **SNW-274. "Snow White And The Seven Dwarfs" Window Card,**
1951. RKO Radio Pictures Inc. 14x22" cardboard for re-release with theater imprint at top. - **$50 $100 $165**

SNOW WHITE AND THE SEVEN DWARFS

SNW-275

SNW-278

❏ **SNW-277. "Snow White And The Seven Dwarfs Paint Book,"**
1952. Whitman. 8.25x10.75" with 128 pages. - **$10 $20 $45**

❏ **SNW-278. "Snow White And The Seven Dwarfs Play Statuettes" Boxed Set,**
1952. Whitman Publishing Co. 7.5x12.5x1" deep box contains statuettes 6" to 8.25" tall with thin layer of wood between cardboard with paper labels for Snow White, the Seven Dwarfs, Wicked Queen, Witch and Prince on solid wood base. - **$50 $100 $200**

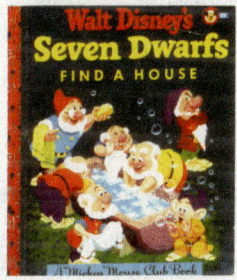

SNW-279

❏ **SNW-279. "Seven Dwarfs Find A House" Book,**
1952. Simon & Schuster. 6.75x8" "Mickey Mouse Club Book" in same format as Little Golden Book, 28 pages. - **$8 $15 $25**

SNW-280

❏ **SNW-280. "Snow White And The Seven Dwarfs Big Golden Book,"**
1952. Simon & Schuster. 9.5x13.25" hardcover with 28 pages. - **$20 $40 $80**

❏ **SNW-275. "Musical Sweeper" Featuring Dopey From Snow White,**
1950. Fisher Price. 7x9x3" tin litho and wood sweeper unit with attached 20" long wood handle. Came in generic Fisher Price design box. Box - **$25 $50 $100**
Sweeper - **$100 $200 $300**

SNW-276

❏ **SNW-276. "Snow White And The Seven Dwarfs/Rinso" Store Sign,**
c. 1951. Sign is 17x22" stiff paper with portrait of Arthur Godfrey with word balloon reading "Play The Rinso Name Game/Just Identify These 4 Walt Disney Characters And Name The Rinso Bird." - **$65 $125 $200**

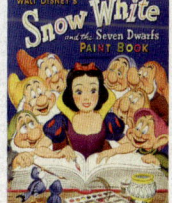

SNW-277

SNW-281

SNW-282

❏ **SNW-281. Movie Re-Release Handout Ink Blotter,**
1952. RKO Radio Pictures. 4x8" vertical format cardboard souvenir for film's second re-release. An 8" ruler design is printed on right edge. - **$20 $40 $60**

❏ **SNW-282. Washing Machine Promotional Folder,**
c. 1952. Bendix Home Appliances. Closed 5.5x8.5" mailer with front cover depiction of housewife whistling "Whistle While It Works." Folder opens first to illustration of "Snow White Automatic Washer" plus images of Doc, Happy and Dopey heating a pan of water with candle for text "Keeps Hot Water Hot...Live Suds Alive." Folder opens once more to additional scene of washing machine surrounded by Snow White, Grumpy, Bashful, Sneezy, plus Bashful and Doc putting a coin in a piggy bank. - **$15 $30 $50**

SNW-283

855

SNOW WHITE AND THE SEVEN DWARFS

❑ **SNW-283. "Snow White Snow Spray Bomb" Can,**
1953. Wilco Co. 6.25" tall metal can with list of uses printed on back of can. Wrap-around art features Snow White and The Seven Dwarfs on a snow-covered landscape. - **$30 $60 $100**

SNW-284

❑ **SNW-284. "Snow White" Boxed Watch With Figure,**
1954. U.S. Time. 4.5x7x1.25" deep box with cellophane display window. Box has plain cardboard slip cover. Issued with either a punch-out cardboard or vacuform plastic Snow White figure. This version is the 6" tall vacuform figure which has a loop at top for hanging.
Near Mint Either Version Boxed - **$400**

SNW-285

❑ **SNW-285. Snow White Watch,**
1954. U.S. Time. 1-1/8" diameter version in plastic case. - **$25 $50 $115**

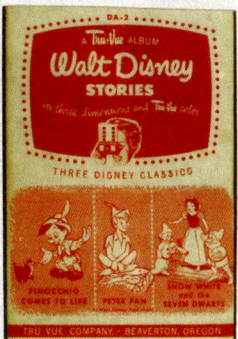
SNW-286

❑ **SNW-286. "Walt Disney Stories" Stereo Cards Set,**
1954. Tru-Vue 4x5.75" envelope containing set "DA-2" of three stereo view cards for Snow White, Pinocchio, Peter Pan. - **$5 $12 $20**

SNW-287

SNW-288

❑ **SNW-287. "Snow White And The Seven Dwarfs In 'The Milky Way'" Premium Comic,**
1955. Comic is 5x7.5" with 16 pages and issued by The American Dairy Assn. - **$12 $36 $120**

❑ **SNW-288. "Snow White Dairy Recipes" Premium Booklet,**
1955. Western Printing. 6x7" with 12 pages of recipes and nice color art. - **$15 $30 $50**

SNW-289

❑ **SNW-289. "Snow White" Watch Figurine,**
1958. US Time. Wristwatch display packaging of 5" tall painted and glazed ceramic, also produced in plastic for same purpose. Ceramic - **$8 $12 $25** Plastic - **$5 $10 $20**

SNW-290

❑ **SNW-290. "Snow White" Boxed Timex Watch With Figure,**
1958. U.S. Time. 4x4.5x6" tall box with top that lifts off to reveal display with attached 4.5" tall hard plastic figure and watch.
Near Mint Boxed - **$500**
Figure Only (Plastic) - **$5 $10 $20**
Figure Only (Ceramic) - **$8 $12 $25**
Watch Only - **$25 $50 $100**

SNW-291

❑ **SNW-291. "Snow White And The Seven Dwarfs" Premium Comic,**
1958. Western Printing. 5x7" with 12 pages. Issued by various food stores. - **$8 $24 $65**

SNW-292

SNOW WHITE AND THE SEVEN DWARFS

❏ **SNW-292. Snow White "Mystery Of The Missing Magic" Premium Comic Book,** 1958. Reynold's Wrap. 5x7" 16-page publication by Western Printing Co. Aluminum foil product is featured in the story. Back cover is an ad for set of Snow White premium plaques available for $1 and Reynolds Wrap seal. - **$15 $30 $60**

SNW-293

❏ **SNW-293. "Snow White And The Seven Dwarfs" Fan Card,** 1950s. Stiff paper 8x10" with scene for "Walt Disney's All-Cartoon Feature." - **$12 $25 $40**

SNW-294

SNW-295

❏ **SNW-294. "Ice Capades" Pennant,** 1950s. Felt fabric 8.5x26" pennant souvenir. - **$15 $30 $50**

❏ **SNW-295. Frame Tray Puzzle,** 1950s. Whitman. 9.25x11.5" inlay jigsaw puzzle. - **$10 $20 $40**

SNW-296

❏ **SNW-296. "Snow White" Figurine,** 1950s. Beswick. 5.25" tall. Underside has markings including incised number "1332." - **$100 $200 $400**

SNW-297

❏ **SNW-297. Snow White And The Seven Dwarfs Figurine Set,** 1950s. Goebel. Set includes 5.5" tall Snow White and Dwarfs are 2.75" tall. Underside of each has full bee marking. Each Dwarf has silver foil label.
Snow White - **$75 $150 $250**
Each Dwarf - **$20 $30 $50**

SNW-298

SNW-299

❏ **SNW-298. "Grumpy" Figurine From Set,** 1950s. Hagen Renaker. 3.25" tall, from set of seven plus Snow White. Each - **$50 $100 $200**
Snow White (not shown) - **$100 $200 $400**

❏ **SNW-299. "Sneezy,"** 1950s. Hagen Renaker. 3.25" tall. - **$40 $75 $150**

SNW-300

❏ **SNW-300. "Sleepy,"** 1950s. Hagen Renaker. 3.25" tall. - **$50 $100 $200**

SNW-301

❏ **SNW-301. "Happy" Large Figurine,** 1950s. Hagen-Renaker. 1.25x2x3.25" tall painted and glazed figurine from larger size Snow White set by this maker. Reverse has foil sticker. Each Dwarf - **$50 $100 $200**

SNW-302

857

SNOW WHITE AND THE SEVEN DWARFS

SNW-303

❑ **SNW-302. Dopey Figurine,**
1950s. Shaw Pottery. 1.75" tall painted and glazed ceramic from small size set of Dwarf figurines. - **$25 $50 $100**

❑ **SNW-303. Bashful Figurine,**
1950s. Shaw Pottery. 1.75" tall painted and glazed ceramic from small size set of Dwarf figurines. - **$25 $50 $100**

SNW-304

SNW-305

❑ **SNW-304. Sneezy Figurine,**
1950s. Shaw Pottery. 1.75" tall painted and glazed ceramic from small size set of Dwarf figurines. -**$25 $50 $100**

❑ **SNW-305. Happy Figurine,**
1950s. Shaw Pottery. 1.75" tall painted and glazed ceramic from small size set of Dwarf figurines. - **$25 $50 $100**

SNW-306

❑ **SNW-306. "Bashful" Figurine,**
1950s. Beswick. 1.75x3x3.5" tall painted and glazed ceramic marked "Beswick England." - **$85 $175 $300**

SNW-307

SNW-308

❑ **SNW-307. "Doc" Figurine,**
1950s. "Beswick-England." 3.5" tall painted and glazed ceramic with underside incised "1329" plus text including his name and copyright. - **$85 $175 $300**

❑ **SNW-308. "Dopey" Figurine,**
1950s. "Beswick-England." 3.5" tall painted and glazed with underside incised "1325" plus text including his name and copyright. - **$85 $175 $300**

SNW-309

❑ **SNW-309. "Sneezy" Figurine,**
1950s. "Beswick-England." 3.5" tall painted and glazed with underside incised name and copyright. - **$85 $175 $300**

SNW-310

❑ **SNW-310. Snow White And Dwarfs Hagen-Renaker Glazed Ceramic Miniatures Set,**
1950s. Each has gold foil sticker copyright Walt Disney Prod. Snow White is 2.25", Dopey is 1-1/8". Other six Dwarfs are of similar size. Snow White - **$50 $100 $150**
Each Dwarf - **$25 $50 $75**

SNW-311

SNOW WHITE AND THE SEVEN DWARFS

❏ **SNW-311. Bashful Figural Clock,**
1950s. "Made In Germany" 7.5x9" painted and glazed ceramic with high relief portrait design, nearly 1.75" at its deepest point. Inset metal clock is marked "Blessing" and has glow-in-the-dark hands and numerals. Reverse has copyright and company name, "J A Sural Hanau/Main." This company produced a series of clocks including those of Donald Duck, Bambi, Pinocchio and other Snow White characters. Each - **$75 $150 $250**

SNW-312

❏ **SNW-312. "Snow White And The Seven Dwarfs 7-Day Illness" Card Set,**
1950s. Gibson Cards. 5x6" stiff paper cover folder containing set of seven 4x4" different Dwarf cards to comply with outer cover instruction, "Send One A Day For A Week." Each card is numbered and different character name appears as part of the get-well wish. The first six cards also note that an additional card was to follow. Set - **$35 $75 $115**

SNW-313

SNW-314

❏ **SNW-313. Bread Labels Set,**
1950s. Eight 2.75x2.75" waxed paper bread wrapper end labels from larger series including other Disney character labels. Each Label - **$3 $6 $12**

❏ **SNW-314. "Snow White" Bread Label Picture,**
1950s. Picture is 11x11.5" with 16 different bread label cut-outs applied. Issued by various bread companies. Picture Sheet Only - **$25 $50 $75**
Completed Sheet - **$50 $100 $200**

SNW-315

SNW-316

❏ **SNW-315. Snow White Uncut Bread Label Strips,**
1950s. Two 2.75x11" waxed paper label strips still uncut for designed individual application on 11x11.5" picture sheet premium offered by various bakeries. Each Label - **$3 $6 $12**

❏ **SNW-316. Snow White And The Seven Dwarfs Boxed German Candy Container Set,**
1950s. Box is 10x10x2.25" deep with eight containers. Snow White is 5.5" tall and dwarfs are 5.25" marked "Made In Germany." All have string hanger and small paper sticker. Box - **$50 $100 $200**
Figure Set - **$100 $200 $300**

SNW-317

❏ **SNW-317. Candy Box With Snow White & Dopey,**
1950s. Super Novelty Candy Co. 1x2.5x3.75" empty "Candy and Toy" box. - **$20 $40 $85**

SNW-318

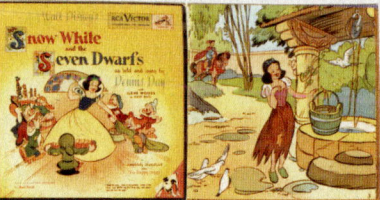
SNW-319

SNOW WHITE AND THE SEVEN DWARFS

❑ **SNW-318. Musical "T.V. Nite Lite,"**
1950s. Hankscraft, Ltd., Toronto. 4x6.25x5" tall hard plastic replica of television set. On back is wind-up key for music box mechanism that chimes Brahm's Lullaby. - **$30 $60 $115**

❑ **SNW-319. "Snow White And The Seven Dwarfs" Book And Record Set,**
1950s. RCA Victor "Little Nipper Series" 7.25x7.25" cardboard album containing bound-in, 24-page book plus pair of 45 rpm records. - **$15 $30 $60**

SNW-320

❑ **SNW-320. "Dopey" Litho Button From Set,**
1950s. From Disney character set with "Donald Duck Peanut Butter" on reverse. 13/16". - **$10 $20 $40**

SNW-321

❑ **SNW-321. "Snow White" Litho Button From Set,**
1950s. From Disney character set with "Donald Duck Peanut Butter" on reverse. 13/16". - **$15 $25 $50**

SNW-322

SNW-323

❑ **SNW-322. Happy Store Sign,**
1950s. Paper poster is 12x19" promoting store specials. Title is "Whistle While You Save On Specials." - **$25 $50 $85**

❑ **SNW-323. Dopey Store Sign,**
1950s. Paper poster is 12.25x20.75" promoting store specials. Title is "Whistle While You Save On Specials." - **$25 $50 $85**

SNW-324

SNW-325

❑ **SNW-324. "Snow White And The Seven Dwarfs" English Hardcover,**
1950s. Collins. 8.25x11" with 80 pages. - **$25 $60 $135**

❑ **SNW-325. European Rug,**
c. 1950s. Unmarked but Belgian large 45x57" fabric rug with woven illustration. - **$40 $75 $150**

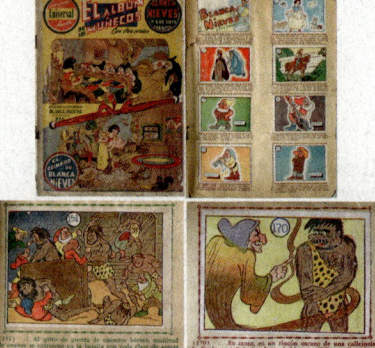

SNW-326

❑ **SNW-326. Cuban Cards Album,**
c. 1950s. "Universal/RKO" Spanish text 8.75x11.5", 24-page album containing 200 numbered 2x3" cards, all neatly mounted at appropriate spots. Content is two separate stories, each illustrated by 100 cards. First story is traditional. Second story introduces various non-traditional characters and plot title that translates to the Reign of Snow White. - **$115 $225 $375**

SNOW WHITE AND THE SEVEN DWARFS

SNW-327

SNW-328

❏ **SNW-327. Austrian Snow White Clock,** c. 1950s. Wood clock designed like a cottage 3.25x7x8.75" tall. Thin die-cut wood figure of Snow white sticks out of die-cut window and she is to move back and forth as seconds tick. Attached along bottom are the Dwarfs in painted pressed cardboard. Marked "Made In Austria." - **$115 $275 $475**

❏ **SNW-328. Snow White Metal Figure Set,** c. 1960. Line Mar. Set of eight painted white metal figures. Snow white is 1.75" and Dwarfs are 1.25". - **$50 $100 $160**

SNW-329

SNW-330

❏ **SNW-329. Snow White Cookie Jar,** c. 1961. Painted and glazed ceramic 5x6x9" tall. Raised Dwarf images around front of dress along with bluebird. - **$200 $400 $700**

❏ **SNW-330. Disney Studio French Card,** 1963. Closed 4x8.5" New Year's greeting folder opening to scene of Snow White, Dwarfs and forest animals carving out wood numbers for the year "1963." Reverse text includes "Walt Disney Mickey Mouse" with Paris offices address. Greeting text is French. - **$12 $25 $50**

SNW-331

SNW-332

❏ **SNW-331. "Snow White And The Seven Dwarfs" Re-Release Lobby Card Set,** 1967. Complete set of nine 11x14" full color glossy stiff paper cards in original envelope. Set is for the Buena Vista re-release of original movie although cards are reprints from an earlier 1958 re-release. Set - **$20 $40 $75**

❏ **SNW-332. "Snow White And The Seven Dwarfs" Re-Release Press Kit,** 1967. Stiff paper folder 11.5x14" containing extensive advance materials for 30th (1968) anniversary re-release of original film. Three inner folders repeat the design of outer folder and hold a total of 23 photos sized either 8x10", 8.5x11.25" or large 10.25x13.5" Other materials are "Production Scenes" 29-page book with related photo on each page and "Production Handbook" with seven pages of credits, movie synopsis and more. Kit - **$40 $65 $125**

SNW-333

❏ **SNW-333. "Snow White And The Seven Dwarfs" Re-Release Pressbook,** 1967. Glossy paper 11x14" "Ad Pad" for Buena Vista re-release of original movie, 16 pages. Content includes newspaper mats and ads in various sizes. - **$8 $12 $25**

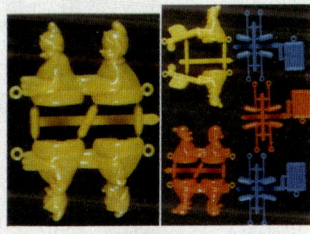

SNW-334

❏ **SNW-334 Dwarf Nabisco Rice Honeys Premium Ramp Walkers,** 1967. Three of four unassembled, each 2" long. Two feature two different and these are Grumpy/Happy and Dopey/Bashful while the third is Doc with wheelbarrow. Missing is Sleepy/Sneezy. Included are plastic tags to be attached to string and then used to pull walker along. Each Unassembled - **$5 $10 $15**
Each Assembled - **$3 $6 $10**

861

SNOW WHITE AND THE SEVEN DWARFS

SNW-335

❏ **SNW-335. "Special Snow White Merchandising Supplement."**
c. 1967. Size is 10.5x14" with 12 pages. Issued in conjunction with re-release of the film. - **$10 $20 $35**

SNW-336

❏ **SNW-336. Snow White And The Seven Dwarfs Disneykin Set,**
1960s. Marx. Set of 1.5" tall painted hard plastic Snow White and 1" tall Dwarfs plus accessories, originally sold as one of the "Disneykin Playsets" boxed sets. Group - **$30 $60 $90**

SNW-337

SNW-338

❏ **SNW-337. "Snow White" Figurine Boxed,**
1960s. Enesco. 3x3.5x4.5" tall painted and glazed ceramic. Box - **$10 $20 $40**
Figure - **$15 $30 $60**

❏ **SNW-338. Disneykins And Disneyking Figures,**
1960s. Marx. Eight hand-painted hard plastic figures including near-set of Disneykins, missing only Bashful. Snow White is 1.5" tall and each Dwarf is 1" tall. Second figure of Snow White is larger 2.25" tall "Disneyking" painted plastic by Marx. Disneyking - **$5 $12 $20**
Each Disneykin - **$3 $5 $8**

SNW-339

SNW-340

❏ **SNW-339. "Disneykins" Set Individually Boxed,**
1960s. Marx. Eight portrait boxes, each containing painted hard plastic miniature figure. Snow White is 1.5" tall and Dwarfs are 1". Boxed Each - **$5 $10 $15**

❏ **SNW-340. Dwarf Figures,**
1960s. Three hard vinyl figures from set about 4.4.5x8" tall. Grumpy and Bashful are movable at the waist and Doc has a movable head. Each is marked with name and number on underside along with "Made In Japan." Each - **$5 $10 $20**

SNW-341

❏ **SNW-341. Disneykins Offer Box,**
1960s. Royal Instant Pudding. 3.25x4x1.25" unopened box with front panel inset text "Special Disneykin Offer (See Back)." Back panel advertises the set of Disneykin Snow White and The Seven Dwarfs figures available for 50 cents and two package backs. - **$20 $40 $75**

SNW-342

SNW-343

❏ **SNW-342. Snow White Candy Dispenser,**
1960s. Pez. 4.25" tall. - **$75 $135 $250**

❏ **SNW-343. "Snow White Soaky,"**
1960s. Hard plastic top and soft plastic bottom 10.5" tall container. - **$10 $20 $40**

SNW-344

❏ **SNW-344. "Dopey" Soap Bottle Variety,**
1960s. "Soaky" 10" tall empty container with soft plastic body and hard plastic head. This example depicts him standing atop a wood fence that has his name in raised lettering. - **$10 $30 $65**

SNOW WHITE AND THE SEVEN DWARFS

SNW-345

SNW-348

❑ **SNW-350. "Snow White" Wall Plaque Boxed,**
1960s. Enesco. 6.5x8.25x.75" deep painted and glazed ceramic centered by high relief image of her. Framing is simulated wood. Box - **$8 $12 $25**
Plaque - **$20 $40 $75**

❑ **SNW-351. Dwarf Cups,**
1960s. Enesco. Five 3.75" tall glazed ceramics from set of eight. Each - **$8 $15 $25**

❑ **SNW-345. "Doc" Toothbrush Holder,**
1960s. Enesco. Unmarked 3x5.5x4.5" tall painted and glazed ceramic figural. Designed for countertop use or wall mounting. - **$20 $40 $75**

❑ **SNW-348 Snow White Night Light Base,**
1960s. Enesco. 3.5x3.5x5.25" painted and glazed ceramic with tree stump designed to hold a small bulb. - **$40 $75 $125**

SNW-352

SNW-346

SNW-349

❑ **SNW-352. "Snow White" Mug,**
1960s. Enesco. 3.75" tall painted and glazed ceramic, from set of eight. - **$10 $20 $30**

SNW-353

SNW-347

❑ **SNW-349. "Snow White" Framed Fabric Picture,**
1960s. 9x11" hard plastic framed texture fabric over cardboard background. - **$5 $10 $15**

SNW-350

❑ **SNW-346. "Secret Storage Box,"**
1960s. 2.25x9.25x1.5" deep wood box with paper label on sliding lid picturing Dwarfs in procession beneath phrase from "Hi-Ho" song. Front has sticker that identifies "Secret Storage Box." Content is total of three partitioned compartments. No copyright. - **$10 $20 $35**

❑ **SNW-347. "Bashful" Oil Lamp,**
1960s. Painted and glazed ceramic 3x3.5x4" tall bust. Underside has copyright and is marked "Crown Lamp Japan." - **$25 $50 $100**

SNW-351

❑ **SNW-353. "Snow White" Pitcher,**
1960s. Enesco. 3x6.25x8.25" tall painted and glazed ceramic. - **$40 $85 $150**

SNW-354

SNOW WHITE AND THE SEVEN DWARFS

SNW-355

❑ **SNW-354. Snow White & Dopey Salt & Pepper Set With Tray,**
1960s. Enesco. Pair of 3.75" tall painted and glazed ceramic shakers on simulated wood grain plastic tray sealed in shrinkwrap with title sticker as issued. Sealed Mint - **$165**
Loose - **$40 $80 $135**

❑ **SNW-355. Snow White Bank,**
1960s. Painted and glazed ceramic 2.5x4.5x5" tall. Raised text on roof is "Wishing And Saving Will Make It So." - **$25 $50 $100**

SNW-356

SNW-357

❑ **SNW-356. Snow White Story Poster With Mailer,**
1960s. Golden Press Div. Of Western Printing Co. Exceptionally large horizontal format glossy paper poster 12.5" tall by just over 6' in width. Bottom center has text story and poster art illustrates pivotal points in chronological order left to right. Poster is rolled in 14" long cardboard mailing tube. Mailer - **$5 $10 $15**
Print - **$25 $50 $75**

❑ **SNW-357. "Dopey" Hand Puppet,**
1960s. Puppet is 10.5" tall with soft vinyl head and printed fabric body with stitched copyright tag. Inside has squeaker mechanism. - **$10 $20 $30**

SNW-358

❑ **SNW-358. "Dopey" Rolykin Boxed,**
1960s. Marx. 1.25" tall painted hard plastic miniature figure with ball bearing roller inserted in base. From a series of Disney character Rolykins. Box - **$5 $10 $20**
Toy - **$5 $10 $20**

SNW-359

❑ **SNW-359. "I'm Dopey" English Button,**
1960s. 1.25". Issued for house cleaning product. - **$3 $8 $15**

SNW-360

❑ **SNW-360. "Snow White" Ceramic Musical Trinket Box,**
c. 1960. Enesco. 6.5" tall. - **$35 $65 $125**

SNW-361

❑ **SNW-361. Ornament Set,**
1960s. "Made In Japan" copyright set of eight hollow vinyl figures finished in felt-covered body/outfit plus lifelike beard on all Dwarfs except Dopey. Snow White is 4" tall and each Dwarf is about 3.75" tall. All have attached string for hanging. Set - **$30 $60 $90**

SNW-362

❑ **SNW-362. Snow White Alarm Clock,**
1960s. By Bayard and marked "Made In France" and more elaborate of two versions. This version features hands designed as tree branches, each with small bird attached, top center has additional bluebird attachment which moves as seconds tick. At center of clock face is image of Snow White with her hand raised in the air so it appears as if moving bird sits on her finger. 2x3.5x4.75" tall. - **$65 $125 $175**

SNW-363

SNOW WHITE AND THE SEVEN DWARFS

☐ **SNW-363. "Snow White" Friction Powered Van Trailer,**
1960s. Line Mar. 12x6" tin toy.
Box - **$100 $200 $400**
Toy - **$200 $400 $800**

SNW-364

☐ **SNW-364. "Snow White And The Seven Dwarfs" Zoetrope,**
1960s. Unmarked but Colorforms visual illusion novelty of,"Canned Movies/Spin And See Magic Movies." Cardboard container 5" tall by 6" diameter with tin lid and wood handle attachment that fits on a rod on underside. Has illustrations of Snow White from waist up and full figure images of the Seven Dwarfs. Set has 12 filmstrips, each 2x18" with single or double images of Snow White, Seven Dwarfs, Prince, Magic Mirror, Wicked Queen. Container has die-cut slots for viewing when spun. - **$100 $200 $350**

SNW-365

☐ **SNW-365. Dwarfs Figural Pencil Holders,**
1960s. Three 2x2.25x4" tall painted and glazed ceramic figures, each on base with opening for pencil or pen placement. Two are identical figures of Bashful although base text is different while the third is of Doc. Doc and one Bashful have "Disneyland" logo and copyright symbol on front and Productions name on underside. The other Bashful is marked on front of base "May I Hold Your Pen" while underside has no Productions marking and a foil sticker "Tilford Japan." Each - **$20 $40 $65**

SNW-366

☐ **SNW-366. Snow White Grocery Store Advertising Lot,**
c. 1960s. Three pieces, 2 stiff glossy paper hangers 18x30" depicting Dopey and a 27x38" poster depicting Dopey and Sleepy. Poster - **$20 $40 $85**
Each Sign - **$10 $20 $50**

SNW-367

☐ **SNW-367. Snow White Rug,**
c. 1960s. Rug is 45x57" and made in Belgium. - **$35 $65 $125**

SNW-368

☐ **SNW-368. Dopey Mexican China Wall Decoration,**
c. 1960s. Bust of Dopey is 5.5x6x1.5" deep marked "Made In Mexico." - **$50 $100 $150**

SNW-369

☐ **SNW-369. "Doc's Storage Barrel" Pencil Sharpener,**
c. 1960s. Painted and glazed ceramic 2.5x4x4.25" three dimensional figure of Doc. Reverse has incised "Crayon/Pencil." - **$25 $65 $115**

SNW-370

☐ **SNW-370. "Snow White And The Seven Dwarfs Turn And Learn Storybook,"**
1971. Ideal Toy Corp. 9x11" vinyl-covered storybook case unfolds to 19". Part of storybook design includes two different "Magic Picture Wheels." Top and bottom inside panels have die-cut window where disks are turned and numbered illustrations are lined up to correspond with story. - **$10 $15 $25**

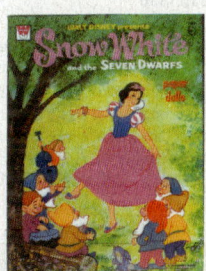
SNW-371

SNW-372

☐ **SNW-371. "Snow White And The Seven Dwarfs Paperdolls,"**
1972. Whitman. 10x12.75" with two stiff pages of punch-outs for Snow White, Seven Dwarfs, Prince and Queen plus six pages of glossy paper outfits and accessories. Uncut - **$20 $40 $65**

☐ **SNW-372. "Snow White" Press Book With Much Merchandise,**
1975. Book is 11.25x15" with 32 pages. Contents include text and photos from the film, promotional contest and much merchandise. - **$10 $20 $40**

SNOW WHITE AND THE SEVEN DWARFS

SNW-373

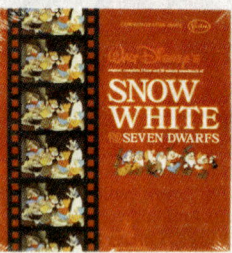

SNW-374

SNW-376

SNW-377

SNW-378

SNW-379

SNW-380

SNW-381

❏ SNW-373. Lunch Box With Thermos,
1975. Aladdin Industries. 7x8x4" deep embossed metal box and 6.5" tall plastic bottle. Box - **$25 $50 $150**
Bottle - **$5 $15 $30**

❏ SNW-374. Commemorative Issue Record Set Boxed,
1975. Buena Vista Records. 12.25x12.25x.5" deep box containing set of three 33-1/3 rpm records to total "Original, Complete 1 Hour And 16 Minutes Soundtrack." Set is accompanied by a poster book. - **$12 $25 $40**

SNW-375

❏ SNW-375. "Snow White And The Seven Dwarfs Mugs" Giant Store Display,
1975. Assembled size is 30x30" by nearly 7' tall. Bottom of display is large bin for placement of store products with wrap-around scene of Snow White, dwarfs and forest animals. Top half has six shelves for holding mugs. There were four mugs made for the set - Snow White, Dopey, Doc and Grumpy and each is 4.25" tall hard plastic. Display - **$65 $135 $250**
Each Mug - **$5 $10 $20**

❏ SNW-376. "Snow White And The Seven Dwarfs" Lunch Box,
c. 1975. Aladdin. 7x9x4" vinyl box with 6.5" plastic thermos. Box - **$20 $40 $80**
Bottle - **$5 $15 $30**

❏ SNW-377. "Snow White Paperdolls" Boxed Set,
1979. Whitman. 5x14.75x1.25" deep box contains a pair of 8.5" dolls of Snow White and the Prince each with plastic stand plus a large glossy sheet with cut-out outfits, accessories and dwarf figures. Uncut - **$15 $30 $60**

❏ SNW-378. Disney Character Cel With Pencil Drawing From Eastern Airlines Commercial,
1970s. Image is 5x9.5" and from a numbered sequence and this is "S-66." Pair Near Mint - **$135**

❏ SNW-379. "Snow White And The Seven Dwarfs" English Lobby Cards,
1970s. Complete set of eight smaller sized 8x10" film scenes for European re-release of original movie. Seven cards prominently feature Snow White and/or Dwarfs and one is image of the Queen. Set - **$20 $40 $65**

❏ SNW-380. "Snow White And The Seven Dwarfs" Re-Release Stills,
1970s. Six 8.25x10" glossy paper film scenes for unspecified re-release date of original movie. Stills come in original manila envelope with "Productions/Burbank" return address. Five stills picture Snow White prominently and the sixth pictures Dopey alone. Each - **$2 $4 $8**

SNOW WHITE AND THE SEVEN DWARFS

❑ **SNW-381. "Snow White" Figurine Boxed,**
1970s. United China & Glass Co. 3.5x4x6" tall box containing 5.5" tall painted and glazed ceramic posed with clasped hands. Boxed - **$30 $40 $60**

SNW-382

SNW-383

❑ **SNW-382. "Snow White Sink,"**
1970s. Wolverine. 11.5x15.5x7.5" deep box holds tin lithographed child's sink. Sink features Snow White portrait along top back edge with illustrations of Doc, Happy and Dopey on cabinet doors and small plastic faucet. Near Mint Boxed - **$60**

❑ **SNW-383. "Snow White" Boxed Doll,**
1970s. Horsman Co. 7.75x10.75x3" deep box containing 8" tall hard vinyl doll with rooted lifelike hair plus glossy fabric gown and hood outfit. Box is designed as a book with display window lid that notes "Walt Disney's Classics" doll series. Boxed - **$20 $40 $60**

SNW-384

❑ **SNW-384. "Snow White And The Seven Dwarfs Paperdolls,"**
1970s. Whitman. 10x13" with two stiff pages of punch-outs for Snow White, Prince, Queen, Seven Dwarfs and outfits. Uncut - **$15 $35 $60**

SNW-385

SNW-386

❑ **SNW-385. Snow White Character Ornaments Set Boxed,**
1970s. Union Wadding Co. 10.5x12x2" deep boxed "Wonderful World of Disney" set of eight hollow soft plastic figures finished in felt and flocking outfits plus string loop for hanging. Snow White ornament is 4.5" tall, others are about 3.75" tall. Boxed - **$10 $25 $40**

❑ **SNW-386. "Snow White And The Seven Dwarfs" Re-Release Poster,**
1983. Poster is 27x41" glossy paper one-sheet for re-release of original movie. Text reads "Still The Fairest Of Them All." - **$5 $15 $25**

SNW-387

❑ **SNW-387. "Snow White And Friends" Porcelain Disk,**
1983. Box 3.25x4x1" deep holds 2.5" diameter disk marked "Designed By Walt Disney Artists/1983 Charter Member Limited Edition." Mint As Issued - **$60**

SNW-388

❑ **SNW-388. "Having Dinner With Snow White and the Seven Dwarfs" Sculpture,**
1984. Disney Capodimonte by master sculptor Enzo Arzenton. Edition of 1000. - **$3500**

867

SNOW WHITE AND THE SEVEN DWARFS

SNW-389

❏ **SNW-389. "Snow White And The Seven Dwarfs" Serigraph,**
1986. "Walt Disney Co." triple matted and metal framed 16x18" display. Reverse has certificate for issuer "Gallery Lainzberg." Mint As Issued - **$135**

SNW-390

❏ **SNW-390. "Walt Disney World/Coca-Cola" Pin Set,**
1986. Clear acrylic plastic case 4.25x6.25x.75" deep holds set of nine different brass/enamel paint pins with needle post and clutch fasteners. Issued for the 15th anniversary of Walt Disney World, each with Coca-Cola logo. Set includes individual pins for Snow White and Seven Dwarfs plus an anniversary logo pin. Mint As Issued - **$65**

SNW-391

❏ **SNW-391. 50th Anniversary Press Kit,**
1987. Folder is 9x12" of publicity materials for golden anniversary re-release of original film. Content is 8.5x11" 24-page booklet and set of six 8x10" glossy black and white publicity photos. Booklet has detailed information on the film and its production. Each photo features multiple images including film scenes and other artwork, Walt with studio models and 'voice' of Snow White, Adriana Caselotti. - **$15 $30 $50**

SNW-392

❏ **SNW-392. 50th Anniversary Ticket & Coin,**
1987. Commemorative for the golden anniversary re-release of original film, comprised of 3.5x7" folder containing 1.5" diameter gold luster coin plus a numbered admission ticket for any movie theater chosen. Both are in mailing envelope. Mint As Issued - **$25**

SNW-393

SNW-394

❏ **SNW-393. "Snow White 50th Anniversary" Silver Medals,**
1987. By Rarities Mint. Each coin comes with 2.25x2.25" laminated card with Snow White illustration and serial number. Embossed character design on front and text on reverse. This is for the "Witch," others for Doc, Sneezy, Grumpy and seven others to make set of 11. Each Mint As Issued - **$25**

❏ **SNW-394. "Snow White" 50th Anniversary Music Box,**
1987. Schmid. 6" tall painted bisque figural on 3.25" diameter base with underside built-in key. Key wind produces tune "Someday My Prince Will Come." Near Mint Boxed - **$35**

SNOW WHITE AND THE SEVEN DWARFS

SNW-395

❑ **SNW-395. Snow White Cel From The Academy Awards,**
1988. Sheet is 10.5x12.5" acetate with 5.25x5.75" painted cel image of her in evening gown for Academy Awards 60th anniversary tribute to her. No. "187" from a numbered sequence. - **$50 $100 $175**

SNW-397

❑ **SNW-397. Dwarfs Publicity Cel,**
1980s. Image is 5.5x6.5". Near Mint - **$135**

SNW-398

SNW-396

❑ **SNW-396. "Doc" Ceramic Music Box,**
c. 1980s. 6-1/4" tall music box by Schmid. NM - **$150**

SNW-399

SNW-400

❑ **SNW-398. "Snow White And The Seven Dwarfs" Movie Theater Standees,**
1980s. Set of four die-cut cardboard standees 19.5x58" with easel on reverse. Each has illustrations including Prince holding Snow White, the Dwarfs, Prince and Snow White on horseback and Queen and Wicked Witch. Each - **$15 $30 $60**

❑ **SNW-399. Snow White Metal Figure,**
1980s. Hudson Pewter Co. 3.25" tall solid pewter figurine with company name and copyright on underside of base. - **$8 $15 $30**

❑ **SNW-400. Snow White Glass Figurine,**
1980s. Frosted glass figurine is 5.75" tall with painted highlights. - **$5 $10 $20**

SNW-401

❑ **SNW-401. "Snow White And The Seven Dwarfs" Lamp,**
1980s. Glass housing 6" diameter at widest point by 11" tall to top of electrical bulb socket. "Disney" copyright. - **$20 $40 $60**

SNW-402

❑ **SNW-402. Snow White And Dopey Teapot,**
1980s. Unmarked 4x8x8" tall painted and glazed ceramic designed like a cottage. - **$40 $85 $150**

SNOW WHITE AND THE SEVEN DWARFS

SNW-403

❏ **SNW-403. "Snow White" Figural Music Box,** 1980s. Schmid. 6" diameter by 8.5" tall painted and glazed ceramic with over-the-glaze paint added on Dopey's long coat. Key-winding plays "Someday My Prince Will Come." - **$12 $25 $45**

SNW-405

❏ **SNW-405. Snow White And Dopey Music Box,** 1980s. Music box is 4.5" diameter by 7" tall painted and glazed ceramic. Key-winding plays "Whistle While You Work." No maker named but underside has Disney copyright. - **$12 $25 $45**

SNW-407

❏ **SNW-407. Snow White Figure Ornament,** 1980s. Schmid. 4.5" tall painted and glazed ceramic with small metal loop attached to head for hanging. - **$5 $12 $20**

SNW-404

❏ **SNW-404. "Snow White" Figural Music Box,** 1980s. Schmid. 4" diameter by 6.5" tall painted and glazed ceramic. Key-winding plays "Some Day My Prince Will Come." - **$12 $25 $45**

SNW-406

❏ **SNW-406. Snow White Figure Ornament,** 1980s. Schmid. 4.75" tall painted bisque with attached hanging cord. Depiction includes bluebird on one hand. - **$10 $20 $30**

SNW-408

❏ **SNW-408. Snow White "Voice" Adriana Caselotti Autographed Photo,** c. 1980s. Publicity photo is 8x10" glossy with vintage image of her beside her inked "Oh Dopey! The Voice Of Snow White/Adriana Caselotti." - **$20 $40 $65**

SNOW WHITE AND THE SEVEN DWARFS

SNW-409

SNW-410

SNW-411

❏ **SNW-411. "Snow White" Limited Edition Employee Watch,**
1993. Velvet pouch is 2.5x9.5" long and contains wristwatch in 1.25" diameter goldtone case. Crystal is designed as the Queen's mirror with image of her peering into it and rim has ornate design of snakes and simulated jewels. As the watch ticks off seconds, the image below the crystal changes from solid black color into a full color Snow White image which then slowly fades out again. These were sold to Disney employees only and this is #162 from limited production of only 750. Mint As Issued - **$165**

SNW-412

❏ **SNW-412. "Old Witch with Apple" Figure,**
1995-96. From the Walt Disney Classics Collection. Made in Thailand. Has to rank as one of the best of the old hag figures. - **$475**

SNW-413

❏ **SNW-413. "The Walt Disney Company Limited Edition Serigraph,"**
1990s. Image is 8.5x9" and shows Snow White with Sleepy, Bashful and Happy. Mint As Issued - **$150**

SNW-414

❏ **SNW-414. Collectors Plate Set,**
1990s. Edwin M. Knowles China Co. Limited edition complete set of twelve numbered 8.5" diameter china plates issued between 1991-1993. Each comes in original generic shipping box, with papers including certificate of authenticity and story folder for each plate. Plates 1-12 consecutively tell the story of Snow White, each by choice color scene. Plates were limited to 150 firing days and marketed originally at $30 each. Each Mint As Issued - **$20**

❏ **SNW-409. "Pelham Puppets" Snow White And The Seven Dwarfs Store Display Marionette Set,**
c. 1980s. Pelham Puppets. Set of eight marionettes. Snow White is 28" tall while dwarfs are each about 19" tall. Head, hands and feet are painted composition. Outfits are cotton and felt. Plain boxes marked only "Pelham Puppets Made In England." Each - **$60 $125 $225**

❏ **SNW-410. Snow White & Grumpy Sculpture,**
c. 1990. "Ron Lee" creation 4x6x5.5" tall of enameled cast metal figures atop a large stone base, believed to be onyx, with nameplate. Front top edge of base is signed by the artist with 1990 date. Reverse has inked edition number/size "59/2750" with Disney copyright. Mint As Issued - **$165**

SNOW WHITE AND THE SEVEN DWARFS

SNW-415

☐ **SNW-415. "Seven Dwarfs" Disneyland Employee Only Watch,**
1990s. Box is 2x9.5x1" deep and holds 1x1.5" diameter watch with black leather straps. Reverse has Company D logo and marked "Limited To 1500." Mint As Issued - **$135**

SNW-416

☐ **SNW-416. The Seven Dwarfs Wristwatch,**
1990s. Goldtone 1.25". Has insert "The Disney Store Exclusive" sticker. Crystal has multifaceted design and dial has illustrations of Dwarfs. Mint As Issued - **$80**

SNW-417

☐ **SNW-417. "Wedding Snow White" Doll in Box,**
2001. - **$40**

SNW-418

☐ **SNW-418. Brass Key Keepsake Collection Snow White Doll,**
2004. Porcelain collectible doll, 7 1/2 " inches high. - **$10**

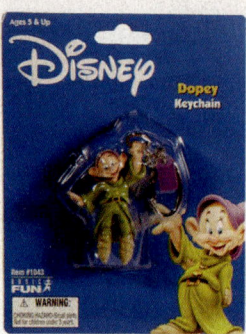

SNW-419

☐ **SNW-419. Dopey Keychain,**
2004. - **$6**

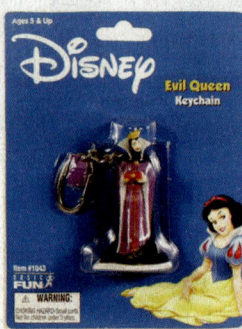

SNW-420

☐ **SNW-420. Evil Queen Keychain,**
2004. - **$6**

SNW-421

☐ **SNW-421. Sparkle Princess Collection Snow White Doll,**
2005. Fashion doll with collectible ring, 11 1/2 " tall. - **$12**

SONG OF THE SOUTH

So Dear To My Heart

A wonderful combination of live-action and animation, this 1949 film is reputed to be one of Walt's personal favorites. It tells the story of a young farm boy named Jeremiah who adopted a young lamb and names him Danny. The name is a tribute to the famous race horse Dan Patch. The lamb is a bit destructive at home, so not too many people think that well of him. One day, Jeremiah is drawing in his scrapbook and as he daydreams, the animals from the pages of his book come to life in an animated sequence. They convince Jeremiah to enter the lamb in the county fair, where the lamb goes on to win a prize.

Directed by Harold Schuster, the cast includes Bobby Driscoll, Burl Ives, Beulah Bondi and Luana Patten. Animators included Marc Davis, Bill Peet, Ken Anderson and Milt Kahl. The song *Lavender Blue* was written by Eliot Daniel and sung in the film by Burl Ives. It was nominated for an Academy Award. Another song, *Stick-to-it-ivity*, entered the language as a popular catchphrase of the time.

The film was re-released theatrically in 1964. Merchandise was limited, but it did include a doll, books, records and a Danny the Lamb watch.

SDE-1

❑ **SDE-1. Danny The Black Lamb Watch,** 1947. Ingersoll/U.S. Time. 1-1/8x1.5" chromed metal case. Dial features full figure image of Danny whose front legs serve as the watch hands. Original black vinyl over leather straps. - $185 $375 $725

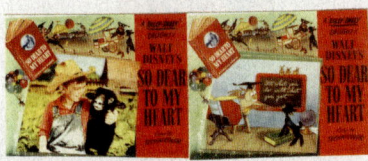
SDE-2

❑ **SDE-2. "So Dear To My Heart" Lobby Cards,** 1948. RKO Radio Pictures Inc. Two, each 11x14". Each - $12 $25 $50

SDE-3

SDE-4

❑ **SDE-3. "So Dear To My Heart" Boxed Record Set,** 1949. Capitol Records. 7.5x7.5x.75" deep box contains complete set of four 45 rpm records. - $15 $30 $60

❑ **SDE-4. "Danny The Little Black Lamb,"** 1949. "Story Hour Series" by Whitman, 5x6.75" hardcover. 32 pages. - $20 $40 $75

SDE-5

❑ **SDE-5. "Danny" The Black Lamb Doll With Button,** 1949. Gund. 12" tall doll with die-cut felt attachment representing blue ribbon centered by 2" button reading "Walt Disney's Danny Special Award Winner." Doll - $50 $100 $150
Felt Blue Ribbon - $5 $12 $25
Button - $15 $25 $50

Song of the South

After World War II, Disney released several films that combined live-action with animation. *Song of the South* (1946), featuring more live action than any Disney film before it, was based on the classic stories of Joel Chandler Harris.

The story is set in the 1870s. Young Johnny's parents are having marital problems and temporarily part ways. Johnny's father will stay in the city while he and his mother will live at Johnny's grandmother's Georgia plantation. Once there Johnny meets wise former slave Uncle Remus, who tells him fables featuring the characters of Brer Rabbit, Brer Bear and Brer Fox. The stories have strong morals that help Johnny in his daily life and lessons that help him when he befriends a young girl named Ginny. When they are bullied by her older brothers, Johnny applies what Uncle Remus has taught him. The tales also serve as inspiration when he is gored by a bull and comes close to death.

Song of the South was directed by Harve Foster. Its cast includes Bobby Driscoll, Johnny Lee, Nicodemus Stewart, and James Baskett as Uncle Remus, a role for which Baskett won an honorary Oscar. Directing the cartoon segments was Wilfred Jackson. Animators included Marc Davis, Les Clark, Ollie Johnston and Eric Larson. The song *Zip-a-Dee-Doo-Dah* won an Academy Award. The film was re-released theatrically four times, the last being in 1986.

Merchandise included books, comics (*Four Color Comics* #129, 208, and 693), records and ceramic figures.

SON-1

❑ **SON-1. "Song Of The South" Concept Art,** 1946. 6.25x7.75" artwork by noted artist Mary Blair. Unique, Near Mint - $4500

SONG OF THE SOUTH

SON-2

❑ **SON-2. "Song Of The South" Lobby Card Set,**
1946. RKO Radio Pictures. Set of eight 11x14" cards. Title card states "Walt Disney's First Live Action Musical Drama Including The Animated Tales Of Uncle Remus." Three cards feature animated scenes with Brer Rabbit, Bear and/or Fox. Three feature live action scenes. One is combination showing Bobby Driscoll and Luana Patton with Mr. Bluebird. Title Card - **$60 $100 $165**
Scene Card - **$45 $75 $135**

SON-3

❑ **SON-3. "Song Of The South" Movie Poster,**
1946. Half sheet 22x28". - **$100 $200 $400**

SON-4

SON-5

❑ **SON-4. "Song Of The South" Movie Program,**
1946. Western Printing. 9.75x12.5" with 16 pages. - **$100 $200 $300**

❑ **SON-5. "Song Of The South" Sheet Music,**
1946. Three, each 9x12". Each is for a different song from the film although cover designs are identical. Music for "Sooner Or Later" and "Uncle Remus Said" is on matte finish paper while "Zip-A-Dee-Doo-Dah" is on glossy paper. Each - **$8 $15 $30**

SON-6

❑ **SON-6. "The Wonderful Tar Baby" Book,**
1946. Grosset & Dunlap. 6.75x8.25" hardcover with 32 pages. - **$55 $110 $165**

 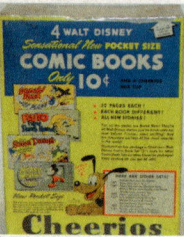

SON-7

❑ **SON-7. Cheerios 7 oz. Cereal Box with Comic Book Offer on Back,**
1946. Brer Rabbit pictured on front. - **$200 $600 $1000**

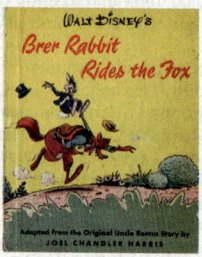

SON-8

❑ **SON-8. "Brer Rabbit Rides The Fox" Australian Book,**
1946. Ayers & Games Pty. Ltd. 6.5x8" hardcover with 32 pages. - **$30 $60 $125**

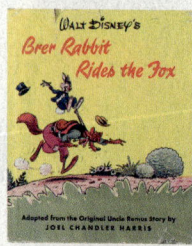

SON-9

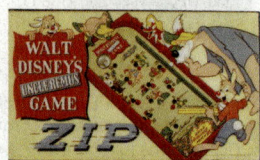

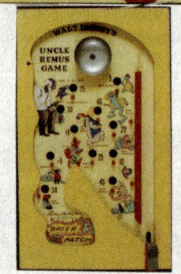

SON-10

SONG OF THE SOUTH

☐ **SON-9. "Brer Rabbit Rides The Fox" Book With Dust Jacket,**
1946. Grosset & Dunlap. 7x8.25" hardcover with 32 pages. Jacket - **$15 $30 $60** Book - **$40 $75 $150**

☐ **SON-10. "Uncle Remus Game" Boxed Bagatelle,**
1946. Parker Brothers. 10x17.5x1.75" deep box contains 9.5x16x.5" deep bagatelle. - **$100 $250 $500**

SON-11

SON-12

☐ **SON-11. Brer Rabbit Bond Bread Employee Patches,**
1947. Each 2.25x3" embroidered fabric patch was used by Bond Bread route men. Each - **$10 $20 $30**

☐ **SON-12. "Brer Rabbit" Better Little Book #1426,**
1947. Whitman. Book #1426. - **$50 $150 $300**

SON-13

☐ **SON-13. Large Painted Solid Plaster Brer Rabbit Figure,**
1940s. Figure is 9x12x13" tall. Totally unmarked but almost certainly used as some type of store display. - **$165 $325 $550**

SON-14

☐ **SON-14. "Br'er Fox" Catalin Plastic Pencil Sharpener,**
1940s. 1.5" with scalloped edge. - **$60 $125 $200**

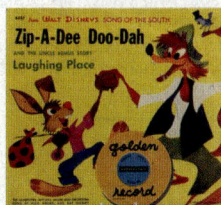
SON-15

SON-16

☐ **SON-15. "Song Of The South" Record,**
1951. Simon & Schuster. "Golden Record" 6.75x7.5" paper sleeve holding yellow vinyl 78 rpm. Record is "RD27" from series with songs "Zip-A-Dee-Doo-Dah/Uncle Remus Story Laughing Place." - **$15 $30 $45**

☐ **SON-16. "The Walt Disney Christmas Show" Publicity Photo,**
1951. Glossy 8x10". Reverse has information on the CBS Christmas Day special that aired in 1951. Characters surrounding Walt include Brer Rabbit and Brer Bear. - **$12 $25 $40**

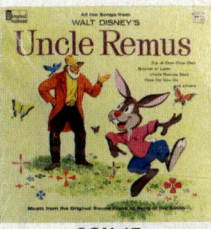
SON-17

☐ **SON-17. "Uncle Remus" Record Album,**
1963. "Disneyland" 12.25" square cardboard cover holding single 33-1/3 rpm original soundtrack. - **$35 $65 $100**

SON-18

☐ **SON-18. "Marx Brer Rabbit Twistable Toy,"**
1960s. Box is 3x7x2" deep with display window and contains 5.5" tall figure, one of four in series that includes Brer Fox. Rabbit or Fox Boxed - **$200 $400 $600**
Unboxed Each - **$100 $200 $300**

SON-19

SON-20

☐ **SON-19. "Song Of The South" Re-Release Lobby Card,**
1972. Card is 11x14" from set of eight. - **$10 $20 $35**

☐ **SON-20. "Song Of The South" Australian Re-Release Poster,**
1970s. Poster is 13.25x26.75" glossy paper insert for reissuance of original 1946 Disney movie. - **$25 $50 $75**

SONG OF THE SOUTH

SON-21

SON-22

❏ SON-21. Brer Rabbit Ceramic Figurine, 1970s. Japan. 2.5x3.5x3.5" tall. - **$15 $30 $60**

❏ SON-22. Brer Bear Figurine, 1970s. "Japan" 3.5x4x7" tall painted and glazed ceramic with copyright marking. - **$12 $25 $50**

Spin and Marty

These two teenage boys were the main characters in a twenty-five episode serial that ran on the original *Mickey Mouse Club* TV show during its first season (1955-56). Set at a western-styled summer camp, the serial starred Tim Considine as regular kid Spin and David Stolley as the spoiled rich kid Marty. The two have numerous personality clashes, but wind up being friends after a rodeo. Among the co-stars in the series were Roy Barcroft and Harry Carey Jr. The serial was based on a book by Lawrence Edward Watkin titled *Marty Markham*. The original was followed by two sequels.
Merchandise included books, comics and several other items.

SPI-1

❏ SPI-1. "Spin And Marty/The Triple 'R' Magic Slate Activities," 1954. Strathmore Co. 6.5x9", 18-page activity book with magic slate back cover. - **$15 $30 $50**

SPI-2

❏ SPI-2. "Spin And Marty/The Triple 'R' Song," Sheet Music, 1955. Published by Walt Disney Music Co./Hanson Publications Inc. - **$20 $40 $60**

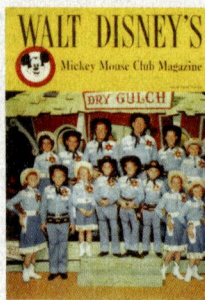

SPI-3

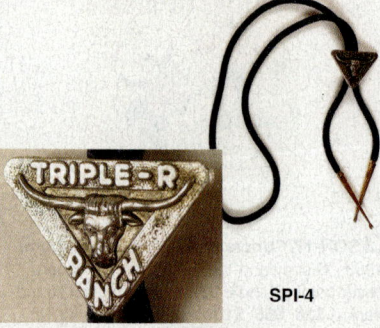

SPI-4

❏ SPI-3. "Walt Disney Magazine," 1956. Volume 1, No. 1 for Spring 1956 with Spin And Marty story. 8.25x11.5". - **$65 $125 $200**

❏ SPI-4. Spin And Marty "Triple-R Ranch" Bolo Tie, 1957. Tie is 15" long rope with 1x1.5" triangular cast metal slide and tips. - **$15 $30 $45**

SPI-5

SPI-6

❏ SPI-5. "Walt Disney's Stars Of Television/Songs About Your Mickey Mouse Favorites" Folio, 1957. Hanson Publications. 9x12" with 16 pages. - **$25 $50 $75**

❏ SPI-6. Walt Disney's Mickey Mouse Club Magazine," 1957. Volume 2, #3. Features a Spin and Marty story. - **$20 $40 $75**

SPI-7

❏ SPI-7. "Spin And Marty" Record, 1975. Disneyland label. 7.25x8" stiff paper sleeve contains 45 rpm. One of six in series. Each - **$12 $25 $40**

SWISS FAMILY ROBINSON

Susie, the Little Blue Coupe

This 1952 cartoon tells the life story of a car named Susie. Her life is traced from the moment she leaves the assembly line until she ends up seemingly abandoned in a junkyard. In between those two points, she has many, many miles put upon her. Just when it all seems over, a teenager finds her in the junkyard and decides to fix her up, giving her one last go-round.

Directed by Clyde Geronomi, the film is narrated by Sterling Holloway. The film makes use of the vocal talents of an un-credited Stan Freberg. Animators included Bob Carlson, Ollie Johnston, Hal King and Cliff Nordberg.

Little merchandise is known for this cartoon.

SUS-1

☐ **SUS-1. "Susie The Little Blue Coupe" Record,** 1952. Decca Records. 10x10" paper sleeve contains 78 rpm record. Story is told by Sterling Holloway with musical accompaniment by Jimmy Carroll. - **$20 $40 $60**

SUS-2

☐ **SUS-2. "Susie The Little Blue Coupe" Figure,** 2000s. Classic Collection. - **$100**

Swamp Fox

Years before *Airplane!* (1980) and *The Naked Gun* (1988) created the image of Leslie Nielsen as a comically oblivious authority figure, Nielsen was respected for playing "serious" roles in films and on TV. In *The Swamp Fox*, a 1959 series of one-hour episodes within the Disney TV show, Nielsen starred as Revolutionary War patriot Francis Marion. Nicknamed "The Swamp Fox," Marion led a band of guerilla fighters, who were based in the Carolina swampland, on various raids during the war. Other cast members included Joy Page and Tim Considine.

The miniseries lasted eight episodes in all. A minor controversy erupted when *The Swamp Fox* was taken off the air in Canada, where representatives in the Canadian House of Commons declared it a distortion of history.

Merchandise included comic books (*Four Color Comics*: #129, 208, and 693.)

SWA-1

☐ **SWA-1. Swamp Fox Publicity Photo From Konetzni Archives,** c. 1959. Glossy 8x10" photo of Leslie Nielson in his Swamp Fox costume surrounded by Disney marketing staff. This is from the archives of "Disney Legend" Al Konetzni who is shown in the photo sitting to the left of Nielsen. At top margin of photo Konetzni has hand-inked notation "Swamp Fox (Leslie Nielson) Visits With Walt Disney Marketing Staff On Madison Avenue New York City." Unique, Near Mint - **$30**

SWA-2

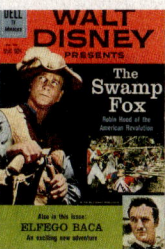
SWA-3

☐ **SWA-2. "Canada Dry/Swamp Fox" Bottle Hanger Paper,** 1960. 3.5x7.25" paper has offer for Swamp Fox flintlock pistol. Top is die-cut for placement over bottle. - **$5 $12 $205**

☐ **SWA-3. "Walt Disney Presents" Comic Book,** 1960. Dell #2. - **$6 $20 $70**

SWA-4

☐ **SWA-4. "Swamp Fox Game,"** 1960. Parker Brothers, 9.5x19x1.5" deep boxed game. - **$12 $25 $50**

Swiss Family Robinson

Considered among the most interesting of Disney's live-action films, *The Swiss Family Robinson* (1960) is based on the book by Johann David Wyss. The plot is simple: a family from Switzerland are the only survivors of a horrible shipwreck. Stranded on a tropical island, they survive through skill and determination. Together, they build a giant house in a tree, grow food and fight pirate raiders. Eventually a ship arrives, and the oldest son of the Robinsons marries the captain's daughter. Given a chance to finally leave, almost everybody elects to stay on the island. Directed by Ken Annakin, the film features John Mills, Dorothy McGuire, James MacArthur, Tommy Kirk, and Janet Munro. The film saw three theatrical re-releases.

Merchandise included books, comics (*Four Color Comics* #1156) and the film's popularity led to a long-lived Swiss Family Robinson Treehouse attraction at the Disney theme parks. Today, the Treehouse has been renamed Tarzan's Treehouse.

SWISS FAMILY ROBINSON

SWI-1

❑ **SWI-1. "Swiss Family Robinson Pirate Pack" Premium,**
1960. Buster Brown Shoes. 4x4" plastic bag contains nicely designed premium set "Inspired By Walt Disney's Movie." Consists of a sheet of twelve tattoos called "Tattoodles" and three-panel sheet of eleven transfers, all with pirate theme including one of Buster and Tige. The other two pieces are a cardboard eye patch and a red plastic "Climbing Pirate" figure. Complete - **$12 $25 $40**

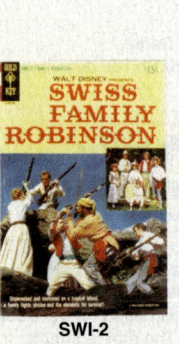

SWI-2

SWI-3

❑ **SWI-2. "Swiss Family Robinson" Movie Comic Book,**
1969. Gold Key reprints of #1156 from 1960. - **$3 $10 $35**

❑ **SWI-3. "Swiss Family Robinson" Movie Poster,**
1975. Re-Release 14x36" glossy full color insert poster. - **$10 $20 $30**

SWI-4

❑ **SWI-4. "Magic Kingdom Super Deluxe Colorforms Playset,"**
c. 1980s. The colorful play board is different from most as it has a gate-fold front that opens to reveal additional play area and graphics. Spotlights Swiss Family Robinson tree house. - **$10 $20 $40**

The Sword in the Stone

A full-length animated feature set in medieval times, this 1963 film was based on the book of the same name by T. H. White. The young orphan Arthur, nicknamed Wart, is out hunting in the woods with his foster brother Kay. They lose an arrow and Wart goes off to find it. There he meets the magician Merlin who decides to give Wart an education. Part of this involves being changed into various animals. At one point Wart runs afoul of the malevolent witch Mad Madam Mim.

Eventually Merlin and Mim duel, with Merlin emerging as the victor. Afterwards there is a tournament to pick a new king. Wart runs to get a sword for Kay, but can't find one. He innocently removes one that he has found embedded in a rock. No one believes that he has done this, so he returns the sword to the rock and removes it again. According to the legend, he is then crowned king. With the coronation, he becomes the King Arthur of fame and legend.

The Sword in the Stone was the first film that Wolfgang Reitherman directed by himself. The story was by Bill Peet. Animators included Ken Anderson, Frank Thomas, Ollie Johnston, Milt Kahl and John Lounsbury.

Vocal talent included Rick Sorenson, Karl Swenson and Richard Reitherman. The film's narration was done by Sebastian Cabot. The music was handled by the same team that had just scored Mary Poppins, Richard M. and Robert B. Sherman. The film was re-released theatrically twice.

Merchandise included books, records, a Sword in the Stone mechanical plastic ring and a ring set. Mad Madam Mim became a long-lived comic book character on her own, appearing in American Disney comics throughout the 1970s and to this day, still appears in some foreign titles.

SWO-1

❑ **SWO-1. "Archimedes" Hand Puppet,**
1962. Gund Mfg. Co. 10.5" tall figure with soft vinyl head and fabric handcover body with inner squeaker mechanism. - **$20 $35 $60**

SWO-2

❑ **SWO-2. "The Sword In The Stone" Insert Poster,**
1963. Glossy 14x36" stiff paper poster. - **$40 $75 $125**

THAT DARN CAT

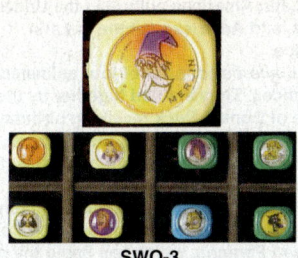

SWO-3

❑ **SWO-3. Sword In The Stone Premium Ring Set,**
1963 Set of nine issued as cereal box inserts. Rings have plastic bases of various colors. Set: Archimedes, Fish, Kay, Madam Mim, Merlin, Sir Ector, Squirrel, Wart, Wolf. Each - **$10 $15 $30**

SWO-4

❑ **SWO-4. Sword In The Stone Ring,**
1963. 3.25" long flexible blue plastic premium ring shown as issued with sword still attached to ring. - **$15 $25 $50**

SWO-5

❑ **SWO-5. "Sword In The Stone Game,"**
1963. Parker Brothers. 9x17x1.5" deep box contains deck of "Merlin's Magic Cards" and different colored hard plastic playing pieces depicting sword in stone plus separate loose sword piece. - **$15 $30 $50**

SWO-6   SWO-7

❑ **SWO-6. "Merlin's Magic Wand" Toy,**
1963. General Electric. 8x17" blister card holding 15" long metal and plastic battery-operated wand designed to light up when "Magic Mercury Switch" is turned on. Bulb is included, three required AAA batteries are not. Carded - **$15 $30 $60**

❑ **SWO-7. "The Sword In The Stone" Paperweight/Letter Opener,**
1963. Cast metal with heavy paperweight base 2x2.75x2.5" tall depicting anvil atop stone block. A 5.5" long cast metal sword fits into a slot on the top of the anvil. Both anvil and sword handle are marked "Walt Disney's The Sword In The Stone." - **$50 $100 $200**

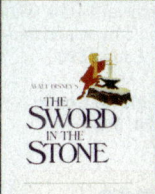 

SWO-8

❑ **SWO-8. "The Sword In The Stone" Press Kit,**
1980s. Re-release 9x12" stiff glossy paper folder contains total of 11 text publicity sheets and five different 8x10" glossy black and white publicity stills. - **$10 $20 $30**

That Darn Cat

This 1965 live-action film is a family favorite and one of the better Disney comedies of the sixties. The Randall family's Siamese cat is out snooping around and wanders into a hideout where bank robbers are holding a teller hostage. In an attempt to contact someone for a rescue, the teller places her wristwatch around the cat's neck. The cat returns home and her owners find the watch. An FBI agent, who happens to be allergic to cats, is put on the case. Eventually, the crooks are caught and it is all due to that darn cat.

Directed by long-time Disney stalwart Robert Stevenson, *That Darn Cat!* features Hayley Mills, Dean Jones, Dorothy Provine, Roddy McDowell, Frank Gorshin and Neville Brand. The film is notable for the strength of the actors' performances. The title song was written by the Sherman Brothers. The film was remade in 1997 with a new cast and released theatrically. In all versions the cat's name is D. C., which stands for Darn Cat.

TDC-1

❑ **TDC-1. Disney Studio Christmas Card,**
1965. Card has folded size of 4.5x8" and opens to 17.5" long. Stiff paper opens to reveal image of Mickey blowing a tuba with different Disney characters popping out of this including Winnie The Pooh, Bambi, That Darn Cat, others. - **$20 $35 $55**

TDC-2

THAT DARN CAT

☐ **TDC-2. "Haley Mills In That Darn Cat" Paperdoll Book,**
1965. 9.25x12" with glossy cardboard cover and 6 paper pages by Whitman #1955. Uncut - **$20 $40 $60**

TDC-3

TDC-4

☐ **TDC-3. That Darn Cat Standee,**
1965. Die-cut 13x16.5" cardboard with easel attached to back. Marked "DC-3" apparently movie theater or store display. - **$20 $40 $65**

☐ **TDC-4. "That Darn Cat" Doll With Tag,**
1965. Gund. 5x8x11.5" tall stuffed plush cat. Attached at neck is a purple ribbon with 4" diameter cardboard tag with same design on each side. Text reads "My Name Is D.C. From Walt Disney's That Darn Cat." Doll - **$12 $25 $50** Tag - **$8 $12 $20**

TDC-5

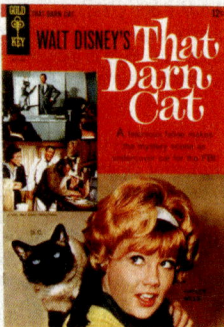
TDC-6

☐ **TDC-5. That Darn Cat Studio Concept Watercolor Portraits,**
c. 1965. Original art done by an unknown Disney artist during "That Darn Cat" production era. From the Al Konetzni archive. 15x20" with art done in black lithographed crayon and tempera paint on thin tan paper. Each - **$90**

☐ **TDC-6. "That Darn Cat" Movie Comic.**
Gold Key from 1966. - **$8 $24 $95**

The Three Caballeros

Set in Latin America, this feature film premiered in Mexico City in December, 1944 and in the United States in February, 1945. *Caballeros*, like *Saludos Amigos (1942)* before it, was created at the request of the American government.
The films were designed as part of the World War II "good neighbor" policy: to promote both Latin American culture in the United States, and American culture in Latin America.

Caballeros consists of four animated sequences. They are tied together by the theme of Donald Duck receiving birthday presents from his friends, José Carioca, the Brazilian parrot, and Panchito Pistoles, the Mexican charro rooster.

Interspersed with live-action segments, the animated sequences include *The Cold-Blooded Penguin*, which has Pablo the penguin trying to find a warmer climate; *The Flying Gauchito*, featuring the eponymous hero and his winged flying donkey; *Baia*, in which Donald dances with a live-action woman, Aurora Miranda; and *La Pinata*, which finds Donald sharing in a south-of-the-border Christmas custom. The film is a feast for fans of Donald.

Some find the entire film to be a bit surreal, especially when Donald is seen dancing with Miranda. The use of Aurora Miranda, who is the sister of the more famous Carmen, marked the first time that Disney had combined real people and cartoon characters on film since the Alice comedies of the early twenties.

The Three Caballeros was directed by Norm Ferguson. Animators included Bill Peet, Ward Kimball, Frank Thomas, Ollie Johnston and Fred Moore. Vocal talent included Clarence Nash, Jose Oliveria and Joaquin Gray. Narrators were Sterling Holloway, Fred Shields and Frank Graham. The multiple narrations confused some movie-goers. The music, among the liveliest to be found in a Disney feature, is by Charles Wolcott, Paul Smith and Ed Plumb. They were nominated for an Academy Award for their work. The film was also nominated for Best Sound.

Merchandise included books, records and most notably ceramic figures. They also appear in *Four Color Comics*: #71.

TCA-1

☐ **TCA-1. "The Three Caballeros" Sheet Music,**
1943. 9x12". - **$10 $20 $35**

THE THREE CABALLEROS

TCA-2

TCA-3

TCA-6

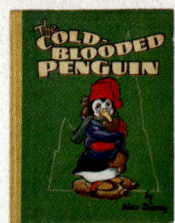

TCA-8

TCA-4

TCA-5

TCA-7

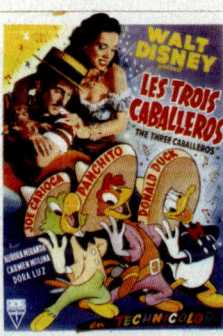

TCA-9

TCA-10

❏ **TCA-2. "The Three Caballeros" Record Set,**
1944. Decca. 10.25x12" thick cardboard cover contains set of three 78 rpm records. - **$50 $100 $150**

❏ **TCA-3. "The Three Caballeros Souvenir Album,"**
1944. Melody Lane Publications. 9x12" song folio with 32 pages. - **$65 $125 $225**

❏ **TCA-4. "The Three Caballeros" Studio Promotional Letterhead,**
1045. Shoot is 8.5x11". - **$10 $20 $35**

❏ **TCA-5. The Three Caballeros Mexican Lobby Card,**
1945. 12.5x16.5" stiff paper card. - **$10 $20 $35**

❏ **TCA-6. "The Three Caballeros" Lobby Cards,**
1945. Pair of 11x14" cards for original release by RKO Radio Pictures Inc. First is title card featuring scene of the Three Cabs along with Aurora Miranda. Second card has film scene of Aurora rubbing Donald on his chin. Title Card - **$40 $85 $150**
Scene Card - **$25 $45 $85**

❏ **TCA-7. "The Flying Donkey and Gauchito" Dolls,**
1945. Cloth-stuffed dolls featured in the animated segment "The Flying Gauchito" from the Disney film "The Three Caballeros." Made in Mexico. - **$200 $400 $750**

❏ **TCA-8. "The Cold Blooded Penguin" English Hardcover,**
1945. Collins Sons & Co. 6.75x8.25" with 24 pages. - **$65 $135 $225**

❏ **TCA-9. "The Three Caballeros" Belgian Movie Poster,**
c. 1946. RKO Radio Films. 14.25x19.25". - **$75 $150 $265**

❏ **TCA-10. Panchito Figurine,**
c. 1946. 3.5x4.25x6.75" tall painted and glazed ceramic with label from American Pottery. - **$75 $125 $250**

THE THREE CABALLEROS

TCA-11

◻ **TCA-11. Joe Carioca Figurine,**
c. 1946. American Pottery. 6.5" tall - **$60 $125 $175**

TCA-12

◻ **TCA-12. Donald From The Three Caballeros Doll,**
c. 1946. 6x7x11" stuffed plush doll with glass eyes wearing felt outfit. Stitched tag. - **$75 $150 $300**

TCA-13

◻ **TCA-13. Donald Duck Three Caballeros Figurine,**
c. 1947. Zaccagnini. 4x4.5x7.5" tall painted glazed ceramic. - **$300 $600 $1000**

TCA-14

◻ **TCA-14. Joe Carioca Ceramic Figurine,**
c. 1947. Zaccagnini. 4x5x7.5" tall painted glazed ceramic. - **$300 $600 $1000**

TCA-15

◻ **TCA-15. Joe Carioca Ceramic Lamp,**
c. 1947. Railley Corp. 5.5" figurine atop 5" diameter base, lamp is a total of 12" tall. Figurine was made by Shaw/American Pottery although lamp issued by Railley Corp. - **$50 $100 $150**

TCA-16

◻ **TCA-16. Donald Duck And Panchito Plaster Bookends,**
1940s. Leonardi Ltd. England. Matching 4.75" tall and each incised "W 78" on base.
Set - **$65 $150 $250**

TCA-17

◻ **TCA-17. Joe Carioca Watch,**
1948. U.S. Time. 1-1/8" diameter chromed metal case. From series of ten birthday watches issued to celebrate Mickey's 20th birthday. - **$75 $150 $250**

THE THREE CABALLEROS

TCA-18

❏ **TCA-18. Joe Carioca Catalin Plastic Pencil Sharpener,**
1940s. 1" round edge variety and white panel around his name. - **$15 $30 $60**

TCA-19

❏ **TCA-19. Joe Carioca Catalin Plastic Pencil Sharpener,**
1940s. 1" round. Edge style variety. - **$20 $40 $75**

TCA-20

❏ **TCA-20. Jose Carioca Composition Wind-Up,**
1940s. Unmarked. 7-3/8" tall with cigar on spring and metal tail feathers. - **$150 $300 $600**

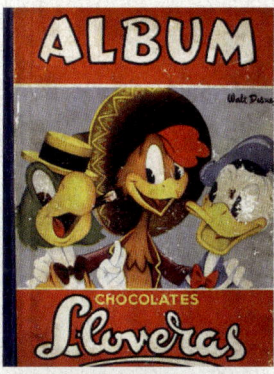

TCA-21

❏ **TCA-21. Spanish Complete Chocolates Card Album Featuring The Three Caballeros,**
1940s. Lloveras Chocolates Barcelona. 8x10.5" hardcover album with 58 pages. Book is complete with 236 cards. There are a total of eight different stories and stories feature between 15-36 cards. Cards are numbered although numbering starts over for each story. Majority of the stories appear to be unique to this album and primarily feature the Three Caballeros as well as Donald's nephews along with other characters including Aracuan Bird, Stromboli, Mickey Mouse, Goofy, a number of others. - **$150 $300 $500**

TCA-22

❏ **TCA-22. Three Caballeros Spanish Fruit Label On Crate Panel,**
1940s. WDP. Danza Melon Fruit. 6.75x16.5x.5" thick wood crate panel with attached 5x10.75" full color paper label. - **$15 $30 $50**

TCA-23

❏ **TCA-23. Joe Carioca Pull Toy,**
1940s. 9.5" tall. Disney copyright but otherwise unmarked. - **$125 $250 $400**

TCA-24

TCA-25

❏ **TCA-24. The Three Caballeros Spanish Sand Pail,**
1940s. Marked along seam "Derechos Exclusivos De Walt Disney, Reservados." 4" diameter by 4" tall tin lithographed pail also came in 4.75" diameter, 5" tall size. Each - **$80 $175 $300**

❏ **TCA-25. The Three Caballeros Foreign Paperback Book,**
1950s. Great Britain. Hazel Watson. 4.5x7" with 112 pages and text in German. - **$8 $12 $25**

THE THREE LITTLE PIGS

The Three Little Pigs

While this 1933 cartoon is technically part of the Silly Symphonies series, its incredible success places it in a category by itself. The heroes are three pigs named Fiddler, Fifer and Practical. The villain is the Big Bad Wolf, who was later given the proper name of Zeke. In order to protect themselves from the wolf, each pig needs to build a house of his own. Fiddler and Fifer would rather play than work, so they quickly design weak houses made of sticks and straw. The third pig, Practical, recognizes Zeke's strength and cunning. He builds his house of bricks. With his incredibly powerful breath, the Wolf blows down Fiddler's and Fifer's houses, but he finds that he can't blow down the house of bricks. What he does do is attempt to go down the chimney. Unfortunately he lands in a pot of boiling water, which sends him howling away into the distance. The pigs gather together for their rallying song: *Who's Afraid of the Big Bad Wolf?*

Not only was *Three Little Pigs* a financial success; its theme song became a rallying cry for theatergoers who were suffering through the Great Depression. The cartoon won an Academy Award. It also inspired three sequels: *The Big Bad Wolf* (1934), *Three Little Wolves* (1936), and *The Practical Pig* (1939). Over the years, all three cartoons were frequently re-released.

Pig and wolf merchandise was extensive throughout the 1930s. In 1945, the characters were revived in the comic book *Walt Disney's Comics and Stories*, whose *Li'l Bad Wolf* stories introduced a new star, the goody-goody Li'l Wolf, to the woodland crew. *L'il Bad Wolf* (2001), a fourth pig cartoon produced for TV, belatedly carried these developments over to animation.

Today the pigs and wolves appear on numerous items specifically released for the collectibles market. Among the most popular are ceramic figures of the pigs.

TPG-1

TPG-2

❑ **TPG-1. "Three Little Pigs" Bisque Toothbrush Holder,**
1933. "Made In Japan" with Disney copyright on back with incised #S165. Depicts Fifer Pig, Fiddler Pig and Practical Pig with trowel and stack of bricks. A second version has Practical Pig with drum. 1.75x3-5/8x4" tall. Bricks Variety - **$60 $115 $175** Drum Variety - **$50 $100 $160**

❑ **TPG-2. "The Three Little Pigs" Toothbrush Holder,**
1933. "Made In Japan" 2x4x3.25" tall painted bisque, scarcest of three different Pig toothbrush holders with Practical seated at piano. Incised on reverse is "The Three Little Pigs," Disney copyright, and Japan origin. - **$60 $125 $250**

TPG-3

❑ **TPG-3. "Who's Afraid Of The Big Bad Wolf Game,"**
1933. Mail premium sponsored by Johnson & Johnson Tek Jr. Toothpaste. Game parts are 14x20" playing board, character disc markers picturing Pigs and Wolf individually, 72 numbered small paper squares. Set With Uncut Sheet - **$50 $85 $175**

TPG-4

❑ **TPG-4. "The Three Little Pigs" And "Mickey Mouse" Record,**
1933. Victor. 10" diameter 78 rpm with Side A title "Who's Afraid Of The Big Bad Wolf?" Side B is "Mickey Mouse And Minnie's In Town." - **$15 $30 $50**

TPG-5

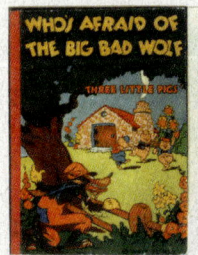 

TPG-6

❑ **TPG-5. "Mickey Mouse Presents Who's Afraid Of The Big Bad Wolf" Sheet Music,**
1933. Irving Berlin Inc. 9x12" complete four-page folder of music and lyrics for song from "The Silly Symphony/The Three Little Pigs." - **$20 $35 $75**

❑ **TPG-6. "Who's Afraid Of The Big Bad Wolf/Three Little Pigs,"**
1933. David McKay Co. 6.25x8.5" with 32 pages. - **$75 $150 $275**

THE THREE LITTLE PIGS

TPG-7

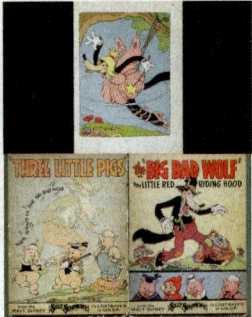
TPG-8

TPG-10

❏ **TPG-10. "Three Little Pigs Game,"**
1933. Einson-Freeman Co. 10.25x14.5x2.5" deep box containing game comprised of 14x20" playing board, four cardboard discs with individual portrait of pigs and Big Bad Wolf, spinner card, instruction sheet. - **$85 $175 $325**

TPG-11

TPG-13

❏ **TPG-13. Enameled Cuff Bracelet,**
1933. - **$100 $200 $425**

TPG-14

❏ **TPG-7. "Three Little Pigs" Book,**
1933. Blue Ribbon Books. 8x10.25" hardcover, 64 pages. - **$100 $200 $400**

❏ **TPG-8. Two-In-One Book,**
1933. Blue Ribbon Books. 7.75x10" hardcover containing two stories, "Three Little Pigs" and "The Big Bad Wolf and Little Red Riding Hood," also published as individual hardcovers. Front and back cover of the 2-in-1 version reflect its contents. Each story is 64 pages. - **$125 $250 $500**

TPG-12

❏ **TPG-11. Bridge Crossing Figurine,**
c. 1933. "Made In Japan" 1.25x6x2.75" tall two-piece display consisting of wood base and solid celluloid bridge with highly detailed three-dimensional figures of Wolf and Pigs. - **$40 $75 $125**

❏ **TPG-12. Three Little Pigs And Big Bad Wolf Figures,**
c. 1933. Unmarked set of four painted solid plaster figures comprised of 4.5" tall Wolf and 3" tall Pigs. Set - **$160 $320 $540**

❏ **TPG-14. "Three Little Pigs" Wash Tub,**
c. 1933. Ohio Art. 6.5" diameter by 3" deep tin litho. - **$200 $400 $750**

TPG-15

❏ **TPG-9. "Red Riding Hood With Big Bad Wolf And 3 Little Pigs" Game,**
1933. Parker Brothers. 13x15.5x1" deep box. Includes gameboard, instruction folder, generic spinner, wax paper bag w/4 wood markers. - **$50 $100 $200**

❏ **TPG-15. Three Little Pigs And Wolf Tin,**
c. 1933. Mickey Mouse Ltd. Great Britain. 6" diameter by 2.25" deep. - **$85 $175 $350**

THE THREE LITTLE PIGS

TPG-16

TPG-18

☐ **TPG-18. The Three Pigs China Mug,**
c. 1933. Patriot China. 3" china with text on underside in silver "Patriot China." - **$40 $90 $165**

TPG-19

☐ **TPG-16. The Three Little Pigs Framed Reverse Painting On Glass,**
c. 1933. 6.5x8.5" framed glass, likely by Reliance Picture Frame Co. although without their name or a copyright. Title is "Who's Afraid Of The Big Bad Wolf" and scene shows the Three Pigs singing and playing their instruments as the Big Bad Wolf peers through their window. Has plain cardboard backing. - **$20 $40 $75**

☐ **TPG-19. Three Little Pigs China Mug,**
c. 1933. Salem China Co. 3" tall mug with wrap-around scene of the Wolf hiding behind a tree and spying on the Pigs. - **$150 $300 $600**

TPG-17

TPG-20

☐ **TPG-17. Big Bad Wolf Glazed Ceramic Figure,**
c. 1933. Faiencerie d'Onnaing Of France. "W. Disney" mark. 8-3/8" tall. - **$550 $1100 $2250**

☐ **TPG-20. Fifer Pig Large Doll,**
c. 1933. Maker Unknown. 7x13.5x18" tall with stuffed cotton body, felt jacket and hat, fabric bow at neck and glass eyes. Has painted facial details. Tail has wire insert. - **$85 $175 $350**

TPG-21

TPG-22

☐ **TPG-21. "The Big Bad Wolf" Canadian Composition Book,**
c. 1933. "Hilroy Series No. 3520" 7x9" unlined paper school use book. - **$15 $30 $65**

☐ **TPG-22. Pencil Drawing,**
1934. Animation paper is 9.5x12" centered right by 3.25x6" image of Fifer Pig, Fiddler Pig, Little Red Riding Hood. Art is for 'Big Bad Wolf' film segment and No. "15" from a numbered sequence. - **$85 $165 $300**

TPG-23

THE THREE LITTLE PIGS

❑ **TPG-23. Three Little Pigs Wooden Utensil Holder,**
1934. Unmarked but by Wm. Rogers & Son. 4.75" wide by 4" tall. Came boxed with utensil. Holder only - **$60 $125 $250**

TPG-24

❑ **TPG-24. Big Bad Wolf Wooden Utensil Holder,**
1934. Wm. Rogers & Son Silverplate. Figure is 9-1/8" tall jigsawed wood holding metal fork, knife and spoon with character images. Photo shows inside of box lid. Box - **$30 $65 $125**
Holder - **$75 $150 $300**
Utensil Set - **$35 $60 $120**

TPG-25

❑ **TPG-25. "Little Red Riding Hood" Wooden Figural Utensil Holder,**
1934. Wm. Rogers Silverplate. Box is 4.75x6.5x2.5" deep. Jigsawed wooden figure is 6.25" tall holding 4" metal pig spoon. Box - **$30 $65 $125**
Figure - **$50 $100 $175**
Spoon - **$12 $20 $45**

TPG-26

❑ **TPG-26. "Little Red Riding Hood And The Big Bad Wolf" Book,**
1934. Book is 7.75x10" cardboard cover book printed in England although no publisher indicated. Content is 32 stiff paper illustrated story pages plus a single full color plate. - **$65 $125 $225**

TPG-27

TPG-28

❑ **TPG-27. Big Bad Wolf Doll,**
1934. Knickerbocker Toy Co. 18" tall plush with felt outfit and glass eyes. - **$350 $1100 $2200**

❑ **TPG-28. Three Little Pigs Animated Alarm Clock,**
1934. Ingersoll. Clock is 2x4.5x4.25" tall in metal case. Wolf's die-cut arms point at numerals and his head moves as if he is opening and closing his mouth as the seconds tick. Red dial color subject to color fade. - **$325 $650 $1200**

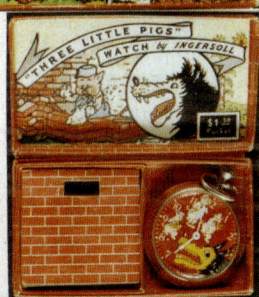

TPG-29

THE THREE LITTLE PIGS

❑ **TPG-29. Three Little Pigs Boxed Watch,**
1934. Ingersoll. 2.5x4.5x1" deep box containing 2" diameter silvered brass case pocket watch. Dial features full figure images of Three Pigs plus Wolf head with separate eye that moves as seconds tick. Back of case is designed as brick wall with door at center incised "May The Big Bad Wolf Never Come To Your Door/Walt Disney." Box has hinged lid over cardboard insert in brick design that holds watch fob, strap and warranty paper. Box - **$250 $500 $1200**
Watch - **$250 $500 $1200**
Fob - **$30 $65 $125**

TPG-30

❑ **TPG-30. Three Little Pigs Pocket Watch Fob,**
1934. 1.5" tall brass fob finished by enamel accents and issued for the 1934 Ingersoll pocket watch. Image is Pigs playing instruments with "Who's Afraid Of The Big Bad Wolf" text above. Top is slotted for insertion of leather strap. - **$30 $65 $125**

TPG-31

❑ **TPG-31. Three Little Pigs Wristwatch With Characters Band,**
1934. Ingersoll. 1.25" diameter metal case on metal link wrist band. Each band has link with character image including one of the Wolf's head with open mouth showing jagged teeth. The other is the Three Little Pigs. Dial face is centered by Wolf image. - **$650 $1300 $2250**

TPG-32

❑ **TPG-32. "The Three Little Pigs Stationery" Boxed Set,**
1934. Powers Paper Co. 6.5x9.5x1" deep box containing complete original set of 24 folder sheets each 4.5x6" with envelope. - **$75 $150 $250**

TPG-33

❑ **TPG-33. Fiddler Pig Rubber Figure,**
c. 1934. Seiberling Latex Products Co. 2.5x3x6" tall painted total rubber likeness. Latex typically deformed and/or hardened. One of three. Each - **$50 $150 $400**

TPG-34

❑ **TPG-34. "Three Little Pigs Composition Book,"**
c. 1934. Powers Paper Co. 6.75x8.25" with glossy stiff paper cover. - **$25 $50 $100**

TPG-35

TPG-36

❑ **TPG-35. "Who's Afraid Of The Big Bad Wolf" Cello Button,**
1935. Kay Kamen backpaper. 1.25". Used as a give-away by toy stores and others. - **$50 $100 $150**

❑ **TPG-36. Toothbrush Holder Set,**
c. 1935. Maw of England. Glazed ceramic each about 4.25" tall and marked on underside with copyright and registration number. Each - **$65 $125 $200**

THE THREE LITTLE PIGS

The year 1933 found Walt and Roy Disney dissatisfied with the Disney character merchandise of the time. Some licensed items featured inferior artwork; others were shoddily constructed. In an effort to establish a consistently high level of quality, the Disneys signed a contract with advertising agent Kay Kamen, a move that turned out brilliantly. Kamen was given the authority to take over the sales campaigns for Mickey, Donald and of course, the Three Little Pigs.

This led to a 1934 deal that Disney arranged with *Good Housekeeping*, then the number-one magazine in the U.S. From 1934 to 1944, the magazine carried a monthly one-page Disney feature, adapting Disney animated films in verse with beautiful painted illustrations. Among the most eye-catching pages were the twenty-one done in 1934 and 1935 by Tom Wood and the two-part 1937 series on *Snow White and the Seven Dwarfs*, featuring artwork by famed children's illustrator Gustaf Tenggren.

❑ **TPG-37. Original Art Scene Panel #1**
1935. Approx. 9 1/4" x 9". - **$13,000**

Aside from featuring some of the finest Disney art of the era, the *GH* pages functioned as previews for cartoons that had not yet been released—and, occasionally, ended up being heavily altered or even shelved after their *GH* pages were published. Apart from this, the *GH* pages functioned as an important advertising outlet. It is interesting to note that by the end of 1935, the profits from Disney character licensing exceeded the income from the theatrical films themselves. Snow White's production was only made possible by funds provided by such merchandising.

Shown on this page is *Three Little Wolves*, the *Good Housekeeping* Disney page for October 1935. Its exquisite watercolor art is the work of Tom Wood.

❑ **TPG-38. Original Art Scene Panel #2**
1935. Approx. 7 1/2" x 8 1/2". - **$6,500**

❑ **TPG-39. Original Art Scene Panel #3**
1935. Approx. 9 1/2" x 9". - **$11,000**

❑ **TPG-40. Original Art Scene Panel #4**
1935. Approx. 7 1/4" x 8". - **$7,500**

❑ **TPG-41. Original Art Scene Panel #5**
1935. Approx. 9 1/2" x 9 1/2". - **$11,000**

The value of several of the **1934** paintings by Disney artist Tom Wood ranges from $45,000 - $75,000 depending on the subject matter. The Wood original paintings produced for Mickey Mouse cartoons done in **1935**, also featured in *Good Housekeeping Magazine,* can bring up to twice that amount.

THE THREE LITTLE PIGS

TPG-42

TPG-43

TPG-44

❏ **TPG-42. Three Little Wolves Ad Page,**
1935. From Good Housekeeping Magazine. Ad was released in 1935 to promote the 1936 film. - **$15 $30 $45**

❏ **TPG-43. Pigs Pencil Drawings From Three Little Pigs,**
1936. Two drawings with each image about 3x3.25" numbered "45" and "47." Each - **$60 $125 $200**

❏ **TPG-44. "1st Little Pig" Glass,**
c. 1936. Glass is 4.25" tall tumbler from the second series of glasses issued by various dairy companies c. 1936-1937. This series has smaller character images in contrast to larger images of the first series. - **$20 $40 $80**

TPG-45

❏ **TPG-45. "Silly Symphony/The Three Little Wolves" Pencil Box,**
c. 1936. Dixon. 6x10.75x1.5" deep box #2908 formed by slightly textured paper over cardboard with snap closure. - **$70 $135 $225**

THE THREE LITTLE PIGS

TPG-46

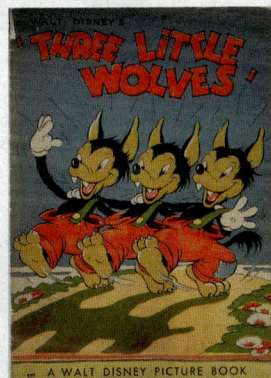

TPG-47

TPG-48

❑ **TPG-48. Three Little Pigs Get Well Card,**
1938. White & Wyckoff Mfg. Co. Closed 4.75x5" folder card in satin paper finish. - **$15 $30 $50**

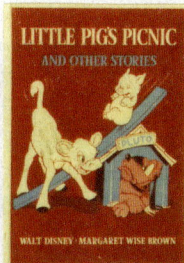

TPG-49

❑ **TPG-49. "Little Pigs" Picnic And Other Stories" Book,**
1939. D.C. Heath & Co. 6.25x8.5" hardcover, 102 pages comprised of ten stories including "The Ugly Duckling, Pluto's Kitten, The Orphan Kittens, The Flying Mouse," others. - **$25 $50 $85**

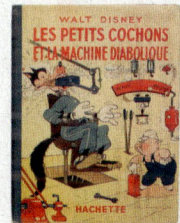

TPG-50

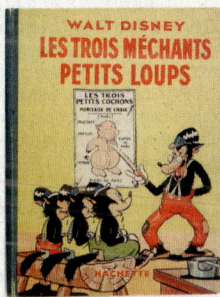

TPG-51

❑ **TPG-46. "Practical Pig" Cel,**
1937. Frame is vintage wood with glass cover over cardboard mat with 8.25x19" opening around the cel. All three Pigs are included with Practical Pig 3.5x4" running behind the other two which have image size of 4.5x6.5" and four small cel images of birds flying around them. Near Mint - **$2750**

❑ **TPG-47. "Three Little Wolves" Book,**
1937. Whitman. 9.5x13" linen-like paper book #895 with 16 pages. - **$65 $125 $250**

THE THREE LITTLE PIGS

❑ **TPG-50. The Three Little Pigs French Hardcover Book With Dust Cover,**
1939. Hachette. 7.25x9" with 48 pages, many full page illustrations. Text is French and title translates to The Three Little Pigs And The Diabolical Machine. Jacket - **$10 $25 $50** Book - **$35 $65 $125**

❑ **TPG-51. The Three Little Pigs French Hardcover Book,**
1939. Hachette. 7.25x9" with 48 pages. Title translates to Three Little Merchant Wolves. - **$35 $65 $125**

TPG-52

TPG-53

❑ **TPG-52. Three Little Pigs Calendar,**
1939. National Life And Accident Insurance Co. 11x14" single sheet thin cardboard premium. Art depicts joyous Pigs celebrating within a room having insurance company's logo on the wall. Seen through the open window is a dejected Big Bad Wolf stalking away. - **$75 $175 $300**

❑ **TPG-53. "The Three Little Pigs Picture Printing Set,"**
1930s. Fulton Specialty Co. 7x8x1" deep box holding contents of wooden stamps of characters, holders, ink pad and type stamps. - **$125 $250 $400**

TPG-54

❑ **TPG-54. Three Little Pigs Decal,**
1930s. Noma Electric Co. 1.75x5" stiff paper sheet. Decal is for application by water transfer to a hard plastic Christmas bulb shade for Noma boxed strand of tree bulbs with shades set. - **$15 $30 $60**

TPG-55

TPG-56

❑ **TPG-55. Three Little Pigs/Wolf/Red Riding Hood Figures Set,**
1930s. "Made In Japan" complete set of five painted bisque replica Disney figures. Big Bad Wolf is 3.5" tall and other four are each about 3" tall. Pink accent color on Wolf and Pigs varies as typically produced. Wolf - **$30 $75 $150** Red - **$100 $200 $300** Each Pig - **$15 $30 $60**

❑ **TPG-56. Practical Pig Figurine,**
1930s. Bisque is 2" tall painted from an unmarked companion set of three. Each - **$25 $50 $75**

TPG-57

❑ **TPG-57. Fifer Pig Figure With Movable Arms,**
1930s. Bisque is 4" tall painted with fabric shirt and neckerchief bow as issued. No maker marking other than "Foreign." - **$35 $75 $125**

TPG-58

❑ **TPG-58. Fiddler Pig Figurine,**
1930s. Bisque is 2" tall painted from an unmarked companion set of three. Each - **$20 $40 $65**

TPG-59

❑ **TPG-59. Fifer Pig Figurine,**
1930s. Bisque is 2" tall painted from an unmarked companion set of three. Each - **$20 $40 $65**

THE THREE LITTLE PIGS

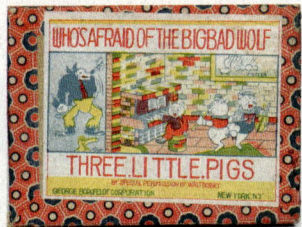

TPG-60

❏ **TPG-60. "Three Little Pigs" Figure Set Boxed,**
1930s. Box containing set is 3.75x5x1.5" deep with complete set of three 3.5" tall painted bisque figures marked "Made In Japan." Box lid label is marked "George Borgfeldt Corp.", a distributor of Disney merchandise. Label also pictures a Wolf vs. Pigs encounter scene.
Boxed - **$150 $275 $450**

TPG-61

TPG-62

❏ **TPG-61. "Three Little Pigs" Fun-E-Flex Figure Set,**
1930s. Set of three figures, each 3.5" tall with wood bodies, stiff twisted paper-covered arms and legs, die-cut stiff paper ears and collars. Each - **$60 $125 $175**

❏ **TPG-62. Practical Pig Cuban Figurine,**
1930s. "Concesionario de Walt Disney-Cuba." 2x2.5x5.5" tall painted solid plaster image. - **$40 $80 $135**

TPG-63

❏ **TPG-63. "The 3 Little Pigs" Candy Wrapper Panel,**
1930s. Waxed paper is 2.5x4.5" center panel only, trimmed from original larger size wrapper by unidentified maker. Non-Disney art. Complete - **$15 $30 $50**

TPG-64

❏ **TPG-64. Three Little Pigs Toothbrush Holder,**
1930s. "Superior Quality/Made In Japan" marked 3x5x3.75" tall china figural inspired by the earliest release of the Disney short but produced without license. Pictured example with green base is the scarcest color variety. - **$60 $125 $175**

TPG-65

❏ **TPG-65. Three Little Pigs Toothbrush Holder,**
1930s. "Superior Quality/Made In Japan" marked 3x5x3.75" tall china figural inspired by the earliest release of the Disney short but produced without license. Front edge of orange base has a recessed tray. - **$50 $85 $150**

TPG-66

❏ **TPG-66. Foreign Framed Fifer Pig Miniature Pictures,**
1930s. Two different images each 1.75x2-3/8". String loops for hanging. From Spain. Each - **$20 $40 $60**

TPG-67

❏ **TPG-67. "Who's Afraid Of The Big Bad Wolf?" Art Glass Picture,**
1930s. Reliance. 7.75x10.75" wood frame holds glass w/painted scene on reverse. - **$65 $125 $250**

TPG-68

THE THREE LITTLE PIGS

☐ **TPG-68. "Three Little Pigs" Glass Picture,**
1930s. Reliance Picture Frame Co. 4.25x5.75" original wood frame around art glass scene. - **$35 $60 $100**

TPG-69

☐ **TPG-69. "The Three Little Pigs" Glass Picture,**
1930s. Reliance Picture Frame Co. 7.75x10.75" original wood frame around art glass scene of non-studio art. - **$30 $60 $90**

TPG-70

TPG-71

☐ **TPG-70. Big Bad Wolf Cello Charm,**
1930s. Japan. 1" tall. - **$5 $10 $20**

☐ **TPG-71. The Three Little Pigs Cake Plates,**
1930s. Faiencerie d'Onnaing China Co. Lot of four 7.25" plates from a set consisting of a serving plate and 12 smaller plates. Reverse is marked with company name and Disney name. Plates are numbered. Serving Plate (not shown) - **$75 $150 $250**
Each Smaller Plate - **$30 $65 $100**

TPG-72

☐ **TPG-72 Big Bad Wolf French Plate,**
1930s. Faiencerie d'Onnaing China Co. of France. 7.25" diameter high gloss ceramic from plate set centered by image of Big Bad Wolf disguised as bearded brush peddler. Title in French is "Il Frappa A La Porte." Reverse has "Walt Disney" name and company mark. - **$35 $65 $100**

TPG-73

TPG-74

☐ **TPG-73. Three Little Pigs Child's Feeding Dish,**
1930s. Patriot China. 7.75" diameter by 1.5" deep three-sectioned china dish. Unmarked. - **$60 $135 $225**

☐ **TPG-74. Fifer Pig Figural Mug,**
1930s. "Patriot China" 4.5" tall painted and glazed ceramic from set of three different companion mugs by Salem China Co. Each - **$15 $30 $60**

TPG-75

☐ **TPG-75. Three Little Pigs Elaborate English Pitcher,**
1930s. Wade-Heath England marked 6x7x10.25" tall painted and glazed ceramic figural Big Bad Wolf handle designed as if he is holding onto the top rim of the pitcher and peering down at the high relief images of the Three Pigs. Pigs are surrounded by trees and flowers with house in the background, all also in relief design. - **$600 $1200 $1800**

TPG-76

☐ **TPG-76. The Three Little Pigs And Big Bad Wolf Figural Ceramic Pitcher,**
1930s. Painted and glazed ceramic measures 4.5x7.5x8" tall, seen both unmarked and with "Shorter & Son England" on underside. - **$85 $175 $300**

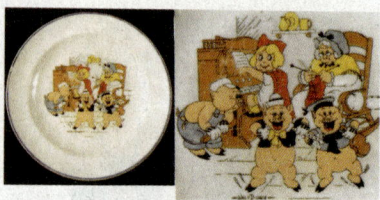

TPG-77

☐ **TPG-77. Three Little Pigs Plate,**
1930s. Salem China Co. 7" diameter plate. - **$30 $60 $90**

894

THE THREE LITTLE PIGS

TPG-78

TPG-79

❑ **TPG-80. "The Big Bad Wolf" Costume,**
1930s. Wornova Mfg. Co. Slick fabric shirt and trouser set totaling about 4' in length. Shirt chest has 3.5" diameter felt fabric patch picturing him. Rear of trousers has a long fabric tail. This example is missing Wolf mask and cap from the original set. Complete - **$50 $100 $165**
As Pictured - **$20 $40 $60**

TPG-81

❑ **TPG-78. Practical Pig Salt And Pepper Set,**
1930s. Pair of 2.25" tall painted and glazed china marked "Japan." - **$40 $75 $135**

❑ **TPG-79. Three Little Pigs Ceramic Bank Set,**
1930s. Likely France or Italy. Three painted and glazed ceramic figural banks, each about 3x3.5x6" tall. Back edge of two bases marked "W. Disney." Underside of one has raised name of "Tomry." Each - **$65 $100 $200**

❑ **TPG-81. Three Little Pigs Ashtray,**
1930s. Three dimensional figures attached to back of ashtray base, 3x4.5x3.25" overall. Marked "Made In Japan." Practical Pig at center with brick stack. - **$60 $115 $225**

TPG-80

TPG-82

❑ **TPG-82. Three Little Pigs Ceramic Ashtray,**
1930s. Scarce version. Practical pig on left with bricks. - **$65 $125 $250**

TPG-83

❑ **TPG-83. Three Little Pigs Matchbox Holder,**
1930s. Enameled brass 1x1x1.5" long depicting Three Pigs singing "Who's Afraid Of The Big Bad Wolf." - **$30 $60 $100**

TPG-84

❑ **TPG-84. Three Pigs Matchbox Holder,**
1930s. Silvered and enameled brass 1x1x1.5" long with wrap-around design of Big Bad Wolf on the front walking toward the Pigs who appear on the back. - **$40 $75 $150**

TPG-85

❑ **TPG-85. "Silly Symphony Lights" Set With Three Little Pigs & Others,**
1930s. Noma Electric Corp. 6.25x16.25x2" deep boxed electrical strand set of hard plastic bulb shades, each finished by wrap-around decal. Each shade has different decal and five shades depict Pigs/Wolves. Remaining three depict Silly Symphony characters Tortoise and Hare, Cock Robin, Orphan Kitten. Box lid and side panel art is Christmas theme with Three Pigs, Big Bad Wolf, Three Little Wolves, Clara Cluck, Tillie, Elmer and Robber Kitten. Box interior has insert with large flip-up top panel with same art that appears on lid. Box - **$100 $200 $300**
Lights Complete - **$50 $100 $200**

THE THREE LITTLE PIGS

TPG-86

❏ **TPG-86. "Three Little Pigs Silly Symphonies Playing Cards" and Box,** 1930s. - **$60 $125 $250**

TPG-87

❏ **TPG-87. "Three Little Pigs" Card Deck,** 1930s. Complete deck of 52 standard playing cards, each 2.25x3.5". - **$25 $50 $100**

TPG-88

TPG-89

❏ **TPG-88. Three Little Pigs "Valentines Day" Fold-Out Card,** 1930s. Hall Brothers Inc. 4x5.25" die-cut stiff paper card opens to 12" image of Pigs. - **$20 $35 $65**

❏ **TPG-89. "The Three Little Pigs" Birthday Card,** 1930s. Hall Brothers. 4x5" folder card. - **$12 $25 $40**

TPG-90

❏ **TPG-90. "Three Little Pigs" Wood Radio,** 1930s. 5x7x9.25" tall with pressed wood attachment depicting the Three Pigs. No Disney markings or company name. - **$500 $1000 $2000**

TPG-91

❏ **TPG-91. "Three Little Pigs" Sand Pail,** 1930s. Unmarked but Ohio Art Co. 5.25" top diameter by 5.5" tall lithographed tin pail with attached carrying handle. Outside is wrap-around scene of Practical Pig outside of his house being passed by Little Red Riding Hood and Fiddler and Fifer Pigs. - **$175 $350 $700**

TPG-92

❏ **TPG-92. "Three Little Pigs" Sand Pail,** 1930s. Chein. Unauthorized non-Disney design. 4.25" tall tin litho. - **$50 $100 $200**

TPG-93

TPG-94

❏ **TPG-93. Three Little Pigs Celluloid Wind-Up Trapeze Toy,** 1930s. "Made In Japan" plus copyright toy with overall size 7.5x11x10.5" tall metal wire frame with attached wind-up mechanism built-in key. - **$350 $700 $1100**

❏ **TPG-94. "Three Little Pigs" Lantern Slide English Set,** 1930s. Ensign Ltd. 3x5.25x1" deep boxed complete set of six 1.5x5.25" glass slides and 2.75x5", 24-page story booklet. - **$60 $125 $200**

THE THREE LITTLE PIGS

TPG-95

☐ **TPG-95. "Three Little Pigs" Boxes Slide Set,**
1930s. Ensign Limited of England. 3.25" square slides in set of 24 with box and papers. - **$30 $60 $100**

TPG-96

☐ **TPG-96. "Who's Afraid Of The Big Bad Wolf" Pencil Box,**
1930s. Dixon. 3.25x8.25x.75" stiff cardboard box with paper covering. Comes with 1.25" eraser picturing the pigs. Box - **$40 $75 $150** Eraser - **$5 $15 $25**

TPG-97

☐ **TPG-97. Three Little Pigs Pencil Holders,**
1930s. Unmarked but known Spanish set of three painted jigsawed wood pencil holders, each about 1.5x4x4" tall. Each has attachment on back for holding pencils. Fiddler Pig has one-row holder for placement of six pencils while the other two have double rows for twelve pencils. Each - **$100 $200 $300**

TPG-98

☐ **TPG-98. Fifer Pig Race Car Pencil Holder,**
1930s. Unmarked but Spanish 2.5x6x3.75" tall jigsawed and painted wood free-wheeling pencil holder. Hood has decal "Concession Walt Disney." - **$150 $300 $500**

TPG-99

☐ **TPG-99. Practical Pig French Pencil Case,**
1930s. A. Fabre. 4x8.5x5" deep with jigsawed wood frame, die-cut cardboard front and back panels. - **$150 $300 $450**

TPG-100

☐ **TPG-100. Fiddler Pig Catalin Plastic Pencil Sharpener,**
1930s. 1-1/8x1-1/8" octagonal. - **$65 $115 $175**

TPG-101

TPG-102

☐ **TPG-101. Big Bad Wolf Story French Postcard Set,**
1930s. Marked "Paris" and "Disney" complete set of twelve numbered 3.5x5.5" French text illustrated postals combining to complete the story of The Big Bad Wolf, also featuring Little Red Riding Hood and The Three Little Pigs. Set - **$150 $300 $600**

☐ **TPG-102. Big Bad Wolf Hand Blown Glass Figure,**
c. 1930s. Unmarked. 2.25" tall. - **$25 $50 $100**

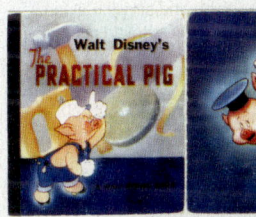
TPG-103

☐ **TPG-103. "The Practical Pig" Book,**
1940. Garden City Publishing Co. 8.75x9.25" hardcover, 24 pages. Content is based on the movie short of same title. - **$60 $125 $250**

TPG-104

897

THE THREE LITTLE PIGS

☐ **TPG-104. "Walt Disney Little Pig" Wrist Watch In Box,**
1947. U.S. Time. 4x7" box complete with price tag, and insert. Box - **$100 $200 $400** Watch - **$85 $175 $300**

TPG-105

☐ **TPG-105. Three Little Pigs Ceramic Figure,**
c. 1947. Zaccagnini. 6x10.5x8" tall. Incredible detailed figurine depicting the Three Pigs huddled together, laughing and strolling along. Underside has mark for this Italian company. - **$1500 $3000 $4750**

TPG-106

☐ **TPG-106. "Three Little Pigs" Record Set,**
1949. Capitol Records. 7.5x8.5" cardboard album containing set of two 45 rpm records designated "CBXF3018" from "Record-Reader" series. Cover has bound-in 40-page full color storybook. - **$50 $100 $150**

TPG-107

☐ **TPG-107. "Erasable Bookmark,"**
1940s. Antioch Bookplate Co. 2x5" cardboard display card holding 4.75" long celluloid bookmark. Card - **$5 $10 $15** Bookmark - **$12 $25 $50**

TPG-108

☐ **TPG-108. "Three Little Pigs" Golden Record,**
1950. Paper sleeve 6.75x7.5" contains vinyl 78 rpm record. - **$8 $15 $25**

TPG-109

TPG-110

☐ **TPG-109. "Three Little Pigs" Scarf,**
1950s. Scarf is 22x24". - **$12 $25 $50**

☐ **TPG-110. Practical Pig Figurine,**
1950s. Shaw Pottery. 1-1/8" tall painted and glazed ceramic miniature with sticker on reverse. - **$30 $60 $90**

TPG-111

☐ **TPG-111. Fiddler Pig Ceramic Figurine,**
1950s. Goebel. 3.75" tall. - **$50 $100 $165**

TPG-112

☐ **TPG-112. Fifer Pig Ceramic Figurine,**
1950s. Goebel. 3.75" tall. - **$50 $100 $165**

THE THREE LITTLE PIGS

TPG-113

TPG-115

❏ **TPG-115. Three Little Pigs Animated Musical Shadow Box,**
1950s. Jaymar Specialty Co./Japan. 9.5x11.75x2.75" deep painted wood shadow box framing 6x8" animated scene comprised of various jigsawed wood movable or stationery pieces. Attached to the bottom of the frame is a pull cord with wood ball knob attachment. When pulled, Fiddler Pig's head and arm move to start the music of "Who's Afraid Of The Big Bad Wolf." Fifer Pig's head also moves slightly. - **$75 $150 $250**

❏ **TPG-113. Practical Pig Ceramic Bank By Hagen-Renaker,**
1950s. 3.5x4x6.5" tall painted and glazed ceramic. Hagen, known for their line of miniature ceramic figurines, also produced a line of larger size Disney character banks, all of which are scarce and include Lady, Dumbo, Figaro and Thumper. Underside, rather than having a trap, had the opening covered by a paper label. - **$200 $400 $700**

TPG-116

TPG-114

❏ **TPG-114. Practical Pig Cookie Jar,**
1950s. Hagen-Renaker. 7.5x7.5x12" tall glazed ceramic. Depicts him holding a L-square ruler. - **$300 $600 $1000**

❏ **TPG-116. The Big Bad Wolf And Three Little Pigs Doll Set,**
1950s. Lars of Italy. Four-piece doll set. Wolf is 7x13x23" tall while each pig is about 6x6x12" tall. Stuffed dolls are primarily felt although Wolf's body has bushy plush covering. Set - **$2200 $4400 $6500**

THE THREE LITTLE PIGS

TPG-117   TPG-118

TPG-121

TPG-123

☐ **TPG-117. Practical Pig Bobbing Head,**
1960s. "Japan" 5.5" tall painted composition figure, likely unauthorized. - **$25 $45 $85**

☐ **TPG-118. Li'l Bad Wolf Candy Dispenser,**
1960s. Pez. 3.75" tall hard plastic. - **$10 $20 $30**

☐ **TPG-121. Big Bad Wolf And Practical Pig Ramp Walker,**
1960s. Marx. 3" tall hard plastic with movable feet. - **$35 $65 $110**

☐ **TPG-123. "Three Little Pigs" Friction Powered Van Trailer,**
1960s. Line Mar. 12x6" tin toy.
Box - **$300 $600 $1000**
Toy - **$1000 $2000 $3000**

TPG-119

TPG-124

☐ **TPG-119. Practical Pig Candy Dispenser,**
1960s. Pez. 4" tall hard plastic variety with crooked cap on head. - **$15 $25 $40**

TPG-120

TPG-122

TPG-125

☐ **TPG-120. Fiddler And Fifer Pigs Ramp Walker,**
1960s. Marx. 3" tall hard plastic with moveable feet. - **$30 $60 $90**

☐ **TPG-122. Big Bad Wolf And Pigs Boxed Wind-ups,**
1960s. Line Mar. Set of four (pigs not shown) each in illustrated box with display window holding 2.25x3.25x4.25" tall lithographed tin figure with built-in key. Box has top back display flap with illustration of Fifer Pig outside of his box (house). This flap folds into the box to turn into a house with peaked roof. Each Box - **$100 $200 $325**
Each Toy - **$100 $200 $300**

☐ **TPG-124. Fiddler Pig Hand Puppet,**
1987. Product from France. - **$25 $50 $75**

☐ **TPG-125. Fifer Pig Hand Puppet,**
1987. Product from France. - **$25 $50 $75**

THE THREE LITTLE PIGS

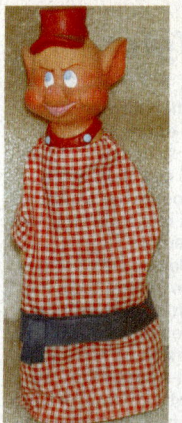

TPG-126   TPG-127

❑ **TPG-126. Practical Pig Hand Puppet,**
1987. Product from France. - **$25 $50 $75**

❑ **TPG-127. Big Bad Wolf Hand Puppet,**
1987. Product from France. - **$25 $50 $80**

TPG-128

❑ **TPG-128. "The Three Little Pigs" Wristwatch,**
c. 1991. "Lorus." Plastic display case for "Disney Character Time Pieces" holding battery-operated watch with dial illustration of the Three Pigs. The second hand disk depicts the Big Bad Wolf huffing and puffing a cloud of air. Boxed - **$20 $40 $60**

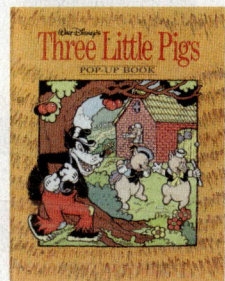

TPG-129

❑ **TPG-129. "Three Little Pigs Pop-Up Book,"**
1993. Disney Press. 8.25x10.25" hardcover with five double-page pop-up/mechanical pages which tell the traditional story. - **$8 $12 $20**

TPG-130

❑ **TPG-130. Big Bad Wolf Statue,**
1995. Walt Disney Classic series. Commemorates 60th anniversary of the Three Little Pigs series. Limited to 7,500 - **$1100**

TPG-131

TPG-132

❑ **TPG-131. Fiddler Plush Doll with Tag,**
1999. From "Three Little Pigs" series sold only at Disneyworld. - **$30**

❑ **TPG-132. Fifer Plush Doll with Tag,**
1999. From "Three Little Pigs" series sold only at Disneyworld. - **$30**

THE THREE LITTLE PIGS

TPG-133

TPG-134

☐ **TPG-133. Practical Pig Plush Doll with Tag,** 1999. From "Three Little Pigs" series sold only at Disneyworld. - **$30**

☐ **TPG-134. Big Bad Wolf Plush Doll with Tag,** 1999. From "Three Little Pigs" series sold only at Disneyworld. - **$40**

TPG-135

☐ **TPG-135. Disney Classic Edition Set,** 1990s. Set - **$450**

The Three Lives of Thomasina

Based on Paul Gallico's best-selling book *Thomasina*, this 1963 full-length live-action feature is set in the Scottish highlands in the year 1912. The ginger cat Thomasina comes to live with a widowed and somewhat bitter veterinary surgeon and his daughter. After Thomasina is injured, the vet attempts to put her to sleep. The cat is found still breathing by a young animal lover who reunites her with her family. Over the course of time, the animal lover and the vet fall in love.

The film was directed by Don Chaffey. Its cast included Patrick McGoohan, Susan Hampshire, Karen Dotrice and Matthew Garber. *Thomasina* marked the first time that Dotrice and Garber would appear in a film together. The pair would next appear as brother and sister in *Mary Poppins* (1964). Terry Gilkyson wrote the song *Thomasina* for the film.

Merchandise seems non-existent.

TLT-1

☐ **TLT-1. Studio Christmas Card,** 1963. Slightly textured paper 7x8" with choice color art. Card opens to reveal calendar for 1964 featuring characters from The Sword In The Stone. Illustration on back is of cat from "The Three Lives Of Thomasina." - **$30 $60 $115**

Toby Tyler

The volume of live-action movies that Disney actually released during the fifties and sixties is something to be marveled at. For every one that sticks out, there are a couple of films that get lost in the shuffle. *Toby Tyler*, from 1960, is one such forgotten film that deserves a better fate.

Based on a story by James Otis Kaler, this full-length live-action feature finds the orphan Toby living with his abusive uncle. One day, the circus comes to town and Toby is dying to go. Unfortunately, he can't afford a ticket. Standing behind a circus tent, he meets a peanut vendor who offers him a job. The only catch is that Toby has to run away and join him on the road.

Despite his uncle's abrasive nature, Toby still feels loyalty and declines the offer. The vendor gives him a free ticket as a consolation. Returning home, Toby finds that he has forgotten to feed the hogs. This drives his uncle over the edge. He rips up the free ticket and sends Toby to bed without dinner. A half-hour later Toby is out the back door and selling peanuts. He becomes integrated with the life that circus folk lead. He ends up friends with an insane monkey named Mr. Stubbs and together, they learn to ride horses. Toby eventually becomes an equestrian and re-unites with his guardians.

The movie was directed by Charles Barton. The cast included Kevin Corcoran, Bob Sweeney, Henry Calvin and Gene Sheldon.

Merchandise was very limited. Toby Tyler appears in *Four Color Comics* #1092.

TOB-1

TOKYO DISNEYLAND

❑ **TOB-1. Disney Studio Christmas Card,** 1959. Card is 7.8" on textured paper. Card opens to reveal Matterhorn bobsled scene with a number of Disney characters including the Seven Dwarfs. Back cover features color photo of Toby Tyler and Mr. Stubbs. - **$35 $65 $125**

TOB-2

❑ **TOB-2. "Toby Tyler" Movie Pressbook,** 1960. 11.5x15" glossy paper book. - **$10 $20 $35**

TOB-3

❑ **TOB-3. "Toby Tyler Frame Tray Puzzle,"** 1960. Whitman. 11.25x14.25". - **$8 $15 $30**

TOB-4

❑ **TOB-4. "Toby Tyler" Hardcover.** 1960. Golden Press. 6.25x9" with 60 pages. - **$5 $12 $20**

TOB-5

❑ **TOB-5. "Toby Tyler" Lobby Card,** 1968. Glossy 11x14" stiff paper card. - **$8 $12 $20**

Tokyo Disneyland

Japanese tourism has always been high at both American Disney theme parks. When the company was looking to expand its theme park business overseas, Tokyo seemed to be the logical first choice. Several areas were surveyed, but eventually Disney settled in the town of Urayasu, thirty miles from a highly populated area.

Tokyo Disneyland officially opened on April 15, 1983. The park is similar in design to the American parks. One major difference is the size of the Japanese park. California's Disneyland is a little over 72 acres; Orlando's Walt Disney World is slightly over 106 acres, but the Japanese park covers 114 acres. Even with the larger space, the park numbers somewhat fewer rides and attractions than the other two. This has made much more free space available. That is space the park needs to accommodate its large crowds. During the summer, it is not unusual for the park to be at capacity by noon. On some days, over a hundred thousand people will file through its gates.

Tokyo Disneyland is known for its immaculate appearance. While the layout of the park is similar to that of its American cousins, cultural differences are noticeable. One of the obvious differences comes at the entrance to the park. Instead of a Main Street, visitors walk through a World Bazaar. Among Tokyo Disneyland's more recent additions is a sister park, Tokyo DisneySeas. Its attractions include Mediterranean Harbor and Mysterious Island, the latter inspired by the work of Jules Verne. The park is heavily attended and it is also a popular tourist attraction for those visiting Japan.

Merchandise includes items manufactured directly for the Japanese market.

TOK-1

❑ **TOK-1. Tokyo Disneyland Patch,** 1983. Opening day patch used by employees; also sold at the Park. - **$115**

TOKYO DISNEYLAND

TOK-2

TOK-4

☐ **TOK-2. "Tokyo Disneyland" Christmas Card With Envelope,** 1984. 4.5x7" stiff textured paper card. - **$10 $20 $40**

☐ **TOK-4. "Tokyo Disneyland" Pin-Back Button Group,** 1980s. Thirteen very graphic designs. Star shapes are 2" each, one Minnie is 2.25" and all others are 3.5". Each - **$5 $10 $15**

TOK-3

TOK-5

☐ **TOK-3. "Christmas Fantasy Tokyo Disneyland" Christmas Card,** 1986. Stiff 4.5x7" textured paper card. - **$10 $20 $40**

☐ **TOK-5. Donald Duck Bean Bag Doll Set,** 1999. Promotes 65th Anniversary. Three sizes only offered in Japan for a short time. Each has its own tags. Set - **$165**

TOK-6

☐ **TOK-6. Donald Duck White Plush,** 1999. From Tokyo Disneyland. With tag. Referred to as "Monochrome Donald." - **$90**

Tonka

Sal Mineo stars as Indian brave White Bull in this live-action 1959 feature. He captures a horse and names him Tonka, but loses him to his cruel cousin. White Bull frees Tonka, who ends up going into battle as the captain's horse at Little Big Horn. The captain is killed in battle, and Tonka is retired by the army to be cared for by White Bull.

Directed by Lewis R. Foster, the film also featured Philip Carey, Jerome Courtland and Joy Page. Merchandise was very limited.

TON-1

☐ **TON-1. "Tonka Little Golden Book,"** 1959. 6.75x8" first printing by Golden Press, 24 pages. - **$10 $20 $35**

TON-2

☐ **TON-2. Movie Herald,** c.1959. From Maryland theater. - **$4 $8 $15**

Toy Story

The first full-length animated feature made completely on computers opened to great reviews and terrific success in 1995. While the film is technically brilliant and ranks as an artistic triumph, the key to its success is its writing. The film operates on several levels: it works perfectly for a three-year-old, engages a twelve-year-old, entertains a 33-year-old and can be easily understood by a 53-year-old.

The film begins with young Andy who has a birthday coming up. His toys are worried that they will be replaced by newer, flashier models. Andy's former favorite toy, a cowboy doll named Woody, tries to do away with Andy's new toy, the futuristic Buzz Lightyear. Woody and Buzz end up away from Andy in the outside world. They have to learn to work together in order to return home to Andy.

The film was directed by John Lasseter. Vocal talent included Tom Hanks, Tim Allen, Jim Varney and Don Rickles. The music was composed by Randy Newman. The film inspired a sequel and also an animated TV show, *Buzz Lightyear of Star Command*.

Merchandise for the film was extensive and it included books, action figures, dolls, watches and various premiums.

TST-1

❑ **TST-1. "Toy Story Limited Edition Collector Card Set,"**
1995. Skybox-Hasbro. 3.5x6x3" deep cardboard replica toy chest containing original 45-card set. Underside has foil sticker with individual issue number and this example is #1160 of 20,000. Mint Boxed - **$25**

TST-2

❑ **TST-2. "Toy Story Rex Squeeze Bottle" Boxed Premium,**
1995. Minute Maid. Figure is 4x3.5x6.75" tall. Near Mint Boxed - **$55**

TST-3

TST-4

❑ **TST-3. "Toy Story" Promotional Poster,**
1995. Burger King. 26x39" stiff glossy paper poster offering character hand puppets available for $1.99 with purchase of any Value Meal. - **$5 $12 $20**

❑ **TST-4. "Toy Story" Translight,**
1995. Burger King 24.5x27" rigid plastic display for use with light box to advertise the six different toys available in "Kids Club Meal." - **$8 $15 $25**

TST-5

TST-6

❑ **TST-5. "Toy Story" French Glass Tumblers Set,**
c. 1995. "VMC" and "Disney Collection" 2x9x4" deep boxed set of three identical 4" tall glasses with Mickey portrait, repeated "Disney" logo and wrap-around images of "Toy Story" logo, Buzz, Woody. Boxed - **$8 $15 $25**

❑ **TST-6. Toy Story Martian Mug,**
c. 1995. Hard plastic 5x6x4.25" tall figural head with hinged lid, sold at Disney's traveling ice show with sticker on back that reads "Walt Disney's World On Ice." Text on underside includes "Manufactured Exclusively For Ringling Brothers And Barnum & Bailey Combined Shows Inc." - **$5 $10 $15**

TST-7

❑ **TST-7. "Toy Story" Japanese Wind-Up Toys,**
c. 1995. "Toy Box" product pair of 4.25x6" blister cards, each containing detailed hard plastic wind-up 2.5" to 3" tall. Most text on packaging is Japanese although some English including toy title "Toko Toko Walker." Figures are Buzz Lightyear and Alien, the only two featured on the packaging including the photo instructions on backs. Both have "White Knob" and attached keychain. Each Packaged - **$10 $18 $30**

TST-8

❑ **TST-8. "Toy Story Express" Electric Train Set,**
1996. International Hobby Corp. 13.5x26.5x2" deep display window box containing HO scale set of locomotive and five freight cars. "Collectors Limited Edition Series One." Also second boxed set of three cars for Mr. Potato Head, Aliens, Rex. Boxed Large - **$20 $40 $80**
Boxed Small - **$10 $20 $30**

TOY STORY

TST-9

TST-10

❏ **TST-9. Buzz Puppet,**
1995. Burger King. - **$6**

❏ **TST-10. Woody Puppet,**
1995. Burger King. - **$6**

TYS-11

❏ **TYS-11. "Buzz" Watch in Tin,**
1996. Fossil. Comes in box inside colorful tin. Limited edition. - **$135**

TYS-12

❏ **TYS-12. Musical Snow Globe,**
1996. - **$100**

TYS-13

❏ **TYS-13. 20" "Woody" Doll with Tags,**
1999. From Toy Story 2. Has two tags. - **$30**

TYS-14

❏ **TYS-14. "Bullseye" Bean Figure with Tag,**
1999. 8" long. Disney Store exclusive. - **$10**

TYS-15

❏ **TYS-15. 9 1/2" "Buzz" Bean Bag Figure with Sound,**
1999. From Toy Story 2. Has two tags. - **$10**

TYS-16

TYS-17

(Figure is identical for both 1999 and 2000. Only tags differ)

906

TOY STORY

❏ **TYS-16. "Jessie Cowgirl" 18" Bean Figure with Tags,**
1999. Disney Store exclusive. One of the hot 1999 Christmas toys, it quickly sold out. Store price was $20 for this first edition. Has felt hat and 2 tags. - **$55**

❏ **TYS-17. Reissued "Jessie Cowgirl" 18" Bean Figure with New Tags,**
2000. Disney Store exclusive. Doll has same felt hat and 2 different tags. Store price was $24 for this second edition. - **$24**

TYS-18

❏ **TYS-18. "Hamm" Bean Bag Figure,**
1999. From Toy Story 2. With tags. - **$12**

TYS-19

❏ **TYS-19. "The Prospector" Star Bean Figure,**
1999. Hat easily chips at edges. - **$15**

TYS-20   TYS-21

❏ **TYS-20. "Tour Guide Barbie" in Box,**
1999. - **$30**

❏ **TYS-21. "Woody and Bo Peep Gift Set",**
1999. In box. - **$40**

TYS-22

❏ **TYS-22. "Jessie the Cowgirl" Figure,**
1999. Base has rollers. - **$3 $6 $12**

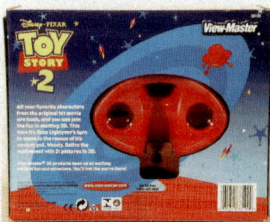
TYS-23

❏ **TYS-23. View-Master With 3-D Pictures,**
1999. Includes 21 photos. - **$25**

TST-24

❏ **TST-24. Jessie Talking Doll,**
1999. Pull-string doll with removable cowgirl hat. - **$25**

TST-25

TST-26

❏ **TST-25. Small Woody Plush,**
1999. From Walt Disney World. - **$10**

❏ **TST-26. Wheezy the Penguin Plush Toy,**
1999. From Walt Disney World. - **$10**

TYS-27

❏ **TYS-27. "Woody" Sprinkler in Box,**
1999. - **$35**

TST-28

TST-29

TOY STORY

☐ **TST-28. Woody and Bullseye Candy Dispenser,** 1999. McDonald's. - **$5**

☐ **TST-29. Bo Peep with Circling Sheep Toy,** 2000. McDonald's. - **$5**

TYS-30   TYS-31

☐ **TYS-30. "Lenny" Bean Figure with Tags,** 2000. - **$10**

☐ **TYS-31. Bear Critter Bean Bag Figure,** 2000. Star Bean. - **$10**

TYS-32

☐ **TYS-32. Cookie Jar,** 2000. - **$60**

TYS-33

☐ **TYS-33. "Hot Wheels" Cars,** 2000. NASCAR 2000 set has 3 cars in box. - **$35**

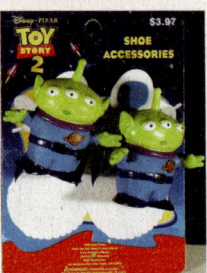

TYS-34

☐ **TYS-34. Aliens Shoe Accessories,** 2000. Two 3-eyed aliens on card. - **$15**

TYS-35

☐ **TYS-35. Buzz Lightyear Blaster in Box,** 2000. Produces cosmic lights and sounds. - **$25**

TST-36

TST-37

☐ **TST-36. View Master Toy,** 2000. McDonald's. Shows movie scenes. - **$20**

☐ **TST-37. Emperor Zurg with Launcher Toy,** 2001. McDonald's. - **$10**

TST-38   TST-39

☐ **TST-38. Buzz Bobble Toy,** 2000s. - **$25**

☐ **TST-39. Woody Bobble Toy,** 2000s. - **$25**

TST-40

☐ **TST-40. Disney Wild Racers,** 2002. Two die-cut car package includes the Lightyear Warpster and the Galaxy Aggressor. - **$15**

TST-41

☐ **TST-41. Mini Bobble Head Figures,** 2004. Kellogg's Frosted Flakes premium. Each - **$7**

Treasure Island

Robert Louis Stevenson's classic novel was the first Disney live-action 1950 film not to contain any animation at all. It was also the first Disney film that was shot in England. After the war, Disney had money tied up in Britain that, due to currency regulations, he could not spend elsewhere. He decided to use the money to begin local film production in the country. Live action films became necessary when Disney couldn't find trained animators in Europe.

Young Jim Hawkins acquires a treasure map and sails to Treasure Island with Squire Trelawney and others. The ship's cook is Long John Silver. Silver plots a mutiny, and kidnaps young Jim when it fails. Jim escapes and with the help of the island's hermit, Ben Gunn, defeats Silver and finds the treasure. Directed by Byron Haskin, the film features Bobby Driscoll, Robert Newton, Basil Sydney and Denis O'Dea.

Merchandise for the film included books and records. *Treasure Island* also appears in *Four Color Comics* # 624.

TRE-1

❏ **TRE-1. Walt Disney's Treasure Island" Half-Sheet Movie Poster,**
1950. RKO Radio Pictures, Inc. 22x28" stiff paper. - **$40 $85 $165**

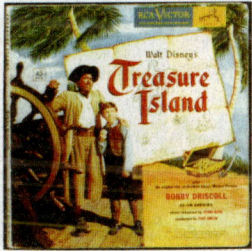
TRE-2

❏ **TRE-2. "Walt Disney's Treasure Island" Record Set,**
1950. RCA. Little Nipper Series. 7.25x7.25" paper sleeve contains set of two yellow vinyl 45 rpm records. - **$10 $20 $35**

TRE-3

❏ **TRE-3. Promotional Handout,**
1950. - **$10 $20 $40**

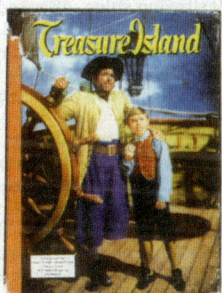
TRE-4

❏ **TRE-4. "Treasure Island" Hardcover,**
1950. Whitman 6x8.25" book with dust jacket from their "Classic Books" series. - **$15 $30 $60**

TRE-5

❏ **TRE-5. "Walt Disney's Treasure Island" Adventure Game,**
c. 1950. Gardner Games. 14x20x1.5" deep box. Parts include board, figural metal ship playing pieces, working compass, sun dial, small treasure chest, three types of cards "Sailing Order, Island Cards, Treasure Maps. - **$50 $100 $150**

TRE-6

❏ **TRE6. "Walt Disney's Treasure Island" Comic Book,**
1962. Dell. "Movie Classics Series." - **$4 $8 $40**

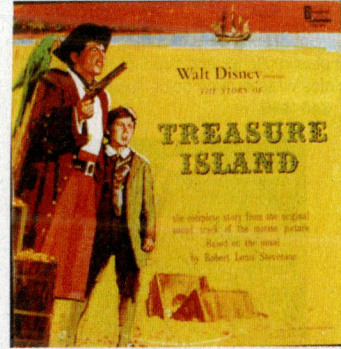
TRE-7

❏ **TRE-7. "Treasure Island" Soundtrack Record Album,**
1964. Disneyland label. 12.25x12.25" cardboard cover contains 33-1/3 rpm. - **$5 $15 $25**

TRON

Tron

This 1982 full-length feature was the first to use extensive computer graphics. It was also one of Disney's rare entries into the genre of science fiction. The director of *Toy Story* (1995), John Lasseter, has said that "without Tron, there would be no *Toy Story*" and he is right. It was a breakthrough in technical abilities as well as in visual style.

A computer programmer is trying to prove himself the true author of some video games whose program code was stolen from him. In order to retrieve the code, he enters a computer world and eventually must compete for his life in an actual video game.

Tron was directed by Steve Lisberger. The cast included Jeff Bridges, Bruce Boxleitner and David Warner. The special effects team included noted comic artist "Moebius" Girard, Syd Mead and Peter Lloyd. The film was nominated for Academy Awards in Sound and Costume Design. The music was by Wendy Carlos.

Merchandising included books, action figures and video games.

TRN-1

❏ **TRN-1. "Tron/Coca-Cola" Pitcher And Cup Set,**
1982. Set of six pieces including 7.5" tall white hard plastic pitcher and five 5.5" tall cups, all with nice wrap-around color illustrations. Set - **$20 $40 $65**

TRN-2

❏ **TRN-2. "Tron Sark" Action Figure,**
1982. Tomy. 6x9" blister card contains 4" tall figure. Back of card includes photo of all four figures in this series as well as the light cycle. Figure comes with glow-in-the-dark accessory disk. Carded - **$25 $50 $80**

Twenty Thousand Leagues Under the Sea

The classic Jules Verne story comes perfectly alive in this entertaining and successful 1954 full-length live-action feature. The evil Captain Nemo is piloting a submarine. While trying to control nuclear energy, he has been destroying ships. Attacked by a giant squid, Nemo is saved by Ned Land, who has been trying to track him down. Land then reveals the location of Nemo's secret island and both Nemo and the island are destroyed.

Highlighted by an impressive set as well as solid special effects (for the time), *20,000 Leagues* was a hit on its first release. The acting was top-rate, especially that of James Mason and Kirk Douglas. The cast also included Peter Lorre and Paul Lucas. The film was directed by Richard Fleischer, the son of animation pioneer Max Fleischer. Norman Gimble and Al Hoffman wrote the signature tune *A Whale of a Tale*, which achieved some level of popularity at the time. The film won Academy Awards for Best Special Effects and Art Decoration/Set Decoration. *20,000 Leagues* was also Disney's first film in Cinemascope.

Merchandising included books, records and *Four Color Comics* #614..

TWE-1

❏ **TWE-1. Studio Christmas Card,**
1954. Slightly textured paper card 7x7.75". Pluto reads "Leagues" book. - **$60 $135 $225**

TWE-2

TWE-3

❏ **TWE-2. "20,000 Leagues Under The Sea" Press Release, Stationery And Fan Card,**
1954. Three sheet press release is 8.5x11". Studio stationery is 8.5x11" and fan card is 8.5x10-1/8". Each - **$8 $15 $25**

❏ **TWE-3. "20,000 Leagues Under The Sea" Frame Tray Puzzle,**
1954. Jaymar. 9.75x12.75". - **$8 $15 $25**

TWE-4

❏ **TWE-4. "20,000 Leagues Under The Sea" Boxed Puzzle,**
1954. Jaymar. 7x10x1.75" deep box contains complete "Vulcania-The Base Of The Nautilus" puzzle. - **$15 $25 $40**

UNCLE SCROOGE

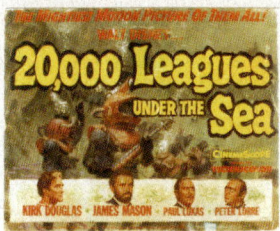

TWE-5

❑ **TWE-5.** "20,000 Leagues Under The Sea" Movie Theater Countertop Standee,
1954. Cardboard 11x14" standee with easel on reverse. - **$110 $225 $325**

TWE-6

❑ **TWE-6.** "Walt Disney's 20,000 Leagues Under The Sea Game,"
1954. Jaymar. 7.75x15x1.25" deep box. Board is 14.5x14.5" with rather simple but colorful design which includes small repeated images of octopus and starfish on the playing area, bottom margin has undersea scene including treasure chest. The 5.5x5.5" cardboard spinner has die-cut Nautilus pointer. Includes instruction sheet. - **$30 $60 $100**

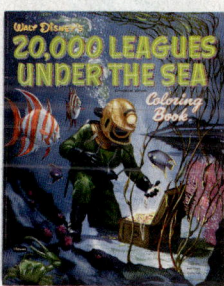

TWE-7

❑ **TWE-7.** "20,000 Leagues Under The Sea" Coloring Book,
1954. Whitman. Large format 11x13.5" - **$25 $60 $125**

TWE-8

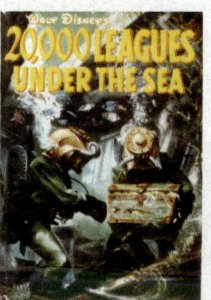

TWE-9

❑ **TWE-8.** "20,000 Leagues Under Sea Nautilus Clockwork Submarine" Boxed English Wind-up,
c. 1954. Sutcliffe Pressings Ltd. 3.75x10.25x2.25" deep box contains 10" long toy. The submarine has high gloss finish paint, complete with four accent decals. The top periscope lifts off for placement of key. Toy is designed to be used in water. Box - **$65 $110 $165**
Toy - **$65 $110 $165**

❑ **TWE-9.** "20,000 Leagues Under The Sea" Hardcover,
1955. Whitman. 5.75x8". - **$8 $15 $25**

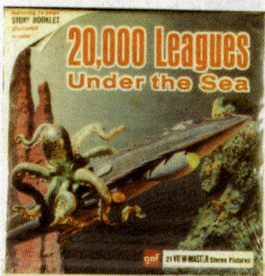

TWE-10

❑ **TWE-10.** "20,000 Leagues Under The Sea" View-Master Set,
1958. Sealed 4.5x4.5" envelope contains non-Disney set of three reels and booklet. - **$8 $15 $25**

Uncle Scrooge

Scrooge was the creation of Carl Barks, legendary comic book artist/writer and former Disney story man. His first appearance came in the Donald Duck one-shot comic book *Four Color* #178 (1947), in a story titled *Christmas on Bear Mountain*. The comic book was published by Dell, who, at the time, had the rights to publish Disney characters in comic book form. Barks' creation of Scrooge was inauspicious; he merely needed a miserly skinflint to propel the story forward. The character next showed up six months later and from there began to appear more and more frequently. With each appearance he became friendlier and friendlier as his bad temper softened. However, his legendary greed and stinginess never died.

In mature form, Scrooge was typically accompanied on adventures by his nephew Donald and grandnephews Huey, Dewey and Louie. Scrooge received his own self-titled comic book in 1952. Carl Barks was the only writer and artist on the title until 1961. He continued to produce the vast majority of the stories until his retirement in 1967. The Scrooge stories Barks created are noted for their adventuresome nature as well as the complexity of the characters. Over time he created an entire universe for Scrooge to operate in. This included Scrooge's enemies the Beagle Boys, Flintheart Glomgold, John D. Rockerduck and Magica De Spell. Other creations included Gyro Gearloose, Gladstone Gander and the Junior Woodchucks.

Scrooge's first animated appearance came in 1955, with a brief cameo in the *Mickey Mouse Club* main titles. His first starring role arrived in a 1967 Disney educational short, *Scrooge McDuck and Money*, directed by longtime Disney animator Hamilton Luske. Scrooge later starred in the animated TV show *DuckTales* (1987). He has also had major roles in *Mickey's Christmas Carol* (1983), *Ducktales: The Movie — Treasure of the Lost Lamp* (1990), and *Mickey's Twice Upon a Christmas* (2004).

Merchandising includes lithographs, banks, figures and books.

UNC-1

UNCLE SCROOGE

❏ **UNC-1. "A Walt Disney's Christmas Coloring Book,"**
1954. Dell. 8.25x10.75" with 80 pages. - **$18 $35 $60**

UNC-2

❏ **UNC-2. Uncle Scrooge Ceramic Figurine,**
1950s. Hagen-Renaker. 1.5" tall. Photo example missing small paper money bill originally glued to cane tip. Near Mint on Card Complete With Money - **$500** Figure Without Card and Money (As Shown) - **$60 $125 $200**

UNC-3

❏ **UNC-3. "Uncle Scrooge The Lemonade King" Book,**
1960. Whitman. Pencils by Carl Barks, finished art adapted by Norman McGary. 32 pages. - **$100 $400 $825**

UNC-4

❏ **UNC-4. "Uncle Scrooge" Bank,**
1961. Don Brechner exclusive.
Bank - **$50 $100 $175**
Box (Not Shown) - **$25 $50 $150**

UNC-5

❏ **UNC-5. "Donald Duck/Mobil" Australian Premium Comic Books,**
1964. Each 5x7.25" with 16 pages on newsprint from a numbered premium series issued weekly by Mobil. #20 and #21, both featuring Carl Barks stories. Each - **$8 $15 $30**

UNC-6

❏ **UNC-6. Large Italian Inflatable Uncle Scrooge,**
1960s. Vinyl figure with detachable travel bag 12x15x25" marked "Made In Italy." - **$100 $200 $300**

UNC-7

❏ **UNC-7. Uncle Scrooge Plaster Figurine,**
1960s. Figure is 2.5x4x6" tall. - **$20 $40 $65**

UNC-8

❏ **UNC-8. Uncle Scrooge Ceramic Bank,**
1960s. Has Disney copyright plus maker's name "Ceranca De Cuernavaca Mexico." 6x7x8" tall large head bank that is painted and glazed ceramic with separate copper wire glasses. - **$100 $200 $300**

UNC-9

❏ **UNC-9. Uncle Scrooge Lunch Box,**
1970s. Likely Italian. 6x9x8" tall. Body is leather with plastic sides that have die-cut hole openings. Front flap features a sewn-in printed cloth insert under clear vinyl cover. - **$65 $110 $165**

UNCLE SCROOGE

UNC-10.

UNC-13

UNC-16

❏ **UNC-10. "Uncle Scrooge" Patch on Card,** 1970s. Tough to find. Near Mint Packaged - **$60** Loose - **$5 $15 $30**

❏ **UNC-12. Uncle Scrooge Composition Bank,** 1970s. Bank is 4x4x8" tall. Marked Korea on underside with Disney copyright. - **$50 $100 $185**

❏ **UNC-13. Uncle Scrooge Squeaker Figure,** 1970s. Soft vinyl with movable head. 5.5x6.5x10" tall. - **$35 $75 $150**

USC-11

UNC-14

UNC-17

❏ **UNC-11. "Uncle Scrooge" Ceramic Bank,** 1970s. - **$30 $55 $110**

❏ **UNC-14. Uncle Scrooge Cel From Mickey's Christmas Carol,** 1983. Acetate sheet is 12x16" with 4x6.5" cel image. #75 from a numbered sequence. - **$60 $115 $175**

❏ **UNC-16. "Uncle Scrooge" Ceramic Music Box,** 1980s. Promotes "Mickey's Christmas Carol." Chair rocks as music plays. - **$30 $65 $135**

❏ **UNC-17. "Uncle Scrooge" Figure,** 1980s. Figure has crystal tummy and glasses. Plated in 14K gold. 2 1/2" tall. Limited edition from Austria. Hard to find. - **$40 $75 $125**

UNC-12

UNC-15

❏ **UNC-15. "DuckTales" 3-D Puzzle,** 1986. Promotes TV show. - **$10 $25 $60**

UNCLE SCROOGE

UNC-18

❑ **UNC-18. "Uncle Scrooge" Ceramic Figure,** 1980s. 5 1/2" tall. From Japan. - **$10 $25 $50**

UNC-19

❑ **UNC-19. Mickey Mouse, Donald Duck And Uncle Scrooge Cel,** 1980s. Pair of 10.5x12.5" acetate sheets with total of three different cel images, each about 2.5x4". - **$60 $125 $175**

UNC-20

UNC-21

❑ **UNC-20. Scrooge McDuck Cel,** 1980s. Acetate sheet is 9x10.5" centered by 7x8" image over laser image window and chair back background. No. "A5" from a numbered sequence. - **$75 $135 $250**

❑ **UNC-21. Uncle Scrooge Cel,** 1980s. Acetate sheet is 9x10.5" centered left by 3.5x4.75" full figure painted image from 'DuckTales' TV show. No. "C-36" from a numbered sequence. - **$65 $125 $175**

UNC-22

❑ **UNC-22. Uncle Scrooge Cel,** 1980s. Acetate sheet is 9x10.5" centered left by 3.5x5.25" full figure painted image of him holding an apparent coin in glass dome. From 'DuckTales' TV show, No. "C89" in a numbered sequence. - **$65 $125 $175**

UNC-23

❑ **UNC-23. Uncle Scrooge Premium Figural Plastic Bank,** 1980s. Bank is 2.5x3.5x6" tall. "MK Made In Finland." Bank premium with no key, designed to be brought to bank and opened by teller for benefit of child's savings account. Full Color - **$20 $40 $100** Bronze Color - **$25 $45 $110**

UNC-24

❑ **UNC-24. Carl Barks Initialed Limited Edition Print,** c. 1980s. Print titled "Which Disney Theme Park Is This?" is 11x11.5" on stiff slightly textured paper. Limited edition of 500. Near Mint - **$115**

UNC-25

❑ **UNC-25. Uncle Scrooge Porcelain Figure,** 1991. Limited edition from the Franklin Mint. Figure has metal glasses, felt clothing and a wooden cane. 14" tall. - **$85 $200 $450**

UNCLE SCROOGE

UNC-26

UNC-27

UNC-29

❏ **UNC-26. Uncle Scrooge Limited Edition Artist Signed Sculpture,**
1990. Metal sculpture with enamel paint and onyx base measuring 5.75" tall. Signed by artist "Ron." Edition #182-2750 with Disney copyright. Mint As Issued - **$450**

❏ **UNC-27. Uncle Scrooge "Merry Christmas" Carl Barks Signed Lithograph Print,**
1995. Original oil painting by Carl Barks for this piece recently sold for $100,000. 11x14". Edition of 500. Mint As Issued - **$425**

❏ **UNC-29. Uncle Scrooge 50th Birthday Original Art,**
1997. Textured stiff art paper is 8.5x11.5" with ink and water color portrait by Patrick Block who does covers for modern Disney comic books by Gemstone Publishing. This piece was done at the time of Scrooge's 50th birthday and is dated November 1, 1997. Image of birthday cake is decorated on sides by coins plus dollar bills on top rather than candles. Signed by Block who added a Disney copyright and "On Scrooge's 50th Birthday." Unique, Near Mint - **$1000**

UNC-30

❏ **UNC-30. "Hands Off My Playthings" Bronze Sculpture,**
1997. Limited edition of 176. Sculpted by Paul Vought. Signed by Carl Barks. Mint as issued - **$600**

UNC-28

UNC-31

❏ **UNC-28. "Sport of Tycoons" Bronze Sculpture,**
1994. Limited edition of 100. Sculpted by Paul Vought. Signed by Carl Barks. - **$5000**

❏ **UNC-31. "Who's Out There" Bronze Sculpture,**
1998. Limited edition of 131. Sculpted by Paul Vought. Signed by Carl Barks. Mint as issued - **$2750**

UNCLE SCROOGE

UNC-32

UNC-33

UNC-34

UNC-35

UNC-36

❑ **UNC-34. Uncle Scrooge Ceramic Bank,** 1998. High quality product. Made in France. - $110

❑ **UNC-35. Uncle Scrooge Star Bean Figure,** 1998. With tag. - $20

❑ **UNC-36. Uncle Scrooge Bean Bag,** 1999. Promotes Christmas Carol film. - $8 $12 $20

❑ **UNC-32. Uncle Scrooge Door Hanger,** 1998. From Disney's Christmas Collection. - $10 $20 $35

❑ **UNC-33. Uncle Scrooge Plush Doll,** 1998. With patch and money sack. - $10 $20 $40

UNC-37

❑ **UNC-37. "This Dollar Saved My Life at Whitehorse" Capodimonte Sculpture,** 1999. Limited edition of 250. - $4000

UNCLE SCROOGE

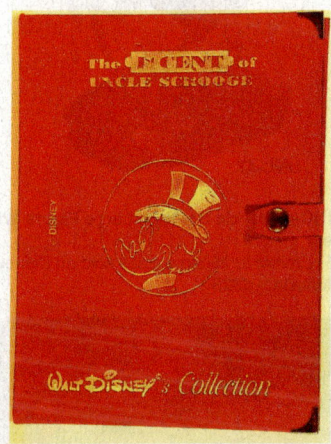

UNC-38

UNC-39

❑ **UNC-39. Uncle Scrooge "Always Another Rainbow" Gold Digger Porcelain Statue,**
1990s. Connoisseur Of Malvern, Great Britain. Edition of 100 pieces which closed at 74 issued and remaining 26 were destroyed. 9-7/8" tall. These statues have sold as high as $10,000. Prices vary widely.

❑ **UNC-38. "The 1st Cent of Uncle Scrooge" Coin Display Book and Coin,**
1990s. Red felt book with snap closure holds coin. Coin is mounted inside a capsule.
Book - $10 $25 $60
Coin - $10 $25 $75

UNC-40

❑ **UNC-40. Uncle Scrooge "Pick And Shovel Laborer" Porcelain Statue,**
1990s. Connoisseur Of Malvern, Great Britain. Edition of 100 with 38 issued, the remaining 62 were destroyed. 10.5" tall. A matching, numbered lithographed was included.
Figure Mint As Issued - **$7500**. Price varies widely.

UNCLE SCROOGE

UNC-41

❑ **UNC-41. Uncle Scrooge Water Globe,** 2000. Plays the tune "Pennies From Heaven." - **$40**

UNC-42

❑ **UNC-42. Uncle Scrooge Figure,** 2001. 18" tall x 15" wide Disneyland Park exclusive. - **$160**

UNC-43

❑ **UNC-43. Uncle Scrooge Figurine,** 2002. Sculpted by David Critchfield and Vic Fortunato. - **$35**

UNC-44

❑ **UNC-44. Uncle Scrooge Snow Globe,** 2004. Limited edition of 250. - **$225**

UNC-45

❑ **UNC-45. Uncle Scrooge Stuffed Doll,** 2004. - **$25**

UNC-46

❑ **UNC-46. Christmas Carol Scrooge Figure,** 2004. - **$20**

UNC-47

❑ **UNC-47. Uncle Scrooge Large Figure With Base,** 2005. Limited to 250 examples sold on Disney's auction site. - **$325**

UNC-48

❑ **UNC-48. Christmas In Uncle Scrooge's Money Bin Original Art,** 2005. Textured stiff art board is 15x22" with ink and watercolor scene by Patrick Block who does covers for modern Disney comic books by Gemstone Publishing. This piece was commisioned from the artist. Unique - **$1750**

UNC-49

❑ **UNC-49. "A Pool of Riches" Statue,** 2000s. Classic Collection. - **$200**

UNCLE SCROOGE COMICS

Uncle Scrooge Comics

Dell began Uncle Scrooge's self-titled book with issue #4. They counted his appearances in Four Color Comics #386, 456, and 495 as the first three issues. The last issue to contain an original work by Barks is #71. The original title was published by Dell until issue #39. Gold Key had the book from issues #40-173. Whitman published the title from #174-209. With issue #210, Gladstone published the book under the title *Walt Disney's Uncle Scrooge* from #210-242. Disney took over publication with #243-280. Gladstone again resumed publication for issues #281-318. Gemstone started their run with issue #319 and continues today under the title *Uncle Scrooge*.

❏ **Four Color Comics #495,** September 1953. Uncle Scrooge by Barks. - $47 $141 $900

❏ **Uncle Scrooge # 6,** June 1854. Barks-a. - $24 $72 $400

❏ **Four Color Comics #386,** March 1952. Uncle Scrooge Barks-a. - $114 $342 $2400

❏ **Uncle Scrooge # 4,** December 1953. Barks-a. - $38 $114 $675

❏ **Uncle Scrooge # 7,** September 1954. Barks-a. - $22 $66 $355

❏ **Four Color Comics #456,** March 1953. Barks-a. - $62 $186 $1300

❏ **Uncle Scrooge # 5,** March 1954. Barks-a. - $31 $93 $550

❏ **Uncle Scrooge # 8,** December 1954. Barks-a. - $18 $54 $300

UNCLE SCROOGE COMICS

❑ **Uncle Scrooge #9,**
March 1955. Barks-a. - **$18 $54 $300**

❑ **Uncle Scrooge #12,**
December 1955. Barks-a. - **$16 $48 $260**

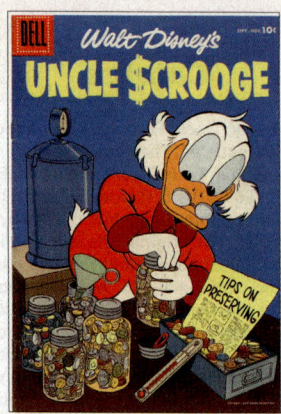

❑ **Uncle Scrooge #15,**
September 1956. Barks-a. - **$16 $48 $260**

❑ **Uncle Scrooge # 10,**
June 1955. Barks-a. - **$18 $54 $300**

❑ **Uncle Scrooge #13,**
March 1956. Barks-a. - **$16 $48 $260**

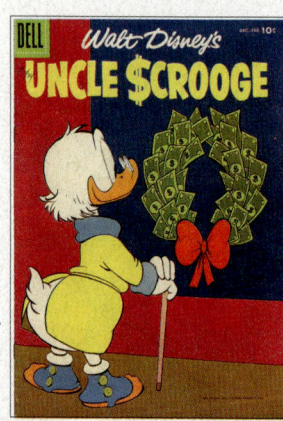

❑ **Uncle Scrooge #16,**
December 1956. Barks-a. - **$16 $48 $260**

❑ **Uncle Scrooge #11,**
September 1955. Barks-a. - **$16 $48 $260**

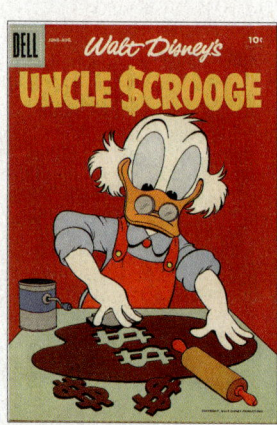

❑ **Uncle Scrooge #14,**
June 1956. Barks-a. - **$16 $48 $260**

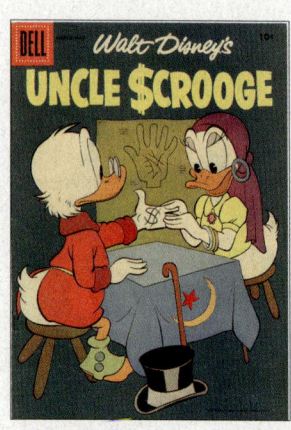

❑ **Uncle Scrooge #17,**
March 1957. Barks-a. - **$16 $48 $260**

UNCLE SCROOGE COMICS

❑ Uncle Scrooge #18,
June 1957, Barks-a. - **$16** **$48** **$260**

❑ Uncle Scrooge #21,
March 1957. Barks-a. - **$13** **$39** **$210**

❑ Uncle Scrooge #24,
December 1958. Barks-a. - **$1v** **$39** **$210**

❑ Uncle Scrooge #19,
September 1957. Barks-a. - **$16** **$48** **$260**

❑ Uncle Scrooge #22,
June 1958. Barks-a. - **$13** **$39** **$210**

❑ Uncle Scrooge #25,
March 1959. Barks-a. - **$13** **$39** **$210**

❑ Uncle Scrooge #20,
December 1957. Barks-a. - **$16** **$48** **$260**

❑ Uncle Scrooge #23,
September 1958. Barks-a. - **$13** **$39** **$210**

❑ Uncle Scrooge #26,
June 1959. Barks-a. - **$13** **$39** **$210**

UNCLE SCROOGE COMICS

❏ **Uncle Scrooge #27,**
September 1959. Barks-a. - **$13 $39 $210**

❏ **Uncle Scrooge #30,**
June 1960. Barks-a. - **$13 $39 $210**

❏ **Uncle Scrooge #33,**
March 1961. Barks-a - **$12 $36 $180**

❏ **Uncle Scrooge #28,**
December 1959. Barks-a. - **$13 $39 $210**

❏ **Uncle Scrooge #31,**
September 1960. Barks-a. - **$12 $36 $180**

❏ **Uncle Scrooge #34,**
June 1961. Barks-a - **$12 $36 $180**

❏ **Uncle Scrooge #29,**
March 1960. Barks-a. - **$13 $39 $210**

❏ **Uncle Scrooge #32,**
December 1960. Barks-a. - **$12 $36 $180**

❏ **Uncle Scrooge #35,**
September 1961. Barks-a. - **$12 $36 $180**

UNCLE SCROOGE COMICS

❏ **Uncle Scrooge #36,** December 1961. Barks-a 1st app. Magica De Spell. - $13 $39 $210

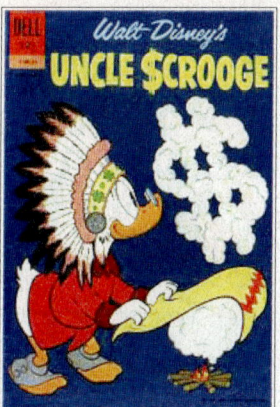
❏ **Uncle Scrooge #39,** September 1962. Barks-a - $12 $36 $180

❏ **Uncle Scrooge #42,** May 1963. Barks-a - $11 $33 $150

❏ **Uncle Scrooge #37,** March 1962. Barks-a - $12 $36 $180

❏ **Uncle Scrooge #40,** December 1962. Barks-a - $12 $36 $180

❏ **Uncle Scrooge #43,** July 1963. Barks-a - $11 $33 $150

❏ **Uncle Scrooge #38,** June 1962. Barks-a - $12 $36 $180

❏ **Uncle Scrooge #41,** March 1963. Barks-a - $11 $33 $150

❏ **Uncle Scrooge #44,** August 1963. Barks-a - $11 $33 $150

UNCLE SCROOGE COMICS

❑ **Uncle Scrooge #45,**
October 1963. Barks-a - **$11** **$33** **$150**

❑ **Uncle Scrooge #48,**
March 1964. Barks-a - **$11** **$33** **$150**

❑ **Uncle Scrooge #51,**
August 1964. Barks-a - **$11** **$33** **$150**

❑ **Uncle Scrooge #46,**
December 1963. Barks-a - **$11** **$33** **$150**

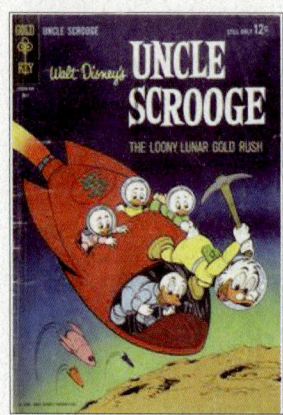

❑ **Uncle Scrooge #49,**
May 1964. Barks-a - **$11** **$33** **$150**

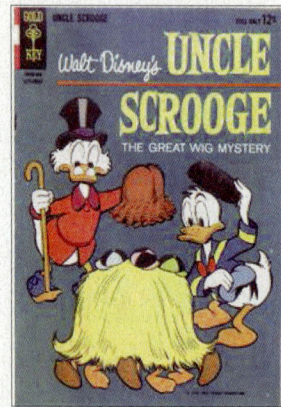

❑ **Uncle Scrooge #52,**
September 1964. Barks-a - **$11** **$33** **$150**

❑ **Uncle Scrooge #47,**
February 1964. Barks-a - **$11** **$33** **$150**

❑ **Uncle Scrooge #50,**
July 1964. Barks-a - **$11** **$33** **$150**

❑ **Uncle Scrooge #53,**
October 1964. Barks-a - **$11** **$33** **$150**

UNCLE SCROOGE COMICS

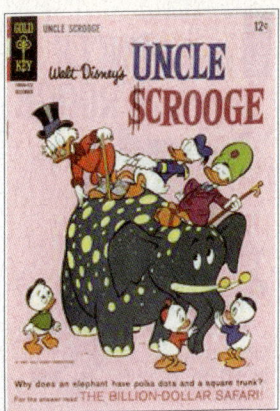

❏ **Uncle Scrooge #54,**
December 1964. Barks-a - **$11 $33 $150**

❏ **Uncle Scrooge #57,**
May 1965. Barks-a - **$11 $33 $150**

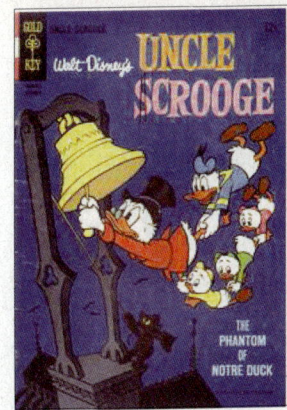

❏ **Uncle Scrooge #60,**
November 1965. Barks-a - **$11 $33 $150**

❏ **Uncle Scrooge #55,**
February 1965. Barks-a - **$11 $33 $150**

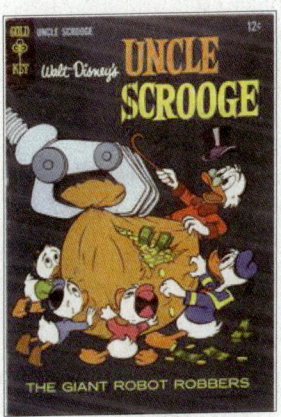

❏ **Uncle Scrooge #58,**
July 1965. Barks-a - **$11 $33 $150**

❏ **Uncle Scrooge #61,**
January 1966. Barks-a - **$10 $30 $130**

❏ **Uncle Scrooge #56,**
March 1965. Barks-a - **$11 $33 $150**

❏ **Uncle Scrooge #59,**
September 1965. Barks-a - **$11 $33 $150**

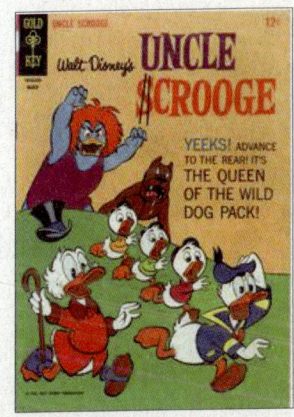

❏ **Uncle Scrooge #62,**
March 1966. Barks-a - **$10 $30 $130**

UNCLE SCROOGE COMICS

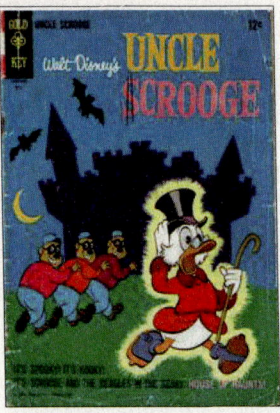

❏ **Uncle Scrooge #63,**
May 1966. - **$10 $30 $130**

❏ **Uncle Scrooge #66,**
November 1966. Barks-a - **$10 $30 $130**

❏ **Uncle Scrooge #69,**
May 1967. Barks-a - **$10 $30 $130**

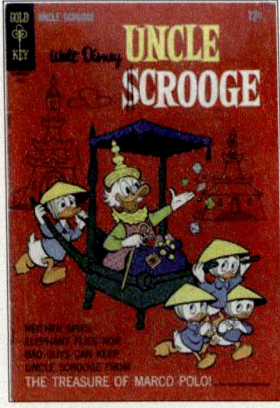

❏ **Uncle Scrooge #64,**
July 1966. Barks-a Barks. - **$13 $39 $200**

❏ **Uncle Scrooge #67,**
January 1967. Barks-r. - **$10 $30 $130**

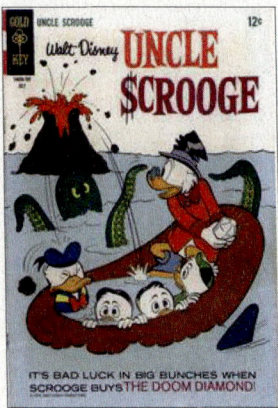

❏ **Uncle Scrooge #70,**
July 1967. Barks-a - **$10 $30 $130**

❏ **Uncle Scrooge #65,**
September 1966. Barks-a - **$10 $30 $130**

❏ **Uncle Scrooge #68,**
March 1967. Barks-a - **$10 $30 $130**

❏ **Uncle Scrooge #71,**
October 1967. Last Barks orig. story, storyboarded script. - **$10 $30 $130**

WALT DISNEY

Walt Disney

Few people in history have ever been blessed with the vision that Walt Disney had. Even fewer have been equally blessed with the ability to follow that vision through. Disney's determination and his innate business skills, combined with his artistic ability, have made him a household name throughout the world.

Born in Chicago in 1901, Walt Disney moved to Missouri with his family a few years later. It was there that Walt developed a great interest in reading, as well as an even greater interest in drawing. At seven he was selling sketches to neighbors. When World War I came around, Walt was too young to join the armed forces. At sixteen, he enlisted in the Red Cross and ended up overseas driving an ambulance.

Returning to Kansas City, Missouri, Walt found work as an advertising cartoonist. It was during this period that Walt developed his first animated films. Together with long-time colleague Ub Iwerks he developed a technique for combining live action and animation. In 1922, Walt opened Laugh-O-Gram Studios and produced six cartoons, but the company was eventually forced to file for bankruptcy. Walt nevertheless knew that animation could be a solid art form and a way to make a living. He set out to join his brother Roy in California. Upon his arrival, the two pooled their resources and, with a little help, were able to set up a studio in an uncle's garage.

Working with the combination of live action and animation he had been developing in Kansas City, Walt coined the concept of the Alice Comedies, in which a live-action human girl explored a cartoon world. On the strength of an Alice pilot short, *Alice's Wonderland* (1923), the two brothers inked a contract with New York film distributor Margaret Winkler. Soon the Alice series was selling and Disney had to hire more staff.

In 1927, the popularity of the Alice Comedies began to fade. Initially, Disney developed the new star character of Oswald the Lucky Rabbit, whose cartoons Disney spent a year producing for Universal Pictures. But when Universal, who was working through a go-between distributor named Charles Mintz, demanded that Disney accept a budget cut or cease to work on the series, Disney relinquished Oswald. With Ub Iwerks, he immediately developed Mickey Mouse.

Mickey's success was the true beginning of the Disney entertainment empire. From there it was on to Academy Awards, feature-length cartoons, live-action movies, theme parks and merchandising opportunities that would make P. T. Barnum green with envy. A true genius and an American icon, Walt Disney worked ceaselessly and deserved every single bit of his success. When he passed away in 1966, the world lost a friend.

WAL-1

❑ **WAL-1. Walt Disney Cigarette Card,** 1935. Imperial Tobacco Premium from England. Tells on back that in 1920 Disney was a hack artist making only 5 pounds a week, then says today he is making 80,000 pounds a year. - **$35 $75 $150**

WAL-2

❑ **WAL-2. "Yearbook Of Motion Pictures,"** 1936. Film Daily. 6x9" hardcover 18th annual edition. Limited distribution. - **$75 $135 $225**

WAL-3

❑ **WAL-3. "Time" With Walt Disney,** 1937. 8.5x11.5" from December 27, 1937 featuring 3-page article on Walt and his business. - **$25 $50 $75**

❑ **WAL-4. "Comics And Their Creators" Illustrated Biography With Dust Jacket,** 1942. Hall, Cushman & Flint Inc. 6.25x9.25" hardcover with 304 black and white pages with numerous self caricatures, specialty drawings and published examples. Includes creators of Superman, Krazy Kat, along with Walt Disney.
Jacket - **$25 $50 $100**
Book - **$20 $40 $75**

WAL-4

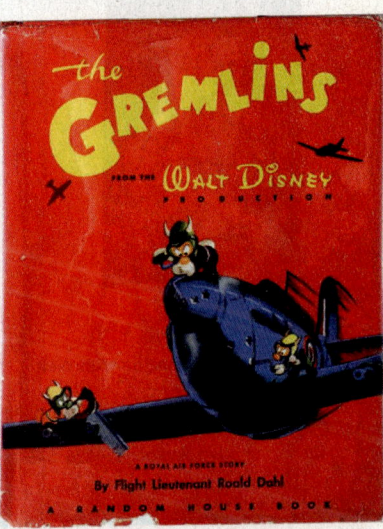

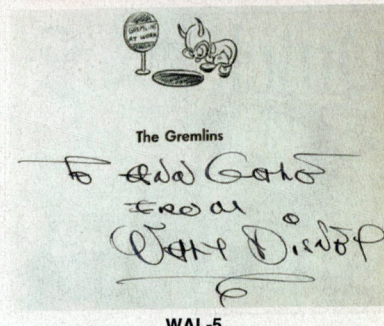

WAL-5

❑ **WAL-5. "The Gremlins" Hardcover Book Signed By Walt Disney,** 1943. Random House. 9x11.25" with 56 pages. Title page has 5.5" long fountain pen signature. Unique, Book Fine - **$2250**

WALT DISNEY

WAL-8

WAL-9

WAL-6

☐ **WAL-8. "TV Forecast" With Disney TV Debut,**
1950. TV Publications of New England. 5.5x8.5", Volume 2, #14 with 20 pages. The Disney front cover was used to promote the first Disney television show "One Hour in Wonderland." - **$150 $300 $600**

☐ **WAL-9. "Electric Trains" Magazine With Walt Disney,**
1951. Volume 1, #3 is 8x11". - **$15 $30 $45**

☐ **WAL-6. "Esquire" Magazine With Walt Disney,**
1945. Volume 23, #2 is 10.5x13.25". This is #4 in the "Esquire Graph" series with brief biography on Disney on preceding page. - **$25 $45 $70**

WAL-7

WAL-10

☐ **WAL-7. "Quick" With Walt Disney/Cinderella,**
1950. Cowles Magazine Inc. 4x6", Volume 2, #17. - **$8 $12 $25**

☐ **WAL-10. "The Story Of Walt Disney" Hardcover Signed By Walt And His Daughter,**
1956. Henry Holt & Co. First edition. 6x8.5" by Diane Disney Miller. The first blank page has been signed "Diane Disney Miller." The next page has a 7" bold Walt Disney signature. Unique, Near Mint - **$2750**

WALT DISNEY

WAL-11

❑ **WAL-11. "Look" Magazine With Walt Disney/Davy Crockett,**
1955. Volume 19, #15 is 10.5x13.5". - **$10 $20 $35**

WAL-12

❑ **WAL-12. "The Saturday Evening Post" Walt Disney,**
1956. 10.75x13.5" issue from November 17, 1956. 8-page article. - **$12 $25 $45**

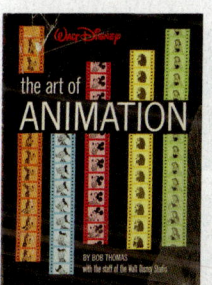
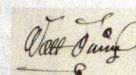

WAL-13

❑ **WAL-13. "The Art Of Animation" Multi-Signed Book,**
1958. Simon & Schuster. 8.25x11.25" with 188 pages. 4.5" signature of Walt Disney on the fly leaf. Also signed by numerous Disney staff including Tom Oreb, Winston Hibler, Joe Rinaldi, Bill Peet, Don DaGradi, Ken Anderson, Xavier Atencio, Bill Justice, Ernest Nordli, Don Griffith, Tom Codrick, Gerry Geronimi, Eric Larson, Milt Kahl, Frank Thomas, Woolie Reitherman, Marc Davis, Les Clark, Ollie Johnson, John Lounsbery, and Ward Kimball. Unique - **$3500**

WAL-14

❑ **WAL-14. "The Story Of Walt Disney" Paperback Book,**
1959. First printing is 4.25x6.5" with 224 pages. - **$20 $35 $60**

WAL-15

WAL-16

❑ **WAL-15. "Walt Disney" Fan Photo,**
1950s. Stiff paper 8-1/8x10-1/8" photo. - **$15 $30 $60**

❑ **WAL-16. Walt Disney And His Train Publicity Photo,**
1950s. Glossy 7.25x9.5" photo. - **$8 $12 $25**

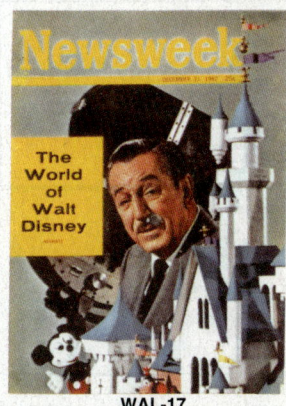

WAL-17

❑ **WAL-17. "Newsweek" With Disney Article,**
1962. 8.25x11" issue from December 31, 1962 featuring 4-page article "The World Of Walt Disney." - **$10 $20 $35**

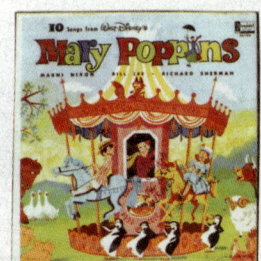

WAL-18

❑ **WAL-18. "Mary Poppins" Record Album Signed By Walt Disney,**
1964. Disneyland label. 12.25x12.25" cardboard album cover contains 33-1/3 rpm. Overall size of Walt's signature is 1x3". Unique, Near Mint - **$3000**

929

WALT DISNEY

WAL-19

❑ **WAL-19. "Walt Disney" First Day Covers,**
1968. 3x6.5" envelopes. Each - **$5 $12 $20**

WAL-20

❑ **WAL-20. Walt Disney Publicity Photos,**
1960s. Each 8x10". Each - **$12 $25 $40**

WAL-21

❑ **WAL-21. Walt Disney Publicity Photos,**
1960s. Each 8x10". Each - **$8 $12 $20**

WAL-22

❑ **WAL-22. Walt Disney Publicity Photo,**
1960s. B&W 8x10". - **$5 $8 $12**

WAL-23

❑ **WAL-23. Walt Disney Publicity Photo,**
1960s. B&W 8x10". - **$5 $8 $12**

WAL-24

❑ **WAL-24. "Walt Disney Productions" Campaign Book,**
1982. Glossy paper 11x15" with 16 pages issued to promote releases. - **$5 $15 $25**

WAL-25

❑ **WAL-25. "Walt and Mickey 2000" Coin and Card,**
2000. Last in series of 55 different. - **$40**

WALT DISNEY'S COMICS AND STORIES

Walt Disney's Comics and Stories

The title first appeared in 1940. Its publication was a logical step in the quickly developing history of books published featuring Disney's name and characters. The first Disney book had appeared in 1930. A few years later, 1933, saw the publication of the first issue of *Mickey Mouse Magazine*. The title was originally seen as a marketing tool, but proved to be very popular. In 1935, the Magazine was made available for newsstand purchase. The content was mixed. Text pieces featuring Mickey and other characters ran next to original comic strips. Soon, half and full-page gag strips began appearing. The Magazine shared some content with its English cousin, *Mickey Mouse Weekly*. Over the next few years, certain characters, such as Donald Duck, rose to prominence and became favorites with readers. The next step in the beginning of WDC&S is an important one. In 1937, the publication of the *Mickey Mouse Magazine* was taken over by a company that had previously only published books, Western Publishing. They were trying to get into the comic market. As a result, the magazine began using more and more newspaper strips and comic art. In 1939 Western than launched a very important comic book, *Dell Four Color*. This title had no regular feature, but instead offered readers a different character, such as Dick Tracy or Don Winslow, in every issue. When Issue #4 of *Four Color* featured Donald Duck, sales went through the roof. An editor at Western figured that since the *Mickey Mouse Magazine* was already gaining comic pages with every issue, why not just make it a regular comic book? The publisher got rid of most of the remaining, non-comic pages, adapted a new masthead, and *Walt Disney's Comics and Stories* was born. Donald Duck greeted readers on the cover of the first issue.

❑ **Walt Disney's Comics and Stories #2,** November 1940. - $618 $1854 $10,500

❑ **Walt Disney's Comics and Stories #3,** December 1940. - $271 $813 $3800

❑ **Walt Disney's Comics and Stories #1** October 1940. (V1#1-c; V2#1-indicia)-Donald Duck strip-r by Al Taliaferro & Gottfredson's Mickey Mouse begin. - $1725 $5175 $30,000

❑ **Walt Disney's Comics and Stories #4,** January 1941. $189 $507 $2650

❑ **Walt Disney's Comics and Stories #5,** February 1941. - $146 $438 $2050

❑ **Walt Disney's Comics and Stories #6,** March 1941. - $118 $354 $1650

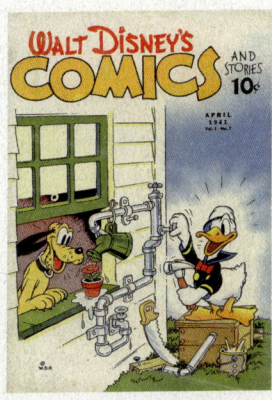
❑ **Walt Disney's Comics and Stories # 7,** April 1941. - $118 $354 $1650

WALT DISNEY'S COMICS AND STORIES

❏ **Walt Disney's Comics and Stories #8,**
May 1941. – **$118 $354 $1650**

❏ **Walt Disney's Comics and Stories #11,**
August 1941. – **$93 $279 $1300**

❏ **Walt Disney's Comics and Stories #14,**
November 1941. - **$93 $279 $1300**

❏ **Walt Disney's Comics and Stories #9,**
June 1941. - **$118 $354 $1650**

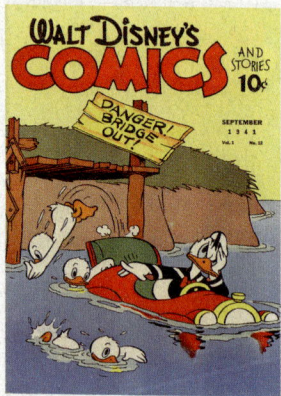
❏ **Walt Disney's Comics and Stories #12,**
September 1941. - **$93 $279 $1300**

❏ **Walt Disney's Comics and Stories #15,**
December 1941. - **$82 $246 $1150**

❏ **Walt Disney's Comics and Stories #10,**
July 1941. - **$118 $354 $1650**

❏ **Walt Disney's Comics and Stories #13,**
October 1941. - **$93 $279 $1300**

❏ **Walt Disney's Comics and Stories #16,**
January 1942. - **$82 $246 $1150**

WALT DISNEY'S COMICS AND STORIES

❏ Walt Disney's Comics and Stories #17, February 1942. - $82 $246 $1150

❏ Walt Disney's Comics and Stories #20, May 1942. - $71 $213 $1000

❏ Walt Disney's Comics and Stories #23, August 1942. - $59 $177 $825

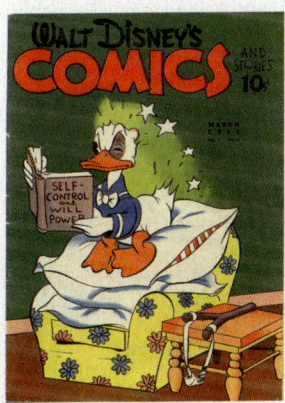
❏ Walt Disney's Comics and Stories #18, March 1942. - $71 $213 $1000

❏ Walt Disney's Comics and Stories #21, June 1942. - $71 $213 $1000

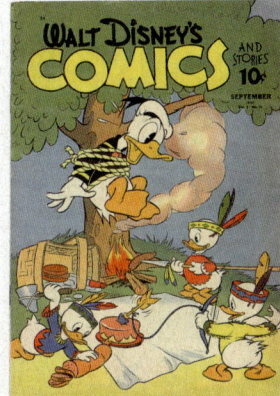
❏ Walt Disney's Comics and Stories #24, September 1942. - $59 $177 $825

❏ Walt Disney's Comics and Stories #19, April 1942. - $71 $213 $1000

❏ Walt Disney's Comics and Stories #22, July 1942. - $59 $177 $825

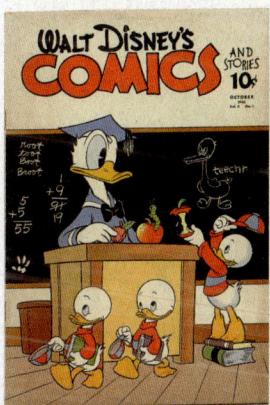
❏ Walt Disney's Comics and Stories #25, October 1942. - $59 $177 $825

WALT DISNEY'S COMICS AND STORIES

❏ Walt Disney's Comics and Stories #26, November 1942. – $59 $177 $825

❏ Walt Disney's Comics and Stories #29, February 1943. - $59 $177 $825

❏ Walt Disney's Comics and Stories #32, May 1943. Barks-a. - $164 $482 $2300

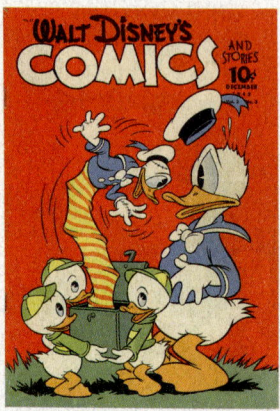
❏ Walt Disney's Comics and Stories #27, December 1942. – $59 $177 $825

❏ Walt Disney's Comics and Stories #30, March 1943. - $59 $177 $825

❏ Walt Disney's Comics and Stories #33, June 1943. Barks-a. - $114 $342 $1600

❏ Walt Disney's Comics and Stories #28, January 1943. - $59 $177 $825

❏ Walt Disney's Comics and Stories #31, April 1943. Donald Duck by Barks begins. - $341 $1023 $5100

❏ Walt Disney's Comics and Stories #34, July 1943. Barks-a. - $93 $279 $1300

WALT DISNEY'S COMICS AND STORIES

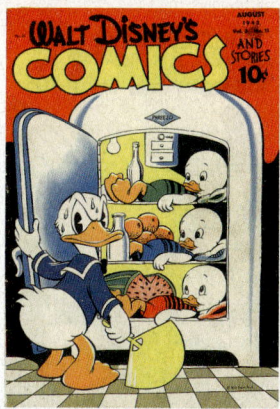

❏ **Walt Disney's Comics and Stories #35,**
August 1943. Barks-a. - $86 $258 $1200

❏ **Walt Disney's Comics and Stories #38,**
November 1943. Barks-a. - $49 $177 $825

❏ **Walt Disney's Comics and Stories #41,**
February 1944. Barks-a. - $48 $144 $650

❏ **Walt Disney's Comics and Stories #36,**
September 1943. Barks-a. - $86 $258 $1200

❏ **Walt Disney's Comics and Stories #39,**
December 1943. Barks-a. - $49 $177 $825

❏ **Walt Disney's Comics and Stories #42,**
March 1944. Barks-a. - $48 $144 $650

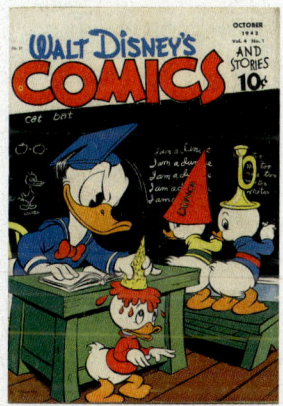

❏ **Walt Disney's Comics and Stories #37,**
October 1943. - $50 $150 $675

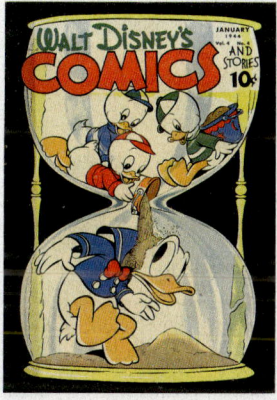

❏ **Walt Disney's Comics and Stories #40,**
January 1944. Barks-a. - $49 $177 $825

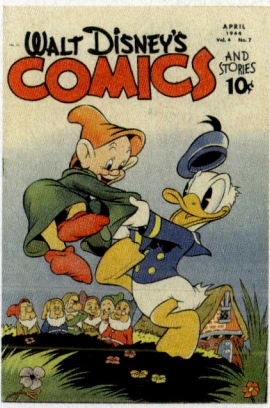

❏ **Walt Disney's Comics and Stories #43,**
April 1944. Barks-a. - $48 $144 $650

WALT DISNEY'S COMICS AND STORIES

❏ **Walt Disney's Comics and Stories #44,** May 1944. Barks-a. - **$48 $144 $650**

❏ **Walt Disney's Comics and Stories #47,** August 1944. Barks-a. - **$48 $144 $650**

❏ **Walt Disney's Comics and Stories #50,** November 1944. Barks-a. – **$48 $144 $650**

❏ **Walt Disney's Comics and Stories #45,** June 1944. Barks-a. - **$48 $144 $650**

❏ **Walt Disney's Comics and Stories #48,** September 1944. Barks-a. - **$48 $144 $650**

❏ **Walt Disney's Comics and Stories #51,** December 1944. - **$29 $87 $470**

❏ **Walt Disney's Comics and Stories #46,** July 1944. Barks-a. - **$48 $144 $650**

❏ **Walt Disney's Comics and Stories #49,** October 1944. Barks-a. - **$48 $144 $650**

❏ **Walt Disney's Comics and Stories #52,** January 1945. Barks-a. - **$29 $87 $470**

WALT DISNEY'S COMICS AND STORIES

❑ **Walt Disney's Comics and Stories #53,** February 1945. Barks-a. - **$29 $87 $470**

❑ **Walt Disney's Comics and Stories #56,** May 1945. Barks-a. - **$29 $87 $470**

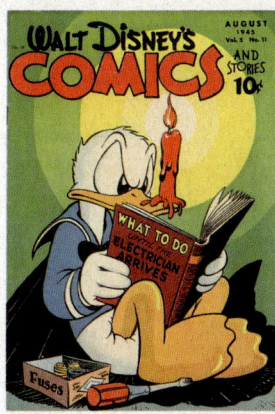
❑ **Walt Disney's Comics and Stories #59,** August 1945. Barks-a. - **$29 $87 $470**

❑ **Walt Disney's Comics and Stories #54,** March 1945. Barks-a. - **$29 $87 $470**

❑ **Walt Disney's Comics and Stories #57,** June 1945. Barks-a. - **$29 $87 $470**

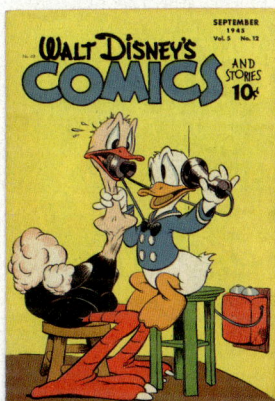
❑ **Walt Disney's Comics and Stories #60,** September 1945. Barks-a. - **$29 $87 $470**

❑ **Walt Disney's Comics and Stories #55,** April 1945. Barks-a. - **$29 $87 $470**

❑ **Walt Disney's Comics and Stories #58,** July 1945. Barks-a. - **$29 $87 $470**

❑ **Walt Disney's Comics and Stories #61,** October 1945. Barks-a. - **$25 $75 $405**

WALT DISNEY'S COMICS AND STORIES

❏ **Walt Disney's Comics and Stories #62,** November 1945. Barks-a. - **$25 $75 $405**

❏ **Walt Disney's Comics and Stories #65,** February 1946. Barks-a. - **$25 $75 $405**

❏ **Walt Disney's Comics and Stories #68,** May 1946. Barks-a. - **$25 $75 $405**

❏ **Walt Disney's Comics and Stories #63,** December 1945. Barks-a. - **$25 $75 $405**

❏ **Walt Disney's Comics and Stories #66,** March 1946. Barks-a. - **$25 $75 $405**

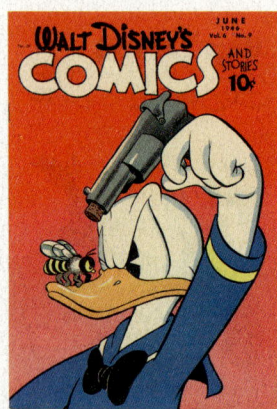

❏ **Walt Disney's Comics and Stories #69,** June 1946. Barks-a. - **$25 $75 $405**

❏ **Walt Disney's Comics and Stories #64,** January 1946. Barks-a. - **$25 $75 $405**

❏ **Walt Disney's Comics and Stories #67,** April 1946. Barks-a. - **$25 $75 $405**

❏ **Walt Disney's Comics and Stories #70,** July 1946. Barks-a. - **$25 $75 $405**

WALT DISNEY'S COMICS AND STORIES

❏ **Walt Disney's Comics and Stories #71,** August 1946. Barks-a. - $19 $57 $305

❏ **Walt Disney's Comics and Stories #74,** November 1946. Barks-a. - $19 $57 $305

❏ **Walt Disney's Comics and Stories #77,** February 1947. Barks-a. - $19 $57 $305

❏ **Walt Disney's Comics and Stories #72,** September 1946. Barks-a. - $19 $57 $305

❏ **Walt Disney's Comics and Stories #75,** December 1946. Barks-a. - $19 $57 $305

❏ **Walt Disney's Comics and Stories #78,** March 1947. Barks-a. - $19 $57 $305

❏ **Walt Disney's Comics and Stories #73,** October 1946. Barks-a. - $19 $57 $305

❏ **Walt Disney's Comics and Stories #76,** January 1947. Barks-a. - $19 $57 $305

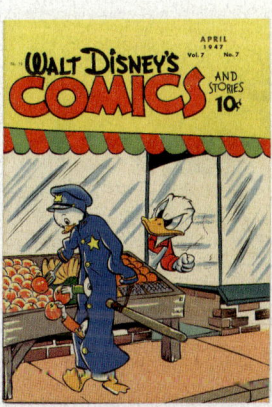

❏ **Walt Disney's Comics and Stories #79,** April 1947. Barks-a. - $19 $57 $305

WALT DISNEY'S COMICS AND STORIES

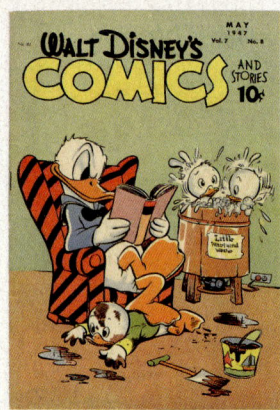

❏ **Walt Disney's Comics and Stories #80,**
May 1947. Barks-a. - **$19 $57 $305**

❏ **Walt Disney's Comics and Stories #83,**
August 1947. Barks-a. - **$16 $48 $260**

❏ **Walt Disney's Comics and Stories #86,**
November 1947. Barks-a. - **$16 $48 $260**

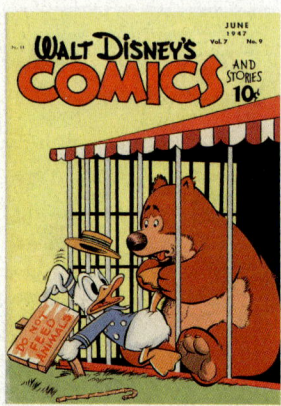

❏ **Walt Disney's Comics and Stories #81,**
June 1947. Barks-a. - **$16 $48 $260**

❏ **Walt Disney's Comics and Stories #84,**
September 1947. Barks-a. - **$16 $48 $260**

❏ **Walt Disney's Comics and Stories #87,**
December 1947. Barks-a. - **$16 $48 $260**

❏ **Walt Disney's Comics and Stories #82,**
July 1947. Barks-a. - **$16 $48 $260**

❏ **Walt Disney's Comics and Stories #85,**
October 1947. Barks-a. – **$16 $48 $260**

❏ **Walt Disney's Comics and Stories #88,**
January 1948. 1st Gladstone Gander by Barks. -
$21 $63 $335

WALT DISNEY'S COMICS AND STORIES

❑ **Walt Disney's Comics and Stories #89,** February 1948. Barks-a. - **$16 $48 $260**

❑ **Walt Disney's Comics and Stories #92,** May 1948. Barks-a. - **$14 $42 $235**

❑ **Walt Disney's Comics and Stories #95,** August 1948. 1st WDC&S Barks-c. - **$14 $42 $235**

❑ **Walt Disney's Comics and Stories #90,** March 1948. Barks-a. - **$16 $48 $260**

❑ **Walt Disney's Comics and Stories #93,** June 1948. Barks-a. - **$14 $42 $235**

❑ **Walt Disney's Comics and Stories #96,** September 1948. Barks-a. - **$14 $42 $235**

❑ **Walt Disney's Comics and Stories #91,** April 1948. Barks-a. - **$14 $42 $235**

❑ **Walt Disney's Comics and Stories #94,** July 1948. Barks-a. - **$14 $42 $235**

❑ **Walt Disney's Comics and Stories #97,** October 1948. Barks-a. - **$14 $42 $235**

WALT DISNEY'S COMICS AND STORIES

❏ **Walt Disney's Comics and Stories #98,** November 1948. 1st Uncle Scrooge in WDC&S. - **$26** **$78** **$420**

❏ **Walt Disney's Comics and Stories #101** February 1949. Barks-a. - **$13** **$39** **$200**

❏ **Walt Disney's Comics and Stories #104** May 1949. Barks-a. - **$13** **$39** **$200**

❏ **Walt Disney's Comics and Stories #99,** December 1948. Barks-a. - **$14** **$42** **$235**

❏ **Walt Disney's Comics and Stories #102** March 1949. Barks-a. - **$13** **$39** **$200**

❏ **Walt Disney's Comics and Stories #105** June 1949. Barks-a. - **$13** **$39** **$200**

❏ **Walt Disney's Comics and Stories #100** January 1949. Barks-a. - **$17** **$51** **$275**

❏ **Walt Disney's Comics and Stories #103** April 1949. Barks-a. - **$13** **$39** **$200**

❏ **Walt Disney's Comics and Stories #106** July 1949. Barks-a. - **$13** **$39** **$200**

WALT DISNEY'S COMICS AND STORIES

❏ **Walt Disney's Comics and Stories #107**
August 1949. Barks-a. - **$13 $39 $200**

❏ **Walt Disney's Comics and Stories #110**
November 1949. Barks-a. - **$13 $39 $200**

❏ **Walt Disney's Comics and Stories #113**
February 1950. - **$9 $27 $110**

❏ **Walt Disney's Comics and Stories #108**
September 1949. Barks-a. - **$13 $39 $200**

❏ **Walt Disney's Comics and Stories #111**
December 1949. Barks-a. - **$12 $36 $170**

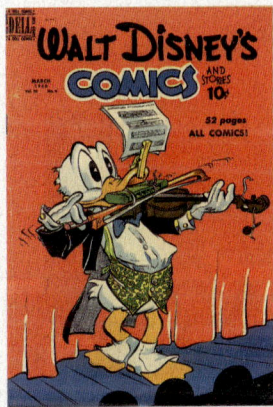

❏ **Walt Disney's Comics and Stories #114**
March 1950. Barks-a. - **$12 $36 $170**

❏ **Walt Disney's Comics and Stories #109**
October 1949. Barks-a. - **$13 $39 $200**

❏ **Walt Disney's Comics and Stories #112**
January 1950. - **$12 $36 $170**

❏ **Walt Disney's Comics and Stories #115**
April 1950. - **$12 $36 $170**

WALT DISNEY'S COMICS AND STORIES

❏ **Walt Disney's Comics and Stories #116**
May 1950. - **$9** **$27** **$110**

❏ **Walt Disney's Comics and Stories #119**
August 1950. - **$9** **$27** **$110**

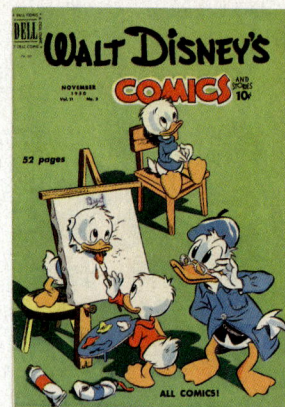
❏ **Walt Disney's Comics and Stories #122**
November 1950. - **$9** **$27** **$110**

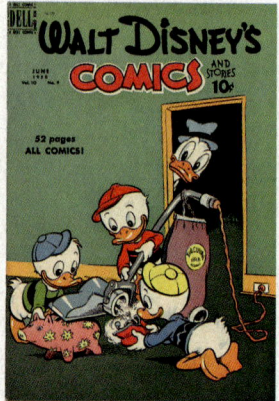
❏ **Walt Disney's Comics and Stories #117**
June 1950. Barks-a. - **$12** **$36** **$170**

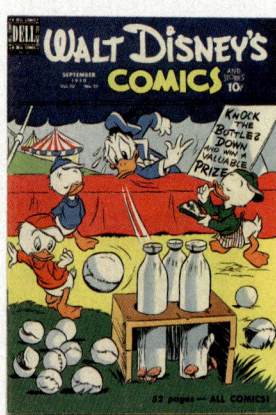
❏ **Walt Disney's Comics and Stories #120**
September 1950. - **$9** **$27** **$110**

❏ **Walt Disney's Comics and Stories #123**
December 1950. - **$9** **$27** **$110**

❏ **Walt Disney's Comics and Stories #118**
July 1950. **$9** **$27** **$110**

❏ **Walt Disney's Comics and Stories #121**
October 1950. - **$9** **$27** **$110**

❏ **Walt Disney's Comics and Stories #124**
January 1951. Barks-a. - **$10** **$30** **$140**

WALT DISNEY'S COMICS AND STORIES

❑ **Walt Disney's Comics and Stories #125**
February 1951. 1st Jr. Woodchucks, Barks-a.
- **$13 $39 $210**

❑ **Walt Disney's Comics and Stories #128**
May 1951. Barks-a. - **$10 $30 $140**

❑ **Walt Disney's Comics and Stories #131**
August 1951. Barks-a. - **$10 $30 $140**

❑ **Walt Disney's Comics and Stories #126**
March 1951. Barks-a. - **$10 $30 $140**

❑ **Walt Disney's Comics and Stories #129**
June 1951. Barks-a. - **$10 $30 $140**

❑ **Walt Disney's Comics and Stories #132**
September 1951. Barks-a. - **$10 $30 $140**

❑ **Walt Disney's Comics and Stories #127**
April 1951. Barks-a. - **$10 $30 $140**

❑ **Walt Disney's Comics and Stories #130**
July 1951. Barks-a. - **$10 $30 $140**

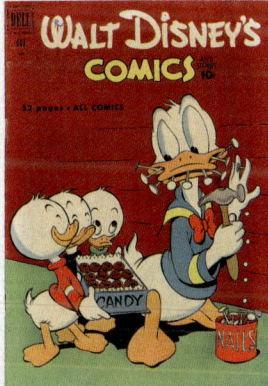

❑ **Walt Disney's Comics and Stories #133**
October 1951. Barks-a. - **$10 $30 $140**

WALT DISNEY'S COMICS AND STORIES

❏ **Walt Disney's Comics and Stories #134**
November 1951. 1st app. Beagle Boys. - $17
$51 $275

❏ **Walt Disney's Comics and Stories #137**
February 1952. Barks-a. - $10 $30 $140

❏ **Walt Disney's Comics and Stories #140**
May 1952. 1st app. Gyro Gearloose by Barks. -
$17 $51 $275

❏ **Walt Disney's Comics and Stories #135**
December 1951. Barks-a. - $10 $30 $140

❏ **Walt Disney's Comics and Stories #138**
March 1952. Classic Scrooge. - $14 $42 $225

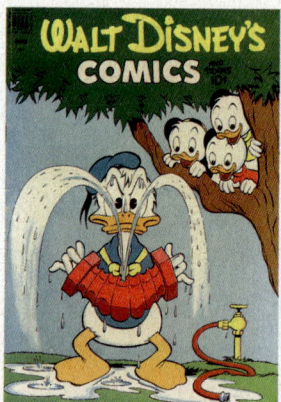

❏ **Walt Disney's Comics and Stories #141**
June 1952. Barks-a. - $8 $24 $105

❏ **Walt Disney's Comics and Stories #136**
January 1952. Barks-a. - $10 $30 $140

❏ **Walt Disney's Comics and Stories #139**
April 1952. Barks-a. - $10 $30 $140

❏ **Walt Disney's Comics and Stories #142**
July 1952. Barks-a. - $8 $24 $105

WALT DISNEY'S COMICS AND STORIES

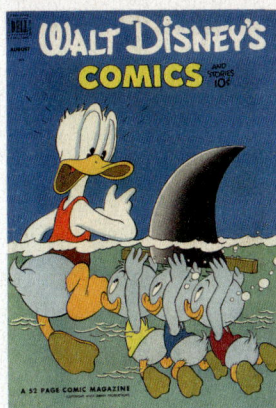

❏ **Walt Disney's Comics and Stories #143**
August 1952. Barks-a. - **$8 $24 $105**

❏ **Walt Disney's Comics and Stories #146**
November 1952. Barks-a. - **$8 $24 $105**

❏ **Walt Disney's Comics and Stories #149**
February 1953. Barks-a. - **$8 $24 $105**

❏ **Walt Disney's Comics and Stories #144**
September 1952. Barks-a. - **$8 $24 $105**

❏ **Walt Disney's Comics and Stories #147**
December 1952. Barks-a. - **$8 $24 $105**

❏ **Walt Disney's Comics and Stories #150**
March 1953. Barks-a. - **$8 $24 $105**

❏ **Walt Disney's Comics and Stories #145**
October 1952. Barks-a. - **$8 $24 $105**

❏ **Walt Disney's Comics and Stories #148**
January 1953. Barks-a. - **$8 $24 $105**

❏ **Walt Disney's Comics and Stories #151**
April 1953. Barks-a. - **$7 $21 $90**

WALT DISNEY'S COMICS AND STORIES

❑ **Walt Disney's Comics and Stories #152**
May 1953. Barks-a. - **$7 $21 $90**

❑ **Walt Disney's Comics and Stories #155**
August 1953. Barks-a. - **$7 $21 $90**

❑ **Walt Disney's Comics and Stories #158**
November 1953. Barks-a. - **$7 $21 $90**

❑ **Walt Disney's Comics and Stories #153**
June 1953. Barks-a. - **$7 $21 $90**

❑ **Walt Disney's Comics and Stories #156**
September 1953. Barks-a. - **$7 $21 $90**

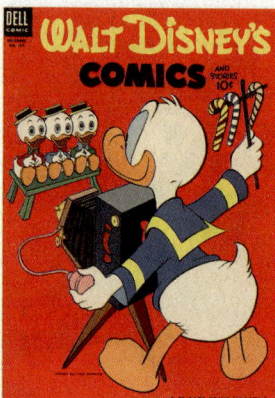

❑ **Walt Disney's Comics and Stories #159**
December 1953. Barks-a. - **$7 $21 $90**

❑ **Walt Disney's Comics and Stories #154**
July 1953. Barks-a. - **$7 $21 $90**

❑ **Walt Disney's Comics and Stories #157**
October 1953. Barks-a. - **$7 $21 $90**

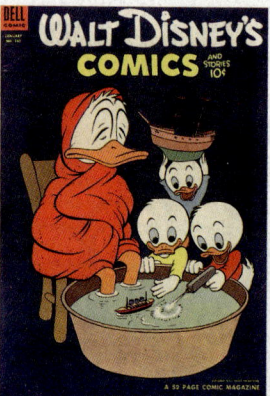

❑ **Walt Disney's Comics and Stories #160**
January 1954. Barks-a. - **$7 $21 $90**

WALT DISNEY'S COMICS AND STORIES

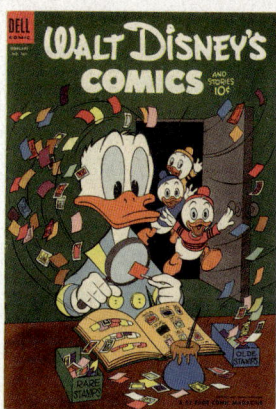
❏ **Walt Disney's Comics and Stories #161**
February 1954. Barks-a. - **$7 $21 $90**

❏ **Walt Disney's Comics and Stories #164**
May 1954. Barks-a. - **$7 $21 $90**

❏ **Walt Disney's Comics and Stories #167**
August 1954. Barks-a. - **$7 $21 $90**

❏ **Walt Disney's Comics and Stories #162**
March 1954. Barks-a. - **$7 $21 $90**

❏ **Walt Disney's Comics and Stories #165**
June 1954. Barks-a. - **$7 $21 $90**

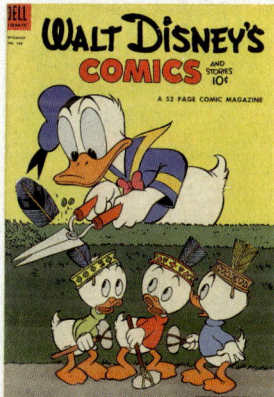
❏ **Walt Disney's Comics and Stories #168**
September 1954. Barks-a. - **$7 $21 $90**

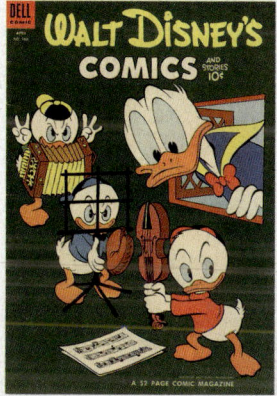
❏ **Walt Disney's Comics and Stories #163**
April 1954. Barks-a. - **$7 $21 $90**

❏ **Walt Disney's Comics and Stories #166**
July 1954. Barks-a. - **$7 $21 $90**

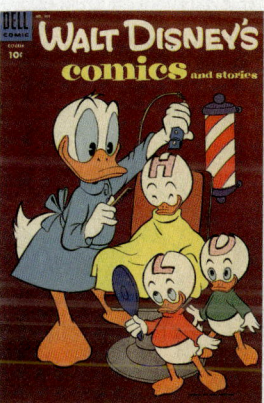
❏ **Walt Disney's Comics and Stories #169**
October 1954. Barks-a. - **$7 $21 $90**

WALT DISNEY'S COMICS AND STORIES

❏ **Walt Disney's Comics and Stories #170**
November 1954. Barks-a. - **$7 $21 $90**

❏ **Walt Disney's Comics and Stories #173**
February 1955. Barks-a. - **$7 $21 $80**

❏ **Walt Disney's Comics and Stories #176**
May 1955. Barks-a. - **$7 $21 $80**

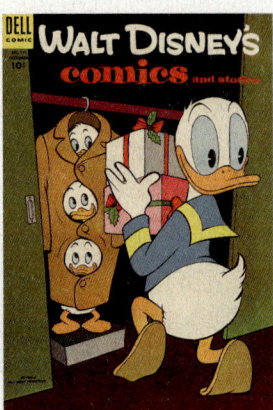
❏ **Walt Disney's Comics and Stories #171**
December 1954. Barks-a. - **$7 $21 $80**

❏ **Walt Disney's Comics and Stories #174**
March 1955. Barks-a. - **$7 $21 $80**

❏ **Walt Disney's Comics and Stories #177**
June 1955. Barks-a. - **$7 $21 $80**

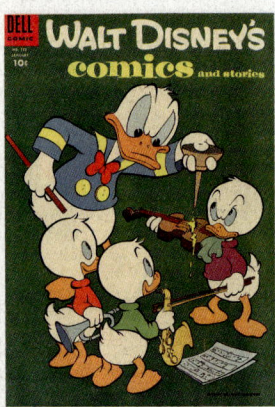
❏ **Walt Disney's Comics and Stories #172**
January 1955. Barks-a. - **$7 $21 $80**

❏ **Walt Disney's Comics and Stories #175**
April 1955. Barks-a. - **$7 $21 $80**

❏ **Walt Disney's Comics and Stories #178**
July 1955. Barks-a. - **$7 $21 $80**

WALT DISNEY'S COMICS AND STORIES

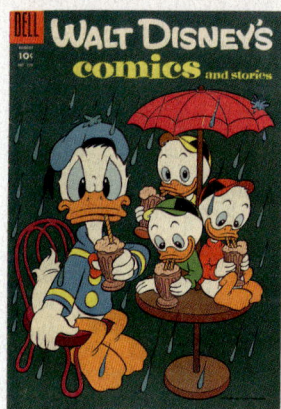
❏ **Walt Disney's Comics and Stories #179**
August 1955. Barks-a. - **$7 $21 $80**

❏ **Walt Disney's Comics and Stories #182**
November 1955. Barks-a. - **$7 $21 $80**

❏ **Walt Disney's Comics and Stories #185**
February 1956. Barks-a. - **$7 $21 $80**

❏ **Walt Disney's Comics and Stories #180**
September 1955. Barks-a. - **$7 $21 $80**

❏ **Walt Disney's Comics and Stories #183**
December 1955. Barks-a. - **$7 $21 $80**

❏ **Walt Disney's Comics and Stories #186**
March 1956. Barks-a. - **$7 $21 $80**

❏ **Walt Disney's Comics and Stories #181**
October 1955. Barks-a. - **$7 $21 $80**

❏ **Walt Disney's Comics and Stories #184**
January 1956. Barks-a. - **$7 $21 $80**

❏ **Walt Disney's Comics and Stories #187**
April 1956. Barks-a. - **$7 $21 $80**

WALT DISNEY'S COMICS AND STORIES

❏ **Walt Disney's Comics and Stories #188**
May 1956. Barks-a. - **$7 $21 $80**

❏ **Walt Disney's Comics and Stories #191**
August 1956. Barks-a. - **$7 $21 $80**

❏ **Walt Disney's Comics and Stories #194**
November 1956. Barks-a. - **$7 $21 $80**

❏ **Walt Disney's Comics and Stories #189**
June 1956. Barks-a. - **$7 $21 $80**

❏ **Walt Disney's Comics and Stories #192**
September 1956. Barks-a. - **$7 $21 $80**

❏ **Walt Disney's Comics and Stories #195**
December 1956. Barks-a. - **$7 $21 $80**

❏ **Walt Disney's Comics and Stories #190**
July 1956. Barks-a. - **$7 $21 $80**

❏ **Walt Disney's Comics and Stories #193**
October 1956. Barks-a. - **$7 $21 $80**

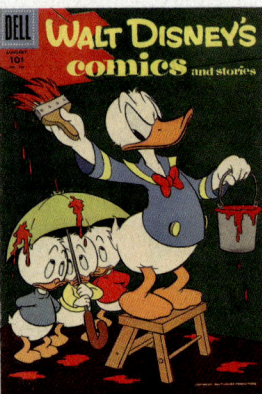
❏ **Walt Disney's Comics and Stories #196**
January 1957. Barks-a. - **$7 $21 $80**

WALT DISNEY'S COMICS AND STORIES

❏ **Walt Disney's Comics and Stories #197**
February 1957. Barks-a. - **$7 $21 $80**

❏ **Walt Disney's Comics and Stories #200,**
May 1957. - **$7 $21 $80**

❏ **Walt Disney's Comics and Stories #203,**
August 1957. Barks-a. - **$6 $18 $70**

❏ **Walt Disney's Comics and Stories #198**
March 1957. Barks-a. - **$7 $21 $80**

❏ **Walt Disney's Comics and Stories # 201,**
June 1957. Barks-a.. - **$6 $18 $70**

❏ **Walt Disney's Comics and Stories #204,**
September 1957. Barks-a. - **$6 $18 $70**

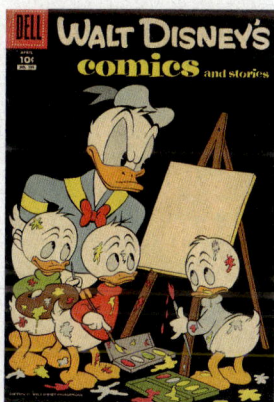
❏ **Walt Disney's Comics and Stories #199**
April 1957. Barks-a. - **$7 $21 $80**

❏ **Walt Disney's Comics and Stories #202,**
July 1957. Barks-a. - **$6 $18 $70**

❏ **Walt Disney's Comics and Stories #205,**
October 1957. Barks-a. - **$6 $18 $70**

WALT DISNEY'S COMICS AND STORIES

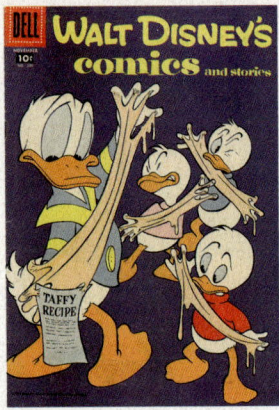
❏ **Walt Disney's Comics and Stories #206,** November 1957. Barks-a. - **$6 $18 $70**

❏ **Walt Disney's Comics and Stories #209,** February 1958. Barks-a. - **$6 $18 $70**

❏ **Walt Disney's Comics and Stories #212,** May 1958. Barks-a. - **$6 $18 $70**

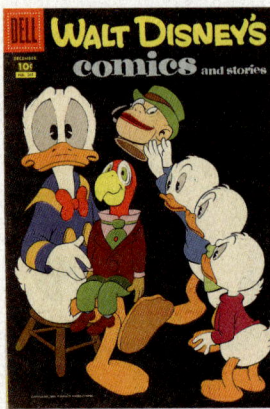
❏ **Walt Disney's Comics and Stories #207,** December 1957. Barks-a. - **$6 $18 $70**

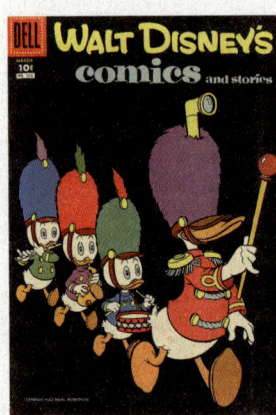
❏ **Walt Disney's Comics and Stories #210,** March 1958. Barks-a. - **$6 $18 $70**

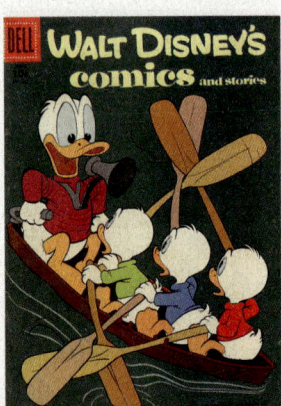
❏ **Walt Disney's Comics and Stories #213,** June 1958. Barks-a. - **$6 $18 $70**

❏ **Walt Disney's Comics and Stories #208,** January 1958. Barks-a. - **$6 $18 $70**

❏ **Walt Disney's Comics and Stories #211,** April 1958. Barks-a. - **$6 $18 $70**

❏ **Walt Disney's Comics and Stories #214,** July 1958. Barks-a. - **$6 $18 $70**

WALT DISNEY'S COMICS AND STORIES

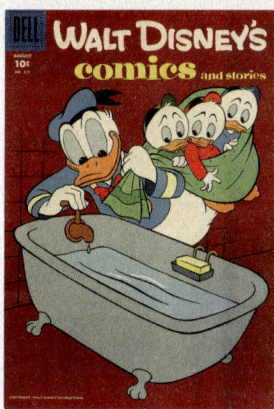
❏ **Walt Disney's Comics and Stories #215,** August 1958. Barks-a. - **$6 $18 $70**

❏ **Walt Disney's Comics and Stories #218,** November 1958. Barks-a. - **$6 $18 $70**

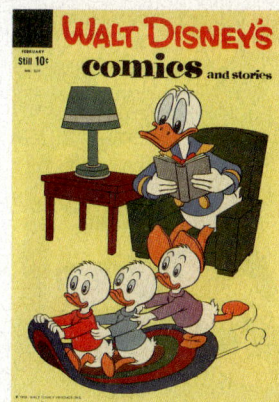
❏ **Walt Disney's Comics and Stories #221,** February 1959. Barks-a. - **$6 $18 $70**

❏ **Walt Disney's Comics and Stories #216,** September 1958. Barks-a. - **$6 $18 $70**

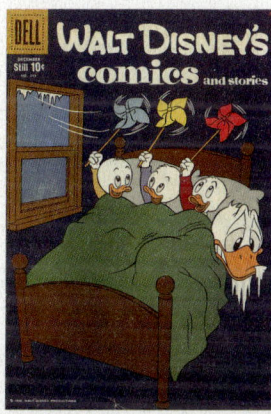
❏ **Walt Disney's Comics and Stories #219,** December 1958. Barks-a. - **$6 $18 $70**

❏ **Walt Disney's Comics and Stories #222,** March 1959. Barks-a. - **$6 $18 $70**

❏ **Walt Disney's Comics and Stories #217,** October 1958. Barks-a. - **$6 $18 $70**

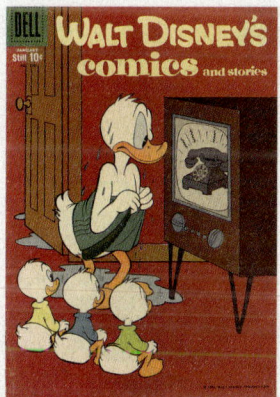
❏ **Walt Disney's Comics and Stories #220,** January 1959. Barks-a. - **$6 $18 $70**

❏ **Walt Disney's Comics and Stories #223,** April 1959. Barks-a. - **$6 $18 $70**

WALT DISNEY'S COMICS AND STORIES

❏ **Walt Disney's Comics and Stories #224,** May 1959. Barks-a. - $6 $18 $70

❏ **Walt Disney's Comics and Stories #227,** August 1959. Barks-a. - $6 $18 $70

❏ **Walt Disney's Comics and Stories #230,** November 1959. Barks-a. - $6 $18 $70

❏ **Walt Disney's Comics and Stories #225,** June 1959. Barks-a. - $6 $18 $70

❏ **Walt Disney's Comics and Stories #228,** September 1959. Barks-a. - $6 $18 $70

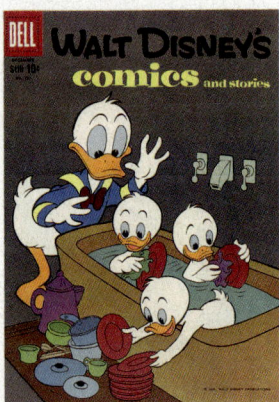
❏ **Walt Disney's Comics and Stories #231,** December 1959. Barks-a. - $6 $18 $70

❏ **Walt Disney's Comics and Stories #226,** July 1959. Barks-a. - $6 $18 $70

❏ **Walt Disney's Comics and Stories #229,** October 1959. Barks-a. - $6 $18 $70

❏ **Walt Disney's Comics and Stories #232,** January 1960. Barks-a. - $6 $18 $70

WALT DISNEY'S COMICS AND STORIES

❑ **Walt Disney's Comics and Stories #233,** February 1960. Barks-a. - **$6 $18 $70**

❑ **Walt Disney's Comics and Stories #236,** May 1960. Barks-a. - **$6 $18 $70**

❑ **Walt Disney's Comics and Stories #239,** August 1960. Barks-a. - **$6 $18 $70**

❑ **Walt Disney's Comics and Stories #234,** March 1960. Barks-a. - **$6 $18 $70**

❑ **Walt Disney's Comics and Stories #237,** June 1960. Barks-a. - **$6 $18 $70**

❑ **Walt Disney's Comics and Stories #240,** September 1960. Barks-a. - **$6 $18 $70**

❑ **Walt Disney's Comics and Stories #235,** April 1960. Barks-a. - **$6 $18 $70**

❑ **Walt Disney's Comics and Stories #238,** July 1960. Barks-a. - **$6 $18 $70**

❑ **Walt Disney's Comics and Stories #241,** October 1960. Barks-a. - **$5 $15 $60**

WALT DISNEY'S COMICS AND STORIES

❑ **Walt Disney's Comics and Stories #242,** November 1960. Barks-a. - **$5 $15 $60**

❑ **Walt Disney's Comics and Stories #245,** February 1961. Barks-a. - **$5 $15 $60**

❑ **Walt Disney's Comics and Stories #248,** May 1961. Barks-a. - **$5 $15 $60**

❑ **Walt Disney's Comics and Stories #243,** December 1960. Barks-a. - **$5 $15 $60**

❑ **Walt Disney's Comics and Stories #246,** March 1961. Barks-a. - **$5 $15 $60**

❑ **Walt Disney's Comics and Stories #249,** June 1961. Barks-a. - **$5 $15 $60**

❑ **Walt Disney's Comics and Stories #244,** January 1961. Barks-a. - **$5 $15 $60**

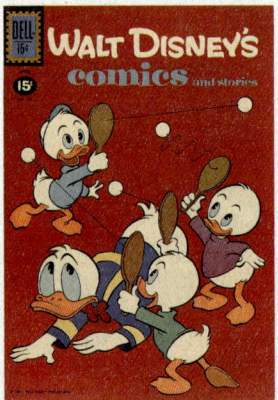
❑ **Walt Disney's Comics and Stories #247,** April 1961. Barks-a. - **$5 $15 $60**

❑ **Walt Disney's Comics and Stories #250,** July 1961. Barks-a. - **$5 $15 $60**

WALT DISNEY'S COMICS AND STORIES

❏ Walt Disney's Comics and Stories #251, August 1961. Barks-a. - $5 $15 $60

❏ Walt Disney's Comics and Stories #254, November 1961. Barks-a. - $5 $15 $60

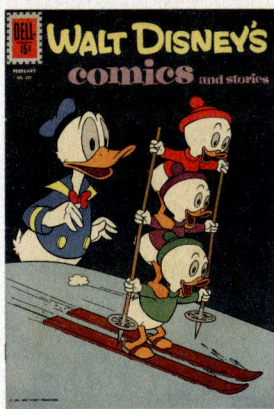
❏ Walt Disney's Comics and Stories #257, February 1962. Barks-a. - $5 $15 $60

❏ Walt Disney's Comics and Stories #252, September 1961. Barks-a. - $5 $15 $60

❏ Walt Disney's Comics and Stories #255, December 1961. Barks-a. - $5 $15 $60

❏ Walt Disney's Comics and Stories #258, March 1962. Barks-a. - $5 $15 $60

❏ Walt Disney's Comics and Stories #253, October 1961. Barks-a. - $5 $15 $60

❏ Walt Disney's Comics and Stories #256, January 1962. Barks-a. - $5 $15 $60

❏ Walt Disney's Comics and Stories #259, April 1962. Barks-a. - $5 $15 $60

WALT DISNEY'S COMICS AND STORIES

❑ Walt Disney's Comics and Stories #260, May 1962. Barks-a. - **$5 $15 $60**

❑ Walt Disney's Comics and Stories #263, August 1962. Barks-a. - **$5 $15 $60**

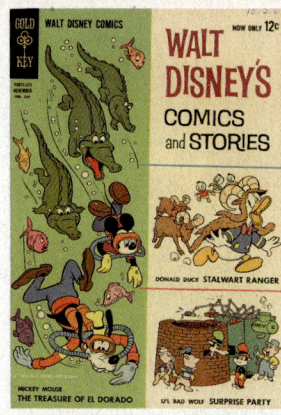
❑ Walt Disney's Comics and Stories #266, November 1962. Barks-a. - **$5 $15 $60**

❑ Walt Disney's Comics and Stories #261, June 1962. Barks-a. - **$5 $15 $60**

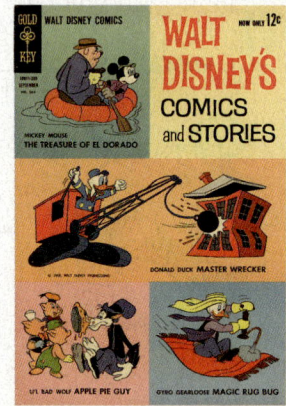
❑ Walt Disney's Comics and Stories #264, September 1962. Barks-a. - **$5 $15 $60**

❑ Walt Disney's Comics and Stories #267, December 1962. Barks-a. - **$5 $15 $60**

❑ Walt Disney's Comics and Stories #262, July 1962. Barks-a. - **$5 $15 $60**

❑ Walt Disney's Comics and Stories #265, October 1962. Barks-a. - **$5 $15 $60**

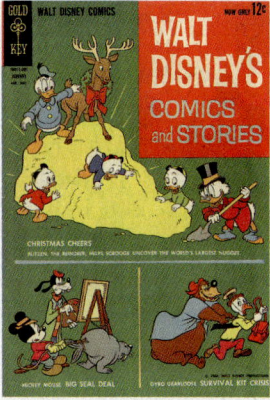
❑ Walt Disney's Comics and Stories #268, January 1963. Barks-a. - **$5 $15 $60**

WALT DISNEY'S COMICS AND STORIES

❑ Walt Disney's Comics and Stories #269, February 1963. Barks-a. - $5 $15 $60

❑ Walt Disney's Comics and Stories #272, May 1963. Barks-a. - $5 $15 $60

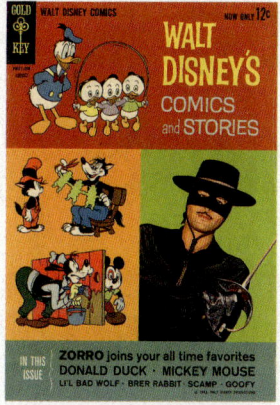
❑ Walt Disney's Comics and Stories #275, August 1963 Barks-a. - $5 $15 $60

❑ Walt Disney's Comics and Stories #270, March 1963. Barks-a. - $5 $15 $60

❑ Walt Disney's Comics and Stories #273, June 1963. Barks-a. - $5 $15 $60

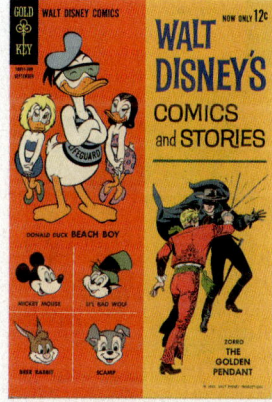
❑ Walt Disney's Comics and Stories #276, September 1963. Barks-a. - $5 $15 $60

❑ Walt Disney's Comics and Stories #271, April 1963. Barks-a. - $5 $15 $60

❑ Walt Disney's Comics and Stories #274, July 1963. Barks-a. - $5 $15 $60

❑ Walt Disney's Comics and Stories #277, October 1963. Barks-a. - $5 $15 $60

WALT DISNEY'S COMICS AND STORIES

❏ Walt Disney's Comics and Stories #278, November 1963. Barks-a. - $5 $15 $60

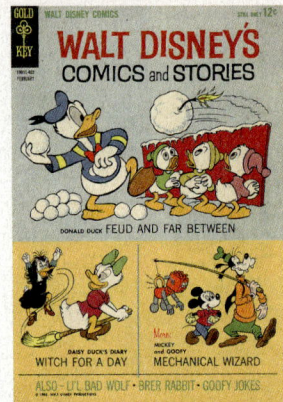
❏ Walt Disney's Comics and Stories #281, February 1964. Barks-a. - $5 $15 $60

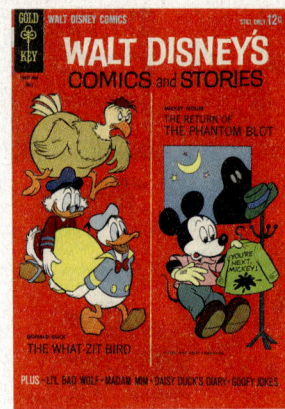
❏ Walt Disney's Comics and Stories #284, May 1964. - $3 $9 $28

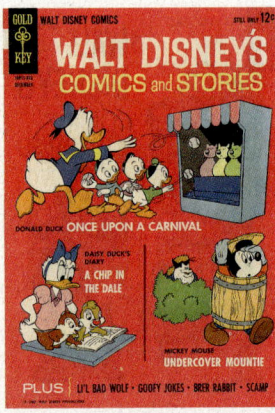
❏ Walt Disney's Comics and Stories #279, December 1963. Barks-a. - $5 $15 $60

❏ Walt Disney's Comics and Stories #282, March 1964. Barks-a. - $5 $15 $60

❏ Walt Disney's Comics and Stories #285, June 1964. - $3 $9 $28

❏ Walt Disney's Comics and Stories #280, January 1964. Barks-a. - $5 $15 $60

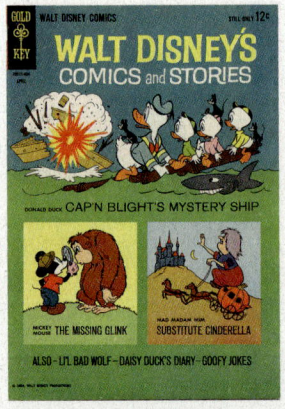
❏ Walt Disney's Comics and Stories #283, April 1964. Barks-a. - $5 $15 $60

❏ Walt Disney's Comics and Stories #286, July 1964. Barks-a. - $3 $10 $35

WALT DISNEY'S COMICS AND STORIES

❏ Walt Disney's Comics and Stories #287, August 1964. $3 $9 $28

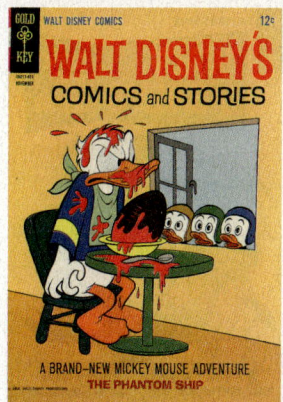
❏ Walt Disney's Comics and Stories #290, November 1964. - $3 $9 $28

❏ Walt Disney's Comics and Stories #293, February 1965. Barks-a. - $3 $10 $35

❏ Walt Disney's Comics and Stories #288, September 1964. Barks-a. - $3 $10 $35

❏ Walt Disney's Comics and Stories #291, December 1964. Barks-a. - $3 $10 $35

❏ Walt Disney's Comics and Stories #294, March 1965. Barks-a. - $3 $10 $35

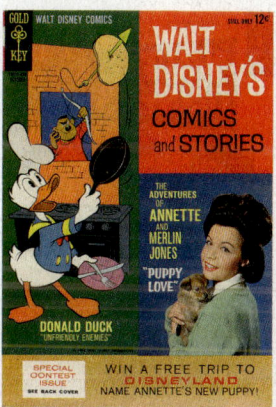
❏ Walt Disney's Comics and Stories #289, October 1964. Barks-a. - $4 $12 $42

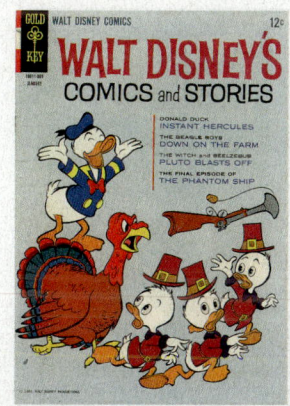
❏ Walt Disney's Comics and Stories #292, January 1965. Barks-a. - $3 $10 $35

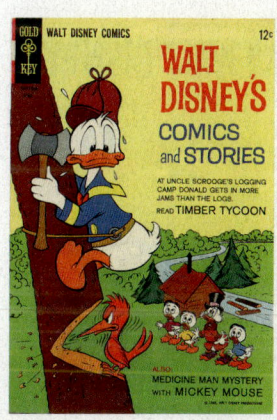
❏ Walt Disney's Comics and Stories #295, April 1965. - $3 $9 $28

WALT DISNEY'S COMICS AND STORIES

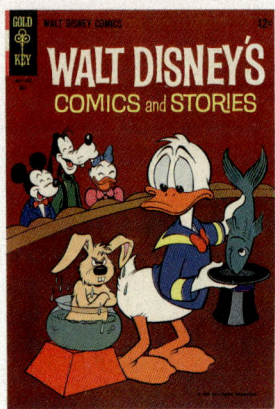

❏ Walt Disney's Comics and Stories #296, May 1965. - **$3 $9 $28**

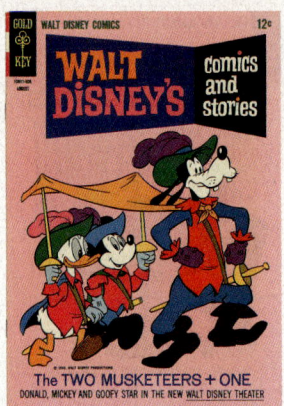

❏ Walt Disney's Comics and Stories #299, August 1965. Barks-r. - **$4 $12 $38**

❏ Walt Disney's Comics and Stories #302, November 1965. Barks-r. - **$4 $12 $38**

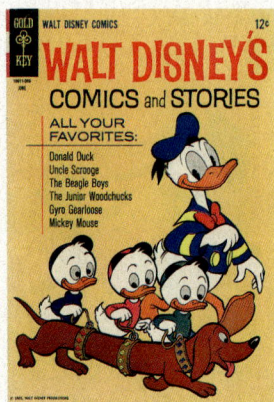

❏ Walt Disney's Comics and Stories #297, June 1965. Barks-a. - **$3 $10 $35**

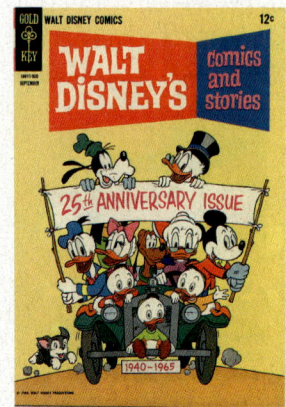

❏ Walt Disney's Comics and Stories #300, September 1965. Barks-r. - **$4 $12 $38**

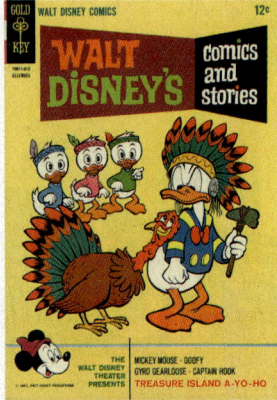

❏ Walt Disney's Comics and Stories #303, December 1965. Barks-r. - **$4 $12 $38**

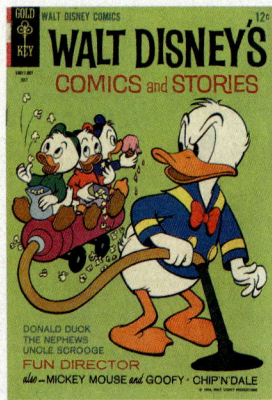

❏ Walt Disney's Comics and Stories #298, July 1965. Barks-a. - **$3 $10 $35**

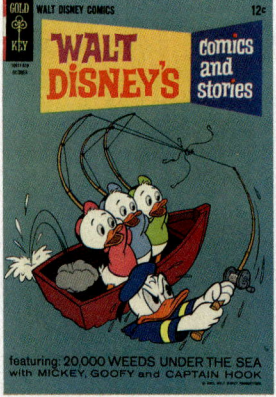

❏ Walt Disney's Comics and Stories #301, October 1965. Barks-r. - **$4 $12 $38**

❏ Walt Disney's Comics and Stories #304, January 1966. Barks-r. - **$4 $12 $38**

WALT DISNEY STUDIO

Walt Disney Studio

Disney's first California studio opened on Hollywood's Kingsley Avenue in 1923. There Walt and his crew produced *Alice Comedies* which combined live-action and animation, as well as various advertising shorts. The studio was moved to Hyperion Avenue in 1926. As the studio staff grew, they needed to find better working space. In 1940, they moved to their current location, South Buena Vista Street in Burbank. The studio presently covers more than forty acres and serves as the company's corporate headquarters. It has five sound stages and is also home to the Walt Disney Archives.

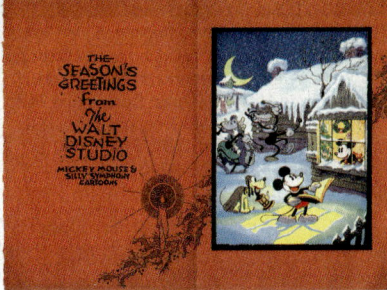
WDS-2

❑ **WDS-2. Walt Disney Studio Christmas Card,**
1931. Card is 5x7.5" closed with tipped-in paper sheet. - **$600 $1600 $3200**

WDS-3

❑ **WDS-3. Walt Disney Studio Christmas Card,**
1932. Mailer card about 8x9" open. This example was sent to a theater in Allentown, PA. - **$500 $1000 $2000**

WDS-4

❑ **WDS-4. Studio Christmas Card,**
1933. Card measures 7-3/16x9-1/8" with image of Mickey, Minnie and Pluto looking through window of Pigs' house as Pigs sing, play instruments and dance on top of grinning (but deceased) Big Bad Wolf who lays on the floor like a bearskin rug. Comes with or without lower right corner text "Printed In USA." - **$200 $500 $800**

WDS-1

❑ **WDS-1. First Walt Disney Studio Christmas Card,**
1930. Card is 6-1/8x4-5/8". Info on the back of the frame reads: "Drawn by Floyd Gottfredson, Disney Christmas Card 1930, Hand Colored in Ink & Paint Dept. Hyperion Studio LA, CA."
- **$1250 $2500 $5000**

WDS-5

❑ **WDS-5. "Modern Mechanix And Inventions" With Mickey Mouse,**
1934. Vol. 11 #6; 6.75x9.5" for April. Article titled "What Makes Mickey Mouse Move?" - **$20 $40 $75**

WDS-6

❑ **WDS-6. Studio Christmas Card,**
1935. Stiff paper cover 8-page card measures 7.25x9.25". Choice color throughout. Pages feature illustrations of many characters and text. - **$150 $300 $600**

WDS-7

❑ **WDS-7. Studio Chirstmas Card Proof,**
1935. 18x12" tall. Printer's proof of studio card. - **$150 $300 $600**

WALT DISNEY STUDIO

WDS-8

WDS-9

❏ **WDS-8. Studio-Issued Publicity Photos,**
1935. Four 8x10" glossy photos. Each - **$20 $35 $65**

❏ **WDS-9. Early Disney Studio Fan Card,**
c. 1935. Stiff paper card measures 7x9.25" **$60 $115 $175**

WDS-10

❏ **WDS-10. Studio Christmas Card,**
1936. Card is 7.25x9.25" stiff linen-like paper. - **$165 $325 $500**

WDS-11

❏ **WDS-11. Studio Christmas Card Set,**
1937. Pair of paper cards, first measuring 7x10" and opens to reveal a tipped-in panel with beautiful Snow White art. Second is a 4x5" insert card picturing Mickey, Minnie, Donald and Pluto with the inscription "-And Greetings From Us Too." Snow White Card - **$80 $160 $300** Mickey Card - **$60 $125 $200**

WDS-12

WDS-13

❏ **WDS-12. 1938 Disney Studio Christmas Card,**
1938. Stiff paper card measuring 6x7.5" with 8 pages. Choice color illustrations of Disney characters sleeping. Text reads "It's The Night Before Christmas And All Through The House Not A Creature Is Stirring Except Mickey Mouse." - **$75 $175 $275**

❏ **WDS-13. "An Introduction To The Walt Disney Studios" New Employee Manual,**
1938. Softcover 6x9" with 32 pages. - **$75 $150 $250**

WDS-14

❏ **WDS-14. Walt Disney Premium Photo,**
1938. Great image of Walt with facsimile signature "Greetings Young America/Walt Disney." Comes with clipping stating that this photo will be mailed to "500 Young America Readers Who Send Only 5 Cents To Cover Handling." Photo - **$50 $85 $175**

WDS-15

❏ **WDS-15. "Walt's Field Day 1938" Complete Program For Studio Employees Picnic,**
1938. 5.75x8.5" with textured stiff paper covers and eight glossy pages. Cover art attributed to Ward Kimball and features Mickey Mouse in golf attire. Art is recognized as the first time Mickey was shown with circles around his pupils. Event was held at the Lake Norconian Hotel in Norco, California on June 4, 1938. Booklet is complete with perforated Dinner/Luncheon coupons. Extremely limited distribution. - **$150 $300 $450**

WDS-16

❏ **WDS-16. "Walt's Field Day" Boating Race Trophy,**
1938. 2" diameter by 6.25" tall metal trophy with engraved text reading "Walt's Field Day 1938 Boating Race/Bud Rickert/Walt Disney Studio." Trophy was made for the rowing race organized by Hal Adelquist for the June 4, 1938 Disney company picnic. Event was won by Douglas "Bud" Rickert. Unique. - **$500**

WALT DISNEY STUDIO

WDS-17

☐ **WDS-17. Studio Christmas Card,**
1939. Booklet format card measuring 6x7.5" with 8 pages. Inside has numerous facsimile signatures of Disney staff and color illustrations and facsimile signatures for Pinocchio characters. - **$60 $125 $200**

WDS-18

☐ **WDS-18. Disney Studio Christmas Card,**
1940. 5.5x6" on stiff textured paper with front design depicting Fantasia fairy spelling out "Greetings" with snowflakes in the background. Card opens once to reveal fairy spelling out "From Walt Disney" and opens one final time for total length of 22". Fully opened reveals an exceptional scene of numerous characters from Fantasia plus the Reluctant Dragon, Donald, Minnie, Goofy, Pinocchio, Snow White and Dopey singing Christmas carols. - **$50 $125 $200**

WDS-19

☐ **WDS-19. "Liberty" Magazine Walt Disney Premium Card,**
c. 1940. 7x7.5" stiff paper card. Text reads "To One Of The Grandest Boys In The World - A Liberty Boy Salesman" with Walt Disney facsimile signature. - **$350 $750 $1500**

WDS-20

WDS-21

☐ **WDS-20. "The Mousetrap" Walt Disney Studio In-House Limited Edition Book,**
1941. Ward Ritchie Press. 9x12" 40-page spiral-bound book. #424 of 500. Humorous writing and much art by the studio employees. - **$225 $450 $850**

☐ **WDS-21. Studio Christmas Card,**
1942. Card is 6.75x8" stiff paper. Rare war years issue. - **$175 $350 $700**

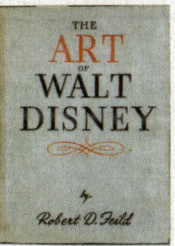

WDS-22

WDS-23

☐ **WDS-22. "The Art Of Walt Disney" Hardcover,**
1942. Collins. 8.5x11" with 290 pages. Reprint of USA edition by MacMillan. England Edition - **$40 $75 $150** USA Edition - **$60 $115 $225**

☐ **WDS-23. Studio Christmas Card For 1943,**
1943. Hallmark. Front of 7.75x10" card has 1944 calendar surrounded by illustrations of Disney characters depicting events to go along with specific months. Marked "A Hallmark Card." - **$100 $200 $350**

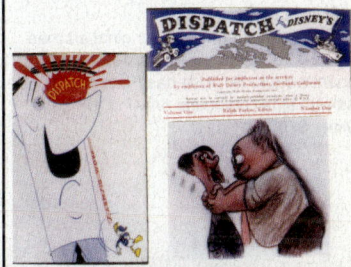
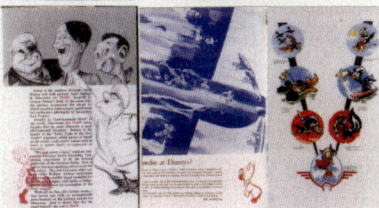

WDS-24

☐ **WDS-24. "Dispatch From Disney's" Publication,**
1943. Volume 1, #1 "Published For Employees In The Services By Employees At Walt Disney Productions, Burbank, California." Contents include one-page introduction from Walt Disney, war-time related articles, features and artwork. 5.5x8". 32 pages. - **$100 $200 $400**

WALT DISNEY STUDIO

WDS-25

WDS-26

WDS-28

❑ **WDS-28. Studio Christmas Card,**
1944. Card is 7.75x10-3/8" stiff paper. Saludos Amigos is featured. - **$75 $150 $300**

❑ **WDS-25. "Pin-Ups For Servicemen From Walt Disney Staff."**
1943. Sheet of 10.5x15.5" textured paper originally came with "Dispatch From Disney's" publication. Reverse includes list of Disney Studio employees in the Armed Forces with three war-related cartoons. - **$60 $135 $225**

❑ **WDS-26. Customized Envelope By Disney Artist "Pinto Colvig,"**
1943. Envelope decorated with original art measures 4.5x10.25". Gold foil letters "R-B" applied to elephant's back. Reverse has Pinto's return address with small outhouse drawing. Unique, Near Mint - **$160**

WDS-29

WDS-30

❑ **WDS-29. Disney War Bond Certificate,**
1944. Issued by "The United States Treasury War Finance Committee"." Center text is surrounded by character portraits. - **$60 $125 $175**

❑ **WDS-30. Disney Studio Christmas Card,**
1945. Three Caballeros is featured. 7.75x10.25" white stiff paper card. - **$65 $135 $200**

WDS-27

❑ **WDS-27. Walt Disney WWII War Workers Nutrition Poster,**
1943. Paper poster measures 12.5x19" and titled "You Can't Breakfast Like A Bird And Work Like A Horse!" and marked "Designed By Walt Disney For The Food And Nutrition Committee California War Council." - **$25 $50 $100**

WDS-31

WDS-32

❑ **WDS-31. Studio Christmas Card,**
1946. Large 7.75x10-1/8" card opens to reveal full color illustrations of characters from several films with 1947 calendar. - **$75 $150 $250**

❑ **WDS-32. Disney Studio Christmas Card,**
1947. 7.25x8" stiff paper card. Card opens to reveal montage of Disney character portraits from films Snow White to the then latest release "Fun And Fancy Free" which is spotlighted at the center. - **$35 $75 $125**

WDS-33

WALT DISNEY STUDIO

❑ **WDS-33. "Walt Disney Character Merchandise 1947-1948" Retailer's Catalogue,**
1947. Covers are 9x12" glossy stiff paper with 100 pages. Items include American Pottery figurines, Ben Cooper costumes, Fisher-Price pull toys, Gund stuffed dolls, Jaymar puzzles, Leeds china items, various store displays, Marx wind-up toys, Sun Rubber toys, Transogram paint sets, US Time watch, various books, sheet music, food-related products, clothing, much more. - **$250 $500 $1000**

WDS-34

WDS-35

❑ **WDS-34. Disney Studio Christmas Card,**
1948. 7x8" on slightly textured paper. - **$55 $115 $185**

❑ **WDS-35. "He Drew As He Pleased A Sketch Book By Albert Hurter,"**
1948. Simon & Schuster. 9.25x12" hardcover with 192 pages. Hurter was long-time Disney animator. Book has Disney and non-Disney content. - **$200 $400 $600**

WDS-36

❑ **WDS-36. Studio Christmas Card,**
1949. Textured paper card measures 7-1/8x8". Inside includes calendar for 1950 plus Fairy Godmother turning a pumpkin into a coach. - **$50 $110 $175**

WDS-37

❑ **WDS-37. Disney Character Fan Card,**
1940s. Stiff paper is 8x10". - **$10 $20 $30**

WDS-38

WDS-39

❑ **WDS-38. 1950 Disney Studio Christmas Card,**
1950. Textured stiff paper card measuring 7x7-7/8". Card opens to reveal calendar for 1951 and Tea Party scene with many characters from the film. - **$65 $150 $225**

❑ **WDS-39. 1951 Disney Studio Christmas Card,**
1951. Card is 7x8" on textured paper. Card opens to reveal scene depicting 12 train cars being pulled by a car. Each car is filled with Disney characters and has a different calendar month for 1952. - **$65 $150 $225**

WALT DISNEY STUDIO

WDS-40

❑ **WDS-40. Studio Christmas Card,** 1952. Features Peter Pan. Card is 7x7.75" slightly textured paper. - **$75 $165 $250**

WDS-42

❑ **WDS-42. "The Sword And The Rose" Theater Handout,** c. 1953. Stiff glossy photo is 8x10" of Richard Todd and Glynis Johns, co-stars of the English historic drama 1953 Disney film released by RKO Radio Pictures. - **$8 $12 $20**

WDS-44

❑ **WDS-44. Studio Christmas Card,** 1955. Slightly textured white paper is 7x7.75". From Disneyland's opening year. - **$100 $225 $350**

WDS-45

WDS-41

❑ **WDS-41. Studio Christmas Card,** 1953. Slightly textured paper is 7.5x7.75". - **$50 $100 $150**

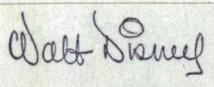

WDS-43

❑ **WDS-43. Studio Christmas Card,** 1954. 7x7.75" slightly textured paper with great illustration on the front of Mickey holding book marked "Noel" while Donald's nephews and Pluto read a copy of "20,000 Leagues Under The Sea." - **$60 $135 $225**

WDS-46

WALT DISNEY STUDIO

❏ **WDS-45. Studio Christmas Card,**
1956. Card is 7x8" on slightly textured paper. - **$50 $85 $150**

❏ **WDS-46. "Westward Ho The Wagons" Movie Poster,**
1956. Poster is 27x41" one-sheet for original release, starring Fess Parker. - **$50 $85 $150**

WDS-47

WDS-48

❏ **WDS-47. Disney Studio Christmas Card,**
1957. 7x8" on slightly textured paper. Front cover scene is of Mickey dressed as Santa filling stockings with books, one of which is "Old Yeller." - **$50 $125 $200**

❏ **WDS-48. 1958 Disney Studio Christmas Card,**
1958. Textured paper 7x8" card that opens to a scene of characters from Sleeping Beauty with monthly calendar for 1959. - **$50 $125 $200**

WDS-49

❏ **WDS-49. Disney Film Rental Catalogue,**
1958. Catalogue is 8.5x11" eight-page titled "1958-59 Catalogue Of Walt Disney 16mm Films." - **$10 $20 $30**

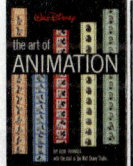 
WDS-50

WDS-51

❏ **WDS-50. "The Art Of Animation" Book,**
1958. Golden Press. 8.25x11.25" with 188 pages. Text describes Disney animation from its earliest days through current production. - **$205 $35 $75**

❏ **WDS-51. Disney Studio Christmas Card,**
1959. 7x8" card on slightly textured paper. Front depicts Disneyland castle with fireworks in the sky. - **$40 $75 $125**

WDS-52

❏ **WDS-52. Disney Publicity Photos,**
c. 1950s. Four 8x10" photos. Typical Example - **$10 $15 $25**

WDS-53

❏ **WDS-53. "Walt Disney's Studio Restaurant" Menu,**
c. 1950s. Stiff cardboard measuring 6.25x9". Inside has many character illustrations. - **$65 $125 $225**

WDS-54

WALT DISNEY STUDIO

WDS-55

WDS-57

❑ **WDS-57. Disney Characters Merchandising Sheet,**
1961. Folder is 7.5x11.75" opening to 44.5" width used as character selection guide for licensees. Front has text about the use of images and includes illustrations of Mickey, Donald, Pluto, large "Wonderful World of Color" logo and Ludwig. Content is 58 additional character illustrations plus two Mouse Club logos. - **$25 $50 $75**

❑ **WDS-54. Disney Studio Christmas Card,**
1960. 7x8" slightly textured paper. - **$10 $20 $40**

❑ **WDS-55. 1961 Disney Studio Christmas Card,**
1961. Textured paper card measures 7x8". Inside holds calendar for 1962 with color scene of "Toyland." Back cover design is for 1962 film "Moon Pilot" with illustrations of smiling moon wearing Santa hat and rocketship. - **$40 $75 $125**

WDS-58

WDS-60

❑ **WDS-58. Studio Christmas Card,**
1963. 7x8" on slightly textured paper. - **$30 $60 $100**

❑ **WDS-59. Studio Christmas Card,**
1964. Slightly textured paper is 5x7" and opens to 28" long. - **$35 $75 $125**

❑ **WDS-60. Disney Studio Christmas Card,**
1965. Card has folded size of 4.5x8" and opens to total of 17.5" long. - **$20 $45 $75**

WDS-56

❑ **WDS-56. Studio Christmas Card,**
1962. Slightly textured paper is 7x8". - **$50 $100 $150**

WDS-59

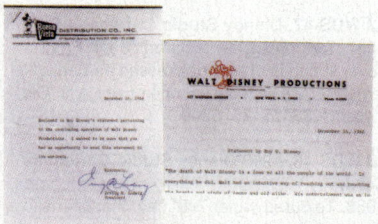
WDS-61

972

WALT DISNEY STUDIO

☐ **WDS-61. Press Release On Walt Disney's Death,**
1966. Three sheets of 8.5x11" paper stapled at top left corner. Top sheet is "Buena Vista Distribution Inc." letterhead with brief statement mentioning statement by Roy Disney. The two-page statement that follows is on "Walt Disney Productions" letterhead by Roy detailing the legacy Walt has left behind. - **$50 $100 $200**

WDS-62

☐ **WDS-62. Studio Christmas Card,**
1967. Stiff paper is 6x7.5". - **$40 $75 $125**

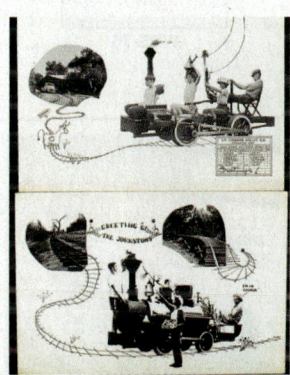

WDS-63

WDS-64

☐ **WDS-63. Ollie Johnston Personal Christmas Cards,**
1967. Two 6x9" one-sided cards, both a limited issue picturing Johnston, long-time Disney artist, and his family. Both designs include train theme photos. One is dated 1967 and other is from similar year. Each - **$10 $20 $30**

☐ **WDS-64. Studio Christmas Card,**
1968. Card is 5.25x7-1/8" on slightly textured stiff paper with diecut design. - **$30 $60 $90**

WDS-65

WDS-66

☐ **WDS-65. 'It's Tough To Be A Bird' Cel,**
1969. Acetate sheet is 12.5x15" centered by 2x4" painted M.C. (Master Of Ceremonies) Bird by animator Ward Kimball for educational short combining animation and live footage description of the evolution and history of birds. Film won an Academy award as best short subject of 1969. - **$75 $150 $225**

☐ **WDS-66. Studio Christmas Card,**
1969. 5.25x7.75" card on slightly textured stiff paper. Card opens to total length of 17.25". - **$30 $60 $90**

WDS-67

☐ **WDS-67. "Mickey And His Friends" Publicity Folder With Photos,**
1960s. Buena Vista Distributing Co. 8.5x11" folder contains six different 6.75x9.25" glossy photos attached to inside pages which have additional description text along bottom margin. Likely issued for Mickey's 40th Birthday in 1968. - **$20 $40 $80**

WDS-68

☐ **WDS-68. "Disney Movie Title Cards" Set,**
1960s. Mailer envelope is 9x12" containing complete set of eight 8.5x11" cards incorporating Disney characters for use as titles for otherwise home movies per instructions "Put Professional-Like Titles In Your Movies Easily/Add Interesting Titles To Your Own Movies." Set - **$10 $20 $40**

WALT DISNEY STUDIO

WDS-69

WDS-72

WDS-75

❑ **WDS-69. Studio Christmas Card,** 1970. 5x5" on stiff textured paper. Card is designed with four panels which fold open in succession. - **$15 $35 $60**

WDS-70

❑ **WDS-70. "Walt Disney Comics" Art,** 1970. Stiff paper comic book page measures 15x22". Total art area is 8.5x15" with image of Scamp playing leap frog with frogs. Used as poster insert in Walt Disney's Comics #358 from May 1970. Unique, Near Mint - **$165**

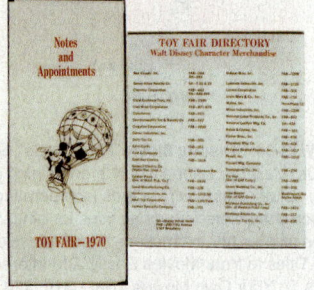

WDS-71

❑ **WDS-71. "Toy Fair-1970 Notes And Appointments" Disney Merchandisers Promotional Folder,** 1970. Folder is 3.5x8.25" and opens to total of 16" long. - **$5 $10 $15**

❑ **WDS-72. "Walt Disney Studios" Licensee Character Guide,** c. 1970. Stiff paper front and back covers measuring 8.5x11" and 12 textured paper sheets. Contains colorful character designs of all the main characters as well as those from Jungle Book, Sword in the Stone, Mary Poppins, Zorro, 101 Dalmations, The Aristocats, Winnie the Pooh, etc. - **$20 $35 $75**

WDS-73

WDS-74

❑ **WDS-73. Disney Studio Christmas Card,** 1971. Full color glossy stiff paper card has folded size of 6x7" and is in the shape of a gift box. Card opens to 17" long. - **$20 $35 $75**

❑ **WDS-74. Disneyland Promotion Christmas Card,** 1972. Slightly textured stiff paper is 4x10". Originally came with admission tickets for "A Christmas Visit To Disneyland." Card Only - **$10 $20 $30**

❑ **WDS-75. Disney Studio Christmas Card,** 1973. 6x9.25" on stiff paper with full color art. Front is die-cut and designed to be folded to give the card three-dimensional effect. - **$12 $25 $40**

WDS-76

WDS-77

❑ **WDS-76. Studio Christmas Card,** 1974. Card is 6x9" and opens to 26" long. - **$15 $30 $50**

❑ **WDS-77. Floyd Gottfredson Signed Photo,** 1974. Photo is 5x5" glossy candid of him at his drawing table with display of four Mickey Mouse daily strips. Same Or Similar - **$30 $65 $125**

WALT DISNEY STUDIO

WDS-78

❏ **WDS-78. "Walt Disney Distributing Company 1974 Merchandise" Catalogue,** 1974. Glossy 8.5x11" catalogue. 76 pages. Filled with hundreds of photos of Disney products. - **$30 $60 $85**

WDS-79

❏ **WDS-79. Studio Christmas Card,** 1976. 6x9" stiff glossy paper card with design on front of large Christmas ball. - **$20 $40 $65**

WDS-80

❏ **WDS-80. Disney Employee Only Christmas Cards,** 1977. Pair of 4x10" cards sent only to Disney employees, retirees and possibly other Disney VIPs. 1977 with silhouette and 1979 with caroling scene. Each - **$8 $12 $20**

WDS-81

WDS-82

❏ **WDS-81. Studio Christmas Card,** 1977. 5.25x7.25" stiff textured paper card. - **$20 $40 $60**

❏ **WDS-82. Disney New Employee Promotional Booklet,** 1977. Stiff glossy paper 8x11.5" with 12 pages. - **$12 $25 $40**

WDS-83

WDS-84

❏ **WDS-83. Signed Studio Christmas Card,** 1978. Mickey's 50th year. Glossy paper card measures 5.25x7.25". Card opens to reveal many illustrations of Mickey through the years. Card is signed by Al Konetzni, former Disney executive for character merchandising. - **$10 $15 $30**

❏ **WDS-84. Disney Studio Christmas Card,** 1979. 6x7.5" on stiff paper. - **$12 $25 $40**

WDS-85

❏ **WDS-85. "Disney's World On Ice" Original Design Art,** 1979. Al Konetzni. 10x25x12.25" sheet. Unique, Near Mint - **$110**

WDS-86

WDS-87

975

WALT DISNEY STUDIO

☐ **WDS-86. "The Apple Dumpling Gang Rides Again" Lobby Card Set,**
1979. Original cover envelope holding set of nine 11x14" full color glossy lobby cards. Eight cards are film scenes including five with both stars Tim Conway and Don Knotts. Title card has movie art. Set - **$15 $25 $45**

☐ **WDS-87. Disney Schmid Music Boxes Publicity Photo,**
1970s. Photo is 8x10" glossy picturing six Disney character music boxes of early 1970s, some of the earliest pieces produced by Schmid. Five are western theme Mickey, Minnie, two of Donald, Goofy with Mickey's nephew. The sixth is Pinocchio with Figaro and Jiminy Cricket. - **$5 $10 $15**

WDS-88

☐ **WDS-88. Disney Studio Christmas Card,**
1980. Disneyland's 25th anniversary. 6x7.5" glossy stiff paper card. - **$10 $20 $30**

WDS-89

WDS-90

☐ **WDS-89. Studio Christmas Card,**
1981. 5.25x7.75" on stiff glossy paper. - **$8 $15 $25**

☐ **WDS-90. Disney Studio Christmas Card,**
1982. 5.25x7.75" stiff paper. - **$10 $20 $30**

WDS-91

WDS-92

☐ **WDS-91. "The Disney Channel" Salesman's Promotional Folder,**
1982. Stiff glossy paper folder is 10x14" with eight pages. - **$6 $12 $20**

☐ **WDS-92. "Disney Newsreel" Publication,**
c. 1982. Weekly publication for employees of Walt Disney Productions and associated companies published in Burbank, Calif. Each is 8.5x11" with eight pages. Each From 1980s - **$1 $2 $3**

WDS-93

☐ **WDS-93. Disney Studio Christmas Card,**
1983. 5.25x7.75" stiff paper card. - **$5 $12 $20**

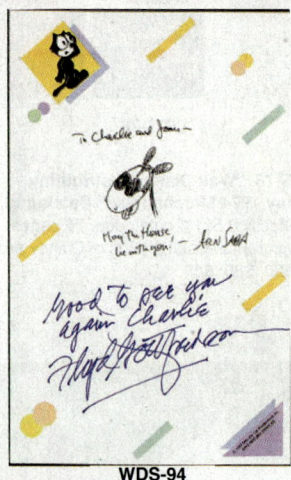

WDS-94

☐ **WDS-94. Floyd Gottfredson/Arn Saba Signatures With Sketch,**
c. 1983. King Features Syndicate. Sheet of Felix the Cat stationery is 5.5x8.5". At top center is inked inscription "To Charlie And Joan-May The Horse Be With You-Arn Saba" with head sketch of Neal the Horse. Saba is the creator of Neal the Horse independent comic book series which started in 1981. Below is inked inscription and signature "Good To See You Again Charlie/Floyd Gottfredson." Long-time Disney employee Gottfredson worked on the Mickey Mouse comic strip from 1930 until his retirement in 1975. Unique, Mint - **$45**

WDS-95

☐ **WDS-95. Disney Studio Christmas Card,**
1984. Features Tokyo Disneyland. Stiff paper 5.25x7.75". - **$5 $10 $15**

WALT DISNEY STUDIO

WDS-96

❏ **WDS-96. "Walt Disney Home Video" Promotional Poster,**
1984. Poster is 23x38.5" glossy paper. - **$10 $15 $25**

WDS-97

WDS-98

❏ **WDS-97. Marc Davis Personal Christmas Cards,**
1987. Three cards, each 5x7" from 1987, 1989 and 1996. Davis was one of the chief designers of the Pirates of The Caribbean ride and is recognized for his work on Bambi plus Cruella DeVil and Maleficent. Each - **$6 $12 $20**

❏ **WDS-98. Disney Studio Christmas Card,**
1987. 4.75x6.5" on stiff glossy paper. - **$8 $15 $25**

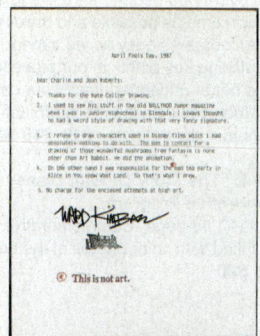

WDS-99

WDS-100

❏ **WDS-99. Ward Kimball Humorous Letter Signed,**
1987. Typewritten letter is 8.5x11" dated "April Fools Day 1987" to Charlie and Joan Roberts. Content is five numbered statements of humorous or tongue-in-cheek nature concerning Disney films and/or his fellow long-time Disney artists who helped develop the films. Letter has inked signature "Ward Kimball" and below this is added ink stamp of a train. Unique, Mint - **$45**

❏ **WDS-100. Disney Corporate Christmas Card,**
1988. Glossy card stock card measures 4.5x6.5". Die-cut illustrations of Roger Rabbit as Santa holding a wreath in front of a lamppost is designed as a 3-D standup. Includes facsimile signatures of Michael Eisner and Frank Wells. - **$10 $20 $30**

WDS-101

❏ **WDS-101. Disney Studio Christmas Card,**
1988. 5x7" on stiff white paper with die-cut design on the front in the shape of Mickey's head. - **$5 $12 $20**

WDS-102

WDS-103

❏ **WDS-102. "Storyboard/The Disneyana Magazine" Issues,**
1988. Two 8.5x11" issues, Vol. 1 #3-4, of publication devoted to collecting of Disney memorabilia, Disney films, stars, animation, many other Disney topics from issue to issue. Each - **$3 $6 $10**

❏ **WDS-103. Disney Corporate Christmas Card,**
c. 1989. Reproduction 4x8.75" of early studio card with facsimile signatures of Michael Eisner and Frank Wells. - **$15 $30 $60**

WDS-104

❏ **WDS-104. "Marc Davis" Cruella DeVil Limited Edition Watch,**
1995. Watch is 1-3/8" diameter and comes in 4.25x8.5x1.5" deep wooden box. Comes with certificate of authenticity. From "Signature Series." Reverse has incised "4343" from an edition of 5000. Mint As Issued - **$135**

WALT DISNEY STUDIO

WDS-105

❑ **WDS-105. Disney Studio/Michael Eisner Christmas Card,**
1998. 5x7" stiff glossy paper. Reverse notes this is a "Reproduction Of Walt Disney Productions 1934 Christmas Card." Inside has text "75 Years Of Love And Laugher...And Here's To 75 More!" along with Eisner facsimile signature. - **$10 $20 $30**

WDS-106

WDS-107

❑ **WDS-106. Signed "Snow White Limited Edition Serigraph,"**
1990s. Image of Snow White is 3x8.5" and image of Sleepy, Bashful and Happy is 5x5.5". Has "Walt Disney Company" seal and signed by long-time Disney animator Marc Davis and "Adriana Caselotti Voice of Snow White." Signed Mint As Issued - **$365**

❑ **WDS-107. Disney Employee Only "Serigraph Cel,"**
1990s. Created for and sold only to "The Walt Disney Company Team Members." Comes with certificate of authenticity and depicts many Disney characters on a movie set. Mint As Issued - **$275**

Walt Disney World Resort

After the success of the first Disney theme park in California, Walt Disney began scanning the East Coast for a place to build a larger vacation resort. He would definitely need more land than Disneyland had occupied and climate was also a major concern. Disney found the location he was looking for in Kissimmee, Florida. Located southwest of Orlando, the location was perfect. The temperature was consistent and the location was already on an established route for tourists. In 1965, Walt and his brother Roy bought twenty-seven thousand acres of land. They felt that left them more than enough room to expand if necessary.

In November 1965, Walt and Roy held the first news conference about the planned resort and theme-park. Sadly, Walt passed away a little over a year later, but Roy went on to finish the project. The grand opening was on October 1, 1971. The Walt Disney World Resort encompasses lakes, lagoons, hotels, golf courses and of course Disney amusement parks.

The first of several parks to be opened is known as the Magic Kingdom. Stylistically, it is akin to Anaheim's Disneyland. It was the first Disney park to host the Country Bear Jamboree, the Hall of Presidents and the Mickey Mouse Revue. The Magic Kingdom was joined in 1983 by EPCOT Center, by the Disney-MGM Studios in 1989, and by Disney's Animal Kingdom in 1998. Well over one billion guests have visited Walt Disney World Resort since its opening.

WDW-1

❑ **WDW-1. "Walt Disney World" Pre-Opening Invitation,**
1970. 4.5x6.25" stiff paper with text "You Are Cordially Invited To Attend A Pre-Opening Presentation Of The Walt Disney World Preview Center" with date of Tuesday, January 13. - **$50 $100 $150**

WDW-2

❑ **WDW-2. "Walt Disney World" Lunch Box With Thermos,**
1970. Aladdin. First issue, later used in 1978 for Mickey's 50th birthday with small birthday logo added to bottom right corner. This 1978 version has either blue or cream rim. 7x8x4" deep embossed metal box and 6.5" tall plastic thermos. First Version Set - **$25 $50 $90**
Birthday Version Set - **$20 $35 $70**

WDW-3

WDW-4

❑ **WDW-3. "Walt Disney World" Pre-Opening Cast Member's Brochure,**
1971. 4x8.5" on slightly textured stiff paper, opens to 25" long. Issued prior to the October 1st opening. Was used to promote jobs at Disney World. Text notes "Since our total cast will reach over 6000 people, we'd like to save you as much time as possible and make the casting procedure as easy as we can for you. We are outlining key points in our procedure to give you a better understanding of our casting process." Includes detailed job information as well as photos/ illustrations. - **$10 $18 $30**

❑ **WDW-4. "The Story Of Walt Disney World" Commemorative Program,**
1971. 11x11", 48-page "Commemorative Edition." Filled with color photos of the park. - **$10 $20 $30**

WALT DISNEY WORLD RESORT

WDW-5

❑ **WDW-5. "Walt Disney World" Pre-Opening Lot,**
1971. Six items issued prior to, and in preparation of October 1 official opening day; all retained by same original owner. Components are 11x17" map, 8.5x11" 20-page "Preview Edition" guide, 4x9" additional information brochure, 2.5x6" booklet of tickets for various attractions, 3.5x11" oversized postcard for local motel in Orlando, plus September 29 edition of "Osceola Sun" newspaper, largely devoted to the park's opening. Group Near Mint - **$90**

WDW-6

❑ **WDW-6. Disney World Christmas Prints,**
c. 1971. Four 7.25" square photo prints for a Christmas season promotion shortly after Walt Disney World opened. Each features same design of wreath with ribbon at top reading "Walt Disney's Magic Kingdom." At center are different Christmas-theme scenes of Mickey, Goofy, Donald, Pinocchio, Jiminy Cricket, Snow White, Pluto, Dopey. Group - **$8 $15 $25**

WDW-7

WDW-8

❑ **WDW-7. "Walt Disney World" Golf-Related Badges,**
1973. First is 2.5" diameter pinback for "1978 PGA Merchandise Show January 28-31, 1978" also marked "PGA Guest" with individual number "1935." Second item is 2.75x3.25" diecut plastic badge with Mickey head design of golf ball with ears for 1973 "Golf Classic." Guest - **$6 $12 $20**
Classic - **$4 $6 $12**

❑ **WDW-8. "Walt Disney World Main Street Electrical Parade" Parade Picture Disk Record,**
1977. Two-sided picture disk in plastic sleeve. - **$15 $30 $50**

WDW-9

❑ **WDW-9. "Disney World" Convention Badges,**
1979. Two issues for specialized events. 4" diameter "110 Club '79/Disney World" has opening on reverse for insertion of name paper visible from front. 3" diameter issue is for "Convention '79 Disney World/Delta Phi Epsilon." Each - **$6 $12 $20**

WDW-10

❑ **WDW-10. "I Like Walt Disney World" Flicker Button Uncut Sheet,**
1970s. Stiff glossy paper sheet is 8x8.25" with nine identical images used to produce individual flicker buttons that alternate image when tilted. - **$10 $20 $30**

WDW-11

WDW-12

WALT DISNEY WORLD RESORT

❏ **WDW-11.** "Walt Disney World" Decorative Wall Plate,
1970s. Plate is 6.75" in diameter. - **$8 $12 $20**

❏ **WDW-12.** "Walt Disney World" Donald Duck Composition Bobbing Head Figure,
1970s. Figure is 3x3x6.5" tall. - **$40 $75 $125**

WDW-13

WDW-14

❏ **WDW-13.** "Walt Disney World Main Street U.S.A." View-Master Reels,
1970s. 4.5x4.5" envelope contains set of three reels. - **$10 $20 $40**

❏ **WDW-14.** "Walt Disney World" Postcard Books,
1970s. Five, each 3.5x8.25" long with eight perforated postcards. Each - **$3 $6 $10**

WDW-15

❏ **WDW-15.** "Walt Disney World Polynesian Village" Large Tiki Mug,
1970s. Glass mug 6" tall by 4" in diameter. - **$5 $10 $20**

WDW-16

WDW-17

❏ **WDW-16.** "Walt Disney World" Ceramic Salt & Pepper Set,
1970s. Each 2.75" tall. - **$5 $10 $15**

❏ **WDW-17.** "Walt Disney World" Metal Coasters,
1970s. Four identical 3.25" diameter. Set - **$6 $12 $20**

WDW-18

❏ **WDW-18.** "Magic Kingdom" TV Tray,
1970s. Lithographed tin tray is 12.75x17.5". - **$10 $18 $30**

WDW-19

❏ **WDW-19.** Goofy "Walt Disney World" Composition Bobbing Head,
1970s. Figure is 2.5x2.5x7.5". - **$40 $65 $100**

WDW-20

WDW-21

❏ **WDW-20.** "Walt Disney World Pencil Sharpener,"
1970s. Alco. 3.5x7.5" blister card contains 3.5" tall figural hard plastic sharpener with tin lithographed globe that spins. Carded - **$5 $10 $15**

❏ **WDW-21.** "Walt Disney World" Souvenir Guides,
1970s. Two 8.75x11.5" editions for 1972 and 1975, each 36 pages. Each has identical front cover. Approximately half of contents between the two are also identical with other half differing in photos and text. Each - **$6 $12 $20**

WALT DISNEY WORLD RESORT

WDW-22

WDW-23

❏ **WDW-22. "Walt Disney World" Decorative Dish Boxed,**
1970s. 7x7x1.5" deep display box with clear plastic lid over 7" diameter glass dish with fluted rim. Boxed - **$6 $12 $20**

❏ **WDW-23. "Disney World" And "Mickey's Christmas Carol" Glasses,**
1970s. "Disney World." 7.5" tall pilsner-style glass illustrating path leading from castle to "Disney Main Gate" to "Holiday Inn" sign. Second glass is non-related 6" tall tumbler from 1982 Coca-Cola series for film "Mickey's Christmas Carol" picturing "Goofy As Marley's Ghost." Each - **$5 $10 $15**

WDW-24

❏ **WDW-24. "Walt Disney World" Tinker Bell Flasher Button,**
1970s. Vari-Vue. 2.5". She says "I Tink It's Great." - **$5 $10 $20**

WDW-25

❏ **WDW-25. "Disney World" Airline Employee Button,**
1970s. Acetate-covered pinback is 4" diameter probably an airline ticket counter promo without any specific airline indicated. Complete text is "Fly To Jacksonville To See Disney World/Between Us You've Got The Best Of Florida." - **$8 $15 $25**

WDW-26

WDW-27

❏ **WDW-26. "Walt Disney World Frontierland" Stereo Reels Set,**
1970s. View-Master. 4.5x4.5" envelope containing descriptive folder and complete three reels of full color photo views. - **$8 $15 $25**

❏ **WDW-27. "Walt Disney World" Postcard Folder,**
1970s. Glossy stiff paper folder is 4x6" opening to 28" length of "14 Colorful Photos Of The Vacation Kingdom." - **$5 $10 $15**

WDW-28

❏ **WDW-28. "Walt Disney World" Keychain And Medallion,**
c. 1970s. Each 1-5/8" diameter marked on rim "C.C. Bronze." Keychain in pewter finish, medallion in bronze finish. Each - **$3 $8 $12**

WDW-29

❏ **WDW-29. "Walt Disney World Eyes & Ears" Publications,**
1983. Sample issues of weekly publication "Prepared By And For The Walt Disney World Cast." Each issue is 11x14.5" with eight pages. Each, Near Mint - **$2**

WDW-30

WDW-31

❏ **WDW-30. "Walt Disney World 15 Years" Commemorative Souvenirs,**
1986. Pendent is 5/8", money clip is 1x2", each boxed. Boxed, Each - **$5 $10 $15**

❏ **WDW-31. "Walt Disney World 15 Years" Anniversary Button,**
1986. Button is 3" diameter pinback depicting "15 Years" logo. - **$6 $12 $20**

WALT DISNEY WORLD RESORT

WDW-32

WDW-33

WDW-35

WDW-36

WDW-38

❑ **WDW-37. "Walt Disney World 25th Anniversary Celebration" Special Event V.I.P. Items,**
1996. Die-cut plastic pass is 5x5.5" and "Coca-Cola Classic" bottle is 7.5" tall with box.
Pass - **$3 $8 $15**
Packaged Coca-Cola - **$10 $20 $30**

❑ **WDW-38. "Walt Disney World" 25th Anniversary Celebration Items,**
1996. Mailing envelope is 9x12" containing four paper items themed by Mickey as Sorcerer's Apprentice with reminder string tied on finger. Contents are announcement folder, eight-page events program, admission ticket. Event was September 30 at Orlando Arena. Set - **$10 $20 $35**

❑ **WDW-32. "Walt Disney World" Decorative China Mug,**
1980s. 6.5" tall mug with foil label "Ceramarte/Made In Brazil." - **$8 $15 $30**

❑ **WDW-33. "Disney World Town Square Playset,"**
1980s. Sealed 20.25x24x3.5" deep sealed box with scale model set sold exclusively at Sears. - **$40 $65 $115**

WDW-34

WDW-37

WDW-39

❑ **WDW-35. Walt Disney World Security Officer" Badge,**
c. 1980s. 2.25"x3" heavy cast metal. - **$40 $75 $150**

❑ **WDW-36. "Splash Mountain" Grand Opening Event Presentation Kit,**
1992. Stiff paper 6.75x9" pop-up folder contains booklet and RSVP card. - **$8 $15 $30**

❑ **WDW-34. "Walt Disney World" License Plate,**
1980s. Embossed tin is 6x12". - **$5 $10 $15**

❑ **WDW-39. "Walt Disney World" 25th Anniversary Celebration Lot,**
1996. Five items including eight-page 5x11" program plus admission ticket, both specifically for the September 30 celebration. Other items are complimentary admission ticket valid September-October, Disney holographic "Press Sample" credit card, identification pass card on neck cord. Likely a kit for news media guest. Set - **$10 $20 $35**

WALT DISNEY'S WONDERFUL WORLD

WDW-40

WDW-41

❑ **WDW-40. "Walt Disney World" Premium 25th Anniversary Watch,**
1997. Made exclusively for Kodak. Packaged Near Mint - **$65**

❑ **WDW-41. Cast Member Birthday Buttons,**
1990s. Three 3" diameter pinbacks issued for 19th, 21st and 26th birthdays from 1990, 1992, 1997 respectively of cast members only. Each includes "Walt Disney World" name and logo. 19th features Pinocchio and Jiminy Cricket; 21st is Splash Mountain ride with Brer Rabbit, Fox and Bear; 26th is Safari scene with Mickey, Donald, Goofy, Pluto. Each - **$2 $4 $8**

Walt Disney's Wonderful World

Walt Disney's first weekly one-hour TV variety show debuted on ABC in 1954. The idea of a TV show was explored for several reasons. Disney had needed a loan to help build the Disneyland park and ABC desperately needed a hit show. In exchange for providing the loan, ABC got the show. The deal worked extremely well for all parties concerned. *Disneyland*, ABC's first top-twenty show, ran under its original name from 1954 until 1958, then as *Walt Disney Presents* from 1958 until 1961.

Always on top of technical innovations, Walt then decided he wanted to broadcast the weekly show in color, but ABC was unable to accommodate his wish. They lacked the technical ability to broadcast color television.

Unable to accept that limitation, Disney moved the show over to NBC in 1961. The show was renamed *Walt Disney's Wonderful World of Color*. Again, everybody was a winner. Disney gained new viewers and his parks gained new visitors. NBC got an immediate hit show that brought in the all-important family demographic. RCA was happy because, all across America, the show boosted the sales of color TVs.

Walt often hosted the show himself. For close to two decades, the show was one of NBC's most consistent performers. In 1981, NBC finally canceled the show. Over the next decade, the same anthology concept that had started in 1954 continued on other networks and eventually onto cable. Each version of the show was known under a new title such as *Disney's Wonderful World* or *The Magical World of Disney*.

WWW-1

❑ **WWW-1. Goofy Cel,**
1961. Walt Disney's Wonderful World Of Color TV show. 12.5x16" acetate sheet with 4x6" cel image with color laser background for "Holiday For Henpecked Husbands." - **$50 $85 $150**

WWW-2

❑ **WWW-2. "Professor Ludwig Von Drake Presents Walt Disney's Wonderful World Of Color Game,"**
1962. Parker Brothers. 9x17x1.5" deep box. - **$15 $30 $60**

WWW-3

❑ **WWW-3. "RCA Silverama Picture Tubes" Store Display,**
c. 1962. Thick die-cut cardboard 8x18x14.5" tall light-up display complete with electric cord and bulb. Attached to the front of the display is a separate 14" tall die-cut figure of Ludwig. Display features a large die-cut "screen" with glossy black and white photo insert of unidentified female actress which can be changed to text promoting picture tubes. - **$150 $300 $500**

WWW-4

❑ **WWW-4. "The Scarecrow Of Romney Marsh" Comic Book/Records,**
1960s. Three items from the mid-1960s for Disney's Wonderful World of Color three-part television show that starred Patrick McGoohan. Gold Key comic #3, the final issue published for this title. First record is 78 rpm in 7x7" stiff paper sleeve photo front of Scarecrow. Second record is 7" diameter, 45 rpm. Both records are on the Disneyland label. Comic - **$3 $10 $35**
Record With Sleeve - **$40 $80 $135**
Record Without Sleeve - **$20 $40 $65**

WHO FRAMED ROGER RABBIT

Who Framed Roger Rabbit

No film in history was as successful in combining live action with animation as *Who Framed Roger Rabbit* (1988). Using Gary Wolf's book *Who Censored Roger Rabbit?* (1981) as the basic outline for the film, it succeeded on both an artistic and financial level.

The movie begins with a short cartoon titled *Somethin's Cookin'*. That cartoon portrays Roger Rabbit's troubles as he tries to baby-sit a child named Baby Herman. Naturally, the baby is placed in every type of danger possible. In his attempts to protect the baby, Roger suffers one humiliating problem after another. The cartoon expertly mimics the energy and style of a classic short.

When the cartoon ends, the camera pulls back to reveal a Hollywood soundstage complete with a live director, stagehands and movie studio surroundings. The cartoon characters revert to lively and more human off-camera personalities. Suddenly, the audience realizes that the characters that were in the cartoon are actually part of the real world. The real-life characters refer to the cartoon characters as "toons."

Roger Rabbit becomes a suspect in the murder of Marvin Acme, the owner of Toontown and a successful prop maker. Roger supposedly did this foul deed because Marvin had been flirting with Roger's wife, the bombshell Jessica. To help prove his innocence, Roger tracks down human detective Eddie Valiant and begs him for help. Eventually the two find the real villain, Judge Doom and his henchmen. In the end, Roger Rabbit is cleared of all wrongdoing.

Who Framed Roger Rabbit was directed by Robert Zemeckis and the animation was directed by Richard Williams. The film was produced by Touchstone Pictures in collaboration with Steven Spielberg. The live cast included Bob Hoskins, Christopher Lloyd, Joanna Cassidy and Stubby Kaye. Charles Fleischer was the voice of Roger Rabbit. The film won Academy Awards for Visual Effects, Film Editing and Sound Effects Editing. Roger Williams was awarded an Oscar for Special Achievement in Animation Directing.

Many of Roger Rabbit's scenes, including the opening short cartoon, were inspired by the classic Warner Brothers and the MGM cartoons of Tex Avery. The film contains cameos from almost every important animated figure of the twentieth century. Some cartoon characters, such as Droopy and Dumbo, made their first memorable appearances in decades. The film was also notable for the number of different companies that allowed their characters to appear together in the film. Roger Rabbit marked the first and only appearance of Mickey Mouse and Bugs Bunny onscreen at the same time. Many fans of animation thought that scene was the highlight of the film.

Who Framed Roger Rabbit inspired three additional cartoon shorts featuring Roger Rabbit, *Tummy Trouble*, *Rollercoaster Rabbit* and *Trail Mix-up*. These were released theatrically as preludes to other full-length Disney features.

Roger Rabbit merchandising included books, comics, figurines, dolls, games and snow globes. Roger was quite a popular character throughout the early 1990s, but corporate differences between Disney and Spielberg's Amblin Entertainment eventually led to his largely being retired.

WHO-1

WHO-2

❑ **WHO-1. Roger Rabbit Black Light Clock,** 1987. Disney/Amblin. 3.5x13x9.5" tall hard plastic. - **$20 $35 $75**

❑ **WHO-2. "Who Framed Roger Rabbit" Watch,** 1987. Disney/Amblin. 1.5" diameter metal case with original leather strap. - **$10 $20 $45**

WHO-3

❑ **WHO-3. Roger Rabbit Animation Cel,** 1988. 7.5x16.5" acetate sheet with pair of 1x2.5" to 3" cel images, one of Jessica Rabbit and the other of Weasel. Includes certificate from Walt Disney Company. - **$60 $125 $225**

WHO-4

❑ **WHO-4. "Who Framed Roger Rabbit" Movie Board Game,** 1988. Hard to find due to low production run. Boxed - **$25 $50 $120**

WHO-5

WHO-6

❑ **WHO-5. Industrial Light And Magic Photos Used For Roger Rabbit Animation,** c. 1988. Two, each 11x14". Each - **$8 $15 $25**

❑ **WHO-6. "Bully" Roger Rabbit Boxed Pen Holder,** c. 1988. German by Bully. 5.5x7x2" deep box contains 2x4x4.5" tall pen holder with hard plastic base and attached hand-painted vinyl figures. Boxed - **$10 $20 $35**

WHO FRAMED ROGER RABBIT

WHO-7

WHO-8

❏ WHO-10. "Max" Italian Magazine With Jessica Rabbit,
1989. 9.25x13.25" from February 1989. 288 pages. Contains large fold-outs of Jessica and Roger. - **$50 $100 $200**

❏ WHO-11. Roger Rabbit Production Test Cel,
1980s. Acetate sheet is 11.5x16.5" with 4x6" cel image. #627 of a numbered sequence with Roger in gray, not white. Mint As Made - **$250**

WHO-15

❏ WHO-7. Roger Rabbit 17" Plush Doll in Benny the Car Cardboard Box,
1988. - **$15 $30 $60**

❏ WHO-8. Roger Rabbit 13 3/4" Super Flex Figure on Card,
1988. - **$10 $25 $50**

WHO-9

❏ WHO-9. "The Art Of Who Framed Roger Rabbit" Sotheby's Auction Catalogue,
1989. Catalogue is 8.25x10.75" with 394 lots of art. - **$5 $10 $20**

WHO-10

WHO-11

WHO-12

❏ WHO-12. Roger Rabbit Consecutively Numbered Production Test Cels,
1980s. Two 11.5x16.5" acetate sheets each with cel image 1.5x3". Numbers are 356 and 357 from a numbered sequence with Roger in gray, not white. Mint As Made Each - **$75**

WHO-13

❏ WHO-13. Roger Rabbit Production Test Cel,
1980s. Acetate sheet is 11.5x16.5" with 3x5" cel image. #736 from a numbered sequence with Roger in gray, not white. Mint As Made - **$300**

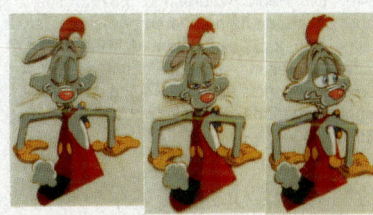

WHO-14

❏ WHO-14. Roger Rabbit Consecutively Numbered Production Test Cels,
1980s. Three 11.5x16.5" acetate sheets, each with cel image about 1.5" to 2.75". Numbers 351, 352, 353 from a numbered sequence with Roger in gray, not white. Mint As Made Each - **$75**

❏ WHO-15. "Who Framed Roger Rabbit" Sign,
1980s. 14x14.5" stiff cardboard. - **$20 $35 $50**

WHO-16

WHO-17

❏ WHO-16. "Who Framed Roger Rabbit" Pin Display,
1980s. 13x18.5" die-cut cardboard with 14 die-cut pins, each 1" tall. (Missing 10 pins). Display - **$12 $35 $50**
Each Pin - **$1 $2 $3**

❏ WHO-17. Roger Rabbit "Pet Toy,"
1980s. Petcrest. 4.5x7" display bag contains 4.5" tall rubber squeaker toy. Packaged - **$8 $12 $20**

WHO FRAMED ROGER RABBIT

WHO-18

❑ **WHO-18. "Who P-P-P-Plugged Roger Rabbit?" Signed And Numbered Limited Edition,** 1991. 5.75x8.5" hardcover with dust jacket by Villard Books. 256 pages signed by author Gary K. Wolf. Number 78 of 500 produced. Mint As Issued - **$265**

WHO-19

❑ **WHO-19. "Roger Rabbit" Snow Globe,** 1999. - **$75**

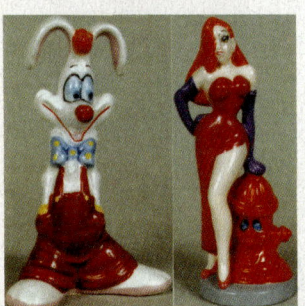
WHO-20

❑ **WHO-20. Who Framed Roger Rabbit Ceramic Figurines,** 1990s. Roger Rabbit is 4.75" tall and Jessica Rabbit is 5.5" tall. Roger - **$15 $25 $45** Jessica - **$25 $40 $80**

Willie the Operatic Whale

Originally part of the 1946 animated feature *Make Mine Music*, this cartoon was re-released on its own in 1954. Willie is a whale who can actually sing, but human onlookers, in particular, theatrical impresario Professor Tetti-Tatti, think that he simply swallowed a few opera singers. As Willie auditions to work as the entertainment for a cruise ship at sea, we see his dreams of one day actually singing at New York's Metropolitan Opera House. Sadly, his dreams are interrupted as he is harpooned. The cartoon ends with Willie's spirit singing at heaven's pearly gates, where a sign reads "Sold Out"!

Directed by Hamilton Luske and Clyde Geronomi, *The Whale Who Wanted to Sing at the Met* was animated by such talents as Ward Kimball, John Lounsbery, Hal King and Fred Moore. The cartoon was based on a story by Irvin Graham. The vocals of the singing whale are handled by Nelson Eddy. Some feel that the cartoon is a sly parody of Orson Welles' film *Citizen Kane* (1941).

Merchandising for the cartoon was limited.

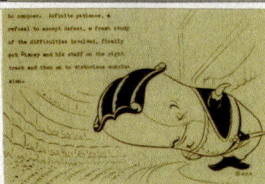
WIL-1

❑ **WIL-1. "Make Mine Music" Movie Reviewer's Promotional Handbook,** 1940. RKO Radio Pictures Inc. 5.5x8.5" stiff paper cover and 32 numbered one-sided pages. Cover is marked "Issued Jan. 15, 1946 by RKO Radio Pictures Inc." Includes detailed information on all aspects of the film along with 12 different illustrations of the film's characters. - **$35 $65 $110**

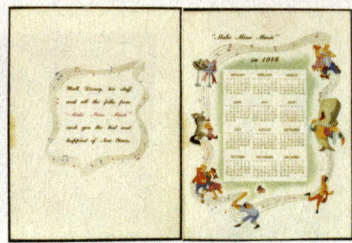
WIL-2

WIL-3

❑ **WIL-2. Disney Studio Christmas Card,** 1945. 7.75x10.25" white stiff paper card. Card opens to reveal calendar for 1946 surrounded by illustrations of characters from the film plus titles "Willie The Whale, Casey At The Bat, Make Mine Music, Peter And The Wolf," three others. - **$65 $135 $200**

❑ **WIL-3. "Make Mine Music" Sheet Music,** 1946. Southern Music Pub. Co. 9x12" with music and words to the song "Blue By You." - **$12 $25 $40**

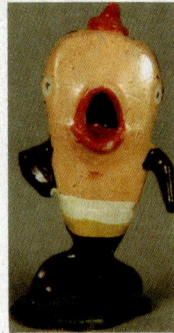
WIL-4

❑ **WIL-4. Willie The Whale Disneykin,** 1968. Marx. 1.5" tall hand-painted hard plastic figure. From the second series by Marx. - **$30 $55 $85**

WINNIE THE POOH

Winnie the Pooh

Walt Disney's daughters were big fans of the Pooh books. A. A. Milne, their author, had even commented that he would be thrilled if Disney were to one day animate his stories. In 1961, Milne's widow, Daphne, sold the rights to Disney. At first, the studio's plan was to create a full-length feature, but Walt then broke the ideas in the books into four separate shorts. While Pooh was incredibly popular in England, at the time, his notoriety stateside was minimal. Disney felt that a gradual introduction to the Hundred Acre Wood characters might help build up a steadier head of steam. This would help create a longer life for the characters.

The first short, *Winnie-the-Pooh and the Honey Tree* (1966), was taken from two book chapters, *In Which We Are Introduced to Winnie-the-Pooh and Some Bees* and *In Which Pooh Goes Visiting and Gets into a Tight Place*.

The second Winnie the Pooh short proved that Walt knew what he was doing. *Winnie-the-Pooh and the Blustery Day* (1968) was very popular with theatergoers. In 1968, it ended up winning an Academy Award for Best Cartoon Short Subject. This cartoon was based on chapters from two Pooh books. It is also the first appearance of Tigger and Piglet in a Disney adaptation.

By the time the third Pooh featurette, *Winnie the Pooh and Tigger Too* (1974) was released, Pooh had become a household name. In 1977, all three featurettes, plus a new climactic sequence, were combined into Disney's 22nd full-length feature, *The Many Adventures of Winnie-the-Pooh*.

In 1983, Disney filmed a final Milne adaptation *Winnie-the-Pooh and a Day for Eeyore*. Since that time, entirely original Disney Pooh material has appeared on video and on TV. In 1987, the TV series *New Adventures of Winnie the Pooh* was launched. In 1997, Disney produced the direct-to-video feature *Pooh's Grand Adventure: The Search for Christopher Robin*. February 2000 saw the theatrical release of a third feature based around Pooh, *The Tigger Movie*.

Disney's animated Pooh cast includes Winnie the Pooh, Christopher Robin, Rabbit, Owl, Kanga, Roo, Piglet, Eeyore, Tigger and Gopher. The last character is an anomaly; proposed for the books by Milne but jettisoned by his publisher in 1926, Disney's films marked his first appearance in any medium.

Longtime Disney director Wolfgang Reitherman directed the first featurette, but did not stick with the series through its development. Vocal talent also changed as the years went by. There has only been one constant: the presence of longtime Disney favorites Sterling Holloway as Pooh and Paul Winchell as Tigger. The skills of those two actors created audience expectations for how the two characters should sound. Disney stayed with that basic feel even when voice artist Jim Cummings had to take over the two roles.

Merchandise has always been extensive. It includes books, records, premiums, dolls, lamps, button sets and comics properties. Winnie the Pooh, the dashes in his name disappeared in the eighties, has become the most lucrative licensed character purchased by Disney.

WTP-1

WTP-2

❑ **WTP-1. "Winnie The Pooh" Promotional Marketing Kit,**
1964. Die-cut stiff glossy paper folder is 5.5x11" and contains fifteen numbered 5.5x7" paper sheets devoted to merchandise or promotion. 1964 copyright but issued in 1965. - **$25 $50 $75**

❑ **WTP-2. "Winnie The Pooh" Variety Promotional Marketing Kit,**
1964. Same as previous "For Extra Profit" kit but this example has different cover design, different colors and is designated "For Christmas." 1964 copyright but issued in 1965. - **$25 $50 $75**

WTP-3

WTP-4

❑ **WTP-3. Christopher Robin Figurine,**
1964. Enesco. 2x2.5x5.5" tall painted and glazed ceramic image of him playing a drum. Has foil-covered cardboard string tag which opens to text "I'm Christopher." Tag - **$3 $6 $10**
Figure - **$30 $55 $95**

❑ **WTP-4. Winnie The Pooh Premium Breakfast Buddies Set,**
1964. Nabisco. Set of seven soft plastic figures 1.2" to 2" tall. Each has slot on underside for placement on a spoon or can be hung off the edge of a cereal bowl by its outstretched arms. Consists of Pooh, Christopher, Owl, Rabbit, Piglet, Eeyore and Kanga with Roo. Each - **$5 $10 $20**

WTP-5

❑ **WTP-5. "Winnie-The-Pooh" Vinyl Lunch Box,**
1964. Aladdin. 7x8.75x3.5" deep. - **$100 $200 $300**

WTP-6

987

WINNIE THE POOH

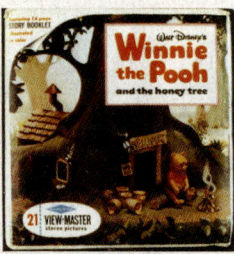

WTP-7

❑ **WTP-6. Ferris Wheel Musical Toy,**
1964. Chein Co. 5x8x10" tall wind-up formed by tin lithographed base and uprights, hard plastic wheel frame and seats. On one side is knob turned to activate winding mechanism. The ferris wheel then spins as the separate seats move slightly and tune 'You Are My Sunshine' is chimed. - **$100 $200 $300**

❑ **WTP-7. "Winnie The Pooh And The Honey Tree" View-Master Set,**
1964. Envelope is 4.5x4.5" and contains complete set of three reels with single inner sleeve, color booklet and catalogue. - **$15 $30 $60**

WTP-8

❑ **WTP-8. "Winnie The Pooh" Boxed Watch With Figure,**
1965. Bradley. 4x4.5x6" tall box with top that lifts off to reveal display with attached 3.5" tall ceramic figure and watch. Bradley watch exclusively for Sears.
Near Mint Boxed - **$75 $150 $250**
Watch Only - **$25 $50 $100**

WTP-9

❑ **WTP-9. "Winnie The Pooh/Honey Munch Cereal" Retailer's Promotional Folder,**
1965. Stiff cardboard folder is 8.5x16" with die-cut design at top. - **$65 $125 $200**

WTP-10

❑ **WTP-10. Winnie The Pooh English Biscuit Tin,**
1965. Huntley & Palmer's. 5" diameter by 1" deep tin litho. - **$35 $70 $115**

WTP-11

WTP-12

❑ **WTP-11. "Pooh As A Cloud" Glass,**
1965. Tumbler is 4.75" tall #1 from a numbered Canadian set of six glasses "Inspired By Walt Disney's Motion Picture." Each - **$20 $40 $60**

❑ **WTP-12. Pooh "North Pole" Glass,**
1965. Tumbler is 4.75" tall tumbler #3 from a numbered Canadian set of six glasses "Inspired By Walt Disney's Motion Picture Winnie The Pooh." Wrap-around scene pictures Pooh and six other characters at North Pole discovery. Each - **$20 $40 $60**

WTP-13

❑ **WTP-13. "Eeyore Has A Birthday" Glass,**
1965. Tumbler is 4.75" tall #5 from a numbered Canadian set of six glasses. - **$20 $40 $60**

WTP-14   WTP-15

❑ **WTP-14. "Winnie The Pooh" Glass,**
1965. Tumbler is 4.75" tall #1 from a numbered single color Canadian set of six glasses "Inspired By Walt Disney's Winnie The Pooh And The Honey Tree." Each - **$20 $40 $60**

❑ **WTP-15. "Kanga And Roo" Glass,**
1965. Tumbler is 4.75" tall #4 from a numbered single color Canadian set of six glasses. - **$20 $40 $60**

WTP-16

❑ **WTP-16. "Owl" Glass,**
1965. Tumbler is 4.75" tall #6 from a numbered single color Canadian set of six glasses "Inspired By Walt Disney's Winnie The Pooh And The Honey Tree." Owl points at chalkboard image of a honey pot. Each - **$20 $40 $60**

WINNIE THE POOH

WTP-17

❏ **WTP-17. "Winnie The Pooh And Piglet" United Kingdom Mug,**
1965. "Keele St. Pty. Co. Ltd." 4" tall glazed ceramic with underside text "From The Cartoon Film Winnie The Pooh And The Honey Tree." - **$12 $25 $40**

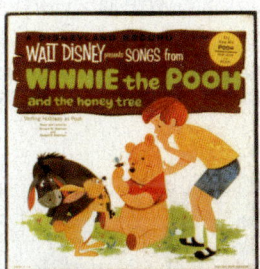

WTP-18

❏ **WTP-18. "Winnie The Pooh And The Honey Tree" Record,**
1965. Paper sleeve is 7x7" holding Disneyland label 45 rpm. - **$5 $12 $20**

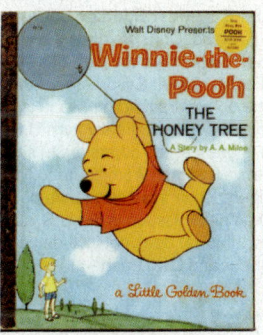

WTP-19

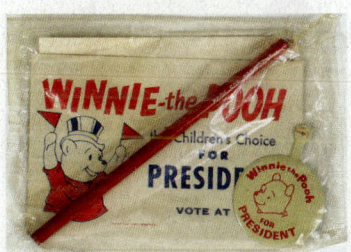

WTP-20

❏ **WTP-19. "Winnie-The-Pooh The Honey Tree" Little Golden Book,**
1965. Golden Press. 6.5x8" with 24 pages. - **$6 $12 $20**

❏ **WTP-20. "Winnie The Pooh For President" Premium,**
1965. Sears. 5.5x7" unopened cellophane pack containing lithographed tin tab, lead pencil, sticker and coloring sheet. Pooh is promoted as "The Children's Choice" presidential candidate. Packaged - **$12 $25 $50**

WTP-21

WTP-22

❏ **WTP-21. Kanga And Roo Doll,**
1966. Gund Mfg. Co. 7" tall sawdust-stuffed felt fabric detailed by separate eye pieces, plastic nose, felt tongue, bow at neck. Separate felt cut-out Roo figure is in Kanga's tummy pouch. - **$10 $20 $40**

❏ **WTP-22. Pooh Characters Original Art,**
c. 1966. Paper sheet is 8x9.5" holding scissored and mounted ink drawings of 4.5x7" Kanga holding Roo plus 1.5x2.25" Piglet. Drawings are by unidentified Disney artist. - **$15 $30 $50**

WTP-23

❏ **WTP-23. Tigger Sketch Signed,**
c. 1966. Small 3.5x4.5" stiff translucent paper nearly filled by marker inks image. Sketch is by "Disney Legend" Al Konetzni, creator of many Disney toys and merchandise items, and signed by him. Unique, Near Mint - **$60**

WTP-24

❏ **WTP-24. "Winnie The Pooh And The Blustery Day" Lobby Cards,**
1968. Set of five 11x14" glossy lobby cards in original envelope. Set - **$30 $60 $120**

WINNIE THE POOH

WTP-25

❑ **WTP-25. "Winnie The Pooh And The Blustery Day" Production Cels,**
1968. Group of four production cels with reproduction background. - **$200 $400 $600**

WTP-26

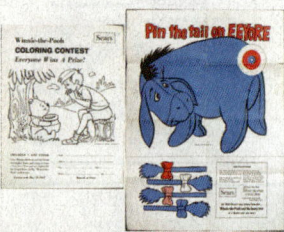

WTP-27

❑ **WTP-26. Tigger Animation Set-Up Art,**
1968. Image is 4.25x6.25" with 10x11.75" reproduction background. Reverse has Art Corner store gold seal. - **$100 $200 $300**

❑ **WTP-27. "Winnie The Pooh" Paper Item Premiums,**
1960s. Sears. 8.5x11" one-sided "Coloring Contest" sheet copyright 1964 although contest deadline date of 1967. Second Sears premium is 17.5x23" sheet picturing Eeyore as the target for tails to be cut from the lower third of the sheet. Contest grand prize was a "Big Winnie The Pooh Stuffed Bear." Game sheet mentions Sears Pooh merchandise based on new cartoon "Winnie The Pooh And The Honey Tree."
Contest - **$5 $10 $15**
Target - **$10 $18 $30**

WTP-28   **WTP-29**

❑ **WTP-28. Owl From Winnie The Pooh Ceramic Figurine,**
1960s. Enesco. Figure is 4.75" tall. - **$15 $30 $50**

❑ **WTP-29. "Owl" From Winnie The Pooh Ceramic Figurine,**
1960s. Beswick England. Figure is 3" tall. - **$20 $40 $65**

WTP-30

WTP-31

❑ **WTP-30. Kanga Figurine,**
1960s. Beswick Of England. 3" tall painted and glazed ceramic. Underside has Beswick name and copyright in gold lettering. - **$15 $35 $45**

❑ **WTP-31. Eeyore Figurine,**
1960s. Beswick Of England. 2" tall painted and glazed ceramic. - **$15 $30 $45**

WTP-32

❑ **WTP-32. Pooh Figurine,**
1960s. Beswick Of England. 2x2x2.5" tall painted and glazed ceramic seated figure. - **$20 $40 $65**

WTP-33

❑ **WTP-33. Winnie The Pooh Canadian Premium Breakfast Buddies Set,**
1960s. Nabisco. Consists of only six vinyl figures, five of which are the same as the U.S.: Pooh, Rabbit, Piglet, Eeyore and Kanga with Roo. The colors are different, each is in a single solid color that differs greatly from U.S. set. Eeyore is orange, the others are in shades of blue that vary slightly from figure to figure. The main difference in this set is figure of Tigger which was never issued in the U.S. set. However, this set does not include figures of Christopher and Owl. Each - **$5 $10 $20**

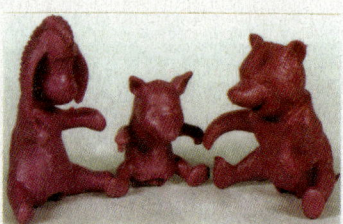

WTP-34

WINNIE THE POOH

❑ **WTP-34. Winnie The Pooh Breakfast Buddies Varieties,**
1960s. Three 1.5" to 2.25" tall figures, identical to 1964 premiums issued by Nabisco Rice Honeys although rather than soft plastic, each of these is soft rubber. Each has slot on underside for placement on a spoon handle tip. Each can also be placed and held on edge of cereal bowl by outstretched arms. Depicted are Eeyore, Piglet, Pooh. Each - **$5 $8 $12**

WTP-37

WTP-40

WTP-35

WTP-38

❑ **WTP-39. Rabbit And Pooh Salt And Pepper Set,**
1960s. Enesco. 2.5x5.5x4" tall painted ceramic tray and figural shakers unit with foil stickers in unopened original cellophane wrap. Set - **$30 $60 $100**

❑ **WTP-40. Winnie The Pooh Animated Ceramic Music Box,**
1960s. Music box is 4x10x7.25" tall. Plays Winnie The Pooh theme song as Tigger spins. Japan. - **$150 $300 $500**

❑ **WTP-35. Winnie The Pooh Ceramic Lamp With Shade,**
1960s. Made in Japan with company logo sticker "MR." 4x5.5x11.5" tall with stiff paper shade 8' tall with 11.5" bottom diameter. Lamp - **$30 $60 $115**
Shade - **$25 $50 $100**

❑ **WTP-37. Winnie The Pooh Pocketknife/Money Clip,**
1960s. Sears promotional. 1.5" square metal. Has knife blade, nail file and screwdriver blade plus money clip attachment on reverse. - **$25 $50 $75**

❑ **WTP-38. Winnie The Pooh Ceramic Mug,**
1960s. Mug is 4" tall. Japan. - **$15 $30 $50**

WTP-36

WTP-39

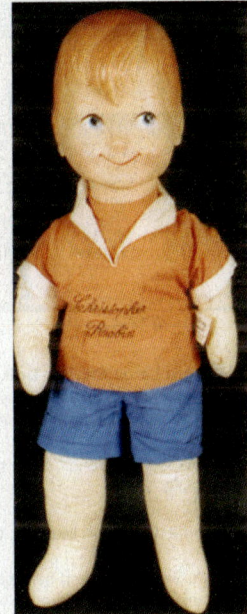

WTP-41

❑ **WTP-36. Winnie The Pooh Ceiling Light Shade,**
1960s. Glass shade is 13.5x13.5x2.5" deep. - **$30 $60 $100**

❑ **WTP-41. "Christopher Robin" Doll,**
1960s. Gund. 4.5x7x18" tall stuffed doll with vinyl head and removable shirt. Originally accompanied by a small Pooh doll. Christopher Only - **$25 $50 $75**

WINNIE THE POOH

WTP-42

WTP-43

WTP-44

WTP-45

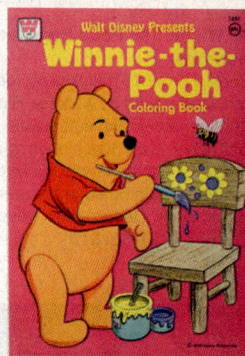

WTP-46

WTP-47

WTP-48

WTP-49

❏ **WTP-42. Eeyore Large English Doll,** 1960s. Stuffed plush doll is 4x13x9" tall with removable snap-on tail. Stitched to one leg is tag for "Merry Thought Iron Bridge/Shrops./Made In England." No Disney markings. - **$25 $50 $85**

❏ **WTP-43. Winnie The Pooh Musical TV Toy,** c. 1970. Ohio Art. 9x10x4.5" deep hard plastic. Knob on top is turned to activate the toy which in turn plays "Winnie The Pooh" as a paper roll with full color illustrations revolves to reveal scenes. - **$20 $40 $60**

❏ **WTP-44. "Winnie The Pooh And Tigger Too" Lobby Card Set,** 1974. Set of six cards in 11.5x14.5" envelope. Includes title card and five with film scenes. Set -**$25 $50 $100**

❏ **WTP-45. "Winnie The Pooh And Tigger Too" Movie Poster,** 1974. Glossy stiff paper is 22x28" half-sheet for original release. Text at top is "It's Pooh-fectly Tigger-ific And It's All New." - **$15 $30 $50**

❏ **WTP-46. "Winnie-The-Pooh Coloring Book,"** 1975. Whitman. 8x11". - **$6 $12 $18**

❏ **WTP-47. "Winnie The Pooh And Tigger Too" Stereo Reels Set,** 1976. View-Master. 4.5" square envelope containing set of three view reels plus story booklet. - **$5 $10 $15**

WINNIE THE POOH

❑ **WTP-48. "Winnie The Pooh" Wristwatch,**
c. 1977. Bradley. 2.5x3x6" deep plastic display case containing watch with 1" diameter chromed metal case. Case - **$10 $20 $40**
Watch - **$35 $60 $100**

❑ **WTP-49. Pooh Characters "Pop-Out" Calendar,**
1979. Random House. 10x15" illustrated envelope containing complete monthly calendar of "12 Dimensional Pictures." Back of calendar has cardboard easel and each month is a separate full color stiff paper sheet with pop-out design of Pooh characters engaged in activities appropriate to that particular month, exemplified by ice skating in January sheet pictured here. - **$5 $12 $20**

WTP-50

❑ **WTP-50. Winnie The Pooh Cel,**
1970s. Acetate sheet is 10x12" with 8x8" image. #37 from a numbered sequence. - **$75 $150 $275**

WTP-51

WTP-52

❑ **WTP-51. Winnie The Pooh Ceramic Figurine,**
1970s. Figure is 2.5" tall. - **$8 $15 $25**

❑ **WTP-52. Tigger Figurine,**
1970s. "Japan." 4" tall painted and glazed ceramic with underside copyright. - **$12 $25 $40**

WTP-53

❑ **WTP-53. Character Figures,**
1970s. Three vinyl figures from apparent different series size scales. Winnie is 6" tall holding a pot of honey and has remnant of string once part of a hanging mobile. Kanga and Roo is 6.5" tall squeaker, Eeyore is 3.5" tall squeaker. Each - **$6 $12 $20**

WTP-54

❑ **WTP-54. "Winnie The Pooh" Lamp With Shade,**
1970s. Lamp is 5.25x9x10.5" tall to top of socket, the glossy stiff paper shade has base diameter of 10" by 7" tall. Lamp base is hard plastic.
Lamp - **$20 $40 $75**
Shade - **$15 $25 $40**

WTP-55

❑ **WTP-55. Figural Bank,**
1970s. 3.5" diameter by 6.5" tall painted hard plastic. - **$12 $20 $40**

WINNIE THE POOH

WTP-56

❑ **WTP-56. "Winnie The Pooh" Doll,**
1970s. Sears. 6.5" tall sawdust-filled with felt body and fabric shirt. - **$20 $40 $60**

WTP-57

❑ **WTP-57. "Tricky Trapeze" Acrobat Toy,**
1970s. Kohner Bros. 2x3x5.25" tall hard plastic with "Disney Toy" logo. - **$12 $25 $40**

WTP-58

❑ **WTP-58. "Pooh's Honey Bank" Ceramics**
1970s. - **$10 $25 $50**

WTP-59

❑ **WTP-59. Winnie The Pooh Cel,**
1980. Acetate sheet ix 10.5x12.5" with 8x8" image. #17 from a numbered sequence. - **$50 $75 $125**

WTP-60

❑ **WTP-60. Pooh's Friends Cel,**
1980s. Acetate sheet is 10.5x12.5" centered by 5.75x10.5" painted image of Christopher Robin, Tigger, Owl and Piglet seated at a table. Laser background depicts forest scene with Pooh's house. From "Many Adventures of Pooh" TV show and No. "48" from a numbered sequence. - **$70 $135 $225**

WTP-61

WTP-62

❑ **WTP-61. Tigger Cel,**
1980s. Acetate sheet is 10.5x14" centered by 5.5x8.5" painted image of Tigger holding sandwich and root beer float. From 'Many Adventures Of Pooh' TV show. - **$65 $125 $200**

❑ **WTP-62. "Winnie The Pooh And The Blustery Day" Serigraph Cel Signed,**
1980s. Mat border is 16x20" around 10.5x13.5" acetate sheet centered by 5.5x7" painted image of Eeyore, Pooh and Piglet in vertical tandem positioning. From a sold-out limited edition of 9500 by Celshop Ltd. authenticated by "Walt Disney Company" seal plus reverse certificate label. Cel is signed by Disney animator/designer Marc Davis. Signed - **$70 $135 $225**

WTP-63

❑ **WTP-63. Pooh And Tigger Serigraph Cel,**
1980s. Acetate sheet is 11x14" centered by 5x7" painted image of Tigger standing on Pooh's stomach. Lower right has Disney Co. seal and text "Serigraph Cel Certified." - **$25 $50 $80**

WINNIE THE POOH

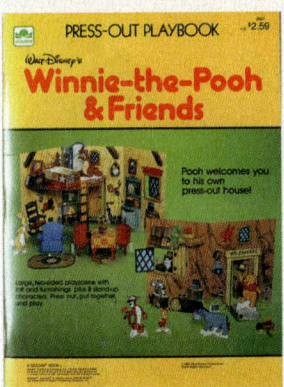

WTP-64

❑ **WTP-64. Pooh Punch-Out Books,**
1980s. Whitman. 8.75x11.25" Christmas theme "Decorate A Tree" book, 1980, six pages; and Western Publishing Co. 10x13.25" Winnie The Pooh & Friends Press-Out Play Book," 1983, eight pages. Each - **$5 $10 $18**

WTP-65

WTP-66

❑ **WTP-65. Pooh And Friends Lunch Box,**
1980s. Thermos Co. 7.5x8.5x4" deep plastic lunch box with high gloss sticker panel on front. - **$10 $20 $35**

❑ **WTP-66. "Walt Disney Television Animation Art" Portfolio,**
1000s. 12x15" portfolio envelope contains "Original Production Art/One Of A Kind Hand-Painted Cel." Image of Rabbit is 3x7.5". Mint As Issued - **$225**

WTP-67

WTP-68

❑ **WTP-67. "The New Adventures Of Winnie The Pooh Walt Disney Television Animation Art" Portfolio,**
1990s. Image of Tigger is 6x8" comes in 12x15" cardboard portfolio envelope. Mint As Issued - **$250**

❑ **WTP-68. "The New Adventures Of Winnie The Pooh Original Production Art" Sealed Portfolio,**
1990s. Walt Disney TV show. 12x15" cardboard portfolio envelope with die-cut windows on front and back contains "Original Production Art/One Of A Kind Hand Painted Cel." Envelope not shown. Near Mint - **$225**

WTP-69

❑ **WTP-69. Hockey Pooh Bean Figure,**
1999. Disney Store exclusive. With tag - **$20**

WTP-70

❑ **WTP-70. Oktoberfest Pooh Bean Figure,**
1999. 8" tall figure with tag. - **$25**

WTP-71

❑ **WTP-71. Baseball Pooh Bean Figure,**
1999. 8" tall figure with tag. - **$25**

WTP-72

❑ **WTP-72. Choo Choo Pooh Bean Figure,**
1999. 8" tall figure with tag. - **$25**

WINNIE THE POOH

WTP-73

❏ **WTP-73. Pilgrim Pooh Bean Figure,** 1999. - **$30**

WTP-74

❏ **WTP-74. Nautical Pooh Bean Figure,** 1999. 8" tall figure with tag. - **$20**

WTP-75

❏ **WTP-75. Choir Angel Pooh Bean Figure,** 2000. 8" tall figure with tag. - **$15**

WTP-76

❏ **WTP-76. Pirate Pooh Figure,** 2000. Star Bean figure with tag. - **$30**

WTP-77

❏ **WTP-77. Tigger Movie Disney Concept Art,** 2000. 10.5x5.25" spectacular watercolor concept painting of Piglet's house by Disney artist Toby Bluth. Unique, Same or Similar - **$300 $600 $1200**

WTP-78

❏ **WTP-78. "Prisoner of Love" Pooh Figure,** 2001. 8" tall figure with tag. - **$15**

WTP-79

❏ **WTP-79. "Robin Hood Pooh" Bean Figure,** 2001. 8" tall figure with tag. - **$15**

WTP-80

WTP-81

❏ **WTP-80. Winnie the Pooh Bobble,** 2004. Hand-painted doll. - **$25**

❏ **WTP-81. Tigger Bobble,** 2004. Hand-painted doll. - **$25**

WORLD WAR TWO DISNEYANA

World War Two Disneyana

Within days of the attack on Pearl Harbor, the Disney Studios shifted into a wartime footing. The studio buildings themselves would be used by the military for maintenance and storage. Meanwhile, the studio's creative push largely moved from the commercial releases to training films.

Studio artists designed over 1,200 insignias for the military, insignias which found their way onto decals, jackets, matchbooks and bomber nose cones. On the home front, Disney began releasing patriotic films. The full-length feature *Victory Through Air Power* was released in July, 1943. Based on the book by Major Alexander D. Seversky, the film was an animated history of airplanes and their wartime applications. David Hand was supervising producer and directing animators were Jack Kinney, Clyde Geronomi and James Alger. The film received an Academy Award for Best Scoring of a Dramatic Picture.

Another wartime production of note was the cartoon *Der Fuehrer's Face* (1943). The short finds Donald Duck having a nightmare that he is living in Nazi Germany. When he awakens, he is overjoyed to see the Statue of Liberty. The cartoon was directed by Jack Kinney. The title song by Oliver Wallace became a huge hit. The cartoon received an Academy Award for Best Cartoon; this was the only time Donald was so honored.

Merchandise from the war period is limited by the very nature of wartime and the material shortages that came with it. They do include books, comics, figures and poster/stamp albums.

WWD-2

WWD-3

WWD-4

WWD-5

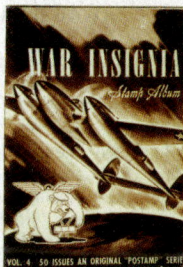
WWD-6

WWD-7

WWD-1

❏ **WWD-1. "The Flight Jacket" Naval Aviation Yearbook With Donald Duck**, 1941. Limited issue 9.25x12.25" hardcover annual with 280 pages for "The Aviation Cadet Regiments Of The U.S. Naval Air Stations at Pensicola and Jacksonville, Florida." Content is largely photos of graduates of flight classes, officers and other staff members, candid photos of cadet life and activities. Throughout are Donald Duck specialty illustrations relating to naval life, apparently done by a class member. - **$60 $135 $200**

❏ **WWD-2. "The Song Of The Seabees" Sheet Music,** 1942. Robbins Music Corp. 9.25x12.25". - **$10 $20 $40**

❏ **WWD-3. "Combat Insignia Stamps Of The United States Army & Navy Air Corps,"** 1942. Disney Studios. Volume 1. Complete set of 50 mounted stamps. 7.5x10.25". 12 pages. - **$50 $100 $150**

❏ **WWD-4. "War Insignia Stamp Album,"** 1942. Disney Studios. Volume #2. Complete set of 50 mounted stamps. 7.5x10.25". 16 pages. - **$65 $125 $200**

❏ **WWD-5. "War Insignia Stamp Album,"** 1942. Disney Studios. Volume 3. Complete set of 50 mounted stamps. 7.5x10.25". 16 pages. - **$75 $150 $250**

❏ **WWD-6. "War Insignia Stamp Album,"** 1942. Disney Studios. Volume 4. Complete set of 50 mounted stamps. 7.5x10.25". 16 pages. - **$100 $200 $300**

❏ **WWD-7. "A War Library Collection Of Combat Insignia" WWII Boxed Set,** 1942. Box is 8x10.75x.5" deep and contains four stamp albums, each 7.5x10.5". Vol. 1 has 12 pages, other three have 16 pages. Each is designed to hold 50 full color gummed stamps. Label on lid states "Designs Are By Walt Disney, Walter Lantz, Pat Sullivan, George McManus and other famous artists.
Box - **$100 $200 $300**
Set - **$290 $575 $900**

WORLD WAR TWO DISNEYANA

WWD-8

WWD-10

WWD-13

❏ **WWD-8. "Der Fuehrer's Face WWII Sheet Music And Record,**
c. 1942. Sheet is 9x12" with six pages of words and music by Oliver Wallace. This came in two versions: earlier had film's original title "Donald Duck In Nutziland" and this version is for film title change to "Der Fuehrer's Face" due to success of the song. Recording "Der Fuehrer's Face" was by multiple artists and this example is by Arthur Fields. Record is 10" diameter 78rpm on the Hit Record label made by Elite Record Manufacturers. Music - **$20 $40 $80** Record - **$15 $25 $50**

❏ **WWD-10. "Liberty" Magazine With Disney WWII Film Article,**
1943. Weekly 8.5x11.25" issue for July 31 containing two-page pictorial montage titled "Victory Through Air Power" based on Disney film of same title. Pictorial shows how long range air power could cause the defeat of the Axis during WWII and includes film scenes. Front cover art is also by Disney Studio. - **$100 $250 $400**

WWD-11

WWD-12

WWD-9

❏ **WWD-9. "Walt Disney Songs From Walt Disney Pictures" WWII Folio,**
1943. Southern Music Publishing Co. 9x12" songbook, 48 pages. Content is words and music to six songs and each also has several pages of black and white photos from film shorts or sketches. Two songs are from Saludos Amigos and the other four are from wartime productions including Der Fuehrer's Face and The Victory March. - **$65 $130 $225**

❏ **WWD-11. "Seabees" Recruitiing Booklet,**
1943. Titled "Build And Fight With The Seabees And Follow Your Trade In The Navy." 6x8.25". - **$20 $40 $80**

❏ **WWD-12. Donald Duck Ink Blotter,**
1943. Sunoco Oil 3.75x6" card picturing Donald in suit of armor driving a jeep under text "Reinforced For Ration Driving." Unused bottom margin is for local dealer imprint. - **$20 $50 $125**

❏ **WWD-13. Women's Defense Corps. Poster,**
c. 1943. Depicts centaurette as a Red Cross worker. 22x28". - **$135 $275 $500**

❏ **WWD-14. Disney Design WWII Insignia Postcard,**
c. 1943. Slightly textured 3.5x5.5" stiff paper front with design not credited but believed by Disney Studio depicting duck landing in water and wearing aviator goggles and helmet. Card also has naval wings with text "Greetings From Pensacola, Florida, Home Of U.S. Naval Air Station." - **$8 $15 $25**

WWD-15

WORLD WAR TWO DISNEYANA

❏ **WWD-15. Disney Design "Seabees" WWII Postcards,**
c. 1943. Two 3.5x5.5" wtih same "Seabees" (construction) insignia design and text "United States Naval Construction Battalions." One has added location "Camp Endicott, Davisville, R.I." The other has added text "We Build And Fight With All Our Might." Each - **$8 $12 $20**

WWD-16

❏ **WWD-16. WWII "What Is Propaganda Education Manual" Featuring Donald Duck,**
1944. Booklet is 5x7.25" with 48 pages by The American Historical Assn. from the "GI Round Table Series" of booklets which "provide material with orientation and education officers may use in conducting group discussions or forms as part of an off-duty education program." This is manual "EM-2" devoted to defining propoganda. Donald also appears on introduction page and inside back cover where he is depicted reading the newspaper "Daily Quack." - **$75 $150 $235**

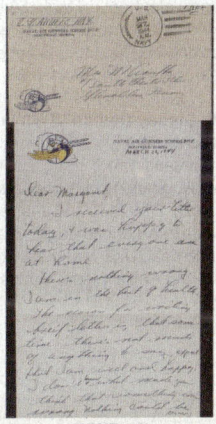

WWD-17

❏ **WWD-17. WWII Era Serviceman's Handwritten Letter With Envelope Featuring Disney Studio Designed Insignia,**
1944. Envelope is 3.5x6.5" and letter is 6x9.5". Both have printed name of "Naval Air Gunners School Hollywood, Florida" and feature insignia design of winged turret being manned by Donald Duck. Envelope has postmark of March 27, 1944. - **$20 $40 $60**

WWD-18

❏ **WWD-18. "Electrical Living,"**
1945. Westinghouse Electric Corp. 8x11" 40 pages. "Adapted From The Film 'The Dawn Of Better Living' By Walt Disney Productions." - **$25 $50 $80**

WWD-19

❏ **WWD-19. "ABC's Of Hand Tools,"**
1945. General Motors Corp. Softcover. 5.25x8". 48 pages. - **$15 $30 $50**

WWD-20

❏ **WWD-20. "The Rain Makers' Log" Seabees Book With Donald Duck,**
c. 1946. Limited issue 9.25x12.25" hardcover with 280-page history of the 133 naval construction battalion of Seabees during WWII covering years 1943-1945. Content is largely photos of staff, officers and platoons, construction activities. The standard Seabees Disney insignia design is on first few pages and a full page Seabees illustration with signature of Walt Disney. Throughout the book are 14 specialty illustrations of Donald Duck in related activities, apparently done by a member of the battalion. - **$40 $80 $135**

WWD-21

❏ **WWD-21. "Seabees" Sign,**
1948. Stiff paper 14x14" sign centered by Disney Studio-designed insignia. Bottom margin has small text "U.S. Government Printing Office." - **$30 $60 $90**

WWD-22

❏ **WWD-22. Disney Studio Designed Insignia Original Art,**
1940s. 9x11" art board sheet in original ship's wardroom metal frame. Pen and ink watercolor art depicts fish wearing a sailor cap and smoking a pipe while holding a hod carrier with torpedo (rather than bricks). Unique, Excellent - **$1000**

WORLD WAR TWO DISNEYANA

WWD-23

WWD-24

WWD-26

WWD-27

WWD-28

WWD-29

WWD-30

❏ **WWD-23. Walt Disney Studio Designed WWII Insignia Hand-Colored Photostat,**
1940s. 8x9" stiff sheet of paper with matte finish. Issued for aero logistics unit devoted to weather forecasting. - **$40 $75 $125**

❏ **WWD-24. "Seabees" Three-Dimensional Insignia Display,**
1940s. Solid rubber figure with translucent thin plastic wings on cast aluminum base inscribed "Seabees 'Can Do'." 3.5x5.7.5" tall. - **$200 $400 $750**

WWD-25

❏ **WWD-25. Disney Design WWII Insignia Glass Tumbler,**
1940s. Weighted bottom glass is 5.5" tall and designed for "503rd Parachute Infantry" depicting parachuting cat. - **$20 $35 $60**

❏ **WWD-26. "Winter Draws On/Meet The "Spandules" WWII Booklet,**
1940s. Publication is 4x6" by The Safety Education Division Flight Control Command/United States Army Air Forces, 20 pages with full page illustrations by Disney Studios of "The Spandules, A Close Relative Of The Gremlin" and text including cold weather tips for airplanes. - **$50 $100 $150**

❏ **WWD-27. "Walt Disney/Pepsi-Cola" Insignia Match Packs,**
1940s. Pepsi-Cola. A numbered series, each pack is 1x2" in red, white and blue. Unused Each - **$5 $10 $15**

❏ **WWD-28. Disney Design WWII Insignia Matchbooks,**
1940s. Pepsi-Cola. Five 1.5x2" unused matchbooks with cover designs from a numbered series with Pepsi logo on front and insignia design on back. Series number and insignia images are #7 Seagull, #9 Lion, #14 Mule, #23 Little Hiawatha, #24 Baby Pegasus. Unused Each - **$5 $10 $15**

❏ **WWD-29. Disney Design WWII Insignia Matchbooks,**
1940s. Five unused 1.5x2" matchbooks with color insignia illustrations on fronts and division names on backs. Divisions and images are 40th Bombardment Group - shotput elephant, 751st Tank Battalion - elephant on tank, 56th Pursuit Squadron - woodpecker cop, 62nd Pursuit Squadron-boxing bulldog, 46th Bombardment Group-kangaroo. Unused Each -$ **$8 $12 $20**

❏ **WWD-30. Disney Design WWII Full Color Insignia Matchbooks,**
1940s. Four unused 1.5x2" matchbooks with color insignia illustrations on fronts and division names on backs. Divisions and images are 23rd Pursuit Squadron-American eagle, Alaska Defense Force-seal, U.S. Mosquito Fleet-mosquito, 165th Field Artillery-Ape. Unused Each - **$8 $12 $20**

WWD-31

WORLD WAR TWO DISNEYANA

☐ **WWD-31. Disney Design WWII Insignia Matchbook Covers,**
1940s. Universal Match Corp. Two oversized 3x4.5" emptied and flattened covers, one for "Banana River, Florida" with designs of a generic owl plus two studio designs of Donald Duck-like character and officer pelican pushing pelican soldier. Second cover design is Jiminy Cricket as a Navy flyer for "U.S. Naval Air Station Hutchinson, Kansas." Both reverses are designed as postcards. Each - **$8 $12 $20**

☐ **WWD-34. Pluto WWII Insignia Decal,**
1940s. Columbia Supply Co. 2.75x3.25" unused decal with Disney copyright and design for "37th Recon. Co." of Pluto listening to radio signal emitted from his tail. - **$10 $20 $40**

WWD-32

☐ **WWD-32. "Seabees" Patch,**
1940s. Fabric patch 2.75" in diameter. - **$25 $45 $85**

WWD-33

☐ **WWD-33. Disney Style WWII Ship Builders Button,**
1940s. 2.25". Produced for the Massachusetts "Fore River" ship building yard during WWII and includes the slogan "Ships For 'V'ictory." No copyright or maker's name. - **$50 $100 $175**

WWD-34

WWD-35

☐ **WWD-35. Disney Insignia Cards,**
1940s. Ten different seen. Each card is 2.25x3.5". Unit or location titles and insignia characters are: 1st Defense Battalion/bulldog, Jack Air Base/Ben Ali Gator, 13th Armor Division/black cat, 751st Tank Battalion/elephant, The Flying Tigers/tiger, 57th Signal Battalion/bumblebee, 67th Bombardment Squadron/pelican, 56th Pursuit Squadron/red bird, Submarine Base /swordfish and octopus, United States Mosquito Fleet/ mosquito. Each - **$8 $12 $25**

WWD-36

☐ **WWD-36. "Seabees" WWI Disney Decal With Mailing Envelope,**
1940s. Unused envelope is 4x5" and contains 3.25x3.75" Disney-designed insignia decal for "Camp Rousseau-Port Hueneme, Calif." Envelope has "War Bonds And Stamps" cachet. Decal - **$10 $20 $30**

WWD-37

WWD-38

☐ **WWD-37. Disney Duck War Insignia Glass,**
c. 1940s. Reads "U.S. Naval Air Station/Jacksonville, Fla." 5.25" tall. - **$65 $125 $175**

☐ **WWD-38. Large Mug With Disney Designed Insignia,**
1965. 7.5" tall heavy ceramic mug with 4.25" diameter and front featuring 3x3" insignia design of a bulldog in uniform holding rifle with tied-on flag reading "3D." Marked "Copyright 1965 Walt Disney Productions." - **$15 $30 $60**

Zorro

Zorro

Don Diego de la Vega, the alter ego of Zorro ("The Fox"), was created by author Johnston McCulley in 1919. Initially, the character's stories were serialized in pulp magazines. Diego posed as a member of high society until it came time to defend the poor. At that point he donned the back cape, took up his sword and put on the famous mask to become Zorro. His black stallion was named Toronado.

After his initial appearance in the pulps, Zorro quickly crossed over into other mediums, most notably film. 1920 saw the release of *The Mark of Zorro*, starring Douglas Fairbanks. Zorro would remain a solid film property for years. In 1944 Republic serialized the character in *Zorro's Black Ship*; 1981 saw *Zorro the Gay Blade* and in 1998, Antonio Banderas played him in *The Mask of Zorro*.

Still, most people remember the Disney TV show of the fifties as a highlight in the character's career. Between 1957 and 1959, ABC aired seventy-eight episodes of the black-and-white show. Starring Guy Williams in the title role, the show was a hit, especially among kids. Joining Williams in the cast were Henry Calvin and Gene Sheldon. A highlight of almost every show was Zorro tormenting Sergeant Garcia by using his sword to slash a "Z" on rotund Garcia's pants. The authenticity of the show was enhanced by the use of outdoor locations, especially the historic San Luis Rey mission near Oceanside, California.

The show generated a large amount of merchandise including capes, masks, books and records. *Zorro* can be seen in *Four Color Comics* #882, 920, 933, 960, 976, 1003 and 1037. He inspired the character of Li'l Zorro, a lightning-fast masked toddler, in 1950s Mickey Mouse newspaper strips.

ZRO-1

❏ **ZRO-1. Television Promo Sign,**
1957. - **$80 $165 $325**

ZRO-2

❏ **ZRO-2. "Zorro ABC TV 7Up" Button,**
1957. 3". Likely used at sales conventions and with limited distribution. - **$60 $125 $225**

ZRO-3

❏ **ZRO-3. Frame Tray Puzzle,**
1957. Whitman. 11.5x14.5" photo scene of Zorro on Tornado as Sgt. Garcia and others look on. - **$10 $20 $35**

ZRO-4

ZRO-5

ZRO-6

❏ **ZRO-4. "Zorro Frame Tray Puzzle,"**
1957. Whitman. 11.5x14.5". - **$15 $25 $40**

❏ **ZRO-5. Frame Tray Puzzle,**
1957. Whitman. 11.5x14.5" vertical format photo scene of Zorro and Captain Ramone sword fighting. - **$15 $25 $40**

❏ **ZRO-6. "Zorro" Frame Tray Puzzle,**
c. 1957. Jaymar. 11x14". - **$10 $20 $30**

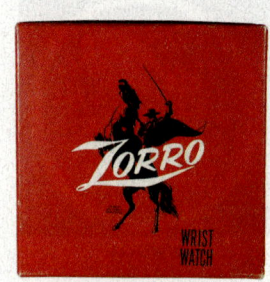

ZRO-7

ZRO-8

❏ **ZRO-7. "Zorro Wristwatch" Boxed Set,**
1957. US Time. 4.5x4.5x2" deep box contains 7/8" diameter watch. As originally packaged, watch is wrapped around a felt-covered hat still sealed by original shrink wrap. Box - **$65 $150 $325**
Watch - **$35 $65 $125**

❏ **ZRO-8. "Zorro" Stereo Reels Set,**
1957. View-Master. 4.5" square envelope containing set of three color photo reels plus related story booklet. - **$15 $30 $50**

ZORRO

ZRO-9

❏ **ZRO-9. "Zorro" Wallet,**
1957. Closed 3.25x4.25" vinyl with dual image front cover panel. Interior is brown vinyl and has snap closure for picture sleeves. - **$45 $75 $125**

ZRO-10

❏ **ZRO-10. Zorro Bracelet in Display Box,**
c. 1957. Box is rare. Bracelet - **$25 $50 $100** Box - **$50 $100 $200**

ZRO-11

❏ **ZRO-11. Zorro Bracelet in Display Box,**
c. 1957. Box is rare. Bracelet - **$25 $50 $100** Box - **$50 $100 $200**

ZRO-12

❏ **ZRO-12. Zorro Tablet With Mask,**
c. 1957. Cut-out mask on front of tablet. Scarce. - **$30 $60 $115**

ZRO-13

ZRO-14

❏ **ZRO-13. "Zorro School Tablet" Publicity Photo,**
c. 1957. Glossy photo is 8x10" picturing four different school tablet covers. - **$10 $20 $30**

❏ **ZRO-14. "Zorro" Felt Hat With Mask,**
1958. Benay Albee. 11x11.5x2.5" tall. Formed and starched felt hat with matching felt mask.
Hat - **$20 $40 $75**
Mask - **$5 $10 $15**

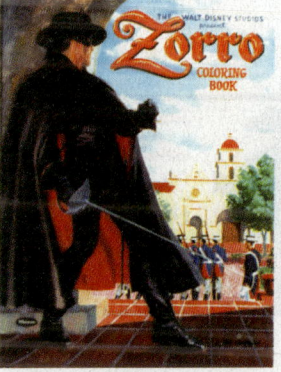

ZRO-15

❏ **ZRO-15. "Zorro Coloring Book,"**
1958. Whitman. 8.5x11". 128 pages. - **$8 $15 $35**

ZRO-16

❏ **ZRO-16. "Zorro" Punch-Out Book,**
1958. Pocket Books Inc. 7.25x13" with four pages. Unpunched - **$50 $100 $150**

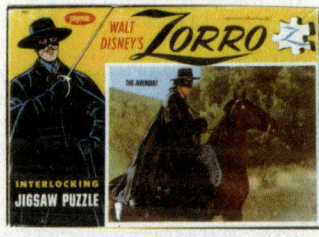

ZRO-17

❏ **ZRO-17. "Zorro" Puzzle,**
1958. Jaymar. 6.75x10x1.75" box holding puzzle titled "The Avenger." - **$10 $20 $40**

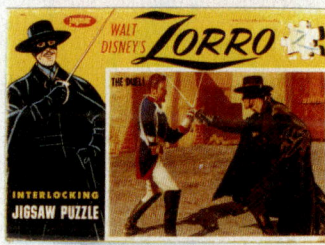

ZRO-18

❏ **ZRO-18. "Zorro" Boxed Puzzle,**
1958. Jaymar. 6.75x10x2" deep boxed jigsaw puzzle with box titled "The Duel" of sword fight between Zorro and Monastario. - **$10 $20 $40**

ZORRO

ZRO-19

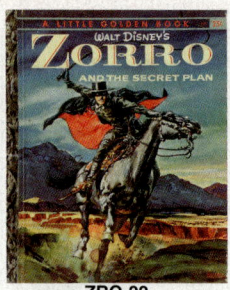

ZRO-22

ZRO-25

❏ **ZRO-25. "Zorro" View-Master Set,**
1958. Envelope is 4.5x4.5" and contains a set of 3 reels and booklet. - **$15 $35 $65**

ZRO-20

ZRO-23

ZRO-26

❏ **ZRO-19. "Zorro" Boxed Puzzle Variation,**
1958. Jaymar. 6.75x10x2" deep boxed "Triple Thick" pieces variety of jigsaw puzzles. Box lid titled "The Duel" of sword fight between Zorro and Monastario. - **$15 $25 $45**

❏ **ZRO-20. "Zorro" Gum Cards,**
1958. Topps. Set of 88 cards each 2.5x3.5" with photos on front and text on back.
Near Mint Set - **$525**
Each Card - **$1 $3 $6**

❏ **ZRO-22. "Zorro And The Secret Plan" Book,**
1958. Simon & Schuster. 6.5x8" Little Golden Book "D77" first edition printing, 24 pages. - **$8 $15 $30**

❏ **ZRO-23. "Walt Disney's Magazine,"**
1958. Vol. 3 #3. 8.25x11.25" with 44 pages. Includes four-page Zorro story with photos from the show. - **$20 $40 $75**

❏ **ZRO-26. "Zorro" Stereo View Card,**
1958. Tru-Vue. 3.75x5.5" film card "D-24" with slipcase paper sleeve. Card has full color photo scenes from the TV show. - **$8 $15 $25**

ZRO-21

ZRO-24

ZRO-27

❏ **ZRO-21. "Zorro Golden Book,"**
1958. Golden Press. 9.25x12.25" with 32 pages. - **$10 $20 $35**

❏ **ZRO-24. "Zorro Game,"**
1958. Whitman. 8.25x15.5x1.75" deep box. - **$20 $40 $75**

❏ **ZRO-27. "Zorro" View-Master Sets Including Belgian Issue,**
1958. Two sets, each 4.5x4.5" three-reel set with full color photos. Each set features the same reels. First set is "Sawyer's" issue. Envelope photo features Zorro on rearing Toronado. Second set is from Belgium, but a "GAF" issue c. late 1960s. Unusual format in which the booklet serves as the envelope with attached sleeve on inside back. 16-page booklet on glossy paper has full color photos along with text detailing scenes from each reel.
USA - **$20 $40 $80**
Belgium - **$15 $30 $50**

ZORRO

ZRO-28

❑ **ZRO-28. "Zorro" School Bag,**
c. 1958. 3.5x13x10" tall vinyl covered canvas with plastic carrying handle. Includes name/address card. - **$100 $200 $300**

ZRO-29

❑ **ZRO-29. Travel Bag,**
c. 1958. Bag is 7x12x4" deep vinyl with pair of carrying handles and zippered top. - **$40 $75 $135**

ZRO-30

❑ **ZRO-30. "Zorro" Hat With Mask,**
c. 1958. Bailey of California. Medium size felt hat with innerband having fabric tag reading "Mouseketeer Mousecap". - **$20 $40 $75**

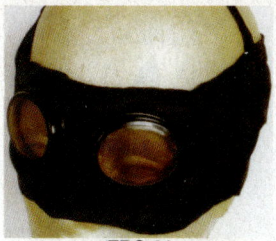

ZRO-31

❑ **ZRO-31. Secret Sight Scarf Mask,**
c. 1958. Mask is 4" wide by 20" long rayon drapery with metal eye lens frames holding plastic lenses. Designed use is a wrap-around mask with metal latch to secure it to the head. Lenses have one-way view reflective coating, easily worn away by use or aging. Mask was originally sold on an illustrated card, "Zorro Secret Sight Scarf Mask" by Westminster Products.
Card - **$12 $25 $50**
Mask - **$20 $35 $65**

ZRO-32

❑ **ZRO-32. "Zorro" Outfit On Card,**
c. 1958. M. Shimmel Sons. 7x24" display card contains four piece set. Includes linen mask, wood/fabric whip, rope lariat and plastic ring with logo. - **$150 $300 $600**

ZRO-33

❑ **ZRO-33. "Zorro Pencil Craft Color By Numbers" Boxed Set,**
c. 1958. Hassenfeld Bros. Inc. 9.75x13.25x1" deep box contains set consisting of six 6x8.25" color-by-number pictures, matching set of six larger 8x10" stiff paper "Art Prints," eight colored pencils, and a die-cut cardboard insert with instructions. - **$30 $60 $100**

ZRO-34

❑ **ZRO-34. "Zorro" Holster/Wrist Cuffs,**
1958. Daisy. Leather holster belt, pair of wrist cuffs. Originally came with Hubley "Coyote" cap pistol. Holster/Belt - **$30 $65 $100**
Cuffs - **$12 $25 $40**

ZRO-35

❑ **ZRO-35. "Zorro" Belt,**
c. 1958. Belt is 31.5" long "Top Grain Cowhide" with 1.25x2.75" enameled metal buckle. - **$15 $30 $60**

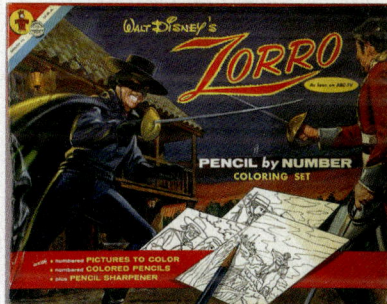

ZRO-36

❑ **ZRO-36. "Pencil By Number Coloring Set,"**
c. 1958. Transogram. 9.25x12.25x1" deep boxed original set of twelve 9x12" pictures to color, ten different colored pencils plus plastic pencil sharpener. - **$35 $70 $115**

ZORRO

ZRO-37

❏ **ZRO-37. "Zorro Spring Action Target" Set,** c. 1958 Knickerbocker. 15x21x2.5" deep box. Die-cut target is 13x19". - **$100 $200 $300**

ZRO-38

❏ **ZRO-38. "Zorro Bean Bag/Dart Game,"** c. 1958. Gardner Games. 14.5x16.5x1.5" deep boxed "2 Complete And Different Games" comprised of two 14x16" rigid cardboard targets, two 4" diameter bean bags, two plastic and rubber suction cup darts. One is designed with five large diecut holes to be used with bean bags; the other has five small point value circles to be used with darts. Box bottom has a built-in easel to keep targets upright. - **$45 $85 $150**

ZRO-39

❏ **ZRO-39. "Zorro Sun Pictures" Kit,** c. 1958. Foil envelope is 2.5x3.75" containing two film negatives, three sheets of photo paper and a cardboard frame for combined use to develop picture by natural light. Negatives are from a numbered series of Zorro images from the TV show. - **$6 $15 $25**

ZRO-40

ZRO-41

❏ **ZRO-40. "Zorro" Hat,** c. 1958. "Benay Albee." 10" diameter by 2.5" tall molded thin plastic with string chin strap adjustable by wooden knob slide. Front of crown has applied fabric patch. - **$20 $35 $60**

❏ **ZRO-41. "Zorro" Proof Sheet,** c. 1958. Proof sheet is 7.25x7.5" glossy one-sided TV show promotion. Text includes show sponsorship names of 7UP and AC Spark Plug Co. Show is described as "A Third Great Family Show From The Walt Disney Studio" with mention of top-rated Disneyland and Mickey Mouse Club shows as well. - **$30 $60 $90**

ZRO-42

❏ **ZRO-42. "Zorro Lido Toy,"** c. 1958. Unopened 3.5x4.75" cellophane bag contains plastic figure of Zorro and his horse. Near Mint Sealed **$60** Loose, No Bag - **$12 $25 $40**

ZRO-43

❏ **ZRO-43. Zorro And Toronado Figure,** c. 1958. Marx. Unmarked hard plastic companion figures, combining to 3.5x12x10.5" overall size with Zorro in place. Soft vinyl accessories are removable hat with chin strap, cape, mask, saddle, bridle, reins, sword, whip. Complete Figure - **$100 $200 $300** Box - **$35 $75 150**

ZORRO

ZRO-44

☐ **ZRO-44. "Zorro Candy" Countertop Display Box,**
c. 1958. Super Novelty Candy Co. 7x11x3" deep. - **$100 $200 $300**

ZRO-45

☐ **ZRO-45. "Zorro Candy And Toy" Box,**
c. 1958. Super Novelty Candy Co. 1x2.5x3.75" deep box only from a series with different comic panel stories on back panel. Pictured panel is "Secret Passage" adventure. Original content was candy and a miniature toy. Each - **$20 $40 $80**

ZRO-46

☐ **ZRO-46. "Zorro" Key Chain Glow-In-Dark Flashlight,**
c. 1958. .5x1x3.25" hard plastic. Hat flips up to reveal Zorro's face. - **$25 $50 $75**

ZRO-47

ZRO-48

☐ **ZRO-47. "Disneyland Rugs" Featuring Zorro,**
c. 1958. 21.5x38" fabric rug, complete with 3.5x5.5" paper label attached to the reverse. This features an illustration of Donald Duck on a flying carpet plus title "Disneyland Rugs" as well as "Made In Belgium." - **$115 $225 $350**

☐ **ZRO-48. "Zorro" Boot Mug,**
c. 1958. Soft plastic 2x6x4.75" tall. - **$15 $30 $50**

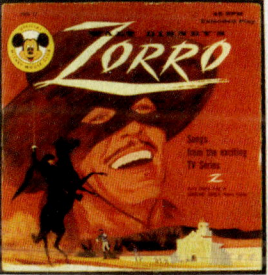

ZRO-49

☐ **ZRO-49. "Zorro" Record,**
c. 1958. Disneyland label. 7x7" glossy paper sleeve contains 45 rpm #DBR 77. - **$20 $40 $65**

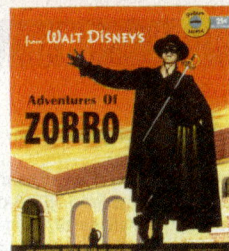

ZRO-50

☐ **ZRO-50. "Adventures Of Zorro" Record,**
c. 1958. Golden Records. 6.75x7.5" paper sleeve contains 78 rpm vinyl record. - **$10 $20 $35**

ZRO-51

☐ **ZRO-51. "Zorro" Complete Cuban Card Album,**
c. 1958. Album is 5.5x8.5" 16-page containing complete set of 100 numbered thin paper cards, all neatly mounted at appropriate spots. Cover title is "La Marca Del Zorro" with illustration of him on rearing Toronado. Back cover has large "Z" at center plus a sword and whip against background of repeated "Z." Pages have text for character cards, rest are picture cards telling a Zorro story. One of two totally different card albums by unidentified sponsor. - **$75 $150 $250**

ZRO-52

ZORRO

ZRO-53

❏ **ZRO-52. "Zorro" Complete Cuban Card Album,**
c. 1958. One of two totally different card albums by unidentified sponsor. 8.5x10.75" 16-page album containing complete set of 108 numbered thin paper cards, all neatly mounted at appropriate spots. Cover title is "Zorro El Vengador" with two action illustrations. Back cover design includes name of Zorro TV portrayer Guy Williams. Pages have text for each card, each 2.5x3". Book starts with seven character cards followed by cards featuring a Zorro story. - **$75 $150 $250**

❏ **ZRO-53. "Zorro" Button Printer's Block,**
c. 1958. 1.5x8x1" thick wood block faced with metal printing plate for production of 3.5" diameter "Zorro" name pinback. Plate has name twice in reversed block letters rather than script style. - **$10 $20 $30**

ZRO-54

❏ **ZRO-54. "Zorro" Large Dry Cleaning Bag Cut-Out Costume,**
c. 1958. White paper bag measuring 23x36". Has ad for dry cleaner plus inscription "Walt Disney Studios Present Zorro On ABC-TV." - **$20 $40 $80**

ZRO-55

❏ **ZRO-55. Zorro Elaborate Playset,**
c. 1958. Marx. 15x24x5" deep and sturdy box containing seven major character figures, 32 Mexican figures, seven saddled horses, tin lithographed building, front gate, plus more than thirty plastic accessory pieces. Playset is "Series 500" #3753. Complete - **$500 $1000 $1500**

ZRO-56

❏ **ZRO-56. "Zorro Playset" With Original Box,**
c. 1958. Marx. 15x24x4" deep. Set "Series 1000" #3754. Complete - **$550 $1100 $2000** Factory Sealed - In 2006, example sold for **$8800**

ZRO-57

ZRO-58

❏ **ZRO-57. Hand Puppet,**
c. 1958. Gund Mfg. Co. 9.5" tall figure with soft vinyl head and fabric hardcover body. Pictured example is missing original separate hat, cape and sword. Complete - **$35 $65 $115**

❏ **ZRO-58. "Zorro Dominos,"**
c. 1958. Halsam Products Co. 4.5x7.5x1" deep box contains complete set of 28 black and white dominos. - **$35 $65 $110**

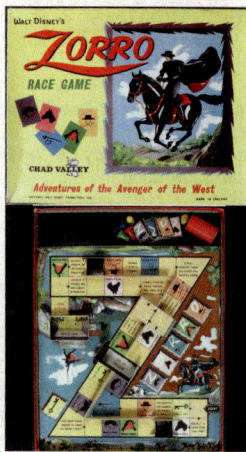
ZRO-59

ZRO-60

❏ **ZRO-59. "Zorro Race Game,"**
c. 1958. Chad Valley Of England. 12.5x16x1.75" deep boxed game with insert playing board featuring "Z" game route plus separate cardboard attachments representing walls, bridge, prison cells. Game includes a deck of cards with letters that spell out "Zorro." - **$50 $80 $140**

❏ **ZRO-60. "Zorro" Pinwheel,**
c. 1958. Wood stick is 16" mounted at top by 7" diameter diecut thin plastic flanges pinwheel with metal bell attachment. At center is separate "Zorro" mask. - **$10 $20 $40**

ZORRO

ZRO-61

❑ **ZRO-61. "Zorro/Sergeant Garcia" Two-Sided Bop Bag,**
c. 1958. Kestral Co. 16x35" inflatable vinyl picturing Zorro with sword on one side and Sgt. Garcia on opposite side with "Z" slashed into his jacket. Bag has weighted bottom to keep it upright. - **$50 $100 $150**

ZRO-62

ZRO-63

❑ **ZRO-62. "Zorro Daisy Big Smoke Rifle,"**
c. 1958. Daisy Manufacturing Co. 25" long blued metal rifle with wood stock featuring silk screened design of "Zorro" logo and image of him on rearing Toronado. Attached to trigger guard is the original string tag "Instruction Manual" which is 2.75x4.5". Includes specific instructions for this "Model 961." Manual notes you can make the rifle smoke by putting "A Few Drops Of Medium-Grade Motor Oil In Muzzle."
Rifle - **$200 $400 $600**
Tag - **$15 $30 $50**

❑ **ZRO-63. "Zorro" Sword,**
c. 1958. Marx. 25" long plastic. - **$25 $50 $100**

ZRO-64

❑ **ZRO-64. "Zorro Target Shoot" Set,**
c. 1958. Lido. 9x10x1.5" deep box with cellophane display window over set consisting of 6" long hard plastic "Pop Gun" with spring-loaded firing mechanism, four corks, set of four different 3.5" tall hard plastic targets of different Spanish soldier. Target bases are domed so that the figures wobble when hit but do not tip over. - **$40 $85 $150**

ZRO-65

❑ **ZRO-65. "Zorro Target Set,"**
c. 1958. Lido. 8x13" display card. Card holds a pair of 4.5" long hard plastic guns, one silver and one gold, each with matching plastic dart. There is a 7.5x8" tin litho bullseye target featuring large "Z" and Zorro on rearing Toronado. Cardboard easel on reverse.
Bagged - **$50 $100 $175**
Target Only - **$20 $40 $75**

ZRO-66

ZRO-67

❑ **ZRO-66. "TV Radio Magazine" With Zorro,**
1959. TV Guide-type regional weekly publication is 5.25x7.25" by "New York Herald Tribune" for January 18-24. Cover article is titled "What's Behind The Man Behind The Mask Of Zorro?"
$20 $40 $65

❑ **ZRO-67. Zorro Outfit On Cardboard Hanger Frame,**
c. 1959. "Lindsay." 16x37" diecut cardboard upper torso Zorro modeling two-piece outfit held in place by scattered original staples as originally displayed. Near Mint Carded - **$165** Complete, No Card - **$20 $40 $75**

ZRO-68

ZRO-69

❑ **ZRO-68. "Zorro" Gloves,**
1950s. Wells Lamont. Each glove is 4.5x7.5" with vinyl cuffs and fabric fingers with "Disneyland" tag. Pair - **$25 $50 $125**

❑ **ZRO-69. "Zorro" Publicity Photo,**
1950s. Glossy 8x10". - **$25 $50 $75**

ZORRO

ZRO-70

❏ **ZRO-70. "Zorro" Standup,**
1950s. Diecut thin cardboard 6x8.25". Unmarked. - **$35 $65 $125**

ZRO-71

❏ **ZRO-71. "Zorro" Ceramic Figurine With Tag,**
1950s. Enesco. 2x4.5x5.75" tall. Figure - **$40 $75 $135**
Tag - **$5 $10 $20**

ZRO-72

❏ **ZRO-72. "Zorro" Figural Ceramic Trinket Dish,**
1950s. Enesco. 9" tall with cardboard string tag and sticker under base. His sword is metal.
Figure - **$100 $200 $300**
Tag - **$5 $10 $20**

ZRO-73

❏ **ZRO-73. "Zorro" Argentina Gum Card Pack,**
1950s. Waxed wrapper is 2.5x3.5" and contains pair of 2.5x3.5" thin glossy pictures with blank backs. Comes with cardboard sheet with two punchouts. - **$15 $30 $60**

ZRO-74

❏ **ZRO-74. "Zorro" Cartoon Portrait Button,**
1950s. 1" litho. - **$15 $30 $50**

ZRO-75

❏ **ZRO-75. "Zorro" Large Litho. Tab,**
1950s. 1.5" tab. - **$15 $30 $50**

ZRO-76

❏ **ZRO-76. "Zorro" TV Channel Promotion Tab,**
1950s. 1.5" lithographed tin plus top stem. Text includes channel number "6," call letters "WDSU-TV" and program time of "5:30 PM Saturday." From New Orleans. - **$25 $50 $75**

ZRO-77

ZRO-78

❏ **ZRO-77. "Zorro" Boxed Wallet,**
1950s. Coyden. 3.5x4.25" vinyl wallet in white box with clear plastic cover. Box - **$5 $10 $15**
Wallet - **$30 $55 $115**

❏ **ZRO-78. "Zorro Costume,"**
1950s. Ben Cooper. 8.25x11x3.5" deep box contains mask, cape and body suit. Boxed - **$25 $50 $90** Loose - **$15 $35 $70**

ZORRO

ZRO-79

ZRO-80

ZRO-83

❏ **ZRO-82. "Zorro" Hat,**
1950s. Starched straw hat measures 12x12.5x3" tall with chin strap and synthetic fabric "Zorro" patch. - **$25 $50 $90**

❏ **ZRO-83. Zorro Figure,**
1950s. Zorro figure is 3.5" tall and horse is 5" long, both in soft plastic. Possibly by Lido, but slightly larger than their standard figure. - **$15 $30 $60**

ZRO-85

❏ **ZRO-85. "The Sign Of Zorro" Movie Poster,**
1960. 27x41" one-sheet. Starred Guy Williams as Zorro and film was "Adapted From The Original Television Series." Text at top reads "Flashings Swords...High Adventure." - **$125 $225 $350**

❏ **ZRO-79. "Zorro Target,"**
1950s. Lido. 7.5x11.75" tin litho. - **$30 $60 $100**

❏ **ZRO-80. "Zorro Magic Slate,"**
1950s. Watkins-Strathmore Co. 10.5x16.5" thick cardboard. - **$20 $40 $70**

ZRO-81

❏ **ZRO-81. "Zorro Pencil Case,"**
1950s. Hassenfeld Brothers Inc. 4x8x1" deep cardboard with paper label on lid. - **$40 $75 $125**

ZRO-84

❏ **ZRO-84. "The Sign Of Zorro" Movie Poster,**
1960. Poster is 14x36" stiff paper insert for original 1960 release "Adapted From The Original Television Series" starring Guy Williams as Zorro. - **$150 $300 $450**

ZRO-86

❏ **ZRO-86. "The Sign Of Zorro" Guy Williams Signed Publicity Still,**
1960. 8x10" glossy still boldly signed by Guy Williams. - **$100 $250 $500**

ZRO-82

1011

ZORRO

ZRO-87

ZRO-89

ZRO-91

ZRO-92

❑ **ZRO-87. Child's Dish And Cup Set,**
c. 1960. "Sun-Valley Melmac." Three-piece hard plastic 7" diameter plate, 5" diameter bowl, 3.5" tall cup. Set - **$15 $30 $60**

❑ **ZRO-89. "Zorro Frame-Tray Puzzle,"**
1965. Whitman. 11.25x14.5". - **$10 $20 $35**

ZRO-88

ZRO-90

❑ **ZRO-88. "Zorro Activity Box,"**
1965. Whitman. 9x11.75x1.75" deep box contains cardboard punch-outs, large paper play mat and box of crayons. - **$40 $75 $150**

❑ **ZRO-90. "Zorro" Model Kit,**
1965-1966. Aurora. 7x13x2.25" deep box. - **$75 $150 $250**

❑ **ZRO-91. "Zorro Game,"**
1965. Whitman. 8x15.5x1" deep boxed game featuring 15.5" square playing board with Z-shaped game route at center surrounded by action illustrations. Other parts are set of picture/individual letter cards plus generic plastic markers. Object is to obtain a set of cards spelling out the name "Zorro." - **$35 $55 $100**

❑ **ZRO-92. "Zorro" Lunch Box,**
1966. Aladdin. 7x8x4" deep embossed metal. The "red sky" version lunch box and the second of two done for Zorro by Aladdin. The first version from 1958 has red, blue and yellow sky.
First - **$100 $225 $350**
Second - **$125 $250 $375**

ZORRO

ZRO-93

◻ **ZRO-93. "Zorro" First Issue Comic Book,**
1966. Gold Key. 1966 reprint of 1957 Dell comic. - **$9 $27 $120**

ZRO-94

◻ **ZRO-94. "Zorro Game,"**
1966. Parker Brothers. 9x17x1.5" boxed game featuring 16.5" square playing board with spinner plus five different illustrated Zorro character cards and four painted metal playing pieces of horseback rider meant to depict Zorro. - **$20 $35 $70**

ZRO-95

ZRO-96

◻ **ZRO-95. Zorro Ceramic Figurine,**
1960s. Enesco. 2.5x3.5x7" tall with metal sword. - **$45 $80 $135**

◻ **ZRO-96. "Zorro" Figurine,**
1960s. Enesco. 2.25x3.5x7.25" tall painted and glazed ceramic from a series of different Zorro figurines by this maker. Underside is marked "WDE 140" with maker's sticker. Complete with original removable metal sword, quite often missing. - **$45 $80 $135**

ZRO-97

◻ **ZRO-97. Zorro Pez Dispenser,**
1960s. Variety that is 4.25" tall with mask that reaches around back of head, dips up over nose, has hatband. - **$40 $80 $135**

ZRO-98

◻ **ZRO-98. "Zorro" Wrist Light,**
1960s. Bantamlite. 2.25" diameter by .5" deep hard plastic light unit with plastic band watch strap. - **$20 $45 $85**

ZRO-99

ZORRO

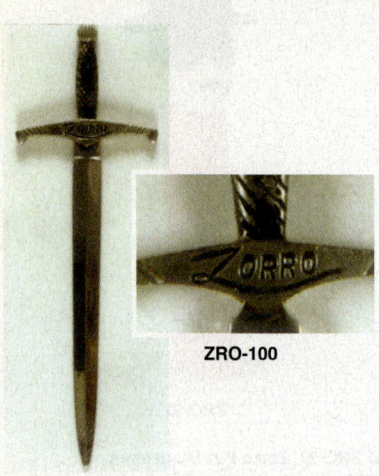

ZRO-100

ZRO-102

ZOR-104

ZRO-101

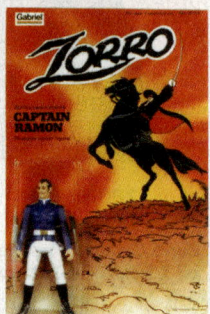

ZRO-103

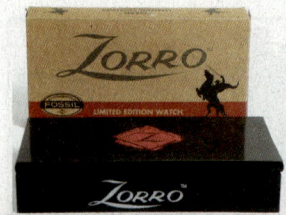

ZRO-105

❑ **ZRO-99. Figural Bookends,**
1960s. Enesco. Set of two 2x4x6" tall painted and glazed ceramics, each with underside flat metal plate. Simulated stone bases each have "Z" initial. Figures differ by one with a whip and one without. Each has foil sticker and set comes with cardboard string tag. Tag - **$5 $10 $20** Pair - **$85 $135 $225**

❑ **ZRO-100. "Zorro" Letter Opener,**
1960s. Dexter Mfg. Co. 5.5" long cast metal designed like a sword. - **$20 $40 $75**

❑ **ZRO-101. "Zorro" Pen,**
1960s. Pen is 5" long hard plastic. - **$20 $35 $60**

❑ **ZRO-102. Zorro Wind-Up,**
1975. Durham Industries Inc. 2x4x4.25" tall hard plastic with built-in key. - **$20 $40 $65**

❑ **ZRO-103. "Zorro" And "Captain Ramone" Action Figures,**
1981. Gabriel/Filmation Associates. Two 6x9" display blister cards, each holding 3.75" tall painted hard plastic poseable figure with accessory weapon piece. Carded, Each - **$6 $12 $20**

❑ **ZOR-104. Zorro Hand Puppet,**
1987. High quality from France. - **$25 $50 $90**

❑ **ZRO-105. "Zorro" Limited Edition Watch,**
1990. Fossil. Double-packaged wristwatch from an edition of 10,000 copyright by Zorro Productions Inc. 4x8x1.5" deep outer cardboard illustrated cover holds same-sized wooden display case with hinged lid. 1.5" diameter watch has silvered metal case and dial face silhouette image of Zorro on rearing Toronado. Back of case has incised issue serial number. Leather straps and is accompanied by 2" diameter pewter replica of Zorro's hat which serves as an ink stamp for "Z" initial. Near Mint As Issued - **$185**

BIBLIOGRAPHY

Atkins, Larry. *Pictorial Price Guide to Metal Lunch Boxes & Thermoses.* Gas City, IN: L-W Book Sales, 1999.

Atkins, Larry. *Pictorial Price Guide to Vinyl & Plastic Lunch Boxes & Thermoses.* Gas City, IN: L-W Book Sales, 1992.

Bertoia, Bill. *Bertoia Auctions Catalogue October 13-14.* Vineland, NJ: 2000.

Blumberg, Arnold T. *The Big Big Little Book Book, An Overstreet Photo-Journal Guide.* Timonium, MD: Gemstone Publishing, 2004.

Brown, Hy. *Comic Character Timepieces: Seven Decades of Memories.* West Chester, PA: Schiffer Publishing, Ltd., 1992.

Farber, R.H. Time to Rewind - A Guide to Collecting Disneyana Ingersoll Wrist Watched 1933-1939. No Publisher Listed (ISBN 0-9736226-0-1) 2004.

Frick, Devin and Hodge, Tamara. *Disneyana Collector Guide To California Pottery.* Orange County, California: Park Place Press, 1998.

Grant, John. *Encyclopedia of Walt Disney Animated Characters.* New York, NY: Harper & Row, 1987.

Hake, Ted. *Hake's Americana & Collectibles Auction Catalogues Nos. 140-190.* York, PA: 1996-2005.

Hake, Ted. *Hake's Price Guide To Character Toys. 6th Edition.* Timonium, MD: Gemstone Publishing, Inc., 2006.

Hake, Ted and King, Russell. *Collectible Pin-Back Buttons 1896-1986.* Radnor, PA: Wallace-Homestead, 1991.

Heide, Robert and Gilman, John. *Mickey The Evolution, The Legend, The Phenomenon.* New York, NY: Disney Editions, 2001.

Lesser, Robert. *A Celebration of Comic Art and Memorabilia.* New York, NY: Hawthorn Books, 1975.

Levin, Marshall N. and Hake, Theodore L. *Buttons In Sets 1896-1972.* York, PA: Hake's Americana & Collectibles Press, 1984.

Maltin, Leonard. *The Disney Films, Fourth Edition.* New York, NY: Disney Editions, 2000.

Munsey, Cecil. *Disneyana.* New York, NY: Hawthorn Books, 1974.

Murray, John J. and Fox, Bruce R. *The Fisher-Price 1931-1963 Toy Book, 3rd Edition.* Florence, AL: Books Americana, 1996.

Pinsky, Maxine A. *Marx Toys: Robots, Space, Comic, Disney & TV Characters.* Atglen, PA: Schiffer Publishing, 1996.

Overstreet, Robert M. *The Overstreet Comic Book Price Guide, 37th Edition.* Timonium, MD: Gemstone Publishing, Inc., 2007.

Rawls, Walton. *Disney Dons Dogtags: The Best of Disney Military Insignia from World War II.* New York, NY: Abbeville, 1992.

Shine, Bernard C. *Mickey Mouse Memorabilia: The Vintage Years 1928-1938.* New York, NY: Harry N. Abrams, 1986.

Smith, Dave. *Disney A to Z: The Updated Official Encyclopedia.* New York, NY: Hyperion, 1998.

Storm, J.P. and Dressler, Mario. *Walt Disney In Deutschland 1927-1945.* Film Museum Potsdam Exhibition Catalogue. Berlin: Henschel Verlag GmbH, 1991.

Thomas, Bob. *Disney's Art of Animation: From Mickey Mouse to Hercules.* New York, NY: Hyperion, 1997.

Thomas, Frank and Ollie Johnston. *The Illusion of Life: Disney Animation.* New York, NY: Hyperion, 1981.

United Artists Corporation. *Exhibitors Complete Campaign for Walt Disney's Mickey Mouse and Silly Symphonies.* New York, NY: United Artists Corporation, 1932.

APPENDIX: DISNEY BOOKS

The following listed books from 1930 through 1950 were produced by Walt Disney Productions and predecessor companies. Included are standard formatted books, Big Little Books, Better Little Books, Fast Action Books, but not comic books. Many titles published in the United States were also distributed in other English-speaking countries and vice versa. This data comes from the Walt Disney Archives and first appeared as an alphabetical title list in *Disneyana* by Cecil Munsey published by Hawthorn Books, 1974. We have re-arranged the list by year of issue in alphabetical order and, in the case of duplicate titles, with lowest to highest page count.

TITLE	PUBLISHER	DATE	REMARKS
Mickey Mouse Book	New York: Bibo and Lang	1930	15 pp. Story and game by Bobette Bibo. On title page: "Hello Everybody."
The Adventures of Mickey Mouse	Philadelphia: McKay	1931	Book 1: 32 pp.
Mickey Mouse	Philadelphia: McKay	1931	48 pp. Book No. 1
Mickey Mouse Movie Stories	Philadelphia: McKay	1931	190 pp.
Mickey Mouse Story Book	Philadelphia: McKay	1931	62 pp. Also in paperback.
The Adventures of Mickey Mouse	Philadelphia: McKay	1932	Book 2: 32 pp.
Mickey Mouse	Philadelphia: McKay	1932	48 pp. Book No. 2
Mickey Mouse	Racine: Whitman	1933	30 pp. No. 948
Mickey Mouse	Philadelphia: McKay	1933	48 pp. Book No. 3
Mickey Mouse	Racine: Whitman	1933	316 pp. Big Little Book No. 717
Mickey Mouse in King Arthur's Court	New York: Blue Ribbon Books	1933	48 pp.
Mickey Mouse Sails for Treasure Island	Racine: Whitman	1933	314 pp. Big Little Book No. 750
Mickey Mouse the Mail Pilot	Racine: Whitman	1933	286 pp. Premium for American Oil Company.
Mickey Mouse the Mail Pilot	Racine: Whitman	1933	296 pp. Big Little Book No. 731
The Pop-Up Mickey Mouse	New York: Blue Ribbon Books	1933	24 pp.
The Pop-Up Minnie Mouse	New York: Blue Ribbon Books	1933	29 pp.
The Pop-Up Silly Symphonies, Containing Babes in the Woods and King Neptune	New York: Blue Ribbon Books	1933	48 pp.
Three Little Pigs	New York: Blue Ribbon Books	1933	62 pp.

APPENDIX: DISNEY BOOKS

TITLE	PUBLISHER	DATE	REMARKS
Who's Afraid of the Big Bad Wolf? Three Little Pigs	Philadelphia: McKay	1933	31 pp.
The Big Bad Wolf and Little Red Riding Hood	New York: Blue Ribbon Books	1934	60 pp.
Little Red Riding Hood and the Big Bad Wolf	Philadelphia: McKay	1934	32 pp.
Mickey and Minnie at the Carnival	Racine: Whitman	1934	38 pp. "Mickey Mouse at the Carnival" on the cover. Wee Little Book Set No. 512.
Mickey Mouse	Philadelphia: McKay	1934	48 pp. Book No. 4
Mickey Mouse and Tanglefoot	Racine: Whitman	1934	40 pp. Wee Little Books, Set No. 512
Mickey Mouse in Blaggard Castle	Racine: Whitman	1934	314 pp. Big Little Book No. 726
Mickey Mouse in Giantland	Philadelphia: McKay	1934	45 pp.
Mickey Mouse in Ye Olden Days, with "Pop-Up Picture"	New York: Blue Ribbon Books	1934	60 pp.
Mickey Mouse Movie Stories	Philadelphia: McKay	1934	196 pp. Book No. 2
Mickey Mouse Presents Walt Disney's Silly Symphonies	Racine: Whitman	1934	234 pp. Big Little Book No. 756
Mickey Mouse Stories	Philadelphia: McKay	1934	62 pp. Book No. 2 (For Book No. 1 see *Mickey Mouse Story Book*.) Also a paperback.
Mickey Mouse the Detective	Racine: Whitman	1934	294 pp. Big Little Book No. 1139
Mickey Mouse Waddle Book	New York: Blue Ribbon Books	1934	33 pp.
Mickey Mouse Will Not Quit	Racine: Whitman	1934	38 pp. Wee Little Books, Set No. 512
Mickey Mouse Wins the Race	Racine: Whitman	1934	38 pp. Wee Little Books, Set No. 512
Mickey Mouse's Misfortune	Racine: Whitman	1934	38 pp. Wee Little Books, Set No. 512
Mickey Mouse's Uphill Fight	Racine: Whitman	1934	38 pp. Wee Little Books, Set No. 512
Peculiar Penguins	Philadelphia: McKay	1934	45 pp.
The Wise Little Hen	Philadelphia: McKay	1934	48 pp.

APPENDIX: DISNEY BOOKS

Donald Duck	Racine: Whitman	1935	14 pp. No. 978. First Donald Duck Book.
Mickey Mouse and Bobo the Elephant	Racine: Whitman	1935	424 pp. Big Little Book No. 1160
Mickey Mouse and Minnie March to Macy's	New York: R.H. Macy	1935	142 pp.
Mickey Mouse and the Bat Bandit	Racine: Whitman	1935	426 pp. Big Little Book No. 1153
Mickey Mouse and the Magic Carpet	New York: Kay Kamen	1935	144 pp.
Mickey Mouse Sails for Treasure Island	Racine: Whitman	1935	192 pp. Premium for Kolynos Dental Cream.
The Robber Kitten	Racine: Whitman	1935	40 pp.
The Robber Kitten	Philadelphia: McKay	1935	46 pp.
The Story of Mickey Mouse and the Smugglers	Racine: Whitman	1935	316 pp. Big Big Book No. 4062. Also a revised edition with a new cover, Mickey and Minnie at the wheel of a boat.
The Three Orphan Kittens	Racine: Whitman	1935	40 pp.
The Three Orphan Kittens	Philadelphia: McKay	1935	46 pp.
The Tortoise and the Hare	Racine: Whitman	1935	40 pp.
The Tortoise and the Hare	Philadelphia: McKay	1935	48 pp.
The Wise Little Hen	Racine: Whitman	1935	40 pp.
ABC Mickey Mouse Alphabet Book	Racine: Whitman	1936	30 pp. No. 936. "A Mickey Mouse Alphabet Book from A to Z" on cover.
Donald Duck	New York: Grosset and Dunlap	1936	33 pp.
Elmer Elephant	Philadelphia: McKay	1936	46 pp.
Forty Big Pages of Mickey Mouse	Racine: Whitman	1936	40 pp. No. 945
Mickey Mouse	Racine: Whitman	1936	29 pp. Stand-Out Book No. 841
A Mickey Mouse ABC Story	Racine: Whitman	1936	31 pp. No. 921
Mickey Mouse and His Friends	Racine: Whitman	1936	12 pp. Linen-like No. 904
Mickey Mouse and His Horse Tanglefoot	Philadelphia: McKay	1936	60 pp.
Mickey Mouse and Pluto	Racine: Whitman	1936	66 pp. No. 2028

APPENDIX: DISNEY BOOKS

Mickey Mouse and Pluto the Racer	Racine: Whitman	1936	424 pp. Big Little Book No. 1128
Mickey Mouse and the Sacred Jewel	Racine: Whitman	1936	424 pp. Big Little Book No. 1187
Mickey Mouse Crusoe	Racine: Whitman	1936	70 pp. No. 711
The Mickey Mouse Fire Brigade	Racine: Whitman	1936	66 pp. No. 2029
Mickey Mouse in Pigmyland	Racine: Whitman	1936	70 pp. No. 711
Mickey Mouse Recipe Scrap Book	Los Angeles: Walt Disney Enterprises	1936	52 pp.
Silly Symphonies: Stories Featuring Donald Duck, Peter Pig, Benny Bird and Bucky Bug	Racine: Whitman	1936	423 pp. Big Little Book No. 1111
The Country Cousin	Philadelphia: McKay	1937	20 pp.
Donald Duck and His Friends	Racine: Whitman	1937	45 pp. Donald Duck Story Book No. 5050
Donald Duck Has His Ups and Downs	Racine: Whitman	1937	16 pp. No. 1077
Donald Duck Has His Ups and Downs	Racine: Whitman	1937	24 pp. Picture Story Book No. 883
The Golden Touch	Racine: Whitman	1937	212 pp.
Hiawatha	Philadelphia: McKay	1937	20 pp.
Mickey Mouse	Racine: Whitman	1937	12 pp. Linen-like No. 973
Mickey Mouse and Donald Duck Gag Book	Racine: Whitman	1937	48 pp. No. 886
Mickey Mouse and His Friends	New York: Nelson	1937	102 pp. By Walt Disney and Jean Ayer.
Mickey Mouse and His Friends Wait for the Country Fair	Racine: Whitman	1937	16 pp. No. 1077
Mickey Mouse and His Friends Wait for the Country Fair	Racine: Whitman	1937	24 pp. Picture Story Book No. 883
Mickey Mouse and Mother Goose	Racine: Whitman	1937	136 pp. No. 4011
Mickey Mouse, Donald Duck and All Their Pals	Racine: Whitman	1937	40 pp. No. 887
Mickey Mouse Has a Busy Day	Racine: Whitman	1937	16 pp. No. 1077
Mickey Mouse Has a Busy Day	Racine: Whitman	1937	24 pp. No. 883
Mickey Mouse Runs His Own Newspaper	Racine: Whitman	1937	424 pp. Big Little Book No. 1409. Also abridged edition of 292 pp.

APPENDIX: DISNEY BOOKS

Mickey's Magic Hat and the Cookie Carnival	Racine: Whitman	1937	24 pp. No. 883
Mickey's Magic Hat; Cookie Carnival	Racine: Whitman	1937	16 pp. No. 1077
Nursery Stories from Walt Disney's Silly Symphony	Racine: Whitman	1937	212 pp.
Pluto and the Puppy	New York: Grosset and Dunlap	1937	36 pp.
Pluto the Pup	Racine: Whitman	1937	12 pp. No. 894
Silly Symphony Featuring Donald Duck	Racine: Whitman	1937	424 pp. Big Little Book No. 1169
Silly Symphony, Featuring Donald Duck and His Misadventures	Racine: Whitman	1937	424 pp. Big Little Book No. 1441
Snow White and the Seven Dwarfs	Philadelphia: McKay	1937	41 pp.
Snow White and the Seven Dwarfs	New York: Harper	1937	79 pp. No. 1
Snow White and the Seven Dwarfs	New York: Grosset and Dunlap	1937	79 pp. Reprint No. 1. Adapted from Grimm's Fairy Tales.
Three Little Wolves	Racine: Whitman	1937	16 pp. Walt Disney Picture Book No. 895
Walt Disney Annual	Racine: Whitman	1937	123 pp. No. 4001
The Wise Little Hen	Racine: Whitman	1937	12 pp. Walt Disney Picture Book No. 888
Animals from Snow White and the Seven Dwarfs	Racine: Whitman	1938	11 pp. No. 922
Brave Little Tailor	Racine: Whitman	1938	24 pp. No. 972
Clock Cleaners	Racine: Whitman	1938	12 pp. Walt Disney Picture Book No. 947. Linen-like.
Donald Duck and the Ducklings	New York: Dell	1938	191 pp. Fast-Action
Donald Duck Hunting for Trouble	Racine: Whitman	1938	424 pp. Better Little Book No. 1478
Dopey: He Don't Talk None	Racine: Whitman	1938	11 pp. No. 955
Edgar Bergen's Charlie McCarthy Meets Walt Disney's Snow White	Racine: Whitman	1938	23 pp. No. 986
Elmer Elephant	Racine: Whitman	1938	12 pp. No. 948. Linen-like.

APPENDIX: DISNEY BOOKS

The Famous Movie Story of Walt Disney's Snow White and the Seven Dwarfs	New York: K.K. Publications	1938	15 pp.
Famous Seven Dwarfs	Racine: Whitman	1938	12 pp. No. 933. Linen-like.
Famous Seven Dwarfs	Racine: Whitman	1938	20 pp. No. 944
Ferdinand the Bull	Racine: Whitman	1938	12 pp. Linen-like No. 903
Ferdinand the Bull	New York: Dell	1938	16 pp.
Ferdinand the Bull	Racine: Whitman	1938	31 pp. No. 842
Forest Friends from Snow White	New York: Grosset and Dunlap	1938	28 pp.
Hiawatha	Racine: Whitman	1938	12 pp. Walt Disney Picture Book No. 924. Linen-like.
A Mickey Mouse Alphabet ABC	Racine: Whitman	1938	16 pp. No. 889
Mickey Mouse; Goofy and Mickey's Nephews	New York: Dell	1938	191 pp. Fast-Action
Mickey Mouse Has a Party	Racine: Whitman	1938	48 pp. No. 798. A School Reader.
Mickey Mouse in Numberland	Racine: Whitman	1938	96 pp. No. 745. "A Very Easy Arithmetic Work Book."
Mickey Mouse in the Race for Riches	Racine: Whitman	1938	424 pp. Better Little Book No. 1476
Mickey Mouse the Boat Builder	New York: Grosset and Dunlap	1938	28 pp. Story Time Book
Mickey Mouse the Sheriff of Nugget Gulch	New York: Dell	1938	192 pp. Fast-Action
Pluto the Pup	Racine: Whitman	1938	424 pp. Big Little Book No. 1467
Snow White and the Seven Dwarfs	Racine: Whitman	1938	11 pp. No. 927
Snow White and the Seven Dwarfs	Racine: Whitman	1938	16 pp. Linen-like No. 925
Snow White and the Seven Dwarfs	New York: Grosset and Dunlap	1938	38 pp.
Snow White and the Seven Dwarfs	Racine: Whitman	1938	63 pp. No. 777
Snow White and the Seven Dwarfs	Racine: Whitman	1938	94 pp. No. 714
Story of Clarabelle Cow	Racine: Whitman	1938	92 pp. No. 1066
Story of Dippy the Goof	Racine: Whitman	1938	92 pp. No. 1066
A Story of Doc	Racine: Whitman	1938	24 pp. Seven Dwarf Books No. 1044
Story of Donald Duck	Racine: Whitman	1938	92 pp. No. 1066

APPENDIX: DISNEY BOOKS

A Story of Dopey	Racine: Whitman	1938	24 pp. Seven Dwarf Books No. 1044
A Story of Grumpy	Racine: Whitman	1938	24 pp. Seven Dwarf Books No. 1044
A Story of Happy	Racine: Whitman	1938	24 pp. Seven Dwarf Books No. 1044
Story of Mickey Mouse	Racine: Whitman	1938	92 pp. No. 1066
Story of Minnie Mouse	Racine: Whitman	1938	92 pp. No. 1066
Story of Pluto the Pup	Racine: Whitman	1938	92 pp. No. 1066
A Story of Sleepy	Racine: Whitman	1938	24 pp. Seven Dwarf Books No. 1044
A Story of Sneezy	Racine: Whitman	1938	24 pp. Seven Dwarf Books No. 1044
A Story of Snow White	Racine: Whitman	1938	24 pp. Seven Dwarf Books No. 1044
The Story of Snow White and the Seven Dwarfs	Racine: Whitman	1938	280 pp. Big Little Book No. 1460. On cover: Snow White and The Seven Dwarfs.
Toby Tortoise and the Hare	Racine: Whitman	1938	10 pp. Walt Disney Picture Book No. 928
Brave Little Tailor	Racine: Whitman	1939	12 pp. Penny Book No. 1145
Brave Little Tailor	Racine: Whitman	1939	64 pp. No. 1058
Donald Duck and His Friends	Boston: Heath	1939	102 pp. By Jean Ayer.
Donald Duck's Cousin Gus	Racine: Whitman	1939	12 pp. Penny Book No. 1145
Donald Forgets to Duck	Racine: Whitman	1939	424 pp. Better Little Book No. 1434
Donald's Better Self	Racine: Whitman	1939	12 pp. Penny Book No. 1145
Donald's Lucky Day	Racine: Whitman	1939	12 pp. Penny Book No. 1145
Donald's Lucky Day	Racine: Whitman	1939	20 pp. No. 897
Farmyard Symphony	Racine: Whitman	1939	12 pp. Penny Book No. 1145
The Farmyard Symphony	Racine: Whitman	1939	64 pp. No. 1058
Goofy and Wilbur	Racine: Whitman	1939	12 pp. Penny Book No. 1145
Little Pig's Picnic and Other Stories	Boston: Heath	1939	102 pp. By Margaret Wise Brown.
Mickey Mouse and the Pirate Submarine	Racine: Whitman	1939	424 pp. Big Little Book No. 1463
Mickey Never Fails	Boston: Heath	1939	102 pp. By Robin Palmer.
Mickey's Gold Rush	Racine: Whitman	1939	12 pp. Penny Book No. 1145

APPENDIX: DISNEY BOOKS

Mother Pluto	Racine: Whitman	1939	64 pp. No. 1058
Pinocchio	New York: Dell	1939	16 pp.
Pinocchio's Christmas Party	New York: Cramer-Tobias-Meyer	1939	16 pp. Christmas give-away.
The Practical Pig	Racine: Whitman	1939	12 pp. Penny Book No. 1145
The Practical Pig	Racine: Whitman	1939	64 pp. No. 1058
School Days in Disneyville	Boston: Heath	1939	102 pp. Told by Caroline D. Emerson.
Society Dog Show	Racine: Whitman	1939	12 pp. Penny Book No. 1145
Such a Life, Says Donald Duck	Racine: Whitman	1939	424 pp. Better Little Book No. 1404
Timid Elmer	Racine: Whitman	1939	64 pp. No. 1058
The Ugly Duckling	Racine: Whitman	1939	12 pp. Penny Book No. 1145
The Ugly Duckling	Philadelphia: Lippincott	1939	40 pp. Adapted from Hans Christian Andersen.
The Ugly Duckling	Racine: Whitman	1939	64 pp. No. 1058
Walt Disney Tells the Story of Pinocchio	Racine: Whitman	1939	144 pp. No. 556
Walt Disney's Version of Pinocchio	New York: Random House	1939	41 numbered leaves including 30 plates. 100 copies printed.
Walt Disney's Version of Pinocchio	New York: Grosset and Dunlap	1939	48 pp.
Walt Disney's Version of Pinocchio	Racine: Whitman	1939	48 pp.
Walt Disney's Version of Pinocchio	New York: Random House	1939	76 pp.
Walt Disney's Version of Pinocchio	Racine: Whitman	1939	95 pp. No. 709. Also revised cover.
Ave Maria: An Interpretation from Fantasia	New York: Random House	1940	36 pp. Inspired by the music of Franz Schubert. Lyrics by Rachel Field.
The Blue Fairy	Racine: Whitman	1940	24 pp. No. 1059. A story paint book from box of six Pinocchio books for reading, coloring and playing.
Dance of the Hours, from Fantasia	New York: Harper	1940	36 pp.
Donald Duck and His Nephews	Boston: Heath	1940	66 pp. By Florence Brumbaugh.
Donald Duck Gets Fed Up	Racine: Whitman	1940	424 pp. Better Little Book No. 1462
Donald Duck Out of Luck	New York: Dell	1940	192 pp. Fast-Action

APPENDIX: DISNEY BOOKS

Donald's Penguin	New York: Garden City	1940	24 pp.
Fantasia	New York: Simon and Schuster	1940	158 pp. By Deems Taylor with foreword by Leopold Stokowski.
Fantasia in Technicolor and Fantasound	New York: Walt Disney Productions	1940	28 pp. Illustrated program.
Figaro and Cleo	New York: Random House	1940	27 pp. Based on the motion picture *Pinocchio*.
Figaro and Cleo: A Story Paint Book	Racine: Whitman	1940	24 pp. No. 1059. From box of 6 Pinocchio books for Reading, Coloring, Playing.
Geppetto: A Story Paint Book	Racine: Whitman	1940	24 pp. No. 1059. From box of 6 Pinocchio books for Reading, Coloring, Playing.
Here They Are	Boston: Heath	1940	56 pp. By Ardra Wavle.
Honest John and Giddy	New York: Random House	1940	27 pp. Based on Pinoccio.
J. Worthington Foulfellow and Gideon: A Story Paint Book	Racine: Whitman	1940	24 pp. No. 1059. From box of 6 Pinocchio books for Reading, Coloring, Playing.
Jiminy Cricket	New York: Random House	1940	27 pp.
Jiminy Cricket: A Story Paint Book	Racine: Whitman	1940	24 pp. No. 1059. From box of 6 Pinocchio books for Reading, Coloring, Playing.
Mickey Mouse and the Seven Ghosts	Racine: Whitman	1940	424 pp. Better Little Book No. 1475
Mickey Mouse in the Foreign Legion	Racine: Whitman	1940	424 pp. Better Little Book No. 1428
The Nutcracker Suite from Walt Disney's Fantasia	Boston: Little, Brown	1940	72 pp. Story and illustrations inspired by the music of Peter Ilich Tchaikovsky. Special arrangements freely transcribed for piano by Frederick Stark.
Pastoral from Walt Disney's Fantasia	New York: Harper	1940	36 pp.
Pinocchio	Racine: Whitman	1940	12 pp. No. 1061
Pinocchio	Racine: Whitman	1940	12 pp. Linen-like No. 1039
Pinocchio	Racine: Whitman	1940	12 pp. No. 6881

APPENDIX: DISNEY BOOKS

Pinocchio	Racine: Whitman	1940	16 pp. No. 846
Pinocchio	Boston: Heath	1940	90 pp. By Dorothy Walter Baruch.
Pinocchio: A Story Paint Book	Racine: Whitman	1940	24 pp. No. 1059. From box of 6 Pinocchio books for Reading, Coloring, Playing.
Pinocchio and Jiminy Cricket	Racine: Whitman	1940	425 pp. Better Little Book No. 1435
Pinocchio Picture Book	New York: Grosset and Dunlap	1940	12 pp.
Pinocchio Picture Book	Racine: Whitman	1940	12 pp. No. 849
Pinocchio: The Story of a Puppet	New York: Dell	1940	192 pp. Fast-Action
The Practical Pig	New York: Garden City	1940	24 pp.
The Sorcerer's Apprentice	New York: Grosset and Dunlap	1940	35 pp.
Stories from Walt Disney's Fantasia	New York: Random House	1940	72 pp.
The Walt Disney Parade	New York: Garden City	1940	176 pp.
Walt Disney's Version of Pinocchio	Racine: Whitman	1940	24 pp.
Walt Disney's Version of Pinocchio	Racine: Whitman	1940	95 pp. No. 6880
Water Babies' Circus and Other Stories	Boston: Heath	1940	78 pp. By Georgiana Browne.
Baby Weems	New York: Doubleday	1941	62 pp. By Joe Grant and Dick Huemer, from the motion picture *The Reluctant Dragon*. Introduction by Robert Benchley.
Bambi	New York: Simon and Schuster	1941	52 pp. Adapted from the novel by Felix Salten.
Donald Duck Says Such Luck	Racine: Whitman	1941	424 pp. Better Little Book No. 1424
Donald Duck Sees Stars	Racine: Whitman	1941	424 pp. Better Little Book No. 1422
Donald Duck Takes it on the Chin	New York: Dell	1941	192 pp. Fast-Action
Dumbo of the Circus	New York: K.K. Publications	1941	48 pp.
Dumbo of the Circus	New York: Garden City	1941	52 pp.
Dumbo of the Circus: Only His Ears Grew	Racine: Whitman	1941	424 pp. Better Little Book No. 1400
Dumbo, the Flying Elephant	Racine: Whitman	1941	32 pp. By Helen Aberson and Harold Pearl.

APPENDIX: DISNEY BOOKS

Dumbo, the Flying Elephant	New York: Dell	1941	192 pp. Fast-Action
Dumbo: The Story of the Little Elephant with the Big Ears	Burbank: Walt Disney Productions	1941	12 pp.
The Life of Donald Duck	New York: Random House	1941	72 pp.
Mickey Mouse in the Treasure Hunt	Racine: Whitman	1941	424 pp. Better Little Book No. 1401
Mickey Mouse on Sky Island	Racine: Whitman	1941	424 pp. Better Little Book No. 1417
The Story of Casey, Jr.	New York: Garden City	1941	28 pp.
Story of the Reluctant Dragon	New York: Garden City	1941	72 pp. Introduced by Robert Benchley. From Kenneth Grahame's *Dream Days*.
The Story of Timothy's House	New York: Garden City	1941	28 pp.
The Art of Walt Disney	New York: Macmillan	1942	290 pp. By Robert Field
Bambi	New York: Grosset and Dunlap	1942	32 pp.
Bambi Picture Book	Racine: Whitman	1942	14 pp. No. 930
Bambi Story Book	Racine: Whitman	1942	96 pp. No. 725
Bambi, the Prince of the Forest	Racine: Whitman	1942	424 pp. Better Little Book No. 1469
Donald Duck Headed for Trouble	Racine: Whitman	1942	424 pp. Better Little Book No. 1430
Dumbo: The Story of the Flying Elephant	Racine: Whitman	1942	24 pp. No. 710
Mickey Mouse and Pluto	New York: Dell	1942	192 pp. Fast-Action No. 16
Mickey Mouse and the Magic Lamp	Racine: Whitman	1942	424 pp. Better Little Book No. 1429
Thumper	New York: Grosset and Dunlap	1942	32 pp.
The Victory March; or the Mystery of the Treasure Chest	New York: Random House	1942	12 pp. By Walt Disney and Chester Williams.
Bambi's Children	Racine: Whitman	1943	424 pp. Better Little Book No. 1497
Donald Duck in the High Andes	New York: Grosset and Dunlap	1943	32 pp. From the Walt Disney feature production *Saludos Amigos*.
Donald Duck Off the Beam	Racine: Whitman	1943	424 pp. Better Little Book No. 1438

APPENDIX: DISNEY BOOKS

Title	Publisher	Year	Notes
The Gremlins	New York: Random House	1943	52 pp. A Royal Air Force story, by Flight Lieutenant Roald Dahl.
Mickey Mouse and the Dude Ranch	Racine: Whitman	1943	424 pp. Better Little Book No. 1471
Mickey's Dog Pluto	Racine: Whitman	1943	187 pp. Tall Comics All-Picture Book No. 532
Pedro: The Story of a Little Airplane	New York: Grosset and Dunlap	1943	32 pp.
Bambi	Boston: Heath	1944	101 pp. Retold by Idella Purnell.
Donald Duck is Here Again	Racine: Whitman	1944	346 pp. Better Little Book No. 1484
Circus	New York: Simon and Schuster	1944	28 pp. Big Golden Book
The Cold-Blooded Penguin	New York: Simon and Schuster	1944	24 pp. Walt Disney's Little Library. Adapted from *The Three Caballeros* by Robert Edmunds.
Mickey Mouse on the Caveman Island	Racine: Whitman	1944	346 pp. Better Little Book No. 1499
Mickey Sees the U.S.A.	Boston: Heath	1944	138 pp. By Caroline D. Emerson.
Surprise Package	New York: Simon and Schuster	1944	90 pp. Giant Golden Book. Abbreviated edition, 1948, 76 pp. Stories adapted by H. Marion Palmer from originals by Hans Christian Andersen and others.
The Three Caballeros	New York: Random House	1944	56 pp. By Marion Palmer.
Through the Picture Frame	New York: Simon and Schuster	1944	24 pp. Walt Disney's Little Library. Adapted by Robert Edmunds from the Hans Christian Andersen story "Ole Lukoie."
Thumper and the Seven Dwarfs	Racine: Whitman	1944	348 pp. Better Little Book No. 1409
ABC's of Hand Tools: Their Correct Usage and Care	Detroit: General Motors Corp.	1945	Later edition, 1967, 47 pp. Also 1971 reprint.
Donald Duck Sees South America	Boston: Heath	1945	137 pp. By Marion Palmer.
Donald Duck Up in the Air	Racine: Whitman	1945	346 pp. Better Little Book No. 1486

APPENDIX: DISNEY BOOKS

Funny Stories About Donald and Mickey	Racine: Whitman	1945	128 pp. No. 714
Mickey Mouse, Bellboy Detective	Racine: Whitman	1945	346 pp. Better Little Book No. 1483
Br'er Rabbit Rides the Fox	New York: Grosset and Dunlap	1946	32 pp. Told by Marion Palmer based on the original stories by Joel Chandler Harris.
Donald Duck and Ghost Morgan's Treasure	Racine: Whitman	1946	348 pp. Better Little Book No. 1411
Mickey Mouse and the 'Lectro Box	Racine: Whitman	1946	346 pp. Better Little Book No. 1413
The Wonderful Tar Baby	New York: Grosset and Dunlap	1946	32 pp. By Marion Palmer. Adapted from the original Uncle Remus story by Joel Chandler Harris.
Bongo	New York: Simon and Schuster	1947	26 pp. Big Golden Book. Based on an adaptation of the original story by Sinclair Lewis. Illustrated by Edgar Starr.
Br'er Rabbit	Racine: Whitman	1947	282 pp. Better Little Book No. 1426
Donald Duck and the Green Serpent	Racine: Whitman	1947	284 pp. Better Little Book No. 1432
Dumbo	New York: Simon and Schuster	1947	42 pp. Little Golden Book No. D3. Also published in 24- and 28-page editions, with several revised covers.
Mickey and the Beanstalk	New York: Grosset and Dunlap	1947	32 pp. Pictures by Campbell Grant. Based on the motion picture *Fun and Fancy Free*.
Mickey Mouse and the Lazy Daisy Mystery	Racine: Whitman	1947	286 pp. Better Little Book No. 1433
Peter and the Wolf	New York: Simon and Schuster	1947	42 pp. Little Golden Book No. D5. Also printed in 1956, 24 pp. as Little Golden Book No. D56. A fairy tale adapted from Serge Prokofieff's musical theme. Pictures by Richard Kelsey. Based on the animated cartoon sequence in *Make Mine Music*.

Uncle Remus	New York: Simon and Schuster	1947	42 pp. Little Golden Book No. D6. Also published in 28- and 24-page editions, the latter in 1959 as Little Golden Book No. D85. Retold by Marion Palmer from the original stories by Joel Chandler Harris. Illustrated by Bob Grant.
Uncle Remus Stories	New York: Simon and Schuster	1947	92 pp. Giant Golden Book. Abridged edition 1959, 57 pp. as Giant Golden Book No. 554. Retold by Marion Palmer. Illustrated by Al Dempster and Bill Justice. Also Nos. 12554, 1962 and 15551, 1966.
Bambi	New York: Simon and Schuster	1948	42 pp. (with later reprints of 28 pp. and 24 pp.) Little Golden Book No. D7. Revised reprint, Golden Press, 1960, Little Golden Book No. D90. A later printing revises the cover, removing a large tree. Illustrated and adapted by Bob Grant.
Bongo	Racine: Whitman	1948	32 pp. Story Hour Series No. 803. Also issued in paperback.
Bongo	New York: Simon and Schuster	1948	42 pp. Little Golden Library No. D9. Revised reprint: 24 pp. 1957. Little Golden Book No. D62. Illustrations adapted by Campbell Grant.
Come Play with Donald Duck	New York: Grosset and Dunlap	1948	32 pp. Walt Disney Picture-Story Books. Adapted by Ernest Terrazas.
Come Play with Mickey Mouse	New York: Grosset and Dunlap	1948	32 pp. Walt Disney Picture-Story Books. Adapted by Manuel Gonzales.

APPENDIX: DISNEY BOOKS

Come Play with Pluto Pup	New York: Grosset and Dunlap	1948	32 pp. Walt Disney Picture-Story Books. Adapted by Julius Svendsen.
Come Play with The Seven Dwarfs	New York: Grosset and Dunlap	1948	32 pp. Walt Disney Picture-Story Books. Adapted by Julius Svendsen.
Donald Duck and His Cat Troubles	Racine: Whitman	1948	95 pp. No. 845
Donald Duck and the Boys	Racine: Whitman	1948	96 pp. No. 845
Donald Duck in Bringing up the Boys	Racine: Whitman	1948	32 pp. Story Hour Series No. 800. Also issued in paperback.
Donald Duck Lays Down the Law	Racine: Whitman	1948	286 pp. Better Little Book No. 1449
Dumbo of the Circus	Boston: Heath	1948	90 pp. By Dorothy Walter Baruch. Illustrations adapted by Melvin Shaw.
He Drew as He Pleased: A Sketchbook	New York: Simon and Schuster	1948	188 pp. By Albert Hurter.
Mickey and the Beanstalk	Racine: Whitman	1948	32 pp. Story Hour Series No. 804. Also in paperback.
Mickey Mouse and the Boy Thursday	Racine: Whitman	1948	96 pp. No. 845
Mickey Mouse and the Desert Palace	Racine: Whitman	1948	286 pp. Better Little Book No. 1451
Mickey Mouse in the World of Tomorrow	Racine: Whitman	1948	286 pp. Better Little Book No. 1444
Mickey Mouse the Miracle Maker	Racine: Whitman	1948	96 pp. No. 845
Mickey Mouse's Summer Vacation	Racine: Whitman	1948	32 pp. Story Hour Series No. 801. Also in paperback.
Minnie Mouse and the Antique Chair	Racine: Whitman	1948	95 pp. No. 845
Pinocchio	New York: Simon and Schuster	1948	42 pp. Little Golden Book No. D8. Also printed in 1962, 24 pp., as Little Golden Book No. D100. Based on the story by Collodi. Adapted by Campbell Grant.
Poor Pluto	Racine: Whitman	1948	96 pp. No. 845

APPENDIX: DISNEY BOOKS

Snow White and The Seven Dwarfs	New York: Simon and Schuster	1948	42 pp. Little Golden Book No. D4. Also published in 1957, 24 pp., as Little Golden Book No. D66. Adapted by Ken O'Brien and Al Dempster.
The Three Little Pigs	New York: Simon and Schuster	1948	42 pp. Little Golden Book No. D10. Also issued in 28- and 24-page editions, the latter in 1958 as Little Golden Book No. D78. Adapted by Milt Banta and Al Dempster.
Treasure Chest	New York: Simon and Schuster	1948	66 pp. Big Golden Book
The Adventures of Mr. Toad	New York: Simon and Schuster	1949	25 pp. Big Golden Book. From the original story *The Wind in the Willows* by Kenneth Grahame. Adapted by John Hench.
Bambi	New York: Simon and Schuster	1949	28 pp. Fuzzy Golden Book No. 443. There is also a version without flocking.
Br'er Rabbit	Racine: Whitman	1949	192 pp. New Better Little Book No. 704
Cinderella Puppet Show	New York: Simon and Schuster	1949	Unpaged. Golden Toy Book.
Danny, the Little Black Lamb	Racine: Whitman	1949	32 pp. Story Hour Series No. 807. Also issued in paperback.
Donald Duck and the Mystery of the Double X	Racine: Whitman	1949	176 pp. New Better Little Book No. 705
Donald Duck in the Great Kite Maker	Racine: Whitman	1949	20 pp. Tiny Tales No. 1030. Also in 1959, Tiny Tales No. 2952.
Donald Duck in Volcano Valley	Racine: Whitman	1949	286 pp. Better Little Book No. 1457
Johnny Appleseed	Racine: Whitman	1949	32 pp. Story Hour Series No. 808. Also issued in paperback.
Johnny Appleseed	New York: Simon and Schuster	1949	42 pp. Little Golden Book No. D11. Illustrations adapted by Ted Parmalee from the motion picture *Melody Time*.

APPENDIX: DISNEY BOOKS

Magnificent Mr. Toad	New York: Grosset and Dunlap	1949	32 pp. Walt Disney Picture Story Book. From the motion picture *Ichabod and Mr. Toad* based on *The Wind in the Willows* by Kenneth Grahame. Illustrations adapted by John Hench.
Mickey Mouse and the Stolen Jewels	Racine: Whitman	1949	286 pp. Better Little Book No. 1464
Mickey Mouse, Goofy and the Night Prowlers	Racine: Whitman	1949	18 pp. Tiny Tales No. 1030. Also in 1959 Tiny Tales No. 2952
Mother Goose	New York: Simon and Schuster	1949	28 pp. Big Golden Book. Reprinted in 1970 as No. 10878, with a new cover. Adapted by Al Dempster.
Mystery in Disneyville	New York: Simon and Schuster	1949	126 pp. Golden Story Book No. 7. Illustrations adapted by Richard Moores and Manuel Gonzales.
The Runaway Lamb at the Country Fair	New York: Grosset and Dunlap	1949	31 pp. Walt Disney Picture Story Book. From the picture *So Dear to My Heart*, based on the original story by Sterling North. Illustrated by Julius Svendsen.
So Dear to My Heart	New York: Dell	1949	191 pp. Dell Book No. 291. By Sterling North.
The Three Orphan Kittens	Racine: Whitman	1949	32 pp. Story Hour Series No. 809. Also issued in paperback.
Bambi Plays Follow the Leader	New York: Simon and Schuster	1950	18 pp. Tiny Golden Book by Jane Werner. Illustrated by Campbell Grant.
Bongo Stars Again	New York: Simon and Schuster	1950	18 pp. Tiny Golden Book. By Jane Werner. Illustrated by Campbell Grant.
Bootle Beetle's Adventures	New York: Simon and Schuster	1950	18 pp. Tiny Golden Book. By Jane Werner. Illustrated by Campbell Grant.
Br'er Rabbit Plays a Trick	New York: Simon and Schuster	1950	18 pp. Tiny Golden Book. By Jane Werner. Illustrated by Campbell Grant.

APPENDIX: DISNEY BOOKS

Cinderella	Racine: Whitman	1950	24 pp. Cozy-Corner Book No. 2416. Also No. 2037, with different end papers and on cheaper paper. Adapted by Julius Svendsen.
Cinderella	New York: Simon and Schuster	1950	26 pp. Big Golden Book No. 425. (There are two versions of No. 425-one is slightly smaller and without the gold plate and tipped in pumpkin.) Reprinted in 1955, Walt Disney Library and 1962, 28 pp. Big Golden Book No. 10425.
Cinderella	New York: Golden Press	1950	28 pp. Little Golden Book No. D13. Revised printings as Little Golden Book No. D59 and D114, 24 pp., the latter in 1964. Illustrations adapted by Campbell Grant.
Cinderella and the Magic Wand	Racine: Whitman	1950	188 pp. New Better Little Book No. 711
Cinderella's Ball Gown	New York: Simon and Schuster	1950	18 pp. Tiny Golden Book. By Jane Werner. Illustrated by Campbell Grant.
Cinderella's Friends	New York: Simon and Schuster	1950	28 pp. Little Golden Book No. D17. Revised reprints, 24 pp. in 1956 as Little Golden Book No. D58 and in 1964 as Little Golden Book No. D115. Told by Jane Werner. Illustrations adapted by Al Dempster.
Donald and Mickey, Cub Scouts	Racine: Whitman	1950	24 pp. Cozy-Corner Book No. 2031
Donald Duck's Adventure	New York: Simon and Schuster	1950	28 pp. Little Golden Book No. D14. Also a Mickey Mouse Club Book and a 24 pp. edition with a new cover, green lettering instead of red. By Annie North Bedford. Illustrations adapted by Campbell Grant.

APPENDIX: DISNEY BOOKS

Donald Duck's Toy Train	New York: Simon and Schuster	1950	28 pp. Little Golden Book No. D18. By Jane Werner. Illustrations adapted by Dick Kelsey and Bill Justice from the movie *Out Of Scale*. Also a 24 pp. edition.
Donald Duck's Wild Goose Chase	New York: Simon and Schuster	1950	18 pp. Tiny Golden Book. By Jane Werner. Illustrated by Campbell Grant.
Dopey and the Wicked Witch	New York: Simon and Schuster	1950	18 pp. Tiny Golden Book. By Jane Werner. Illustrated by Campbell Grant.
Dumbo's Magic Feather	New York: Simon and Schuster	1950	18 pp. Tiny Golden Book. By Jane Werner. Illustrated by Campbell Grant.
Mickey Mouse on the Haunted Island	Racine: Whitman	1950	188 pp. New Better Little Book No. 708
Mickey Mouse's Picnic	New York: Simon and Schuster	1950	28 pp. Little Golden Book No. D15. Story by Jane Werner. Also 24 pp. versions.
Mickey's New Car	New York: Simon and Schuster	1950	18 pp. Tiny Golden Book. By Jane Werner. Illustrated by Campbell Grant.
Once Upon a Wintertime	New York: Simon and Schuster	1950	42 pp. Little Golden Book No. D12. Adapted by Tom Oreb from the motion picture *Melody Time*.
Pablo the Penguin Takes a Trip	New York: Simon and Schuster	1950	18 pp. Tiny Golden Book. By Jane Werner. Illustrated by Campbell Grant.
Pinocchio's Surprise	New York: Simon and Schuster	1950	18 pp. Tiny Golden Book. By Jane Werner. Illustrated by Campbell Grant.
Santa's Toy Shop	New York: Simon and Schuster	1950	28 pp. Little Golden Book No. D16. Illustrations adapted by Al Dempster. Also 24 pp. edition and revised cover.
So Dear to My Heart	New York: Simon and Schuster	1950	125 pp. Golden Story Book No. 12. Story adapted by Helen Palmer. Illustrations adapted by Bill Peet. Based on the novel by Sterling North.
Three Little Pigs Fool a Wolf	New York: Simon and Schuster	1950	18 pp. Tiny Golden Book. By Jane Werner. Illustrated by Campbell Grant.

More Disney Entertainment from GEMSTONE PUBLISHING

In addition to our monthly Disney comic publications, be sure to check out our periodical one-shots—special publications you'll only see once in a blue moon; like *Walt Disney's Mickey and the Gang; The Life and Times of Scrooge McDuck; Walt Disney Treasures; Christmas Parade; Vacation Parade; Mickey Mouse and Blotman in Blotman Returns; The Life and Times of Scrooge McDuck Companion.*

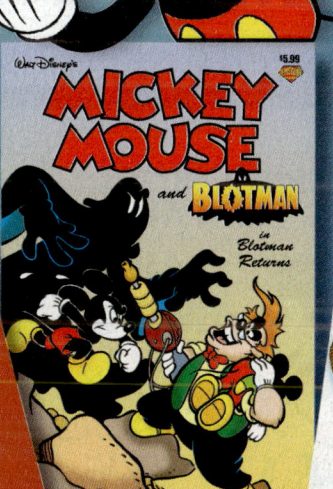

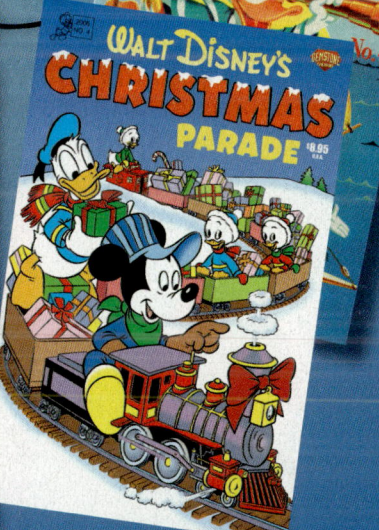

WWW.GEMSTONEPUB.COM/DISNEY

The leader in character collectibles for more than 40 years!

CONSIGNMENTS WANTED • ALWAYS BUYING

ONE ITEM OR ENTIRE COLLECTIONS

AUCTIONS • SALES • EBAY

NO BUYER'S PREMIUM

HAKE'S AMERICANA & COLLECTIBLES • 1966 GREENSPRING DRIVE, SUITE 400 ✤ TIMONIUM,

A division of Diamond International Galleries

HAKE'S
AMERICANA & COLLECTIBLES

MD 21093 ✦ TOLL FREE (866) 404-9800 ✦ PHONE (410) 427-9440 ✦ WWW.HAKES.COM

What would happen if...

Thousands of fine people lost their lifetime hobbies in the 2004-05 hurricane seasons. Collectibles ranging from rare and cherished books and paper ephemera, to munuscripts, autographs, basement model railroad layouts and cut glass were sadly destroyed. Did insurance help many of these victims? In too many cases, the answer was, "NO."

We know what it's like to lose the treasures of a lifetime hobby. Here's a lesson we'd like to pass along to you: Homeowners insurance is rarely, if ever, adequate for your collectibles. Take a minute now and call, write or e-mail us for brochures that can help your peace of mind.

We INSURE Disney Collectibles at Attractive Rates.

- **Our insurance carrier** is AM Best's rated A+ (Superior).
- **We insure scores of major collectibles** from Disney memorabilia to toys and books. "One-stop" service for practically everything you collect.
- **Personal Attention.** Consumer friendly service. Dedicated staff. Network of expert assistance in valuing collectibles at time of loss. You won't deal with someone who doesn't know the collectibles business.
- **Detailed inventory** and/or professional appraisal not required. Collectors list items over $5,000, dealers no listing required.
- **See our website** (or call, fax, e-mail us) for full information, including standard exclusions.

Get A Rate Quote!
Call Toll Free:
1-888-837-9537
Fax: (410) 876-9233

CIA Collectibles Insurance Agency
11350 McCormick Road • Suite 700
Hunt Valley, MD 21031
E-Mail: info@insurecollectibles.com
www.collectinsure.com

YOUR AD HERE!

The Overstreet Price Guide to Disney Collectibles helps you reach collectors, dealers, and anyone else serious about Disney collectibles. E-mail ads@gemstonepub.com to find out about next time!

IT'S LIKE MONEY IN THE BANK!

INVEST IN ONE OF THESE COLLECTIBLES TODAY!

COMIC BOOKS
ORIGINAL STRIP ART
COMIC BOOK ART
AND MUCH MORE!

DIAMOND INTERNATIONAL GALLERIES
INTERNET WEB STORE

WWW.DIAMONDGALLERIES.COM

Gemstone Publishing presents More Life and Times of $crooge McDuck

You asked for them, and here they are… the prequels, the sequels, and the in-between-quels to Don Rosa's *Life and Times of Scrooge McDuck!* Filling in the gaps between the twelve original chapters are "The Cowboy Captain of the Cutty Sark" (Chapter 3B/*Uncle Scrooge* 318), "The Vigilante of Pizen Bluff" (Chapter 6B/*US* 306), "The Prisoner of White Agony Creek" (the all-new Chapter 8B!), "Hearts of the Yukon" (Chapter 8C/*Walt Disney Giant* 1) and "The Sharpie of the Culebra Cut" (Chapter 10B/*US* 332).

But wait… there's more! We've got Don's first look at Scrooge's youth—the famous flashback from "Last Sled to Dawson" (*Uncle Scrooge Adventures* 5). We've got the apocrypha: "Of Ducks and Dimes and Destinies" (Chapter 0/*US* 297) and "The Dream of a Lifetime!" (*US* 329), with the modern-day Magica De Spell and Beagle Boys wreaking havoc in Scrooge's past. And we've got the commentary—more than a dozen pages of Rosa recollections on how these classics came to be, all for only $16.99!

STILL ON SALE (AT A TIGHTWAD-FRIENDLY PRICE!)

It's Rosa's original twelve-chapter quest into Scrooge's life—presented in a 264-page volume replete with extensive authorial commentary. From Scrooge's Scottish childhood to his worldwide quest for gold; from his ill-starred romances to his meetings with history's heroes, this classic biography marked a milestone in duck comics. Annotated by Rosa himself and full of new-to-North-America art, Gemstone's $16.99 collected edition belongs on every Disney fan's bookshelf.

COLLECTORS:
Make Your Next Big Find a Great Comics Shop!

COMIC SHOP LOCATOR SERVICE
888-COMIC-BOOK
comicshoplocator.com

By phone and online, millions of people around the world have used the Comic Shop Locator Service to find comic book specialty stores in their areas!

Sponsored By

FREE COMIC BOOK DAY
1st Saturday In May
www.freecomicbookday.com

OCT 18 2007